OA 3116359

A CONCORDANCE
TO THE ENGLISH POEMS
OF ANDREW MARVELL

Compiled and Edited by
GEORGE R. GUFFEY

The University of North Carolina Press
Chapel Hill

CC

Copyright©1974 by
The University of North Carolina Press
All rights reserved
Manufactured in the United States of America
ISBN 0-8078-1230-7
Library of Congress Catalog Card Number 73-21550

Library of Congress Cataloging in Publication Data

Guffey, George Robert.
  A concordance to the English poems of Andrew Marvell.

  "Based on . . . volume 1 of the second edition of H. M. Margoliouth's The poems &
letters of Andrew Marvell, 2 vols. (...1952)"
  Includes bibliographical references.
  1. Marvell, Andrew, 1621-1678—Concordances.
I. Marvell, Andrew, 1621-1678. Poems & letters.
II. Title.
PR3546.G77   821'.4   73-21550
ISBN 0-8078-1230-7

Contents

Preface

i. *The Poems Concorded*

This concordance to the English poems of Andrew Marvell is based on a copy of Volume I of the second edition of H. M. Margoliouth's *The Poems & Letters of Andrew Marvell*, 2 vols. (Oxford: Clarendon Press, 1952).[1] After the computer cards for the concordance had been punched and verified, Pierre Legouis and E. E. Duncan-Jones published a third, expanded edition[2] based on Margoliouth's second edition. Although Legouis and Duncan-Jones added a great deal of material to Margoliouth's commentaries on the poems, the texts they printed are essentially those printed by Margoliouth: "This is still Margoliouth's edition, not one on new lines. It has established itself over forty years among scholars: from it quotations are made, it is the primary resort for annotation, whether the borrowings are made with or without acknowledgement. I have preserved almost all it contained, for the convenience of those who will seek references in this reset edition" (p. v). A collation of the texts of the English poems of Margoliouth's second edition against the same poems of the Legouis edition reveals very few substantive variants.[3] Given the essential similarities between the texts of the second and third editions and the established position of the texts of Margoliouth's second edition (as Legouis has pointed out), the second

1. Although the title page labels this the second edition of the work, comparison with the first edition of 1927 indicates that the text was not reset in 1952 and that what is called the "second edition" is, more properly speaking, a second issue of the first edition.

2. *The Poems and Letters of Andrew Marvell*, ed. H. M. Margoliouth, 3rd ed., revised by Pierre Legouis, with the collaboration of E. E. Duncan-Jones (Oxford: Clarendon Press, 1971).

3. The most significant variants between the English poems of Margoliouth's second edition (M) and the same poems in Legouis's third edition (L) are the following—"The Definition of Love," l. 29: bind.] M; bind, L; "Upon Appleton House," l. 556: *Sin.*] M; *Sin.*) L; "Two Songs at the Marriage of the Lord Fauconberg and the Lady Mary Cromwell," "Second Song," l. 3: *Son.*] M; *Son* L; "A Poem upon the Death of O. C.," l. 276: greate;] M; greate. L; "The Last Instructions to a Painter," l. 160: Thought] M; Though L; "The Loyall Scot," l. 118: mistook] M; forsook L; "The Loyall Scot," l. 132: Bishop . . . soe!] M; Bishop? . . . soe, L; "The Loyall Scot," l. 204: even bishops] M; bishops even L; "The Statue at Charing Cross," l. 4: Puchinello] M (*but* Punchinello *in the commentary*); Punchinello L; "An Historicall Poem," l. 63: grate.] M; grate, L.

edition still appears to be the most practical one on which to base a concordance.[4]

A somewhat knottier problem, however, is that of the Marvell canon. Scholars have debated the authenticity of a number of the satires for more than a hundred years. In his edition of the poems and satires (1892), G. A. Aitken, following A. B. Grosart's earlier edition (1872), relegated six satires previously attributed to Marvell to an appendix containing "unauthenticated" poems. Margoliouth accepted one of the six as authentic ("The King's Vowes") but agreed that the other five ("Hodge's Vision from the Monument," "Oceana and Britannia," "Upon the Cutting of Sir John Coventry's Nose," "The Ballad Call'd the Chequer Inn," "The Doctor Turn'd Justice") were spurious: "Aitken followed Grosart and put these six satires in an appendix. Grosart's reasons for rejecting ["The King's Vowes"] no longer hold good and I have therefore printed it. . . . But I have not printed any of the others in the text, as it seems to me a great mistake to continue to print among Marvell's poems inferior stuff which has long been considered spurious" (I, 214). Although he excluded "The Chequer Inn" from the text proper, Margoliouth did print it "as illustrative matter in the notes to *The Statue at Charing Cross*" (I, 215).

In addition, Margoliouth had serious reservations about the authenticity of some of the poems he admitted into his text proper. Certainly spurious, in his opinion, were "Advice to a Painter to Draw the Duke by" and "An Historicall Poem"; "I have, of course, had to print them, for they have hitherto been considered genuine. I am quite sure that some of the others are not Marvell's, but I have discussed the authenticity of each separately in the notes." In his notes, Margoliouth expresses strong doubt about the authenticity of "Nostradamus's Prophecy" and varying degrees of doubt about "Clarindon's House-Warming," lines 87-177 and 186-235 of "The Loyall Scot," "The Statue in Stocks-Market," "Upon His Majesties Being Made Free of the Citty," "Britannia and Rawleigh," "The Statue at Charing Cross," and "A Dialogue Between the Two Horses." Finally, in an appendix he printed "An Elegy upon the Death of My Lord Francis Villiers," a poem for which very slight evidence existed, either for or against authorship by Marvell.

In 1958 George de Forest Lord argued that two additional poems should be accepted into the canon—"The Second Advice to a Painter" and "The Third Advice to a Painter," first published (1667) as written by

4. Since the lineation of the poems of Legouis's third edition is identical with that of Margoliouth's second edition, readers who wish to use the concordance with the third edition can, of course, do so (although pagination differences become greater as one nears the end of the books).

Sir John Denham.[5] During the decade that followed, Lord's two attributions were spiritedly debated by Lord and a number of other scholars,[6] but in 1968 he was still sufficiently enough convinced of Marvell's authorship to print them in his Modern Library edition of Marvell's poems (*Andrew Marvell: Complete Poetry* [New York: Random House]). On the other hand, he decided not to include a great deal of the English poetry that Margoliouth had printed in his edition: "Advice to a Painter to Draw the Duke by," "Britannia and Rawleigh," "Upon His House," "Upon His Grand-Children," "Further Advice to a Painter," "The Chequer Inn," "Nostradamus's Prophecy," "A Dialogue Between the Two Horses," "An Historicall Poem," and parts of "The Loyall Scot" (ll. 63-64, 73-74, and 89-233). In an appendix ("Poems of Doubtful Authorship," pp. 255-70), Lord printed four poems ("An Elegy upon the Death of My Lord Francis Villiers," "A Dialogue Between Thyrsis and Dorinda," "Tom May's Death," and "On the Victory Obtained by Blake") that he felt were of questionable authenticity.

In preparing his revision of Margoliouth's edition, Professor Legouis, of course, took the foregoing debate into consideration; and, although he too felt some doubts about some of the poems Margoliouth had printed, he decided to make only one change in the canon: "The canon of the *Poems*, still abundant in uncertainties, has not been altered, save that one satire ['A Ballad Call'd the Chequer Inn'] has been promoted from the Commentary to a place among the others. Even the order of the poems has been preserved . . ." (I, v). Legouis, like Margoliouth, placed "An Elegy upon the Death of My Lord Francis Villiers" in an appendix, rather than in the book proper. This concordance to the English poems of Marvell reflects the change in the canon made by Professor Legouis. It includes all the poems printed by Margoliouth, plus "The Chequer Inn"; it does not include the more doubtful poem

5. "Two New Poems by Marvell?" *Bulletin of The New York Public Library* 62 (1958): 551-70.
6. See, for example, David V. Erdman, "The Signature of Style," *Bulletin of The New York Public Library* 63 (1959): 88-109; Ephim G. Fogel, "Salmons in Both, or Some Caveats for Canonical Scholars," *Bulletin of The New York Public Library* 63 (1959): 223-36, 292-308; George de Forest Lord, "Comments on the Canonical Caveat," *Bulletin of The New York Public Library* 63 (1959): 355-66; John M. Wallace, "The Date of John Tatham's *The Distracted State*," *Bulletin of The New York Public Library* 64 (1960), 29-40; John M. Wallace, "Restoration Satire," *The Yale Review* 53 (1964): 608-13; Ephim G. Fogel, "On 'Multiple Rhymes': Some Clarifications," in *Evidence for Authorship: Essays on Problems of Attribution*, ed. David V. Erdman and Ephim G. Fogel (Ithaca, N.Y.: Cornell University Press, 1966), pp. 121-27; and George de Forest Lord, "A Comment on the 'Multiple Rhymes' Question," in *Evidence for Authorship: Essays on Problems of Attribution*, ed. David V. Erdman and Ephim G. Fogel (Ithaca, N.Y.: Cornell University Press, 1966), pp. 128-29.

("Villiers"), which both Margoliouth and Legouis relegated to an appendix.

ii. *Index Words*

Since the index words of this concordance reflect the spelling anomalies of Margoliouth's edition (and, of course, the seventeenth-century copy texts), a number of cross-references (i.e., "See" and "See also") seemed necessary.

Although context lines have not been given for some relatively insignificant words ("of," "for," etc.), frequency and relative frequency numbers (to the fourth decimal place) have been indicated for each of them. A magnetic tape record of the data used in the generation of this concordance will be kept permanently on file at the UCLA Campus Computing Center; any such word and its context line(s) can, therefore, be easily retrieved in the future if the need arises. The following list indicates all the words that were counted but not concorded:

a	beene	don
again	bee'st	done
againe	be'nt	dos [does]
agen	both	dost
ah	but	do'st
alas	by	do't
although		doth
am	can	durst
among	cannot	
amongst	canst	each
an	can'st	either
and	can't	else
another	cou'd	em
anothers	could	'em
any	couldst	every
are	could'st	ev'ry
as		
as't	did	for
at	didst	for's
att	did'st	for't
	do	from
be	does	
because	doeth	ha'
been	doing	had

hadst	i'th	should'st
has	i'th'	so
hath	its	soe
have	it's	soever
having	itself	such
he	I've	
he'd		t'
hee	me	than
hee'l	mee	that
hence	must	thats
henceforth	my	that's
her		t'have
here	nay	the
here's	no	thee
heretofore	noe	their
hers	nor	theire
he's	not	theirs
him		them
himself	o	themselves
himselfe	o'	then
his	of	thence
how	oh	thenceforth
howeere	on	there
however	on't	thereat
howso'ere	or	thereby
	o're	therefore
I	our	therein
if	ours	ther's [there's]
if't	ourselves	theres
Ile [I'll]	o'th	these
I'le [I'll]	out	they
I'll	over	they'l
I'lle [I'll]		they've
I'm	shall	thine
I'me [I'm]	shalt	this
in	she	thither
in's	shee	tho
into	shee'l	tho'
is	shold	thorough
is't	shou'd	thorow
it	should	those
itt	shouldst	thou

though	was	whoever
thro	we	who'ld
thro'	we'd	whom
through	wee	whose
throughout	weel	whosoe're
th'row	wee'l	whosoever
thus	were	why
thy	wer't	with
tis	we've	wou'd
'tis	what	would
to	whats	wouldst
too	what's	would'st
towards	whatsoever	
twas	when	y'
'twas	whence	ye
'twere	where	yea
'twill	whereat	yee
twixt	wheres	you
'twixt	wheres'ere	youl
'twould	wheresoe're	you'l
	wherewith	your
under	whether	yours
unto	which	
upon	whither	
us	who	

iii. *Context Lines*

Poem titles, lines of poetry, and other lines containing that word (or variant spelling) are printed below each index word. Each of these context lines has two parts: a location reference (page number, poem title, line number) followed by a line of poetry (or poem title or other matter). In the case of a line of poetry, in other words, the location reference lists in succession the page number in Margoliouth's edition (1952, Vol. I), the title (sometimes abbreviated) of the poem in which the line occurs, and the line number in the poem; an example follows:

[Page]	[Title]	[Line]	[Line of Poetry]
P. 13	DROP OF DEW	36	It all about does upwards bend.

In cases in which the location reference involves a poem title of one line or less in length, the abbreviation "t" appears in the "Line" column:

[Page]	[Title]	[Line]	[Poem Title]
P. 48	THE GARDEN	t	The Garden.

In a few cases in which the location reference involves a poem title longer than a single line, the abbreviation "t1," "t2," or "t3" (first, second, or third printed line of the title) appears in the "Line" column, indicating that the "poem title" given in that context line is only part of the full title of the poem; for example:

[Page]	[Title]	[Line]	[Part of the Poem Title]
P. 93	DR. WITTY	t2	Translation of the Popular Errors.

Finally, a few context lines contain matter that can be neither classified as a line of poetry nor title material; where such matter is being reproduced but no line number was supplied by Margoliouth, symbols such as "t+" and "8+" appear in the "Line" column, indicating that the material being referred to follows the title ("t") or indicated line of poetry ("8"). For example, some of the context lines containing the speech heading "Ametas" appear in the concordance as follows:

[Page]	[Title]	[Line]	[Speech Heading]
P. 46	AMETAS	t+	Ametas.
P. 46	AMETAS	8+	Ametas.

iv. *Titles*

Most of the titles of Marvell's poems were too long to be given in full in the context lines of this concordance; where necessary, appropriate abbreviated titles have been substituted for the full titles. The following list indicates all the titles used in the context lines of the concordance, the corresponding titles appearing in the Margoliouth edition, and the locations (page numbers) of each of the poems in that edition:

Title in the Concordance	Title in Margoliouth	Page Number[s]
ADVICE	*Further Advice to a Painter.*	168-69
A. HOUSE	*Upon Appleton House, to my Lord* Fairfax.	59-83
AMETAS	Ametas *and* Thestylis *making Hay-Ropes.*	46
ANNIVERSARY	THE FIRST ANNIVERSARY *Of the Government under* O.C.	103-13
BERMUDAS	*Bermudas.*	17-18
BILL-BOROW	*Upon the Hill and Grove at* Bill-borow.	56-58

v. *Acknowledgments*

In the preparation of this concordance, I was fortunate to have the dedicated assistance of the following people: Jeanette Wallin and Cyndia Goodman, who punched the IBM cards; Diane Eliel and Achsah Guibbory, who helped verify them; and Sidney Orr, who helped to de-bug the program and expedite various production runs of the concordance. I am especially indebted to Vinton A. Dearing, who wrote the computer program.

G. R. G.

A CONCORDANCE
TO THE ENGLISH POEMS
OF ANDREW MARVELL

A Concordance to the English Poems of Andrew Marvell

a   frequency: 727   relative frequency: 0.0151

aaron   frequency: 1   relative frequency: 0.0000
     P. 175 LOYALL SCOT   135 Aaron Casts Calves but Moses them Calcines.

abandon   frequency: 1   relative frequency: 0.0000
     P. 168 KINGS VOWES   64 I wholly will abandon State affaires,

abandoning   frequency: 1   relative frequency: 0.0000
     P.   79 A. HOUSE   643 Abandoning my lazy Side,

abate   frequency: 1   relative frequency: 0.0000
     P. 108 ANNIVERSARY   195 See how they each his towring Crest abate,

abbess   frequency: 2   relative frequency: 0.0000
     P.   63 A. HOUSE   157 'Our Abbess too, now far in Age,
     P.   66 A. HOUSE   253 While the disjcinted Abbess threads

abbot   frequency: 1   relative frequency: 0.0000
     P. 175 LOYALL SCCT   164 Abbot one Buck, but he shot many a Doe,

abbyss   frequency: 1   relative frequency: 0.0000
     P.   70 A. HOUSE   369 And' now to the Abbyss I pass

abednego   frequency: 1   relative frequency: 0.0000
     P. 156 INSTRUCTIONS 648 Like Shadrack, Mesheck, and Abednego.

abhoring   frequency: 1   relative frequency: 0.0000
     P. 197 DUKE   4 Abhoring wisdome and dispising witt,

abhors   frequency: 2   relative frequency: 0.0000
     P. 152 INSTRUCTIONS 451 The first instructs our (Verse the Name abhors)
     P. 160 INSTRUCTIONS 814 But with a Parliament abhors to meet,

abide   frequency: 1   relative frequency: 0.0000
     P. 140 HOUSEWARMING 101 Now some (as all Buildings must censure abide)

abject   frequency: 1   relative frequency: 0.0000
     P.   28 LOVER   30 Th' unfortunate and abject Heir:

abjured   frequency: 1   relative frequency: 0.0000
     P. 198 DUKE   38 He who longe since abjured the Royall line

able   frequency: 2   relative frequency: 0.0000
     P. 142 INSTRUCTIONS   59 Happy'st of Women, if she were but able
     P. 171 PROPHECY   37 A Minister able only in his Tongue

ablest   frequency: 1   relative frequency: 0.0000
     P. 160 INSTRUCTIONS 802 And ablest Speaker, who cf Law has least;

abortive   frequency: 1   relative frequency: 0.0000
     P. 142 INSTRUCTIONS   72 And Fawns, that from the womb abortive fled.

abound   frequency: 1   relative frequency: 0.0000

                 P. 177 LOYALL SCOT   232 -leness and all the vice that did abound,

about   frequency: 27   relative frequency: 0.0005
    P.   13 DROP OF DEW   36 It all about does upwards bend.
    P.   14 THE CORONET   15 About the flow'rs disguis'd does fold,
    P.   43 DAMON   64 About me they contract their Ring.
    P.   49 THE GARDEN   34 Ripe Apples drop about my head;
    P.   62 A. HOUSE   100 'But hedge our Liberty about.
    P.   63 A. HOUSE   143 'And round about you Glory breaks,
    P.   68 A. HOUSE   314 Of Stars walks round about the Pole,
    P.   74 A. HOUSE   512 Echo about their tuned Fires.
    P.   78 A. HOUSE   610 Curle me about ye gadding Vines,
    P.   80 A. HOUSE   704 The Wood about her draws a Skreen.
    P.   105 ANNIVERSARY   100 He hurles e'r since the World about him round;
    P.   106 ANNIVERSARY   141 But a thick Cloud about that Morning lyes,
    P.   108 ANNIVERSARY   203 And all about was heard a Panique groan,
    P.   124 O.C.   50 Hanging about her neck or at his knees.
    P.   129 O.C.   232 To fetch day, presse about his chamber-door;
    P.   130 O.C.   300 Wander like ghosts about thy loved tombe;
    P.   144 INSTRUCTIONS   158 But knew the Word and well could face about;
    P.   154 INSTRUCTIONS   535 His sporting Navy all about him swim,
    P.   157 INSTRUCTIONS   681 Round the transparent Fire about him glows,
    P.   158 INSTRUCTIONS   736 Was led about in sport, the publick scorn.
    P.   163 INSTRUCTIONS   922 The purple thread about his Neck does show:
    P.   164 INSTRUCTIONS   970 About the Common Prince have rais'd a Fence;
    P.   169 ADVICE   31 At Arlingtons, and round about it sate
    P.   173 LOYALL SCOT   47 Round the Transparent fire about him Glowes
    P.   194 TWO HORSES   112 And returns to remount about break of Day.
    P.   197 DUKE   3 Who all in triumph shall about him sitte
    P.   316 CHEQUER INN   145 They talkt about and made such Din

above   frequency: 26   relative frequency: 0.0005
    P.   4 HASTINGS   17 For, there above, They number not as here,
    P.   4 LOVELACE   48 Above their envy, or mine aid doth clime.
    P.   9 DIALOGUE   17 I sup above, and cannot stay
    P.   12 DROP OF DEW   31 Dark beneath, but bright above:
    P.   50 THE GARDEN   67 Where from above the milder Sun
    P.   73 A. HOUSE   464 As Constellations do above.
    P.   85 FLECKNO   75 And above that yet casts an antick Cloak,
    P.   103 ANNIVERSARY   6 While flowing Time above his Head does close.
    P.   104 ANNIVERSARY   37 No other care they bear of things above,
    P.   108 ANNIVERSARY   217 From the low World, and thankless Men above,
    P.   108 ANNIVERSARY   226 Then ought below, or yet above a King:
    P.   112 ANNIVERSARY   386 'Where below Earth, or where above the Sphere?
    P.   113 ANNIVERSARY   400 As far above their Malice as my Praise.
    P.   114 BLAKE   26 Above both Worlds, since 'tis above the rest.
    P.   116 BLAKE   82 A grief, above the cure of Grapes best juice.
    P.   120 TWO SONGS   24 Securing their Repose above.
    P.   121 TWO SONGS   56 His Progeny above the Air;
    P.   125 O.C.   104 What they above cannot prevent, foretell;
    P.   127 O.C.   158 Have such high honours from above been shown:
    P.   130 O.C.   296 (Farr better known above than here below;)
    P.   132 PARADISE   37 And above a humane flight dost soar aloft,
    P.   200 DUKE   112 Bribed by a croune on earth and one above,
    P.   203 HISTORICALL   99 And never durst their tricks above board shew.
    P.   205 HISTORICALL   170 And Monarchs are above all human Lawes.
    P.   316 CHEQUER INN   138 And made above a Hundred.

abroad   frequency: 6   relative frequency: 0.0001
    P.   32 MOURNING   27 But casts abroad these Donatives,
    P.   98 HOLLAND   102 What then are their confederacies abroad?
    P.   99 HOLLAND   148 Watchful abroad, and honest still within.
    P.   112 ANNIVERSARY   389 'Abroad a King he seems, and something more,
    P.   138 HOUSEWARMING   55 Unless all abroad he divulg'd the design,
    P.   193 TWO HORSES   65 Ch. And our few ships abroad become Tripoly's
                                    scorn

abrupter   frequency: 1   relative frequency: 0.0000
    P.   56 BILL-BOROW   10 Which to abrupter greatness thrust,

abruptly   frequency: 1   relative frequency: 0.0000
    P.   172 LOYALL SCOT   13 Abruptly he began disguising art,

absence   frequency: 2   relative frequency: 0.0000
    P.   35 DAPHNIS   61 Absence is too much alone:
    P.   145 INSTRUCTIONS   194 Or in his absence him that first it lay'd.

absent   frequency: 2   relative frequency: 0.0000
    P.   118 BLAKE   147 So prosperous Stars, though absent to the sence,
    P.   194 TWO HORSES   107 Our riders are absent; who is't that can hear?

absolute   frequency: 1   relative frequency: 0.0000

P. 185 BRITANNIA   32 Leviathans and absolute comands.

absolved   frequency: 1   relative frequency: 0.0000
    P. 179 STOCKSMARKET   8 He that vows for a calm is absolved by a wreck.

absurdityes   frequency: 1   relative frequency: 0.0000
    P. 86 FLECKNO   146 Absurdityes in them then were before.

abyss. See "abbyss," "abysse."

abysse   frequency: 2   relative frequency: 0.0000
    P. 127 O.C.   168 Of your Abysse, with cover'd Head bewail
    P. 130 O.C.   290 Plunging dost bathe and tread the bright abysse:

accent   frequency: 1   relative frequency: 0.0000
    P. 177 LOYALL SCOT   247 Where a Mistaken accent Causeth death.

accents   frequency: 2   relative frequency: 0.0000
    P. 106 ANNIVERSARY   121 Then shall I once with graver Accents shake
    P. 111 ANNIVERSARY   338 And with such accents, as Despairing, mourn'd:

accept   frequency: 1   relative frequency: 0.0000
    P. 146 INSTRUCTIONS   229 They both accept the Charge with merry glee,

access   frequency: 1   relative frequency: 0.0000
    P. 57 BILL-BOROW   17 See what a soft access and wide

accidents   frequency: 1   relative frequency: 0.0000
    P. 146 INSTRUCTIONS   227 Nor better choice all accidents could hit;

accomptants   frequency: 2   relative frequency: 0.0000
    P. 146 INSTRUCTIONS   203 Carteret the rich did the Accomptants guide,
    P. 147 INSTRUCTIONS   261 And surly Williams, the Accomptants bane:

according   frequency: 1   relative frequency: 0.0000
    P. 36 DAPHNIS   107 For, according to the Lawes,

account   frequency: 1   relative frequency: 0.0000
    P. 149 INSTRUCTIONS   343 What an Account to Carteret; that and more

accumulate   frequency: 1   relative frequency: 0.0000
    P. 159 INSTRUCTIONS   763 But Fate does still accumulate our Woes,

accurs'd   frequency: 2   relative frequency: 0.0000
    P. 158 INSTRUCTIONS   737 Black Day accurs'd! On thee let no man hale
    P. 164 INSTRUCTIONS   967 Bold and accurs'd are they, that all this while

accursed   frequency: 1   relative frequency: 0.0000
    See also "accurs'd," "accurst."
    P. 111 ANNIVERSARY   311 Accursed Locusts, whom your King does spit

accurst   frequency: 1   relative frequency: 0.0000
    P. 140 HOUSEWARMING   98 Where this Idol of State sits ador'd and
                               accurst:

accus'd   frequency: 2   relative frequency: 0.0000
    P.   3 LOVELACE   26 You shall for being faultlesse be accus'd.
    P. 159 INSTRUCTIONS   766 Some one must be accus'd by Punishment.

accuse   frequency: 2   relative frequency: 0.0000
    P. 111 ANNIVERSARY   348 And credulous Ambassadors accuse.
    P. 148 INSTRUCTIONS   314 To cheat their Pay, feign want, the House
                               accuse.

achieved. See "atchiev'd."

acquainted   frequency: 1   relative frequency: 0.0000
    P. 313 CHEQUER INN   12 They seem'd so well acquainted

acre   frequency: 1   relative frequency: 0.0000
    P. 165 KINGS VOWES   4 Then Charles without acre

act   frequency: 11   relative frequency: 0.0002
    P. 89 ODE   76 That does both act and know.
    P. 111 ANNIVERSARY   319 Well may you act the Adam and the Eve;
    P. 115 BLAKE   66 Shall conquests act, your present are unsung.
    P. 116 BLAKE   92 They build and act all that can make them strong.
    P. 123 O.C.   9 And blame the last Act, like Spectators vain,
    P. 139 HOUSEWARMING   71 Since the Act of Oblivion was never such
                               selling,
    P. 145 INSTRUCTIONS   198 Mourning his Countess, anxious for his Act.

```
        P.  170 PROPHECY        15 When Players shall use to act the parts of
                                   Queens
        P.  176 LOYALL SCOT     189 Where but two hands to Act, two feet to goe.
        P.  199 DUKE            58 But when he came to act upon the stage,
        P.  199 DUKE            71 Although no scholler, yet can act the cooke:

acted                              frequency:    1      relative frequency: 0.0000
        P.  113 BLAKE            4 Frayted with acted Guilt, and Guilt to come:

acte's                             frequency:    1      relative frequency: 0.0000
        P.  189 BRITANNIA      171 Poppea, Tegeline and Acte's name

action                             frequency:    2      relative frequency: 0.0000
        P.  148 INSTRUCTIONS   291 To speak not forward, but in Action brave;
        P.  168 ADVICE          14 Whose life does scarce one Generous Action own,

active                             frequency:    5      relative frequency: 0.0001
        P.    5 HASTINGS        32 There better recreates his active Minde.
        P.   87 ODE             12 Urged his active Star.
        P.  104 ANNIVERSARY     23 Yet some more active for a Frontier Town
        P.  117 BLAKE          130 As Oakes did then, Urg'd by the active fire.
        P.  186 BRITANNIA       77 Dastards the hearts and active heat controules.

actor                              frequency:    1      relative frequency: 0.0000
        P.   88 ODE             53 That thence the Royal Actor born

acts                               frequency:    8      relative frequency: 0.0001
        P.   58 BILL-BOROW      64 Those Acts that swell'd the Cheek of Fame.
        P.   73 A. HOUSE       465 Then, to conclude these pleasant Acts,
        P.  103 ANNIVERSARY     14 And in one Year the work of Ages acts:
        P.  129 O.C.           241 Whose meanest acts he would himself advance,
        P.  145 INSTRUCTIONS   191 Then marcht the Troop, whose valiant Acts
                                   before,
        P.  145 INSTRUCTIONS   192 (Their publick Acts) oblig'd them still to more.
        P.  152 INSTRUCTIONS   478 Their Acts to vitiate, and them over-awe.
        P.  317 CHEQUER INN    179 And the whole business of their Acts

adam                               frequency:    1      relative frequency: 0.0000
        P.  111 ANNIVERSARY    319 Well may you act the Adam and the Eve;

adam's                             frequency:    1      relative frequency: 0.0000
        P.  203 HISTORICALL    107 The chiefest blessings Adam's Chaplin got.

adapt                              frequency:    1      relative frequency: 0.0000
        P.  175 LOYALL SCOT    170 A Congruous Dress they to themselves Adapt,

add                                frequency:    3      relative frequency: 0.0000
        See also "adde."
        P.   63 A. HOUSE       129 'But much it to our work would add
        P.   94 DR. WITTY       10 To add such lustre, and so many rayes,
        P.  169 ADVICE          46 And add new Beams to Sands's former Glory.

adde                               frequency:    1      relative frequency: 0.0000
        P.  193 TWO HORSES      75 W. To the bold talking members if the Bastards
                                   you adde,

added                              frequency:    1      relative frequency: 0.0000
        P.   94 DR. WITTY       16 That mends; and added beauties are but spots.

addeth                             frequency:    1      relative frequency: 0.0000
        P.   94 DR. WITTY       13 He is Translations thief that addeth more,

addle-brain'd                      frequency:    1      relative frequency: 0.0000
        P.  181 MADE FREE       13 Oh you Addle-Brain'd Citts

addleheaded                        frequency:    1      relative frequency: 0.0000
        P.  194 TWO HORSES      94 With an Addleheaded Knight and a Lord without
                                   Brains.

address.  See "adress."

addresses.  See "adresses."

addrest                            frequency:    1      relative frequency: 0.0000
        P.  172 LOYALL SCOT      7 Hee Understood and Willingly Addrest

adds                               frequency:    1      relative frequency: 0.0000
        P.  124 O.C.            38 And ev'ry minute adds a Lustre new;

adieu                              frequency:    2      relative frequency: 0.0000
        P.   20 THYRSIS         42 By bidding, with mee, all adieu.
```

P. 164 INSTRUCTIONS 943 Painter adieu, how will our Arts agree;

adjourn   frequency: 2   relative frequency: 0.0000
  P. 145 INSTRUCTIONS 201 Thence fell to Words, but, quarrel to adjourn,
  P. 161 INSTRUCTIONS 840 And for three days, thence moves them to adjourn.

adjusts. See "re-adjusts."

adjutant-general   frequency: 1   relative frequency: 0.0000
  P. 148 INSTRUCTIONS 300 Adjutant-General was still at hand.

admirable   frequency: 1   relative frequency: 0.0000
  P. 60 A. HOUSE   42 Those short but admirable Lines,

admiral   frequency: 1   relative frequency: 0.0000
  P. 155 INSTRUCTIONS 615 And thence the Brittish Admiral became;

admir'd   frequency: 2   relative frequency: 0.0000
  P. 123 O.C.   18 For what he least affected was admir'd,
  P. 160 INSTRUCTIONS 795 All men admir'd he to that pitch could fly:

admire   frequency: 5   relative frequency: 0.0001
  P. 115 BLAKE   75 The Peek's proud height, the Spaniards all
                           admire,
  P. 116 BLAKE   80 Make them admire, so much as they did fear.
  P. 153 INSTRUCTIONS 515 Whether his Valour they so much admire,
  P. 163 INSTRUCTIONS 917 While, the pale Ghosts, his Eye does fixt
                           admire
  P. 189 BRITANNIA   173 Make 'em admire the Sidnies, Talbots, Veres,

admires   frequency: 1   relative frequency: 0.0000
  P. 158 INSTRUCTIONS 730 And all admires, but most his easie Prey.

admiring   frequency: 1   relative frequency: 0.0000
  P. 79 A. HOUSE   672 Admiring Nature does benum.

admit. See "t'admit."

adoe   frequency: 1   relative frequency: 0.0000
  P. 177 LOYALL SCOT   227 With much adoe preserves his postern Chast.

ador'd   frequency: 1   relative frequency: 0.0000
  P. 140 HOUSEWARMING   98 Where this Idol of State sits ador'd and
                           accurst:

adore   frequency: 4   relative frequency: 0.0000
  P. 26 MISTRESS   15 Two hundred to adore each Breast:
  P. 60 A. HOUSE   35 These sacred Places to adore,
  P. 106 ANNIVERSARY   114 And her whom they should Massacre adore:
  P. 187 BRITANNIA   125 Mack James the Irish Pagod does Adore,

adoreing   frequency: 1   relative frequency: 0.0000
  P. 198 DUKE   8 Adoreing Roome, this labell in his mouth.

adores   frequency: 1   relative frequency: 0.0000
  P. 175 LOYALL SCOT   150 None knows what god our Flamen now Adores;

adoring. See "adoreing."

adorn   frequency: 5   relative frequency: 0.0001
  P. 41 THE MOWER   38 May to adorn the Gardens stand:
  P. 46 MOWER'S SONG   28 With which I shall adorn my Tomb;
  P. 88 ODE   54 The Tragick Scaffold might adorn:
  P. 157 INSTRUCTIONS 684 His burning Locks adorn his Face Divine.
  P. 173 LOYALL SCOT   50 His burning Locks Adorn his face divine.

adorn'd   frequency: 1   relative frequency: 0.0000
  P. 14 THE CORONET   8 That once adorn'd my Shepherdesses head.

adorned   frequency: 1   relative frequency: 0.0000
     See also "adorn'd."
  P. 29 THE GALLERY   14 Adorned Tyrants Cabinet;

adorns   frequency: 2   relative frequency: 0.0000
  P. 61 A. HOUSE   66 Adorns without the open Door:
  P. 75 A. HOUSE   515 Low Shrubs she sits in, and adorns

adress   frequency: 1   relative frequency: 0.0000
  P. 204 HISTORICALL   148 Bold Irish Ruffins to his Court adress:

adresses   frequency: 1   relative frequency: 0.0000

          P. 187 BRITANNIA   115 Frequent adresses to my Charles I send,

adulterate. See "adult'rate."

adulterers. See "adult'rers."

adultery   frequency: 1   relative frequency: 0.0000
          P. 152 INSTRUCTIONS   454 Cessation, as the look Adultery.

adult'rate   frequency: 1   relative frequency: 0.0000
          P. 41 THE MOWER   25 That the uncertain and adult'rate fruit

adult'rers   frequency: 1   relative frequency: 0.0000
          P. 111 ANNIVERSARY   313 Wand'rers, Adult'rers, Lyers, Munser's rest,

adust   frequency: 1   relative frequency: 0.0000
          P. 161 INSTRUCTIONS   833 And all with Sun and Choler come adust;

advance   frequency: 4   relative frequency: 0.0000
          P. 129 O.C.   241 Whose meanest acts he would himself advance,
          P. 167 KINGS VOWES   58 Some one I will advance from mean descent,
          P. 184 MADE FREE   118 Who still doth advance
          P. 204 HISTORICALL   121 Taxes Excise and Armyes dos advance.

advanced   frequency: 1   relative frequency: 0.0000
          P. 179 STOCKSMARKET   3 So Sir Robert advanced the King's statue, in
                                     token

advancement   frequency: 1   relative frequency: 0.0000
          P. 58 BILL-BOROW   54 And in their Lord's advancement grow;

advances   frequency: 1   relative frequency: 0.0000
          P. 145 INSTRUCTIONS   181 C-------n advances next, whose Coife dos awe

advantage   frequency: 2   relative frequency: 0.0000
          P. 31 FAIR SINGER   16 Who has th' advantage both of Eyes and Voice,
          P. 143 INSTRUCTIONS   113 But here the Court does its advantage know,

advent'ring   frequency: 1   relative frequency: 0.0000
          P. 143 INSTRUCTIONS   110 These now advent'ring how to win it back.

adventrous   frequency: 1   relative frequency: 0.0000
          P. 87 ODE   11 But through adventrous War

adventur'd   frequency: 2   relative frequency: 0.0000
          P. 128 O.C.   214 For these his life adventur'd every day:
          P. 156 INSTRUCTIONS   631 Daniel had there adventur'd, Man of might;

adventures   frequency: 2   relative frequency: 0.0000
          P. 153 INSTRUCTIONS   512 Why he should still b'on all adventures us'd.
          P. 181 MADE FREE   27 Tho he has past through so many Adventures;

adventuring. See "advent'ring."

adventurous. See "adventrous."

adverse   frequency: 2   relative frequency: 0.0000
          P. 128 O.C.   196 Yet him the adverse steel could never pierce.
          P. 147 INSTRUCTIONS   268 The adverse Troops, and hold them all at Bay.

advice   frequency: 5   relative frequency: 0.0001
          P. 139 HOUSEWARMING   61 He lik'd the advice, and then soon it assay'd;
          P. 168 ADVICE   t Further Advice to a Painter.
          P. 197 DUKE   t Advice to a Painter to draw the Duke by.
          P. 200 DUKE   81 And soe should wee, were his advice obey'd.
          P. 204 HISTORICALL   155 From Tybur came the advice boat Monthly home,

advis'd   frequency: 1   relative frequency: 0.0000
          P. 128 O.C.   223 Oh! ill advis'd, if not for love, for shame,

advise   frequency: 1   relative frequency: 0.0000
          P. 159 INSTRUCTIONS   779 Who did advise no Navy out to set?

aeolus   frequency: 1   relative frequency: 0.0000
          P. 154 INSTRUCTIONS   547 Aeolus their Sails inspires with Eastern Wind,

aesculapius   frequency: 1   relative frequency: 0.0000
          P.   5 HASTINGS   47 And Aesculapius, who, asham'd and stern,

aeson   frequency: 1   relative frequency: 0.0000
          P. 149 INSTRUCTIONS   337 Not so decrepid Aeson, hash'd and stew'd

aetna   frequency: 1   relative frequency: 0.0000
    P. 139 HOUSEWARMING   77 Like Jove under Aetna o'erwhelming the Gyant,

afar.   See "afarr."

afarr   frequency: 1   relative frequency: 0.0000
    P. 189 BRITANNIA   188 In Triumph lead chaind tyrants from afarr.

afeard   frequency: 1   relative frequency: 0.0000
    P. 193 TWO HORSES   70 But Tyrants ingratefull are always afeard.

affaires   frequency: 1   relative frequency: 0.0000
    P. 168 KINGS VOWES   64 I wholly will abandon State affaires,

affairs   frequency: 2   relative frequency: 0.0000
    See also "affaires."
    P. 143 INSTRUCTIONS   119 For so too Rubens, with affairs of State,
    P. 153 INSTRUCTIONS   509 The State Affairs thus Marshall'd, for the
                              rest

affect   frequency: 1   relative frequency: 0.0000
    P. 81 A. HOUSE   711 Nor yet that Wisdome would affect,

affected   frequency: 2   relative frequency: 0.0000
    P. 123 O.C.   18 For what he least affected was admir'd,
    P. 128 O.C.   208 Yet still affected most what best deserv'd.

affection   frequency: 2   relative frequency: 0.0000
    P. 124 O.C.   43 Then might y' ha' daily his Affection spy'd,
    P. 178 LOYALL SCOT   263 Hee our Affection both and will Comands,

affections   frequency: 1   relative frequency: 0.0000
    P. 128 O.C.   207 More strong affections never reason serv'd,

affirm   frequency: 3   relative frequency: 0.0000
    P. 32 MOURNING   13 Yet some affirm, pretending Art,
    P. 89 ODE   77 They can affirm his Praises best,
    P. 179 STOCKSMARKET   14 Yet all do affirm that the king is much worse,

affirms   frequency: 1   relative frequency: 0.0000
    P. 180 STOCKSMARKET   53 But Sir Robert affirms we do him much wrong;

afflictions   frequency: 1   relative frequency: 0.0000
    P. 169 ADVICE   64 Tis by afflictions passive men grow great.

afford   frequency: 5   relative frequency: 0.0001
    P. 114 BLAKE   41 And these want nothing Heaven can afford,
    P. 161 INSTRUCTIONS   845 True Trojan! while this Town can Girls afford,
    P. 168 ADVICE   29 Change once again and let the next afford
    P. 180 STOCKSMARKET   52 They will scarce afford him a rag to his breech.
    P. 314 CHEQUER INN   69 She might it well afford

affronted   frequency: 1   relative frequency: 0.0000
    P. 85 FLECKNO   91 He thought himself affronted; and reply'd,

afraid   frequency: 2   relative frequency: 0.0000
    P. 194 TWO HORSES   105 W. Truth 's as Bold as a Lyon, I am not
                              afraid;
    P. 316 CHEQUER INN   142 Twas such a Feast that I'm afraid

african   frequency: 1   relative frequency: 0.0000
    P. 137 HOUSEWARMING   22 Of African Poultney, and Tyrian Did'

after   frequency: 22   relative frequency: 0.0004
    P. 40 THE MOWER   2 Did after him the World seduce:
    P. 44 GLO-WORMS   12 And after foolish Fires do stray;
    P. 48 THE GARDEN   31 And Pan did after Syrinx speed,
    P. 49 THE GARDEN   59 After a Place so pure, and sweet,
    P. 60 A. HOUSE   33 And surely when the after Age
    P. 72 A. HOUSE   433 When after this 'tis pil'd in Cocks,
    P. 86 FLECKNO   120 After th' Assizes dinner mild appear,
    P. 86 FLECKNO   136 At ordinaries after dinner show'th,
    P. 86 FLECKNO   138 Yet he first kist them, and after takes pains
    P. 97 HOLLAND   55 'Tis probable Religion after this
    P. 117 BLAKE   121 The Air was soon after the fight begun,
    P. 129 O.C.   271 So shall his praise to after times encrease,
    P. 141 INSTRUCTIONS   1 After two sittings, now our Lady State,
    P. 142 INSTRUCTIONS   54 How after Childbirth to renew a Maid,
    P. 156 INSTRUCTIONS   624 After the Robbers, for her Whelps does yell:
    P. 159 INSTRUCTIONS   765 After this loss, to rellish discontent,
    P. 169 ADVICE   41 And after him a brave Bregade of Hors

```
      P. 178 LOYALL SCOT     283 After such Frankness shown to bee his friend,
      P. 191 STATUE           53 So the Statue up after all this delay,
      P. 192 TWO HORSES       33 And that the two Jades after mutuall Salutes
      P. 193 TWO HORSES       72 Was after rewarded with losing his own.
      P. 201 HISTORICALL      19 And his Dutch Sister quickly after dy'd,
```

again   frequency: 28   relative frequency: 0.0005
      See also "againe," "agen."

againe   frequency: 6   relative frequency: 0.0001

against   frequency: 28   relative frequency: 0.0005
      See also "'gainst."
```
      P.   3 LOVELACE         14 And against others Fame his owne employs.
      P.   3 LOVELACE         18 Of Insects which against you rise in arms.
      P.   9 DIALOGUE          4 Ballance thy Sword against the Fight.
      P.  19 THYRSIS          17 Till it hit, against the pole,
      P.  27 LOVER            15 And there she split against the Stone,
      P.  30 THE GALLERY      33 But, against that, thou sit'st a float
      P.  31 FAIR SINGER      15 But all resistance against her is vain,
      P.  40 THE MOWER         t The Mower against Gardens.
      P.  66 A. HOUSE        247 Yet, against Fate, his Spouse they kept;
      P.  66 A. HOUSE        249 Some to the Breach against their Foes
      P.  81 A. HOUSE        714 Those Trains by Youth against thee meant;
      P.  87 FLECKNO         161 Against the Rebel; who, at this struck dead,
      P.  88 ODE              37 Though Justice against Fate complain,
      P.  92 MAY'S DEATH      87 Against thee, and expels thee from their side,
      P. 104 ANNIVERSARY      28 And only are against their Subjects strong;
      P. 115 BLAKE            50 Peace, against you, was the sole strength of
                                 Spain.
      P. 116 BLAKE            85 To fight against such Foes, was vain they knew,
      P. 143 INSTRUCTIONS    108 On opposite points, the black against the white.
      P. 148 INSTRUCTIONS    325 Long thus they could against the House conspire,
      P. 152 INSTRUCTIONS    464 For Sin against th' Eleventh Commandment.
      P. 153 INSTRUCTIONS    510 Monk in his Shirt against the Dutch is prest.
      P. 176 LOYALL SCOT     202 The Mitred Hubbub against Pluto Moot
      P. 178 LOYALL SCOT     259 That senseless Rancour against Interest.
      P. 178 LOYALL SCOT     278 I single did against a Nation write,
      P. 178 LOYALL SCOT     279 Against a Nation thou didst singly fight.
      P. 187 BRITANNIA        88 Thus Heavens designs against heavens self youl
                                 turn
      P. 196 TWO HORSES      187 Then, Charles, thy edict against Coffee recall;
      P. 314 CHEQUER INN      56 Mannerly rear'd against the Wall
```

age   frequency: 27   relative frequency: 0.0005
```
      P.   3 LOVELACE         5 That candid Age no other way could tell
      P.   4 HASTINGS        10 Needs must he die, that doth out-run his Age.
      P.  26 MISTRESS        17 An Age at least to every part,
      P.  26 MISTRESS        18 And the last Age should show your Heart.
      P.  38 PICTURE         32 That Violets may a longer Age endure.
      P.  54 THYESTE          7 Pass away my silent Age.
      P.  55 EPITAPH         10 In this Age loose and all unlac't;
      P.  59 A. HOUSE        28 Of that more sober Age and Mind,
      P.  60 A. HOUSE        33 And surely when the after Age
      P.  63 A. HOUSE       157 'Our Abbess too, now far in Age,
      P.  74 A. HOUSE       496 Will in green Age her Hearse expect.
      P. 106 ANNIVERSARY    146 Who in his Age has always forward prest:
      P. 107 ANNIVERSARY    162 Live out an Age, long as a Pedigree;
      P. 110 ANNIVERSARY    294 The Shame and Plague both of the Land and
                                Age,
      P. 112 ANNIVERSARY    382 'Courage with Age, Maturity with Hast:
      P. 118 BLAKE          159 And in one War the present age may boast,
      P. 125 O.C.            89 So have I seen a Vine, whose lasting Age
      P. 141 INSTRUCTIONS    37 But Age, allaying now that youthful heat,
      P. 142 INSTRUCTIONS    47 But thought the Golden Age was now restor'd,
      P. 149 INSTRUCTIONS   339 And with fresh Age felt his glad Limbs unite;
      P. 175 LOYALL SCOT    162 How oft hath age his hallowing hands Misled
      P. 177 LOYALL SCOT    226 Ev'n Father Dis tho so with Age defac'd
      P. 188 BRITANNIA      163 Watch and Preside over their tender age
      P. 196 TWO HORSES     163 If Speech from Brute Animals in Romes first
                                age
      P. 199 DUKE            51 You might have lingred out a lazy age,
      P. 199 DUKE            59 He proved the mad Cethegus of his age.
      P. 312 CHEQUER INN      5 In any Age on English ground
```

aged   frequency: 3   relative frequency: 0.0000
```
      P.  25 YOUNG LOVE       3 Clear thine aged Fathers brow
      P.  57 BILL-BOROW      34 A Plump of aged Trees does wave.
      P. 159 INSTRUCTIONS    743 When aged Thames was bound with Fetters base,
```

agen   frequency: 5   relative frequency: 0.0001

ages   frequency: 7   relative frequency: 0.0001
    P.   79 A. HOUSE   656 Of all her Sex, her Ages Aw.
    P.   83 FLECKNO   30 The future Ages how I did indure:
    P. 103 ANNIVERSARY   14 And in one Year the work of Ages acts:
    P. 118 BLAKE   157 Ages to come, your conquering Arms will bless,
    P. 123 O.C.   27 And leave succeeding Ages cause to mourn,
    P. 130 O.C.   277 Thee, many ages hence, in martial verse
    P. 200 DUKE   114 See in all ages what examples are

aghast   frequency: 1   relative frequency: 0.0000
    P.   34 DAPHNIS   38 With the shrieks of Friends aghast,

agitation   frequency: 1   relative frequency: 0.0000
    P.   98 HOLLAND   133 Besides that very Agitation laves,

ago   frequency: 1   relative frequency: 0.0000
    P.   97 HOLLAND   83 Some Fifteen hundred and more years ago;

agree   frequency: 9   relative frequency: 0.0001
    P.   31 FAIR SINGER   3 In whom both Beauties to my death agree,
    P.   47 EMPIRE   5 Jubal first made the wilder Notes agree;
    P.   91 MAY'S DEATH   52 How ill the measures of these States agree.
    P. 105 ANNIVERSARY   98 Knit by the Roofs Protecting weight agree.
    P. 160 INSTRUCTIONS   821 All to agree the Articles were clear,
    P. 161 INSTRUCTIONS   856 No Dial more could with the Sun agree.
    P. 162 INSTRUCTIONS   892 Though ill agree her Posture, Hour, or Place:
    P. 164 INSTRUCTIONS   943 Painter adieu, how will our Arts agree;
    P. 179 STOCKSMARKET   19 And so loose in his seat that all men agree

agreed   frequency: 4   relative frequency: 0.0000
    P. 128 O.C.   218 To keep so deare, so diff'ring minds agreed?
    P. 145 INSTRUCTIONS   202 Their Friends agreed they should command by
                               turn.
    P. 192 TWO HORSES   30 One night came togeather by all is agreed,
    P. 192 TWO HORSES   38 When both knaves agreed to be each others
                               brother.

agree't   frequency: 1   relative frequency: 0.0000
    P. 190 STATUE   15 Or the Bishops and Treasurer did they Agree't

ah   frequency: 11   relative frequency: 0.0002

aid   frequency: 3   relative frequency: 0.0000
    See also "aide."
    P.   4 LOVELACE   48 Above their envy, or mine aid doth clime.
    P. 147 INSTRUCTIONS   259 Keen Whorwood next, in aid of Damsel frail,
    P. 155 INSTRUCTIONS   592 For its last aid: Hold Chain or we are broke.

aide   frequency: 1   relative frequency: 0.0000
    P. 205 HISTORICALL   159 Tells him the holy Church demands his aide,

aim   frequency: 4   relative frequency: 0.0000
    See also "aime."
    P.   18 CLORINDA   5 The Grass I aim to feast thy Sheep:
    P.   44 GLO-WORMS   11 That in the Night have lost their aim,
    P.   92 MAY'S DEATH   60 Because a Gazet writer mist his aim?
    P. 141 INSTRUCTIONS   16 With Hook then, through the microscope, take aim

aime   frequency: 1   relative frequency: 0.0000
    P. 169 ADVICE   50 That aime at mountains and bring forth a Mous,

aiming   frequency: 2   relative frequency: 0.0000
    P.   67 A. HOUSE   288 As aiming one for ev'ry Sense.
    P.   77 A. HOUSE   603 Where Beauty, aiming at the Heart,

air   frequency: 30   relative frequency: 0.0006
    See also "aire."
    P.   9 DIALOGUE   6 With silken Banners spreads the air.
    P.   17 BERMUDAS   16 On daily Visits through the Air.
    P.   28 LOVER   33 They fed him up with Hopes and Air,
    P.   30 THE GALLERY   36 Betwixt the Air and Water fly.
    P.   30 THE GALLERY   54 Hangs loosely playing in the Air,
    P.   31 FAIR SINGER   12 My Fetters of the very Air I breath?
    P.   36 DAPHNIS   104 And but rid to take the Air.
    P.   40 THE MOWER   6 A dead and standing pool of Air:
    P.   47 EMPIRE   17 Then Musick, the Mosaique of the Air,
    P.   76 A. HOUSE   566 Streight floting on the Air shall fly:
    P.   77 A. HOUSE   596 Flatters with Air my panting Brows.
    P.   80 A. HOUSE   673 The viscous Air, wheres'ere She fly,
    P.   84 FLECKNO   40 Mov'd by the Air and hidden Sympathies;
    P.   84 FLECKNO   68 Should leave his Soul to wander in the Air,

P. 88 ODE   21 Then burning through the Air he went,
P. 98 HOLLAND   129 As the obsequious Air and Waters rest,
P. 108 ANNIVERSARY   197 Nor through wide Nostrils snuffe the wanton air,
P. 109 ANNIVERSARY   235 Then did thick Mists and Winds the air deform,
P. 112 ANNIVERSARY   372 'Can quickly leave us neither Earth nor Air.
P. 114 BLAKE   34 Where still the Earth is moist, the Air still
                          dry;
P. 117 BLAKE   121 The Air was soon after the fight begun,
P. 121 TWO SONGS   56 His Progeny above the Air;
P. 124 O.C.   70 Devides the Air, and opens all the Skyes:
P. 126 O.C.   131 And as through Air his wasting Spirits flow'd,
P. 138 HOUSEWARMING   31 He himself would not dwell in a Castle of air,
P. 153 INSTRUCTIONS   530 He finds the Air, and all things, sweeter here.
P. 154 INSTRUCTIONS   538 And with inveigling Colours Court the Air.
P. 158 INSTRUCTIONS   733 Then with rude shouts, secure, the Air they vex;
P. 174 LOYALL SCOT   85 That between us the Common Air shold bar
P. 176 LOYALL SCOT   201 Shattering the silent Air disturbs our Joys!

aire   frequency: 2   relative frequency: 0.0000
P. 129 O.C.   235 Yet always temper'd with an aire so mild,
P. 129 O.C.   265 When angry Jove darts lightning through the
                          aire,

aires   frequency: 1   relative frequency: 0.0000
P. 10 DIALOGUE   38 For thy Stay these charming Aires;

airs   frequency: 1   relative frequency: 0.0000
See also "aires."
P. 172 LOYALL SCOT   11 For those soft Airs had temper'd every thought,

air's. See "ayre's."

airy   frequency: 4   relative frequency: 0.0000
P. 125 O.C.   82 Or fan with airy plumes so soft an heat.
P. 126 O.C.   118 And thrash'd the Harvest in the airy floore;
P. 154 INSTRUCTIONS   554 The airy Sterns the Sun behind does guild;
P. 163 INSTRUCTIONS   904 And th' airy Picture vanisht from his hold.

ajax   frequency: 1   relative frequency: 0.0000
P. 28 LOVER   48 Like Ajax, the mad Tempest braves.

alabaster   frequency: 1   relative frequency: 0.0000
P. 24 NYMPH   120 Of purest Alabaster made:

alamode   frequency: 1   relative frequency: 0.0000
P. 204 HISTORICALL   120 Sets up in Scotland alamode de France,

alarm   frequency: 1   relative frequency: 0.0000
P. 147 INSTRUCTIONS   247 First spy'd the Enemy and gave th' Alarm:

alarms   frequency: 2   relative frequency: 0.0000
P. 112 ANNIVERSARY   375 'That one Man still, although but nam'd, alarms
P. 169 ADVICE   36 Frightens all Christendome with fresh Alarms,

alas   frequency: 14   relative frequency: 0.0002

alban   frequency: 1   relative frequency: 0.0000
P. 142 INSTRUCTIONS   46 Two Saints at once, St. German, St. Alban.

albans   frequency: 7   relative frequency: 0.0001
P. 141 INSTRUCTIONS   29 Paint then St. Albans full of soup and gold,
P. 141 INSTRUCTIONS   35 Well he the Title of St. Albans bore,
P. 148 INSTRUCTIONS   311 St. Albans straight is sent to, to forbear,
P. 149 INSTRUCTIONS   365 France had St. Albans promis'd (so they sing)
P. 149 INSTRUCTIONS   366 St Albans promis'd him, and he the King.
P. 151 INSTRUCTIONS   427 St. Albans writ to that he may bewail
P. 151 INSTRUCTIONS   440 And to St. Albans too undutiful;

albemarle   frequency: 1   relative frequency: 0.0000
P. 146 INSTRUCTIONS   222 To rescue Albemarle from the Sea-Cod:

albemarles   frequency: 1   relative frequency: 0.0000
P. 158 INSTRUCTIONS   725 And spight of Ruperts and of Albemarles,

alce   frequency: 1   relative frequency: 0.0000
P. 166 KINGS VOWES   38 As bold as Alce Pierce and as faire as Jane
                          Shore;

alcides   frequency: 2   relative frequency: 0.0000
P. 157 INSTRUCTIONS   695 When Oeta and Alcides are forgot,
P. 173 LOYALL SCOT   61 When Oeta and Alcides are forgott,

alcorand   frequency: 1   relative frequency: 0.0000
    P. 110 ANNIVERSARY   310 For prophecies fit to be Alcorand.

ale   frequency: 2   relative frequency: 0.0000
    P. 196 TWO HORSES   188 Theres ten times more Treason in Brandy and
                               ale.
    P. 312 CHEQUER INN   3 The Choyce of Ale and Beere

alexander   frequency: 2   relative frequency: 0.0000
    P. 143 INSTRUCTIONS   103 Ah Painter, now could Alexander live,
    P. 171 PROPHECY   32 A Greater Thief then Alexander was.

alexanders   frequency: 1   relative frequency: 0.0000
    P.   72 A. HOUSE   428 Smells like an Alexanders sweat.

aley. See "aly."

algeryne   frequency: 1   relative frequency: 0.0000
    P. 199 DUKE   79 Rich with the Spoile of a poore Algeryne,

alien   frequency: 1   relative frequency: 0.0000
    P. 184 MADE FREE   117 To colour the good of an Alien,

alike   frequency: 3   relative frequency: 0.0000
    P. 113 ANNIVERSARY   398 So that we both alike may miss our End:
    P. 145 INSTRUCTIONS   168 And both of them alike French Martyrs were.
    P. 195 TWO HORSES   126 And Free men alike value life and Estate.

alive   frequency: 5   relative frequency: 0.0001
    P.   22 NYMPH   4 To kill thee. Thou neer didst alive
    P.   59 A. HOUSE   18 Demands more room alive then dead.
    P.   70 A. HOUSE   378 We wonder how they rise alive.
    P. 111 ANNIVERSARY   323 And, to your spight, returning yet alive
    P. 195 TWO HORSES   142 W. But hee 's buryed alive in lust and in
                              sloath.

all   frequency: 383   relative frequency: 0.0080
    See also "clowns-all-heal."
    P.   3 LOVELACE   25 Till when in vaine they have thee all perus'd,
    P.   4 LOVELACE   39 They all in mutiny though yet undrest
    P.   5 HASTINGS   26 And all that Worth from hence did Ostracize.
    P.   5 HASTINGS   36 Of all these Sublunary Elements.
    P.   5 HASTINGS   39 And gladly there can all his Kinred claim,
    P.   5 HASTINGS   56 All Herbs, and them a thousand ways infus'd?
    P.   5 HASTINGS   57 All he had try'd, but all in vain, he saw,
    P.   10 DIALOGUE   36 The rest is all but Earth disguis'd.
    P.   10 DIALOGUE   42 On this I would it all dispose.
    P.   11 DIALOGUE   51 All this fair, and soft, and sweet,
    P.   11 DIALOGUE   59 Till thou purchase all below,
    P.   11 DIALOGUE   63 Wilt thou all the Glory have
    P.   13 DROP OF DEW   36 It all about does upwards bend.
    P.   14 THE CORONET   7 Dismantling all the fragrant Towers
    P.   14 THE CORONET   9 And now when I have summ'd up all my store,
    P.   14 THE CORONET   21 And disintangle all his winding Snare:
    P.   15 EYES   7 These Tears which better measure all,
    P.   15 EYES   12 Are the true price of all my Joyes.
    P.   15 EYES   15 And all the Jewels which we prize,
    P.   15 EYES   19 And yet, from all the flow'rs I saw,
    P.   18 BERMUDAS   39 And all the way, to guide their Chime,
    P.   18 CLORINDA   4 Where Flora blazons all her pride.
    P.   18 CLORINDA   30 For all the World is our Pan's Quire.
    P.   20 THYRSIS   42 By bidding, with mee, all adieu.
    P.   21 SOUL & BODY   25 And all my Care its self employes,
    P.   22 NYMPH   8 Nor do I for all this; nor will:
    P.   23 NYMPH   75 And all the Spring time of the year
    P.   24 NYMPH   87 But all its chief delight was still
    P.   25 YOUNG LOVE   28 So all Forraign Claims to drown,
    P.   26 MISTRESS   23 And yonder all before us lye
    P.   26 MISTRESS   30 And into ashes all my Lust.
    P.   26 YOUNG LOVE   29 So, to make all Rivals vain,
    P.   27 MISTRESS   41 Let us roll all our Strength, and all
    P.   28 LOVER   44 At sharp before it all the day:
    P.   28 LOVER   46 With all his wing'd Artillery.
    P.   28 LOVER   55 And all he saies, a Lover drest
    P.   29 THE GALLERY   3 Now all its several lodgings lye
    P.   29 THE GALLERY   7 That, for all furniture, you'l find
    P.   29 THE GALLERY   21 While all the morning Quire does sing,
    P.   30 THE GALLERY   35 The Halcyons, calming all that's nigh,
    P.   30 THE GALLERY   43 In all the Forms thou can'st invent
    P.   31 FAIR SINGER   1 To make a final conquest of all me,
    P.   31 FAIR SINGER   15 But all resistance against her is vain,

```
P.  31 FAIR SINGER      17 And all my Forces needs must be undone,
P.  33 DAPHNIS           3 That must all his Hopes devour,
P.  33 DAPHNIS           4 All his Labour, all his Art.
P.  33 DAPHNIS          11 And would gladly yield to all,
P.  33 DAPHNIS          17 He, well read in all the wayes
P.  34 DAPHNIS          52 More than all thy Cruelty?
P.  34 DAPHNIS          55 And allow him all he will,
P.  35 DAPHNIS          74 All th' Enjoyment of our Love
P.  36 DAPHNIS          89 Farewel therefore all the fruit
P.  36 DAPHNIS          95 Yet bring with me all the Fire
P.  36 DAPHNIS         101 But hence Virgins all beware.
P.  37 DEFINITION       23 And, us to joyn, the World should all
P.  39 PICTURE          40 Nip in the blossome all our hopes and Thee.
P.  39 THE MATCH         2 Of all her choisest store;
P.  39 THE MATCH         8 All as she thought secure.
P.  40 THE MATCH        24 And all that burns the Mind.
P.  40 THE MATCH        28 All Nature could inflame.
P.  40 THE MATCH        33 Thus all his fewel did unite
P.  40 THE MATCH        38 Whilst all the World is poor,
P.  40 THE MATCH        40 All Love's and Nature's store.
P.  41 THE MOWER        31 'Tis all enforc'd; the Fountain and the Grot;
P.  41 THE MOWER        33 Where willing Nature does to all dispence
P.  43 DAMON            42 Through all the Meadows I have mown.
P.  43 DAMON            52 More ground then all his Sheep do hide.
P.  43 DAMON            54 Of all these Closes ev'ry Year.
P.  43 DAMON            67 But now I all the day complain,
P.  44 DAMON            74 Depopulating all the Ground,
P.  44 GLO-WORMS         3 And studying all the Summer-night,
P.  45 MOWER'S SONG      2 Of all these Medows fresh and gay;
P.  45 MOWER'S SONG     21 And Flow'rs, and Grass, and I and all,
P.  47 EMPIRE            3 All Musick was a solitary sound,
P.  47 EMPIRE           18 Did of all these a solemn noise prepare:
P.  47 EMPIRE           20 Including all between the Earth and Sphear.
P.  48 THE GARDEN        7 While all Flow'rs and all Trees do close
P.  48 THE GARDEN       15 Society is all but rude,
P.  49 THE GARDEN       47 Annihilating all that's made
P.  54 THYESTE           3 All I seek is to lye still.
P.  55 EPITAPH          10 In this Age loose and all unlac't;
P.  55 EPITAPH          19 'Tis true: but all so weakly said;
P.  55 THYESTE           9 I have liv'd out all my span,
P.  57 BILL-BOROW       22 And all the way it rises bends;
P.  57 BILL-BOROW       25 Yet thus it all the field commands,
P.  57 BILL-BOROW       40 Ratling through all the Grove and Hill.
P.  58 BILL-BOROW       69 For all the Civick Garlands due
P.  59 A. HOUSE          9 Why should of all things Man unrul'd
P.  59 A. HOUSE         21 What need of all this Marble Crust
P.  59 A. HOUSE         25 But all things are composed here
P.  61 A. HOUSE         87 And all that Neighbour-Ruine shows
P.  62 A. HOUSE        121 'When we have prayed all our Beads,
P.  62 A. HOUSE        123 'While all the rest with Needles paint
P.  63 A. HOUSE        145 'All Beauty, when at such a height,
P.  64 A. HOUSE        165 'Those Virtues to us all so dear,
P.  64 A. HOUSE        177 'For such indeed are all our Arts;
P.  64 A. HOUSE        191 'All Night embracing Arm in Arm,
P.  65 A. HOUSE        193 'But what is this to all the store
P.  65 A. HOUSE        215 'For like themselves they alter all,
P.  66 A. HOUSE        242 Shall fight through all the Universe;
P.  69 A. HOUSE        332 And all the Garrisons were Flowrs,
P.  69 A. HOUSE        339 The Nursery of all things green
P.  69 A. HOUSE        343 But war all this doth overgrow:
P.  71 A. HOUSE        397 The Edge all bloody from its Breast
P.  74 A. HOUSE        487 And where all Creatures might have shares,
P.  74 A. HOUSE        500 To one great Trunk them all did mold.
P.  74 A. HOUSE        505 Dark all without it knits; within
P.  75 A. HOUSE        541 And all the way, to keep it clean,
P.  77 A. HOUSE        580 Like Mexique Paintings, all the Plumes.
P.  77 A. HOUSE        587 The Oak-Leaves me embroyder all,
P.  77 A. HOUSE        608 And gaul its Horsemen all the Day.
P.  78 A. HOUSE        637 Where all things gaze themselves, and doubt
P.  79 A. HOUSE        656 Of all her Sex, her Ages Aw.
P.  80 A. HOUSE        702 Where She may all her Beautyes look;
P.  81 A. HOUSE        708 In all the Languages as hers;
P.  81 A. HOUSE        717 True Praise (That breaks through all defence;)
P.  81 A. HOUSE        730 Do all your useless Study place,
P.  81 A. HOUSE        736 And Virtue all those Furrows till'd.
P.  82 A. HOUSE        751 That, as all Virgins She precedes,
P.  82 A. HOUSE        752 So you all Woods, Streams, Gardens, Meads.
P.  82 A. HOUSE        763 All negligently overthrown,
P.  85 FLECKNO          73 Thus armed underneath, he over all
P.  86 FLECKNO         129 Of all his Poems there he stands ungirt
P.  86 FLECKNO         141 But all his praises could not now appease
```

P.	87	ODE	17	For 'tis all one to Courage high
P.	88	ODE	45	What Field of all the Civil Wars,
P.	90	MAY'S DEATH	9	At last while doubtfully he all compares,
P.	90	ODE	103	And to all States not free
P.	91	MAY'S DEATH	30	Sworn Enemy to all that do pretend,
P.	91	MAY'S DEATH	46	Until you all grow Consuls in your wine.
P.	91	MAY'S DEATH	58	The sacred Laurel, hence are all these teares?
P.	91	MAY'S DEATH	59	Must therefore all the World be set on flame,
P.	92	MAY'S DEATH	91	The Cerberus with all his Jawes shall gnash,
P.	92	MAY'S DEATH	92	Magaera thee with all her Serpents lash.
P.	94	DR. WITTY	31	Now I reform, and surely so will all
P.	97	HOLLAND	80	Themselves the Hogs as all their Subjects Bores!
P.	98	HOLLAND	95	Tunn'd up with all their sev'ral Towns of Beer;
P.	98	HOLLAND	103	Let this one court'sie witness all the rest;
P.	98	HOLLAND	107	No, but all ancient Rights and Leagues must vail,
P.	98	HOLLAND	130	Till the dear Halcyon hatch out all its nest.
P.	99	HOLLAND	140	Their Navy all our Conquest or our Wreck:
P.	103	ANNIVERSARY	17	And though they all Platonique years should raign,
P.	105	ANNIVERSARY	77	All other Matter yields, and may be rul'd;
P.	105	ANNIVERSARY	85	Yet all compos'd by his attractive Song,
P.	105	ANNIVERSARY	87	The Common-wealth does through their Centers all
P.	107	ANNIVERSARY	150	Look on, all unconcern'd, or unprepar'd;
P.	107	ANNIVERSARY	173	Thee proof beyond all other Force or Skill,
P.	107	ANNIVERSARY	176	At once assay'd to overturn us all.
P.	108	ANNIVERSARY	203	And all about was heard a Panique groan,
P.	108	ANNIVERSARY	221	For all delight of Life thou then didst lose,
P.	109	ANNIVERSARY	259	Though why should others all thy Labor spoil,
P.	110	ANNIVERSARY	271	The Passengers all wearyed out before,
P.	110	ANNIVERSARY	279	'Tis not a Freedome, that where All command;
P.	111	ANNIVERSARY	324	Does with himself all that is good revive.
P.	111	ANNIVERSARY	327	All day he follow'd with unwearied sight,
P.	112	ANNIVERSARY	367	'Needs must we all their Tributaries be,
P.	112	ANNIVERSARY	376	'More then all Men, all Navies, and all Arms.
P.	112	ANNIVERSARY	377	'Him, all the Day, Him, in late Nights I dread,
P.	112	ANNIVERSARY	384	'And still his Fauchion all our Knots unties.
P.	113	ANNIVERSARY	366	'Whose watry Leaguers all the world surround?
P.	113	BLAKE	11	Wealth which all others Avarice might cloy,
P.	114	BLAKE	39	Your worth to all these Isles, a just right brings,
P.	114	BLAKE	46	Have broken all her Swords, then this one Peace,
P.	115	BLAKE	56	All that is good, and are not curst with Gold.
P.	115	BLAKE	70	That place saluted, where they all must dye.
P.	115	BLAKE	75	The Peek's proud height, the Spaniards all admire,
P.	116	BLAKE	88	To all besides, triumphantly do live.
P.	116	BLAKE	89	With hast they therefore all their Gallions moar,
P.	116	BLAKE	91	Forts, Lines, and Sconces all the Bay along,
P.	116	BLAKE	92	They build and act all that can make them strong.
P.	117	BLAKE	114	And all assumes your courage, in your cause.
P.	118	BLAKE	161	All the Foes Ships destroy'd, by Sea or fire,
P.	120	TWO SONGS	23	My wakeful Lamp all night must move,
P.	122	TWO SONGS	14	There is Bayes enough for all.
P.	122	TWO SONGS	32	Whil'st all the Nymphs on Damon's choice attend?
P.	122	TWO SONGS	28+	All.
P.	123	O.C.	3	Now in its self (the Glass where all appears)
P.	123	O.C.	15	And he whom Nature all for Peace had made,
P.	124	O.C.	70	Devides the Air, and opens all the Skyes:
P.	126	O.C.	129	Such Tortures all the Elements unfix'd,
P.	126	O.C.	142	Of honour; all the Year was Cromwell's day:
P.	126	O.C.	143	But this, of all the most auspicious found,
P.	127	O.C.	155	Here ended all his mortal toyles: He lay'd
P.	127	O.C.	163	As jealous only here lest all be less,
P.	127	O.C.	183	Those Strokes he said will pierce through all below
P.	128	O.C.	193	In all his warrs needs must he triumph, when
P.	128	O.C.	204	His tendernesse extended unto all.
P.	128	O.C.	222	All law is uselesse, all reward is due.
P.	128	O.C.	228	At once with him, and all that's good beside;
P.	129	O.C.	243	All, all is gone of ours or his delight
P.	129	O.C.	253	All wither'd, all discolour'd, pale and wan,
P.	129	O.C.	267	(It groanes, and bruises all below that stood
P.	131	PARADISE	5	Heav'n, Hell, Earth, Chaos, All; the Argument
P.	132	PARADISE	28	And all that was improper dost omit:

P. 132 PARADISE	47 While the Town-Bays writes all the while and spells,
P. 138 HOUSEWARMING	26 And all for to save the expences of Brickbat,
P. 138 HOUSEWARMING	29 But while these devices he all doth compare,
P. 138 HOUSEWARMING	33 Already he had got all our Money and Cattel,
P. 138 HOUSEWARMING	55 Unless all abroad he divulg'd the design,
P. 139 HOUSEWARMING	68 As all Chedder Dairys club to the incorporate Cheese
P. 139 HOUSEWARMING	89 And upon the Tarras, to consummate all,
P. 140 HIS HOUSE	8 The Queens Marriage and all;
P. 140 HOUSEWARMING	101 Now some (as all Buildings must censure abide)
P. 141 INSTRUCTIONS	17 Where, like the new Controller, all men laugh
P. 141 INSTRUCTIONS	28 What all thy softest touches cannot do.
P. 144 INSTRUCTIONS	122 And thought all lost that goest not to the Cheats:
P. 144 INSTRUCTIONS	136 And on all Trade like Casawar she feeds:
P. 144 INSTRUCTIONS	138 Else swallows all down her indented maw.
P. 144 INSTRUCTIONS	139 She stalks all day in Streets conceal'd from sight,
P. 144 INSTRUCTIONS	143 Black Birch, of all the Earth-born race most hot,
P. 145 INSTRUCTIONS	171 His Birth, his Youth, his Brokage all dispraise,
P. 145 INSTRUCTIONS	175 Bronkard Loves Squire; through all the field array'd,
P. 145 INSTRUCTIONS	177 Then march't the Troop of Clarendon, all full,
P. 145 INSTRUCTIONS	193 For Chimney's sake they all Sir Pool obey'd,
P. 146 INSTRUCTIONS	204 And in ill English all the World defy'd,
P. 146 INSTRUCTIONS	217 The Lords Sons, last, all these did reinforce:
P. 146 INSTRUCTIONS	225 All the two Coventrys their Gen'rals chose:
P. 146 INSTRUCTIONS	227 Nor better choice all accidents could hit;
P. 146 INSTRUCTIONS	230 To fight a Battel, from all Gun-shot free.
P. 146 INSTRUCTIONS	236 The Speaker early, when they all fell in.
P. 146 INSTRUCTIONS	238 Excise had got the day, and all been lost.
P. 146 INSTRUCTIONS	239 For th' other side all in loose Quarters lay,
P. 147 INSTRUCTIONS	245 But Strangeways, that all Night still walk'd the round,
P. 147 INSTRUCTIONS	252 And all to pattern his Example boast.
P. 147 INSTRUCTIONS	268 The adverse Troops, and hold them all at Bay.
P. 147 INSTRUCTIONS	283 And, charging all their Pikes, a sullen Band
P. 148 INSTRUCTIONS	285 Nor could all these the Field have long maintain'd,
P. 148 INSTRUCTIONS	297 Then closing, all in equal Front fall on,
P. 148 INSTRUCTIONS	317 Mean time through all the Yards their Orders run
P. 148 INSTRUCTIONS	322 The Stores and Wages all are mine and thine.
P. 149 INSTRUCTIONS	334 But all the Members Lives, consulting, spare.
P. 149 INSTRUCTIONS	346 But blooms all Night, and shoots its branches high.
P. 149 INSTRUCTIONS	367 The Count forthwith is order'd all to close,
P. 150 INSTRUCTIONS	374 All to new Sports their wanton fears release.
P. 150 INSTRUCTIONS	400 And thought all safe if they were so far off.
P. 151 INSTRUCTIONS	416 Change all for Guinea's, and a Crown for each:
P. 151 INSTRUCTIONS	419 White-hall's unsafe, the Court all meditates
P. 151 INSTRUCTIONS	421 Each does the other blame, and all distrust;
P. 151 INSTRUCTIONS	426 Orders, amaz'd at last gives none at all.
P. 152 INSTRUCTIONS	462 Their Fleet, to threaten, we will give them all.
P. 152 INSTRUCTIONS	486 Now thinks all but too little for their Fear.
P. 153 INSTRUCTIONS	512 Why he should still b'on all adventures us'd.
P. 153 INSTRUCTIONS	516 Or that for Cowardice they all retire.
P. 153 INSTRUCTIONS	519 All Causes sure concur, but most they think
P. 153 INSTRUCTIONS	528 Bosomes, and all which from themselves they hide.
P. 153 INSTRUCTIONS	530 He finds the Air, and all things, sweeter here.
P. 154 INSTRUCTIONS	535 His sporting Navy all about him swim,
P. 154 INSTRUCTIONS	549 With Pearly Shell the Tritons all the while
P. 154 INSTRUCTIONS	556 When, all on sudden, their calm bosome rives
P. 155 INSTRUCTIONS	578 That rul'd all Seas, and did our Channel grace.
P. 155 INSTRUCTIONS	586 And all our hopes now on frail Chain depend:
P. 156 INSTRUCTIONS	638 And all those lines by which men are mistook.
P. 156 INSTRUCTIONS	645 Captain, Lieutenant, Ensign, all make haste,
P. 158 INSTRUCTIONS	701 Of all our Navy none should now survive,
P. 158 INSTRUCTIONS	729 Her moving Shape; all these he does survey,
P. 158 INSTRUCTIONS	730 And all admires, but most his easie Prey.
P. 158 INSTRUCTIONS	731 The Seamen search her all, within, without:
P. 159 INSTRUCTIONS	748 When all the Rivers grac'd their Nuptial Bed;
P. 159 INSTRUCTIONS	767 All our miscarriages on Pett must fall:
P. 159 INSTRUCTIONS	768 His Name alone seems fit to answer all.
P. 159 INSTRUCTIONS	770 Who all Commands sold thro' the Navy? Pett.
P. 159 INSTRUCTIONS	777 Who all our Seamen cheated of their Debt?
P. 159 INSTRUCTIONS	778 And all our Prizes who did swallow? Pett.
P. 160 INSTRUCTIONS	783 Who all our Ships expos'd in Chathams Net?

```
P. 160 INSTRUCTIONS   786 Was the first cause of all these Naval slips:
P. 160 INSTRUCTIONS   795 All men admir'd he to that pitch could fly:
P. 160 INSTRUCTIONS   801 Who hath no Chimneys, to give all is best,
P. 160 INSTRUCTIONS   810 All Arts they try how to prolong its Date.
P. 160 INSTRUCTIONS   821 All to agree the Articles were clear,
P. 161 INSTRUCTIONS   823 Yet Harry must job back and all mature,
P. 161 INSTRUCTIONS   833 And all with Sun and Choler come adust;
P. 162 INSTRUCTIONS   870 But all the while his Private-Bill's in sight.
P. 162 INSTRUCTIONS   889 There, as in the calm horrour all alone,
P. 163 INSTRUCTIONS   915 Shake then the room, and all his Curtains tear,
P. 164 INSTRUCTIONS   966 And, where all England serves, themselves would
                          reign.
P. 164 INSTRUCTIONS   967 Bold and accurs'd are they, that all this while
P. 165 KINGS VOWES      7 I will have a Religion then all of my owne,
P. 165 KINGS VOWES     15 But if they displease me, I will have all their
                          Lands.
P. 165 KINGS VOWES     16 I will have a fine Chancelor beare all the sway,
P. 166 KINGS VOWES     32 I will winke all the while my Revenue is stole,
P. 167 KINGS VOWES     60 And all their bills for publike good prevent.
P. 168 ADVICE          24 All looking this way how to give their votes,
P. 168 KINGS VOWES     62 That all his dareing crimes, what ere they be,
P. 169 ADVICE          36 Frightens all Christendome with fresh Alarms,
P. 169 ADVICE          42 Arm'd at all points ready to reinforce
P. 169 ADVICE          57 Thus all imploy themselves, and without pitty
P. 171 PROPHECY        41 When Bishops shall lay all Religion by
P. 174 LOYALL SCOT     91 All Letanies in this have wanted faith:
P. 174 LOYALL SCOT    108 Instead of all the Plagues had Bishops come,
P. 174 LOYALL SCOT    114 Their Rank Ambition all this heat hath stir'd
P. 175 LOYALL SCOT    134 All Mischeifs Moulded by those state divines:
P. 175 LOYALL SCOT    167 And their Religion all but Masquerade.
P. 176 LOYALL SCOT    213 But to reform is all Indifferent
P. 177 LOYALL SCOT    222 Incorrigible among all their paines
P. 177 LOYALL SCOT    232 -leness and all the vice that did abound,
P. 177 LOYALL SCOT    236 The world in all doth but two Nations bear,
P. 177 LOYALL SCOT    246 Nation is all but name as Shibboleth,
P. 178 LOYALL SCOT    261 English and Scotch, 'tis all but Crosse and
                          Pile
P. 178 LOYALL SCOT    271 And all themselves in meal and friendship close.
P. 179 STOCKSMARKET    10 To be all a revenge and a malice forecast,
P. 179 STOCKSMARKET    14 Yet all do affirm that the king is much worse,
P. 179 STOCKSMARKET    19 And so loose in his seat that all men agree
P. 179 STOCKSMARKET    26 Than all the Dutch pictures that caused the war,
P. 180 STOCKSMARKET    29 But Sir Robert to take all the scandal away
P. 180 STOCKSMARKET    50 Whose loyalty now all expires with his spankers.
P. 180 STOCKSMARKET    57 But with all his faults restore us our King,
P. 181 MADE FREE       21 That all the World there did leave him;
P. 181 MADE FREE       31 He spends all his Days
P. 181 MADE FREE       34 And wasts all his Nights
P. 182 MADE FREE       48 And his Creditors all left to Sorrow.
P. 182 MADE FREE       60 They had Burglard all your Propriety.
P. 182 MADE FREE       63 As had cancelld all former Disasters
P. 182 MADE FREE       64 All your Wives had been Strumpetts
P. 182 MADE FREE       66 And the Souldiers had all beene your Masters.
P. 182 MADE FREE       69 Which must all be defrayd by London,
P. 183 MADE FREE       84 For his virtues exceed all his vices.
P. 184 MADE FREE      112 When in Heart you all knew
P. 184 MADE FREE      121 But all ye Blind Apes,
P. 184 MADE FREE      132 Unless you all burne again, burne again.
P. 187 BRITANNIA       90 When all their Gobling Intrest in Mankind
P. 187 BRITANNIA      106 Of French, Scots, Irish (all my mortall foes):
P. 187 BRITANNIA      118 Had lost all sense of Honour, Justice, fame;
P. 188 BRITANNIA      128 Fiend Lauderdale, with ordure all defiles.
P. 189 BRITANNIA      172 Yeild to all these in Lewdness, lust, and shame.
P. 189 BRITANNIA      176 On whose fam'd Deeds all tongues, all writers
                          wait.
P. 189 STATUE           3 Dear Wheeler impart, for wee're all at a loss
P. 191 STATUE          53 So the Statue will up after all this delay,
P. 191 TWO HORSES      15 All Popish beleivers think something divine,
P. 192 TWO HORSES      30 One night came togeather by all is agreed,
P. 192 TWO HORSES      31 When both the Kings weary of Sitting all day
P. 193 TWO HORSES      60 And yet all his Court be as poore as Church
                          Ratts;
P. 195 TWO HORSES     136 Under all that shall Reign of the false
                          Scottish race.
P. 195 TWO HORSES     148 Wee must all to the Stake or be Converts to
                          Rome.
P. 196 TWO HORSES     165 That shall come to pass all mankind may swear
P. 196 TWO HORSES     170 Than all that the beasts had spoken before.
P. 197 DUKE             3 Who all in triumph shall about him sitte
P. 198 DUKE             5 Hateing all justice and resolv'd to fight
P. 198 DUKE            14 Till all this nation to thy footstoole bend.
```

P. 199	DUKE	55	The Counsellors of all this villany.
P. 199	DUKE	70	His sword is all his argument, and his book;
P. 200	DUKE	93	Defying all their heads and all their hands.
P. 200	DUKE	107	What all thy subjects doe each minute feare:
P. 200	DUKE	109	Ends all the Joys of England and thy life.
P. 200	DUKE	114	See in all ages what examples are
P. 201	HISTORICALL	4	And kept his Fathers Asses all the while.
P. 201	HISTORICALL	8	And cloath him all from head to foot anew;
P. 203	HISTORICALL	80	All but religious cheats might justly sweare
P. 203	HISTORICALL	83	Who with vain Faith made all their Reason blind:
P. 203	HISTORICALL	87	And practise all the Vices they araigne:
P. 204	HISTORICALL	126	Of all the Miscreants ever went to hell
P. 204	HISTORICALL	140	T'hunt down 's Prey and hope to master all.
P. 205	HISTORICALL	161	Bid him be bold all dangers to defye,
P. 205	HISTORICALL	164	All England strait should fall beneath his yoake,
P. 205	HISTORICALL	170	And Monarchs are above all human Lawes.
P. 205	HISTORICALL	176	And all the People been in blood embru'd,
P. 313	CHEQUER INN	8	Where all the Berties make their Hay
P. 313	CHEQUER INN	18	The way they all have rosen.
P. 313	CHEQUER INN	21	And heapes up all our Treasure
P. 313	CHEQUER INN	29	For all his slender Quarter Staffe
P. 313	CHEQUER INN	34	And tho' by selling of Us all
P. 313	CHEQUER INN	45	Tho' all Men blusht that heard it
P. 313	CHEQUER INN	47	They all deserv'd to have been fin'd
P. 314	CHEQUER INN	49	And now they march't all Tagg and Ragg
P. 314	CHEQUER INN	83	All of 'em of the Grand Inquest
P. 314	CHEQUER INN	85	Wild with his Tongue did all outrun
P. 315	CHEQUER INN	106	And Berkenhead of all the Rout
P. 315	CHEQUER INN	112	Nay Portman tho' all men cry'd shame
P. 315	CHEQUER INN	131	And sweeping all our Chimney Stacks
P. 316	CHEQUER INN	136	The tale of all that there did sup
P. 316	CHEQUER INN	163	They all said I who had said noe
P. 316	CHEQUER INN	168	The Guests tooke all away
P. 317	CHEQUER INN	176	They sell us all our Barnes and Wives

all-seeing   frequency: 2   relative frequency: 0.0000
     P. 15 EYES   21 So the all-seeing Sun each day
     P. 118 BLAKE   137 Th' all-seeing Sun, neer gaz'd on such a sight,

allan   frequency: 1   relative frequency: 0.0000
     P. 91 MAY'S DEATH   41 Polydore, Lucan, Allan, Vandale, Goth,

allaying   frequency: 1   relative frequency: 0.0000
     P. 141 INSTRUCTIONS 37 But Age, allaying now that youthful heat,

alledge   frequency: 1   relative frequency: 0.0000
     P.   3 LOVELACE   27 Some reading your Lucasta, will alledge

allege. See "alledge."

alleges   frequency: 1   relative frequency: 0.0000
     P. 180 STOCKSMARKET 31 And alleges the workmanship was not his own

allens   frequency: 5   relative frequency: 0.0001
     P. 138 HOUSEWARMING 49 To proceed in the Model he call'd in his Allens,
     P. 138 HOUSEWARMING 50 The two Allens when jovial, who ply him with gallons,
     P. 138 HOUSEWARMING 51 The two Allens who serve his blind Justice for ballance,
     P. 138 HOUSEWARMING 52 The two Allens who serve his Injustice for Tallons.

allied. See "ally'd."

allies   frequency: 1   relative frequency: 0.0000
     P. 68 A. HOUSE   291 The Bee through these known Allies hums,

allow   frequency: 2   relative frequency: 0.0000
     P. 34 DAPHNIS   55 And allow him all he will,
     P. 85 FLECKNO   84 His Chamber, whose compactness did allow

allow'd   frequency: 4   relative frequency: 0.0000
     P. 41 THE MOWER   19 And yet these Rarities might be allow'd,
     P. 55 EPITAPH   11 Nor was, when Vice is so allow'd,
     P. 129 O.C.   272 When truth shall be allow'd, and faction cease,
     P. 138 HOUSEWARMING 38 To make Mortar and Brick, yet allow'd them no straw,

allowed   frequency: 1   relative frequency: 0.0000

```
           See also "allow'd."
           P. 316 CHEQUER INN     148 On them she was allowed to raile

allows                                  frequency:    1    relative frequency: 0.0000
     P.  88 ODE                    42 Allows of penetration less:

allur'd                                 frequency:    1    relative frequency: 0.0000
     P. 144 INSTRUCTIONS          159 Expectants pale, with hopes of spoil allur'd,

allure                                  frequency:    3    relative frequency: 0.0000
     P.  40 THE MOWER              3 And from the fields the Flow'rs and Plants
                                       allure,
     P.  84 FLECKNO               36 Left off, and try'd t' allure me with his Lute.
     P. 132 PARADISE              45 Well mightst thou scorn thy Readers to allure

alluring                                frequency:    1    relative frequency: 0.0000
     P.  10 DIALOGUE              47 The Batteries of alluring Sense,

alluvion                                frequency:    1    relative frequency: 0.0000
     P.  95 HOLLAND                5 Or what by th' Oceans slow alluvion fell,

allwayes                                frequency:    3    relative frequency: 0.0000
     P. 165 KINGS VOWES           10 I will have a fine Parliament allwayes to
                                       Friend,
     P. 166 KINGS VOWES           29 And allwayes who beards me shall have the next
                                       Grace,
     P. 166 KINGS VOWES           34 I will have a Privy Councell to sit allwayes
                                       still,

ally                                    frequency:    2    relative frequency: 0.0000
     P.   5 HASTINGS              28 Secures his neerest and most lov'd Ally;
     P.  90 MAY'S DEATH            6 For whence in Stevens ally Trees or Grass?

ally'd                                  frequency:    1    relative frequency: 0.0000
     P. 157 INSTRUCTIONS          700 Ally'd in Fate, increase, with theirs, her
                                       Flames.

almighty                                frequency:    2    relative frequency: 0.0000
     P.  13 DROP OF DEW           40 Into the Glories of th' Almighty Sun.
     P. 205 HISTORICALL          177 Had not Almighty Providence drawne neere,

almond-milk                             frequency:    1    relative frequency: 0.0000
     P.  94 DR. WITTY             30 Stint them to Cawdles, Almond-milk, and Broth.

almost                                  frequency:    2    relative frequency: 0.0000
     P. 107 ANNIVERSARY          179 When thou hadst almost quit thy Mortal cares,
     P. 161 INSTRUCTIONS          862 And had almost mistook and call'd them Rogues.

aloft                                   frequency:    2    relative frequency: 0.0000
     P. 132 PARADISE              37 And above humane flight dost soar aloft,
     P. 137 HOUSEWARMING          18 Made Thebes dance aloft while he fidled and
                                       sung,

alone                                   frequency:   19    relative frequency: 0.0003
     P.  30 THE GALLERY           45 For thou alone to people me,
     P.  35 DAPHNIS               61 Absence is too much alone:
     P.  37 DEFINITION             5 Magnanimous Despair alone
     P.  40 THE MATCH             37 So we alone the happy rest,
     P.  44 DAMON                 87 'Tis death alone that this must do:
     P.  49 THE GARDEN            64 To live in Paradise alone.
     P.  57 BILL-BOROW            46 Such Wounds alone these Woods became:
     P.  60 A. HOUSE             41 Humility alone designs
     P.  84 FLECKNO              48 For he has this of gen'rous, that alone
     P. 103 ANNIVERSARY            7 Cromwell alone with greater Vigour runs,
     P. 103 ANNIVERSARY           11 Cromwell alone doth with new Lustre spring,
     P. 106 ANNIVERSARY          127 And in dark Nights, and in cold Dayes alone
     P. 115 BLAKE                 51 By that alone those Islands she secures,
     P. 155 INSTRUCTIONS          599 Leave him alone when first they hear the Gun;
     P. 159 INSTRUCTIONS          768 His Name alone seems fit to answer all.
     P. 162 INSTRUCTIONS          889 There, as in the calm horrour all alone,
     P. 174 LOYALL SCOT          100 Stretch for your Line their Circingle Alone,
     P. 175 LOYALL SCOT          138 That power Alone Can Loose this spell that
                                       tyes,
     P. 177 LOYALL SCOT          228 The Innocentest mind their thirst alone

along                                   frequency:   10    relative frequency: 0.0002
     P.  17 BERMUDAS               3 From a small Boat, that row'd along,
     P.  71 A. HOUSE             394 These Massacre the Grass along:
     P. 109 ANNIVERSARY          270 And Corposants along the Tacklings slide.
     P. 116 BLAKE                 91 Forts, Lines, and Sconces all the Bay along,
     P. 129 O.C.                 252 Loose and depriv'd of vigour, stretch'd along:
```

```
P.  148 INSTRUCTIONS  323 Along the Coast and Harbours they take care
P.  154 INSTRUCTIONS  548 Puffs them along, and breathes upon them kind.
P.  154 INSTRUCTIONS  552 A Fleet of Clouds, sailing along the Skies:
P.  162 INSTRUCTIONS  887 And those bright gleams that dart along and glare
P.  168 ADVICE         22 The spoyls of England; and along that side
```

alpes   frequency: 1   relative frequency: 0.0000
```
P.  174 LOYALL SCOT    98 Nothing, not Boggs, not Sands, not seas, not
                          Alpes
```

alps. See "alpes."

already   frequency: 11   relative frequency: 0.0002
```
P.    3 LOVELACE       17 The Ayre's already tainted with the swarms
P.    4 HASTINGS       16 Are hurried hence, as if already old.
P.   57 BILL-BOROW     48 'Twas writ already in their Heart.
P.   63 A. HOUSE      146 'Is so already consecrate.
P.   76 A. HOUSE      569 Already I begin to call
P.   79 A. HOUSE      655 She that already is the Law
P.   86 FLECKNO       116 Said 'twas too late, he was already both.
P.  131 O.C.          319 We find already what those omens mean,
P.  138 HOUSEWARMING   33 Already he had got all our Money and Cattel,
P.  190 STATUE         20 Have wee not had enough already of one?
P.  194 TWO HORSES     96 When one already hath made him soe poor.
```

altar   frequency: 2   relative frequency: 0.0000
```
P.   67 A. HOUSE      264 That weeping at the Altar waites.
P.  140 HOUSEWARMING   99 And to handsel his Altar and Nostrils divine,
```

altars   frequency: 2   relative frequency: 0.0000
```
P.   64 A. HOUSE      179 'Flow'rs dress the Altars; for the Clothes,
P.   97 HOLLAND        89 Each to the Temple with these Altars tend,
```

altar's   frequency: 1   relative frequency: 0.0000
```
P.   62 A. HOUSE      128 'That serves for Altar's Ornaments.
```

alter   frequency: 2   relative frequency: 0.0000
```
P.    3 LOVELACE        3 And as complexions alter with the Climes,
P.   65 A. HOUSE      215 'For like themselves they alter all,
```

alter'd   frequency: 2   relative frequency: 0.0000
```
P.  104 ANNIVERSARY    54 As he the Treble alter'd, or the Base:
P.  129 O.C.          259 And in his alter'd face you something faigne
```

altered. See "alter'd," "altred."

altering. See "alt'ring."

although   frequency: 6   relative frequency: 0.0001

altred   frequency: 1   relative frequency: 0.0000
```
P.  173 LOYALL SCOT    52 His Altred form and sodred Limbs to Melt,
```

alt'ring   frequency: 1   relative frequency: 0.0000
```
P.  157 INSTRUCTIONS  686 His alt'ring Form, and soder'd Limbs to melt;
```

alwaies   frequency: 5   relative frequency: 0.0001
```
P.   26 MISTRESS       21 But at my back I alwaies hear
P.   27 LOVER          18 Which at his Eyes he alwaies bears.
P.   37 DEFINITION     12 And alwaies crouds it self betwixt.
P.   57 BILL-BOROW     37 For something alwaies did appear
P.  132 PARADISE       40 So never Flags, but alwaies keeps on Wing.
```

alwayes   frequency: 4   relative frequency: 0.0000
```
P.   20 THYRSIS        35 There, alwayes is, a rising Sun,
P.  103 ANNIVERSARY     3 So Man, declining alwayes, disappears
P.  131 PARADISE       19 (Such as disquiet alwayes what is well,
P.  174 LOYALL SCOT    95 For Becketts sake Kent alwayes shall have
                          tails.
```

always   frequency: 11   relative frequency: 0.0002
See also "allwayes," "alwaies," "alwayes."
```
P.   75 A. HOUSE      525 Yet always, for some Cause unknown,
P.  106 ANNIVERSARY   146 Who in his Age has always forward prest:
P.  107 ANNIVERSARY   168 And always hast thy Tongue from fraud refrain'd;
P.  129 O.C.          235 Yet always temper'd with an aire so mild,
P.  130 O.C.          286 Always thy honour, praise and name, shall last.
P.  145 INSTRUCTIONS  172 In vain, for always he commands that pays.
P.  152 INSTRUCTIONS  485 And the wise Court, that always lov'd it dear,
P.  161 INSTRUCTIONS  842 Trusty as Steel, that always ready hung;
P.  161 INSTRUCTIONS  847 The Girls shall always kiss thee, though grown
                          old,
```

```
P. 193 TWO HORSES      70 But Tyrants ingratefull are always afeard.
P. 313 CHEQUER INN     23 He dandles always in his Hand
```

aly   frequency: 1   relative frequency: 0.0000
```
P. 141 INSTRUCTIONS    10 The Aly roof, with snuff of Candle dimm,
```

am   frequency: 10   relative frequency: 0.0002

amaz'd   frequency: 2   relative frequency: 0.0000
```
P.  90 MAY'S DEATH      3 But was amaz'd on the Elysian side,
P. 151 INSTRUCTIONS   426 Orders, amaz'd at last gives none at all.
```

amaze   frequency: 1   relative frequency: 0.0000
```
P.  48 THE GARDEN       1 How vainly men themselves amaze
```

amazons   frequency: 1   relative frequency: 0.0000
```
P.  62 A. HOUSE       106 'Like Virgin Amazons do fight.
```

ambassadors   frequency: 3   relative frequency: 0.0000
```
    See also "embassadors."
P. 111 ANNIVERSARY    348 And credulous Ambassadors accuse.
P. 150 INSTRUCTIONS   369 While Chain'd together two Ambassadors
P. 152 INSTRUCTIONS   452 Plenipotentiary Ambassadors,
```

amber   frequency: 4   relative frequency: 0.0000
```
P.  24 NYMPH          100 Melt in such Amber Tears as these.
P.  64 A. HOUSE       180 'The Sea-born Amber we compose;
P. 157 INSTRUCTIONS   682 As the clear Amber on the Bee does close:
P. 173 LOYALL SCOT     48 As the Clear Amber on the bee doth Close;
```

ambergreece   frequency: 1   relative frequency: 0.0000
```
P.  95 HOLLAND         12 Of Earth, as if't had been of Ambergreece;
```

ambergris   frequency: 2   relative frequency: 0.0000
```
    See also "ambergreece."
P.  17 BERMUDAS        28 Proclaime the Ambergris on shoar.
P.  30 THE GALLERY     38 A Mass of Ambergris it bears.
```

ambigue   frequency: 1   relative frequency: 0.0000
```
P. 175 LOYALL SCOT    141 Fish and flesh Bishops are the Ambigue.
```

ambition   frequency: 7   relative frequency: 0.0001
```
P.   3 LOVELACE         9 Modest ambition studi'd only then,
P.  70 A. HOUSE       354 Ambition weed, but Conscience till.
P.  70 A. HOUSE       366 Th' Ambition of its Prelate great.
P.  83 FLECKNO         27 Only this frail Ambition did remain,
P. 174 LOYALL SCOT    114 Their Rank Ambition all this heat hath stir'd
P. 177 LOYALL SCOT    231 Oppression Avarice Ambition Id--
P. 205 HISTORICALL    173 Fiends of Ambition here his Soul possesst,
```

ambitious   frequency: 2   relative frequency: 0.0000
```
P. 109 ANNIVERSARY    264 Th' ambitious Shrubs thou in just time didst aw.
P. 200 DUKE           111 But to a zealous and ambitious minde,
```

ambles   frequency: 1   relative frequency: 0.0000
```
P. 161 INSTRUCTIONS   827 Up ambles Ccuntry Justice on his Pad,
```

ambush   frequency: 1   relative frequency: 0.0000
```
P.  81 A. HOUSE       719 But knowing where this Ambush lay,
```

america. See "t'america."

ametas   frequency: 4   relative frequency: 0.0000
```
P.  46 AMETAS           t Ametas and Thestylis making Hay-Ropes.
P.  46 AMETAS          t+ Ametas.
P.  46 AMETAS          8+ Ametas.
P.  46 AMETAS         14+ Ametas.
```

amity   frequency: 1   relative frequency: 0.0000
```
P.  98 HOLLAND        101 But when such Amity at home is show'd;
```

ammunition   frequency: 1   relative frequency: 0.0000
```
P. 155 INSTRUCTIONS   608 Now needful, dces for Ammunition call.
```

among   frequency: 22   relative frequency: 0.0004

amongst   frequency: 6   relative frequency: 0.0001

amorous. See "am'rous."

amphibii   frequency: 1   relative frequency: 0.0000
```
```

       P. 83 A. HOUSE   774 These rational Amphibii go?

amphibium   frequency: 1   relative frequency: 0.0000
       P. 28 LOVER   40 Th' Amphibium of Life and Death.

amphion   frequency: 2   relative frequency: 0.0000
    See also "amphyon."
       P. 104 ANNIVERSARY   49 So when Amphion did the Lute command,
       P. 105 ANNIVERSARY   73 Then our Amphion issues out and sings,

amphitrio   frequency: 1   relative frequency: 0.0000
       P. 203 HISTORICALL   95 Becomes the Priests Amphitrio dureing Life.

amphyon   frequency: 1   relative frequency: 0.0000
       P. 137 HOUSEWARMING   17 But then recollecting how the Harper Amphyon

am'rous   frequency: 5   relative frequency: 0.0001
       P. 27 MISTRESS   38 And now, like am'rous birds of prey,
       P. 32 MOURNING   19 She courts her self in am'rous Rain;
       P. 41 DAMON   6 But scorching like his am'rous Care.
       P. 48 THE GARDEN   18 So am'rous as this lovely green.
       P. 153 INSTRUCTIONS   533 Like am'rous Victors he begins to shave,

amsterdam   frequency: 1   relative frequency: 0.0000
       P. 97 HOLLAND   71 Hence Amsterdam, Turk-Christian-Pagan-Jew,

an   frequency: 88   relative frequency: 0.0018

anathama   frequency: 1   relative frequency: 0.0000
       P. 174 LOYALL SCOT   111 A Bishops self is an Anathama.

anathema. See "anathama."

anatomists   frequency: 1   relative frequency: 0.0000
       P. 173 LOYALL SCOT   77 Anatomists may Sooner fix the Cells

anchises   frequency: 1   relative frequency: 0.0000
       P. 120 TWO SONGS   30 Anchises was a Shepheard too;

anchor   frequency: 4   relative frequency: 0.0000
       P. 112 ANNIVERSARY   364 'And sink the Earth that does at Anchor ride.
       P. 115 BLAKE   68 And safely there casts Anchor in the Bay.
       P. 117 BLAKE   111 Behold their Navy does at Anchor lye,
       P. 118 BLAKE   138 Two dreadful Navies there at Anchor Fight.

ancient   frequency: 8   relative frequency: 0.0001
    See also "antient."
       P. 41 THE MOWER   37 Their Statues polish'd by some ancient hand,
       P. 74 A. HOUSE   489 The double Wood of ancient Stocks
       P. 90 MAY'S DEATH   15 Sounding of ancient Heroes, such as were
       P. 92 MAY'S DEATH   69 Sings still of ancient Rights and better Times,
       P. 98 HOLLAND   107 No, but all ancient Rights and Leagues must
                                 vail,
       P. 111 ANNIVERSARY   318 Bent to reduce us to the ancient Pict;
       P. 155 INSTRUCTIONS   577 Those Oaken Gyants of the ancient Race,
       P. 157 INSTRUCTIONS   673 Much him the Honours of his ancient Race

ancients   frequency: 1   relative frequency: 0.0000
    See also "antients."
       P. 164 INSTRUCTIONS   947 His Master-hand the Ancients shall out-do

and   frequency: 1789   relative frequency: 0.0373

anew   frequency: 1   relative frequency: 0.0000
       P. 201 HISTORICALL   8 And cloath him all from head to foot anew;

angel   frequency: 1   relative frequency: 0.0000
    See also "angell."
       P. 113 ANNIVERSARY   401 And as the Angel of our Commonweal,

angelic. See "angelique."

angelique   frequency: 1   relative frequency: 0.0000
       P. 106 ANNIVERSARY   126 Angelique Cromwell who outwings the wind;

angell   frequency: 2   relative frequency: 0.0000
       P. 187 BRITANNIA   122 Resigns his Crcwn to Angell Carwells trust.
       P. 200 DUKE   96 And can her Guardian Angell lett her stoope

angells   frequency: 1   relative frequency: 0.0000
       P. 173 LOYALL SCOT   49 And as on Angells head their Glories shine

angels   frequency: 4   relative frequency: 0.0000
  See also "angells."
  P.   5 HASTINGS   34 The armed Angels hold their Carouzels;
  P.   63 A. HOUSE   141 'I see the Angels in a Crown
  P. 131 PARADISE   4 Rebelling Angels, the Forbidden Tree,
  P. 157 INSTRUCTIONS   683 And, as on Angels Heads their Glories shine,

anger   frequency: 4   relative frequency: 0.0000
  P.   86 FLECKNO   151 Thereat the Poet swell'd, with anger full,
  P.   87 FLECKNO   166 Ere the fierce Poets anger turn'd to rime.
  P. 141 INSTRUCTIONS   24 His Anger reacht that rage which past his Art;
  P. 163 INSTRUCTIONS   939 But in wise anger he their Crimes forbears,

angle   frequency: 2   relative frequency: 0.0000
  P.   15 EYES   6 In a false Angle takes each hight;
  P.   37 DEFINITION   26 Themselves in every Angle greet:

angles   frequency: 1   relative frequency: 0.0000
  P.   79 A. HOUSE   650 And Angles, idle Utensils.

anglesey   frequency: 1   relative frequency: 0.0000
  P. 187 BRITANNIA   124 False Finch, Krave Anglesey misguide the
                              seals;

angry   frequency: 7   relative frequency: 0.0001
  P.   28 LOVER   41 And now, when angry Heaven wou'd
  P.   39 PICTURE   36 Lest Flora angry at thy crime,
  P.   88 ODE   26 The force of angry Heavens flame:
  P. 106 ANNIVERSARY   106 Kiss the approaching, nor yet angry Son;
  P. 123 O.C.   16 But angry Heaven unto War had sway'd,
  P. 129 O.C.   265 When angry Jove darts lightning through the
                              aire,
  P. 147 INSTRUCTIONS   254 And to new edge their angry Courage grind.

anguish   frequency: 1   relative frequency: 0.0000
  P. 162 INSTRUCTIONS   897 And silent tears her secret anguish speak,

animals   frequency: 1   relative frequency: 0.0000
  P. 196 TWO HORSES   163 If Speech from Brute Animals in Romes first
                              age

animated   frequency: 1   relative frequency: 0.0000
  P. 105 ANNIVERSARY   86 Into the Animated City throng.

animates   frequency: 1   relative frequency: 0.0000
  P. 112 ANNIVERSARY   380 'Moves the great Bulk, and animates the whole.

ankle   frequency: 1   relative frequency: 0.0000
  P.   44 DAMON   78 Did into his own Ankle glance;

annext   frequency: 1   relative frequency: 0.0000
  P. 175 LOYALL SCOT   130 A higher work is to their Court Annext:

annihilating   frequency: 1   relative frequency: 0.0000
  P.   49 THE GARDEN   47 Annihilating all that's made

anniversary   frequency: 1   relative frequency: 0.0000
  P. 103 ANNIVERSARY   t1 THE FIRST ANNIVERSARY

annual   frequency: 1   relative frequency: 0.0000
  P. 203 HISTORICALL   77 And annual Stypends for their guilt recieve:

anointed   frequency: 1   relative frequency: 0.0000
  P. 109 ANNIVERSARY   260 And Brambles be ancinted with thine Oyl,

another   frequency: 16   relative frequency: 0.0003

anothers   frequency: 1   relative frequency: 0.0000

answer   frequency: 5   relative frequency: 0.0001
  P.   60 A. HOUSE   62 Where ev'ry Thing does answer Use?
  P. 151 INSTRUCTIONS   443 The gravell'd Ccunt did with the Answer faint:
  P. 159 INSTRUCTIONS   768 His Name alone seems fit to answer all.
  P. 166 KINGS VOWES   33 And if any be Questiond, I'lle answer the
                              whole.
  P. 317 CHEQUER INN   2t The Answer.

answer'd   frequency: 1   relative frequency: 0.0000
  P.   85 FLECKNO   89 I answer'd he is here Sir; but you see

answered   frequency: 1   relative frequency: 0.0000

        See also "answer'd."
        P. 84 FLECKNO   47 He answered yes; with such, and such an one.

answers   frequency: 3   relative frequency: 0.0000
        P. 124 O.C.   60 Answers the touch in Notes more sad more true.
        P. 191 TWO HORSES   14 Have to Questions return'd oracular Answers:
        P. 192 TWO HORSES   18 When Shrines give Answers, say a knave 's in
                                  the Roode;

antedate   frequency: 1   relative frequency: 0.0000
        P. 25 YOUNG LOVE   23 We that Good shall antedate,

antick   frequency: 2   relative frequency: 0.0000
        P. 77 A. HOUSE   591 Under this antick Cope I move
        P. 85 FLECKNO   75 And above that yet casts an antick Cloak,

antidate   frequency: 1   relative frequency: 0.0000
        P. 20 THYRSIS   28 By silent thinking, Antidate:

antidote   frequency: 1   relative frequency: 0.0000
        P. 188 BRITANNIA   148 It 's by noe Potent Antidote withstood.

antient   frequency: 4   relative frequency: 0.0000
        P. 88 ODE   38 And plead the antient Rights in vain:
        P. 167 KINGS VOWES   55 The Antient Nobility I will lay by,
        P. 172 LOYALL SCOT   39 Much him the glories of his Antient Race
        P. 186 BRITANNIA   62 Her left Arm bears, the Antient Gallick shield

antients   frequency: 1   relative frequency: 0.0000
        P. 188 BRITANNIA   157 With her the Prudence of the Antients read

antioch   frequency: 1   relative frequency: 0.0000
        P. 85 FLECKNO   76 Worn at the first Counsel of Antioch;

antipodes   frequency: 1   relative frequency: 0.0000
        P. 83 A. HOUSE   771 And, like Antipodes in Shoes,

antique   frequency: 2   relative frequency: 0.0000
        See also "antick."
        P. 141 INSTRUCTIONS   9 Or hast thou mark't how antique Masters limn
        P. 175 LOYALL SCOT   158 Seth's Pillars are noe Antique Brick and stone

antiquity   frequency: 1   relative frequency: 0.0000
        P. 150 INSTRUCTIONS   387 Prudent Antiquity, that knew by Shame,

ants   frequency: 1   relative frequency: 0.0000
        P. 183 MADE FREE   89 Like Ants at a Straw,

anxious   frequency: 1   relative frequency: 0.0000
        P. 145 INSTRUCTIONS   198 Mourning his Countess, anxious for his Act.

anxiously   frequency: 1   relative frequency: 0.0000
        P. 96 HOLLAND   13 Collecting anxiously small Loads of Clay,

any   frequency: 25   relative frequency: 0.0005

apartment. See "appartement."

apeare   frequency: 1   relative frequency: 0.0000
        P. 202 HISTORICALL   42 Death and the Duke so terrible apeare.

apelles   frequency: 1   relative frequency: 0.0000
        P. 143 INSTRUCTIONS   104 And this Campaspe thee Apelles give!

apes   frequency: 1   relative frequency: 0.0000
        P. 184 MADE FREE   121 But all ye Blind Apes,

apochriphall   frequency: 1   relative frequency: 0.0000
        P. 176 LOYALL SCOT   176 But an Apochriphall Archbishopp Bell

apocryphal. See "apochriphall."

apollo   frequency: 2   relative frequency: 0.0000
        P. 48 THE GARDEN   29 Apollo hunted Daphne so,
        P. 137 HOUSEWARMING   5 Us Mars, and Apollo, and Vulcan consume;

apostatizing   frequency: 1   relative frequency: 0.0000
        P. 92 MAY'S DEATH   73 Apostatizing from our Arts and us,

apostles   frequency: 1   relative frequency: 0.0000
        P. 97 HOLLAND   58 Th' Apostles were so many Fishermen?

apothecary. See "pothecare."

appartement   frequency: 1   relative frequency: 0.0000
     P. 83 FLECKNO   18 He'd Stanza's for a whole Appartement.

appear   frequency: 13   relative frequency: 0.0002
     See also "apeare," "appeare."
     P. 35 DAPHNIS   77 And I parting should appear
     P. 57 BILL-BOROW   37 For something alwaies did appear
     P. 70 A. HOUSE   371 Where Men like Grashoppers appear,
     P. 83 A. HOUSE   776 Does now like one of them appear.
     P. 86 FLECKNO   120 After th' Assizes dinner mild appear,
     P. 87 ODE   1 The forward Youth that would appear
     P. 117 BLAKE   107 Those Forts, which there, so high and strong
                               appear,
     P. 132 PARADISE   49 Their Fancies like our bushy Points appear,
     P. 145 INSTRUCTIONS   185 Next th' Lawyers Mercenary Band appear:
     P. 148 INSTRUCTIONS   312 Lest the sure Peace, forsooth, too soon appear.
     P. 152 INSTRUCTIONS   488 Of current Myrmidons appear in Arms.
     P. 169 ADVICE   51 Who make it by their mean retreat appear
     P. 193 TWO HORSES   62 No token should appear but a poor Copper
                               farthing;

appear'd   frequency: 2   relative frequency: 0.0000
     P. 67 A. HOUSE   259 Then th' unfrequented Vault appear'd,
     P. 73 A. HOUSE   455 Such, in the painted World, appear'd

appeare   frequency: 1   relative frequency: 0.0000
     P. 171 PROPHECY   48 And Magna Carta shall no more appeare,

appeared   frequency: 1   relative frequency: 0.0000
     See also "appear'd."
     P. 199 DUKE   56 Clifford, who first appeared in humble guise,

appeares   frequency: 1   relative frequency: 0.0000
     P. 200 DUKE   106 Observe the danger that appeares soe neare,

appears   frequency: 5   relative frequency: 0.0001
     See also "appeares."
     P. 15 EYES   13 What in the World most fair appears,
     P. 30 THE GALLERY   37 Or, if some rowling Wave appears,
     P. 74 A. HOUSE   491 It like two Pedigrees appears,
     P. 123 O.C.   3 Now in its self (the Glass where all appears)
     P. 179 STOCKSMARKET   9 But now it appears from the first to the last

appeas'd   frequency: 1   relative frequency: 0.0000
     P. 10 DIALOGUE   26 Such as oft the Gods appeas'd,

appease   frequency: 3   relative frequency: 0.0000
     P. 38 PICTURE   16 Appease this virtuous Enemy of Man!
     P. 86 FLECKNO   141 But all his praises could not now appease
     P. 185 BRITANNIA   48 As the Jessean Herce did appease

appetites   frequency: 1   relative frequency: 0.0000
     P. 175 LOYALL SCOT   144 If Wealth or vice can tempt your appetites,

applaud   frequency: 1   relative frequency: 0.0000
     P. 123 O.C.   10 Unless the Prince whom they applaud be slain.

applause   frequency: 1   relative frequency: 0.0000
     P. 117 BLAKE   113 This said, the whole Fleet gave it their
                               applause,

apple   frequency: 1   relative frequency: 0.0000
     P. 69 A. HOUSE   327 What luckless Apple did we tast,

apples   frequency: 2   relative frequency: 0.0000
     P. 17 BERMUDAS   23 But Apples plants of such a price,
     P. 49 THE GARDEN   34 Ripe Apples drop about my head;

appleton   frequency: 1   relative frequency: 0.0000
     P. 59 A. HOUSE   t Upon Appleton House, to my Lord Fairfax.

applied. See "apply'd."

apply   frequency: 1   relative frequency: 0.0000
     P. 109 ANNIVERSARY   229 For, neither didst thou from the first apply

apply'd   frequency: 2   relative frequency: 0.0000
     P. 104 ANNIVERSARY   58 And still new Stopps to various Time apply'd:
     P. 164 INSTRUCTIONS   949 So his bold Tube, Man, to the Sun apply'd,

appoint   frequency: 1   relative frequency: 0.0000
     P. 64 A. HOUSE   186 'Appcint a fresh and Virgin Bride;

apprenticeships. See "prentiships."

approach   frequency: 1   relative frequency: 0.0000
     P. 73 A. HOUSE   461 Such Pleas, ere they approach the Eye,

approaching   frequency: 1   relative frequency: 0.0000
     P. 106 ANNIVERSARY   106 Kiss the approaching, nor yet angry Son;

approacht   frequency: 1   relative frequency: 0.0000
     P. 185 BRITANNIA   27 Such slimy Monsters ne're approacht a throne

approve   frequency: 2   relative frequency: 0.0000
     P.   4 LOVELACE   49 Him, valianst men, and fairest Nymphs approve,
     P. 138 HOUSEWARMING   53 They approve it thus far, and said it was fine;

approves   frequency: 1   relative frequency: 0.0000
     P. 121 TWO SONGS   53 And Jove himself approves

april   frequency: 1   relative frequency: 0.0000
     P. 129 O.C.   236 No April sunns that e'er so gently smil'd;

april's   frequency: 1   relative frequency: 0.0000
     P. 154 INSTRUCTIONS   551 So have I seen in April's bud, arise

apron   frequency: 1   relative frequency: 0.0000
     P. 162 INSTRUCTIONS   872 And a Poll-Bill does like his Apron look.

apsley   frequency: 1   relative frequency: 0.0000
     P. 146 INSTRUCTIONS   212 Apsley and Brotherick, marching hand in hand.

araigne   frequency: 1   relative frequency: 0.0000
     P. 203 HISTORICALL   87 And practise all the Vices they araigne:

aranjuez   frequency: 1   relative frequency: 0.0000
     P. 82 A. HOUSE   755 Aranjuez, as less, disdain'd;

arch   frequency: 1   relative frequency: 0.0000
     P. 59 A. HOUSE   8 To arch the Brows that on them gaz'd.

arch-bishops   frequency: 1   relative frequency: 0.0000
     P. 194 TWO HORSES   121 Arch-Bishops and Bishops, Arch-Deacons and
                               Deans

arch-deacons   frequency: 1   relative frequency: 0.0000
     P. 194 TWO HORSES   121 Arch-Bishops and Bishops, Arch-Deacons and
                               Deans

archbishop. See "archbishopp."

archbishopp   frequency: 1   relative frequency: 0.0000
     P. 176 LOYALL SCOT   176 But an Apochriphall Archbishopp Bell

archbishoprick   frequency: 1   relative frequency: 0.0000
     P. 175 LOYALL SCOT   155 But will Transform for an Archbishoprick.

arched   frequency: 1   relative frequency: 0.0000
     P. 56 BILL-BOROW   1 See how the arched Earth does here

arches   frequency: 1   relative frequency: 0.0000
     P. 105 ANNIVERSARY   96 The Fabrick as with Arches stronger binds,

archimedes   frequency: 1   relative frequency: 0.0000
     P. 142 INSTRUCTIONS   51 She, nak'd, can Archimedes self put down,

arching   frequency: 1   relative frequency: 0.0000
     P. 74 A. HOUSE   509 The arching Boughs unite between

architect   frequency: 5   relative frequency: 0.0001
     P. 59 A. HOUSE   2 Work of no Forrain Architect;
     P. 91 MAY'S DEATH   51 Foul Architect that hadst not Eye to see
     P. 105 ANNIVERSARY   84 And some fall back upon the Architect;
     P. 137 HOUSEWARMING   4 'Twas the season he thought to turn Architect.
     P. 160 INSTRUCTIONS   785 Pett, the Sea Architect, in making Ships,

architects   frequency: 2   relative frequency: 0.0000
     P. 21 SOUL & BODY   43 So Architects do square and hew,
     P. 89 ODE   70 Did fright the Architects to run;

ardour   frequency: 1   relative frequency: 0.0000

P. 189 BRITANNIA   177 When with fierce Ardour their brave souls do
                            burn,

are   frequency: 110   relative frequency: 0.0022
    See also "finly'r," "wee're."

ares   frequency: 1   relative frequency: 0.0000
    P. 90 MAY'S DEATH   10 He saw near hand, as he imagin'd Ares.

argu'd   frequency: 1   relative frequency: 0.0000
    P. 152 INSTRUCTIONS 459 But, would they not be argu'd back from Sea,

argument   frequency: 2   relative frequency: 0.0000
    P. 131 PARADISE   5 Heav'n, Hell, Earth, Chaos, All; the
                              Argument
    P. 199 DUKE   70 His sword is all his argument, and his book;

arise   frequency: 2   relative frequency: 0.0000
    P. 154 INSTRUCTIONS 551 So have I seen in April's bud, arise
    P. 184 BRITANNIA   7 Awake, arise, from thy long blest repose;

ark   frequency: 2   relative frequency: 0.0000
    See also "arke."
    P. 74 A. HOUSE   484 In this yet green, yet growing Ark;
    P. 97 HOLLAND   68 And from the East would Westward steer its
                             Ark,

arke   frequency: 1   relative frequency: 0.0000
    P. 129 O.C.   242 As ungirt David to the arke did dance.

arks   frequency: 1   relative frequency: 0.0000
    P. 112 ANNIVERSARY   357 'Theirs are not Ships, but rather Arks of War,

arlington   frequency: 2   relative frequency: 0.0000
    P. 150 INSTRUCTIONS 399 Bab May and Arlington did wisely scoff,
    P. 163 INSTRUCTIONS 933 False to his Master Bristol, Arlington,

arlingtons   frequency: 1   relative frequency: 0.0000
    P. 169 ADVICE   31 At Arlingtons, and round about it sate

arm   frequency: 6   relative frequency: 0.0001
    P. 64 A. HOUSE   191 'All Night embracing Arm in Arm,
    P. 129 O.C.   238 Whose force oft spar'd the labour of his arm:
    P. 147 INSTRUCTIONS 248 Fighting it single till the rest might arm.
    P. 156 INSTRUCTIONS 627 At her own Breast her useless claws does arm;
    P. 186 BRITANNIA   62 Her left Arm bears, the Antient Gallick shield

armado   frequency: 1   relative frequency: 0.0000
    P. 190 STATUE   14 When the King in Armado to Portsmouth should
                             saile,

arm'd   frequency: 2   relative frequency: 0.0000
    P. 112 ANNIVERSARY   362 'Arm'd with three Tire of brazen Hurricans;
    P. 169 ADVICE   42 Arm'd at all pcints ready to reinforce

armed   frequency: 7   relative frequency: 0.0001
    See also "arm'd."
    P.   5 HASTINGS   34 The armed Angels hold their Carouzels;
    P. 85 FLECKNO   73 Thus armed underneath, he over all
    P. 88 ODE   55 While round the armed Bands
    P. 98 HOLLAND   135 And now again our armed Bucentore
    P. 126 O.C.   145 When up the armed Mountains of Dunbar
    P. 154 INSTRUCTIONS 557 With Thunder and Lightning from each armed
                             Cloud;
    P. 198 DUKE   15 Armed with boold zeale and blessing with thy
                             hands

armepitts   frequency: 1   relative frequency: 0.0000
    P. 175 LOYALL SCCT   163 Confirming breasts and Armepitts for the head.

armes   frequency: 8   relative frequency: 0.0001
    P. 98 HOLLAND   100 The Armes of the United Frovinces.
    P. 117 BLAKE   106 And a third World seek out our Armes to shun.
    P. 120 TWO SONGS   38 Have I not Armes that reach to thee?
    P. 127 O.C.   179 He first put Armes into Religions hand,
    P. 169 ADVICE   35 Thus whilst the King of France with powerfull
                             Armes
    P. 185 BRITANNIA   44 How Spaines prow'd power her Virgin Armes
                             contrould
    P. 187 BRITANNIA   96 Shake of those Baby bonds from your strong
                             Armes,
    P. 189 BRITANNIA   183 Greek arts and Roman armes in her conjoynd

armies   frequency: 2   relative frequency: 0.0000
    See also "armyes," "standing-armies."
    P. 74 A. HOUSE   488 Although in Armies, not in Paires.
    P. 144 INSTRUCTIONS   127 Should pay Land Armies, should dissolve the
                               vain

armless   frequency: 1   relative frequency: 0.0000
    P. 155 INSTRUCTIONS   580 Flies to the Wood, and hides his armless Head.

armour   frequency: 3   relative frequency: 0.0000
    P. 57 BILL-BOROW   39 And Men could hear his Armour still
    P. 62 A. HOUSE   105 'Here we, in shining Armour white,
    P. 129 O.C.   244 In horses fierce, wild deer, or armour bright;

armours   frequency: 1   relative frequency: 0.0000
    P. 87 ODE   6 And oyl th' unused Armours rust:

armpit   frequency: 1   relative frequency: 0.0000
    P. 145 INSTRUCTIONS   164 And under's Armpit he defends his Head.

armpits. See "armepitts."

arms   frequency: 9   relative frequency: 0.0001
    See also "armes."
    P.   3 LOVELACE   18 Of Insects which against you rise in arms.
    P. 69 A. HOUSE   333 When Roses only Arms might bear,
    P. 112 ANNIVERSARY   376 'More then all Men, all Navies, and all Arms.
    P. 118 BLAKE   157 Ages to come, your conquering Arms will bless,
    P. 124 O.C.   32 He oft would flourish in his mighty Arms;
    P. 152 INSTRUCTIONS   455 And that by Law of Arms, in Martial strife,
    P. 152 INSTRUCTIONS   488 Of current Myrmidons appear in Arms.
    P. 162 INSTRUCTIONS   893 Naked as born, and her round Arms behind,
    P. 189 BRITANNIA   165 Tell 'em how arts and Arms in thy young dayes

army   frequency: 8   relative frequency: 0.0001
    P.   9 DIALOGUE   5 See where an Army, strong as fair,
    P. 110 ANNIVERSARY   299 Whose frantique Army should they want for Men
    P. 147 INSTRUCTIONS   271 Believes himself an Army, theirs one Man,
    P. 151 INSTRUCTIONS   414 And the French Army one from Calais spies.
    P. 152 INSTRUCTIONS   480 To raise a two-edg'd Army for's defence.
    P. 160 INSTRUCTIONS   818 The Peace not sure, new Army must be paid.
    P. 161 INSTRUCTIONS   844 Th' Army soon rais'd, he doth as soon disarm.
    P. 190 STATUE   26 Had within it an Army that burnt up the Town:

armyes   frequency: 4   relative frequency: 0.0000
    P. 127 O.C.   185 Astonish'd armyes did their flight prepare,
    P. 130 O.C.   280 And with the name cf Cromwell, armyes fright.
    P. 199 DUKE   63 Then Fleets and Armyes, battles, blood and
                               wounds;
    P. 204 HISTORICALL   121 Taxes Excise and Armyes dos advance.

arose   frequency: 1   relative frequency: 0.0000
    P. 104 ANNIVERSARY   60 And joyning streight the Theban Tow'r arose;

around   frequency: 1   relative frequency: 0.0000
    P. 186 BRITANNIA   67 Around her Joves lou'd ravenous Currs complain;

arraign. See "araigne."

arraigns   frequency: 1   relative frequency: 0.0000
    P. 92 MAY'S DEATH   70 Seeks wretched good, arraigns successful Crimes.

arras-hangings   frequency: 1   relative frequency: 0.0000
    P. 29 THE GALLERY   5 And the great Arras-hangings, made

array'd   frequency: 1   relative frequency: 0.0000
    P. 145 INSTRUCTIONS   175 Bronkard Loves Squire; through all the field
                               array'd,

arrear   frequency: 1   relative frequency: 0.0000
    P. 138 HOUSEWARMING   57 His Rent would no more in arrear run to
                               Worster;

arrest   frequency: 1   relative frequency: 0.0000
    P.   4 HASTINGS   6 And, ere they fall, arrest the early Showers.

arrius   frequency: 1   relative frequency: 0.0000
    P. 175 LOYALL SCOT   153 Whilst Arrius stands at th' Athanasian Creed.

arrive   frequency: 3   relative frequency: 0.0000
    P. 18 BERMUDAS   34 Till it arrive at Heavens Vault:

```
         P.  37 DEFINITION      9 And yet I quickly might arrive
         P. 180 STOCKSMARKET   55 But alas! he will never arrive at his end,

arrives                           frequency:   1    relative frequency: 0.0000
         P. 161 INSTRUCTIONS  849 Mean while the certain News of Peace arrives

arsenic. See "ars'nick."

ars'nick                          frequency:   1    relative frequency: 0.0000
         P. 149 INSTRUCTIONS  341 What Frosts to Fruit, what Ars'nick to the
                                  Rat,

art                               frequency:  25    relative frequency: 0.0005
         P.   3 LOVELACE       13 He highest builds, who with most Art destroys,
         P.   5 HASTINGS       60 And Art indeed is Long, but Life is Short.
         P.   9 DIALOGUE        9 And shew that Nature wants an Art
         P.  24 NYMPH         114 Th' Engraver sure his Art may spare;
         P.  29 THE GALLERY     9 Here Thou art painted in the Dress
         P.  29 THE GALLERY    17 But, on the other side, th' art drawn
         P.  30 THE GALLERY    46 Art grown a num'rous Colony;
         P.  31 FAIR SINGER    11 Whose subtile Art invisibly can wreath
         P.  32 MOURNING       13 Yet some affirm, pretending Art,
         P.  33 DAPHNIS         4 All his Labour, all his Art.
         P.  44 DAMON          88 For Death thou art a Mower too.
         P.  61 A. HOUSE       77 Art would more neatly have defac'd
         P.  65 A. HOUSE      204 'An Art by which you finly'r cheat?
         P.  84 FLECKNO        38 Being tun'd by Art, if the one touched be
         P.  88 ODE            48 He had of wiser Art.
         P. 115 BLAKE          49 Forces and art, she soon will feel, are vain,
         P. 130 O.C.          299 For we, since thou art gone, with heavy doome,
         P. 130 O.C.          303 Since thou art gone, who best that way could'st
                                  teach,
         P. 141 INSTRUCTIONS   24 His Anger reacht that rage which past his Art;
         P. 141 INSTRUCTIONS   25 Chance finisht that which Art could but begin,
         P. 157 INSTRUCTIONS  672 Or with known Art to try the gentle Wave.
         P. 172 LOYALL SCOT    13 Abruptly he began disguising art,
         P. 172 LOYALL SCOT    38 Or with known art to try the Gentle Wave.
         P. 173 LOYALL SCOT    75 Prick down the point whoever has the Art
         P. 199 DUKE           76 Let the beholder by thy Art descrey

arteries                          frequency:   1    relative frequency: 0.0000
         P.  20 SOUL & BODY     8 Of Nerves, and Arteries, and Veins.

artfull                           frequency:   1    relative frequency: 0.0000
         P. 186 BRITANNIA      50 Soe the learn'd Bard with Artfull song represt

arthur's                          frequency:   1    relative frequency: 0.0000
         P. 127 O.C.          177 And in a valour less'ning Arthur's deeds,

articles                          frequency:   1    relative frequency: 0.0000
         P. 160 INSTRUCTIONS  821 All to agree the Articles were clear,

articulate                        frequency:   1    relative frequency: 0.0000
         P. 191 TWO HORSES      2 Of Beasts that have uttered Articulate words:

artificer                         frequency:   1    relative frequency: 0.0000
         P. 180 STOCKSMARKET   30 Does the fault upon the artificer lay,

artilery                          frequency:   1    relative frequency: 0.0000
         P.  70 A. HOUSE      362 Th' invisible Artilery;

artillery                         frequency:   1    relative frequency: 0.0000
         See also "artilery."
         P.  28 LOVER          46 With all his wing'd Artillery.

artless                           frequency:   1    relative frequency: 0.0000
         P. 110 ANNIVERSARY   275 The Helm does from the artless Steersman
                                  strain,

arts                              frequency:  14    relative frequency: 0.0002
         P.  29 THE GALLERY    12 Thy fertile Shop of cruel Arts:
         P.  64 A. HOUSE      177 'For such indeed are all our Arts;
         P.  87 ODE            10 In the inglorious Arts of Peace,
         P.  90 ODE           119 The same Arts that did gain
         P.  92 MAY'S DEATH    73 Apostatizing from our Arts and us,
         P. 112 ANNIVERSARY   385 'Where did he learn those Arts that cost us dear?
         P. 142 INSTRUCTIONS   73 Not unprovok'd she trys forbidden Arts,
         P. 143 INSTRUCTIONS  118 With what small Arts the publick game they play.
         P. 160 INSTRUCTIONS  810 All Arts they try how to prolong its Date.
         P. 164 INSTRUCTIONS  943 Painter adieu, how will our Arts agree;
         P. 185 BRITANNIA      29 I'th sacred ear Tyranick Arts they Croak,
```

```
        P.  186 BRITANNIA       84 Are proper arts, the long-eard rout t'enslave:
        P.  189 BRITANNIA      165 Tell 'em how arts and Arms in thy young dayes
        P.  189 BRITANNIA      183 Greek arts and Roman armes in her conjoynd

arundells                        frequency:    1    relative frequency: 0.0000
        P.  199 DUKE            75 Letts see the nuntio Arundells sweete face;

as                               frequency:  367    relative frequency: 0.0076

ascend                           frequency:    4    relative frequency: 0.0000
        P.   13 DROP OF DEW     34 How girt and ready to ascend.
        P.   60 A. HOUSE        60 But low Things clownishly ascend.
        P.  157 INSTRUCTIONS   664 Then, lest Heav'n fall, e're thither he ascend.
        P.  172 LOYALL SCOT     30 Then least Heaven fall ere thither hee Ascend.

ascended                         frequency:    1    relative frequency: 0.0000
        P.  104 ANNIVERSARY     56 And the great Work ascended while he play'd.

ascends                          frequency:    1    relative frequency: 0.0000
        P.   57 BILL-BOROW      21 See then how courteous it ascends,

ascent                           frequency:    1    relative frequency: 0.0000
        P.  108 ANNIVERSARY    219 We only mourn'd our selves, in thine Ascent,

asham'd                          frequency:    4    relative frequency: 0.0000
        P.    5 HASTINGS        47 And Aesculapius, who, asham'd and stern,
        P.   55 EPITAPH         12 Of Virtue or asham'd, or proud;
        P.   89 ODE             73 And now the Irish are asham'd
        P.   96 HOLLAND         35 Nature, it seem'd, asham'd of her mistake,

ashburnham                       frequency:    1    relative frequency: 0.0000
        P.  144 INSTRUCTIONS   156 That sold their Master, led by Ashburnham.

ashen-wood                       frequency:    1    relative frequency: 0.0000
        P.  153 INSTRUCTIONS   513 If they for nothing ill, like Ashen-wood,

ashes                            frequency:    6    relative frequency: 0.0001
        P.   26 MISTRESS        30 And into ashes all my Lust.
        P.   75 A. HOUSE       533 The Heron from the Ashes top,
        P.  139 HOUSEWARMING    94 Like vain Chymists, a flower from its ashes
                                     returning;
        P.  157 INSTRUCTIONS   692 And the sad Stream beneath his Ashes drinks.
        P.  158 INSTRUCTIONS   708 Ev'n London's Ashes had been then destroy'd.
        P.  173 LOYALL SCOT     58 And the sad stream beneath his Ashes drinks.

aside                            frequency:    6    relative frequency: 0.0001
        P.    9 DIALOGUE        13 Lay aside that Warlike Crest,
        P.   49 THE GARDEN      51 Casting the Bodies Vest aside,
        P.   67 A. HOUSE       257 But, waving these aside like Flyes,
        P.  108 ANNIVERSARY    192 What could they more? shrunk guiltily aside.
        P.  110 ANNIVERSARY    296 Rejoycing when thy Foot had slipt aside;
        P.  314 CHEQUER INN     62 Her Forehead Cloath had laid aside

ask                              frequency:    2    relative frequency: 0.0000
        P.  142 INSTRUCTIONS    40 That, disavowing Treaty, ask supply.
        P.  152 INSTRUCTIONS   491 Of the whole Nation now to ask a Loan.

ask'd                            frequency:    6    relative frequency: 0.0001
        P.   84 FLECKNO         34 Ask'd still for more, and pray'd him to repeat:
        P.   84 FLECKNO         46 Ask'd civilly if he had eat this Lent.
        P.   84 FLECKNO         51 I ask'd if he eat flesh. And he, that was
        P.   85 FLECKNO        105 He ask'd me pardon; and to make me way
        P.  108 ANNIVERSARY    200 And with shrill Neighings ask'd him of the
                                     Wood.
        P.  151 INSTRUCTIONS   442 But ask'd him bluntly for his Character.

asked. See "ask'd," "ask't."

askes                            frequency:    1    relative frequency: 0.0000
        P.   68 A. HOUSE       320 She runs you through, or askes the Word.

asks. See "askes."

ask't                            frequency:    1    relative frequency: 0.0000
        P.  182 MADE FREE       46 But when they ask't for their owne

asleep                           frequency:    2    relative frequency: 0.0000
        P.   79 A. HOUSE       665 So when the Shadows laid asleep
        P.  129 O.C.           246 Nor with soft notes shall sing his cares asleep.

asparagus. See "sparagus."

aspect                           frequency:    3    relative frequency: 0.0000
```

P. 38 PICTURE   4 And there with her fair Aspect tames
P. 124 O.C.   48 And at her Aspect calms his growing Cares;
P. 145 INSTRUCTIONS   184 And bid much Fraud under an aspect grim.

aspects   frequency: 1   relative frequency: 0.0000
P. 105 ANNIVERSARY   101 And in his sev'ral Aspects, like a Star,

aspire   frequency: 2   relative frequency: 0.0000
P. 19 THYRSIS   16 Hath no wings, yet doth aspire
P. 117 BLAKE   129 Nature ne'r made Cedars so high aspire,

aspireing   frequency: 1   relative frequency: 0.0000
P. 170 PROPHECY   6 With high aspireing head towards those Skyes

aspiring. See "aspireing."

assault   frequency: 2   relative frequency: 0.0000
P. 116 BLAKE   98 Wish then for that assault he lately fear'd.
P. 169 ADVICE   44 In this Assault upon a single man.

assay'd   frequency: 4   relative frequency: 0.0000
P. 107 ANNIVERSARY   176 At once assay'd to overturn us all.
P. 139 HOUSEWARMING   61 He lik'd the advice, and then soon it assay'd;
P. 142 INSTRUCTIONS   53 She perfected that Engine, oft assay'd,
P. 143 INSTRUCTIONS   89 Fears lest he scorn a Woman once assay'd,

asse   frequency: 2   relative frequency: 0.0000
P. 191 TWO HORSES   12 And Balam the Prophet was reprov'd by his
                            Asse:
P. 194 TWO HORSES   101 When the Asse so bouldly rebuked the Prophet,

assembly   frequency: 1   relative frequency: 0.0000
P. 197 DUKE   2 The great assembly and the numerous traine,

asses   frequency: 1   relative frequency: 0.0000
P. 201 HISTORICALL   4 And kept his Fathers Asses all the while.

assist   frequency: 2   relative frequency: 0.0000
P. 80 A. HOUSE   679 And Men the silent Scene assist,
P. 169 ADVICE   53 These must assist her in her countermines

assizes   frequency: 1   relative frequency: 0.0000
P. 86 FLECKNO   120 After th' Assizes dinner mild appear,

associates   frequency: 1   relative frequency: 0.0000
P. 198 DUKE   12 I and the wise associates of my vow,

assumed   frequency: 1   relative frequency: 0.0000
P. 168 ADVICE   15 Unless it be his late Assumed grief

assumes   frequency: 1   relative frequency: 0.0000
P. 117 BLAKE   114 And all assumes your courage, in your cause.

assur'd   frequency: 1   relative frequency: 0.0000
P. 89 ODE   66 Which first assur'd the forced Pow'r.

assure   frequency: 2   relative frequency: 0.0000
P. 83 FLECKNO   29 That there had been some present to assure
P. 151 INSTRUCTIONS   411 Fresh Messengers still the sad News assure,

assures   frequency: 1   relative frequency: 0.0000
P. 130 O.C.   307 Revives; and by his milder beams assures;

as't   frequency: 2   relative frequency: 0.0000

astonish'd   frequency: 2   relative frequency: 0.0000
P. 73 A. HOUSE   472 And Isl's th' astonish'd Cattle round.
P. 127 O.C.   185 Astonish'd armyes did their flight prepare,

astray   frequency: 2   relative frequency: 0.0000
P. 18 CLORINDA   2 D. No: 'tis too late they went astray.
P. 164 INSTRUCTIONS   959 Kings in the Country oft have gone astray,

astride   frequency: 1   relative frequency: 0.0000
P. 204 HISTORICALL   137 His meager Highness now had got astride,

astrologers   frequency: 2   relative frequency: 0.0000
P. 104 ANNIVERSARY   38 But with Astrologers divine, and Jove,
P. 119 TWO SONGS   1 Th' Astrologers own Eyes are set,

at   frequency: 196   relative frequency: 0.0040

See also "att."

at-home   frequency: 1   relative frequency: 0.0000
    P. 138 HOUSEWARMING   58 He should dwell more noble, and cheap too
                               at-home,

atchiev'd   frequency: 1   relative frequency: 0.0000
    P. 127 O.C.   152 Yet joy'd remembring what he once atchiev'd.

athanasian   frequency: 1   relative frequency: 0.0000
    P. 175 LOYALL SCOT   153 Whilst Arrius stands at th' Athanasian Creed.

atheist   frequency: 1   relative frequency: 0.0000
    P. 185 BRITANNIA   19 Till Atheist Lauderdale shall leave this Land,

atheists   frequency: 1   relative frequency: 0.0000
    P. 111 ANNIVERSARY   314 Sorcerers, Atheists, Jesuites, Possest;

athens   frequency: 1   relative frequency: 0.0000
    P. 202 HISTORICALL   70 As they att Athens, we att Dover meet,

athos   frequency: 1   relative frequency: 0.0000
    P. 98 HOLLAND   98 Cut out each others Athos to a Man:

atome   frequency: 2   relative frequency: 0.0000
    P. 138 HOUSEWARMING   60 As by hook and by crook the world cluster'd of
                               Atome.
    P. 200 DUKE   91 The smalest atome of an English soul.

atomes   frequency: 1   relative frequency: 0.0000
    P. 86 FLECKNO   150 Confus'der then the atomes in the Sun.

atone   frequency: 1   relative frequency: 0.0000
    P. 178 LOYALL SCOT   264 And, where twin Simpathies cannot atone,

atonement.   See "attonement."

att   frequency: 10   relative frequency: 0.0002

attempt   frequency: 2   relative frequency: 0.0000
    P. 98 HOLLAND   119 Yet of his vain Attempt no more he sees
    P. 177 LOYALL SCOT   224 Others Attempt, to Cool their fervent Chine,

attend   frequency: 3   relative frequency: 0.0000
    P. 122 TWO SONGS   32 Whil'st all the Nymphs on Damon's choice
                               attend?
    P. 123 O.C.   5 And thenceforth onely did attend to trace,
    P. 155 INSTRUCTIONS   585 Our wretched Ships within their Fate attend,

attended   frequency: 2   relative frequency: 0.0000
    P. 118 BLAKE   144 And was attended by as high success.
    P. 202 HISTORICALL   72 What sad events attended on the same

attentive   frequency: 1   relative frequency: 0.0000
    P. 76 A. HOUSE   573 And more attentive there doth sit

attonement   frequency: 1   relative frequency: 0.0000
    P. 85 FLECKNO   109 Together our attonement: so increas'd

attorney   frequency: 1   relative frequency: 0.0000
    P. 168 ADVICE   20 Sate by the worst Attorney of the Nacion,

attract   frequency: 1   relative frequency: 0.0000
    P. 10 DIALOGUE   32 Which should first attract thine Eye:

attractive   frequency: 1   relative frequency: 0.0000
    P. 105 ANNIVERSARY   85 Yet all compos'd by his attractive Song,

augment   frequency: 1   relative frequency: 0.0000
    P. 158 INSTRUCTIONS   710 Our loss, does so much more our loss augment.

augments   frequency: 1   relative frequency: 0.0000
    P. 194 TWO HORSES   92 Which Augments and secures his own profitt and
                               peace.

aurelius   frequency: 1   relative frequency: 0.0000
    P. 168 ADVICE   3 There holy Charles, here good Aurelius Sate,

aurora   frequency: 1   relative frequency: 0.0000
    P. 29 THE GALLERY   18 Like to Aurora in the Dawn;

auspicious   frequency: 1   relative frequency: 0.0000

          P. 126 O.C.   143 But this, of all the most auspicious found,

austere   frequency: 1   relative frequency: 0.0000
     P. 88 ODE   30 He liv'd reserved and austere,

authentic. See "authentik."

authentik   frequency: 1   relative frequency: 0.0000
     P. 204 HISTORICALL   119 The most authentik Statutes of the Land,

author   frequency: 2   relative frequency: 0.0000
     See also "authour."
     P. 86 FLECKNO   142 The provok't Author, whom it did displease
     P. 94 DR. WITTY   15 Of the first Author. Here he maketh blots

authors   frequency: 3   relative frequency: 0.0000
     P. 94 DR. WITTY   7 So of Translators they are Authors grown,
     P. 107 ANNIVERSARY   158 And good Designes still with their Authors
                               lost.
     P. 191 TWO HORSES   9 Phalaris had a Bull which grave Authors tell ye

authour   frequency: 1   relative frequency: 0.0000
     See also "author."
     P.   3 LOVELACE   32 Their first Petition by the Authour sent.

autumn   frequency: 1   relative frequency: 0.0000
     P. 125 O.C.   100 Frustrates the Autumn and the hopes of Wine.

autumnall   frequency: 1   relative frequency: 0.0000
     P. 199 DUKE   78 Let Belassis Autumnall face be seene,

avant   frequency: 1   relative frequency: 0.0000
     P. 65 A. HOUSE   205 'Hypocrite Witches, hence avant,

avarice   frequency: 4   relative frequency: 0.0000
     P. 113 BLAKE   11 Wealth which all others Avarice might cloy,
     P. 144 INSTRUCTIONS 129 Hyde's Avarice, Bennet's Luxury should
                               suffice,
     P. 177 LOYALL SCOT   231 Oppression Avarice Ambition Id--
     P. 203 HISTORICALL   86 'Gainst Avarice and Luxury complaine,

avaunt. See "avant."

avoid   frequency: 1   relative frequency: 0.0000
     P. 31 FAIR SINGER   10 But how should I avoid to be her Slave,

aw   frequency: 2   relative frequency: 0.0000
     P. 79 A. HOUSE   656 Of all her Sex, her Ages Aw.
     P. 109 ANNIVERSARY   264 Th' ambitious Shrubs thou in just time didst aw.

awake   frequency: 1   relative frequency: 0.0000
     P. 184 BRITANNIA   7 Awake, arise, from thy long blest repose;

aware   frequency: 1   relative frequency: 0.0000
     P. 79 A. HOUSE   661 The Sun himself, of Her aware,

away   frequency: 46   relative frequency: 0.0009
     P.   12 DROP OF DEW   28 Every way it turns away:
     P.   19 THYRSIS   20 Pass Eternity away?
     P.   19 THYRSIS   24 Our Lightfoot we may give away;
     P.   20 THYRSIS   48 So shall we smoothly pass away in sleep.
     P.   22 NYMPH   38 My solitary time away,
     P.   23 NYMPH   67 And when 'thad left me far away,
     P.   25 YOUNG LOVE   18 Thee before thy time away:
     P.   27 LOVER   12 And, e're brought forth, was cast away:
     P.   30 THE GALLERY   31 And (when inform'd) them throw'st away,
     P.   32 MOURNING   10 Slow drops unty themselves away;
     P.   35 DAPHNIS   69 Rather I away will pine
     P.   36 DAPHNIS   97 At these words away he broke;
     P.   54 THYESTE   7 Pass away my silent Age.
     P.   67 A. HOUSE   265 But the glad Youth away her bears,
     P.   73 A. HOUSE   470 It try's t'invite him thus away.
     P.   79 A. HOUSE   649 But now away my Hooks, my Quills,
     P.   94 DR. WITTY   12 Much of the precious Metal rub away.
     P.   96 HOLLAND   14 Less then what building Swallows bear away;
     P.   96 HOLLAND   36 Would throw their Land away at Duck and Drake.
     P. 108 ANNIVERSARY 193 First winged Fear transports them far away,
     P. 121 TWO SONGS   1 Phillis, Tomalin, away:
     P. 126 O.C.   141 No part of time but bore his mark away
     P. 127 O.C.   171 Since him away the dismal Tempest rent,
     P. 142 INSTRUCTIONS 77 And nightly hears the hated Guards away

```
P. 156 INSTRUCTIONS   647 Three Children tall, unsing'd, away they row,
P. 157 INSTRUCTIONS   662 And wondred much at those that run away
P. 160 INSTRUCTIONS   789 But, his great Crime, one Boat away he sent;
P. 165 KINGS VOWES     17 Yet if Men should clammor I'le pack him away:
P. 170 PROPHECY        10 Hir'd for their share to give the rest away
P. 172 LOYALL SCOT     28 And wonder'd much at those that Runne away,
P. 174 LOYALL SCOT    110 From Church they need not Censure men Away,
P. 180 STOCKSMARKET    29 But Sir Robert to take all the scandal away
P. 180 STOCKSMARKET    37 Hath Blood him away (as his crown once)
                          conveyed?
P. 185 BRITANNIA       13 I stole away; and never will return
P. 185 BRITANNIA       33 Thus Fayry like the King they steal away
P. 191 STATUE          55 Tho of Brass, yet with grief it would melt him
                          away,
P. 193 TWO HORSES      78 Should give away Millions at every Summons.
P. 194 TWO HORSES     111 On ocasions like these he oft steals away
P. 201 HISTORICALL     27 She chants Te Deum and so comes away
P. 201 HISTORICALL     36 So slips away and leaves us in the lurch.
P. 202 HISTORICALL     75 Let loose the Raines and give the Realme away:
P. 204 HISTORICALL    127 This Villin Rampant bares away the bell.
P. 204 HISTORICALL    142 One hang'd himself, the other fled away:
P. 314 CHEQUER INN     60 None went away unhir'd.
P. 314 CHEQUER INN     74 And was as soone sent for away
P. 316 CHEQUER INN    168 The Guests tooke all away
```

aw'd   frequency: 1   relative frequency: 0.0000
```
P. 186 BRITANNIA       82 If not ore aw'd by new found holy cheat.
```

awe   frequency: 2   relative frequency: 0.0000
See also "aw," "over-awe."
```
P. 145 INSTRUCTIONS   181 C-------n advances next, whose Coife dos awe
P. 150 INSTRUCTIONS   377 A Punishment invented first to awe
```

awful   frequency: 1   relative frequency: 0.0000
See also "awfull."
```
P.  91 MAY'S DEATH     34 The awful Sign of his supream command.
```

awfull   frequency: 1   relative frequency: 0.0000
```
P. 129 O.C.           233 From which he issu'd with that awfull state,
```

ax   frequency: 2   relative frequency: 0.0000
```
P.  76 A. HOUSE       546 As if he mark'd them with the Ax.
P. 148 INSTRUCTIONS   319 The Timber rots, and useless Ax does rust,
```

axel   frequency: 1   relative frequency: 0.0000
```
P.  92 MAY'S DEATH     68 And though the World's disjointed Axel crack,
```

axes   frequency: 1   relative frequency: 0.0000
```
P.  88 ODE             60 The Axes edge did try:
```

axle. See "axel."

ay   frequency: 1   relative frequency: 0.0000
```
P. 111 ANNIVERSARY    320 Ay, and the Serpent too that did deceive.
```

ayre's   frequency: 1   relative frequency: 0.0000
```
P.   3 LOVELACE        17 The Ayre's already tainted with the swarms
```

azure   frequency: 2   relative frequency: 0.0000
```
P.  80 A. HOUSE       674 Follows and sucks her Azure dy;
P. 186 BRITANNIA       61 Faire flower-deluces in an Azure field
```

baals   frequency: 1   relative frequency: 0.0000
```
P. 203 HISTORICALL     98 Baals wretched Curates Legerdemain'd it so,
```

bab   frequency: 1   relative frequency: 0.0000
```
P. 150 INSTRUCTIONS   399 Bab May and Arlington did wisely scoff,
```

babel   frequency: 2   relative frequency: 0.0000
See also "rebabel."
```
P.  96 HOLLAND         21 Building their watry Babel far more high
P. 177 LOYALL SCOT    249 At Babel names from pride and discord flow'd,
```

baby   frequency: 1   relative frequency: 0.0000
```
P. 187 BRITANNIA       96 Shake of those Baby bonds from your strong
                          Armes,
```

bacchanals   frequency: 1   relative frequency: 0.0000
See also "backanalls."
```
P. 169 ADVICE          37 Wee in our Glorious Bacchanals dispose
```

bacchus   frequency: 2   relative frequency: 0.0000

P. 164 INSTRUCTIONS   974 Bacchus is Wine, the Country is the King.)
P. 196 TWO HORSES   186 Tis Bacchus and the Brewer swear Dam 'um and
                          sink 'um.

back   frequency: 26   relative frequency: 0.0005
P. 12 DROP OF DEW   11 But gazing back upon the Skies,
P. 12 DROP OF DEW   18 And to the Skies exhale it back again.
P. 15 EYES   24 Which straight in pity back he powers.
P. 26 MISTRESS   21 But at my back I alwaies hear
P. 34 DAPHNIS   39 Looks distracted back in hast,
P. 78 A. HOUSE   635 And its yet muddy back doth lick,
P. 91 MAY'S DEATH   39 Far from these blessed shades tread back agen
P. 92 MAY'S DEATH   67 He, when the wheel of Empire, whirleth back,
P. 105 ANNIVERSARY   70 Framing a Liberty that still went back;
P. 105 ANNIVERSARY   84 And some fall back upon the Architect;
P. 110 ANNIVERSARY   276 And doubles back unto the safer Main.
P. 127 O.C.   167 Stand back ye Seas, and shrunk beneath the vail
P. 138 HOUSEWARMING   43 Nay ev'n from Tangier have sent back for the
                          mold,
P. 143 INSTRUCTIONS   110 These now advent'ring how to win it back.
P. 147 INSTRUCTIONS   279 Ev'n Iron Strangeways, chafing yet gave back,
P. 152 INSTRUCTIONS   459 But, would they not be argu'd back from Sea,
P. 156 INSTRUCTIONS   653 His yellow Locks curl back themselves to seek,
P. 161 INSTRUCTIONS   823 Yet Harry must job back and all mature,
P. 163 INSTRUCTIONS   903 But soon shrunk back, chill'd with her touch so
                          cold,
P. 171 PROPHECY   34 And pray to Jove to take him back againe.
P. 172 LOYALL SCOT   19 His shady locks Curl back themselves to seek
P. 174 LOYALL SCOT   124 Ah! like Lotts wife they still look Back and
                          Halt
P. 179 STOCKSMARKET   7 When with honour he might from his word have gone
                          back;
P. 189 BRITANNIA   178 Back to my dearest Country I'le return:
P. 195 TWO HORSES   124 Ch. The King on thy Back is a Lamentable
                          Tool.
P. 316 CHEQUER INN   159 And clap't 'em on the Back

backanalls   frequency: 1   relative frequency: 0.0000
P. 187 BRITANNIA   109 With fury drunke like Backanalls they roar

backs   frequency: 1   relative frequency: 0.0000
P. 17 BERMUDAS   10 That lift the Deep upon their Backs.

backside   frequency: 2   relative frequency: 0.0000
P. 140 HOUSEWARMING   103 And others as much reprehend his Backside,
P. 314 CHEQUER INN   52 On backside of their Letter some

bacon   frequency: 2   relative frequency: 0.0000
P. 141 INSTRUCTIONS   36 For never Bacon study'd Nature more.
P. 191 TWO HORSES   11 Fryar Bacon had a head that spoke made of
                          Brass,

bad   frequency: 2   relative frequency: 0.0000
P. 177 LOYALL SCOT   237 The good, the bad, and those mixt every where.
P. 177 LOYALL SCOT   239 The good will bravely, bad will basely doe;

badgers   frequency: 1   relative frequency: 0.0000
P. 174 LOYALL SCOT   112 Where Foxes Dung their earths the Badgers
                          yeild;

bag. See "black-bag."

baggage   frequency: 1   relative frequency: 0.0000
P. 151 INSTRUCTIONS   446 Trusses his baggage, and the Camp does fly.

bailes   frequency: 1   relative frequency: 0.0000
P. 315 CHEQUER INN   116 The Landlord Bailes, out eate, out roar'd

bairns. See "barnes."

bait   frequency: 2   relative frequency: 0.0000
P.   9 DIALOGUE   18 To bait so long upon the way.
P. 96 HOLLAND   20 Where barking Waves still bait the forced
                          Ground;

baits   frequency: 1   relative frequency: 0.0000
P. 64 A. HOUSE   182 'We mold, as Baits for curious tasts.

balaam. See "balam."

balam   frequency: 2   relative frequency: 0.0000

P. 191 TWO HORSES   12 And Balam the Prophet was reprov'd by his
                          Asse:
P. 194 TWO HORSES   104 Insted of a Cudgell Balam wish't for a Sword.

balance. See "ballance."

baleful   frequency: 1   relative frequency: 0.0000
    P. 109 ANNIVERSARY   269 While baleful Tritons to the shipwrack guide.

ball   frequency: 2   relative frequency: 0.0000
    P. 27 MISTRESS   42 Our sweetness, up into one Ball:
    P. 139 HOUSEWARMING   91 And shews on the top by the Regal Gilt Ball,

ballad   frequency: 1   relative frequency: 0.0000
    P. 312 CHEQUER INN   t A Ballad call'd the Chequer Inn.

ballance   frequency: 2   relative frequency: 0.0000
    P.   9 DIALOGUE   4 Ballance thy Sword against the Fight.
    P. 138 HOUSEWARMING   51 The two Allens who serve his blind Justice for
                             ballance,

ballating   frequency: 1   relative frequency: 0.0000
    P. 183 MADE FREE   106 In Ballating it use

balloting. See "ballating."

balls   frequency: 1   relative frequency: 0.0000
    P. 174 LOYALL SCOT   107 Shews you first one, then makes that one two
                             Balls.

balm   frequency: 1   relative frequency: 0.0000
    P. 189 BRITANNIA   182 Balm in their wounds, will fleeting life restore.

balms   frequency: 1   relative frequency: 0.0000
    P. 64 A. HOUSE   181 'Balms for the griv'd we draw; and Pasts

balsam. See "balsome."

balsam-tree   frequency: 1   relative frequency: 0.0000
    P.   5 HASTINGS   54 Had they been planted on that Balsam-tree!

balsome   frequency: 1   relative frequency: 0.0000
    P. 24 NYMPH   97 So weeps the wounded Balsome: so

band   .frequency: 7   relative frequency: 0.0001
    P. 110 ANNIVERSARY   309 As thou must needs have own'd them of thy band
    P. 145 INSTRUCTIONS 185 Next th' Lawyers Mercenary Band appear:
    P. 147 INSTRUCTIONS 283 And, charging all their Pikes, a sullen Band
    P. 168 ADVICE   25 Their new made Band of Pentioners
    P. 200 DUKE   99 This band of traytors hang'd in Effigie.
    P. 315 CHEQUER INN   98 Had Mortgag'd of his Two, one Band
    P. 315 CHEQUER INN   102 That Band with Sawce too dasht.

bands   frequency: 3   relative frequency: 0.0000
    P. 88 ODE   55 While round the armed Bands
    P. 98 HOLLAND   105 Not Christian Captives to redeem from Bands:
    P. 198 DUKE   16 Ile raise my papist and my Irish bands,

bane   frequency: 1   relative frequency: 0.0000
    P. 147 INSTRUCTIONS 261 And surly Williams, the Accomptants bane:

banish   frequency: 3   relative frequency: 0.0000
    P. 64 A. HOUSE   170 'Delight to banish as a Vice.
    P. 122 TWO SONGS   30 Whose Hopes united banish our Despair.
    P. 123 TWO SONGS   48 Whose Hopes united banish our Despair.

banish'd   frequency: 1   relative frequency: 0.0000
    P. 98 HOLLAND   125 While half their banish'd keels the Tempest
                             tost,

banished. See "banish'd," "banisht."

banishing   frequency: 1   relative frequency: 0.0000
    P. 164 INSTRUCTIONS 962 Banishing Love, Trust, Ornament and Use;

banisht   frequency: 2   relative frequency: 0.0000
    P.   3 LOVELACE   11 These vertues now are banisht out of Towne,
    P.   5 HASTINGS   31 So he, not banisht hence, but there confin'd,

bank   frequency: 8   relative frequency: 0.0001
    P. 23 NYMPH   82 It like a bank of Lillies laid.

```
P.   79 A. HOUSE        644 Stretcht as a Bank unto the Tide;
P.   96 HOLLAND          47 To make a Bank was a great Plot of State;
P.   97 HOLLAND          73 That Bank of Conscience, where not one so
                            strange
P.  155 INSTRUCTIONS    596 Monk from the bank the dismal sight does view.
P.  156 INSTRUCTIONS    623 Such from Euphrates bank, a Tygress fell,
P.  173 LOYALL SCOT      82 Whose one bank vertue, th' other vice doth breed?
P.  193 TWO HORSES       55 W. That the bank should be seiz'd yet the
                            Chequer so poor;
```

bankers   frequency: 2   relative frequency: 0.0000
    See also "banquers," "banquiers."
```
P.  179 STOCKSMARKET      4 Of bankers defeated and Lombard-street broken.
P.  180 STOCKSMARKET     49 Sure the king will ne'er think of repaying his
                            bankers,
```

bankrupt. See "banquerout."

banks   frequency: 3   relative frequency: 0.0000
```
P.   77 A. HOUSE        597 Thanks for my Rest ye Mossy Banks,
P.   79 A. HOUSE        666 From underneath these Banks do creep,
P.  153 INSTRUCTIONS    525 Survey'd their Crystal Streams, and Banks so
                            green,
```

bann'd   frequency: 1   relative frequency: 0.0000
```
P.  152 INSTRUCTIONS    471 His Writing-Master many a time he bann'd,
```

banneret   frequency: 1   relative frequency: 0.0000
```
P.   29 LOVER            57 This is the only Banneret
```

banners   frequency: 1   relative frequency: 0.0000
```
P.    9 DIALOGUE          6 With silken Banners spreads the air.
```

banquerout   frequency: 1   relative frequency: 0.0000
```
P.  153 INSTRUCTIONS    494 In rescue of the Banquiers Banquerout:
```

banquers   frequency: 1   relative frequency: 0.0000
```
P.  139 HOUSEWARMING     66 Sinners, Governors, Farmers, Banquers,
                            Patentees.
```

banquet   frequency: 1   relative frequency: 0.0000
```
P.    9 DIALOGUE         14 And of Nature's banquet share:
```

banquiers   frequency: 1   relative frequency: 0.0000
```
P.  153 INSTRUCTIONS    494 In rescue of the Banquiers Banquerout:
```

baptize. See "re-baptize."

bar   frequency: 2   relative frequency: 0.0000
    See also "barr."
```
P.  161 INSTRUCTIONS    859 But like his Pris'ners to the Bar them led,
P.  174 LOYALL SCOT      85 That between us the Common Air shold bar
```

barbed   frequency: 1   relative frequency: 0.0000
```
P.    3 LOVELACE        21 The barbed Censurers begin to looke
```

bard   frequency: 1   relative frequency: 0.0000
```
P.  186 BRITANNIA        50 Soe the learn'd Bard with Artfull song represt
```

bare   frequency: 4   relative frequency: 0.0000
    See also "thread-bare," "thred-bare."
```
P.  145 INSTRUCTIONS    187 The Troop of Priviledge, a Rabble bare
P.  170 PROPHECY         13 When bare fac'd Villany shall not blush to cheat
P.  171 PROPHECY         44 Make him self rich, his king and People bare,
P.  195 TWO HORSES      134 I had rather Bare Nero than Sardanapalus.
```

bares   frequency: 1   relative frequency: 0.0000
```
P.  204 HISTORICALL     127 This Villin Rampant bares away the bell.
```

barge. See "tower-barge."

bark   frequency: 6   relative frequency: 0.0001
```
P.   41 THE MOWER        21 Had he not dealt between the Bark and Tree,
P.   75 A. HOUSE        542 Doth from the Bark the Wood-moths glean.
P.  109 ANNIVERSARY     266 Hurry the Bark, but more the Seamens minds,
P.  157 INSTRUCTIONS    669 The fatal Bark him boards with grappling fire,
P.  164 INSTRUCTIONS    972 And peal the Bark to burn at last the Tree.
P.  172 LOYALL SCOT      35 The fatall bark him boards with Grapling fire
```

barkes   frequency: 1   relative frequency: 0.0000
```
P.   48 THE GARDEN       23 Fair Trees! where s'eer your barkes I wound,
```

barking   frequency: 1   relative frequency: 0.0000
     P. 96 HOLLAND   20 Where barking Waves still bait the forced
                              Ground;

barks   frequency: 1   relative frequency: 0.0000
     See also "barkes."
     P. 57 BILL-BOROW   47 But ere he well the Barks could part

barne   frequency: 1   relative frequency: 0.0000
     P. 316 CHEQUER INN   139 Our greatest Barne cou'd not have held

barnes   frequency: 1   relative frequency: 0.0000
     P. 317 CHEQUER INN   176 They sell us all our Barnes and Wives

baron   frequency: 1   relative frequency: 0.0000
     P. 175 LOYALL SCOT   146 And in a Baron Bishop you have both

barr   frequency: 1   relative frequency: 0.0000
     P. 168 ADVICE   17 And place me by the Barr on the left hand

barr'd   frequency: 2   relative frequency: 0.0000
     P. 69 A. HOUSE   335 Tulips, in several Colours barr'd,
     P. 182 MADE FREE   58 And the House was well barr'd,

bars   frequency: 1   relative frequency: 0.0000
     P. 62 A. HOUSE   101 'These Bars inclose that wider Den

barties   frequency: 2   relative frequency: 0.0000
     P. 189 BRITANNIA   170 The Cleavelands, Osbornes, Barties,
                              Lauderdales.
     P. 191 STATUE   45 Where for so many Barties there are to provide,

base   frequency: 5   relative frequency: 0.0001
     P. 47 EMPIRE   10 And Virgin Trebles wed the manly Base.
     P. 92 MAY'S DEATH   71 But thou base man first prostituted hast
     P. 104 ANNIVERSARY   54 As he the Treble alter'd, or the Base:
     P. 159 INSTRUCTIONS 743 When aged Thames was bound with Fetters base,
     P. 187 BRITANNIA   112 And from my Charles to a base Goal me drew,

basely   frequency: 2   relative frequency: 0.0000
     P. 177 LOYALL SCOT   239 The good will travely, bad will basely doe;
     P. 203 HISTORICALL   110 Till native Reason's basely forct to yield

baser   frequency: 1   relative frequency: 0.0000
     P. 193 TWO HORSES   85 Ch. Yet baser the souls of those low priced
                              Sinners,

basest   frequency: 1   relative frequency: 0.0000
     P. 193 TWO HORSES   69 Ch. The basest Ingratitude ever was heard;

bashful   frequency: 2   relative frequency: 0.0000
     P. 76 A. HOUSE   556 Tempts impotent and bashful Sin.
     P. 153 INSTRUCTIONS 527 Through the vain sedge the bashful Nymphs he
                              ey'd;

basis   frequency: 3   relative frequency: 0.0000
     See also "bassis."
     P. 105 ANNIVERSARY   97 Which on the Basis of a Senate free,
     P. 140 HIS HOUSE   6 Fixt on an Eccentrick Basis;
     P. 200 DUKE   94 Its steady Basis never could bee shooke,

basket   frequency: 1   relative frequency: 0.0000
     P. 92 MAY'S DEATH   62 As for the Basket Guelphs and Gibellines be?

bassis   frequency: 1   relative frequency: 0.0000
     P. 188 BRITANNIA   136 (The Bassis of his throne and Government);

basso   frequency: 1   relative frequency: 0.0000
     P. 84 FLECKNO   63 This Basso Relievo of a Man,

bastard   frequency: 1   relative frequency: 0.0000
     P. 187 BRITANNIA   120 Beseig'd by 's whores, Buffoones, and Bastard
                              Chitts;

bastards   frequency: 2   relative frequency: 0.0000
     P. 182 MADE FREE   68 And the Bastards he gets
     P. 193 TWO HORSES   75 W. To the bold talking members if the Bastards
                              you adde,

bastion   frequency: 1   relative frequency: 0.0000
     P. 164 INSTRUCTIONS 976 Nor Powder so the vaulted Bastion tear;

bastions   frequency: 2   relative frequency: 0.0000
   P. 67 A. HOUSE   287 And with five Bastions it did fence,
   P. 70 A. HOUSE   361 The sight does from these Bastions ply,

batavian   frequency: 1   relative frequency: 0.0000
   P. 202 HISTORICALL   40 With the Batavian common Wealth to fight.

bath   frequency: 2   relative frequency: 0.0000
   P. 16 EYES   28 Bath still their Eyes in their own Dew.
   P. 18 CLORINDA   15 D. Might a Soul bath there and be clean,

bathe   frequency: 1   relative frequency: 0.0000
   P. 130 O.C.   290 Plunging dost bathe and tread the bright abysse:

bathes   frequency: 1   relative frequency: 0.0000
   P. 43 DAMON   48 In cowslip-water bathes my feet.

bats. See "batts."

battail   frequency: 1   relative frequency: 0.0000
   P. 72 A. HOUSE   420 A Camp of Battail newly fought:

battel   frequency: 3   relative frequency: 0.0000
   P. 146 INSTRUCTIONS   230 To fight a Battel, from all Gun-shot free.
   P. 147 INSTRUCTIONS   274 That each, tho' Duelling, a Battel fights.
   P. 148 INSTRUCTIONS   295 The Van and Battel, though retiring, falls

batteries   frequency: 1   relative frequency: 0.0000
   P. 10 DIALOGUE   47 The Batteries of alluring Sense,

battery   frequency: 1   relative frequency: 0.0000
   P. 70 A. HOUSE   364 To point the Battery of its Beams.

battle   frequency: 1   relative frequency: 0.0000
   See also "battail," "battel," "sea-battel."
   P. 128 O.C.   195 Hence, though in battle none so brave or fierce,

battlement   frequency: 1   relative frequency: 0.0000
   P. 126 O.C.   114 The Signal from the starry Battlement.

battles   frequency: 1   relative frequency: 0.0000
   P. 199 DUKE   63 Then Fleets and Armyes, battles, blood and
                         wounds;

batts   frequency: 1   relative frequency: 0.0000
   P. 144 INSTRUCTIONS   140 And flies like Batts with leathern Wings by
                         Night.

bawd   frequency: 1   relative frequency: 0.0000
   P. 167 KINGS VOWES   44 My Bawd shall Embassadors send farr and neare,

bawds   frequency: 1   relative frequency: 0.0000
   P. 187 BRITANNIA   114 To Boys, Bawds, whores, and made a Publick
                         game.

bay   frequency: 7   relative frequency: 0.0001
   P. 18 BERMUDAS   36 Eccho beyond the Mexique Bay.
   P. 113 BLAKE   t2 in the Bay of Sanctacruze, in the Island of
   P. 115 BLAKE   68 And safely there casts Anchor in the Bay.
   P. 116 BLAKE   91 Forts, Lines, and Sconces all the Bay along,
   P. 117 BLAKE   115 That Bay they enter, which unto them owes,
   P. 118 BLAKE   162 Victorious Blake, does from the Bay retire,
   P. 147 INSTRUCTIONS   268 The adverse Troops, and hold them all at Bay.

bayes   frequency: 5   relative frequency: 0.0001
   P.   3 LOVELACE   8 Twas more esteemd to give, then weare the Bayes:
   P. 48 THE GARDEN   2 To win the Palm, the Oke, or Bayes;
   P. 91 MAY'S DEATH   32 Shook his gray locks, and his own Bayes did tear
   P. 122 TWO SONGS   14 There is Bayes enough for all.
   P. 122 TWO SONGS   16 But when Old he planted Bayes.

bays. See "bayes," "town-bays."

be   frequency: 209   relative frequency: 0.0043
   See also "bee," "king-wou'd-be."

bead   frequency: 1   relative frequency: 0.0000
   P. 150 INSTRUCTIONS   408 And on Pasiphae's Tomb to drop a Bead.

beads   frequency: 2   relative frequency: 0.0000
   P. 62 A. HOUSE   121 'When we have prayed all our Beads,

```
      P.  66 A. HOUSE      254 The gingling Chain-shot of her Beads.

beak                             frequency:    2    relative frequency: 0.0000
      P.  75 A. HOUSE      543 He, with his Beak, examines well
      P.  76 A. HOUSE      547 But where he, tinkling with his Beak,

beaked                           frequency:    1    relative frequency: 0.0000
      P. 112 ANNIVERSARY   358 'And beaked Promontories sail'd from far;

beakns                           frequency:    1    relative frequency: 0.0000
      P. 139 HOUSEWARMING   69 Bulteales, Beakns, Morley, Wrens fingers with
                               telling

beams                            frequency:    9    relative frequency: 0.0001
      P.   5 HASTINGS       42 But draw their Veils, and their pure Beams
                               reveal:
      P.  42 DAMON          24 But Juliana's scorching beams.
      P.  70 A. HOUSE      364 To point the Battery of its Beams.
      P. 105 ANNIVERSARY   103 While by his Beams observing Princes steer,
      P. 106 ANNIVERSARY   142 And intercepts the Beams of Mortal eyes,
      P. 111 ANNIVERSARY   329 But thought him when he miss'd his setting beams,
      P. 130 O.C.          307 Revives; and by his milder beams assures;
      P. 169 ADVICE         46 And add new Beams to Sands's former Glory.
      P. 180 STOCKSMARKET   45 Or do you his teams out of modesty veil

bear                             frequency:   12    relative frequency: 0.0002
      See also "beare."
      P.  17 BERMUDAS       24 No Tree could ever bear them twice.
      P.  19 THYRSIS        22 Ther's no Wolf, no Fox, nor Bear.
      P.  20 THYRSIS        37 Shepheards there, bear equal sway,
      P.  58 BILL-BOROW     71 Nor are our Trunks enow to bear
      P.  69 A. HOUSE      333 When Roses only Arms might bear,
      P.  96 HOLLAND        14 Less then what building Swallows bear away;
      P.  96 HOLLAND        54 Nor bear strict service, nor pure Liberty.
      P.  97 HOLLAND        75 In vain for Catholicks our selves we bear;
      P. 104 ANNIVERSARY    37 No other care they bear of things above,
      P. 145 INSTRUCTIONS  167 Headless St. Dennis so his Head does bear;
      P. 175 LOYALL SCOT   148 How can you bear such Miscreants shold live,
      P. 177 LOYALL SCOT   236 The world in all doth but two Nations bear,

beards                           frequency:    1    relative frequency: 0.0000
      P. 166 KINGS VOWES    29 And allwayes who beards me shall have the next
                               Grace,

beare                            frequency:    2    relative frequency: 0.0000
      P. 165 KINGS VOWES    16 I will have a fine Chancelor beare all the sway,
      P. 313 CHEQUER INN    26 And beare himself on such a Twigg

beares                           frequency:    1    relative frequency: 0.0000
      P. 184 MADE FREE     126 London beares the Crosse with the Dagger.

bearing. See "tankard-bearing."

bears                            frequency:   10    relative frequency: 0.0002
      See also "bares," "beares."
      P.  17 EYES           55 And each the other's difference bears;
      P.  27 LOVER          18 Which at his Eyes he alwaies bears.
      P.  30 THE GALLERY    38 A Mass of Ambergris it bears.
      P.  60 A. HOUSE       57 So Honour better Lowness bears,
      P.  67 A. HOUSE      265 But the glad Youth away her bears,
      P.  70 A. HOUSE      357 A prickling leaf it bears, and such
      P.  92 MAY'S DEATH   100 Such as unto the Sabboth bears the Witch.
      P. 105 ANNIVERSARY    79 No Quarry bears a Stone so hardly wrought,
      P. 186 BRITANNIA      62 Her left Arm bears, the Antient Gallick shield
      P. 186 BRITANNIA      65 Her Towry front a fiery Meteor bears

beast                            frequency:    6    relative frequency: 0.0001
      P.  23 NYMPH          46 Unkind, t' a Beast that loveth me.
      P.  73 A. HOUSE      454 Is pincht yet nearer by the Beast.
      P. 106 ANNIVERSARY   124 Winding his Horn to Kings that chase the
                               Beast.
      P. 144 INSTRUCTIONS  146 Bugger'd in Incest with the mungrel Beast.
      P. 194 TWO HORSES    100 Bold speaking hath done both man and beast wrong.
      P. 194 TWO HORSES    103 Tho' the beast gave his Master ne're an ill
                               word,

beasts                           frequency:    7    relative frequency: 0.0001
      P.  22 NYMPH          16 Ev'n Beasts must be with justice slain;
      P.  59 A. HOUSE       11 The Beasts are by their Denns exprest:
      P. 108 ANNIVERSARY   191 But the poor Beasts wanting their noble Guide,
      P. 191 TWO HORSES      2 Of Beasts that have uttered Articulate words:
```

```
        P. 192 TWO HORSES      22 To beleive men and beasts have spoke in effigie,
        P. 196 TWO HORSES     170 Than all that the beasts had spoken before.
        P. 196 TWO HORSES     177 Yet the beasts of the field or the stones in the
                                  wall

beat                             frequency:    5    relative frequency: 0.0001
        See also "beate."
        P. 125 O.C.            81 No downy breast did ere so gently beat,
        P. 151 INSTRUCTIONS   430 Threaten to beat us, and are naughty Boys.
        P. 163 INSTRUCTIONS   914 And finds the Drums Lewis's March did beat.
        P. 166 KINGS VOWES     21 But if they should beat me, I will doe what they
                                  please.
        P. 169 ADVICE          58 Leave Temple Single to be beat in the Citty.

beate                            frequency:    1    relative frequency: 0.0000
        P. 182 MADE FREE       52 And when he was beate,

beaten.   See "weather-beaten."

beating                          frequency:    1    relative frequency: 0.0000
        P.  68 A. HOUSE       292 Beating the Dian with its Drums.

beats                            frequency:    2    relative frequency: 0.0000
        P. 130 O.C.           306 Beats on the rugged track: he, vertue dead,
        P. 150 INSTRUCTIONS   380 And beats the Husband till for peace he prays:

beauteous                        frequency:    2    relative frequency: 0.0000
        P.   3 LOVELACE        33 But when the beauteous Ladies came to know
        P. 187 BRITANNIA      104 Strong as your Raigne and beauteous as your
                                  mind.'

beauties                         frequency:    8    relative frequency: 0.0001
        See also "beautyes."
        P.  25 YOUNG LOVE       9 Common Beauties stay fifteen;
        P.  31 FAIR SINGER      3 In whom both Beauties to my death agree,
        P.  48 THE GARDEN      22 How far these Beauties Hers exceed!
        P.  81 A. HOUSE       705 For She, to higher Beauties rais'd,
        P.  94 DR. WITTY       16 That mends; and added beauties are but spots.
        P. 122 TWO SONGS       35 Now lesser Beauties may take place,
        P. 123 TWO SONGS       43 But Virtue shall be Beauties hire,
        P. 153 INSTRUCTIONS   526 And Beauties e're this never naked seen.

beauty                           frequency:   18    relative frequency: 0.0003
        P.  11 DIALOGUE        53 Shall within one Beauty meet,
        P.  26 MISTRESS        25 Thy Beauty shall no more be found;
        P.  38 PICTURE         26 It self does at thy Beauty charm,
        P.  39 PICTURE         33 But O young beauty of the Woods,
        P.  39 THE MATCH       15 Of which one perfect Beauty grew,
        P.  42 DAMON           19 It from an higher Beauty grow'th,
        P.  48 THE GARDEN      27 The Gods, that mortal Beauty chase,
        P.  63 A. HOUSE       135 'And in one Beauty we would take
        P.  63 A. HOUSE       145 'All Beauty, when at such a height,
        P.  77 A. HOUSE       603 Where Beauty, aiming at the Heart,
        P.  80 A. HOUSE       690 That wondrous Beauty which they have;
        P.  81 A. HOUSE       707 She counts her Beauty to converse
        P.  82 A. HOUSE       760 Yet nor to them your Beauty yields.
        P. 124 O.C.            39 When with meridian height her Beauty shin'd,
        P. 143 INSTRUCTIONS    88 Her looks, and oft-try'd Beauty now distrusts:
        P. 156 INSTRUCTIONS   651 And modest Beauty yet his Sex did Veil,
        P. 162 INSTRUCTIONS   902 Whose Beauty greater seem'd by her distress;
        P. 172 LOYALL SCOT     17 And modest beauty yet his sex did vail,

beautyes                         frequency:    1    relative frequency: 0.0000
        P.  80 A. HOUSE       702 Where She may all her Beautyes look;

beauty's                         frequency:    1    relative frequency: 0.0000
        P.  94 DR. WITTY       23 Her native beauty's not Italianated,

beaver                           frequency:    1    relative frequency: 0.0000
        P. 145 INSTRUCTIONS   183 He March'd with Beaver cock'd of Bishop's
                                  brim,

became                           frequency:    3    relative frequency: 0.0000
        P.  57 BILL-BOROW      46 Such Wounds alone these Woods became:
        P. 116 BLAKE           95 Yet they by restless toyl, became at Length,
        P. 155 INSTRUCTIONS   615 And thence the Brittish Admiral became;

because                          frequency:    7    relative frequency: 0.0001

becketts                         frequency:    1    relative frequency: 0.0000
        P. 174 LOYALL SCOT     95 For Becketts sake Kent alwayes shall have
```

tails.

become   frequency: 4   relative frequency: 0.0000
   P.   5 HASTINGS   24 Lest He become like Them, taste more then one.
   P.   46 MOWER'S SONG   27 Shall now the Heraldry become
   P. 185 BRITANNIA   21 Till Kate a happy mother shall become,
   P. 193 TWO HORSES   65 Ch. And our few ships abroad become Tripoly's
                         scorn

becomes   frequency: 3   relative frequency: 0.0000
   P.   38 PICTURE   8 What Colour best becomes them, and what Smell.
   P. 131 O.C.   313 How he becomes that seat, how strongly streigns,
   P. 203 HISTORICALL   95 Becomes the Priests Amphitrio dureing Life.

bed   frequency: 14   relative frequency: 0.0002
   P.   64 A. HOUSE   189 'Where you may lye as chast in Bed,
   P.   67 A. HOUSE   281 From that blest Bed the Heroe came,
   P.   75 A. HOUSE   529 Then as I carless on the Bed
   P.   79 A. HOUSE   663 And lest She see him go to Bed;
   P.   83 PLECKNO   16 There being no Bed where he entertain'd:
   P.   89 ODE   64 Down as upon a Bed.
   P. 144 INSTRUCTIONS   153 In Loyal haste they left young Wives in Bed,
   P. 157 INSTRUCTIONS   690 As one that's warm'd himself and gone to Bed.
   P. 159 INSTRUCTIONS   748 When all the Rivers grac'd their Nuptial Bed;
   P. 163 INSTRUCTIONS   912 But again thunders when he lyes in Bed;
   P. 173 LOYALL SCOT   56 As one that Huggs himself in a Warm bed.
   P. 177 LOYALL SCOT   219 Indifferent to have a Wench in bed.
   P. 187 BRITANNIA   100 Three spotless virgins to your bed I bring,
   P. 314 CHEQUER INN   70 For ev'n at Bed the time has beene

bedeckt   frequency: 1   relative frequency: 0.0000
   P. 186 BRITANNIA   60 Entred a Dame bedeckt with spotted pride;

beds   frequency: 1   relative frequency: 0.0000
   P.   23 NYMPH   77 Among the beds of Lillyes, I

bee   frequency: 16   relative frequency: 0.0003
   P.   50 THE GARDEN   69 And, as it works, th' industrious Bee
   P.   68 A. HOUSE   291 The Bee through these known Allies hums,
   P.   68 A. HOUSE   318 Each Bee as Sentinel is shut;
   P. 157 INSTRUCTIONS   682 As the clear Amber on the Bee does close:
   P. 172 LOYALL SCOT   23 Among the Beeds to bee espy'd by him
   P. 173 LOYALL SCOT   48 As the Clear Amber on the bee doth Close;
   P. 174 LOYALL SCOT   93 Never shall Calvin Pardoned bee for Sales,
   P. 174 LOYALL SCOT   121 A shorter Way's to bee by Clergie sav'd.
   P. 175 LOYALL SCOT   132 Noe Bishop Rather then it shold bee soe!
   P. 175 LOYALL SCOT   140 Will you bee treated Princes? here fall to:
   P. 176 LOYALL SCOT   212 To conform's necessary or bee shent,
   P. 177 LOYALL SCOT   242 The Tryell would however bee too nice
   P. 178 LOYALL SCOT   269 The hive a comb case, every bee a drone,
   P. 178 LOYALL SCOT   283 After such Frankness shown to bee his friend,
   P. 199 DUKE   72 And will cutt throats againe if he bee paid:
   P. 200 DUKE   94 Its steady Basis never could bee shooke,

bee-like   frequency: 1   relative frequency: 0.0000
   P.   60 A. HOUSE   40 As Romulus his Bee-like Cell.

beef   frequency: 1   relative frequency: 0.0000
   P. 146 INSTRUCTIONS   208 And old Fitz-Harding of the Eaters Beef.

been   frequency: 33   relative frequency: 0.0006
   See also "beene," "bin."

beene   frequency: 6   relative frequency: 0.0001

beer   frequency: 1   relative frequency: 0.0000
   See also "beere."
   P.   98 HOLLAND   95 Tunn'd up with all their sev'ral Towns of Beer;

beere   frequency: 1   relative frequency: 0.0000
   P. 312 CHEQUER INN   3 The Choyce of Ale and Beere

bees   frequency: 2   relative frequency: 0.0000
   P. 147 INSTRUCTIONS   273 With Heart of Bees so full, and Head of
                         Mites,
   P. 178 LOYALL SCOT   267 The Idle tumult of his factious bees,

bee'st   frequency: 2   relative frequency: 0.0000

beetles   frequency: 1   relative frequency: 0.0000
   P.   96 HOLLAND   15 Or then those Pills which sordid Beetles roul,

```
before                              frequency:    43    relative frequency: 0.0008
   P.    4 HASTINGS         4 Of Tears untoucht, and never wept before.
   P.    5 HASTINGS        33 Before the Chrystal Palace where he dwells,
   P.   23 NYMPH           80 Find it, although before mine Eyes.
   P.   25 YOUNG LOVE      18 Thee before thy time away:
   P.   25 YOUNG LOVE      20 And learn Love before we may.
   P.   26 MISTRESS         8 Love you ten years before the Flood:
   P.   26 MISTRESS        23 And yonder all before us lye
   P.   28 LOVER           44 At sharp before it all the day:
   P.   33 DAPHNIS         26 Words she never spake before;
   P.   43 DAMON           44 Before her darling Daffadils.
   P.   60 A. HOUSE        36 By Vere and Fairfax trod before,
   P.   73 A. HOUSE       468 (What it but seem'd before) a Sea.
   P.   78 A. HOUSE       620 The Trees before their Lord divide;
   P.   84 FLECKNO         53 Would break his fast before, said he was Sick,
   P.   86 FLECKNO        146 Absurdityes in them then were before.
   P.   92 MAY'S DEATH     76 Before thou couldst great Charles his death
                             relate.
   P.   97 HOLLAND         63 Faith, that could never Twins conceive before,
   P.  103 ANNIVERSARY     10 Is the just Wonder of the Day before.
   P.  109 ANNIVERSARY    240 Still from behind, and it before him rush'd,
   P.  110 ANNIVERSARY    271 The Passengers all wearyed out before,
   P.  122 TWO SONGS       34 Before Marina's turn were sped?
   P.  126 O.C.           148 That had before immortaliz'd his Name?
   P.  144 INSTRUCTIONS   131 Excise, a Monster worse than e're before
   P.  145 INSTRUCTIONS   191 Then marcht the Troop, whose valiant Acts
                             before,
   P.  145 INSTRUCTIONS   197 Before them Higgins rides with brow compact,
   P.  146 INSTRUCTIONS   211 Before them enter'd, equal in Command,
   P.  146 INSTRUCTIONS   216 That 'twas so long before he could be drest.
   P.  146 INSTRUCTIONS   218 Cornbury before them manag'd Hobby-horse.
   P.  146 INSTRUCTIONS   219 Never, before nor since, an Host so steel'd
   P.  147 INSTRUCTIONS   249 Such Roman Cocles strid: before the Foe,
   P.  151 INSTRUCTIONS   418 In Holland theirs had lodg'd before, and
                             France.
   P.  159 INSTRUCTIONS   744 And Medway chast ravish'd before his Face,
   P.  162 INSTRUCTIONS   895 Her mouth lockt up, a blind before her Eyes,
   P.  173 LOYALL SCOT     74 And Joyn those Lands that seemed to part
                             before.
   P.  175 LOYALL SCOT    161 Neither before to trust him nor behind.
   P.  181 MADE FREE       23 Much worse than before;
   P.  196 TWO HORSES     167 But I should have told you, before the Jades
                             parted,
   P.  196 TWO HORSES     170 Than all that the beasts had spoken before.
   P.  199 DUKE            43 That sent Nan Hide before her under ground,
   P.  199 DUKE            53 Dy before twenty, or rott before sixteene.
   P.  204 HISTORICALL    141 Clifford and Hide before had lost the day,
   P.  315 CHEQUER INN    123 Before he'd sell the Nation,

beforehand                          frequency:     1    relative frequency: 0.0000
   P.  138 HOUSEWARMING    1 When Clarindon has discern'd beforehand,

beg                                 frequency:     4    relative frequency: 0.0000
   P.   39 THE MATCH        4 To beg in vain for more.
   P.  149 INSTRUCTIONS   328 Is brought to beg in publick and to chide.
   P.  150 INSTRUCTIONS   370 Like Slaves, shall beg for Peace at Hollands
                             doors.
   P.  155 INSTRUCTIONS   606 Cannon and Powder, but in vain, to beg:

began                               frequency:     5    relative frequency: 0.0001
   P.  143 INSTRUCTIONS    82 Discern'd Love's Cause, and a new Flame began.
   P.  172 LOYALL SCOT     13 Abruptly he began disguising art,
   P.  181 MADE FREE       19 Beyond Sea he began,
   P.  201 HISTORICALL     10 But in his thirtieth yeare began to Raigne.
   P.  313 CHEQUER INN     16 And for his Countrey first began

begery                              frequency:     1    relative frequency: 0.0000
   P.  192 TWO HORSES      51 W. That Bondage and Begery should be brought
                             on the Nacion

beget                               frequency:     1    relative frequency: 0.0000
   P.  159 INSTRUCTIONS   769 Whose Counsel first did this mad War beget?

beggar                              frequency:     1    relative frequency: 0.0000
   P.  193 TWO HORSES      53 Ch. To see a white staffe make a Beggar a Lord

beggarly.  See "beggerly."

beggars.  See "beggers."

beggary.  See "begery."

begg'd                              frequency:     2    relative frequency: 0.0000
```

P.   99 HOLLAND   144 The War, (but who would) Peace if begg'd
                             refuse.
P. 137 HOUSEWARMING   23 That he begg'd for a Pallace so much of his
                             ground,

beggerly   frequency: 1   relative frequency: 0.0000
   P. 193 TWO HORSES   79 W. Yet some of those givers such beggerly
                             Villains

beggers   frequency: 1   relative frequency: 0.0000
   P. 193 TWO HORSES   81 Ch. No wonder that Beggers should still be for
                             giving

beggs   frequency: 1   relative frequency: 0.0000
   P. 104 ANNIVERSARY   24 Took in by Proxie, beggs a false Renown;

begin   frequency: 12   relative frequency: 0.0002
   P.   3 LOVELACE   21 The barbed Censurers begin to looke
   P.   35 DAPHNIS   57 But I will not now begin
   P.   65 A. HOUSE   199 Which She hence forward does begin;
   P.   76 A. HOUSE   569 Already I begin to call
   P.   79 A. HOUSE   668 With Eben Shuts begin to close;
   P.   83 A. HOUSE   770 Their Leathern Boats begin to hoist;
   P. 104 ANNIVERSARY   36 Much less themselves to perfect them begin;
   P. 141 INSTRUCTIONS   25 Chance finisht that which Art could but begin,
   P. 156 INSTRUCTIONS   650 The early Down but newly did begin;
   P. 160 INSTRUCTIONS   808 Hyde and the Court again begin to mourn.
   P. 172 LOYALL SCOT   16 The Early down but newly did begin,
   P. 183 MADE FREE   93 Hee is too farr gone to begin it;

begins   frequency: 5   relative frequency: 0.0001
   P.   38 PICTURE   2 This Nimph begins her golden daies!
   P.   83 FLECKNO   21 Begins to exercise; as if I were
   P. 117 BLAKE   119 The Thund'ring Cannon now begins the Fight,
   P. 153 INSTRUCTIONS   533 Like am'rous Victors he begins to shave,
   P. 178 LOYALL SCOT   272 The Insect Kingdome streight begins to thrive

begot   frequency: 1   relative frequency: 0.0000
   P. 144 INSTRUCTIONS   144 And most rapacicus, like himself begot.

begotten   frequency: 1   relative frequency: 0.0000
   P.   36 DEFINITION   3 It was begotten by despair

begs. See "beggs."

beguil'd   frequency: 3   relative frequency: 0.0000
   P.   4 HASTINGS   13 What man is he, that hath not Heaven beguil'd,
   P.   22 NYMPH   33 But Sylvio soon had me beguil'd.
   P.   25 YOUNG LOVE   6 By young Love old Time beguil'd:

begun   frequency: 6   relative frequency: 0.0001
   P.   20 THYRSIS   36 And day is ever, but begun.
   P.   89 ODE   69 A bleeding Head where they begun,
   P. 117 BLAKE   121 The Air was soon after the fight begun,
   P. 143 INSTRUCTIONS   97 But envious Fame, too soon, begun to note
   P. 148 INSTRUCTIONS   318 To lay the Ships up, cease the Keels begun.
   P. 186 BRITANNIA   54 Then, to confirm the cure so well begun,

behaviour   frequency: 1   relative frequency: 0.0000
   P. 150 INSTRUCTIONS   382 Nor partial Justice her Behaviour binds;

beheld   frequency: 1   relative frequency: 0.0000
   P. 131 PARADISE   1 When I beheld the Poet blind, yet bold,

behemoth   frequency: 1   relative frequency: 0.0000
   P. 175 LOYALL SCOT   147 Leviathen served up and Behemoth.

behind   frequency: 19   relative frequency: 0.0003
   P.   64 A. HOUSE   188 'Yet Neither should be left behind.
   P.   77 A. HOUSE   601 How safe, methinks, and strong, behind
   P.   78 A. HOUSE   630 Remains behind our little Nile;
   P.   92 MAY'S DEATH   78 Hast left surviving Davenant still behind
   P. 106 ANNIVERSARY   125 Till then my Muse shall Parliament kiss him behind
   P. 109 ANNIVERSARY   240 Still from behind, and it before him rush'd,
   P. 111 ANNIVERSARY   341 When streight the Sun behind him he descry'd,
   P. 128 O.C.   230 To loathsome life, alas! are left behind.
   P. 137 HOUSEWARMING   9 But observing that Mortals run often behind,
   P. 139 HOUSEWARMING   76 No, would the whole Parliament kiss him behind.
   P. 142 INSTRUCTIONS   64 There, not behind the Coach, her Pages jump.
   P. 147 INSTRUCTIONS   250 The falling Bridge behind, the Stream below.
   P. 154 INSTRUCTIONS   554 The airy Sterns the Sun behind does guild;

```
      P. 162 INSTRUCTIONS   893 Naked as born, and her round Arms behind,
      P. 170 PROPHECY        16 Within the Curtains and behind the Scenes,
      P. 175 LOYALL SCOT    161 Neither before to trust him nor behind.
      P. 183 MADE FREE       98 Leave his freedome behind
      P. 194 TWO HORSES     114 With an Harlot got up on my Crupper behind him.
      P. 196 TWO HORSES     174 Have the spirit of Prophecy likewise behind?


behold                          frequency:    7    relative frequency: 0.0001
      P.   5 HASTINGS        37 But most he doth th' Eternal Book behold,
      P.  28 LOVER           42 Behold a spectacle of Blood,
      P.  62 A. HOUSE       119 'And can in Heaven hence behold
      P. 114 BLAKE           19 They dreaded to behold, Least the Sun's light,
      P. 114 BLAKE           24 For they behold the sweet Canary Isles;
      P. 117 BLAKE          111 Behold their Navy does at Anchor lye,
      P. 191 STATUE          56 To behold every day such a Court, such a son.


beholder.  See "behoulder."


behoulder                       frequency:    1    relative frequency: 0.0000
      P. 199 DUKE            76 Let the behoulder by thy Art descrey


being                           frequency:    7    relative frequency: 0.0001
      P.   3 LOVELACE        26 You shall for being faultlesse be accus'd.
      P.  83 FLECKNO         16 There being no Bed where he entertain'd:
      P.  84 FLECKNO         38 Being tun'd by Art, if the one touched be
      P. 181 MADE FREE        t Upon his Majesties being made free of the Citty
      P. 194 TWO HORSES      98 Yet truth many times being punisht for Treason,
      P. 198 DUKE             9 Most holy Father, being joyned in league
      P. 199 DUKE            52 Then in false hopes of being once a Queene


bel-retiro                      frequency:    1    relative frequency: 0.0000
      P.  82 A. HOUSE       756 The Bel-Retiro as constrain'd;


belassis                        frequency:    1    relative frequency: 0.0000
      P. 199 DUKE            78 Let Belassis Autumnall face be seene,


beleive                         frequency:    2    relative frequency: 0.0000
      P. 174 LOYALL SCOT    122 Beleive but onely as the Church beleives
      P. 192 TWO HORSES      22 To beleive men and beasts have spoke in effigie,


beleivers                       frequency:    1    relative frequency: 0.0000
      P. 191 TWO HORSES      15 All Popish beleivers think something divine,


beleives                        frequency:    2    relative frequency: 0.0000
      P. 174 LOYALL SCOT    122 Beleive but onely as the Church beleives
      P. 192 TWO HORSES      46 Who beleives not a word, the word of God saith;


belgick                         frequency:    2    relative frequency: 0.0000
      P. 127 O.C.           154 Gave chase to Ligny on the Belgick Coast.
      P. 154 INSTRUCTIONS   559 Such up the stream the Belgick Navy glides,


belgium                         frequency:    1    relative frequency: 0.0000
      P. 171 PROPHECY        55 Then They with envious Eyes shall Belgium See


belides.  See "bellydes."


believe                         frequency:    3    relative frequency: 0.0000
      See also "beleive."
      P.  32 MOURNING        34 Disputing not what they believe
      P. 200 DUKE           116 Hard fate of princes, who will nere believe,
      P. 203 HISTORICALL     96 Who would such men Heavens messengers believe,


believers.  See "beleivers."


believes                        frequency:    1    relative frequency: 0.0000
      See also "beleives."
      P. 147 INSTRUCTIONS   271 Believes himself an Army, theirs one Man,


believing                       frequency:    2    relative frequency: 0.0000
      P. 147 INSTRUCTIONS   272 As eas'ly Conquer'd, and believing can.
      P. 151 INSTRUCTIONS   413 False Terrors our believing Fears devise:


bell                            frequency:    5    relative frequency: 0.0001
      P.  18 CLORINDA        13 C. Near this, a Fountaines liquid Bell
      P.  22 NYMPH           28 Ty'd in this silver Chain and Bell,
      P. 104 ANNIVERSARY     42 And with vain Scepter, strike the hourly Bell;
      P. 176 LOYALL SCOT    176 But an Apochriphall Archbishopp Bell
      P. 204 HISTORICALL    127 This Villin Rampant bares away the bell.


belli                           frequency:    1    relative frequency: 0.0000
      P.  98 HOLLAND        113 Was this Jus Belli <and> Pacis; could this be
```

bellona   frequency: 1   relative frequency: 0.0000
      P. 202 HISTORICALL   51 Foil'd thus by Venus he Bellona woes,

bellow   frequency: 1   relative frequency: 0.0000
      P. 73 A. HOUSE   474 How Eels now bellow in the Ox;

bellow'd   frequency: 1   relative frequency: 0.0000
      P. 191 TWO HORSES   8 That a sacraficed ox, when his Gutts were out,
                                 Bellow'd:

bells   frequency: 1   relative frequency: 0.0000
      P. 132 PARADISE   48 And like a Pack-Horse tires without his Bells.

belly   frequency: 4   relative frequency: 0.0000
      P. 84 FLECKNO   42 Over the Lute, his murmuring Belly calls,
      P. 142 INSTRUCTIONS   63 With Chanc'lor's Belly, and so large a Rump.
      P. 191 TWO HORSES   10 Would roar like a Devill with a man in his
                                 belly:
      P. 316 CHEQUER INN   140 The Belly Timber that they fell'd

bellydes   frequency: 1   relative frequency: 0.0000
      P. 171 PROPHECY   53 But like the Bellydes shall toyle in vaine

belov'd   frequency: 1   relative frequency: 0.0000
      P. 168 ADVICE   9 Do to their more belov'd delights repair,

beloved   frequency: 3   relative frequency: 0.0000
      See also "belov'd."
      P. 63 A. HOUSE   153 'Here live beloved, and obey'd:
      P. 68 A. HOUSE   317 Then in some Flow'rs beloved Hut
      P. 139 HOUSEWARMING   74 Nor would take his beloved Canary in kind:

below   frequency: 17   relative frequency: 0.0003
      P. 10 DIALOGUE   28 Like another God below.
      P. 11 DIALOGUE   59 Till thou purchase all below,
      P. 13 DROP OF DEW   35 Moving but on a point below,
      P. 48 THE GARDEN   13 Your sacred Plants, if here below,
      P. 70 A. HOUSE   367 But ore the Meads below it plays,
      P. 71 A. HOUSE   410 To build below the Grasses Root;
      P. 73 A. HOUSE   453 And what below the Sith increast
      P. 80 A. HOUSE   675 The gellying Stream compacts below,
      P. 85 FLECKNO   108 Oblig'd us, when below, to celebrate
      P. 108 ANNIVERSARY   226 Then ought below, or yet above a King:
      P. 111 ANNIVERSARY   330 Sunk in the Hills, or plung'd below the
                                 Streams.
      P. 112 ANNIVERSARY   386 'Where below Earth, or where above the Sphere?
      P. 120 TWO SONGS   36 How far below thine Orbe sublime?
      P. 127 O.C.   183 Those Strokes he said will pierce through all
                                 below
      P. 129 O.C.   267 (It groanes, and bruises all below that stood
      P. 130 O.C.   296 (Farr better known above than here below;)
      P. 147 INSTRUCTIONS   250 The falling Bridge behind, the Stream below.

bemoan   frequency: 1   relative frequency: 0.0000
      See also "bemoane."
      P. 67 A. HOUSE   267 Who guiltily their Prize bemoan,

bemoane   frequency: 1   relative frequency: 0.0000
      P. 24 NYMPH   115 For I so truly thee bemoane,

ben   frequency: 2   relative frequency: 0.0000
      P. 90 MAY'S DEATH   13 'Twas Ben that in the dusky Laurel shade
      P. 91 MAY'S DEATH   29 But Ben, who knew not neither foe nor friend,

bend   frequency: 6   relative frequency: 0.0001
      P. 13 DROP OF DEW   36 It all about does upwards bend.
      P. 42 DAMON   28 Or to what gelid Fountain bend?
      P. 60 A. HOUSE   59 Height with a certain Grace does bend,
      P. 63 A. HOUSE   156 'The Rule it self to you shall bend.
      P. 106 ANNIVERSARY   134 Should bend to his, as he to Heavens will,
      P. 198 DUKE   14 Till all this nation to thy footstoole bend.

bending   frequency: 1   relative frequency: 0.0000
      P. 31 MOURNING   7 Seem bending upwards, to restore

bends   frequency: 3   relative frequency: 0.0000
      P. 57 BILL-BOROW   22 And all the way it rises bends;
      P. 77 A. HOUSE   604 Bends in some Tree its useless Dart;
      P. 105 ANNIVERSARY   81 None to be sunk in the Foundation bends,

beneath   frequency: 8   relative frequency: 0.0001

P.	12	DROP OF DEW	31 Dark beneath, but bright above:
P.	108	ANNIVERSARY	220 Whom thou hadst left beneath with Mantle rent.
P.	126	O.C.	132 The Universe labour'd beneath their load.
P.	127	O.C.	167 Stand back ye Seas, and shrunk beneath the vail
P.	157	INSTRUCTIONS	692 And the sad Stream beneath his Ashes drinks.
P.	162	INSTRUCTIONS	896 Yet from beneath the Veil her blushes rise;
P.	173	LOYALL SCOT	58 And the sad stream beneath his Ashes drinks.
P.	205	HISTORICALL	164 All England strait should fall beneath his yoake,

benefits   frequency: 1   relative frequency: 0.0000
   P. 114 BLAKE   32 The benefits without the ills of rain.

benevolence   frequency: 1   relative frequency: 0.0000
   P. 139 HOUSEWARMING 72 As at this Benevolence out of the Snips.

bennet   frequency: 2   relative frequency: 0.0000
   P. 151 INSTRUCTIONS 415 Bennet and May, and those of shorter reach,
   P. 163 INSTRUCTIONS 928 Bennet and Coventry, as't were design'd.

bennet's   frequency: 1   relative frequency: 0.0000
   P. 144 INSTRUCTIONS 129 Hyde's Avarice, Bennet's Luxury should suffice,

bent   frequency: 2   relative frequency: 0.0000
   P. 55 EPITAPH   13 That her Soul was on Heaven so bent
   P. 111 ANNIVERSARY   318 Bent to reduce us to the ancient Pict;

be'nt   frequency: 1   relative frequency: 0.0000

benum   frequency: 1   relative frequency: 0.0000
   P. 79 A. HOUSE   672 Admiring Nature does benum.

benumb. See "benum."

bequeath'd   frequency: 1   relative frequency: 0.0000
   P. 33 DAPHNIS   28 To a dying Man bequeath'd.

bequeaths   frequency: 1   relative frequency: 0.0000
   P. 67 A. HOUSE   266 And to the Nuns bequeaths her Tears:

bergamot   frequency: 1   relative frequency: 0.0000
   P. 88 ODE   32 To plant the Bergamot,

bergen   frequency: 1   relative frequency: 0.0000
   P. 159 INSTRUCTIONS 772 Who treated out the time at Bergen? Pett.

berkenhead   frequency: 1   relative frequency: 0.0000
   P. 315 CHEQUER INN   106 And Berkenhead of all the Rout

bermudas   frequency: 2   relative frequency: 0.0000
   P. 17 BERMUDAS   t Bermudas.
   P. 17 BERMUDAS   1 Where the remote Bermudas ride

berries. See "straw-berryes."

berties   frequency: 1   relative frequency: 0.0000
   P. 313 CHEQUER INN   8 Where all the Berties make their Hay

beseig'd   frequency: 1   relative frequency: 0.0000
   P. 187 BRITANNIA   120 Beseig'd by 's whores, Buffoones, and Bastard Chitts;

beside   frequency: 1   relative frequency: 0.0000
   P. 128 O.C.   228 At once with him, and all that's good beside;

besides   frequency: 7   relative frequency: 0.0001
   P. 20 SOUL & BODY   9 Tortur'd, besides each other part,
   P. 90 ODE   117 Besides the force it has to fright
   P. 97 HOLLAND   59 Besides the Waters of themselves did rise,
   P. 98 HOLLAND   133 Besides that very Agitation laves,
   P. 116 BLAKE   88 To all besides, triumphantly do live.
   P. 190 STATUE   7 Besides the injustice it were to eject
   P. 313 CHEQUER INN   44 Besides a good Freind in the Chair

besieged. See "beseig'd."

bespeak   frequency: 1   relative frequency: 0.0000
   P. 24 NYMPH   110 Will but bespeak thy Grave, and dye.

bespeaks   frequency: 1   relative frequency: 0.0000

P. 161 INSTRUCTIONS   828 And Vest bespeaks to be more seemly clad.

besse   frequency: 1   relative frequency: 0.0000
      P. 195 TWO HORSES   150 None ever Reign'd like old Besse in the Ruffe.

best   frequency: 24   relative frequency: 0.0005
      P.   3 LOVELACE   7 Who best could prayse, had then the greatest
                              prayse,
      P.   3 LOVELACE   36 He who lov'd best and them defended best.
      P. 28 LOVER   56 In his own Blocd does relish best.
      P. 30 THE GALLERY   50 That at the Entrance likes me best:
      P. 38 PICTURE   8 What Colour best becomes them, and what Smell.
      P. 48 THE GARDEN   26 Love hither makes his best retreat.
      P. 62 A. HOUSE   127 'This Work the Saints best represents;
      P. 74 A. HOUSE   485 Where the first Carpenter might best
      P. 89 ODE   77 They can affirm his Praises best,
      P. 95 DR. WITTY   39 You have Translaticns statutes best fulfil'd.
      P. 96 HOLLAND   39 For as with Pygmees who best kills the Crane,
      P. 96 HOLLAND   45 Who best could know to pump an Earth so leak
      P. 112 ANNIVERSARY   393 'But let them write his Praise that love him
                              best,
      P. 114 BLAKE   40 The best of Lands should have the best of
                              Kings.
      P. 116 BLAKE   82 A grief, above the cure of Grapes best juice.
      P. 128 O.C.   208 Yet still affected most what best deserv'd.
      P. 130 O.C.   303 Since thou art gone, who best that way could'st
                              teach,
      P. 153 INSTRUCTIONS 504 (This lik'd him best) his Cash beyond Sea whip.
      P. 160 INSTRUCTIONS 801 Who hath nc Chimneys, to give all is best,
      P. 178 LOYALL SCOT   281 And such my Rashness best thy valour praise.
      P. 198 DUKE   35 You and I say itt: therefore its the best.
      P. 201 HISTORICALL   17 But the best times have ever some mishap;

bestow   frequency: 1   relative frequency: 0.0000
      P. 91 MAY'S DEATH   47 Or thou Dictator of the glass bestow

bestow'd   frequency: 1   relative frequency: 0.0000
      P. 63 A. HOUSE   134 'Through ev'ry Shrine should be bestow'd.

bestows   frequency: 2   relative frequency: 0.0000
      P. 80 A. HOUSE   691 She streightness on the Woods bestows;
      P. 117 BLAKE   116 The noblest wreaths, that Victory bestows.

bestride   frequency: 1   relative frequency: 0.0000
      P. 192 TWO HORSES   28 For the two mighty Monarchs that doe now
                              bestride 'um.

bet   frequency: 1   relative frequency: 0.0000
      P. 159 INSTRUCTIONS 771 Who would not follow when the Dutch were bet?

bethlehem's. See "bethlem's."

bethlem's   frequency: 1   relative frequency: 0.0000
      P. 91 MAY'S DEATH   50 As Bethlem's Hcuse did to Loretto walk.

betray   frequency: 4   relative frequency: 0.0000
      P. 130 O.C.   298 Which in expressing, we curselves betray.
      P. 163 INSTRUCTIONS 935 Who to the Brother, Brother would betray;
      P. 170 PROPHECY   9 When Legislators shall their trust betray
      P. 203 HISTORICALL   104 His God and Lord this preacher did betray.

betray'd   frequency: 4   relative frequency: 0.0000
      P. 139 HOUSEWARMING   63 So the Bribes overlaid her that Rome once
                              betray'd:
      P. 182 MADE FREE   62 Had it not been betray'd,
      P. 187 BRITANNIA   92 And by imposters Gcd and man betray'd,
      P. 200 DUKE   80 Who trusting in him was by him betray'd,

betrayer   frequency: 1   relative frequency: 0.0000
      P. 137 HOUSEWARMING   6 While he the Betrayer of England and Flander,

better   frequency: 23   relative frequency: 0.0004
      P.   5 HASTINGS   32 There better recreates his active Minde.
      P. 15 EYES   7 These Tears which better measure all,
      P. 23 NYMPH   53 Thy Love was far more better then
      P. 33 DAPHNIS   20 Better 'twas the Siege to raise.
      P. 35 DAPHNIS   62 Better 'tis to go in peace,
      P. 60 A. HOUSE   57 So Honour better Lowness bears,
      P. 61 A. HOUSE   74 Or Bilbrough, better hold then they:
      P. 67 A. HOUSE   276 'Tis likely better thus fulfill'd.
      P. 77 A. HOUSE   585 And see how Chance's better Wit

P. 92 MAY'S DEATH   69 Sings still of ancient Rights and better Times,
P. 99 HOLLAND   142 Would render fain unto our better Rome.
P. 107 ANNIVERSARY   160 A Mold was chosen cut of better Earth;
P. 114 BLAKE   45 For Spain had better, Shee'l ere long confess,
P. 130 O.C.   296 (Farr better known above than here below;)
P. 130 O.C.   310 In private, to be view'd by better light;
P. 145 INSTRUCTIONS   176 No Troop was better clad nor so well pay'd.
P. 146 INSTRUCTIONS   227 Nor better choice all accidents could hit;
P. 146 INSTRUCTIONS   232 They feign a parly, better to surprize:
P. 150 INSTRUCTIONS   388 Better than Law, Domestick Crimes to tame
P. 164 INSTRUCTIONS   963 Better it were to live in Cloysters Lock,
P. 173 LOYALL SCOT   64 Sometimes the Gall'way Proves the better Nagg.
P. 180 STOCKSMARKET   60 Yet we'd better by far have him than his brother.
P. 199 DUKE   48 Better some jealous neighbour of your owne

between   frequency: 17   relative frequency: 0.0003
   See also "betweene."
P.   9 DIALOGUE   t1 A DIALOGUE BETWEEN
P. 19 THYRSIS   t A Dialogue between Thyrsis and Dorinda.
P. 20 SOUL & BODY   t A Dialogue between the Soul and Body.
P. 34 DAPHNIS   32 Between Joy and Sorrow rent.
P. 41 THE MOWER   21 Had he not dealt between the Bark and Tree,
P. 44 DAMON   76 Each stroke between the Earth and Root,
P. 47 EMPIRE   20 Including all between the Earth and Sphear.
P. 74 A. HOUSE   509 The arching Boughs unite between
P. 77 A. HOUSE   588 Between which Caterpillars crawl:
P. 117 BLAKE   125 Fate these two Fleets, between both Worlds had
                          brought.
P. 127 O.C.   190 The sea between, yet hence his pray'r prevail'd.
P. 156 INSTRUCTIONS   625 But sees, inrag'd, the River flow between.
P. 170 PROPHECY   20 And practise Incest between Seven and Eight,
P. 174 LOYALL SCOT   85 That between us the Common Air shold bar
P. 191 TWO HORSES   t1 A Dialogue between the Two Horses.
P. 192 TWO HORSES   24 Of a Dialogue lately between the two Horses,
P. 195 TWO HORSES   128 Between the two Scourges wee find little odds.

betweene   frequency: 1   relative frequency: 0.0000
P. 314 CHEQUER INN   71 When noe one could see Sun betweene

betwixt   frequency: 11   relative frequency: 0.0002
   See also "twixt," "'twixt."
P.   4 HASTINGS   5 Go, stand betwixt the Morning and the Flowers;
P. 28 LOVER   47 Whilst he, betwixt the Flames and Waves,
P. 30 THE GALLERY   36 Betwixt the Air and Water fly.
P. 37 DEFINITION   12 And alwaies crouds it self betwixt.
P. 78 A. HOUSE   622 Betwixt two Labyrinths does lead.
P. 79 A. HOUSE   670 Flying betwixt the Day and Night;
P. 85 FLECKNO   110 Betwixt us two the Dinner to a Feast.
P. 109 ANNIVERSARY   244 But walk still middle betwixt War and Peace;
P. 143 INSTRUCTIONS   111 The Dice betwixt them must the Fate divide,
P. 176 LOYALL SCOT   188 And wild disputes betwixt those heads must Grow,
P. 176 LOYALL SCOT   191 What Brittain was, betwixt two Kings distrest.

bewail   frequency: 2   relative frequency: 0.0000
P. 127 O.C.   168 Of your Abysse, with cover'd Head bewail
P. 151 INSTRUCTIONS   427 St. Albans writ to that he may bewail

beware   frequency: 1   relative frequency: 0.0000
P. 36 DAPHNIS   101 But hence Virgins all beware.

beyond   frequency: 11   relative frequency: 0.0002
P. 12 DIALOGUE   77 The rest does lie beyond the Pole,
P. 18 BERMUDAS   36 Eccho beyond the Mexique Bay.
P. 49 THE GARDEN   61 But 'twas beyond a Mortal's share
P. 61 A. HOUSE   91 Fair beyond Measure, and an Heir
P. 82 A. HOUSE   738 Supplies beyond her Sex the Line;
P. 107 ANNIVERSARY   173 Thee proof beyond all other Force or Skill,
P. 130 O.C.   287 Thou in a pitch how farre beyond the sphere
P. 142 INSTRUCTIONS   50 Philosopher beyond Newcastle's Wife.
P. 153 INSTRUCTIONS   504 (This lik'd him best) his Cash beyond Sea whip.
P. 181 MADE FREE   19 Beyond Sea he began,
P. 204 HISTORICALL   118 Declares the Councel Edicts are beyond

bias. See "biass."

biass   frequency: 1   relative frequency: 0.0000
P. 177 LOYALL SCOT   234 Had it not been for such a Biass Strong,

bible   frequency: 1   relative frequency: 0.0000
P. 174 LOYALL SCOT   119 The Bible and Grammar for the service Book.

bid   frequency: 3   relative frequency: 0.0000

```
        P. 153 INSTRUCTIONS  499 The Kingdoms Farm he lets to them bid least:
        P. 205 HISTORICALL   161 Bid him be bold all dangers to defye,
        P. 314 CHEQUER INN     54 The rest were bid by Cooper.
```

bidding   frequency: 1   relative frequency: 0.0000
        P. 20 THYRSIS   42 By bidding, with mee, all adieu.

big   frequency: 1   relative frequency: 0.0000
    See also "bigg."
        P. 156 INSTRUCTIONS 633 Paint him of Person tall, and big of bone,

bigg   frequency: 1   relative frequency: 0.0000
        P. 313 CHEQUER INN   25 And tho' he now do looke so bigg

bilbrough   frequency: 1   relative frequency: 0.0000
        P. 61 A. HOUSE   74 Or Bilbrough, better hold then they:

bill   frequency: 1   relative frequency: 0.0000
    See also "poll-bill."
        P. 28 LOVER   36 Another on his Heart did bill.

bill-borow   frequency: 1   relative frequency: 0.0000
        P. 56 BILL-BOROW   t1 Upon the Hill and Grove at Bill-borow.

billeted   frequency: 1   relative frequency: 0.0000
        P. 64 A. HOUSE   190 'As Pearls together billeted.

bills   frequency: 1   relative frequency: 0.0000
        P. 167 KINGS VOWES   60 And all their bills for publike good prevent.

bill's. See "private-bill's."

bin   frequency: 1   relative frequency: 0.0000
        P. 160 INSTRUCTIONS 787 Had he not built, none of these faults had bin;

bind   frequency: 6   relative frequency: 0.0001
        P. 10 DIALOGUE   44 Whom this sweet Chordage cannot bind.
        P. 31 FAIR SINGER   5 That while she with her Eyes my Heart does
                                  bind,
        P. 37 DEFINITION   29 Therefore the love which us doth bind.
        P. 58 BILL-BOROW   52 The Genius of the house do bind.
        P. 78 A. HOUSE   609 Bind me ye Woodbines in your 'twines,
        P. 183 MADE FREE   74 Cannot bind him to Troth,

binders   frequency: 1   relative frequency: 0.0000
        P. 126 O.C.   117 Out of the Binders Hand the Sheaves they tore,

binding   frequency: 1   relative frequency: 0.0000
        P. 161 INSTRUCTIONS 824 Binding, e're th' Houses meet, the Treaty sure.

binds   frequency: 5   relative frequency: 0.0001
        P. 46 AMETAS   4 Love binds Love as Hay binds Hay.
        P. 105 ANNIVERSARY   96 The Fabrick as with Arches stronger binds,
        P. 150 INSTRUCTIONS 382 Nor partial Justice her Behaviour binds;
        P. 165 INSTRUCTIONS 984 Nor Guilt to flatt'ry binds, nor want to
                                  stealth;

birch   frequency: 1   relative frequency: 0.0000
        P. 144 INSTRUCTIONS 143 Black Birch, of all the Earth-born race most
                                  hot,

bird   frequency: 4   relative frequency: 0.0000
        P. 49 THE GARDEN   53 There like a Bird it sits, and sings,
        P. 76 A. HOUSE   572 The Bird upon the Bough divines;
        P. 132 PARADISE   39 The Bird nam'd from that Paradise you sing
        P. 313 CHEQUER INN   36 And looks like Bird of Goale

birding   frequency: 2   relative frequency: 0.0000
        P. 157 INSTRUCTIONS 666 With birding at the Dutch, as if in sport:
        P. 172 LOYALL SCOT   31 With birding at the Dutch, as though in sport,

birds   frequency: 8   relative frequency: 0.0001
        P. 19 THYRSIS   13 Dorinda. There Birds may nest, but how can I,
        P. 20 THYRSIS   33 There, birds sing Consorts, garlands grow,
        P. 27 MISTRESS   38 And now, like am'rous birds of prey,
        P. 59 A. HOUSE   12 And Birds contrive an equal Nest;
        P. 71 A. HOUSE   409 Unhappy Birds! what does it boot
        P. 76 A. HOUSE   562 Among the Birds and Trees confer:
        P. 92 MAY'S DEATH   88 As th' Eagles Plumes from other birds divide.
        P. 191 TWO HORSES   4 It is a clear proofe that birds too may talke;

birth   frequency: 7   relative frequency: 0.0001

P. 28 LOVER   25 While Nature to his Birth presents
P. 36 DEFINITION   1 My Love is of a birth as rare
P. 61 A. HOUSE   85 A Nunnery first gave it birth.
P. 107 ANNIVERSARY   159 And thou, great Cromwell, for whose happy birth
P. 145 INSTRUCTIONS   171 His Birth, his Youth, his Brokage all
                          dispraise,
P. 147 INSTRUCTIONS   265 Of Birth, State, Wit, Strength, Courage,
                          How'rd presumes,
P. 158 INSTRUCTIONS   716 Unloaded here the Birth of either Pole;

birthday   frequency: 1   relative frequency: 0.0000
P. 179 STOCKSMARKET   11 Upon the King's birthday to set up a thing

birthright   frequency: 1   relative frequency: 0.0000
P. 198 DUKE   27 It is our birthright to have Power to kill.

bishop   frequency: 5   relative frequency: 0.0001
P. 174 LOYALL SCOT   104 A Bishop will like Mahomet tear the Moon
P. 175 LOYALL SCOT   132 Noe Bishop Rather then it shold bee soe!
P. 175 LOYALL SCOT   146 And in a Baron Bishop you have both
P. 176 LOYALL SCOT   175 Eating their brethren Bishop Turn and Cat
P. 194 TWO HORSES   109 Where is thy King gone? Ch. To see Bishop
                          Laud.

bishoprick   frequency: 1   relative frequency: 0.0000
P. 175 LOYALL SCOT   127 A Bishoprick is a great sine-Cure.

bishops   frequency: 25   relative frequency: 0.0005
P. 139 HOUSEWARMING   65 Straight Judges, Priests, Bishops, true sons
                          of the Seal,
P. 165 KINGS VOWES   13 I will have as fine Bishops as were ere made
                          with hands,
P. 171 PROPHECY   41 When Bishops shall lay all Religion by
P. 174 LOYALL SCOT   90 Noe Scotch was ever like a Bishops feud.
P. 174 LOYALL SCOT   92 Theres noe 'deliver us from a Bishops Wrath'.
P. 174 LOYALL SCOT   99 Seperate the world soe as the Bishops scalpes.
P. 174 LOYALL SCOT   103 Then Bishops Crampt the Comerce of Mankind.
P. 174 LOYALL SCOT   108 Instead of all the Plagues had Bishops come,
P. 174 LOYALL SCOT   111 A Bishops self is an Anathama.
P. 174 LOYALL SCOT   113 At Bishops Dung the Foxes quit the feild.
P. 174 LOYALL SCOT   115 A Bishops Bennett makes the strongest Curd.
P. 175 LOYALL SCOT   137 One Bishops fiend spirits a whole Diocesse.
P. 175 LOYALL SCOT   139 For only Kings can Bishops Exercise.
P. 175 LOYALL SCOT   141 Fish and flesh Bishops are the Ambigue.
P. 175 LOYALL SCOT   143 Bishops are very good when in Commendum.
P. 176 LOYALL SCOT   185 A Bishops Cruelty, the Crown had gone.
P. 176 LOYALL SCOT   193 The Bishops Nodle Perks up cheek by Jowle.
P. 176 LOYALL SCOT   196 Kings head saith this, But Bishops head that
                          doe.
P. 176 LOYALL SCOT   198 Well that Scotch monster and our Bishops sort
P. 176 LOYALL SCOT   204 Strange boldness! even bishops there rebell
P. 177 LOYALL SCOT   214 'Tis necessary Bishops have their rent,
P. 177 LOYALL SCOT   220 Such Bishops are Without a Complement
P. 190 STATUE   15 Or the Bishops and Treasurer did they Agree't
P. 194 TWO HORSES   121 Arch-Bishops and Bishops, Arch-Deacons and
                          Deans
P. 201 HISTORICALL   13 Bishops and Deanes, Peeres, Pimps and Knights
                          he made,

bishop's   frequency: 1   relative frequency: 0.0000
P. 145 INSTRUCTIONS   183 He March'd with Beaver cock'd of Bishop's
                          brim,

bishops-hill   frequency: 1   relative frequency: 0.0000
P. 61 A. HOUSE   73 Him Bishops-Hill, or Denton may,

bitter   frequency: 2   relative frequency: 0.0000
P. 27 LOVER   17 The Sea him lent these bitter Tears
P. 195 TWO HORSES   153 Ch. Troth, Brother, well said, but thats
                          somewhat bitter:

bitterly   frequency: 1   relative frequency: 0.0000
P. 87 FLECKNO   162 Wept bitterly as disinherited.

black   frequency: 11   relative frequency: 0.0002
P. 28 LOVER   27 A num'rous fleet of Corm'rants black,
P. 29 THE GALLERY   16 Black Eyes, red Lips, and curled Hair.
P. 71 A. HOUSE   400 To him a Fate as black forebode.
P. 85 FLECKNO   79 But were he not in this black habit deck't,
P. 86 FLECKNO   123 And draws out of the black box of his Breast
P. 143 INSTRUCTIONS   108 On opposite points, the black against the white.

P. 144 INSTRUCTIONS   143 Black Birch, of all the Earth-born race most
                          hot,
P. 156 INSTRUCTIONS   635 Scarce can burnt Iv'ry feign an Hair so black,
P. 158 INSTRUCTIONS   737 Black Day accurs'd! On thee let no man hale
P. 185 BRITANNIA   49 Sauls stormy rage and Check his black disease,
P. 203 HISTORICALL   79 To the black Idol for an Offering.

black-bag   frequency: 1   relative frequency: 0.0000
  P. 81 A. HOUSE   734 Thorough the Black-bag of your Skin;

blackest   frequency: 1   relative frequency: 0.0000
  P. 199 DUKE   54 Now, Painter, shew us in the blackest dye

blackheath   frequency: 1   relative frequency: 0.0000
  P. 202 HISTORICALL   61 Should we the Blackheath Project here relate,

blacks   frequency: 1   relative frequency: 0.0000
  P. 111 ANNIVERSARY   331 While dismal blacks hung round the Universe,

blade   frequency: 1   relative frequency: 0.0000
  P. 45 MOWER'S SONG   9 That not one Blade of Grass you spy'd,

blake   frequency: 5   relative frequency: 0.0001
  P. 99 HOLLAND   150 Steel'd with those piercing Heads, Dean, Monck
                          and Blake.
  P. 113 BLAKE   t1 On the Victory obtained by Blake over the
                          Spaniards,
  P. 116 BLAKE   99 His wish he has, for now undaunted Blake,
  P. 118 BLAKE   162 Victorious Blake, does from the Bay retire,
  P. 189 BRITANNIA   174 Blake, Candish, Drake, (men void of slavish
                          fears)

blame   frequency: 5   relative frequency: 0.0001
  P. 88 ODE   25 'Tis Madness to resist or blame
  P. 123 O.C.   9 And blame the last Act, like Spectators vain,
  P. 140 HOUSEWARMING 102 Throw dust in its Front, and blame situation:
  P. 151 INSTRUCTIONS 421 Each does the other blame, and all distrust;
  P. 164 INSTRUCTIONS 957 Blame not the Muse that brought those spots to
                          sight,

blames   frequency: 3   relative frequency: 0.0000
  P. 152 INSTRUCTIONS 483 Then, from the usual Common-place, he blames
  P. 160 INSTRUCTIONS 812 Blames the last Session, and this more does
                          fear.
  P. 164 INSTRUCTIONS 965 She blames them only who the Court restrain,

blast   frequency: 1   relative frequency: 0.0000
  P. 88 ODE   24 Did through his Laurels blast.

blasted   frequency: 1   relative frequency: 0.0000
  P. 149 INSTRUCTIONS 358 Blasted with Lightning, struck with Thunder
                          fell.

blazons   frequency: 1   relative frequency: 0.0000
  P. 18 CLORINDA   4 Where Flora blazons all her pride.

bleacht   frequency: 1   relative frequency: 0.0000
  P. 161 INSTRUCTIONS 838 With Face new bleacht, smoothen'd and stiff with
                          starch.

bleating   frequency: 1   relative frequency: 0.0000
  P. 188 BRITANNIA   146 To the Bleating Flock by him so lately torn.

bleed   frequency: 2   relative frequency: 0.0000
  P. 24 NYMPH   84 Until its Lips ev'n seem'd to bleed:
  P. 175 LOYALL SCOT   152 Noe Wonder if the Orthodox doe Bleed,

bleeding   frequency: 2   relative frequency: 0.0000
  P. 89 ODE   69 A bleeding Head where they begun,
  P. 125 O.C.   80 Of Halcyons kind, or bleeding Pelicans?

bleeds   frequency: 2   relative frequency: 0.0000
  P. 125 O.C.   96 And through the Wound its vital humour bleeds;
  P. 204 HISTORICALL   133 For one man's weakeness a whole Nation bleeds

blemishes   frequency: 1   relative frequency: 0.0000
  P. 202 HISTORICALL   62 Or count the various blemishes of State--

bless   frequency: 4   relative frequency: 0.0000
  P. 16 EYES   25 Yet happy they whom Grief doth bless,
  P. 23 NYMPH   43 Me to its game: it seem'd to bless

```
P. 118 BLAKE          148 Bless those they shine for, by their Influence.
P. 118 BLAKE          157 Ages to come, your conquering Arms will bless,

blessed                    frequency:    1    relative frequency: 0.0000
  See also "blest."
P.  91 MAY'S DEATH     39 Far from these blessed shades tread back agen

blessing                   frequency:    1    relative frequency: 0.0000
P. 198 DUKE            15 Armed with boold zeale and blessing with thy
                          hands

blessings                  frequency:    2    relative frequency: 0.0000
P. 184 BRITANNIA        6 Those would be Blessings in this spurious reign,
P. 203 HISTORICALL    107 The chiefest blessings Adam's Chaplin got.

blest                      frequency:   10    relative frequency: 0.0002
P.  33 DAPHNIS         24 As to see he might be blest.
P.  67 A. HOUSE       281 From that blest Bed the Heroe came,
P.  81 A. HOUSE       713 Blest Nymph! that couldst so soon prevent
P. 107 ANNIVERSARY    155 Hence that blest Day still counterpoysed wastes,
P. 108 ANNIVERSARY    218 Unto the Kingdom blest of Peace and Love:
P. 114 BLAKE           25 One of which doubtless is by Nature blest
P. 184 BRITANNIA        7 Awake, arise, from thy long blest repose;
P. 185 BRITANNIA       43 In Lofty Notes Tudors blest reign to sing,
P. 189 BRITANNIA      191 Freed by thy labours, Fortunate blest Isle,
P. 192 TWO HORSES      52 By a Curst hous of Commons and a blest
                          Restauracion;

blew                       frequency:    2    relative frequency: 0.0000
P.  85 FLECKNO         82 As the Chamelion, yellow, blew, or green.
P. 160 INSTRUCTIONS   796 Powder ne're blew man up so soon so high.

blind                      frequency:    8    relative frequency: 0.0001
  See also "blinde."
P.  96 HOLLAND         41 Among the blind the one-ey'd blinkard reigns,
P. 109 ANNIVERSARY    241 Though undiscern'd among the tumult blind,
P. 131 PARADISE         1 When I beheld the Poet blind, yet bold,
P. 131 PARADISE        14 O're which lame Faith leads Understanding
                          blind;
P. 138 HOUSEWARMING    51 The two Allens who serve his blind Justice for
                          ballance,
P. 162 INSTRUCTIONS   895 Her mouth lockt up, a blind before her Eyes,
P. 184 MADE FREE      121 But all ye Blind Apes,
P. 203 HISTORICALL     83 Who with vain Faith made all their Reason
                          blind:

blinde                     frequency:    1    relative frequency: 0.0000
P. 130 O.C.           302 To guide us upward through this region blinde.

blinded                    frequency:    3    relative frequency: 0.0000
P.  20 SOUL & BODY      5 Here blinded with an Eye; and there
P. 158 INSTRUCTIONS   735 Such the fear'd Hebrew, captive, blinded, shorn,
P. 189 STATUE           2 This five moneths continues still blinded with
                          board?

blinkard                   frequency:    1    relative frequency: 0.0000
P.  96 HOLLAND         41 Among the blind the one-ey'd blinkard reigns,

blisse                     frequency:    1    relative frequency: 0.0000
P. 130 O.C.           289 Despoyl'd of mortall robes, in seas of blisse,

blither                    frequency:    1    relative frequency: 0.0000
P. 149 INSTRUCTIONS   335 Blither than Hare that hath escap'd the Hounds,

bloated                    frequency:    1    relative frequency: 0.0000
P. 145 INSTRUCTIONS   180 And bloated Wren conducts them to their seats.

blood                      frequency:   14    relative frequency: 0.0002
  See also "bloud," "life-blocd."
P.   5 HASTINGS        52 Had Mayern once been mixt with Hastings blood!
P.  28 LOVER           42 Behold a spectacle of Blood,
P.  28 LOVER           56 In his own Blocd does relish best.
P.  44 DAMON           84 The Blood I stanch, and Wound I seal.
P.  84 FLECKNO         62 Hath sure more flesh and blood then he can boast.
P. 153 INSTRUCTIONS   532 Swells his old Veins with fresh Blood, fresh
                          Delight.
P. 170 PROPHECY         1 The blood of the Just London's firm Doome
                          shall fix
P. 176 LOYALL SCOT    178 When daring Blocd to have his rents regain'd
P. 180 STOCKSMARKET    37 Hath Blood him away (as his crown once)
                          conveyed?
P. 184 BRITANNIA        4 Of Earles, of Dukes, and Princes of the blood,
```

P. 188 BRITANNIA	147	If this Imperiall cyl cnce taint the Blood,
P. 198 DUKE	26	And thinke a prince oth blood can ere doe Ill?
P. 199 DUKE	63	Then Fleets and Armyes, battles, blood and wounds;
P. 205 HISTORICALL	176	And all the People been in blood embru'd,

bloods   frequency: 1   relative frequency: 0.0000
   P. 125 O.C.   92 At its rich bloods expence their Sorrows chear,

bloodworth-chanc'lor   frequency: 1   relative frequency: 0.0000
   P. 151 INSTRUCTIONS 425 The Bloodworth-Chanc'lor gives, then does recal

bloody   frequency: 5   relative frequency: 0.0001
   See also "bloudy."
   P. 71 A. HOUSE   397 The Edge all blcody from its Breast
   P. 71 A. HOUSE   401 But bloody Thestylis, that waites
   P. 88 ODE   56 Did clap their bloody hands.
   P. 185 BRITANNIA 39 The Bloody scottish Chronicle turnd o're
   P. 195 TWO HORSES 133 The Debauch'd and the Bloody since they Equally Gall us,

blooming   frequency: 1   relative frequency: 0.0000
   P. 61 A. HOUSE   90 There dwelt the blcoming Virgin Thwates;

blooms   frequency: 1   relative frequency: 0.0000
   P. 149 INSTRUCTIONS 346 But blooms all Night, and shoots its branches high.

blossome   frequency: 3   relative frequency: 0.0000
   P. 3 LOVELACE   16 On the faire blcssome cf each growing wit.
   P. 39 PICTURE   40 Nip in the blossome all our hopes and Thee.
   P. 107 ANNIVERSARY 164 T'have smelt the Blossome, and not eat the Fruit;

blossoms   frequency: 2   relative frequency: 0.0000
   P. 12 DROP OF DEW 23 Shuns the sweat leaves and blossoms green;
   P. 25 YOUNG LOVE 11 Whcse fair Blossoms are too green

blot   frequency: 1   relative frequency: 0.0000
   P. 203 HISTORICALL 106 Hence Death and Sin did human Nature blot:

blots   frequency: 1   relative frequency: 0.0000
   P. 94 DR. WITTY 15 Cf the first Author. Here he maketh blots

bloud   frequency: 2   relative frequency: 0.0000
   P. 186 BRITANNIA 66 From Exhalation bred of bloud and tears.
   P. 188 BRITANNIA 144 With the Doggs bloud his gentle kind convey

bloudy   frequency: 1   relative frequency: 0.0000
   P. 186 BRITANNIA 63 (By her usurpt), her right a bloudy sword

blow   frequency: 3   relative frequency: 0.0000
   P. 127 O.C.   184 Where those that strike from Heaven fetch their Blcw.
   P. 141 INSTRUCTIONS 27 So may'st thou perfect, by a lucky blow,
   P. 145 INSTRUCTIONS 163 Still his Hook-shoulder seems the blcw to dread,

blowes   frequency: 1   relative frequency: 0.0000
   P. 119 BLAKE   167 Whilst fame in every place, her Trumpet blowes,

blowing   frequency: 1   relative frequency: 0.0000
   P. 12 DROP OF DEW 3 Into the blowing Rcses,

blown   frequency: 1   relative frequency: 0.0000
   See also "blowne."
   P. 117 BLAKE   128 Some Ships are sunk, some blown up in the skie.

blowne   frequency: 1   relative frequency: 0.0000
   P. 171 PROPHECY 28 Then London lately burnt shall be blowne up,

blows   frequency: 1   relative frequency: 0.0000
   See also "blowes."
   P. 30 THE GALLERY 39 Nor blows more Wind than what may well

blue   frequency: 1   relative frequency: 0.0000
   See also "blew."
   P. 163 INSTRUCTIONS 916 And with blue streaks infect the Taper clear:

blunter   frequency: 1   relative frequency: 0.0000
   P. 43 DAMON   71 But, when the Iron blunter grows,

bluntly   frequency: 1   relative frequency: 0.0000

P. 151 INSTRUCTIONS 442 But ask'd him bluntly for his Character.

blush   frequency: 1   relative frequency: 0.0000
    P. 170 PROPHECY   13 When bare fac'd Villany shall not blush to cheat

blushes   frequency: 1   relative frequency: 0.0000
    P. 162 INSTRUCTIONS   896 Yet from beneath the Veil her blushes rise;

blushing   frequency: 1   relative frequency: 0.0000
    P. 79 A. HOUSE   664 In blushing Clouds conceales his Head.

blusht   frequency: 2   relative frequency: 0.0000
    P. 23 NYMPH   60 I blusht to see its foot more soft,
    P. 313 CHEQUER INN   45 Tho' all Men blusht that heard it

board   frequency: 9   relative frequency: 0.0001
    P. 155 INSTRUCTIONS   603 Or to their fellows swim on board the Dutch,
    P. 155 INSTRUCTIONS   614 His exil'd Sov'raign on its happy Board;
    P. 156 INSTRUCTIONS   639 But when, by shame constrain'd to go on Board,
    P. 169 ADVICE   30 The figure of a Drunken Councell board
    P. 169 ADVICE   34 To make them th' other Councell board forgett.
    P. 189 STATUE   2 This five moneths continues still blinded with
                              board?
    P. 193 TWO HORSES   54 And scarce a wise man at a long Councell board;
    P. 203 HISTORICALL   99 And never durst their tricks above board shew.
    P. 314 CHEQUER INN   67 Wheeler at Board, then next her set,

boards   frequency: 2   relative frequency: 0.0000
    P. 157 INSTRUCTIONS   669 The fatal Bark him boards with grappling fire,
    P. 172 LOYALL SCOT   35 The fatall bark him boards with Grapling fire

boast   frequency: 4   relative frequency: 0.0000
    P. 17 BERMUDAS   29 He cast (of which we rather boast)
    P. 84 FLECKNO   62 Hath sure more flesh and blood then he can boast.
    P. 118 BLAKE   159 And in one War the present age may boast,
    P. 147 INSTRUCTIONS   252 And all to pattern his Example boast.

boasting   frequency: 1   relative frequency: 0.0000
    P. 116 BLAKE   97 That they with joy their boasting General heard,

boat   frequency: 6   relative frequency: 0.0001
    See also "cock-boat," "packet-boat,"
             "pleasure-boat."
    P. 17 BERMUDAS   3 From a small Boat, that row'd along,
    P. 18 BERMUDAS   37 Thus sung they, in the English boat,
    P. 30 THE GALLERY   34 Like Venus in her pearly Boat.
    P. 158 INSTRUCTIONS   739 Or row a Boat in thy unlucky hour:
    P. 160 INSTRUCTIONS   789 But, his great Crime, one Boat away he sent;
    P. 204 HISTORICALL   155 From Tybur came the advice boat Monthly home,

boats   frequency: 3   relative frequency: 0.0000
    P. 72 A. HOUSE   436 How Boats among them safely steer.
    P. 73 A. HOUSE   477 How Boats can over Bridges sail;
    P. 83 A. HOUSE   770 Their Leathern Boats begin to hoist;

bodies   frequency: 7   relative frequency: 0.0001
    P. 49 THE GARDEN   51 Casting the Bodies Vest aside,
    P. 59 A. HOUSE   16 Their Bodies measure out their Place.
    P. 72 A. HOUSE   422 Lyes quilted ore with Bodies slain:
    P. 98 HOLLAND   99 And carve in their large Bodies, where they
                              please,
    P. 118 BLAKE   135 Scarce souls from bodies sever'd are so far,
    P. 118 BLAKE   136 By death, as bodies there were by the War.
    P. 145 INSTRUCTIONS   179 Gross Bodies, grosser Minds, and grossest
                              Cheats;

boding   frequency: 1   relative frequency: 0.0000
    P. 125 O.C.   102 Fore boding Princes falls, and seldom vain.

body   frequency: 13   relative frequency: 0.0002
    P. 20 SOUL & BODY   t A Dialogue between the Scul and Body.
    P. 21 SOUL & BODY   19 A Body that could never rest,
    P. 21 SOUL & BODY   10+ Body.
    P. 21 SOUL & BODY   30+ Body.
    P. 35 DAPHNIS   76 Of a Body dead while warm.
    P. 84 FLECKNO   58 But till he had himself a Body made.
    P. 84 FLECKNO   67 Lest his too suttle Body, growing rare,
    P. 85 FLECKNO   98 Delightful, said there can no Body pass
    P. 109 ANNIVERSARY   232 An healthful Mind within a Body strong;
    P. 146 INSTRUCTIONS   241 A scatter'd Body, which the Foe ne'r try'd,
    P. 162 INSTRUCTIONS   865 That may his Body, this his Mind explain.

```
          P. 169 ADVICE          43 The body of foot that was to have the van
          P. 176 LOYALL SCOT     187 With single body like the two Neckt Swan,


boggs                                   frequency:    1    relative frequency: 0.0000
          P. 174 LOYALL SCOT     98 Nothing, not Boggs, not Sands, not seas, not
                                    Alpes


bogs.  See "boggs."

boil.  See "boyl."

boiling.  See "boyling."


bold                                    frequency:   15    relative frequency: 0.0003
     See also "boold."
          P.   4 HASTINGS        15 While those of growth more sudden, and more bold,
          P. 117 BLAKE           117 Bold Stainer Leads, this Fleets design'd by
                                    fate,
          P. 131 PARADISE         1 When I beheld the Poet blind, yet bold,
          P. 146 INSTRUCTIONS    207 Bold Duncombe next, of the Projectors chief:
          P. 164 INSTRUCTIONS    949 So his bold Tube, Man, to the Sun apply'd,
          P. 164 INSTRUCTIONS    967 Bold and accurs'd are they, that all this while
          P. 166 KINGS VOWES      38 As bold as Alce Pierce and as faire as Jane
                                    Shore;
          P. 166 KINGS VOWES      40 Which if any bold Commoner dare to oppose,
          P. 193 TWO HORSES       75 W. To the bold talking members if the Bastards
                                    you adde,
          P. 194 TWO HORSES      100 Bold speaking hath done both man and beast wrong.
          P. 194 TWO HORSES      105 W. Truth 's as Bold as a Lyon, I am not
                                    afraid;
          P. 201 HISTORICALL      21 Bold James survives, no dangers make him flinch,
          P. 201 HISTORICALL      30 Why not with easy Youngsters make as bold?
          P. 204 HISTORICALL     148 Bold Irish Ruffins to his Court adress:
          P. 205 HISTORICALL     161 Bid him be bold all dangers to defye,


bolder                                  frequency:    2    relative frequency: 0.0000
          P.  32 MOURNING        21 Nay others, bolder, hence esteem
          P.  66 A. HOUSE       251 Another bolder stands at push


boldly                                  frequency:    2    relative frequency: 0.0000
     See also "bouldly."
          P.  24 NYMPH           85 And then to me 'twould boldly trip,
          P. 120 TWO SONGS       29 Courage, Endymicn, boldly Woo,


boldness                                frequency:    1    relative frequency: 0.0000
          P. 176 LOYALL SCOT    204 Strange boldness! even bishops there rebell


bolts                                   frequency:    1    relative frequency: 0.0000
          P.  20 SOUL & BODY      3 With bolts of Bcnes, that fetter'd stands


b'on                                    frequency:    1    relative frequency: 0.0000
          P. 153 INSTRUCTIONS   512 Why he should still b'on all adventures us'd.


bondage                                 frequency:    2    relative frequency: 0.0000
          P.  78 A. HOUSE       614 Ere I your Silken Bondage break,
          P. 192 TWO HORSES      51 W. That Bondage and Begery should be brought
                                    on the Nacion


bonds                                   frequency:    2    relative frequency: 0.0000
          P.  21 SOUL & BODY     12 From bonds of this Tyrannic Soul?
          P. 187 BRITANNIA       96 Shake of those Baby bonds from your strong
                                    Armes,


bone                                    frequency:    2    relative frequency: 0.0000
          P. 156 INSTRUCTIONS   633 Paint him of Person tall, and big of bone,
          P. 175 LOYALL SCOT    159 But of the Choicest Modern flesh and Bone.


bones                                   frequency:    2    relative frequency: 0.0000
          P.  20 SOUL & BODY      3 With bolts of Bcnes, that fetter'd stands
          P. 140 HIS HOUSE        1 Here lies the sacred Bones


bonne                                   frequency:    1    relative frequency: 0.0000
          P.  79 A. HOUSE       660 Starts forth with to its Bonne Mine.


book                                    frequency:    9    relative frequency: 0.0001
     See also "booke."
          P.   3 LOVELACE        31 And one the Bock prohibits, because Kent
          P.   5 HASTINGS        37 But most he doth th' Eternal Book behold,
          P.  77 A. HOUSE       584 Hath read in Natures mystick Book.
          P.  94 DR. WITTY        8 For ill Translators make the Book their own.
          P.  94 DR. WITTY       33 I see the people hastning to thy Book,
```

```
      P.  94 DR. WITTY       36 Now worth the liking, but thy Book and thee.
      P. 131 PARADISE         2 In slender Book his vast Design unfold,
      P. 174 LOYALL SCOT    119 The Bible and Grammar for the service Book.
      P. 199 DUKE            70 His sword is all his argument, and his book;

book-scorpions                   frequency:    1    relative frequency: 0.0000
      P.   3 LOVELACE        19 Word-peckers, Paper-rats, Book-scorpions,

booke                            frequency:    2    relative frequency: 0.0000
      P.   3 LOVELACE        22 Like the grim consistory on thy Booke;
      P.   4 LOVELACE        50 His Booke in them finds Judgement, with you
                                Love.

books                            frequency:    1    relative frequency: 0.0000
      See also "news-books."
      P.  87 ODE             5 'Tis time to leave the Books in dust,

boold                            frequency:    1    relative frequency: 0.0000
      P. 198 DUKE            15 Armed with boold zeale and blessing with thy
                                hands

boot                             frequency:    1    relative frequency: 0.0000
      P.  71 A. HOUSE       409 Unhappy Birds! what does it boot

bore                             frequency:    4    relative frequency: 0.0000
      P.  27 LOVER           19 And from the Winds the Sighs he bore,
      P. 126 O.C.           141 No part of time but bore his mark away
      P. 141 INSTRUCTIONS    35 Well he the Title of St. Albans bore,
      P. 164 INSTRUCTIONS   979 And through the Palace's Foundations bore,

bores                            frequency:    1    relative frequency: 0.0000
      P.  97 HOLLAND         80 Themselves the Hogs as all their Subjects
                                Bores!

born                             frequency:   10    relative frequency: 0.0002
      See also "borne," "earth-born," "new-born," "sea-born."
      P.  12 DROP OF DEW      5 For the clear Region where 'twas born
      P.  38 PICTURE         10 This Darling of the Gods was born!
      P.  88 ODE             53 That thence the Royal Actor born
      P. 107 ANNIVERSARY    170 Hast born securely thine undaunted Head,
      P. 108 ANNIVERSARY    216 And firy Steeds had born out of the Warr,
      P. 112 ANNIVERSARY    387 'He seems a King by long Succession born,
      P. 148 INSTRUCTIONS   287 A Gross of English Gentry, nobly born,
      P. 162 INSTRUCTIONS   893 Naked as born, and her round Arms behind,
      P. 165 INSTRUCTIONS   983 But they whom born to Virtue and to Wealth,
      P. 180 STOCKSMARKET    48 The day that he was both restored and born?

borne                            frequency:    1    relative frequency: 0.0000
      P. 199 DUKE            46 Poore princess, borne under a sullen starr

borrow                           frequency:    1    relative frequency: 0.0000
      P. 182 MADE FREE       45 He wou'd run on the score and borrow;

bosom                            frequency:    1    relative frequency: 0.0000
      See also "bosome."
      P.  12 DROP OF DEW      2 Shed from the Bosom of the Morn

bosome                           frequency:    6    relative frequency: 0.0001
      P.  17 BERMUDAS         2 In th' Oceans bosome unespy'd,
      P.  18 CLORINDA        11 C. In whose cool bosome we may lye
      P.  30 THE GALLERY     56 To crown her Head, and Bosome fill.
      P.  32 MOURNING        14 Her Eyes have so her Bosome drown'd,
      P.  86 FLECKNO        128 Picks out the tender bosome to its young.
      P. 154 INSTRUCTIONS   556 When, all on sudden, their calm bosome rives

bosomes                          frequency:    1    relative frequency: 0.0000
      P. 153 INSTRUCTIONS   528 Bosomes, and all which from themselves they hide.

bosoms.  See "bosomes."

both                             frequency:   60    relative frequency: 0.0012

bottle                           frequency:    1    relative frequency: 0.0000
      P. 316 CHEQUER INN    154 But downe the Visick Bottle threw

bottom                           frequency:    2    relative frequency: 0.0000
      See also "bottome."
      P.  32 MOURNING        32 And not of one the bottom sound.
      P.  70 A. HOUSE       384 And prove they've at the Bottom been.

bottome                          frequency:    1    relative frequency: 0.0000
```

P. 184 MADE FREE   125 I'th' bottome of the Box,

bough   frequency: 1   relative frequency: 0.0000
     P. 76 A. HOUSE   572 The Bird upon the Bough divines;

boughs   frequency: 4   relative frequency: 0.0000
     P. 49 THE GARDEN   52 My Soul into the boughs does glide:
     P. 74 A. HOUSE   509 The arching Boughs unite between
     P. 77 A. HOUSE   595 While the Wind, cooling through the Boughs,
     P. 129 O.C.   263 Whose spacious boughs are hung with trophies
                              round,

bought   frequency: 2   relative frequency: 0.0000
     P. 149 INSTRUCTIONS 332 Bought off with Eighteen hundred thousand pound.
     P. 179 STOCKSMARKET   24 Say his Majesty himself is bought too and sold.

bouldly   frequency: 1   relative frequency: 0.0000
     P. 194 TWO HORSES   101 When the Asse so bouldly rebuked the Prophet,

bound   frequency: 6   relative frequency: 0.0001
     P. 47 EMPIRE   4 To hollow Rocks and murm'ring Fountains bound.
     P. 96 HOLLAND   19 And to the stake a strugling Country bound,
     P. 98 HOLLAND   126 Half bound at home in Prison to the frost:
     P. 159 INSTRUCTIONS 743 When aged Thames was bound with Fetters base,
     P. 181 MADE FREE   28 But e're since he was bound
     P. 182 MADE FREE   49 Tho' oft bound to the Peace

bounders   frequency: 1   relative frequency: 0.0000
     P. 110 ANNIVERSARY   281 But who of both the Bounders knows to lay

boundless   frequency: 2   relative frequency: 0.0000
     P. 113 BLAKE   14 That boundless Empire, where you give the Law,
     P. 187 BRITANNIA   94 So boundless Lewis in full Glory shines,

bow   frequency: 5   relative frequency: 0.0001
     P. 38 PICTURE   14 See his Bow broke and Ensigns torn.
     P. 56 BILL-BOROW   6 So equal as this Hill does bow.
     P. 89 ODE   94 But on the next green Bow to pearch;
     P. 192 TWO HORSES   41 To see Church and state bow down to a whore
     P. 198 DUKE   11 Throwne att thy sacred feete I humbly bow,

bow'd   frequency: 1   relative frequency: 0.0000
     P. 89 ODE   63 But bow'd his comely Head,

bowel   frequency: 1   relative frequency: 0.0000
     P. 139 HOUSEWARMING   78 For foundation he Bristol sunk in the Earth's
                              bowel;

bowels   frequency: 1   relative frequency: 0.0000
     P. 91 MAY'S DEATH   24 In his own Bowels sheath'd the conquering
                              health.

bower. See "bowr."

bowles   frequency: 1   relative frequency: 0.0000
     P. 169 ADVICE   33 Capacious Bowles with Lusty wine repleat

bowls. See "bowles."

bowr   frequency: 1   relative frequency: 0.0000
     P. 32 MOURNING   18 Within her solitary Bowr,

bows   frequency: 1   relative frequency: 0.0000
     P. 147 INSTRUCTIONS 277 But strength at last still under number bows,

box   frequency: 7   relative frequency: 0.0001
     P. 86 FLECKNO   123 And draws out of the black box of his Breast
     P. 181 MADE FREE   3 In a Box the Citty Maggott;
     P. 181 MADE FREE   10 In a Golden Box
     P. 183 MADE FREE   91 If a Box of Pills
     P. 183 MADE FREE   99 And in this Box you have sent it;
     P. 183 MADE FREE   105 It might deserve a Box and a Gold one;
     P. 184 MADE FREE   125 I'th' bottome of the Box,

boxes   frequency: 1   relative frequency: 0.0000
     P. 143 INSTRUCTIONS 115 As some from Boxes, he so from the Chair

boy   frequency: 5   relative frequency: 0.0001
     P. 157 INSTRUCTIONS 659 They sigh'd and said, Fond Boy, why so untame,
     P. 157 INSTRUCTIONS 693 Fortunate Boy! if either Pencil's Fame,
     P. 170 PROPHECY   19 A Boy shall take his Sister for his Mate

P. 172 LOYALL SCOT   25 They sigh'd and said 'fond boy why soe Untame,
P. 173 LOYALL SCOT   59 Fortunate Boy, if ere my verse may Claim

boyl   frequency: 2   relative frequency: 0.0000
P. 64 A. HOUSE   173 'So through the mortal fruit we boyl
P. 96 HOLLAND   27 A daily deluge over them does boyl;

boyling   frequency: 1   relative frequency: 0.0000
P. 199 DUKE   62 Their boyling heads can hear no other sounds

boynton   frequency: 1   relative frequency: 0.0000
P. 160 INSTRUCTIONS   813 With Boynton or with Middleton 'twere sweet;

boys   frequency: 4   relative frequency: 0.0000
P. 150 INSTRUCTIONS   386 And Boys and Girls in Troops run houting by;
P. 151 INSTRUCTIONS   430 Threaten to beat us, and are naughty Boys.
P. 154 INSTRUCTIONS   542 And wanton Boys on every Rope do cling.
P. 187 BRITANNIA   114 To Boys, Bawds, whores, and made a Publick
                         game.

brag. See "bragg."

bragg   frequency: 2   relative frequency: 0.0000
P. 173 LOYALL SCOT   63 Skip Sadles: Pegasus thou needst not Bragg,
P. 314 CHEQUER INN   50 Each of his Handyworke to bragg

brain   frequency: 3   relative frequency: 0.0000
P. 59 A. HOUSE   6 Did for a Model vault his Brain,
P. 83 FLECKNO   28 The last distemper of the sober Brain,
P. 162 INSTRUCTIONS   866 Paint him in Golden Gown, with Mace's Brain:

brain'd   frequency: 1   relative frequency: 0.0000
P. 138 HOUSEWARMING   27 That Engine so fatal, which Denham had brain'd,

braine   frequency: 2   relative frequency: 0.0000
P. 165 KINGS VOWES   3 Our Pockets as empty as braine;
P. 315 CHEQUER INN   103 His Braine and Face Tredenham wrung

brains   frequency: 1   relative frequency: 0.0000
P. 194 TWO HORSES   94 With an Addleheaded Knight and a Lord without
                         Brains.

brake   frequency: 1   relative frequency: 0.0000
P. 90 ODE   109 Happy if in the tufted brake

brambles   frequency: 2   relative frequency: 0.0000
P. 78 A. HOUSE   615 Do you, O Brambles, chain me too,
P. 109 ANNIVERSARY   260 And Brambles be anointed with thine Oyl,

branch   frequency: 3   relative frequency: 0.0000
P. 83 FLECKNO   3 I for some branch of Melchizedeck took,
P. 125 O.C.   93 If some dear branch where it extends its life
P. 166 KINGS VOWES   42 Tho' for't I a branch of Prerogative lose.

branches   frequency: 4   relative frequency: 0.0000
P. 58 BILL-BOROW   70 To him our Branches are but few.
P. 79 A. HOUSE   647 And in its Branches tough to hang,
P. 129 O.C.   262 To Heav'n its branches, and through earth its
                         roots:
P. 149 INSTRUCTIONS   346 But blooms all Night, and shoots its branches
                         high.

brand   frequency: 2   relative frequency: 0.0000
P.   4 LOVELACE   37 Whose hand so rudely grasps the steely brand,
P. 98 HOLLAND   115 Ram'd with Gun-powder, flaming with Brand wine,

brandish   frequency: 1   relative frequency: 0.0000
P. 141 INSTRUCTIONS   18 To see a tall Lowse brandish the white Staff.

brandy   frequency: 1   relative frequency: 0.0000
P. 196 TWO HORSES   188 Theres ten times more Treason in Brandy and
                         ale.

brantford   frequency: 1   relative frequency: 0.0000
P. 170 PROPHECY   25 When two good Kings shall be att Brantford
                         knowne

brass   frequency: 6   relative frequency: 0.0001
P. 112 ANNIVERSARY   374 'Through double Oak, <and> lin'd with treble
                         Brass;
P. 190 STATUE   25 The Trojan Horse, tho' not of Brass but of wood,

```
          P. 191 STATUE        55 Tho of Brass, yet with grief it would melt him
                                  away,
          P. 191 TWO HORSES    11 Fryar Bacon had a head that spoke made of
                                  Brass,
          P. 192 TWO HORSES    29 The stately Brass Stallion and the white marble
                                  Steed
          P. 192 TWO HORSES    40 My Brass is provok't as much as thy stone
```

brat   frequency: 1   relative frequency: 0.0000
```
          P. 144 INSTRUCTIONS 145 And, of his Brat enamour'd, as't increast,
```

brav'd   frequency: 1   relative frequency: 0.0000
```
          P. 149 INSTRUCTIONS 361 But still he car'd, while in Revenge he brav'd,
```

brave   frequency: 14   relative frequency: 0.0002
```
          P.  10 DIALOGUE      45 Earth cannot shew so brave a Sight
          P. 128 O.C.         195 Hence, though in battle none so brave or fierce,
          P. 148 INSTRUCTIONS 291 To speak not forward, but in Action brave;
          P. 156 INSTRUCTIONS 649 Not so brave Douglas; on whose lovely chin
          P. 167 KINGS VOWES   59 So high that he shall brave the Parliament,
          P. 168 ADVICE         7 Whilest the brave youths tired with the work of
                                  State
          P. 169 ADVICE        41 And after him a brave Bregade of Hors
          P. 169 ADVICE        59 What Scandal's this! Temple, the wise, the
                                  Brave,
          P. 172 LOYALL SCOT   15 Not so brave Douglass, on whose Lovely Chin
          P. 173 LOYALL SCOT   67 Such in the Roman forum Curtius brave
          P. 186 BRITANNIA     83 These pious frauds (too slight t'ensnare the
                                  brave)
          P. 189 BRITANNIA    177 When with fierce Ardour their brave souls do
                                  burn,
          P. 195 TWO HORSES   137 Ch. De Witt and Cromwell had each a brave
                                  soul.
          P. 202 HISTORICALL   56 Whilst the brave Tudors wore th' Imperial
                                  Crowne:
```

bravely   frequency: 1   relative frequency: 0.0000
```
          P. 177 LOYALL SCOT  239 The good will bravely, bad will basely doe;
```

braves   frequency: 2   relative frequency: 0.0000
```
          P.  28 LOVER         48 Like Ajax, the mad Tempest braves.
          P. 204 HISTORICALL  150 From hence he picks and calls his murd'ring
                                  braves:
```

bravo's   frequency: 1   relative frequency: 0.0000
```
          P. 166 KINGS VOWES   41 I'll order my Bravo's to cutt off his Nose,
```

brawny   frequency: 2   relative frequency: 0.0000
```
          P. 143 INSTRUCTIONS  85 His brazen Calves, his brawny Thighs, (the
                                  Face
          P. 150 INSTRUCTIONS 379 Where when the brawny Female disobeys,
```

brazen   frequency: 2   relative frequency: 0.0000
```
          P. 112 ANNIVERSARY  362 'Arm'd with three Tire of brazen Hurricans;
          P. 143 INSTRUCTIONS  85 His brazen Calves, his brawny Thighs, (the
                                  Face
```

breach   frequency: 1   relative frequency: 0.0000
```
          P.  66 A. HOUSE     249 Some to the Breach against their Foes
```

breaches   frequency: 1   relative frequency: 0.0000
```
          P. 173 LOYALL SCOT   66 Unite our distance, fill the breaches old?
```

bread   frequency: 3   relative frequency: 0.0000
```
          P. 181 MADE FREE      9 And your Orphans want Bread to feed on,
          P. 198 DUKE          30 Shall they presume to say that bread is bread,
```

breadth   frequency: 1   relative frequency: 0.0000
See also "bredth."
```
          P.  59 A. HOUSE      23 That thinks by Breadth the World t'unite
```

break   frequency: 9   relative frequency: 0.0001
```
          P.  78 A. HOUSE     614 Ere I your Silken Bondage break,
          P.  84 FLECKNO       53 Would break his fast before, said he was Sick,
          P.  88 ODE           39 But those do hold or break
          P.  92 MAY'S DEATH   94 Shalt break, and the perpetual Vulture feel.
          P. 108 ANNIVERSARY  214 Break up each Deck, and rip the Oaken seams.
          P. 151 INSTRUCTIONS 447 Yet Lewis writes, and lest our Hearts should
                                  break,
          P. 162 INSTRUCTIONS 898 Her heart throbs, and with very shame would break.
```

```
    P. 192 TWO HORSES      36 To see a Lord Major and a Lumbard Street
                              break,
    P. 194 TWO HORSES     112 And returns to remount about break of Day.

breaking                        frequency:    4    relative frequency: 0.0000
    P.  31 FAIR SINGER      9 Breaking the curled trammels of her hair.
    P.  87 ODE             14 Breaking the Clouds where it was nurst,
    P. 142 INSTRUCTIONS    66 Can without breaking venom'd juice convey.
    P. 200 DUKE            83 He gott his wealth by breaking of his word;

breaks                          frequency:    4    relative frequency: 0.0000
    P.  28 LOVER           21 No Day he saw but that which breaks,
    P.  63 A. HOUSE       143 'And round about you Glory breaks,
    P.  81 A. HOUSE       717 True Praise (That breaks through all defence;)
    P. 144 INSTRUCTIONS   134 Breaks into Shops, and into Cellars prys.

breast                          frequency:   16    relative frequency: 0.0003
See also "brest."
    P.  14 THE CORONET     14 That, twining in his speckled breast,
    P.  24 NYMPH          118 My breast, themselves engraving there.
    P.  26 MISTRESS        15 Two hundred to adore each Breast:
    P.  27 LOVER           20 Which through his surging Breast do roar.
    P.  42 DAMON           32 Nor Cold but in her Icy Breast.
    P.  71 A. HOUSE       397 The Edge all bloody from its Breast
    P.  83 FLECKNO         25 Calm'd the disorders of my youthful Breast,
    P.  86 FLECKNO        123 And draws out of the black box of his Breast
    P. 123 O.C.            25 That they, to whom his Breast still open lyes,
    P. 125 O.C.            81 No downy breast did ere so gently beat,
    P. 142 INSTRUCTIONS    74 But in her soft Breast Loves hid Cancer
                              smarts.
    P. 147 INSTRUCTIONS   266 And in his Breast wears many Montezumes.
    P. 156 INSTRUCTIONS   627 At her own Breast her useless claws does arm;
    P. 186 BRITANNIA       51 The swelling Passions of his Cankred breast,
    P. 201 HISTORICALL     33 Her mischiefbreeding breast did so prevaile
    P. 205 HISTORICALL    174 And thirst of Empire Calentur'd his Breast.

breasts                         frequency:    1    relative frequency: 0.0000
See also "brests."
    P. 175 LOYALL SCOT    163 Confirming breasts and Armepitts for the head.

breath                          frequency:   10    relative frequency: 0.0002
    P.  23 NYMPH           59 It had so sweet a Breath! And oft
    P.  28 LOVER           39 And languished with doubtful Breath,
    P.  31 FAIR SINGER     12 My Fetters of the very Air I breath?
    P.  68 A. HOUSE       304 With Breath so sweet, or Cheek so faire.
    P. 125 O.C.            71 And now his Life, suspended by her breath,
    P. 142 INSTRUCTIONS    61 Paint her with Oyster Lip, and breath of Fame,
    P. 146 INSTRUCTIONS   224 Shall with one Breath like thistle-down
                              disperse.
    P. 147 INSTRUCTIONS   280 Spent with fatigue, to breath a while Toback.
    P. 154 INSTRUCTIONS   539 While the red Flags breath on their Top-masts
                              high
    P. 184 BRITANNIA        1 Brit: Ah! Rawleigh, when thy Breath thou didst
                              resign

breath'd                        frequency:    1    relative frequency: 0.0000
    P.  33 DAPHNIS         25 Till Love in her Language breath'd

breathes                        frequency:    1    relative frequency: 0.0000
    P. 154 INSTRUCTIONS   548 Puffs them along, and breathes upon them kind.

breathing                       frequency:    1    relative frequency: 0.0000
    P.  58 BILL-BOROW      62 Discourses with the breathing Trees;

breathless                      frequency:    1    relative frequency: 0.0000
    P.  57 BILL-BOROW      20 The feet of breathless Travellers.

breaths                         frequency:    1    relative frequency: 0.0000
    P.  62 A. HOUSE       109 'Our Orient Breaths perfumed are

bred                            frequency:    6    relative frequency: 0.0001
    P.  66 A. HOUSE       232 First from a Judge, then Souldier bred.
    P.  76 A. HOUSE       554 A Traitor-worm, within it bred.
    P. 106 ANNIVERSARY    117 Unhappy Princes, ignorantly bred,
    P. 186 BRITANNIA       53 Of Countryes love (by truth and Justice bred).
    P. 186 BRITANNIA       66 From Exhalation bred of bloud and tears.
    P. 202 HISTORICALL     53 But here his french bred Prowes provd in Vain,

breda                           frequency:    1    relative frequency: 0.0000
    P. 151 INSTRUCTIONS   449 Two Letters next unto Breda are sent,
```

bredth   frequency: 1   relative frequency: 0.0000
        P. 109 ANNIVERSARY   246 Trying the Measures of the Bredth and Height;

breech   frequency: 1   relative frequency: 0.0000
        P. 180 STOCKSMARKET   52 They will scarce afford him a rag to his breech.

breeches   frequency: 3   relative frequency: 0.0000
        P. 142 INSTRUCTIONS   42 Whose Breeches were the Instrument of Peace.
        P. 196 TWO HORSES   172 As learned men say, came out of their breeches,
        P. 315 CHEQUER INN   92 The Cheere into his Breeches ram'd

breed   frequency: 2   relative frequency: 0.0000
        P. 112 ANNIVERSARY   356 'Of shedding Leaves, that with their Ocean
                                   breed.
        P. 173 LOYALL SCOT   82 Whose one bank vertue, th' other vice doth breed?

breeding   frequency: 1   relative frequency: 0.0000
        P. 181 MADE FREE   18 Yet know both his Freinds and his Breeding.

breeds   frequency: 1   relative frequency: 0.0000
        P. 115 BLAKE   53 There the indulgent Soil that rich Grape
                                   breeds,

breez   frequency: 1   relative frequency: 0.0000
        P.   58 BILL-BOROW   61 Onely sometimes a flutt'ring Breez

breeze. See "breez."

bregade   frequency: 1   relative frequency: 0.0000
        P. 169 ADVICE   41 And after him a brave Bregade of Hors

brest   frequency: 7   relative frequency: 0.0001
        P.   3 LOVELACE   35 Lovelace that thaw'd the most congealed brest,
        P.   28 LOVER   45 And Tyrant Love his brest does ply
        P. 107 ANNIVERSARY   171 Thy Brest through ponyarding Conspiracies,
        P. 120 TWO SONGS   27 Shine thorough this obscurer Brest,
        P. 124 O.C.   35 Then to the Mothers brest her softly move,
        P. 125 O.C.   73 Like polish'd Mirrcurs, so his steely Brest
        P. 178 LOYALL SCOT   258 For shame extirpate from each loyall brest

brests   frequency: 1   relative frequency: 0.0000
        P. 115 BLAKE   76 Yet in their brests, carry a pride much higher.

brethren   frequency: 1   relative frequency: 0.0000
        P. 176 LOYALL SCOT   175 Eating their brethren Bishop Turn and Cat

brewer   frequency: 1   relative frequency: 0.0000
        P. 196 TWO HORSES   186 Tis Bacchus and the Brewer swear Dam 'um and
                                   sink 'um.

brewers   frequency: 1   relative frequency: 0.0000
        P. 169 ADVICE   56 Contriving Projects with a Brewers Clerk.

briars   frequency: 2   relative frequency: 0.0000
        P.   78 A. HOUSE   616 And courteous Briars nail me through.
        P. 109 ANNIVERSARY   254 With Thorns and Briars of the Wilderness.

brib'd   frequency: 1   relative frequency: 0.0000
        P. 193 TWO HORSES   77 Ch. That Traitors to their Country in a
                                   Brib'd Hous of Commons

bribe   frequency: 3   relative frequency: 0.0000
        P. 153 INSTRUCTIONS   500 Greater the Bribe, and that's at Interest.
        P. 185 BRITANNIA   17 Till Howard and Garway shall a bribe reject,
        P. 186 BRITANNIA   85 Bribe hungry Priests to deify your might,

bribed   frequency: 1   relative frequency: 0.0000
    See also "brib'd."
        P. 200 DUKE   112 Bribed by a croune on earth and one above,

briberies   frequency: 1   relative frequency: 0.0000
        P. 140 HIS HOUSE   3 Here lie Golden Briberies,

bribes   frequency: 1   relative frequency: 0.0000
        P. 139 HOUSEWARMING   63 So the Bribes overlaid her that Rome once
                                   betray'd:

brick   frequency: 2   relative frequency: 0.0000
        P. 138 HOUSEWARMING   38 To make Mortar and Brick, yet allow'd them no
                                   straw,
        P. 175 LOYALL SCOT   158 Seth's Pillars are noe Antique Brick and stone

brickbat   frequency: 1   relative frequency: 0.0000
    P. 138 HOUSEWARMING   26 And all for to save the expences of Brickbat,

bride   frequency: 4   relative frequency: 0.0000
    P. 64 A. HOUSE   186 'Appoint a fresh and Virgin Bride;
    P. 121 TWO SONGS   6 In a Garland for the Bride.
    P. 198 DUKE   37 Conveying his Religion and his bride:
    P. 314 CHEQUER INN   61 The Lady drest like any Bride

bridegroom   frequency: 1   relative frequency: 0.0000
    P. 62 A. HOUSE   108 'Lest the great Bridegroom find them dim.

bridge   frequency: 2   relative frequency: 0.0000
    P. 147 INSTRUCTIONS   250 The falling Bridge behind, the Stream below.
    P. 158 INSTRUCTIONS   705 Up to the Bridge contagious Terrour strook:

bridges   frequency: 1   relative frequency: 0.0000
    P. 73 A. HOUSE   477 How Boats can over Bridges sail;

bridle   frequency: 1   relative frequency: 0.0000
    P. 194 TWO HORSES   99 Wee ought to be wary and Bridle our Tongue;

brigade. See "bregade."

brigades   frequency: 1   relative frequency: 0.0000
    P. 147 INSTRUCTIONS   276 Broach'd whole Brigades like Larks upon his
                             Lance.

bright   frequency: 18   relative frequency: 0.0003
    P.   9 DIALOGUE   3 Close on thy Head thy Helmet bright.
    P. 12 DROP OF DEW   31 Dark beneath, but bright above:
    P. 17 BERMUDAS   17 He hangs in shades the Orange bright,
    P. 40 THE MATCH   35 None ever burn'd so hot, so bright;
    P. 55 EPITAPH   17 Modest as Morn; as Mid-day bright;
    P. 67 A. HOUSE   263 But truly bright and holy Thwaites
    P. 93 DR. WITTY   6 That sence in English which was bright and pure
    P. 111 ANNIVERSARY   326 See the bright Sun his shining Race pursue,
    P. 111 ANNIVERSARY   339 Why did mine Eyes once see so bright a Ray;
    P. 120 TWO SONGS   26 Can make a Night more bright then Day;
    P. 129 O.C.   244 In horses fierce, wild deer, or armour bright;
    P. 130 O.C.   290 Plunging dost bathe and tread the bright abysse:
    P. 157 INSTRUCTIONS   679 His shape exact, which the bright flames infold,
    P. 162 INSTRUCTIONS   867 Bright Hair, fair Face, obscure and dull of
                             Head;
    P. 162 INSTRUCTIONS   887 And those bright gleams that dart along and glare
    P. 164 INSTRUCTIONS   950 And Spots unknown to the bright Star descry'd;
    P. 173 LOYALL SCOT   45 His shape Exact which the bright flames enfold
    P. 186 BRITANNIA   69 From th' easie King she truthes bright Mirrour
                             took,

brighter   frequency: 2   relative frequency: 0.0000
    P. 62 A. HOUSE   120 'Our brighter Robes and Crowns of Gold?
    P. 153 INSTRUCTIONS   529 The Sun much brighter, and the Skies more
                             clear,

brightness   frequency: 1   relative frequency: 0.0000
    P. 58 BILL-BOROW   78 From his own Brightness he retreats:

brim   frequency: 1   relative frequency: 0.0000
    P. 145 INSTRUCTIONS   183 He March'd with Beaver cock'd of Bishop's
                             brim,

bring   frequency: 20   relative frequency: 0.0004
    P. 36 DAPHNIS   95 Yet bring with me all the Fire
    P. 40 THE MOWER   1 Luxurious Man, to bring his Vice in use,
    P. 42 DAMON   35 To Thee the harmless Snake I bring,
    P. 70 A. HOUSE   383 They bring up Flow'rs so to be seen,
    P. 71 A. HOUSE   402 To bring the mowing Camp their Cates,
    P. 109 ANNIVERSARY   237 Which to the thirsty Land did plenty bring,
    P. 121 TWO SONGS   7 If thou would'st a Garland bring,
    P. 139 HOUSEWARMING   67 Bring in the whole Milk of a year at a meal,
    P. 148 INSTRUCTIONS   315 Each day they bring the Tale, and that too true,
    P. 167 KINGS VOWES   51 And who knowes but the Mode may soon bring in
                             the rest?
    P. 169 ADVICE   50 That aime at mountains and bring forth a Mous,
    P. 170 PROPHECY   8 Tho the Walls stand to bring the Citty lower;
    P. 183 MADE FREE   86 Is this that you bring,
    P. 185 BRITANNIA   42 The other day fam'd Spencer I did bring
    P. 187 BRITANNIA   100 Three spotless virgins to your bed I bring,
    P. 189 BRITANNIA   180 With me I'le bring to dry my peoples tears:
    P. 203 HISTORICALL   78 Corrupt with Gold they Wives and Daughters bring

P. 204 HISTORICALL   123 To bring upon our Necks the heavier yoke:
P. 205 HISTORICALL   181 If a Kings Brother can such mischief bring,
P. 316 CHEQUER INN   162 He'd bring him off i' fack.

brings   frequency: 5   relative frequency: 0.0001
P. 72 A. HOUSE   441 This Scene again withdrawing brings
P. 96 HOLLAND   38 Something like Government among them brings.
P. 114 BLAKE   39 Your worth to all these Isles, a just right
                           brings,
P. 119 BLAKE   164 And there first brings of his success the news;
P. 201 HISTORICALL   31 From the french Court she haughty Topiks
                           brings,

brisk   frequency: 1   relative frequency: 0.0000
P. 162 INSTRUCTIONS   883 At night, than Canticleer more brisk and hot,

bristol   frequency: 2   relative frequency: 0.0000
P. 139 HOUSEWARMING   78 For foundation he Bristol sunk in the Earth's
                           bowel;
P. 163 INSTRUCTIONS   933 False to his Master Bristol, Arlington,

brit.   frequency: 4   relative frequency: 0.0000
P. 184 BRITANNIA   1 Brit: Ah! Rawleigh, when thy Breath thou didst
                           resign
P. 184 BRITANNIA   11 Brit: Favour'd by night, conceald by this
                           disguise,
P. 185 BRITANNIA   25 Brit: A Colony of French Possess the Court;
P. 188 BRITANNIA   141 Brit: Rawleigh, nce more; too long in vain I've
                           try'd

britain   frequency: 2   relative frequency: 0.0000
See also "brittain."
P. 66 A. HOUSE   246 His Horse through conquer'd Britain ride?
P. 205 HISTORICALL   160 Heaven had him Chieftain of great Britain made,

britain's. See "brittains."

britannia   frequency: 1   relative frequency: 0.0000
See also "brit.," "brittannia."
P. 184 BRITANNIA   t BRITANNIA and RAWLEIGH.

british   frequency: 1   relative frequency: 0.0000
See also "brittish."
P. 127 O.C.   176 Whether of British Saints or Worthy's told;

brittain   frequency: 2   relative frequency: 0.0000
P. 168 ADVICE   6 The Brittain Jigging it in Mascarade;
P. 176 LOYALL SCOT   191 What Brittain was, betwixt two Kings distrest.

brittains   frequency: 1   relative frequency: 0.0000
P. 195 TWO HORSES   147 If e're he be King I know Brittains Doome;

brittania   frequency: 1   relative frequency: 0.0000
P. 204 HISTORICALL   138 Dos on Brittania as on Churchill ride:

brittish   frequency: 3   relative frequency: 0.0000
P. 95 HOLLAND   2 As but th' Off-scouring of the Brittish Sand;
P. 155 INSTRUCTIONS   615 And thence the Brittish Admiral became;
P. 314 CHEQUER INN   80 The Foreman of the Brittish Crew

brittle   frequency: 2   relative frequency: 0.0000
P. 103 ANNIVERSARY   20 More slow and brittle then the China clay:
P. 155 INSTRUCTIONS   594 Snapping the brittle links, does thorow reel;

broach'd   frequency: 2   relative frequency: 0.0000
P. 147 INSTRUCTIONS   276 Broach'd whole Brigades like Larks upon his
                           Lance.
P. 149 INSTRUCTIONS   354 Be Broach'd again, for the great Holy-day

broak   frequency: 1   relative frequency: 0.0000
P. 186 BRITANNIA   70 And on the ground in spitefull rage it broak,

brokage   frequency: 1   relative frequency: 0.0000
P. 145 INSTRUCTIONS   171 His Birth, his Youth, his Brokage all
                           dispraise,

broke   frequency: 8   relative frequency: 0.0001
See also "broak."
P. 36 DAPHNIS   97 At these words away he broke;
P. 38 PICTURE   14 See his Bow broke and Ensigns torn.

P. 125 O.C.	78 But the dear Image fled the Mirrour broke.
P. 129 O.C.	234 It seem'd Mars broke through Janus' double gate;
P. 155 INSTRUCTIONS	592 For its last aid: Hold Chain or we are broke.
P. 181 MADE FREE	30 Has every Day broke his Indentures.
P. 192 TWO HORSES	39 Ch. Here Charing broke silence and thus he went on:
P. 204 HISTORICALL	122 This Saracen his Ccuntryes freedom broke

broken   frequency: 4   relative frequency: 0.0000
See also "brooken."
P. 114 BLAKE	46 Have broken all her Swords, then this one Peace,
P. 148 INSTRUCTIONS	307 Broken in Courage, yet the Men the same,
P. 179 STOCKSMARKET	4 Of bankers defeated and Lombard-street broken.
P. 182 MADE FREE	47 He was broken and gone

bronkard   frequency: 1   relative frequency: 0.0000
| P. 145 INSTRUCTIONS | 175 Bronkard Loves Squire; through all the field array'd, |

brood   frequency: 2   relative frequency: 0.0000
| P. 184 BRITANNIA | 3 Cubbs, didst thou call 'um? hadst thou seen this Brood |
| P. 188 BRITANNIA | 153 And shall this stinking Scottish brood evade |

brook   frequency: 2   relative frequency: 0.0000
| P. 42 DAMON | 13 But in the brook the green Frog wades; |
| P. 80 A. HOUSE | 701 And for a Glass the limpid Brook, |

brooke   frequency: 1   relative frequency: 0.0000
| P. 83 FLECKNO | 4 (Though he derives himself from my Lcrd Brooke) |

brooken   frequency: 1   relative frequency: 0.0000
| P. 190 STATUE | 38 Not Viner delayed us sc, tho' he was brooken |

broom   frequency: 1   relative frequency: 0.0000
| P. 137 HOUSEWARMING | 7 Like the King-fisher chuseth to build in the Broom, |

broth   frequency: 1   relative frequency: 0.0000
| P. 94 DR. WITTY | 30 Stint them to Cawdles, Almond-milk, and Broth. |

brother   frequency: 14   relative frequency: 0.0002
P. 160 INSTRUCTIONS	805 But the true cause was, that, in 's Erother May,
P. 163 INSTRUCTIONS	935 Who to the Brother, Brother would betray;
P. 180 STOCKSMARKET	60 Yet we'd better by far have him than his brother.
P. 192 TWO HORSES	38 When both knaves agreed to be each others brother.
P. 194 TWO HORSES	97 Ch. Enough, dear Brcther, for tho' we have reason,
P. 194 TWO HORSES	115 Ch. Pause, Brother, a while and calmly consider:
P. 195 TWO HORSES	153 Ch. Troth, Brother, well said, but thats somewhat bitter:
P. 200 DUKE	105 Destroyd by a false brcther and false friend.
P. 201 HISTORICALL	18 His younger Brcther perisht by a clap.
P. 205 HISTORICALL	162 His Brother sneaking Heretik should dye,
P. 205 HISTORICALL	172 Who strait design'd his Brother to supplant.
P. 205 HISTORICALL	181 If a Kings Brother can such mischief bring,
P. 315 CHEQUER INN	109 Old Hobbs's Brcther, Cheney there

brother-in-law's   frequency: 1   relative frequency: 0.0000
| P. 190 STATUE | 29 But his brother-in-law's horse had gain'd such repute |

brotherick   frequency: 1   relative frequency: 0.0000
| P. 146 INSTRUCTIONS | 212 Apsley and Brotherick, marching hand in hand. |

brotherless   frequency: 1   relative frequency: 0.0000
| P. 24 NYMPH | 99 The brotherless Heliades |

brothers   frequency: 1   relative frequency: 0.0000
| P. 200 DUKE | 110 Brothers, its true, by nature should be kinde: |

brought   frequency: 17   relative frequency: 0.0003
P. 27 LOVER	12 And, e're brought forth, was cast away:
P. 42 DAMON	40 Nor what they are, nor whc them brought.
P. 61 A. HOUSE	86 For Virgin Buildings oft brought forth.
P. 83 FLECKNO	22 Possest; and sure the Devil brought me there.

```
P.   83 PLECKNO        23 But I, who now imagin'd my self brought
P.  105 ANNIVERSARY    80 Nor with such labour from its Center brought;
P.  115 BLAKE          61 Ah, why was thither brought that cause of War,
P.  117 BLAKE         125 Fate these two Fleets, between both Worlds had
                          brought.
P.  119 BLAKE         165 The saddest news that ere to Spain was brought,
P.  149 INSTRUCTIONS  328 Is brought to beg in publick and to chide.
P.  164 INSTRUCTIONS  957 Blame not the Muse that brought those spots to
                          sight,
P.  180 STOCKSMARKET   34 That when to the scaffold your liege you had
                          brought
P.  192 TWO HORSES     51 W. That Bondage and Begery should be brought
                          on the Nacion
P.  194 TWO HORSES     87 W. 'Tis they who brought on us the Scandalous
                          Yoak
P.  204 HISTORICALL   125 First brought his Mother for a Prostitute:
P.  205 HISTORICALL   156 And brought new Lessons to the Duke from Rome.
P.  314 CHEQUER INN    78 From thence he brought his Seeds.
```

brow   frequency: 3   relative frequency: 0.0000
```
P.   25 YOUNG LOVE      3 Clear thine aged Fathers brow
P.   56 BILL-BOROW      5 Nor softest Pensel draw a Brow
P.  145 INSTRUCTIONS  197 Before them Higgins rides with brow compact,
```

brows   frequency: 5   relative frequency: 0.0001
```
P.   59 A. HOUSE        8 To arch the Brows that on them gaz'd.
P.   77 A. HOUSE      596 Flatters with Air my panting Brows.
P.   81 A. HOUSE      731 Nor once at Vice your Brows dare knit
P.  131 O.C.          318 His brows, like an imperiall jewell grac'd.
P.  147 INSTRUCTIONS  278 And the faint sweat trickled down Temples
                          Brows.
```

bruis'd   frequency: 1   relative frequency: 0.0000
```
P.    5 HASTINGS       55 But what could he, good man, although he bruis'd
```

bruises   frequency: 1   relative frequency: 0.0000
```
P.  129 O.C.          267 (It groanes, and bruises all below that stood
```

brush   frequency: 1   relative frequency: 0.0000
```
P.   66 A. HOUSE      252 With their old Holy-Water Brush.
```

brute   frequency: 1   relative frequency: 0.0000
```
P.  196 TWO HORSES    163 If Speech from Brute Animals in Romes first
                          age
```

brutish   frequency: 1   relative frequency: 0.0000
```
P.  107 ANNIVERSARY   177 Our brutish fury strugling to be Free,
```

brutus   frequency: 1   relative frequency: 0.0000
```
P.   90 MAY'S DEATH    18 Brutus and Cassius the Peoples cheats.
```

bucentore   frequency: 1   relative frequency: 0.0000
```
P.   98 HOLLAND       135 And now again our armed Bucentore
```

buck   frequency: 1   relative frequency: 0.0000
```
P.  175 LOYALL SCOT   164 Abbot one Buck, but he shot many a Doe,
```

buckingham   frequency: 1   relative frequency: 0.0000
```
P.  149 INSTRUCTIONS  357 First Buckingham, that durst to him Rebel,
```

buckingham's   frequency: 1   relative frequency: 0.0000
```
P.  140 HOUSEWARMING  100 Great Buckingham's Sacrifice must be the first.
```

bud   frequency: 2   relative frequency: 0.0000
```
P.   82 A. HOUSE      742 The Priest shall cut the sacred Bud;
P.  154 INSTRUCTIONS  551 So have I seen in April's bud, arise
```

buds   frequency: 1   relative frequency: 0.0000
```
P.   39 PICTURE        35 Gather the Flow'rs, but spare the Buds;
```

buff   frequency: 1   relative frequency: 0.0000
```
P.   84 FLECKNO        71 Wears a close Jacket of poetick Buff,
```

buffoones   frequency: 2   relative frequency: 0.0000
```
P.  185 BRITANNIA      26 Pimps, Priests, Buffoones i'th privy chamber
                          sport.
P.  187 BRITANNIA     120 Beseig'd by 's whores, Buffoones, and Bastard
                          Chitts:
```

buffoons   frequency: 1   relative frequency: 0.0000
See also "buffoones."
```
P.  203 HISTORICALL    90 As Killegrew buffoons his Master, they
```

bugger'd   frequency: 1   relative frequency: 0.0000
    P. 144 INSTRUCTIONS 146 Bugger'd in Incest with the mungrel Beast.

build   frequency: 12   relative frequency: 0.0002
    P. 21 SOUL & BODY   42 To build me up for Sin so fit?
    P. 59 A. HOUSE   10 Such unproporticn'd dwellings build?
    P. 71 A. HOUSE   410 To build below the Grasses Root;
    P. 72 A. HOUSE   417 Or sooner hatch or higher build:
    P. 104 ANNIVERSARY   33 They neither build the Temple in their dayes,
    P. 105 ANNIVERSARY   78 But who the Minds of stubborn Men can build?
    P. 116 BLAKE   92 They build and act all that can make them strong.
    P. 137 HOUSEWARMING   7 Like the King-fisher chuseth to build in the
                               Broom,
    P. 137 HOUSEWARMING   20 To build with the Jews-trump of his cwn tongue.
    P. 138 HOUSEWARMING   40 So he could to build but make Policy Law.
    P. 166 KINGS VOWES   24 But if they build it too fast, I will soon make
                               them hold.
    P. 179 STOCKSMARKET   2 Do at their own charge their citadels build,

builders   frequency: 1   relative frequency: 0.0000
    P. 59 A. HOUSE   24 Though the first Builders fail'd in Height?

building   frequency: 4   relative frequency: 0.0000
    P. 76 A. HOUSE   549 That for his building he designs,
    P. 96 HOLLAND   14 Less then what building Swallows bear away;
    P. 96 HOLLAND   21 Building their watry Babel far more high
    P. 139 HOUSEWARMING   81 For surveying the building, Prat did the feat,

buildings   frequency: 3   relative frequency: 0.0000
    P. 61 A. HOUSE   86 For Virgin Buildings oft brought forth.
    P. 65 A. HOUSE   217 'But sure those Buildings last not long,
    P. 140 HOUSEWARMING   101 Now some (as all Buildings must censure abide)

builds   frequency: 2   relative frequency: 0.0000
    P.   3 LOVELACE   13 He highest builds, who with most Art destroys,
    P. 139 HOUSEWARMING   93 Fond City, its Rubbish and Ruines that builds,

built   frequency: 6   relative frequency: 0.0001
    P. 47 EMPIRE   8 And built the Organs City where they dwell.
    P. 61 A. HOUSE   69 The House was built upcn the Place
    P. 138 HOUSEWARMING   32 Though he had built full many a one for his
                               Master
    P. 140 HOUSEWARMING   109 Or rather how wisely his Stall was built near,
    P. 160 INSTRUCTIONS   787 Had he not built, ncne of these faults had bin;
    P. 175 LOYALL SCOT   169 When for a Church hee built a Theatre.

bulk   frequency: 3   relative frequency: 0.0000
    P. 74 A. HOUSE   501 There the huge Bulk takes place, as ment
    P. 112 ANNIVERSARY   380 'Moves the great Bulk, and animates the whole.
    P. 154 INSTRUCTIONS   575 For whose strong bulk Earth scarce could Timber
                               find,

bull   frequency: 4   relative frequency: 0.0000
    P. 25 YOUNG LOVE   15 As the lusty Bull or Ram,
    P. 86 FLECKNO   152 And roar'd cut, like Perillus in's own Bull;
    P. 145 INSTRUCTICNS   178 Haters of Fowl, tc Teal preferring Bull.
    P. 191 TWO HORSES   9 Phalaris had a Bull which grave Authors tell ye

bullet   frequency: 1   relative frequency: 0.0000
    P. 154 INSTRUCTIONS   566 Through the Walls untight, and Bullet show'rs:

bullet-cheese   frequency: 1   relative frequency: 0.0000
    P. 98 HOLLAND   120 Then of Case-Butter shot and Bullet-Cheese.

bulls   frequency: 2   relative frequency: 0.0000
    P. 72 A. HOUSE   448 Ere the Bulls enter at Madril.
    P. 150 INSTRUCTIONS   407 With the Bulls Horn to measure his own Head,

bulteales   frequency: 1   relative frequency: 0.0000
    P. 139 HOUSEWARMING   69 Bulteales, Beakns, Morley, Wrens fingers with
                               telling

bun   frequency: 1   relative frequency: 0.0000
    P. 201 HISTORICALL   24 Was thus enamour'd with a butterd bun,

buoy'd   frequency: 1   relative frequency: 0.0000
    P. 98 HOLLAND   112 We buoy'd so often up their sinking State.

burden. See "burthen."

burger   frequency: 1   relative frequency: 0.0000

P.   96 HOLLAND   29 The Fish oft-times the Burger dispossest,

burgess   frequency: 1   relative frequency: 0.0000
     See also "burgesse."
     P. 161 INSTRUCTIONS 831 The portly Burgess, through the Weather hot,

burgesse   frequency: 1   relative frequency: 0.0000
     P. 313 CHEQUER INN   15 Till he was Burgesse chosen

burglard   frequency: 1   relative frequency: 0.0000
     P. 182 MADE FREE   60 They had Burglard all your Propriety.

burglared. See "burglard."

burgomaster   frequency: 1   relative frequency: 0.0000
     P. 98 HOLLAND   114 Cause why their Burgomaster of the Sea

buried   frequency: 1   relative frequency: 0.0000
     See also "bury'd," "buryed."
     P. 118 BLAKE   155 Wars chief support with them would buried be,

burn   frequency: 9   relative frequency: 0.0001
     See also "burne."
     P. 75 A. HOUSE   528 That in so equal Flames do burn!
     P. 92 MAY'S DEATH   90 Where Sulphrey Phlegeton does ever burn.
     P. 106 ANNIVERSARY   116 Nor teach, but traffique with, or burn the Jew.
     P. 123 O.C.   28 As long as Grief shall weep, or Love shall
                              burn.
     P. 158 INSTRUCTIONS 712 Our Merchant-men, lest they should burn, we
                              drown.
     P. 158 INSTRUCTIONS 723 Now (nothing more at Chatham left to burn)
     P. 164 INSTRUCTIONS 972 And peal the Bark to burn at last the Tree.
     P. 185 BRITANNIA   14 Till England knowes who did her Citty burn,
     P. 189 BRITANNIA   177 When with fierce Ardour their brave souls do
                              burn,

burn'd   frequency: 2   relative frequency: 0.0000
     P. 40 THE MATCH   35 None ever burn'd so hot, so bright;
     P. 111 ANNIVERSARY   332 And Stars (like Tapers) burn'd upon his Herse:

burne   frequency: 4   relative frequency: 0.0000
     P. 170 PROPHECY   5 To burne the Cittye which againe shall rise
     P. 184 MADE FREE   132 Unless you all burne again, burne again.
     P. 204 HISTORICALL   154 Hee'l burne a Citty or destroy a King.

burned. See "burn'd," "sun-burn'd."

burnes   frequency: 1   relative frequency: 0.0000
     P. 173 LOYALL SCOT   57 The ship burnes down and with his reliques sinks,

burnetts   frequency: 1   relative frequency: 0.0000
     P. 174 LOYALL SCOT   94 Never for Burnetts sake the Lauderdales,

burning   frequency: 6   relative frequency: 0.0001
     P. 84 FLECKNO   31 And how I, silent, turn'd my burning Ear
     P. 88 ODE   21 Then burning through the Air he went,
     P. 117 BLAKE   123 Never so burning was that Climate known,
     P. 139 HOUSEWARMING   96 And till there you remove, you shall never leave
                              burning
     P. 157 INSTRUCTIONS 684 His burning Locks adorn his Face Divine.
     P. 173 LOYALL SCOT   50 His burning Locks Adorn his face divine.

burnish'd   frequency: 1   relative frequency: 0.0000
     P. 157 INSTRUCTIONS 680 Like the Sun's Statue stands of burnish'd
                              Gold.

burnished. See "burnish'd," "burnisht."

burnisht   frequency: 1   relative frequency: 0.0000
     P. 173 LOYALL SCOT   46 Like the sun's Statue stands of burnisht Gold:

burns   frequency: 6   relative frequency: 0.0001
     See also "burnes."
     P. 40 THE MATCH   24 And all that burns the Mind.
     P. 42 DAMON   20 Which burns the Fields and Mower both:
     P. 119 TWO SONGS   16 That burns with an immortal Flame.
     P. 149 INSTRUCTIONS 348 The Comet dread, and Earth and Heaven burns.
     P. 157 INSTRUCTIONS 691 His Ship burns down, and with his Relicks
                              sinks,
     P. 157 INSTRUCTIONS 698 The Loyal-london, now a third time burns.

burnt   frequency: 7   relative frequency: 0.0001

P.	139	HOUSEWARMING	90 A Lanthorn, like Faux's surveys the burnt Town,
P.	156	INSTRUCTIONS	635 Scarce can burnt Iv'ry feign an Hair so black,
P.	159	INSTRUCTIONS	756 And were it burnt, yet less would be their pain.
P.	171	LOYALL SCOT	t2 Upon The occasion of the death of Captain Douglas burnt in one
P.	171	PROPHECY	28 Then London lately burnt shall be blowne up,
P.	190	STATUE	26 Had within it an Army that burnt up the Town:
P.	202	HISTORICALL	50 Burnt downe the Pallace of Persepolis.

burrough   frequency: 1   relative frequency: 0.0000
     P. 312 CHEQUER INN   6 In Burrough or in Shire.

burrowing. See "burr'wing."

burr'wing   frequency: 1   relative frequency: 0.0000
     P. 164 INSTRUCTIONS 980 Burr'wing themselves to hoard their guilty Store.

burthen   frequency: 1   relative frequency: 0.0000
     P. 124 O.C.   33 And, lest their force the tender burthen wrong,

bury'd   frequency: 1   relative frequency: 0.0000
     P. 148 INSTRUCTIONS 320 The unpractis'd Saw lyes bury'd in its Dust;

buryed   frequency: 2   relative frequency: 0.0000
     P. 118 BLAKE   154 Were buryed in as large, and deep a grave,
     P. 195 TWO HORSES   142 W. But hee 's buryed alive in lust and in sloath.

bushes   frequency: 2   relative frequency: 0.0000
     P. 82 A. HOUSE   745 Mean time ye Fields, Springs, Bushes, Flow'rs,
     P. 154 INSTRUCTIONS 558 Shepherds themselves in vain in bushes shrowd.

bushy   frequency: 1   relative frequency: 0.0000
     P. 132 PARADISE   49 Their Fancies like our bushy Points appear,

busie   frequency: 2   relative frequency: 0.0000
     P. 48 THE GARDEN   12 In busie Companies of Men.
     P. 148 INSTRUCTIONS 321 The busie Hammer sleeps, the Ropes untwine;

business   frequency: 1   relative frequency: 0.0000
     P. 317 CHEQUER INN   179 And the whole business of their Acts

busy. See "busie."

but   frequency: 489   relative frequency: 0.0102

butchers   frequency: 1   relative frequency: 0.0000
     P. 141 INSTRUCTIONS   33 Paint him with Drayman's Shoulders, butchers Mien,

butter. See "case-butter."

butter-coloss   frequency: 1   relative frequency: 0.0000
     P. 97 HOLLAND   94 A Water-Hercules Butter-Coloss,

butterd   frequency: 1   relative frequency: 0.0000
     P. 201 HISTORICALL   24 Was thus enamour'd with a butterd bun,

buttered. See "butterd."

buttery. See "buttry."

buttry   frequency: 1   relative frequency: 0.0000
     P. 315 CHEQUER INN   93 Which Buttry were and Larder

buy   frequency: 5   relative frequency: 0.0001
     P. 11 DIALOGUE   60 And want new Worlds to buy.
     P. 138 HOUSEWARMING   34 To buy us for Slaves, and purchase our Lands;
     P. 166 KINGS VOWES   30 And I either will vacate, or buy him a place.
     P. 191 STATUE   46 To buy a King is not so wise as to sell,
     P. 192 TWO HORSES   27 Since Viner and Osburn did buy and provide 'um

buy-at   frequency: 1   relative frequency: 0.0000
     P. 137 HOUSEWARMING   10 (So unreasonable are the rate they buy-at)

buys   frequency: 1   relative frequency: 0.0000
     P. 179 STOCKSMARKET   22 Who the Parliament buys and revenues does sell,

by   frequency: 244   relative frequency: 0.0050

c.   frequency: 14   relative frequency: 0.0002
P. 18 CLORINDA   1 C. Damon come drive thy flocks this way.
P. 18 CLORINDA   3 C. I have a grassy Scutcheon spy'd,
P. 18 CLORINDA   8 C. Seize the short Joyes then, ere they vade.
P. 18 CLORINDA   10 D. That den? C. Loves Shrine. D. But
                           Virtue's Grave.
P. 18 CLORINDA   11 C. In whose cool bosome we may lye
P. 18 CLORINDA   13 C. Near this, a Fountaines liquid Bell
P. 18 CLORINDA   16 Or slake its Drought? C. What is't you mean?
P. 18 CLORINDA   19 C. And what late change? D. The other day
P. 18 CLORINDA   20 Pan met me. C. What did great Pan say?
P. 18 CLORINDA   24 C. Sweet must Pan sound in Damons Note.
P. 18 CLORINDA   26 C. Who would not in Pan's Praises meet?
P. 38 PICTURE   t1 The Picture of little T. C. in a Prospect
P. 103 ANNIVERSARY   t2 Of The Government under O. C.
P. 123 O.C.   t A Poem upon the Death of O. C.

c-------n   frequency: 1   relative frequency: 0.0000
P. 145 INSTRUCTICNS   181 C-------n advances next, whose Coife dos awe

cabal   frequency: 2   relative frequency: 0.0000
P. 144 INSTRUCTIONS   121 The close Cabal mark'd how the Navy eats,
P. 180 STOCKSMARKET   39 Or is he in cabal in his cabinet set?

cabillau   frequency: 1   relative frequency: 0.0000
P. 96 HOLLAND   32 Whole sholes of Dutch serv'd up for Cabillau;

cabinet   frequency: 2   relative frequency: 0.0000
P. 29 THE GALLERY   14 Adorned Tyrants Cabinet;
P. 180 STOCKSMARKET   39 Or is he in cabal in his cabinet set?

cacao   frequency: 1   relative frequency: 0.0000
P. 142 INSTRUCTICNS   68 Out of the cordial meal of the Cacao.

caelia   frequency: 2   relative frequency: 0.0000
P. 94 DR. WITTY   17 Caelia whose English doth more richly flow
P. 94 DR. WITTY   21 But she is Caelia still: no other grace

caesar   frequency: 1   relative frequency: 0.0000
P. 90 ODE   101 A Caesar he ere long to Gaul,

caesars   frequency: 1   relative frequency: 0.0000
P. 88 ODE   23 And Caesars head at last

calais   frequency: 1   relative frequency: 0.0000
P. 151 INSTRUCTIONS   414 And the French Army one from Calais spies.

calcines   frequency: 1   relative frequency: 0.0000
P. 175 LOYALL SCOT   135 Aaron Casts Calves but Moses them Calcines.

caledonian   frequency: 1   relative frequency: 0.0000
P. 90 ODE   112 The Caledonian Deer.

calentur'd   frequency: 1   relative frequency: 0.0000
P. 205 HISTORICALL   174 And thirst of Empire Calentur'd his Breast.

call   frequency: 12   relative frequency: 0.0002
P. 70 A. HOUSE   376 Of the green spir's, to us do call.
P. 71 A. HOUSE   413 And now your Orphan Parents Call
P. 76 A. HOUSE   569 Already I begin to call
P. 110 ANNIVERSARY   301 What thy Misfortune, they the Spirit call,
P. 152 INSTRUCTIONS   477 Or in their hasty Call to find a flaw,
P. 153 INSTRUCTIONS   517 As Heav'n in Storms, they call, in gusts of
                           State,
P. 155 INSTRUCTIONS   608 Now needful, does for Ammunition call.
P. 165 KINGS VOWES   18 And yet call him home again, soon as I may.
P. 177 LOYALL SCOT   251 First call each other names and then they fight.
P. 184 BRITANNIA   3 Cubbs, didst thou call 'um? hadst thou seen this
                           Brood
P. 201 HISTORICALL   6 The People call him home to helpe the State,
P. 314 CHEQUER INN   65 That she was forc't to call for Groome

call'd   frequency: 8   relative frequency: 0.0001
P. 28 LOVER   43 Fortune and He are call'd to play
P. 47 EMPIRE   7 He call'd the Ecchoes from their sullen Cell,
P. 71 A. HOUSE   406 And cryes, he call'd us Israelites;
P. 89 ODE   61 Nor call'd the Gods with vulgar spight
P. 97 HOLLAND   82 That it had one Civilis call'd by Name,
P. 138 HOUSEWARMING   49 To proceed in the Model he call'd in his
                           Allens,
P. 161 INSTRUCTICNS   862 And had almost mistook and call'd them Rogues.

P. 312 CHEQUER INN   t A Ballad call'd the Chequer Inn.

called   frequency: 2   relative frequency: 0.0000
    See also "call'd."
    P. 62 A. HOUSE   102 'Of those wild Creatures, called Men.
    P. 199 DUKE   49 Had called you to a sound though petty Throne,

calls   frequency: 4   relative frequency: 0.0000
    P. 84 FLECKNO   42 Over the Lute, his murmuring Belly calls,
    P. 86 FLECKNO   126 Then Nero's Poem he calls charity:
    P. 174 LOYALL SCOT 106 The Jugling Prelate on his hocus calls,
    P. 204 HISTORICALL 150 From hence he picks and calls his murd'ring
                            traves:

calm   frequency: 9   relative frequency: 0.0001
    See also "calme."
    P. 54 THYESTE   5 In calm Leisure let me rest;
    P. 62 A. HOUSE   114 'With which calm Pleasure overflows;
    P. 72 A. HOUSE   434 Like a calm Sea it shews the Rocks:
    P. 79 A. HOUSE   671 And such an horror calm and dumb,
    P. 98 HOLLAND   128 In a calm Winter, under Skies Serene.
    P. 154 INSTRUCTIONS 556 When, all on sudden, their calm bosome rives
    P. 157 INSTRUCTIONS 675 And secret Joy, in his calm Soul does rise,
    P. 162 INSTRUCTIONS 889 There, as in the calm horrour all alone,
    P. 179 STOCKSMARKET   8 He that vows for a calm is absolved by a wreck.

calm'd   frequency: 1   relative frequency: 0.0000
    P. 83 FLECKNO   25 Calm'd the disorders of my youthful Breast,

calme   frequency: 1   relative frequency: 0.0000
    P. 131 O.C.   321 Cease now our griefs, calme peace succeeds a war,

calmely   frequency: 1   relative frequency: 0.0000
    'P. 24 NYMPH   94 And dye as calmely as a Saint.

calming   frequency: 1   relative frequency: 0.0000
    P. 30 THE GALLERY   35 The Halcyons, calming all that's nigh,

calmly   frequency: 1   relative frequency: 0.0000
    See also "calmely."
    P. 194 TWO HORSES   115 Ch. Pause, Brother, a while and calmly
                            consider:

calms   frequency: 1   relative frequency: 0.0000
    P. 124 O.C.   48 And at her Aspect calms his growing Cares;

calves   frequency: 2   relative frequency: 0.0000
    P. 143 INSTRUCTIONS 85 His brazen Calves, his brawny Thighs, (the
                            Face
    P. 175 LOYALL SCOT 135 Aaron Casts Calves but Moses them Calcines.

calvin   frequency: 1   relative frequency: 0.0000
    P. 174 LOYALL SCOT   93 Never shall Calvin Pardoned bee for Sales,

cambridge   frequency: 1   relative frequency: 0.0000
    P. 140 G.-CHILDREN   1 Kendal is dead, and Cambridge riding post.

came   frequency: 25   relative frequency: 0.0005
    P.   3 LOVELACE   33 But when the beauteous Ladies came to know
    P. 31 MOURNING   8 To Heaven, whence it came, their Woe.
    P. 33 DAPHNIS   21 But he came so full possest
    P. 40 THE MATCH   26 And rarely thither came;
    P. 41 THE MOWER   23 No Plant now knew the Stock from which it came;
    P. 45 MOWER'S SONG   5 When Juliana came, and She
    P. 45 MOWER'S SONG 11 When Juliana came, and She
    P. 45 MOWER'S SONG 17 When Juliana came, and She
    P. 55 EPITAPH   14 No Minute but it came and went;
    P. 67 A. HOUSE   281 From that blest Bed the Heroe came,
    P. 85 FLECKNO   86 But who came last is forc'd first to go out;
    P. 86 FLECKNO   117 But now, Alas, my first Tormentor came,
    P. 97 HOLLAND   56 Came next in order; which they could not miss.
    P. 105 ANNIVERSARY   75 The Commonwealth then first together came,
    P. 144 INSTRUCTIONS 155 Of the old Courtiers next a Squadron came,
    P. 152 INSTRUCTIONS 469 But when he came the odious Clause to Pen,
    P. 155 INSTRUCTIONS 597 Our feather'd Gallants, which came down that day
    P. 160 INSTRUCTIONS 820 Harry came Post just as he shew'd his Watch.
    P. 192 TWO HORSES   30 One night came togeather by all is agreed,
    P. 196 TWO HORSES   172 As learned men say, came out of their breeches,
    P. 199 DUKE   58 But when he came to act upon the stage,
    P. 201 HISTORICALL   11 In a slasht doublet then he came to shoare,
    P. 202 HISTORICALL   57 But since the ill gott race of Stewarts came,

```
        P. 204 HISTORICALL    155 From Tybur came the advice boat Monthly home,
        P. 315 CHEQUER INN     113 And Cholmley of Vale Royall came

camel                              frequency:    1    relative frequency: 0.0000
        P.  84 FLECKNO          64 Who as a Camel tall, yet easly can

came't                             frequency:    1    relative frequency: 0.0000
        P. 180 STOCKSMARKET     33 But, Sir Knight of the Vine, how came't in
                                   your thought

camp                               frequency:    3    relative frequency: 0.0000
        P.  71 A. HOUSE        402 To bring the mowing Camp their Cates,
        P.  72 A. HOUSE        420 A Camp of Battail newly fought:
        P. 151 INSTRUCTIONS    446 Trusses his baggage, and the Camp does fly.

campaspe                           frequency:    1    relative frequency: 0.0000
        P. 143 INSTRUCTIONS    104 And this Campaspe thee Apelles give!

camps                              frequency:    1    relative frequency: 0.0000
        P.  72 A. HOUSE        439 And such the Roman Camps do rise

can                                frequency:   89    relative frequency: 0.0018

canary                             frequency:    2    relative frequency: 0.0000
        P. 114 BLAKE            24 For they behold the sweet Canary Isles;
        P. 139 HOUSEWARMING     74 Nor would take his beloved Canary in kind:

canary-patent                      frequency:    1    relative frequency: 0.0000
        P. 149 INSTRUCTIONS    353 And now, now, the Canary-Patent may

cancelld                           frequency:    1    relative frequency: 0.0000
        P. 182 MADE FREE        63 As had cancelld all former Disasters

cancelled. See "cancelld."

cancer                             frequency:    1    relative frequency: 0.0000
        P. 142 INSTRUCTIONS     74 But in her soft Breast Loves hid Cancer
                                   smarts.

candid                             frequency:    1    relative frequency: 0.0000
        P.   3 LOVELACE          5 That candid Age no other way could tell

candidly                           frequency:    1    relative frequency: 0.0000
        P. 148 INSTRUCTIONS    293 Candidly credulous for once, nay twice;

candish                            frequency:    1    relative frequency: 0.0000
        P. 189 BRITANNIA       174 Blake, Candish, Drake, (men void of slavish
                                   fears)

candle                             frequency:    1    relative frequency: 0.0000
        P. 141 INSTRUCTIONS     10 The Aly roof, with snuff of Candle dimm,

candlesticks                       frequency:    1    relative frequency: 0.0000
        P. 316 CHEQUER INN     169 Candlesticks, Forkes, Saltes Plates Spoones
                                   Knives

candy                              frequency:    2    relative frequency: 0.0000
        P. 150 INSTRUCTIONS    398 Off, at the Isle of Candy, Dutch and ships.
        P. 150 INSTRUCTIONS    410 This Isle of Candy was on Essex Coast.

cane                               frequency:    2    relative frequency: 0.0000
        P. 144 INSTRUCTIONS    162 Wood these commands, Knight of the Horn and
                                   Cane.
        P. 147 INSTRUCTIONS    262 And Lovelace young, of Chimney-men the Cane.

canibal                            frequency:    1    relative frequency: 0.0000
        P.  35 DAPHNIS          72 For the Canibal to dine.

cankered. See "cankred."

cankred                            frequency:    1    relative frequency: 0.0000
        P. 186 BRITANNIA        51 The swelling Passions of his Cankred breast,

cannon                             frequency:    8    relative frequency: 0.0001
        See also "canon."
        P.  66 A. HOUSE        255 But their lowd'st Cannon were their Lungs;
        P.  81 A. HOUSE        716 And Sighs (Loves Cannon charg'd with Wind;)
        P. 116 BLAKE            90 And flank with Cannon from the Neighbouring
                                   shore.
        P. 117 BLAKE           119 The Thund'ring Cannon now begins the Fight,
        P. 118 BLAKE           149 Our Cannon now tears every Ship and Sconce,
```

```
P. 154 INSTRUCTIONS  565 No man can sit there safe, the Cannon pow'rs
P. 155 INSTRUCTIONS  606 Cannon and Powder, but in vain, to beg:
P. 156 INSTRUCTIONS  640 He heard how the wild Cannon nearer roar'd;
```

cannot   frequency: 27   relative frequency: 0.0005

canoes. See "canoos."

canon   frequency: 1   relative frequency: 0.0000
```
P. 163 INSTRUCTIONS  909 With Canon, Trumpets, Drums, his door
                         surround,
```

canoos   frequency: 1   relative frequency: 0.0000
```
P.  83 A. HOUSE      772 Have shod their Heads in their Canoos.
```

canst   frequency: 4   relative frequency: 0.0000

can'st   frequency: 1   relative frequency: 0.0000
    See also "canst."

can't   frequency: 1   relative frequency: 0.0000

canticleer   frequency: 1   relative frequency: 0.0000
```
P. 162 INSTRUCTIONS  883 At night, than Canticleer more brisk and hot,
```

canvas   frequency: 1   relative frequency: 0.0000
    See also "canvass."
```
P. 180 STOCKSMARKET   35 With canvas and deals you e'er since do him
                         cloud,
```

canvass   frequency: 1   relative frequency: 0.0000
```
P. 197 DUKE            1 Spread a large canvass, Painter, to containe
```

capacious   frequency: 1   relative frequency: 0.0000
    See also "capatious."
```
P. 169 ADVICE         33 Capacious Bowles with Lusty wine repleat
```

capatious   frequency: 1   relative frequency: 0.0000
```
P. 113 BLAKE           7 Every capatious Gallions womb was fill'd,
```

capitols   frequency: 1   relative frequency: 0.0000
```
P.  89 ODE            68 The Capitols first Line,
```

captain   frequency: 5   relative frequency: 0.0001
```
P. 106 ANNIVERSARY   109 How might they under such a Captain raise
P. 111 ANNIVERSARY   321 But the great Captain, now the danger's ore,
P. 111 ANNIVERSARY   350 'Spent with both Wars, under a Captain dead?
P. 156 INSTRUCTIONS  645 Captain, Lieutenant, Ensign, all make haste,
P. 171 LOYALL SCOT    t2 Upon The occasion of the death of Captain
                         Douglas burnt in one
```

captivate   frequency: 2   relative frequency: 0.0000
```
P.  31 FAIR SINGER     6 She with her Voice might captivate my Mind.
P. 155 INSTRUCTIONS  588 It fitter seem'd to captivate a Flea.
```

captivating   frequency: 1   relative frequency: 0.0000
```
P.  16 EYES           30 Dissolv'd those captivating Eyes,
```

captive   frequency: 3   relative frequency: 0.0000
```
P.  11 DIALOGUE       68 What Slaves, unless I captive you?
P. 158 INSTRUCTIONS  726 To Ruyter's Triumph lead the captive Charles.
P. 158 INSTRUCTIONS  735 Such the fear'd Hebrew, captive, blinded, shorn,
```

captives   frequency: 2   relative frequency: 0.0000
```
P.  98 HOLLAND       105 Not Christian Captives to redeem from Bands:
P. 112 ANNIVERSARY   370 'But that once took, we Captives are on Land.
```

captivity   frequency: 1   relative frequency: 0.0000
```
P.  87 FLECKNO       168 As one scap't strangely from Captivity,
```

car   frequency: 1   relative frequency: 0.0000
    See also "carr."
```
P. 186 BRITANNIA      57 Shee mounted up on a triumphall Car
```

car'd   frequency: 3   relative frequency: 0.0000
```
P. 107 ANNIVERSARY   149 But Men alas, as if they nothing car'd,
P. 138 HOUSEWARMING   39 He car'd not though Egypt's Ten Plagues us
                         distrest,
P. 149 INSTRUCTIONS  361 But still he car'd, while in Revenge he brav'd,
```

cards   frequency: 1   relative frequency: 0.0000

    P. 141 INSTRUCTIONS   38 Fits him in France to play at Cards and treat.

care   frequency: 22   relative frequency: 0.0004
    P.   15 THE CORONET   24 Though set with Skill and chosen out with Care.
    P.   17 BERMUDAS   15 And sends the Fowl's to us in care,
    P.   21 SOUL & BODY   25 And all my Care its self employes,
    P.   28 LOVER   29 Receiv'd into their cruel Care,
    P.   30 THE GALLERY   29 Divining thence, with horrid Care,
    P.   39 THE MATCH   10 But with the nicest care;
    P.   41 DAMON   6 But scorching like his am'rous Care.
    P.   75 A. HOUSE   538 Who here has the Holt-felsters care.
    P.   79 A. HOUSE   662 Seems to descend with greater Care.
    P.   99 HOLLAND   146 Darling of Heaven, and of Men the Care;
    P. 104 ANNIVERSARY   37 No other care they bear of things above,
    P. 120 TWO SONGS   20 On Sublunary things thy care;
    P. 123 O.C.   1 That Providence which had so long the care
    P. 127 O.C.   161 Which with more Care set forth his Obsequies
    P. 145 INSTRUCTIONS   188 Of Debtors deep, fell to Trelawny's care.
    P. 148 INSTRUCTIONS   323 Along the Coast and Harbours they take care
    P. 160 INSTRUCTIONS   793 Southampton dead, much of the Treasure's care,
    P. 162 INSTRUCTICNS   888 From his clear Eyes, yet these too dark with
                                Care.
    P. 165 INSTRUCTICNS   987 That serve the King with their Estates and
                                Care,
    P. 182 MADE FREE   70 That Notwithstanding the Care
    P. 187 BRITANNIA   116 And to his care did my sad state commend.
    P. 316 CHEQUER INN   153 Nor of his owne took care

careen   frequency: 1   relative frequency: 0.0000
    P.   98 HOLLAND   127 That ours mean time at leizure might careen,

career   frequency: 1   relative frequency: 0.0000
    See also "careere."
    P. 164 INSTRUCTIONS   954 And hurls them off, e're since, in his Career.

careere   frequency: 1   relative frequency: 0.0000
    P. 205 HISTORICALL   178 And stopt his Malice in its full Careere.

careful   frequency: 1   relative frequency: 0.0000
    P. 110 ANNIVERSARY   273 Some lusty Mate, who with more careful Eye

careless   frequency: 3   relative frequency: 0.0000
    See also "carless."
    P.   12 DROP OF DEW   4 Yet careless of its Mansion new;
    P.   44 DAMON   77 The edged Stele by careless chance
    P.   72 A. HOUSE   425 And now the careless Victors play,

cares   frequency: 3   relative frequency: 0.0000
    P. 107 ANNIVERSARY   179 When thou hadst almost quit thy Mortal cares,
    P. 124 O.C.   48 And at her Aspect calms his growing Cares;
    P. 129 O.C.   246 Nor with soft notes shall sing his cares asleep.

caresbrooks   frequency: 1   relative frequency: 0.0000
    P.   88 ODE   52 To Caresbrooks narrow case.

carillo   frequency: 1   relative frequency: 0.0000
    P.   20 THYRSIS   45 Chorus. Then let us give Carillo charge o'th
                                Sheep,

carless   frequency: 1   relative frequency: 0.0000
    P.   75 A. HOUSE   529 Then as I carless on the Bed

carnegie's. See "coneig's."

carol   frequency: 1   relative frequency: 0.0000
    P. 122 TWO SONGS   27 Come, lets in some Carol new

carousels. See "carouzels."

carouzels   frequency: 1   relative frequency: 0.0000
    P.   5 HASTINGS   34 The armed Angels hold their Carouzels;

carpenter   frequency: 1   relative frequency: 0.0000
    P.   74 A. HOUSE   485 Where the first Carpenter might best

carpets   frequency: 1   relative frequency: 0.0000
    P.   80 A. HOUSE   699 The Meadow Carpets where to tread;

carr   frequency: 1   relative frequency: 0.0000
    P. 108 ANNIVERSARY   215 But thee triumphant hence the firy Carr,

carriage   frequency: 1   relative frequency: 0.0000

P. 183 MADE FREE   90 Tho' too small for the Carriage of Starling.

carry   frequency: 3   relative frequency: 0.0000
P. 115 BLAKE   76 Yet in their brests, carry a pride much higher.
P. 137 HOUSEWARMING   24 As might carry the measure and name of an Hyde.
P. 314 CHEQUER INN   66 To carry up her Taile.

carta   frequency: 1   relative frequency: 0.0000
P. 171 PROPHECY   48 And Magna Carta shall no more appeare,

carteret   frequency: 2   relative frequency: 0.0000
P. 146 INSTRUCTIONS   203 Carteret the rich did the Accomptants guide,
P. 149 INSTRUCTIONS   343 What an Account to Carteret; that and more

carthage   frequency: 1   relative frequency: 0.0000
P. 99 HOLLAND   141 Or, what is left, their Carthage overcome

carve   frequency: 1   relative frequency: 0.0000
P. 98 HOLLAND   99 And carve in their large Bodies, where they
                            please,

carves   frequency: 1   relative frequency: 0.0000
P. 71 A. HOUSE   395 While one, unknowing, carves the Rail,

carvells   frequency: 3   relative frequency: 0.0000
P. 182 MADE FREE   54 To his Cleavelands, his Nells and his
                            Carwells.
P. 187 BRITANNIA   122 Resigns his Crown to Angell Carwells trust.
P. 189 BRITANNIA   169 Teach 'em to scorn the Carwells, Pembrookes,
                            Nells,

casawar   frequency: 1   relative frequency: 0.0000
P. 144 INSTRUCTIONS   136 And on all Trade like Casawar she feeds:

case   frequency: 3   relative frequency: 0.0000
P. 88 ODE   52 To Caresbrooks narrow case.
P. 178 LOYALL SCOT   269 The hive a comb case, every bee a drone,
P. 195 TWO HORSES   135 W. One of the two Tyrants must still be our
                            case

case-butter   frequency: 1   relative frequency: 0.0000
P. 98 HOLLAND   120 Then of Case-Butter shot and Bullet-Cheese.

cases   frequency: 1   relative frequency: 0.0000
See also "stair-cases."
P. 59 A. HOUSE   14 In cases fit of Tortoise-shell:

cash   frequency: 2   relative frequency: 0.0000
P. 153 INSTRUCTIONS   504 (This lik'd him best) his Cash beyond Sea whip.
P. 182 MADE FREE   38 Intrusted him with Cash,

cassius   frequency: 1   relative frequency: 0.0000
P. 90 MAY'S DEATH   18 Brutus and Cassius the Peoples cheats.

cassock   frequency: 1   relative frequency: 0.0000
P. 176 LOYALL SCOT   180 Hee Chose the Cassock Circingle and Gown,

cast   frequency: 12   relative frequency: 0.0002
P.   3 LOVELACE   23 And on each line cast a reforming eye,
P. 17 BERMUDAS   29 He cast (of which we rather boast)
P. 27 LOVER   12 And, e're brought forth, was cast away:
P. 65 A. HOUSE   208 'As rob though in the Dungeon cast.
P. 88 ODE   35 And cast the Kingdome old
P. 91 MAY'S DEATH   44 On them some Romane cast similitude,
P. 92 MAY'S DEATH   97 Thus by irrevocable Sentence cast,
P. 115 BLAKE   48 She cast off that which only made her strong.
P. 126 O.C.   139 Which, since they might not hinder, yet they cast
P. 128 O.C.   215 And 'twould be found, could we his thoughts have
                            cast,
P. 156 INSTRUCTIONS   646 E're in the Firy Furnace they be cast.
P. 188 BRITANNIA   130 And none are left these furyes to cast out.

caster   frequency: 1   relative frequency: 0.0000
P. 138 HOUSEWARMING   30 None sollid enough seem'd for his Thong Caster;

casting   frequency: 2   relative frequency: 0.0000
P. 49 THE GARDEN   51 Casting the Bodies Vest aside,
P. 115 BLAKE   47 Casting that League off, which she held so long,

castle   frequency: 4   relative frequency: 0.0000
P. 67 A. HOUSE   270 The Castle vanishes or rends)
P. 70 A. HOUSE   363 And at proud Cawood Castle seems

P. 138 HOUSEWARMING   31 He himself would not dwell in a Castle of air,
P. 149 INSTRUCTIONS   349 Now Mordant may, within his Castle Tow'r,

castlemain   frequency: 2   relative frequency: 0.0000
    P. 163 INSTRUCTIONS   927 At his first step, he Castlemain does find,
    P. 163 INSTRUCTIONS   932 To her own Husband, Castlemain, untrue.

castlemaine   frequency: 1   relative frequency: 0.0000
    See also "castlemain."
    P. 143 INSTRUCTIONS   79 Paint Castlemaine in Colours that will hold,

castle's. See "upnor-castle's."

casts   frequency: 5   relative frequency: 0.0001
    P. 32 MOURNING   27 But casts abroad these Donatives,
    P. 35 DAPHNIS   83 In one minute casts the Seed,
    P. 85 FLECKNO   75 And above that yet casts an antick Cloak,
    P. 115 BLAKE   68 And safely there casts Anchor in the Bay.
    P. 175 LOYALL SCOT   135 Aaron Casts Calves but Moses them Calcines.

cat   frequency: 1   relative frequency: 0.0000
    See also "catt."
    P. 176 LOYALL SCOT   175 Eating their brethren Bishop Turn and Cat

cataracts   frequency: 1   relative frequency: 0.0000
    P. 73 A. HOUSE   466 Denton sets ope its Cataracts;

catched. See "new-catched."

catching   frequency: 1   relative frequency: 0.0000
    P. 122 TWO SONGS   18 Far more catching then my Hook.

caterpillar   frequency: 1   relative frequency: 0.0000
    P.   3 LOVELACE   15 I see the envicus Caterpillar sit

caterpillars   frequency: 1   relative frequency: 0.0000
    P. 77 A. HOUSE   588 Between which Caterpillars crawl:

cates   frequency: 1   relative frequency: 0.0000
    P. 71 A. HOUSE   402 To bring the mowing Camp their Cates,

catholick   frequency: 1   relative frequency: 0.0000
    P. 192 TWO HORSES   17 But they that faith Catholick ne're understood,

catholicks   frequency: 1   relative frequency: 0.0000
    P. 97 HOLLAND   75 In vain for Catholicks our selves we bear;

cato   frequency: 1   relative frequency: 0.0000
    P. 91 MAY'S DEATH   48 On him the Cato, this the Cicero.

catt   frequency: 1   relative frequency: 0.0000
    P. 313 CHEQUER INN   17 But quickly turn'd Catt i'th' Pan

cattel   frequency: 1   relative frequency: 0.0000
    P. 138 HOUSEWARMING   33 Already he had got all our Money and Cattel,

cattle   frequency: 2   relative frequency: 0.0000
    See also "cattel," "irish-cattel."
    P. 73 A. HOUSE   452 Their Cattle, which it closer rase;
    P. 73 A. HOUSE   472 And Isl's th' astonish'd Cattle round.

caudles. See "cawdles."

caus'd   frequency: 1   relative frequency: 0.0000
    P. 113 BLAKE   12 But yet in them caus'd as much fear, as Joy.

cause   frequency: 21   relative frequency: 0.0004
    P.   4 LOVELACE   46 In your defence, or in his cause would dy.
    P. 11 DIALOGUE   69 Thou shalt know each hidden Cause;
    P. 36 DAPHNIS   106 Nor indeed without a Cause.
    P. 38 PICTURE   9 Who can foretel for what high cause
    P. 75 A. HOUSE   525 Yet always, for some Cause unknown,
    P. 92 MAY'S DEATH   66 And single fights forsaken Vertues cause.
    P. 98 HOLLAND   114 Cause why their Burgomaster of the Sea
    P. 115 BLAKE   61 Ah, why was thither brought that cause of War,
    P. 117 BLAKE   114 And all assumes your courage, in your cause.
    P. 118 BLAKE   152 The only place where it can cause no Ill.
    P. 123 O.C.   27 And leave succeeding Ages cause to mourn,
    P. 125 O.C.   101 A secret Cause does sure those Signs ordain
    P. 137 HOUSEWARMING   2 (As the Cause can eas'ly foretel the Effect)
    P. 143 INSTRUCTIONS   82 Discern'd Love's Cause, and a new Flame began.

```
        P.  148 INSTRUCTIONS  290 For Countrys Cause, that Glorious think and
                                  sweet:
        P.  160 INSTRUCTIONS  786 Was the first cause of all these Naval slips:
        P.  160 INSTRUCTIONS  805 But the true cause was, that, in 's Brother
                                  May,
        P.  177 LOYALL SCOT   252 Scotland and England cause of Just uproar!
        P.  198 DUKE           21 I nere can fight in a more glorious Cause
        P.  205 HISTORICALL   165 God did renounce him and his Cause disowne
        P.  205 HISTORICALL   169 The holy Scripture vindicates his Cause,

caused                            frequency:    1    relative frequency: 0.0000
     See also "caus'd."
        P.  179 STOCKSMARKET   26 Than all the Dutch pictures that caused the war,

causeless                         frequency:    1    relative frequency: 0.0000
        P.  131 PARADISE       24 My causeless, yet not impious, surmise.

causes                            frequency:    2    relative frequency: 0.0000
        P.  153 INSTRUCTIONS  519 All Causes sure concur, but most they think
        P.  176 LOYALL SCOT   195 And in their Causes think themselves supream.

causeth                           frequency:    2    relative frequency: 0.0000
        P.   42 DAMON          23 Not July causeth these Extremes,
        P.  177 LOYALL SCOT   247 Where a Mistaken accent Causeth death.

caution                           frequency:    1    relative frequency: 0.0000
        P.  166 KINGS VOWES    20 And the Dutch shall give Caution for their
                                  Provinces;

cavaleer                          frequency:    1    relative frequency: 0.0000
        P.  190 STATUE         17 No, to comfort the hearts of the poor Cavaleer

cavaleers                         frequency:    1    relative frequency: 0.0000
        P.  185 BRITANNIA      15 Till Cavaleers shall favorites be Deem'd

cavalier                          frequency:    1    relative frequency: 0.0000
     See also "cavaleer."
        P.  152 INSTRUCTIONS  458 The second Coventry the Cavalier.

cavaliers                         frequency:    1    relative frequency: 0.0000
     See also "cavaleers."
        P.  140 HIS HOUSE       5 The Cavaliers Debenter-Wall,

cave                              frequency:    5    relative frequency: 0.0001
        P.   18 CLORINDA        9 Seest thou that unfrequented Cave?
        P.   30 THE GALLERY    28 Over his Entrails, in the Cave;
        P.   42 DAMON          27 To what cool Cave shall I descend,
        P.  121 TWO SONGS      49 That Cave is dark. Endymion. Then none can
                                  spy:
        P.  173 LOYALL SCOT    68 Galloping down Clos'd up the Gaping Cave.

caves                             frequency:    3    relative frequency: 0.0000
        P.   18 CLORINDA       18 Clorinda, Pastures, Caves, and Springs.
        P.   18 CLORINDA       28 Caves eccho, and the Fountains ring.
        P.   59 A. HOUSE        3 That unto Caves the Quarries drew,

cawdles                           frequency:    1    relative frequency: 0.0000
        P.   94 DR. WITTY      30 Stint them to Cawdles, Almond-milk, and Broth.

cawood                            frequency:    1    relative frequency: 0.0000
        P.   70 A. HOUSE      363 And at proud Cawood Castle seems

ceas'd                            frequency:    1    relative frequency: 0.0000
        P.  105 ANNIVERSARY    65 Thus, ere he ceas'd, his sacred Lute creates

cease                             frequency:   11    relative frequency: 0.0002
        P.   10 DIALOGUE       43 Cease Tempter. None can chain a mind
        P.   67 A. HOUSE      284 His warlike Studies could not cease;
        P.   85 FLECKNO       112 And that both Poems did and Quarrels cease
        P.   87 ODE            9 So restless Cromwel could not cease
        P.  109 ANNIVERSARY   243 'Twas Heav'n would not that his Pow'r should
                                  cease,
        P.  129 O.C.          272 When truth shall be allow'd, and faction cease,
        P.  131 O.C.          321 Cease now our griefs, calme peace succeeds a war,
        P.  148 INSTRUCTIONS  318 To lay the Ships up, cease the Keels begun.
        P.  151 INSTRUCTIONS  437 Pray him to make De-Witte, and Ruyter cease,
        P.  182 MADE FREE      50 He never wou'd cease
        P.  194 TWO HORSES     91 W. That a King shou'd endavour to make a warr
                                  cease

cedars                            frequency:    2    relative frequency: 0.0000
```

```
          P.  17 BERMUDAS       25 With Cedars, chosen by his hand,
          P. 117 BLAKE         129 Nature ne'r made Cedars so high aspire,
```

cedar's   frequency: 1   relative frequency: 0.0000
          P. 109 ANNIVERSARY   262 Had quickly Levell'd every Cedar's top.

ceiling. See "seeling."

celebrate   frequency: 1   relative frequency: 0.0000
          P. 85 FLECKNO   108 Oblig'd us, when below, to celebrate

celebrates   frequency: 1   relative frequency: 0.0000
          P. 125 O.C.   108 Their fun'rals celebrates while it decrees.

celestial. See "celestiall."

celestiall   frequency: 1   relative frequency: 0.0000
          P. 186 BRITANNIA   81 Should drive them from their proud Celestiall
                                   seat,

celia   frequency: 2   relative frequency: 0.0000
          P. 39 THE MATCH   16 And that was Celia.
          P. 40 THE MATCH   36 And Celia that am I.

cell   frequency: 4   relative frequency: 0.0000
          P. 19 THYRSIS   8 Is our cell Elizium?
          P. 47 EMPIRE   7 He call'd the Ecchoes from their sullen Cell,
          P. 60 A. HOUSE   40 As Romulus his Bee-like Cell.
          P. 83 FLECKNO   17 And though within one Cell so narrow pent,

cellars   frequency: 1   relative frequency: 0.0000
          P. 144 INSTRUCTIONS 134 Breaks into Shops, and into Cellars prys.

cells   frequency: 2   relative frequency: 0.0000
          P. 40 THE MATCH   21 He kept the several Cells repleat
          P. 173 LOYALL SCOT   77 Anatomists may Sconer fix the Cells

cemented   frequency: 1   relative frequency: 0.0000
          P. 139 HOUSEWARMING   86 And with matter profane, cemented with holy,

censure   frequency: 3   relative frequency: 0.0000
          P. 95 DR. WITTY   37 And (if I Judgment have) I censure right;
          P. 140 HOUSEWARMING 101 Now some (as all Buildings must censure abide)
          P. 174 LOYALL SCOT   110 From Church they need not Censure men Away,

censurers   frequency: 1   relative frequency: 0.0000
          P.   3 LOVELACE   21 The barbed Censurers begin to looke

center   frequency: 8   relative frequency: 0.0001
          See also "centre."
          P. 19 THYRSIS   18 Heaven's the Center of the Soul.
          P. 56 BILL-BOROW   14 Nature must a new Center find,
          P. 82 A. HOUSE   767 You Heaven's Center, Nature's Lap.
          P. 96 HOLLAND   18 Thorough the Center their new-catched Miles;
          P. 105 ANNIVERSARY   80 Nor with such labour from its Center brought;
          P. 108 ANNIVERSARY   205 It seem'd the Earth did from the Center tear;
          P. 111 ANNIVERSARY   312 Out of the Center of th' unbottom'd Pit;
          P. 112 ANNIVERSARY   363 'That through the Center shoot their thundring
                                   side

centers   frequency: 1   relative frequency: 0.0000
          P. 105 ANNIVERSARY   87 The Common-wealth does through their Centers
                                   all

centre   frequency: 1   relative frequency: 0.0000
          P. 11 DIALOGUE   71 Try what depth the Centre draws;

cerberus   frequency: 2   relative frequency: 0.0000
          P. 92 MAY'S DEATH   91 The Cerberus with all his Jawes shall gnash,
          P. 171 PROPHECY   30 When Cerberus shall be the Treasurer.

ceremonies   frequency: 1   relative frequency: 0.0000
          See also "ceremonyes."
          P. 195 TWO HORSES   123 W. He that dyes for Ceremonies dyes like a
                                   fool.

ceremonyes   frequency: 1   relative frequency: 0.0000
          P. 176 LOYALL SCOT   207 Of Ceremonyes Wrangle in the Crow'd,

ceres   frequency: 1   relative frequency: 0.0000
          P. 164 INSTRUCTIONS 973 (But Ceres Corn, and Flora is the Spring,

certain   frequency: 5   relative frequency: 0.0001
   P. 58 BILL-BOROW   74 More certain Oracles in Oak.
   P. 60 A. HOUSE   59 Height with a certain Grace does bend,
   P. 77 A. HOUSE   605 And where the World no certain Shot
   P. 118 BLAKE   160 The certain seeds of many Wars are lost.
   P. 161 INSTRUCTIONS   849 Mean while the certain News of Peace arrives

cesarian   frequency: 1   relative frequency: 0.0000
   P. 27 LOVER   16 In a Cesarian Section.

cesar's   frequency: 1   relative frequency: 0.0000
   P. 189 BRITANNIA   179 Tarquins just judge and Cesar's Equall Peers

cess. See "sesse."

cessation   frequency: 1   relative frequency: 0.0000
   P. 152 INSTRUCTIONS   454 Cessation, as the look Adultery.

cethegus   frequency: 1   relative frequency: 0.0000
   P. 199 DUKE   59 He proved the mad Cethegus of his age.

ch.   frequency: 28   relative frequency: 0.0005
   P. 192 TWO HORSES   39 Ch. Here Charing broke silence and thus he went
                             on:
   P. 192 TWO HORSES   45 Ch. That he should be styled defender o' th
                             faith,
   P. 192 TWO HORSES   49 Ch. Tho he chang'd his Religion I hope hee 's
                             so civill
   P. 193 TWO HORSES   53 Ch. To see a white staffe make a Beggar a Lord
   P. 193 TWO HORSES   57 Ch. That a Million and half should be his
                             revenue,
   P. 193 TWO HORSES   61 Ch. That of four Seas dominion and Guarding
   P. 193 TWO HORSES   65 Ch. And our few ships abroad become Tripoly's
                             scorn
   P. 193 TWO HORSES   69 Ch. The basest Ingratitude ever was heard;
   P. 193 TWO HORSES   73 Ch. That Parliament men should rail at the
                             Court,
   P. 193 TWO HORSES   77 Ch. That Traitors to their Country in a
                             Brib'd Hous of Commons
   P. 193 TWO HORSES   81 Ch. No wonder that Beggers should still be for
                             giving
   P. 193 TWO HORSES   85 Ch. Yet baser the souls of those low priced
                             Sinners,
   P. 194 TWO HORSES   89 Ch. But thanks to the whores who have made the
                             King Dogged
   P. 194 TWO HORSES   93 Ch. And Plenipotentiaryes send into France
   P. 194 TWO HORSES   97 Ch. Enough, dear Brother, for tho' we have
                             reason,
   P. 194 TWO HORSES   109 Where is thy King gone? Ch. To see Bishop
                             Laud.
   P. 194 TWO HORSES   115 Ch. Pause, Brother, a while and calmly
                             consider:
   P. 194 TWO HORSES   122 Ch. Thy King will ne're fight unless't be for
                             Queans.
   P. 195 TWO HORSES   124 Ch. The King on thy Back is a Lamentable
                             Tool.
   P. 195 TWO HORSES   131 Ch. More Tolerable are the Lion Kings
                             Slaughters
   P. 195 TWO HORSES   137 Ch. De Witt and Cromwell had each a brave
                             soul.
   P. 195 TWO HORSES   141 Ch. Thy Ryder puts no man to death in his
                             wrath,
   P. 195 TWO HORSES   143 Ch. What is thy opinion of James Duke of
                             York?
   P. 195 TWO HORSES   151 Ch. Her Walsingham could dark Councells
                             unriddle,
   P. 195 TWO HORSES   153 Ch. Troth, Brother, well said, but thats
                             somewhat bitter:
   P. 195 TWO HORSES   155 Ch. Yet have wee one Secretary honest and wise:
   P. 195 TWO HORSES   157 Ch. But canst thou Divine when things shall be
                             mended?
   P. 195 TWO HORSES   159 Ch. Then, England, Rejoyce, thy Redemption
                             draws nigh;

chaff   frequency: 1   relative frequency: 0.0000
   P. 77 A. HOUSE   600 And winnow from the Chaff my Head.

chafing   frequency: 1   relative frequency: 0.0000
   P. 147 INSTRUCTIONS   279 Ev'n Iron Strangeways, chafing yet gave back,

chafing-dish   frequency: 1   relative frequency: 0.0000

P.   97 HOLLAND   86 Reeking at Church over the Chafing-Dish.

chain   frequency: 6   relative frequency: 0.0001
      P.   10 DIALOGUE   43 Cease Tempter. None can chain a mind
      P.   22 NYMPH   28 Ty'd in this silver Chain and Bell,
      P.   78 A. HOUSE   615 Do you, O Brambles, chain me too,
      P.   78 A. HOUSE   617 Here in the Morning tye my Chain,
      P. 155 INSTRUCTIONS   586 And all our hopes now on frail Chain depend:
      P. 155 INSTRUCTIONS   592 For its last aid: Hold Chain or we are broke.

chain-shot   frequency: 1   relative frequency: 0.0000
      P.   66 A. HOUSE   254 The gingling Chain-shot of her Beads.

chaind   frequency: 1   relative frequency: 0.0000
      P. 189 BRITANNIA   188 In Triumph lead chaind tyrants from afarr.

chain'd   frequency: 1   relative frequency: 0.0000
      P. 150 INSTRUCTIONS   369 While Chain'd together two Ambassadors

chained. See "chaind," "chain'd."

chaines   frequency: 2   relative frequency: 0.0000
      P.   16 EYES   31 Whose liquid Chaines could flowing meet
      P. 181 MADE FREE   12 You in Chaines offer your freedome.

chains   frequency: 2   relative frequency: 0.0000
      P.   20 SOUL & BODY   7 A Soul hung up, as 'twere, in Chains
      P. 156 INSTRUCTIONS   629 The Guards, plac'd for the Chains and Fleets
                                    defence,

chair   frequency: 4   relative frequency: 0.0000
      P. 143 INSTRUCTIONS   115 As some from Boxes, he so from the Chair
      P. 162 INSTRUCTIONS   871 In Chair, he smoaking sits like Master-Cook,
      P. 168 ADVICE   28 For money comes when Seymour leaves the Chair.
      P. 313 CHEQUER INN   44 Besides a good Freind in the Chair

chairs   frequency: 1   relative frequency: 0.0000
      P. 174 LOYALL SCOT   97 Or to the Joynt stooles reconcile the Chairs?

challenge   frequency: 1   relative frequency: 0.0000
      P.   23 NYMPH   66 It oft would challenge me the Race:

chamber   frequency: 4   relative frequency: 0.0000
      P.   83 FLECKNO   9 I found at last a Chamber, as 'twas said,
      P.   85 FLECKNO   84 His Chamber, whose compactness did allow
      P. 182 MADE FREE   72 Your Chamber must needs be undone.
      P. 185 BRITANNIA   26 Pimps, Priests, Buffoones i'th privy chamber
                                    sport.

chamber-door   frequency: 1   relative frequency: 0.0000
      P. 129 O.C.   232 To fetch day, presse about his chamber-door;

chameleon. See "chamelion."

chameleons   frequency: 1   relative frequency: 0.0000
      P.   42 DAMON   37 To Thee Chameleons changing-hue,

chamelion   frequency: 1   relative frequency: 0.0000
      P.   85 FLECKNO   82 As the Chamelion, yellow, blew, or green.

chammish   frequency: 1   relative frequency: 0.0000
      P. 110 ANNIVERSARY   293 Yet such a Chammish issue still does rage,

champion   frequency: 2   relative frequency: 0.0000
      P. 169 ADVICE   40 Draw me a Champion mounted on his steed,
      P. 171 PROPHECY   40 The Champion of the English Hierarchye,

chanc'd   frequency: 1   relative frequency: 0.0000
      P. 182 MADE FREE   57 But he chanc'd to have more Sobriety,

chance   frequency: 11   relative frequency: 0.0002
      P.   44 DAMON   77 The edged Stele by careless chance
      P.   61 A. HOUSE   96 (As 'twere by Chance) Thoughts long conceiv'd.
      P.   71 A. HOUSE   412 And Chance o'retakes what scapeth spight?
      P.   87 FLECKNO   169 Have made the Chance be painted; and go now
      P. 125 O.C.   94 Chance to be prun'd by an untimely knife,
      P. 141 INSTRUCTIONS   25 Chance finisht that which Art could but begin,
      P. 143 INSTRUCTIONS   112 As Chance does still in Multitudes decide.
      P. 147 INSTRUCTIONS   251 Each ran, as chance him guides, to sev'ral Post:
      P. 148 INSTRUCTIONS   303 See sudden chance of War! To Paint or Write,
      P. 151 INSTRUCTIONS   417 But wiser Men, and well foreseen in chance,

P. 183 MADE FREE   102 The whole Nation may chance to repent it.

chancellor   frequency: 2   relative frequency: 0.0000
    See also "chancelor."
    P. 149 INSTRUCTIONS 336 The House Prorogu'd, the Chancellor rebounds.
    P. 149 INSTRUCTIONS 344 A Parliament is to the Chancellor.

chancellor's. See "chancellours," "chanc'lor's."

chancellours   frequency: 1   relative frequency: 0.0000
    P. 139 HOUSEWARMING   84 But receiv'd now and paid the Chancellours
                             Custome.

chancelor   frequency: 1   relative frequency: 0.0000
    P. 165 KINGS VOWES   16 I will have a fine Chancelor beare all the sway,

chance's   frequency: 1   relative frequency: 0.0000
    P. 77 A. HOUSE   585 And see how Chance's better Wit

chanc'lor's   frequency: 1   relative frequency: 0.0000
    P. 142 INSTRUCTIONS   63 With Chanc'lor's Belly, and so large a Rump.

chancres   frequency: 1   relative frequency: 0.0000
    P. 86 FLECKNO   137 When they compare their Chancres and Poulains.

chang'd   frequency: 2   relative frequency: 0.0000
    P. 96 HOLLAND   34 For pickled Herring, pickled Heeren chang'd.
    P. 192 TWO HORSES   49 Ch. Tho he chang'd his Religion I hope hee 's
                             so civill

change   frequency: 11   relative frequency: 0.0002
    P. 18 CLORINDA   19 C. And what late change? D. The other day
    P. 40 THE MOWER   10 The nutriment did change the kind.
    P. 71 A. HOUSE   386 Does oftner then these Meadows change.
    P. 131 PARADISE   22 To change in Scenes, and show it in a Play.
    P. 151 INSTRUCTIONS 416 Change all for Guinea's, and a Crown for each:
    P. 153 INSTRUCTIONS 531 The sudden change, and such a tempting sight,
    P. 159 INSTRUCTIONS 747 Sad change, since first that happy pair was wed,
    P. 168 ADVICE   11 Then change the scene and let the next present
    P. 168 ADVICE   29 Change once again and let the next afford
    P. 180 STOCKSMARKET   42 That to change him into a Jack-pudding you mean,
    P. 200 DUKE   89 And change the order of a nation's fate?

changing   frequency: 1   relative frequency: 0.0000
    P. 93 DR. WITTY   5 Changing the Latine, but do more obscure

changing-hue   frequency: 1   relative frequency: 0.0000
    P. 42 DAMON   37 To Thee Chamelecns changing-hue,

changling   frequency: 1   relative frequency: 0.0000
    P. 185 BRITANNIA   34 And in his place a Lewis Changling lay.

channel   frequency: 1   relative frequency: 0.0000
    See also "channell."
    P. 155 INSTRUCTIONS 578 That rul'd all Seas, and did our Channel grace.

channell   frequency: 1   relative frequency: 0.0000
    P. 128 O.C.   205 And that deep soule through every channell flows,

chant. See "chaunt."

chanticleer. See "canticleer."

chants   frequency: 1   relative frequency: 0.0000
    P. 201 HISTORICALL   27 She chants Te Deum and so comes away

chaos   frequency: 2   relative frequency: 0.0000
    P. 126 O.C.   122 And pour the Deluge ore the Chaos head.
    P. 131 PARADISE   5 Heav'n, Hell, Earth, Chaos, All; the
                             Argument

chaplain   frequency: 1   relative frequency: 0.0000
    See also "chaplin."
    P. 176 LOYALL SCOT   174 A Hungry Chaplain and a Starved Rat

chaplet   frequency: 1   relative frequency: 0.0000
    P. 14 THE CORONET   11 So rich a Chaplet thence to weave

chaplin   frequency: 1   relative frequency: 0.0000
    P. 203 HISTORICALL   107 The chiefest blessings Adam's Chaplin got.

chapt. See "slow-chapt."

character   frequency: 3   relative frequency: 0.0000

```
        P.  95 HOLLAND         t The Character cf Holland
        P. 151 INSTRUCTIONS   442 But ask'd him bluntly for his Character.
        P. 151 INSTRUCTIONS   444 (His Character was that which thou didst paint)

chareing                          frequency:   1    relative frequency: 0.0000
        P. 313 CHEQUER INN      7 At Chareing Crosse hard by the way

charg'd                           frequency:   1    relative frequency: 0.0000
        P.  81 A. HOUSE       716 And Sighs (Loves Cannon charg'd with Wind;)

charge                            frequency:   6    relative frequency: 0.0001
        P.  20 THYRSIS         45 Chorus. Then let us give Carillo charge o'th
                                  Sheep,
        P.  68 A. HOUSE       300 Again as great a charge they press:
        P. 130 O.C.           278 Shall th' English souldier, ere he charge,
                                  rehearse;
        P. 146 INSTRUCTIONS   229 They both accept the Charge with merry glee,
        P. 148 INSTRUCTIONS   305 At the first Charge the Enemy give out;
        P. 179 STOCKSMARKET     2 Do at their own charge their citadels build,

charges                           frequency:   1    relative frequency: 0.0000
        P.  10 DIALOGUE        49 Then persevere: for still new Charges sound:

charging                          frequency:   1    relative frequency: 0.0000
        P. 147 INSTRUCTIONS   283 And, charging all their Pikes, a sullen Band

charing                           frequency:   4    relative frequency: 0.0000
        See also "ch.," "chareing."
        P. 189 STATUE          t The Statue at Charing Cross.
        P. 189 STATUE          1 What can be the Mistery why Charing Cross
        P. 192 TWO HORSES      25 The Horses I mean cf Woolchurch and Charing,
        P. 192 TWO HORSES      39 Ch. Here Charing broke silence and thus he went
                                  cn:

chariot.  See "charriot."

charioteer                        frequency:   1    relative frequency: 0.0000
        P. 108 ANNIVERSARY    224 To turn the headstrong Peoples Charioteer;

charity                           frequency:   1    relative frequency: 0.0000
        P.  86 FLECKNO        126 Then Nero's Poem he calls charity:

charles                           frequency:  21    relative frequency: 0.0004
        P.  88 ODE            51 That Charles himself might chase
        P.  92 MAY'S DEATH    76 Before thou couldst great Charles his death
                                  relate.
        P. 155 INSTRUCTIONS   611 But when the Royal Charles, what Rage, what
                                  Grief,
        P. 158 INSTRUCTIONS   726 To Ruyter's Triumph lead the captive Charles.
        P. 159 INSTRUCTIONS   755 But most they for their Darling Charles
                                  complain:
        P. 163 INSTRUCTIONS   918 Of Grandsire Harry, and of Charles his Sire.
        P. 163 INSTRUCTIONS   921 And ghastly Charles, turning his Collar low,
        P. 164 INSTRUCTIONS   946 And henceforth Charles only to Charles shall
                                  sit.
        P. 164 INSTRUCTIONS   956 Sun of our World, as he the Charles is there.
        P. 165 KINGS VOWES      4 Then Charles without acre
        P. 168 ADVICE           3 There holy Charles, here good Aurelius Sate,
        P. 176 LOYALL SCOT    197 Doth Charles the second rain or Charles the
                                  two?
        P. 178 LOYALL SCOT    262 Charles our great soul this onely Understands:
        P. 185 BRITANNIA       22 Till Charles loves Parliaments, till James
                                  hates Rome.
        P. 187 BRITANNIA      112 And from my Charles to a base Goal me drew,
        P. 187 BRITANNIA      115 Frequent adresses to my Charles I send,
        P. 196 TWO HORSES     187 Then, Charles, thy edict against Coffee recall;
        P. 200 DUKE           100 Great Charles, who full of mercy wouldst command
        P. 201 HISTORICALL     26 To fetch for Charles the floury Lisbon Kate,

charm                             frequency:   2    relative frequency: 0.0000
        P.  38 PICTURE         26 It self does at thy Beauty charm,
        P. 129 O.C.           237 No more shall heare that powerful language charm,

charm'd                           frequency:   1    relative frequency: 0.0000
        P.  80 A. HOUSE       680 Charm'd with the Saphir-winged Mist.

charmes                           frequency:   1    relative frequency: 0.0000
        P. 187 BRITANNIA       97 Henceforth be deaf to that old witches charmes,

charming                          frequency:   2    relative frequency: 0.0000
        P.  10 DIALOGUE        38 For thy Stay these charming Aires;
```

P. 168 ADVICE   18 Circean Clifford with his charming Wand,

charms   frequency: 2   relative frequency: 0.0000
    See also "charmes."
    P.   5 HASTINGS   30 And in the choicest Pleasures charms his Pains:
    P. 124 O.C.   31 Her when an infant, taken with her Charms,

charriot   frequency: 1   relative frequency: 0.0000
    P.   26 MISTRESS   22 Times winged Charriot hurrying near:

charta   frequency: 1   relative frequency: 0.0000
    P. 187 BRITANNIA   110 'Down with that common Magna Charta whore.'

charters   frequency: 1   relative frequency: 0.0000
    P. 184 MADE FREE   114 To Charters, our King and Soveraigne.

chase   frequency: 6   relative frequency: 0.0001
    P.   48 THE GARDEN   27 The Gods, that mortal Beauty chase,
    P.   73 A. HOUSE   451 The Villagers in common chase
    P.   88 ODE   51 That Charles himself might chase
    P. 106 ANNIVERSARY 124 Winding his Horn to Kings that chase the
                             Beast.
    P. 127 O.C.   154 Gave chase to Ligny on the Belgick Coast.
    P. 173 LOYALL SCOT   70 Nor Chaunt the fabulous hunt of Chivy Chase:

chast   frequency: 10   relative frequency: 0.0002
    P.   16 EYES   34 Nor the chast Ladies pregnant Womb,
    P.   19 THYRSIS   6 Thyrsis. A Chast Soul, can never mis't.
    P.   55 EPITAPH   9 To say she liv'd a Virgin chast,
    P.   62 A. HOUSE   107 'And our chast Lamps we hourly trim,
    P.   64 A. HOUSE   189 'Where you may lye as chast in Bed,
    P.   75 A. HOUSE   524 With Nuptial Rings their Ensigns chast;
    P.   92 MAY'S DEATH   72 Our spotless knowledge and the studies chast.
    P.   94 DR. WITTY   24 Nor her chast mind into the French translated:
    P. 159 INSTRUCTIONS 744 And Medway chast ravish'd before his Face,
    P. 177 LOYALL SCOT 227 With much adoe preserves his postern Chast.

chaste. See "chast."

chaster   frequency: 1   relative frequency: 0.0000
    P.   38 PICTURE   11 Yet this is She whose chaster Laws

chatham   frequency: 4   relative frequency: 0.0000
    P. 154 INSTRUCTIONS 572 March straight to Chatham, to increase the fear.
    P. 158 INSTRUCTIONS 723 Now (nothing more at Chatham left to burn)
    P. 171 LOYALL SCOT   t3 of his Majesties shipps at Chatham.
    P. 193 TWO HORSES   63 W. Our worm-eaten Navy be laid up at Chatham,

chathams   frequency: 1   relative frequency: 0.0000
    P. 160 INSTRUCTIONS 783 Who all our Ships expos'd in Chathams Net?

chaucer   frequency: 1   relative frequency: 0.0000
    P.   92 MAY'S DEATH   86 And reverend Chaucer, but their dust does rise

chaunt   frequency: 1   relative frequency: 0.0000
    P. 173 LOYALL SCOT   70 Nor Chaunt the fabulous hunt of Chivy Chase:

cheap   frequency: 2   relative frequency: 0.0000
    P. 138 HOUSEWARMING 58 He should dwell more noble, and cheap too
                             at-home,
    P. 156 INSTRUCTIONS 619 Now a cheap spoil, and the mean Victor's Slave,

chear   frequency: 2   relative frequency: 0.0000
    P. 125 O.C.   92 At its rich bloods expence their Sorrows chear,
    P. 140 HOUSEWARMING 111 When like the good Oxe, for publick good chear,

chearful   frequency: 2   relative frequency: 0.0000
    P.   18 BERMUDAS   38 An holy and a chearful Note,
    P.   21 SOUL & BODY   37 Joy's chearful Madness does perplex:

cheat   frequency: 8   relative frequency: 0.0001
    See also "godly-cheat."
    P.   65 A. HOUSE   204 'An Art by which you finly'r cheat?
    P. 143 INSTRUCTIONS 114 For the Cheat Turnor for them both must throw.
    P. 148 INSTRUCTIONS 294 But sure the Devil cannot cheat them thrice.
    P. 148 INSTRUCTIONS 314 To cheat their Pay, feign want, the House
                             accuse.
    P. 170 PROPHECY   13 When bare fac'd Villany shall not blush to cheat
    P. 177 LOYALL SCOT 215 To cheat the Plague money Indifferent.
    P. 186 BRITANNIA   82 If not ore aw'd by new found holy cheat.
    P. 192 TWO HORSES   37 Thy founder and mine to Cheat one another,

cheated   frequency: 2   relative frequency: 0.0000
     P. 155 INSTRUCTIONS   584 Cheated of Pay, was he that show'd them in.
     P. 159 INSTRUCTIONS   777 Who all our Seamen cheated of their Debt?

cheating   frequency: 1   relative frequency: 0.0000
     P. 185 BRITANNIA   18 Till Golden Osborn cheating shall detect,

cheats   frequency: 4   relative frequency: 0.0000
     P. 90 MAY'S DEATH   18 Brutus and Cassius the Peoples cheats.
     P. 144 INSTRUCTIONS   122 And thought all lost that goest not to the
                               Cheats:
     P. 145 INSTRUCTIONS   179 Gross Bodies, grosser Minds, and grossest
                               Cheats;
     P. 203 HISTORICALL   80 All but religious cheats might justly sweare

check   frequency: 1   relative frequency: 0.0000
     P. 185 BRITANNIA   49 Sauls stormy rage and Check his black disease,

checker. See "checquer," "chequer."

checquer   frequency: 2   relative frequency: 0.0000
     P. 170 PROPHECY   14 And Checquer dores shall shut up Lombard
                               street,
     P. 170 PROPHECY   22 When even to rob the Checquer shall be Just,

cheddar. See "chedder."

chedder   frequency: 1   relative frequency: 0.0000
     P. 139 HOUSEWARMING   68 As all Chedder Dairys club to the incorporate
                               Cheese

cheek   frequency: 6   relative frequency: 0.0001
     P. 41 THE MOWER   14 And learn'd to interline its cheek:
     P. 58 BILL-BOROW   64 Those Acts that swell'd the Cheek of Fame.
     P. 68 A. HOUSE   304 With Breath so sweet, or Cheek so faire.
     P. 156 INSTRUCTIONS   654 Nor other Courtship knew but to his Cheek.
     P. 172 LOYALL SCOT   20 Nor other Courtship knew but to his Cheek.
     P. 176 LOYALL SCOT   193 The Bishops Nodle Ferks up cheek by Jowle.

cheer. See "chear," "cheere."

cheere   frequency: 2   relative frequency: 0.0000
     P. 315 CHEQUER INN   92 The Cheere into his Breeches ram'd
     P. 315 CHEQUER INN   114 For something more then Chop Cheere.

cheerful. See "chearful."

cheese   frequency: 1   relative frequency: 0.0000
     See also "bullet-cheese."
     P. 139 HOUSEWARMING   68 As all Chedder Dairys club to the incorporate
                               Cheese

chemist. See "chymist."

chemists. See "chymists."

cheney   frequency: 1   relative frequency: 0.0000
     P. 315 CHEQUER INN   109 Old Hobbs's Brother, Cheney there

chequer   frequency: 3   relative frequency: 0.0000
     See also "checquer."
     P. 193 TWO HORSES   55 W. That the bank should be seiz'd yet the
                               Chequer so poor;
     P. 312 CHEQUER INN   t A Ballad call'd the Chequer Inn.
     P. 316 CHEQUER INN   137 On Chequer Tally was scor'd up

cherry   frequency: 1   relative frequency: 0.0000
     P. 41 THE MOWER   29 And in the Cherry he does Nature vex,

chevy. See "chivy."

chide   frequency: 2   relative frequency: 0.0000
     P. 149 INSTRUCTIONS   328 Is brought to beg in publick and to chide.
     P. 179 STOCKSMARKET   17 To see him so disfigured the herbwomen chide,

chief   frequency: 3   relative frequency: 0.0000
     See also "chiefe."
     P. 24 NYMPH   87 But all its chief delight was still
     P. 118 BLAKE   155 Wars chief support with them would buried be,
     P. 146 INSTRUCTIONS   207 Bold Duncombe next, of the Projectors chief:

chiefe   frequency: 2   relative frequency: 0.0000

    P. 169 ADVICE   61 Whom France Esteem'd our Chiefe in
                              Parliament,
    P. 192 TWO HORSES   42 And the King's Chiefe minister holding the
                              doore:

chiefest   frequency: 1   relative frequency: 0.0000
    P. 203 HISTORICALL   107 The chiefest blessings Adam's Chaplin got.

chieftain   frequency: 1   relative frequency: 0.0000
    P. 205 HISTORICALL   160 Heaven had him Chieftain of great Britain made,

child   frequency: 4   relative frequency: 0.0000
    See also "childe."
    P. 25 YOUNG LOVE   8 As the Nurses with the Child.
    P. 67 A. HOUSE   268 Like Gipsies that a Child hath stoln.
    P. 149 INSTRUCTIONS   350 Imprison Parents, and the Child deflowre.
    P. 200 DUKE   84 And now hath gott his Daughter gott with Child,

childbirth   frequency: 1   relative frequency: 0.0000
    P. 142 INSTRUCTIONS   54 How after Childbirth to renew a Maid.

childe   frequency: 1   relative frequency: 0.0000
    P.   4 HASTINGS   14 And is not thence mistaken for a Childe?

children   frequency: 3   relative frequency: 0.0000
    See also "grand-children."
    P. 124 O.C.   49 Or with a Grandsire's joy her Children sees
    P. 128 O.C.   212 To him the children of the Highest were?
    P. 156 INSTRUCTIONS   647 Three Children tall, unsing'd, away they row,

chill   frequency: 3   relative frequency: 0.0000
    P. 13 DROP OF DEW   38 White, and intire, though congeal'd and chill.
    P. 156 INSTRUCTIONS   655 Oft has he in chill Eske or Seine, by night,
    P. 172 LOYALL SCCT   21 Oft as hee in Chill Eske or Seyne by night

chill'd   frequency: 1   relative frequency: 0.0000
    P. 163 INSTRUCTIONS   903 But soon shrunk back, chill'd with her touch so
                              cold,

chime   frequency: 1   relative frequency: 0.0000
    P. 18 BERMUDAS   39 And all the way, to guide their Chime,

chimney   frequency: 1   relative frequency: 0.0000
    P. 315 CHEQUER INN   131 And sweeping all our Chimney Stacks

chimney-contractors. See "chimny-contractors."

chimney-men   frequency: 1   relative frequency: 0.0000
    P. 147 INSTRUCTIONS   262 And Lovelace young, of Chimney-men the Cane.

chimneys   frequency: 1   relative frequency: 0.0000
    P. 160 INSTRUCTIONS   801 Who hath no Chimneys, to give all is best,

chimney's   frequency: 1   relative frequency: 0.0000
    P. 145 INSTRUCTIONS   193 For Chimney's sake they all Sir Pool obey'd,

chimny-contractors   frequency: 1   relative frequency: 0.0000
    P. 139 HOUSEWARMING   73 'Twas then that the Chimny-Contractors he smoakd,

chin   frequency: 2   relative frequency: 0.0000
    P. 156 INSTRUCTIONS   649 Not so brave Douglas; on whose lovely chin
    P. 172 LOYALL SCOT   15 Not so brave Douglass, on whose Lovely Chin

china   frequency: 1   relative frequency: 0.0000
    P. 103 ANNIVERSARY   20 More slow and brittle then the China clay:

china-clay   frequency: 1   relative frequency: 0.0000
    P. 142 INSTRUCTIONS   65 Express her studying now, if China-clay,

chine   frequency: 2   relative frequency: 0.0000
    P. 141 INSTRUCTIONS   34 Member'd like Mules, with Elephantine chine.
    P. 177 LOYALL SCOT   224 Others Attempt, to Ccol their fervent Chine,

chisel   frequency: 1   relative frequency: 0.0000
    P. 180 STOCKSMARKET   56 For 'tis such a king as no chisel can mend.

chits. See "chitts."

chitts   frequency: 1   relative frequency: 0.0000
    P. 187 BRITANNIA   120 Beseig'd by 's whores, Buffoones, and Bastard
                              Chitts;

chivy   frequency: 1   relative frequency: 0.0000

          P. 173 LOYALL SCOT   70 Nor Chaunt the fabulous hunt of Chivy Chase:

chloe   frequency: 4   relative frequency: 0.0000
          P. 33 DAPHNIS   t Daphnis and Chloe.
          P. 33 DAPHNIS   1 Daphnis must from Chloe part:
          P. 34 DAPHNIS   49 Ah my Chloe how have I
          P. 36 DAPHNIS   108 Why did Chloe once refuse?

chlora's   frequency: 1   relative frequency: 0.0000
          P. 31 MOURNING   4 Spring from the Starrs of Chlora's Eyes?

choak   frequency: 1   relative frequency: 0.0000
          P. 185 BRITANNIA   30 Pervert his mind, his good Intencions Choak,

chocolat   frequency: 1   relative frequency: 0.0000
          P. 149 INSTRUCTIONS   342 What to fair Denham mortal Chocolat;

chocolate. See "chocolat," "chocolatte," "chocolet."

chocolatte   frequency: 1   relative frequency: 0.0000
          P. 138 HOUSEWARMING   28 And too much resembled his Wives Chocolatte.

chocolet   frequency: 1   relative frequency: 0.0000
          P. 196 TWO HORSES   184 Chocolet Tea and Coffee are liquors of peace.

choice   frequency: 10   relative frequency: 0.0002
          See also "choyce."
          P. 31 FAIR SINGER   14 Where Victory might hang in equal choice,
          P. 75 A. HOUSE   513 The Nightingale does here make choice
          P. 82 A. HOUSE   744 And make their Destiny their Choice.
          P. 107 ANNIVERSARY   147 And knowing not where Heavens choice may light,
          P. 118 BLAKE   142 Necessity did them, but Choice did us.
          P. 118 BLAKE   143 A choice which did the highest worth express,
          P. 122 TWO SONGS   32 Whil'st all the Nymphs on Damon's choice
                                    attend?
          P. 131 O.C.   315 Heav'n to this choice prepar'd a diadem,
          P. 146 INSTRUCTIONS   227 Nor better choice all accidents could hit;
          P. 165 INSTRUCTIONS   989 (Where few the number, choice is there less hard)

choicer   frequency: 1   relative frequency: 0.0000
          P. 30 THE GALLERY   47 And a Collection choicer far

choicest   frequency: 2   relative frequency: 0.0000
          See also "choisest."
          P.   5 HASTINGS   30 And in the choicest Pleasures charms his Pains:
          P. 175 LOYALL SCOT   159 But of the Choicest Modern flesh and Bone.

choir. See "quire."

choirs. See "quires."

choisest   frequency: 1   relative frequency: 0.0000
          P. 39 THE MATCH   2 Of all her choisest store;

choke. See "choak."

choler   frequency: 1   relative frequency: 0.0000
          P. 161 INSTRUCTIONS   833 And all with Sun and Choler come adust;

cholmley   frequency: 1   relative frequency: 0.0000
          P. 315 CHEQUER INN   113 And Cholmley of Vale Royall came

choose   frequency: 2   relative frequency: 0.0000
          See also "chuse."
          P. 114 BLAKE   21 In thickest darkness they would choose to steer,
          P. 183 MADE FREE   107 A new Duke to choose,

chooseth. See "chuseth."

choosing   frequency: 1   relative frequency: 0.0000
          P. 109 ANNIVERSARY   245 Choosing each Stone, and poysing every weight,

chop   frequency: 1   relative frequency: 0.0000
          P. 315 CHEQUER INN   114 For something more then Chop Cheere.

choppes   frequency: 1   relative frequency: 0.0000
          P. 314 CHEQUER INN   88 The Pelletts which his Choppes did dart

chops   frequency: 1   relative frequency: 0.0000
          See also "choppes."
          P. 144 INSTRUCTIONS   137 Chops off the piece where e're she close the Jaw,

chor.   frequency: 1   relative frequency: 0.0000
    P. 54 THYESTE   t Senec. Traged. ex Thyeste Chor. 2.

chordage   frequency: 1   relative frequency: 0.0000
    P. 10 DIALOGUE   44 Whom this sweet Chordage cannot bind.

chorus   frequency: 10   relative frequency: 0.0002
    P. 10 DIALOGUE   44+ Chorus.
    P. 12 DIALOGUE   74+ Chorus.
    P. 18 CLORINDA   26+ Chorus.
    P. 20 THYRSIS   45 Chorus. Then let us give Carillo charge o'th
                                 Sheep,
    P. 90 MAY'S DEATH   14 Amongst the Chorus of old Poets laid,
    P. 108 ANNIVERSARY   211 Such as the dying Chorus sings by turns,
    P. 119 TWO SONGS   t4 Chorus. Endymion. Luna.
    P. 119 TWO SONGS   t4+ Chorus.
    P. 120 TWO SONGS   28+ Chorus.
    P. 121 TWO SONGS   50+ Chorus.

chose   frequency: 9   relative frequency: 0.0001
    P.   3 LOVELACE   2 Which your sweet Muse which your fair Fortune
                                 chose,
    P. 47 EMPIRE   14 And others chose the Cornet eloquent.
    P. 97 HOLLAND   78 Where wisely for their Court they chose a
                                 Village.
    P. 141 INSTRUCTIONS   32 But Fortune chose him for her pleasure salt.
    P. 146 INSTRUCTIONS   225 All the two Coventrys their Gen'rals chose:
    P. 150 INSTRUCTIONS   393 With homely sight, they chose thus to relax
    P. 172 LOYALL SCOT   5 And (as a favourable Pennance) Chose
    P. 176 LOYALL SCOT   180 Hee Chose the Cassock Circingle and Gown,
    P. 315 CHEQUER INN   107 There was but one cou'd be chose out

chosen   frequency: 5   relative frequency: 0.0001
    P. 15 THE CORONET   24 Though set with Skill and chosen out with Care.
    P. 17 BERMUDAS   25 With Cedars, chosen by his hand,
    P. 107 ANNIVERSARY   160 A Mold was chosen out of better Earth;
    P. 121 TWO SONGS   9 They ha' chosen such an hour
    P. 313 CHEQUER INN   15 Till he was Burgesse chosen

choyce   frequency: 3   relative frequency: 0.0000
    P. 183 MADE FREE   80 In thy fortunate Choyce
    P. 312 CHEQUER INN   3 The Choyce of Ale and Beere
    P. 312 CHEQUER INN   4 But such a Choyce as ne're was found

christendome   frequency: 1   relative frequency: 0.0000
    P. 169 ADVICE   36 Frightens all Christendome with fresh Alarms,

christian   frequency: 2   relative frequency: 0.0000
    See also "turk-christian-pagan-jew."
    P. 98 HOLLAND   105 Not Christian Captives to redeem from Bands:
    P. 142 INSTRUCTIONS   45 Nor fears he the most Christian should trepan

christians   frequency: 1   relative frequency: 0.0000
    P. 192 TWO HORSES   21 If the Roman Church, good Christians, oblige
                                 yee

chronicle   frequency: 1   relative frequency: 0.0000
    P. 185 BRITANNIA   39 The Bloody scottish Chronicle turnd o're

chronicler   frequency: 1   relative frequency: 0.0000
    P. 92 MAY'S DEATH   74 To turn the Chronicler to Spartacus.

chrystal   frequency: 4   relative frequency: 0.0000
    P.   5 HASTINGS   33 Before the Chrystal Palace where he dwells,
    P. 64 A. HOUSE   192 'Like Chrystal pure with Cotton warm.
    P. 78 A. HOUSE   636 Till as a Chrystal Mirrour slick;
    P. 80 A. HOUSE   678 As Flies in Chrystal overt'ane;

chrystal-pure   frequency: 1   relative frequency: 0.0000
    P. 80 A. HOUSE   694 So Chrystal-pure but only She;

church   frequency: 16   relative frequency: 0.0003
    P. 97 HOLLAND   76 The universal Church is onely there.
    P. 97 HOLLAND   86 Reeking at Church over the Chafing-Dish.
    P. 167 KINGS VOWES   48 And I'lle first put the Church then my Crowne
                                 in Commission.
    P. 174 LOYALL SCOT   110 From Church they need not Censure men Away,
    P. 174 LOYALL SCOT   122 Beleive but onely as the Church beleives
    P. 175 LOYALL SCOT   133 Noe Church! noe Trade! noe king! noe people! noe!

```
P. 175 LOYALL SCOT   169 When for a Church hee built a Theatre.
P. 187 BRITANNIA      93 The Church and state you safely may invade.
P. 192 TWO HORSES     21 If the Roman Church, good Christians, oblige
                         yee
P. 192 TWO HORSES     41 To see Church and state bow down to a whore
P. 192 TWO HORSES     47 W. That the Duke should turne Papist and that
                         Church defy
P. 193 TWO HORSES     60 And yet all his Court be as poore as Church
                         Ratts;
P. 194 TWO HORSES    120 By Knaves who cry'd themselves up for the
                         Church,
P. 199 DUKE           69 But nere can make a piller for a church;
P. 201 HISTORICALL    35 For those and Germin's sins she founds a
                         Church,
P. 205 HISTORICALL   159 Tells him the holy Church demands his aide,
```

churches   frequency: 3   relative frequency: 0.0000
```
P. 177 LOYALL SCOT   217 Indifferent to Bob Churches of their Coals.
P. 181 MADE FREE       7 Whil'st your Churches unbuilt
P. 190 STATUE         16 To repair with such riffe raffe our Churches old
                         Pale?
```

churchill   frequency: 2   relative frequency: 0.0000
```
P. 199 DUKE           44 The wound of which now tainted Churchill faids,
P. 204 HISTORICALL   138 Dos on Brittania as on Churchill ride:
```

churchmen   frequency: 1   relative frequency: 0.0000
```
P.  92 MAY'S DEATH    64 And fear has Coward Churchmen silenced,
```

chuse   frequency: 2   relative frequency: 0.0000
```
P. 126 O.C.          140 To chuse it worthy of his Glories past.
P. 152 INSTRUCTIONS  468 None but himself must chuse the King a Queen.)
```

chuseth   frequency: 1   relative frequency: 0.0000
```
P. 137 HOUSEWARMING    7 Like the King-fisher chuseth to build in the
                         Broom,
```

chymick   frequency: 1   relative frequency: 0.0000
```
P.  15 EYES           22 Distills the World with Chymick Ray;
```

chymist   frequency: 1   relative frequency: 0.0000
```
P.   5 HASTINGS       49 Like some sad Chymist, who, prepar'd to reap
```

chymists   frequency: 2   relative frequency: 0.0000
```
P. 139 HOUSEWARMING   94 Like vain Chymists, a flower from its ashes
                         returning;
P. 176 LOYALL SCOT   208 And would like Chymists fixing Mercury
```

cicero   frequency: 1   relative frequency: 0.0000
```
P.  91 MAY'S DEATH    48 On him the Cato, this the Cicero.
```

cider   frequency: 1   relative frequency: 0.0000
```
P. 161 INSTRUCTIONS  846 And long as Cider lasts in Hereford;
```

cinque   frequency: 1   relative frequency: 0.0000
```
P.  69 A. HOUSE      349 But he preferr'd to the Cinque Ports
```

cipher   frequency: 1   relative frequency: 0.0000
```
P. 151 INSTRUCTIONS  450 In Cipher one to Harry Excellent.
```

circean   frequency: 1   relative frequency: 0.0000
```
P. 168 ADVICE         18 Circean Clifford with his charming Wand,
```

circingle   frequency: 2   relative frequency: 0.0000
```
P. 174 LOYALL SCOT   100 Stretch for your Line their Circingle Alone,
P. 176 LOYALL SCOT   180 Hee Chose the Cassock Circingle and Gown,
```

circle   frequency: 3   relative frequency: 0.0000
```
P.  60 A. HOUSE       46 The Circle in the Quadrature!
P. 157 INSTRUCTIONS  668 Within its circle, knows himself secure.
P. 172 LOYALL SCOT    34 Within its Circle knows himselfe secure.
```

circles   frequency: 3   relative frequency: 0.0000
```
P.  72 A. HOUSE      430 Which they in Fairy Circles tread:
P.  78 A. HOUSE      611 And Oh so close your Circles lace,
P. 103 ANNIVERSARY     4 In the weak Circles of increasing Years;
```

circling   frequency: 2   relative frequency: 0.0000
```
P.  12 DROP OF DEW    25 Does, in its pure and circling thoughts, express
P. 153 INSTRUCTIONS  497 Horse-leeches circling at the Hem'roid Vein;
```

circular   frequency: 1   relative frequency: 0.0000
    P. 56 BILL-BOROW   4 A Line more circular and like;

circumcised   frequency: 1   relative frequency: 0.0000
    P. 98 HOLLAND   118 Our sore new circumcised Common wealth.

circumference. See "circumf'rence."

circumf'rence   frequency: 1   relative frequency: 0.0000
    P. 105 ANNIVERSARY   88 Draw the Circumf'rence of the publique Wall;

circumscribes   frequency: 1   relative frequency: 0.0000
    P. 84 FLECKNO   69 He therefore circumscribes himself in rimes;

citadels   frequency: 1   relative frequency: 0.0000
    P. 179 STOCKSMARKET   2 Do at their own charge their citadels build,

cited   frequency: 1   relative frequency: 0.0000
    P. 314 CHEQUER INN   53 For surenesse Cited were to come

cities   frequency: 2   relative frequency: 0.0000
    See also "cittyes," "cityes."
    P. 144 INSTRUCTIONS 141 She wastes the Country and on Cities preys.
    P. 179 STOCKSMARKET   1 As cities that to the fierce conquerors yield

citizens   frequency: 1   relative frequency: 0.0000
    P. 147 INSTRUCTIONS 282 Of Citizens and Merchants held dispute:

citts   frequency: 1   relative frequency: 0.0000
    P. 181 MADE FREE   13 Oh you Addle-Brain'd Citts

citty   frequency: 8   relative frequency: 0.0001
    P. 169 ADVICE   58 Leave Temple Single to be beat in the Citty.
    P. 170 PROPHECY   8 Tho the Walls stand to bring the Citty lower;
    P. 181 MADE FREE   t Upon his Majesties being made free of the Citty
    P. 181 MADE FREE   3 In a Box the Citty Maggott;
    P. 185 BRITANNIA   14 Till England knowes who did her Citty burn,
    P. 196 TWO HORSES   181 Let the Citty drink Coffee and Quietly groan
    P. 202 HISTORICALL   48 He sells the Citty where 'twas sett on fire.
    P. 204 HISTORICALL   154 Hee'l burne a Citty or destroy a King.

cittye   frequency: 1   relative frequency: 0.0000
    P. 170 PROPHECY   5 To burne the Cittye which againe shall rise

cittyes   frequency: 1   relative frequency: 0.0000
    P. 204 HISTORICALL   146 Our fleets our Ports our Cittyes and our
                              Townes

city   frequency: 7   relative frequency: 0.0001
    See also "citty," "cittye."
    P. 47 EMPIRE   8 And built the Organs City where they dwell.
    P. 105 ANNIVERSARY   66 Th' harmonicus City of the seven Gates.
    P. 105 ANNIVERSARY   86 Into the Animated City throng.
    P. 139 HOUSEWARMING   93 Fond City, its Rubbish and Ruines that builds,
    P. 154 INSTRUCTIONS 570 Until the City put it in repair.
    P. 165 INSTRUCTIONS 982 And a poor Warren once a City ras'd.
    P. 179 STOCKSMARKET   6 Obliging the city with a king and a steed,

cityes   frequency: 1   relative frequency: 0.0000
    P. 127 O.C.   186 And cityes strong were stormed by his prayer;

civic. See "civick," "civicke."

civick   frequency: 1   relative frequency: 0.0000
    P. 58 BILL-BOROW   69 For all the Civick Garlands due

civicke   frequency: 1   relative frequency: 0.0000
    P.   3 LOVELACE   12 Our Civill Wars have lost the Civicke crowne.

civil   frequency: 2   relative frequency: 0.0000
    See also "civill."
    P. 88 ODE   45 What Field of all the Civil Wars,
    P. 91 MAY'S DEATH   21 Cups more then civil of Emathian wine,

civilis   frequency: 1   relative frequency: 0.0000
    P. 97 HOLLAND   82 That it had one Civilis call'd by Name,

civility   frequency: 1   relative frequency: 0.0000
    P. 97 HOLLAND   77 Nor can Civility there want for Tillage,

civill   frequency: 2   relative frequency: 0.0000

```
     P.   3 LOVELACE      12 Our Civill Wars have lost the Civicke crowne.
     P. 192 TWO HORSES     49 Ch. Tho he chang'd his Religion I hope hee 's
                              so civill
```

civilly   frequency: 1   relative frequency: 0.0000
```
     P.  84 FLECKNO        46 Ask'd civilly if he had eat this Lent.
```

clad   frequency: 2   relative frequency: 0.0000
```
     P. 145 INSTRUCTIONS  176 No Troop was better clad nor so well pay'd.
     P. 161 INSTRUCTIONS  828 And Vest bespeaks to be more seemly clad.
```

claim   frequency: 3   relative frequency: 0.0000
     See also "claime."
```
     P.   5 HASTINGS       39 And gladly there can all his Kinred claim,
     P.  96 HOLLAND        23 Yet still his claim the Injur'd Ocean laid,
     P. 173 LOYALL SCOT     59 Fortunate Boy, if ere my verse may Claim
```

claime   frequency: 1   relative frequency: 0.0000
```
     P. 128 O.C.          201 Friendship, that sacred virtue, long dos claime
```

claims   frequency: 1   relative frequency: 0.0000
```
     P.  25 YOUNG LOVE     28 So all Forraign Claims to drown,
```

clamerous   frequency: 1   relative frequency: 0.0000
```
     P. 176 LOYALL SCOT    206 Those whom you hear more Clamerous Yet and
                              Loud
```

clammor   frequency: 1   relative frequency: 0.0000
```
     P. 165 KINGS VOWES    17 Yet if Men should clammor I'le pack him away:
```

clamor. See "clammor," "clamour."

clamorous. See "clamerous."

clamour   frequency: 1   relative frequency: 0.0000
```
     P. 148 INSTRUCTIONS  313 The Seamens Clamour to three ends they use;
```

clap   frequency: 2   relative frequency: 0.0000
```
     P.  88 ODE           56 Did clap their bloody hands.
     P. 201 HISTORICALL    18 His younger Brother perisht by a clap.
```

claps   frequency: 1   relative frequency: 0.0000
```
     P. 202 HISTORICALL    54 De Ruyter claps him in Solbay again.
```

clap't   frequency: 1   relative frequency: 0.0000
```
     P. 316 CHEQUER INN   159 And clap't 'em on the Back
```

clarendon   frequency: 2   relative frequency: 0.0000
     See also "clarindon."
```
     P. 145 INSTRUCTIONS  177 Then march't the Troop of Clarendon, all full,
     P. 153 INSTRUCTIONS  508 Pain of Displeasure of great Clarendon.
```

clarendon's. See "clarindon's."

clarindon   frequency: 1   relative frequency: 0.0000
```
     P. 138 HOUSEWARMING    1 When Clarindon has discern'd beforehand,
```

clarindon's   frequency: 1   relative frequency: 0.0000
```
     P. 137 HOUSEWARMING    t Clarindon's House-Warming.
```

clasps   frequency: 1   relative frequency: 0.0000
```
     P.  77 A. HOUSE      590 Me licks, and clasps, and curles, and hales.
```

clattering. See "clatt'ring."

clatt'ring   frequency: 1   relative frequency: 0.0000
```
     P. 143 INSTRUCTIONS  106 The House of Commons clatt'ring like the Men.
```

clause   frequency: 1   relative frequency: 0.0000
```
     P. 152 INSTRUCTIONS  469 But when he came the odious Clause to Pen,
```

claw   frequency: 1   relative frequency: 0.0000
```
     P. 313 CHEQUER INN    28 Then oh how cou'd I claw him off
```

claws   frequency: 3   relative frequency: 0.0000
```
     P.  75 A. HOUSE      520 Within the Skin its shrunken claws.
     P. 156 INSTRUCTIONS  627 At her own Breast her useless claws does arm;
     P. 204 HISTORICALL   116 This haughty Monster with his ugly claws
```

clay   frequency: 2   relative frequency: 0.0000
     See also "china-clay."
```
     P.  96 HOLLAND        13 Collecting anxiously small Loads of Clay,
```

     P. 103 ANNIVERSARY   20 More slow and brittle then the China clay:

clayton's   frequency: 1   relative frequency: 0.0000
     P. 180 STOCKSMARKET   38 Or is he to Clayton's gone in masquerade?

clean   frequency: 5   relative frequency: 0.0001
     P. 18 CLORINDA   15 D. Might a Soul bath there and be clean,
     P. 22 NYMPH   21 Yet could they not be clean: their Stain
     P. 75 A. HOUSE   541 And all the way, to keep it clean,
     P. 86 FLECKNO   131 Yet these he promises as soon as clean.
     P. 174 LOYALL SCOT   117 How a Clean Laundress and noe sermons please.

clear   frequency: 16   relative frequency: 0.0003
     See also "cleare."
     P. 12 DROP OF DEW   5 For the clear Region where 'twas born
     P. 12 DROP OF DEW   20 Of the clear Fountain of Eternal Day,
     P. 25 YOUNG LOVE   3 Clear thine aged Fathers brow
     P. 64 A. HOUSE   176 'Is thus preserved clear and full.
     P. 104 ANNIVERSARY   47 Learning a Musique in the Region clear,
     P. 119 TWO SONGS   6 Thorough the clear and silent Night.
     P. 148 INSTRUCTIONS   288 Of clear Estates, and to no Faction sworn;
     P. 152 INSTRUCTIONS   457 Presbyter Hollis the first point should clear;
     P. 153 INSTRUCTIONS   529 The Sun much brighter, and the Skies more
                                    clear,
     P. 157 INSTRUCTIONS   682 As the clear Amber on the Bee does close:
     P. 160 INSTRUCTIONS   821 All to agree the Articles were clear,
     P. 162 INSTRUCTIONS   888 From his clear Eyes, yet these too dark with
                                    Care.
     P. 163 INSTRUCTIONS   916 And with blue streaks infect the Taper clear:
     P. 165 INSTRUCTIONS   986 Does with clear Counsels their large Souls
                                    supply;
     P. 173 LOYALL SCOT   48 As the Clear Amber on the bee doth Close;
     P. 191 TWO HORSES   4 It is a clear proofe that birds too may talke;

clear'd   frequency: 1   relative frequency: 0.0000
     P. 66 A. HOUSE   228 And dazled not but clear'd his sight.

cleare   frequency: 1   relative frequency: 0.0000
     P. 313 CHEQUER INN   41 To cleare him wou'd have been the first

clearly   frequency: 1   relative frequency: 0.0000
     P. 172 LOYALL SCOT   10 Hee Judg'd more Clearly now and saw more plain.

clears   frequency: 1   relative frequency: 0.0000
     P. 62 A. HOUSE   112 'Most strangly our Complexion clears.

cleavelands   frequency: 2   relative frequency: 0.0000
     P. 182 MADE FREE   54 To his Cleavelands, his Nells and his
                                    Carwells.
     P. 189 BRITANNIA   170 The Cleavelands, Osbornes, Barties,
                                    Lauderdales.

cleaves   frequency: 1   relative frequency: 0.0000
     P. 154 INSTRUCTIONS   545 And, where the deep Keel on the shallow cleaves,

cleavland   frequency: 1   relative frequency: 0.0000
     P. 172 LOYALL SCOT   6 Cleavland on whom they would the Task Impose.

clemency   frequency: 2   relative frequency: 0.0000
     P. 123 O.C.   14 In danger him, or Clemency that would.
     P. 131 O.C.   323 Tempt not his clemency to try his pow'r,

clergie   frequency: 2   relative frequency: 0.0000
     P. 174 LOYALL SCOT   89 Nothing but Clergie cold us two seclude:
     P. 174 LOYALL SCOT   121 A shorter Way's to bee by Clergie sav'd.

clerick   frequency: 1   relative frequency: 0.0000
     P. 139 HOUSEWARMING   85 By Subsidies thus both Clerick and Laick,

clerk   frequency: 1   relative frequency: 0.0000
     P. 169 ADVICE   56 Contriving Projects with a Brewers Clerk.

cleveland. See "cleavland."

clevelands. See "cleavelands."

cliff   frequency: 1   relative frequency: 0.0000
     P. 57 BILL-BOROW   27 Discerning further then the Cliff

clifford   frequency: 3   relative frequency: 0.0000
     P. 168 ADVICE   18 Circean Clifford with his charming Wand,

```
P. 199 DUKE          56 Clifford, who first appeared in humble guise,
P. 204 HISTORICALL  141 Clifford and Hide before had lost the day,
```

climacteric. See "clymacterick."

climate   frequency: 1   relative frequency: 0.0000
    P. 117 BLAKE   123 Never so burning was that Climate known,

climb   frequency: 3   relative frequency: 0.0000
    See also "climbe," "clime."
    P. 11 DIALOGUE   72 And then to Heaven climb.
    P. 27 LOVER   7 Nor can they to that Region climb,
    P. 54 THYESTE   1 Climb at Court for me that will

climbe   frequency: 2   relative frequency: 0.0000
    P. 88 ODE   33 Could by industrious Valour climbe
    P. 120 TWO SONGS   35 Here unto Latmos Top I climbe:

climbing   frequency: 1   relative frequency: 0.0000
    P. 109 ANNIVERSARY 261 Whose climbing Flame, without a timely stop,

clime   frequency: 1   relative frequency: 0.0000
    P.   4 LOVELACE   48 Above their envy, or mine aid doth clime.

climes   frequency: 2   relative frequency: 0.0000
    P.   3 LOVELACE   3 And as complexions alter with the Climes,
    P. 117 LOYALL SCOT 240 And few indeed can paralell our Climes

cling   frequency: 1   relative frequency: 0.0000
    P. 154 INSTRUCTIONS 542 And wanton Boys on every Rope do cling.

cloak   frequency: 1   relative frequency: 0.0000
    P. 85 FLECKNO   75 And above that yet casts an antick Cloak,

cloath   frequency: 2   relative frequency: 0.0000
    P. 201 HISTORICALL   8 And cloath him all from head to foot anew;
    P. 314 CHEQUER INN   62 Her Forehead Cloath had laid aside

cloaths   frequency: 1   relative frequency: 0.0000
    P. 315 CHEQUER INN 122 But wou'd as well as Meate have Cloaths

cloister   frequency: 1   relative frequency: 0.0000
    See also "cloyster."
    P. 67 A. HOUSE   271 The wasting Cloister with the rest

cloisters. See "cloysters."

clonmell   frequency: 1   relative frequency: 0.0000
    P. 127 O.C.   188 The story, and impregnable Clonmell.

clora   frequency: 1   relative frequency: 0.0000
    P. 29 THE GALLERY   1 Clora come view my Soul, and tell

clorinda   frequency: 2   relative frequency: 0.0000
    See also "c."
    P. 18 CLORINDA   t Clorinda and Damon.
    P. 18 CLORINDA   18 Clorinda, Pastures, Caves, and Springs.

clorinda's   frequency: 1   relative frequency: 0.0000
    P. 18 CLORINDA   25 D. Clorinda's voice might make it sweet.

clos'd   frequency: 2   relative frequency: 0.0000
    P. 85 FLECKNO   96 But himself there clos'd in a Scabbard saw
    P. 173 LOYALL SCOT   68 Galloping down Clos'd up the Gaping Cave.

close   frequency: 16   relative frequency: 0.0003
    P.   9 DIALOGUE   3 Close on thy Head thy Helmet bright.
    P. 17 BERMUDAS   19 And does in the Pomgranates close,
    P. 37 DEFINITION   14 Two perfect Loves; nor lets them close:
    P. 48 THE GARDEN   7 While all Flow'rs and all Trees do close
    P. 78 A. HOUSE   611 And Oh so close your Circles lace,
    P. 79 A. HOUSE   668 With Eben Shuts begin to close;
    P. 84 FLECKNO   71 Wears a close Jacket of poetick Buff,
    P. 103 ANNIVERSARY   6 While flowing Time above his Head does close.
    P. 144 INSTRUCTIONS 121 The close Cabal mark'd how the Navy eats,
    P. 144 INSTRUCTIONS 137 Chops off the piece where e're she close the
                            Jaw,
    P. 149 INSTRUCTIONS 367 The Count forthwith is order'd all to close,
    P. 153 INSTRUCTIONS 521 Soon then the Independent Troops would close,
    P. 157 INSTRUCTIONS 682 As the clear Amber on the Bee does close:
    P. 173 LOYALL SCOT   48 As the Clear Amber on the bee doth Close;
```
```

```
       P. 178 LOYALL SCOT     271 And all themselves in meal and friendship close.
       P. 200 DUKE             98 Noe, Painter, noe; close up this peice and see

closely                          frequency:    1    relative frequency: 0.0000
       P.  74 A. HOUSE         503 And stretches still so closely wedg'd

closer                           frequency:    2    relative frequency: 0.0000
       P.  33 DAPHNIS           16 Sudden Parting closer glews.
       P.  73 A. HOUSE         452 Their Cattle, which it closer rase;

closes                           frequency:    1    relative frequency: 0.0000
       P.  43 DAMON             54 Of all these Closes ev'ry Year.

closing                          frequency:    1    relative frequency: 0.0000
       P. 148 INSTRUCTIONS     297 Then closing, all in equal Front fall on,

cloth                            frequency:    1    relative frequency: 0.0000
       See also "cloath."
       P. 141 INSTRUCTIONS      21 The Painter so, long having vext his cloth,

clothe.  See "cloath."

clothes                          frequency:    3    relative frequency: 0.0000
       See also "cloaths."
       P.  64 A. HOUSE         179 'Plow'rs dress the Altars; for the Clothes,
       P.  72 A. HOUSE         444 As Clothes for Lilly strecht to stain.
       P.  97 HOLLAND           79 How fit a Title clothes their Governours,

cloud                            frequency:    5    relative frequency: 0.0001
       P.  92 MAY'S DEATH       99 And streight he vanisht in a Cloud of pitch,
       P. 106 ANNIVERSARY      141 But a thick Cloud about that Morning lyes,
       P. 109 ANNIVERSARY      234 As a small Cloud, like a Mans hand didst rise;
       P. 154 INSTRUCTIONS     557 With Thunder and Lightning from each armed
                                   Cloud;
       P. 180 STOCKSMARKET      35 With canvas and deals you e'er since do him
                                   cloud,

clouds                           frequency:    8    relative frequency: 0.0001
       P.  10 DIALOGUE          27 Thou in fragrant Clouds shalt show
       P.  16 EYES              49 Now like two Clouds dissolving, drop,
       P.  28 LOVER             22 Through frighted Clouds in forked streaks.
       P.  79 A. HOUSE         664 In blushing Clouds conceales his Head.
       P.  87 ODE               14 Breaking the Clouds where it was nurst,
       P. 114 BLAKE             28 Trees there the duty of the Clouds supply;
       P. 119 TWO SONGS         10 The fleecy Clouds with silver wand.
       P. 154 INSTRUCTIONS     552 A Fleet of Clouds, sailing along the Skies:

clouts                           frequency:    1    relative frequency: 0.0000
       P. 180 STOCKSMARKET      44 As if we'd as good have a king made of clouts.

cloven                           frequency:    2    relative frequency: 0.0000
       P. 176 LOYALL SCOT      203 That Cloven head must Govern Cloven foot.

clownishly                       frequency:    1    relative frequency: 0.0000
       P.  60 A. HOUSE          60 But low Things clownishly ascend.

clowns-all-heal                  frequency:    1    relative frequency: 0.0000
       P.  44 DAMON             83 With Shepherds-purse, and Clowns-all-heal,

cloy                             frequency:    1    relative frequency: 0.0000
       P. 113 BLAKE             11 Wealth which all others Avarice might cloy,

cloy'd                           frequency:    1    relative frequency: 0.0000
       P. 158 INSTRUCTIONS     707 And were not Ruyters maw with ravage cloy'd,

cloyster                         frequency:    2    relative frequency: 0.0000
       P.  62 A. HOUSE         103 'The Cloyster outward shuts its Gates,
       P.  67 A. HOUSE         278 The Cloyster yet remained hers.

cloysters                        frequency:    2    relative frequency: 0.0000
       P.  61 A. HOUSE          89 Near to this gloomy Cloysters Gates
       P. 164 INSTRUCTIONS     963 Better it were to live in Cloysters Lock,

club                             frequency:    1    relative frequency: 0.0000
       P. 139 HOUSEWARMING      68 As all Chedder Dairys club to the incorporate
                                   Cheese

cluster'd                        frequency:    1    relative frequency: 0.0000
       P. 138 HOUSEWARMING      60 As by hook and by crook the world cluster'd of
                                   Atome.

clusters                         frequency:    1    relative frequency: 0.0000
```

          P. 49 THE GARDEN   35 The Luscious Clusters of the Vine

clutch   frequency: 1   relative frequency: 0.0000
          P. 155 INSTRUCTIONS 604 Which show the tempting metal in their clutch.

clutterbuck   frequency: 1   relative frequency: 0.0000
          P. 139 HOUSEWARMING   70 Were shriveled, and Clutterbuck, Eagers <and>
                                   Kips;

clymacterick   frequency: 1   relative frequency: 0.0000
          P. 90 ODE   104 Shall Clymacterick be.

coach   frequency: 1   relative frequency: 0.0000
          See also "stage-coach."
          P. 142 INSTRUCTIONS   64 There, not behind the Coach, her Pages jump.

coals   frequency: 1   relative frequency: 0.0000
          P. 177 LOYALL SCOT   217 Indifferent to Rob Churches of their Coals.

coast   frequency: 4   relative frequency: 0.0000
          P. 17 BERMUDAS   30 The Gospels Pearl upon our Coast.
          P. 127 O.C.   154 Gave chase to Ligny on the Belgick Coast.
          P. 148 INSTRUCTIONS 323 Along the Coast and Harbours they take care
          P. 150 INSTRUCTIONS 410 This Isle of Candy was on Essex Coast.

coat   frequency: 1   relative frequency: 0.0000
          See also "saffron-coat."
          P. 143 INSTRUCTIONS   98 More gold in's Fob, more Lace upon his Coat

coates   frequency: 1   relative frequency: 0.0000
          P. 168 ADVICE   23 Place Falstaffs Regement of Thread-bare
                                   Coates

coats. See "coates."

cock-boat   frequency: 1   relative frequency: 0.0000
          P. 98 HOLLAND   111 A Cock-boat tost with the same wind and fate;

cock-horse   frequency: 1   relative frequency: 0.0000
          P. 146 INSTRUCTIONS 221 Not the first Cock-horse, that with Cork were
                                   shod

cock'd   frequency: 1   relative frequency: 0.0000
          P. 145 INSTRUCTIONS 183 He March'd with Beaver cock'd of Bishop's
                                   brim,

cockle   frequency: 1   relative frequency: 0.0000
          P. 95 HOLLAND   6 Of shipwrackt Cockle and the Muscle-shell;

cocks   frequency: 1   relative frequency: 0.0000
          P. 72 A. HOUSE   433 When after this 'tis pil'd in Cocks,

cocles   frequency: 1   relative frequency: 0.0000
          P. 147 INSTRUCTIONS 249 Such Roman Cocles strid: before the Foe,

cod. See "sea-cod."

coffee   frequency: 3   relative frequency: 0.0000
          P. 196 TWO HORSES   181 Let the Citty drink Coffee and Quietly groan
          P. 196 TWO HORSES   184 Chocolet Tea and Coffee are liquors of peace.
          P. 196 TWO HORSES   187 Then, Charles, thy edict against Coffee recall;

coffin   frequency: 2   relative frequency: 0.0000
          P. 83 FLECKNO   10 But seem'd a Coffin set on the Stairs head.
          P. 180 STOCKSMARKET   36 As if you had meant it his coffin and shroud?

coife   frequency: 1   relative frequency: 0.0000
          P. 145 INSTRUCTIONS 181 C-------n advances next, whose Coife dos awe

cold   frequency: 9   relative frequency: 0.0001
          P. 24 NYMPH   90 In whitest sheets of Lillies cold.
          P. 25 YOUNG LOVE   4 From cold Jealousie and Fears.
          P. 39 THE MATCH   20 To save him from the cold.
          P. 42 DAMON   32 Nor Cold but in her Icy Breast.
          P. 106 ANNIVERSARY   127 And in dark Nights, and in cold Dayes alone
          P. 163 INSTRUCTIONS 903 But soon shrunk back, chill'd with her touch so
                                   cold,
          P. 172 LOYALL SCOT   29 Nor other fear himself cold Comprehend
          P. 172 LOYALL SCOT   40 Inspire, nor cold hee his own Deeds deface;
          P. 174 LOYALL SCOT   89 Nothing but Clergie cold us two seclude:

collar   frequency: 1   relative frequency: 0.0000

```
        P. 163 INSTRUCTIONS  921 And ghastly Charles, turning his Collar low,

collecting                        frequency:    1    relative frequency: 0.0000
        P.  96 HOLLAND         13 Collecting anxiously small Loads of Clay,

collection                        frequency:    1    relative frequency: 0.0000
        P.  30 THE GALLERY     47 And a Collection choicer far

colonies                          frequency:    1    relative frequency: 0.0000
        P.  47 EMPIRE          12 Into harmonious Colonies withdrew.

colony                            frequency:    3    relative frequency: 0.0000
        P.  30 THE GALLERY     46 Art grown a num'rous Colony;
        P. 185 BRITANNIA       25 Brit: A Colony of French Possess the Court;
        P. 204 HISTORICALL    149 This is the Colony to plant his knaves:

colored.  See "party-colour'd."

colossus                          frequency:    1    relative frequency: 0.0000
        P. 173 LOYALL SCOT     72 Our nations Melting thy Colossus Frame,

colour                            frequency:    4    relative frequency: 0.0000
        P.  38 PICTURE          8 What Colour best becomes them, and what Smell.
        P.  78 A. HOUSE       627 Whose Grass, with moister colour dasht,
        P.  85 FLECKNO         81 Each colour that he past by; and be seen,
        P. 184 MADE FREE      117 To colour the good of an Alien,

coloured.  See "party-colour'd."

colours                           frequency:    8    relative frequency: 0.0001
        P.  39 THE MATCH        5 Her Orientest Colours there,
        P.  68 A. HOUSE       290 Hangs out the Colours of the Day,
        P.  68 A. HOUSE       310 Under their Colours stand displaid:
        P.  69 A. HOUSE       335 Tulips, in several Colours barr'd,
        P. 141 INSTRUCTIONS     5 Canst thou paint without Colours? Then 'tis
                                  right:
        P. 143 INSTRUCTIONS    79 Paint Castlemaine in Colours that will hold,
        P. 154 INSTRUCTIONS   538 And with inveigling Colours Court the Air.
        P. 156 INSTRUCTIONS   620 Taught the Dutch Colours from its top to wave;

columnes                          frequency:    2    relative frequency: 0.0000
        P.  59 A. HOUSE         7 Whose Columnes should so high be rais'd
        P.  74 A. HOUSE       510 The Columnes of the Temple green;

columns                           frequency:    1    relative frequency: 0.0000
        See also "columnes."
        P. 105 ANNIVERSARY     64 Therefore the Temples rear'd their Columns
                                  high:

comand                            frequency:    1    relative frequency: 0.0000
        P. 187 BRITANNIA      126 His French and Teagues comand on sea and shoar.

comands                           frequency:    2    relative frequency: 0.0000
        P. 178 LOYALL SCOT    263 Hee our Affection both and will Comands,
        P. 185 BRITANNIA       32 Leviathans and absolute comands.

comb                              frequency:    1    relative frequency: 0.0000
        P. 178 LOYALL SCOT    269 The hive a comb case, every bee a drone,

combat                            frequency:    2    relative frequency: 0.0000
        P.   9 DIALOGUE         8 In this day's Combat let it shine:
        P. 147 INSTRUCTIONS   264 This Combat truer than the Naval Fight.

combin'd                          frequency:    1    relative frequency: 0.0000
        P. 174 LOYALL SCOT    102 The friendly Loadstone hath not more Combin'd

combine                           frequency:    1    relative frequency: 0.0000
        P.  46 AMETAS          7 Where both parties so combine,

combs                             frequency:    1    relative frequency: 0.0000
        P.  49 THE GARDEN      54 Then whets, and combs its silver Wings;

come                              frequency:   38    relative frequency: 0.0007
        P.  18 CLORINDA         1 C. Damon come drive thy flocks this way.
        P.  20 THYRSIS         29 I prethee let us spend our time to come
        P.  24 NYMPH           95 See how it weeps. The Tears do come
        P.  25 YOUNG LOVE       1 Come little Infant, Love me now,
        P.  29 THE GALLERY      1 Clora come view my Soul, and tell
        P.  33 DAPHNIS          2 Now is come the dismal Hour
        P.  36 DAPHNIS         93 Fate I come, as dark, as sad,
        P.  45 GLO-WORMS       14 Since Juliana here is come,
        P.  60 A. HOUSE        34 Shall hither come in Pilgrimage,
```

```
P.  81 A. HOUSE      725 Where not one object can come nigh
P.  83 FLECKNO        13 Save that th' ingenious Door did as you come
P.  88 ODE            44 Where greater Spirits come.
P.  91 MAY'S DEATH    25 By this May to himself and them was come,
P.  92 MAY'S DEATH    83 And with the publick gravity would come,
P.  96 HOLLAND        25 As if on purpose it on Land had come
P. 113 BLAKE           4 Frayted with acted Guilt, and Guilt to come:
P. 118 BLAKE         157 Ages to come, your conquering Arms will bless,
P. 121 TWO SONGS      46 And cannot, though they would, come near.
P. 122 TWO SONGS      27 Come, lets in some Carol new
P. 122 TWO SONGS      36 And meaner Virtues come in play;
P. 138 HOUSEWARMING   45 His Wood would come in at the easier rate,
P. 143 INSTRUCTIONS  102 And Jermyn straight has leave to come agen.
P. 152 INSTRUCTIONS  475 But still in hope he solac'd, e're they come,
P. 161 INSTRUCTIONS  826 Let them come up so to go down agen.
P. 161 INSTRUCTIONS  833 And all with Sun and Choler come adust;
P. 161 INSTRUCTIONS  851 Hyde orders Turner that he should come late,
P. 161 INSTRUCTIONS  855 At last together Eaton come and he:
P. 171 PROPHECY       29 And Wooden shoos shall come to be the weare
P. 171 PROPHECY       31 London shall then see, for it will come to pass,
P. 174 LOYALL SCOT   108 Instead of all the Plagues had Bishops come,
P. 181 MADE FREE      22 And now he's come ore,
P. 188 BRITANNIA     131 Oh Vindex, come, and purge the Poyson'd state;
P. 193 TWO HORSES     64 Not our trade to secure but foes to come at 'um,
P. 194 TWO HORSES    102 Thou knowest what danger was like to come of it;
P. 196 TWO HORSES    165 That shall come to pass all mankind may swear
P. 199 DUKE           47 To finde such wellcome when you come soe farr.
P. 314 CHEQUER INN    53 For surenesse Cited were to come
P. 317 CHEQUER INN   182 Wee poure in Water when it won't come
```

comeing   frequency: 1   relative frequency: 0.0000
```
P. 316 CHEQUER INN   167 The paines of comeing in agen
```

comely   frequency: 1   relative frequency: 0.0000
```
P.  89 ODE            63 But bow'd his comely Head,
```

comerce   frequency: 1   relative frequency: 0.0000
```
P. 174 LOYALL SCOT   103 Then Bishops Crampt the Comerce of Mankind.
```

comes   frequency: 11   relative frequency: 0.0002
```
P.  45 MOWER'S SONG   23 For Juliana comes, and She
P.  46 MOWER'S SONG   29 For Juliana comes, and She
P.  60 A. HOUSE       51 But where he comes the swelling Hall
P.  79 A. HOUSE      669 The modest Halcyon comes in sight,
P. 122 TWO SONGS      17 Here She comes; but with a Look
P. 140 HOUSEWARMING  112 He comes to be roasted next St. James's Fair.
P. 145 INSTRUCTIONS  195 Then comes the thrifty Troop of Privateers,
P. 149 INSTRUCTIONS  351 The Irish-Herd is now let loose, and comes
P. 150 INSTRUCTIONS  376 Comes news of Pastime, Martial and old:
P. 168 ADVICE         28 For money comes when Seymour leaves the Chair.
P. 201 HISTORICALL    27 She chants Te Deum and so comes away
```

comet   frequency: 2   relative frequency: 0.0000
```
P.  80 A. HOUSE      683 No new-born Comet such a Train
P. 149 INSTRUCTIONS  348 The Comet dread, and Earth and Heaven burns.
```

comets   frequency: 1   relative frequency: 0.0000
```
P.  44 GLO-WORMS       5 Ye Country Comets, that portend
```

comfort   frequency: 1   relative frequency: 0.0000
```
P. 190 STATUE         17 No, to comfort the hearts of the poor Cavaleer
```

coming. See "comeing."

command   frequency: 18   relative frequency: 0.0003
See also "comand," "sea-command."
```
P.  38 PICTURE        13 And, under her command severe,
P.  69 A. HOUSE      352 Pow'r which the Ocean might command.
P.  89 ODE            81 Nor yet grown stiffer with Command,
P.  91 MAY'S DEATH    34 The awful Sign of his supream command.
P. 104 ANNIVERSARY    49 So when Amphion did the Lute command,
P. 108 ANNIVERSARY   222 When to Command, thou didst thy self Depose;
P. 110 ANNIVERSARY   279 'Tis not a Freedome, that where All command;
P. 112 ANNIVERSARY   369 'The Ocean is the Fountain of Command,
P. 119 TWO SONGS       9 As we our Flocks, so you command
P. 145 INSTRUCTIONS  200 For the command of Politicks or Sotts.
P. 145 INSTRUCTIONS  202 Their Friends agreed they should command by
                         turn.
P. 146 INSTRUCTIONS  211 Before them enter'd, equal in Command,
P. 146 INSTRUCTIONS  240 Without Intelligence, Command, or Pay:
P. 148 INSTRUCTIONS  299 Lee, equal to obey or to command,
```

P. 151 INSTRUCTIONS	434	Our Money spent; else 'twere at his command.
P. 154 INSTRUCTIONS	561	Sprag there, the practic'd in the Sea command,
P. 200 DUKE	100	Great Charles, who full of mercy wouldst command
P. 204 HISTORICALL	153	At his Command Mack will doe any thing,

commanded   frequency: 1   relative frequency: 0.0000
P. 128 O.C.   192 Since the commanded sun o're Gibeon stay'd?

commandment   frequency: 1   relative frequency: 0.0000
P. 152 INSTRUCTIONS   464 For Sin against th' Eleventh Commandment.

commands   frequency: 8   relative frequency: 0.0001
See also "comands."
P. 57 BILL-BOROW   25 Yet thus it all the field commands,
P. 72 A. HOUSE   418 The Mower now commands the Field;
P. 96 HOLLAND   43 Not who first see the rising Sun commands,
P. 144 INSTRUCTIONS   162 Wood these commands, Knight of the Horn and
                              Cane.
P. 145 INSTRUCTIONS   172 In vain, for always he commands that pays.
P. 159 INSTRUCTIONS   764 And Richmond here commands, as Ruyter those.
P. 159 INSTRUCTIONS   770 Who all Commands sold thro' the Navy? Pett.
P. 165 KINGS VOWES   14 With Consciences flexible to my Commands;

commend   frequency: 8   relative frequency: 0.0001
P. 11 DIALOGUE   64 That War or Peace commend?
P. 55 EPITAPH   2 'Tis to commend her but to name.
P. 55 EPITAPH   8 Without Detracting, her commend.
P. 87 FLECKNO   163 Who should commend his Mistress now? Or who
P. 94 DR. WITTY   22 But her own smiles commend that lovely face;
P. 132 PARADISE   52 And while I meant to Praise thee, must
                              Commend.
P. 187 BRITANNIA   116 And to his care did my sad state commend.
P. 315 CHEQUER INN   128 Which shoud the other most commend

commends   frequency: 1   relative frequency: 0.0000
P. 61 A. HOUSE   67 Nor less the Rooms within commends

commendum   frequency: 1   relative frequency: 0.0000
P. 175 LOYALL SCOT   143 Bishops are very good when in Commendum.

comments   frequency: 1   relative frequency: 0.0000
P. 110 ANNIVERSARY   306 Have writ the Comments of thy sacred Foame:

commerce. See "comerce."

commission   frequency: 3   relative frequency: 0.0000
P. 96 HOLLAND   52 Who look like a Commission of the Sewers.
P. 142 INSTRUCTIONS   39 Draw no Commission lest the Court should lye,
P. 167 KINGS VOWES   48 And I'lle first put the Church then my Crowne
                              in Commission.

common   frequency: 15   relative frequency: 0.0003
P. 25 YOUNG LOVE   9 Common Beauties stay fifteen;
P. 45 MOWER'S SONG   22 Will in one common Ruine fall.
P. 73 A. HOUSE   451 The Villagers in common chase
P. 88 ODE   57 He nothing common did or mean
P. 98 HOLLAND   118 Our sore new circumcised Common wealth.
P. 98 HOLLAND   131 The Common wealth doth by its losses grow;
P. 104 ANNIVERSARY   30 This Common Enemy is still opprest;
P. 164 INSTRUCTIONS   970 About the Common Prince have rais'd a Fence;
P. 174 LOYALL SCOT   85 That between us the Common Air shold bar
P. 178 LOYALL SCOT   273 And Each works hony for the Common Hive.
P. 187 BRITANNIA   110 'Down with that common Magna Charta whore.'
P. 198 DUKE   20 That common sense is my eternall foe.
P. 198 DUKE   32 That extreame unction is but common oyle
P. 202 HISTORICALL   40 With the Batavian common Wealth to fight.
P. 202 HISTORICALL   73 We leave to the report of Common fame.

common-place   frequency: 1   relative frequency: 0.0000
P. 152 INSTRUCTIONS   483 Then, from the usual Common-place, he blames

common-wealth   frequency: 3   relative frequency: 0.0000
P. 91 MAY'S DEATH   23 Where the Historian of the Common-wealth
P. 105 ANNIVERSARY   87 The Common-wealth does through their Centers
                              all
P. 195 TWO HORSES   161 W. A Commonwealth a Common-wealth wee proclaim
                              to the Nacion;

commoner   frequency: 1   relative frequency: 0.0000
P. 166 KINGS VOWES   40 Which if any bold Commoner dare to opose,

commons   frequency: 10   relative frequency: 0.0002

```
P.  89 ODE           85 He to the Commons Feet presents
P. 143 INSTRUCTIONS 106 The House of Commons clatt'ring like the Men.
P. 144 INSTRUCTIONS 128 Commons, and ever such a Court maintain,
P. 149 INSTRUCTIONS 333 Thus, like fair Thieves, the Commons Purse
                        they share,
P. 149 INSTRUCTIONS 359 Next the Twelve Commons are condemn'd to groan,
P. 161 INSTRUCTIONS 858 Nor gave the Commons leave to say their
                        Pray'rs:
P. 185 BRITANNIA     20 Till commons votes shall cut-nose guards disband,
P. 192 TWO HORSES    52 By a Curst hous of Commons and a blest
                        Restauracion;
P. 193 TWO HORSES    77 Ch. That Traitors to their Country in a
                        Brib'd Hous of Commons
P. 198 DUKE          23 Theire house of Commons and their house of
                        Lords,
```

commonweal   frequency: 1   relative frequency: 0.0000
```
P. 113 ANNIVERSARY  401 And as the Angel of our Commonweal,
```

commonwealth   frequency: 2   relative frequency: 0.0000
```
P. 105 ANNIVERSARY   75 The Commonwealth then first together came,
P. 195 TWO HORSES   161 W. A Commonwealth a Common-wealth wee proclaim
                        to the Nacion;
```

compact   frequency: 1   relative frequency: 0.0000
```
P. 145 INSTRUCTIONS 197 Before them Higgins rides with brow compact,
```

compactness   frequency: 1   relative frequency: 0.0000
```
P.  85 FLECKNO       84 His Chamber, whose compactness did allow
```

compacts   frequency: 1   relative frequency: 0.0000
```
P.  80 A. HOUSE     675 The gellying Stream compacts below,
```

companies   frequency: 1   relative frequency: 0.0000
See also "companyes."
```
P.  48 THE GARDEN    12 In busie Companies of Men.
```

companions   frequency: 1   relative frequency: 0.0000
```
P.  46 MOWER'S SONG  26 Companions of my thoughts more green,
```

company   frequency: 1   relative frequency: 0.0000
```
P. 182 MADE FREE     55 Nay his Company lewd
```

companyes   frequency: 1   relative frequency: 0.0000
```
P. 175 LOYALL SCOT  166 Their Companyes the worst that ever playd
```

compar'd   frequency: 1   relative frequency: 0.0000
```
P. 156 INSTRUCTIONS 622 With present shame compar'd, his mind distraught.
```

compare   frequency: 5   relative frequency: 0.0001
```
P.  68 A. HOUSE     303 And think so still! though not compare
P.  86 FLECKNO      137 When they compare their Chancres and Poulains.
P. 108 ANNIVERSARY  198 Nor their round Hoofs, or curled Mane's
                        compare;
P. 138 HOUSEWARMING  29 But while these devices he all doth compare,
P. 314 CHEQUER INN   58 And simper'd (justly to compare)
```

compares   frequency: 1   relative frequency: 0.0000
```
P.  90 MAY'S DEATH    9 At last while doubtfully he all compares,
```

compass   frequency: 3   relative frequency: 0.0000
```
P.  56 BILL-BOROW     3 The stiffest Compass could not strike
P. 127 O.C.         170 To compass in our Isle; our Tears suffice;
P. 132 PARADISE      41 Where couldst thou Words of such a compass find?
```

compassion   frequency: 2   relative frequency: 0.0000
```
P.  45 MOWER'S SONG  19 But what you in Compassion ought,
P. 125 O.C.          88 Yet in compassion of another dy'd.
```

compendious   frequency: 1   relative frequency: 0.0000
```
P. 141 INSTRUCTIONS  15 Or if to score out our compendious Fame,
```

complain   frequency: 11   relative frequency: 0.0002
See also "complaine."
```
P.  15 EYES           4 They might be ready to complain.
P.  21 SOUL & BODY   23 Where whatsoever it complain,
P.  26 MISTRESS       7 Of Humber would complain. I would
P.  42 DAMON         30 When Remedies themselves complain.
P.  43 DAMON         67 But now I all the day complain,
P.  65 A. HOUSE     202 Yet would he valiantly complain.
P.  88 ODE           37 Though Justice against Fate complain,
```

P. 123 TWO SONGS   42 No more shall need of Love complain;
P. 159 INSTRUCTIONS   755 But most they for their Darling Charles
                          complain:
P. 184 BRITANNIA   5 No more of Scottish race thou wouldst complain;
P. 186 BRITANNIA   67 Around her Joves lou'd ravenous Currs complain;

complain'd   frequency: 2   relative frequency: 0.0000
P. 83 FLECKNO   15 Yet of his State no man could have complain'd;
P. 151 INSTRUCTIONS   424 At London's Flame, nor so the Court
                          complain'd.

complaine   frequency: 1   relative frequency: 0.0000
P. 203 HISTORICALL   86 'Gainst Avarice and Luxury complaine,

complaining   frequency: 1   relative frequency: 0.0000
P. 22 NYMPH   t The Nymph complaining for the death of her
                          Faun.

complaint   frequency: 1   relative frequency: 0.0000
P. 41 DAMON   4 The Scene more fit for his complaint.

complaisence   frequency: 1   relative frequency: 0.0000
P. 154 INSTRUCTIONS   536 And witness their complaisence in their trim.

compleat   frequency: 1   relative frequency: 0.0000
P. 201 HISTORICALL   3 Twelve Yeares compleat he suffer'd in Exile

complement   frequency: 1   relative frequency: 0.0000
P. 177 LOYALL SCOT   220 Such Bishops are Without a Complement

complementing   frequency: 1   relative frequency: 0.0000
P. 85 FLECKNO   85 No empty place for complementing doubt,

complete. See "compleat."

complexion   frequency: 2   relative frequency: 0.0000
P. 41 THE MOWER   13 The Tulip, white, did for complexion seek;
P. 62 A. HOUSE   112 'Most strangly our Complexion clears.

complexions   frequency: 1   relative frequency: 0.0000
P.   3 LOVELACE   3 And as complexions alter with the Climes,

compliant   frequency: 1   relative frequency: 0.0000
P. 139 HOUSEWARMING   79 And St. John must now for the Leads be
                          compliant,

complying   frequency: 1   relative frequency: 0.0000
P. 81 A. HOUSE   718 And feign'd complying Innocence;

compos'd   frequency: 3   relative frequency: 0.0000
P. 29 THE GALLERY   4 Compos'd into one Gallery;
P. 105 ANNIVERSARY   85 Yet all compos'd by his attractive Song,
P. 124 O.C.   59 No trembling String compos'd to numbers new,

compose   frequency: 3   relative frequency: 0.0000
P. 31 FAIR SINGER   2 Love did compose so sweet an Enemy,
P. 64 A. HOUSE   180 'The Sea-born Amber we compose;
P. 103 ANNIVERSARY   5 And his short Tumults of themselves Compose,

composed   frequency: 1   relative frequency: 0.0000
P. 59 A. HOUSE   25 But all things are composed here

compound   frequency: 1   relative frequency: 0.0000
P. 38 PICTURE   17 O then let me in time compound,

comprehend   frequency: 3   relative frequency: 0.0000
P. 124 O.C.   45 While they by sence, not knowing, comprehend
P. 157 INSTRUCTIONS   663 Nor other fear himself could comprehend,
P. 172 LOYALL SCOT   29 Nor other fear himself cold Comprehend

compriz'd   frequency: 1   relative frequency: 0.0000
P. 33 DAPHNIS   12 So it had his stay compriz'd.

compter   frequency: 1   relative frequency: 0.0000
P. 180 STOCKSMARKET   40 Or have you to the Compter removed him for debt?

computes   frequency: 1   relative frequency: 0.0000
P. 50 THE GARDEN   70 Computes its time as well as we.

concave   frequency: 1   relative frequency: 0.0000
P. 18 CLORINDA   14 Tinkles within the concave Shell.

```
conceal                            frequency:   3    relative frequency: 0.0000
    P.    5 HASTINGS       41 The gods themselves cannot their Joy conceal,
    P.  143 INSTRUCTIONS  100 No lcnger could conceal his Fortune sweet.
    P.  196 TWO HORSES    176 To conceal their own crimes and cover their
                              shame,

conceald                           frequency:   1    relative frequency: 0.0000
    P.  184 BRITANNIA      11 Brit: Favour'd by night, conceald by this
                              disguise,

conceal'd                          frequency:   3    relative frequency: 0.0000
    P.   65 A. HOUSE      220 'When they it think by Night conceal'd.
    P.  124 O.C.           63 Yet both perceiv'd, yet both conceal'd their
                              Skills,
    P.  144 INSTRUCTIONS  139 She stalks all day in Streets conceal'd from
                              sight,

concealed.  See "conceald," "conceal'd."

conceales                          frequency:   1    relative frequency: 0.0000
    P.   79 A. HOUSE      664 In blushing Clouds conceales his Head.

conceals.  See "conceales."

conceiv'd                          frequency:   1    relative frequency: 0.0000
    P.   61 A. HOUSE       96 (As 'twere by Chance) Thoughts long conceiv'd.

conceive                           frequency:   1    relative frequency: 0.0000
    P.   97 HOLLAND        63 Faith, that could never Twins conceive before,

concern'd                          frequency:   1    relative frequency: 0.0000
    P.  150 INSTRUCTIONS  381 No concern'd Jury for him Damage finds,

conclude                           frequency:   1    relative frequency: 0.0000
    P.   73 A. HOUSE      465 Then, to conclude these pleasant Acts,

conclusion                         frequency:   2    relative frequency: 0.0000
    P.  195 TWO HORSES     2t Conclusion.
    P.  196 TWO HORSES    162 Conclusion.

concur                             frequency:   1    relative frequency: 0.0000
    P.  153 INSTRUCTIONS  519 All Causes sure concur, but most they think

condemn                            frequency:   2    relative frequency: 0.0000
    See also "contemn."
    P.   60 A. HOUSE       63 Where neatness nothing can condemn,
    P.   86 FLECKNO       121 And on full stomach do condemn but few:

condemn'd                          frequency:   2    relative frequency: 0.0000
    P.   86 FLECKNO       144 That were ill made condemn'd to be read worse:
    P.  149 INSTRUCTIONS  359 Next the Twelve Commons are condemn'd to groan,

condemned                          frequency:   1    relative frequency: 0.0000
    See also "condemn'd."
    P.   34 DAPHNIS        53 So to the condemned Wight

condemneth                         frequency:   1    relative frequency: 0.0000
    P.    5 HASTINGS       48 Himself at once condemneth, and Mayern;

condition                          frequency:   1    relative frequency: 0.0000
    P.  167 KINGS VOWES    46 If this please not I'lle Raigne upon any
                              Condition,

conducts                           frequency:   1    relative frequency: 0.0000
    P.  145 INSTRUCTIONS  180 And bloated Wren conducts them to their seats.

coneig's                           frequency:   1    relative frequency: 0.0000
    P.  202 HISTORICALL    46 With Denham and Coneig's infected pot,

confederacies                      frequency:   1    relative frequency: 0.0000
    P.   98 HOLLAND       102 What then are their confederacies abroad?

confer                             frequency:   1    relative frequency: 0.0000
    P.   76 A. HOUSE      562 Among the Birds and Trees confer:

confess                            frequency:   3    relative frequency: 0.0000
    P.   64 A. HOUSE      184 'These as sweet Sins we should confess.
    P.  114 BLAKE          45 For Spain had better, Shee'l ere long confess,
    P.  130 O.C.          276 Seeing how little we confess, how greate;

confessor                          frequency:   1    relative frequency: 0.0000
```

P. 127 O.C.   178 For Holyness the Confessor exceeds.

confest   frequency: 3   relative frequency: 0.0000
    P. 89 ODE   78 And have, though overcome, confest
    P. 112 ANNIVERSARY 394 'It grieves me sore to have thus much confest.
    P. 146 INSTRUCTIONS 215 He, to excuse his slowness, truth confest

confident   frequency: 1   relative frequency: 0.0000
    P. 116 BLAKE   96 So proud and confident of their made strength,

confind   frequency: 1   relative frequency: 0.0000
    P. 199 DUKE   61 To be by justice and by laws confind:

confin'd   frequency: 3   relative frequency: 0.0000
    P.   5 HASTINGS   31 So he, not banisht hence, but there confin'd,
    P. 128 O.C.   229 And we death's refuse nature's dregs confin'd
    P. 156 INSTRUCTIONS 641 And saw himself confin'd, like Sheep in Pen;

confine   frequency: 1   relative frequency: 0.0000
    P. 21 SOUL & BODY   21 What Magick could me thus confine

confined. See "confind," "confin'd."

confines   frequency: 1   relative frequency: 0.0000
    P. 60 A. HOUSE   38 Within such dwarfish Confines went:

confirm   frequency: 1   relative frequency: 0.0000
    P. 186 BRITANNIA   54 Then, to confirm the cure so well begun,

confirming   frequency: 1   relative frequency: 0.0000
    P. 175 LOYALL SCOT   163 Confirming breasts and Armepitts for the head.

confiscate   frequency: 2   relative frequency: 0.0000
    P. 153 INSTRUCTIONS 502 Their Money lodge; confiscate when he please.
    P. 179 STOCKSMARKET   28 May be henceforth confiscate for reasons more
                             just.

conform's   frequency: 1   relative frequency: 0.0000
    P. 176 LOYALL SCOT   212 To conform's necessary or bee shent,

confus'd   frequency: 2   relative frequency: 0.0000
    P. 31 MOURNING   5 Her Eyes confus'd, and doubled ore,
    P. 187 BRITANNIA   105 When she had spoke, a confus'd murmur rose

confus'der   frequency: 1   relative frequency: 0.0000
    P. 86 FLECKNO   150 Confus'der then the atomes in the Sun.

confuseder. See "confus'der."

confusion   frequency: 1   relative frequency: 0.0000
    P. 155 INSTRUCTIONS 610 Confusion, folly, treach'ry, fear, neglect.

conge   frequency: 1   relative frequency: 0.0000
    P. 167 KINGS VOWES   45 And my Wench shall dispose of the Conge
                             d'eslire.

congeal'd   frequency: 2   relative frequency: 0.0000
    P. 13 DROP OF DEW   38 White, and intire, though congeal'd and chill.
    P. 13 DROP OF DEW   39 Congeal'd on Earth: but does, dissolving, run

congealed   frequency: 1   relative frequency: 0.0000
    See also "congeal'd."
    P.   3 LOVELACE   35 Lovelace that thaw'd the most congealed brest,

congruous   frequency: 1   relative frequency: 0.0000
    P. 175 LOYALL SCOT   170 A Congruous Dress they to themselves Adapt,

conjoined. See "conjoynd."

conjoynd   frequency: 1   relative frequency: 0.0000
    P. 189 BRITANNIA   183 Greek arts and Roman armes in her conjoynd

conjunction   frequency: 1   relative frequency: 0.0000
    P. 37 DEFINITION   31 Is the Conjunction of the Mind,

conjuncture   frequency: 1   relative frequency: 0.0000
    P. 106 ANNIVERSARY   136 From such a wish'd Conjuncture might reflect.

conjure   frequency: 2   relative frequency: 0.0000
    P. 157 INSTRUCTIONS 667 Or Waves his Sword, and could he them conjure
    P. 172 LOYALL SCOT   33 Or waves his swcrd and, Cou'd hee them Conjure,

conquer   frequency: 3   relative frequency: 0.0000
    P.   9 DIALOGUE   10 To conquer one resolved Heart.
    P. 118 BLAKE   140 There one must Conquer, or there both must dye.
    P. 166 KINGS VOWES   19 I will have a fine Navy to Conquer the Seas,

conquer'd   frequency: 3   relative frequency: 0.0000
    P. 66 A. HOUSE   246 His Horse through conquer'd Britain ride?
    P. 128 O.C.   194 He conquer'd God, still ere he fought with men:
    P. 147 INSTRUCTIONS   272 As eas'ly Conquer'd, and believing can.

conquered   frequency: 2   relative frequency: 0.0000
    See also "conquer'd."
    P. 104 ANNIVERSARY   32 If Conquered, on them they wreak their Spight:
    P. 196 TWO HORSES   182 They that Conquered the Father won't be slaves
                             to the Son:

conquering   frequency: 5   relative frequency: 0.0001
    P. 38 PICTURE   18 And parly with those conquering Eyes;
    P. 91 MAY'S DEATH   24 In his own Bowels sheath'd the conquering
                             health.
    P. 114 BLAKE   44 Your Conquering Sword will soon that want
                             remove.
    P. 116 BLAKE   101 For your renown, his conquering Fleet does ride,
    P. 118 BLAKE   157 Ages to come, your conquering Arms will bless,

conqueror   frequency: 2   relative frequency: 0.0000
    P. 47 EMPIRE   22 Unto a gentler Conqueror then you;
    P. 147 INSTRUCTIONS   255 First enter'd forward Temple, Conqueror

conquerors   frequency: 2   relative frequency: 0.0000
    P. 104 ANNIVERSARY   31 If Conquerors, on them they turn their might;
    P. 179 STOCKSMARKET   1 As cities that to the fierce conquerors yield

conquest   frequency: 4   relative frequency: 0.0000
    P. 31 FAIR SINGER   1 To make a final conquest of all me,
    P. 99 HOLLAND   140 Their Navy all our Conquest or our Wreck:
    P. 109 ANNIVERSARY   250 Yet by the Conquest of two Kings grown great,
    P. 158 INSTRUCTIONS   732 Viewing her strength, they yet their Conquest
                             doubt.

conquests   frequency: 1   relative frequency: 0.0000
    P. 115 BLAKE   66 Shall conquests act, your present are unsung.

conscience   frequency: 6   relative frequency: 0.0001
    P. 70 A. HOUSE   354 Ambition weed, but Conscience till.
    P. 70 A. HOUSE   355 Conscience, that Heaven-nursed Plant,
    P. 97 HOLLAND   73 That Bank of Conscience, where not one so
                             strange
    P. 127 O.C.   180 And tim'rous Conscience unto Courage man'd:
    P. 165 INSTRUCTIONS   985 Whose gen'rous Conscience and whose Courage
                             high
    P. 193 TWO HORSES   84 For selling their Conscience were Liberally
                             paid.

consciences   frequency: 1   relative frequency: 0.0000
    P. 165 KINGS VOWES   14 With Consciences flexible to my Commands;

conscious   frequency: 4   relative frequency: 0.0000
    P. 10 DIALOGUE   24 Conscious of doing what I ought.
    P. 128 O.C.   219 The worser sort, so conscious of their ill,
    P. 155 INSTRUCTIONS   579 The conscious Stag, so once the Forests dread,
    P. 175 LOYALL SCOT   168 The Conscious Prelate therefore did not Err,

consecrate   frequency: 2   relative frequency: 0.0000
    P. 63 A. HOUSE   146 'Is so already consecrate.
    P. 65 A. HOUSE   222 'Not Thee, that they would consecrate.

consecrated   frequency: 1   relative frequency: 0.0000
    P. 84 FLECKNO   61 With consecrated Wafers: and the Host

consent   frequency: 4   relative frequency: 0.0000
    P. 105 ANNIVERSARY   67 Such was that wondrous Order and Consent,
    P. 125 O.C.   105 Or the great World do by consent presage,
    P. 144 INSTRUCTIONS   154 And Denham these by one consent did head.
    P. 187 BRITANNIA   111 With Joynt consent on helpless me they flew,

consenting   frequency: 1   relative frequency: 0.0000
    P. 152 INSTRUCTIONS   474 Consenting, for his Rupture, to be Gelt;

consider   frequency: 2   relative frequency: 0.0000
    P. 140 HOUSEWARMING   105 But do not consider how in process of times,

```
             P. 194 TWO HORSES    115 Ch. Pause, Brother, a while and calmly
                                        consider:

considers                            frequency:    1    relative frequency: 0.0000
   P. 174 LOYALL SCOT     87 But who Considers well will find indeed

consist                              frequency:    1    relative frequency: 0.0000
   P.  85 FLECKNO        101 Consist but in one substance. Then, to fit

consistory                           frequency:    1    relative frequency: 0.0000
   P.   3 LOVELACE        22 Like the grim consistory on thy Booke;

consoles                             frequency:    1    relative frequency: 0.0000
   P. 151 INSTRUCTIONS   448 Consoles us morally out of Seneque.

consort                              frequency:    1    relative frequency: 0.0000
   P.  47 EMPIRE          9 Each sought a consort in that lovely place;

consorts                             frequency:    1    relative frequency: 0.0000
   P.  20 THYRSIS        33 There, birds sing Consorts, garlands grow,

conspiracies                         frequency:    1    relative frequency: 0.0000
   P. 107 ANNIVERSARY    171 Thy Brest through ponyarding Conspiracies,

conspire                             frequency:    1    relative frequency: 0.0000
   P. 148 INSTRUCTIONS   325 Long thus they could against the House conspire,

constant                             frequency:    4    relative frequency: 0.0000
   P.  46 AMETAS          13 What you cannot constant hope
   P. 159 INSTRUCTIONS   741 And constant Time, to keep his course yet right,
   P. 181 MADE FREE       35 In his constant Delights
   P. 203 HISTORICALL     76 With lavish hands they constant Tributes give

constellations                       frequency:    1    relative frequency: 0.0000
   P.  73 A. HOUSE       464 As Constellations do above.

constrain'd                          frequency:    3    relative frequency: 0.0000
   P.  21 SOUL & BODY     27 Constrain'd not only to indure
   P.  82 A. HOUSE       756 The Bel-Retiro as constrain'd;
   P. 156 INSTRUCTIONS   639 But when, by shame constrain'd to go on Board,

consuls                              frequency:    1    relative frequency: 0.0000
   P.  91 MAY'S DEATH     46 Until you all grow Consuls in your wine.

consult                              frequency:    1    relative frequency: 0.0000
   P. 104 ANNIVERSARY     35 Nor sacred Prophecies consult within,

consulting                           frequency:    2    relative frequency: 0.0000
   P. 149 INSTRUCTIONS   334 But all the Members Lives, consulting, spare.
   P. 171 LOYALL SCOT      3 They streight Consulting gather'd in a Ring

consume                              frequency:    2    relative frequency: 0.0000
   P. 137 HOUSEWARMING     5 Us Mars, and Apollo, and Vulcan consume;
   P. 193 TWO HORSES      59 W. That a King should consume three Realms
                             whole Estates

consumed                             frequency:    1    relative frequency: 0.0000
   P.  28 LOVER           38 He both consumed, and increast:

consumes                             frequency:    1    relative frequency: 0.0000
   P.  77 A. HOUSE       579 And in one History consumes,

consummate                           frequency:    1    relative frequency: 0.0000
   P. 139 HOUSEWARMING    89 And upon the Tarras, to consummate all,

contagion                            frequency:    2    relative frequency: 0.0000
   P. 188 BRITANNIA      150 Must be immur'd, lest their contagion steal
   P. 204 HISTORICALL    131 Nothing the dire Contagion can opose.

contagious                           frequency:    1    relative frequency: 0.0000
   P. 158 INSTRUCTIONS   705 Up to the Bridge contagious Terrour strook:

contain'd                            frequency:    1    relative frequency: 0.0000
   P.  60 A. HOUSE        44 Things greater are in less contain'd.

containe                             frequency:    1    relative frequency: 0.0000
   P. 197 DUKE            1 Spread a large canvass, Painter, to containe

contains                             frequency:    1    relative frequency: 0.0000
   P.  82 A. HOUSE       765 Your lesser World contains the same.

contemn                              frequency:    2    relative frequency: 0.0000
```

    P. 60 A. HOUSE   64 Nor Pride invent what to contemn?
    P. 70 A. HOUSE   373 They, in there squeking Laugh, contemn

contempt   frequency: 1   relative frequency: 0.0000
    P. 204 HISTORICALL   135 Let Cromwells Ghost smile with Contempt to see

contend   frequency: 2   relative frequency: 0.0000
    P. 113 ANNIVERSARY   397 I yield, nor further will the Prize contend;
    P. 315 CHEQUER INN   127 Sir Courtney Poole and he contend

contends   frequency: 1   relative frequency: 0.0000
    P. 105 ANNIVERSARY   82 Each in the House the highest Place contends,

content   frequency: 3   relative frequency: 0.0000
    P. 22 NYMPH   39 With this: and very well content,
    P. 76 A. HOUSE   559 While the Oake seems to fall content,
    P. 149 INSTRUCTIONS 330 They with the first days proffer seem content:

contented   frequency: 1   relative frequency: 0.0000
    P. 58 BILL-BOROW   58 Contented if they fix their Root.

contest   frequency: 2   relative frequency: 0.0000
    P.   4 LOVELACE   40 Sally'd, and would in his defence contest.
    P. 104 ANNIVERSARY   29 Their other Wars seem but a feign'd contest,

contignation   frequency: 1   relative frequency: 0.0000
    P. 105 ANNIVERSARY   90 Fast'ning the Contignation which they thwart;

continent   frequency: 1   relative frequency: 0.0000
    P. 127 O.C.   172 Who once more joyn'd us to the Continent;

continue   frequency: 2   relative frequency: 0.0000
    P. 30 THE GALLERY   30 How long thou shalt continue fair;
    P. 91 MAY'S DEATH   54 Those but to Lucan do continue May.

continued   frequency: 1   relative frequency: 0.0000
    P. 174 LOYALL SCOT   84 Up from her Stream Continued to the Sky's,

continues   frequency: 1   relative frequency: 0.0000
    P. 189 STATUE   2 This five moneths continues still blinded with
                             board?

contract   frequency: 1   relative frequency: 0.0000
    P. 43 DAMON   64 About me they contract their Ring.

contractors. See "chimny-contractors."

contracts   frequency: 1   relative frequency: 0.0000
    P. 103 ANNIVERSARY   13 'Tis he the force of scatter'd Time contracts,

contradict   frequency: 1   relative frequency: 0.0000
    P. 198 DUKE   25 Shall these men dare to contradict my will

contrary   frequency: 1   relative frequency: 0.0000
    P. 86 FLECKNO   154 Should know the contrary. Whereat, I, now

contribute   frequency: 1   relative frequency: 0.0000
    P. 104 ANNIVERSARY   43 Nor more contribute to the state of Things,

contributed   frequency: 2   relative frequency: 0.0000
    P. 95 HOLLAND   3 And so much Earth as was contributed
    P. 139 HOUSEWARMING   64 The Tribes ne'er contributed so to the Temple.

contriv'd   frequency: 1   relative frequency: 0.0000
    P. 29 THE GALLERY   2 Whether I have contriv'd it well.

contrive   frequency: 1   relative frequency: 0.0000
    P. 59 A. HOUSE   12 And Birds contrive an equal Nest;

contrived   frequency: 1   relative frequency: 0.0000
    See also "contriv'd."
    P. 198 DUKE   17 And by a noble well contrived plott,

contriving   frequency: 1   relative frequency: 0.0000
    P. 169 ADVICE   56 Contriving Projects with a Brewers Clerk.

control. See "controll," "controule."

controll   frequency: 1   relative frequency: 0.0000
    P. 166 KINGS VOWES   31 I will have a Privy-purse without a Controll,

controlled. See "contrould."

controller   frequency: 1   relative frequency: 0.0000

P. 141 INSTRUCTIONS   17 Where, like the new Controller, all men laugh

controls. See "controules."

contrould   frequency: 1   relative frequency: 0.0000
    P. 185 BRITANNIA   44 How Spaines prow'd power her Virgin Armes
                             contrould

controule   frequency: 2   relative frequency: 0.0000
    P. 176 LOYALL SCOT   192 But now, when one Head doeth both Realmes
                             controule,
    P. 200 DUKE   90 Ten thousand such as these can nere controule

controules   frequency: 1   relative frequency: 0.0000
    P. 186 BRITANNIA   77 Dastards the hearts and active heat controules.

convenience   frequency: 1   relative frequency: 0.0000
    P. 140 HOUSEWARMING   107 And with that convenience he soon for his Crimes

convenient   frequency: 2   relative frequency: 0.0000
    P. 153 INSTRUCTIONS   506 How can he Engines so convenient spare?
    P. 191 STATUE   43 She thinks not convenient to goe to the price,

converse   frequency: 1   relative frequency: 0.0000
    P. 81 A. HOUSE   707 She counts her Beauty to converse

conversion   frequency: 1   relative frequency: 0.0000
    P. 26 MISTRESS   10 Till the Conversion of the Jews.

convert   frequency: 1   relative frequency: 0.0000
    P. 106 ANNIVERSARY   115 But Indians whom they shculd convert, subdue;

converted   frequency: 1   relative frequency: 0.0000
    P. 97 HOLLAND   57 How could the Dutch but be converted, when

converts   frequency: 1   relative frequency: 0.0000
    P. 195 TWO HORSES   148 Wee must all tc the Stake or be Converts to
                             Rome.

convey   frequency: 2   relative frequency: 0.0000
    P. 142 INSTRUCTIONS   66 Can without breaking venom'd juice ccnvey.
    P. 188 BRITANNIA   144 With the Doggs bloud his gentle kind convey

conveyed   frequency: 1   relative frequency: 0.0000
    P. 180 STOCKSMARKET   37 Hath Blood him away (as his crown once)
                             conveyed?

conveying   frequency: 1   relative frequency: 0.0000
    P. 198 DUKE   37 Conveying his Religion and his bride:

convinc'd   frequency: 1   relative frequency: 0.0000
    P. 131 PARADISE   25 But I am now convinc'd, and none will dare

convince   frequency: 1   relative frequency: 0.0000
    P. 20 THYRSIS   41 Convince me now, that this is true;

convocation   frequency: 1   relative frequency: 0.0000
    P. 160 INSTRUCTIONS   816 Till it be govern'd by a Convocation.

convoy   frequency: 1   relative frequency: 0.0000
    P. 30 THE GALLERY   40 Convoy the Perfume to the Smell.

convulsion   frequency: 1   relative frequency: 0.0000
    P. 37 DEFINITION   22 And Earth some new Convulsicn tear;

cook. See "cooke," "master-cook."

cooke   frequency: 1   relative frequency: 0.0000
    P. 199 DUKE   71 Although no schcller, yet can act the cooke:

cool   frequency: 7   relative frequency: 0.0001
    P. 18 CLORINDA   11 C. In whose cool bcsome we may lye
    P. 20 THYRSIS   34 Cocl winds do whisper, springs do flow.
    P. 27 LOVER   4 By Fountains cool, and Shadows green.
    P. 42 DAMON   27 To what cool Cave shall I descend,
    P. 55 EPITAPH   18 Gentle as Ev'ning; cool as Night;
    P. 77 A. HOUSE   598 And unto you cocl Zephyr's Thanks,
    P. 177 LOYALL SCOT   224 Others Attempt, to Cool their fervent Chine,

cool'd   frequency: 3   relative frequency: 0.0000
    P. 108 ANNIVERSARY   208 Courage disheartned, and Religion cool'd.

```
          P. 156 INSTRUCTIONS  656 Harden'd and cool'd his Limbs, so soft, so
                                   white,
          P. 172 LOYALL SCOT    22 Hardned and Cool'd those Limbs soe soft, soe
                                   white,

cooling                           frequency:   1   relative frequency: 0.0000
          P.  77 A. HOUSE       595 While the Wind, cooling through the Boughs,

coolness                          frequency:   1   relative frequency: 0.0000
          P. 114 BLAKE           37 And coolness there, with heat doth never fight,

cooper                            frequency:   1   relative frequency: 0.0000
          P. 314 CHEQUER INN     54 The rest were bid by Cooper.

cope                              frequency:   1   relative frequency: 0.0000
          P.  77 A. HOUSE       591 Under this antick Cope I move

copes                             frequency:   1   relative frequency: 0.0000
          P. 176 LOYALL SCOT    173 Of Rochets Tippets Copes, and wheres theire
                                   Grace?

copies                            frequency:   1   relative frequency: 0.0000
          P.  86 FLECKNO        130 Save only two foul copies for his shirt:

copper                            frequency:   2   relative frequency: 0.0000
          P. 190 STATUE          39 Tho' the King be of Copper and Danby of Gold,
          P. 193 TWO HORSES      62 No token should appear but a poor Copper
                                   farthing;

cordage                           frequency:   1   relative frequency: 0.0000
          P. 158 INSTRUCTIONS   728 Her Masts erect, tough Cordage, Timbers
                                   strong,

cordial                           frequency:   1   relative frequency: 0.0000
          P. 142 INSTRUCTIONS    68 Out of the cordial meal of the Cacao.

corinthean                        frequency:   1   relative frequency: 0.0000
          P.  74 A. HOUSE       508 As the Corinthean Porticoes.

corinthian                        frequency:   1   relative frequency: 0.0000
          See also "corinthean."
          P. 173 LOYALL SCOT     71 Mixt in Corinthian Mettall at thy Flame

cork                              frequency:   1   relative frequency: 0.0000
          P. 146 INSTRUCTIONS   221 Not the first Cock-horse, that with Cork were
                                   shod

cormorant.  See "corm'rant."

cormorants.  See "corm'rants."

corm'rant                         frequency:   1   relative frequency: 0.0000
          P.  28 LOVER           35 And as one Corm'rant fed him, still

corm'rants                        frequency:   1   relative frequency: 0.0000
          P.  28 LOVER           27 A num'rous fleet of Corm'rants black,

corn                              frequency:   2   relative frequency: 0.0000
          P. 160 INSTRUCTIONS   799 And who the Forts would not vouchsafe a corn,
          P. 164 INSTRUCTIONS   973 (But Ceres Corn, and Flora is the Spring,

cornbry                           frequency:   1   relative frequency: 0.0000
          P. 155 INSTRUCTIONS   600 (Cornbry the fleetest) and to London run.

cornbury                          frequency:   1   relative frequency: 0.0000
          See also "cornbry."
          P. 146 INSTRUCTIONS   218 Cornbury before them manag'd Hobby-horse.

cornet                            frequency:   1   relative frequency: 0.0000
          P.  47 EMPIRE          14 And others chose the Cornet eloquent.

coronet                           frequency:   1   relative frequency: 0.0000
          P.  14 THE CORONET      t The Coronet.

corporation                       frequency:   1   relative frequency: 0.0000
          P. 161 INSTRUCTIONS   832 Does for his Corporation sweat and trot.

corposants                        frequency:   1   relative frequency: 0.0000
          P. 109 ANNIVERSARY    270 And Corposants along the Tacklings slide.

corpulence                        frequency:   1   relative frequency: 0.0000
```

P. 90 MAY'S DEATH   11 Such did he seem for corpulence and port,

corrode   frequency: 1   relative frequency: 0.0000
    P. 164 INSTRUCTIONS 958 Which, in your Splendor hid, Corrode your
                             Light;

corrupcions   frequency: 1   relative frequency: 0.0000
    P. 188 BRITANNIA   164 Least Court corrupcions should their souls
                             engage.

corrupt   frequency: 2   relative frequency: 0.0000
    P. 76 A. HOUSE   555 (As first our Flesh corrupt within
    P. 203 HISTORICALL   78 Corrupt with Gold they Wives and Daughters
                             bring

corrupted   frequency: 1   relative frequency: 0.0000
    P.   3 LOVELACE   20 Of wit corrupted, the unfashion'd Sons.

corruptible   frequency: 1   relative frequency: 0.0000
    P. 98 HOLLAND   134 And purges out the corruptible waves.

corruptions. See "corrupcions."

corslet   frequency: 1   relative frequency: 0.0000
    P. 87 ODE   8 The Corslet of the Hall.

cost   frequency: 4   relative frequency: 0.0000
    P. 104 ANNIVERSARY   25 Another triumphs at the publick Cost,
    P. 112 ANNIVERSARY   385 'Where did he learn those Arts that cost us dear?
    P. 126 O.C.   112 But oh what pangs that Death did Nature cost!
    P. 166 KINGS VOWES   37 But what ever it cost I will have a fine Whore,

costly   frequency: 1   relative frequency: 0.0000
    P. 107 ANNIVERSARY   183 Like skilful Looms which through the costly
                             thred

costs   frequency: 1   relative frequency: 0.0000
    P. 65 A. HOUSE   196 'The Tryal neither Costs, nor Tyes.

cotton   frequency: 1   relative frequency: 0.0000
    P. 64 A. HOUSE   192 'Like Chrystal pure with Cotton warm.

cou'd   frequency: 9   relative frequency: 0.0001

could   frequency: 95   relative frequency: 0.0019
    See also "cou'd."

couldst   frequency: 5   relative frequency: 0.0001

could'st   frequency: 2   relative frequency: 0.0000
    See also "couldst."

councel   frequency: 1   relative frequency: 0.0000
    P. 204 HISTORICALL   118 Declares the Councel Edicts are beyond

councell   frequency: 5   relative frequency: 0.0001
    P. 166 KINGS VOWES   34 I will have a Privy Councell to sit allwayes
                             still,
    P. 169 ADVICE   30 The figure of a Drunken Councell board
    P. 169 ADVICE   34 To make them th' other Councell board forgett.
    P. 169 ADVICE   47 Draw our Olimpia next in Councell Sate
    P. 193 TWO HORSES   54 And scarce a wise man at a long Councell board;

councells   frequency: 1   relative frequency: 0.0000
    P. 195 TWO HORSES   151 Ch. Her Walsingham could dark Councells
                             unriddle,

councels   frequency: 1   relative frequency: 0.0000
    P. 205 HISTORICALL   157 Here with curst precepts and with Councels dire

council. See "councel," "councell," "counsel," "counsell."

councils. See "councells," "councels," "counsels."

counsel   frequency: 5   relative frequency: 0.0001
    P. 85 FLECKNO   76 Worn at the first Counsel of Antioch;
    P. 148 INSTRUCTIONS 292 In giving Gen'rous, but in Counsel Grave;
    P. 159 INSTRUCTIONS 769 Whose Counsel first did this mad War beget?
    P. 160 INSTRUCTIONS 794 And place in Counsel fell to Duncombes share.
    P. 160 INSTRUCTIONS 809 Frequent in Counsel, earnest in Debate,

counsell   frequency: 1   relative frequency: 0.0000

P. 129 O.C.   240 In warre, in counsell, or in pray'r, and praise;

counsell'd   frequency: 1   relative frequency: 0.0000
    P. 87 FLECKNO   165 With truth. I counsell'd him to go in time,

counselled. See "counsell'd," "ill-counsell'd."

counsellor. See "couns'llor."

counsellors   frequency: 2   relative frequency: 0.0000
    P. 111 ANNIVERSARY   347 Who their suspected Counsellors refuse,
    P. 199 DUKE   55 The Counsellors of all this villany.

counsels   frequency: 1   relative frequency: 0.0000
    P. 165 INSTRUCTIONS   986 Does with clear Counsels their large Souls
                              supply;

couns'llor   frequency: 1   relative frequency: 0.0000
    P. 160 INSTRUCTIONS   804 And for a Couns'llor, he that has least Wit.

count   frequency: 4   relative frequency: 0.0000
    P. 149 INSTRUCTIONS   367 The Count forthwith is order'd all to close,
    P. 151 INSTRUCTIONS   443 The gravell'd Count did with the Answer faint:
    P. 175 LOYALL SCOT   128 Enough for them, God knows, to Count their
                              Wealth,
    P. 202 HISTORICALL   62 Or count the various blemishes of State--

counted   frequency: 1   relative frequency: 0.0000
    P. 110 ANNIVERSARY   274 Counted the Hours, and ev'ry Star did spy,

counterfeit   frequency: 1   relative frequency: 0.0000
    P. 22 NYMPH   26 I had not found him counterfeit,

counterfeits   frequency: 1   relative frequency: 0.0000
    P. 180 STOCKSMARKET   32 For he counterfeits only in gold, not in stone.

countermines   frequency: 1   relative frequency: 0.0000
    P. 169 ADVICE   53 These must assist her in her countermines

counterpoised. See "counterpoysed."

counterpoysed   frequency: 1   relative frequency: 0.0000
    P. 107 ANNIVERSARY   155 Hence that blest Day still counterpoysed wastes,

countess   frequency: 1   relative frequency: 0.0000
    P. 145 INSTRUCTIONS   198 Mourning his Countess, anxious for his Act.

countrey   frequency: 2   relative frequency: 0.0000
    P. 198 DUKE   6 To robb their native countrey of its right.
    P. 313 CHEQUER INN   16 And for his Countrey first began

country   frequency: 11   relative frequency: 0.0002
    See also "countrey."
    P. 44 GLO-WORMS   5 Ye Country Comets, that portend
    P. 55 THYESTE   11 An old honest Country man.
    P. 96 HOLLAND   19 And to the stake a strugling Country bound,
    P. 97 HOLLAND   81 Let it suffice to give their Country Fame
    P. 143 INSTRUCTIONS   107 Describe the Court and Country, both set right,
    P. 144 INSTRUCTIONS   141 She wastes the Country and on Cities preys.
    P. 161 INSTRUCTIONS   827 Up ambles Country Justice on his Pad,
    P. 164 INSTRUCTIONS   959 Kings in the Country oft have gone astray,
    P. 164 INSTRUCTIONS   974 Bacchus is Wine, the Country is the King.)
    P. 189 BRITANNIA   178 Back to my dearest Country I'le return:
    P. 193 TWO HORSES   77 Ch. That Traitors to their Country in a
                              Brib'd Hous of Commons

country-host   frequency: 1   relative frequency: 0.0000
    P. 162 INSTRUCTIONS   881 At Table, jolly as a Country-Host,

countryes   frequency: 2   relative frequency: 0.0000
    P. 186 BRITANNIA   53 Of Countryes love (by truth and Justice bred).
    P. 204 HISTORICALL   122 This Saracen his Countryes freedom broke

countrys   frequency: 1   relative frequency: 0.0000
    P. 148 INSTRUCTIONS   290 For Countrys Cause, that Glorious think and
                              sweet:

country's   frequency: 1   relative frequency: 0.0000
    See also "countryes," "countrys."
    P. 96 HOLLAND   46 Him they their Lord and Country's Father
                              speak.

counts   frequency: 1   relative frequency: 0.0000

P. 81 A. HOUSE   707 She counts her Beauty to converse

coupl'd   frequency: 1   relative frequency: 0.0000
P. 316 CHEQUER INN   134 Fathers and Sons like Coupl'd Slaves

couple   frequency: 3   relative frequency: 0.0000
P. 75 A. HOUSE   527 O why should such a Couple mourn,
P. 150 INSTRUCTIONS   384 Mounting the neighbour Couple on lean Jade.
P. 159 INSTRUCTIONS   753 And to each other helpless couple moan,

courage   frequency: 16   relative frequency: 0.0003
P.   9 DIALOGUE   1 Courage my Soul, now learn to wield
P. 58 BILL-BOROW   76 That Courage its own Praises flies.
P. 66 A. HOUSE   231 For Justice still that Courage led;
P. 87 ODE   17 For 'tis all one to Courage high
P. 108 ANNIVERSARY   208 Courage disheartned, and Religion cool'd.
P. 112 ANNIVERSARY   382 'Courage with Age, Maturity with Hast:
P. 117 BLAKE   114 And all assumes your courage, in your cause.
P. 120 TWO SONGS   29 Courage, Endymion, boldly Woo,
P. 127 O.C.   180 And tim'rous Conscience unto Courage man'd:
P. 141 INSTRUCTIONS   31 Him neither Wit nor Courage did exalt,
P. 147 INSTRUCTIONS   246 (For Vigilance and Courage both renown'd)
P. 147 INSTRUCTIONS   254 And to new edge their angry Courage grind.
P. 147 INSTRUCTIONS   265 Of Birth, State, Wit, Strength, Courage,
                               How'rd presumes,
P. 148 INSTRUCTIONS   307 Broken in Courage, yet the Men the same,
P. 165 INSTRUCTIONS   985 Whose gen'rous Conscience and whose Courage
                               high
P. 204 HISTORICALL   143 'Twas want of Wit and Courage made them fail,

course   frequency: 4   relative frequency: 0.0000
P. 106 ANNIVERSARY   139 Fore-shortned Time its useless Course would
                               stay,
P. 109 ANNIVERSARY   267 Who with mistaken Course salute the Sand,
P. 127 O.C.   165 Then let us to our course of Mourning keep:
P. 159 INSTRUCTIONS   741 And constant Time, to keep his course yet right,

courser   frequency: 1   relative frequency: 0.0000
P. 58 BILL-BOROW   51 And underneath the Courser Rind

court   frequency: 40   relative frequency: 0.0008
P. 54 THYESTE   1 Climb at Court for me that will
P. 66 A. HOUSE   234 The Court him grants the lawful Form;
P. 97 HOLLAND   78 Where wisely for their Court they chose a
                               Village.
P. 105 ANNIVERSARY   104 And wisely court the Influence they fear;
P. 142 INSTRUCTIONS   39 Draw no Commission lest the Court should lye,
P. 143 INSTRUCTIONS   83 Her wonted joys thenceforth and Court she shuns,
P. 143 INSTRUCTIONS   107 Describe the Court and Country, both set right,
P. 143 INSTRUCTIONS   113 But here the Court does its advantage know,
P. 144 INSTRUCTIONS   128 Commons, and ever such a Court maintain,
P. 150 INSTRUCTIONS   373 The Court, as once of War, now fond of Peace,
P. 151 INSTRUCTIONS   419 White-hall's unsafe, the Court all meditates
P. 151 INSTRUCTIONS   424 At London's Flame, nor so the Court
                               complain'd.
P. 152 INSTRUCTIONS   485 And the wise Court, that always lov'd it dear,
P. 154 INSTRUCTIONS   538 And with inveigling Colours Court the Air.
P. 159 INSTRUCTIONS   761 The Court in Farthing yet it self does please,
P. 160 INSTRUCTIONS   808 Hyde and the Court again begin to mourn.
P. 161 INSTRUCTIONS   850 At Court, and so reprieves their guilty Lives.
P. 164 INSTRUCTIONS   965 She flames them only who the Court restrain,
P. 165 INSTRUCTIONS   990 Give us this Court, and rule without a Guard.
P. 166 KINGS VOWES   28 I will have a fine Court with ne'er an old face,
P. 170 PROPHECY   18 And whoreing shall be the least sin att Court,
P. 170 PROPHECY   24 Shall be in use at Court but faith and Troth,
P. 172 LOYALL SCOT   8 His ready muse to Court the Warlike Guest.
P. 175 LOYALL SCOT   130 A higher work is to their Court Annext:
P. 176 LOYALL SCOT   199 It was Musitian too and dwelt at Court.
P. 185 BRITANNIA   12 Whilest the Lew'd Court in drunken slumbers
                               lyes,
P. 185 BRITANNIA   16 And loyall sufferings by the Court esteem'd,
P. 185 BRITANNIA   24 Your own lov'd Court and Masters Progeny?
P. 185 BRITANNIA   25 Brit: A Colony of French Possess the Court;
P. 188 BRITANNIA   127 The scotch scabbado of one Court, two Isles,
P. 188 BRITANNIA   164 Least Court corrupcions should their souls
                               engage.
P. 190 STATUE   11 And soe near to the Court they will never indure
P. 191 STATUE   56 To behold every day such a Court, such a son.
P. 193 TWO HORSES   60 And yet all his Court be as poore as Church
                               Ratts;
P. 193 TWO HORSES   73 Ch. That Parliament men should rail at the Court,

```
        P. 193 TWO HORSES       86 Who vote with the Court for drink and for
                                   Dinners.
        P. 201 HISTORICALL      31 From the french Court she haughty Topiks
                                   brings,
        P. 202 HISTORICALL      37 Now the Court Sins did every place defile,
        P. 202 HISTORICALL      67 Outdoes Tiberius and his Goatish Court:
        P. 204 HISTORICALL     148 Bold Irish Ruffins to his Court adress:
```

```
court-mushrumps                    frequency:    1    relative frequency: 0.0000
        P. 162 INSTRUCTIONS    876 Court-mushrumps ready are sent in in pickle.
```

```
court-officers                     frequency:    1    relative frequency: 0.0000
        P. 145 INSTRUCTIONS    169 Court-Officers, as us'd, the next place took,
```

```
courteous                          frequency:    3    relative frequency: 0.0000
        P.  45 GLO-WORMS        13 Your courteous Lights in vain you wast,
        P.  57 BILL-BOROW       21 See then how courteous it ascends,
        P.  78 A. HOUSE        616 And courteous Briars nail me through.
```

```
courtesy.  See "court'sie."
```

```
courtiers                          frequency:    4    relative frequency: 0.0000
        P. 144 INSTRUCTIONS    155 Of the old Courtiers next a Squadron came,
        P. 161 INSTRUCTIONS    835 But, fresh as from the Mint, the Courtiers fine
        P. 164 INSTRUCTIONS    952 And seem his Courtiers, are but his disease.
        P. 164 INSTRUCTIONS    978 As scratching Courtiers undermine a Realm:
```

```
courtney                           frequency:    1    relative frequency: 0.0000
        P. 315 CHEQUER INN     127 Sir Courtney Poole and he contend
```

```
courts                             frequency:    3    relative frequency: 0.0000
        P.  32 MOURNING         19 She courts her self in am'rous Rain;
        P.  39 PICTURE          34 Whom Nature courts with fruits and flow'rs,
        P. 141 INSTRUCTIONS     30 The new Courts pattern, Stallion of the old.
```

```
courtship                          frequency:    3    relative frequency: 0.0000
        P.  55 EPITAPH           3 Courtship, which living she declin'd,
        P. 156 INSTRUCTIONS    654 Nor other Courtship knew but to his Cheek.
        P. 172 LOYALL SCOT      20 Nor other Courtship knew but to his Cheek.
```

```
court'sie                          frequency:    1    relative frequency: 0.0000
        P.  98 HOLLAND         103 Let this one court'sie witness all the rest;
```

```
covenanter                         frequency:    1    relative frequency: 0.0000
        P. 171 PROPHECY         39 When an old Scotch Covenanter shall be
```

```
coventry                           frequency:    3    relative frequency: 0.0000
        P. 152 INSTRUCTIONS    458 The second Coventry the Cavalier.
        P. 163 INSTRUCTIONS    928 Bennet and Coventry, as't were design'd.
        P. 163 INSTRUCTIONS    934 And Coventry, falser than any one,
```

```
coventrys                          frequency:    1    relative frequency: 0.0000
        P. 146 INSTRUCTIONS    225 All the two Coventrys their Gen'rals chose:
```

```
cover                              frequency:    2    relative frequency: 0.0000
        P. 170 PROPHECY          2 And cover it in flames in sixty six;
        P. 196 TWO HORSES      176 To conceal their own crimes and cover their
                                   shame,
```

```
cover'd                            frequency:    1    relative frequency: 0.0000
        P. 127 O.C.            168 Of your Abysse, with cover'd Head bewail
```

```
coward                             frequency:    2    relative frequency: 0.0000
        P.  92 MAY'S DEATH      64 And fear has Coward Churchmen silenced,
        P. 151 INSTRUCTIONS    428 To Master Lewis, and tell Coward tale,
```

```
cowardice                          frequency:    1    relative frequency: 0.0000
        P. 153 INSTRUCTIONS    516 Or that for Cowardice they all retire.
```

```
cowards                            frequency:    1    relative frequency: 0.0000
        P. 144 INSTRUCTIONS    161 Then damming Cowards rang'd the vocal Plain,
```

```
cowslip-water                      frequency:    1    relative frequency: 0.0000
        P.  43 DAMON            48 In cowslip-water bathes my feet.
```

```
coy                                frequency:    5    relative frequency: 0.0001
        P.  12 DROP OF DEW      27 In how coy a Figure wound,
        P.  26 MISTRESS          t To his Coy Mistress.
        P.  33 DAPHNIS           6 Long had taught her to be coy:
        P. 123 TWO SONGS        45 Marina yields. Who dares be coy?
```

P. 162 INSTRUCTIONS 901 And with kind hand does the coy Vision press,

coyness   frequency: 1   relative frequency: 0.0000
    P. 26 MISTRESS   2 This coyness Lady were no crime.

crack   frequency: 1   relative frequency: 0.0000
    P. 92 MAY'S DEATH   68 And though the World's disjointed Axel crack,

craddle   frequency: 1   relative frequency: 0.0000
    P. 25 YOUNG LOVE   27 In the craddle crown their King,

cradle   frequency: 1   relative frequency: 0.0000
    See also "craddle."
    P. 74 A. HOUSE   495 And, as they Natures Cradle deckt,

crambo   frequency: 1   relative frequency: 0.0000
    P. 203 HISTORICALL   89 And with dull Crambo feed the silly sheep.

cram'd   frequency: 1   relative frequency: 0.0000
    P. 315 CHEQUER INN   91 But King (God save him) tho' so cram'd

crammed. See "cram'd."

cramp   frequency: 1   relative frequency: 0.0000
    P. 21 SOUL & BODY   33 Whom first the Cramp of Hope does Tear:

cramp'd   frequency: 1   relative frequency: 0.0000
    P. 37 DEFINITION   24 Be cramp'd into a Planisphere.

cramped. See "cramp'd," "crampt."

crampt   frequency: 1   relative frequency: 0.0000
    P. 174 LOYALL SCOT 103 Then Bishops Crampt the Comerce of Mankind.

crane   frequency: 2   relative frequency: 0.0000
    P. 96 HOLLAND   39 For as with Pygmees who best kills the Crane,
    P. 171 PROPHECY   33 The Frogs shall then grow weary of their Crane

craules   frequency: 1   relative frequency: 0.0000
    P. 84 FLECKNO   41 So while he with his gouty Fingers craules

crave   frequency: 1   relative frequency: 0.0000
    P. 110 ANNIVERSARY 290 That they enjoy, but more they vainly crave:

crawl   frequency: 1   relative frequency: 0.0000
    P. 77 A. HOUSE   588 Between which Caterpillars crawl:

crawls. See "craules."

creak   frequency: 1   relative frequency: 0.0000
    P. 71 A. HOUSE   415 Death-Trumpets creak in such a Note,

create   frequency: 2   relative frequency: 0.0000
    P. 137 HOUSEWARMING 12 How he might create a House with a Fiat.
    P. 167 KINGS VOWES   56 And new Ones Create Great Places to supplye,

created   frequency: 4   relative frequency: 0.0000
    P.   9 DIALOGUE   t2 The Resolved Soul, and Created Pleasure.
    P. 29 LOVER   58 That ever Love created yet:
    P. 72 A. HOUSE   445 The World when first created sure
    P. 132 PARADISE   53 Thy verse created like thy Theme sublime,

creates   frequency: 3   relative frequency: 0.0000
    P. 49 THE GARDEN   45 Yet it creates, transcending these,
    P. 105 ANNIVERSARY   65 Thus, ere he ceas'd, his sacred Lute creates
    P. 117 BLAKE   120 And though it be at Noon, creates a Night.

creation   frequency: 1   relative frequency: 0.0000
    P. 160 INSTRUCTIONS 788 If no Creation, there had been no Sin.

creations   frequency: 2   relative frequency: 0.0000
    P.   9 DIALOGUE   11 Welcome the Creations Guest,
    P. 131 PARADISE   21 Might hence presume the whole Creations day

creator's   frequency: 1   relative frequency: 0.0000
    P. 10 DIALOGUE   35 When the Creator's skill is priz'd,

creature   frequency: 2   relative frequency: 0.0000
    P. 59 A. HOUSE   15 No Creature loves an empty space;
    P. 187 BRITANNIA   123 Her Creature Osborn the Revenue steals;

creatures   frequency: 2   relative frequency: 0.0000

```
        P.   62 A. HOUSE        102 'Of those wild Creatures, called Men.
        P.   74 A. HOUSE        487 And where all Creatures might have shares,

credible                              frequency:    1    relative frequency: 0.0000
        P.   58 BILL-BOROW       49 For they ('tis credible) have sense,

credit                                frequency:    3    relative frequency: 0.0000
        P.   97 HOLLAND          74 Opinion but finds Credit, and Exchange.
        P.  183 MADE FREE        75 He values not Credit nor Hist'ry,
        P.  192 TWO HORSES       23 Why should wee not credit the publique discourses

creditors                             frequency:    1    relative frequency: 0.0000
        P.  182 MADE FREE        48 And his Creditors all left to Sorrow.

credulous                             frequency:    2    relative frequency: 0.0000
        P.  111 ANNIVERSARY     348 And credulous Ambassadors accuse.
        P.  148 INSTRUCTIONS    293 Candidly credulous for once, nay twice;

creed                                 frequency:    1    relative frequency: 0.0000
        P.  175 LOYALL SCOT     153 Whilst Arrius stands at th' Athanasian Creed.

creek                                 frequency:    1    relative frequency: 0.0000
        P.  158 INSTRUCTIONS    703 And the kind River in its Creek them hides,

creep                                 frequency:    1    relative frequency: 0.0000
        P.   79 A. HOUSE        666 From underneath these Banks do creep,

crescent                              frequency:    2    relative frequency: 0.0000
        P.   43 DAMON            60 As in a crescent Moon the Sun.
        P.  189 BRITANNIA       190 The Turkish Crescent and the Persian sun.

crest                                 frequency:    5    relative frequency: 0.0001
        P.    9 DIALOGUE         13 Lay aside that Warlike Crest,
        P.   57 BILL-BOROW       33 Upon its crest this Mountain grave
        P.   89 ODE              98 While Victory his Crest does plume!
        P.  108 ANNIVERSARY     195 See how they each his towring Crest abate,
        P.  110 ANNIVERSARY     284 Left by the Wars Flood on the Mountains crest:

crew                                  frequency:    2    relative frequency: 0.0000
        P.  182 MADE FREE        40 And amongst his Wild Crew
        P.  314 CHEQUER INN      80 The Foreman of the Brittish Crew

cried. See "cry'd."

crime                                 frequency:    5    relative frequency: 0.0001
        P.   26 MISTRESS          2 This coyness Lady were no crime.
        P.   39 PICTURE          36 Lest Flora angry at thy crime,
        P.  143 INSTRUCTIONS     95 And washing (lest the scent her Crime disclose)
        P.  160 INSTRUCTIONS    789 But, his great Crime, one Boat away he sent;
        P.  178 LOYALL SCOT     280 My differing Crime doth more thy vertue raise

crimes                                frequency:    9    relative frequency: 0.0001
        P.   92 MAY'S DEATH      70 Seeks wretched good, arraigns successful Crimes.
        P.  140 HOUSEWARMING    107 And with that convenience he soon for his Crimes
        P.  141 INSTRUCTIONS     13 But if to match our Crimes thy skill presumes,
        P.  150 INSTRUCTIONS    388 Better than Law, Domestick Crimes to tame
        P.  163 INSTRUCTIONS    939 But in wise anger he their Crimes forbears,
        P.  168 KINGS VOWES      62 That all his dareing crimes, what ere they be,
        P.  177 LOYALL SCOT     241 For Worth Heroick or Heroick Crimes.
        P.  185 BRITANNIA        23 Bawl: What fatall crimes make you forever fly
        P.  196 TWO HORSES      176 To conceal their own crimes and cover their
                                    shame,

croak                                 frequency:    2    relative frequency: 0.0000
        P.  162 INSTRUCTIONS    878 Frisks like a Frog to croak a Taxes load.
        P.  185 BRITANNIA        29 I'th sacred ear Tyranick Arts they Croak,

crocodile                             frequency:    1    relative frequency: 0.0000
        P.   78 A. HOUSE        629 No Serpent new nor Crocodile

cromwel                               frequency:    1    relative frequency: 0.0000
        P.   87 ODE               9 So restless Cromwel could not cease

cromwell                              frequency:   13    relative frequency: 0.0002
        See also "cromwel."
        P.  103 ANNIVERSARY       7 Cromwell alone with greater Vigour runs,
        P.  103 ANNIVERSARY      11 Cromwell alone doth with new Lustre spring,
        P.  104 ANNIVERSARY      45 While indefatigable Cromwell hyes,
        P.  105 ANNIVERSARY      68 When Cromwell tun'd the ruling Instrument;
        P.  106 ANNIVERSARY     126 Angelique Cromwell who outwings the wind;
        P.  107 ANNIVERSARY     159 And thou, great Cromwell, for whose happy birth
```

P. 108 ANNIVERSARY   201 Thou Cromwell falling, not a stupid Tree,
P. 108 ANNIVERSARY   225 For to be Cromwell was a greater thing,
P. 119 TWO SONGS   t2 and the Lady Mary Cromwell.
P. 127 O.C.   157 O Cromwell, Heavens Favorite! To none
P. 130 O.C.   280 And with the name of Cromwell, armyes fright.
P. 130 O.C.   312 A Cromwell in an houre a prince will grow.
P. 195 TWO HORSES   137 Ch. De Witt and Cromwell had each a brave
                          soul.

cromwells   frequency: 1   relative frequency: 0.0000
    P. 204 HISTORICALL   135 Let Cromwells Ghost smile with Contempt to see

cromwell's   frequency: 2   relative frequency: 0.0000
    See also "cromwells," "cromwel's."
    P. 123 O.C.   2 Of Cromwell's head, and numbered ev'ry hair,
    P. 126 O.C.   142 Of honour; all the Year was Cromwell's day:

cromwel's   frequency: 1   relative frequency: 0.0000
    P. 87 ODE   t An Horatian Ode upon Cromwel's Return from
                              Ireland.

crook   frequency: 1   relative frequency: 0.0000
    P. 138 HOUSEWARMING   60 As by hook and by crook the world cluster'd of
                              Atome.

cross   frequency: 4   relative frequency: 0.0000
    See also "crosse."
    P. 189 STATUE   t The Statue at Charing Cross.
    P. 189 STATUE   1 What can be the Mistery why Charing Cross
    P. 193 TWO HORSES   56 Lord a Mercy and a Cross might be set on the
                              doore;
    P. 194 TWO HORSES   118 For the Surplice, Lawn-Sleeves, the Cross and
                              the mitre,

crosse   frequency: 3   relative frequency: 0.0000
    P. 178 LOYALL SCOT   261 English and Scotch, 'tis all but Crosse and
                              Pile
    P. 184 MADE FREE   126 London beares the Crosse with the Dagger.
    P. 313 CHEQUER INN   7 At Chareing Crosse hard by the way

crossed. See "crost."

crossest   frequency: 1   relative frequency: 0.0000
    P. 105 ANNIVERSARY   89 The crossest Spirits here do take their part,

crost   frequency: 2   relative frequency: 0.0000
    P. 126 O.C.   111 He unconcern'd the dreadful passage crost;
    P. 146 INSTRUCTIONS 237 Propitious Heavens, had not you them crost,

croud   frequency: 1   relative frequency: 0.0000
    P. 139 HOUSEWARMING   62 And Presents croud headlong to give good
                              example:

crouds   frequency: 1   relative frequency: 0.0000
    P. 37 DEFINITION   12 And alwaies crouds it self betwixt.

croune   frequency: 1   relative frequency: 0.0000
    P. 200 DUKE   112 Bribed by a croune on earth and one above,

crowd   frequency: 2   relative frequency: 0.0000
    See also "croud," "crow'd."
    P. 71 A. HOUSE   392 And crowd a Lane to either Side.
    P. 85 FLECKNO   100 Two make a crowd, nor can three Persons here

crow'd   frequency: 1   relative frequency: 0.0000
    P. 176 LOYALL SCOT   207 Of Ceremonyes Wrangle in the Crow'd,

crowder   frequency: 1   relative frequency: 0.0000
    P. 142 INSTRUCTIONS   57 Hence Crowder made the rare Inventress free,

crowding   frequency: 1   relative frequency: 0.0000
    P. 313 CHEQUER INN   10 Where I cou'd see 'em Crowding in

crowds   frequency: 1   relative frequency: 0.0000
    See also "crouds."
    P. 91 MAY'S DEATH   37 As he crowds in he whipt him ore the pate

crown   frequency: 22   relative frequency: 0.0004
    See also "croune," "crowne."
    P. 15 THE CORONET   26 May crown thy Feet, that could not crown thy
                              Head.
    P. 25 YOUNG LOVE   26 Other Titles to their Crown,
    P. 25 YOUNG LOVE   27 In the craddle crown their King,

```
P.   26 YOUNG LOVE      30 Now I crown thee with my Love:
P.   26 YOUNG LOVE      31 Crown me with thy Love again,
P.   30 THE GALLERY     56 To crown her Head, and Bosome fill.
P.   63 A. HOUSE       141 'I see the Angels in a Crown
P.   80 A. HOUSE       700 The Garden Flow'rs to Crown Her Head;
P.   89 ODE            100 If thus he crown each Year!
P.  107 ANNIVERSARY    180 And soyl'd in Dust thy Crown of silver Hairs.
P.  139 HOUSEWARMING    92 Where you are to expect the Scepter and Crown.
P.  142 INSTRUCTIONS    52 For an Experiment upon the Crown.
P.  151 INSTRUCTIONS   416 Change all for Guinea's, and a Crown for each:
P.  158 INSTRUCTIONS   711 The Dutch had robb'd those Jewels of the
                           Crown:
P.  164 INSTRUCTIONS   971 The Kingdom from the Crown distinct would see,
P.  176 LOYALL SCOT    181 The fittest Mask for one that Robs a Crown.
P.  176 LOYALL SCOT    185 A Bishops Cruelty, the Crown had gone.
P.  180 STOCKSMARKET    37 Hath Blood him away (as his crown once)
                           conveyed?
P.  185 BRITANNIA       28 Since Pharoh's Reign nor so Defild a Crown.
P.  187 BRITANNIA      122 Resigns his Crown to Angell Carwells trust.
P.  193 TWO HORSES      71 W. On Seventh Harry's head he that placed the
                           Crown
```

```
crown'd                        frequency:   9   relative frequency: 0.0001
P.   10 DIALOGUE        50 And if thou overcom'st thou shalt be crown'd.
P.   14 THE CORONET      3 My Saviours head have crown'd,
P.   48 THE GARDEN       4 Crown'd from some single Herb or Tree.
P.  124 O.C.            55 So the Flowr with'ring which the Garden
                           crown'd,
P.  126 O.C.           144 Twice had in open field him Victor crown'd:
P.  129 O.C.           264 And honour'd wreaths have oft the victour
                           crown'd.
P.  131 PARADISE         3 Messiah Crown'd, Gods Reconcil'd Decree,
P.  155 INSTRUCTIONS   616 Crown'd, for that Merit, with their Masters
                           Name.
P.  181 MADE FREE       29 ('tis the same to be Crown'd)
```

```
crowne                         frequency:   4   relative frequency: 0.0000
P.    3 LOVELACE        12 Our Civill Wars have lost the Civicke crowne.
P.  167 KINGS VOWES     48 And I'lle first put the Church then my Crowne
                           in Commission.
P.  200 DUKE           104 Let not thy life and crowne togeather end,
P.  202 HISTORICALL     56 Whilst the brave Tudors wore th' Imperial
                           Crowne:
```

```
crowne's                       frequency:   1   relative frequency: 0.0000
P.  171 PROPHECY        45 When the Crowne's Heir shall English Men
                           dispise
```

```
crowns                         frequency:   2   relative frequency: 0.0000
P.   62 A. HOUSE       120 'Our brighter Robes and Crowns of Gold?
P.   70 A. HOUSE       360 That in the Crowns of Saints do shine.
```

crown's. See "crowne's."

```
crows                          frequency:   1   relative frequency: 0.0000
P.  202 HISTORICALL     65 Lookes as one sett up for to scare the Crows.
```

crowther. See "crowder."

```
cruel                          frequency:   5   relative frequency: 0.0001
P.   23 NYMPH           54 The love of false and cruel men.
P.   28 LOVER           29 Receiv'd into their cruel Care,
P.   29 THE GALLERY     12 Thy fertile Shop of cruel Arts:
P.   34 DAPHNIS         36 And his cruel Fate forswear.
P.   48 THE GARDEN      19 Fond Lovers, cruel as their Flame,
```

```
cruelty                        frequency:   3   relative frequency: 0.0000
P.   34 DAPHNIS         52 More than all thy Cruelty?
P.   86 FLECKNO        125 Yet that which was a greater cruelty
P.  176 LOYALL SCOT    185 A Bishops Cruelty, the Crown had gone.
```

```
crupper                        frequency:   2   relative frequency: 0.0000
P.  191 STATUE          44 And wee've lost both our King, our Hors and our
                           Crupper.
P.  194 TWO HORSES     114 With an Harlot got up on my Crupper behind him.
```

```
crusado                        frequency:   1   relative frequency: 0.0000
P.  189 BRITANNIA      189 Her true Crusado shall at last pull down
```

```
crush                          frequency:   1   relative frequency: 0.0000
P.   49 THE GARDEN      36 Upon my Mouth do crush their Wine;
```

crust   frequency: 1   relative frequency: 0.0000
   P.   59 A. HOUSE   21 What need of all this Marble Crust

cry   frequency: 3   relative frequency: 0.0000
   P.   20 THYRSIS   39 Dorinda. Ah me, ah me. (Thyrsis.) Dorinda, why
                               do'st Cry?
   P. 115 BLAKE   69 Never so many with one joyful cry,
   P. 191 TWO HORSES   3 When Magpyes and Parratts cry 'walke Knave
                               walk',

cry'd   frequency: 2   relative frequency: 0.0000
   P. 194 TWO HORSES   120 By Knaves who cry'd themselves up for the
                               Church,
   P. 315 CHEQUER INN   112 Nay Portman tho' all men cry'd shame

cryes   frequency: 1   relative frequency: 0.0000
   P.   71 A. HOUSE   406 And cryes, he call'd us Israelites;

crys. See "cryes."

crystal   frequency: 3   relative frequency: 0.0000
   See also "chrystal."
   P.   10 DIALOGUE   34 In this Crystal view thy face.
   P.   24 NYMPH   102 Keep these two crystal Tears; and fill
   P. 153 INSTRUCTIONS   525 Survey'd their Crystal Streams, and Banks so
                               green,

crystal-pure. See "chrystal-pure."

cubbs   frequency: 1   relative frequency: 0.0000
   P. 184 BRITANNIA   3 Cubbs, didst thou call 'um? hadst thou seen this
                               Brood

cubs. See "cubbs."

cuckold   frequency: 1   relative frequency: 0.0000
   P. 194 TWO HORSES   110 W. To Cuckold a Scrivener mine's in
                               Masquerade.

cudgell   frequency: 1   relative frequency: 0.0000
   P. 194 TWO HORSES   104 Insted of a Cudgell Balam wish't for a Sword.

cuffing   frequency: 1   relative frequency: 0.0000
   P.   28 LOVER   50 Cuffing the Thunder with one hand;

culminant   frequency: 1   relative frequency: 0.0000
   P. 149 INSTRUCTIONS   355 See how he Reigns in his new Palace culminant,

cup   frequency: 2   relative frequency: 0.0000
   P.   34 DAPHNIS   54 The delicious Cup we fill;
   P. 314 CHEQUER INN   81 (His Cup he never failes)

cupid   frequency: 1   relative frequency: 0.0000
   P. 169 ADVICE   48 With Cupid Seymour and the Tool of State,

cups   frequency: 2   relative frequency: 0.0000
   P.   91 MAY'S DEATH   21 Cups more then civil of Emathian wine,
   P. 194 TWO HORSES   88 Of Exciseing our Cups and Taxing our Smoak.

curates   frequency: 2   relative frequency: 0.0000
   P. 175 LOYALL SCOT   131 The Nation they devide, their Curates Text.
   P. 203 HISTORICALL   98 Baals wretched Curates Legerdemain'd it so,

curb'd   frequency: 1   relative frequency: 0.0000
   P. 153 INSTRUCTIONS   523 Ruyter the while, that had our Ocean curb'd,

curd   frequency: 1   relative frequency: 0.0000
   P. 174 LOYALL SCOT   115 A Bishops Bennett makes the strongest Curd.

cur'd   frequency: 2   relative frequency: 0.0000
   P. 125 O.C.   76 Had drawn such staines as were not to be cur'd.
   P. 172 LOYALL SCOT   9 Much had hee Cur'd the Humor of his vein:

cure   frequency: 5   relative frequency: 0.0001
   P.   21 SOUL & BODY   28 Diseases, but, whats worse, the Cure:
   P.   44 DAMON   85 Only for him no Cure is found,
   P. 116 BLAKE   82 A grief, above the cure of Grapes best juice.
   P. 183 MADE FREE   92 To cure the Dukes ills,
   P. 186 BRITANNIA   54 Then, to confirm the cure so well begun,

cures   frequency: 1   relative frequency: 0.0000

```
        P.  188 BRITANNIA      132 Descend, descend, ere the Cures desperate.

curious                            frequency:    3    relative frequency: 0.0000
        P.   14 THE CORONET     22 Or shatter too with him my curious frame:
        P.   49 THE GARDEN      37 The Nectaren, and curious Peach,
        P.   64 A. HOUSE       182 'We mold, as Baits for curious tasts.

curl                               frequency:    2    relative frequency: 0.0000
    See also "curle."
        P.  156 INSTRUCTIONS    653 His yellow Locks curl back themselves to seek,
        P.  172 LOYALL SCOT      19 His shady locks Curl back themselves to seek

curl'd                             frequency:    2    relative frequency: 0.0000
        P.   68 A. HOUSE        315 Their Leaves, that to the stalks are curl'd,
        P.  122 TWO SONGS        22 Curl'd so lovely as her Hair:

curle                              frequency:    1    relative frequency: 0.0000
        P.   78 A. HOUSE        610 Curle me about ye gadding Vines,

curled                             frequency:    3    relative frequency: 0.0000
    See also "curl'd."
        P.   29 THE GALLERY      16 Black Eyes, red Lips, and curled Hair.
        P.   31 FAIR SINGER       9 Breaking the curled trammels of her hair.
        P.  108 ANNIVERSARY     198 Nor their round Hoofs, or curled Mane's
                                    compare;

curles                             frequency:    1    relative frequency: 0.0000
        P.   77 A. HOUSE        590 Me licks, and clasps, and curles, and hales.

curlings                           frequency:    1    relative frequency: 0.0000
        P.  103 ANNIVERSARY       1 Like the vain Curlings of the Watry maze,

curls.  See "curles."

current                            frequency:    1    relative frequency: 0.0000
        P.  152 INSTRUCTIONS    488 Of current Myrmidons appear in Arms.

currs                              frequency:    1    relative frequency: 0.0000
        P.  186 BRITANNIA        67 Around her Joves lou'd ravenous Currs complain;

curs.  See "currs."

curs'd                             frequency:    1    relative frequency: 0.0000
        P.  152 INSTRUCTIONS    490 With that curs'd Quill pluck'd from a Vulture's
                                    Wing:

curse                              frequency:    4    relative frequency: 0.0000
        P.   86 FLECKNO         143 To hear his Verses, by so just a curse
        P.  141 INSTRUCTIONS     19 Else shalt thou oft thy guiltless Pencil curse,
        P.  317 CHEQUER INN     175 Curse on such Representatives
        P.  317 CHEQUER INN     190 But sure this is a heavier Curse

cursed.  See "curs'd," "curst."

curst                              frequency:    4    relative frequency: 0.0000
        P.  115 BLAKE            56 All that is good, and are not curst with Gold.
        P.  149 INSTRUCTIONS    340 His Gout (yet still he curst) had left him
                                    quite.
        P.  192 TWO HORSES       52 By a Curst hous of Commons and a blest
                                    Restauracion;
        P.  205 HISTORICALL     157 Here with curst precepts and with Councels dire

curtains                           frequency:    2    relative frequency: 0.0000
        P.  163 INSTRUCTIONS    915 Shake then the room, and all his Curtains tear,
        P.  170 PROPHECY         16 Within the Curtains and behind the Scenes,

curtius                            frequency:    1    relative frequency: 0.0000
        P.  173 LOYALL SCOT      67 Such in the Roman forum Curtius brave

curvets                            frequency:    1    relative frequency: 0.0000
        P.  152 INSTRUCTIONS    465 Hyde's flippant Stile there pleasantly curvets:

custome                            frequency:    1    relative frequency: 0.0000
        P.  139 HOUSEWARMING     84 But receiv'd now and paid the Chancellours
                                    Custome.

cut                                frequency:    9    relative frequency: 0.0001
    See also "cutt."
        P.   24 NYMPH           112 Be cut in Marble; and withal,
        P.   43 DAMON            69 And with my Sythe cut down the Grass,
        P.   44 DAMON            75 And, with his whistling Sythe, does cut
```

```
       P.   48 THE GARDEN      20 Cut in these Trees their Mistress name.
       P.   82 A. HOUSE       742 The Priest shall cut the sacred Bud;
       P.   98 HOLLAND         98 Cut out each others Athos to a Man:
       P.  139 HOUSEWARMING    80 Or his right hand shall else be cut off with the
                                  Trowel.
       P.  163 INSTRUCTIONS   938 That who does cut his Purse will cut his
                                  Throat.

cut-nose                         frequency:    1    relative frequency: 0.0000
       P.  185 BRITANNIA        20 Till commons votes shall cut-nose guards disband,

cuts                             frequency:    1    relative frequency: 0.0000
       P.  104 ANNIVERSARY      46 And cuts his way still nearer to the Skyes,

cutt                             frequency:    2    relative frequency: 0.0000
       P.  166 KINGS VOWES      41 I'll order my Bravo's to cutt off his Nose,
       P.  199 DUKE             72 And will cutt throats againe if he bee paid:

cutting                          frequency:    1    relative frequency: 0.0000
       P.  195 TWO HORSES      130 This for picking our Pocketts, that for cutting
                                  our Throats.

cyclops                          frequency:    1    relative frequency: 0.0000
       P.  150 INSTRUCTIONS    371 This done, among his Cyclops he retires,

cymbal                           frequency:    1    relative frequency: 0.0000
       P.   47 EMPIRE            1 First was the World as one great Cymbal made,

cynthia                          frequency:   11    relative frequency: 0.0002
       P.   16 EYES             35 Nor Cynthia Teeming show's so fair,
       P.  119 TWO SONGS         7 Cynthia, O Cynthia, turn thine Ear,
       P.  119 TWO SONGS       10+ Cynthia,.
       P.  120 TWO SONGS        33 And Cynthia, though the strongest,
       P.  120 TWO SONGS       16+ Cynthia.
       P.  120 TWO SONGS       22+ Cynthia.
       P.  120 TWO SONGS       38+ Cynthia.
       P.  121 TWO SONGS       42+ Cynthia.
       P.  121 TWO SONGS       48+ Cynthia.
       P.  130 O.C.            282 As long as Cynthia shall relieve the sunne,

cynthia's                        frequency:    1    relative frequency: 0.0000
       P.  121 TWO SONGS        52 For he has Cynthia's favour won.

cypress                          frequency:    1    relative frequency: 0.0000
       P.   93 DR. WITTY         4 Take off the Cypress vail, but leave a mask,

d.                               frequency:   10    relative frequency: 0.0002
       P.   18 CLORINDA          2 D. No: 'tis too late they went astray.
       P.   18 CLORINDA          7 D. Grass withers; and the Flow'rs too fade.
       P.   18 CLORINDA         10 D. That den? C. Loves Shrine. D. But
                                  Virtue's Grave.
       P.   18 CLORINDA         12 Safe from the Sun. D. not Heaven's Eye.
       P.   18 CLORINDA         15 D. Might a Soul bath there and be clean,
       P.   18 CLORINDA         17 D. These once had been enticing things,
       P.   18 CLORINDA         19 C. And what late change? D. The other day
       P.   18 CLORINDA         21 D. Words that transcend poor Shepherds skill,
       P.   18 CLORINDA         25 D. Clorinda's voice might make it sweet.

d----s                           frequency:    1    relative frequency: 0.0000
       P.  142 INSTRUCTIONS     60 To make her glassen D----s once malleable!

daffadils                        frequency:    1    relative frequency: 0.0000
       P.   43 DAMON            44 Before her darling Daffadils.

dagger                           frequency:    1    relative frequency: 0.0000
       P.  184 MADE FREE       126 London beares the Crosse with the Dagger.

daies                            frequency:    1    relative frequency: 0.0000
       P.   38 PICTURE           2 This Nimph begins her golden daies!

daily                            frequency:    4    relative frequency: 0.0000
       See also "dayly."
       P.   17 BERMUDAS         16 On daily Visits through the Air.
       P.   61 A. HOUSE         68 Daily new Furniture of Friends.
       P.   96 HOLLAND          27 A daily deluge over them does boyl;
       P.  124 O.C.             43 Then might y' ha' daily his Affection spy'd,

dairys                           frequency:    1    relative frequency: 0.0000
       P.  139 HOUSEWARMING     68 As all Chedder Dairys club to the incorporate
                                  Cheese

dam                              frequency:    2    relative frequency: 0.0000
```

```
       P. 158 INSTRUCTIONS   740 Thee, the Year's monster, let thy Dam devour.
       P. 196 TWO HORSES     186 Tis Bacchus and the Brewer swear Dam 'um and
                                 sink 'um.

damage                           frequency:    1    relative frequency: 0.0000
       P. 150 INSTRUCTIONS   381 No concern'd Jury for him Damage finds,

dame                             frequency:    2    relative frequency: 0.0000
       P. 186 BRITANNIA       60 Entred a Dame bedeckt with spotted pride;
       P. 187 BRITANNIA      117 But his fair soul, transform'd by that French
                                 Dame,

damming                          frequency:    1    relative frequency: 0.0000
       P. 144 INSTRUCTIONS   161 Then damming Cowards rang'd the vocal Plain,

damnacion                        frequency:    1    relative frequency: 0.0000
       P. 186 BRITANNIA       87 To sound damnacion to those dare deny't.

damon                            frequency:    6    relative frequency: 0.0001
       P.  18 CLORINDA        t Clorinda and Damon.
       P.  18 CLORINDA        1 C. Damon come drive thy flocks this way.
       P.  41 DAMON           t Damon the Mower.
       P.  41 DAMON           1 Heark how the Mower Damon Sung,
       P.  43 DAMON          41 I am the Mower Damon, known
       P. 123 TWO SONGS      46 Or who despair, now Damon does enjoy?

damons                           frequency:    1    relative frequency: 0.0000
       P.  18 CLORINDA       24 C. Sweet must Pan sound in Damons Note.

damon's                          frequency:    1    relative frequency: 0.0000
       See also "damons."
       P. 122 TWO SONGS      32 Whil'st all the Nymphs on Damon's choice
                                 attend?

damp                             frequency:    1    relative frequency: 0.0000
       P. 125 O.C.           75 And with the damp of her last Gasps obscur'd,

damsel                           frequency:    1    relative frequency: 0.0000
       P. 147 INSTRUCTIONS  259 Keen Whorwood next, in aid of Damsel frail,

danae                            frequency:    1    relative frequency: 0.0000
       P.  32 MOURNING       20 Her self both Danae and the Showr.

danby                            frequency:    2    relative frequency: 0.0000
       P. 190 STATUE         39 Tho' the King be of Copper and Danby of Gold,
       P. 204 HISTORICALL   139 White liverd Danby for his swift Jacall

dance                            frequency:    3    relative frequency: 0.0000
       P.  42 DAMON          12 And hamstring'd Frogs can dance no more.
       P. 129 O.C.          242 As ungirt David to the arke did dance.
       P. 137 HOUSEWARMING   18 Made Thebes dance aloft while he fidled and
                                 sung,

danced.  See "dans'd."

dances                           frequency:    1    relative frequency: 0.0000
       See also "danses."
       P.  72 A. HOUSE      431 When at their Dances End they kiss,

dancing                          frequency:    1    relative frequency: 0.0000
       P.  72 A. HOUSE      426 Dancing the Triumphs of the Hay;

dandles                          frequency:    1    relative frequency: 0.0000
       P. 313 CHEQUER INN    23 He dandles always in his Hand

danger                           frequency:    5    relative frequency: 0.0001
       P.  98 HOLLAND       124 A wholesome Danger drove us to our Ports.
       P. 128 O.C.          199 Danger itself refusing to offend
       P. 158 INSTRUCTIONS  706 The Tow'r it self with the near danger shook.
       P. 194 TWO HORSES    102 Thou knowest what danger was like to come of it;
       P. 200 DUKE          106 Observe the danger that appeares soe neare,

dangers                          frequency:    4    relative frequency: 0.0000
       P. 155 INSTRUCTIONS  601 Our Seamen, whom no Dangers shape could fright,
       P. 185 BRITANNIA      37 Taught him their use, what dangers would ensue
       P. 201 HISTORICALL    21 Bold James survives, no dangers make him flinch,
       P. 205 HISTORICALL   161 Bid him be bold all dangers to defye,

danger's                         frequency:    1    relative frequency: 0.0000
       P. 111 ANNIVERSARY   321 But the great Captain, now the danger's ore,

daniel                           frequency:    2    relative frequency: 0.0000
```

P. 156 INSTRUCTIONS   631 Daniel had there adventur'd, Man of might;
P. 156 INSTRUCTIONS   642 Daniel then thought he was in Lyons Den.

dank   frequency: 1   relative frequency: 0.0000
    P. 68 A. HOUSE   295 And dries its Pan yet dank with Dew,

dans'd   frequency: 1   relative frequency: 0.0000
    P. 104 ANNIVERSARY 52 Dans'd up in order from the Quarreys rude;

danses   frequency: 1   relative frequency: 0.0000
    P. 43 DAMON   62 To lead them in their Danses soft;

daphne   frequency: 1   relative frequency: 0.0000
    P. 48 THE GARDEN   29 Apollo hunted Daphne so,

daphnis   frequency: 4   relative frequency: 0.0000
    P. 33 DAPHNIS   t Daphnis and Chloe.
    P. 33 DAPHNIS   1 Daphnis must from Chloe part:
    P. 34 DAPHNIS   31 When poor Daphnis is undone,
    P. 34 DAPHNIS   41 So did wretched Daphnis look,

darby   frequency: 2   relative frequency: 0.0000
    P. 169 ADVICE   54 To overthrow the Darby Hous designes,
    P. 198 DUKE   10 With Father Patricke Darby and with Teage,

dare   frequency: 11   relative frequency: 0.0002
    P. 63 A. HOUSE   137 'And (for I dare not quench the Fire
    P. 81 A. HOUSE   731 Nor once at Vice your Brows dare knit
    P. 122 TWO SONGS   19 'Twas those Eyes, I now dare swear,
    P. 128 O.C.   225 Least others dare to think your zeale a maske,
    P. 131 PARADISE   25 But I am now convinc'd, and none will dare
    P. 158 INSTRUCTIONS 738 Out of the Port, or dare to hoise a Sail,
    P. 166 KINGS VOWES 40 Which if any bold Commoner dare to opose,
    P. 186 BRITANNIA   87 To scund damnacion to those dare deny't.
    P. 198 DUKE   25 Shall these men dare to contradict my will
    P. 198 DUKE   28 Shall these men dare to thinke, shall these
                          decide
    P. 203 HISTORICALL 97 Who from the sacred Pulpit dare decieve?

dareing   frequency: 1   relative frequency: 0.0000
    P. 168 KINGS VOWES 62 That all his dareing crimes, what ere they be,

dares   frequency: 1   relative frequency: 0.0000
    P. 123 TWO SONGS   45 Marina yields. Who dares be coy?

daring   frequency: 2   relative frequency: 0.0000
See also "dareing," "heaven-daring."
    P. 147 INSTRUCTIONS 257 Then daring Seymour, that with Spear and
                           Shield,
    P. 176 LOYALL SCOT 178 When daring Blood to have his rents regain'd

dark   frequency: 10   relative frequency: 0.0002
    P. 12 DROP OF DEW 31 Dark beneath, but bright above:
    P. 36 DAPHNIS   93 Fate I come, as dark, as sad,
    P. 74 A. HOUSE   505 Dark all without it knits; within
    P. 83 A. HOUSE   775 Let's in: for the dark Hemisphere
    P. 106 ANNIVERSARY 127 And in dark Nights, and in cold Dayes alone
    P. 121 TWO SONGS   49 That Cave is dark. Endymion. Then none can
                          spy:
    P. 162 INSTRUCTIONS 888 From his clear Eyes, yet these too dark with
                           Care.
    P. 169 ADVICE   55 Whilst Positive walks Woodcock in the dark,
    P. 194 TWO HORSES 113 In every dark night you are sure to find him
    P. 195 TWO HORSES 151 Ch. Her Walsingham could dark Councells
                          unriddle,

darken   frequency: 1   relative frequency: 0.0000
    P. 188 BRITANNIA 160 Shall darken story, Ingross loudmouthd fame.

darkness   frequency: 3   relative frequency: 0.0000
    P. 114 BLAKE   21 In thickest darkness they would choose to steer,
    P. 114 BLAKE   22 So that such darkness might suppress their fear;

darling   frequency: 7   relative frequency: 0.0001
    P. 38 PICTURE   10 This Darling of the Gods was born!
    P. 43 DAMON   44 Before her darling Daffadils.
    P. 99 HOLLAND   146 Darling of Heaven, and of Men the Care;
    P. 123 O.C.   30 Eliza, Natures and his darling, seize.
    P. 159 INSTRUCTIONS 755 But most they for their Darling Charles
                           complain:
    P. 183 MADE FREE   87 To the Duke the Kingdoms Darling?

    P. 188 BRITANNIA   133 Rawl: Once more, great Queen, thy darling try
                               to save;

darlings   frequency: 1   relative frequency: 0.0000
    P.   5 HASTINGS   46 Reversed, at his Darlings Funeral.

dart   frequency: 5   relative frequency: 0.0001
    P. 77 A. HOUSE   604 Bends in some Tree its useless Dart;
    P. 84 FLECKNO   50 With gristly Tongue to dart the passing Flyes.
    P. 141 INSTRUCTIONS   23 His desperate Pencil at the work did dart,
    P. 162 INSTRUCTIONS   887 And those bright gleams that dart along and glare
    P. 314 CHEQUER INN   88 The Pelletts which his Choppes did dart

darts   frequency: 2   relative frequency: 0.0000
    P. 111 ANNIVERSARY   345 Up from the other World his Flame he darts,
    P. 129 O.C.   265 When angry Jove darts lightning through the
                               aire,

dasht   frequency: 2   relative frequency: 0.0000
    P. 78 A. HOUSE   627 Whose Grass, with moister colour dasht,
    P. 315 CHEQUER INN   102 That Band with Sawce too dasht.

dastards   frequency: 1   relative frequency: 0.0000
    P. 186 BRITANNIA   77 Dastards the hearts and active heat controules.

date   frequency: 1   relative frequency: 0.0000
    P. 160 INSTRUCTIONS   810 All Arts they try how to prolong its Date.

daub. See "dawb."

daughter   frequency: 3   relative frequency: 0.0000
    P. 121 TWO SONGS   4 Has Menalca's daughter wcn.
    P. 137 HOUSEWARMING   15 And wish'd that his Daughter had had as much
                               grace
    P. 200 DUKE   84 And now hath gott his Daughter gott with Child,

daughters   frequency: 2   relative frequency: 0.0000
    P. 195 TWO HORSES   132 Than the Goats making whores of our wives and
                               our Daughters.
    P. 203 HISTORICALL   78 Corrupt with Gold they Wives and Daughters
                               bring

davenant   frequency: 2   relative frequency: 0.0000
    P. 73 A. HOUSE   456 Davenant with th' Universal Heard.
    P. 92 MAY'S DEATH   78 Hast left surviving Davenant still behind

david   frequency: 2   relative frequency: 0.0000
    P. 129 O.C.   242 As ungirt David to the arke did dance.
    P. 130 O.C.   294 And David, for the sword and harpe renown'd;

dawb   frequency: 1   relative frequency: 0.0000
    P. 141 INSTRUCTIONS   7 Or canst thou dawb a Sign-post, and that ill?

dawn   frequency: 1   relative frequency: 0.0000
    P. 29 THE GALLERY   18 Like to Aurora in the Dawn;

day   frequency: 59   relative frequency: 0.0012
See also "holy-day," "mid-day."
    P.   4 HASTINGS   11 The Phlegmatick and Slowe prolongs his day,
    P. 12 DROP OF DEW   20 Of the clear Fountain of Eternal Day,
    P. 12 DROP OF DEW   30 Yet receiving in the Day.
    P. 15 EYES   21 So the all-seeing Sun each day
    P. 18 CLORINDA   19 C. And what late change? D. The other day
    P. 19 THYRSIS   12 That leads to Everlasting day.
    P. 20 THYRSIS   36 And day is ever, but begun.
    P. 23 NYMPH   57 And as it grew, so every day
    P. 26 MISTRESS   4 To walk, and pass our long Loves Day.
    P. 28 LOVER   21 No Day he saw but that which breaks,
    P. 28 LOVER   44 At sharp before it all the day:
    P. 38 PICTURE   12 The wanton Love shall one day fear,
    P. 41 DAMON   5 Like her fair Eyes the day was fair;
    P. 42 DAMON   26 Of the hot day, or hot desires.
    P. 43 DAMON   67 But now I all the day complain,
    P. 55 EPITAPH   16 She summ'd her Life up ev'ry day;
    P. 57 BILL-BOROW   32 Directs, and this no less by Day.
    P. 68 A. HOUSE   290 Hangs out the Colours of the Day,
    P. 77 A. HOUSE   608 And gaul its Horsemen all the Day.
    P. 79 A. HOUSE   670 Flying betwixt the Day and Night;
    P. 103 ANNIVERSARY   9 And still the Day which he doth next restore,
    P. 103 ANNIVERSARY   10 Is the just Wonder of the Day before.
    P. 106 ANNIVERSARY   140 And soon precipitate the latest Day.

P. 107 ANNIVERSARY   155 Hence that blest Day still counterpoysed wastes,
P. 107 ANNIVERSARY   174 Our Sins endanger, and shall one day kill.
P. 111 ANNIVERSARY   327 All day he follow'd with unwearied sight,
P. 111 ANNIVERSARY   340 Or why Day last no longer then a Day?
P. 112 ANNIVERSARY   377 'Him, all the Day, Him, in late Nights I
                          dread,

P. 114 BLAKE   17 Day, that to those who sail upon the deep,
P. 114 BLAKE   38 This only rules by day, and that by Night.
P. 120 TWO SONGS   26 Can make a Night more bright then Day;
P. 121 TWO SONGS   2 Never such a merry day.
P. 124 O.C.   47 With her each day the pleasing Hours he shares,
P. 126 O.C.   142 Of honour; all the Year was Cromwell's day:
P. 126 O.C.   147 What day should him eternize but the same
P. 128 O.C.   214 For these his life adventur'd every day:
P. 129 O.C.   232 To fetch day, presse about his chamber-door;
P. 130 O.C.   297 And in those joyes dost spend the endlesse day,
P. 131 PARADISE   21 Might hence presume the whole Creations day
P. 144 INSTRUCTIONS   139 She stalks all day in Streets conceal'd from
                          sight,
P. 146 INSTRUCTIONS   238 Excise had got the day, and all been lost.
P. 148 INSTRUCTIONS   315 Each day they bring the Tale, and that too true,
P. 155 INSTRUCTIONS   597 Our feather'd Gallants, which came down that day
P. 157 INSTRUCTIONS   661 on his Ship, he fac'd that horrid Day,
P. 157 INSTRUCTIONS   697 Each doleful day still with fresh loss returns;
P. 158 INSTRUCTIONS   737 Black Day accurs'd! On thee let no man hale
P. 161 INSTRUCTIONS   853 The King, that day rais'd early from his rest,
P. 162 INSTRUCTIONS   875 Whence ev'ry day, the Palat more to tickle;
P. 172 LOYALL SCOT   27 Fix'd on his ship hee fac'd the horrid day
P. 180 STOCKSMARKET   48 The day that he was both restored and born?
P. 181 MADE FREE   30 Has every Day broke his Indentures.
P. 185 BRITANNIA   42 The other day fam'd Spencer I did bring
P. 191 STATUE   56 To behold every day such a Court, such a son.
P. 192 TWO HORSES   31 When both the Kings weary of Sitting all day
P. 194 TWO HORSES   112 And returns to remount about break of Day.
P. 201 HISTORICALL   16 His jolly Vassalls treat him day and Night.
P. 204 HISTORICALL   141 Clifford and Hide before had lost the day,
P. 315 CHEQUER INN   129 For what that Day they spoke

dayes   frequency: 8   relative frequency: 0.0001
P. 27 LOVER   1 Alas, how pleasant are their dayes
P. 42 DAMON   18 Nor Dog-star so inflame's the dayes.
P. 104 ANNIVERSARY   33 They neither build the Temple in their dayes,
P. 106 ANNIVERSARY   110 The great Designes kept for the latter Dayes!
P. 106 ANNIVERSARY   127 And in dark Nights, and in cold Dayes alone
P. 129 O.C.   239 No more shall follow where he spent the dayes
P. 185 BRITANNIA   45 And Golden dayes in peacefull order rould,
P. 189 BRITANNIA   165 Tell 'em how arts and Arms in thy young dayes

dayly   frequency: 1   relative frequency: 0.0000
P. 138 HOUSEWARMING   25 Thus dayly his Gouty Inventions he pain'd,

days   frequency: 4   relative frequency: 0.0000
See also "daies," "dayes."
P. 144 INSTRUCTIONS   142 Her, of a female Harpy, in Dog Days:
P. 149 INSTRUCTIONS   330 They with the first days proffer seem content:
P. 161 INSTRUCTIONS   840 And for three days, thence moves them to adjourn.
P. 181 MADE FREE   31 He spends all his Days

day's   frequency: 1   relative frequency: 0.0000
See also "days."
P.   9 DIALOGUE   8 In this day's Combat let it shine:

dazle   frequency: 1   relative frequency: 0.0000
P. 203 HISTORICALL   93 They dazle both the Prince and Peasants sight.

dazled   frequency: 1   relative frequency: 0.0000
P. 66 A. HOUSE   228 And dazled not but clear'd his sight.

de   frequency: 4   relative frequency: 0.0000
P. 160 INSTRUCTIONS   817 But in the Thames mouth still de Ruyter laid,
P. 195 TWO HORSES   137 Ch. De Witt and Cromwell had each a brave
                          soul.
P. 202 HISTORICALL   54 De Ruyter claps him in Solbay again.
P. 204 HISTORICALL   120 Sets up in Scotland alamode de France,

de-ruyter's   frequency: 1   relative frequency: 0.0000
P. 159 INSTRUCTIONS   758 Now in the Ravisher De-Ruyter's hand,

de-witte   frequency: 1   relative frequency: 0.0000
P. 151 INSTRUCTIONS   437 Pray him to make De-Witte, and Ruyter cease,

dead   frequency: 21   relative frequency: 0.0004

```
P.    4 HASTINGS          3 Hastings is dead, and we must finde a Store
P.    4 HASTINGS          7 Hastings is dead; and we, disconsolate,
P.   32 MOURNING         26 To her dead Love this Tribute due;
P.   34 DAPHNIS          37 As the Soul of one scarce dead,
P.   35 DAPHNIS          76 Of a Body dead while warm.
P.   35 DAPHNIS          78 Like the Gourmand Hebrew dead,
P.   40 THE MOWER         6 A dead and standing pool of Air:
P.   55 EPITAPH           4 When dead to offer were unkind.
P.   55 EPITAPH          20 'Twere more Significant, She's Dead.
P.   59 A. HOUSE         18 Demands more room alive then this dead.
P.   87 FLECKNO         161 Against the Rebel; who, at this struck dead,
P.  108 ANNIVERSARY     188 And speak as of the Dead the Praises due:
P.  111 ANNIVERSARY     350 'Spent with both Wars, under a Captain dead?
P.  129 O.C.            247 I saw him dead, a leaden slumber lyes,
P.  129 O.C.            258 That still though dead, greater than death he
                            lay'd;
P.  130 O.C.            306 Beats on the rugged track: he, vertue dead,
P.  140 G.-CHILDREN       1 Kendal is dead, and Cambridge riding post.
P.  160 INSTRUCTIONS    793 Southampton dead, much of the Treasure's care,
P.  162 INSTRUCTIONS    885 Paint last the King, and a dead Shade of
                            Night,
P.  188 BRITANNIA       137 In his deaf ear sound his dead Fathers name;
P.  198 DUKE             31 Or that theres not a purgatory for the dead?
```

dead's   frequency: 1   relative frequency: 0.0000
```
P.   82 A. HOUSE        759 Much less the Dead's Elysian Fields,
```

deaf   frequency: 6   relative frequency: 0.0001
```
P.   20 SOUL & BODY       6 Deaf with the drumming of an Ear.
P.   86 FLECKNO         148 As a deaf Man upon a Viol playes,
P.  108 ANNIVERSARY     212 And to deaf Seas, and ruthless Tempests mourns,
P.  155 INSTRUCTIONS    591 Th' English from shore the Iron deaf invoke
P.  187 BRITANNIA        97 Henceforth be deaf to that old witches charmes,
P.  188 BRITANNIA       137 In his deaf ear sound his dead Fathers name;
```

deal   frequency: 1   relative frequency: 0.0000
```
P.  138 HOUSEWARMING     46 So long as the Yards had a Deal or a Spar:
```

deales   frequency: 1   relative frequency: 0.0000
```
P.  190 STATUE           13 Were these Deales kept in store for sheathing
                            our fleet
```

deals   frequency: 1   relative frequency: 0.0000
```
      See also "deales."
P.  180 STOCKSMARKET     35 With canvas and deals you e'er since do him
                            cloud,
```

dealt   frequency: 1   relative frequency: 0.0000
```
      See also "delt."
P.   41 THE MOWER        21 Had he not dealt between the Bark and Tree,
```

dean   frequency: 1   relative frequency: 0.0000
```
P.   99 HOLLAND         150 Steel'd with those piercing Heads, Dean, Monck
                            and Blake.
```

deanes   frequency: 1   relative frequency: 0.0000
```
P.  201 HISTORICALL      13 Bishops and Deanes, Peeres, Pimps and Knights
                            he made,
```

deans   frequency: 1   relative frequency: 0.0000
```
      See also "deanes."
P.  194 TWO HORSES      121 Arch-Bishops and Bishops, Arch-Deacons and
                            Deans
```

dear   frequency: 26   relative frequency: 0.0005
```
      See also "deare."
P.   16 EYES            41 The Incense was to Heaven dear,
P.   22 NYMPH           32 Hath taught a Faun to hunt his Dear.
P.   34 DAPHNIS         33 At that Why, that Stay my Dear,
P.   44 GLO-WORMS        1 Ye living Lamps, by whose dear light
P.   48 THE GARDEN      10 And Innocence thy Sister dear!
P.   64 A. HOUSE       165 'Those Virtues to us all so dear,
P.   69 A. HOUSE       321 Oh Thou, that dear and happy Isle
P.   87 ODE             2 Must now forsake his Muses dear,
P.   98 HOLLAND        130 Till the dear Halcyon hatch out all its nest.
P.  108 ANNIVERSARY    223 Resigning up thy Privacy so dear,
P.  112 ANNIVERSARY    385 'Where did he learn those Arts that cost us dear?
P.  124 O.C.            51 Hold fast dear Infants, hold them both or none;
P.  125 O.C.            78 But the dear Image fled the Mirrour broke.
P.  125 O.C.            93 If some dear branch where it extends its life
P.  148 INSTRUCTIONS   289 Dear Lovers of their King, and Death to meet,
```

```
P. 150 INSTRUCTIONS   390 So thou and I, dear Painter, represent
P. 152 INSTRUCTIONS   485 And the wise Court, that always lov'd it dear,
P. 153 INSTRUCTIONS   511 Often, dear Painter, have I sate and mus'd
P. 156 INSTRUCTIONS   617 That Pleasure-boat of War, in whose dear side
P. 157 INSTRUCTIONS   688 With his dear Sword reposing by his Side.
P. 159 INSTRUCTIONS   745 And their dear Off-spring murder'd in their
                          sight;
P. 162 INSTRUCTIONS   863 Dear Painter, draw this Speaker to the foot:
P. 168 ADVICE          27 And of his dear Reward let none dispair,
P. 173 LOYALL SCOT     54 With his dear sword reposing by his side,
P. 189 STATUE           3 Dear Wheeler impart, for wee're all at a loss
P. 194 TWO HORSES      97 Ch. Enough, dear Brother, for tho' we have
                          reason,
```

```
deare                      frequency:   3    relative frequency: 0.0000
P.   3 LOVELACE        34 That their deare Lovelace was endanger'd so:
P. 128 O.C.           211 If so indulgent to his own, how deare
P. 128 O.C.           218 To keep so deare, so diff'ring minds agreed?
```

```
dearest                    frequency:   1    relative frequency: 0.0000
P. 189 BRITANNIA      178 Back to my dearest Country I'le return:
```

```
death                      frequency:  36    relative frequency: 0.0007
P.   4 HASTINGS         t Upon the Death of the Lord Hastings.
P.   4 HASTINGS         9 Alas, his Vertues did his Death presage:
P.  19 THYRSIS          1 Dorinda. When Death, shall part us from these
                          Kids,
P.  22 NYMPH            t The Nymph complaining for the death of her
                          Faun.
P.  22 NYMPH            6 Thy death yet do them any good.
P.  28 LOVER          40 Th' Amphibium of Life and Death.
P.  31 FAIR SINGER      3 In whom both Beauties to my death agree,
P.  44 DAMON          87 'Tis death alone that this must do:
P.  44 DAMON          88 For Death thou art a Mower too.
P.  55 THYESTE        14 Death to him 's a Strange surprise.
P.  65 A. HOUSE      207 'Death only can such Theeves make fast,
P.  90 MAY'S DEATH      t Tom May's Death.
P.  92 MAY'S DEATH    76 Before thou couldst great Charles his death
                          relate.
P.  92 MAY'S DEATH    79 Who laughs to see in this thy death renew'd,
P. 118 BLAKE         136 By death, as bodies there were by the War.
P. 123 O.C.            t A Poem upon the Death of O. C.
P. 123 O.C.            6 What death might least so fair a Life deface.
P. 123 O.C.            8 Death when more horrid so more noble deem;
P. 123 O.C.           26 In gentle Passions should his Death disguise:
P. 125 O.C.           72 Ran out impetuously to hasting Death.
P. 126 O.C.          112 But oh what pangs that Death did Nature cost!
P. 126 O.C.          128 And hasten not to see his Death their own.
P. 126 O.C.          149 That so who ere would at his Death have joy'd,
P. 129 O.C.          255 Oh! humane glory, vaine, oh! death, oh! wings,
P. 129 O.C.          258 That still though dead, greater than death he
                          lay'd;
P. 129 O.C.          260 That threatens death, he yet will live again.
P. 130 O.C.          275 But when death takes them from that envy'd seate,
P. 148 INSTRUCTIONS  289 Dear Lovers of their King, and Death to meet,
P. 171 LOYALL SCOT    t2 Upon The occasion of the death of Captain
                          Douglas burnt in one
P. 173 LOYALL SCOT    65 Shall not a death soe Generous now when told
P. 177 LOYALL SCOT   247 Where a Mistaken accent Causeth death.
P. 178 LOYALL SCOT   275 Thy death more noble did the same Extort.
P. 186 BRITANNIA      68 Pale death, lusts, Horrour fill her pompous
                          train.
P. 195 TWO HORSES    141 Ch. Thy Ryder puts no man to death in his
                          wrath,
P. 202 HISTORICALL    42 Death and the Duke so terrible apeare.
P. 203 HISTORICALL   106 Hence Death and Sin did human Nature blot:
```

```
death-trumpets             frequency:   1    relative frequency: 0.0000
P.  71 A. HOUSE      415 Death-Trumpets creak in such a Note,
```

```
deathless                  frequency:   1    relative frequency: 0.0000
P.  43 DAMON          61 The deathless Fairyes take me oft
```

```
death's                    frequency:   1    relative frequency: 0.0000
P. 128 O.C.          229 And we death's refuse nature's dregs confin'd
```

```
debar'd                    frequency:   1    relative frequency: 0.0000
P.  66 A. HOUSE      237 Yet still the Nuns his Right debar'd,
```

debarred. See "debar'd."

```
debarrs                    frequency:   1    relative frequency: 0.0000
```

P.   37 DEFINITION   30 But Fate so enviously debarrs,

debars. See "debarrs."

debase   frequency: 1   relative frequency: 0.0000
     P.   14 THE CORONET   17 Ah, foolish Man, that would'st debase with them,

debate   frequency: 4   relative frequency: 0.0000
     P. 144 INSTRUCTIONS   149 Who, in an English Senate, fierce debate,
     P. 160 INSTRUCTIONS   809 Frequent in Counsel, earnest in Debate,
     P. 161 INSTRUCTIONS   852 Lest some new Tomkins spring a fresh debate.
     P. 169 ADVICE   32 Our mighty Masters in a warme debate:

debauch   frequency: 1   relative frequency: 0.0000
     P. 141 INSTRUCTIONS   8 'Twill suit our great debauch and little skill.

debauch'd   frequency: 1   relative frequency: 0.0000
     P. 195 TWO HORSES   133 The Debauch'd and the Bloody since they
                              Equally Gall us,

debenter-wall   frequency: 1   relative frequency: 0.0000
     P. 140 HIS HOUSE   5 The Cavaliers Debenter-Wall,

debt   frequency: 4   relative frequency: 0.0000
     P.   35 DAPHNIS   58 Such a Debt unto my Foe;
     P.   55 EPITAPH   15 That ready her last Debt to pay
     P. 159 INSTRUCTIONS 777 Who all our Seamen cheated of their Debt?
     P. 180 STOCKSMARKET   40 Or have you to the Compter removed him for debt?

debtors   frequency: 1   relative frequency: 0.0000
     P. 145 INSTRUCTIONS 188 Of Debtors deep, fell to Trelawny's Care.

debts   frequency: 2   relative frequency: 0.0000
     P. 182 MADE FREE   67 So many are the Debts
     P. 193 TWO HORSES   58 Yet the King of his debts pay no man a penny;

decay'd   frequency: 2   relative frequency: 0.0000
     P.   39 THE MATCH   3 Fearing, when She should be decay'd,
     P. 129 O.C.   257 Yet dwelt that greatnesse in his shape decay'd,

deceiv'd   frequency: 1   relative frequency: 0.0000
     P. 108 ANNIVERSARY   189 While impious Men deceiv'd with pleasure short,

deceive   frequency: 2   relative frequency: 0.0000
See also "decieve."
     P.   14 THE CORONET   10 Thinking (so I my self deceive)
     P. 111 ANNIVERSARY   320 Ay, and the Serpent too that did deceive.

december   frequency: 1   relative frequency: 0.0000
     P. 180 STOCKSMARKET   58 As ever you hope in December for Spring,

decent   frequency: 1   relative frequency: 0.0000
     P.   82 A. HOUSE   766 But in more decent Order tame;

decently   frequency: 1   relative frequency: 0.0000
     P. 179 STOCKSMARKET   18 Who upon their panniers more decently ride,

decide   frequency: 2   relative frequency: 0.0000
     P. 143 INSTRUCTIONS 112 As Chance does still in Multitudes decide.
     P. 198 DUKE   28 Shall these men dare to thinke, shall these
                              decide

decieve   frequency: 1   relative frequency: 0.0000
     P. 203 HISTORICALL   97 Who from the sacred Pulpit dare decieve?

decipher   frequency: 1   relative frequency: 0.0000
     P.   31 MOURNING   1 You, that decipher out the Fate

deciple   frequency: 1   relative frequency: 0.0000
     P. 195 TWO HORSES   146 Father Patricks Deciple will make England
                              smart.

deck   frequency: 3   relative frequency: 0.0000
     P. 108 ANNIVERSARY   214 Break up each Deck, and rip the Oaken seams.
     P. 157 INSTRUCTIONS 687 Down on the Deck he laid himself, and dy'd,
     P. 173 LOYALL SCOT   53 Down on the Deck hee laid him down and dy'd

decked. See "deckt," "deck't."

decks   frequency: 1   relative frequency: 0.0000
     P. 158 INSTRUCTIONS 734 With Gamesome Joy insulting on her Decks.

deckt   frequency: 1   relative frequency: 0.0000
    P. 74 A. HOUSE   495 And, as they Natures Cradle deckt,

deck't   frequency: 1   relative frequency: 0.0000
    P. 85 FLECKNO   79 But were he not in this black habit deck't,

declaims   frequency: 1   relative frequency: 0.0000
    P. 152 INSTRUCTIONS 484 These; and in Standing-Armies praise declaims.

declarations   frequency: 1   relative frequency: 0.0000
    P. 170 PROPHECY   23 When Declarations lye, when every Oath

declare   frequency: 2   relative frequency: 0.0000
    P. 195 TWO HORSES   138 W. I freely declare it, I am for old Noll.
    P. 196 TWO HORSES   166 Which two inanimate Horses declare.

declares   frequency: 1   relative frequency: 0.0000
    P. 204 HISTORICALL   118 Declares the Councel Edicts are beyond

declin'd   frequency: 1   relative frequency: 0.0000
    P. 55 EPITAPH   3 Courtship, which living she declin'd,

declining   frequency: 1   relative frequency: 0.0000
    P. 103 ANNIVERSARY   3 So Man, declining alwayes, disappears

decoy   frequency: 1   relative frequency: 0.0000
    P. 167 KINGS VOWES   52 I will have a fine pond and a pretty decoy,

decrease   frequency: 1   relative frequency: 0.0000
    P. 126 O.C.   127 Numbers of Men decrease with pains unknown,

decree   frequency: 3   relative frequency: 0.0000
    P. 15 EYES   1 How wisely Nature did decree,
    P. 123 O.C.   23 From which those Powers that issu'd the Decree,
    P. 131 PARADISE   3 Messiah Crown'd, Gods Reconcil'd Decree,

decreed   frequency: 2   relative frequency: 0.0000
    P. 169 ADVICE   39 Which to effect when thus it was decreed
    P. 184 MADE FREE   131 You for Slaves are decreed,

decrees   frequency: 4   relative frequency: 0.0000
    P. 37 DEFINITION   17 And therefore her Decrees of Steel
    P. 109 ANNIVERSARY   242 Who think those high Decrees by Man design'd.
    P. 125 O.C.   108 Their fun'rals celebrates while it decrees.
    P. 144 INSTRUCTIONS 123 So therefore secretly for Peace decrees,

decrepid   frequency: 1   relative frequency: 0.0000
    P. 149 INSTRUCTIONS 337 Not so decrepid Aescn, hash'd and stew'd

decrepit. See "decrepid."

deed   frequency: 1   relative frequency: 0.0000
    P. 179 STOCKSMARKET   5 Some thought it a knightly and generous deed,

deeds   frequency: 6   relative frequency: 0.0001
    P. 127 O.C.   177 And in a valour less'ning Arthur's deeds,
    P. 157 INSTRUCTIONS 674 Inspire, nor would he his own deeds deface.
    P. 172 LOYALL SCOT   40 Inspire, ncr cold hee his own Deeds deface;
    P. 185 BRITANNIA   47 Full of Gray Hairs, good deeds, endless renown.
    P. 189 BRITANNIA   176 On whose fam'd Deeds all tongues, all writers
                             wait.
    P. 314 CHEQUER INN   75 Tho' not for his good Deeds:

deem   frequency: 1   relative frequency: 0.0000
    P. 123 O.C.   8 Death when more horrid so more noble deem;

deem'd   frequency: 1   relative frequency: 0.0000
    P. 185 BRITANNIA   15 Till Cavaleers shall favorites be Deem'd

deep   frequency: 12   relative frequency: 0.0002
    P. 17 BERMUDAS   10 That lift the Deep upon their Backs.
    P. 61 A. HOUSE   80 Deep Meadows, and transparent Floods.
    P. 114 BLAKE   17 Day, that to those who sail upon the deep,
    P. 118 BLAKE   154 Were buryed in as large, and deep a grave,
    P. 120 TWO SONGS   28 With shades of deep Despair opprest.
    P. 126 O.C.   120 The deep foundations open'd to the Skyes.
    P. 126 O.C.   146 He march'd, and through deep Severn ending war.
    P. 128 O.C.   205 And that deep scule through every channell flows,
    P. 145 INSTRUCTIONS 188 Of Debtors deep, fell to Trelawny's Care.
    P. 154 INSTRUCTIONS 545 And, where the deep Keel on the shallow cleaves,
    P. 158 INSTRUCTIONS 721 Once a deep River, now with Timber floor'd,

P. 163 INSTRUCTIONS   905 In his deep thoughts the wonder did increase,

deeper   frequency: 2   relative frequency: 0.0000
    P. 32 MOURNING   31 Would find her Tears yet deeper Waves
    P. 92 MAY'S DEATH   77 But what will deeper wound thy little mind,

deepest   frequency: 2   relative frequency: 0.0000
    P. 88 ODE   46 Where his were not the deepest Scars?
    P. 128 O.C.   216 Their griefs struck deepest, if Eliza's last.

deeps   frequency: 1   relative frequency: 0.0000
    P. 71 A. HOUSE   391 To them the Grassy Deeps divide,

deer   frequency: 2   relative frequency: 0.0000
    See also "dear."
    P. 90 ODE   112 The Caledonian Deer.
    P. 129 O.C.   244 In horses fierce, wild deer, or armour bright;

defac'd   frequency: 2   relative frequency: 0.0000
    P. 61 A. HOUSE   77 Art would more neatly have defac'd
    P. 177 LOYALL SCOT   226 Ev'n Father Dis tho so with Age defac'd

deface   frequency: 4   relative frequency: 0.0000
    P. 111 ANNIVERSARY   315 You who the Scriptures and the Laws deface
    P. 123 O.C.   6 What death might least so fair a Life deface.
    P. 157 INSTRUCTIONS 674 Inspire, nor would he his own deeds deface.
    P. 172 LOYALL SCOT   40 Inspire, nor cold hee his own Deeds deface;

defeated   frequency: 1   relative frequency: 0.0000
    P. 179 STOCKSMARKET   4 Of bankers defeated and Lombard-street broken.

defence   frequency: 5   relative frequency: 0.0001
    P.   4 LOVELACE   40 Sally'd, and would in his defence contest.
    P.   4 LOVELACE   46 In your defence, or in his cause would dy.
    P. 81 A. HOUSE   717 True Praise (That breaks through all defence;)
    P. 152 INSTRUCTIONS 480 To raise a two-edg'd Army for's defence.
    P. 156 INSTRUCTIONS 629 The Guards, plac'd for the Chains and Fleets
                             defence,

defend   frequency: 1   relative frequency: 0.0000
    P. 190 STATUE   10 Since the privy garden could not it defend,

defended   frequency: 1   relative frequency: 0.0000
    P.   3 LOVELACE   36 He who lov'd best and them defended best.

defender   frequency: 1   relative frequency: 0.0000
    P. 192 TWO HORSES   45 Ch. That he should be styled defender o' th
                             faith,

defends   frequency: 1   relative frequency: 0.0000
    P. 145 INSTRUCTIONS 164 And under's Armpit he defends his Head.

defied. See "defy'd."

defild   frequency: 1   relative frequency: 0.0000
    P. 185 BRITANNIA   28 Since Pharoh's Reign nor so Defild a Crown.

defil'd   frequency: 1   relative frequency: 0.0000
    P. 200 DUKE   85 And Pimpt to have his family defil'd.

defile   frequency: 1   relative frequency: 0.0000
    P. 202 HISTORICALL   37 Now the Court Sins did every place defile,

defiled. See "defild," "defil'd."

defiles   frequency: 1   relative frequency: 0.0000
    P. 188 BRITANNIA   128 Fiend Lauderdale, with ordure all defiles.

definition   frequency: 1   relative frequency: 0.0000
    P. 36 DEFINITION   t The Definition of Love.

deflower   frequency: 1   relative frequency: 0.0000
    See also "deflowre."
    P. 187 BRITANNIA   99 'Tis Royall Game whole Kingdomes to deflower.

deflowre   frequency: 1   relative frequency: 0.0000
    P. 149 INSTRUCTIONS 350 Imprison Parents, and the Child deflowre.

deform   frequency: 2   relative frequency: 0.0000
    P. 56 BILL-BOROW   12 The Earth deform and Heaven fright,
    P. 109 ANNIVERSARY   235 Then did thick Mists and Winds the air deform,

deform'd   frequency: 1   relative frequency: 0.0000
    P. 43 DAMON   57 Nor am I so deform'd to sight,

deformity   frequency: 1   relative frequency: 0.0000
    P. 61 A. HOUSE   92 Which might Deformity make fair.

defray   frequency: 1   relative frequency: 0.0000
    P. 144 INSTRUCTIONS 130 And what can these defray but the Excise?

defrayd   frequency: 1   relative frequency: 0.0000
    P. 182 MADE FREE   69 Which must all be defrayd by London,

defrayed. See "defrayd."

defy   frequency: 1   relative frequency: 0.0000
    See also "defye."
    P. 192 TWO HORSES   47 W. That the Duke should turne Papist and that
                           Church defy

defy'd   frequency: 2   relative frequency: 0.0000
    P. 146 INSTRUCTIONS 204 And in ill English all the World defy'd.
    P. 156 INSTRUCTIONS 618 Secure so oft he had this Foe defy'd:

defye   frequency: 1   relative frequency: 0.0000
    P. 205 HISTORICALL 161 Bid him be bold all dangers to defye,

defying   frequency: 1   relative frequency: 0.0000
    P. 200 DUKE   93 Defying all their heads and all their hands.

degenerate   frequency: 2   relative frequency: 0.0000
    P.   3 LOVELACE   1 Our times are much degenerate from those
    P. 168 ADVICE   4 Weeping to see their Sonns degenerate,

degree   frequency: 3   relative frequency: 0.0000
    P. 11 DIALOGUE   73 None thither mounts by the degree
    P. 128 O.C.   209 If he Eliza lov'd to that degree,
    P. 168 KINGS VOWES 61 And I will take his part to that degree,

dei   frequency: 1   relative frequency: 0.0000
    P. 192 TWO HORSES   43 W. To see dei Gratia writ on the Throne,

deify   frequency: 1   relative frequency: 0.0000
    P. 186 BRITANNIA   85 Bribe hungry Priests to deify your might,

deities. See "deityes."

deityes   frequency: 1   relative frequency: 0.0000
    P. 121 TWO SONGS   58 Makes Mortals matches fit for Deityes.

delay   frequency: 3   relative frequency: 0.0000
    P. 46 AMETAS   10 Which your selve and us delay:
    P. 148 INSTRUCTIONS 310 And what haste lost, recover by delay.
    P. 191 STATUE   53 So the Statue will up after all this delay,

delayed   frequency: 1   relative frequency: 0.0000
    P. 190 STATUE   38 Not Viner delayed us so, tho' he was brooken

delaying   frequency: 1   relative frequency: 0.0000
    P. 107 ANNIVERSARY 156 The Ill delaying, what th'elected hastes;

delicious   frequency: 3   relative frequency: 0.0000
    P. 34 DAPHNIS   54 The delicious Cup we fill;
    P. 48 THE GARDEN   16 To this delicious Solitude.
    P. 187 BRITANNIA   98 Tast the delicious sweets of sovereign power,

delight   frequency: 12   relative frequency: 0.0002
    P. 10 DIALOGUE   48 And Heaven views it with delight.
    P. 24 NYMPH   87 But all its chief delight was still
    P. 34 DAPHNIS   56 For his last and short Delight.
    P. 64 A. HOUSE   170 'Delight to banish as a Vice.
    P. 108 ANNIVERSARY 221 For all delight of Life thou then didst lose,
    P. 119 TWO SONGS   5 Heark how he sings, with sad delight,
    P. 129 O.C.   243 All, all is gone of ours or his delight
    P. 130 O.C.   284 While sheep delight the grassy downs to pick,
    P. 132 PARADISE   35 At once delight and horrour on us seize,
    P. 153 INSTRUCTIONS 532 Swells his old Veins with fresh Blood, fresh
                           Delight.
    P. 201 HISTORICALL 15 With Women, Wine and Vyands of delight
    P. 202 HISTORICALL 39 Pride nourisht folly, folly a Delight

delightful   frequency: 1   relative frequency: 0.0000

       P.   85 FLECKNO   98 Delightful, said there can no Body pass

delights   frequency: 4   relative frequency: 0.0000
       P.   60 A. HOUSE   56 That in it self which him delights.
       P. 168 ADVICE   9 Do to their more belov'd delights repair,
       P. 181 MADE FREE   35 In his constant Delights
       P. 202 HISTORICALL   68 In Loves delights none did him ere excell

deliver   frequency: 2   relative frequency: 0.0000
       P.   21 SOUL & BODY   11 O who shall me deliver whole,
       P. 174 LOYALL SCOT   92 Theres noe 'deliver us from a Bishops Wrath'.

delphick   frequency: 1   relative frequency: 0.0000
       P. 196 TWO HORSES   171 If the Delphick Sybills cracular speeches,

delphos   frequency: 1   relative frequency: 0.0000
       P. 191 TWO HORSES   13 At Delphos and Rome Stocks and Stones now and
                                   then, sirs,

delt   frequency: 1   relative frequency: 0.0000
       P. 128 O.C.   198 Each wound himself which he to others delt;

deluded   frequency: 1   relative frequency: 0.0000
       P. 115 BLAKE   71 Deluded men! Fate with you did but sport,

deluders   frequency: 1   relative frequency: 0.0000
       P. 203 HISTORICALL   82 Priests were the first deluders of Mankind,

deludes   frequency: 1   relative frequency: 0.0000
       P. 201 HISTORICALL   32 Deludes their plyant Nature with Vain things,

deluding. See "self-deluding."

deluge   frequency: 3   relative frequency: 0.0000
       P.   96 HOLLAND   27 A daily deluge over them does boyl;
       P. 126 O.C.   122 And pour the Deluge ore the Chaos head.
       P. 131 O.C.   324 He threats no deluge, yet foretells a showre.

deluges   frequency: 2   relative frequency: 0.0000
       P. 120 TWO SONGS   22 Mine Eyes uncessant deluges.
       P. 137 HOUSEWARMING   3 At once three Deluges threatning our Land;

demand   frequency: 3   relative frequency: 0.0000
       P.   85 FLECKNO   88 Stopping the passage, and did him demand:
       P. 127 O.C.   169 Your Monarch: We demand not your supplies
       P. 153 INSTRUCTIONS   507 Let no Man touch them, or demand his own,

demanded   frequency: 1   relative frequency: 0.0000
       P. 169 ADVICE   52 Five members need not be demanded here.

demands   frequency: 2   relative frequency: 0.0000
       P.   59 A. HOUSE   18 Demands more rocm alive then dead.
       P. 205 HISTORICALL   159 Tells him the hcly Church demands his aide,

democratick   frequency: 1   relative frequency: 0.0000
       P.   5 HASTINGS   25 Therefore the Democratick Stars did rise,

demolish'd   frequency: 1   relative frequency: 0.0000
       P. 158 INSTRUCTIONS   714 The Houses were demolish'd near the Tow'r.

demolished. See "demolish'd," "demolisht."

demolishing   frequency: 1   relative frequency: 0.0000
       P.   67 A. HOUSE   273 At the demolishing, this Seat

demolisht   frequency: 1   relative frequency: 0.0000
       P. 138 HOUSEWARMING   42 He would have demclisht to raise up his Walls;

demonstrates   frequency: 1   relative frequency: 0.0000
       P. 150 INSTRUCTIONS   409 But Morrice learn'd demonstrates, by the Post,

den   frequency: 5   relative frequency: 0.0001
       P.   18 CLORINDA   10 D. That den? C. Loves Shrine. D. But
                                   Virtue's Grave.
       P.   62 A. HOUSE   101 'These Bars inclose that wider Den
       P. 106 ANNIVERSARY   129 Which shrinking to her Rcman Den impure,
       P. 143 INSTRUCTIONS   101 Justly the Rogue was whipt in Porter's Den:
       P. 156 INSTRUCTIONS   642 Daniel then thought he was in Lyons Den.

denham   frequency: 4   relative frequency: 0.0000
       P. 138 HOUSEWARMING   27 That Engine so fatal, which Denham had brain'd,

P. 144 INSTRUCTIONS 154 And Denham these by one consent did head.
P. 149 INSTRUCTIONS 342 What to fair Denham mortal Chocolat;
P. 202 HISTORICALL   46 With Denham and Coneig's infected pot,

denham's   frequency: 2   relative frequency: 0.0000
P. 140 G.-CHILDREN   2 What fitter Sacrifice for Denham's Ghost?
P. 142 INSTRUCTIONS 76 And her self sccrn'd for emulous Denham's Face;

denied. See "deny'd," "denyed."

dennis   frequency: 1   relative frequency: 0.0000
P. 145 INSTRUCTIONS 167 Headless St. Dennis so his Head does bear;

denns   frequency: 1   relative frequency: 0.0000
P. 59 A. HOUSE   11 The Beasts are by their Denns exprest:

dens. See "denns."

denton   frequency: 2   relative frequency: 0.0000
P. 61 A. HOUSE   73 Him Bishops-Hill, cr Denton may,
P. 73 A. HOUSE   466 Denton sets ope its Cataracts;

deny   frequency: 1   relative frequency: 0.0000
P. 114 BLAKE   33 Both health and profit, Fate cannot deny;

deny'd   frequency: 2   relative frequency: 0.0000
P. 85 FLECKNO   92 I whom the Pallace never has deny'd
P. 149 INSTRUCTIONS 327 And the lov'd King, and never yet deny'd,

denyed   frequency: 1   relative frequency: 0.0000
P. 191 STATUE   47 And however, she said, it could not be denyed

deny't   frequency: 1   relative frequency: 0.0000
P. 186 BRITANNIA   87 To sound damnacicn to those dare deny't.

deodands   frequency: 1   relative frequency: 0.0000
P. 22 NYMPH   17 Else Men are made their Deodands.

departure   frequency: 3   relative frequency: 0.0000
P. 34 DAPHNIS   47 Could departure not suffice,
P. 35 DAPHNIS   59 Nor to my Departure owe
P. 127 O.C.   151 But those that sadly his departure griev'd,

depend   frequency: 2   relative frequency: 0.0000
P. 124 O.C.   46 How on each other both their Fates depend.
P. 155 INSTRUCTIONS 586 And.all our hopes now on frail Chain depend:

deplore   frequency: 1   relative frequency: 0.0000
P. 204 HISTORICALL   128 Now must my Muse deplore the Nations fate,

depopulating   frequency: 1   relative frequency: 0.0000
P. 44 DAMON   74 Depopulating all the Ground,

depose   frequency: 2   relative frequency: 0.0000
P. 37 DEFINITION   16 And her Tyrannick pow'r depose.
P. 108 ANNIVERSARY   222 When to Command, thou didst thy self Depose;

deprav'd   frequency: 1   relative frequency: 0.0000
P. 174 LOYALL SCOT   120 Religion has the World tco Long deprav'd

depress   frequency: 1   relative frequency: 0.0000
P. 108 ANNIVERSARY   227 Therefore thou rather didst thy Self depress,

depriv'd   frequency: 1   relative frequency: 0.0000
P. 129 O.C.   252 Loose and depriv'd cf vigour, stretch'd along:

depth   frequency: 1   relative frequency: 0.0000
P. 11 DIALOGUE   71 Try what depth the Centre draws;

depths   frequency: 1   relative frequency: 0.0000
P. 163 INSTRUCTIONS 930 Which his hid mind did in its depths inclose.

deputy-lieutenants   frequency: 1   relative frequency: 0.0000
P. 161 INSTRUCTIONS 830 And Deputy-Lieutenants in their own.

deride   frequency: 1   relative frequency: 0.0000
P. 110 ANNIVERSARY   295 Who watch'd thy halting, and thy Fall deride,

derives   frequency: 1   relative frequency: 0.0000
P. 83 FLECKNC   4 (Though he derives himself frcm my Lord Brooke)

desarts   frequency: 1   relative frequency: 0.0000

```
        P.  26 MISTRESS        24 Desarts of vast Eternity.

descend                      frequency:   6    relative frequency: 0.0001
        P.  42 DAMON           27 To what cool Cave shall I descend,
        P.  79 A. HOUSE       662 Seems to descend with greater Care;
        P. 120 TWO SONGS       42 It is the same so you descend.
        P. 126 O.C.           136 As silent Suns to meet the Night descend.
        P. 188 BRITANNIA      132 Descend, descend, ere the Cures desperate.

descent                      frequency:   1    relative frequency: 0.0000
        P. 167 KINGS VOWES     58 Some one I will advance from mean descent,

descrey                      frequency:   1    relative frequency: 0.0000
        P. 199 DUKE            76 Let the beholder by thy Art descrey

describe                     frequency:   1    relative frequency: 0.0000
        P. 143 INSTRUCTIONS   107 Describe the Court and Country, both set right,

descry. See "descrey."

descry'd                     frequency:   2    relative frequency: 0.0000
        P. 111 ANNIVERSARY    341 When streight the Sun behind him he descry'd,
        P. 164 INSTRUCTIONS   950 And Spots unknown to the bright Star descry'd;

desert                       frequency:   3    relative frequency: 0.0000
        P.  35 DAPHNIS         80 He does through the Desert err.
        P.  72 A. HOUSE       437 Or, like the Desert Memphis Sand,
        P.  93 DR. WITTY        2 Where just desert enrolles thy honour'd Name

deserted. See "ill-deserted."

deserts                      frequency:   1    relative frequency: 0.0000
        See also "desarts."
        P.  82 A. HOUSE       764 Gulfes, Deserts, Precipices, Stone.

deserv'd                     frequency:   2    relative frequency: 0.0000
        P. 128 O.C.           208 Yet still affected most what best deserv'd.
        P. 313 CHEQUER INN     47 They all deserv'd to have been fin'd

deserve                      frequency:   2    relative frequency: 0.0000
        P.  26 MISTRESS        19 For Lady you deserve this State;
        P. 183 MADE FREE      105 It might deserve a Box and a Gold one;

deserved                     frequency:   2    relative frequency: 0.0000
        See also "deserv'd."
        P. 104 ANNIVERSARY     40 From the deserved Fate their guilty lives:
        P. 123 O.C.            19 Deserved yet an End whose ev'ry part

deserves                     frequency:   2    relative frequency: 0.0000
        P.  10 DIALOGUE        33 But since none deserves that grace,
        P.  95 HOLLAND          1 Holland, that scarce deserves the name of Land,

design                       frequency:   5    relative frequency: 0.0001
        P.  59 A. HOUSE         5 Who of his great Design in pain
        P.  89 ODE             67 So when they did design
        P. 131 PARADISE         2 In slender Book his vast Design unfold,
        P. 138 HOUSEWARMING    55 Unless all abroad he divulg'd the design,
        P. 161 INSTRUCTIONS    836 Salute them, smiling at their vain design.

design'd                     frequency:   6    relative frequency: 0.0001
        P.  56 BILL-BOROW      13 For whose excrescence ill design'd,
        P. 109 ANNIVERSARY    242 Who think those high Decrees by Man design'd.
        P. 117 BLAKE          117 Bold Stainer Leads, this Fleets design'd by
                                  fate,
        P. 137 HOUSEWARMING    11 His Omnipotence therfore much rather design'd
        P. 163 INSTRUCTIONS   928 Bennet and Coventry, as't were design'd.
        P. 205 HISTORICALL    172 Who strait design'd his Brother to supplant.

designes                     frequency:   4    relative frequency: 0.0000
        P. 106 ANNIVERSARY    110 The great Designes kept for the latter Dayes!
        P. 107 ANNIVERSARY    158 And good Designes still with their Authors
                                  lost.
        P. 112 ANNIVERSARY    354 'What Mints of Men, what Union of Designes!
        P. 169 ADVICE          54 To overthrow the Darby Hous designes,

designment                   frequency:   1    relative frequency: 0.0000
        P. 150 INSTRUCTIONS   397 But a fresh News, the great designment nips,

designs                      frequency:   3    relative frequency: 0.0000
        See also "designes."
        P.  60 A. HOUSE        41 Humility alone designs
        P.  76 A. HOUSE       549 That for his building he designs,
```

P. 187 BRITANNIA   88 Thus Heavens designs against heavens self youl
                             turn

desir'd   frequency: 2   relative frequency: 0.0000
    P. 123 O.C.   17 And so less useful where he most desir'd,
    P. 314 CHEQUER INN   57 Till to sit downe were desir'd

desire   frequency: 2   relative frequency: 0.0000
    P. 16 EYES   37 The sparkling Glance that shoots Desire,
    P. 36 DAPHNIS   94 As thy Malice could desire;

desires   frequency: 1   relative frequency: 0.0000
    P. 42 DAMON   26 Of the hot day, or hot desires.

d'eslire   frequency: 1   relative frequency: 0.0000
    P. 167 KINGS VOWES   45 And my Wench shall dispose of the Conge
                             d'eslire.

despair   frequency: 8   relative frequency: 0.0001
    See also "dispair."
    P. 28 LOVER   34 Which soon digested to Despair.
    P. 36 DEFINITION   3 It was begotten by despair
    P. 37 DEFINITION   5 Magnanimous Despair alone
    P. 99 HOLLAND   145 For now of nothing may our State despair,
    P. 120 TWO SONGS   28 With shades of deep Despair opprest.
    P. 122 TWO SONGS   30 Whose Hopes united banish our Despair.
    P. 123 TWO SONGS   46 Or who despair, now Damon does enjoy?
    P. 123 TWO SONGS   48 Whose Hopes united banish our Despair.

despairing   frequency: 1   relative frequency: 0.0000
    P. 111 ANNIVERSARY   338 And with such accents, as Despairing, mourn'd:

desperate   frequency: 3   relative frequency: 0.0000
    P. 141 INSTRUCTIONS   23 His desperate Pencil at the work did dart,
    P. 188 BRITANNIA   132 Descend, descend, ere the Cures desperate.
    P. 194 TWO HORSES   117 W. Thy Priest-ridden King turn'd desperate
                             Fighter

desperately   frequency: 1   relative frequency: 0.0000
    P. 95 HOLLAND   11 And div'd as desperately for each piece

despicable   frequency: 1   relative frequency: 0.0000
    P. 144 INSTRUCTIONS 157 To them succeeds a despicable Rout,

despight   frequency: 1   relative frequency: 0.0000
    P. 44 DAMON   82 To those that dye by Loves despight.

despise   frequency: 2   relative frequency: 0.0000
    See also "dispise."
    P. 38 PICTURE   22 And them that yield but more despise.
    P. 131 PARADISE   23 Pardon me, mighty Poet, nor despise

despising. See "dispising."

despite. See "despight."

despoiled. See "despoyl'd."

despoyl'd   frequency: 1   relative frequency: 0.0000
    P. 130 O.C.   289 Despoyl'd of mortall robes, in seas of blisse,

destil   frequency: 1   relative frequency: 0.0000
    P. 13 DROP OF DEW   37 Such did the Manna's sacred Dew destil;

destiny   frequency: 2   relative frequency: 0.0000
    P. 82 A. HOUSE   744 And make their Destiny their Choice.
    P. 124 O.C.   44 Doubling that knot which Destiny had ty'd.

destroy   frequency: 5   relative frequency: 0.0001
    P. 118 BLAKE   158 There they destroy, what had destroy'd their
                             Peace.
    P. 198 DUKE   22 Then to destroy their liberty and laws,
    P. 199 DUKE   64 And to destroy our libertyes they hope
    P. 204 HISTORICALL   117 First temper'd Poison to destroy our Lawes,
    P. 204 HISTORICALL   154 Hee'l burne a Citty or destroy a King.

destroyd   frequency: 1   relative frequency: 0.0000
    P. 200 DUKE   105 Destroyd by a false brother and false friend.

destroy'd   frequency: 3   relative frequency: 0.0000
    P. 118 BLAKE   158 There they destroy, what had destroy'd their
                                                                    Peace.

P. 118 BLAKE   161 All the Foes Ships destroy'd, by Sea or fire,
P. 158 INSTRUCTIONS   708 Ev'n London's Ashes had been then destroy'd.

destroyed. See "destroyd," "destroy'd."

destroys   frequency: 2   relative frequency: 0.0000
    P.   3 LOVELACE   13 He highest builds, who with most Art destroys,
    P. 21 SOUL & BODY 26 That to preserve, which me destroys:

destruction   frequency: 1   relative frequency: 0.0000
    P. 205 HISTORICALL 175 Hence Ruine and Destruction had ensu'd,

detect   frequency: 2   relative frequency: 0.0000
    P. 132 PARADISE   30 But to detect their Ignorance or Theft.
    P. 185 BRITANNIA   18 Till Golden Osborn cheating shall detect,

determine   frequency: 3   relative frequency: 0.0000
    P. 90 MAY'S DEATH 5 Could not determine in what place he was,
    P. 106 ANNIVERSARY 143 That 'tis the most which we determine can,
    P. 126 O.C.   138 Left to determine now his fatal Hour;

deterring   frequency: 1   relative frequency: 0.0000
    P. 132 PARADISE   32 Draws the Devout, deterring the Profane.

deterrs   frequency: 1   relative frequency: 0.0000
    P. 57 BILL-BOROW 19 Nor with the rugged path deterrs

deters. See "deterrs."

detest   frequency: 2   relative frequency: 0.0000
    P. 71 A. HOUSE   398 He draws, and does his stroke detest;
    P. 203 HISTORICALL 108 Thrice wretched they who natures Lawes detest

detracting   frequency: 1   relative frequency: 0.0000
    P. 55 EPITAPH   8 Without Detracting, her commend.

detracts   frequency: 1   relative frequency: 0.0000
    P. 130 O.C.   274 Detracts from objects than itself more high:

deum   frequency: 1   relative frequency: 0.0000
    P. 201 HISTORICALL 27 She chants Te Deum and so comes away

devices   frequency: 1   relative frequency: 0.0000
    P. 138 HOUSEWARMING 29 But while these devices he all doth compare,

devide   frequency: 3   relative frequency: 0.0000
    P. 168 ADVICE   21 This great triumvirate that can devide
    P. 175 LOYALL SCOT 131 The Nation they devide, their Curates Text.
    P. 188 BRITANNIA   142 The Stuart from the Tyrant to devide.

devides   frequency: 2   relative frequency: 0.0000
    P. 124 O.C.   70 Devides the Air, and opens all the Skyes:
    P. 178 LOYALL SCOT 255 That syllable like a Picts wall devides.

devil   frequency: 3   relative frequency: 0.0000
    See also "devill."
    P. 83 FLECKNO   22 Possest; and sure the Devil brought me there.
    P. 148 INSTRUCTIONS 294 But sure the Devil cannot cheat them thrice.
    P. 175 LOYALL SCOT 136 The Legion Devil did but one man possess:

devill   frequency: 3   relative frequency: 0.0000
    P. 191 TWO HORSES 10 Would roar like a Devill with a man in his
                          belly:
    P. 192 TWO HORSES 20 By the Devill, a Priest, a Fryar, or Nun.
    P. 192 TWO HORSES 50 Not to think his own Father is gone to the
                          Devill.

devise   frequency: 1   relative frequency: 0.0000
    P. 151 INSTRUCTIONS 413 False Terrors our believing Fears devise:

devoto   frequency: 1   relative frequency: 0.0000
    P. 63 A. HOUSE   152 'He your Devoto were, then Love.

devour   frequency: 5   relative frequency: 0.0001
    P. 27 MISTRESS   39 Rather at once our Time devour,
    P. 33 DAPHNIS   3 That must all his Hopes devour,
    P. 105 ANNIVERSARY 72 That Island, which the Sea cannot devour:
    P. 158 INSTRUCTIONS 713 So when the Fire did not enough devour,
    P. 158 INSTRUCTIONS 740 Thee, the Year's monster, let thy Dam devour.

devout   frequency: 1   relative frequency: 0.0000

```
       P. 132 PARADISE        32 Draws the Devout, deterring the Profane.

dew                            frequency:    8   relative frequency: 0.0001
       P.  12 DROP OF DEW      t On a Drop of Dew.
       P.  12 DROP OF DEW      1 See how the Orient Dew,
       P.  13 DROP OF DEW     37 Such did the Manna's sacred Dew destil;
       P.  16 EYES            28 Bath still their Eyes in their own Dew.
       P.  27 MISTRESS        34 Sits on thy skin like morning dew,
       P.  43 DAMON           43 On me the Morn her dew distills
       P.  68 A. HOUSE       295 And dries its Pan yet dank with Dew,
       P.  71 A. HOUSE       408 Rails rain for Quails, for Manna Dew.

dews                           frequency:    1   relative frequency: 0.0000
       P. 178 LOYALL SCCT    268 The morning dews and flowers Neglected grown,

diadem                         frequency:    3   relative frequency: 0.0000
       P.  14 THE CORONET     18 And mortal Glory, Heavens Diadem!
       P. 131 O.C.           315 Heav'n to this choice prepar'd a diadem,
       P. 176 LOYALL SCOT    179 Upon the English Diadem distrain'd,

dial                           frequency:    2   relative frequency: 0.0000
       See also "diall."
       P.  50 THE GARDEN      66 Of flow'rs and herbes this Dial new;
       P. 161 INSTRUCTIONS   856 No Dial more could with the Sun agree.

dialect                        frequency:    1   relative frequency: 0.0000
       P.  81 A. HOUSE       712 But as 'tis Heavens Dialect.

diall                          frequency:    1   relative frequency: 0.0000
       P. 190 STATUE          9 For a Diall the place is too unsecure

dialogue                       frequency:    6   relative frequency: 0.0001
       P.   9 DIALOGUE        t1 A DIALOGUE BETWEEN
       P.  19 THYRSIS         t A Dialogue between Thyrsis and Dorinda.
       P.  20 SOUL & BODY     t A Dialogue between the Soul and Body.
       P. 191 TWO HORSES     t1 A Dialogue between the Two Horses.
       P. 192 TWO HORSES     24 Of a Dialogue lately between the twc Horses,
       P. 192 TWO HORSES    34+ Dialcgue.

diamonds                       frequency:    1   relative frequency: 0.0000
       P. 181 MADE FREE       16 When in Diamonds and Gold

dian                           frequency:    1   relative frequency: 0.0000
       P.  68 A. HOUSE       292 Beating the Dian with its Drumms.

diana's                        frequency:    1   relative frequency: 0.0000
       P.  24 NYMPH          104 Then place it in Diana's Shrine.

dice                           frequency:    1   relative frequency: 0.0000
       P. 143 INSTRUCTIONS   111 The Dice betwixt them must the Fate divide,

dick                           frequency:    4   relative frequency: 0.0000
       P. 312 CHEQUER INN      1 I'll tell thee Dick where I have beene
       P. 313 CHEQUER INN     32 And leaner Dick then any Rake
       P. 315 CHEQUER INN    120 But who can helpe it Dick.
       P. 317 CHEQUER INN    177 Quoth Dick with Indignation

dictator                       frequency:    1   relative frequency: 0.0000
       P.  91 MAY'S DEATH     47 Or thou Dictator of the glass bestow

did                            frequency:  184   relative frequency: 0.0038

did'                           frequency:    1   relative frequency: 0.0000
       P. 137 HOUSEWARMING    22 Cf African Poultney, and Tyrian Did'

dido.  See "did'."

didst                          frequency:   13   relative frequency: 0.0002

did'st                         frequency:    1   relative frequency: 0.0000
       See also "didst."

die                            frequency:    3   relative frequency: 0.0000
       See also "dy," "dye."
       P.   4 HASTINGS        10 Needs must he die, that doth out-run his Age.
       P.  15 THE CORONET     23 And let these wither, so that he may die,
       P. 143 INSTRUCTIONS   116 Can strike the Die, and still with them goes
                                 share.

died.  See "dy'd."

dies                           frequency:    3   relative frequency: 0.0000
```

See also "dyes."
P. 34 DAPHNIS   46 More to torture him that dies?
P. 157 INSTRUCTIONS   676 That Monk looks on to see how Douglas dies.
P. 172 LOYALL SCOT   42 That Monk lookes on to see how Douglass dies.

difference   frequency: 1   relative frequency: 0.0000
P. 17 EYES   55 And each the other's difference bears;

different   frequency: 2   relative frequency: 0.0000
P. 118 BLAKE   141 Far different Motives yet, engag'd them thus,
P. 195 TWO HORSES   127 Tho Father and Sonne are different Rodds,

differing   frequency: 1   relative frequency: 0.0000
See also "diff'ring."
P. 178 LOYALL SCOT   280 My differing Crime doth more thy vertue raise

difficult   frequency: 1   relative frequency: 0.0000
P. 87 FLECKNO   164 Praise him? both difficult indeed to do

diff'ring   frequency: 1   relative frequency: 0.0000
P. 128 O.C.   218 To keep so deare, so diff'ring minds agreed?

diffus'd   frequency: 1   relative frequency: 0.0000
P. 39 THE MATCH   11 For, with one grain of them diffus'd,

dig'd   frequency: 1   relative frequency: 0.0000
P. 137 HOUSEWARMING   14 Who was dig'd up so often ere she did marry;

digested   frequency: 1   relative frequency: 0.0000
P. 28 LOVER   34 Which soon digested to Despair.

digestion   frequency: 1   relative frequency: 0.0000
P. 162 INSTRUCTIONS   874 And make a sawce fit for Whitehall's digestion:

digged. See "dig'd."

digress   frequency: 1   relative frequency: 0.0000
P. 203 HISTORICAIL   112 My Muse presum'd a litle to digress

dike-grave. See "dyke-grave."

diligence   frequency: 1   relative frequency: 0.0000
P. 144 INSTRUCTIONS   152 For Diligence renown'd, and Discipline:

dim   frequency: 1   relative frequency: 0.0000
P. 62 A. HOUSE   108 'Lest the great Bridegroom find them dim.

dimension   frequency: 1   relative frequency: 0.0000
P. 85 FLECKNO   72 With which he doth his third Dimension Stuff.

dimensions   frequency: 1   relative frequency: 0.0000
P. 59 A. HOUSE   27 In which we the Dimensions find

diminishing   frequency: 1   relative frequency: 0.0000
P. 124 O.C.   64 And so diminishing increast their ills:

dimm   frequency: 1   relative frequency: 0.0000
P. 141 INSTRUCTIONS   10 The Aly roof, with snuff of Candle dimm,

din   frequency: 1   relative frequency: 0.0000
P. 316 CHEQUER INN   145 They talkt about and made such Din

dine   frequency: 2   relative frequency: 0.0000
P. 35 DAPHNIS   72 For the Canibal to dine.
P. 112 ANNIVERSARY   352 'And ere we Dine, rase and rebuild their State.

dinner   frequency: 4   relative frequency: 0.0000
P. 84 FLECKNO   57 And Silent. Nothing now Dinner stay'd
P. 85 FLECKNO   110 Betwixt us two the Dinner to a Feast.
P. 86 FLECKNO   120 After th' Assizes dinner mild appear,
P. 86 FLECKNO   136 At ordinaries after dinner show'th,

dinners   frequency: 1   relative frequency: 0.0000
P. 193 TWO HORSES   86 Who vote with the Court for drink and for
                           Dinners.

diocesse   frequency: 2   relative frequency: 0.0000
P. 175 LOYALL SCOT   137 One Bishops fiend spirits a whole Diocesse.
P. 176 LOYALL SCOT   211 To preach in diccesse Indifferent.

dire   frequency: 2   relative frequency: 0.0000

P. 204 HISTORICALL   131 Nothing the dire Contagion can opose.
P. 205 HISTORICALL   157 Here with curst precepts and with Councels dire

direct   frequency: 2   relative frequency: 0.0000
P. 105 ANNIVERSARY   83 And each the Hand that lays him will direct,
P. 203 HISTORICALL   114 Now to the State she tends againe direct,

directs   frequency: 1   relative frequency: 0.0000
P. 57 BILL-BOROW   32 Directs, and this no less by Day.

dirted   frequency: 1   relative frequency: 0.0000
P. 314 CHEQUER INN   64 Tho they had dirted so the Roome

dis   frequency: 1   relative frequency: 0.0000
P. 177 LOYALL SCOT   226 Ev'n Father Dis tho so with Age defac'd

dis-intanfled   frequency: 1   relative frequency: 0.0000
P. 31 FAIR SINGER   8 My dis-intangled Soul it self might save,

disabled   frequency: 1   relative frequency: 0.0000
P. 159 INSTRUCTIONS 773 Who the Dutch Fleet with Storms disabled met,

disappear'd   frequency: 1   relative frequency: 0.0000
P. 163 INSTRUCTIONS 924 Through the lock'd door both of them disappear'd.

disappears   frequency: 1   relative frequency: 0.0000
P. 103 ANNIVERSARY   3 So Man, declining alwayes, disappears

disarm   frequency: 3   relative frequency: 0.0000
P. 35 DAPHNIS   73 Whilst this grief does thee disarm,
P. 38 PICTURE   30 And Roses of their thorns disarm:
P. 161 INSTRUCTIONS 844 Th' Army soon rais'd, he doth as soon disarm.

disarmed   frequency: 1   relative frequency: 0.0000
P. 42 DAMON   36 Disarmed of its teeth and sting.

disasters   frequency: 1   relative frequency: 0.0000
P. 182 MADE FREE   63 As had cancelld all former Disasters

disavowing   frequency: 1   relative frequency: 0.0000
P. 142 INSTRUCTIONS   40 That, disavowing Treaty, ask supply.

disband   frequency: 2   relative frequency: 0.0000
P. 46 AMETAS   3 Love unpaid does soon disband:
P. 185 BRITANNIA   20 Till commons votes shall cut-nose guards disband,

discern   frequency: 2   relative frequency: 0.0000
P. 96 HOLLAND   44 But who could first discern the rising Lands.
P. 178 LOYALL SCOT   270 Powders them ore till none discern their foes

discern'd   frequency: 2   relative frequency: 0.0000
P. 138 HOUSEWARMING   1 When Clarindon has discern'd beforehand,
P. 143 INSTRUCTIONS   82 Discern'd Love's Cause, and a new Flame began.

discerning   frequency: 1   relative frequency: 0.0000
P. 57 BILL-BOROW   27 Discerning further then the Cliff

discipline   frequency: 2   relative frequency: 0.0000
P. 81 A. HOUSE   723 Under the Discipline severe
P. 144 INSTRUCTIONS 152 For Diligence renown'd, and Discipline:

disclose   frequency: 1   relative frequency: 0.0000
P. 143 INSTRUCTIONS   95 And washing (lest the scent her Crime disclose)

discolour'd   frequency: 1   relative frequency: 0.0000
P. 129 O.C.   253 All wither'd, all discolour'd, pale and wan,

disconsolate   frequency: 1   relative frequency: 0.0000
P.   4 HASTINGS   7 Hastings is dead; and we, disconsolate,

discontent   frequency: 2   relative frequency: 0.0000
P. 110 ANNIVERSARY   277 What though a while they grumble discontent,
P. 159 INSTRUCTIONS 765 After this loss, to rellish discontent,

discord   frequency: 2   relative frequency: 0.0000
P. 114 BLAKE   35 The jarring Elements no discord know,
P. 177 LOYALL SCOT   249 At Babel names from pride and discord flow'd,

discourse   frequency: 1   relative frequency: 0.0000
P. 173 LOYALL SCOT   69 Noe more discourse of Scotch or English Race

discoursed   frequency: 1   relative frequency: 0.0000

    P. 192 TWO HORSES   34 Not onely discoursed but fell to disputes.

discourses   frequency: 2   relative frequency: 0.0000
    P. 58 BILL-BOROW   62 Discourses with the breathing Trees;
    P. 192 TWO HORSES   23 Why should wee not credit the publique discourses

discoursing   frequency: 1   relative frequency: 0.0000
    P. 61 A. HOUSE   94 Discoursing with the Suttle Nunns.

discovers   frequency: 1   relative frequency: 0.0000
    P. 43 DAMON   51 This Sithe of mine discovers wide

discreet   frequency: 1   relative frequency: 0.0000
    P. 124 O.C.   41 When She with Smiles serene and Words discreet

disdain   frequency: 3   relative frequency: 0.0000
    P. 143 INSTRUCTIONS 92 That to a Groom couldst humble her disdain!
    P. 186 BRITANNIA   71 And, frowning, thus with proud disdain she spoke.
    P. 201 HISTORICALL   9 Nor did he such small favours then disdain

disdain'd   frequency: 1   relative frequency: 0.0000
    P. 82 A. HOUSE   755 Aranjuez, as less, disdain'd;

disdaines   frequency: 1   relative frequency: 0.0000
    P. 172 LOYALL SCOT 37 That pretious life hee yet disdaines to save

disdainful   frequency: 2   relative frequency: 0.0000
    P. 87 FLECKNO   159 For the disdainful Poet was retir'd
    P. 145 INSTRUCTIONS 170 And follow'd Fox, but with disdainful look.

disdaining   frequency: 1   relative frequency: 0.0000
    P. 12 DROP OF DEW 32 Here disdaining, there in Love.

disdains   frequency: 2   relative frequency: 0.0000
    See also "disdaines."
    P. 81 A. HOUSE   706 Disdains to be for lesser prais'd.
    P. 157 INSTRUCTIONS 671 That precious life he yet disdains to save,

disdain'st   frequency: 1   relative frequency: 0.0000
    P. 120 TWO SONGS   19 Since thou disdain'st not then to share

disease   frequency: 3   relative frequency: 0.0000
    P. 123 O.C.   29 Streight does a slow and languishing Disease
    P. 164 INSTRUCTIONS 952 And seem his Courtiers, are but his disease.
    P. 185 BRITANNIA   49 Sauls stormy rage and Check his black disease,

diseases   frequency: 1   relative frequency: 0.0000
    P. 21 SOUL & BODY 28 Diseases, but, whats worse, the Cure:

disentangle. See "disintangle."

disentangled. See "dis-intangled."

disesteem   frequency: 1   relative frequency: 0.0000
    P. 63 A. HOUSE   150 'For whom you Heav'n should disesteem?

disesteem'd   frequency: 1   relative frequency: 0.0000
    P. 85 FLECKNO   77 Which by the Jews long hid, and Disesteem'd,

disfigured   frequency: 1   relative frequency: 0.0000
    P. 179 STOCKSMARKET 17 To see him so disfigured the herbwomen chide,

disfurnish   frequency: 1   relative frequency: 0.0000
    P. 85 FLECKNO   83 He drest, and ready to disfurnish now

disgrace   frequency: 2   relative frequency: 0.0000
    P. 142 INSTRUCTIONS 75 While she revolves, at once, Sidney's disgrace,
    P. 163 INSTRUCTIONS 926 And rising, straight on Hyde's Disgrace
                           resolves.

disguis'd   frequency: 3   relative frequency: 0.0000
    P. 10 DIALOGUE   36 The rest is all but Earth disguis'd.
    P. 14 THE CORONET 15 About the flow'rs disguis'd does fold,
    P. 187 BRITANNIA   107 Some English too disguis'd (oh shame) I spy'd

disguise   frequency: 2   relative frequency: 0.0000
    P. 123 O.C.   26 In gentle Passions should his Death disguise:
    P. 184 BRITANNIA   11 Brit: Favour'd by night, conceald by this
                           disguise,

disguising   frequency: 1   relative frequency: 0.0000

P. 172 LOYALL SCOT   13 Abruptly he began disguising art,

dish. See "chafing-dish."

disheartned   frequency: 1   relative frequency: 0.0000
    P. 108 ANNIVERSARY   208 Courage disheartned, and Religion cool'd.

dishonour'd   frequency: 1   relative frequency: 0.0000
    P. 159 INSTRUCTIONS   752 Themselves dishonour'd, and the Gods untrue:

disinherited   frequency: 1   relative frequency: 0.0000
    P. 87 FLECKNO   162 Wept bitterly as disinherited.

disintangle   frequency: 1   relative frequency: 0.0000
    P. 14 THE CORONET   21 And disintangle all his winding Snare:

disjointed   frequency: 2   relative frequency: 0.0000
    P. 66 A. HOUSE   253 While the disjointed Abbess threads
    P. 92 MAY'S DEATH   68 And though the World's disjointed Axel crack,

disliking   frequency: 1   relative frequency: 0.0000
    P. 94 DR. WITTY   35 And so disliking, that they nothing see

dismal   frequency: 6   relative frequency: 0.0001
    P. 33 DAPHNIS   2 Now is come the dismal Hour
    P. 83 FLECKNO   20 In hideous verse, he, and a dismal tone,
    P. 108 ANNIVERSARY   209 A dismal Silence through the Palace went,
    P. 111 ANNIVERSARY   331 While dismal blacks hung round the Universe,
    P. 127 O.C.   171 Since him away the dismal Tempest rent,
    P. 155 INSTRUCTIONS   596 Monk from the bank the dismal sight does view.

dismantling   frequency: 1   relative frequency: 0.0000
    P. 14 THE CORONET   7 Dismantling all the fragrant Towers

disobedient   frequency: 1   relative frequency: 0.0000
    P. 151 INSTRUCTIONS   431 Now Doleman's disobedient, and they still

disobeys   frequency: 1   relative frequency: 0.0000
    P. 150 INSTRUCTIONS   379 Where when the trawny Female disobeys,

disorder   frequency: 1   relative frequency: 0.0000
    P. 148 INSTRUCTIONS   296 Without disorder in their Intervals:

disorder'd   frequency: 2   relative frequency: 0.0000
    P. 34 DAPHNIS   34 His disorder'd Locks he tare;
    P. 146 INSTRUCTIONS   209 Late and disorder'd out the Drinkers drew;

disorders   frequency: 1   relative frequency: 0.0000
    P. 83 FLECKNO   25 Calm'd the disorders of my youthful Breast,

disowne   frequency: 1   relative frequency: 0.0000
    P. 205 HISTORICALL   165 God did renounce him and his Cause disowne

dispair   frequency: 2   relative frequency: 0.0000
    P. 87 FLECKNO   158 But saw with sad dispair that 'twas too late.
    P. 168 ADVICE   27 And of his dear Reward let none dispair,

dispatch   frequency: 1   relative frequency: 0.0000
    P. 160 INSTRUCTIONS   819 Hyde saith he hourly waits for a Dispatch;

dispence   frequency: 1   relative frequency: 0.0000
    P. 41 THE MOWER   33 Where willing Nature does to all dispence

dispensed   frequency: 1   relative frequency: 0.0000
    P. 65 A. HOUSE   198 Religion that dispensed hath;

dispers'd   frequency: 1   relative frequency: 0.0000
    P. 162 INSTRUCTIONS   886 Only dispers'd by a weak Tapers light;

disperse   frequency: 1   relative frequency: 0.0000
    P. 146 INSTRUCTIONS   224 Shall with one Breath like thistle-down
                               disperse.

dispise   frequency: 1   relative frequency: 0.0000
    P. 171 PROPHECY   45 When the Crowne's Heir shall English Men
                               dispise

dispising   frequency: 1   relative frequency: 0.0000
    P. 197 DUKE   4 Abhoring wisdome and dispising witt,

displac'd   frequency: 1   relative frequency: 0.0000

```
       P.  45 GLO-WORMS      15 For She my Mind hath so displac'd

displaid                        frequency:    1    relative frequency: 0.0000
       P.  68 A. HOUSE       310 Under their Colcurs stand displaid:

displayed.  See "displaid."

displayes                       frequency:    1    relative frequency: 0.0000
       P.  68 A. HOUSE       294 Their Silken Ensigns each displayes,

displaying                      frequency:    1    relative frequency: 0.0000
       P. 148 INSTRUCTIONS  301 The martial Standard Sands displaying, shows

displays.  See "displayes."

displease                       frequency:    2    relative frequency: 0.0000
       P.  86 FLECKNO       142 The provok't Author, whom it did displease
       P. 165 KINGS VOWES    15 But if they displease me, I will have all their
                               Lands.

displeasure                     frequency:    1    relative frequency: 0.0000
       P. 153 INSTRUCTIONS  508 Pain of Displeasure of great Clarendon.

dispose                         frequency:    5    relative frequency: 0.0001
       P.  10 DIALOGUE       42 On this I would it all dispose.
       P. 153 INSTRUCTIONS  522 And Hyde's last Project would his Place
                               dispose.
       P. 167 KINGS VOWES    45 And my Wench shall dispose of the Conge
                               d'eslire.
       P. 169 ADVICE         37 Wee in our Glorious Bacchanals dispose
       P. 315 CHEQUER INN     94 And cf more Prcvant to dispose

dispossest                      frequency:    2    relative frequency: 0.0000
       P.  67 A. HOUSE       272 Was in one instant dispossest.
       P.  96 HOLLAND        29 The Fish oft-times the Burger dispossest,

dispraise                       frequency:    1    relative frequency: 0.0000
       P. 145 INSTRUCTIONS  171 His Birth, his Youth, his Brokage all
                               dispraise,

dispute                         frequency:    6    relative frequency: 0.0001
       P.  41 THE MOWER      26 Might put the Palate in dispute.
       P.  60 A. HOUSE       37 Men will dispute how their Extent
       P. 107 ANNIVERSARY   163 That she might seem, could we the Fall dispute,
       P. 142 INSTRUCTIONS   43 Who, if the French dispute his Pow'r, from
                               thence
       P. 147 INSTRUCTIONS  282 Of Citizens and Merchants held dispute:
       P. 204 HISTORICAIL   124 This is the Savage Pimp without dispute

disputes                        frequency:    2    relative frequency: 0.0000
       P. 176 LOYALL SCCT   188 And wild disputes betwixt those heads must Grow,
       P. 192 TWO HORSES     34 Not cnely discoursed but fell to disputes.

disputing                       frequency:    1    relative frequency: 0.0000
       P.  32 MOURNING       34 Disputing not what they believe

disquiet                        frequency:    1    relative frequency: 0.0000
       P. 131 PARADISE       19 (Such as disquiet alwayes what is well,

disrespect                      frequency:    1    relative frequency: 0.0000
       P. 190 STATUE          5 'Twere to Scaramuchio too great disrespect

dissensions.  See "dissentions."

dissentions                     frequency:    1    relative frequency: 0.0000
       P. 178 LOYALL SCCT   257 Perverted serve dissentions to increase.

dissolv'd                       frequency:    1    relative frequency: 0.0000
       P.  16 EYES           30 Dissolv'd those captivating Eyes,

dissolve                        frequency:    1    relative frequency: 0.0000
       P. 144 INSTRUCTIONS  127 Should pay Land Armies, should dissolve the
                               vain

dissolved                       frequency:    1    relative frequency: 0.0000
       See also "dissolv'd."
       P.  94 DR. WITTY      18 Then Tagus, purer then dissolved snow,

dissolving                      frequency:    2    relative frequency: 0.0000
       P.  13 DROP OF DEW    39 Congeal'd on Earth: but does, dissolving, run
       P.  16 EYES           49 Now like two Clouds dissolving, drop,
```

distaff   frequency: 1   relative frequency: 0.0000
    P. 150 INSTRUCTIONS   385 The Distaff knocks, the Grains from Kettle
                             fly,

distance   frequency: 3   relative frequency: 0.0000
    P. 16 EYES   50 And at each Tear in distance stop:
    P. 173 LOYALL SCOT   66 Unite our distance, fill the breaches old?
    P. 176 LOYALL SCOT   200 Hark! tho' at such a Distance what a Noise

distant   frequency: 1   relative frequency: 0.0000
    P. 37 DEFINITION   18 Us as the distant Poles have plac'd,

distemper   frequency: 1   relative frequency: 0.0000
    P. 83 FLECKNO   28 The last distemper of the sober Brain,

distill. See "destil."

distills   frequency: 2   relative frequency: 0.0000
    P. 15 EYES   22 Distills the World with Chymick Bay;
    P. 43 DAMON   43 On me the Morn her dew distills

distinct   frequency: 1   relative frequency: 0.0000
    P. 164 INSTRUCTIONS   971 The Kingdom from the Crown distinct would see,

distracted   frequency: 1   relative frequency: 0.0000
    P. 34 DAPHNIS   39 Looks distracted back in hast,

distrain'd   frequency: 1   relative frequency: 0.0000
    P. 176 LOYALL SCOT   179 Upon the English Diadem distrain'd,

distraught   frequency: 1   relative frequency: 0.0000
    P. 156 INSTRUCTIONS   622 With present shame compar'd, his mind distraught.

distress   frequency: 1   relative frequency: 0.0000
    P. 162 INSTRUCTICNS   902 Whose Beauty greater seem'd by her distress;

distrest   frequency: 3   relative frequency: 0.0000
    P. 60 A. HOUSE   53 More by his Magnitude distrest,
    P. 138 HOUSEWARMING   39 He car'd not though Egypt's Ten Plagues us
                             distrest,
    P. 176 LOYALL SCOT   191 What Brittain was, betwixt two Kings distrest.

distrust   frequency: 2   relative frequency: 0.0000
    P. 151 INSTRUCTIONS   421 Each does the other blame, and all distrust;
    P. 183 MADE FREE   82 Yet I doe not distrust

distrusts   frequency: 1   relative frequency: 0.0000
    P. 143 INSTRUCTIONS   88 Her looks, and oft-try'd Beauty now distrusts:

disturbs   frequency: 1   relative frequency: 0.0000
    P. 176 LOYALL SCOT   201 Shattering the silent Air disturbs our Joys!

disuse   frequency: 1   relative frequency: 0.0000
    P. 99 HOLLAND   143 Unless our Senate, lest their Youth disuse,

div'd   frequency: 1   relative frequency: 0.0000
    P. 95 HOLLAND   11 And div'd as desperately for each piece

dive   frequency: 2   relative frequency: 0.0000
    P. 70 A. HOUSE   377 To see Men through this Meadow Dive,
    P. 158 INSTRUCTIONS   702 But that the Ships themselves were taught to
                             dive:

divide   frequency: 7   relative frequency: 0.0001
    See also "devide."
    P. 71 A. HOUSE   391 To them the Grassy Deeps divide,
    P. 78 A. HOUSE   620 The Trees before their Lord divide;
    P. 87 ODE   16 His fiery way divide.
    P. 92 MAY'S DEATH   88 As th' Eagles Plumes from other birds divide.
    P. 105 ANNIVERSARY   91 And they, whose Nature leads them to divide,
    P. 143 INSTRUCTIONS   111 The Dice betwixt them must the Fate divide,
    P. 146 INSTRUCTIONS   242 But oftner did among themselves divide.

divided   frequency: 4   relative frequency: 0.0000
    P. 12 DROP OF DEW   14 Because so long divided from the Sphear.
    P. 19 THYRSIS   2 And shut up our divided Lids,
    P. 150 INSTRUCTIONS   404 The next divided, and the third we've none.
    P. 159 INSTRUCTIONS   776 The Fleet divided? Writ for Rupert? Pett.

divides. See "devides."

divin'd   frequency: 1   relative frequency: 0.0000

P. 163 INSTRUCTIONS   906 And be Divin'd 'twas England or the Peace.

divine   frequency: 13   relative frequency: 0.0002
    P.   9 DIALOGUE   7 Now, if thou bee'st that thing Divine,
    P.   37 DEFINITION   6 Could show me so divine a thing,
    P.   70 A. HOUSE   359 But Flowrs eternal, and divine,
    P.   82 A. HOUSE   737 Hence She with Graces more divine
    P.   83 FLECKNO   6 Of the sad Pelican; Subject divine
    P. 104 ANNIVERSARY   38 But with Astrolcgers divine, and Jove,
    P. 132 PARADISE   33 And things divine thou treatst of in such state
    P. 140 HOUSEWARMING   99 And to handsel his Altar and Nostrils divine,
    P. 149 INSTRUCTIONS   356 And sits in State Divine like Jove the
                               fulminant!
    P. 157 INSTRUCTIONS   684 His burning Locks adorn his Face Divine.
    P. 173 LOYALL SCOT   50 His burning Locks Adorn his face divine.
    P. 191 TWO HORSES   15 All Popish beleivers think something divine,
    P. 195 TWO HORSES   157 Ch. But canst thou Divine when things shall be
                               mended?

divines   frequency: 2   relative frequency: 0.0000
    P.   76 A. HOUSE   572 The Bird upon the Eough divines;
    P. 175 LOYALL SCOT   134 All Mischeifs Mculded by those state divines:

divining   frequency: 1   relative frequency: 0.0000
    P.   30 THE GALLERY   29 Divining thence, with horrid Care,

divinum   frequency: 1   relative frequency: 0.0000
    P. 176 LOYALL SCOT   205 And plead their Jus Divinum tho' in Hell.

divorce   frequency: 1   relative frequency: 0.0000
    P.   66 A. HOUSE   236 To hinder the unjust Divorce.

divulg'd   frequency: 1   relative frequency: 0.0000
    P. 138 HOUSEWARMING   55 Unless all abroad he divulg'd the design,

do   frequency: 101   relative frequency: 0.0021
    See also "doe," "out-do," "out-doe."

doctor   frequency: 2   relative frequency: 0.0000
    P.   93 DR. WITTY   t1 To his worthy Friend Doctor Witty upon his
    P.   94 DR. WITTY   29 Women must not teach here: the Doctor doth

doe   frequency: 19   relative frequency: 0.0003
    P. 166 KINGS VOWES   21 But if they shculd beat me, I will doe what they
                               please.
    P. 166 KINGS VOWES   35 I will have a fine Junto to doe what I will,
    P. 175 LOYALL SCOT   152 Noe Wonder if the Crthodox doe Bleed,
    P. 175 LOYALL SCOT   164 Abbot one Buck, but he shot many a Doe,
    P. 176 LOYALL SCOT   172 Doe but their Pyebald Lordships once Uncase
    P. 176 LOYALL SCOT   196 Kings head saith this, But Bishops head that
                               doe.
    P. 177 LOYALL SCOT   239 The good will kravely, bad will basely doe;
    P. 181 MADE FREE   2 To the King doe present
    P. 183 MADE FREE   82 Yet I doe not distrust
    P. 186 BRITANNIA   74 Doe Monarchs rise by vertues or the sword?
    P. 190 STATUE   19 What a doe with the Kings and the Statues is
                               here:
    P. 190 STATUE   34 Such things you should never or Suddainly doe.
    P. 191 STATUE   48 That a Monarch cf Gingerbread would doe as
                               well.
    P. 191 TWO HORSES   6 Have spoken as plainly as men doe with Tongues:
    P. 192 TWO HORSES   28 For the two mighty Monarchs that dce now
                               bestride 'um.
    P. 198 DUKE   26 And thinke a prince oth blood can ere doe Ill?
    P. 200 DUKE   107 What all thy subjects doe each minute feare:
    P. 204 HISTORICALL   153 At his Command Mack will doe any thing,
    P. 205 HISTORICALL   163 A Priest should dce it, from whose sacred stroke

does   frequency: 156   relative frequency: 0.0032
    See also "dos," "do's."

doeth   frequency: 1   relative frequency: 0.0000

dog   frequency: 4   relative frequency: 0.0000
    P.   19 THYRSIS   23 No need of Dog to fetch our stray,
    P.   42 DAMON   21 Which made the Dog, and makes the Sun
    P. 141 INSTRUCTIONS   26 And he sat smiling how his Dog did grinn.
    P. 144 INSTRUCTIONS   142 Her, of a female Harpy, in Dog Days:

dog-star   frequency: 1   relative frequency: 0.0000
    P.   42 DAMON   18 Nor Dog-star so inflame's the dayes.

dogged   frequency: 1   relative frequency: 0.0000
   P. 194 TWO HORSES   89 Ch. But thanks to the whores who have made the
                              King Dogged

doggs   frequency: 1   relative frequency: 0.0000
   P. 188 BRITANNIA   144 With the Doggs bloud his gentle kind convey

dogs. See "doggs."

doing   frequency: 1   relative frequency: 0.0000

doleful   frequency: 2   relative frequency: 0.0000
   P. 111 ANNIVERSARY   335 His weeping Eyes the doleful Vigils keep,
   P. 157 INSTRUCTIONS 697 Each doleful day still with fresh loss returns;

doleman   frequency: 1   relative frequency: 0.0000
   P. 315 CHEQUER INN   110 Throgmorton, Nevill, Doleman were

doleman's   frequency: 1   relative frequency: 0.0000
   P. 151 INSTRUCTIONS 431 Now Doleman's disobedient, and they still

domestick   frequency: 2   relative frequency: 0.0000
   P. 81 A. HOUSE   722 In a Domestick Heaven nurst,
   P. 150 INSTRUCTIONS 388 Better than Law, Domestick Crimes to tame

domineer   frequency: 1   relative frequency: 0.0000
   P. 99 HOLLAND   152 Vainly in Hell let Pluto domineer.

dominion   frequency: 1   relative frequency: 0.0000
   P. 193 TWO HORSES   61 Ch. That of four Seas dominion and Guarding

don   frequency: 1   relative frequency: 0.0000

donatives   frequency: 1   relative frequency: 0.0000
   P. 32 MOURNING   27 But casts abroad these Donatives,

done   frequency: 7   relative frequency: 0.0001
   See also "don."

doome   frequency: 3   relative frequency: 0.0000
   P. 130 O.C.   299 For we, since thou art gone, with heavy doome,
   P. 170 PROPHECY   1 The blood of the Just London's firm Doome
                              shall fix
   P. 195 TWO HORSES   147 If e're he be King I know Brittains Doome;

door   frequency: 5   relative frequency: 0.0001
   See also "chamber-door," "doore."
   P. 61 A. HOUSE   66 Adorns without the open Door:
   P. 83 FLECKNO   13 Save that th' ingenious Door did as you come
   P. 86 FLECKNO   127 And so the Pelican at his door hung
   P. 163 INSTRUCTIONS 909 With Canon, Trumpets, Drums, his door
                              surround,
   P. 163 INSTRUCTIONS 924 Through the lock'd door both of them disappear'd.

doore   frequency: 3   relative frequency: 0.0000
   P. 192 TWO HORSES   42 And the King's Chiefe minister holding the
                              doore:
   P. 193 TWO HORSES   56 Lord a Mercy and a Cross might be set on the
                              doore;
   P. 315 CHEQUER INN   124 And wisely lodging at next Doore

doors   frequency: 2   relative frequency: 0.0000
   P. 59 A. HOUSE   31 As practising, in doors so strait,
   P. 150 INSTRUCTIONS 370 Like Slaves, shall beg for Peace at Hollands
                              doors.

dores   frequency: 1   relative frequency: 0.0000
   P. 170 PROPHECY   14 And Checquer dores shall shut up Lombard
                              street,

dorinda   frequency: 11   relative frequency: 0.0002
   P.   19 THYRSIS   t A Dialogue between Thyrsis and Dorinda.
   P.   19 THYRSIS   1 Dorinda. When Death, shall part us from these
                              Kids,
   P.   19 THYRSIS   5 Thyrsis. To the Elizium: (Dorinda) oh where
                              i'st?
   P.   19 THYRSIS   7 Dorinda. I know no way, but one, our home;
   P.   19 THYRSIS   13 Dorinda. There Birds may nest, but how can I,
   P.   19 THYRSIS   19 Dorinda. But in Elizium how do they
   P.   20 THYRSIS   27 Dorinda. Oh sweet! oh sweet! How I my future
                              state
   P.   20 THYRSIS   39 Dorinda. Ah me, ah me. (Thyrsis.) Dorinda, why
                              do'st Cry?

P. 20 THYRSIS	40	Dorinda. I'm sick, I'm sick, and fain would dye:
P. 36 DAPHNIS	103	This night for Dorinda kept;

dos   frequency: 5   relative frequency: 0.0001

do's   frequency: 1   relative frequency: 0.0000
　　P. 198 DUKE   39 Do's now in popery with his Master joyne.

dost   frequency: 10   relative frequency: 0.0002

do'st   frequency: 1   relative frequency: 0.0000
　　See also "dost."

do't   frequency: 1   relative frequency: 0.0000

doth   frequency: 50   relative frequency: 0.0010
　　See also "doeth."

doting   frequency: 1   relative frequency: 0.0000
　　P. 199 DUKE   65 By Irish fools and by a doting pope.

double   frequency: 10   relative frequency: 0.0002
　　P. 16 EYES   45 Ope then mine Eyes your double Sluice,
　　P. 20 SOUL & BODY   10 In a vain Head, and double Heart.
　　P. 40 THE MATCH   25 He fortifi'd the double Gate,
　　P. 40 THE MOWER   9 The Pink grew then as double as his Mind;
　　P. 74 A. HOUSE   489 The double Wood of ancient Stocks
　　P. 90 MAY'S DEATH   17 But how a double headed Vulture Eats,
　　P. 112 ANNIVERSARY   374 'Through double Oak, <and> lin'd with treble Brass;
　　P. 120 TWO SONGS   21 Rather restrain these double Seas,
　　P. 129 O.C.   234 It seem'd Mars broke through Janus' double gate;
　　P. 315 CHEQUER INN   95 Had sowd on too his double Hose

doubled   frequency: 2   relative frequency: 0.0000
　　P. 31 MOURNING   5 Her Eyes confus'd, and doubled ore,
　　P. 124 O.C.   57 Each Groan he doubled and each Sigh he sigh'd,

doubles   frequency: 1   relative frequency: 0.0000
　　P. 110 ANNIVERSARY   276 And doubles back unto the safer Main.

doublet   frequency: 1   relative frequency: 0.0000
　　P. 201 HISTORICALL   11 In a slasht doublet then he came to shoare,

doubling   frequency: 1   relative frequency: 0.0000
　　P. 124 O.C.   44 Doubling that knot which Destiny had ty'd.

doubt   frequency: 4   relative frequency: 0.0000
　　P. 78 A. HOUSE   637 Where all things gaze themselves, and doubt
　　P. 85 FLECKNO   85 No empty place for complementing doubt,
　　P. 117 BLAKE   109 Of Speedy Victory let no man doubt,
　　P. 158 INSTRUCTIONS 732 Viewing her strength, they yet their Conquest doubt.

doubtful   frequency: 2   relative frequency: 0.0000
　　P. 25 YOUNG LOVE   21 So we win of doubtful Fate;
　　P. 28 LOVER   39 And languished with doubtful Breath,

doubtfully   frequency: 1   relative frequency: 0.0000
　　P. 90 MAY'S DEATH   9 At last while doubtfully he all compares,

doubtless   frequency: 1   relative frequency: 0.0000
　　P. 114 BLAKE   25 One of which doubtless is by Nature blest

douglas   frequency: 4   relative frequency: 0.0000
　　See also "douglass."
　　P. 156 INSTRUCTIONS 649 Not so brave Douglas; on whose lovely chin
　　P. 157 INSTRUCTIONS 676 That Monk looks on to see how Douglas dies.
　　P. 171 LOYALL SCOT   t2 Upon The occasion of the death of Captain Douglas burnt in one
　　P. 178 LOYALL SCOT   282 Here Douglas smileing said hee did Intend

douglass   frequency: 3   relative frequency: 0.0000
　　P. 171 LOYALL SCOT   2 Saw Douglass Marching on the Elisian Glades,
　　P. 172 LOYALL SCOT   15 Not so brave Douglass, on whose Lovely Chin
　　P. 172 LOYALL SCOT   42 That Monk lookes on to see how Douglass dies.

dover   frequency: 2   relative frequency: 0.0000

```
        P.  168 ADVICE        19 Our Pig-eyed Duncomb in his Dover Fashion
        P.  202 HISTORICALL   70 As they att Athens, we att Dover meet,

doves                            frequency:    1     relative frequency: 0.0000
        See also "stock-doves."
        P.   29 THE GALLERY   23 And, at thy Feet, the wooing Doves

down                             frequency:   33     relative frequency: 0.0006
        See also "downe," "thistle-down."
        P.   16 EYES          51 Now like two Fountains trickle down:
        P.   26 MISTRESS       3 We would sit down, and think which way
        P.   43 DAMON         69 And with my Sythe cut down the Grass,
        P.   44 DAMON         79 And there among the Grass fell down,
        P.   63 A. HOUSE     142 'On you the Lillies show'ring down:
        P.   75 A. HOUSE     517 But highest Oakes stoop down to hear,
        P.   78 A. HOUSE     624 There at the Ev'ning stake me down.
        P.   85 FLECKNO      106 Went down, as I him follow'd to obey.
        P.   89 ODE           64 Down as upon a Bed.
        P.   94 DR. WITTY     28 Down into Error with the Vulgar tide;
        P.   97 HOLLAND       65 More pregnant then their Marg'ret, that laid
                                 down
        P.  109 ANNIVERSARY  236 And down at last thou pow'rdst the fertile
                                 Storm;
        P.  109 ANNIVERSARY  247 Here pulling down, and there erecting New,
        P.  142 INSTRUCTIONS  51 She, nak'd, can Archimedes self put down,
        P.  143 INSTRUCTIONS  94 Nor scorns to rub him down with those fair
                                 Hands;
        P.  144 INSTRUCTIONS 138 Else swallows all down her indented maw.
        P.  147 INSTRUCTIONS 278 And the faint sweat trickled down Temples
                                 Brows.
        P.  155 INSTRUCTIONS 597 Our feather'd Gallants, which came down that day
        P.  156 INSTRUCTIONS 650 The early Down but newly did begin;
        P.  157 INSTRUCTIONS 687 Down on the Deck he laid himself, and dy'd,
        P.  157 INSTRUCTIONS 691 His Ship burns down, and with his Relicks
                                 sinks,
        P.  161 INSTRUCTIONS 826 Let them come up so to go down agen.
        P.  163 INSTRUCTIONS 919 Harry sits down, and in his open side
        P.  172 LOYALL SCOT   16 The Early down but newly did begin,
        P.  173 LOYALL SCOT   53 Down on the Deck hee laid him down and dy'd
        P.  173 LOYALL SCOT   57 The ship burnes down and with his reliques sinks,
        P.  173 LOYALL SCOT   68 Galloping down Clos'd up the Gaping Cave.
        P.  173 LOYALL SCOT   75 Prick down the point whoever has the Art
        P.  187 BRITANNIA    110 'Down with that common Magna Charta whore.'
        P.  189 BRITANNIA    189 Her true Crusado shall at last pull down
        P.  192 TWO HORSES    41 To see Church and state bow down to a whore
        P.  204 HISTORICALL  140 T' hunt down 's Prey and hope to master all.

downe                            frequency:    3     relative frequency: 0.0000
        P.  202 HISTORICALL   50 Burnt downe the Pallace of Persepolis.
        P.  314 CHEQUER INN   57 Till to sit downe were desir'd
        P.  316 CHEQUER INN  154 But downe the Visick Bottle threw

downfall                         frequency:    1     relative frequency: 0.0000
        P.  196 TWO HORSES   169 Which Monarchys downfall portended much more

downs                            frequency:    1     relative frequency: 0.0000
        P.  130 O.C.         284 While sheep delight the grassy downs to pick,

downy                            frequency:    2     relative frequency: 0.0000
        P.    9 DIALOGUE      19 On these downy Pillows lye,
        P.  125 O.C.          81 No downy breast did ere so gently beat,

drag. See "dragg."

dragg                            frequency:    1     relative frequency: 0.0000
        P.  181 MADE FREE      6 Of the whole Guild-Hall Teame to dragg it.

dragon                           frequency:    1     relative frequency: 0.0000
        P.  176 LOYALL SCOT  177 Like Snake that Swallowes toad doth Dragon
                                 swell.

dragons                          frequency:    1     relative frequency: 0.0000
        P.  107 ANNIVERSARY  151 And Stars still fall, and still the Dragons
                                 Tail

drain'd                          frequency:    1     relative frequency: 0.0000
        P.  124 O.C.          36 Which while she drain'd of Milk she fill'd with
                                 Love.

draine                           frequency:    1     relative frequency: 0.0000
        P.  317 CHEQUER INN  191 That suck and draine thus ev'ry Purse
```

draines   frequency: 1   relative frequency: 0.0000
     P. 96 HOLLAND   42 So rules among the drowned he that draines.

drains. See "draines."

drake   frequency: 2   relative frequency: 0.0000
     P. 96 HOLLAND   36 Would throw their Land away at Duck and Drake.
     P. 189 BRITANNIA   174 Blake, Candish, Drake, (men void of slavish
                              fears)

drakes   frequency: 1   relative frequency: 0.0000
     P. 167 KINGS VOWES   53 Where the Ducks and the Drakes may their
                              freedomes enjoy,

draught   frequency: 1   relative frequency: 0.0000
     P. 172 LOYALL SCOT   12 And of wise Lethe hee had took a draught.

drave   frequency: 1   relative frequency: 0.0000
     P. 27 LOVER   14 Upon the Rock his Mother drave;

draw   frequency: 28   relative frequency: 0.0005
     P.   5 HASTINGS   42 But draw their Veils, and their pure Beams
                              reveal:
     P. 15 EYES   20 No Hony, but these Tears could draw.
     P. 56 BILL-BOROW   5 Nor softest Pensel draw a Brow
     P. 64 A. HOUSE   162 'Shall draw Heav'n nearer, raise us higher.
     P. 64 A. HOUSE   181 'Balms for the griv'd we draw; and Pasts
     P. 85 FLECKNO   95 He gathring fury still made sign to draw;
     P. 105 ANNIVERSARY   88 Draw the Circumf'rence of the publique Wall;
     P. 115 BLAKE   65 But whilst I draw that Scene, where you ere
                              long,
     P. 141 INSTRUCTIONS   14 As th' Indians, draw our Luxury in Plumes.
     P. 142 INSTRUCTIONS   39 Draw no Commission lest the Court should lye,
     P. 142 INSTRUCTIONS   67 Or how a mortal Poyson she may draw,
     P. 143 INSTRUCTIONS   105 Draw next a Pair of Tables op'ning, then
     P. 144 INSTRUCTIONS   148 (And Painter, wanting other, draw this Fight.)
     P. 145 INSTRUCTIONS   199 Sir Frederick and Sir Salomon draw Lotts
     P. 156 INSTRUCTIONS   632 Sweet Painter draw his Picture while I write.
     P. 156 INSTRUCTIONS   644 Pregnant with Sulphur, to him nearer draw
     P. 162 INSTRUCTIONS   863 Dear Painter, draw this Speaker to the foot:
     P. 163 INSTRUCTIONS   910 But let some other Painter draw the sound:
     P. 168 ADVICE   2 And draw me in one Scene London and Rome,
     P. 168 ADVICE   13 Where draw Sir Edward mounted on his throne,
     P. 169 ADVICE   40 Draw me a Champion mounted on his steed,
     P. 169 ADVICE   47 Draw our Olimpia next in Councell Sate
     P. 183 MADE FREE   88 How you hugg it and draw,
     P. 197 DUKE   t Advice to a Painter to draw the Duke by.
     P. 198 DUKE   7 First draw him falling prostrate to the South,
     P. 198 DUKE   36 Next, Painter, draw his Mordant by his side,
     P. 198 DUKE   40 Then draw the princesse with her golden locks,
     P. 200 DUKE   86 Next, Painter, draw the Rabble of the plott,

drawen   frequency: 1   relative frequency: 0.0000
     P. 73 A. HOUSE   458 A Landskip drawen in Looking-Glass.

drawers   frequency: 1   relative frequency: 0.0000
     P. 143 INSTRUCTIONS   81 She through her Lacquies Drawers as he ran,

drawes   frequency: 1   relative frequency: 0.0000
     P. 92 MAY'S DEATH   65 Then is the Poets time, 'tis then he drawes,

drawn   frequency: 3   relative frequency: 0.0000
     See also "drawen," "drawne."
     P. 29 THE GALLERY   17 But, on the other side, th' art drawn
     P. 107 ANNIVERSARY   172 Drawn from the Sheath of lying Prophecies;
     P. 125 O.C.   76 Had drawn such staines as were not to be cur'd.

drawne   frequency: 2   relative frequency: 0.0000
     P.   3 LOVELACE   4 Our wits have drawne th' infection of our times.
     P. 205 HISTORICALL   177 Had not Almighty Providence drawne neere,

draws   frequency: 10   relative frequency: 0.0002
     See also "drawes."
     P. 11 DIALOGUE   71 Try what depth the Centre draws;
     P. 66 A. HOUSE   229 Sometimes resolv'd his Sword he draws,
     P. 71 A. HOUSE   398 He draws, and does his stroke detest;
     P. 75 A. HOUSE   519 The Thorn, lest it should hurt her, draws
     P. 80 A. HOUSE   684 Draws through the Skie, nor Star new-slain.
     P. 80 A. HOUSE   704 The Wood about her draws a Skreen.
     P. 86 FLECKNO   123 And draws out of the black box of his Breast
     P. 132 PARADISE   32 Draws the Devout, deterring the Profane.

```
        P. 160 INSTRUCTIONS   807 But now draws near the Parliament's return;
        P. 195 TWO HORSES     159 Ch. Then, England, Rejoyce, thy Redemption
                                  draws nigh;

drayman's                        frequency:   1   relative frequency: 0.0000
        P. 141 INSTRUCTIONS    33 Paint him with Drayman's Shoulders, butchers
                                  Mien,

dread                            frequency:   5   relative frequency: 0.0001
        P.  91 MAY'S DEATH     35 At whose dread Whisk Virgil himself does quake,
        P. 112 ANNIVERSARY    377 'Him, all the Day, Him, in late Nights I
                                  dread,
        P. 145 INSTRUCTIONS   163 Still his Hook-shoulder seems the blow to dread,
        P. 149 INSTRUCTIONS   348 The Comet dread, and Earth and Heaven burns.
        P. 155 INSTRUCTIONS   579 The conscious Stag, so once the Forests dread,

dreaded                          frequency:   1   relative frequency: 0.0000
        P. 114 BLAKE           19 They dreaded to behold, Least the Sun's light,

dreadful                         frequency:   2   relative frequency: 0.0000
        See also "dreadfull."
        P. 118 BLAKE          138 Two dreadful Navies there at Anchor Fight.
        P. 126 O.C.           111 He unconcern'd the dreadful passage crost;

dreadfull                        frequency:   1   relative frequency: 0.0000
        P. 202 HISTORICALL     43 The dreadfull Victor tooke his soft repose,

dream                            frequency:   2   relative frequency: 0.0000
        P.  32 MOURNING        29 How wide they dream! The Indian Slaves
        P. 176 LOYALL SCOT    194 They, tho' nce poets, on Parnassus dream,

dregs                            frequency:   1   relative frequency: 0.0000
        P. 128 O.C.           229 And we death's refuse nature's dregs confin'd

drench'd                         frequency:   1   relative frequency: 0.0000
        P.  16 EYES            38 Drench'd in these Waves, does lose it fire.

dress                            frequency:   4   relative frequency: 0.0000
        P.  29 THE GALLERY      9 Here Thou art painted in the Dress
        P.  64 A. HOUSE       179 'Flow'rs dress the Altars; for the Clothes,
        P. 112 ANNIVERSARY    351 'Yet rig a Navy while we dress us late;
        P. 175 LOYALL SCOT    170 A Congruous Dress they to themselves Adapt,

drest                            frequency:   9   relative frequency: 0.0001
        P.  28 LOVER           55 And all he saies, a Lover drest
        P.  84 FLECKNO         59 I mean till he were drest: for else so thin
        P.  85 FLECKNO         83 He drest, and ready to disfurnish now
        P.  86 FLECKNO        124 Ten quire of paper in which he was drest.
        P. 146 INSTRUCTIONS   216 That 'twas so long before he could be drest.
        P. 161 INSTRUCTIONS   854 Expects as at a Play till Turner's drest.
        P. 167 KINGS VOWES     50 Tho' not rule like the Turk yet I will be so
                                  drest,
        P. 184 BRITANNIA       10 Ah! mighty Queen, why so unsemly drest?
        P. 314 CHEQUER INN     61 The Lady drest like any Bride

drew                             frequency:   6   relative frequency: 0.0001
        P.  39 THE MATCH       13 But likeness soon together drew
        P.  50 THE GARDEN      65 How well the skilful Gardner drew
        P.  59 A. HOUSE         3 That unto Caves the Quarries drew,
        P. 146 INSTRUCTIONS   209 Late and disorder'd out the Drinkers drew;
        P. 161 INSTRUCTIONS   841 Not so, quoth Tomkins; and straight drew his
                                  Tongue,
        P. 187 BRITANNIA      112 And from my Charles to a base Goal me drew,

dried.  See "dry'd."

dries                            frequency:   1   relative frequency: 0.0000
        P.  68 A. HOUSE       295 And dries its Pan yet dank with Dew,

drink                            frequency:   6   relative frequency: 0.0001
        P.  20 THYRSIS         47 In wine, and drink on't even till we weep,
        P. 115 BLAKE           54 Which of the Gods the fancied drink exceeds;
        P. 193 TWO HORSES      86 Who vote with the Court for drink and for
                                  Dinners.
        P. 196 TWO HORSES     181 Let the Citty drink Coffee and Quietly groan
        P. 196 TWO HORSES     183 'Tis wine and Strong drink makes tumults
                                  increase;
        P. 196 TWO HORSES     185 No Quarrells or oathes amongst those that drink
                                  'um;

drinkers                         frequency:   1   relative frequency: 0.0000
```

```
          P. 146 INSTRUCTIONS   209 Late and disorder'd out the Drinkers drew;

drinking                          frequency:    1    relative frequency: 0.0000
          P. 181 MADE FREE        36 Of Revelling, Drinking and Whoreing.

drinks                            frequency:    2    relative frequency: 0.0000
          P. 157 INSTRUCTIONS   692 And the sad Stream beneath his Ashes drinks.
          P. 173 LOYALL SCOT     58 And the sad stream beneath his Ashes drinks.

drive                             frequency:    4    relative frequency: 0.0000
          P.  18 CLORINDA         1 C. Damon come drive thy flocks this way.
          P.  37 DEFINITION      11 But Fate does Iron wedges drive
          P.  38 PICTURE         20 Ere, with their glancing wheels, they drive
          P. 186 BRITANNIA       81 Should drive them from their proud Celestiall
                                    seat,

drives                            frequency:    1    relative frequency: 0.0000
          P. 154 INSTRUCTIONS   555 And gentle Gales them steer, and Heaven drives,

driving                           frequency:    1    relative frequency: 0.0000
          P. 140 HOUSEWARMING   110 Lest with driving too far his Tallow impair;

droll                             frequency:    1    relative frequency: 0.0000
          P. 203 HISTORICALL     91 Droll on their God but a much duller way:

drone                             frequency:    1    relative frequency: 0.0000
          P. 178 LOYALL SCOT    269 The hive a comb case, every bee a drone,

drooping                          frequency:    1    relative frequency: 0.0000
          P.   5 HASTINGS        43 Onely they drooping Hymeneus note,

drop                              frequency:    6    relative frequency: 0.0001
        See also "droppe."
          P.  12 DROP OF DEW      t On a Drop of Dew.
          P.  12 DROP OF DEW     19 So the Soul, that Drop, that Ray
          P.  16 EYES            49 Now like two Clouds dissolving, drop,
          P.  49 THE GARDEN      34 Ripe Apples drop about my head;
          P.  75 A. HOUSE       534 The eldest of its young lets drop,
          P. 150 INSTRUCTIONS   408 And on Pasiphae's Tomb to drop a Bead.

droppe                            frequency:    1    relative frequency: 0.0000
          P. 200 DUKE           108 A droppe of poisone or a papish knife

dropping                          frequency:    2    relative frequency: 0.0000
          P.  24 NYMPH           96 Sad, slowly dropping like a Gumme.
          P.  24 NYMPH          117 Until my Tears, still dropping, wear

drops                             frequency:    2    relative frequency: 0.0000
          P.  32 MOURNING        10 Slow drops unty themselves away;
          P. 125 O.C.            97 Trickling in watry drops, whose flowing shape

dropt                             frequency:    1    relative frequency: 0.0000
          P. 185 BRITANNIA       46 How, like ripe fruit, she dropt from of the
                                    Throne

drought                           frequency:    1    relative frequency: 0.0000
          P.  18 CLORINDA        16 Or slake its Drought? C. What is't you mean?

drove                             frequency:    1    relative frequency: 0.0000
        See also "drave."
          P.  98 HOLLAND        124 A wholesome Danger drove us to our Ports.

drown                             frequency:    4    relative frequency: 0.0000
          P.  16 EYES            52 Now like two floods o'return and drown.
          P.  25 YOUNG LOVE      28 So all Forraign Claims to drown,
          P.  78 A. HOUSE       623 But, where the Floods did lately drown,
          P. 158 INSTRUCTIONS   712 Our Merchant-men, lest they should burn, we
                                    drown.

drown'd                           frequency:    2    relative frequency: 0.0000
          P.  32 MOURNING        14 Her Eyes have so her Bosome drown'd,
          P.  73 A. HOUSE       471 The River in it self is drown'd,

drowned                           frequency:    1    relative frequency: 0.0000
        See also "drown'd."
          P.  96 HOLLAND         42 So rules among the drowned he that draines.

drowsie                           frequency:    1    relative frequency: 0.0000
          P.  68 A. HOUSE       293 Then Flow'rs their drowsie Eylids raise,

drowsy.  See "drowsie."

drumming                          frequency:    1    relative frequency: 0.0000
```

P. 20 SOUL & BODY   6 Deaf with the drumming of an Ear.

drumms   frequency: 1   relative frequency: 0.0000
    P. 68 A. HOUSE   292 Beating the Dian with its Drumms.

drums   frequency: 2   relative frequency: 0.0000
    See also "drumms."
    P. 163 INSTRUCTIONS   909 With Canon, Trumpets, Drums, his door
                               surround,
    P. 163 INSTRUCTIONS   914 And finds the Drums Lewis's March did beat.

drunk   frequency: 2   relative frequency: 0.0000
    See also "drunke."
    P. 90 MAY'S DEATH   1 As one put drunk into the Packet-boat,
    P. 92 MAY'S DEATH   84 When thou hadst drunk thy last to lead thee home.

drunkards   frequency: 1   relative frequency: 0.0000
    P. 141 INSTRUCTIONS   12 'Twill serve this race of Drunkards, Pimps, and
                               Fools.

drunke   frequency: 2   relative frequency: 0.0000
    P. 187 BRITANNIA   109 With fury drunke like Backanalls they roar
    P. 316 CHEQUER INN   157 They drunke, I know not who had most

drunken   frequency: 3   relative frequency: 0.0000
    P. 110 ANNIVERSARY   288 Of Liberty, not drunken with its Wine.
    P. 169 ADVICE   30 The figure of a Drunken Councell board
    P. 185 BRITANNIA   12 Whilest the Lew'd Court in drunken slumbers
                               lyes,

dry   frequency: 4   relative frequency: 0.0000
    See also "half-dry."
    P. 96 HOLLAND   53 For these Half-anders, half wet, and half dry,
    P. 114 BLAKE   34 Where still the Earth is moist, the Air still
                               dry;
    P. 125 O.C.   99 So the dry Stock, no more that spreading Vine,
    P. 189 BRITANNIA   180 With me I'le bring to dry my peoples tears:

dry'd   frequency: 1   relative frequency: 0.0000
    P. 78 A. HOUSE   625 For now the Waves are fal'n and dry'd,

dubbed. See "dubd."

dubd   frequency: 1   relative frequency: 0.0000
    P. 201 HISTORICALL   12 And dubd poore Palmer's wife his Royall Whore.

duck   frequency: 1   relative frequency: 0.0000
    P. 96 HOLLAND   36 Would throw their Land away at Duck and Drake.

ducks   frequency: 1   relative frequency: 0.0000
    P. 167 KINGS VOWES   53 Where the Ducks and the Drakes may their
                               freedomes enjoy,

due   frequency: 8   relative frequency: 0.0001
    P. 32 MOURNING   26 To her dead Love this Tribute due;
    P. 42 DAMON   38 And Oak leaves tipt with hony due.
    P. 58 BILL-BOROW   69 For all the Civick Garlands due
    P. 88 ODE   28 Much to the Man is due.
    P. 108 ANNIVERSARY   188 And speak as of the Dead the Praises due:
    P. 122 TWO SONGS   28 Pay to Love and Them their due.
    P. 128 O.C.   222 All law is uselesse, all reward is due.
    P. 316 CHEQUER INN   155 And tooke his Wine when it was due

duelling   frequency: 1   relative frequency: 0.0000
    P. 147 INSTRUCTIONS   274 That each, tho' Duelling, a Battel fights.

duke   frequency: 11   relative frequency: 0.0002
    P. 142 INSTRUCTIONS   78 Galloping with the Duke to other Prey.
    P. 183 MADE FREE   87 To the Duke the Kingdoms Darling?
    P. 183 MADE FREE   107 A new Duke to choose,
    P. 192 TWO HORSES   47 W. That the Duke should turne Papist and that
                               Church defy
    P. 195 TWO HORSES   143 Ch. What is thy opinion of James Duke of
                               York?
    P. 197 DUKE   t Advice to a Painter to draw the Duke by.
    P. 199 DUKE   60 He and his Duke had both to great a minde
    P. 202 HISTORICALL   42 Death and the Duke so terrible apeare.
    P. 204 HISTORICALL   144 But Osborn and the Duke must needs prevail.
    P. 204 HISTORICALL   145 The Duke now vaunts, with popish Myrmidons;
    P. 205 HISTORICALL   156 And brought new Lessons to the Duke from Rome.

dukes   frequency: 2   relative frequency: 0.0000

```
           P. 183 MADE FREE     92 To cure the Dukes ills,
           P. 184 BRITANNIA      4 Of Earles, of Dukes, and Princes of the blood,

dull                             frequency:    4    relative frequency: 0.0000
           P. 151 INSTRUCTIONS 439 But Lewis was of Memory but dull,
           P. 162 INSTRUCTIONS 867 Bright Hair, fair Face, obscure and dull of
                                    Head;
           P. 198 DUKE          24 Theire parchment presidents and dull records.
           P. 203 HISTORICALL   89 And with dull Crambo feed the silly sheep.

duller                           frequency:    1    relative frequency: 0.0000
           P. 203 HISTORICALL   91 Drcll on their God but a much duller way:

dumb                             frequency:    2    relative frequency: 0.0000
           P.  79 A. HOUSE     671 And such an horror calm and dumb,
           P. 144 INSTRUCTIONS 126 Should Goodrick silence, and strike Paston
                                    dumb;

dunbar                           frequency:    1    relative frequency: 0.0000
           P. 126 O.C.         145 When up the armed Mountains of Dunbar

duncomb                          frequency:    1    relative frequency: 0.0000
           P. 168 ADVICE        19 Our Pig-eyed Duncomb in his Dover Fashion

duncombe                         frequency:    2    relative frequency: 0.0000
           See also "duncomb."
           P. 146 INSTRUCTIONS 207 Bold Duncome next, of the Projectors chief:
           P. 155 INSTRUCTIONS 605 Oft had he sent, cf Duncombe and of Legg

duncombes                        frequency:    1    relative frequency: 0.0000
           P. 160 INSTRUCTIONS 794 And place in Counsel fell to Duncombes share.

dung                             frequency:    2    relative frequency: 0.0000
           P. 174 LOYALL SCOT  112 Where Foxes Dung their earths the Badgers
                                    yeild;
           P. 174 LOYALL SCOT  113 At Bishops Dung the Foxes quit the feild.

dungeon                          frequency:    2    relative frequency: 0.0000
           P.  20 SOUL & BODY    1 O who shall, from this Dungeon, raise
           P.  65 A. HOUSE     208 'As rob though in the Dungeon cast.

dunghil                          frequency:    1    relative frequency: 0.0000
           P.  96 HOLLAND       16 Tranfusing into them their Dunghil Scul.

dunghill.  See "dunghil."

dunkirk                          frequency:    1    relative frequency: 0.0000
           P. 138 HOUSEWARMING  41 The Scotch Forts <and> Dunkirk, but that they
                                    were sold,

dunkirk-town                     frequency:    1    relative frequency: 0.0000
           P. 140 HIS HOUSE      7 Here's Dunkirk-Town and Tangier-Hall,

dunstan                          frequency:    1    relative frequency: 0.0000
           P. 148 INSTRUCTIONS 302 St. Dunstan in it, tweaking Satan's Nose.

dureing                          frequency:    1    relative frequency: 0.0000
           P. 203 HISTORICALL   95 Becomes the Priests Amphitric dureing Life.

during                           frequency:    1    relative frequency: 0.0000
           See also "dureing."
           P.  86 FLECKNO      113 During the Table; though my new made Friend

durst                            frequency:    7    relative frequency: 0.0001

dusky                            frequency:    1    relative frequency: 0.0000
           P.  90 MAY'S DEATH   13 'Twas Ben that in the dusky Laurel shade

dust                             frequency:    8    relative frequency: 0.0001
           P.  26 MISTRESS      29 And your quaint Honour turn to dust;
           P.  59 A. HOUSE      22 T'impark the wanton Mote cf Dust,
           P.  87 ODE            5 'Tis time to leave the Books in dust,
           P.  92 MAY'S DEATH   86 And reverend Chaucer, but their dust does rise
           P. 107 ANNIVERSARY  180 And soyl'd in Dust thy Crown of silver Hairs.
           P. 140 HOUSEWARMING 102 Throw dust in its Front, and blame situation:
           P. 148 INSTRUCTIONS 320 The unpractis'd Saw lyes bury'd in its Dust;
           P. 161 INSTRUCTIONS 834 And threaten Hyde to raise a greater Dust.

dutch                            frequency:   26    relative frequency: 0.0005
           P.  95 HOLLAND        8 Fell to the Dutch by just Propriety.
           P.  96 HOLLAND       32 Whole sholes of Dutch serv'd up for Cabillau;
```

P.	97	HOLLAND	57	How could the Dutch but be converted, when
P.	146	INSTRUCTIONS	233	They, that e're long shall the rude Dutch upbraid,
P.	148	INSTRUCTIONS	316	How strong the Dutch their Equipage renew.
P.	150	INSTRUCTIONS	398	Off, at the Isle of Candy, Dutch and ships.
P.	151	INSTRUCTIONS	438	And whip the Dutch, unless they'l hold their peace.
P.	152	INSTRUCTIONS	463	The Dutch are then in Proclamation shent,
P.	152	INSTRUCTIONS	479	But most rely'd upon this Dutch pretence,
P.	152	INSTRUCTIONS	482	(As if, alas, we Ships or Dutch had Horse.)
P.	153	INSTRUCTIONS	505	When Dutch Invade, when Parliament prepare,
P.	153	INSTRUCTIONS	510	Monk in his Shirt against the Dutch is prest.
P.	155	INSTRUCTIONS	603	Or to their fellows swim on board the Dutch,
P.	156	INSTRUCTIONS	620	Taught the Dutch Colours from its top to wave;
P.	157	INSTRUCTIONS	666	With birding at the Dutch, as if in sport:
P.	157	INSTRUCTIONS	670	And safely through its Port the Dutch retire:
P.	158	INSTRUCTIONS	711	The Dutch had robb'd those Jewels of the Crown:
P.	159	INSTRUCTIONS	771	Who would not follow when the Dutch were bet?
P.	159	INSTRUCTIONS	773	Who the Dutch Fleet with Storms disabled met,
P.	166	KINGS VOWES	20	And the Dutch shall give Caution for their Provinces;
P.	172	LOYALL SCOT	31	With birding at the Dutch, as though in sport,
P.	172	LOYALL SCOT	36	And safely through its ports the Dutch retire.
P.	179	STOCKSMARKET	26	Than all the Dutch pictures that caused the war,
P.	201	HISTORICALL	19	And his Dutch Sister quickly after dy'd,
P.	202	HISTORICALL	41	But the Dutch fleet fled suddainly with feare;
P.	202	HISTORICALL	52	And with the Dutch a second Warr renews.

dutches   frequency: 1   relative frequency: 0.0000
P. 202 HISTORICALL 71 And gentlier farre the Orleans Dutches treat.

dutchman's   frequency: 1   relative frequency: 0.0000
P. 140 HIS HOUSE   9 The Dutchman's Templum Pacis.

duty   frequency: 3   relative frequency: 0.0000
P. 113 ANNIVERSARY 396 More then our Love and Duty do thee Right.
P. 114 BLAKE   28 Trees there the duty of the Clouds supply;
P. 125 O.C.   83 For he no duty by his height excus'd,

dwarfish   frequency: 1   relative frequency: 0.0000
P.   60 A. HOUSE   38 Within such dwarfish Confines went:

dwell   frequency: 7   relative frequency: 0.0001
P.   41 THE MOWER   40 The Gods themselves with us do dwell.
P.   47 EMPIRE   8 And built the Organs City where they dwell.
P.   59 A. HOUSE   13 The low roof'd Tortoises do dwell
P.   92 MAY'S DEATH 89 Nor here thy shade must dwell, Return, Return,
P. 138 HOUSEWARMING 31 He himself would not dwell in a Castle of air,
P. 138 HOUSEWARMING 58 He should dwell more noble, and cheap too at-home,
P. 154 INSTRUCTIONS 569 And swore that he would never more dwell there

dwelling   frequency: 1   relative frequency: 0.0000
P.   61 A. HOUSE   88 The Quarries whence this dwelling rose.

dwellings   frequency: 1   relative frequency: 0.0000
P.   59 A. HOUSE   10 Such unproportion'd dwellings build?

dwells   frequency: 4   relative frequency: 0.0000
P.   5 HASTINGS   33 Before the Chrystal Palace where he dwells,
P. 170 PROPHECY   7 Where Vengeance dwells, but there is one trick more
P. 173 LOYALL SCOT 78 Where life resides or Understanding dwells:
P. 313 CHEQUER INN 13 The Host, that dwells in that same House

dwelt   frequency: 3   relative frequency: 0.0000
P.   61 A. HOUSE   90 There dwelt the blooming Virgin Thwates;
P. 129 O.C.   257 Yet dwelt that greatnesse in his shape decay'd,
P. 176 LOYALL SCOT 199 It was Musitian too and dwelt at Court.

dy   frequency: 3   relative frequency: 0.0000
P.   4 LOVELACE   46 In your defence, or in his cause would dy.
P.   80 A. HOUSE   674 Follows and sucks her Azure dy;
P. 199 DUKE   53 Dy before twenty, or rott before sixteene.

dy'd   frequency: 9   relative frequency: 0.0001
P.   22 NYMPH   22 Is dy'd in such a Purple Grain.
P.   78 A. HOUSE   626 And now the Meadows fresher dy'd;
P. 125 O.C.   88 Yet in compassion of another dy'd.
P. 128 O.C.   227 Valour, religion, friendship, prudence dy'd

```
          P. 157 INSTRUCTIONS   687 Down on the Deck he laid himself, and dy'd,
          P. 159 INSTRUCTIONS   760 And were they mortal, both for grief had dy'd.
          P. 163 INSTRUCTIONS   920 The grizly Wound reveals, of which he dy'd.
          P. 173 LOYALL SCOT     53 Down on the Deck hee laid him down and dy'd
          P. 201 HISTORICALL     19 And his Dutch Sister quickly after dy'd,
```

dye   frequency: 20   relative frequency: 0.0004
```
          P.  20 THYRSIS          40 Dorinda. I'm sick, I'm sick, and fain would
                                     dye:
          P.  20 THYRSIS          44 Will for thee, much more with thee dye.
          P.  21 SOUL & BODY      18 Has made me live to let me dye.
          P.  22 NYMPH             2 Have shot my Faun and it will dye.
          P.  22 NYMPH            13 It cannot dye so. Heavens King
          P.  24 NYMPH            94 And dye as calmely as a Saint.
          P.  24 NYMPH           110 Will but bespeak thy Grave, and dye.
          P.  44 DAMON            82 To those that dye by Loves despight.
          P.  55 THYESTE          10 I shall dye, without a groan,
          P. 112 ANNIVERSARY     392 'So should I hope yet he might Dye as wee.
          P. 115 BLAKE            70 That place saluted, where they all must dye.
          P. 115 BLAKE            73 'Twas more for Englands fame you should dye
                                     there,
          P. 117 BLAKE           127 Thousands of wayes, Thousands of men there dye,
          P. 118 BLAKE           140 There one must Conquer, or there both must dye.
          P. 123 O.C.             12 To those that liv'd in War, to dye in Fight.
          P. 126 O.C.            134 He with Eliza, It with him would dye.
          P. 192 TWO HORSES       48 For which his own Father a Martyr did dye.
          P. 195 TWO HORSES      160 Thy oppression together with Kingship shall
                                     dye.
          P. 199 DUKE             54 Now, Painter, shew us in the blackest dye
          P. 205 HISTORICALL     162 His Brother sneaking Heretik should dye,
```

dyes   frequency: 2   relative frequency: 0.0000
```
          P. 195 TWO HORSES      123 W. He that dyes for Ceremonies dyes like a
                                     fool.
```

dying   frequency: 5   relative frequency: 0.0001
```
          P.  29 LOVER            61 Yet dying leaves a Perfume here,
          P.  33 DAPHNIS          28 To a dying Man bequeath'd.
          P.  58 BILL-BOROW       68 And Mountains rais'd of dying Men.
          P. 108 ANNIVERSARY     211 Such as the dying Chorus sings by turns,
          P. 204 HISTORICALL     129 Like a true Lover for her dying Mate.
```

dyke-grave   frequency: 1   relative frequency: 0.0000
```
          P.  96 HOLLAND          49 Hence some small Dyke-grave unperceiv'd invades
```

each   frequency: 68   relative frequency: 0.0014

eagers   frequency: 1   relative frequency: 0.0000
```
          P. 139 HOUSEWARMING     70 Were shriveled, and Clutterbuck, Eagers <and>
                                     Kips;
```

eagles   frequency: 1   relative frequency: 0.0000
```
          P.  92 MAY'S DEATH      88 As th' Eagles Plumes from other birds divide.
```

ear   frequency: 10   relative frequency: 0.0002
```
          P.  20 SOUL & BODY       6 Deaf with the drumming of an Ear.
          P.  29 LOVER            62 And Musick within every Ear:
          P.  47 EMPIRE           19 With which She gain'd the Empire of the Ear,
          P.  68 A. HOUSE        307 Whose shrill report no Ear can tell,
          P.  75 A. HOUSE        518 And listning Elders prick the Ear.
          P.  84 FLECKNO          31 And how I, silent, turn'd my burning Ear
          P. 119 TWO SONGS         7 Cynthia, O Cynthia, turn thine Ear,
          P. 163 INSTRUCTIONS    907 Express him startling next with listning ear,
          P. 185 BRITANNIA         29 I'th sacred ear Tyranick Arts they Croak,
          P. 188 BRITANNIA       137 In his deaf ear sound his dead Fathers name;
```

eared. See "long-eard."

earles   frequency: 1   relative frequency: 0.0000
```
          P. 184 BRITANNIA         4 Of Earles, of Dukes, and Princes of the blood,
```

earls. See "earles."

early   frequency: 8   relative frequency: 0.0001
```
          P.   4 HASTINGS          6 And, ere they fall, arrest the early Showers.
          P.   4 HASTINGS          8 With early Tears must mourn his early Fate.
          P. 144 INSTRUCTIONS    151 Of early Wittals first the Troop march'd in,
          P. 146 INSTRUCTIONS    236 The Speaker early, when they all fell in.
          P. 156 INSTRUCTIONS    650 The early Down but newly did begin;
          P. 161 INSTRUCTIONS    853 The King, that day rais'd early from his rest,
          P. 172 LOYALL SCOT      16 The Early down but newly did begin,
```

earnest   frequency: 1   relative frequency: 0.0000
    P. 160 INSTRUCTIONS 809 Frequent in Counsel, earnest in Debate,

ears   frequency: 3   relative frequency: 0.0000
    P.   19 THYRSIS   25 No Oat-pipe's needfull, there thine Ears
    P. 108 ANNIVERSARY   199 With wandring Eyes, and restless Ears they
                              stood,
    P. 168 ADVICE   26 That give their votes more by their eyes than
                              ears:

earth   frequency: 30   relative frequency: 0.0006
    P.   4 HASTINGS   22 To Earth, and then what Jealousies to Heaven!
    P.   9 DIALOGUE   12 Lord of Earth, and Heavens Heir.
    P.   10 DIALOGUE   36 The rest is all but Earth disguis'd.
    P.   10 DIALOGUE   45 Earth cannot shew so brave a Sight
    P.   13 DROP OF DEW   39 Congeal'd on Earth: but does, dissolving, run
    P.   37 DEFINITION   22 And Earth some new Convulsion tear;
    P.   40 THE MOWER   7 And a more luscious Earth for them did knead,
    P.   44 DAMON   76 Each stroke between the Earth and Root,
    P.   47 EMPIRE   20 Including all between the Earth and Sphear.
    P.   56 BILL-BOROW   1 See how the arched Earth does here
    P.   56 BILL-BOROW   12 The Earth deform and Heaven fright,
    P.   80 A. HOUSE   686 Which from the putrid Earth exhale,
    P.   95 HOLLAND   3 And so much Earth as was contributed
    P.   95 HOLLAND   12 Of Earth, as if't had been of Ambergreece;
    P.   96 HOLLAND   28 The Earth and Water play at Level-coyl;
    P.   96 HOLLAND   45 Who best could know to pump an Earth so leak
    P. 107 ANNIVERSARY   160 A Mold was chosen out of better Earth;
    P. 108 ANNIVERSARY   205 It seem'd the Earth did from the Center tear;
    P. 112 ANNIVERSARY   364 'And sink the Earth that does at Anchor ride.
    P. 112 ANNIVERSARY   372 'Can quickly leave us neither Earth nor Air.
    P. 112 ANNIVERSARY   386 'Where below Earth, or where above the Sphere?
    P. 114 BLAKE   34 Where still the Earth is moist, the Air still
                              dry;
    P. 116 BLAKE   78 At once both to Inhabit Earth and Heaven.
    P. 129 O.C.   262 To Heav'n its branches, and through earth its
                              roots:
    P. 131 O.C.   320 Earth ne'er more glad, nor Heaven more serene.
    P. 131 PARADISE   5 Heav'n, Hell, Earth, Chaos, All; the
                              Argument
    P. 149 INSTRUCTIONS 348 The Comet dread, and Earth and Heaven burns.
    P. 154 INSTRUCTIONS 575 For whose strong bulk Earth scarce could Timber
                              find,
    P. 189 BRITANNIA   192 The Earth shall rest, the Heavens shall on thee
                              smile,
    P. 200 DUKE   112 Bribed by a croune on earth and one above,

earth-born   frequency: 1   relative frequency: 0.0000
    P. 144 INSTRUCTIONS 143 Black Birch, of all the Earth-born race most
                              hot,

earthen   frequency: 1   relative frequency: 0.0000
    P.   97 HOLLAND   87 A vestal Turf enshrin'd in Earthen Ware

earthly   frequency: 1   relative frequency: 0.0000
    P.   70 A. HOUSE   356 Which most our Earthly Gardens want.

earthquake   frequency: 1   relative frequency: 0.0000
    P. 164 INSTRUCTIONS 977 Nor Earthquake so an hollow Isle overwhelm,

earths   frequency: 1   relative frequency: 0.0000
    P. 174 LOYALL SCOT   112 Where Foxes Dung their earths the Badgers
                              yeild;

earth's   frequency: 1   relative frequency: 0.0000
    P. 139 HOUSEWARMING   78 For foundation he Bristol sunk in the Earth's
                              bowel;

earthy   frequency: 1   relative frequency: 0.0000
    P. 103 ANNIVERSARY   19 Their earthy Projects under ground they lay,

ease   frequency: 5   relative frequency: 0.0001
    P.   42 DAMON   29 Alas! I look for Ease in vain,
    P.   77 A. HOUSE   593 Then, languishing with ease, I toss
    P. 132 PARADISE   36 Thou singst with so much gravity and ease;
    P. 153 INSTRUCTIONS 501 Here Men induc'd by Safety, Gain, and Ease,
    P. 174 LOYALL SCOT   116 How Reverend things are 'lord', Lawn Sleeves
                              and Ease!

easie   frequency: 8   relative frequency: 0.0001
    P.   13 DROP OF DEW   33 How loose and easie hence to go:

```
P.  31 FAIR SINGER    13 It had been easie fighting in some plain,
P.  76 A. HOUSE      561 Thus I, easie Philcsopher,
P. 131 PARADISE       16 And what was easie he should render vain.
P. 154 INSTRUCTIONS  574 Like molting Fowl, a weak and easie Prey.
P. 158 INSTRUCTIONS  730 And all admires, but most his easie Prey.
P. 164 INSTRUCTIONS  964 Or in fair Fields to rule the easie Flock.
P. 186 BRITANNIA      69 From th' easie King she truthes bright Mirrour
                         took,
```

easier   frequency: 1   relative frequency: 0.0000
```
   P. 138 HOUSEWARMING   45 His Wood would come in at the easier rate,
```

easily   frequency: 1   relative frequency: 0.0000
See also "easly," "eas'ly."
```
   P. 188 BRITANNIA      143 As easily learn'd Virtuoso's may
```

easly   frequency: 1   relative frequency: 0.0000
```
   P.  84 FLECKNO         64 Who as a Camel tall, yet easly can
```

eas'ly   frequency: 2   relative frequency: 0.0000
```
   P. 137 HOUSEWARMING    2 (As the Cause can eas'ly foretel the Effect)
   P. 147 INSTRUCTIONS  272 As eas'ly Ccnquer'd, and believing can.
```

east   frequency: 5   relative frequency: 0.0001
```
   P.  29 THE GALLERY     19 When in the East she slumb'ring lyes,
   P.  68 A. HOUSE       289 When in the East the Morning Ray
   P.  97 HOLLAND         68 And from the East would Westward steer its
                            Ark,
   P. 106 ANNIVERSARY    123 Like the shrill Huntsman that prevents the
                            East,
   P. 158 INSTRUCTIONS  718 From the South Perfumes, Spices from the
                            East;
```

eastern   frequency: 2   relative frequency: 0.0000
```
   P. 131 O.C.           316 Richer than any eastern silk, or gemme;
   P. 154 INSTRUCTIONS  547 Aeolus their Sails inspires with Eastern Wind,
```

easy   frequency: 2   relative frequency: 0.0000
See also "easie."
```
   P. 128 O.C.           220 Lye weak and easy to the ruler's will;
   P. 201 HISTORICALL     30 Why not with easy Youngsters make as bold?
```

eat   frequency: 5   relative frequency: 0.0001
See also "eate."
```
   P.  21 SOUL & BODY     36 Or Hatred's hidden Ulcer eat.
   P.  84 FLECKNO         46 Ask'd civilly if he had eat this Lent.
   P.  84 FLECKNO         51 I ask'd if he eat flesh. And he, that was
   P.  85 FLECKNO        111 Let it suffice that we could eat in peace;
   P. 107 ANNIVERSARY    164 T'have smelt the Blosscme, and not eat the
                            Fruit;
```

eate   frequency: 2   relative frequency: 0.0000
```
   P. 315 CHEQUER INN    100 And tho' his Sweate the while he eate
   P. 315 CHEQUER INN    116 The Landlord Bailes, cut eate, out roar'd
```

eaten. See "worm-eaten."

eaters   frequency: 1   relative frequency: 0.0000
```
   P. 146 INSTRUCTICNS  208 And old Fitz-Harding cf the Eaters Beef.
```

eating   frequency: 2   relative frequency: 0.0000
```
   P.  86 FLECKNO        118 Who satisfy'd with eating, but not tame
   P. 176 LOYALL SCCT    175 Eating their brethren Bishop Turn and Cat
```

eaton   frequency: 1   relative frequency: 0.0000
```
   P. 161 INSTRUCTIONS  855 At last together Eaton come and he:
```

eats   frequency: 2   relative frequency: 0.0000
```
   P.  90 MAY'S DEATH     17 But how a double headed Vulture Eats,
   P. 144 INSTRUCTIONS  121 The close Cabal mark'd how the Navy eats,
```

ebb   frequency: 2   relative frequency: 0.0000
```
   P. 120 TWO SONGS       18 Ruling the Waves that Ebb and flow.
   P. 165 KINGS VOWES      1 When the Plate was at pawne, and the fobb att
                            low Ebb,
```

ebbs   frequency: 1   relative frequency: 0.0000
```
   P.  98 HOLLAND        132 And, like its cwn Seas, only Ebbs to flow.
```

eben   frequency: 1   relative frequency: 0.0000
```
   P.  79 A. HOUSE       668 With Eben Shuts begin to close;
```

eccentrick   frequency: 1   relative frequency: 0.0000
  P. 140 HIS HOUSE   6 Fixt on an Eccentrick Basis;

eccho   frequency: 2   relative frequency: 0.0000
  P. 18 BERMUDAS   36 Eccho beyond the Mexique Bay.
  P. 18 CLORINDA   28 Caves eccho, and the Fountains ring.

ecchoes   frequency: 2   relative frequency: 0.0000
  P. 47 EMPIRE   7 He call'd the Ecchoes from their sullen Cell,
  P. 68 A. HOUSE   308 But Ecchoes to the Eye and smell.

ecchoing   frequency: 1   relative frequency: 0.0000
  P. 26 MISTRESS   27 My ecchoing Song: then Worms shall try

echo   frequency: 2   relative frequency: 0.0000
  See also "eccho."
  P. 74 A. HOUSE   512 Echo about their tuned Fires.
  P. 84 FLECKNO   44 In Echo to the trembling Strings repin'd.

echoes. See "ecchoes."

echoing. See "ecchoing."

eclipse. See "eclypse."

eclypse   frequency: 1   relative frequency: 0.0000
  P. 121 TWO SONGS   48 While Stars Eclypse by mixing Rayes.

edge   frequency: 5   relative frequency: 0.0001
  P. 71 A. HOUSE   397 The Edge all bloody from its Breast
  P. 88 ODE   60 The Axes edge did try:
  P. 147 INSTRUCTIONS   254 And to new edge their angry Courage grind.
  P. 162 INSTRUCTIONS   868 Like Knife with Iv'ry haft, and edge of Lead.
  P. 316 CHEQUER INN   146 That scarce the Lady cou'd edge in

edged   frequency: 1   relative frequency: 0.0000
  See also "two-edg'd."
  P. 44 DAMON   77 The edged Stele by careless chance

edict   frequency: 1   relative frequency: 0.0000
  P. 196 TWO HORSES   187 Then, Charles, thy edict against Coffee recall;

edicts   frequency: 1   relative frequency: 0.0000
  P. 204 HISTORICALL   118 Declares the Councel Edicts are beyond

edward   frequency: 1   relative frequency: 0.0000
  P. 168 ADVICE   13 Where draw Sir Edward mounted on his throne,

eels   frequency: 1   relative frequency: 0.0000
  P. 73 A. HOUSE   474 How Eels now bellow in the Ox;

e'er   frequency: 2   relative frequency: 0.0000
  P. 129 O.C.   236 No April sunns that e'er so gently smil'd;
  P. 180 STOCKSMARKET   35 With canvas and deals you e'er since do him
                    cloud,

effect   frequency: 5   relative frequency: 0.0001
  P. 90 ODE   115 And for the last effect
  P. 106 ANNIVERSARY   135 What we might hope, what wonderful Effect
  P. 137 HOUSEWARMING   2 (As the Cause can eas'ly foretel the Effect)
  P. 169 ADVICE   39 Which to effect when thus it was decreed
  P. 177 LOYALL SCOT   245 From Scotch or English heart the same effect.

effects   frequency: 1   relative frequency: 0.0000
  P. 188 BRITANNIA   139 Who knows what good effects from thence may
                    spring;

effigie   frequency: 2   relative frequency: 0.0000
  P. 192 TWO HORSES   22 To beleive men and beasts have spoke in effigie,
  P. 200 DUKE   99 This band of traytors hang'd in Effigie.

effigy   frequency: 1   relative frequency: 0.0000
  See also "effigie."
  P. 150 INSTRUCTIONS   391 In quick Effigy, others Faults, and feign

egypt's   frequency: 1   relative frequency: 0.0000
  P. 138 HOUSEWARMING   39 He car'd not though Egypt's Ten Plagues us
                    distrest,

eight   frequency: 3   relative frequency: 0.0000
  P. 110 ANNIVERSARY   283 Thou, and thine House, like Noah's Eight did rest,

```
        P. 170 PROPHECY        20 And practise Incest between Seven and Eight,
        P. 190 STATUE          24 Hee'l shortly reduce us to fourty and eight.

eighteen                       frequency:    2    relative frequency: 0.0000
        P. 149 INSTRUCTIONS   332 Bought off with Eighteen hundred thousand pound.
        P. 152 INSTRUCTIONS   492 (The Eighteen hundred thousand pound was gone.)

either                         frequency:   16    relative frequency: 0.0003

eject                          frequency:    1    relative frequency: 0.0000
        P. 190 STATUE          7 Besides the injustice it were to eject

elbow                          frequency:    3    relative frequency: 0.0000
        P.  44 DAMON           73 While thus he threw his Elbow round,
        P.  71 A. HOUSE       393 With whistling Sithe, and Elbow strong,
        P. 145 INSTRUCTIONS   166 Hid with his Elbow like the Spice he stole.

elder                          frequency:    1    relative frequency: 0.0000
        P. 314 CHEQUER INN     86 And popping like an Elder Gun

elders                         frequency:    2    relative frequency: 0.0000
        P.  75 A. HOUSE       518 And listning Elders prick the Ear.
        P. 109 ANNIVERSARY    253 And how he Succoths Elders durst suppress,

eldest                         frequency:    1    relative frequency: 0.0000
        P.  75 A. HOUSE       534 The eldest of its young lets drop,

elect                          frequency:    1    relative frequency: 0.0000
        P. 188 BRITANNIA      151 Over the whole: the elect Jessean line

elected. See "th'elected."

element                        frequency:    3    relative frequency: 0.0000
        P.  12 DROP OF DEW      8 Frames as it can its native Element.
        P.  74 A. HOUSE       502 To thrust up a Fifth Element;
        P. 117 BLAKE          132 That it return'd to its own Element.

elements                       frequency:    7    relative frequency: 0.0001
        P.   5 HASTINGS        36 Of all these Sublunary Elements.
        P.  28 LOVER           26 This masque of quarrelling Elements;
        P. 114 BLAKE           35 The jarring Elements no discord know,
        P. 116 BLAKE           86 Which did the rage of Elements subdue.
        P. 118 BLAKE          150 And o're two Elements Triumphs at once.
        P. 126 O.C.           129 Such Tortures all the Elements unfix'd,
        P. 127 O.C.           159 For whom the Elements we Mourners see,

elephantine                    frequency:    1    relative frequency: 0.0000
        P. 141 INSTRUCTIONS    34 Member'd like Mules, with Elephantine chine.

eleventh                       frequency:    1    relative frequency: 0.0000
        P. 152 INSTRUCTIONS   464 For Sin against th' Eleventh Commandment.

elisian                        frequency:    1    relative frequency: 0.0000
        P. 171 LOYALL SCOT      2 Saw Douglass Marching on the Elisian Glades,

eliza                          frequency:    3    relative frequency: 0.0000
        P. 123 O.C.            30 Eliza, Natures and his darling, seize.
        P. 126 O.C.           134 He with Eliza, It with him would dye.
        P. 128 O.C.           209 If he Eliza lov'd to that degree,

eliza's                        frequency:    3    relative frequency: 0.0000
        P. 124 O.C.            67 And now Eliza's purple Locks were shorn,
        P. 125 O.C.            85 But rather then in his Eliza's pain
        P. 128 O.C.           216 Their griefs struck deepest, if Eliza's last.

elizium                        frequency:    5    relative frequency: 0.0001
        P.  19 THYRSIS         5 Thyrsis. To the Elizium: (Dorinda) oh where
                                  i'st?
        P.  19 THYRSIS         8 Is our cell Elizium?
        P.  19 THYRSIS        19 Dorinda. But in Elizium how do they
        P.  20 THYRSIS        30 In talking of Elizium.
        P.  24 NYMPH         107 In fair Elizium to endure,

elms                           frequency:    2    relative frequency: 0.0000
        P.  75 A. HOUSE       526 Sad pair unto the Elms they moan.
        P. 142 INSTRUCTIONS    71 Ye neighb'ring Elms, that your green leaves did
                                  shed,

eloquent                       frequency:    1    relative frequency: 0.0000
        P.  47 EMPIRE          14 And others chose the Cornet eloquent.
```

else   frequency: 11   relative frequency: 0.0002

elysian   frequency: 2   relative frequency: 0.0000
     See also "elisian," "elyzean."
     P. 82 A. HOUSE   759 Much less the Dead's Elysian Fields,
     P. 90 MAY'S DEATH   3 But was amaz'd on the Elysian side,

elysium. See "elizium."

elyzean   frequency: 1   relative frequency: 0.0000
     P. 177 LOYALL SCOT   223 Some sue for tyth of the Elyzean plaines:

em   frequency: 1   relative frequency: 0.0000

'em   frequency: 7   relative frequency: 0.0001

emathian   frequency: 1   relative frequency: 0.0000
     P. 91 MAY'S DEATH   21 Cups more then civil of Emathian wine,

embark. See "imbark."

embassadors   frequency: 1   relative frequency: 0.0000
     P. 167 KINGS VOWES   44 My Bawd shall Embassadors send farr and neare,

embleme   frequency: 1   relative frequency: 0.0000
     P. 176 LOYALL SCOT   190 Nature in Living Embleme there Exprest

embrac'd   frequency: 1   relative frequency: 0.0000
     P. 37 DEFINITION   20 Not by themselves to be embrac'd.

embrace   frequency: 1   relative frequency: 0.0000
     P. 26 MISTRESS   32 But none I think do there embrace.

embraces   frequency: 1   relative frequency: 0.0000
     See also "imbraces."
     P. 157 INSTRUCTIONS   678 And tries his first embraces in their Sheets.

embracing   frequency: 1   relative frequency: 0.0000
     P. 64 A. HOUSE   191 'All Night embracing Arm in Arm,

embroider. See "embroyder."

embroyder   frequency: 1   relative frequency: 0.0000
     P. 77 A. HOUSE   587 The Oak-Leaves me embroyder all,

embru'd   frequency: 1   relative frequency: 0.0000
     P. 205 HISTORICALL   176 And all the People been in blood embru'd,

empire   frequency: 7   relative frequency: 0.0001
     P. 47 EMPIRE   t Musicks Empire.
     P. 47 EMPIRE   19 With which She gain'd the Empire of the Ear,
     P. 92 MAY'S DEATH   67 He, when the wheel of Empire, whirleth back,
     P. 113 BLAKE   14 That boundless Empire, where you give the Law,
     P. 159 INSTRUCTIONS   750 His Empire old, to their immortal Line!
     P. 164 INSTRUCTIONS   955 And you, Great Sir, that with him Empire
                                    share,
     P. 205 HISTORICALL   174 And thirst of Empire Calentur'd his Breast.

empires   frequency: 1   relative frequency: 0.0000
     P. 26 MISTRESS   12 Vaster then Empires, and more slow.

employ   frequency: 3   relative frequency: 0.0000
     See also "imploy."
     P. 82 A. HOUSE   749 Employ the means you have by Her,
     P. 107 ANNIVERSARY   185 So shall the Tears we on past Grief employ,
     P. 183 MADE FREE   104 You would wisely employ,

employed. See "imployd," "imploy'd."

employes   frequency: 1   relative frequency: 0.0000
     P. 21 SOUL & BODY   25 And all my Care its self employes,

employs   frequency: 1   relative frequency: 0.0000
     See also "employes," "imployes."
     P.   3 LOVELACE   14 And against others Fame his owne employs.

emptiness   frequency: 1   relative frequency: 0.0000
     P. 88 ODE   41 Nature that hateth emptiness,

empty   frequency: 5   relative frequency: 0.0001
     P. 59 A. HOUSE   15 No Creature loves an empty space;

```
          P.   72 A. HOUSE          442 A new and empty Face of things;
          P.   85 FLECKNO            85 No empty place for complementing doubt,
          P.  165 KINGS VOWES         3 Our Pockets as empty as braine;
          P.  171 PROPHECY           38 To make starcht empty Speeches two hours long.

emulous                             frequency:    2     relative frequency: 0.0000
          P.   87 ODE               18 The Emulous or Enemy;
          P.  142 INSTRUCTIONS      76 And her self scorn'd for emulous Denham's Face;

enamells                            frequency:    1     relative frequency: 0.0000
          P.   17 BERMUDAS          14 Which here enamells every thing;

enamels.  See "enamells."

enamour'd                           frequency:    2     relative frequency: 0.0000
          P.  144 INSTRUCTIONS     145 And, of his Brat enamour'd, as't increast,
          P.  201 HISTORICALL       24 Was thus enamour'd with a butterd bun,

encamped.  See "incamp'd."

enchant.  See "inchant."

enchantment.  See "inchantment."

enchantress                         frequency:    1     relative frequency: 0.0000
          P.   30 THE GALLERY       25 Like an Enchantress here thou show'st,

enclos'd                            frequency:    1     relative frequency: 0.0000
          P.   40 THE MOWER          5 He first enclos'd within the Gardens square

encrease                            frequency:    1     relative frequency: 0.0000
          P.  129 O.C.             271 So shall his praise to after times encrease,

end                                 frequency:   14     relative frequency: 0.0002
          P.   44 GLO-WORMS          7 Shining unto no higher end
          P.   48 THE GARDEN        28 Still in a Tree did end their race.
          P.   72 A. HOUSE         431 When at their Dances End they kiss,
          P.   97 HOLLAND           90 But still does place it at her Western End:
          P.  113 ANNIVERSARY      398 So that we both alike may miss our End:
          P.  123 O.C.              19 Deserved yet an End whose ev'ry part
          P.  126 O.C.             135 He without noise still travell'd to his End,
          P.  141 INSTRUCTIONS       2 To end her Picture, does the third time wait.
          P.  165 KINGS VOWES       12 But when they will not, they shall be att an end.
          P.  180 STOCKSMARKET      55 But alas! he will never arrive at his end,
          P.  182 MADE FREE         42 As if he shou'd ne're see an end on't.
          P.  198 DUKE              13 A vow that fire and sword shall never end
          P.  200 DUKE             104 Let not thy life and crowne togeather end,
          P.  316 CHEQUER INN      151 The Host that sate at lower end

endanger                            frequency:    1     relative frequency: 0.0000
          See also "indanger."
          P.  107 ANNIVERSARY      174 Our Sins endanger, and shall one day kill.

endanger'd                          frequency:    1     relative frequency: 0.0000
          P.    3 LOVELACE          34 That their deare Lovelace was endanger'd so:

endavour                            frequency:    1     relative frequency: 0.0000
          P.  194 TWO HORSES        91 W. That a King shou'd endavour to make a warr
                                       cease

endeavour.  See "endavour."

ended                               frequency:    2     relative frequency: 0.0000
          P.  127 O.C.             155 Here ended all his mortal toyles: He lay'd
          P.  195 TWO HORSES       158 W. When the Reign of the Line of the Stuarts
                                       is ended.

ending                              frequency:    1     relative frequency: 0.0000
          P.  126 O.C.             146 He march'd, and through deep Severn ending war.

endless                             frequency:    1     relative frequency: 0.0000
          See also "endlesse."
          P.  185 BRITANNIA         47 Full of Gray Hairs, good deeds, endless renown.

endlesse                            frequency:    1     relative frequency: 0.0000
          P.  130 O.C.             297 And in those joyes dost spend the endlesse day,

ends                                frequency:    3     relative frequency: 0.0000
          P.   67 A. HOUSE        269 Thenceforth (as when th' Inchantment ends
          P.  148 INSTRUCTIONS     313 The Seamens Clamour to three ends they use;
          P.  200 DUKE             109 Ends all the Joys of England and thy life.
```

```
endure                        frequency:    2    relative frequency: 0.0000
     See also "indure."
     P.  24 NYMPH         107 In fair Elizium to endure,
     P.  38 PICTURE        32 That Violets may a longer Age endure.

endured.  See "indur'd."

endures                       frequency:    1    relative frequency: 0.0000
     See also "indures."
     P.  96 HOLLAND        51 But for less envy some joynt States endures,

endymion                      frequency:   11    relative frequency: 0.0002
     P. 119 TWO SONGS      t4 Chorus. Endymion. Luna.
     P. 119 TWO SONGS      6+ Endymion.
     P. 119 TWO SONGS     12+ Endymion.
     P. 120 TWO SONGS      29 Courage, Endymion, boldly Woo,
     P. 120 TWO SONGS     18+ Endymion.
     P. 120 TWO SONGS     24+ Endymion.
     P. 120 TWO SONGS     34+ Endymion.
     P. 120 TWO SONGS     40+ Endymion.
     P. 121 TWO SONGS      49 That Cave is dark. Endymion. Then none can
                             spy:
     P. 121 TWO SONGS      51 Joy to Endymion,
     P. 121 TWO SONGS     44+ Endymion.

endymions                     frequency:    1    relative frequency: 0.0000
     P. 119 TWO SONGS       8 Nor scorn Endymions plaints to hear.

enemies                       frequency:    1    relative frequency: 0.0000
     P. 195 TWO HORSES    140 Hee made England great and it's enemies tremble.

enemy                         frequency:   10    relative frequency: 0.0002
     P.  31 FAIR SINGER     2 Love did compose so sweet an Enemy,
     P.  38 PICTURE        16 Appease this virtucus Enemy of Man!
     P.  87 ODE            18 The Emulous or Enemy;
     P.  91 MAY'S DEATH    30 Sworn Enemy to all that do pretend,
     P. 104 ANNIVERSARY    30 This Common Enemy is still opprest;
     P. 128 O.C.          200 So lcose an enemy, so fast a friend.
     P. 147 INSTRUCTIONS  247 First spy'd the Enemy and gave th' Alarm:
     P. 148 INSTRUCTIONS  305 At the first Charge the Enemy give out;
     P. 151 INSTRUCTIONS  445 And so enforc'd, like Enemy or Spy,
     P. 154 INSTRUCTIONS  540 Terrour and War, but want an Enemy.

enflam'd                      frequency:    2    relative frequency: 0.0000
     P. 117 BLAKE         122 Far more enflam'd by it, then by the Sun.
     P. 202 HISTORICALL    47 Which with Religicn so enflam'd his ire

enflamed                      frequency:    1    relative frequency: 0.0000
     P. 202 HISTORICALL    49 So Philips Son enflamed with a Miss

enfold                        frequency:    1    relative frequency: 0.0000
     See also "infold."
     P. 173 LOYALL SCOT    45 His shape Exact which the bright flames enfold

enforc'd                      frequency:    2    relative frequency: 0.0000
     P.  41 THE MOWER      31 'Tis all enforc'd; the Fountain and the Grot;
     P. 151 INSTRUCTIONS  445 And so enforc'd, like Enemy or Spy,

engag'd                       frequency:    1    relative frequency: 0.0000
     P. 118 BLAKE         141 Far different Motives yet, engag'd them thus,

engage                        frequency:    1    relative frequency: 0.0000
     See also "ingage."
     P. 188 BRITANNIA     164 Least Court corrupcions should their souls
                             engage.

engine                        frequency:    3    relative frequency: 0.0000
     P. 138 HOUSEWARMING   27 That Engine so fatal, which Denham had brain'd,
     P. 142 INSTRUCTIONS   53 She perfected that Engine, oft assay'd,
     P. 155 INSTRUCTIONS  587 Engine so slight tc guard us from the Sea,

engines                       frequency:    4    relative frequency: 0.0000
     P.  29 THE GALLEBY    13 Engines more keen than ever yet
     P.  71 A. HOUSE      385 No Scene that turns with Engines strange
     P. 153 INSTRUCTIONS  506 How can he Engines so convenient spare?
     P. 317 CHEQUER INN   178 They are but Engines to raise Tax

england                       frequency:   21    relative frequency: 0.0004
     P.  91 MAY'S DEATH    53 And who by Romes example England lay,
     P. 127 O.C.          173 Who planted England on the Flandrick shoar,
     P. 137 HOUSEWARMING    6 While he the Betrayer of England and Flander,
```

```
P. 163 INSTRUCTIONS    906 And he Divin'd 'twas England or the Peace.
P. 164 INSTRUCTICNS    966 And, where all England serves, themselves would
                           reign.
P. 165 KINGS VOWES       6 If ere I see England againe,
P. 168 ADVICE           22 The spoyls of England; and along that side
P. 173 LOYALL SCOT      76 Where Nature Scotland doth from England part.
P. 177 LOYALL SCOT     252 Scotland and England cause of Just uproar!
P. 184 MADE FREE       123 Never think in England to swagger,
P. 185 BRITANNIA        14 Till England knowes who did her Citty burn,
P. 189 BRITANNIA       184 Shall England raise, releive opprest mankind.
P. 189 BRITANNIA       187 Soe shall my England by a Holy Warr
P. 195 TWO HORSES      140 Hee made England great and it's enemies tremble.
P. 195 TWO HORSES      146 Father Patricks Deciple will make England
                           smart.
P. 195 TWO HORSES      159 Ch. Then, England, Rejoyce, thy Redemption
                           draws nigh;
P. 198 DUKE             19 Prove to the world Ile have ould England know
P. 200 DUKE             92 Old England on its strong foundations stands,
P. 200 DUKE            109 Ends all the Jcys cf England and thy life.
P. 204 HISTORICALL     136 Old England truckling under slavery.
P. 205 HISTORICALL     164 All England strait should fall beneath his
                           yoake,
```

englands   frequency: 1   relative frequency: 0.0000
```
P. 115 BLAKE            73 'Twas more for Englands fame you shculd dye
                           there,
```

english   frequency: 30   relative frequency: 0.0006
```
P.  18 BERMUDAS         37 Thus sung they, in the English boat,
P.  83 FLECKNO           t Fleckno, an English Priest at Rome.
P.  90 ODE             110 The English Hunter him mistake;
P.  93 DR. WITTY         6 That sence in English which was bright and pure
P.  94 DR. WITTY        17 Caelia whose English dcth more richly flow
P.  94 DR. WITTY        25 Her thoughts are English, though her sparkling
                           wit
P.  95 HOLLAND           4 By English Pilcts when they heav'd the Lead;
P.  98 HOLLAND         108 Rather then to the English strike their sail;
P. 114 BLAKE            20 With English Streamers, should salute their
                           sight:
P. 130 O.C.            278 Shall th' English souldier, ere he charge,
                           rehearse;
P. 144 INSTRUCTIONS    149 Who, in an English Senate, fierce debate,
P. 146 INSTRUCTIONS    204 And in ill English all the World defy'd.
P. 148 INSTRUCTIONS    287 A Gross of English Gentry, nobly born,
P. 153 INSTRUCTIONS    534 And his new Face locks in the English Wave.
P. 155 INSTRUCTIONS    583 An English Pilot tco, (O Shame, O Sin!)
P. 155 INSTRUCTIONS    591 Th' English frcm shore the Iron deaf invoke
P. 157 INSTRUCTIONS    696 Our English youth shall sing the Valiant Scot.
P. 171 PROPHECY         40 The Champion of the English Hierarchye,
P. 171 PROPHECY         45 When the Crowne's Heir shall English Men
                           dispise
P. 171 PROPHECY         47 Then wooden Shcos shall be the English weare
P. 171 PROPHECY         49 Then the English shall a Greater Tyrant Know
P. 173 LOYALL SCOT      62 Our English youth shall sing the valiant Scott.
P. 173 LOYALL SCOT      69 Noe more discourse of Scotch or English Race
P. 176 LOYALL SCOT     179 Upon the English Diadem distrain'd,
P. 177 LOYALL SCCT     243 Which stronger were, a Scotch or English vice,
P. 177 LOYALL SCCT     245 From Scotch or English heart the same effect.
P. 178 LOYALL SCOT     261 English and Scctch, 'tis all but Crosse and
                           Pile
P. 187 BRITANNIA       107 Some English tco disguis'd (oh shame) I spy'd
P. 200 DUKE             91 The smalest atcme cf an English soul.
P. 312 CHEQUER INN       5 In any Age on English ground
```

engraved. See "ingrav'd."

engraver   frequency: 1   relative frequency: 0.0000
```
P.  24 NYMPH           114 Th' Engraver sure his Art may spare;
```

engraver's. See "graver's."

engraving   frequency: 1   relative frequency: 0.0000
```
P.  24 NYMPH           118 My breast, themselves engraving there.
```

engross. See "ingross."

enjoy   frequency: 3   relative frequency: 0.0000
```
See also "t'enjoy."
P. 110 ANNIVERSARY     290 That they enjoy, but more they vainly crave:
P. 123 TWO SONGS        46 Cr who despair, ncw Damon does enjoy?
P. 167 KINGS VOWES      53 Where the Ducks and the Drakes may their
                           freedomes enjoy,
```

enjoyment   frequency: 1   relative frequency: 0.0000
   P. 35 DAPHNIS   74 All th' Enjoyment of our Love

enlarge   frequency: 1   relative frequency: 0.0000
   P. 140 HOUSEWARMING   106 That for Name-sake he may with Hyde Park it
        enlarge,

enough   frequency: 15   relative frequency: 0.0003
   See also "enow."
   P. 26 MISTRESS   1 Had we but World enough, and Time,
   P. 55 EPITAPH   1 Enough: and leave the rest to Fame.
   P. 63 A. HOUSE   136 'Enough a thousand Saints to make.
   P. 120 TWO SONGS   17 I have enough for me to do,
   P. 122 TWO SONGS   14 There is Bayes enough for all.
   P. 130 O.C.   292 Spacious enough, and pure enough for thee.
   P. 138 HOUSEWARMING   30 None sollid enough seem'd for his Thong Caster;
   P. 149 INSTRUCTIONS   329 But when this fail'd, and Months enough were
        spent,
   P. 158 INSTRUCTIONS   713 So when the Fire did not enough devour,
   P. 175 LOYALL SCCT   128 Enough for them, God knows, to Count their
        Wealth,
   P. 190 STATUE   20 Have wee not had enough already of one?
   P. 194 TWO HORSES   97 Ch. Enough, dear Brother, for tho' we have
        reason,
   P. 195 TWO HORSES   149 A Tudor a Tudor! wee've had Stuarts enough;
   P. 313 CHEQUER INN   43 But he had Men enough to spare

enow   frequency: 1   relative frequency: 0.0000
   P. 58 BILL-BOROW   71 Nor are our Trunks enow to bear

enraged. See "inrag'd."

enrich   frequency: 2   relative frequency: 0.0000
   P. 35 DAPHNIS   65 Why should I enrich my Fate?
   P. 180 STOCKSMARKET   51 If the Indies and Smyrna do not him enrich,

enroll'd   frequency: 2   relative frequency: 0.0000
   P.   5 HASTINGS   38 On which the happie Names do stand enroll'd;
   P. 181 MADE FREE   17 You have him thus enroll'd,

enrolles   frequency: 1   relative frequency: 0.0000
   P. 93 DR. WITTY   2 Where just desert enrolles thy honour'd Name

enrolls. See "enrolles."

enshrin'd   frequency: 1   relative frequency: 0.0000
   P. 97 HOLLAND   87 A vestal Turf enshrin'd in Earthen Ware

ensign   frequency: 1   relative frequency: 0.0000
   P. 156 INSTRUCTIONS   645 Captain, Lieutenant, Ensign, all make haste,

ensignes   frequency: 1   relative frequency: 0.0000
   P. 204 HISTORICALL   151 Here for an Ensignes or Lieutenants place

ensigns   frequency: 4   relative frequency: 0.0000
   P. 38 PICTURE   14 See his Bow broke and Ensigns torn.
   P. 68 A. HOUSE   294 Their Silken Ensigns each displayes,
   P. 68 A. HOUSE   316 Seem to their Staves the Ensigns furl'd.
   P. 75 A. HOUSE   524 With Nuptial Rings their Ensigns chast;

ensign's. See "ensignes."

enslave. See "t'enslave."

enslaved. See "inslav'd."

ensnare. See "t'ensnare."

ensnared. See "insnar'd."

ensu'd   frequency: 1   relative frequency: 0.0000
   P. 205 HISTORICALL   175 Hence Ruine and Destruction had ensu'd,

ensue   frequency: 1   relative frequency: 0.0000
   P. 185 BRITANNIA   37 Taught him their use, what dangers would ensue

entail. See "intail."

enter   frequency: 4   relative frequency: 0.0000

```
       P.  59 A. HOUSE      30 To enter at a narrow loop;
       P.  71 A. HOUSE     388 The tawny Mowers enter next;
       P.  72 A. HOUSE     448 Ere the Bulls enter at Madril.
       P. 117 BLAKE        115 That Bay they enter, which unto them owes,
```

enter'd   frequency: 4   relative frequency: 0.0000
```
       P. 105 ANNIVERSARY    76 And each one enter'd in the willing Frame;
       P. 146 INSTRUCTIONS  211 Before them enter'd, equal in Command,
       P. 147 INSTRUCTIONS  255 First enter'd forward Temple, Conqueror
       P. 314 CHEQUER INN    55 They stood (when enter'd in the Hall)
```

entered. See "enter'd," "entred."

enterfeers   frequency: 1   relative frequency: 0.0000
```
       P. 145 INSTRUCTIONS  196 Whose Horses each with other enterfeers.
```

entertain   frequency: 2   relative frequency: 0.0000
```
       P.  28 LOVER          31 Guardians most fit to entertain
       P.  61 A. HOUSE       71 And for an Inn to entertain
```

entertain'd   frequency: 1   relative frequency: 0.0000
```
       P.  83 FLECKNO        16 There being no Bed where he entertain'd:
```

entertains   frequency: 3   relative frequency: 0.0000
```
       P.   5 HASTINGS       29 His Thought with richest Triumphs entertains,
       P. 157 INSTRUCTIONS  665 But entertains, the while, his time too short
       P. 172 LOYALL SCOT    32 Hee entertains the while his life too short,
```

enticing   frequency: 1   relative frequency: 0.0000
```
       P.  18 CLORINDA       17 D. These once had been enticing things,
```

entire. See "intire."

entrails   frequency: 1   relative frequency: 0.0000
See also "intrails."
```
       P.  30 THE GALLERY    28 Over his Entrails, in the Cave;
```

entrance   frequency: 1   relative frequency: 0.0000
```
       P.  30 THE GALLERY    50 That at the Entrance likes me best:
```

entred   frequency: 1   relative frequency: 0.0000
```
       P. 186 BRITANNIA      60 Entred a Dame bedeckt with spotted pride;
```

entrust. See "intrust."

entrusted. See "intrusted."

envenomed. See "invenom'd."

envied. See "envy'd."

envious   frequency: 5   relative frequency: 0.0001
```
       P.   3 LOVELACE       15 I see the envious Caterpillar sit
       P. 143 INSTRUCTIONS   97 But envious Fame, too soon, begun to note
       P. 156 INSTRUCTIONS  652 While envious Virgins hope he is a Male.
       P. 171 PROPHECY       55 Then They with envious Eyes shall Belgium See
       P. 172 LOYALL SCOT    18 Whilst Envious virgins hope hee is a Male.
```

enviously   frequency: 1   relative frequency: 0.0000
```
       P.  37 DEFINITION     30 But Fate so enviously debarrs,
```

envy   frequency: 4   relative frequency: 0.0000
```
       P.   4 LOVELACE       48 Above their envy, or mine aid doth clime.
       P.  96 HCLLAND        51 But for less envy some joynt States endures,
       P. 148 INSTRUCTIONS  326 Load them with Envy, and with Sitting tire:
       P. 313 CHEQUER INN    33 Envy is not so pale;
```

envy'd   frequency: 1   relative frequency: 0.0000
```
       P. 130 O.C.          275 But when death takes them from that envy'd seate,
```

epitaph   frequency: 1   relative frequency: 0.0000
```
       P.  55 EPITAPH         t An Epitaph upon----
```

equal   frequency: 20   relative frequency: 0.0004
See also "equall."
```
       P.  15 EYES           11 And then paid out in equal Poise,
       P.  20 THYRSIS        37 Shepheards there, bear equal sway,
       P.  31 FAIR SINGER    14 Where Victory might reign in equal choice,
       P.  56 BILL-BOROW      6 So equal as this Hill does bow.
       P.  59 A. HOUSE       12 And Birds contrive an equal Nest;
       P.  60 A. HOUSE       48 In ev'ry Figure equal Man.
       P.  68 A. HOUSE      306 And round your equal Fires do meet;
```

P. 73 A. HOUSE   449 For to this naked equal Flat,
P. 75 A. HOUSE   528 That in so equal Flames do burn!
P. 78 A. HOUSE   621 This, like a long and equal Thread,
P. 92 MAY'S DEATH   75 Yet wast thou taken hence with equal fate,
P. 105 ANNIVERSARY   93 But the most Equal still sustein the Height,
P. 112 ANNIVERSARY   390 'At Home a Subject on the equal Floor.
P. 123 TWO SONGS   44 And those be equal that have equal Fire.
P. 132 PARADISE   38 With Plume so strong, so equal, and so soft.
P. 146 INSTRUCTIONS   211 Before them enter'd, equal in Command,
P. 148 INSTRUCTIONS   297 Then closing, all in equal Front fall on,
P. 148 INSTRUCTIONS   299 Lee, equal to obey or to command,
P. 160 INSTRUCTIONS   792 And march with Punishment in equal pace;

equall   frequency: 1   relative frequency: 0.0000
P. 189 BRITANNIA   179 Tarquins just judge and Cesar's Equall Peers

equally   frequency: 2   relative frequency: 0.0000
P. 195 TWO HORSES   125 W. The Goat and the Lyon I Equally hate,
P. 195 TWO HORSES   133 The Debauch'd and the Bloody since they
                           Equally Gall us,

equipage   frequency: 2   relative frequency: 0.0000
P. 148 INSTRUCTIONS   316 How strong the Dutch their Equipage renew.
P. 180 STOCKSMARKET   41 Methinks by the equipage of this vile scene

e'r   frequency: 1   relative frequency: 0.0000
P. 105 ANNIVERSARY   100 He hurles e'r since the World about him round;

ere   frequency: 40   relative frequency: 0.0008
P.   4 HASTINGS   6 And, ere they fall, arrest the early Showers.
P. 18 CLORINDA   8 C. Seize the short Joyes then, ere they vade.
P. 18 CLORINDA   22 But He ere since my Songs does fill:
P. 31 MOURNING   6 With Tears suspended ere they flow;
P. 38 PICTURE   19 Ere they have try'd their force to wound,
P. 38 PICTURE   20 Ere, with their glancing wheels, they drive
P. 39 PICTURE   39 And, ere we see,
P. 57 BILL-BOROW   35 No hostile hand durst ere invade
P. 57 BILL-BOROW   47 But ere he well the Barks could part
P. 63 A. HOUSE   147 'Fairfax I know; and long ere this
P. 69 A. HOUSE   322 The Garden of the World ere while,
P. 72 A. HOUSE   448 Ere the Bulls enter at Madril.
P. 73 A. HOUSE   461 Such Fleas, ere they approach the Eye,
P. 77 A. HOUSE   581 What Rome, Greece, Palestine, ere said
P. 78 A. HOUSE   614 Ere I your Silken Bondage break,
P. 86 FLECKNO   114 Did, as he threatned, ere 'twere long intend
P. 87 FLECKNO   166 Ere the fierce Poets anger turn'd to rime.
P. 90 ODE   101 A Caesar he ere long to Gaul,
P. 92 MAY'S DEATH   95 'Tis just what Torments Poets ere did feign,
P. 105 ANNIVERSARY   65 Thus, ere he ceas'd, his sacred Lute creates
P. 112 ANNIVERSARY   352 'And ere we Dine, rase and rebuild their State.
P. 114 BLAKE   45 For Spain had better, Shee'l ere long confess,
P. 115 BLAKE   65 But whilst I draw that Scene, where you ere
                           long,
P. 119 BLAKE   165 The saddest news that ere to Spain was brought,
P. 125 O.C.   81 No downy breast did ere so gently beat,
P. 125 O.C.   98 Weeps that it falls ere fix'd into a Grape.
P. 126 O.C.   149 That so who ere would at his Death have joy'd,
P. 128 O.C.   194 He conquer'd God, still ere he fought with men:
P. 129 O.C.   269 The tree ere while foreshortned to our view,
P. 130 O.C.   278 Shall th' English souldier, ere he charge,
                           rehearse;
P. 137 HOUSEWARMING   14 Who was dig'd up so often ere she did marry;
P. 165 KINGS VOWES   6 If ere I see England againe,
P. 165 KINGS VOWES   13 I will have as fine Bishops as were ere made
                           with hands,
P. 168 KINGS VOWES   62 That all his dareing crimes, what ere they be,
P. 172 LOYALL SCOT   30 Then least Heaven fall ere thither hee Ascend.
P. 173 LOYALL SCOT   59 Fortunate Boy, if ere my verse may Claim
P. 174 LOYALL SCOT   96 Who sermons ere can pacifie and prayers?
P. 188 BRITANNIA   132 Descend, descend, ere the Cures desperate.
P. 198 DUKE   26 And thinke a prince oth blood can ere doe Ill?
P. 202 HISTORICAIL   68 In Loves delights none did him ere excell

e're   frequency: 20   relative frequency: 0.0004
P.   4 LOVELACE   41 And one the loveliest that was yet e're seen,
P. 11 DIALOGUE   57 Where so e're thy Foot shall go
P. 27 LOVER   12 And, e're brought forth, was cast away:
P. 141 INSTRUCTIONS   3 But er'e thou fal'st to work, first Painter see
P. 143 INSTRUCTIONS   90 And now first, wisht she e're had been a Maid.
P. 144 INSTRUCTIONS   131 Excise, a Monster worse than e're before
P. 144 INSTRUCTIONS   137 Chops off the piece where e're she close the Jaw,

P. 146 INSTRUCTIONS 233 They, that e're long shall the rude Dutch
                            upbraid,
P. 146 INSTRUCTIONS 244 And undescry'd return'd e're morning peep.
P. 152 INSTRUCTIONS 475 But still in hope he solac'd, e're they come,
P. 153 INSTRUCTIONS 526 And Beauties e're this never naked seen.
P. 156 INSTRUCTIONS 646 E're in the Firy Furnace they be cast.
P. 157 INSTRUCTIONS 664 Then, lest Heav'n fall, e're thither he ascend.
P. 161 INSTRUCTIONS 824 Binding, e're th' Houses meet, the Treaty sure.
P. 164 INSTRUCTIONS 954 And hurls them off, e're since, in his Career.
P. 181 MADE FREE   28 But e're since he was bound
P. 184 MADE FREE   130 I see who e're is freed,
P. 186 BRITANNIA   75 Who e're grew great by keeping of his word?
P. 195 TWO HORSES   147 If e're he be King I know Brittains Doome;
P. 313 CHEQUER INN   37 And where he might e're now have laid

erect   frequency: 4   relative frequency: 0.0000
P. 90 ODE   116 Still keep thy Sword erect:
P. 137 HOUSEWARMING   16 To erect him a Pyramid out of her Quarry.
P. 158 INSTRUCTIONS 728 Her Masts erect, tough Cordage, Timbers
                            strong,
P. 179 STOCKSMARKET   16 That he did for the King his own statue erect.

erecting   frequency: 1   relative frequency: 0.0000
P. 109 ANNIVERSARY   247 Here pulling dcwn, and there erecting New,

ermines. See "ermins."

ermins   frequency: 1   relative frequency: 0.0000
P. 24 NYMPH   108 With milk-white Lambs, and Ermins pure.

err   frequency: 2   relative frequency: 0.0000
P. 35 DAPHNIS   80 He does through the Desert err.
P. 175 LOYALL SCOT   168 The Conscious Prelate therefore did not Err,

erring   frequency: 1   relative frequency: 0.0000
P. 188 BRITANNIA   138 Perhaps that spell may his Erring soul reclaim.

erroneous. See "erronious."

erronious   frequency: 1   relative frequency: 0.0000
P. 175 LOYALL SCOT   156 In faith Erronicus and in life Prophane

error   frequency: 2   relative frequency: 0.0000
See also "errour."
P. 94 DR. WITTY   28 Down into Error with the Vulgar tide;
P. 145 INSTRUCTIONS 189 Their Fortune's error they supply'd in rage,

errors   frequency: 1   relative frequency: 0.0000
See also "errours."
P. 93 DR. WITTY   t2 Translation of the Popular Errors.

errour   frequency: 1   relative frequency: 0.0000
See also "error."
P. 106 ANNIVERSARY   118 By Malice some, by Errour more misled;

errours   frequency: 2   relative frequency: 0.0000
See also "errors."
P. 38 PICTURE   27 Reform the errours cf the Spring;
P. 203 HISTORICALL   111 And hosts of upstart Errours gaine the field.

escap'd   frequency: 1   relative frequency: 0.0000
P. 149 INSTRUCTIONS 335 Blither than Hare that hath escap'd the Hounds,

escape   frequency: 3   relative frequency: 0.0000
P. 112 ANNIVERSARY   365 'What refuge to escape them can be found,
P. 144 INSTRUCTIONS 147 Say Muse, for ncthing can escape thy sight,
P. 152 INSTRUCTIONS 467 (So Spain could not escape his Laughters
                            spleen:

escaped. See "escap'd," "scap'd," "scap't."

escheat   frequency: 1   relative frequency: 0.0000
P. 67 A. HOUSE   274 To Fairfax fell as by Escheat.

eske   frequency: 2   relative frequency: 0.0000
P. 156 INSTRUCTIONS 655 Oft has he in chill Eske or Seine, by night,
P. 172 LOYALL SCOT   21 Cft as hee in Chill Eske or Seyne by night

espie   frequency: 1   relative frequency: 0.0000
P. 23 NYMPH   52 Could in so short a time espie,

espied. See "espy'd."

espy   frequency: 1   relative frequency: 0.0000
   See also "espie."
   P. 75 A. HOUSE   531 And through the Hazles thick espy

espy'd   frequency: 2   relative frequency: 0.0000
   P. 156 INSTRUCTIONS 657 Among the Reeds, to be espy'd by him,
   P. 172 LOYALL SCOT   23 Among the Reeds to bee espy'd by him

essence   frequency: 1   relative frequency: 0.0000
   P. 15 EYES   23 But finds the Essence only Showers,

essences   frequency: 1   relative frequency: 0.0000
   P. 39 THE MATCH   6 And Essences most pure,

essex   frequency: 1   relative frequency: 0.0000
   P. 150 INSTRUCTIONS 410 This Isle of Candy was on Essex Coast.

establish. See "'stablish."

estate   frequency: 2   relative frequency: 0.0000
   P. 160 INSTRUCTIONS 803 Who less Estate, for Treasurer most fit;
   P. 195 TWO HORSES   126 And Free men alike value life and Estate.

estates   frequency: 3   relative frequency: 0.0000
   P. 148 INSTRUCTIONS 288 Of clear Estates, and to no Faction sworn;
   P. 165 INSTRUCTIONS 987 That serve the King with their Estates and
                            Care,
   P. 193 TWO HORSES   59 W. That a King should consume three Realms
                            whole Estates

esteem   frequency: 3   relative frequency: 0.0000
   P. 32 MOURNING   21 Nay others, bolder, hence esteem
   P. 42 DAMON   34 Esteem me, and my Presents less?
   P. 123 O.C.   7 The People, which what most they fear esteem,

esteemd   frequency: 1   relative frequency: 0.0000
   P.   3 LOVELACE   8 Twas more esteemd to give, then weare the Bayes:

esteem'd   frequency: 2   relative frequency: 0.0000
   P. 169 ADVICE   61 Whom France Esteem'd our Chiefe in
                            Parliament,
   P. 185 BRITANNIA   16 And loyall sufferings by the Court esteem'd,

esteemed. See "esteemd," "esteem'd."

eternal   frequency: 5   relative frequency: 0.0001
   See also "eternall."
   P.   5 HASTINGS   37 But most he doth th' Eternal Book behold,
   P. 12 DROP OF DEW   20 Of the clear Fountain of Eternal Day,
   P. 17 BERMUDAS   13 He gave us this eternal Spring,
   P. 70 A. HOUSE   359 But Flowrs eternal, and divine,
   P. 161 INSTRUCTIONS 848 And in eternal Healths thy Name be trowl'd.

eternall   frequency: 2   relative frequency: 0.0000
   P. 188 BRITANNIA   154 Eternall Lawes by God for mankind made? Noe!
   P. 198 DUKE   20 That common sense is my eternall foe.

eternity   frequency: 2   relative frequency: 0.0000
   P. 19 THYRSIS   20 Pass Eternity away?
   P. 26 MISTRESS   24 Desarts of vast Eternity.

eternize   frequency: 1   relative frequency: 0.0000
   P. 126 O.C.   147 What day should him eternize but the same

ethick   frequency: 1   relative frequency: 0.0000
   P. 173 LOYALL SCOT   81 What Ethick River is this Wondrous Tweed

eunuchs   frequency: 1   relative frequency: 0.0000
   P. 41 THE MOWER   27 His green Seraglio has its Eunuchs too;

euphrates   frequency: 1   relative frequency: 0.0000
   P. 156 INSTRUCTIONS 623 Such from Euphrates bank, a Tygress fell,

evade   frequency: 1   relative frequency: 0.0000
   P. 188 BRITANNIA   153 And shall this stinking Scottish brood evade

evangelist   frequency: 1   relative frequency: 0.0000
   P. 97 HOLLAND   62 And Poor-John to have been th' Evangelist.

eve   frequency: 2   relative frequency: 0.0000

        P. 111 ANNIVERSARY   319 Well may you act the Adam and the Eve;
        P. 203 HISTORICALL   102 Fond Eve did for this subtle Tempters sake

even   frequency: 6   relative frequency: 0.0001
    See also "ev'n."
        P. 15 EYES   14 Yea even Laughter, turns to Tears:
        P. 20 THYRSIS   47 In wine, and drink on't even till we weep,
        P. 119 TWO SONGS   2 And even Wolves the Sheep forget;
        P. 170 PROPHECY   22 When even to rob the Checquer shall be Just,
        P. 176 LOYALL SCOT   204 Strange boldness! even bishops there rebell
        P. 179 STOCKSMARKET   20 Even Sir William Peake sits much firmer than
                                     he.

evening. See "ev'ning."

events   frequency: 2   relative frequency: 0.0000
        P. 196 TWO HORSES   164 Prodigious events did surely presage,
        P. 202 HISTORICALL   72 What sad events attended on the same

ever   frequency: 25   relative frequency: 0.0005
    See also "e'er," "e'r," "ere," "e're," "s'eer."
        P. 17 BERMUDAS   24 No Tree could ever bear them twice.
        P. 20 THYRSIS   36 And day is ever, but begun.
        P. 29 LOVER   58 That ever Love created yet:
        P. 29 THE GALLERY   13 Engines more keen than ever yet
        P. 40 THE MATCH   35 None ever burn'd so hot, so bright;
        P. 48 THE GARDEN   17 No white nor red was ever seen
        P. 58 BILL-BOROW   73 'Tis true, ye Trees nor ever spoke
        P. 91 MAY'S DEATH   31 Rose more then ever he was seen severe,
        P. 92 MAY'S DEATH   90 Where Sulphrey Phlegeton does ever burn.
        P. 109 ANNIVERSARY   255 No King might ever such a Force have done;
        P. 127 O.C.   187 Of that for ever Preston's field shall tell
        P. 128 O.C.   191 What man was ever so in Heav'n obey'd
        P. 144 INSTRUCTIONS   128 Commons, and ever such a Court maintain,
        P. 166 KINGS VOWES   37 But what ever it cost I will have a fine Whore,
        P. 174 LOYALL SCOT   90 Noe Scotch was ever like a Bishops feud.
        P. 175 LOYALL SCOT   166 Their Companyes the worst that ever playd
        P. 177 LOYALL SCOT   250 And ever since men with a female spite
        P. 180 STOCKSMARKET   58 As ever you hope in December for Spring,
        P. 183 MADE FREE   100 But if ever he get,
        P. 193 TWO HORSES   69 Ch. The basest Ingratitude ever was heard;
        P. 195 TWO HORSES   150 None ever Reign'd like old Besse in the Ruffe.
        P. 201 HISTORICALL   17 But the best times have ever some mishap;
        P. 203 HISTORICALL   94 Who ever has an over zealous wife
        P. 204 HISTORICALL   126 Of all the Miscreants ever went to hell
        P. 313 CHEQUER INN   19 And ever since he did so wex

everlasting   frequency: 2   relative frequency: 0.0000
        P. 12 DIALOGUE   78 And is thine everlasting Store.
        P. 19 THYRSIS   12 That leads to Everlasting day.

every   frequency: 36   relative frequency: 0.0007
    See also "ev'ry."

evil   frequency: 3   relative frequency: 0.0000
        P. 107 ANNIVERSARY   167 Though thou thine Heart from Evil still
                                     unstain'd,
        P. 204 HISTORICALL   130 The Royal Evil so malignant growes,
        P. 204 HISTORICALL   134 Ill luck starts up and thrives like Evil weeds.

ev'n   frequency: 8   relative frequency: 0.0001
        P. 22 NYMPH   16 Ev'n Beasts must be with justice slain;
        P. 24 NYMPH   84 Until its Lips ev'n seem'd to bleed:
        P. 118 BLAKE   146 By which we Laurels reapt ev'n on the Mayn.
        P. 138 HOUSEWARMING   43 Nay ev'n from Tangier have sent back for the
                                     mold,
        P. 147 INSTRUCTIONS   279 Ev'n Iron Strangeways, chafing yet gave back,
        P. 158 INSTRUCTIONS   708 Ev'n London's Ashes had been then destroy'd.
        P. 177 LOYALL SCOT   226 Ev'n Father Dis tho so with Age defac'd
        P. 314 CHEQUER INN   70 For ev'n at Bed the time has beene

ev'ning   frequency: 4   relative frequency: 0.0000
        P. 43 DAMON   47 While, going home, the Ev'ning sweet
        P. 55 EPITAPH   18 Gentle as Ev'ning; cool as Night;
        P. 78 A. HOUSE   624 There at the Ev'ning stake me down.
        P. 80 A. HOUSE   682 The World, and through the Ev'ning rush.

ev'ry   frequency: 18   relative frequency: 0.0003

ex   frequency: 1   relative frequency: 0.0000
        P. 54 THYESTE   t Senec. Traged. ex Thyeste Chor. 2.

exact   frequency: 2   relative frequency: 0.0000
    P. 157 INSTRUCTIONS   679 His shape exact, which the bright flames infold,
    P. 173 LOYALL SCOT   45 His shape Exact which the bright flames enfold

exactly   frequency: 1   relative frequency: 0.0000
    P. 126 O.C.   130 Troubled to part where so exactly mix'd.

exalt   frequency: 3   relative frequency: 0.0000
    P.   18 BERMUDAS   33 Oh let our Voice his Praise exalt,
    P. 116 BLAKE   94 They only Labour to exalt your praise.
    P. 141 INSTRUCTIONS   31 Him neither Wit nor Courage did exalt,

examines   frequency: 1   relative frequency: 0.0000
    P.   75 A. HOUSE   543 He, with his Beak, examines well

examining   frequency: 1   relative frequency: 0.0000
    P.   29 THE GALLERY   11 Examining upon our Hearts

example   frequency: 6   relative frequency: 0.0001
    P.   39 PICTURE   38 Do quickly make th' Example Yours;
    P.   64 A. HOUSE   163 'And your Example, if our Head,
    P.   91 MAY'S DEATH   53 And who by Romes example England lay,
    P. 110 ANNIVERSARY   298 And make the World, by his Example, Quake:
    P. 139 HOUSEWARMING   62 And Presents croud headlong to give good
                              example:
    P. 147 INSTRUCTIONS   252 And all to pattern his Example boast.

examples   frequency: 1   relative frequency: 0.0000
    P. 200 DUKE   114 See in all ages what examples are

exceed   frequency: 4   relative frequency: 0.0000
    P.   48 THE GARDEN   22 How far these Beauties Hers exceed!
    P. 173 LOYALL SCOT   79 But this wee know, tho' that Exceed their skill,
    P. 175 LOYALL SCOT   145 These Templar Lords Exceed the Templar
                              Knights,
    P. 183 MADE FREE   84 For his virtues exceed all his vices.

exceeds   frequency: 3   relative frequency: 0.0000
    P. 115 BLAKE   54 Which of the Gods the fancied drink exceeds;
    P. 127 O.C.   178 For Holyness the Confessor exceeds.
    P. 144 INSTRUCTIONS   135 With hundred rows of Teeth the Shark exceeds,

excel   frequency: 1   relative frequency: 0.0000
    See also "excell."
    P.   41 THE MOWER   39 But howso'ere the Figures do excel,

excell   frequency: 2   relative frequency: 0.0000
    P. 131 PARADISE   20 And by ill imitating would excell)
    P. 202 HISTORICALL   68 In Loves delights none did him ere excell

excellent   frequency: 2   relative frequency: 0.0000
    P. 139 HOUSEWARMING   88 By a Model more excellent than Lesly's Folly.
    P. 151 INSTRUCTIONS   450 In Cipher one to Harry Excellent.

except   frequency: 1   relative frequency: 0.0000
    P.   85 FLECKNO   99 Except by penetration hither, where

exchange   frequency: 1   relative frequency: 0.0000
    P.   97 HOLLAND   74 Opinion but finds Credit, and Exchange.

exchequer   frequency: 3   relative frequency: 0.0000
    P. 160 INSTRUCTIONS   798 Show'd him to manage the Exchequer meeter:
    P. 160 INSTRUCTIONS   806 The Exchequer might the Privy-purse obey.
    P. 179 STOCKSMARKET   27 And what the exchequer for that took on trust

excise   frequency: 7   relative frequency: 0.0001
    P. 144 INSTRUCTIONS   130 And what can these defray but the Excise?
    P. 144 INSTRUCTIONS   131 Excise, a Monster worse than e're before
    P. 146 INSTRUCTIONS   238 Excise had got the day, and all been lost.
    P. 148 INSTRUCTIONS   306 And the Excise receives a total Rout.
    P. 149 INSTRUCTIONS   331 And to Land-tax from the Excise turn round,
    P. 204 HISTORICALL   121 Taxes Excise and Armyes dos advance.
    P. 315 CHEQUER INN   132 Excise Us for our Smoake.

exciseing   frequency: 1   relative frequency: 0.0000
    P. 194 TWO HORSES   88 Of Exciseing our Cups and Taxing our Smoak.

excising. See "exciseing."

exclude   frequency: 1   relative frequency: 0.0000
    P.   69 A. HOUSE   325 But, to exclude the World, did guard

excluding   frequency: 1   relative frequency: 0.0000
    P. 12 DROP OF DEW   29 So the World excluding round,

excommunicate   frequency: 1   relative frequency: 0.0000
    P. 175 LOYALL SCOT   129 To Excommunicate and Study health.

excrescence   frequency: 1   relative frequency: 0.0000
    P. 56 BILL-BOROW   13 For whose excrescence ill design'd,

excus'd   frequency: 1   relative frequency: 0.0000
    P. 125 O.C.   83 For he no duty by his height excus'd,

excuse   frequency: 3   relative frequency: 0.0000
    P. 36 DAPHNIS   105 Yet he does himself excuse;
    P. 60 A. HOUSE   61 And yet what needs there here Excuse,
    P. 146 INSTRUCTIONS 215 He, to excuse his slowness, truth confest

excuses   frequency: 1   relative frequency: 0.0000
    P. 46 AMETAS   9 Thus you vain Excuses find,

executioner   frequency: 1   relative frequency: 0.0000
    P. 35 DAPHNIS   67 For my Executioner,

executioners   frequency: 1   relative frequency: 0.0000
    P. 163 INSTRUCTIONS 940 As Thieves repriev'd for Executioners;

exercise   frequency: 2   relative frequency: 0.0000
    P. 83 FLECKNO   21 Begins to exercise; as if I were
    P. 175 LOYALL SCOT   139 For only Kings can Bishops Exercise.

exercisedst   frequency: 1   relative frequency: 0.0000
    P. 109 ANNIVERSARY   231 But in thine own Fields exercisedst long,

exhalation   frequency: 1   relative frequency: 0.0000
    P. 186 BRITANNIA   66 From Exhalation bred of bloud and tears.

exhale   frequency: 2   relative frequency: 0.0000
    P. 12 DROP OF DEW   18 And to the Skies exhale it back again.
    P. 80 A. HOUSE   686 Which from the putrid Earth exhale,

exhibition   frequency: 1   relative frequency: 0.0000
    P. 167 KINGS VOWES   47 Miss and I will both learne to live on
                            Exhibition,

exil'd   frequency: 1   relative frequency: 0.0000
    P. 155 INSTRUCTIONS 614 His exil'd Sov'raign on its happy Board;

exile   frequency: 2   relative frequency: 0.0000
    P. 150 INSTRUCTIONS 406 Where Pilgrim Palmer travell'd in Exile,
    P. 201 HISTORICALL   3 Twelve Yeares compleat he suffer'd in Exile

expatiation   frequency: 1   relative frequency: 0.0000
    P. 140 HOUSEWARMING 104 As too narrow by far for his expatiation,

expect   frequency: 4   relative frequency: 0.0000
    P. 59 A. HOUSE   1 Within this sober Frame expect
    P. 74 A. HOUSE   496 Will in green Age her Hearse expect.
    P. 139 HOUSEWARMING   92 Where you are to expect the Scepter and Crown.
    P. 155 INSTRUCTIONS 609 He finds wheresoe're he succour might expect,

expectants   frequency: 1   relative frequency: 0.0000
    P. 144 INSTRUCTIONS 159 Expectants pale, with hopes of spoil allur'd,

expects   frequency: 1   relative frequency: 0.0000
    P. 161 INSTRUCTIONS 854 Expects as at a Play till Turner's drest.

expels   frequency: 1   relative frequency: 0.0000
    P. 92 MAY'S DEATH   87 Against thee, and expels thee from their side,

expence   frequency: 2   relative frequency: 0.0000
    P. 125 O.C.   92 At its rich bloods expence their Sorrows chear,
    P. 139 HOUSEWARMING   82 But for the expence he rely'd upon Worstenholm,

expences   frequency: 1   relative frequency: 0.0000
    P. 138 HOUSEWARMING   26 And all for to save the expences of Brickbat,

expense   frequency: 1   relative frequency: 0.0000
    See also "expence."
    P. 132 PARADISE   42 Whence furnish such a vast expense of Mind?

expenses. See "expences."

experiment   frequency: 1   relative frequency: 0.0000

P. 142 INSTRUCTIONS   52 For an Experiment upon the Crown.

expires   frequency: 1   relative frequency: 0.0000
     P. 180 STOCKSMARKET   50 Whose loyalty now all expires with his spankers.

explain   frequency: 2   relative frequency: 0.0000
     P. 131 PARADISE   15 Lest he perplext the things he would explain,
     P. 162 INSTRUCTIONS   865 That may his Body, this his Mind explain.

expos'd   frequency: 4   relative frequency: 0.0000
     P. 55 THYESTE   12 Who expos'd to others Ey's,
     P. 160 INSTRUCTIONS   783 Who all our Ships expos'd in Chathams Net?
     P. 171 PROPHECY   51 Their Wives to his Lust expos'd, their Wealth
                              to his spoyle
     P. 187 BRITANNIA   113 My reverend head expos'd to scorn and shame,

expose   frequency: 1   relative frequency: 0.0000
     P. 180 STOCKSMARKET   43 Or else thus expose him to popular flouts,

express   frequency: 7   relative frequency: 0.0001
     P. 12 DROP OF DEW   25 Does, in its pure and circling thoughts, express
     P. 35 DAPHNIS   71 Than be fatted up express
     P. 118 BLAKE   143 A choice which did the highest worth express,
     P. 127 O.C.   164 That we could to his Memory express.
     P. 142 INSTRUCTIONS   65 Express her studying now, if China-clay,
     P. 163 INSTRUCTIONS   907 Express him startling next with listning ear,
     P. 180 STOCKSMARKET   47 To express how his navy was shattered and torn

expressing   frequency: 1   relative frequency: 0.0000
     P. 130 O.C.   298 Which in expressing, we ourselves betray.

exprest   frequency: 3   relative frequency: 0.0000
     P. 59 A. HOUSE   11 The Beasts are by their Denns exprest:
     P. 125 O.C.   74 Had ev'ry figure of her woes exprest;
     P. 176 LOYALL SCOT   190 Nature in Living Embleme there Exprest

extend   frequency: 1   relative frequency: 0.0000
     P. 107 ANNIVERSARY   154 The World by Sin, does by the same extend.

extended   frequency: 2   relative frequency: 0.0000
     P. 37 DEFINITION   10 Where my extended Soul is fixt,
     P. 128 O.C.   204 His tendernesse extended unto all.

extends   frequency: 2   relative frequency: 0.0000
     P. 109 ANNIVERSARY   251 He on the Peace extends a Warlike power,
     P. 125 O.C.   93 If some dear branch where it extends its life

extent   frequency: 2   relative frequency: 0.0000
     P. 12 DROP OF DEW   7 And in its little Globes Extent,
     P. 60 A. HOUSE   37 Men will dispute how their Extent

extirpate   frequency: 1   relative frequency: 0.0000
     P. 178 LOYALL SCOT   258 For shame extirpate from each loyall brest

extort   frequency: 1   relative frequency: 0.0000
     P. 178 LOYALL SCOT   275 Thy death more noble did the same Extort.

extreame   frequency: 1   relative frequency: 0.0000
     P. 198 DUKE   32 That extreame unction is but common oyle

extreme. See "extreame."

extremes   frequency: 1   relative frequency: 0.0000
     P. 42 DAMON   23 Not July causeth these Extremes,

ey'd   frequency: 2   relative frequency: 0.0000
     P. 104 ANNIVERSARY   57 The listning Structures he with Wonder ey'd,
     P. 153 INSTRUCTIONS   527 Through the vain sedge the bashful Nymphs he
                              ey'd;

eye   frequency: 22   relative frequency: 0.0004
     P.   3 LOVELACE   23 And on each line cast a reforming eye,
     P. 10 DIALOGUE   32 Which should first attract thine Eye:
     P. 15 EYES   10 Within the Scales of either Eye,
     P. 18 CLORINDA   12 Safe from the Sun. D. not Heaven's Eye.
     P. 19 THYRSIS   9 Thyrsis. Turn thine Eye to yonder Skie,
     P. 20 SOUL & BODY   5 Here blinded with an Eye; and there
     P. 37 DEFINITION   13 For Fate with jealous Eye does see
     P. 68 A. HOUSE   308 But Ecchoes to the Eye and smell.
     P. 73 A. HOUSE   461 Such Fleas, ere they approach the Eye,
     P. 74 A. HOUSE   497 When first the Eye this Forrest sees

P.	75	A. HOUSE	532	The hatching Thrastles shining Eye,
P.	81	A. HOUSE	726	But pure, and spotless as the Eye;
P.	84	FLECKNO	65	The Needles Eye thread without any stich,
P.	88	ODE	59	But with his keener Eye
P.	90	MAY'S DEATH	4	And with an Eye uncertain, gazing wide,
P.	91	MAY'S DEATH	51	Foul Architect that hadst not Eye to see
P.	110	ANNIVERSARY	273	Some lusty Mate, who with more careful Eye
P.	122	TWO SONGS	40	Our Flocks and us with a propitious Eye.
P.	130	O.C.	273	And his own shadows with him fall; the eye
P.	149	INSTRUCTIONS	345	So the sad Tree shrinks from the Mornings Eye;
P.	163	INSTRUCTIONS	917	While, the pale Ghosts, his Eye does fixt admire
P.	199	DUKE	77	His sense, his soul as squinting as his eye.

eyed.   See "ey'd," "one-ey'd," "pig-eyed."

eyelids.   See "eylids."

eyes   frequency: 45   relative frequency: 0.0009
      See also "ey's."

P.	4	LOVELACE	43	Mine eyes invaded with a female spight,
P.	15	EYES	t	Eyes and Tears.
P.	15	EYES	2	With the same Eyes to weep and see!
P.	15	EYES	16	Melt in these Pendants of the Eyes.
P.	16	EYES	28	Bath still their Eyes in their own Dew.
P.	16	EYES	30	Dissolv'd those captivating Eyes,
P.	16	EYES	36	As two Eyes swoln with weeping are.
P.	16	EYES	45	Ope then mine Eyes your double Sluice,
P.	16	EYES	48	But only humane Eyes can weep.
P.	17	EYES	54	Till Eyes and Tears be the same things:
P.	17	EYES	56	These weeping Eyes, those seeing Tears.
P.	23	NYMPH	80	Find it, although before mine Eyes.
P.	26	MISTRESS	14	Thine Eyes, and on thy Forehead Gaze.
P.	27	LOVER	18	Which at his Eyes he alwaies bears.
P.	29	THE GALLERY	16	Black Eyes, red Lips, and curled Hair.
P.	31	FAIR SINGER	5	That while she with her Eyes my Heart does bind,
P.	31	FAIR SINGER	16	Who has th' advantage both of Eyes and Voice,
P.	31	MOURNING	4	Spring from the Starrs of Chlora's Eyes?
P.	31	MOURNING	5	Her Eyes confus'd, and doubled ore,
P.	32	MOURNING	14	Her Eyes have so her Bosome drown'd,
P.	34	DAPHNIS	35	And with rowling Eyes did glare,
P.	38	PICTURE	18	And parly with those conquering Eyes;
P.	41	DAMON	5	Like her fair Eyes the day was fair;
P.	44	DAMON	86	Whom Julianas Eyes do wound.
P.	61	A. HOUSE	81	While with slow Eyes we these survey,
P.	79	A. HOUSE	653	'Twere shame that such judicious Eyes
P.	94	DR. WITTY	32	Whose happy Eyes on thy Translation fall,
P.	97	HOLLAND	92	Fills the Priests Nostrils and puts out his Eyes.
P.	106	ANNIVERSARY	142	And intercepts the Beams of Mortal eyes,
P.	108	ANNIVERSARY	199	With wandring Eyes, and restless Ears they stood,
P.	111	ANNIVERSARY	335	His weeping Eyes the doleful Vigils keep,
P.	111	ANNIVERSARY	339	Why did mine Eyes once see so bright a Ray;
P.	119	TWO SONGS	1	Th' Astrologers own Eyes are set,
P.	119	TWO SONGS	13	The Shepheard, since he saw thine Eyes,
P.	120	TWO SONGS	22	Mine Eyes uncessant deluges.
P.	120	TWO SONGS	37	O why, as well as Eyes to see,
P.	122	TWO SONGS	19	'Twas those Eyes, I now dare swear,
P.	127	O.C.	162	Then those of Moses hid from humane Eyes;
P.	129	O.C.	248	And mortal sleep over those wakeful eyes:
P.	144	INSTRUCTIONS	133	A thousand Hands she has and thousand Eyes,
P.	162	INSTRUCTIONS	869	At Pray'rs, his Eyes turn up the Pious white,
P.	162	INSTRUCTIONS	888	From his clear Eyes, yet these too dark with Care.
P.	162	INSTRUCTIONS	895	Her mouth lockt up, a blind before her Eyes,
P.	168	ADVICE	26	That give their votes more by their eyes than ears:
P.	171	PROPHECY	55	Then They with envious Eyes shall Belgium See

eylids   frequency: 1   relative frequency: 0.0000
      P.   68 A. HOUSE   293 Then Flow'rs their drowsie Eylids raise,

ey's   frequency: 1   relative frequency: 0.0000
      P.   55 THYESTE   12 Who expos'd to others Ey's,

fable   frequency: 1   relative frequency: 0.0000
      P. 131 PARADISE   8 The sacred Truths to Fable and old Song,

fables   frequency: 1   relative frequency: 0.0000

P. 127 O.C.   175 Whose greater Truths obscure the Fables old,

fabrick   frequency: 2   relative frequency: 0.0000
P. 105 ANNIVERSARY   96 The Fabrick as with Arches stronger binds,
P. 138 HOUSEWARMING   59 While into a fabrick the Presents would muster;

fabulous   frequency: 1   relative frequency: 0.0000
P. 173 LOYALL SCOT   70 Nor Chaunt the fabulous hunt of Chivy Chase:

fac'd   frequency: 3   relative frequency: 0.0000
P. 157 INSTRUCTIONS   661 Fixt on his Ship, he fac'd that horrid Day,
P. 170 PROPHECY   13 When bare fac'd Villany shall not blush to cheat
P. 172 LOYALL SCOT   27 Fix'd on his ship hee fac'd the horrid day

face   frequency: 24   relative frequency: 0.0005
P. 10 DIALOGUE   34 In this Crystal view thy face.
P. 62 A. HOUSE   124 'The Face and Graces of the Saint.
P. 63 A. HOUSE   130 'If here your hand, your Face we had:
P. 72 A. HOUSE   442 A new and empty Face of things;
P. 81 A. HOUSE   729 Go now fond Sex that on your Face
P. 81 A. HOUSE   733 Yet your own Face shall at you grin,
P. 94 DR. WITTY   22 But her own smiles commend that lovely face;
P. 129 O.C.   259 And in his alter'd face you something faigne
P. 142 INSTRUCTIONS   76 And her self scorn'd for emulous Denham's Face;
P. 143 INSTRUCTIONS   85 His brazen Calves, his brawny Thighs, (the
                               Face
P. 144 INSTRUCTIONS   158 But knew the Word and well could face about;
P. 153 INSTRUCTIONS   534 And his new Face looks in the English Wave.
P. 156 INSTRUCTIONS   636 Or Face so red thine Oker and thy Lack.
P. 157 INSTRUCTIONS   684 His burning Locks adorn his Face Divine.
P. 159 INSTRUCTIONS   744 And Medway chast ravish'd before his Face,
P. 161 INSTRUCTIONS   838 With Face new bleacht, smoothen'd and stiff with
                               starch.
P. 162 INSTRUCTIONS   867 Bright Hair, fair Face, obscure and dull of
                               Head;
P. 162 INSTRUCTIONS   891 Raise up a sudden Shape with Virgins Face,
P. 166 KINGS VOWES   28 I will have a fine Court with ne'er an old face,
P. 173 LOYALL SCOT   50 His burning Locks Adorn his face divine.
P. 191 STATUE   54 But to turn the face to Whitehall you must
                               Shun,
P. 199 DUKE   75 Letts see the nuntio Arundells sweete face;
P. 199 DUKE   78 Let Belassis Autumnall face be seene,
P. 315 CHEQUER INN   103 His Braine and Face Tredenham wrung

faces   frequency: 2   relative frequency: 0.0000
P. 29 THE GALLERY   6 Of various Faces, by are laid;
P. 73 A. HOUSE   460 As Spots, so shap'd, on Faces do.

fack   frequency: 1   relative frequency: 0.0000
P. 316 CHEQUER INN   162 He'd bring him off i' fack.

fact. See "fack."

faction   frequency: 2   relative frequency: 0.0000
P. 129 O.C.   272 When truth shall be allow'd, and faction cease,
P. 148 INSTRUCTIONS   288 Of clear Estates, and to no Faction sworn;

factious   frequency: 1   relative frequency: 0.0000
P. 178 LOYALL SCOT   267 The Idle tumult of his factious bees,

fade   frequency: 1   relative frequency: 0.0000
P. 18 CLORINDA   7 D. Grass withers; and the Flow'rs too fade.

fades. See "faids."

faids   frequency: 1   relative frequency: 0.0000
P. 199 DUKE   44 The wound of which now tainted Churchill faids,

faigne   frequency: 1   relative frequency: 0.0000
P. 129 O.C.   259 And in his alter'd face you something faigne

fail   frequency: 5   relative frequency: 0.0001
See also "faile."
P. 22 NYMPH   12 Rather then fail. But, O my fears!
P. 71 A. HOUSE   396 Whose yet unfeather'd Quils her fail.
P. 80 A. HOUSE   685 For streight those giddy Rockets fail,
P. 142 INSTRUCTIONS   70 Moon, that o'rcome with the sick steam did'st
                               fail;
P. 204 HISTORICALL   143 'Twas want of Wit and Courage made them fail,

fail'd   frequency: 5   relative frequency: 0.0001

P. 59 A. HOUSE   24 Though the first Builders fail'd in Height?
P. 107 ANNIVERSARY   175 How near they fail'd, and in thy sudden Fall
P. 148 INSTRUCTIONS   309 Where force had fail'd with Stratagem to play,
P. 149 INSTRUCTIONS   329 But when this fail'd, and Months enough were
                          spent,
P. 176 LOYALL SCOT   183 And while hee spared the keepers life hee fail'd.

faile   frequency: 1   relative frequency: 0.0000
P. 313 CHEQUER INN   27 'Twill faile him in a yeare

failes   frequency: 1   relative frequency: 0.0000
P. 314 CHEQUER INN   81 (His Cup he never failes)

fails. See "failes."

fain   frequency: 2   relative frequency: 0.0000
P. 20 THYRSIS   40 Dorinda. I'm sick, I'm sick, and fain would
                          dye:
P. 99 HOLLAND   142 Would render fain unto our better Rome.

faint   frequency: 3   relative frequency: 0.0000
See also "faint-green-sickness."
P. 24 NYMPH   93 O help! O help! I see it faint:
P. 147 INSTRUCTIONS   278 And the faint sweat trickled down Temples
                          Brows.
P. 151 INSTRUCTIONS   443 The gravell'd Count did with the Answer faint:

faint-green-sickness   frequency: 1   relative frequency: 0.0000
P. 186 BRITANNIA   76 Virtues a faint-green-sickness of the souls,

fair   frequency: 34   relative frequency: 0.0007
See also "faire," "fayre."
P.   3 LOVELACE   2 Which your sweet Muse which your fair Fortune
                          chose,
P.   9 DIALOGUE   5 See where an Army, strong as fair,
P. 11 DIALOGUE   51 All this fair, and soft, and sweet,
P. 15 EYES   13 What in the World most fair appears,
P. 16 EYES   35 Nor Cynthia Teeming show's so fair,
P. 19 THYRSIS   15 Thyrsis. Do not sigh (fair Nimph) for fire
P. 24 NYMPH   107 In fair Elizium to endure,
P. 25 YOUNG LOVE   11 Whose fair Blossoms are too green
P. 30 THE GALLERY   30 How long thou shalt continue fair;
P. 31 FAIR SINGER   t The Fair Singer.
P. 31 FAIR SINGER   7 I could have fled from One but singly fair:
P. 38 PICTURE   4 And there with her fair Aspect tames
P. 38 PICTURE   29 Of sweetness, seeing they are fair;
P. 41 DAMON   5 Like her fair Eyes the day was fair;
P. 42 DAMON   33 How long wilt Thou, fair Shepheardess,
P. 48 THE GARDEN   9 Fair quiet, have I found thee here,
P. 48 THE GARDEN   23 Fair Trees! where s'eer your barkes I wound,
P. 61 A. HOUSE   91 Fair beyond Measure, and an Heir
P. 61 A. HOUSE   92 Which might Deformity make fair.
P. 63 A. HOUSE   160 'Might such fair Hands as yours it tye!
P. 75 A. HOUSE   523 The Stock-doves, whose fair necks are grac'd
P. 80 A. HOUSE   695 She yet more Pure, Sweet, Streight, and Fair,
P. 113 BLAKE   3 But though the wind was fair, they slowly swoome
P. 123 O.C.   6 What death might least so fair a Life deface.
P. 140 HOUSEWARMING   112 He comes to be roasted next St. James's Fair.
P. 143 INSTRUCTIONS   94 Nor scorns to rub him down with those fair
                          Hands;
P. 149 INSTRUCTIONS   333 Thus, like fair Thieves, the Commons Purse
                          they share,
P. 149 INSTRUCTIONS   342 What to fair Denham mortal Chocolat;
P. 154 INSTRUCTIONS   537 Their streaming Silks play through the weather
                          fair,
P. 162 INSTRUCTIONS   867 Bright Hair, fair Face, obscure and dull of
                          Head;
P. 164 INSTRUCTIONS   964 Or in fair Fields to rule the easie Flock.
P. 187 BRITANNIA   117 But his fair soul, transform'd by that French
                          Dame,
P. 314 CHEQUER INN   59 Like Maidens at a Statute Fair,

faire   frequency: 5   relative frequency: 0.0001
P.   3 LOVELACE   16 On the faire blossome of each growing wit.
P. 68 A. HOUSE   304 With Breath so sweet, or Cheek so faire.
P. 129 O.C.   245 Francisca faire can nothing now but weep,
P. 166 KINGS VOWES   38 As bold as Alce Pierce and as faire as Jane
                          Shore;
P. 186 BRITANNIA   61 Faire flower-deluces in an Azure field

fairer   frequency: 1   relative frequency: 0.0000

```
     P. 124 O.C.            40 And thorough that sparkled her fairer Mind;

fairest                        frequency:   1    relative frequency: 0.0000
     P.   4 LOVELACE         49 Him, valianst men, and fairest Nymphs approve,

fairfacian                     frequency:   1    relative frequency: 0.0000
     P.  82 A. HOUSE        740 On the Fairfacian Oak does grow;

fairfax                        frequency:  10    relative frequency: 0.0002
     P.  56 BILL-BOROW       t2 To the Lord Fairfax.
     P.  59 A. HOUSE          t Upon Appleton House, to my Lord Fairfax.
     P.  60 A. HOUSE         36 By Vere and Fairfax trod before,
     P.  63 A. HOUSE        147 'Fairfax I know; and long ere this
     P.  65 A. HOUSE        197 Now Fairfax seek her promis'd faith:
     P.  67 A. HOUSE        258 Young Fairfax through the Wall does rise.
     P.  67 A. HOUSE        274 To Fairfax fell as by Escheat.
     P.  74 A. HOUSE        492 On one hand Fairfax, th' other Veres:
     P.  81 A. HOUSE        724 Of Fairfax, and the starry Vere;
     P.  82 A. HOUSE        748 And find a Fairfax for our Thwaites)

fairies. See "fairyes," "faryes."

fairy                          frequency:   1    relative frequency: 0.0000
     See also "fayry."
     P.  72 A. HOUSE        430 Which they in Fairy Circles tread:

fairyes                        frequency:   1    relative frequency: 0.0000
     P.  43 DAMON            61 The deathless Fairyes take me oft

faith                          frequency:  14    relative frequency: 0.0002
     P.  65 A. HOUSE        197 Now Fairfax seek her promis'd faith:
     P.  65 A. HOUSE        212 'Who first Thee from thy Faith misled.
     P.  97 HOLLAND          63 Faith, that could never Twins conceive before,
     P. 131 PARADISE         14 O're which lame Faith leads Understanding
                               blind;
     P. 170 PROPHECY         24 Shall be in use at Court but faith and Troth,
     P. 170 PROPHECY         27 When publike faith and Vowes and Payments stop,
     P. 174 LOYALL SCOT      91 All Letanies in this have wanted faith:
     P. 174 LOYALL SCOT     123 And learn to pin your faith upon their sleeves.
     P. 175 LOYALL SCOT     156 In faith Erronicus and in life Prophane
     P. 175 LOYALL SCOT     157 These Hypocrites their faith and Linnen stain.
     P. 178 LOYALL SCOT     260 One King, one faith, one Language and one Ile:
     P. 192 TWO HORSES       17 But they that faith Catholick ne're understood,
     P. 192 TWO HORSES       45 Ch. That he should be styled defender o' th
                               faith,
     P. 203 HISTORICALL      83 Who with vain Faith made all their Reason
                               blind:

falchion. See "fauchion."

falckner                       frequency:   1    relative frequency: 0.0000
     P.  89 ODE              96 The Falckner has her sure.

falcon                         frequency:   1    relative frequency: 0.0000
     P.  89 ODE              91 So when the Falcon high

falconer. See "falckner."

fall                           frequency:  33    relative frequency: 0.0006
     P.   4 HASTINGS          6 And, ere they fall, arrest the early Showers.
     P.  10 DIALOGUE         40 And suspend the Rivers Fall.
     P.  15 EYES              8 Like wat'ry Lines and Plummets fall.
     P.  33 DAPHNIS          10 Soon she let that Niceness fall;
     P.  37 DEFINITION       21 Unless the giddy Heaven fall,
     P.  44 GLO-WORMS         8 Then to presage the Grasses fall;
     P.  45 MOWER'S SONG     22 Will in one common Ruine fall.
     P.  49 THE GARDEN       40 Insnar'd with Flow'rs, I fall on Grass.
     P.  70 A. HOUSE        380 Whether he fall through it or go.
     P.  76 A. HOUSE        552 Should fall by such a feeble Strok'!
     P.  76 A. HOUSE        559 While the Oake seems to fall content,
     P.  85 FLECKNO          74 Does make a primitive Sotana fall;
     P.  86 FLECKNO         147 For he his untun'd voice did fall or raise
     P.  94 DR. WITTY        32 Whose happy Eyes on thy Translation fall,
     P. 105 ANNIVERSARY      84 And some fall back upon the Architect;
     P. 107 ANNIVERSARY     151 And Stars still fall, and still the Dragons
                               Tail
     P. 107 ANNIVERSARY     163 That she might seem, could we the Fall dispute,
     P. 107 ANNIVERSARY     175 How near they fail'd, and in thy sudden Fall
     P. 108 ANNIVERSARY     190 On their own Hopes shall find the Fall retort.
     P. 110 ANNIVERSARY     295 Who watch'd thy halting, and thy Fall deride,
     P. 110 ANNIVERSARY     302 And their Religion only is to Fall.
```

```
        P. 126 O.C.            125 With pensive head towards the ground they fall,
        P. 128 O.C.            203 But within one its narrow limits fall,
        P. 130 O.C.            273 And his own shadows with him fall; the eye
        P. 148 INSTRUCTIONS    297 Then closing, all in equal Front fall on,
        P. 157 INSTRUCTIONS    664 Then, lest Heav'n fall, e're thither he ascend.
        P. 159 INSTRUCTIONS    767 All our miscarriages on Pett must fall:
        P. 172 LOYALL SCOT      30 Then least Heaven fall ere thither hee Ascend.
        P. 175 LOYALL SCOT     140 Will you bee treated Princes? here fall to:
        P. 178 LOYALL SCOT     254 Say but a Scot and  treight wee fall to sides:
        P. 196 TWO HORSES      178 Will publish their faults and prophesy their
                                   fall.
        P. 196 TWO HORSES      180 They teach them the Sooner to fall to their
                                   Swords.
        P. 205 HISTORICALL     164 All England strait should fall beneath his
                                   yoake,


fallen.  See "fall'n," "faln," "fal'n."


fallest.  See "fal'st."


falling                        frequency:    5    relative frequency: 0.0001
        P.  18 BERMUDAS         40 With falling Oars they kept the time.
        P. 108 ANNIVERSARY     201 Thou Cromwell falling, not a stupid Tree,
        P. 147 INSTRUCTIONS    250 The falling Bridge behind, the Stream below.
        P. 188 BRITANNIA       140 'Tis god-like-good to save a falling King.
        P. 198 DUKE              7 First draw him falling prostrate to the South,


falling-sickness               frequency:    1    relative frequency: 0.0000
        P. 110 ANNIVERSARY     304 Thy Falling-sickness should have made thee
                                   Reign,


fall'n                         frequency:    2    relative frequency: 0.0000
        P.  65 A. HOUSE        211 'It must have fall'n upon her Head
        P. 129 O.C.            270 When fall'n shews taller yet than as it grew:


falls                          frequency:    5    relative frequency: 0.0001
        P.  29 THE GALLERY      22 And Manna falls, and Roses spring;
        P.  89 ODE              92 Falls heavy from the Sky,
        P. 125 O.C.             98 Weeps that it falls ere fix'd into a Grape.
        P. 125 O.C.            102 Fore boding Princes falls, and seldom vain.
        P. 148 INSTRUCTIONS    295 The Van and Battel, though retiring, falls


falmouths                      frequency:    1    relative frequency: 0.0000
        P. 201 HISTORICALL      22 He marry'd Minhier Falmouths pregnant wench.


faln                           frequency:    1    relative frequency: 0.0000
        P. 108 ANNIVERSARY     206 It seem'd the Sun was faln out of the Sphere:


fal'n                          frequency:    1    relative frequency: 0.0000
        P.  78 A. HOUSE        625 For now the Waves are fal'n and dry'd,


false                          frequency:   17    relative frequency: 0.0003
        P.  15 EYES              6 In a false Angle takes each hight;
        P.  23 NYMPH            50 Perhaps as false or more than he.
        P.  23 NYMPH            54 The love of false and cruel men.
        P.  67 A. HOUSE        261 The Relicks false were set to view;
        P.  86 FLECKNO         153 Sir you read false. That any one but you
        P.  87 FLECKNO         156 To say that you read false Sir is no Lye.
        P. 104 ANNIVERSARY      24 Took in by Proxie, beggs a false Renown;
        P. 151 INSTRUCTIONS    413 False Terrors our believing Fears devise:
        P. 159 INSTRUCTIONS    775 Who with false News prevented the Gazette?
        P. 163 INSTRUCTIONS    933 False to his Master Bristol, Arlington,
        P. 164 INSTRUCTIONS    969 And to improve themselves, on false pretence,
        P. 170 PROPHECY         11 And those false Men the Soveraign People sent
        P. 187 BRITANNIA       124 False Finch, Knave Anglesey misguide the
                                   seals;
        P. 195 TWO HORSES      136 Under all that shall Reign of the false
                                   Scottish race.
        P. 199 DUKE             52 Then in false hopes of being once a Queene
        P. 200 DUKE            105 Destroyd by a false brother and false friend.


falser                         frequency:    1    relative frequency: 0.0000
        P. 163 INSTRUCTIONS    934 And Coventry, falser than any one,


fal'st                         frequency:    1    relative frequency: 0.0000
        P. 141 INSTRUCTIONS      3 But er'e thou fal'st to work, first Painter see


falstaffs                      frequency:    1    relative frequency: 0.0000
        P. 168 ADVICE           23 Place Falstaffs Regement of Thread-bare
                                   Coates


fam'd                          frequency:    3    relative frequency: 0.0000
```

```
P.  185  BRITANNIA        42  The other day fam'd Spencer I did bring
P.  188  BRITANNIA       156  From her sage mouth fam'd Principles to know,
P.  189  BRITANNIA       176  On whose fam'd Deeds all tongues, all writers
                              wait.
```

fame   frequency: 19   relative frequency: 0.0003
```
P.    3  LOVELACE         14  And against others Fame his owne employs.
P.   14  THE CORONET      16  With wreaths of Fame and Interest.
P.   55  EPITAPH           1  Enough: and leave the rest to Fame.
P.   58  BILL-BOROW       64  Those Acts that swell'd the Cheek of Fame.
P.   67  A. HOUSE        282  Whom France and Poland yet does fame:
P.   89  ODE              88  His Fame to make it theirs:
P.   93  DR. WITTY         1  Sit further, and make room for thine own fame,
P.   97  HOLLAND          81  Let it suffice to give their Country Fame
P.  115  BLAKE            73  'Twas more for Englands fame you should dye
                              there,
P.  119  BLAKE           167  Whilst fame in every place, her Trumpet blowes,
P.  128  O.C.            224  Spare yet your own, if you neglect his fame;
P.  141  INSTRUCTIONS     15  Or if to score cut our compendious Fame,
P.  142  INSTRUCTIONS     61  Paint her with Oyster Lip, and breath of Fame,
P.  143  INSTRUCTIONS     97  But envious Fame, too soon, begun to note
P.  157  INSTRUCTIONS    693  Fortunate Boy! if either Pencil's Fame,
P.  173  LOYALL SCOT      60  That Matchless grace to propagate thy fame,
P.  187  BRITANNIA       118  Had lost all sense of Honour, Justice, fame;
P.  188  BRITANNIA       160  Shall darken story, Ingross loudmouthd fame.
P.  202  HISTORICALL      73  We leave to the report of Common fame.
```

familiar   frequency: 1   relative frequency: 0.0000
```
P.   77  A. HOUSE        589  And Ivy, with familiar trails,
```

families   frequency: 1   relative frequency: 0.0000
```
P.  140  HIS HOUSE         4  The price of ruin'd Families:
```

family   frequency: 1   relative frequency: 0.0000
```
P.  200  DUKE             85  And Pimpt to have his family defil'd.
```

famine   frequency: 1   relative frequency: 0.0000
```
P.  138  HOUSEWARMING     35  What Joseph by Famine, he wrought by
                              Sea-Battel;
```

famish   frequency: 1   relative frequency: 0.0000
```
P.   28  LOVER            37  Thus while they famish him, and feast,
```

famous   frequency: 1   relative frequency: 0.0000
```
P.  147  INSTRUCTIONS    275  Such once Orlando, famous in Romance,
```

fan   frequency: 1   relative frequency: 0.0000
```
P.  125  O.C.             82  Or fan with airy plumes so soft an heat.
```

fancied   frequency: 1   relative frequency: 0.0000
```
P.  115  BLAKE            54  Which of the Gods the fancied drink exceeds;
```

fancies   frequency: 1   relative frequency: 0.0000
```
P.  132  PARADISE         49  Their Fancies like our bushy Points appear,
```

fancy. See "phancy."

fantastic. See "phantastik."

far   frequency: 30   relative frequency: 0.0006
See also "farr," "farre."
```
P.   17  BERMUDAS          8  And yet far kinder than our own?
P.   23  NYMPH            53  Thy Love was far more better then
P.   23  NYMPH            67  And when 'thad left me far away,
P.   30  THE GALLERY      47  And a Collection choicer far
P.   43  DAMON            56  Yet am I richer far in Hay.
P.   48  THE GARDEN       22  How far these Beauties Hers exceed!
P.   49  THE GARDEN       46  Far other Worlds, and other Seas;
P.   54  THYESTE           6  And far of the publick Stage
P.   58  BILL-BOROW       60  Their prudent Heads too far intrust.
P.   63  A. HOUSE        157  'Our Abbess too, now far in Age,
P.   91  MAY'S DEATH      39  Far from these blessed shades tread back agen
P.   96  HOLLAND          21  Building their watry Babel far more high
P.  106  ANNIVERSARY     125  Till then my Muse shall hollow far behind
P.  108  ANNIVERSARY     193  First winged Fear transports them far away,
P.  112  ANNIVERSARY     358  'And beaked Promontories sail'd from far;
P.  113  ANNIVERSARY     400  As far above their Malice as my Praise.
P.  115  BLAKE            62  Kind Nature had from thence remov'd so far.
P.  117  BLAKE           122  Far more enflam'd by it, then by the Sun.
P.  118  BLAKE           135  Scarce souls from bodies sever'd are so far,
P.  118  BLAKE           141  Far different Motives yet, engag'd them thus,
```

P.	120	TWO SONGS	36 How far below thine Orbe sublime?
P.	122	TWO SONGS	18 Far more catching then my Hook.
P.	138	HOUSEWARMING	53 They approve it thus far, and said it was fine;
P.	140	HOUSEWARMING	104 As too narrow by far for his expatiation,
P.	140	HOUSEWARMING	110 Lest with driving too far his Tallow impair;
P.	150	INSTRUCTIONS	400 And thought all safe if they were so far off.
P.	179	STOCKSMARKET	25 This statue is surely more scandalous far
P.	180	STOCKSMARKET	60 Yet we'd better by far have him than his brother.
P.	186	BRITANNIA	56 How by her Peoples lookes persued from far
P.	190	STATUE	36 Will you venture soe far to Prorogue the King too?

farewel   frequency: 1   relative frequency: 0.0000
    P. 36 DAPHNIS   89 Farewel therefore all the fruit

farewell. See "farewel."

farm   frequency: 1   relative frequency: 0.0000
    P. 153 INSTRUCTIONS 499 The Kingdoms Farm he lets to them bid least:

farmers   frequency: 1   relative frequency: 0.0000
    P. 139 HOUSEWARMING   66 Sinners, Governors, Farmers, Banquers, Patentees.

farr   frequency: 5   relative frequency: 0.0001
    P. 130 O.C.   296 (Farr better known above than here below;)
    P. 167 KINGS VOWES   44 My Bawd shall Embassadors send farr and neare,
    P. 170 PROPHECY   4 As farr as from Whitehall to Pudden lane
    P. 183 MADE FREE   93 Hee is too farr gone to begin it:
    P. 199 DUKE   47 To finde such wellcome when you come soe farr.

farre   frequency: 2   relative frequency: 0.0000
    P. 130 O.C.   287 Thou in a pitch how farre beyond the sphere
    P. 202 HISTORICALL   71 And gentlier farre the Orleans Dutches treat.

farted   frequency: 1   relative frequency: 0.0000
    P. 196 TWO HORSES   168 Both Gallopt to Whitehall and there Horribly farted,

farthing   frequency: 2   relative frequency: 0.0000
    P. 159 INSTRUCTIONS 761 The Court in Farthing yet it self does please,
    P. 193 TWO HORSES   62 No token should appear but a poor Copper farthing;

faryes   frequency: 1   relative frequency: 0.0000
    P. 41 THE MOWER   35 And Fauns and Faryes do the Meadows till,

fashion   frequency: 2   relative frequency: 0.0000
    P. 132 PARADISE   50 The Poets tag them; we for fashion wear.
    P. 168 ADVICE   19 Our Pig-eyed Duncomb in his Dover Fashion

fast   frequency: 9   relative frequency: 0.0001
    P. 24 NYMPH   109 O do not run too fast: for I
    P. 64 A. HOUSE   167 'And that, once sprung, increase so fast
    P. 65 A. HOUSE   207 'Death only can such Theeves make fast,
    P. 84 FLECKNO   53 Would break his fast before, said he was Sick,
    P. 124 O.C.   51 Hold fast dear Infants, hold them both or none;
    P. 128 O.C.   200 So loose an enemy, so fast a friend.
    P. 165 KINGS VOWES   11 That shall furnish me Treasure as fast as I spend;
    P. 166 KINGS VOWES   24 But if they build it too fast, I will soon make them hold.
    P. 171 PROPHECY   54 For that still fill'd runs out as fast againe;

fastening. See "fast'ning."

fast'ning   frequency: 1   relative frequency: 0.0000
    P. 105 ANNIVERSARY   90 Fast'ning the Contignation which they thwart;

fat   frequency: 1   relative frequency: 0.0000
    P. 97 HOLLAND   91 While the fat steam of Female Sacrifice

fatal   frequency: 9   relative frequency: 0.0001
    See also "fatall."
    P. 31 FAIR SINGER   4 Joyning themselves in fatal Harmony;
    P. 110 ANNIVERSARY   272 Giddy, and wishing for the fatal Shore;
    P. 115 BLAKE   57 With fatal Gold, for still where that does grow,
    P. 123 O.C.   21 To Love and Grief the fatal Writ was sign'd;
    P. 126 O.C.   138 Left to determine now his fatal Hour;
    P. 138 HOUSEWARMING   27 That Engine so fatal, which Denham had brain'd,
    P. 151 INSTRUCTIONS 423 Not such a fatal stupefaction reign'd

P. 157 INSTRUCTIONS 669 The fatal Bark him boards with grappling fire,
P. 159 INSTRUCTIONS 757 To see that fatal Pledge of Sea-command,

fatall   frequency: 2   relative frequency: 0.0000
P. 172 LOYALL SCOT   35 The fatall bark him boards with Grapling fire
P. 185 BRITANNIA   23 Bawl: What fatall crimes make you forever fly

fate   frequency: 36   relative frequency: 0.0007
P.   4 HASTINGS   8 With early Tears must mourn his early Fate.
P. 25 YOUNG LOVE   21 So we win of doubtful Fate;
P. 31 MOURNING   1 You, that decipher out the Fate
P. 34 DAPHNIS   36 And his cruel Fate forswear.
P. 35 DAPHNIS   65 Why should I enrich my Fate?
P. 36 DAPHNIS   93 Fate I come, as dark, as sad,
P. 37 DEFINITION   11 But Fate does Iron wedges drive,
P. 37 DEFINITION   13 For Fate with jealous Eye does see
P. 37 DEFINITION   30 But Fate so enviously debarrs,
P. 61 A. HOUSE   84 The Progress of this Houses Fate.
P. 66 A. HOUSE   247 Yet, against Fate, his Spouse they kept;
P. 71 A. HOUSE   400 To him a Fate as black forebode.
P. 82 A. HOUSE   747 (Till Fate her worthily translates,
P. 88 ODE   37 Though Justice against Fate complain,
P. 89 ODE   72 Foresaw it's happy Fate.
P. 92 MAY'S DEATH   75 Yet wast thou taken hence with equal fate,
P. 98 HOLLAND   111 A Cock-boat tost with the same wind and fate;
P. 104 ANNIVERSARY   40 From the deserved Fate their guilty lives:
P. 114 BLAKE   33 Both health and profit, Fate cannot deny;
P. 115 BLAKE   71 Deluded men! Fate with you did but sport,
P. 117 BLAKE   105 Wer't not for that, they from their Fate would
                        run,
P. 117 BLAKE   117 Bold Stainer Leads, this Fleets design'd by
                        fate,
P. 117 BLAKE   125 Fate these two Fleets, between both Worlds had
                        brought.
P. 123 O.C.   11 Nor Fate indeed can well refuse that right
P. 124 O.C.   68 Where She so long her Fathers fate had worn:
P. 125 O.C.   77 Fate could not either reach with single stroke,
P. 125 O.C.   109 But never yet was any humane Fate
P. 143 INSTRUCTIONS 111 The Dice betwixt them must the Fate divide,
P. 155 INSTRUCTIONS 585 Our wretched Ships within their Fate attend,
P. 157 INSTRUCTIONS 700 Ally'd in Fate, increase, with theirs, her
                        Flames.
P. 159 INSTRUCTIONS 763 But Fate does still accumulate our Woes,
P. 169 ADVICE   38 The humble fate of a Plebeian nose;
P. 200 DUKE   89 And change the order of a nation's fate?
P. 200 DUKE   116 Hard fate of princes, who will nere believe,
P. 201 HISTORICALL   5 At length by wonderfull impulse of Fate
P. 204 HISTORICALL 128 Now must my Muse deplore the Nations fate,

fates   frequency: 1   relative frequency: 0.0000
P. 124 O.C.   46 How on each other both their Fates depend.

father   frequency: 12   relative frequency: 0.0002
P. 96 HOLLAND   46 Him they their Lord and Country's Father
                        speak.
P. 110 ANNIVERSARY 282 Him as their Father must the State obey.
P. 130 O.C.   309 He, as his father, long was kept from sight
P. 159 INSTRUCTIONS 749 And Father Neptune promis'd to resign
P. 177 LOYALL SCOT 226 Ev'n Father Dis tho so with Age defac'd
P. 192 TWO HORSES   48 For which his own Father a Martyr did dye.
P. 192 TWO HORSES   50 Not to think his own Father is gone to the
                        Devill.
P. 195 TWO HORSES   127 Tho Father and Sonne are different Bodds,
P. 195 TWO HORSES   146 Father Patricks Deciple will make England
                        smart.
P. 196 TWO HORSES   182 They that Conquered the Father won't be slaves
                        to the Son:
P. 198 DUKE   9 Most holy Father, being joyned in league
P. 198 DUKE   10 With Father Patricke Darby and with Teage,

fathers   frequency: 6   relative frequency: 0.0001
P. 25 YOUNG LOVE   3 Clear thine aged Fathers brow
P. 124 O.C.   68 Where She so long her Fathers fate had worn:
P. 163 INSTRUCTIONS 937 His Fathers Ghost too whisper'd him one Note,
P. 188 BRITANNIA   137 In his deaf ear sound his dead Fathers name;
P. 201 HISTORICALL   4 And kept his Fathers Asses all the while.
P. 316 CHEQUER INN 134 Fathers and Sons like Coupl'd Slaves

fatigue   frequency: 1   relative frequency: 0.0000
P. 147 INSTRUCTIONS 280 Spent with fatigue, to breath a while Toback.

fatted   frequency: 1   relative frequency: 0.0000

```
        P.  35 DAPHNIS         71 Than be fatted up express

fauchion                          frequency:    1    relative frequency: 0.0000
        P. 112 ANNIVERSARY    384 'And still his Fauchion all our Knots unties.

fauconberg                        frequency:    1    relative frequency: 0.0000
        P. 119 TWO SONGS      t1 Two Songs at the Marriage of the Lord
                                 Fauconberg

fault                             frequency:    2    relative frequency: 0.0000
        P. 179 STOCKSMARKET   13 When each one that passes finds fault with the
                                 horse,
        P. 180 STOCKSMARKET   30 Does the fault upon the artificer lay,

faultlesse                        frequency:    1    relative frequency: 0.0000
        P.   3 LOVELACE       26 You shall for being faultlesse be accus'd.

faults                            frequency:    5    relative frequency: 0.0001
        P. 150 INSTRUCTIONS  391 In quick Effigy, others Faults, and feign
        P. 160 INSTRUCTIONS  787 Had he not built, none of these faults had bin;
        P. 180 STOCKSMARKET   57 But with all his faults restore us our King,
        P. 196 TWO HORSES    178 Will publish their faults and prophesy their
                                 fall.
        P. 200 DUKE          103 Shooke by the faults of others, not thine owne.

faun                              frequency:    5    relative frequency: 0.0001
        P.  22 NYMPH          t The Nymph complaining for the death of her
                                 Faun.
        P.  22 NYMPH          2 Have shot my Faun and it will dye.
        P.  22 NYMPH         32 Hath taught a Faun to hunt his Dear.
        P.  22 NYMPH         36 Left me his Faun, but took his Heart.
        P.  24 NYMPH        105 Now my Sweet Faun is vanish'd to

fauns                             frequency:    1    relative frequency: 0.0000
        P.  41 THE MOWER     35 And Fauns and Faryes do the Meadows till,

faux's                            frequency:    1    relative frequency: 0.0000
        P. 139 HOUSEWARMING  90 A Lanthorn, like Faux's surveys the burnt
                                 Town,

favor.  See "favour."

favorable.  See "favourable."

favored.  See "favour'd."

favorite                          frequency:    1    relative frequency: 0.0000
        P. 127 O.C.         157 O Cromwell, Heavens Favorite! To none

favorites                         frequency:    1    relative frequency: 0.0000
        P. 185 BRITANNIA     15 Till Cavaleers shall favorites be Deem'd

favors                            frequency:    1    relative frequency: 0.0000
        See also "favours."
        P.  54 THYESTE        2 Tottering favors Pinacle;

favour                            frequency:    3    relative frequency: 0.0000
        P.  58 BILL-BOROW    75 But Peace (if you his favour prize)
        P.  85 FLECKNO       94 Me a great favour, for I seek to go.
        P. 121 TWO SONGS     52 For he has Cynthia's favour won.

favourable                        frequency:    1    relative frequency: 0.0000
        P. 172 LOYALL SCOT    5 And (as a favourable Pennance) Chose

favour'd                          frequency:    1    relative frequency: 0.0000
        P. 184 BRITANNIA     11 Brit: Favour'd by night, conceald by this
                                 disguise,

favoured.  See "favour'd."

favourite.  See "favorite."

favourites.  See "favorites."

favours                           frequency:    2    relative frequency: 0.0000
        See also "favors."
        P.  34 DAPHNIS       51 When thy Favours should me wound
        P. 201 HISTORICALL    9 Nor did he such small favours then disdain

fawn.  See "faun."

fawns                             frequency:    1    relative frequency: 0.0000
```

P. 142 INSTRUCTIONS   72 And Fawns, that from the womb abortive fled.

fayre   frequency: 1   relative frequency: 0.0000
    P. 183 MADE FREE   94 Or does your fayre show

fayry   frequency: 2   relative frequency: 0.0000
    P. 185 BRITANNIA   31 Tell him of Golden Indies, Fayry Lands,
    P. 185 BRITANNIA   33 Thus Fayry like the King they steal away

feake   frequency: 1   relative frequency: 0.0000
    P. 110 ANNIVERSARY   305 While Peake and Simpson would in many a Tome,

fear   frequency: 31   relative frequency: 0.0006
    See also "feare."
    P. 19 THYRSIS   21 Thyrsis. Oh, ther's, neither hope nor fear
    P. 21 SOUL & BODY   34 And then the Palsie Shakes of Fear.
    P. 38 PICTURE   12 The wanton Love shall one day fear,
    P. 57 BILL-BOROW   41 Fear of the Master, and respect
    P. 65 A. HOUSE   223 'Fly from their Ruine. How I fear
    P. 89 ODE   99 What may not others fear
    P. 90 MAY'S DEATH   16 The Subjects Safety, and the Rebel's Fear.
    P. 92 MAY'S DEATH   64 And fear has Coward Churchmen silenced,
    P. 105 ANNIVERSARY   104 And wisely court the Influence they fear;
    P. 108 ANNIVERSARY   193 First winged Fear transports them far away,
    P. 113 ANNIVERSARY   395 Pardon, great Prince, if thus their Fear or
                              Spight
    P. 113 BLAKE   12 But yet in them caus'd as much fear, as Joy.
    P. 114 BLAKE   22 So that such darkness might suppress their fear;
    P. 115 BLAKE   74 Where you had most of strength, and least of
                              fear.
    P. 116 BLAKE   80 Make them admire, so much as they did fear.
    P. 117 BLAKE   108 Do not so much suppress, as shew their fear.
    P. 122 TWO SONGS   13 Fear not; at Menalca's Hall
    P. 123 O.C.   7 The People, which what most they fear esteem,
    P. 127 O.C.   182 And fearing God how they should nothing fear.
    P. 131 PARADISE   12 I lik'd his Project, the success did fear;
    P. 152 INSTRUCTIONS   486 Now thinks all but too little for their Fear.
    P. 154 INSTRUCTIONS   572 March straight to Chatham, to increase the fear.
    P. 155 INSTRUCTIONS   610 Confusion, folly, treach'ry, fear, neglect.
    P. 157 INSTRUCTIONS   663 Nor other fear himself could comprehend,
    P. 158 INSTRUCTIONS   709 Officious fear, however, to prevent
    P. 160 INSTRUCTIONS   812 Blames the last Session, and this more does
                              fear.
    P. 161 INSTRUCTIONS   861 Trembling with joy and fear, Hyde them
                              Prorogues,
    P. 172 LOYALL SCOT   29 Nor other fear himself cold Comprehend
    P. 187 BRITANNIA   89 And they will fear those powers they once did
                              scorn.
    P. 194 TWO HORSES   108 Letts be true to ourselves; whom then need wee
                              fear?

fear'd   frequency: 3   relative frequency: 0.0000
    P. 67 A. HOUSE   260 And superstitions vainly fear'd.
    P. 116 BLAKE   98 Wish then for that assault he lately fear'd.
    P. 158 INSTRUCTIONS   735 Such the fear'd Hebrew, captive, blinded, shorn,

feare   frequency: 2   relative frequency: 0.0000
    P. 200 DUKE   107 What all thy subjects doe each minute feare:
    P. 202 HISTORICALL   41 But the Dutch fleet fled suddainly with feare;

fearful   frequency: 2   relative frequency: 0.0000
    P. 114 BLAKE   15 Of winds and waters rage, they fearful be,
    P. 114 BLAKE   16 But much more fearful are your Flags to see.

fearing   frequency: 4   relative frequency: 0.0000
    P. 39 THE MATCH   3 Fearing, when She should be decay'd,
    P. 71 A. HOUSE   399 Fearing the Flesh untimely mow'd
    P. 127 O.C.   182 And fearing God how they should nothing fear.
    P. 186 BRITANNIA   80 Fearing the mighty Projects of the great

fears   frequency: 9   relative frequency: 0.0001
    P. 22 NYMPH   12 Rather then fail. But, O my fears!
    P. 25 YOUNG LOVE   4 From cold Jealousie and Fears.
    P. 88 ODE   49 Where, twining subtile fears with hope,
    P. 112 ANNIVERSARY   373 'Yet if through these our Fears could find a
                              pass;
    P. 142 INSTRUCTIONS   45 Nor fears he the most Christian should trepan
    P. 143 INSTRUCTIONS   89 Fears lest he scorn a Woman once assay'd,
    P. 150 INSTRUCTIONS   374 All to new Sports their wanton fears release.
    P. 151 INSTRUCTIONS   413 False Terrors our believing Fears devise:
    P. 189 BRITANNIA   174 Blake, Candish, Drake, (men void of slavish fears)

feast   frequency: 6   relative frequency: 0.0001
    P.   4 HASTINGS   20 And on the Tree of Life once made a Feast,
    P.   18 CLORINDA   5 The Grass I aim to feast thy Sheep:
    P.   19 THYRSIS   26 May feast with Musick of the Spheres.
    P.   28 LOVER   37 Thus while they famish him, and feast,
    P.   85 FLECKNO   110 Betwixt us two the Dinner to a Feast.
    P. 316 CHEQUER INN   142 Twas such a Feast that I'm afraid

feat   frequency: 1   relative frequency: 0.0000
    P. 139 HOUSEWARMING   81 For surveying the building, Prat did the feat,

feather-men   frequency: 1   relative frequency: 0.0000
    P. 146 INSTRUCTIONS   223 Nor the late Feather-men, whom Tomkins fierce

feather'd   frequency: 1   relative frequency: 0.0000
    P. 155 INSTRUCTIONS   597 Our feather'd Gallants, which came down that day

features   frequency: 1   relative frequency: 0.0000
    P.   63 A. HOUSE   133 'Some of your Features, as we sow'd,

fed   frequency: 6   relative frequency: 0.0001
    P.   28 LOVER   33 They fed him up with Hopes and Air,
    P.   28 LOVER   35 And as one Corm'rant fed him, still
    P.   35 DAPHNIS   79 While with Quailes and Manna fed,
    P.   40 THE MOWER   8 Which stupifi'd them while it fed.
    P.   76 A. HOUSE   553 Nor would it, had the Tree not fed
    P.   84 FLECKNO   60 He stands, as if he only fed had been

feeble   frequency: 2   relative frequency: 0.0000
    P.   37 DEFINITION   7 Where feeble Hope could ne'r have flown
    P.   76 A. HOUSE   552 Should fall by such a feeble Strok'!

feed   frequency: 6   relative frequency: 0.0001
    P.   24 NYMPH   83 Upon the Roses it would feed,
    P.   73 A. HOUSE   463 They feed so wide, so slowly move,
    P.   76 A. HOUSE   558 But serves to feed the Hewels young.
    P. 181 MADE FREE   9 And your Orphans want Bread to feed on,
    P. 203 HISTORICALL   89 And with dull Crambo feed the silly sheep.
    P. 314 CHEQUER INN   89 Did feed his Neighbour over-thwart

feeds   frequency: 2   relative frequency: 0.0000
    P.   84 FLECKNO   49 He never feeds; save only when he tryes
    P. 144 INSTRUCTIONS   136 And on all Trade like Casawar she feeds:

feel   frequency: 4   relative frequency: 0.0000
    P.   21 SOUL & BODY   24 I feel, that cannot feel, the pain.
    P.   92 MAY'S DEATH   94 Shalt break, and the perpetual Vulture feel.
    P. 115 BLAKE   49 Forces and art, she soon will feel, are vain,

feet   frequency: 14   relative frequency: 0.0002
    See also "feete."
    P.   15 THE CORONET   26 May crown thy Feet, that could not crown thy
                               Head.
    P.   16 EYES   32 To fetter her Redeemers feet.
    P.   17 BERMUDAS   22 And throws the Melons at our feet.
    P.   20 SOUL & BODY   4 In Feet; and manacled in Hands.
    P.   23 NYMPH   64 'Twas on those little silver feet.
    P.   24 NYMPH   119 There at my feet shalt thou be laid,
    P.   29 THE GALLERY   23 And, at thy Feet, the wooing Doves
    P.   43 DAMON   48 In cowslip-water bathes my feet.
    P.   45 MOWER'S SONG   16 While I lay trodden under feet?
    P.   57 BILL-BOROW   20 The feet of breathless Travellers.
    P.   83 FLECKNO   11 Not higher then Seav'n, nor larger then three
                               feet;
    P.   89 ODE   85 He to the Commons Feet presents
    P. 143 INSTRUCTIONS   86 She slights) his Feet shapt for a smoother race.
    P. 176 LOYALL SCOT   189 Where but two hands to Act, two feet to goe.

feete   frequency: 1   relative frequency: 0.0000
    P. 198 DUKE   11 Throwne att thy sacred feete I humbly bow,

feign   frequency: 6   relative frequency: 0.0001
    See also "faigne."
    P.   92 MAY'S DEATH   95 'Tis just what Torments Poets ere did feign,
    P. 141 INSTRUCTIONS   22 Of his Hound's Mouth to feign the raging froth,
    P. 146 INSTRUCTIONS   232 They feign a parly, better to surprize:
    P. 148 INSTRUCTIONS   314 To cheat their Pay, feign want, the House
                               accuse.
    P. 150 INSTRUCTIONS   391 In quick Effigy, others Faults, and feign

P. 156 INSTRUCTIONS 635 Scarce can burnt Iv'ry feign an Hair so black,

feign'd   frequency: 5   relative frequency: 0.0001
  P. 81 A. HOUSE   718 And feign'd complying Innocence;
  P. 98 HOLLAND   117 While, with feign'd Treaties, they invade by
                           stealth
  P. 104 ANNIVERSARY   29 Their other Wars seem but a feign'd contest,
  P. 156 INSTRUCTIONS 630 Long since were fled on many a feign'd pretence.
  P. 163 INSTRUCTIONS 931 Through their feign'd speech their secret hearts
                           he knew;

feigns   frequency: 1   relative frequency: 0.0000
  P. 124 O.C.   62 And He to lessen hers his Sorrow feigns:

feild   frequency: 1   relative frequency: 0.0000
  P. 174 LOYALL SCOT   113 At Bishops Dung the Foxes quit the feild.

fell   frequency: 15   relative frequency: 0.0003
  P. 44 DAMON   79 And there among the Grass fell down,
  P. 67 A. HOUSE   274 To Fairfax fell as by Escheat.
  P. 74 A. HOUSE   493 Of whom though many fell in War,
  P. 75 A. HOUSE   544 Which fit to stand and which to fell.
  P. 95 HOLLAND   5 Or what by th' Oceans slow alluvion fell,
  P. 95 HOLLAND   8 Fell to the Dutch by just Propriety.
  P. 124 O.C.   65 That whether by each others grief they fell,
  P. 145 INSTRUCTIONS 188 Of Debtors deep, fell to Trelawny's Care.
  P. 145 INSTRUCTIONS 201 Thence fell to Words, but, quarrel to adjourn,
  P. 146 INSTRUCTIONS 236 The Speaker early, when they all fell in.
  P. 149 INSTRUCTIONS 358 Blasted with Lightning, struck with Thunder
                           fell.
  P. 156 INSTRUCTIONS 623 Such from Euphrates bank, a Tygress fell,
  P. 160 INSTRUCTIONS 794 And place in Counsel fell to Duncombes share.
  P. 192 TWO HORSES   34 Not onely discoursed but fell to disputes.
  P. 202 HISTORICALL   38 And Plague and Warre fell heavye on our Isle.

fell'd   frequency: 1   relative frequency: 0.0000
  P. 316 CHEQUER INN   140 The Belly Timber that they fell'd

fellow'd   frequency: 1   relative frequency: 0.0000
  P. 191 TWO HORSES   7 Livy tells a strang story can hardly be fellow'd

fellows   frequency: 2   relative frequency: 0.0000
  P. 155 INSTRUCTIONS 603 Or to their fellows swim on board the Dutch,
  P. 159 INSTRUCTIONS 746 Thou, and thy Fellows, held'st the odious
                           Light.

fellowship   frequency: 1   relative frequency: 0.0000
  P. 45 MOWER'S SONG   14 A fellowship so true forego,

felt   frequency: 5   relative frequency: 0.0001
  P. 128 O.C.   197 Pity it seem'd to hurt him more that felt
  P. 149 INSTRUCTIONS 339 And with fresh Age felt his glad Limbs unite;
  P. 152 INSTRUCTIONS 473 Never old Letcher more repugnance felt,
  P. 157 INSTRUCTIONS 685 But, when in his immortal Mind he felt
  P. 173 LOYALL SCOT   51 But when in his Imortall mind hee felt

female   frequency: 6   relative frequency: 0.0001
  P.   4 LOVELACE   43 Mine eyes invaded with a female spight,
  P. 97 HOLLAND   91 While the fat steam of Female Sacrifice
  P. 144 INSTRUCTIONS 142 Her, of a female Harpy, in Dog Days:
  P. 150 INSTRUCTIONS 379 Where when the brawny Female disobeys,
  P. 159 INSTRUCTIONS 762 And female Stewart, there, Rules the four
                           Seas.
  P. 177 LOYALL SCOT   250 And ever since men with a female spite

females   frequency: 2   relative frequency: 0.0000
  P. 72 A. HOUSE   429 Their Females fragrant as the Mead
  P. 81 A. HOUSE   728 On Females, if there want a Male.

fence   frequency: 3   relative frequency: 0.0000
  P. 10 DIALOGUE   46 As when a single Soul does fence
  P. 67 A. HOUSE   287 And with five Bastions it did fence,
  P. 164 INSTRUCTIONS 970 About the Common Prince have rais'd a Fence;

fencers   frequency: 1   relative frequency: 0.0000
  P. 168 ADVICE   5 The Roman takeing up the fencers trade,

fenwick   frequency: 1   relative frequency: 0.0000
  P. 127 O.C.   189 And where the sandy mountain Fenwick scal'd,

fern   frequency: 1   relative frequency: 0.0000

P. 35 DAPHNIS   82 For the Fern, whose magick Weed

fertile   frequency: 5   relative frequency: 0.0001
P. 29 THE GALLERY   12 Thy fertile Shop of cruel Arts:
P. 58 BILL-BOROW   72 The Trophees of one fertile Year.
P. 97 HOLLAND   64 Never so fertile, spawn'd upon this shore:
P. 109 ANNIVERSARY   236 And down at last thou pow'rdst the fertile
                          Storm;
P. 114 BLAKE   30 Fertile to be, yet never need her showres.

fervent   frequency: 1   relative frequency: 0.0000
P. 177 LOYALL SCOT   224 Others Attempt, to Cool their fervent Chine,

fetch   frequency: 4   relative frequency: 0.0000
P. 19 THYRSIS   23 No need of Dog to fetch our stray,
P. 127 O.C.   184 Where those that strike from Heaven fetch their
                          Blow.
P. 129 O.C.   232 To fetch day, presse about his chamber-door;
P. 201 HISTORICALL   26 To fetch for Charles the floury Lisbon Kate,

fetter   frequency: 1   relative frequency: 0.0000
P. 16 EYES   32 To. fetter her Redeemers feet.

fetter'd   frequency: 1   relative frequency: 0.0000
P. 20 SOUL & BODY   3 With bolts of Bones, that fetter'd stands

fetters   frequency: 4   relative frequency: 0.0000
P. 31 FAIR SINGER   12 My Fetters of the very Air I breath?
P. 78 A. HOUSE   613 But, lest your Fetters prove too weak,
P. 159 INSTRUCTIONS   743 When aged Thames was bound with Fetters base,
P. 187 BRITANNIA   95 Whilst your starv'd power in Legall fetters
                          pines.

feud   frequency: 1   relative frequency: 0.0000
P. 174 LOYALL SCOT   90 Noe Scotch was ever like a Bishops feud.

fever   frequency: 1   relative frequency: 0.0000
P. 21 SOUL & BODY   16 (A Fever could but do the same.)

few   frequency: 8   relative frequency: 0.0001
P. 58 BILL-BOROW   70 To him our Branches are but few.
P. 86 FLECKNO   121 And on full stomach do condemn but few:
P. 97 HOLLAND   61 Though Herring for their God few voices mist,
P. 117 LOYALL SCOT   240 And few indeed can paralell our Climes
P. 128 O.C.   221 But to the good (too many or too few)
P. 165 INSTRUCTIONS   989 (Where few the number, choice is there less hard)
P. 170 PROPHECY   3 Firetalls shall flye and but few see the traine
P. 193 TWO HORSES   65 Ch. And our few ships abroad become Tripoly's
                          scorn

fewel   frequency: 2   relative frequency: 0.0000
P. 40 THE MATCH   33 Thus all his fewel did unite
P. 114 BLAKE   36 Fewel and Rain together kindly grow;

fewer   frequency: 1   relative frequency: 0.0000
P. 142 INSTRUCTIONS   56 In fewer months than Mothers once indur'd.

fiat   frequency: 1   relative frequency: 0.0000
P. 137 HOUSEWARMING   12 How he might create a House with a Fiat.

fiddle   frequency: 1   relative frequency: 0.0000
P. 195 TWO HORSES   152 W. And our Sir Joseph write news-books, and
                          fiddle.

fiddled. See "fidled."

fidled   frequency: 1   relative frequency: 0.0000
P. 137 HOUSEWARMING   18 Made Thebes dance aloft while he fidled and
                          sung,

field   frequency: 13   relative frequency: 0.0002
See also "feild," "tuttle-field."
P. 29 LOVER   64 In a Field Sable a Lover Gules.
P. 57 BILL-BOROW   25 Yet thus it all the field commands,
P. 72 A. HOUSE   418 The Mower now commands the Field;
P. 88 ODE   45 What Field of all the Civil Wars,
P. 126 O.C.   144 Twice had in open field him Victor crown'd:
P. 127 O.C.   187 Of that for ever Preston's field shall tell
P. 131 PARADISE   13 Through that wide Field how he his way should
                          find
P. 145 INSTRUCTIONS   175 Bronkard Loves Squire; through all the field
                                                         array'd,

P. 147 INSTRUCTIONS 258 Had strecht the monster Patent on the Field.
P. 148 INSTRUCTIONS 285 Nor could all these the Field have long
                         maintain'd,
P. 186 BRITANNIA   61 Faire flower-deluces in an Azure field
P. 196 TWO HORSES   177 Yet the beasts of the field or the stones in the
                         wall
P. 203 HISTORICALL   111 And hosts of upstart Errours gaine the field.

fields   frequency: 8   relative frequency: 0.0001
P. 40 THE MOWER   3 And from the fields the Flow'rs and Plants
                         allure,
P. 41 THE MOWER   32 While the sweet Fields do lye forgot:
P. 42 DAMON   20 Which burns the Fields and Mower both:
P. 82 A. HOUSE   745 Mean time ye Fields, Springs, Bushes,
                         Flow'rs,
P. 82 A. HOUSE   759 Much less the Dead's Elysian Fields,
P. 109 ANNIVERSARY   231 But in thine own Fields exercisedst long,
P. 139 HOUSEWARMING   95 Your Metropolis House is in St. James's
                         Fields,
P. 164 INSTRUCTIONS 964 Or in fair Fields to rule the easie Flock.

fiend   frequency: 2   relative frequency: 0.0000
P. 175 LOYALL SCOT   137 One Bishops fiend spirits a whole Diocesse.
P. 188 BRITANNIA   128 Fiend Lauderdale, with ordure all defiles.

fiends   frequency: 1   relative frequency: 0.0000
P. 205 HISTORICALL   173 Fiends of Ambition here his Soul possesst,

fierce   frequency: 11   relative frequency: 0.0002
P. 28 LOVER   49 See how he nak'd and fierce does stand,
P. 66 A. HOUSE   241 Is not this he whose Offspring fierce
P. 87 FLECKNO   166 Ere the fierce Poets anger turn'd to rime.
P. 128 O.C.   195 Hence, though in battle none so brave or fierce,
P. 129 O.C.   244 In horses fierce, wild deer, or armour bright;
P. 144 INSTRUCTIONS 149 Who, in an English Senate, fierce debate,
P. 146 INSTRUCTIONS 223 Nor the late Feather-men, whom Tomkins fierce
P. 157 INSTRUCTIONS 677 Like a glad Lover, the fierce Flames he meets,
P. 172 LOYALL SCOT   43 Like a glad lover the fierce Flames hee meets
P. 179 STOCKSMARKET   1 As cities that to the fierce conquerors yield
P. 189 BRITANNIA   177 When with fierce Ardour their brave souls do
                         burn,

fiery   frequency: 2   relative frequency: 0.0000
See also "firy."
P. 87 ODE   16 His fiery way divide.
P. 186 BRITANNIA   65 Her Towry front a fiery Meteor bears

fifteen   frequency: 2   relative frequency: 0.0000
P. 25 YOUNG LOVE   9 Common Beauties stay fifteen;
P. 97 HOLLAND   83 Some Fifteen hundred and more years ago;

fifth   frequency: 2   relative frequency: 0.0000
P. 74 A. HOUSE   502 To thrust up a Fifth Element;
P. 110 ANNIVERSARY   297 That their new King might the fifth Scepter
                         shake,

fifty   frequency: 1   relative frequency: 0.0000
P. 193 TWO HORSES   80 As not to be trusted for twice fifty shillings.

fight   frequency: 24   relative frequency: 0.0005
P.   9 DIALOGUE   4 Ballance thy Sword against the Fight.
P. 62 A. HOUSE   106 'Like Virgin Amazons do fight.
P. 66 A. HOUSE   242 Shall fight through all the Universe;
P. 104 ANNIVERSARY   27 They fight by Others, but in Person wrong,
P. 107 ANNIVERSARY   148 Girds yet his Sword, and ready stands to fight;
P. 114 BLAKE   37 And coolness there, with heat doth never fight,
P. 116 BLAKE   85 To fight against such Foes, was vain they knew,
P. 117 BLAKE   119 The Thund'ring Cannon now begins the Fight,
P. 117 BLAKE   121 The Air was soon after the fight begun,
P. 117 BLAKE   126 Who fight, as if for both those Worlds they
                         fought.
P. 118 BLAKE   138 Two dreadful Navies there at Anchor Fight.
P. 123 O.C.   12 To those that liv'd in War, to dye in Fight.
P. 130 O.C.   279 Singing of thee, inflame themselves to fight,
P. 141 INSTRUCTIONS   6 For so we too without a Fleet can fight.
P. 144 INSTRUCTIONS 148 (And Painter, wanting other, draw this Fight.)
P. 146 INSTRUCTIONS 230 To fight a Battel, from all Gun-shot free.
P. 147 INSTRUCTIONS 264 This Combat truer than the Naval Fight.
P. 148 INSTRUCTIONS 304 Is longer Work, and harder than to fight.
P. 177 LOYALL SCOT   251 First call each other names and then they fight.

P.	178 LOYALL SCOT	279	Against a Nation thou didst singly fight.
P.	194 TWO HORSES	122	Ch. Thy King will ne're fight unless't be for Queans.
P.	198 DUKE	5	Hateing all justice and resolv'd to fight
P.	198 DUKE	21	I nere can fight in a more glorious Cause
P.	202 HISTORICALL	40	With the Batavian common Wealth to fight.

fighter   frequency: 1   relative frequency: 0.0000
```
     P.  194 TWO HORSES   117 W. Thy Priest-ridden King turn'd desperate
                              Fighter
```

fighting   frequency: 2   relative frequency: 0.0000
```
     P.   31 FAIR SINGER    13 It had been easie fighting in some plain,
     P.  147 INSTRUCTIONS  248 Fighting it single till the rest might arm.
```

fights   frequency: 2   relative frequency: 0.0000
```
     P.   92 MAY'S DEATH    66 And single fights forsaken Vertues cause.
     P.  147 INSTRUCTIONS  274 That each, tho' Duelling, a Battel fights.
```

figs   frequency: 1   relative frequency: 0.0000
```
     P.   17 BERMUDAS       21 He makes the Figs our mouths to meet;
```

figure   frequency: 5   relative frequency: 0.0001
```
     P.   12 DROP OF DEW    27 In how coy a Figure wound,
     P.   60 A. HOUSE       48 In ev'ry Figure equal Man.
     P.   67 A. HOUSE      286 In the just Figure of a Fort;
     P.  125 O.C.           74 Had ev'ry figure of her woes exprest;
     P.  169 ADVICE         30 The figure of a Drunken Councell board
```

figures   frequency: 1   relative frequency: 0.0000
```
     P.   41 THE MOWER      39 But howso'ere the Figures do excel,
```

fil'd   frequency: 1   relative frequency: 0.0000
```
     P.  145 INSTRUCTIONS  173 Then the Procurers under Progers fil'd,
```

fill   frequency: 11   relative frequency: 0.0002
```
     P.   18 CLORINDA       22 But He ere since my Songs does fill:
     P.   24 NYMPH          88 On Roses thus its self to fill:
     P.   24 NYMPH         102 Keep these two crystal Tears; and fill
     P.   30 THE GALLERY    56 To crown her Head, and Bosome fill.
     P.   34 DAPHNIS        54 The delicious Cup we fill;
     P.  118 BLAKE         151 Their Gallions sunk, their wealth the Sea does
                              fill,
     P.  159 INSTRUCTIONS  742 Fill up thy space with a redoubled Night.
     P.  171 PROPHECY       52 With groans to fill his Treasure they must
                              toyle,
     P.  173 LOYALL SCOT    66 Unite our distance, fill the breaches old?
     P.  186 BRITANNIA      68 Pale death, lusts, Horrour fill her pompous
                              train.
     P.  199 DUKE           68 He's of a size indeed to fill a porch,
```

fill'd   frequency: 6   relative frequency: 0.0001
```
     P.   81 A. HOUSE      735 When knowledge only could have fill'd
     P.  113 BLAKE           7 Every capatious Gallions womb was fill'd,
     P.  124 O.C.           36 Which while she drain'd of Milk she fill'd with
                              Love.
     P.  154 INSTRUCTIONS  553 The liquid Region with their Squadrons fill'd,
     P.  171 PROPHECY       54 For that still fill'd runs out as fast againe;
     P.  315 CHEQUER INN   101 With his owne Gravy fill'd his Plate
```

filling   frequency: 1   relative frequency: 0.0000
```
     P.  155 INSTRUCTIONS  590 Filling his Sails, more force to recollect.
```

fills   frequency: 2   relative frequency: 0.0000
```
     P.   68 A. HOUSE      296 And fills its Flask with Odours new.
     P.   97 HOLLAND        92 Fills the Priests Nostrils and puts out his
                              Eyes.
```

final   frequency: 1   relative frequency: 0.0000
```
     P.   31 FAIR SINGER     1 To make a final conquest of all me,
```

finally. See "finly'r."

finch   frequency: 2   relative frequency: 0.0000
```
     P.  145 INSTRUCTIONS  186 Finch, in the Front, and Thurland in the Rear.
     P.  187 BRITANNIA     124 False Finch, Knave Anglesey misguide the
                              seals;
```

find   frequency: 33   relative frequency: 0.0006
```
     See also "finde."
     P.   14 THE CORONET    13 Alas I find the Serpent old
     P.   23 NYMPH          80 Find it, although before mine Eyes.
```

```
P.   26 MISTRESS        6 Should'st Rubies find: I by the Tide
P.   29 THE GALLERY     7 That, for all furniture, you'l find
P.   32 MOURNING       31 Would find her Tears yet deeper Waves
P.   41 THE MOWER      18 To find the Marvel of Peru.
P.   45 GLO-WORMS      16 That I shall never find my home.
P.   46 AMETAS          9 Thus you vain Excuses find,
P.   49 THE GARDEN     44 Does streight its own resemblance find;
P.   56 BILL-BOROW     14 Nature must a new Center find,
P.   59 A. HOUSE       27 In which we the Dimensions find
P.   62 A. HOUSE      108 'Lest the great Bridegroom find them dim.
P.   64 A. HOUSE      187 'Whom if our Lord at midnight find,
P.   76 A. HOUSE      548 Does find the hollow Oak to speak,
P.   76 A. HOUSE      576 Which I returning cannot find.
P.   82 A. HOUSE      748 And find a Fairfax for our Thwaites)
P.   90 ODE          105 The Pict no shelter now shall find
P.  108 ANNIVERSARY   190 On their own Hopes shall find the Fall retort.
P.  112 ANNIVERSARY   373 'Yet if through these our Fears could find a
                          pass;
P.  126 O.C.          150 In their own Griefs might find themselves
                          imploy'd;
P.  131 O.C.          319 We find already what those omens mean,
P.  131 PARADISE       13 Through that wide Field how he his way should
                          find
P.  132 PARADISE       41 Where couldst thou Words of such a compass find?
P.  152 INSTRUCTIONS  477 Or in their hasty Call to find a flaw,
P.  154 INSTRUCTIONS  575 For whose strong bulk Earth scarce could Timber
                          find,
P.  163 INSTRUCTIONS  927 At his first step, he Castlemain does find,
P.  174 LOYALL SCOT    87 But who Considers well will find indeed
P.  175 LOYALL SCOT   160 Who views but Gilberts Toyls will reason find
P.  183 MADE FREE      97 You durst not I find
P.  184 MADE FREE     124 He will find who unlocks,
P.  187 BRITANNIA     103 Rack nature till new pleasures she shall find,
P.  194 TWO HORSES    113 In every dark night you are sure to find him
P.  195 TWO HORSES    128 Between the two Scourges wee find little odds.
```

fin'd   frequency: 1   relative frequency: 0.0000
```
P.  313 CHEQUER INN    47 They all deserv'd to have been fin'd
```

finde   frequency: 2   relative frequency: 0.0000
```
P.    4 HASTINGS        3 Hastings is dead, and we must finde a Store
P.  199 DUKE           47 To finde such wellcome when you come soe farr.
```

finding   frequency: 1   relative frequency: 0.0000
```
P.   87 FLECKNO       167 He hasted; and I, finding my self free,
```

finds   frequency: 8   relative frequency: 0.0001
```
P.    4 LOVELACE       50 His Booke in them finds Judgement, with you
                          Love.
P.   15 EYES           23 But finds the Essence only Showers,
P.   97 HOLLAND        74 Opinion but finds Credit, and Exchange.
P.  150 INSTRUCTIONS  381 No concern'd Jury for him Damage finds,
P.  153 INSTRUCTIONS  530 He finds the Air, and all things, sweeter here.
P.  155 INSTRUCTIONS  609 He finds wheresoe're he succour might expect,
P.  163 INSTRUCTIONS  914 And finds the Drums Lewis's March did beat.
P.  179 STOCKSMARKET   13 When each one that passes finds fault with the
                          horse,
```

fine   frequency: 17   relative frequency: 0.0003
```
P.   26 MISTRESS       31 The Grave's a fine and private place,
P.   45 MOWER'S SONG    8 Grew more luxuriant still and fine;
P.   79 A. HOUSE      659 And every thing so whisht and fine,
P.   91 MAY'S DEATH    45 Tell them of Liberty, the Stories fine,
P.  138 HOUSEWARMING   53 They approve it thus far, and said it was fine;
P.  161 INSTRUCTIONS  835 But, fresh as from the Mint, the Courtiers fine
P.  165 KINGS VOWES    10 I will have a fine Parliament allwayes to
                          Friend,
P.  165 KINGS VOWES    13 I will have as fine Bishops as were ere made
                          with hands,
P.  165 KINGS VOWES    16 I will have a fine Chancelor beare all the sway,
P.  166 KINGS VOWES    19 I will have a fine Navy to Conquer the Seas,
P.  166 KINGS VOWES    25 I will have a fine Son in makeing the marrd,
P.  166 KINGS VOWES    28 I will have a fine Court with ne'er an old face,
P.  166 KINGS VOWES    35 I will have a fine Junto to doe what I will,
P.  166 KINGS VOWES    36 I will have two fine Secretaryes pisse thro one
                          Quill.
P.  166 KINGS VOWES    37 But what ever it cost I will have a fine Whore,
P.  167 KINGS VOWES    49 I will have a fine Tunick a Sash and a Vest,
P.  167 KINGS VOWES    52 I will have a fine pond and a pretty decoy,
```

finest   frequency: 1   relative frequency: 0.0000

         P. 64 A. HOUSE   178 'Still handling Natures finest Parts.

fingers   frequency: 3   relative frequency: 0.0000
    P.   23 NYMPH   56 I it at mine own fingers nurst.
    P.   84 FLECKNO   41 So while he with his gouty Fingers craules
    P. 139 HOUSEWARMING   69 Bulteales, Beakns, Morley, Wrens fingers with
                                telling

finish   frequency: 2   relative frequency: 0.0000
    P. 106 ANNIVERSARY   138 Would forthwith finish under such a Hand:
    P. 138 HOUSEWARMING   54 Yet his Lordship to finish it would be unable;

finish'd   frequency: 1   relative frequency: 0.0000
    P. 139 HOUSEWARMING   87 He finish'd at last his Palace Mosaick,

finished. See "finish'd," "finisht."

finisht   frequency: 1   relative frequency: 0.0000
    P. 141 INSTRUCTIONS   25 Chance finisht that which Art could but begin,

finly'r   frequency: 1   relative frequency: 0.0000
    P.   65 A. HOUSE   204 'An Art by which you finly'r cheat?

fir'd   frequency: 1   relative frequency: 0.0000
    P.   87 FLECKNO   160 Home, his most furious Satyr to have fir'd

fire   frequency: 16   relative frequency: 0.0003
    P.   16 EYES   38 Drench'd in these Waves, does lose it fire.
    P.   19 THYRSIS   15 Thyrsis. Do not sigh (fair Nimph) for fire
    P.   36 DAPHNIS   95 Yet bring with me all the Fire
    P.   40 THE MATCH   34 To make one fire high:
    P.   63 A. HOUSE   137 'And (for I dare not quench the Fire
    P. 117 BLAKE   130 As Oakes did then, Urg'd by the active fire.
    P. 118 BLAKE   161 All the Foes Ships destroy'd, by Sea or fire,
    P. 123 TWO SONGS   44 And those be equal that have equal Fire.
    P. 124 O.C.   53 A silent fire now wasts those Limbs of Wax,
    P. 157 INSTRUCTIONS   669 The fatal Bark him boards with grappling fire,
    P. 157 INSTRUCTIONS   681 Round the transparent Fire about him glows,
    P. 158 INSTRUCTIONS   713 So when the Fire did not enough devour,
    P. 172 LOYALL SCOT   35 The fatall bark him boards with Grapling fire
    P. 173 LOYALL SCOT   47 Round the Transparent fire about him Gloves
    P. 198 DUKE   13 A vow that fire and sword shall never end
    P. 202 HISTORICALL   48 He sells the Citty where 'twas sett on fire.

fire-ships   frequency: 1   relative frequency: 0.0000
    P. 156 INSTRUCTIONS   643 But when the frightful Fire-ships he saw,

fireballs   frequency: 1   relative frequency: 0.0000
    P. 170 PROPHECY   3 Fireballs shall flye and but few see the traine

firemen   frequency: 1   relative frequency: 0.0000
    P.   68 A. HOUSE   305 Well shot ye Firemen! Oh how sweet,

fires   frequency: 8   relative frequency: 0.0001
    P.   27 MISTRESS   36 At every pore with instant Fires,
    P.   42 DAMON   25 Tell me where I may pass the Fires.
    P.   44 GLC-WORMS   12 And after foolish Fires do stray;
    P.   68 A. HOUSE   306 And round your equal Fires do meet;
    P.   74 A. HOUSE   512 Echo about their tuned Fires.
    P. 150 INSTRUCIONS   372 To forge new Thunder, and inspect their Fires.
    P. 157 INSTRUCTIONS   660 That fly'st Love Fires, reserv'd for other
                                Flame?
    P. 172 LOYALL SCOT   26 That flyst loves fires reserv'd for other flame?'

firm   frequency: 3   relative frequency: 0.0000
    P. 109 ANNIVERSARY   248 Founding a firm State by Proportions true.
    P. 170 PROPHECY   1 The blood of the Just London's firm Doome
                                shall fix
    P. 188 BRITANNIA   152 To this firm Law their scepter did resign:

firmer   frequency: 1   relative frequency: 0.0000
    P. 179 STOCKSMARKET   20 Even Sir William Peake sits much firmer than
                                he.

first   frequency: 90   relative frequency: 0.0018
    P.   3 LOVELACE   32 Their first Petition by the Authour sent.
    P.   10 DIALOGUE   32 Which should first attract thine Eye:
    P.   21 SOUL & BODY   33 Whom first the Cramp of Hope does Tear:
    P.   23 NYMPH   55 With sweetest milk, and sugar, first
    P.   24 NYMPH   111 First my unhappy Statue shall
    P.   30 THE GALLERY   52 Remains, with which I first was took.

P.	40	THE MOWER	5	He first enclos'd within the Gardens square
P.	47	EMPIRE	1	First was the World as one great Cymbal made,
P.	47	EMPIRE	5	Jubal first made the wilder Notes agree;
P.	59	A. HOUSE	24	Though the first Builders fail'd in Height?
P.	61	A. HOUSE	85	A Nunnery first gave it birth.
P.	65	A. HOUSE	212	'Who first Thee from thy Faith misled.
P.	66	A. HOUSE	227	For first Religion taught him Right,
P.	66	A. HOUSE	232	First from a Judge, then Souldier bred.
P.	72	A. HOUSE	445	The World when first created sure
P.	74	A. HOUSE	485	Where the first Carpenter might best
P.	74	A. HOUSE	497	When first the Eye this Forrest sees
P.	76	A. HOUSE	555	(As first our Flesh corrupt within
P.	80	A. HOUSE	697	Therefore what first She on them spent,
P.	81	A. HOUSE	721	This 'tis to have been from the first
P.	85	FLECKNO	76	Worn at the first Counsel of Antioch:
P.	85	FLECKNO	86	But who came last is forc'd first to go out;
P.	86	FLECKNO	117	But now, Alas, my first Tormentor came,
P.	86	FLECKNO	138	Yet he first kist them, and after takes pains
P.	87	ODE	13	And, like the three-fork'd Lightning, first
P.	89	ODE	66	Which first assur'd the forced Pow'r.
P.	89	ODE	68	The Capitols first Line,
P.	89	ODE	86	A Kingdome, for his first years rents:
P.	89	ODE	95	Where, when he first does lure,
P.	92	MAY'S DEATH	71	But thou base man first prostituted hast
P.	92	MAY'S DEATH	96	Thou first Historically shouldst sustain.
P.	94	DR. WITTY	15	Of the first Author. Here he maketh blots
P.	96	HOLLAND	37	Therefore Necessity, that first made Kings,
P.	96	HOLLAND	43	Not who first see the rising Sun commands,
P.	96	HOLLAND	44	But who could first discern the rising Lands.
P.	97	HOLLAND	70	Each one thence pillag'd the first piece he found:
P.	103	ANNIVERSARY	t1	THE FIRST ANNIVERSARY
P.	105	ANNIVERSARY	75	The Commonwealth then first together came,
P.	107	ANNIVERSARY	153	For the great Justice that did first suspend
P.	108	ANNIVERSARY	193	First winged Fear transports them far away,
P.	109	ANNIVERSARY	229	For, neither didst thou from the first apply
P.	109	ANNIVERSARY	263	Therefore first growing to thy self a Law,
P.	111	ANNIVERSARY	325	So when first Man did through the Morning new
P.	119	BLAKE	164	And there first brings of his success the news;
P.	119	TWO SONGS	t3	First.
P.	126	O.C.	113	First the great Thunder was shot off, and sent
P.	127	O.C.	179	He first put Armes into Religions hand,
P.	128	O.C.	202	The first foundation of his house and name:
P.	140	HOUSEWARMING	100	Great Buckingham's Sacrifice must be the first.
P.	141	INSTRUCTIONS	3	But er'e thou fal'st to work, first Painter see
P.	143	INSTRUCTIONS	90	And now first, wisht she e're had been a Maid.
P.	144	INSTRUCTIONS	151	Of early Wittals first the Troop march'd in,
P.	145	INSTRUCTIONS	194	Or in his absence him that first it lay'd.
P.	146	INSTRUCTIONS	221	Not the first Cock-horse, that with Cork were shod
P.	147	INSTRUCTIONS	247	First spy'd the Enemy and gave th' Alarm:
P.	147	INSTRUCTIONS	255	First enter'd forward Temple, Conqueror
P.	148	INSTRUCTIONS	305	At the first Charge the Enemy give out;
P.	149	INSTRUCTIONS	330	They with the first days proffer seem content:
P.	149	INSTRUCTIONS	357	First Buckingham, that durst to him Rebel,
P.	150	INSTRUCTIONS	377	A Punishment invented first to awe
P.	150	INSTRUCTIONS	403	While the first year our Navy is but shown,
P.	151	INSTRUCTIONS	412	More tim'rous now we are, than first secure.
P.	152	INSTRUCTIONS	451	The first instructs our (Verse the Name abhors)
P.	152	INSTRUCTIONS	457	Presbyter Hollis the first point should clear;
P.	152	INSTRUCTIONS	481	First, then he march'd our whole Militia's force,
P.	154	INSTRUCTIONS	568	So at the first Salute resolves Retreat,
P.	155	INSTRUCTIONS	599	Leave him alone when first they hear the Gun;
P.	157	INSTRUCTIONS	678	And tries his first embraces in their Sheets.
P.	159	INSTRUCTIONS	747	Sad change, since first that happy pair was wed,
P.	159	INSTRUCTIONS	769	Whose Counsel first did this mad War beget?
P.	160	INSTRUCTIONS	786	Was the first cause of all these Naval slips:
P.	162	INSTRUCTIONS	900	He wonder'd first, then pity'd, then he lov'd:
P.	163	INSTRUCTIONS	927	At his first step, he Castlemain does find,
P.	167	KINGS VOWES	48	And I'lle first put the Church then my Crowne in Commission.
P.	172	LOYALL SCOT	44	And tries his first Imbraces in their sheets.
P.	174	LOYALL SCOT	107	Shews you first one, then makes that one two Balls.
P.	174	LOYALL SCOT	109	Pharoah at first would have sent Israell home.
P.	177	LOYALL SCOT	251	First call each other names and then they fight.
P.	179	STOCKSMARKET	9	But now it appears from the first to the last
P.	184	MADE FREE	109	The very First Head
P.	196	TWO HORSES	163	If Speech from Brute Animals in Romes first age
P.	198	DUKE	7	First draw him falling prostrate to the South,

```
        P. 199 DUKE           56 Clifford, who first appeared in humble guise,
        P. 199 DUKE           73 I'th Irish shambles he first learn'd the trade.
        P. 203 HISTORICALL    82 Priests were the first deluders of Mankind,
        P. 203 HISTORICALL   100 When our first Parents Paradice did grace,
        P. 204 HISTORICALL   117 First temper'd Poison to destroy our Lawes,
        P. 204 HISTORICALL   125 First brought his Mother for a Prostitute:
        P. 313 CHEQUER INN    16 And for his Countrey first began
        P. 313 CHEQUER INN    41 To cleare him wou'd have been the first
```

firy   frequency: 3   relative frequency: 0.0000
```
        P. 108 ANNIVERSARY   215 But thee triumphant hence the firy Carr,
        P. 108 ANNIVERSARY   216 And firy Steeds had born out of the Warr,
        P. 156 INSTRUCTIONS  646 E're in the Firy Furnace they be cast.
```

fish   frequency: 4   relative frequency: 0.0000
```
        P.  96 HOLLAND        29 The Fish oft-times the Burger dispossest,
        P.  97 HOLLAND        85 See but their Mairmaids with their Tails of
                                 Fish,
        P. 154 INSTRUCTIONS  562 With panting Heart, lay like a fish on Land,
        P. 175 LOYALL SCOT   141 Fish and flesh Bishops are the Ambigue.
```

fish'd   frequency: 1   relative frequency: 0.0000
```
        P.  95 HOLLAND        10 They with mad labour fish'd the Land to Shoar;
```

fishermen   frequency: 1   relative frequency: 0.0000
```
        P.  97 HOLLAND        58 Th' Apostles were so many Fishermen?
```

fishers. See "salmon-fishers."

fishes   frequency: 3   relative frequency: 0.0000
```
        P.  73 A. HOUSE      478 And Fishes do the Stables scale.
        P.  79 A. HOUSE      648 While at my Lires the Fishes twang!
        P.  80 A. HOUSE      677 The stupid Fishes hang, as plain
```

fit   frequency: 22   relative frequency: 0.0004
    See also "fitt."
```
        P.  21 SOUL & BODY    42 To build me up for Sin so fit?
        P.  28 LOVER          31 Guardians most fit to entertain
        P.  41 DAMON           4 The Scene more fit for his complaint.
        P.  59 A. HOUSE       14 In cases fit of Tortoise-shell.
        P.  63 A. HOUSE      140 'To holy things, for Heaven fit.
        P.  74 A. HOUSE      486 Fit Timber for his Keel have Prest.
        P.  75 A. HOUSE      544 Which fit to stand and which to fell.
        P.  85 FLECKNO       101 Consist but in one substance. Then, to fit
        P.  89 ODE            80 And fit for highest Trust:
        P.  89 ODE            83 How fit he is to sway
        P.  94 DR. WITTY      26 With other Language doth them fitly fit.
        P.  97 HOLLAND        79 How fit a Title clothes their Governours,
        P. 110 ANNIVERSARY   310 For prophecies fit to be Alcorand.
        P. 111 ANNIVERSARY   322 Makes you for his sake Tremble one fit more;
        P. 121 TWO SONGS      58 Makes Mortals matches fit for Deityes.
        P. 122 TWO SONGS      25 He so looks as fit to keep
        P. 132 PARADISE       27 Thou hast not miss'd one thought that could be
                                 fit,
        P. 159 INSTRUCTIONS  768 His Name alone seems fit to answer all.
        P. 160 INSTRUCTIONS  803 Who less Estate, for Treasurer most fit;
        P. 162 INSTRUCTIONS  874 And make a sawce fit for Whitehall's digestion:
        P. 164 INSTRUCTIONS  945 But this great work is for our Monarch fit,
        P. 184 MADE FREE     111 Shews how fit he is to Governe;
```

fitly   frequency: 1   relative frequency: 0.0000
```
        P.  94 DR. WITTY      26 With other Language doth them fitly fit.
```

fits   frequency: 1   relative frequency: 0.0000
    See also "fitts."
```
        P. 141 INSTRUCTIONS   38 Fits him in France to play at Cards and treat.
```

fitt   frequency: 2   relative frequency: 0.0000
```
        P. 199 DUKE           74 Then, Painter, shew thy skill and in fitt place
        P. 200 DUKE           88 Are these fitt hands to overturne a State
```

fitter   frequency: 4   relative frequency: 0.0000
```
        P. 137 HOUSEWARMING   21 Yet a President fitter in Virgil he found,
        P. 140 G.-CHILDREN     2 What fitter Sacrifice for Denham's Ghost?
        P. 155 INSTRUCTIONS  588 It fitter seem'd to captivate a Flea.
        P. 195 TWO HORSES    154 W. His perfum'd predecessor was never much
                                 fitter.
```

fittest   frequency: 1   relative frequency: 0.0000
```
        P. 176 LOYALL SCOT   181 The fittest Mask for one that Robs a Crown.
```

fitting   frequency: 1   relative frequency: 0.0000
```
```

```
        P. 201 HISTORICALL      14 Things highly fitting for a Monarchs trade.

fitts                              frequency:   1     relative frequency: 0.0000
        P. 175 LOYALL SCOT      151 One Mytre fitts the Heads of full four Moors.

fitz-harding                       frequency:   1     relative frequency: 0.0000
        P. 146 INSTRUCTIONS     208 And old Fitz-Harding of the Eaters Beef.

fitzgerald                         frequency:   1     relative frequency: 0.0000
        See also "fitzgerard."
        P. 200 DUKE             87 Jermyne, Fitzgerald, Loftus, Porter, Scot.

fitzgerard                         frequency:   1     relative frequency: 0.0000
        P. 198 DUKE             18 Manag'd by wise Fitzgerard and by Scott,

five                               frequency:   5     relative frequency: 0.0001
        P.  67 A. HOUSE         287 And with five Bastions it did fence,
        P.  69 A. HOUSE         350 These five imaginary Forts:
        P. 169 ADVICE           49 Two of the five recanters of the Hous
        P. 169 ADVICE           52 Five members need not be demanded here.
        P. 189 STATUE            2 This five moneths continues still blinded with
                                   board?

fix                                frequency:   7     relative frequency: 0.0001
        P.  32 MOURNING         16 A place to fix another Wound.
        P.  58 BILL-BOROW       58 Contented if they fix their Root.
        P.  80 A. HOUSE         676 If it might fix her shadow so;
        P. 144 INSTRUCTIONS     125 And fix to the Revenue such a Summ,
        P. 170 PROPHECY          1 The blood of the Just London's firm Doome
                                   shall fix
        P. 173 LOYALL SCOT      73 Shall fix a foot cn either neighbouring Shore
        P. 173 LOYALL SCOT      77 Anatomists may Sconer fix the Cells

fix'd                              frequency:   3     relative frequency: 0.0000
        P. 121 TWO SONGS        45 The Stars are fix'd unto their Sphere,
        P. 125 O.C.             98 Weeps that it falls ere fix'd into a Grape.
        P. 172 LOYALL SCOT      27 Fix'd on his ship hee fac'd the horrid day

fixed.  See "fix'd," "fixt."

fixing                             frequency:   1     relative frequency: 0.0000
        P. 176 LOYALL SCOT      208 And would like Chymists fixing Mercury

fixt                               frequency:   5     relative frequency: 0.0001
        P.  37 DEFINITION       10 Where my extended Soul is fixt,
        P.  91 MAY'S DEATH      56 Misled, but malice fixt and understood.
        P. 140 HIS HOUSE         6 Fixt on an Eccentrick Basis;
        P. 157 INSTRUCTIONS     661 Fixt on his Ship, he fac'd that horrid Day,
        P. 163 INSTRUCTIONS     917 While, the pale Ghosts, his Eye does fixt
                                   admire

flags                              frequency:   3     relative frequency: 0.0000
        P. 114 BLAKE            16 But much more fearful are your Flags to see.
        P. 132 PARADISE         40 So never Flags, but alwaies keeps on Wing.
        P. 154 INSTRUCTIONS     539 While the red Flags breath on their Top-masts
                                   high

flail                              frequency:   1     relative frequency: 0.0000
        P. 107 ANNIVERSARY      152 Swinges the Volumes of its horrid Flail.

flakes.  See "fleaks."

flame                              frequency:  12     relative frequency: 0.0002
        P.  44 GLC-WORMS         9 Ye Glo-worms, whose officious Flame
        P.  48 THE GARDEN       19 Fond Lovers, cruel as their Flame,
        P.  88 ODE              26 The force of angry Heavens flame:
        P.  91 MAY'S DEATH      59 Must therefore all the World be set on flame,
        P. 109 ANNIVERSARY      261 Whose climbing Flame, without a timely stop,
        P. 111 ANNIVERSARY      345 Up from the other World his Flame he darts,
        P. 119 TWO SONGS        16 That burns with an immortal Flame.
        P. 143 INSTRUCTIONS     82 Discern'd Love's Cause, and a new Flame began.
        P. 151 INSTRUCTIONS     424 At London's Flame, nor so the Court
                                   complain'd.
        P. 157 INSTRUCTIONS     660 That fly'st Love Fires, reserv'd for other
                                   Flame?
        P. 172 LOYALL SCOT      26 That flyst loves fires reserv'd for other flame?'
        P. 173 LOYALL SCOT      71 Mixt in Corinthian Mettall at thy Flame

flamen                             frequency:   1     relative frequency: 0.0000
        P. 175 LOYALL SCOT      150 None knows what god our Flamen now Adores;

flames                             frequency:  12     relative frequency: 0.0002
```

```
       P.   27 LOVER            5 But soon these Flames do lose their light,
       P.   28 LOVER           47 Whilst he, betwixt the Flames and Waves,
       P.   28 LOVER           54 Torn into Flames, and ragg'd with Wounds.
       P.   75 A. HOUSE       528 That in so equal Flames do burn!
       P.   80 A. HOUSE       687 But by her Flames, in Heaven try'd,
       P.  137 HOUSEWARMING     8 And nestles in flames like the Salamander.
       P.  157 INSTRUCTIONS   677 Like a glad Lover, the fierce Flames he meets,
       P.  157 INSTRUCTIONS   679 His shape exact, which the bright flames infold,
       P.  157 INSTRUCTIONS   700 Ally'd in Fate, increase, with theirs, her
                                  Flames.
       P.  170 PROPHECY         2 And cover it in flames in sixty six;
       P.  172 LOYALL SCOT     43 Like a glad lover the fierce Flames hee meets
       P.  173 LOYALL SCOT     45 His shape Exact which the bright flames enfold
```

```
flaming                          frequency:    4    relative frequency: 0.0000
       P.   69 A. HOUSE       326 With watry if not flaming Sword;
       P.   98 HOLLAND        115 Ram'd with Gun-powder, flaming with Brand wine,
       P.  157 INSTRUCTIONS   689 And, on the flaming Plank, so rests his Head,
       P.  173 LOYALL SCOT     55 And on his flaming Planks soe rests his head
```

```
flander                          frequency:    1    relative frequency: 0.0000
       P.  137 HOUSEWARMING     6 While he the Betrayer of England and Flander,
```

```
flanders                         frequency:    2    relative frequency: 0.0000
       See also "flander."
       P.  149 INSTRUCTIONS   368 To play for Flanders, and the stake to lose.
       P.  150 INSTRUCTIONS   396 And our next neighbours France and Flanders
                                  ride.
```

```
flandrick                        frequency:    1    relative frequency: 0.0000
       P.  127 O.C.           173 Who planted England on the Flandrick shoar,
```

```
flank                            frequency:    1    relative frequency: 0.0000
       P.  116 BLAKE           90 And flank with Cannon from the Neighbouring
                                  shore.
```

```
flapt                            frequency:    1    relative frequency: 0.0000
       P.   37 DEFINITION       8 But vainly flapt its Tinsel Wing.
```

```
flask                            frequency:    1    relative frequency: 0.0000
       P.   68 A. HOUSE       296 And fills its Flask with Odours new.
```

```
flat                             frequency:    1    relative frequency: 0.0000
       P.   73 A. HOUSE       449 For to this naked equal Flat,
```

```
flatters                         frequency:    1    relative frequency: 0.0000
       P.   77 A. HOUSE       596 Flatters with Air my panting Brows.
```

```
flattery                         frequency:    1    relative frequency: 0.0000
       See also "flatt'ry."
       P.  189 BRITANNIA      168 To Flattery, Pimping, and a gawdy shew:
```

```
flatt'ry                         frequency:    1    relative frequency: 0.0000
       P.  165 INSTRUCTIONS   984 Nor Guilt to flatt'ry binds, nor want to
                                  stealth;
```

```
flaw                             frequency:    1    relative frequency: 0.0000
       P.  152 INSTRUCTIONS   477 Or in their hasty Call to find a flaw,
```

```
flaxen                           frequency:    1    relative frequency: 0.0000
       P.   23 NYMPH           81 For, in the flaxen Lillies shade,
```

```
flea                             frequency:    1    relative frequency: 0.0000
       P.  155 INSTRUCTIONS   588 It fitter seem'd to captivate a Flea.
```

```
fleaks                           frequency:    1    relative frequency: 0.0000
       P.   86 FLECKNO        134 Like white fleaks rising from a Leaper's skin!
```

```
fleas                            frequency:    1    relative frequency: 0.0000
       P.   73 A. HOUSE       461 Such Fleas, ere they approach the Eye,
```

```
fleckno                          frequency:    1    relative frequency: 0.0000
       P.   83 FLECKNO          t Fleckno, an English Priest at Rome.
```

```
fled                             frequency:    9    relative frequency: 0.0001
       P.   31 FAIR SINGER      7 I could have fled from One but singly fair:
       P.   34 DAPHNIS         40 And then streight again is fled.
       P.  125 O.C.            78 But the dear Image fled the Mirrour broke.
       P.  129 O.C.           249 Those gentle rays under the lids were fled,
       P.  142 INSTRUCTIONS    72 And Fawns, that from the womb abortive fled.
       P.  156 INSTRUCTIONS   630 Long since were fled on many a feign'd pretence.
```

```
          P. 163 INSTRUCTIONS  911 Thrice did he rise, thrice the vain Tumult fled,
          P. 202 HISTORICALL    41 But the Dutch fleet fled suddainly with feare;
          P. 204 HISTORICALL   142 One hang'd himself, the other fled away:
```

fleece   frequency: 1   relative frequency: 0.0000
```
          P.  43 DAMON          53 With this the golden fleece I shear
```

fleeces   frequency: 1   relative frequency: 0.0000
```
          P. 122 TWO SONGS      21 Not our Lambs own Fleeces are
```

fleecy   frequency: 1   relative frequency: 0.0000
```
          P. 119 TWO SONGS      10 The fleecy Clouds with silver wand.
```

fleet   frequency: 21   relative frequency: 0.0004
```
          P.  23 NYMPH          63 It is a wond'rous thing, how fleet
          P.  28 LOVER          27 A num'rous fleet of Corm'rants black,
          P. 112 ANNIVERSARY   360 'A Fleet of Worlds, of other Worlds in quest;
          P. 113 BLAKE           1 Now does Spains Fleet her spatious wings
                                    unfold,
          P. 115 BLAKE          67 For Sanctacruze the glad Fleet takes her way,
          P. 116 BLAKE          84 Nor Winters storms, had made your Fleet
                                    retreat.
          P. 116 BLAKE         101 For your renown, his conquering Fleet does ride,
          P. 116 BLAKE         103 Whose Fleet and Trenches view'd, he soon did
                                    say,
          P. 117 BLAKE         113 This said, the whole Fleet gave it their
                                    applause,
          P. 119 BLAKE         166 Their rich Fleet sunk, and ours with Lawrel
                                    fraught.
          P. 141 INSTRUCTIONS    6 For so we too without a Fleet can fight.
          P. 143 INSTRUCTIONS   99 And he, unwary, and of Tongue too fleet,
          P. 152 INSTRUCTIONS  462 Their Fleet, to threaten, we will give them all.
          P. 154 INSTRUCTIONS  552 A Fleet of Clouds, sailing along the Skies:
          P. 159 INSTRUCTIONS  773 Who the Dutch Fleet with Storms disabled met,
          P. 159 INSTRUCTIONS  776 The Fleet divided? Writ for Rupert? Pett.
          P. 160 INSTRUCTIONS  790 That lost our Fleet, and did our Flight
                                    prevent.
          P. 160 INSTRUCTIONS  822 The Holland Fleet and Parliament so near.
          P. 190 STATUE         13 Were these Deales kept in store for sheathing
                                    our fleet
          P. 201 HISTORICALL    25 And that the Fleet was gone in Pompe and state
          P. 202 HISTORICALL    41 But the Dutch fleet fled suddainly with feare;
```

fleetest   frequency: 1   relative frequency: 0.0000
```
          P. 155 INSTRUCTIONS  600 (Cornbry the fleetest) and to London run.
```

fleeting   frequency: 1   relative frequency: 0.0000
```
          P. 189 BRITANNIA     182 Balm in their wounds, will fleeting life restore.
```

fleets   frequency: 5   relative frequency: 0.0001
```
          P. 117 BLAKE         117 Bold Stainer Leads, this Fleets design'd by
                                    fate,
          P. 117 BLAKE         125 Fate these two Fleets, between both Worlds had
                                    brought.
          P. 156 INSTRUCTIONS  629 The Guards, plac'd for the Chains and Fleets
                                    defence,
          P. 199 DUKE           63 Then Fleets and Armyes, battles, blood and
                                    wounds;
          P. 204 HISTORICALL   146 Our fleets our Ports our Cittyes and our
                                    Townes
```

flemish   frequency: 1   relative frequency: 0.0000
```
          P. 201 HISTORICALL    34 The new got flemish Towne was sett to sale.
```

flesh   frequency: 7   relative frequency: 0.0001
```
          P.  71 A. HOUSE      399 Fearing the Flesh untimely mow'd
          P.  76 A. HOUSE      555 (As first our Flesh corrupt within
          P.  84 FLECKNO        51 I ask'd if he eat flesh. And he, that was
          P.  84 FLECKNO        62 Hath sure more flesh and blood then he can boast.
          P. 175 LOYALL SCOT   141 Fish and flesh Bishops are the Ambigue.
          P. 175 LOYALL SCOT   159 But of the Choicest Modern flesh and Bone.
          P. 199 DUKE           67 Laden with folly, flesh and Ill got land:
```

fleurs-de-lis. See "flower-deluces."

flew   frequency: 1   relative frequency: 0.0000
```
          P. 187 BRITANNIA     111 With Joynt consent on helpless me they flew,
```

flexible   frequency: 1   relative frequency: 0.0000
```
          P. 165 KINGS VOWES    14 With Consciences flexible to my Commands;
```

flies   frequency: 5   relative frequency: 0.0001

See also "flyes."
P. 47 EMPIRE   23 Who though He flies the Musick of his praise,
P. 58 BILL-BOROW   76 That Courage its own Praises flies.
P. 80 A. HOUSE   678 As Flies in Chrystal overt'ane;
P. 144 INSTRUCTIONS   140 And flies like Batts with leathern Wings by
                             Night.
P. 155 INSTRUCTIONS   580 Flies to the Wood, and hides his armless Head.

flight   frequency: 5   relative frequency: 0.0001
P. 49 THE GARDEN   55 And, till prepar'd for longer flight,
P. 108 ANNIVERSARY   194 And leaden Sorrow then their flight did stay.
P. 127 O.C.   185 Astonish'd armyes did their flight prepare,
P. 132 PARADISE   37 And above humane flight dost soar aloft,
P. 160 INSTRUCTIONS   790 That lost our Fleet, and did our Flight
                             prevent.

flinch   frequency: 1   relative frequency: 0.0000
P. 201 HISTORICALL   21 Bold James survives, no dangers make him flinch,

fling   frequency: 1   relative frequency: 0.0000
P. 72 A. HOUSE   423 The Women that with forks it fling,

flippant   frequency: 1   relative frequency: 0.0000
P. 152 INSTRUCTIONS   465 Hyde's flippant Stile there pleasantly curvets;

float   frequency: 1   relative frequency: 0.0000
P. 30 THE GALLERY   33 But, against that, thou sit'st a float

floating. See "floting."

flock   frequency: 3   relative frequency: 0.0000
P. 43 DAMON   50 The plains with an unnum'red Flock,
P. 164 INSTRUCTIONS   964 Or in fair Fields to rule the easie Flock.
P. 188 BRITANNIA   146 To the Bleating Flock by him so lately torn.

flocking   frequency: 1   relative frequency: 0.0000
P. 104 ANNIVERSARY   62 The flocking Marbles in a Palace meet;

flocks   frequency: 3   relative frequency: 0.0000
P. 18 CLORINDA   1 C. Damon come drive thy flocks this way.
P. 119 TWO SONGS   9 As we our Flocks, so you command
P. 122 TWO SONGS   40 Our Flocks and us with a propitious Eye.

flood   frequency: 3   relative frequency: 0.0000
P. 26 MISTRESS   8 Love you ten years before the Flood:
P. 74 A. HOUSE   481 But I, retiring from the Flood,
P. 110 ANNIVERSARY   284 Left by the Wars Flood on the Mountains crest:

floods   frequency: 3   relative frequency: 0.0000
P. 16 EYES   52 Now like two floods o'return and drown.
P. 61 A. HOUSE   80 Deep Meadows, and transparent Floods.
P. 78 A. HOUSE   623 But, where the Floods did lately drown,

floor   frequency: 1   relative frequency: 0.0000
See also "floore."
P. 112 ANNIVERSARY   390 'At Home a Subject on the equal Floor.

floor'd   frequency: 1   relative frequency: 0.0000
P. 158 INSTRUCTIONS   721 Once a deep River, now with Timber floor'd,

floore   frequency: 1   relative frequency: 0.0000
P. 126 O.C.   118 And thrash'd the Harvest in the airy floore;

flora   frequency: 3   relative frequency: 0.0000
P. 18 CLORINDA   4 Where Flora blazons all her pride.
P. 39 PICTURE   36 Lest Flora angry at thy crime,
P. 164 INSTRUCTIONS   973 (But Ceres Corn, and Flora is the Spring,

floting   frequency: 3   relative frequency: 0.0000
P. 27 LOVER   11 That my poor Lover floting lay,
P. 76 A. HOUSE   566 Streight floting on the Air shall fly:
P. 112 ANNIVERSARY   359 'Of floting Islands a new Hatched Nest;

flourish   frequency: 1   relative frequency: 0.0000
P. 124 O.C.   32 He oft would flourish in his mighty Arms;

flourishing   frequency: 1   relative frequency: 0.0000
P. 69 A. HOUSE   348 Fresh as his own and flourishing.

floury   frequency: 1   relative frequency: 0.0000
P. 201 HISTORICALL   26 To fetch for Charles the floury Lisbon Kate,

flouts   frequency: 1   relative frequency: 0.0000
    P. 180 STOCKSMARKET   43 Or else thus expose him to popular flouts,

flow   frequency: 7   relative frequency: 0.0001
    P. 20 THYRSIS   34 Cool winds do whisper, springs do flow.
    P. 24 NYMPH   98 The holy Frankincense doth flow.
    P. 31 MOURNING   6 With Tears suspended ere they flow;
    P. 94 DR. WITTY   17 Caelia whose English doth more richly flow
    P. 98 HOLLAND   132 And, like its own Seas, only Ebbs to flow.
    P. 120 TWO SONGS   18 Ruling the Waves that Ebb and flow.
    P. 156 INSTRUCTIONS   625 But sees, inrag'd, the River flow between.

flow'd   frequency: 2   relative frequency: 0.0000
    P. 126 O.C.   131 And as through Air his wasting Spirits flow'd,
    P. 177 LOYALL SCOT   249 At Babel names from pride and discord flow'd,

flower   frequency: 2   relative frequency: 0.0000
    See also "flowr," "flow'r."
    P. 45 MOWER'S SONG   10 But had a Flower on either side;
    P. 139 HOUSEWARMING   94 Like vain Chymists, a flower from its ashes
                              returning;

flower-deluces   frequency: 1   relative frequency: 0.0000
    P. 186 BRITANNIA   61 Faire flower-deluces in an Azure field

flowers   frequency: 3   relative frequency: 0.0000
    See also "flowrs," "flow'rs."
    P.   4 HASTINGS   5 Go, stand betwixt the Morning and the Flowers;
    P. 38 PICTURE   t2 of Flowers.
    P. 178 LOYALL SCOT   268 The morning dews and flowers Neglected grown,

flowery. See "floury," "flowry."

flowing   frequency: 3   relative frequency: 0.0000
    P. 16 EYES   31 Whose liquid Chaines could flowing meet
    P. 103 ANNIVERSARY   6 While flowing Time above his Head does close.
    P. 125 O.C.   97 Trickling in watry drops, whose flowing shape

flown   frequency: 1   relative frequency: 0.0000
    P. 37 DEFINITION   7 Where feeble Hope could ne'r have flown

flowr   frequency: 1   relative frequency: 0.0000
    P. 124 O.C.   55 So the Flowr with'ring which the Garden
                              crown'd,

flow'r   frequency: 4   relative frequency: 0.0000
    P. 12 DROP OF DEW   9 How it the purple flow'r does slight,
    P. 12 DROP OF DEW   21 Could it within the humane flow'r be seen,
    P. 68 A. HOUSE   302 Seems with the Flow'rs a Flow'r to be.
    P. 121 TWO SONGS   10 When She is the only flow'r.

flowrs   frequency: 2   relative frequency: 0.0000
    P. 69 A. HOUSE   332 And all the Garrisons were Flowrs,
    P. 70 A. HOUSE   359 But Flowrs eternal, and divine,

flow'rs   frequency: 27   relative frequency: 0.0005
    P.   9 DIALOGUE   15 Where the Souls of fruits and flow'rs
    P. 14 THE CORONET   6 I gather flow'rs (my fruits are only flow'rs)
    P. 14 THE CORONET   15 About the flow'rs disguis'd does fold,
    P. 15 EYES   19 And yet, from all the flow'rs I saw,
    P. 18 CLORINDA   6 The Flow'rs I for thy Temples keep.
    P. 18 CLORINDA   7 D. Grass withers; and the Flow'rs too fade.
    P. 30 THE GALLERY   55 Transplanting Flow'rs from the green Hill,
    P. 38 PICTURE   5 The Wilder flow'rs, and gives them names:
    P. 39 PICTURE   34 Whom Nature courts with fruits and flow'rs,
    P. 39 PICTURE   35 Gather the Flow'rs, but spare the Buds;
    P. 40 THE MOWER   3 And from the fields the Flow'rs and Plants
                              allure,
    P. 41 THE MOWER   12 And Flow'rs themselves were taught to paint.
    P. 45 MOWER'S SONG   21 And Flow'rs, and Grass, and I and all,
    P. 48 THE GARDEN   7 While all Flow'rs and all Trees do close
    P. 49 THE GARDEN   40 Insnar'd with Flow'rs, I fall on Grass.
    P. 50 THE GARDEN   66 Of flow'rs and herbes this Dial new;
    P. 50 THE GARDEN   72 Be reckon'd but with herbs and flow'rs!
    P. 64 A. HOUSE   179 'Flow'rs dress the Altars; for the Clothes,
    P. 68 A. HOUSE   293 Then Flow'rs their drowsie Eylids raise,
    P. 68 A. HOUSE   302 Seems with the Flow'rs a Flow'r to be.
    P. 68 A. HOUSE   309 See how the Flow'rs, as at Parade,
    P. 68 A. HOUSE   317 Then in some Flow'rs beloved Hut
    P. 70 A. HOUSE   383 They bring up Flow'rs so to be seen,
    P. 80 A. HOUSE   700 The Garden Flow'rs to Crown Her Head;

```
    P.   82 A. HOUSE      745 Mean time ye Fields, Springs, Bushes,
                              Flow'rs,
    P.  121 TWO SONGS        5 Stay till I some flow'rs ha' ty'd

flowry                       frequency:    1    relative frequency: 0.0000
    P.   18 CLORINDA        27 Of Pan the flowry Pastures sing,

flows                        frequency:    2    relative frequency: 0.0000
    P.   79 A. HOUSE       667 And on the River as it flows
    P.  128 O.C.           205 And that deep scule through every channell flows,

fluttering.  See "flutt'ring."

flutt'ring                   frequency:    1    relative frequency: 0.0000
    P.   58 BILL-BOROW      61 Onely sometimes a flutt'ring Breez

fly                          frequency:   17    relative frequency: 0.0003
    See also "flye."
    P.    9 DIALOGUE        20 Whose soft Plumes will thither fly:
    P.   19 THYRSIS         14 That have no wings and cannot fly?
    P.   30 THE GALLERY     36 Betwixt the Air and Water fly.
    P.   65 A. HOUSE       221 'Fly from their Vices. 'tis thy state,
    P.   65 A. HOUSE       223 'Fly from their Ruine. How I fear
    P.   68 A. HOUSE       298 In fragrant Vollyes they let fly;
    P.   76 A. HOUSE       566 Streight floting on the Air shall fly:
    P.   80 A. HOUSE       673 The viscous Air, wheres'ere She fly,
    P.  117 BLAKE          112 And they are ours, for now they cannot fly.
    P.  118 BLAKE          133 Torn Limbs some leagues into the Island fly,
    P.  118 BLAKE          139 And neither have, or power, or will to fly,
    P.  130 O.C.           283 While staggs shall fly unto the forests thick,
    P.  150 INSTRUCTIONS   385 The Distaff knocks, the Grains from Kettle
                              fly,
    P.  151 INSTRUCTIONS   420 To fly to Windsor, and mure up the Gates.
    P.  151 INSTRUCTIONS   446 Trusses his baggage, and the Camp does fly.
    P.  160 INSTRUCTIONS   795 All men admir'd he to that pitch could fly:
    P.  185 BRITANNIA       23 Rawl: What fatall crimes make you forever fly

flye                         frequency:    1    relative frequency: 0.0000
    P.  170 PROPHECY         3 Fireballs shall flye and but few see the traine

flyes                        frequency:    3    relative frequency: 0.0000
    P.   67 A. HOUSE       257 But, waving these aside like Flyes,
    P.   84 FLECKNO         50 With gristly Tongue to dart the passing Flyes.
    P.  124 O.C.            69 And frequent lightning to her Soul that flyes,

flyest.  See "flyst," "fly'st."

flying                       frequency:    1    relative frequency: 0.0000
    P.   79 A. HOUSE       670 Flying betwixt the Day and Night;

flyst                        frequency:    1    relative frequency: 0.0000
    P.  172 LOYALL SCOT     26 That flyst loves fires reserv'd for other flame?'

fly'st                       frequency:    1    relative frequency: 0.0000
    P.  157 INSTRUCTIONS   660 That fly'st Love Fires, reserv'd for other
                              Flame?

foam                         frequency:    1    relative frequency: 0.0000
    See also "foame."
    P.   98 HOLLAND        122 While the Sea laught it self into a foam,

foame                        frequency:    1    relative frequency: 0.0000
    P.  110 ANNIVERSARY    306 Have writ the Comments of thy sacred Foame:

foaming                      frequency:    1    relative frequency: 0.0000
    P.  163 INSTRUCTIONS   941 While Hyde provok'd his foaming tusk does whet,

fob                          frequency:    1    relative frequency: 0.0000
    See also "fobb."
    P.  143 INSTRUCTIONS    98 More gold in's Fob, more Lace upon his Coat

fobb                         frequency:    1    relative frequency: 0.0000
    P.  165 KINGS VOWES      1 When the Plate was at pawne, and the fobb att
                              low Ebb,

foe                          frequency:    7    relative frequency: 0.0001
    P.   33 DAPHNIS          5 Nature her own Sexes foe,
    P.   35 DAPHNIS         58 Such a Debt unto my Foe;
    P.   91 MAY'S DEATH     29 But Ben, who knew not neither foe nor friend,
    P.  146 INSTRUCTIONS   241 A scatter'd Body, which the Foe ne'r try'd,
    P.  147 INSTRUCTIONS   249 Such Roman Cocles strid: before the Foe,
```

```
        P. 156 INSTRUCTIONS   618 Secure so oft he had this Foe defy'd:
        P. 198 DUKE            20 That common sense is my eternall foe.

foes                          frequency:    7   relative frequency: 0.0001
        P.  66 A. HOUSE       249 Some to the Breach against their Foes
        P. 116 BLAKE           85 To fight against such Foes, was vain they knew,
        P. 118 BLAKE          161 All the Foes Ships destroy'd, by Sea or fire,
        P. 178 LOYALL SCOT    270 Powders them ore till none discern their foes
        P. 187 BRITANNIA      106 Of French, Scots, Irish (all my mortall foes):
        P. 193 TWO HORSES      64 Not our trade to secure but foes to come at 'um,
        P. 202 HISTORICALL     44 Scorning the persuit of such recreant foes.

foil'd                        frequency:    1   relative frequency: 0.0000
        P. 202 HISTORICALL     51 Foil'd thus by Venus he Bellona woes,

fold                          frequency:    3   relative frequency: 0.0000
        P.  14 THE CORONET     15 About the flow'rs disguis'd does fold,
        P.  24 NYMPH           89 And its pure virgin Limbs to fold
        P. 184 MADE FREE      128 Goe fold up your Furrs,

folds                         frequency:    1   relative frequency: 0.0000
        P.  78 A. HOUSE       633 See in what wanton harmless folds

folk.   See "volke."

follow                        frequency:    2   relative frequency: 0.0000
        P. 129 O.C.           239 No more shall follow where he spent the dayes
        P. 159 INSTRUCTIONS   771 Who would not follow when the Dutch were bet?

follow'd                      frequency:    3   relative frequency: 0.0000
        P.  85 FLECKNO        106 Went down, as I him follow'd to obey.
        P. 111 ANNIVERSARY    327 All day he follow'd with unwearied sight,
        P. 145 INSTRUCTIONS   170 And follow'd Fox, but with disdainful look.

follows                       frequency:    1   relative frequency: 0.0000
        P.  80 A. HOUSE       674 Follows and sucks her Azure dy;

folly                         frequency:    6   relative frequency: 0.0001
        P.  65 A. HOUSE       218 'Founded by Folly, kept by Wrong.
        P. 139 HOUSEWARMING    88 By a Model more excellent than Lesly's Folly.
        P. 155 INSTRUCTIONS   610 Confusion, folly, treach'ry, fear, neglect.
        P. 199 DUKE            67 Laden with folly, flesh and Ill got land:
        P. 202 HISTORICALL     39 Pride nourisht folly, folly a Delight

fond                          frequency:    8   relative frequency: 0.0001
        P.  48 THE GARDEN      19 Fond Lovers, cruel as their Flame,
        P.  81 A. HOUSE       729 Go now fond Sex that on your Face
        P. 116 BLAKE           93 Fond men who know not whilst such works they
                                  raise,
        P. 139 HOUSEWARMING    93 Fond City, its Rubbish and Ruines that builds,
        P. 150 INSTRUCTIONS   373 The Court, as once of War, now fond of Peace,
        P. 157 INSTRUCTIONS   659 They sigh'd and said, Fond Boy, why so untame,
        P. 172 LOYALL SCOT     25 They sigh'd and said 'fond boy why soe Untame,
        P. 203 HISTORICALL    102 Fond Eve did for this subtle Tempters sake

fool                          frequency:    2   relative frequency: 0.0000
        P. 171 PROPHECY        35 When the Seal's given to a talking fool
        P. 195 TWO HORSES     123 W. He that dyes for Ceremonies dyes like a
                                  fool.

fool'd                        frequency:    2   relative frequency: 0.0000
        P. 108 ANNIVERSARY    207 Justice obstructed lay, and Reason fool'd;
        P. 190 STATUE          22 When their Pensions are stopt to be fool'd with
                                  a sight?

fooles                        frequency:    1   relative frequency: 0.0000
        P. 181 MADE FREE       24 Oh what Fooles were you to receive him.

foolish                       frequency:    2   relative frequency: 0.0000
        P.  14 THE CORONET     17 Ah, foolish Man, that would'st debase with them,
        P.  44 GLO-WORMS       12 And after foolish Fires do stray;

fools                         frequency:    3   relative frequency: 0.0000
        See also "fooles."
        P. 141 INSTRUCTIONS    12 'Twill serve this race of Drunkards, Pimps, and
                                  Fools.
        P. 199 DUKE            65 By Irish fools and by a doting pope.
        P. 200 DUKE            97 At last to fools and mad men and the pope?

foot                          frequency:   16   relative frequency: 0.0003
        P.  11 DIALOGUE        57 Where so e're thy Foot shall go
```

P.   23 NYMPH   42 Of foot, and heart; and did invite,
P.   23 NYMPH   60 I blusht to see its foot more soft,
P.   49 THE GARDEN   49 Here at the Fountains sliding foot,
P.   71 A. HOUSE   390 Walking on foot through a green Sea.
P.   75 A. HOUSE   540 Meas'ring the Timber with his Foot;
P.   79 A. HOUSE   645 Or to suspend my sliding Foot
P.   91 MAY'S DEATH   27 Yet then with foot as stumbling as his tongue
P. 105 ANNIVERSARY   99 When for his Foot he thus a place had found,
P. 110 ANNIVERSARY   296 Rejoycing when thy Foot had slipt aside;
P. 162 INSTRUCTIONS   863 Dear Painter, draw this Speaker to the foot:
P. 169 ADVICE   43 The body of foot that was to have the van
P. 173 LOYALL SCOT   73 Shall fix a foot on either neighbouring Shore
P. 176 LOYALL SCOT   203 That Cloven head must Govern Cloven foot.
P. 193 TWO HORSES   67 W. That makeing us slaves by hors and foot
                            Guards
P. 201 HISTORICALL   8 And cloath him all from head to foot anew;

footman   frequency: 1   relative frequency: 0.0000
P. 143 INSTRUCTIONS   84 And still within her mind the Footman runs:

footstep   frequency: 1   relative frequency: 0.0000
P.   61 A. HOUSE   82 And on each pleasant footstep stay,

footsteps   frequency: 1   relative frequency: 0.0000
P. 106 ANNIVERSARY   107 And in their numbred Footsteps humbly tread

footstoole   frequency: 1   relative frequency: 0.0000
P. 198 DUKE   14 Till all this nation to thy footstoole bend.

for   frequency: 416   relative frequency: 0.0086
See also "for's," "for't."

forbear   frequency: 1   relative frequency: 0.0000
See also "forbeare."
P. 148 INSTRUCTIONS   311 St. Albans straight is sent to, to forbear,

forbeare   frequency: 1   relative frequency: 0.0000
P. 184 MADE FREE   116 That he would forbeare

forbears   frequency: 2   relative frequency: 0.0000
P.   89 ODE   87 And, what he may, forbears
P. 163 INSTRUCTIONS   939 But in wise anger he their Crimes forbears,

forbidden   frequency: 4   relative frequency: 0.0000
P.   41 THE MOWER   22 Forbidden mixtures there to see.
P. 131 PARADISE   4 Retelling Angels, the Forbidden Tree,
P. 142 INSTRUCTIONS   73 Not unprovok'd she trys forbidden Arts,
P. 203 HISTORICALL   103 From the forbidden tree the Pipin take:

forc'd   frequency: 2   relative frequency: 0.0000
P.   85 FLECKNO   86 But who came last is forc'd first to go out;
P. 184 BRITANNIA   9 Raw: What mighty power has forc'd me from my
                            rest?

force   frequency: 15   relative frequency: 0.0003
P.   38 PICTURE   19 Ere they have try'd their force to wound,
P.   66 A. HOUSE   235 Which licens'd either Peace or Force,
P.   88 ODE   26 The force of angry Heavens flame:
P.   90 ODE   117 Besides the force it has to fright
P. 103 ANNIVERSARY   13 'Tis he the force of scatter'd Time contracts,
P. 107 ANNIVERSARY   173 Thee proof beyond all other Force or Skill,
P. 109 ANNIVERSARY   239 What since he did, an higher Force him push'd
P. 109 ANNIVERSARY   255 No King might ever such a Force have done;
P. 117 BLAKE   131 Which by quick powders force, so high was sent,
P. 124 O.C.   33 And, lest their force the tender burthen wrong,
P. 126 O.C.   115 The Winds receive it, and its force out-do,
P. 129 O.C.   238 Whose force oft spar'd the labour of his arm:
P. 148 INSTRUCTIONS   309 Where force had fail'd with Stratagem to play,
P. 152 INSTRUCTIONS   481 First, then he march'd our whole Militia's
                            force,
P. 155 INSTRUCTIONS   590 Filling his Sails, more force to recollect.

forced   frequency: 4   relative frequency: 0.0000
See also "forc'd," "forct," "forc't."
P.   29 LOVER   60 Forced to live in Storms and Warrs:
P.   89 ODE   66 Which first assur'd the forced Pow'r.
P.   94 DR. WITTY   9 Others do strive with words and forced phrase
P.   96 HOLLAND   20 Where barking Waves still bait the forced
                            Ground;

forces   frequency: 3   relative frequency: 0.0000

P. 21 SOUL & BODY   39 Which Knowledge forces me to know;
P. 31 FAIR SINGER   17 And all my Forces needs must be undone,
P. 115 BLAKE   49 Forces and art, she soon will feel, are vain,

forct   frequency: 1   relative frequency: 0.0000
P. 203 HISTORICALL   110 Till native Reason's basely forct to yield

forc't   frequency: 1   relative frequency: 0.0000
P. 314 CHEQUER INN   65 That she was forc't to call for Grocme

ford   frequency: 2   relative frequency: 0.0000
P. 158 INSTRUCTIONS   722 And shrunk, lest Navigable, to a Ford.
P. 315 CHEQUER INN   115 The Westerne Glcry, Harry Ford

fore   frequency: 1   relative frequency: 0.0000
P. 125 O.C.   102 Fore boding Princes falls, and seldom vain.

fore-seen   frequency: 1   relative frequency: 0.0000
P. 39 THE MATCH   17 Love wisely had of long fore-seen

fore-shortned   frequency: 1   relative frequency: 0.0000
P. 106 ANNIVERSARY   139 Fore-shortned Time its useless Course would
                           stay,

forebode   frequency: 1   relative frequency: 0.0000
P. 71 A. HOUSE   400 To him a Fate as black forebode.

forecast   frequency: 1   relative frequency: 0.0000
P. 179 STOCKSMARKET   10 To be all a revenge and a malice forecast,

forego   frequency: 1   relative frequency: 0.0000
P. 45 MOWER'S SONG   14 A fellowship so true forego,

foregoe   frequency: 1   relative frequency: 0.0000
P. 21 SOUL & BODY   40 And Memory will not foregoe.

forehead   frequency: 3   relative frequency: 0.0000
P. 26 MISTRESS   14 Thine Eyes, and on thy Forehead Gaze.
P. 81 A. HOUSE   732 Lest the smooth Forehead wrinkled sit:
P. 314 CHEQUER INN   62 Her Forehead Cloath had laid aside

foreign. See "forraign," "forrain."

foreman   frequency: 1   relative frequency: 0.0000
P. 314 CHEQUER INN   80 The Foreman of the Brittish Crew

foresaw   frequency: 1   relative frequency: 0.0000
P. 89 ODE   72 Foresaw it's happy Fate.

foreseen   frequency: 1   relative frequency: 0.0000
P. 151 INSTRUCTIONS   417 But wiser Men, and well foreseen in chance,

foresees   frequency: 1   relative frequency: 0.0000
P. 125 O.C.   107 Or rather Heav'n, which us so long foresees,

foreshortned   frequency: 1   relative frequency: 0.0000
P. 129 O.C.   269 The tree ere while foreshortned to our view,

forest   frequency: 1   relative frequency: 0.0000
   See also "forrest."
P. 21 SOUL & BODY   44 Green Trees that in the Forest grew.

forests   frequency: 2   relative frequency: 0.0000
   See also "forrests."
P. 130 O.C.   283 While staggs shall fly unto the forests thick,
P. 155 INSTRUCTIONS   579 The conscious Stag, so once the Forests dread,

foretel   frequency: 2   relative frequency: 0.0000
P. 38 PICTURE   9 Who can foretel for what high cause
P. 137 HOUSEWARMING   2 (As the Cause can eas'ly foretel the Effect)

foretell   frequency: 1   relative frequency: 0.0000
   See also "foretel."
P. 125 O.C.   104 What they above cannot prevent, foretell;

foretells   frequency: 1   relative frequency: 0.0000
P. 131 O.C.   324 He threats no deluge, yet foretells a showre.

forever   frequency: 1   relative frequency: 0.0000
P. 185 BRITANNIA   23 Bawl: What fatall crimes make you forever fly

forewarn'd   frequency: 1   relative frequency: 0.0000

P. 109 ANNIVERSARY   238 But though forewarn'd, o'r-took and wet the
                           King.

forge   frequency: 1   relative frequency: 0.0000
     P. 150 INSTRUCTIONS 372 To forge new Thunder, and inspect their Fires.

forget   frequency: 4   relative frequency: 0.0000
     See also "forgett."
     P. 22 NYMPH   10 Prevail with Heaven to forget
     P. 119 TWO SONGS   2 And even Wolves the Sheep forget;
     P. 159 INSTRUCTIONS 781 Who to supply with Powder, did forget
     P. 178 LOYALL SCOT   276 My former satyr for this verse forget,

forgett   frequency: 1   relative frequency: 0.0000
     P. 169 ADVICE   34 To make them th' other Councell board forgett.

forgot   frequency: 2   relative frequency: 0.0000
     See also "forgott."
     P. 41 THE MOWER   32 While the sweet Fields do lye forgot:
     P. 157 INSTRUCTIONS 695 When Oeta and Alcides are forgot,

forgott   frequency: 1   relative frequency: 0.0000
     P. 173 LOYALL SCOT   61 When Oeta and Alcides are forgott,

forked   frequency: 1   relative frequency: 0.0000
     See also "three-fork'd."
     P. 28 LOVER   22 Through frighted Clouds in forked streaks.

forkes   frequency: 1   relative frequency: 0.0000
     P. 316 CHEQUER INN   169 Candlesticks, Forkes, Saltes Plates Spoones
                              Knives

forks   frequency: 1   relative frequency: 0.0000
     See also "forkes."
     P. 72 A. HOUSE   423 The Women that with forks it fling,

form   frequency: 3   relative frequency: 0.0000
     P. 66 A. HOUSE   234 The Court him grants the lawful Form;
     P. 157 INSTRUCTIONS 686 His alt'ring Form, and soder'd Limbs to melt;
     P. 173 LOYALL SCOT   52 His Altred form and scored Limbs to Melt,

former   frequency: 6   relative frequency: 0.0001
     P. 12 DROP OF DEW   22 Remembring still its former height,
     P. 147 INSTRUCTIONS 253 Their former Trophees they recal to mind,
     P. 156 INSTRUCTIONS 621 Of former Glories the reproachful thought,
     P. 169 ADVICE   46 And add new Beams to Sands's former Glory.
     P. 178 LOYALL SCOT   276 My former satyr for this verse forget,
     P. 182 MADE FREE   63 As had cancelld all former Disasters

forms   frequency: 1   relative frequency: 0.0000
     P. 30 THE GALLERY   43 In all the Forms thou can'st invent

forraign   frequency: 1   relative frequency: 0.0000
     P. 25 YOUNG LOVE   28 So all Forraign Claims to drown,

forrain   frequency: 1   relative frequency: 0.0000
     P. 59 A. HOUSE   2 Work of no Forrain Architect;

forrest   frequency: 1   relative frequency: 0.0000
     P. 74 A. HOUSE   497 When first the Eye this Forrest sees

forrests   frequency: 2   relative frequency: 0.0000
     P. 59 A. HOUSE   4 And Forrests did to Pastures hew;
     P. 112 ANNIVERSARY   353 'What Oaken Forrests, and what golden Mines!

for's   frequency: 1   relative frequency: 0.0000

forsake   frequency: 1   relative frequency: 0.0000
     P. 87 ODE   2 Must now forsake his Muses dear,

forsaken   frequency: 1   relative frequency: 0.0000
     P. 92 MAY'S DEATH   66 And single fights forsaken Vertues cause.

forsooth   frequency: 1   relative frequency: 0.0000
     P. 148 INSTRUCTIONS 312 Lest the sure Peace, forsooth, too soon appear.

forswear   frequency: 1   relative frequency: 0.0000
     P. 34 DAPHNIS   36 And his cruel Fate forswear.

fort   frequency: 3   relative frequency: 0.0000
     P. 33 DAPHNIS   19 Knew not that the Fort to gain
     P. 67 A. HOUSE   286 In the just Figure of a Fort;
     P. 154 INSTRUCTIONS 563 And quickly judg'd the Fort was not tenable,

for't   frequency: 2   relative frequency: 0.0000

forth   frequency: 5   relative frequency: 0.0001
    P.   27 LOVER   12 And, e're brought forth, was cast away:
    P.   61 A. HOUSE   86 For Virgin Buildings oft brought forth.
    P.   79 A. HOUSE   660 Starts forth with to its Bonne Mine.
    P.   127 O.C.   161 Which with more Care set forth his Obsequies
    P.   169 ADVICE   50 That aime at mountains and bring forth a Mous,

forthwith   frequency: 4   relative frequency: 0.0000
    P.   71 A. HOUSE   404 And forthwith means on it to sup:
    P.   106 ANNIVERSARY   138 Would forthwith finish under such a Hand:
    P.   149 INSTRUCTIONS 367 The Count forthwith is order'd all to close,
    P.   155 INSTRUCTIONS 581 Ruyter forthwith a Squadron does untack,

fortifi'd   frequency: 1   relative frequency: 0.0000
    P.   40 THE MATCH   25 He fortifi'd the double Gate,

fortified. See "fortifi'd."

forts   frequency: 9   relative frequency: 0.0001
    P.   69 A. HOUSE   338 And his more gentle Forts did trace.
    P.   69 A. HOUSE   350 These five imaginary Forts:
    P.   116 BLAKE   91 Forts, Lines, and Sconces all the Bay along,
    P.   117 BLAKE   107 Those Forts, which there, so high and strong
                               appear,
    P.   138 HOUSEWARMING   41 The Scotch Forts <and> Dunkirk, but that they
                               were sold,
    P.   148 INSTRUCTIONS 324 That Money lack, nor Forts be in repair.
    P.   151 INSTRUCTIONS 433 Tell him our Ships unrigg'd, our Forts unman'd,
    P.   159 INSTRUCTIONS 780 And who the Forts left unrepair'd? Pett.
    P.   160 INSTRUCTIONS 799 And who the Forts would not vouchsafe a corn,

fortunate   frequency: 4   relative frequency: 0.0000
    P.   157 INSTRUCTIONS 693 Fortunate Boy! if either Pencil's Fame,
    P.   173 LOYALL SCOT   59 Fortunate Boy, if ere my verse may Claim
    P.   183 MADE FREE   80 In thy fortunate Choyce
    P.   189 BRITANNIA   191 Freed by thy labours, Fortunate blest Isle,

fortune   frequency: 7   relative frequency: 0.0001
    P.   3 LOVELACE   2 Which your sweet Muse which your fair Fortune
                               chose,
    P.   28 LOVER   43 Fortune and He are call'd to play
    P.   98 HOLLAND   123 'Tis true since that (as fortune kindly sports,)
    P.   114 BLAKE   23 At length theirs vanishes, and fortune smiles;
    P.   115 BLAKE   64 If fortune can make guilty what she will.
    P.   141 INSTRUCTIONS   32 But Fortune chose him for her pleasure salt.
    P.   143 INSTRUCTIONS 100 No longer could conceal his Fortune sweet.

fortunes   frequency: 2   relative frequency: 0.0000
    P.   90 ODE   113 But thou the Wars and Fortunes Son
    P.   167 KINGS VOWES   57 That they may raise Fortunes to my owne frye.

fortune's   frequency: 1   relative frequency: 0.0000
    P.   145 INSTRUCTIONS 189 Their Fortune's error they supply'd in rage,

forty. See "fourty."

forum   frequency: 1   relative frequency: 0.0000
    P.   173 LOYALL SCOT   67 Such in the Roman forum Curtius brave

forward   frequency: 7   relative frequency: 0.0001
    P.   65 A. HOUSE   199 Which She hence forward does begin;
    P.   87 ODE   1 The forward Youth that would appear
    P.   106 ANNIVERSARY   146 Who in his Age has always forward prest:
    P.   147 INSTRUCTIONS 255 First enter'd forward Temple, Conqueror
    P.   148 INSTRUCTIONS 291 To speak not forward, but in Action brave;
    P.   156 INSTRUCTIONS 658 The Nymphs would rustle; he would forward swim.
    P.   172 LOYALL SCOT   24 The Nymphs would Rustle, hee would forward
                               swim:

forwarn'd   frequency: 1   relative frequency: 0.0000
    P.   178 LOYALL SCOT   284 Forwarn'd him therefore lest in time he were

fought   frequency: 5   relative frequency: 0.0001
    P.   72 A. HOUSE   420 A Camp of Battail newly fought:
    P.   117 BLAKE   126 Who fight, as if for both those Worlds they
                               fought.
    P.   126 O.C.   137 The Stars that for him fought had only pow'r
    P.   128 O.C.   194 He conquer'd God, still ere he fought with men:
    P.   150 INSTRUCTIONS 402 Where Venice twenty years the Turk had fought:

```
foul                               frequency:    2    relative frequency: 0.0000
    P.  86 FLECKNO        130 Save only two foul copies for his shirt:
    P.  91 MAY'S DEATH     51 Foul Architect that hadst not Eye to see

found                              frequency:   25    relative frequency: 0.0005
    P.  22 NYMPH           26 I had not found him counterfeit,
    P.  26 MISTRESS        25 Thy Beauty shall no more be found;
    P.  34 DAPHNIS         50 Such a wretched minute found,
    P.  44 DAMON           85 Only for him no Cure is found,
    P.  48 THE GARDEN       9 Fair quiet, have I found thee here,
    P.  48 THE GARDEN      24 No Name shall but your own be found.
    P.  73 A. HOUSE       479 How Salmons trespassing are found;
    P.  75 A. HOUSE       521 But I have for my Musick found
    P.  83 FLECKNO          9 I found at last a Chamber, as 'twas said,
    P.  90 MAY'S DEATH      8 Signs by which itt he found and lost his way.
    P.  91 MAY'S DEATH     26 He found he was translated, and by whom.
    P.  95 HOLLAND          9 Glad then, as Miners that have found the Oar,
    P.  97 HOLLAND         70 Each one thence pillag'd the first piece he
                              found:
    P. 103 ANNIVERSARY     18 In the same Posture would be found again.
    P. 105 ANNIVERSARY     99 When for his Foot he thus a place had found,
    P. 112 ANNIVERSARY    365 'What refuge to escape them can be found,
    P. 117 BLAKE          110 Our worst works past, now we have found them out.
    P. 123 O.C.            24 Although immortal, found they were not free.)
    P. 126 O.C.           143 But this, of all the most auspicious found,
    P. 128 O.C.           215 And 'twould be found, could we his thoughts have
                              cast,
    P. 130 O.C.           293 How soon thou Moses hast, and Joshua found,
    P. 137 HOUSEWARMING    21 Yet a President fitter in Virgil he found,
    P. 142 INSTRUCTIONS    55 And found how Royal Heirs might be matur'd,
    P. 186 BRITANNIA       82 If not ore aw'd by new found holy cheat.
    P. 312 CHEQUER INN      4 But such a Choyce as ne're was found

foundation                         frequency:    3    relative frequency: 0.0000
    P. 105 ANNIVERSARY     81 None to be sunk in the Foundation bends,
    P. 128 O.C.           202 The first foundation of his house and name:
    P. 139 HOUSEWARMING    78 For foundation he Bristol sunk in the Earth's
                              bowel;

foundations                        frequency:    3    relative frequency: 0.0000
    P. 126 O.C.           120 The deep foundations open'd to the Skyes.
    P. 164 INSTRUCTIONS   979 And through the Palace's Foundations bore,
    P. 200 DUKE            92 Old England on its strong foundations stands,

founded                            frequency:    1    relative frequency: 0.0000
    P.  65 A. HOUSE       218 'Founded by Folly, kept by Wrong.

founder                            frequency:    1    relative frequency: 0.0000
    P. 192 TWO HORSES      37 Thy founder and mine to Cheat one another,

founders                           frequency:    2    relative frequency: 0.0000
    P.  67 A. HOUSE       275 And what both Nuns and Founders will'd
    P. 104 ANNIVERSARY     34 Nor Matter for succeeding Founders raise;

founding                           frequency:    1    relative frequency: 0.0000
    P. 109 ANNIVERSARY    248 Founding a firm State by Proportions true.

founds                             frequency:    1    relative frequency: 0.0000
    P. 201 HISTORICALL     35 For those and Germin's sins she founds a
                              Church,

fountain                           frequency:    5    relative frequency: 0.0001
    P.   4 HASTINGS         1 Go, intercept some Fountain in the Vein,
    P.  12 DROP OF DEW     20 Of the clear Fountain of Eternal Day,
    P.  41 THE MOWER       31 'Tis all enforc'd; the Fountain and the Grot;
    P.  42 DAMON           28 Or to what gelid Fountain bend?
    P. 112 ANNIVERSARY    369 'The Ocean is the Fountain of Command,

fountaines                         frequency:    1    relative frequency: 0.0000
    P.  18 CLORINDA        13 C. Near this, a Fountaines liquid Bell

fountains                          frequency:    5    relative frequency: 0.0001
    P.  16 EYES            51 Now like two Fountains trickle down:
    P.  18 CLORINDA        28 Caves eccho, and the Fountains ring.
    P.  27 LOVER            4 By Fountains cool, and Shadows green.
    P.  47 EMPIRE           4 To hollow Rocks and murm'ring Fountains bound.
    P.  49 THE GARDEN      49 Here at the Fountains sliding foot,

fountain's.  See "fountaines," "fountains."

four                               frequency:    6    relative frequency: 0.0001
```

```
P.   23 NYMPH         70 And trod, as on the four Winds.
P.   69 A. HOUSE     323 Thou Paradise cf four Seas,
P.  159 INSTRUCTICNS 762 And female Stewart, there, Rules the four
                        Seas.
P.  175 LOYALL SCCT  151 One Mytre fitts the Heads of full four Moors.
P.  193 TWO HORSES    61 Ch. That of four Seas dcminion and Guarding
P.  193 TWO HORSES    83 W. Four Knights and a Knave, who were
                        Publicans made,
```

fourty   frequency: 2   relative frequency: 0.0000
```
P.  190 STATUE        23 And 'tis fourty to one if he Play the old Game
P.  190 STATUE        24 Hee'l shortly reduce us to fourty and eight.
```

fowl   frequency: 2   relative frequency: 0.0000
  See also "fowle."
```
P.  145 INSTRUCTICNS 178 Haters of Fowl, to Teal preferring Bull.
P.  154 INSTRUCTICNS 574 Like molting Fcwl, a weak and easie Prey.
```

fowle   frequency: 1   relative frequency: 0.0000
```
P.  112 ANNIVERSARY  355 'Unless their Ships, dc, as their Fcwle proceed
```

fowles   frequency: 1   relative frequency: 0.0000
```
P.   76 A. HOUSE     564 Cr of the Fowles, or of the Plants.
```

fowls. See "fowles," "fowl's."

fowl's   frequency: 1   relative frequency: 0.0000
```
P.   17 BERMUDAS      15 And sends the Fcwl's to us in care,
```

fox   frequency: 2   relative frequency: 0.0000
```
P.   19 THYRSIS       22 Ther's no Wolf, no Fox, nor Bear.
P.  145 INSTRUCTICNS 170 And follow'd Fcx, but with disdainful look.
```

foxes   frequency: 2   relative frequency: 0.0000
```
P.  174 LOYALL SCCT  112 Where Foxes Dung their earths the Badgers
                        yeild;
P.  174 LOYALL SCCT  113 At Bishops Dung the Foxes quit the feild.
```

fragrant   frequency: 7   relative frequency: 0.0001
```
P.   10 DIALOGUE      27 Thou in fragrant Clouds shalt show
P.   14 THE CORONET    7 Dismantling all the fragrant Towers
P.   41 THE MOWER     34 A wild and fragrant Innocence:
P.   50 THE GARDEN    68 Does through a fragrant Zodiack run;
P.   61 A. HOUSE      79 In fragrant Gardens, shaddy Woods,
P.   68 A. HOUSE     298 In fragrant Vollyes they let fly;
P.   72 A. HOUSE     429 Their Females fragrant as the Mead
```

frail   frequency: 3   relative frequency: 0.0000
```
P.   83 FLECKNO       27 Only this frail Ambition did remain,
P.  147 INSTRUCTIONS 259 Keen Whorwood next, in aid of Damsel frail,
P.  155 INSTRUCTICNS 586 And all our hopes now cn frail Chain depend:
```

fram'd   frequency: 1   relative frequency: 0.0000
```
P.  138 HOUSEWARMING  48 To grudge him scme Timber who fram'd them the
                        War.
```

frame   frequency: 7   relative frequency: 0.0001
```
P.   14 THE CORONET   22 Or shatter too with him my curious frame:
P.   18 BERMUDAS      31 And in these Rocks for us did frame
P.   21 SOUL & BODY   15 And warms and mcves this needless Frame:
P.   59 A. HOUSE       1 Within this sober Frame expect
P.  105 ANNIVERSARY   76 And each one enter'd in the willing Frame;
P.  173 LOYALL SCOT   72 Our nations Melting thy Colossus Frame,
P.  188 BRITANNIA    159 By those great Patterns such a state I'le frame
```

frames   frequency: 1   relative frequency: 0.0000
```
P.   12 DROP OF DEW    8 Frames as it can its native Element.
```

framing   frequency: 1   relative frequency: 0.0000
```
P.  105 ANNIVERSARY   70 Framing a Liberty that still went back;
```

france   frequency: 12   relative frequency: 0.0002
```
P.   66 A. HOUSE     244 France, Poland, either Germany;
P.   67 A. HOUSE     282 Whcm France and Poland yet dces fame:
P.   94 DR. WITTY     20 Now learns the tongues of France and Italy;
P.  141 INSTRUCTIONS  38 Fits him in France to play at Cards and treat.
P.  149 INSTRUCTIONS 365 France had St. Albans prcmis'd (sc they sing)
P.  150 INSTRUCTIONS 396 And our next neighbcurs France and Flanders
                        ride.
P.  151 INSTRUCTIONS 418 In Holland theirs had lodg'd before, and
                        France.
P.  169 ADVICE        35 Thus whilst the King cf France with powerfull
```

		Armes
P. 169 ADVICE	61	Whom France Esteem'd our Chiefe in Parliament,
P. 184 MADE FREE	119	The Government cf France
P. 194 TWO HORSES	93	Ch. And Plenipotentiaryes send into France
P. 204 HISTORICALL	120	Sets up in Scotland alamode de France,

francisca   frequency: 1   relative frequency: 0.0000
    P. 129 O.C.   245 Francisca faire can nothing now but weep,

frankincense   frequency: 1   relative frequency: 0.0000
    P. 24 NYMPH   98 The holy Frankincense doth flow.

frankness   frequency: 1   relative frequency: 0.0000
    P. 178 LOYALL SCOT 283 After such Frankness shown to bee his friend,

frantic. See "frantique."

frantique   frequency: 1   relative frequency: 0.0000
    P. 110 ANNIVERSARY 299 Whose frantique Army should they want for Men

fraud   frequency: 2   relative frequency: 0.0000
    P. 107 ANNIVERSARY 168 And always hast thy Tongue from fraud refrain'd;
    P. 145 INSTRUCTIONS 184 And hid much Fraud under an aspect grim.

frauds   frequency: 1   relative frequency: 0.0000
    P. 186 BRITANNIA   83 These pious frauds (toc slight t'ensnare the brave)

fraudulent   frequency: 1   relative frequency: 0.0000
    P. 65 A. HOUSE   214 'With them 'twould scon grow fraudulent:

fraught   frequency: 1   relative frequency: 0.0000
    P. 119 BLAKE   166 Their rich Fleet sunk, and ours with Lawrel fraught.

fraughting   frequency: 1   relative frequency: 0.0000
    P. 158 INSTRUCTIONS 704 Fraughting their pierced Keels with Oosy Tides.

frayted   frequency: 1   relative frequency: 0.0000
    P. 113 BLAKE   4 Frayted with acted Guilt, and Guilt to come:

frederick   frequency: 1   relative frequency: 0.0000
    P. 145 INSTRUCTIONS 199 Sir Frederick and Sir Salcmon draw Lotts

free   frequency: 15   relative frequency: 0.0003

P. 25 YOUNG LOVE	7	While our Sportings are as free
P. 61 A. HOUSE	75	But Nature here hath been so free
P. 87 FLECKNO	167	He hasted; and I, finding my self free,
P. 90 ODE	103	And to all States nct free
P. 105 ANNIVERSARY	97	Which on the Basis of a Senate free,
P. 107 ANNIVERSARY	177	Our brutish fury strugling to be Free,
P. 115 BLAKE	63	In vain doth she those Islands free from Ill,
P. 123 O.C.	24	Although immcrtal, found they were not free.)
P. 137 HOUSEWARMING	19	He thought (as an Instrument he was most free on)
P. 142 INSTRUCTIONS	57	Hence Crowder made the rare Inventress free,
P. 146 INSTRUCTIONS	230	To fight a Battel, from all Gun-shot free.
P. 181 MADE FREE	t	Upon his Majesties being made free of the Citty
P. 181 MADE FREE	26	How to serve or be free,
P. 189 BRITANNIA	185	As Joves great sunn the infested globe did free
P. 195 TWO HORSES	126	And Free men alike value life and Estate.

freed   frequency: 2   relative frequency: 0.0000
    P. 184 MADE FREE   130 I see who e're is freed,
    P. 189 BRITANNIA   191 Freed by thy labours, Fortunate blest Isle,

freedom   frequency: 1   relative frequency: 0.0000
See also "freedome."
    P. 204 HISTORICALL 122 This Saracen his Ccuntryes freedom broke

freedome   frequency: 4   relative frequency: 0.0000
    P. 110 ANNIVERSARY 279 'Tis not a Freedome, that where All command;
    P. 181 MADE FREE   12 You in Chaines cffer your freedome.
    P. 183 MADE FREE   98 Leave his freedcme behind
    P. 196 TWO HORSES   179 When they take from the people the freedcme of words,

freedomes   frequency: 1   relative frequency: 0.0000
    P. 167 KINGS VOWES 53 Where the Ducks and the Drakes may their freedomes enjoy,

freedoms. See "freedomes."

freely   frequency: 1   relative frequency: 0.0000
      P. 195 TWO HORSES   138 W. I freely declare it, I am for old Noll.

freeman   frequency: 1   relative frequency: 0.0000
      P. 183 MADE FREE   81 To have made this Freeman of Spices;

freighted. See "frayted."

freind   frequency: 1   relative frequency: 0.0000
      P. 313 CHEQUER INN   44 Besides a good Freind in the Chair

freinds   frequency: 1   relative frequency: 0.0000
      P. 181 MADE FREE   18 Yet know both his Freinds and his Breeding.

french   frequency: 14   relative frequency: 0.0002
      P. 86 FLECKNO   135 More odious then those raggs which the French
                              youth
      P. 94 DR. WITTY   24 Nor her chast mind into the French translated:
      P. 142 INSTRUCTIONS   43 Who, if the French dispute his Pow'r, from
                              thence
      P. 145 INSTRUCTIONS 168 And both of them alike French Martyrs were.
      P. 146 INSTRUCTIONS 214 Led the French Standard, weltring in his
                              stride,
      P. 151 INSTRUCTIONS 414 And the French Army one from Calais spies.
      P. 171 PROPHECY   46 And think French onely Loyall, Irish wise,
      P. 185 BRITANNIA   25 Brit: A Colony of French Possess the Court;
      P. 187 BRITANNIA   106 Of French, Scots, Irish (all my mortall foes):
      P. 187 BRITANNIA   117 But his fair soul, transform'd by that French
                              Dame,
      P. 187 BRITANNIA   126 His French and Teagues comand on sea and shoar.
      P. 194 TWO HORSES   95 W. That the King should send for another
                              French whore,
      P. 201 HISTORICALL   31 From the french Court she haughty Topiks
                              brings,
      P. 202 HISTORICALL   53 But here his french bred Prowes provd in Vain,

frenches   frequency: 1   relative frequency: 0.0000
      P. 316 CHEQUER INN   147 The Papist and the Frenches

frequent   frequency: 4   relative frequency: 0.0000
      P. 83 FLECKNO   1 Oblig'd by frequent visits of this man,
      P. 124 O.C.   69 And frequent lightning to her Soul that flyes,
      P. 160 INSTRUCTIONS 809 Frequent in Counsel, earnest in Debate,
      P. 187 BRITANNIA   115 Frequent adresses to my Charles I send,

fresh   frequency: 12   relative frequency: 0.0002
      P. 45 MOWER'S SONG   2 Of all these Medows fresh and gay;
      P. 64 A. HOUSE   186 'Appoint a fresh and Virgin Bride;
      P. 69 A. HOUSE   348 Fresh as his own and flourishing.
      P. 149 INSTRUCTIONS 339 And with fresh Age felt his glad Limbs unite;
      P. 150 INSTRUCTIONS 397 But a fresh News, the great designment nips,
      P. 151 INSTRUCTIONS 411 Fresh Messengers still the sad News assure,
      P. 153 INSTRUCTIONS 532 Swells his old Veins with fresh Blood, fresh
                              Delight.
      P. 157 INSTRUCTIONS 697 Each doleful day still with fresh loss returns;
      P. 161 INSTRUCTIONS 835 But, fresh as from the Mint, the Courtiers fine
      P. 161 INSTRUCTIONS 852 Lest some new Tomkins spring a fresh debate.
      P. 169 ADVICE   36 Frightens all Christendome with fresh Alarms,

fresher   frequency: 1   relative frequency: 0.0000
      P. 78 A. HOUSE   626 And now the Meadows fresher dy'd;

friar. See "fryar."

friend   frequency: 10   relative frequency: 0.0002
      See also "freind."
      P.   3 LOVELACE   t1 To his Noble Friend Mr. Richard Lovelace,
      P. 11 DIALOGUE   66 The other half thy Friend.
      P. 55 EPITAPH   7 Nor can the truest Wit or Friend,
      P. 86 FLECKNO   113 During the Table: though my new made Friend
      P. 91 MAY'S DEATH   29 But Ben, who knew not neither foe nor friend,
      P. 93 DR. WITTY   t1 To his worthy Friend Doctor Witty upon his
      P. 128 O.C.   200 So loose an enemy, so fast a friend.
      P. 165 KINGS VOWES   10 I will have a fine Parliament allwayes to
                              Friend,
      P. 178 LOYALL SCOT   283 After such Frankness shown to bee his friend,
      P. 200 DUKE   105 Destroyd by a false brother and false friend.

friendly   frequency: 1   relative frequency: 0.0000
     P. 174 LOYALL SCOT   102 The friendly Loadstone hath not more Combin'd

friends   frequency: 5   relative frequency: 0.0001
     See also "freinds."
     P. 11 DIALOGUE   67 What Friends, if to my self untrue?
     P. 34 DAPHNIS   38 With the shrieks of Friends aghast,
     P. 61 A. HOUSE   68 Daily new Furniture of Friends.
     P. 138 HOUSEWARMING   47 His Friends in the Navy would not be ingrate,
     P. 145 INSTRUCTIONS   202 Their Friends agreed they should command by
                               turn.

friendship   frequency: 4   relative frequency: 0.0000
     P. 128 O.C.   201 Friendship, that sacred virtue, long dos claime
     P. 128 O.C.   227 Valour, religion, friendship, prudence dy'd
     P. 178 LOYALL SCOT   271 And all themselves in meal and friendship close.
     P. 200 DUKE   113 There is no friendship, tenderness nor love:

fright   frequency: 5   relative frequency: 0.0001
     P. 56 BILL-BOROW   12 The Earth deform and Heaven fright,
     P. 89 ODE   70 Did fright the Architects to run;
     P. 90 ODE   117 Besides the force it has to fright
     P. 130 O.C.   280 And with the name of Cromwell, armyes fright.
     P. 155 INSTRUCTIONS 601 Our Seamen, whom no Dangers shape could fright,

frighted   frequency: 2   relative frequency: 0.0000
     P. 28 LOVER   22 Through frighted Clouds in forked streaks.
     P. 144 INSTRUCTIONS 132 Frighted the Midwife, and the Mother tore.

frightening. See "frighting."

frightens   frequency: 1   relative frequency: 0.0000
     P. 169 ADVICE   36 Frightens all Christendome with fresh Alarms,

frightful   frequency: 1   relative frequency: 0.0000
     P. 156 INSTRUCTIONS 643 But when the frightful Fire-ships he saw,

frighting   frequency: 1   relative frequency: 0.0000
     P. 34 DAPHNIS   42 Frighting her he loved most.

frisks   frequency: 1   relative frequency: 0.0000
     P. 162 INSTRUCTIONS 878 Frisks like a Frog to croak a Taxes load.

frog   frequency: 2   relative frequency: 0.0000
     See also "leap-frog."
     P. 42 DAMON   13 But in the brook the green Frog wades;
     P. 162 INSTRUCTIONS 878 Frisks like a Frog to croak a Taxes load.

froggs   frequency: 1   relative frequency: 0.0000
     P. 195 TWO HORSES   144 W. The Same that the Froggs had of Jupiters
                              Stork.

frogs   frequency: 2   relative frequency: 0.0000
     See also "froggs."
     P. 42 DAMON   12 And hamstring'd Frogs can dance no more.
     P. 171 PROPHECY   33 The Frogs shall then grow weary of their Crane

from   frequency: 182   relative frequency: 0.0038

front   frequency: 5   relative frequency: 0.0001
     P. 140 HOUSEWARMING 102 Throw dust in its Front, and blame situation:
     P. 145 INSTRUCTIONS 186 Finch, in the Front, and Thurland in the Rear.
     P. 148 INSTRUCTIONS 297 Then closing, all in equal Front fall on,
     P. 154 INSTRUCTIONS 571 So he in Front, his Garrison in Rear,
     P. 186 BRITANNIA   65 Her Towry front a fiery Meteor bears

frontier   frequency: 1   relative frequency: 0.0000
     See also "frontire."
     P. 104 ANNIVERSARY   23 Yet some more active for a Frontier Town

frontire   frequency: 1   relative frequency: 0.0000
     P. 127 O.C.   174 And stretch'd our frontire to the Indian Ore;

frontispice   frequency: 1   relative frequency: 0.0000
     P. 61 A. HOUSE   65 A Stately Frontispice of Poor

frontispiece. See "frontispice."

frost   frequency: 1   relative frequency: 0.0000
     P. 98 HOLLAND   126 Half bound at home in Prison to the frost:

frosts   frequency: 1   relative frequency: 0.0000

P. 149 INSTRUCTIONS   341 What Frosts to Fruit, what Ars'nick to the
                          Rat,

froth   frequency: 1   relative frequency: 0.0000
   P. 141 INSTRUCTIONS   22 Of his Hound's Mouth to feign the raging froth,

frowning   frequency: 1   relative frequency: 0.0000
   P. 186 BRITANNIA   71 And, frowning, thus with proud disdain she spoke.

fruit   frequency: 8   relative frequency: 0.0001
   See also "fruit-trees."
   P. 36 DAPHNIS   89 Farewel therefore all the fruit
   P. 41 THE MOWER   25 That the uncertain and adult'rate fruit
   P. 64 A. HOUSE   173 'So through the mortal fruit we boyl
   P. 65 A. HOUSE   219 'I know what Fruit their Gardens yield,
   P. 107 ANNIVERSARY   164 T'have smelt the Blosscme, and not eat the
                             Fruit;
   P. 149 INSTRUCTIONS   341 What Frosts to Fruit, what Ars'nick to the
                             Rat,
   P. 185 BRITANNIA   46 How, like ripe fruit, she dropt from of the
                             Throne
   P. 190 STATUE   31 And instead of that markett of herbs and of fruit

fruit-trees   frequency: 1   relative frequency: 0.0000
   P. 49 THE GARDEN   50 Or at some Fruit-trees mossy root,

fruition   frequency: 1   relative frequency: 0.0000
   P. 35 DAPHNIS   64 By a late Fruition.

fruits   frequency: 3   relative frequency: 0.0000
   P.   9 DIALOGUE   15 Where the Souls of fruits and flow'rs
   P. 14 THE CORONET   6 I gather flow'rs (my fruits are only flow'rs)
   P. 39 PICTURE   34 Whom Nature courts with fruits and flow'rs,

frustrate   frequency: 1   relative frequency: 0.0000
   P. 156 INSTRUCTIONS   626 Frustrate Revenge, and Love, by loss more keen,

frustrates   frequency: 1   relative frequency: 0.0000
   P. 125 O.C.   100 Frustrates the Autumn and the hopes cf Wine.

frustrating   frequency: 1   relative frequency: 0.0000
   P. 25 YOUNG LOVE   25 Thus as Kingdomes, frustrating

fryar   frequency: 2   relative frequency: 0.0000
   P. 191 TWO HORSES   11 Fryar Bacon had a head that spoke made of
                             Brass,
   P. 192 TWO HORSES   20 By the Devill, a Priest, a Fryar, or Nun.

frye   frequency: 1   relative frequency: 0.0000
   P. 167 KINGS VOWES   57 That they may raise Fortunes to my owne frye.

fuel. See "fewel."

fulfil'd   frequency: 1   relative frequency: 0.0000
   P. 95 DR. WITTY   39 You have Translaticns statutes best fulfil'd.

fulfill'd   frequency: 1   relative frequency: 0.0000
   P. 67 A. HOUSE   276 'Tis likely better thus fulfill'd.

fulfilled. See "fulfil'd," "fulfill'd."

full   frequency: 17   relative frequency: 0.0003
   P. 16 EYES   33 Not full sailes hasting loaden home,
   P. 20 THYRSIS   31 Thyrsis. Then I'le go on: There, sheep are
                             full
   P. 23 NYMPH   41 For it was full cf sport; and light
   P. 33 DAPHNIS   21 But he came so full possest
   P. 64 A. HOUSE   176 'Is thus preserved clear and full.
   P. 86 FLECKNO   121 And on full stomach do condemn but few:
   P. 86 FLECKNO   151 Thereat the Poet swell'd, with anger full,
   P. 138 HOUSEWARMING   32 Though he had built full many a one for his
                             Master
   P. 141 INSTRUCTICNS   29 Faint then St. Albans full cf soup and gold,
   P. 145 INSTRUCTIONS   177 Then march't the Trcop of Clarendon, all full,
   P. 147 INSTRUCTIONS   273 With Heart of Bees so full, and Head of
                             Mites,
   P. 175 LOYALL SCOT   151 One Mytre fitts the Heads of full four Moors.
   P. 185 BRITANNIA   47 Full of Gray Hairs, good deeds, endless renown.
   P. 187 BRITANNIA   94 So boundless Lewis in full Glory shines,
   P. 200 DUKE   100 Great Charles, who full of mercy wouldst command
   P. 205 HISTORICALL   178 And stopt his Malice in its full Careere.

P. 317 CHEQUER INN   186 And then it runs full spout

fulminant   frequency: 1   relative frequency: 0.0000
    P. 149 INSTRUCTIONS 356 And sits in State Divine like Jove the
                             fulminant!

fumes   frequency: 1   relative frequency: 0.0000
    P. 97 HCLLAND   88 Fumes through the loop-holes of a wooden Square.

function   frequency: 1   relative frequency: 0.0000
    P. 203 HISTORICALL   113 And touch the holy function with her Verse:

funeral   frequency: 3   relative frequency: 0.0000
    See also "fun'ral."
    P.   5 HASTINGS   46 Reversed, at his Darlings Funeral.
    P. 44 GLO-WORMS   6 No War, nor Princes funeral,
    P. 71 A. HOUSE   414 Sounds your untimely Funeral.

funerals. See "fun'rals."

fun'ral   frequency: 1   relative frequency: 0.0000
    P. 28 LOVER   24 As at the Fun'ral of the World.

fun'rals   frequency: 2   relative frequency: 0.0000
    P. 111 ANNIVERSARY   334 Did make the Fun'rals sadder by their Joyes.
    P. 125 O.C.   108 Their fun'rals celetrates while it decrees.

furies. See "furyes."

furious   frequency: 1   relative frequency: 0.0000
    P. 87 FLECKNO   160 Home, his most furious Satyr to have fir'd

furl'd   frequency: 1   relative frequency: 0.0000
    P. 68 A. HOUSE   316 Seem to their Staves the Ensigns furl'd.

furnace   frequency: 1   relative frequency: 0.0000
    P. 156 INSTRUCTIONS 646 E're in the Firy Furnace they be cast.

furnish   frequency: 2   relative frequency: 0.0000
    P. 132 PARADISE   42 Whence furnish such a vast expense of Mind?
    P. 165 KINGS VOWES   11 That shall furnish me Treasure as fast as I
                             spend;

furniture   frequency: 2   relative frequency: 0.0000
    P. 29 THE GALLERY   7 That, for all furniture, you'l find
    P. 61 A. HOUSE   68 Daily new Furniture of Friends.

furrows   frequency: 1   relative frequency: 0.0000
    P. 81 A. HOUSE   736 And Virtue all those Furrows till'd.

furrs   frequency: 2   relative frequency: 0.0000
    P. 158 INSTRUCTIONS 717 Furrs from the North, and Silver from the
                             West,
    P. 184 MADE FREE   128 Goe fold up your Furrs,

furs. See "furrs."

further   frequency: 8   relative frequency: 0.0001
    P. 57 BILL-BOROW   27 Discerning further then the Cliff
    P. 58 BILL-BOROW   57 Yet now no further strive to shoot,
    P. 83 FLECKNO   19 Straight without further information,
    P. 93 DR. WITTY   1 Sit further, and make room for thine own fame,
    P. 111 ANNIVERSARY   342 Smiling serenely from the further side.
    P. 113 ANNIVERSARY   397 I yield, nor further will the Prize contend;
    P. 145 INSTRUCTIONS 190 Nor any further would then these ingage.
    P. 168 ADVICE   t Further Advice to a Painter.

fury   frequency: 3   relative frequency: 0.0000
    P. 85 FLECKNO   95 He gathring fury still made sign to draw;
    P. 107 ANNIVERSARY   177 Our brutish fury strugling to be Free,
    P. 187 BRITANNIA   109 With fury drunke like Backanalls they roar

furyes   frequency: 1   relative frequency: 0.0000
    P. 188 BRITANNIA   130 And none are left these furyes to cast out.

future   frequency: 5   relative frequency: 0.0001
    P. 11 DIALOGUE   70 And see the future Time:
    P. 20 THYRSIS   27 Dorinda. Oh sweet! oh sweet! How I my future
                             state
    P. 83 FLECKNO   30 The future Ages how I did indure:
    P. 125 O.C.   106 As hollow Seas with future Tempests rage:

```
        P. 130 O.C.            285 As long as future time succeeds the past,

gadding                            frequency:   1    relative frequency: 0.0000
        P.  78 A. HOUSE         610 Curle me about ye gadding Vines,

gain                               frequency:   8    relative frequency: 0.0001
        See also "gaine."
        P.  21 SOUL & BODY       29 And ready oft the Port to gain,
        P.  33 DAPHNIS           19 Knew not that the Port to gain
        P.  57 BILL-BOROW        23 Nor for it self the height does gain,
        P.  90 ODE              119 The same Arts that did gain
        P. 114 BLAKE             31 A happy People, which at once do gain
        P. 149 INSTRUCTIONS     363 Gain and Revenge, Revenge and Gain are sweet:
        P. 153 INSTRUCTIONS     501 Here Men induc'd by Safety, Gain, and Ease,

gaind                              frequency:   1    relative frequency: 0.0000
        P. 202 HISTORICALL       55 This Isle was well reform'd and gaind renowne,

gain'd                             frequency:   2    relative frequency: 0.0000
        P.  47 EMPIRE            19 With which She gain'd the Empire of the Ear,
        P. 190 STATUE            29 But his brother-in-law's horse had gain'd such
                                    repute

gaine                              frequency:   1    relative frequency: 0.0000
        P. 203 HISTORICALL      111 And hosts of upstart Errours gaine the field.

gained                             frequency:   1    relative frequency: 0.0000
        See also "gaind," "gain'd."
        P.  31 FAIR SINGER       18 She having gained both the Wind and Sun.

'gainst                            frequency:   2    relative frequency: 0.0000
        P. 178 LOYALL SCOT      277 The hare's head 'gainst the goose gibletts sett.
        P. 203 HISTORICALL       86 'Gainst Avarice and Luxury complaine,

gales                              frequency:   1    relative frequency: 0.0000
        P. 154 INSTRUCTIONS     555 And gentle Gales them steer, and Heaven drives,

gall                               frequency:   1    relative frequency: 0.0000
        P. 195 TWO HORSES       133 The Debauch'd and the Bloody since they
                                    Equally Gall us,

gallant                            frequency:   2    relative frequency: 0.0000
        P. 205 HISTORICALL      171 Thus said the Scarlet Whore to her gallant,
        P. 314 CHEQUER INN       51 Over a Gallant Supper

gallants                           frequency:   1    relative frequency: 0.0000
        P. 155 INSTRUCTIONS     597 Our feather'd Gallants, which came down that day

galleons.  See "gallions."

gallery                            frequency:   3    relative frequency: 0.0000
        P.  29 THE GALLERY        t The Gallery.
        P.  29 THE GALLERY        4 Compos'd into one Gallery;
        P.  30 THE GALLERY       42 Of Thee, my Gallery do store;

gallick                            frequency:   2    relative frequency: 0.0000
        P. 171 PROPHECY          50 Then either Greek or Gallick Story shew,
        P. 186 BRITANNIA         62 Her left Arm bears, the Antient Gallick shield

gallions                           frequency:   3    relative frequency: 0.0000
        P. 113 BLAKE              7 Every capatious Gallions womb was fill'd,
        P. 116 BLAKE             89 With hast they therefore all their Gallions
                                    moar,
        P. 118 BLAKE            151 Their Gallions sunk, their wealth the Sea does
                                    fill,

gallons                            frequency:   2    relative frequency: 0.0000
        P. 138 HOUSEWARMING      50 The two Allens when jovial, who ply him with
                                    gallons,

galloping                          frequency:   2    relative frequency: 0.0000
        P. 142 INSTRUCTIONS      78 Galloping with the Duke to other Prey.
        P. 173 LOYALL SCOT       68 Galloping down Clos'd up the Gaping Cave.

gallopt                            frequency:   1    relative frequency: 0.0000
        P. 196 TWO HORSES       168 Both Gallopt to Whitehall and there Horribly
                                    farted,

galloway.  See "gall'way."

gall'way                           frequency:   1    relative frequency: 0.0000
```

         P. 173 LOYALL SCOT   64 Sometimes the Gall'way Proves the better Nagg.

gambia. See "gambo."

gambo   frequency: 1   relative frequency: 0.0000
         P. 158 INSTRUCTIONS   719 From Gambo Gold, and from the Ganges Gems;

game   frequency: 6   relative frequency: 0.0001
         P. 23 NYMPH   43 Me to its game: it seem'd to bless
         P. 143 INSTRUCTIONS   118 With what small Arts the publick game they play.
         P. 148 INSTRUCTIONS   308 Resolve henceforth upon their other Game:
         P. 187 BRITANNIA   99 'Tis Royall Game whole Kingdomes to deflower.
         P. 187 BRITANNIA   114 To Boys, Bawds, whores, and made a Publick
                                    game.
         P. 190 STATUE   23 And 'tis fourty to one if he Play the old Game

games. See "may-games."

gamesome   frequency: 1   relative frequency: 0.0000
         P. 158 INSTRUCTIONS   734 With Gamesome Joy insulting on her Decks.

ganges   frequency: 2   relative frequency: 0.0000
         P. 26 MISTRESS   5 Thou by the Indian Ganges side
         P. 158 INSTRUCTIONS   719 From Gambo Gold, and from the Ganges Gems;

gap'd   frequency: 1   relative frequency: 0.0000
         P. 314 CHEQUER INN   90 That gap'd to heare him sputter

gaping   frequency: 1   relative frequency: 0.0000
         P. 173 LOYALL SCOT   68 Galloping down Clos'd up the Gaping Cave.

garden   frequency: 8   relative frequency: 0.0001
         P. 14 THE CORONET   5 Through every Garden, every Mead,
         P. 15 EYES   17 I have through every Garden been,
         P. 23 NYMPH   71 I have a Garden of my own,
         P. 48 THE GARDEN   t The Garden.
         P. 69 A. HOUSE   322 The Garden of the World ere while,
         P. 80 A. HOUSE   700 The Garden Flow'rs to Crown Her Head;
         P. 124 O.C.   55 So the Flowr with'ring which the Garden
                                    crown'd,
         P. 190 STATUE   10 Since the privy garden could not it defend,

garden-state   frequency: 1   relative frequency: 0.0000
         P. 49 THE GARDEN   57 Such was that happy Garden-state,

gardener. See "gardiner," "gardner."

gardens   frequency: 13   relative frequency: 0.0002
         P. 40 THE MOWER   t The Mower against Gardens.
         P. 40 THE MOWER   5 He first enclos'd within the Gardens square
         P. 41 THE MOWER   38 May to adorn the Gardens stand:
         P. 61 A. HOUSE   79 In fragrant Gardens, shaddy Woods,
         P. 65 A. HOUSE   219 'I know what Fruit their Gardens yield,
         P. 67 A. HOUSE   285 But laid these Gardens out in sport
         P. 69 A. HOUSE   331 When Gardens only had their Towrs,
         P. 69 A. HOUSE   347 Might once have made our Gardens spring
         P. 70 A. HOUSE   356 Which most our Earthly Gardens want.
         P. 80 A. HOUSE   689 'Tis She that to these Gardens gave
         P. 80 A. HOUSE   696 Then Gardens, Woods, Meads, Rivers are.
         P. 82 A. HOUSE   752 So you all Woods, Streams, Gardens, Meads.
         P. 88 ODE   29 Who, from his private Gardens, where

gardiner   frequency: 1   relative frequency: 0.0000
         P. 69 A. HOUSE   337 The Gardiner had the Souldiers place,

gardner   frequency: 1   relative frequency: 0.0000
         P. 50 THE GARDEN   65 How well the skilful Gardner drew

garland   frequency: 2   relative frequency: 0.0000
         P. 121 TWO SONGS   6 In a Garland for the Bride.
         P. 121 TWO SONGS   7 If thou would'st a Garland bring,

garlands   frequency: 5   relative frequency: 0.0001
         P. 14 THE CORONET   4 I seek with Garlands to redress that Wrong:
         P. 20 THYRSIS   33 There, birds sing Consorts, garlands grow,
         P. 48 THE GARDEN   8 To weave the Garlands of repose.
         P. 58 BILL-BOROW   69 For all the Civick Garlands due
         P. 69 A. HOUSE   334 And Men did rosie Garlands wear?

garrison   frequency: 1   relative frequency: 0.0000
         P. 154 INSTRUCTIONS   571 So he in Front, his Garrison in Rear,

garrisons   frequency: 1   relative frequency: 0.0000
     P.   69 A. HOUSE   332 And all the Garrisons were Flowrs,

garroway. See "garrway," "garway."

garrway   frequency: 1   relative frequency: 0.0000
     P. 148 INSTRUCTIONS 298 Led by great Garrway, and great Littleton.

garway   frequency: 1   relative frequency: 0.0000
     P. 185 BRITANNIA   17 Till Howard and Garway shall a bribe reject,

gasps   frequency: 1   relative frequency: 0.0000
     P. 125 O.C.   75 And with the damp of her last Gasps obscur'd,

gate   frequency: 3   relative frequency: 0.0000
     P.   40 THE MATCH   25 He fortifi'd the double Gate,
     P.   59 A. HOUSE   32 To strain themselves through Heavens Gate.
     P. 129 O.C.   234 It seem'd Mars broke through Janus' double
                            gate;

gates   frequency: 5   relative frequency: 0.0001
     P.   27 MISTRESS   44 Thorough the Iron gates of Life.
     P.   61 A. HOUSE   89 Near to this gloomy Cloysters Gates
     P.   62 A. HOUSE   103 'The Cloyster outward shuts its Gates,
     P. 105 ANNIVERSARY 66 Th' harmonious City of the seven Gates.
     P. 151 INSTRUCTIONS 420 To fly to Windsor, and more up the Gates.

gather   frequency: 3   relative frequency: 0.0000
     P.   14 THE CORONET   6 I gather flow'rs (my fruits are only flow'rs)
     P.   36 DAPHNIS   87 Gather Roses in the rain,
     P.   39 PICTURE   35 Gather the Flow'rs, but spare the Buds;

gather'd   frequency: 1   relative frequency: 0.0000
     P. 171 LOYALL SCOT   3 They streight Consulting gather'd in a Ring

gathering. See "gathring."

gathring   frequency: 1   relative frequency: 0.0000
     P.   85 FLECKNO   95 He gathring fury still made sign to draw;

gaudy. See "gawdy."

gaul   frequency: 2   relative frequency: 0.0000
     P.   77 A. HOUSE   608 And gaul its Horsemen all the Day.
     P.   90 ODE   101 A Caesar he ere long to Gaul,

gave   frequency: 12   relative frequency: 0.0002
     P.   17 BERMUDAS   13 He gave us this eternal Spring,
     P.   22 NYMPH   29 Gave it to me: nay and I know
     P.   61 A. HOUSE   85 A Nunnery first gave it birth.
     P.   80 A. HOUSE   689 'Tis She that to these Gardens gave
     P. 104 ANNIVERSARY 50 Which the God gave him, with his gentle hand,
     P. 117 BLAKE   113 This said, the whole Fleet gave it their
                            applause,
     P. 127 O.C.   154 Gave chase to Ligny on the Belgick Coast.
     P. 147 INSTRUCTIONS 247 First spy'd the Enemy and gave th' Alarm:
     P. 147 INSTRUCTIONS 279 Ev'n Iron Strangeways, chafing yet gave back,
     P. 161 INSTRUCTIONS 858 Nor gave the Commons leave to say their
                            Pray'rs:
     P. 194 TWO HORSES 103 Tho' the beast gave his Master ne're an ill
                            word,
     P. 315 CHEQUER INN 130 The Man that gave a woefull Tax

gawdy   frequency: 2   relative frequency: 0.0000
     P.   45 MOWER'S SONG 15 And in your gawdy May-games meet,
     P. 189 BRITANNIA   168 To Flattery, Pimping, and a gawdy shew:

gay   frequency: 2   relative frequency: 0.0000
     P.   45 MOWER'S SONG 2 Of all these Medows fresh and gay;
     P. 161 INSTRUCTIONS 837 And Turner gay up to his Pearch does march,

gaz'd   frequency: 2   relative frequency: 0.0000
     P.   59 A. HOUSE   8 To arch the Brows that on them gaz'd.
     P. 118 BLAKE   137 Th' all-seeing Sun, neer gaz'd on such a sight,

gaze   frequency: 3   relative frequency: 0.0000
     P.   26 MISTRESS   14 Thine Eyes, and on thy Forehead Gaze.
     P.   70 A. HOUSE   368 Or innocently seems to gaze.
     P.   78 A. HOUSE   637 Where all things gaze themselves, and doubt

gazet   frequency: 1   relative frequency: 0.0000

P. 92 MAY'S DEATH   60 Because a Gazet writer mist his aim?

gazette   frequency: 1   relative frequency: 0.0000
       See also "gazet."
P. 159 INSTRUCTIONS   775 Who with false News prevented the Gazette?

gazing   frequency: 2   relative frequency: 0.0000
P. 12 DROP OF DEW   11 But gazing back upon the Skies,
P. 90 MAY'S DEATH   4 And with an Eye uncertain, gazing wide,

gelded   frequency: 1   relative frequency: 0.0000
       See also "gelt."
P. 140 HIS HOUSE   2 Of Paul late gelded of his Stones.

gelid   frequency: 2   relative frequency: 0.0000
P. 42 DAMON   28 Or to what gelid Fountain bend?
P. 75 A. HOUSE   530 Of gelid Straw-berryes do tread,

gellying   frequency: 1   relative frequency: 0.0000
P. 80 A. HOUSE   675 The gellying Stream compacts below,

gelt   frequency: 1   relative frequency: 0.0000
P. 152 INSTRUCTIONS   474 Consenting, for his Rupture, to be Gelt;

gem. See "gemme."

gemme   frequency: 1   relative frequency: 0.0000
P. 131 O.C.   316 Richer than any eastern silk, or gemme;

gems   frequency: 1   relative frequency: 0.0000
P. 158 INSTRUCTIONS   719 From Gambo Gold, and from the Ganges Gems;

general   frequency: 1   relative frequency: 0.0000
       See also "trumpet-gen'ral."
P. 116 BLAKE   97 That they with joy their boasting General heard,

generals. See "gen'rals."

generation   frequency: 1   relative frequency: 0.0000
P. 315 CHEQUER INN   126 With his whole Generation

generous   frequency: 4   relative frequency: 0.0000
       See also "gen'rous."
P. 168 ADVICE   14 Whose life does scarce one Generous Action own,
P. 173 LOYALL SCOT   65 Shall not a death soe Generous now when told
P. 179 STOCKSMARKET   5 Some thought it a knightly and generous deed,
P. 189 BRITANNIA   167 Tell em the Generous scorn their Rise to owe

genious   frequency: 1   relative frequency: 0.0000
P. 118 BLAKE   145 For your resistless genious there did Raign,

genitalls   frequency: 1   relative frequency: 0.0000
P. 202 HISTORICALL   45 But now Yorkes Genitalls grew over hot

genitals. See "genitalls."

genius   frequency: 1   relative frequency: 0.0000
       See also "genious."
P. 58 BILL-BOROW   52 The Genius of the house do bind.

gen'rals   frequency: 1   relative frequency: 0.0000
P. 146 INSTRUCTIONS   225 All the two Coventrys their Gen'rals chose:

gen'rous   frequency: 3   relative frequency: 0.0000
P. 84 FLECKNO   48 For he has this of gen'rous, that alone
P. 148 INSTRUCTIONS   292 In giving Gen'rous, but in Counsel Grave;
P. 165 INSTRUCTIONS   985 Whose gen'rous Conscience and whose Courage
                          high

gent   frequency: 1   relative frequency: 0.0000
P. 181 MADE FREE   1 The Londoners Gent,

gentle   frequency: 10   relative frequency: 0.0002
P. 55 EPITAPH   18 Gentle as Ev'ning; cool as Night;
P. 69 A. HOUSE   338 And his more gentle Forts did trace.
P. 104 ANNIVERSARY   50 Which the God gave him, with his gentle hand,
P. 123 O.C.   26 In gentle Passions should his Death disguise:
P. 123 TWO SONGS   41 But what is most, the gentle Swain
P. 129 O.C.   249 Those gentle rays under the lids were fled,
P. 154 INSTRUCTIONS   555 And gentle Gales them steer, and Heaven drives,
P. 157 INSTRUCTIONS   672 Or with known Art to try the gentle Wave.

```
         P. 172 LOYALL SCOT    38 Or with known art to try the Gentle Wave.
         P. 188 BRITANNIA     144 With the Doggs bloud his gentle kind convey

gentlemen                        frequency:    1    relative frequency: 0.0000
         P. 161 INSTRUCTIONS  829 Plain Gentlemen are in Stage-Coach o'rethrown,

gentler                          frequency:    3    relative frequency: 0.0000
         P.  10 DIALOGUE       23 My gentler Rest is on a Thought,
         P.  36 DAPHNIS        85 Gentler times for Love are ment
         P.  47 EMPIRE         22 Unto a gentler Conqueror then you;

gentlest                         frequency:    1    relative frequency: 0.0000
         P. 145 INSTRUCTIONS  174 Gentlest of men, and his Lieutenant mild,

gentlier                         frequency:    1    relative frequency: 0.0000
         P. 202 HISTORICALL    71 And gentlier farre the Orleans Dutches treat.

gently                           frequency:    5    relative frequency: 0.0001
         P.   4 LOVELACE       38 Whose hand so gently melts the Ladies hand.
         P.  91 MAY'S DEATH    20 Gently to signifie that he was wrong.
         P. 125 O.C.           81 No downy breast did ere so gently beat,
         P. 129 O.C.          236 No April sunns that e'er so gently smil'd;
         P. 131 O.C.          314 How gently winds at once the ruling reins?

gentry                           frequency:    1    relative frequency: 0.0000
         P. 148 INSTRUCTIONS  287 A Gross of English Gentry, nobly born,

geographers                      frequency:    1    relative frequency: 0.0000
         P. 150 INSTRUCTIONS  401 Modern Geographers, 'twas there they thought,

geometrick                       frequency:    1    relative frequency: 0.0000
         P.   4 HASTINGS       18 But weigh to Man the Geometrick yeer.

george                           frequency:    1    relative frequency: 0.0000
         P. 314 CHEQUER INN    79 And next him sate George Mountague

german                           frequency:    1    relative frequency: 0.0000
         P. 142 INSTRUCTIONS   46 Two Saints at once, St. German, St. Alban.

germany                          frequency:    1    relative frequency: 0.0000
         P.  66 A. HOUSE      244 France, Poland, either Germany;

germin's                         frequency:    1    relative frequency: 0.0000
         P. 201 HISTORICALL    35 For those and Germin's sins she founds a
                                  Church,

gerrard                          frequency:    1    relative frequency: 0.0000
         P. 166 KINGS VOWES    27 And Successor be, if not to me, to Gerrard.

get                              frequency:    4    relative frequency: 0.0000
         P. 183 MADE FREE     100 But if ever he get,
         P. 193 TWO HORSES     74 And get good preferment Imediately for't.
         P. 193 TWO HORSES     82 Who out of what 's given do get a good living.
         P. 317 CHEQUER INN   183 And that way get more cut

gets                             frequency:    1    relative frequency: 0.0000
         P. 182 MADE FREE      68 And the Bastards he gets

ghastly                          frequency:    1    relative frequency: 0.0000
         P. 163 INSTRUCTIONS  921 And ghastly Charles, turning his Collar low,

ghibellines.  See "gibellines."

ghost                            frequency:    6    relative frequency: 0.0001
         P.  30 THE GALLERY    26 Vexing thy restless Lover's Ghost;
         P.  34 DAPHNIS        43 At the last, this Lovers Ghost
         P. 127 O.C.          153 And the last minute his victorious Ghost
         P. 140 G.-CHILDREN     2 What fitter Sacrifice for Denham's Ghost?
         P. 163 INSTRUCTIONS  937 His Fathers Ghost too whisper'd him one Note,
         P. 204 HISTORICALL   135 Let Cromwells Ghost smile with Contempt to see

ghosts                           frequency:    2    relative frequency: 0.0000
         P. 130 O.C.          300 Wander like ghosts about thy loved tombe;
         P. 163 INSTRUCTIONS  917 While, the pale Ghosts, his Eye does fixt
                                  admire

giant.  See "gyant."

giants.  See "gyants."

gibellines                       frequency:    1    relative frequency: 0.0000
```

P. 92 MAY'S DEATH   62 As for the Basket Guelphs and Gibellines be?

gibeon   frequency: 1   relative frequency: 0.0000
   P. 128 O.C.   192 Since the commanded sun o're Gibeon stay'd?

giblets. See "gibletts."

gibletts   frequency: 1   relative frequency: 0.0000
   P. 178 LOYALL SCOT   277 The hare's head 'gainst the goose gibletts sett.

giddy   frequency: 3   relative frequency: 0.0000
   P. 37 DEFINITION   21 Unless the giddy Heaven fall,
   P. 80 A. HOUSE   685 For streight those giddy Rockets fail,
   P. 110 ANNIVERSARY   272 Giddy, and wishing for the fatal Shore;

gideon   frequency: 1   relative frequency: 0.0000
   P. 109 ANNIVERSARY   249 When Gideon so did from the War retreat,

gifts   frequency: 1   relative frequency: 0.0000
   P. 23 NYMPH   49 As Sylvio did: his Gifts might be

gigantick   frequency: 1   relative frequency: 0.0000
   P. 96 HOLLAND   17 How did they rivet, with Gigantick Piles,

gilberts   frequency: 1   relative frequency: 0.0000
   P. 175 LOYALL SCOT   160 Who views but Gilberts Toyls will reason find

gilt   frequency: 1   relative frequency: 0.0000
   P. 139 HOUSEWARMING   91 And shews on the top by the Regal Gilt Ball,

gingerbread   frequency: 1   relative frequency: 0.0000
   P. 191 STATUE   48 That a Monarch of Gingerbread would doe as
                             well.

gingling   frequency: 1   relative frequency: 0.0000
   P. 66 A. HOUSE   254 The gingling Chain-shot of her Beads.

gipsies   frequency: 1   relative frequency: 0.0000
   P. 67 A. HOUSE   268 Like Gipsies that a Child hath stoln.

girds   frequency: 1   relative frequency: 0.0000
   P. 107 ANNIVERSARY   148 Girds yet his Sword, and ready stands to fight;

girles   frequency: 1   relative frequency: 0.0000
   P. 316 CHEQUER INN   170 Like Sweat Meates, for their Girles and Wives

girls   frequency: 3   relative frequency: 0.0000
   See also "girles."
   P. 150 INSTRUCTIONS   386 And Boys and Girls in Troops run houting by;
   P. 161 INSTRUCTIONS   845 True Trojan! while this Town can Girls afford,
   P. 161 INSTRUCTIONS   847 The Girls shall always kiss thee, though grown
                             old,

girt   frequency: 1   relative frequency: 0.0000
   P. 13 DROP OF DEW   34 How girt and ready to ascend.

give   frequency: 28   relative frequency: 0.0005
   P.   3 LOVELACE   8 Twas more esteem'd to give, then weare the Bayes:
   P. 19 THYRSIS   24 Our Lightfoot we may give away;
   P. 20 THYRSIS   45 Chorus. Then let us give Carillo charge o'th
                             Sheep,
   P. 76 A. HOUSE   565 Give me but Wings as they, and I
   P. 97 HOLLAND   81 Let it suffice to give their Country Fame
   P. 106 ANNIVERSARY   119 If gracious Heaven to my Life give length,
   P. 113 BLAKE   14 That boundless Empire, where you give the Law,
   P. 116 BLAKE   87 Who on the Ocean that does horror give,
   P. 117 BLAKE   118 To give him Lawrel, as the Last did Plate.
   P. 139 HOUSEWARMING   62 And Presents croud headlong to give good
                             example:
   P. 143 INSTRUCTIONS   104 And this Campaspe thee Apelles give!
   P. 148 INSTRUCTIONS   305 At the first Charge the Enemy give out;
   P. 152 INSTRUCTIONS   462 Their Fleet, to threaten, we will give them all.
   P. 155 INSTRUCTIONS   612 He saw seiz'd, and could give her no Relief!
   P. 160 INSTRUCTIONS   801 Who hath no Chimneys, to give all is best,
   P. 165 INSTRUCTIONS   990 Give us this Court, and rule without a Guard.
   P. 166 KINGS VOWES   20 And the Dutch shall give Caution for their
                             Provinces;
   P. 168 ADVICE   24 All looking this way how to give their votes,
   P. 168 ADVICE   26 That give their votes more by their eyes than
                             ears:
   P. 170 PROPHECY   10 Hir'd for their share to give the rest away

```
   P. 170 PROPHECY        12 Give Taxes to the King and Parliament.
   P. 175 LOYALL SCOT     149 And holy Ordure Holy orders give?
   P. 189 BRITANNIA       193 And this kind secret for reward shall give:
   P. 192 TWO HORSES      18 When Shrines give Answers, say a knave 's in
                             the Roode;
   P. 193 TWO HORSES      78 Should give away Millions at every Summons.
   P. 202 HISTORICALL     75 Let loose the Raines and give the Realme away:
   P. 203 HISTORICALL     76 With lavish hands they constant Tributes give
   P. 205 HISTORICALL     180 To give you kings in's Wrath to vex you sore:
```

given   frequency: 4   relative frequency: 0.0000
```
   P.   4 HASTINGS        21 As that of Knowledge; what Loves had he given
   P. 116 BLAKE           77 And to this vast hill a power is given,
   P. 171 PROPHECY        35 When the Seal's given to a talking fool
   P. 193 TWO HORSES      82 Who out of what 's given do get a good living.
```

givers   frequency: 1   relative frequency: 0.0000
```
   P. 193 TWO HORSES      79 W. Yet some of those givers such beggerly
                             Villains
```

gives   frequency: 7   relative frequency: 0.0001
```
   P.  38 PICTURE          5 The Wilder flow'rs, and gives them names:
   P.  42 DAMON           11 The Grass-hopper its pipe gives ore;
   P. 111 ANNIVERSARY     343 So while our Star that gives us Light and
                             Heat,
   P. 145 INSTRUCTIONS    182 The Miter Troop, and with his looks gives Law.
   P. 151 INSTRUCTIONS    425 The Bloodworth-Chanc'lor gives, then does recal
   P. 151 INSTRUCTIONS    426 Orders, amaz'd at last gives none at all.
   P. 317 CHEQUER INN     185 He Money gives amongst this Pack
```

giving   frequency: 3   relative frequency: 0.0000
```
   P. 148 INSTRUCTIONS    292 In giving Gen'rous, but in Counsel Grave;
   P. 193 TWO HORSES      81 Ch. No wonder that Beggers should still be for
                             giving
   P. 194 TWO HORSES      90 For giving noe more the Rogues are prorogued.
```

glad   frequency: 10   relative frequency: 0.0002
```
   P.  57 BILL-BOROW      29 How glad the weary Seamen hast
   P.  67 A. HOUSE        265 But the glad Youth away her bears,
   P.  82 A. HOUSE        743 While her glad Parents most rejoice,
   P.  95 HOLLAND          9 Glad then, as Miners that have found the Oar,
   P. 115 BLAKE           67 For Sanctacruze the glad Fleet takes her way,
   P. 131 O.C.            320 Earth ne'er more glad, nor Heaven more serene.
   P. 149 INSTRUCTIONS    339 And with fresh Age felt his glad Limbs unite;
   P. 157 INSTRUCTIONS    677 Like a glad Lover, the fierce Flames he meets,
   P. 172 LOYALL SCOT     43 Like a glad lover the fierce Flames hee meets
   P. 186 BRITANNIA       59 Whilst in truthes Mirror this Glad scene he
                             spy'd,
```

glades   frequency: 1   relative frequency: 0.0000
```
   P. 171 LOYALL SCOT      2 Saw Douglass Marching on the Elisian Glades,
```

gladly   frequency: 2   relative frequency: 0.0000
```
   P.   5 HASTINGS        39 And gladly there can all his Kinred claim,
   P.  33 DAPHNIS         11 And would gladly yield to all,
```

glance   frequency: 2   relative frequency: 0.0000
```
   P.  16 EYES            37 The sparkling Glance that shoots Desire,
   P.  44 DAMON           78 Did into his own Ankle glance;
```

glancing   frequency: 1   relative frequency: 0.0000
```
   P.  38 PICTURE         20 Ere, with their glancing wheels, they drive
```

glare   frequency: 2   relative frequency: 0.0000
```
   P.  34 DAPHNIS         35 And with rouling Eyes did glare,
   P. 162 INSTRUCTIONS    887 And those bright gleams that dart along and glare
```

glass   frequency: 5   relative frequency: 0.0001
```
   P.  45 MOWER'S SONG     4 Did see its Hopes as in a Glass;
   P.  80 A. HOUSE        701 And for a Glass the limpid Brook,
   P.  91 MAY'S DEATH     47 Or thou Dictator of the glass bestow
   P. 123 O.C.             3 Now in its self (the Glass where all appears)
   P. 143 INSTRUCTIONS    87 Poring within her Glass she re-adjusts
```

glassen   frequency: 1   relative frequency: 0.0000
```
   P. 142 INSTRUCTIONS    60 To make her glassen D----s once malleable!
```

glasses   frequency: 2   relative frequency: 0.0000
```
   P.   5 HASTINGS        50 The Golden Harvest, sees his Glasses leap.
   P.  73 A. HOUSE        462 In Multiplying Glasses lye.
```

gleams   frequency: 1   relative frequency: 0.0000
```
```

```
        P. 162 INSTRUCTIONS  887 And those bright gleams that dart along and glare

glean                                frequency:   2    relative frequency: 0.0000
        P.  75 A. HOUSE      542 Doth from the Bark the Wood-moths glean.
        P.  86 FLECKNO       132 But how I loath'd to see my Neighbour glean

glee                                 frequency:   1    relative frequency: 0.0000
        P. 146 INSTRUCTIONS  229 They both accept the Charge with merry glee,

glews                                frequency:   1    relative frequency: 0.0000
        P.  33 DAPHNIS        16 Sudden Parting closer glews.

glide                                frequency:   1    relative frequency: 0.0000
        P.  49 THE GARDEN     52 My Soul into the boughs does glide:

glides                               frequency:   1    relative frequency: 0.0000
        P. 154 INSTRUCTIONS  559 Such up the stream the Belgick Navy glides,

glitter                              frequency:   1    relative frequency: 0.0000
        P. 107 ANNIVERSARY   186 Still as they trickle, glitter in our Joy.

glitters                             frequency:   2    relative frequency: 0.0000
        P.  42 DAMON          16 Now glitters in its second skin.
        P.  92 MAY'S DEATH    63 When the Sword glitters ore the Judges head,

glo-worms                            frequency:   2    relative frequency: 0.0000
        P.  44 GLO-WORMS       t The Mower to the Glo-Worms.
        P.  44 GLO-WORMS       9 Ye Glo-worms, whose officious Flame

globe                                frequency:   1    relative frequency: 0.0000
        P. 189 BRITANNIA     185 As Joves great sunn the infested globe did free

globes                               frequency:   1    relative frequency: 0.0000
        P.  12 DROP OF DEW     7 And in its little Globes Extent,

gloominess                           frequency:   1    relative frequency: 0.0000
        P. 114 BLAKE          27 For least some Gloominess might stain her sky,

gloomy                               frequency:   2    relative frequency: 0.0000
        P.  61 A. HOUSE       89 Near to this gloomy Cloysters Gates
        P. 111 ANNIVERSARY   344 Seem'd now a long and gloomy Night to threat,

glories                              frequency:   8    relative frequency: 0.0001
        P.  13 DROP OF DEW    40 Into the Glories of th' Almighty Sun.
        P.  38 PICTURE        24 Where I may see thy Glories from some shade.
        P. 107 ANNIVERSARY   182 The other Glories of our yearly Song.
        P. 126 O.C.          140 To chuse it worthy of his Glories past.
        P. 156 INSTRUCTIONS  621 Of former Glories the reproachful thought,
        P. 157 INSTRUCTIONS  683 And, as on Angels Heads their Glories shine,
        P. 172 LOYALL SCOT    39 Much him the glories of his Antient Race
        P. 173 LOYALL SCOT    49 And as on Angells head their Glories shine

glorious                             frequency:   4    relative frequency: 0.0000
        P. 148 INSTRUCTIONS  290 For Countrys Cause, that Glorious think and
                                 sweet:
        P. 169 ADVICE         37 Wee in our Glorious Bacchanals dispose
        P. 186 BRITANNIA      55 To him I shew'd this Glorious setting sun,
        P. 198 DUKE           21 I nere can fight in a more glorious Cause

glory                                frequency:  12    relative frequency: 0.0002
        P.   4 LOVELACE       47 But he secure of glory and of time
        P.  11 DIALOGUE       63 Wilt thou all the Glory have
        P.  14 THE CORONET    12 As never yet the king of Glory wore:
        P.  14 THE CORONET    18 And mortal Glory, Heavens Diadem!
        P.  56 BILL-BOROW     16 Which to securer Glory lead.
        P.  63 A. HOUSE      143 'And round about you Glory breaks,
        P. 129 O.C.          255 Oh! humane glory, vaine, oh! death, oh! wings,
        P. 130 O.C.          288 Of humane glory tow'rst, and raigning there
        P. 130 ADVICE         46 And add new Beams to Sands's former Glory.
        P. 187 BRITANNIA      94 So boundless Lewis in full Glory shines,
        P. 189 BRITANNIA     175 True sons of Glory, Pillars of the state,
        P. 315 CHEQUER INN   115 The Westerne Glory, Harry Ford

glowes                               frequency:   1    relative frequency: 0.0000
        P. 173 LOYALL SCOT    47 Round the Transparent fire about him Glowes

glows                                frequency:   1    relative frequency: 0.0000
        See also "glowes."
        P. 157 INSTRUCTIONS  681 Round the transparent Fire about him glows,

glues.  See "glews."

gnash                                frequency:   1    relative frequency: 0.0000
```

P.   92 MAY'S DEATH   91 The Cerberus with all his Jawes shall gnash,

gnashes   frequency: 1   relative frequency: 0.0000
P. 106 ANNIVERSARY   130 Gnashes her Goary teeth; nor there secure.

go   frequency: 23   relative frequency: 0.0004
See also "goe."
P.   4 HASTINGS   1 Go, intercept scme Fountain in the Vein,
P.   4 HASTINGS   5 Go, stand betwixt the Mcrning and the Flowers;
P.   11 DIALOGUE   57 Where so e're thy Foot shall go
P.   13 DROP OF DEW   33 How loose and easie hence to go:
P.   19 THYRSIS   4 Whither thou and I must go.
P.   20 THYRSIS   31 Thyrsis. Then I'le go on: There, sheep are
                             full
P.   21 SOUL & BODY   14 That mine own Precipice I go;
P.   24 NYMPH   106 Whether the Swans and Turtles go:
P.   26 MISTRESS   13 An hundred years should go to praise
P.   33 DAPHNIS   8 Nor yet let her Lover go.
P.   35 DAPHNIS   62 Better 'tis to go in peace,
P.   46 AMETAS   16 And go kiss within the Hay.
P.   70 A. HOUSE   380 Whether he fall through it or go.
P.   79 A. HOUSE   663 And lest She see him go to Bed;
P.   81 A. HOUSE   729 Go now fond Sex that on your Face
P.   83 A. HOUSE   774 These rational Amphibii go?
P.   85 FLECKNC   86 But who came last is forc'd first to go out;
P.   85 FLECKNO   94 Me a great favour, for I seek to go.
P.   87 FLECKNO   165 With truth. I counsell'd him to go in time,
P.   87 FLECKNO   169 Have made the Chance be painted; and go now
P.   91 MAY'S DEATH   43 Go seek the novice Statesmen, and obtrude
P. 156 INSTRUCTIONS   639 But when, by shame constrain'd to go on Board,
P. 161 INSTRUCTICNS   826 Let them come up sc to go down agen.

goal   frequency: 1   relative frequency: 0.0000
P. 187 BRITANNIA   112 And from my Charles to a base Goal me drew,

goale   frequency: 1   relative frequency: 0.0000
P. 313 CHEQUER INN   36 And looks like Bird of Goale

goary   frequency: 1   relative frequency: 0.0000
P. 106 ANNIVERSARY   130 Gnashes her Goary teeth; nor there secure.

goat   frequency: 1   relative frequency: 0.0000
P. 195 TWO HORSES   125 W. The Goat and the Lyon I Equally hate,

goatish   frequency: 1   relative frequency: 0.0000
P. 202 HISTORICALL   67 Outdoes Tiberius and his Goatish Court:

goats   frequency: 1   relative frequency: 0.0000
P. 195 TWO HORSES   132 Than the Goats making whores of our wives and
                             our Daughters.

gobling   frequency: 1   relative frequency: 0.0000
P. 187 BRITANNIA   90 When all their Gcbling Intrest in Mankind

god   frequency: 18   relative frequency: 0.0003
P.   10 DIALOGUE   28 Like another Gcd below.
P.   69 A. HOUSE   346 Who, had it pleased him and God,
P.   97 HOLLAND   61 Though Herring for their God few voices mist,
P. 104 ANNIVERSARY   50 Which the God gave him, with his gentle hand,
P. 127 O.C.   182 And fearing God how they should nothing fear.
P. 128 O.C.   194 He conquer'd Gcd, still ere he fought with men:
P. 175 LOYALL SCCT   128 Enough for them, Gcd knows, to Count their
                             Wealth,
P. 175 LOYALL SCCT   150 None knows what god our Flamen now Adores;
P. 187 BRITANNIA   92 And by imposters Gcd and man betray'd,
P. 187 BRITANNIA   101 A sacrafice to you, their God and King.
P. 188 BRITANNIA   154 Eternall Lawes by God for mankind made? Noe!
P. 192 TWO HORSES   44 And the Kings wicked life say God there is
                             none;
P. 192 TWO HORSES   46 Who beleives not a word, the word of God saith;
P. 203 HISTORICALL   91 Drcll on their Gcd but a much duller way:
P. 203 HISTORICALL   104 His God and Lord this preacher did betray.
P. 205 HISTORICALL   165 Gocd did renounce him and his Cause disowne
P. 205 HISTORICALL   179 Be wise ye Sons of Men tempt God no more
P. 315 CHEQUER INN   91 But King (Gcd save him) tho' so cram'd

god-like-good   frequency: 1   relative frequency: 0.0000
P. 188 BRITANNIA   140 'Tis god-like-gocd to save a falling King.

godly-cheat   frequency: 1   relative frequency: 0.0000
P. 205 HISTORICAIL   158 The Godly-cheat King-wou'd-be did inspire,

gods   frequency: 12   relative frequency: 0.0002
    P.   5 HASTINGS   41 The gods themselves cannot their Joy conceal,
    P.   10 DIALOGUE   26 Such as oft the Gods appeas'd,
    P.   38 PICTURE   10 This Darling of the Gods was born!
    P.   41 THE MOWER   40 The Gods themselves with us do dwell.
    P.   48 THE GARDEN   27 The Gods, that mortal Beauty chase,
    P.   89 ODE   61 Nor call'd the Gods with vulgar spight
    P. 115 BLAKE   54 Which of the Gods the fancied drink exceeds;
    P. 131 PARADISE   3 Messiah Crown'd, Gods Reconcil'd Decree,
    P. 154 INSTRUCTIONS   544 (The Gods themselves do help the provident.)
    P. 159 INSTRUCTIONS   752 Themselves dishonour'd, and the Gods untrue:
    P. 186 BRITANNIA   78 The Rivall Gods, Monarchs of th' other world,
    P. 196 TWO HORSES   162 The Gods have repented the Kings Restoration.

goe   frequency: 7   relative frequency: 0.0001
    P. 130 O.C.   295 How streight canst to each happy mansion goe?
    P. 176 LOYALL SCOT   189 Where but two hands to Act, two feet to goe.
    P. 183 MADE FREE   95 A Processioning goe,
    P. 184 MADE FREE   128 Goe fold up your Furrs,
    P. 188 BRITANNIA   155 To the serene Venetian state I'le goe
    P. 191 STATUE   43 She thinks not convenient to goe to the price,
    P. 316 CHEQUER INN   164 And now (who wou'd) twas tyme to goe

goes   frequency: 3   relative frequency: 0.0000
    P.   59 A. HOUSE   19 And in his hollow Palace goes
    P.   68 A. HOUSE   297 These, as their Governour goes by,
    P. 143 INSTRUCTIONS   116 Can strike the Die, and still with them goes
                               share.

goest   frequency: 1   relative frequency: 0.0000
    P. 144 INSTRUCTIONS   122 And thought all lost that goest not to the
                               Cheats:

going   frequency: 2   relative frequency: 0.0000
    P.   3 LOVELACE   30 Because you write when going to the Warre,
    P.   43 DAMON   47 While, going home, the Ev'ning sweet

gold   frequency: 15   relative frequency: 0.0003
    P.   11 DIALOGUE   58 The minted Gold shall lie;
    P.   11 DIALOGUE   61 Wer't not a price who'ld value Gold?
    P.   62 A. HOUSE   120 'Our brighter Robes and Crowns of Gold?
    P. 115 BLAKE   56 All that is good, and are not curst with Gold.
    P. 115 BLAKE   57 With fatal Gold, for still where that does grow,
    P. 141 INSTRUCTIONS   29 Paint then St. Albans full of soup and gold,
    P. 143 INSTRUCTIONS   98 More gold in's Fob, more Lace upon his Coat
    P. 157 INSTRUCTIONS   680 Like the Sun's Statue stands of burnish'd
                               Gold.
    P. 158 INSTRUCTIONS   719 From Gambo Gold, and from the Ganges Gems;
    P. 173 LOYALL SCOT   46 Like the sun's Statue stands of burnisht Gold:
    P. 180 STOCKSMARKET   32 For he counterfeits only in gold, not in stone.
    P. 181 MADE FREE   16 When in Diamonds and Gold
    P. 183 MADE FREE   105 It might deserve a Box and a Gold one;
    P. 190 STATUE   39 Tho' the King be of Copper and Danby of Gold,
    P. 203 HISTORICALL   78 Corrupt with Gold they Wives and Daughters
                               bring

golden   frequency: 16   relative frequency: 0.0003
    P.   5 HASTINGS   50 The Golden Harvest, sees his Glasses leap.
    P.   17 BERMUDAS   18 Like golden Lamps in a green Night.
    P.   24 NYMPH   101 I in a golden Vial will
    P.   38 PICTURE   2 This Nimph begins her golden daies!
    P.   43 DAMON   53 With this the golden fleece I shear
    P.   98 HOLLAND   106 Or intercept the Western golden Sands:
    P. 112 ANNIVERSARY   353 'What Oaken Forrests, and what golden Mines!
    P. 123 O.C.   4 Had seen the period of his golden Years:
    P. 140 HIS HOUSE   3 Here lie Golden Briberies,
    P. 142 INSTRUCTIONS   47 But thought the Golden Age was now restor'd,
    P. 162 INSTRUCTIONS   866 Paint him in Golden Gown, with Mace's Brain:
    P. 181 MADE FREE   10 In a Golden Box
    P. 185 BRITANNIA   18 Till Golden Osborn cheating shall detect,
    P. 185 BRITANNIA   31 Tell him of Golden Indies, Fayry Lands,
    P. 185 BRITANNIA   45 And Golden dayes in peacefull order rould,
    P. 198 DUKE   40 Then draw the princesse with her golden locks,

gone   frequency: 15   relative frequency: 0.0003
    P. 124 O.C.   52 This will not stay when once the other's gone.
    P. 129 O.C.   243 All, all is gone of ours or his delight
    P. 130 O.C.   299 For we, since thou art gone, with heavy doome,
    P. 130 O.C.   303 Since thou art gone, who best that way could'st
                               teach,
    P. 152 INSTRUCTIONS   492 (The Eighteen hundred thousand pound was gone.)

P. 157 INSTRUCTIONS 690 As one that's warm'd himself and gone to Bed.
P. 164 INSTRUCTIONS 959 Kings in the Country oft have gone astray,
P. 176 LOYALL SCOT   185 A Bishops Cruelty, the Crown had gone.
P. 179 STOCKSMARKET   7 When with honour he might from his word have gone
                          back;
P. 180 STOCKSMARKET   38 Or is he to Clayton's gone in masquerade?
P. 182 MADE FREE   47 He was broken and gone
P. 183 MADE FREE   93 Hee is too farr gone to begin it;
P. 192 TWO HORSES   50 Not to think his own Father is gone to the
                          Devill.
P. 194 TWO HORSES   109 Where is thy King gone? Ch. To see Bishop
                          Laud.
P. 201 HISTORICALL   25 And that the Fleet was gone in Pompe and state

good   frequency: 38   relative frequency: 0.0007
    See also "god-like-good."
P.   5 HASTINGS   55 But what could he, good man, although he bruis'd
P.   22 NYMPH   6 Thy death yet do them any good.
P.   25 YOUNG LOVE   22 And, if good she to us meant,
P.   25 YOUNG LOVE   23 We that Good shall antedate,
P.   63 A. HOUSE   138 'That me does for your good inspire)
P.   76 A. HOUSE   545 The good he numbers up, and hacks;
P.   82 A. HOUSE   741 Whence, for some universal good,
P.   86 FLECKNO   140 Not one Word, thought and swore that they were
                          good.
P.   89 ODE   79 How good he is, how just,
P.   91 MAY'S DEATH   55 But the nor Ignorance nor seeming good
P.   92 MAY'S DEATH   70 Seeks wretched good, arraigns successful Crimes.
P.   93 DR. WITTY   3 The good Interpreter. Some in this task
P. 107 ANNIVERSARY   158 And good Designes still with their Authors
                          lost.
P. 111 ANNIVERSARY   324 Does with himself all that is good revive.
P. 115 BLAKE   56 All that is good, and are not curst with Gold.
P. 128 O.C.   221 But to the good (too many or too few)
P. 128 O.C.   228 At once with him, and all that's good beside;
P. 139 HOUSEWARMING   62 And Presents croud headlong to give good
                          example:
P. 140 HOUSEWARMING   111 When like the good Oxe, for publick good chear,
P. 153 INSTRUCTIONS   514 Or think him, like Herb-John, for nothing good.
P. 160 INSTRUCTIONS   797 But sure his late good Husbandry in Peeter,
P. 167 KINGS VOWES   60 And all their bills for publike good prevent.
P. 168 ADVICE   3 There holy Charles, here good Aurelius Sate,
P. 170 PROPHECY   25 When two good Kings shall be att Brantford
                          knowne
P. 175 LOYALL SCOT   143 Bishops are very good when in Commendum.
P. 177 LOYALL SCOT   237 The good, the bad, and those mixt every where.
P. 177 LOYALL SCOT   239 The good will travely, bad will basely doe;
P. 180 STOCKSMARKET   44 As if we'd as good have a king made of clouts.
P. 184 MADE FREE   117 To colour the good of an Alien,
P. 185 BRITANNIA   30 Pervert his mind, his good Intencions Choak,
P. 185 BRITANNIA   47 Full of Gray Hairs, good deeds, endless renown.
P. 188 BRITANNIA   139 Who knows what good effects from thence may
                          spring;
P. 192 TWO HORSES   21 If the Roman Church, good Christians, oblige
                          yee
P. 193 TWO HORSES   74 And get good preferment Imediately for't.
P. 193 TWO HORSES   82 Who out of what 's given do get a good living.
P. 313 CHEQUER INN   44 Besides a good Freind in the Chair
P. 314 CHEQUER INN   75 Tho' not for his good Deeds:

goodness   frequency: 1   relative frequency: 0.0000
P.   81 A. HOUSE   727 And Goodness doth it self intail

goodrick   frequency: 1   relative frequency: 0.0000
P. 144 INSTRUCTIONS   126 Should Goodrick silence, and strike Paston
                          dumb;

goose   frequency: 1   relative frequency: 0.0000
P. 178 LOYALL SCOT   277 The hare's head 'gainst the goose gibletts sett.

gore   frequency: 1   relative frequency: 0.0000
P. 185 BRITANNIA   40 Shew'd him how many Kings in Purple Gore

gorge   frequency: 1   relative frequency: 0.0000
P. 105 ANNIVERSARY   71 Whose num'rous Gorge could swallow in an hour

gory. See "goary."

gospels   frequency: 1   relative frequency: 0.0000
P.   17 BERMUDAS   30 The Gospels Pearl upon our Coast.

got   frequency: 7   relative frequency: 0.0001

```
          See also "gott."
          P. 138 HOUSEWARMING    33 Already he had got all our Money and Cattel,
          P. 146 INSTRUCTIONS   238 Excise had got the day, and all been lost.
          P. 194 TWO HORSES     114 With an Harlot got up on my Crupper behind him.
          P. 199 DUKE            67 Laden with folly, flesh and Ill got land:
          P. 201 HISTORICALL     34 The new got flemish Towne was sett to sale.
          P. 203 HISTORICALL    107 The chiefest blessings Adam's Chaplin got.
          P. 204 HISTORICALL    137 His meager Highness now had got astride,

goth                            frequency:   1    relative frequency: 0.0000
          P.  91 MAY'S DEATH     41 Polydore, Lucan, Allan, Vandale, Goth,

gott                            frequency:   5    relative frequency: 0.0001
          P. 200 DUKE            82 The Hero once gott honour by the sword;
          P. 200 DUKE            83 He gott his wealth by breaking of his word;
          P. 200 DUKE            84 And now hath gott his Daughter gott with Child,
          P. 202 HISTORICALL     57 But since the ill gctt race of Stewarts came,

gourmand                        frequency:   1    relative frequency: 0.0000
          P.  35 DAPHNIS         78 Like the Gourmand Hebrew dead,

gout                            frequency:   2    relative frequency: 0.0000
          P. 149 INSTRUCTIONS   340 His Gout (yet still he curst) had left him
                                   quite.
          P. 152 INSTRUCTIONS   472 And wish'd himself the Gout, to seize his hand.

gouty                           frequency:   2    relative frequency: 0.0000
          P.  84 FLECKNO         41 So while he with his gouty Fingers craules
          P. 138 HOUSEWARMING    25 Thus dayly his Gouty Inventions he pain'd,

govern                          frequency:   2    relative frequency: 0.0000
          See also "governe."
          P. 128 O.C.           226 And you to govern only Heaven's taske.
          P. 176 LOYALL SCOT    203 That Cloven head must Govern Cloven foot.

govern'd                        frequency:   1    relative frequency: 0.0000
          P. 160 INSTRUCTIONS   816 Till it be govern'd by a Convocation.

governe                         frequency:   1    relative frequency: 0.0000
          P. 184 MADE FREE      111 Shews how fit he is to Governe;

governess                       frequency:   1    relative frequency: 0.0000
          P.  68 A. HOUSE       299 And to salute their Governess

government                      frequency:   7    relative frequency: 0.0001
          P.  96 HOLLAND         38 Something like Government among them brings.
          P. 103 ANNIVERSARY     t2 Of The Government under O. C.
          P. 184 MADE FREE      119 The Government cf France
          P. 188 BRITANNIA      136 (The Bassis of his throne and Government);
          P. 195 TWO HORSES     139 Tho' his Government did a Tyrants resemble,
          P. 205 HISTORICALL    168 And Jesse's son plac'd in the Government:
          P. 314 CHEQUER INN     77 To Plant with Us his Government

governor.  See "governour."

governors                       frequency:   1    relative frequency: 0.0000
          See also "governours."
          P. 139 HOUSEWARMING    66 Sinners, Governors, Farmers, Banquers,
                                   Patentees.

governour                       frequency:   1    relative frequency: 0.0000
          P.  68 A. HOUSE       297 These, as their Governour goes by,

governours                      frequency:   1    relative frequency: 0.0000
          See also "governors."
          P.  97 HCLLAND         79 How fit a Title clothes their Governours,

governs                         frequency:   1    relative frequency: 0.0000
          P.  99 HOLLAND        151 And while Jove governs in the highest Sphere,

gown                            frequency:   2    relative frequency: 0.0000
          P. 162 INSTRUCTIONS   866 Paint him in Golden Gown, with Mace's Brain:
          P. 176 LOYALL SCOT    180 Hee Chose the Cassock Circingle and Gown,

grac'd                          frequency:   3    relative frequency: 0.0000
          P.  75 A. HOUSE       523 The Stock-doves, whose fair necks are grac'd
          P. 131 O.C.           318 His brows, like an imperiall jewell grac'd.
          P. 159 INSTRUCTIONS   748 When all the Rivers grac'd their Nuptial Bed;

grace                           frequency:  14    relative frequency: 0.0002
          P.  10 DIALOGUE        33 But since ncne deserves that grace,
```

P. 23 NYMPH   65 With what a pretty skipping grace,
P. 60 A. HOUSE   59 Height with a certain Grace does bend,
P. 61 A. HOUSE   70 Only as for a Mark of Grace;
P. 94 DR. WITTY   21 But she is Caelia still: no other grace
P. 106 ANNIVERSARY   132 High Grace should meet in one with highest
                          Pow'r,
P. 122 TWO SONGS   39 Shall grace
P. 137 HOUSEWARMING   15 And wish'd that his Daughter had had as much
                          grace
P. 155 INSTRUCTIONS   578 That rul'd all Seas, and did our Channel grace.
P. 166 KINGS VOWES   29 And allwayes who beards me shall have the next
                          Grace,
P. 173 LOYALL SCOT   60 That Matchless grace to propagate thy fame,
P. 176 LOYALL SCOT   173 Of Rochets Tippets Copes, and wheres theire
                          Grace?
P. 203 HISTORICALL   100 When our first Parents Paradice did grace,
P. 316 CHEQUER INN   165 For Grace they did not stay

graces   frequency: 2   relative frequency: 0.0000
P. 62 A. HOUSE   124 'The Face and Graces of the Saint.
P. 82 A. HOUSE   737 Hence She with Graces more divine

gracious   frequency: 1   relative frequency: 0.0000
P. 106 ANNIVERSARY   119 If gracious Heaven to my Life give length,

grafts   frequency: 1   relative frequency: 0.0000
P. 41 THE MOWER   24 He grafts upon the Wild the Tame:

grain   frequency: 3   relative frequency: 0.0000
P. 22 NYMPH   22 Is dy'd in such a Purple Grain.
P. 39 THE MATCH   11 For, with one grain of them diffus'd,
P. 96 HOLLAND   40 Among the hungry he that treasures Grain,

grains   frequency: 1   relative frequency: 0.0000
P. 150 INSTRUCTIONS   385 The Distaff knocks, the Grains from Kettle
                          fly,

grammar   frequency: 1   relative frequency: 0.0000
P. 174 LOYALL SCOT   119 The Bible and Grammar for the service Book.

grand   frequency: 1   relative frequency: 0.0000
P. 314 CHEQUER INN   83 All of 'em of the Grand Inquest

grand-children   frequency: 1   relative frequency: 0.0000
P. 140 G.-CHILDREN   t Upon his Grand-Children.

grandsire   frequency: 1   relative frequency: 0.0000
P. 163 INSTRUCTIONS   918 Of Grandsire Harry, and of Charles his Sire.

grandsire's   frequency: 1   relative frequency: 0.0000
P. 124 O.C.   49 Or with a Grandsire's joy her Children sees

grants   frequency: 1   relative frequency: 0.0000
P. 66 A. HOUSE   234 The Court him grants the lawful Form;

grape   frequency: 2   relative frequency: 0.0000
P. 115 BLAKE   53 There the indulgent Soil that rich Grape
                          breeds,
P. 125 O.C.   98 Weeps that it falls ere fix'd into a Grape.

grapes   frequency: 1   relative frequency: 0.0000
P. 116 BLAKE   82 A grief, above the cure of Grapes best juice.

grapling   frequency: 1   relative frequency: 0.0000
P. 172 LOYALL SCOT   35 The fatall bark him boards with Grapling fire

grapple   frequency: 1   relative frequency: 0.0000
P. 28 LOVER   52 And grapple, with the stubborn Rock:

grappling   frequency: 1   relative frequency: 0.0000
See also "grapling."
P. 157 INSTRUCTIONS   669 The fatal Bark him boards with grappling fire,

grashoppers   frequency: 2   relative frequency: 0.0000
P. 70 A. HOUSE   371 Where Men like Grashoppers appear,
P. 70 A. HOUSE   372 But Grashoppers are Gyants there:

grasps   frequency: 1   relative frequency: 0.0000
P.   4 LOVELACE   37 Whose hand so rudely grasps the steely brand,

grass   frequency: 23   relative frequency: 0.0004

```
P.  18 CLORINDA          5 The Grass I aim to feast thy Sheep:
P.  18 CLORINDA          7 C. Grass withers; and the Flow'rs too fade.
P.  20 THYRSIS          32 Of sweetest grass, and softest wooll;
P.  38 PICTURE           3 In the green Grass she loves to lie,
P.  41 DAMON             8 And wither'd like his Hopes the Grass.
P.  43 DAMON            69 And with my Sythe cut down the Grass,
P.  44 DAMON            79 And there among the Grass fell down,
P.  45 MOWER'S SONG      3 And in the greenness of the Grass
P.  45 MOWER'S SONG      6 What I do to the Grass, does to my Thoughts
                           and Me.
P.  45 MOWER'S SONG      9 That not one Blade of Grass you spy'd,
P.  45 MOWER'S SONG     12 What I do to the Grass, does to my Thoughts
                           and Me.
P.  45 MOWER'S SONG     18 What I do to the Grass, does to my Thoughts
                           and Me.
P.  45 MOWER'S SONG     21 And Flow'rs, and Grass, and I and all,
P.  45 MOWER'S SONG     24 What I do to the Grass, does to my Thoughts
                           and Me.
P.  46 MOWER'S SONG     30 What I do to the Grass, does to my Thoughts
                           and Me.
P.  49 THE GARDEN       40 Insnar'd with Flow'rs, I fall on Grass.
P.  70 A. HOUSE        370 Of that unfathomable Grass,
P.  71 A. HOUSE        387 For when the Sun the Grass hath vext,
P.  71 A. HOUSE        394 These Massacre the Grass along:
P.  73 A. HOUSE        457 They seem within the polisht Grass
P.  78 A. HOUSE        627 Whose Grass, with moister colour dasht,
P.  90 MAY'S DEATH       6 For whence in Stevens ally Trees or Grass?
P. 108 ANNIVERSARY     196 And the green Grass, and their known Mangers
                           hate,
```

```
grass-hopper                          frequency:    1    relative frequency: 0.0000
P.  42 DAMON            11 The Grass-hopper its pipe gives ore;

grass-hoppers                         frequency:    1    relative frequency: 0.0000
P.  42 DAMON            14 And Grass-hoppers seek out the shades.

grasses                               frequency:    2    relative frequency: 0.0000
P.  44 GLO-WORMS        8 Then to presage the Grasses fall;
P.  71 A. HOUSE       410 To build below the Grasses Root;
```

grasshoppers. See "grashoppers," "grass-hoppers."

```
grassy                                frequency:    5    relative frequency: 0.0001
P.  17 BERMUDAS        11 He lands us on a grassy Stage;
P.  18 CLORINDA         3 C. I have a grassy Scutcheon spy'd,
P.  57 BILL-BOROW      18 Lyes open to its grassy side;
P.  71 A. HOUSE       391 To them the Grassy Deeps divide,
P. 130 O.C.           284 While sheep delight the grassy downs to pick,
```

```
grate                                 frequency:    1    relative frequency: 0.0000
P. 202 HISTORICALL     63 Our muse would on the Readers patience grate.

grateful                              frequency:    1    relative frequency: 0.0000
P.  92 MAY'S DEATH     81 Poor Poet thou, and grateful Senate they,

gratefully                            frequency:    1    relative frequency: 0.0000
P.  80 A. HOUSE       698 They gratefully again present.

grates                                frequency:    1    relative frequency: 0.0000
P.  62 A. HOUSE       104 'And, from us, locks on them the Grates.

gratia                                frequency:    1    relative frequency: 0.0000
P. 192 TWO HORSES      43 W. To see dei Gratia writ on the Throne,

gratitude                             frequency:    1    relative frequency: 0.0000
P.  92 MAY'S DEATH     80 Right Romane poverty and gratitude.

grave                                 frequency:    8    relative frequency: 0.0001
See also "dyke-grave," "grave's."
P.  18 CLORINDA        10 D. That den? C. Loves Shrine. D. But
                          Virtue's Grave.
P.  24 NYMPH          110 Will but bespeak thy Grave, and dye.
P.  57 BILL-BOROW      33 Upon its crest this Mountain grave
P. 118 BLAKE          154 Were buryed in as large, and deep a grave,
P. 148 INSTRUCTIONS   292 In giving Gen'rous, but in Counsel Grave;
P. 160 INSTRUCTIONS   811 Grave Primate Shelden (much in Preaching
                          there)
P. 188 BRITANNIA      134 Rescue him again from scandall and the Grave.
P. 191 TWO HORSES       9 Phalaris had a Bull which grave Authors tell ye

gravell'd                             frequency:    1    relative frequency: 0.0000
```

P. 151 INSTRUCTIONS 443 The gravell'd Ccunt did with the Answer faint:

graver   frequency: 2   relative frequency: 0.0000
    P. 105 ANNIVERSARY   63 But, for he most the graver Notes did try,
    P. 106 ANNIVERSARY 121 Then shall I once with graver Accents shake

graver's   frequency: 1   relative frequency: 0.0000
    P. 180 STOCKSMARKET   54 For the graver's at work to reform him thus long.

grave's   frequency: 1   relative frequency: 0.0000
    P. 26 MISTRESS   31 The Grave's a fine and private place,

gravesend   frequency: 1   relative frequency: 0.0000
    P. 159 INSTRUCTIONS 782 Languard, Sheerness, Gravesend, and Upnor?
                             Pett.

gravity   frequency: 2   relative frequency: 0.0000
    P. 92 MAY'S DEATH   83 And with the publick gravity would come,
    P. 132 PARADISE   36 Thou singst with sc much gravity and ease;

gravy   frequency: 1   relative frequency: 0.0000
    P. 315 CHEQUER INN   101 With his owne Gravy fill'd his Plate

gray   frequency: 2   relative frequency: 0.0000
    P. 91 MAY'S DEATH   32 Shook his gray locks, and his own Bayes did tear
    P. 185 BRITANNIA   47 Full of Gray Hairs, good deeds, endless renown.

graze   frequency: 1   relative frequency: 0.0000
    P. 122 TWO SONGS   15 He when Young as we did graze,

great   frequency: 62   relative frequency: 0.0012
    See also "greate."
    P. 18 CLORINDA   20 Pan met me. C. What did great Pan say?
    P. 29 THE GALLERY   5 And the great Arras-hangings, made
    P. 47 EMPIRE   1 First was the World as one great Cymbal made,
    P. 57 BILL-BOROW   38 Of the great Masters terrour there:
    P. 57 BILL-BOROW   42 Of the great Nymph did it protect;
    P. 59 A. HOUSE   5 Who cf his great Design in pain
    P. 60 A. HOUSE   50 And scarce indures the Master great:
    P. 62 A. HOUSE   108 'Lest the great Bridegroom find them dim.
    P. 65 A. HOUSE   203 'Is this that Sanctity so great,
    P. 66 A. HOUSE   248 And the great Race would intercept.
    P. 68 A. HOUSE   300 Again as great a charge they press:
    P. 70 A. HOUSE   366 Th' Ambition of its Prelate great.
    P. 74 A. HOUSE   500 To one great Trunk them all did mold.
    P. 77 A. HOUSE   592 Like some great Prelate of the Grove,
    P. 85 FLECKNO   94 Me a great favour, for I seek to go.
    P. 88 ODE   34 To ruine the great Work of Time,
    P. 92 MAY'S DEATH   76 Before thou couldst great Charles his death
                             relate.
    P. 96 HOLLAND   47 To make a Bank was a great Plot of State;
    P. 104 ANNIVERSARY   56 And the great Work ascended while he play'd.
    P. 106 ANNIVERSARY   110 The great Designes kept for the latter Dayes!
    P. 107 ANNIVERSARY   153 For the great Justice that did first suspend
    P. 107 ANNIVERSARY   159 And thou, great Cromwell, for whose happy birth
    P. 109 ANNIVERSARY   250 Yet by the Conquest of two Kings grown great,
    P. 111 ANNIVERSARY   321 But the great Captain, now the danger's ore,
    P. 112 ANNIVERSARY   380 'Moves the great Bulk, and animates the whole.
    P. 113 ANNIVERSARY   395 Pardon, great Prince, if thus their Fear or
                             Spight
    P. 114 BLAKE   43 But this great want, will not a long one prove,
    P. 125 O.C.   105 Or the great World do by consent presage,
    P. 126 O.C.   113 First the great Thunder was shot off, and sent
    P. 127 O.C.   160 And Heav'n it self would the great Herald be;
    P. 130 O.C.   291 There thy great soule at once a world does see,
    P. 130 O.C.   305 And Richard yet, where his great parent led,
    P. 140 HOUSEWARMING 100 Great Buckingham's Sacrifice must be the first.
    P. 141 INSTRUCTIONS   8 'Twill suit our great debauch and little skill.
    P. 143 INSTRUCTIONS   91 Great Love, how dost thou triumph, and how
                             reign,
    P. 148 INSTRUCTIONS 298 Led by great Garrway, and great Littleton.
    P. 149 INSTRUCTIONS 354 Be Broach'd again, for the great Holy-day
    P. 150 INSTRUCTIONS 397 But a fresh News, the great designment nips,
    P. 153 INSTRUCTIONS 508 Pain of Displeasure of great Clarendon.
    P. 154 INSTRUCTIONS 546 With Trident's Leaver, and great Shoulder
                             heaves.
    P. 160 INSTRUCTIONS 789 For, his great Crime, one Boat away he sent;
    P. 164 INSTRUCTIONS 945 But this great work is for our Monarch fit,
    P. 164 INSTRUCTIONS 955 And you, Great Sir, that with him Empire
                             share,
    P. 167 KINGS VOWES   56 And new Ones Create Great Places to supplye,

```
P.  168 ADVICE          21 This great triumvirate that can devide
P.  169 ADVICE          45 Tis this must make Obryan great in Story,
P.  169 ADVICE          64 Tis by afflictions passive men grow great.
P.  175 LOYALL SCOT    127 A Bishoprick is a great sine-Cure.
P.  178 LOYALL SCOT    262 Charles our great soul this onely Understands:
P.  186 BRITANNIA       75 Who e're grew great by keeping of his word?
P.  186 BRITANNIA       80 Fearing the mighty Projects of the great
P.  188 BRITANNIA      133 Rawl: Once more, great Queen, thy darling try
                            to save;
P.  188 BRITANNIA      159 By those great Patterns such a state I'le frame
P.  189 BRITANNIA      185 As Joves great sunn the infested globe did free
P.  190 STATUE           5 'Twere to Scaramuchio too great disrespect
P.  195 TWO HORSES     140 Hee made England great and it's enemies tremble.
P.  197 DUKE             2 The great assembly and the numerous traine,
P.  199 DUKE            60 He and his Duke had both to great a minde
P.  199 DUKE            66 Now Talbott must by his great master stand,
P.  200 DUKE           100 Great Charles, who full of mercy wouldst command
P.  205 HISTORICALL    160 Heaven had him Chieftain of great Britain made,
```

greate   frequency: 2   relative frequency: 0.0000
```
P.  130 O.C.           276 Seeing how little we confess, how greate;
P.  315 CHEQUER INN    118 What pitty 'tis a Witt so greate
```

greater   frequency: 17   relative frequency: 0.0003
```
P.   12 DROP OF DEW     26 The greater Heaven in an Heaven less.
P.   60 A. HOUSE        44 Things greater are in less contain'd.
P.   79 A. HOUSE       662 Seems to descend with greater Care;
P.   86 FLECKNO        125 Yet that which was a greater cruelty
P.   88 ODE            44 Where greater Spirits come.
P.   98 HOLLAND       110 It self, when as some greater Vessel tows
P.  103 ANNIVERSARY      7 Cromwell alone with greater Vigour runs,
P.  108 ANNIVERSARY    225 For to be Cromwell was a greater thing,
P.  127 O.C.           175 Whose greater Truths obscure the Fables old,
P.  129 O.C.           258 That still though dead, greater than death he
                            lay'd;
P.  153 INSTRUCTIONS   500 Greater the Bribe, and that's at Interest.
P.  161 INSTRUCTIONS   834 And threaten Hyde to raise a greater Dust.
P.  162 INSTRUCTIONS   902 Whose Beauty greater seem'd by her distress;
P.  171 PROPHECY        32 A Greater Thief then Alexander was.
P.  171 PROPHECY        49 Then the English shall a Greater Tyrant Know
P.  205 HISTORICALL    182 Then how much greater Mischiefe as a King.
P.  315 CHEQUER INN    108 That was a greater Lyar.
```

greatest   frequency: 3   relative frequency: 0.0000
```
P.    3 LOVELACE         7 Who best could prayse, had then the greatest
                            prayse,
P.  165 INSTRUCTIONS   981 The smallest Vermin make the greatest waste,
P.  316 CHEQUER INN    139 Our greatest Barne cou'd not have held
```

greatness   frequency: 3   relative frequency: 0.0000
See also "greatnesse."
```
P.   56 BILL-BOROW      10 Which to abrupter greatness thrust,
P.   57 BILL-BOROW      26 And in unenvy'd Greatness stands,
P.   60 A. HOUSE        58 Then That unwonted Greatness wears.
```

greatnesse   frequency: 1   relative frequency: 0.0000
```
P.  129 O.C.           257 Yet dwelt that greatnesse in his shape decay'd,
```

greece   frequency: 1   relative frequency: 0.0000
```
P.   77 A. HOUSE       581 What Rome, Greece, Palestine, ere said
```

greedy   frequency: 2   relative frequency: 0.0000
```
P.   30 THE GALLERY     32 To be the greedy Vultur's prey.
P.   71 A. HOUSE       403 Greedy as Kites has trust it up,
```

greek   frequency: 2   relative frequency: 0.0000
```
P.  171 PROPHECY        50 Then either Greek cr Gallick Story shew,
P.  189 BRITANNIA      183 Greek arts and Roman armes in her conjoynd
```

green   frequency: 28   relative frequency: 0.0005
See also "faint-green-sickness."
```
P.   12 DROP OF DEW     23 Shuns the sweat leaves and blossoms green;
P.   15 EYES            18 Amongst the Red, the White, the Green;
P.   17 BERMUDAS        18 Like golden Lamps in a green Night.
P.   21 SOUL & BODY     44 Green Trees that in the Forest grew.
P.   25 YOUNG LOVE      11 Whose fair Blossoms are too green
P.   27 LOVER            4 By Fountains cool, and Shadows green.
P.   30 THE GALLERY     55 Transplanting Flow'rs from the green Hill,
P.   38 PICTURE          3 In the green Grass she loves to lie,
P.   41 THE MOWER       27 His green Seraglio has its Eunuchs too;
P.   42 DAMON           13 But in the brock the green Frog wades;
```

P.	46	MOWER'S SONG	26	Companions of my thoughts more green,
P.	48	THE GARDEN	18	So am'rous as this lovely green.
P.	49	THE GARDEN	48	To a green Thought in a green Shade.
P.	58	BILL-BOROW	56	As under this so streight and green.
P.	69	A. HOUSE	339	The Nursery of all things green
P.	70	A. HOUSE	376	Of the green spir's, to us do call.
P.	71	A. HOUSE	390	Walking on foot through a green Sea.
P.	74	A. HOUSE	484	In this yet green, yet growing Ark;
P.	74	A. HOUSE	496	Will in green Age her Hearse expect.
P.	74	A. HOUSE	510	The Columnes of the Temple green;
P.	78	A. HOUSE	628	Seems as green Silks but newly washt.
P.	85	FLECKNO	82	As the Chamelion, yellow, blew, or green.
P.	89	ODE	94	But on the next green Bow to pearch;
P.	108	ANNIVERSARY	196	And the green Grass, and their known Mangers hate,
P.	122	TWO SONGS	12	Without each a Sprig of Green.
P.	142	INSTRUCTIONS	71	Ye neighb'ring Elms, that your green leaves did shed,
P.	153	INSTRUCTIONS	525	Survey'd their Crystal Streams, and Banks so green,

greenness   frequency: 1   relative frequency: 0.0000
   P. 45 MOWER'S SONG   3 And in the greenness of the Grass

greenwich   frequency: 1   relative frequency: 0.0000
   P. 150 INSTRUCTIONS 375 From Greenwich (where Intelligence they hold)

greet   frequency: 1   relative frequency: 0.0000
   P. 37 DEFINITION   26 Themselves in every Angle greet:

grew   frequency: 12   relative frequency: 0.0002
   P. 21 SOUL & BODY   44 Green Trees that in the Forest grew.
   P. 22 NYMPH   34 This waxed tame, while he grew wild,
   P. 23 NYMPH   57 And as it grew, so every day
   P. 39 THE MATCH   15 Of which one perfect Beauty grew,
   P. 40 THE MOWER   9 The Pink grew then as double as his Mind;
   P. 45 MOWER'S SONG   8 Grew more luxuriant still and fine;
   P. 97 HOLLAND   72 Staple of Sects and Mint of Schisme grew;
   P. 124 O.C.   37 But as with riper Years her Virtue grew,
   P. 129 O.C.   270 When fall'n shews taller yet than as it grew:
   P. 186 BRITANNIA   75 Who e're grew great by keeping of his word?
   P. 202 HISTORICALL   45 But now Yorkes Genitalls grew over hot
   P. 315 CHEQUER INN   96 For tymes thou know'st grew harder.

grief   frequency: 19   relative frequency: 0.0003
   See also "griefe."
   P. 16 EYES   25 Yet happy they whom Grief doth bless,
   P. 21 SOUL & BODY   22 Within anothers Grief to pine?
   P. 32 MOURNING   24 Like Grief, is from her Windows thrown.
   P. 33 DAPHNIS   22 With the Grief of Parting thence,
   P. 35 DAPHNIS   73 Whilst this grief does thee disarm,
   P. 36 DAPHNIS   92 Nor will I this Grief pollute.
   P. 43 DAMON   70 Yet still my Grief is where it was:
   P. 62 A. HOUSE   113 'Not Tears of Grief; but such as those
   P. 107 ANNIVERSARY   185 So shall the Tears we on past Grief employ,
   P. 116 BLAKE   82 A grief, above the cure of Grapes best juice.
   P. 123 O.C.   21 To Love and Grief the fatal Writ was sign'd;
   P. 123 O.C.   28 As long as Grief shall weep, or Love shall burn.
   P. 124 O.C.   65 That whether by each others grief they fell,
   P. 125 O.C.   95 The Parent-Tree unto the Grief succeeds,
   P. 155 INSTRUCTIONS 611 But when the Royal Charles, what Rage, what Grief,
   P. 159 INSTRUCTIONS 751 Now with vain grief their vainer hopes they rue,
   P. 159 INSTRUCTIONS 760 And were they mortal, both for grief had dy'd.
   P. 168 ADVICE   15 Unless it be his late Assumed grief
   P. 191 STATUE   55 Tho of Brass, yet with grief it would melt him away,

griefe   frequency: 1   relative frequency: 0.0000
   P. 130 O.C.   308 And yet how much of them his griefe obscures.

griefs   frequency: 3   relative frequency: 0.0000
   P. 126 O.C.   150 In their own Griefs might find themselves imploy'd;
   P. 128 O.C.   216 Their griefs struck deepest, if Eliza's last.
   P. 131 O.C.   321 Cease now our griefs, calme peace succeeds a war,

grievance   frequency: 1   relative frequency: 0.0000
   P. 162 INSTRUCTIONS 877 When Grievance urg'd, he swells like squatted Toad,

griev'd   frequency: 1   relative frequency: 0.0000

P. 127 O.C.   151 But those that sadly his departure griev'd,

grieve   frequency: 4   relative frequency: 0.0000
    P.   32 MOURNING   36 It is to be suppos'd they grieve.
    P.   62 A. HOUSE   117 'How should we grieve that must be seen
    P. 124 O.C.   61 She lest He grieve hides what She can her
                             pains,
    P. 125 O.C.   86 Not love, not grieve, would neither live nor
                             reign:

grieves   frequency: 1   relative frequency: 0.0000
    P. 112 ANNIVERSARY 394 'It grieves me sore to have thus much confest.

grim   frequency: 2   relative frequency: 0.0000
    P.   3 LOVELACE   22 Like the grim consistory on thy Booke;
    P. 145 INSTRUCTIONS 184 And hid much Fraud under an aspect grim.

grin   frequency: 1   relative frequency: 0.0000
    See also "grinn."
    P.   81 A. HOUSE   733 Yet your own Face shall at you grin,

grind   frequency: 1   relative frequency: 0.0000
    P. 147 INSTRUCTIONS 254 And to new edge their angry Courage grind.

grinn   frequency: 1   relative frequency: 0.0000
    P. 141 INSTRUCTIONS 26 And he sat smiling how his Dog did grinn.

gristly   frequency: 1   relative frequency: 0.0000
    P.   84 FLECKNO   50 With gristly Tongue to dart the passing Flyes.

griv'd   frequency: 1   relative frequency: 0.0000
    P.   64 A. HOUSE   181 'Balms for the griv'd we draw; and Pasts

grizly   frequency: 1   relative frequency: 0.0000
    P. 163 INSTRUCTIONS 920 The grizly Wound reveals, of which he dy'd.

grizzly. See "grizly."

groan   frequency: 6   relative frequency: 0.0001
    P.   55 THYESTE   10 I shall dye, without a groan,
    P. 108 ANNIVERSARY 203 And all about was heard a Panique groan,
    P. 124 O.C.   57 Each Groan he doubled and each Sigh he sigh'd,
    P. 149 INSTRUCTIONS 359 Next the Twelve Commons are condemn'd to groan,
    P. 159 INSTRUCTIONS 754 As the sad Tortoise for the Sea does groan.
    P. 196 TWO HORSES   181 Let the Citty drink Coffee and Quietly groan

groan'd   frequency: 1   relative frequency: 0.0000
    P. 317 CHEQUER INN 189 Wee groan'd under the Rump

groanes   frequency: 1   relative frequency: 0.0000
    P. 129 O.C.   267 (It groanes, and bruises all below that stood

groans   frequency: 1   relative frequency: 0.0000
    See also "groanes."
    P. 171 PROPHECY   52 With groans to fill his Treasure they must
                             toyle,

groap'd   frequency: 1   relative frequency: 0.0000
    P. 131 PARADISE   9 (So Sampson groap'd the Temples Posts in
                             spight)

groom   frequency: 1   relative frequency: 0.0000
    See also "groome."
    P. 143 INSTRUCTIONS 92 That to a Groom couldst humble her disdain!

groome   frequency: 1   relative frequency: 0.0000
    P. 314 CHEQUER INN   65 That she was forc't to call for Groome

groped. See "groap'd."

gross   frequency: 3   relative frequency: 0.0000
    P.   97 HOLLAND   93 Or what a Spectacle the Skipper gross,
    P. 145 INSTRUCTIONS 179 Gross Bodies, grosser Minds, and grossest
                             Cheats;
    P. 148 INSTRUCTIONS 287 A Gross of English Gentry, nobly born,

grosser   frequency: 1   relative frequency: 0.0000
    P. 145 INSTRUCTIONS 179 Gross Bodies, grosser Minds, and grossest
                             Cheats;

grossest   frequency: 1   relative frequency: 0.0000

P. 145 INSTRUCTIONS 179 Gross Bodies, grosser Minds, and grossest
                         Cheats;

grot   frequency: 1   relative frequency: 0.0000
    P. 41 THE MOWER   31 'Tis all enforc'd; the Fountain and the Grot;

grotto. See "grot."

ground   frequency: 15   relative frequency: 0.0003
    P. 32 MOURNING   12 Would strow the ground where Strephon lay.
    P. 43 DAMON   52 More ground then all his Sheep do hide.
    P. 44 DAMON   74 Depopulating all the Ground,
    P. 70 A. HOUSE   382 And show upon their Lead the Ground,
    P. 96 HOLLAND   20 Where barking Waves still bait the forced
                            Ground;
    P. 97 HOLLAND   69 It struck, and splitting on this unknown ground,
    P. 103 ANNIVERSARY   19 Their earthy Projects under ground they lay,
    P. 124 O.C.   56 The sad Root pines in secret under ground.
    P. 126 O.C.   125 With pensive head towards the ground they fall,
    P. 137 HOUSEWARMING 23 That he begg'd for a Pallace so much of his
                            ground,
    P. 152 INSTRUCTIONS 487 Hyde Stamps, and straight upon the ground the
                            swarms
    P. 186 BRITANNIA   70 And on the ground in spitefull rage it broak,
    P. 189 BRITANNIA   194 No Poisonous tyrant on thy ground shall live.
    P. 199 DUKE   43 That sent Nan Hide before her under ground,
    P. 312 CHEQUER INN   5 In any Age on English ground

grove   frequency: 4   relative frequency: 0.0000
    P. 56 BILL-BOROW   t1 Upon the Hill and Grove at Bill-borow.
    P. 57 BILL-BOROW   40 Ratling through all the Grove and Hill.
    P. 77 A. HOUSE   592 Like some great Prelate of the Grove,
    P. 82 A. HOUSE   757 But name not the Idalian Grove,

groves   frequency: 3   relative frequency: 0.0000
    P. 58 BILL-BOROW   65 Much other Groves, say they, then these
    P. 58 BILL-BOROW   67 Through Groves of Pikes he thunder'd then,
    P. 58 BILL-BOROW   79 Nor he the Hills without the Groves,

grow   frequency: 25   relative frequency: 0.0005
    P. 12 DROP OF DEW   16 Trembling lest it grow impure:
    P. 20 THYRSIS   33 There, birds sing Consorts, garlands grow,
    P. 26 MISTRESS   11 My vegetable Love should grow
    P. 34 DAPHNIS   48 But that you must then grow kind?
    P. 39 THE MATCH   18 That he must once grow old;
    P. 48 THE GARDEN   14 Only among the Plants will grow.
    P. 48 THE GARDEN   30 Only that She might Laurel grow.
    P. 58 BILL-BOROW   54 And in their Lord's advancement grow;
    P. 64 A. HOUSE   166 'Will straight grow Sanctity when here:
    P. 65 A. HOUSE   214 'With them 'twould soon grow fraudulent:
    P. 82 A. HOUSE   740 On the Fairfacian Oak does grow;
    P. 91 MAY'S DEATH   46 Until you all grow Consuls in your wine.
    P. 98 HOLLAND   131 The Common wealth doth by its losses grow;
    P. 107 ANNIVERSARY 165 Though none does of more lasting Parents grow,
    P. 114 BLAKE   36 Fewel and Rain together kindly grow;
    P. 115 BLAKE   57 With fatal Gold, for still where that does grow,
    P. 130 O.C.   312 A Cromwell in an houre a prince will grow.
    P. 138 HOUSEWARMING 56 For his House then would grow like a Vegetable.
    P. 165 KINGS VOWES   9 But if it grow troublesome, I will have none.
    P. 169 ADVICE   64 Tis by afflictions passive men grow great.
    P. 171 PROPHECY   33 The Frogs shall then grow weary of their Crane
    P. 176 LOYALL SCOT 188 And wild disputes betwixt those heads must Grow,
    P. 187 BRITANNIA   102 As these grow stale weel Harass humankind,
    P. 317 CHEQUER INN 188 Parli'ments grow nought as they grow old

growes   frequency: 1   relative frequency: 0.0000
    P. 204 HISTORICALL 130 The Royal Evil so malignant growes,

groweth. See "grow'th."

growing   frequency: 6   relative frequency: 0.0001
    P.   3 LOVELACE   16 On the faire blossome of each growing wit.
    P. 74 A. HOUSE   484 In this yet green, yet growing Ark;
    P. 84 FLECKNO   67 Lest his too suttle Body, growing rare,
    P. 109 ANNIVERSARY 263 Therefore first growing to thy self a Law,
    P. 124 O.C.   48 And at her Aspect calms his growing Cares;
    P. 131 PARADISE   11 Yet as I read, soon growing less severe,

grown   frequency: 11   relative frequency: 0.0002
    See also "growne."
    P. 23 NYMPH   72 But so with Roses over grown,
    P. 30 THE GALLERY   46 Art grown a num'rous Colony;
    P. 32 MOURNING   22 Joy now so much her Master grown,

```
P.   40 THE MATCH       31 And, grown magnetically strong,
P.   89 ODE             81 Nor yet grown stiffer with Command,
P.   94 DR. WITTY        7 So of Translators they are Authors grown,
P.  109 ANNIVERSARY    250 Yet by the Conquest of two Kings grown great,
P.  141 INSTRUCTIONS     4 It be'nt too slight grown, or too hard for thee.
P.  161 INSTRUCTIONS   847 The Girls shall always kiss thee, though grown
                          old,
P.  178 LOYALL SCOT    268 The morning dews and flowers Neglected grown,
P.  191 STATUE          41 The Huswifely Treasuress sure is grown nice
```

growne   frequency: 1   relative frequency: 0.0000
```
P.  182 MADE FREE       56 Were thrice growne so rude,
```

grows   frequency: 6   relative frequency: 0.0001
See also "growes."
```
P.   43 DAMON           71 But, when the Iron blunter grows,
P.   60 A. HOUSE        52 Stirs, and the Square grows Spherical;
P.   68 A. HOUSE       311 Each Regiment in order grows,
P.   74 A. HOUSE       507 And in as loose an order grows,
P.   96 HOLLAND         50 The Pow'r, and grows as 'twere a King of
                          Spades.
P.  143 INSTRUCTIONS    80 Her, not her Picture, for she now grows old.
```

growth   frequency: 2   relative frequency: 0.0000
```
P.    4 HASTINGS        15 While those of growth more sudden, and more bold,
P.  126 O.C.           119 Or of huge Trees, whose growth with his did
                          rise,
```

grow'th   frequency: 1   relative frequency: 0.0000
```
P.   42 DAMON           19 It from an higher Beauty grow'th,
```

grudge   frequency: 2   relative frequency: 0.0000
```
P.  138 HOUSEWARMING    48 To grudge him some Timber who fram'd them the
                          War.
P.  190 STATUE          40 Shall a Treasurer of Guinny a Prince Grudge
                          of Token?
```

grumble   frequency: 1   relative frequency: 0.0000
```
P.  110 ANNIVERSARY    277 What though a while they grumble discontent,
```

guard   frequency: 9   relative frequency: 0.0001
```
P.   66 A. HOUSE       238 Standing upon their holy Guard.
P.   69 A. HOUSE       325 But, to exclude the World, did guard
P.   69 A. HOUSE       336 Were then the Switzers of our Guard.
P.   78 A. HOUSE       619 While, like a Guard on either side,
P.  155 INSTRUCTIONS   587 Engine so slight to guard us from the Sea,
P.  165 INSTRUCTIONS   990 Give us this Court, and rule without a Guard.
P.  166 KINGS VOWES     26 If not o're a Kingdome, to raigne ore my Guard;
P.  182 MADE FREE       59 Else with Guard upon Guard
```

guardian   frequency: 2   relative frequency: 0.0000
```
P.  188 BRITANNIA      145 Into the Wolf and make him Guardian turn
P.  200 DUKE            96 And can her Guardian Angell lett her stoope
```

guardians   frequency: 1   relative frequency: 0.0000
```
P.   28 LOVER           31 Guardians most fit to entertain
```

guarding   frequency: 1   relative frequency: 0.0000
```
P.  193 TWO HORSES      61 Ch. That of four Seas dominion and Guarding
```

guards   frequency: 4   relative frequency: 0.0000
```
P.  142 INSTRUCTIONS    77 And nightly hears the hated Guards away
P.  156 INSTRUCTIONS   629 The Guards, plac'd for the Chains and Fleets
                          defence,
P.  185 BRITANNIA       20 Till commons votes shall cut-nose guards disband,
P.  193 TWO HORSES      67 W. That makeing us slaves by hors and foot
                          Guards
```

guelphs   frequency: 1   relative frequency: 0.0000
```
P.   92 MAY'S DEATH     62 As for the Basket Guelphs and Gibellines be?
```

guess   frequency: 1   relative frequency: 0.0000
```
P.   23 NYMPH           73 And lillies, that you would it guess
```

guest   frequency: 4   relative frequency: 0.0000
```
P.    9 DIALOGUE        11 Welcome the Creations Guest,
P.   96 HOLLAND         30 And sat not as a Meat but as a Guest;
P.  106 ANNIVERSARY    145 And well he therefore does, and well has guest,
P.  172 LOYALL SCOT      8 His ready muse to Court the Warlike Guest.
```

guests   frequency: 1   relative frequency: 0.0000

```
         P. 316 CHEQUER INN    168 The Guests tooke all away

guide                          frequency:     7    relative frequency: 0.0001
    P.  18 BERMUDAS             39 And all the way, to guide their Chime,
    P. 108 ANNIVERSARY         191 But the poor Beasts wanting their noble Guide,
    P. 109 ANNIVERSARY         269 While baleful Tritons to the shipwrack guide.
    P. 130 O.C.                302 To guide us upward through this region blinde.
    P. 146 INSTRUCTIONS        203 Carteret the rich did the Accomptants guide,
    P. 154 INSTRUCTIONS        550 Sound the Sea-march, and guide to Sheppy Isle.
    P. 198 DUKE                 29 The way to heaven and who shall be my guide?

guides                         frequency:     2    relative frequency: 0.0000
    P.  95 DR. WITTY            38 For something guides my hand that I must write.
    P. 147 INSTRUCTIONS        251 Each ran, as chance him guides, to sev'ral Post:

guild                          frequency:     2    relative frequency: 0.0000
    P.  95 DR. WITTY            40 That handling neither sully nor would guild.
    P. 154 INSTRUCTIONS        554 The airy Sterns the Sun behind does guild;

guild-hall                     frequency:     1    relative frequency: 0.0000
    P. 181 MADE FREE            6 Of the whole Guild-Hall Teame to dragg it.

guilt                          frequency:     4    relative frequency: 0.0000
    P. 113 BLAKE                4 Frayted with acted Guilt, and Guilt to come:
    P. 165 INSTRUCTIONS        984 Nor Guilt to flatt'ry binds, nor want to
                                   stealth;
    P. 203 HISTORICALL         77 And annual Stypends for their guilt recieve:

guiltily                       frequency:     2    relative frequency: 0.0000
    P.  67 A. HOUSE           267 Who guiltily their Prize bemoan,
    P. 108 ANNIVERSARY        192 What could they more? shrunk guiltily aside.

guiltless                      frequency:     2    relative frequency: 0.0000
    P.  65 A. HOUSE           224 'Though guiltless lest thou perish there.
    P. 141 INSTRUCTIONS        19 Else shalt thou oft thy guiltless Pencil curse,

guilty                         frequency:     5    relative frequency: 0.0001
    P.  22 NYMPH               18 Though they should wash their guilty hands
    P. 104 ANNIVERSARY         40 From the deserved Fate their guilty lives:
    P. 115 BLAKE               64 If fortune can make guilty what she will.
    P. 161 INSTRUCTIONS       850 At Court, and so reprieves their guilty Lives.
    P. 164 INSTRUCTIONS       980 Burr'wing themselves to hoard their guilty
                                   Store.

guinea.  See "guinny."

guinea's                       frequency:     1    relative frequency: 0.0000
    P. 151 INSTRUCTIONS       416 Change all for Guinea's, and a Crown for each:

guinny                         frequency:     1    relative frequency: 0.0000
    P. 190 STATUE              40 Shall a Treasurer of Guinny a Prince Grudge
                                  of Token?

guise                          frequency:     1    relative frequency: 0.0000
    P. 199 DUKE                56 Clifford, who first appeared in humble guise,

gules                          frequency:     1    relative frequency: 0.0000
    P.  29 LOVER               64 In a Field Sable a Lover Gules.

gulfes                         frequency:     1    relative frequency: 0.0000
    P.  82 A. HOUSE           764 Gulfes, Deserts, Precipices, Stone.

gulfs.  See "gulfes."

gum.  See "gumme."

gumme                          frequency:     1    relative frequency: 0.0000
    P.  24 NYMPH               96 Sad, slowly dropping like a Gumme.

gun                            frequency:     2    relative frequency: 0.0000
    P. 155 INSTRUCTIONS       599 Leave him alone when first they hear the Gun;
    P. 314 CHEQUER INN         86 And popping like an Elder Gun

gun-powder                     frequency:     1    relative frequency: 0.0000
    P.  98 HOLLAND            115 Ram'd with Gun-powder, flaming with Brand wine,

gun-shot                       frequency:     1    relative frequency: 0.0000
    P. 146 INSTRUCTIONS       230 To fight a Battel, from all Gun-shot free.

guns                           frequency:     1    relative frequency: 0.0000
    P. 193 TWO HORSES          66 By pawning for Victualls their Guns at Legorne;
```

gust   frequency: 1   relative frequency: 0.0000
     P. 58 BILL-BOROW   59 Nor to the winds uncertain gust,

gusts   frequency: 1   relative frequency: 0.0000
     P. 153 INSTRUCTIONS 517 As Heav'n in Storms, they call, in gusts of
                             State,

guts   frequency: 1   relative frequency: 0.0000
     See also "gutts."
     P. 84 FLECKNO   43 Whose hungry Guts to the same streightness
                             twin'd

gutts   frequency: 1   relative frequency: 0.0000
     P. 191 TWO HORSES   8 That a sacraficed ox, when his Gutts were out,
                             Bellow'd:

gyant   frequency: 3   relative frequency: 0.0000
     P. 139 HOUSEWARMING 77 Like Jove under Aetna o'erwhelming the Gyant,
     P. 147 INSTRUCTIONS 260 That pierc't the Gyant Mordant through his
                             Mail.
     P. 203 HISTORICALL 115 And dos on Gyant Lauderdale reflect.

gyants   frequency: 2   relative frequency: 0.0000
     P. 70 A. HOUSE   372 But Grashoppers are Gyants there:
     P. 155 INSTRUCTIONS 577 Those Oaken Gyants of the ancient Race,

gypsies. See "gipsies."

ha'   frequency: 3   relative frequency: 0.0000

habit   frequency: 1   relative frequency: 0.0000
     P. 85 FLECKNO   79 But were he not in this black habit deck't,

hack   frequency: 1   relative frequency: 0.0000
     P. 105 ANNIVERSARY 69 While tedious Statesmen many years did hack,

hacks   frequency: 1   relative frequency: 0.0000
     P. 76 A. HOUSE   545 The good he numbers up, and hacks;

had   frequency: 151   relative frequency: 0.0031

hadst   frequency: 5   relative frequency: 0.0001

haft   frequency: 1   relative frequency: 0.0000
     P. 162 INSTRUCTIONS 868 Like Knife with Iv'ry haft, and edge of Lead.

hair   frequency: 8   relative frequency: 0.0001
     P. 29 THE GALLERY   16 Black Eyes, red Lips, and curled Hair.
     P. 30 THE GALLERY   53 A tender Shepherdess, whose Hair
     P. 31 FAIR SINGER   9 Breaking the curled trammels of her hair.
     P. 77 A. HOUSE   599 Who, as my Hair, my Thoughts too shed,
     P. 122 TWO SONGS   22 Curl'd so lovely as her Hair:
     P. 123 O.C.   2 Of Cromwell's head, and numbered ev'ry hair,
     P. 156 INSTRUCTIONS 635 Scarce can burnt Iv'ry feign an Hair so black,
     P. 162 INSTRUCTIONS 867 Bright Hair, fair Face, obscure and dull of
                             Head;

hairs   frequency: 2   relative frequency: 0.0000
     P. 107 ANNIVERSARY 180 And soyl'd in Dust thy Crown of silver Hairs.
     P. 185 BRITANNIA   47 Full of Gray Hairs, good deeds, endless renown.

halcyon   frequency: 2   relative frequency: 0.0000
     P. 79 A. HOUSE   669 The modest Halcyon comes in sight,
     P. 98 HOLLAND   130 Till the dear Halcyon hatch out all its nest.

halcyons   frequency: 2   relative frequency: 0.0000
     P. 30 THE GALLERY   35 The Halcyons, calming all that's nigh,
     P. 125 O.C.   80 Of Halcyons kind, or bleeding Pelicans?

hale   frequency: 1   relative frequency: 0.0000
     P. 158 INSTRUCTIONS 737 Black Day accurs'd! On thee let no man hale

hales   frequency: 1   relative frequency: 0.0000
     P. 77 A. HOUSE   590 Me licks, and clasps, and curles, and hales.

half   frequency: 12   relative frequency: 0.0002
     P. 11 DIALOGUE   65 Half the World shall be thy Slave
     P. 11 DIALOGUE   66 The other half thy Friend.
     P. 83 FLECKNO   14 Turn in, and shew to Wainscot half the Room.

P.   85 FLECKNO   80 This half transparent Man would soon reflect
P.   86 FLECKNO   149 Making the half points and the periods run
P.   96 HOLLAND   53 For these Half-anders, half wet, and half dry,
P.   98 HOLLAND   125 While half their banish'd keels the Tempest
                         tost,
P.   98 HOLLAND   126 Half bound at home in Prison to the frost:
P. 122 TWO SONGS   24 Half so white or sweet as She.
P. 174 LOYALL SCOT 105 And slip one Half into his sleeve as soon.
P. 193 TWO HORSES   57 Ch. That a Million and half should be his
                         revenue.

half-anders   frequency: 1   relative frequency: 0.0000
      P.   96 HOLLAND   53 For these Half-anders, half wet, and half dry,

half-dry   frequency: 1   relative frequency: 0.0000
      P.   69 A. HOUSE   351 And, in those half-dry Trenches, spann'd

halfecrown   frequency: 1   relative frequency: 0.0000
      P. 190 STATUE   28 For the old King on Horseback is but an
                            Halfecrown.

hall   frequency: 5   relative frequency: 0.0001
      See "guild-hall," "tangier-hall."
      P.   5 HASTINGS   45 And trails his Torches th'row the Starry Hall
      P.   60 A. HOUSE   51 But where he comes the swelling Hall
      P.   87 ODE   8 The Corslet of the Hall.
      P. 122 TWO SONGS   13 Fear not; at Menalca's Hall
      P. 314 CHEQUER INN 55 They stood (when enter'd in the Hall)

hallelujahs   frequency: 1   relative frequency: 0.0000
      P.   47 EMPIRE   24 Would with you Heavens Hallelujahs raise.

hallowing   frequency: 1   relative frequency: 0.0000
      P. 175 LOYALL SCOT 162 How oft hath age his hallowing hands Misled

halt   frequency: 1   relative frequency: 0.0000
      P. 174 LOYALL SCOT 124 Ah! like Lotts wife they still look Back and
                            Halt

halting   frequency: 1   relative frequency: 0.0000
      P. 110 ANNIVERSARY 295 Who watch'd thy halting, and thy Fall deride,

hammer   frequency: 1   relative frequency: 0.0000
      P. 148 INSTRUCTIONS 321 The busie Hammer sleeps, the Ropes untwine;

hampton   frequency: 1   relative frequency: 0.0000
      P.   88 ODE   47 And Hampton shows what part

hamstring'd   frequency: 1   relative frequency: 0.0000
      P.   42 DAMON   12 And hamstring'd Frogs can dance no more.

hand   frequency: 34   relative frequency: 0.0007
      See also "master-hand."
      P.   4 LOVELACE   37 Whose hand so rudely grasps the steely brand,
      P.   4 LOVELACE   38 Whose hand so gently melts the Ladies hand.
      P.   17 BERMUDAS   25 With Cedars, chosen by his hand,
      P.   23 NYMPH   61 And white, (shall I say then my hand?)
      P.   28 LOVER   50 Cuffing the Thunder with one hand;
      P.   41 THE MOWER   37 Their Statues polish'd by some ancient hand,
      P.   57 BILL-BOROW   35 No hostile hand durst ere invade
      P.   63 A. HOUSE   130 'If here your hand, your Face we had:
      P.   65 A. HOUSE   210 'One Stone that a just Hand had laid,
      P.   74 A. HOUSE   492 On one hand Fairfax, th' other Veres:
      P.   89 ODE   82 But still in the Republick's hand:
      P.   90 MAY'S DEATH 10 He saw near hand, as he imagin'd Ares.
      P.   95 DR. WITTY   38 For something guides my hand that I must write.
      P. 104 ANNIVERSARY 50 Which the God gave him, with his gentle hand,
      P. 105 ANNIVERSARY 83 And each the Hand that lays him will direct,
      P. 106 ANNIVERSARY 138 Would forthwith finish under such a Hand:
      P. 109 ANNIVERSARY 234 As a small Cloud, like a Mans hand didst rise;
      P. 126 O.C.   117 Out of the Binders Hand the Sheaves they tore,
      P. 127 O.C.   179 He first put Armes into Religions hand,
      P. 131 PARADISE   18 Jealous I was that some less skilful hand
      P. 139 HOUSEWARMING 80 Or his right hand shall else be cut off with the
                            Trowel.
      P. 146 INSTRUCTIONS 212 Apsley and Brotherick, marching hand in hand.
      P. 148 INSTRUCTIONS 300 Adjutant-General was still at hand.
      P. 152 INSTRUCTIONS 472 And wish'd himself the Gout, to seize his hand.
      P. 159 INSTRUCTIONS 758 Now in the Ravisher De-Ruyter's hand,
      P. 162 INSTRUCTIONS 901 And with kind hand does the coy Vision press,
      P. 168 ADVICE   17 And place me by the Barr on the left hand

```
        P. 168 KINGS VOWES      63 Under my hand and Seal shall have Indemnity.
        P. 185 BRITANNIA        36 In 's left the scales, in 's right hand plac'd
                                   the sword,
        P. 189 BRITANNIA       181 Publicola with healing hand shall power
        P. 190 STATUE           35 As the Parliament twice was prorogued by your
                                   hand,
        P. 313 CHEQUER INN      23 He dandles always in his Hand

handling                        frequency:   2    relative frequency: 0.0000
        P.  64 A. HOUSE        178 'Still handling Natures finest Parts.
        P.  95 DR. WITTY        40 That handling neither sully nor would guild.

hands                           frequency:  15    relative frequency: 0.0003
        P.  20 SOUL & BODY       4 In Feet; and manacled in Hands.
        P.  22 NYMPH            18 Though they should wash their guilty hands
        P.  49 THE GARDEN       38 Into my hands themselves do reach;
        P.  63 A. HOUSE        160 'Might such fair Hands as yours it tye!
        P.  88 ODE              56 Did clap their bloody hands.
        P. 138 HOUSEWARMING     36 Nay scarce the Priests portion could scape from
                                   his hands.
        P. 143 INSTRUCTIONS     94 Nor scorns to rub him down with those fair
                                   Hands;
        P. 144 INSTRUCTIONS    133 A thousand Hands she has and thousand Eyes,
        P. 165 KINGS VOWES      13 I will have as fine Bishops as were ere made
                                   with hands,
        P. 175 LOYALL SCOT     162 How oft hath age his hallowing hands Misled
        P. 176 LOYALL SCOT     189 Where but two hands to Act, two feet to goe.
        P. 198 DUKE             15 Armed with boold zeale and blessing with thy
                                   hands
        P. 200 DUKE             88 Are these fitt hands to overturne a State
        P. 200 DUKE             93 Defying all their heads and all their hands.
        P. 203 HISTORICALL      76 With lavish hands they constant Tributes give

handsel                         frequency:   1    relative frequency: 0.0000
        P. 140 HOUSEWARMING     99 And to handsel his Altar and Nostrils divine,

handyworke                      frequency:   1    relative frequency: 0.0000
        P. 314 CHEQUER INN      50 Each of his Handyworke to bragg

hang                            frequency:   5    relative frequency: 0.0001
        See also "hange."
        P.  31 FAIR SINGER      14 Where Victory might hang in equal choice,
        P.  73 A. HOUSE        476 Turn'd as they hang to Leeches quick;
        P.  79 A. HOUSE        647 And in its Branches tough to hang,
        P.  80 A. HOUSE        677 The stupid Fishes hang, as plain
        P.  87 FLECKNO         170 To hang it in Saint Peter's for a Vow.

hang'd                          frequency:   2    relative frequency: 0.0000
        P. 200 DUKE             99 This band of traytors hang'd in Effigie.
        P. 204 HISTORICALL     142 One hang'd himself, the other fled away:

hange                           frequency:   1    relative frequency: 0.0000
        P. 316 CHEQUER INN     149 But (and thereby doth hange a Tale)

hanging                         frequency:   2    relative frequency: 0.0000
        P. 112 ANNIVERSARY     378 'And still his Sword seems hanging o're my head.
        P. 124 O.C.             50 Hanging about her neck or at his knees.

hangings. See "arras-hangings."

hangs                           frequency:   3    relative frequency: 0.0000
        P.  17 BERMUDAS         17 He hangs in shades the Orange bright,
        P.  30 THE GALLERY      54 Hangs loosely playing in the Air,
        P.  68 A. HOUSE        290 Hangs out the Colours of the Day,

hanmers                         frequency:   1    relative frequency: 0.0000
        P. 316 CHEQUER INN     133 The Hanmers, Herberts, Sandys, Musgraves

hannibal                        frequency:   1    relative frequency: 0.0000
        P.  90 ODE             102 To Italy an Hannibal,

hans-in-kelder                  frequency:   1    relative frequency: 0.0000
        P.  97 HOLLAND          66 For Hans-in-Kelder of a whole Hans-Town.

hans-town                       frequency:   1    relative frequency: 0.0000
        P.  97 HOLLAND          66 For Hans-in-Kelder of a whole Hans-Town.

happie                          frequency:   1    relative frequency: 0.0000
        P.   5 HASTINGS         38 On which the happie Names do stand enroll'd;

happiest. See "happy'st."

happiness                       frequency:   1    relative frequency: 0.0000
```

P. 49 THE GARDEN   42 Withdraws into its happiness:

happy   frequency: 21   relative frequency: 0.0004
    See also "happie."
    P. 16 EYES   25 Yet happy they whom Grief doth bless,
    P. 38 PICTURE   15 Happy, who can
    P. 40 THE MATCH   37 So we alone the happy rest,
    P. 43 DAMON   65 How happy might I still have mow'd,
    P. 49 THE GARDEN   57 Such was that happy Garden-state,
    P. 62 A. HOUSE   116 'That live without this happy Vow.
    P. 69 A. HOUSE   321 Oh Thou, that dear and happy Isle
    P. 77 A. HOUSE   583 Thrice happy he who, not mistook,
    P. 84 FLECKNO   56 Happy at once to make him Protestant,
    P. 89 ODE   72 Foresaw it's happy Fate.
    P. 90 ODE   109 Happy if in the tufted brake
    P. 94 DR. WITTY   32 Whose happy Eyes on thy Translation fall,
    P. 106 ANNIVERSARY 131 Hence oft I think, if in some happy Hour
    P. 107 ANNIVERSARY 159 And thou, great Cromwell, for whose happy birth
    P. 114 BLAKE   31 A happy People, which at once do gain
    P. 122 TWO SONGS   29 Joy to that happy Pair,
    P. 123 TWO SONGS   47 Joy to that happy Pair,
    P. 130 O.C.   295 How streight canst to each happy mansion goe?
    P. 155 INSTRUCTIONS 614 His exil'd Sov'raign on its happy Board;
    P. 159 INSTRUCTIONS 747 Sad change, since first that happy pair was wed,
    P. 185 BRITANNIA   21 Till Kate a happy mother shall become,

happy'st   frequency: 1   relative frequency: 0.0000
    P. 142 INSTRUCTIONS 59 Happy'st of Women, if she were but able

harass   frequency: 1   relative frequency: 0.0000
    P. 187 BRITANNIA   102 As these grow stale weel Harass humankind,

harbours   frequency: 1   relative frequency: 0.0000
    P. 148 INSTRUCTIONS 323 Along the Coast and Harbours they take care

hard   frequency: 5   relative frequency: 0.0001
    P. 141 INSTRUCTIONS   4 It be'nt too slight grown, or too hard for thee.
    P. 165 INSTRUCTIONS 989 (Where few the number, choice is there less hard)
    P. 169 ADVICE   63 Tis hard; yet this he has for safe retreat:
    P. 200 DUKE   116 Hard fate of princes, who will nere believe,
    P. 313 CHEQUER INN   7 At Chareing Crosse hard by the way

harden'd   frequency: 1   relative frequency: 0.0000
    P. 156 INSTRUCTIONS 656 Harden'd and cool'd his Limbs, so soft, so
                            white,

hardened. See "harden'd," "hardned."

harder   frequency: 2   relative frequency: 0.0000
    P. 148 INSTRUCTIONS 304 Is longer Work, and harder than to fight.
    P. 315 CHEQUER INN   96 For tymes thou know'st grew harder.

hardly   frequency: 2   relative frequency: 0.0000
    P. 105 ANNIVERSARY   79 No Quarry bears a Stone so hardly wrought,
    P. 191 TWO HORSES   7 Livy tells a strang story can hardly be fellow'd

hardned   frequency: 1   relative frequency: 0.0000
    P. 172 LOYALL SCOT   22 Hardned and Cool'd those limbs soe soft, soe
                            white,

hare   frequency: 1   relative frequency: 0.0000
    P. 149 INSTRUCTIONS 335 Blither than Hare that hath escap'd the Hounds,

hare's   frequency: 1   relative frequency: 0.0000
    P. 178 LOYALL SCOT 277 The hare's head 'gainst the goose gibletts sett.

hark   frequency: 1   relative frequency: 0.0000
    See also "heark."
    P. 176 LOYALL SCOT 200 Hark! tho' at such a Distance what a Noise

harlot   frequency: 1   relative frequency: 0.0000
    P. 194 TWO HORSES   114 With an Harlot got up on my Crupper behind him.

harm   frequency: 2   relative frequency: 0.0000
    P. 22 NYMPH   5 Them any harm: alas nor cou'd
    P. 156 INSTRUCTIONS 628 She tears herself since him she cannot harm.

harmless   frequency: 3   relative frequency: 0.0000
    P. 29 THE GALLERY   24 Sit perfecting their harmless Loves.
    P. 42 DAMON   35 To Thee the harmless Snake I bring,
    P. 78 A. HOUSE   633 See in what wanton harmless folds

harmonious   frequency: 2   relative frequency: 0.0000
    P.   47 EMPIRE   12 Into harmonious Colonies withdrew.
    P. 105 ANNIVERSARY   66 Th' harmonious City of the seven Gates.

harmony   frequency: 1   relative frequency: 0.0000
    P.   31 FAIR SINGER   4 Joyning themselves in fatal Harmony;

harpe   frequency: 1   relative frequency: 0.0000
    P. 130 O.C.   294 And David, for the sword and harpe renown'd;

harper   frequency: 1   relative frequency: 0.0000
    P. 137 HOUSEWARMING   17 But then recollecting how the Harper Amphyon

harpy   frequency: 1   relative frequency: 0.0000
    P. 144 INSTRUCTIONS   142 Her, of a female Harpy, in Dog Days:

harry   frequency: 7   relative frequency: 0.0001
    P. 146 INSTRUCTIONS   228 While Hector Harry steers by Will the Wit:
    P. 151 INSTRUCTIONS   450 In Cipher one to Harry Excellent.
    P. 160 INSTRUCTIONS   820 Harry came Post just as he shew'd his Watch.
    P. 161 INSTRUCTIONS   823 Yet Harry must job back and all mature,
    P. 163 INSTRUCTIONS   918 Of Grandsire Harry, and of Charles his Sire.
    P. 163 INSTRUCTIONS   919 Harry sits down, and in his open side
    P. 315 CHEQUER INN   115 The Westerne Glcry, Harry Ford

harry's   frequency: 2   relative frequency: 0.0000
    P. 152 INSTRUCTIONS   461 But Harry's Order, if they won't recal
    P. 193 TWO HORSES   71 W. On Seventh Harry's head he that placed the
                                  Crown

harvest   frequency: 2   relative frequency: 0.0000
    P.   5 HASTINGS   50 The Golden Harvest, sees his Glasses leap.
    P. 126 O.C.   118 And thrash'd the Harvest in the airy floore;

has   frequency: 37   relative frequency: 0.0007

hash'd   frequency: 1   relative frequency: 0.0000
    P. 149 INSTRUCTIONS   337 Not so decrepid Aescn, hash'd and stew'd

hast   frequency: 13   relative frequency: 0.0002
    P.   34 DAPHNIS   39 Looks distracted back in hast,
    P.   42 DAMON   39 Yet Thou ungrateful hast not sought
    P.   57 BILL-BOROW   29 How glad the weary Seamen hast
    P.   92 MAY'S DEATH   71 But thou base man first prostituted hast
    P.   92 MAY'S DEATH   78 Hast left surviving Davenant still behind
    P. 107 ANNIVERSARY   168 And always hast thy Tongue from fraud refrain'd;
    P. 107 ANNIVERSARY   170 Hast born securely thine undaunted Head,
    P. 112 ANNIVERSARY   382 'Courage with Age, Maturity with Hast:
    P. 116 BLAKE   89 With hast they therefore all their Gallions
                                  roar,
    P. 130 O.C.   293 How soon thou Mcses hast, and Joshua found,
    P. 132 PARADISE   27 Thou hast not miss'd one thought that could be
                                  fit,
    P. 141 INSTRUCTIONS   9 Or hast thou mark't how antique Masters limn
    P. 194 TWO HORSES   116 What hast thou to say cf my Royall Rider?

haste   frequency: 3   relative frequency: 0.0000
    See also "hast."
    P. 144 INSTRUCTIONS   153 In Lcyal haste they left young Wives in Bed,
    P. 148 INSTRUCTIONS   310 And what haste lcst, recover by delay.
    P. 156 INSTRUCTIONS   645 Captain, Lieutenant, Ensign, all make haste,

hasted   frequency: 1   relative frequency: 0.0000
    P.   87 FLECKNO   167 He hasted; and I, finding my self free,

hasten   frequency: 1   relative frequency: 0.0000
    P. 126 O.C.   128 And hasten not to see his Death their cwn.

hastening. See "hastning."

hastens   frequency: 1   relative frequency: 0.0000
    P. 113 BLAKE   2 Leaves the new World and hastens for the old:

hastes   frequency: 1   relative frequency: 0.0000
    P. 107 ANNIVERSARY   156 The Ill delaying, what th'elected hastes;

hasting   frequency: 2   relative frequency: 0.0000
    P.   16 EYES   33 Not full sailes hasting lcaden home,
    P. 125 O.C.   72 Ran cut impetucusly to hasting Death.

hastings   frequency: 4   relative frequency: 0.0000

```
P.   4 HASTINGS        t Upon the Death of the Lord Hastings.
P.   4 HASTINGS        3 Hastings is dead, and we must finde a Store
P.   4 HASTINGS        7 Hastings is dead; and we, disconsolate,
P.   5 HASTINGS       52 Had Mayern once been mixt with Hastings blood!

hastning                 frequency:    2    relative frequency: 0.0000
P.  94 DR. WITTY       33 I see the people hastning to thy Book,
P. 198 DUKE            41 Hastning to be invenom'd with the pox

hasty                    frequency:    1    relative frequency: 0.0000
P. 152 INSTRUCTIONS   477 Or in their hasty Call to find a flaw,

hatch                    frequency:    2    relative frequency: 0.0000
P.  72 A. HOUSE       417 Or sooner hatch or higher build:
P.  98 HOLLAND        130 Till the dear Halcyon hatch out all its nest.

hatched                  frequency:    1    relative frequency: 0.0000
P. 112 ANNIVERSARY    359 'Of floting Islands a new Hatched Nest;

hatching                 frequency:    1    relative frequency: 0.0000
P.  75 A. HOUSE       532 The hatching Thrastles shining Eye,

hate                     frequency:    4    relative frequency: 0.0000
P. 106 ANNIVERSARY    112 They know them not, and what they know not, hate.
P. 108 ANNIVERSARY    196 And the green Grass, and their known Mangers
                          hate,
P. 153 INSTRUCTIONS   518 On Monk and Parliament, yet both do hate.
P. 195 TWO HORSES     125 W. The Goat and the Lyon I Equally hate,

hated                    frequency:    1    relative frequency: 0.0000
P. 142 INSTRUCTIONS    77 And nightly hears the hated Guards away

hateing                  frequency:    1    relative frequency: 0.0000
P. 198 DUKE             5 Hateing all justice and resolv'd to fight

haters                   frequency:    1    relative frequency: 0.0000
P. 145 INSTRUCTIONS   178 Haters of Fowl, to Teal preferring Bull.

hates                    frequency:    1    relative frequency: 0.0000
P. 185 BRITANNIA       22 Till Charles loves Parliaments, till James
                          hates Rome.

hateth                   frequency:    1    relative frequency: 0.0000
P.  88 ODE             41 Nature that hateth emptiness,

hath                     frequency:   21    relative frequency: 0.0004

hating.  See "hateing."

hatred's                 frequency:    1    relative frequency: 0.0000
P.  21 SOUL & BODY     36 Or Hatred's hidden Ulcer eat.

haughty                  frequency:    2    relative frequency: 0.0000
P. 201 HISTORICALL     31 From the french Court she haughty Topiks
                          brings,
P. 204 HISTORICALL    116 This haughty Monster with his ugly claws

haunts                   frequency:    1    relative frequency: 0.0000
P. 177 LOYALL SCOT    233 While they liv'd here, still Haunts them
                          Underground.

have                     frequency:  167    relative frequency: 0.0035
   See also "ha'," "i've," "t'have,"
           "they've," "wee've." "we've."

having                   frequency:    6    relative frequency: 0.0001

hay                      frequency:   11    relative frequency: 0.0002
P.  43 DAMON           56 Yet am I richer far in Hay.
P.  46 AMETAS           4 Love binds Love as Hay binds Hay.
P.  46 AMETAS           8 Neither Love will twist nor Hay.
P.  46 AMETAS          12 Looser then with Ropes of Hay.
P.  46 AMETAS          16 And go kiss within the Hay.
P.  72 A. HOUSE       421 Where, as the Meads with Hay, the Plain
P.  72 A. HOUSE       426 Dancing the Triumphs of the Hay;
P.  72 A. HOUSE       432 Their new-made Hay not sweeter is.
P.  72 A. HOUSE       438 Short Pyramids of Hay do stand.
P. 313 CHEQUER INN      8 Where all the Berties make their Hay

hay-ropes                frequency:    1    relative frequency: 0.0000
P.  46 AMETAS           t Ametas and Thestylis making Hay-Ropes.
```

hazels.   See "hazles."

hazles   frequency: 1   relative frequency: 0.0000
       P.   75 A. HOUSE   531 And through the Hazles thick espy

he   frequency: 472   relative frequency: 0.0098
       See also "he'd," "hee," "hee'l," "he's."

head   frequency: 49   relative frequency: 0.0010
       P.   9 DIALOGUE   3 Close on thy Head thy Helmet bright.
       P.   14 THE CORONET   3 My Saviours head have crown'd,
       P.   14 THE CORONET   8 That once adorn'd my Shepherdesses head.
       P.   15 THE CORONET   26 May crown thy Feet, that could not crown thy
                                    Head.
       P.   20 SOUL & BODY   10 In a vain Head, and double Heart.
       P.   30 THE GALLERY   56 To crown her Head, and Bosome fill.
       P.   49 THE GARDEN   34 Ripe Apples drop about my head;
       P.   64 A. HOUSE   163 'And your Example, if our Head,
       P.   65 A. HOUSE   211 'It must have fall'm upon her Head
       P.   77 A. HOUSE   600 And winnow from the Chaff my Head.
       P.   79 A. HOUSE   664 In blushing Clouds conceales his Head.
       P.   80 A. HOUSE   700 The Garden Flow'rs to Crown Her Head;
       P.   83 FLECKNO   10 But seem'd a Coffin set on the Stairs head.
       P.   88 ODE   23 And Caesars head at last
       P.   89 ODE   63 But bow'd his comely Head,
       P.   89 ODE   69 A bleeding Head where they begun,
       P.   90 MAY'S DEATH   7 Nor where the Popes head, nor the Mitre lay,
       P.   92 MAY'S DEATH   63 When the Sword glitters ore the Judges head,
       P. 103 ANNIVERSARY   6 While flowing Time above his Head does close.
       P. 107 ANNIVERSARY   170 Hast born securely thine undaunted Head,
       P. 112 ANNIVERSARY   378 'And still his Sword seems hanging o're my head.
       P. 113 ANNIVERSARY   399 While thou thy venerable Head dost raise
       P. 123 O.C.   2 Of Cromwell's head, and numbered ev'ry hair,
       P. 126 O.C.   122 And pour the Deluge ore the Chaos head.
       P. 126 O.C.   125 With pensive head towards the ground they fall,
       P. 127 O.C.   168 Of your Abysse, with cover'd Head bewail
       P. 144 INSTRUCTIONS   154 And Denham these by one consent did head.
       P. 145 INSTRUCTIONS   164 And under's Armpit he defends his Head.
       P. 145 INSTRUCTIONS   167 Headless St. Dennis so his Head does bear;
       P. 147 INSTRUCTIONS   273 With Heart of Bees so full, and Head of
                                    Mites,
       P. 150 INSTRUCTIONS   407 With the Bulls Horn to measure his own Head,
       P. 155 INSTRUCTIONS   580 Flies to the Wood, and hides his armless Head.
       P. 157 INSTRUCTIONS   689 And, on the flaming Plank, so rests his Head,
       P. 162 INSTRUCTIONS   867 Bright Hair, fair Face, obscure and dull of
                                    Head;
       P. 170 PROPHECY   6 With high aspireing head towards those Skyes
       P. 173 LOYALL SCOT   49 And as on Angells head their Glories shine
       P. 173 LOYALL SCOT   55 And on his flaming Planks soe rests his head
       P. 175 LOYALL SCOT   163 Confirming breasts and Armepitts for the head.
       P. 176 LOYALL SCOT   192 But now, when one Head doeth both Realmes
                                    controule,
       P. 176 LOYALL SCOT   196 Kings head saith this, But Bishops head that
                                    doe.
       P. 176 LOYALL SCOT   203 That Cloven head must Govern Cloven foot.
       P. 178 LOYALL SCOT   277 The hare's head 'gainst the goose gibletts sett.
       P. 184 MADE FREE   109 The very First Head
       P. 187 BRITANNIA   113 My reverend head expos'd to scorn and shame,
       P. 191 TWO HORSES   11 Fryar Bacon had a head that spoke made of
                                    Brass,
       P. 193 TWO HORSES   71 W. On Seventh Harry's head he that placed the
                                    Crown
       P. 195 TWO HORSES   145 With the Turk in his head and the Pope in his
                                    heart
       P. 201 HISTORICALL   8 And cloath him all from head to foot anew;

headed   frequency: 2   relative frequency: 0.0000
       P.   90 MAY'S DEATH   17 But how a double headed Vulture Eats,
       P. 176 LOYALL SCOT   186 Strange was the Sight the scotch Twin headed
                                    man

headless   frequency: 1   relative frequency: 0.0000
       P. 145 INSTRUCTIONS   167 Headless St. Dennis so his Head does bear;

headlong   frequency: 1   relative frequency: 0.0000
       P. 139 HOUSEWARMING   62 And Presents croud headlong to give good
                                    example:

heads   frequency: 9   relative frequency: 0.0001
       P.   58 BILL-BOROW   60 Their prudent Heads too far intrust.
       P.   83 A. HOUSE   772 Have shod their Heads in their Canoos.

```
        P.   99 HOLLAND          150 Steel'd with these piercing Heads, Dean, Monck
                                     and Blake.
        P.  104 ANNIVERSARY       44 Then wooden Heads unto the Viols strings.
        P.  157 INSTRUCTIONS     683 And, as on Angels Heads their Glories shine,
        P.  175 LOYALL SCOT      151 One Mytre fitts the Heads of full four Moors.
        P.  176 LOYALL SCOT      188 And wild disputes betwixt those heads must Grow,
        P.  199 DUKE              62 Their boyling heads can hear no other sounds
        P.  200 DUKE              93 Defying all their heads and all their hands.

heads-man                            frequency:    1    relative frequency: 0.0000
        P.   36 DAPHNIS           99 To his Heads-man makes the Sign,

headstrong                           frequency:    2    relative frequency: 0.0000
        P.  108 ANNIVERSARY      224 To turn the headstrong Peoples Chariteer;
        P.  202 HISTORICALL       74 The Senate which should headstrong Princes stay

heal                                 frequency:    1    relative frequency: 0.0000
      See also "clowns-all-heal."
        P.  113 ANNIVERSARY      402 Troubling the Waters, yearly mak'st them Heal.

healing                              frequency:    1    relative frequency: 0.0000
        P.  189 BRITANNIA        181 Publicola with healing hand shall power

health                               frequency:    4    relative frequency: 0.0000
        P.   21 SOUL & BODY       30 Am Shipwrackt into Health again.
        P.   91 MAY'S DEATH       24 In his own Bowels sheath'd the conquering
                                     health.
        P.  114 BLAKE             33 Both health and profit, Fate cannot deny;
        P.  175 LOYALL SCOT      129 To Excommunicate and Study health.

healthful                            frequency:    1    relative frequency: 0.0000
        P.  109 ANNIVERSARY      232 An healthful Mind within a Body strong;

healths                              frequency:    3    relative frequency: 0.0000
        P.  161 INSTRUCTIONS     848 And in eternal Healths thy Name be trowl'd.
        P.  177 LOYALL SCOT      229 And Uninforc'd Quaff healths in Phlegethon.
        P.  316 CHEQUER INN      152 The Healths in Order did up send

heap                                 frequency:    1    relative frequency: 0.0000
        P.   82 A. HOUSE         762 But a rude heap together hurl'd;

heapes                               frequency:    1    relative frequency: 0.0000
        P.  313 CHEQUER INN       21 And heapes up all our Treasure

heaps.  See "heapes."

hear                                 frequency:   13    relative frequency: 0.0002
      See also "heare."
        P.   26 MISTRESS          21 But at my back I alwaies hear
        P.   57 BILL-BOROW        39 And Men could hear his Armour still
        P.   75 A. HOUSE         517 But highest Oakes stoop down to hear,
        P.   84 FLECKNO           32 Towards the Verse; and when that could not hear,
        P.   86 FLECKNO          143 To hear his Verses, by so just a curse
        P.  119 TWO SONGS          8 Nor scorn Endymicns plaints to hear.
        P.  155 INSTRUCTIONS     599 Leave him alone when first they hear the Gun;
        P.  161 INSTRUCTIONS     860 Where mute they stand to hear their Sentence
                                     read;
        P.  163 INSTRUCTIONS     908 As one that some unusual noise does hear.
        P.  164 INSTRUCTIONS     953 Through Optick Trunk the Planet seem'd to
                                     hear,
        P.  176 LOYALL SCOT      206 Those whom you hear more Clamerous Yet and
                                     Loud
        P.  194 TWO HORSES       107 Our riders are absent; who is't that can hear?
        P.  199 DUKE              62 Their boyling heads can hear no other sounds

heard                                frequency:    7    relative frequency: 0.0001
        P.   73 A. HOUSE         456 Davenant with th' Universal Heard.
        P.   85 FLECKNO           78 He heard of by Traditicn, and redeem'd.
        P.  108 ANNIVERSARY      203 And all about was heard a Panique groan,
        P.  116 BLAKE             97 That they with joy their boasting General heard,
        P.  156 INSTRUCTIONS     640 He heard how the wild Cannon nearer roar'd;
        P.  193 TWO HORSES        69 Ch. The basest Ingratitude ever was heard;
        P.  313 CHEQUER INN       45 Tho' all Men blusht that heard it

heare                                frequency:    2    relative frequency: 0.0000
        P.  129 O.C.             237 No more shall heare that powerful language charm,
        P.  314 CHEQUER INN       90 That gap'd to heare him sputter

heareing                             frequency:    1    relative frequency: 0.0000
        P.  201 HISTORICALL       23 The pious Mother Queen heareing her Son

hearing                              frequency:    1    relative frequency: 0.0000
```

See also "heareing."
P. 192 TWO HORSES   26 Who have told many truths well worth a mans
                          hearing,

hear k   frequency: 3   relative frequency: 0.0000
P. 10 DIALOGUE   37 Heark how Musick then prepares,
P. 41 DAMON   1 Heark how the Mower Damon Sung,
P. 119 TWO SONGS   5 Heark how he sings, with sad delight,

hears   frequency: 1   relative frequency: 0.0000
P. 142 INSTRUCTIONS   77 And nightly hears the hated Guards away

hearse   frequency: 1   relative frequency: 0.0000
See also "herse."
P. 74 A. HOUSE   496 Will in green Age her Hearse expect.

heart   frequency: 22   relative frequency: 0.0004
P.   9 DIALOGUE   10 To conquer one resolved Heart.
P. 20 SOUL & BODY   10 In a vain Head, and double Heart.
P. 22 NYMPH   20 From thine, and wound me to the Heart,
P. 22 NYMPH   36 Left me his Faun, but took his Heart.
P. 23 NYMPH   42 Of foot, and heart; and did invite,
P. 26 MISTRESS   18 And the last Age should show your Heart.
P. 28 LOVER   36 Another on his Heart did bill.
P. 31 FAIR SINGER   5 That while she with her Eyes my Heart does
                          bind,
P. 32 MOURNING   15 Only to soften near her Heart
P. 55 THYESTE   13 Into his own Heart ne'r pry's,
P. 57 BILL-BOROW   48 'Twas writ already in their Heart.
P. 77 A. HOUSE   603 Where Beauty, aiming at the heart,
P. 107 ANNIVERSARY   167 Though thou thine Heart from Evil still
                          unstain'd,
P. 109 ANNIVERSARY   257 Thou with the same strength, and an Heart as
                          plain,
P. 123 O.C.   20 Should speak the wondrous softness of his Heart.
P. 147 INSTRUCTIONS   273 With Heart of Bees so full, and Head of
                          Mites,
P. 154 INSTRUCTIONS   562 With panting Heart, lay like a fish on Land,
P. 162 INSTRUCTIONS   898 Her heart throbs, and with very shame would
                          break.
P. 177 LOYALL SCOT   245 From Scotch or English heart the same effect.
P. 184 MADE FREE   112 When in Heart you all knew
P. 186 BRITANNIA   52 And in his heart kind influences shed
P. 195 TWO HORSES   145 With the Turk in his head and the Pope in his
                          heart

hearts   frequency: 6   relative frequency: 0.0001
P. 29 THE GALLERY   11 Examining upon our Hearts
P. 38 PICTURE   21 In Triumph over Hearts that strive,
P. 151 INSTRUCTIONS   447 Yet Lewis writes, and lest our Hearts should
                          break,
P. 163 INSTRUCTIONS   931 Through their feign'd speech their secret hearts
                          he knew;
P. 186 BRITANNIA   77 Dastards the hearts and active heat controules.
P. 190 STATUE   17 No, to comfort the hearts of the poor Cavaleer

heat   frequency: 13   relative frequency: 0.0002
P. 21 SOUL & BODY   35 The Pestilence of Love does heat:
P. 40 THE MATCH   23 The Naphta's and the Sulphurs heat,
P. 42 DAMON   17 This heat the Sun could never raise,
P. 43 DAMON   45 And, if at Noon my toil me heat,
P. 48 THE GARDEN   25 When we have run our Passions heat,
P. 72 A. HOUSE   427 Where every Mowers wholesome Heat
P. 111 ANNIVERSARY   343 So while our Star that gives us Light and
                          Heat,
P. 114 BLAKE   37 And coolness there, with heat doth never fight,
P. 116 BLAKE   83 They learn'd with Terrour, that nor Summers
                          heat,
P. 125 O.C.   82 Or fan with airy plumes so soft an heat.
P. 141 INSTRUCTIONS   37 But Age, allaying now that youthful heat,
P. 174 LOYALL SCOT   114 Their Rank Ambition all this heat hath stir'd
P. 186 BRITANNIA   77 Dastards the hearts and active heat controules.

heats   frequency: 1   relative frequency: 0.0000
P. 42 DAMON   9 Oh what unusual Heats are here,

heav'd   frequency: 1   relative frequency: 0.0000
P. 95 HOLLAND   4 By English Pilots when they heav'd the Lead;

heaven   frequency: 34   relative frequency: 0.0007
See also "heav'n."
P.   4 HASTINGS   13 What man is he, that hath not Heaven beguil'd,

P.	4 HASTINGS	22 To Earth, and then what Jealousies to Heaven!
P.	10 DIALOGUE	48 And Heaven views it with delight.
P.	11 DIALOGUE	72 And then to Heaven climb.
P.	12 DROP OF DEW	26 The greater Heaven in an Heaven less.
P.	16 EYES	41 The Incense was to Heaven dear,
P.	22 NYMPH	10 Prevail with Heaven to forget
P.	28 LOVER	41 And now, when angry Heaven wou'd
P.	31 MOURNING	8 To Heaven, whence it came, their Woe.
P.	34 DAPHNIS	45 Are my Hell and Heaven Joyn'd
P.	37 DEFINITION	21 Unless the giddy Heaven fall,
P.	55 EPITAPH	13 That her Soul was on Heaven so bent
P.	56 BILL-BOROW	12 The Earth deform and Heaven fright,
P.	62 A. HOUSE	119 'And can in Heaven hence behold
P.	63 A. HOUSE	140 'To holy things, for Heaven fit.
P.	69 A. HOUSE	324 Which Heaven planted us to please,
P.	74 A. HOUSE	494 Yet more to Heaven shooting are:
P.	80 A. HOUSE	687 But by her Flames, in Heaven try'd,
P.	81 A. HOUSE	722 In a Domestick Heaven nurst,
P.	99 HOLLAND	146 Darling of Heaven, and of Men the Care;
P.	106 ANNIVERSARY	119 If gracious Heaven to my Life give length,
P.	114 BLAKE	29 O noble Trust which Heaven on this Isle poures,
P.	114 BLAKE	41 And these want nothing Heaven can afford,
P.	116 BLAKE	78 At once both to Inhabit Earth and Heaven.
P.	123 O.C.	16 But angry Heaven unto War had sway'd,
P.	127 O.C.	166 Where Heaven leads, 'tis Piety to weep.
P.	127 O.C.	184 Where those that strike from Heaven fetch their Blow.
P.	131 O.C.	320 Earth ne'er more glad, nor Heaven more serene.
P.	149 INSTRUCTIONS	348 The Comet dread, and Earth and Heaven burns.
P.	154 INSTRUCTIONS	555 And gentle Gales them steer, and Heaven drives,
P.	172 LOYALL SCOT	30 Then least Heaven fall ere thither hee Ascend.
P.	198 DUKE	29 The way to heaven and who shall be my guide?
P.	205 HISTORICALL	160 Heaven had him Chieftain of great Britain made,

heaven-daring   frequency: 1   relative frequency: 0.0000
   P.   57 BILL-BOROW   28 Of Heaven-daring Teneriff.

heaven-nursed   frequency: 1   relative frequency: 0.0000
   P.   70 A. HOUSE   355 Conscience, that Heaven-nursed Plant,

heavenly   frequency: 1   relative frequency: 0.0000
   P. 203 HISTORICALL   92 With hocus pocus and their heavenly slight

heavens   frequency: 21   relative frequency: 0.0004

P.	5 HASTINGS	59 For Man (alas) is but the Heavens sport;
P.	9 DIALOGUE	12 Lord of Earth, and Heavens Heir.
P.	11 DIALOGUE	55 If things of Sight such Heavens be,
P.	11 DIALOGUE	56 What Heavens are those we cannot see?
P.	14 THE CORONET	18 And mortal Glory, Heavens Diadem!
P.	18 BERMUDAS	34 Till it arrive at Heavens Vault:
P.	22 NYMPH	13 It cannot dye so. Heavens King
P.	47 EMPIRE	16 To sing Mens Triumphs, or in Heavens quire.
P.	47 EMPIRE	24 Would with you Heavens Hallelujahs raise.
P.	59 A. HOUSE	32 To strain themselves through Heavens Gate.
P.	81 A. HOUSE	712 But as 'tis Heavens Dialect.
P.	88 ODE	26 The force of angry Heavens flame:
P.	106 ANNIVERSARY	134 Should bend to his, as he to Heavens will,
P.	107 ANNIVERSARY	147 And knowing not where Heavens choice may light,
P.	127 O.C.	157 O Cromwell, Heavens Favorite! To none
P.	146 INSTRUCTIONS	237 Propitious Heavens, had not you them crost,
P.	154 INSTRUCTIONS	576 The Ocean Water, or the Heavens Wind.
P.	187 BRITANNIA	88 Thus Heavens designs against heavens self youl turn
P.	189 BRITANNIA	192 The Earth shall rest, the Heavens shall on thee smile,
P.	203 HISTORICALL	96 Who would such men Heavens messengers believe,

heaven's   frequency: 5   relative frequency: 0.0001
   See also "heavens."
P.	10 DIALOGUE	30 Is Heaven's and its own perfume.
P.	18 CLORINDA	12 Safe from the Sun. D. not Heaven's Eye.
P.	19 THYRSIS	18 Heaven's the Center of the Soul.
P.	82 A. HOUSE	767 You Heaven's Center, Nature's Lap.
P.	128 O.C.	226 And you to govern only Heaven's taske.

heaves   frequency: 1   relative frequency: 0.0000
   P. 154 INSTRUCTIONS   546 With Trident's Leaver, and great Shoulder heaves.

heavier   frequency: 2   relative frequency: 0.0000

```
       P. 204 HISTORICALL   123 To bring upon our Necks the heavier yoke:
       P. 317 CHEQUER INN    190 But sure this is a heavier Curse

heav'n                       frequency:   12   relative frequency: 0.0002
       P.  63 A. HOUSE       150 'For whom you Heav'n should disesteem?
       P.  64 A. HOUSE       162 'Shall draw Heav'n nearer, raise us higher.
       P. 109 ANNIVERSARY    243 'Twas Heav'n would not that his Pow'r should
                                 cease,
       P. 125 O.C.           107 Or rather Heav'n, which us so long foresees,
       P. 127 O.C.           160 And Heav'n it self would the great Herald be;
       P. 128 O.C.           191 What man was ever so in Heav'n obey'd
       P. 129 O.C.           262 To Heav'n its branches, and through earth its
                                 roots:
       P. 131 O.C.           315 Heav'n to this choice prepar'd a diadem,
       P. 131 PARADISE         5 Heav'n, Hell, Earth, Chaos, All; the
                                 Argument
       P. 132 PARADISE        43 Just Heav'n Thee, like Tiresias, to requite,
       P. 153 INSTRUCTIONS   517 As Heav'n in Storms, they call, in gusts of
                                 State,
       P. 157 INSTRUCTIONS   664 Then, lest Heav'n fall, e're thither he ascend.

heavy                        frequency:    5   relative frequency: 0.0001
       See also "heavye."
       P.  79 A. HOUSE       642 My Temples here with heavy sedge;
       P.  89 ODE             92 Falls heavy from the Sky,
       P. 103 ANNIVERSARY     15 While heavy Monarchs make a wide Return,
       P. 126 O.C.           121 Then heavy Showres the winged Tempests lead,
       P. 130 O.C.           299 For we, since thou art gone, with heavy doome,

heavye                       frequency:    1   relative frequency: 0.0000
       P. 202 HISTORICALL     38 And Plague and Warre fell heavye on our Isle.

hebrew                       frequency:    2   relative frequency: 0.0000
       P.  35 DAPHNIS         78 Like the Gourmand Hebrew dead,
       P. 158 INSTRUCTIONS   735 Such the fear'd Hebrew, captive, blinded, shorn,

hecatomb                     frequency:    1   relative frequency: 0.0000
       P. 126 O.C.           124 Offer themselves in many an Hecatomb;

hecatombs                    frequency:    1   relative frequency: 0.0000
       P. 149 INSTRUCTIONS   352 By Millions over, not by Hecatombs.

hector                       frequency:    1   relative frequency: 0.0000
       P. 146 INSTRUCTIONS   228 While Hector Harry steers by Will the Wit:

he'd                         frequency:    4   relative frequency: 0.0000

hedg'd                       frequency:    1   relative frequency: 0.0000
       P.  74 A. HOUSE       504 As if the Night within were hedg'd.

hedge                        frequency:    2   relative frequency: 0.0000
       P.  62 A. HOUSE       100 'But hedge our Liberty about.
       P.  79 A. HOUSE       641 Oh what a Pleasure 'tis to hedge

hee                          frequency:   28   relative frequency: 0.0005

heed                         frequency:    1   relative frequency: 0.0000
       P.  48 THE GARDEN      21 Little, Alas, they know, or heed,

heeding                      frequency:    1   relative frequency: 0.0000
       P. 181 MADE FREE       15 Wou'd intrust their youth to your heeding?

hee'l                        frequency:    2   relative frequency: 0.0000

heeren                       frequency:    1   relative frequency: 0.0000
       P.  96 HOLLAND         34 For pickled Herring, pickled Heeren chang'd.

height                       frequency:   12   relative frequency: 0.0002
       See also "hight."
       P.  12 DROP OF DEW     22 Remembring still its former height,
       P.  56 BILL-BOROW      11 That do with your hook-shoulder'd height
       P.  57 BILL-BOROW      23 Nor for it self the height does gain,
       P.  58 BILL-BOROW      80 Nor Height but with Retirement loves.
       P.  59 A. HOUSE        24 Though the first Builders fail'd in Height?
       P.  60 A. HOUSE        59 Height with a certain Grace does bend,
       P.  63 A. HOUSE       145 'All Beauty, when at such a height,
       P. 105 ANNIVERSARY     93 But the most Equal still sustein the Height,
       P. 109 ANNIVERSARY    246 Trying the Measures of the Bredth and Height;
       P. 115 BLAKE           75 The Peek's proud height, the Spaniards all
                                 admire,
       P. 124 O.C.            39 When with meridian height her Beauty shin'd,
```

P. 125 O.C.   83 For he no duty by his height excus'd,

heighten   frequency: 1   relative frequency: 0.0000
   P.   9 DIALOGUE   16 Stand prepar'd to heighten yours.

heir   frequency: 5   relative frequency: 0.0001
   P.   9 DIALOGUE   12 Lord of Earth, and Heavens Heir.
   P. 28 LOVER   30 Th' unfortunate and abject Heir:
   P. 61 A. HOUSE   91 Fair beyond Measure, and an Heir
   P. 171 PROPHECY   45 When the Crowne's Heir shall English Men
                              dispise
   P. 200 DUKE   115 Of Monarchs murthered by the Impatient heir:

heirs   frequency: 1   relative frequency: 0.0000
   P. 142 INSTRUCTIONS   55 And found how Royal Heirs might be matur'd,

held   frequency: 6   relative frequency: 0.0001
   P. 84 FLECKNO   33 Held him the other; and instead yet,
   P. 115 BLAKE   47 Casting that League off, which she held so long,
   P. 120 TWO SONGS   34 Seeks but the honour to have held out longest.
   P. 131 PARADISE   6 Held me a while misdoubting his Intent,
   P. 147 INSTRUCTIONS   282 Of Citizens and Merchants held dispute:
   P. 316 CHEQUER INN   139 Our greatest Barne cou'd not have held

heldest. See "held'st."

held'st   frequency: 1   relative frequency: 0.0000
   P. 159 INSTRUCTIONS   746 Thou, and thy Fellows, held'st the odious
                              Light.

heliades   frequency: 1   relative frequency: 0.0000
   P. 24 NYMPH   99 The brotherless Heliades

hell   frequency: 7   relative frequency: 0.0001
   P. 34 DAPHNIS   45 Are my Hell and Heaven Joyn'd
   P. 99 HOLLAND   152 Vainly in Hell let Pluto domineer.
   P. 131 PARADISE   5 Heav'n, Hell, Earth, Chaos, All; the
                              Argument
   P. 176 LOYALL SCOT   205 And plead their Jus Divinum tho' in Hell.
   P. 184 MADE FREE   122 Led in Hell by the Papes,
   P. 185 BRITANNIA   41 Were Hurl'd to Hell by Learning Tyrants
                              Lore.
   P. 204 HISTORICALL   126 Of all the Miscreants ever went to hell

hellborn   frequency: 1   relative frequency: 0.0000
   P. 189 BRITANNIA   186 From Noxious Monsters, Hellborn tyranny,

hellish   frequency: 1   relative frequency: 0.0000
   P. 188 BRITANNIA   129 Thus the state's night-Mard by this Hellish rout

helm   frequency: 1   relative frequency: 0.0000
   P. 110 ANNIVERSARY   275 The Helm does from the artless Steersman
                              strain,

helmet   frequency: 1   relative frequency: 0.0000
   P.   9 DIALOGUE   3 Close on thy Head thy Helmet bright.

help   frequency: 4   relative frequency: 0.0000
   See also "helpe."
   P. 24 NYMPH   93 O help! O help! I see it faint:
   P. 49 THE GARDEN   60 What other Help could yet be meet!
   P. 154 INSTRUCTIONS   544 (The Gods themselves do help the provident.)

helpe   frequency: 2   relative frequency: 0.0000
   P. 201 HISTORICALL   6 The People call him home to helpe the State,
   P. 315 CHEQUER INN   120 But who can helpe it Dick.

helpless   frequency: 4   relative frequency: 0.0000
   P. 89 ODE   62 To vindicate his helpless Right,
   P. 126 O.C.   126 And helpless languish at the tainted Stall.
   P. 159 INSTRUCTIONS   753 And to each other helpless couple moan,
   P. 187 BRITANNIA   111 With Joynt consent on helpless me they flew,

hemisphere   frequency: 2   relative frequency: 0.0000
   P. 56 BILL-BOROW   2 Rise in a perfect Hemisphere!
   P. 83 A. HOUSE   775 Let's in: for the dark Hemisphere

hemorrhoid. See "hem'roid."

hem'roid   frequency: 1   relative frequency: 0.0000
   P. 153 INSTRUCTIONS   497 Horse-leeches circling at the Hem'roid Vein;

hen   frequency: 1   relative frequency: 0.0000
     P. 162 INSTRUCTIONS 880 An Urinal, and sit like any Hen.

hence   frequency: 30   relative frequency: 0.0006

henceforth   frequency: 5   relative frequency: 0.0001

her   frequency: 208   relative frequency: 0.0043

herald   frequency: 1   relative frequency: 0.0000
     P. 127 O.C.   160 And Heav'n it self would the great Herald be;

heraldry   frequency: 1   relative frequency: 0.0000
     P. 46 MOWER'S SONG   27 Shall now the Heraldry become

herb   frequency: 1   relative frequency: 0.0000
     P. 48 THE GARDEN   4 Crown'd from some single Herb or Tree.

herb-john   frequency: 1   relative frequency: 0.0000
     P. 153 INSTRUCTIONS 514 Or think him, like Herb-John, for nothing good.

herberts   frequency: 1   relative frequency: 0.0000
     P. 316 CHEQUER INN   133 The Hanmers, Herberts, Sandys, Musgraves

herbes   frequency: 1   relative frequency: 0.0000
     P. 50 THE GARDEN   66 Of flow'rs and herbes this Dial new;

herbs   frequency: 4   relative frequency: 0.0000
     See also "herbes."
     P.   5 HASTINGS   56 All Herbs, and them a thousand ways infus'd?
     P. 50 THE GARDEN   72 Be reckon'd but with herbs and flow'rs!
     P. 149 INSTRUCTIONS 338 With Magic Herbs, rose from the Pot renew'd:
     P. 190 STATUE   31 And instead of that markett of herbs and of fruit

herbwomen   frequency: 1   relative frequency: 0.0000
     P. 179 STOCKSMARKET   17 To see him so disfigured the herbwomen chide,

herculean   frequency: 1   relative frequency: 0.0000
     P. 153 INSTRUCTIONS 520 Under Herculean Labours he may sink.

hercules   frequency: 1   relative frequency: 0.0000
     See also "water-hercules."
     P. 99 HOLLAND   138 Is strangled by our Infant Hercules.

herd. See "irish-herd."

here   frequency: 73   relative frequency: 0.0015
     See also "here's."

hereford   frequency: 1   relative frequency: 0.0000
     P. 161 INSTRUCTIONS 846 And long as Cider lasts in Hereford;

here's   frequency: 1   relative frequency: 0.0000

heresies   frequency: 1   relative frequency: 0.0000
     P. 110 ANNIVERSARY   300 Might muster Heresies, so one were ten.

heretic. See "heretick," "heretique."

heretik   frequency: 1   relative frequency: 0.0000
     P. 205 HISTORICALL   162 His Brother sneaking Heretik should dye,

heretique   frequency: 1   relative frequency: 0.0000
     P. 175 LOYALL SCOT   154 What soe obdurate Pagan Heretique

heretofore   frequency: 1   relative frequency: 0.0000

hero   frequency: 1   relative frequency: 0.0000
     See also "heroe."
     P. 200 DUKE   82 The Hero once gett honour by the sword;

heroe   frequency: 3   relative frequency: 0.0000
     P. 67 A. HOUSE   281 From that blest Bed the Heroe came,
     P. 178 LOYALL SCOT   274 Pardon, Young Heroe, this soe long Transport;
     P. 185 BRITANNIA   48 As the Jessean Herce did appease

heroes   frequency: 2   relative frequency: 0.0000
     P. 90 MAY'S DEATH   15 Sounding of ancient Heroes, such as were
     P. 171 LOYALL SCOT   1 Of the old Herces when the Warlike shades

heroick   frequency: 2   relative frequency: 0.0000

    P. 177 LOYALL SCOT   241 For Worth Heroick or Heroick Crimes.

heron   frequency: 1   relative frequency: 0.0000
    P.   75 A. HOUSE   533 The Heron from the Ashes top,

herring   frequency: 2   relative frequency: 0.0000
    P.   96 HOLLAND   34 For pickled Herring, pickled Heeren chang'd.
    P.   97 HOLLAND   61 Though Herring for their God few voices mist,

hers   frequency: 5   relative frequency: 0.0001

herse   frequency: 1   relative frequency: 0.0000
    P. 111 ANNIVERSARY 332 And Stars (like Tapers) burn'd upon his Herse:

herself   frequency: 1   relative frequency: 0.0000
    P. 156 INSTRUCTIONS 628 She tears herself since him she cannot harm.

he's   frequency: 2   relative frequency: 0.0000

hew   frequency: 3   relative frequency: 0.0000
    P.   21 SOUL & BODY   43 So Architects do square and hew,
    P.   27 MISTRESS   33 Now therefore, while the youthful hew
    P.   59 A. HOUSE   4 And Forrests did to Pastures hew;

hew'd   frequency: 1   relative frequency: 0.0000
    P. 104 ANNIVERSARY   51 The rougher Stones, unto his Measures hew'd,

hewels   frequency: 1   relative frequency: 0.0000
    P.   76 A. HOUSE   558 But serves to feed the Hewels young.

hewel's   frequency: 1   relative frequency: 0.0000
    P.   75 A. HOUSE   537 But most the Hewel's wonders are,

hid   frequency: 7   relative frequency: 0.0001
    P.   85 FLECKNO   77 Which by the Jews long hid, and Disesteem'd,
    P. 127 O.C.   162 Then those of Moses hid from humane Eyes;
    P. 142 INSTRUCTIONS 74 But in her soft Breast Loves hid Cancer
                                smarts.
    P. 145 INSTRUCTIONS 166 Hid with his Elbow like the Spice he stole.
    P. 145 INSTRUCTIONS 184 And hid much Fraud under an aspect grim.
    P. 163 INSTRUCTIONS 930 Which his hid mind did in its depths inclose.
    P. 164 INSTRUCTIONS 958 Which, in your Splendor hid, Corrode your
                                  Light;

hidden   frequency: 4   relative frequency: 0.0000
    P.   11 DIALOGUE   69 Thou shalt know each hidden Cause;
    P.   21 SOUL & BODY   36 Or Hatred's hidden Ulcer eat.
    P.   84 FLECKNO   40 Mov'd by the Air and hidden Sympathies;
    P. 124 O.C.   42 His hidden Soul at ev'ry turn could meet;

hide   frequency: 6   relative frequency: 0.0001
    P.   43 DAMON   52 More ground then all his Sheep do hide.
    P.   79 A. HOUSE   652 Hide trifling Youth thy Pleasures slight.
    P. 153 INSTRUCTIONS 528 Bosomes, and all which from themselves they hide.
    P. 187 BRITANNIA   108 Led up by the wise son-in-law of Hide.
    P. 199 DUKE   43 That sent Nan Hide before her under ground,
    P. 204 HISTORICALL 141 Clifford and Hide before had lost the day,

hideous   frequency: 2   relative frequency: 0.0000
    P.   83 FLECKNO   20 In hideous verse, he, and a dismal tone,
    P. 112 ANNIVERSARY 361 'An hideous shole of wood-Leviathans,

hides   frequency: 3   relative frequency: 0.0000
    P. 124 O.C.   61 She lest He grieve hides what She can her
                                pains,
    P. 155 INSTRUCTIONS 580 Flies to the Wood, and hides his armless Head.
    P. 158 INSTRUCTIONS 703 And the kind River in its Creek them hides,

hierarchye   frequency: 1   relative frequency: 0.0000
    P. 171 PROPHECY   40 The Champion of the English Hierarchye,

hies. See "hyes."

higgins   frequency: 1   relative frequency: 0.0000
    P. 145 INSTRUCTIONS 197 Before them Higgins rides with brow compact,

high   frequency: 29   relative frequency: 0.0006
    P.   35 DAPHNIS   68 Jewels of so high a rate.
    P.   36 DEFINITION   2 As 'tis for object strange and high:
    P.   38 PICTURE   9 Who can foretel for what high cause
    P.   40 THE MATCH   34 To make one fire high:
    P.   41 THE MOWER   15 Its Onion root they then so high did hold,

```
P.  59 A. HOUSE          7 Whose Columnes should so high be rais'd
P.  75 A. HOUSE        516 With Musick high the squatted Thorns.
P.  83 FLECKNO           7 For Poetry: There three Stair-Cases high,
P.  87 ODE              17 For 'tis all one to Courage high
P.  89 ODE              91 So when the Falcon high
P.  96 HOLLAND          21 Building their watry Babel far more high
P. 105 ANNIVERSARY      64 Therefore the Temples rear'd their Columns
                           high:
P. 106 ANNIVERSARY     132 High Grace should meet in one with highest
                           Pow'r,
P. 109 ANNIVERSARY     230 Thy sober Spirit unto things too High,
P. 109 ANNIVERSARY     242 Who think those high Decrees by Man design'd.
P. 117 BLAKE           107 Those Forts, which there, so high and strong
                           appear,
P. 117 BLAKE           129 Nature ne'r made Cedars so high aspire,
P. 117 BLAKE           131 Which by quick powders force, so high was sent,
P. 118 BLAKE           144 And was attended by as high success.
P. 120 TWO SONGS        41 Though I so high may not pretend,
P. 122 TWO SONGS        38 Looking from high,
P. 127 O.C.            158 Have such high honours from above been shown:
P. 130 O.C.            274 Detracts from objects than itself more high:
P. 149 INSTRUCTIONS    346 But blooms all Night, and shoots its branches
                           high.
P. 154 INSTRUCTIONS    539 While the red Flags breath on their Top-masts
                           high
P. 160 INSTRUCTIONS    796 Powder ne're blew man up so soon so high.
P. 165 INSTRUCTIONS    985 Whose gen'rous Conscience and whose Courage
                           high
P. 167 KINGS VOWES      59 So high that he shall brave the Parliament,
P. 170 PROPHECY          6 With high aspireing head towards those Skyes
```

higher   frequency: 11   relative frequency: 0.0002
```
P.  42 DAMON            19 It from an higher Beauty grow'th,
P.  44 GLO-WORMS         7 Shining unto no higher end
P.  64 A. HOUSE        162 'Shall draw Heav'n nearer, raise us higher.
P.  72 A. HOUSE        417 Or sooner hatch or higher build:
P.  81 A. HOUSE        705 For She, to higher Beauties rais'd,
P.  83 FLECKNO          11 Not higher then Seav'n, nor larger then three
                           feet;
P. 104 ANNIVERSARY      48 To tune this lower to that higher Sphere.
P. 104 ANNIVERSARY      53 This took a Lower, that an Higher place,
P. 109 ANNIVERSARY     239 What since he did, an higher Force him push'd
P. 115 BLAKE            76 Yet in their brests, carry a pride much higher.
P. 175 LOYALL SCOT     130 A higher work is to their Court Annext:
```

highest   frequency: 9   relative frequency: 0.0001
```
P.   3 LOVELACE         13 He highest builds, who with most Art destroys,
P.  75 A. HOUSE        517 But highest Oakes stoop down to hear,
P.  88 ODE              31 As if his highest plot
P.  89 ODE              80 And fit for highest Trust:
P.  99 HOLLAND         151 And while Jove governs in the highest Sphere,
P. 105 ANNIVERSARY      82 Each in the House the highest Place contends,
P. 106 ANNIVERSARY     132 High Grace should meet in one with highest
                           Pow'r,
P. 118 BLAKE           143 A choice which did the highest worth express,
P. 128 O.C.            212 To him the children of the Highest were?
```

highly   frequency: 1   relative frequency: 0.0000
```
P. 201 HISTORICALL      14 Things highly fitting for a Monarchs trade.
```

highness   frequency: 2   relative frequency: 0.0000
```
P. 142 INSTRUCTIONS     49 Paint then again Her Highness to the life,
P. 204 HISTORICALL     137 His meager Highness now had got astride,
```

highnesses   frequency: 1   relative frequency: 0.0000
```
P. 142 INSTRUCTIONS     58 Of's Highnesses Royal Society.
```

highnesses's   frequency: 1   relative frequency: 0.0000
```
P. 182 MADE FREE        65 To his Highnesses's Trumpetts
```

highness's. See "highnesses," "highnesses's."

hight   frequency: 2   relative frequency: 0.0000
```
P.  15 EYES              6 In a false Angle takes each hight;
P.  71 A. HOUSE        411 When Lowness is unsafe as Hight,
```

hill   frequency: 6   relative frequency: 0.0001
```
P.  30 THE GALLERY      55 Transplanting Flow'rs from the green Hill,
P.  56 BILL-BOROW        6 So equal as this Hill does bow.
P.  56 BILL-BOROW       t1 Upon the Hill and Grove at Bill-borow.
P.  57 BILL-BOROW       40 Ratling through all the Grove and Hill.
```

```
        P. 116 BLAKE         77 Onely to this vast hill a power is given,
        P. 119 TWO SONGS      4 Upon this Hill outwakes the Moon.

hills                          frequency:    4     relative frequency: 0.0000
        P.  58 BILL-BOROW    66 And other Hills him once did please.
        P.  58 BILL-BOROW    79 Nor he the Hills without the Groves,
        P.  72 A. HOUSE     440 In Hills for Soldiers Obsequies.
        P. 111 ANNIVERSARY  330 Sunk in the Hills, or plung'd below the
                                Streams.

him                            frequency:  186     relative frequency: 0.0038

himself                        frequency:   40     relative frequency: 0.0008
        See also "himselfe."

himselfe                       frequency:    2     relative frequency: 0.0000

hinder                         frequency:    2     relative frequency: 0.0000
        P.  66 A. HOUSE     236 To hinder the unjust Divorce.
        P. 126 O.C.         139 Which, since they might nct hinder, yet they cast

hindes                         frequency:    1     relative frequency: 0.0000
        P.  23 NYMPH         69 For it was nimbler much than Hindes;

hinds.  See "hindes."

hir'd                          frequency:    1     relative frequency: 0.0000
        P. 170 PROPHECY      10 Hir'd for their share to give the rest away

hire                           frequency:    1     relative frequency: 0.0000
        P. 123 TWO SONGS     43 But Virtue shall be Beauties hire,

hirelings                      frequency:    1     relative frequency: 0.0000
        P. 187 BRITANNIA     91 By hirelings sould to you shall be resign'd

his                            frequency:  648     relative frequency: 0.0135
        See also "of's," "'s," "under's."

hissing                        frequency:    1     relative frequency: 0.0000
        P.  16 EYES          40 And here the hissing Lightning slakes.

historian                      frequency:    2     relative frequency: 0.0000
        P.  91 MAY'S DEATH   23 Where the Historian of the Common-wealth
        P.  91 MAY'S DEATH   42 Malignant Poet and Historian both.

historical.  See "historicall."

historicall                    frequency:    1     relative frequency: 0.0000
        P. 201 HISTORICALL    t An Historicall Poem.

historically                   frequency:    1     relative frequency: 0.0000
        P.  92 MAY'S DEATH   96 Thou first Histcrically shouldst sustain.

history                        frequency:    1     relative frequency: 0.0000
        See also "hist'ry."
        P.  77 A. HOUSE     579 And in one Histcry consumes,

hist'ry                        frequency:    1     relative frequency: 0.0000
        P. 183 MADE FREE     75 He values not Credit nor Hist'ry,

hit                            frequency:    3     relative frequency: 0.0000
        P.  19 THYRSIS       17 Till it hit, against the pole,
        P.  77 A. HOUSE     586 Could with a Mask my studies hit!
        P. 146 INSTRUCTICNS 227 Nor better choice all accidents could hit;

hither                         frequency:    5     relative frequency: 0.0001
        P.  48 THE GARDEN    26 Love hither makes his best retreat.
        P.  60 A. HOUSE      34 Shall hither ccme in Pilgrimage,
        P.  85 FLECKNO       99 Except by penetration hither, where
        P.  91 MAY'S DEATH   49 Transferring old Rome hither in your talk,
        P. 316 CHEQUER INN  172 I saw no more but hither ran

hive                           frequency:    2     relative frequency: 0.0000
        P. 178 LOYALL SCOT  269 The hive a comb case, every bee a drone,
        P. 178 LOYALL SCOT  273 And Each works hony fcr the Common Hive.

hoard                          frequency:    1     relative frequency: 0.0000
        P. 164 INSTRUCTICNS 980 Burr'wing themselves to hoard their guilty
                                Store.

hoarded                        frequency:    1     relative frequency: 0.0000
```

```
      P.  39 THE MATCH       7 With sweetest Perfumes hoarded were,

hobbinol                       frequency:    5    relative frequency: 0.0001
      P. 121 TWO SONGS       t5+ Hobbinol. Phillis. Tomalin. Hobbinol.
      P. 122 TWO SONGS       12+ Hobbinol.
      P. 122 TWO SONGS       20+ Hobbinol.
      P. 122 TWO SONGS       26+ Hobbinol.

hobbs's                        frequency:    1    relative frequency: 0.0000
      P. 315 CHEQUER INN     109 Old Hobbs's Brother, Cheney there

hobby-horse                    frequency:    1    relative frequency: 0.0000
      P. 146 INSTRUCTIONS    218 Cornbury before them manag'd Hobby-horse.

hocus                          frequency:    2    relative frequency: 0.0000
      P. 174 LOYALL SCOT     106 The Jugling Prelate on his hocus calls,
      P. 203 HISTORICALL     92 With hocus pocus and their heavenly slight

hogs                           frequency:    1    relative frequency: 0.0000
      P.  97 HOLLAND         80 Themselves the Hogs as all their Subjects
                                Bores!

hoise                          frequency:    1   relative frequency: 0.0000
      P. 158 INSTRUCTIONS    738 Out of the Port, or dare to hoise a Sail,

hoist                          frequency:    1    relative frequency: 0.0000
      See also "hoise."
      P.  83 A. HOUSE        770 Their Leathern Boats begin to hoist;

hold                           frequency:   17    relative frequency: 0.0003
      P.   5 HASTINGS        34 The armed Angels hold their Carouzels;
      P.  41 THE MOWER       15 Its Onion root they then so high did hold,
      P.  61 A. HOUSE        74 Or Bilbrough, better hold then they:
      P.  88 ODE             39 But those do hold or break
      P.  98 HOLLAND         116 Should raging hold his Linstock to the Mine?
      P. 112 ANNIVERSARY     368 'Whose Navies hold the Sluces of the Sea.
      P. 124 O.C.            51 Hold fast dear Infants, hold them both or none;
      P. 143 INSTRUCTIONS    79 Paint Castlemaine in Colours that will hold,
      P. 147 INSTRUCTIONS    268 The adverse Troops, and hold them all at Bay.
      P. 150 INSTRUCTIONS    375 From Greenwich (where Intelligence they hold)
      P. 151 INSTRUCTIONS    438 And whip the Dutch, unless they'l hold their
                                 peace.
      P. 155 INSTRUCTIONS    592 For its last aid: Hold Chain or we are broke.
      P. 162 INSTRUCTIONS    879 His patient Piss, he could hold longer then
      P. 163 INSTRUCTIONS    904 And th' airy Picture vanisht from his hold.
      P. 166 KINGS VOWES     24 But if they build it too fast, I will soon make
                                them hold.
      P. 179 STOCKSMARKET    23 And others to make the similitude hold

holding                        frequency:    1    relative frequency: 0.0000
      P. 192 TWO HORSES      42 And the King's Chiefe minister holding the
                                doore:

holds                          frequency:    1    relative frequency: 0.0000
      P.  78 A. HOUSE        634 It ev'ry where the Meadow holds;

holes.  See "loop-holes."

holiness                       frequency:    1    relative frequency: 0.0000
      See also "holyness."
      P. 204 HISTORICALL     147 Are man'd by him or by his Holiness.

holland                        frequency:    7    relative frequency: 0.0001
      P.  95 HOLLAND          t The Character of Holland
      P.  95 HOLLAND          1 Holland, that scarce deserves the name of Land,
      P. 150 INSTRUCTIONS    395 So Holland with us had the Mast'ry try'd,
      P. 151 INSTRUCTIONS    418 In Holland theirs had lodg'd before, and
                                 France.
      P. 155 INSTRUCTIONS    593 But with her Sailing weight, the Holland Keel
      P. 158 INSTRUCTIONS    724 The Holland Squadron leisurely return:
      P. 160 INSTRUCTIONS    822 The Holland Fleet and Parliament so near.

hollanders                     frequency:    1    relative frequency: 0.0000
      P. 151 INSTRUCTIONS    429 How yet the Hollanders do make a noise,

hollands                       frequency:    1    relative frequency: 0.0000
      P. 150 INSTRUCTIONS    370 Like Slaves, shall beg for Peace at Hollands
                                 doors.

hollis                         frequency:    1    relative frequency: 0.0000
      P. 152 INSTRUCTIONS    457 Presbyter Hollis the first point should clear;
```

```
hollow                                  frequency:    7    relative frequency: 0.0001
     P.   17 BERMUDAS      27 And makes the hollow Seas, that roar,
     P.   47 EMPIRE         4 To hollow Rocks and murm'ring Fountains bound.
     P.   59 A. HOUSE      19 And in his hollow Palace goes
     P.   76 A. HOUSE     548 Does find the hollow Oak to speak,
     P.  106 ANNIVERSARY  125 Till then my Muse shall hollow far behind
     P.  125 O.C.         106 As hollow Seas with future Tempests rage:
     P.  164 INSTRUCTIONS 977 Nor Earthquake so an hollow Isle overwhelm,

holt                                    frequency:    1    relative frequency: 0.0000
     P.  315 CHEQUER INN   97 Holt out of Linnen (as for Land)

holt-felsters                           frequency:    1    relative frequency: 0.0000
     P.   75 A. HOUSE     538 Who here has the Holt-felsters care.

holy                                    frequency:   21    relative frequency: 0.0004
     P.   18 BERMUDAS      38 An holy and a chearful Note,
     P.   24 NYMPH         98 The holy Frankincense doth flow.
     P.   60 A. HOUSE      47 These holy Mathematicks can
     P.   62 A. HOUSE      97 'Within this holy leisure we
     P.   62 A. HOUSE     122 'Some One the holy Legend reads;
     P.   63 A. HOUSE     140 'To holy things, for Heaven fit.
     P.   66 A. HOUSE     238 Standing upon their holy Guard.
     P.   67 A. HOUSE     263 But truly bright and holy Thwaites
     P.  106 ANNIVERSARY  108 The path where holy Oracles do lead;
     P.  139 HOUSEWARMING  86 And with matter profane, cemented with holy,
     P.  168 ADVICE         3 There holy Charles, here good Aurelius Sate,
     P.  174 LOYALL SCOT   88 'Tis Holy Island parts us not the Tweed.
     P.  175 LOYALL SCOT  149 And holy Ordure Holy orders give?
     P.  186 BRITANNIA     82 If not ore aw'd by new found holy cheat.
     P.  188 BRITANNIA    162 To love sobriety and holy truth,
     P.  189 BRITANNIA    187 Soe shall my England by a Holy Warr
     P.  198 DUKE           9 Most holy Father, being joyned in league
     P.  203 HISTORICALL  113 And touch the holy function with her Verse:
     P.  205 HISTORICALL  159 Tells him the holy Church demands his aide,
     P.  205 HISTORICALL  169 The holy Scripture vindicates his Cause,

holy-day                                frequency:    1    relative frequency: 0.0000
     P.  149 INSTRUCTIONS 354 Be Broach'd again, for the great Holy-day

holy-water                              frequency:    2    relative frequency: 0.0000
     P.   62 A. HOUSE     111 'And Holy-water of our Tears
     P.   66 A. HOUSE     252 With their old Holy-Water Brush.

holyness                                frequency:    1    relative frequency: 0.0000
     P.  127 O.C.         178 For Holyness the Confessor exceeds.

homage                                  frequency:    1    relative frequency: 0.0000
     P.   47 EMPIRE        21 Victorious sounds! yet here your Homage do

home                                    frequency:   19    relative frequency: 0.0003
     See also "at-home."
     P.   16 EYES          33 Not full sailes hasting loaden home,
     P.   19 THYRSIS        7 Dorinda. I know no way, but one, our home;
     P.   43 DAMON         47 While, going home, the Ev'ning sweet
     P.   45 GLO-WORMS     16 That I shall never find my home.
     P.   87 FLECKNO      160 Home, his most furious Satyr to have fir'd
     P.   92 MAY'S DEATH   84 When thou hadst drunk thy last to lead thee home.
     P.   92 MAY'S DEATH   85 If that can be thy home where Spencer lyes
     P.   98 HOLLAND      101 But when such Amity at home is show'd;
     P.   98 HOLLAND      121 And the torn Navy stagger'd with him home,
     P.   98 HOLLAND      126 Half bound at home in Prison to the frost:
     P.  112 ANNIVERSARY  390 'At Home a Subject on the equal Floor.
     P.  152 INSTRUCTIONS 460 Then to return home straight infecta re.
     P.  152 INSTRUCTIONS 476 To work the Peace, and so to send them home.
     P.  165 KINGS VOWES   18 And yet call him home again, soon as I may.
     P.  169 ADVICE        62 To be at home made such a presedent!
     P.  174 LOYALL SCOT  109 Pharoah at first would have sent Israell home.
     P.  201 HISTORICALL    6 The People call him home to helpe the State,
     P.  204 HISTORICALL  155 From Tybur came the advice boat Monthly home,
     P.  317 CHEQUER INN  181 Just like our Rotten Pump at home

homely                                  frequency:    1    relative frequency: 0.0000
     P.  150 INSTRUCTIONS 393 With homely sight, they chose thus to relax

honest                                  frequency:    4    relative frequency: 0.0000
     P.   55 THYESTE       11 An old honest Country man.
     P.   99 HOLLAND      148 Watchful abroad, and honest still within.
     P.  121 TWO SONGS     57 But to be honest, valiant, wise,
     P.  195 TWO HORSES   155 Ch. Yet have wee one Secretary honest and wise:

honey.  See "hony."

honor                                   frequency:    1    relative frequency: 0.0000
```

```
      See also "honour."
      P. 107 ANNIVERSARY      166 But never any did them Honor so;

honored.  See "honour'd."

honors.  See "honours."

honour                          frequency:   12   relative frequency: 0.0002
      See also "honor."
      P.   3 LOVELACE          10 To honour not her selfe, but worthy men.
      P.  26 MISTRESS          29 And your quaint Honour turn to dust;
      P.  60 A. HOUSE          57 So Honour better Lowness bears,
      P.  63 A. HOUSE         151 'Ah, no! and 'twould more Honour prove
      P.  66 A. HOUSE         233 Small Honour would be in the Storm.
      P. 120 TWO SONGS         34 Seeks but the honour to have held out longest.
      P. 126 O.C.             142 Of honour; all the Year was Cromwell's day:
      P. 130 O.C.             286 Always thy honour, praise and name, shall last.
      P. 179 STOCKSMARKET       7 When with honour he might from his word have gone
                                  back;
      P. 187 BRITANNIA        118 Had lost all sense of Honour, Justice, fame;
      P. 200 DUKE              82 The Hero once gett honour by the sword;
      P. 203 HISTORICALL       88 Riches and honour they from Lay-men reap,

honour'd                        frequency:    2   relative frequency: 0.0000
      P.  93 DR. WITTY          2 Where just desert enrolles thy honour'd Name
      P. 129 O.C.             264 And honour'd wreaths have oft the victour
                                  crown'd.

honours                         frequency:    2   relative frequency: 0.0000
      P. 127 O.C.             158 Have such high honours from above been shown:
      P. 157 INSTRUCTIONS     673 Much him the Honours of his ancient Race

hony                            frequency:    3   relative frequency: 0.0000
      P.  15 EYES              20 No Hony, but these Tears could draw.
      P.  42 DAMON             38 And Oak leaves tipt with hony due.
      P. 178 LOYALL SCOT      273 And Each works hony for the Common Hive.

hoofs                           frequency:    1   relative frequency: 0.0000
      P. 108 ANNIVERSARY      198 Nor their round Hoofs, or curled Mane's
                                  compare;

hook                            frequency:    3   relative frequency: 0.0000
      P. 122 TWO SONGS         18 Far more catching then my Hook.
      P. 138 HOUSEWARMING      60 As by hook and by crook the world cluster'd of
                                  Atome.
      P. 141 INSTRUCTIONS      16 With Hook then, through the microscope, take aim

hook-shoulder                   frequency:    1   relative frequency: 0.0000
      P. 145 INSTRUCTIONS     163 Still his Hook-shoulder seems the blow to dread,

hook-shoulder'd                 frequency:    1   relative frequency: 0.0000
      P.  56 BILL-BOROW        11 That do with your hook-shoulder'd height

hooks                           frequency:    1   relative frequency: 0.0000
      P.  79 A. HOUSE         649 But now away my Hooks, my Quills,

hooting.  See "houting."

hooves                          frequency:    1   relative frequency: 0.0000
      P. 143 INSTRUCTIONS      96 His sweaty Hooves, tickles him 'twixt the Toes.

hope                            frequency:   15   relative frequency: 0.0003
      P.  19 THYRSIS           21 Thyrsis. Oh, ther's, neither hope nor fear
      P.  21 SOUL & BODY       33 Whom first the Cramp of Hope does Tear:
      P.  37 DEFINITION         7 Where feeble Hope could ne'r have flown
      P.  46 AMETAS            13 What you cannot constant hope
      P.  88 ODE               49 Where, twining subtile fears with hope,
      P. 106 ANNIVERSARY      135 What we might hope, what wonderful Effect
      P. 112 ANNIVERSARY      392 'So should I hope yet he might Dye as wee.
      P. 122 TWO SONGS         33 What Shepherdess could hope to wed
      P. 152 INSTRUCTIONS     475 But still in hope he solac'd, e're they come,
      P. 156 INSTRUCTIONS     652 While envious Virgins hope he is a Male.
      P. 172 LOYALL SCOT       18 Whilst Envious virgins hope hee is a Male.
      P. 180 STOCKSMARKET      58 As ever you hope in December for Spring,
      P. 192 TWO HORSES        49 Ch. Tho he chang'd his Religion I hope hee 's
                                  so civill
      P. 199 DUKE              64 And to destroy our libertyes they hope
      P. 204 HISTORICALL      140 T'hunt down 's Prey and hope to master all.

hopeful                         frequency:    1   relative frequency: 0.0000
      P. 201 HISTORICALL       28 To wish her hopeful Issue timely Joy.
```

hopes   frequency: 13   relative frequency: 0.0002
    P.   28 LOVER   33 They fed him up with Hopes and Air,
    P.   33 DAPHNIS   3 That must all his Hopes devour,
    P.   39 PICTURE   40 Nip in the blossome all our hopes and Thee.
    P.   41 DAMON   8 And wither'd like his Hopes the Grass.
    P.   45 MOWER'S SONG   4 Did see its Hopes as in a Glass;
    P. 108 ANNIVERSARY   190 On their own Hopes shall find the Fall retort.
    P. 122 TWO SONGS   30 Whose Hopes united banish our Despair.
    P. 123 TWO SONGS   48 Whose Hopes united banish our Despair.
    P. 125 O.C.   100 Frustrates the Autumn and the hopes of Wine.
    P. 144 INSTRUCTIONS 159 Expectants pale, with hopes of spoil allur'd,
    P. 155 INSTRUCTIONS 586 And all our hopes now on frail Chain depend:
    P. 159 INSTRUCTIONS 751 Now with vain grief their vainer hopes they rue,
    P. 199 DUKE   52 Then in false hopes of being once a Queene

horace   frequency: 1   relative frequency: 0.0000
    P.   91 MAY'S DEATH   36 And Horace patiently its stroke does take,

horatian   frequency: 1   relative frequency: 0.0000
    P.   87 ODE   t An Horatian Ode upon Cromwel's Return from
                             Ireland.

horn   frequency: 3   relative frequency: 0.0000
    P. 106 ANNIVERSARY   124 Winding his Horn to Kings that chase the
                             Beast.
    P. 144 INSTRUCTIONS 162 Wood these commands, Knight of the Horn and
                             Cane.
    P. 150 INSTRUCTIONS 407 With the Bulls Horn to measure his own Head,

horribly   frequency: 1   relative frequency: 0.0000
    P. 196 TWO HORSES   168 Both Gallopt to Whitehall and there Horribly
                             farted,

horrid   frequency: 5   relative frequency: 0.0001
    P.   30 THE GALLERY   29 Divining thence, with horrid Care,
    P. 107 ANNIVERSARY   152 Swinges the Volumes of its horrid Flail.
    P. 123 O.C.   8 Death when more horrid so more noble deem;
    P. 157 INSTRUCTIONS 661 Fixt on his Ship, he fac'd that horrid Day,
    P. 172 LOYALL SCOT   27 Fix'd on his ship hee fac'd the horrid day

horror   frequency: 2   relative frequency: 0.0000
    See also "horrour."
    P.   79 A. HOUSE   671 And such an horror calm and dumb,
    P. 116 BLAKE   87 Who on the Ocean that does horror give,

horrour   frequency: 3   relative frequency: 0.0000
    See also "horror."
    P. 132 PARADISE   35 At once delight and horrour on us seize,
    P. 162 INSTRUCTIONS 889 There, as in the calm horrour all alone,
    P. 186 BRITANNIA   68 Pale death, lusts, Horrour fill her pompous
                             train.

hors   frequency: 4   relative frequency: 0.0000
    P. 169 ADVICE   41 And after him a brave Bregade of Hors
    P. 191 STATUE   44 And wee've lost both our King, our Hors and our
                             Crupper.
    P. 192 TWO HORSES   35 W. Quoth the marble white Hors: 'twould make a
                             stone speak
    P. 193 TWO HORSES   67 W. That makeing us slaves by hors and foot
                             Guards

horsback   frequency: 1   relative frequency: 0.0000
    P. 190 STATUE   18 The late King on Horsback is here to be shown:

horse   frequency: 5   relative frequency: 0.0001
    See also "cock-horse," "hobby-horse," "hors,"
             "pack-horse."
    P.   66 A. HOUSE   246 His Horse through conquer'd Britain ride?
    P. 152 INSTRUCTIONS 482 (As if, alas, we Ships or Dutch had Horse.)
    P. 179 STOCKSMARKET   13 When each one that passes finds fault with the
                             horse,
    P. 190 STATUE   25 The Trojan Horse, tho' not of Brass but of
                             wood,
    P. 190 STATUE   29 But his brother-in-law's horse had gain'd such
                             repute

horse-leeches   frequency: 1   relative frequency: 0.0000
    P. 153 INSTRUCTIONS 497 Horse-leeches circling at the Hem'roid Vein;

horseback   frequency: 1   relative frequency: 0.0000
    See also "horsback."
    P. 190 STATUE   28 For the old King on Horseback is but an
                                                      Halfecrown.

horsemen   frequency: 1   relative frequency: 0.0000
    P.   77 A. HOUSE   608 And gaul its Horsemen all the Day.

horses   frequency: 10   relative frequency: 0.0002
    P.   73 A. HOUSE   475 How Horses at their Tails do kick,
    P. 107 ANNIVERSARY   178 Hurry'd thy Horses while they hurry'd thee.
    P. 126 O.C.   123 The Race of warlike Horses at his Tomb
    P. 129 O.C.   244 In horses fierce, wild deer, or armour bright;
    P. 145 INSTRUCTIONS   196 Whose Horses each with other enterfeers.
    P. 191 TWO HORSES   t1 A Dialogue between the Two Horses.
    P. 192 TWO HORSES   24 Of a Dialogue lately between the two Horses,
    P. 192 TWO HORSES   25 The Horses I mean of Woolchurch and Charing,
    P. 196 TWO HORSES   166 Which two inanimate Horses declare.
    P. 196 TWO HORSES   173 Why might not our Horses, since words are but
                                wind,

hosanna   frequency: 1   relative frequency: 0.0000
    P. 106 ANNIVERSARY   113 Hence still they sing Hosanna to the Whore,

hose   frequency: 1   relative frequency: 0.0000
    P. 315 CHEQUER INN   95 Had sowd on too his double Hose

host   frequency: 7   relative frequency: 0.0001
    See also "country-host."
    P.   84 FLECKNO   61 With consecrated Wafers: and the Host
    P. 146 INSTRUCTIONS   219 Never, before nor since, an Host so steel'd
    P. 183 MADE FREE   96 With the Pox and the Host within it?
    P. 313 CHEQUER INN   13 The Host, that dwells in that same House
    P. 316 CHEQUER INN   151 The Host that sate at Lower end
    P. 316 CHEQUER INN   158 Till King both Hostesse kist and Host
    P. 317 CHEQUER INN   184 Soe when mine Host doth Money lack

hostesse   frequency: 1   relative frequency: 0.0000
    P. 316 CHEQUER INN   158 Till King both Hostesse kist and Host

hostile   frequency: 1   relative frequency: 0.0000
    P.   57 BILL-BOROW   35 No hostile hand durst ere invade

hosts   frequency: 1   relative frequency: 0.0000
    P. 203 HISTORICALL   111 And hosts of upstart Errours gaine the field.

hot   frequency: 7   relative frequency: 0.0001
    P.   40 THE MATCH   35 None ever burn'd so hot, so bright;
    P.   42 DAMON   26 Of the hot day, or hot desires.
    P. 144 INSTRUCTIONS   143 Black Birch, of all the Earth-born race most
                                hot,
    P. 161 INSTRUCTIONS   831 The portly Burgess, through the Weather hot,
    P. 162 INSTRUCTIONS   883 At night, than Canticleer more brisk and hot,
    P. 202 HISTORICALL   45 But now Yorkes Genitalls grew over hot

hotter   frequency: 1   relative frequency: 0.0000
    P.   42 DAMON   22 Hotter then his own Phaeton.

hounds   frequency: 2   relative frequency: 0.0000
    P.   90 ODE   111 Nor lay his Hounds in near
    P. 149 INSTRUCTIONS   335 Blither than Hare that hath escap'd the Hounds,

hound's   frequency: 1   relative frequency: 0.0000
    P. 141 INSTRUCTIONS   22 Of his Hound's Mouth to feign the raging froth,

hour   frequency: 8   relative frequency: 0.0001
    See also "houre."
    P.   33 DAPHNIS   2 Now is come the dismal Hour
    P.   89 ODE   65 This was that memorable Hour
    P. 105 ANNIVERSARY   71 Whose num'rous Gorge could swallow in an hour
    P. 106 ANNIVERSARY   131 Hence oft I think, if in some happy Hour
    P. 121 TWO SONGS   9 They ha' chosen such an hour
    P. 126 O.C.   138 Left to determine now his fatal Hour;
    P. 158 INSTRUCTIONS   739 Or row a Boat in thy unlucky hour:
    P. 162 INSTRUCTIONS   892 Though ill agree her Posture, Hour, or Place:

houre   frequency: 1   relative frequency: 0.0000
    P. 130 O.C.   312 A Cromwell in an houre a prince will grow.

hourly   frequency: 3   relative frequency: 0.0000
    P.   62 A. HOUSE   107 'And our chast Lamps we hourly trim,
    P. 104 ANNIVERSARY   42 And with vain Scepter, strike the hourly Bell;
    P. 160 INSTRUCTIONS   819 Hyde saith he hourly waits for a Dispatch;

hours   frequency: 5   relative frequency: 0.0001

P.	50	THE GARDEN	71 How could such sweet and wholsome Hours
P.	82	A. HOUSE	746 Where yet She leads her studious Hours,
P.	110	ANNIVERSARY	274 Counted the Hours, and ev'ry Star did spy,
P.	124	O.C.	47 With her each day the pleasing Hours he shares,
P.	171	PROPHECY	38 To make starcht empty Speeches two hours long.

hous   frequency: 4   relative frequency: 0.0000
P.	169	ADVICE	49 Two of the five recanters of the Hous
P.	169	ADVICE	54 To overthrow the Darby Hous designes,
P.	192	TWO HORSES	52 By a Curst hous of Commons and a blest Restauracion;
P.	193	TWO HORSES	77 Ch. That Traitors to their Country in a Erib'd Hous of Commons

house   frequency: 27   relative frequency: 0.0005
See also "hous."
P.	58	BILL-BOROW	52 The Genius of the house do bind.
P.	59	A. HOUSE	t Upon Appleton House, to my Lord Fairfax.
P.	60	A. HOUSE	49 Yet thus the laden House does sweat,
P.	61	A. HOUSE	69 The House was built upon the Place
P.	65	A. HOUSE	209 'Were there but, when this House was made,
P.	67	A. HOUSE	280 'Twas no Religious House till now.
P.	91	MAY'S DEATH	50 As Bethlem's House did to Loretto walk.
P.	105	ANNIVERSARY	82 Each in the House the highest Place contends,
P.	110	ANNIVERSARY	283 Thou, and thine House, like Noah's Eight did rest,
P.	128	O.C.	202 The first foundation of his house and name:
P.	137	HOUSEWARMING	12 How he might create a House with a Fiat.
P.	138	HOUSEWARMING	56 For his House then would grow like a Vegetable.
P.	139	HOUSEWARMING	95 Your Metropolis House is in St. James's Fields,
P.	140	HIS HOUSE	t Upon his House.
P.	143	INSTRUCTIONS	106 The House of Commons clatt'ring like the Men.
P.	146	INSTRUCTIONS	205 The Papists, but of those the House had none:
P.	146	INSTRUCTIONS	235 Thick was the Morning, and the House was thin,
P.	148	INSTRUCTIONS	314 To cheat their Pay, feign want, the House accuse.
P.	148	INSTRUCTIONS	325 Long thus they could against the House conspire,
P.	149	INSTRUCTIONS	336 The House Prorogu'd, the Chancellor rebounds.
P.	150	INSTRUCTIONS	383 But the just Street does the next House invade,
P.	154	INSTRUCTIONS	564 Which, if a House, yet were not tenantable.
P.	182	MADE FREE	58 And the House was well barr'd,
P.	198	DUKE	23 Theire house of Commons and their house of Lords,
P.	313	CHEQUER INN	9 There stands a House new Painted
P.	313	CHEQUER INN	13 The Host, that dwells in that same House

house-warming   frequency: 1   relative frequency: 0.0000
P.	137	HOUSEWARMING	t Clarindon's House-Warming.

houses   frequency: 5   relative frequency: 0.0001
P.	3	LOVELACE	28 You wrong'd in her the Houses Priviledge.
P.	61	A. HOUSE	84 The Progress of this Houses Fate.
P.	158	INSTRUCTIONS	714 The Houses were demolish'd near the Tow'r.
P.	161	INSTRUCTIONS	824 Binding, e're th' Houses meet, the Treaty sure.
P.	181	MADE FREE	8 And your Houses undwelt

houting   frequency: 1   relative frequency: 0.0000
P. 150 INSTRUCTIONS 386 And Boys and Girls in Troops run houting by;

how   frequency: 128   relative frequency: 0.0026

howard   frequency: 1   relative frequency: 0.0000
See also "how'rd."
P. 185 BRITANNIA   17 Till Howard and Garway shall a bribe reject,

howere   frequency: 1   relative frequency: 0.0000

however   frequency: 4   relative frequency: 0.0000
See also "howere."

howl   frequency: 1   relative frequency: 0.0000
P. 158 INSTRUCTIONS 715 Those Ships, that yearly from their teeming Howl,

how'rd   frequency: 1   relative frequency: 0.0000
P. 147 INSTRUCTIONS 265 Of Birth, State, Wit, Strength, Courage, How'rd presumes,

howso'ere   frequency: 1   relative frequency: 0.0000

howsoever. See "howso'ere."

hubbub   frequency: 1   relative frequency: 0.0000

P. 176 LOYALL SCOT   202 The Mitred Hubbub against Pluto Moot

hue   frequency: 1   relative frequency: 0.0000
    See also "changing-hue."
    P. 201 HISTORICALL   1 Of a tall Stature and of sable hue,

hug. See "hugg."

huge   frequency: 4   relative frequency: 0.0000
    P. 17 BERMUDAS   9 Where he the huge Sea-Monsters wracks,
    P. 73 A. HOUSE   459 And shrunk in the huge Pasture show
    P. 74 A. HOUSE   501 There the huge Bulk takes place, as ment
    P. 126 O.C.   119 Or of huge Trees, whose growth with his did
                              rise,

hugg   frequency: 1   relative frequency: 0.0000
    P. 183 MADE FREE   88 How you hugg it and draw,

huggs   frequency: 1   relative frequency: 0.0000
    P. 173 LOYALL SCOT   56 As one that Huggs himself in a Warm bed.

hugs. See "huggs."

human   frequency: 2   relative frequency: 0.0000
    See also "humane."
    P. 203 HISTORICALL   106 Hence Death and Sin did human Nature blot:
    P. 205 HISTORICALL   170 And Monarchs are above all human Lawes.

humane   frequency: 11   relative frequency: 0.0002
    P. 12 DROP OF DEW   21 Could it within the humane flow'r be seen,
    P. 16 EYES   48 But only humane Eyes can weep.
    P. 31 MOURNING   2 Of humane Off-springs from the Skies,
    P. 63 A. HOUSE   144 'That something more then humane speaks.
    P. 123 O.C.   22 (Those nobler weaknesses of humane Mind,
    P. 125 O.C.   109 But never yet was any humane Fate
    P. 127 O.C.   162 Then those of Moses hid from humane Eyes;
    P. 128 O.C.   217 What prudence more than humane did he need
    P. 129 O.C.   255 Oh! humane glory, vaine, oh! death, oh! wings,
    P. 130 O.C.   288 Of humane glory tow'rst, and raigning there
    P. 132 PARADISE   37 And above humane flight dost soar aloft,

humankind   frequency: 1   relative frequency: 0.0000
    P. 187 BRITANNIA   102 As these grow stale weel Harass humankind,

humber   frequency: 1   relative frequency: 0.0000
    P. 26 MISTRESS   7 Of Humber would complain. I would

humble   frequency: 4   relative frequency: 0.0000
    P. 56 BILL-BOROW   15 Learn here those humble steps to tread,
    P. 143 INSTRUCTIONS   92 That to a Groom couldst humble her disdain!
    P. 169 ADVICE   38 The humble fate of a Plebeian nose;
    P. 199 DUKE   56 Clifford, who first appeared in humble guise,

humbly   frequency: 2   relative frequency: 0.0000
    P. 106 ANNIVERSARY   107 And in their numbred Footsteps humbly tread
    P. 198 DUKE   11 Throwne att thy sacred feete I humbly bow,

humility   frequency: 2   relative frequency: 0.0000
    P. 11 DIALOGUE   74 Of Knowledge, but Humility.
    P. 60 A. HOUSE   41 Humility alone designs

humor   frequency: 1   relative frequency: 0.0000
    See also "humour."
    P. 172 LOYALL SCOT   9 Much had hee Cur'd the Humor of his vein:

humour   frequency: 1   relative frequency: 0.0000
    See also "humor."
    P. 125 O.C.   96 And through the Wound its vital humour bleeds;

hums   frequency: 1   relative frequency: 0.0000
    P. 68 A. HOUSE   291 The Bee through these known Allies hums,

hundred   frequency: 7   relative frequency: 0.0001
    P. 26 MISTRESS   13 An hundred years should go to praise
    P. 26 MISTRESS   15 Two hundred to adore each Breast:
    P. 97 HOLLAND   83 Some Fifteen hundred and more years ago;
    P. 144 INSTRUCTIONS 135 With hundred rows of Teeth the Shark exceeds,
    P. 149 INSTRUCTIONS 332 Bought off with Eighteen hundred thousand pound.
    P. 152 INSTRUCTIONS 492 (The Eighteen hundred thousand pound was gone.)
    P. 316 CHEQUER INN   138 And made above a Hundred.

hung   frequency: 5   relative frequency: 0.0001

```
P.   20 SOUL & BODY      7 A Soul hung up, as 'twere, in Chains
P.   86 FLECKNO        127 And so the Pelican at his door hung
P.  111 ANNIVERSARY    331 While dismal blacks hung round the Universe,
P.  129 O.C.           263 Whose spacious boughs are hung with trophies
                           round,
P.  161 INSTRUCTIONS   842 Trusty as Steel, that always ready hung;
```

hungry   frequency: 5   relative frequency: 0.0001
```
P.   84 FLECKNO         43 Whose hungry Guts to the same streightness
                           twin'd
P.   84 FLECKNO         52 So hungry that though ready to say Mass
P.   96 HOLLAND        40 Among the hungry he that treasures Grain,
P.  176 LOYALL SCOT    174 A Hungry Chaplain and a Starved Rat
P.  186 BRITANNIA       85 Bribe hungry Priests to deify your might,
```

hunt   frequency: 2   relative frequency: 0.0000
```
P.   22 NYMPH          32 Hath taught a Faun to hunt his Dear.
P.  173 LOYALL SCOT    70 Nor Chaunt the fabulous hunt of Chivy Chase:
```

hunted   frequency: 1   relative frequency: 0.0000
```
P.   48 THE GARDEN     29 Apollo hunted Daphne so,
```

hunter   frequency: 1   relative frequency: 0.0000
```
P.   90 ODE           110 The English Hunter him mistake;
```

huntsman   frequency: 2   relative frequency: 0.0000
```
P.   22 NYMPH          31 Said He, look how your Huntsman here
P.  106 ANNIVERSARY   123 Like the shrill Huntsman that prevents the
                          East,
```

hurld   frequency: 1   relative frequency: 0.0000
```
P.  186 BRITANNIA      79 This Mortall poyson amongst Princes hurld,
```

hurl'd   frequency: 3   relative frequency: 0.0000
```
P.   28 LOVER         23 While round the ratling Thunder hurl'd,
P.   82 A. HOUSE     762 But a rude heap together hurl'd;
P.  185 BRITANNIA     41 Were Hurl'd to Hell by Learning Tyrants
                         Lore.
```

hurled. See "hurld," "hurl'd."

hurles   frequency: 1   relative frequency: 0.0000
```
P.  105 ANNIVERSARY   100 He hurles e'r since the World about him round;
```

hurls   frequency: 1   relative frequency: 0.0000
See also "hurles."
```
P.  164 INSTRUCTIONS   954 And hurls them off, e're since, in his Career.
```

hurricane   frequency: 1   relative frequency: 0.0000
```
P.   28 LOVER         32 The Orphan of the Hurricane.
```

hurricans   frequency: 1   relative frequency: 0.0000
```
P.  112 ANNIVERSARY   362 'Arm'd with three Tire of brazen Hurricans;
```

hurried   frequency: 1   relative frequency: 0.0000
See also "hurry'd."
```
P.    4 HASTINGS      16 Are hurried hence, as if already old.
```

hurry   frequency: 1   relative frequency: 0.0000
```
P.  109 ANNIVERSARY   266 Hurry the Bark, but more the Seamens minds,
```

hurry'd   frequency: 3   relative frequency: 0.0000
```
P.   90 MAY'S DEATH    2 Tom May was hurry'd hence and did not know't.
P.  107 ANNIVERSARY   178 Hurry'd thy Horses while they hurry'd thee.
```

hurrying   frequency: 1   relative frequency: 0.0000
```
P.   26 MISTRESS      22 Times winged Charriot hurrying near:
```

hurt   frequency: 2   relative frequency: 0.0000
```
P.   75 A. HOUSE     519 The Thorn, lest it should hurt her, draws
P.  128 O.C.         197 Pity it seem'd to hurt him more that felt
```

hurts   frequency: 1   relative frequency: 0.0000
```
P.   44 DAMON        81 Alas! said He, these hurts are slight
```

husband   frequency: 3   relative frequency: 0.0000
```
P.  150 INSTRUCTIONS  380 And beats the Husband till for peace he prays:
P.  163 INSTRUCTIONS  932 To her own Husband, Castlemain, untrue.
P.  199 DUKE          50 Where twixt a wholsome husband and a page
```

husbandman   frequency: 2   relative frequency: 0.0000

P. 110 ANNIVERSARY   286 Which thou but as an Husbandman wouldst Till:
P. 178 LOYALL SCOT   266 Just soe the prudent Husbandman who sees

husbandry   frequency: 1   relative frequency: 0.0000
     P. 160 INSTRUCTIONS   797 But sure his late good Husbandry in Peeter,

hush   frequency: 1   relative frequency: 0.0000
     P. 80 A. HOUSE   681 Maria such, and so doth hush

huswifely   frequency: 1   relative frequency: 0.0000
     P. 191 STATUE   41 The Huswifely Treasuress sure is grown nice

hut   frequency: 1   relative frequency: 0.0000
     P. 68 A. HOUSE   317 Then in some Flow'rs beloved Hut

hyde   frequency: 9   relative frequency: 0.0001
     P. 137 HOUSEWARMING   24 As might carry the measure and name of an Hyde.
     P. 140 HOUSEWARMING   106 That for Name-sake he may with Hyde Park it
                                  enlarge,
     P. 152 INSTRUCTIONS   487 Hyde Stamps, and straight upon the ground the
                                  swarms
     P. 160 INSTRUCTIONS   808 Hyde and the Court again begin to mourn.
     P. 160 INSTRUCTIONS   819 Hyde saith he hourly waits for a Dispatch;
     P. 161 INSTRUCTIONS   834 And threaten Hyde to raise a greater Dust.
     P. 161 INSTRUCTIONS   851 Hyde orders Turner that he should come late,
     P. 161 INSTRUCTIONS   861 Trembling with joy and fear, Hyde them
                                  Prorogues,
     P. 163 INSTRUCTIONS   941 While Hyde provok'd his foaming tusk does whet,

hyde's   frequency: 4   relative frequency: 0.0000
     P. 144 INSTRUCTIONS   129 Hyde's Avarice, Bennet's Luxury should
                                  suffice,
     P. 152 INSTRUCTIONS   465 Hyde's flippant Stile there pleasantly curvets;
     P. 153 INSTRUCTIONS   522 And Hyde's last Project would his Place
                                  dispose.
     P. 163 INSTRUCTIONS   926 And rising, straight on Hyde's Disgrace
                                  resolves.

hydra   frequency: 1   relative frequency: 0.0000
     P. 99 HOLLAND   137 And now the Hydra of seaven Provinces

hyes   frequency: 1   relative frequency: 0.0000
     P. 104 ANNIVERSARY   45 While indefatigable Cromwell hyes,

hymeneus   frequency: 1   relative frequency: 0.0000
     P.   5 HASTINGS   43 Onely they drooping Hymeneus note,

hypocrite   frequency: 1   relative frequency: 0.0000
     P. 65 A. HOUSE   205 'Hypocrite Witches, hence avant,

hypocrites   frequency: 1   relative frequency: 0.0000
     P. 175 LOYALL SCOT   157 These Hypocrites their faith and Linnen stain.

hypocritically   frequency: 1   relative frequency: 0.0000
     P. 111 ANNIVERSARY   317 Oh Race most hypocritically strict!

i   frequency: 269   relative frequency: 0.0056
     See also "ile," "i'le," "i'll," "i'lle," "i'm," "i'me," "i've."

i'   frequency: 1   relative frequency: 0.0000
     P. 316 CHEQUER INN   162 He'd bring him off i' fack.

icy   frequency: 1   relative frequency: 0.0000
     P. 42 DAMON   32 Nor Cold but in her Icy Breast.

id--   frequency: 1   relative frequency: 0.0000
     P. 177 LOYALL SCOT   231 Oppression Avarice Ambition Id--

idalian   frequency: 1   relative frequency: 0.0000
     P. 82 A. HOUSE   757 But name not the Idalian Grove,

ida's   frequency: 1   relative frequency: 0.0000
     P. 120 TWO SONGS   32 Sporting with him in Ida's shade:

idle   frequency: 3   relative frequency: 0.0000
     P. 22 NYMPH   40 Could so mine idle Life have spent.
     P. 79 A. HOUSE   650 And Angles, idle Utensils.
     P. 178 LOYALL SCOT   267 The Idle tumult of his factious bees,

idleness. See "id--" and "leness."

idol   frequency: 2   relative frequency: 0.0000

```
       P. 140 HOUSEWARMING    98 Where this Idol of State sits ador'd and
                                 accurst:
       P. 203 HISTORICALL     79 To the black Idol for an Offering.

idolls                            frequency:    1    relative frequency: 0.0000
       P. 192 TWO HORSES      19 Those Idolls ne're speak, but the miracle 's
                                 done

idols.  See "idolls."

if                                frequency:  121    relative frequency: 0.0025
       See also "if't."

if't                              frequency:    1    relative frequency: 0.0000

ignorance                         frequency:    2    relative frequency: 0.0000
       P.  91 MAY'S DEATH     55 But the nor Ignorance nor seeming good
       P. 132 PARADISE        30 But to detect their Ignorance or Theft.

ignorantly                        frequency:    1    relative frequency: 0.0000
       P. 106 ANNIVERSARY    117 Unhappy Princes, ignorantly bred,

ile                               frequency:    4    relative frequency: 0.0000

i'le                              frequency:    9    relative frequency: 0.0001

ill                               frequency:   25    relative frequency: 0.0005
       P.  21 SOUL & BODY     20 Since this ill Spirit it possest.
       P.  22 NYMPH            7 I'me sure I never wisht them ill;
       P.  25 YOUNG LOVE      24 Or, if ill, that Ill prevent.
       P.  55 EPITAPH          5 Where never any could speak ill,
       P.  56 BILL-BOROW      13 For whose excrescence ill design'd,
       P.  86 FLECKNO        144 That were ill made condemn'd to be read worse:
       P.  91 MAY'S DEATH     52 How ill the measures of these States agree.
       P.  94 DR. WITTY        8 For ill Translators make the Book their own.
       P. 107 ANNIVERSARY    156 The Ill delaying, what th'elected hastes;
       P. 115 BLAKE           63 In vain doth she those Islands free from Ill,
       P. 118 BLAKE          152 The only place where it can cause no Ill.
       P. 128 O.C.           219 The worser sort, so conscious of their ill,
       P. 128 O.C.           223 Oh! ill advis'd, if not for love, for shame,
       P. 131 PARADISE        20 And by ill imitating would excell)
       P. 141 INSTRUCTIONS     7 Or canst thou dawb a Sign-post, and that ill?
       P. 146 INSTRUCTIONS   204 And in ill English all the World defy'd.
       P. 153 INSTRUCTIONS   513 If they for nothing ill, like Ashen-wood,
       P. 154 INSTRUCTIONS   567 The neighbr'hood ill, and an unwholesome seat.
       P. 162 INSTRUCTIONS   892 Though ill agree her Posture, Hour, or Place:
       P. 194 TWO HORSES     103 Tho' the beast gave his Master ne're an ill
                                 word,
       P. 198 DUKE            26 And thinke a prince oth blood can ere doe Ill?
       P. 199 DUKE            67 Laden with folly, flesh and Ill got land:
       P. 202 HISTORICALL     57 But since the ill gott race of Stewarts came,
       P. 204 HISTORICALL    134 Ill luck starts up and thrives like Evil weeds.

i'll                              frequency:    2    relative frequency: 0.0000
       See also "ile," "i'le," "i'lle."

ill-counsell'd                    frequency:    1    relative frequency: 0.0000
       P.  66 A. HOUSE       239 Ill-counsell'd Women, do you know

ill-deserted                      frequency:    1    relative frequency: 0.0000
       P. 155 INSTRUCTIONS   607 And Upnor-Castle's ill-deserted Wall,

i'lle                             frequency:    3    relative frequency: 0.0000

ills                              frequency:    3    relative frequency: 0.0000
       P. 114 BLAKE           32 The benefits without the ills of rain.
       P. 124 O.C.            64 And so diminishing increast their ills:
       P. 183 MADE FREE       92 To cure the Dukes ills,

i'm                               frequency:    3    relative frequency: 0.0000
       See also "i'me."

image                             frequency:    3    relative frequency: 0.0000
       P.  24 NYMPH          121 For I would have thine Image be
       P. 124 O.C.            54 And him within his tortur'd Image racks.
       P. 125 O.C.            78 But the dear Image fled the Mirrour broke.

image-like                        frequency:    1    relative frequency: 0.0000
       P. 104 ANNIVERSARY     41 Thus (Image-like) an useless time they tell,

images                            frequency:    1    relative frequency: 0.0000
```

        P. 191 TWO HORSES   16 When Images speak, possesses the shrine:

imaginary   frequency: 1   relative frequency: 0.0000
        P. 69 A. HOUSE   350 These five imaginary Forts:

imagin'd   frequency: 2   relative frequency: 0.0000
        P. 83 FLECKNO   23 But I, who now imagin'd my self brought
        P. 90 MAY'S DEATH   10 He saw near hand, as he imagin'd Ares.

imbark   frequency: 2   relative frequency: 0.0000
        P. 74 A. HOUSE   483 And, while it lasts, my self imbark
        P. 97 HOLLAND   67 Sure when Religion did it self imbark,

imbraces   frequency: 1   relative frequency: 0.0000
        P. 172 LOYALL SCOT   44 And tries his first Imbraces in their sheets.

i'me   frequency: 2   relative frequency: 0.0000

imediately   frequency: 1   relative frequency: 0.0000
        P. 193 TWO HORSES   74 And get good preferment Imediately for't.

imitating   frequency: 1   relative frequency: 0.0000
        P. 131 PARADISE   20 And by ill imitating would excell)

immediately. See "imediately."

immortal   frequency: 7   relative frequency: 0.0001
        See also "imortall."
        P.   5 HASTINGS   51 For, how Immortal must their race have stood,
        P.   9 DIALOGUE   2 The weight of thine immortal Shield.
        P. 119 TWO SONGS   16 That burns with an immortal Flame.
        P. 123 O.C.   24 Although immortal, found they were not free.)
        P. 125 O.C.   87 And in himself so oft immortal try'd,
        P. 157 INSTRUCTIONS 685 But, when in his immortal Mind he felt
        P. 159 INSTRUCTIONS 750 His Empire old, to their immortal Line!

immortaliz'd   frequency: 1   relative frequency: 0.0000
        P. 126 O.C.   148 That had before immortaliz'd his Name?

immur'd   frequency: 1   relative frequency: 0.0000
        P. 188 BRITANNIA   150 Must be immur'd, lest their contagion steal

immure. See "t'immure."

imortall   frequency: 1   relative frequency: 0.0000
        P. 173 LOYALL SCOT   51 But when in his Imortall mind hee felt

impair   frequency: 1   relative frequency: 0.0000
        P. 140 HOUSEWARMING 110 Lest with driving too far his Tallow impair;

impales   frequency: 1   relative frequency: 0.0000
        P. 21 SOUL & BODY   13 Which, stretcht upright, impales me so,

impark. See "t'impark."

impart   frequency: 1   relative frequency: 0.0000
        P. 189 STATUE   3 Dear Wheeler impart, for wee're all at a loss

impatient   frequency: 1   relative frequency: 0.0000
        P. 200 DUKE   115 Of Monarchs murthered by the Impatient heir:

imperial   frequency: 1   relative frequency: 0.0000
        See also "imperiall."
        P. 202 HISTORICALL   56 Whilst the brave Tudors wore th' Imperial
                                 Crowne:

imperiall   frequency: 2   relative frequency: 0.0000
        P. 131 O.C.   318 His brows, like an imperiall jewell grac'd.
        P. 188 BRITANNIA   147 If this Imperiall cyl once taint the Blood,

impetuous   frequency: 1   relative frequency: 0.0000
        P. 202 HISTORICALL   60 Tainted with Pride or with impetuous lust.

impetuously   frequency: 1   relative frequency: 0.0000
        P. 125 O.C.   72 Ran out impetucusly to hasting Death.

impious   frequency: 3   relative frequency: 0.0000
        P. 57 BILL-BOROW   36 With impious Steel the sacred Shade.
        P. 108 ANNIVERSARY   189 While impious Men deceiv'd with pleasure short,
        P. 131 PARADISE   24 My causeless, yet not impious, surmise.

imploy   frequency: 1   relative frequency: 0.0000

P. 169 ADVICE   57 Thus all imploy themselves, and withcut pitty

imployd   frequency: 1   relative frequency: 0.0000
    P. 189 BRITANNIA   166 Imployd the Youth, not Taverns, Stewes and
                             playes:

imploy'd   frequency: 1   relative frequency: 0.0000
    P. 126 O.C.   150 In their own Griefs might find themselves
                             imploy'd;

imployes   frequency: 1   relative frequency: 0.0000
    P. 81 A. HOUSE   709 Nor yet in those her self imployes

imply   frequency: 1   relative frequency: 0.0000
    P. 152 INSTRUCTIONS 453 To prove by Scripture, Treaty does imply

impose   frequency: 1   relative frequency: 0.0000
    P. 172 LOYALL SCOT   6 Cleavland on whom they would the Task Impose.

impossibility   frequency: 1   relative frequency: 0.0000
    P. 36 DEFINITION   4 Upon Impossibility.

impossible   frequency: 2   relative frequency: 0.0000
    P. 84 FLECKNO   66 (His only impossible is to be rich)
    P. 86 FLECKNO   145 And how (impossible) he made yet more

imposters   frequency: 1   relative frequency: 0.0000
    P. 187 BRITANNIA   92 And by imposters Gcd and man betray'd,

impotent   frequency: 1   relative frequency: 0.0000
    P. 76 A. HOUSE   556 Tempts impotent and bashful Sin.

impregnable   frequency: 1   relative frequency: 0.0000
    P. 127 O.C.   188 The story, and impregnable Clonmell.

impression   frequency: 1   relative frequency: 0.0000
    P. 27 LOVER   8 To make impression upon Time.

imprison   frequency: 1   relative frequency: 0.0000
    P. 149 INSTRUCTIONS 350 Imprison Parents, and the Child deflowre.

improper   frequency: 1   relative frequency: 0.0000
    P. 132 PARADISE   28 And all that was improper dost omit:

improve   frequency: 1   relative frequency: 0.0000
    P. 164 INSTRUCTIONS 969 And to improve themselves, cn false pretence,

imps   frequency: 1   relative frequency: 0.0000
    P. 153 INSTRUCTIONS 495 His minion Imps that, in his secret part,

impulse   frequency: 1   relative frequency: 0.0000
    P. 201 HISTORICALL   5 At length by wcnderfull impulse of Fate

impure   frequency: 2   relative frequency: 0.0000
    P. 12 DROP OF DEW   16 Trembling lest it grow impure:
    P. 106 ANNIVERSARY   129 Which shrinking to her Rcman Den impure,

in   frequency: 682   relative frequency: 0.0142
    See also "i'," "in's," "i'th," "i'th'."

inanimate   frequency: 1   relative frequency: 0.0000
    P. 196 TWO HORSES   166 Which two inanimate Horses declare.

incamp'd   frequency: 1   relative frequency: 0.0000
    P. 77 A. HOUSE   602 These Trees have I incamp'd my Mind;

incased. See "inchas'd."

incense   frequency: 1   relative frequency: 0.0000
    See also "insense."
    P. 16 EYES   41 The Incense was to Heaven dear,

incessant   frequency: 1   relative frequency: 0.0000
    P. 62 A. HOUSE   110 'With insense of incessant Pray'r.

incest   frequency: 2   relative frequency: 0.0000
    P. 144 INSTRUCTIONS 146 Bugger'd in Incest with the mungrel Beast.
    P. 170 PROPHECY   20 And practise Incest between Seven and Eight,

inchant   frequency: 1   relative frequency: 0.0000
    P. 65 A. HOUSE   206 'Who though in prison yet inchant!

```
inchantment                        frequency:     1    relative frequency: 0.0000
     P.  67 A. HOUSE       269 Thenceforth (as when th' Inchantment ends

inchas'd                           frequency:     2    relative frequency: 0.0000
     P. 112 ANNIVERSARY    381 'He Secrecy with Number hath inchas'd,
     P. 131 O.C.           317 A pearly rainbow, where the sun inchas'd

inclose                            frequency:     3    relative frequency: 0.0000
     P.  62 A. HOUSE       101 'These Bars inclose that wider Den
     P.  87 ODE             19 And with such to inclose
     P. 163 INSTRUCTIONS   930 Which his hid mind did in its depths inclose.

incloses                           frequency:     1    relative frequency: 0.0000
     P.  12 DROP OF DEW      6 Round in its self incloses:

including                          frequency:     1    relative frequency: 0.0000
     P.  47 EMPIRE          20 Including all between the Earth and Sphear.

incognito                          frequency:     1    relative frequency: 0.0000
     P. 192 TWO HORSES      32 Were stolne of Incognito each his own way,

incorporate                        frequency:     1    relative frequency: 0.0000
     P. 139 HOUSEWARMING    68 As all Chedder Dairys club to the incorporate
                               Cheese

incorrigible                       frequency:     1    relative frequency: 0.0000
     P. 177 LOYALL SCOT    222 Incorrigible among all their paines

increas'd                          frequency:     1    relative frequency: 0.0000
     P.  85 FLECKNO        109 Together our attonement: so increas'd

increase                           frequency:     7    relative frequency: 0.0001
     See also "encrease."
     P.  35 DAPHNIS         63 Than my Losses to increase
     P.  64 A. HOUSE       167 'And that, once sprung, increase so fast
     P. 154 INSTRUCTIONS   572 March straight to Chatham, to increase the fear.
     P. 157 INSTRUCTIONS   700 Ally'd in Fate, increase, with theirs, her
                               Flames.
     P. 163 INSTRUCTIONS   905 In his deep thoughts the wonder did increase,
     P. 178 LOYALL SCOT    257 Perverted serve dissentions to increase.
     P. 196 TWO HORSES     183 'Tis wine and Strong drink makes tumults
                               increase;

increasing                         frequency:     1    relative frequency: 0.0000
     P. 103 ANNIVERSARY      4 In the weak Circles of increasing Years;

increast                           frequency:     5    relative frequency: 0.0001
     P.   4 HASTINGS        19 Had he but at this Measure still increast,
     P.  28 LOVER           38 He both consumed, and increast:
     P.  73 A. HOUSE       453 And what below the Sith increast
     P. 124 O.C.            64 And so diminishing increast their ills:
     P. 144 INSTRUCTIONS   145 And, of his Brat enamour'd, as't increast,

indanger                           frequency:     1    relative frequency: 0.0000
     P. 123 O.C.            14 Indanger him, or Clemency that would.

indeed                             frequency:     9    relative frequency: 0.0001
     P.   5 HASTINGS        60 And Art indeed is Long, but Life is Short.
     P.  36 DAPHNIS        106 Nor indeed without a Cause.
     P.  64 A. HOUSE       177 'For such indeed are all our Arts;
     P.  74 A. HOUSE       498 It seems indeed as Wood not Trees:
     P.  87 FLECKNO        164 Praise him? both difficult indeed to do
     P. 117 LOYALL SCOT    240 And few indeed can paralell our Climes
     P. 123 O.C.            11 Nor Fate indeed can well refuse that right
     P. 174 LOYALL SCOT     87 But who Considers well will find indeed
     P. 199 DUKE            68 He's of a size indeed to fill a porch,

indefatigable                      frequency:     1    relative frequency: 0.0000
     P. 104 ANNIVERSARY     45 While indefatigable Cromwell hyes,

indefatigably                      frequency:     1    relative frequency: 0.0000
     P.  90 ODE            114 March indefatigably on;

indemnity                          frequency:     1    relative frequency: 0.0000
     P. 168 KINGS VOWES     63 Under my hand and Seal shall have Indemnity.

indented                           frequency:     1    relative frequency: 0.0000
     P. 144 INSTRUCTIONS   138 Else swallows all down her indented maw.

indentures                         frequency:     1    relative frequency: 0.0000
     P. 181 MADE FREE       30 Has every Day broke his Indentures.
```

independent   frequency: 1   relative frequency: 0.0000
    P. 153 INSTRUCTIONS   521 Soon then the Independent Troops would close,

indian   frequency: 3   relative frequency: 0.0000
    P. 26 MISTRESS   5 Thou by the Indian Ganges side
    P. 32 MOURNING   29 How wide they dream! The Indian Slaves
    P. 127 O.C.   174 And stretch'd our frontire to the Indian Ore;

indians   frequency: 2   relative frequency: 0.0000
    P. 106 ANNIVERSARY   115 But Indians whom they should convert, subdue;
    P. 141 INSTRUCTIONS   14 As th' Indians, draw our Luxury in Plumes.

indicted   frequency: 1   relative frequency: 0.0000
    P. 313 CHEQUER INN   39 For some had been Indicted

indies   frequency: 3   relative frequency: 0.0000
    P. 118 BLAKE   153 Ah would those Treasures which both Indies
                               have,
    P. 180 STOCKSMARKET   51 If the Indies and Smyrna do not him enrich,
    P. 185 BRITANNIA   31 Tell him of Golden Indies, Fayry Lands,

indiferrence   frequency: 1   relative frequency: 0.0000
    P. 176 LOYALL SCOT   209 Transfuse Indiferrence with necessity.

indifferent   frequency: 6   relative frequency: 0.0001
    P. 176 LOYALL SCOT   211 To preach in diccesse Indifferent.
    P. 176 LOYALL SCOT   213 But to reform is all Indifferent
    P. 177 LOYALL SCOT   215 To cheat the Plague money Indifferent.
    P. 177 LOYALL SCOT   217 Indifferent to Rob Churches of their Coals.
    P. 177 LOYALL SCOT   219 Indifferent to have a Wench in bed.
    P. 177 LOYALL SCOT   221 Not necessary nor Indifferent.

indigested   frequency: 1   relative frequency: 0.0000
    P. 95 HOLLAND   7 This indigested vomit of the Sea

indignation   frequency: 1   relative frequency: 0.0000
    P. 317 CHEQUER INN   177 Quoth Dick with Indignation

indite   frequency: 1   relative frequency: 0.0000
    P. 316 CHEQUER INN   161 Shou'd they Indite him o're and o're

induc'd   frequency: 1   relative frequency: 0.0000
    P. 153 INSTRUCTIONS   501 Here Men induc'd by Safety, Gain, and Ease,

indulgent   frequency: 2   relative frequency: 0.0000
    P. 115 BLAKE   53 There the indulgent Soil that rich Grape
                               breeds,
    P. 128 O.C.   211 If so indulgent to his own, how deare

indur'd   frequency: 1   relative frequency: 0.0000
    P. 142 INSTRUCTIONS   56 In fewer months than Mothers once indur'd.

indure   frequency: 4   relative frequency: 0.0000
    P. 21 SOUL & BOLY   27 Constrain'd not only to indure
    P. 83 FLECKNO   30 The future Ages how I did indure:
    P. 175 LOYALL SCOT   126 Who that is wise would pulpit Toyl Indure?
    P. 190 STATUE   11 And soe near to the Court they will never indure

indures   frequency: 1   relative frequency: 0.0000
    P. 60 A. HOUSE   50 And scarce indures the Master great:

industrious   frequency: 2   relative frequency: 0.0000
    P. 50 THE GARDEN   69 And, as it works, th' industrious Bee
    P. 88 ODE   33 Could by industrious Valour climbe

infallible   frequency: 1   relative frequency: 0.0000
    P. 198 DUKE   33 And not Infallible the Roman Soyle?

infamous   frequency: 1   relative frequency: 0.0000
    P. 195 TWO HORSES   129 Both Infamous Stand in three Kingdoms votes,

infant   frequency: 5   relative frequency: 0.0001
    P. 25 YOUNG LOVE   1 Come little Infant, love me now,
    P. 27 LOVER   2 With whom the Infant Love yet playes!
    P. 47 EMPIRE   2 Where Jarring Windes to infant Nature plaid.
    P. 99 HOLLAND   138 Is strangled by our Infant Hercules.
    P. 124 O.C.   31 Her when an infant, taken with her Charms,

infants   frequency: 3   relative frequency: 0.0000
    P. 31 MOURNING   3 What mean these Infants which of late
    P. 39 PICTURE   37 To kill her Infants in their prime,

P. 124 O.C.   51 Hold fast dear Infants, hold them both or none;

infect   frequency: 1   relative frequency: 0.0000
     P. 163 INSTRUCTIONS 916 And with blue streaks infect the Taper clear:

infecta   frequency: 1   relative frequency: 0.0000
     P. 152 INSTRUCTIONS 460 Then to return home straight infecta re.

infected   frequency: 1   relative frequency: 0.0000
     P. 202 HISTORICALL   46 With Denham and Coneig's infected pot,

infection   frequency: 1   relative frequency: 0.0000
     P.   3 LOVELACE   4 Our wits have drawne th' infection of our times.

infects   frequency: 1   relative frequency: 0.0000
     P. 65 A. HOUSE   216 'And vice infects the very Wall.

infested   frequency: 1   relative frequency: 0.0000
     P. 189 BRITANNIA   185 As Joves great sunn the infested globe did free

infinite   frequency: 2   relative frequency: 0.0000
     P. 37 DEFINITION   28 Though infinite can never meet.
     P. 131 PARADISE   17 Or if a Work so infinite he spann'd,

inflame   frequency: 2   relative frequency: 0.0000
     P. 40 THE MATCH   28 All Nature could inflame.
     P. 130 O.C.   279 Singing of thee, inflame themselves to fight,

inflamed. See "enflam'd," "enflamed."

inflame's   frequency: 1   relative frequency: 0.0000
     P. 42 DAMON   18 Nor Dog-star so inflame's the dayes.

influence   frequency: 4   relative frequency: 0.0000
     P. 105 ANNIVERSARY   104 And wisely court the Influence they fear;
     P. 118 BLAKE   148 Bless those they shine for, by their Influence.
     P. 121 TWO SONGS   54 With his serenest influence their Loves.
     P. 174 LOYALL SCOT   86 And split the Influence of Every star?

influences   frequency: 1   relative frequency: 0.0000
     P. 186 BRITANNIA   52 And in his heart kind influences shed

infold   frequency: 1   relative frequency: 0.0000
     See also "enfold."
     P. 157 INSTRUCTIONS 679 His shape exact, which the bright flames infold,

information   frequency: 1   relative frequency: 0.0000
     P. 83 FLECKNO   19 Straight without further information,

inform'd   frequency: 1   relative frequency: 0.0000
     P. 30 THE GALLERY   31 And (when inform'd) them throw'st away,

infus'd   frequency: 1   relative frequency: 0.0000
     P.   5 HASTINGS   56 All Herbs, and them a thousand ways infus'd?

ingage   frequency: 1   relative frequency: 0.0000
     P. 145 INSTRUCTIONS 190 Nor any further would then these ingage.

ingenious   frequency: 2   relative frequency: 0.0000
     P.   3 LOVELACE   6 To be ingenious, but by speaking well.
     P. 83 FLECKNO   13 Save that th' ingenious Door did as you come

inglorious   frequency: 1   relative frequency: 0.0000
     P. 87 ODE   10 In the inglorious Arts of Peace,

ingrate   frequency: 1   relative frequency: 0.0000
     P. 138 HOUSEWARMING   47 His Friends in the Navy would not be ingrate,

ingratefull   frequency: 1   relative frequency: 0.0000
     P. 193 TWO HORSES   70 But Tyrants ingratefull are always afeard.

ingratitude   frequency: 1   relative frequency: 0.0000
     P. 193 TWO HORSES   69 Ch. The basest Ingratitude ever was heard;

ingrav'd   frequency: 1   relative frequency: 0.0000
     P. 57 BILL-BOROW   45 And on these Okes ingrav'd her Name;

ingross   frequency: 1   relative frequency: 0.0000
     P. 188 BRITANNIA   160 Shall darken story, Ingross loudmouthd fame.

inhabit   frequency: 1   relative frequency: 0.0000

P. 116 BLAKE   78 At once both to Inhabit Earth and Heaven.

inhabitable   frequency: 1   relative frequency: 0.0000
    P. 174 LOYALL SCOT   101 'Twill make a more Inhabitable zone.

inhumane   frequency: 1   relative frequency: 0.0000
    P. 29 THE GALLERY   10 Of an Inhumane Murtheress;

injur'd   frequency: 1   relative frequency: 0.0000
    P. 96 HOLLAND   23 Yet still his claim the Injur'd Ocean laid,

injustice   frequency: 2   relative frequency: 0.0000
    P. 138 HOUSEWARMING   52 The two Allens who serve his Injustice for
                              Tallons.
    P. 190 STATUE   7 Besides the injustice it were to eject

inn   frequency: 2   relative frequency: 0.0000
    P. 61 A. HOUSE   71 And for an Inn to entertain
    P. 312 CHEQUER INN   t A Ballad call'd the Chequer Inn.

innocence   frequency: 3   relative frequency: 0.0000
    P. 41 THE MOWER   34 A wild and fragrant Innocence:
    P. 48 THE GARDEN   10 And Innocence thy Sister dear!
    P. 81 A. HOUSE   718 And feign'd complying Innocence;

innocent   frequency: 1   relative frequency: 0.0000
    P. 150 INSTRUCTIONS   389 And taught Youth by Spectacle Innocent!

innocentest   frequency: 1   relative frequency: 0.0000
    P. 177 LOYALL SCOT   228 The Innocentest mind their thirst alone

innocently   frequency: 2   relative frequency: 0.0000
    P. 62 A. HOUSE   98 'Live innocently as you see.
    P. 70 A. HOUSE   368 Or innocently seems to gaze.

inquest   frequency: 1   relative frequency: 0.0000
    P. 314 CHEQUER INN   83 All of 'em of the Grand Inquest

inrag'd   frequency: 1   relative frequency: 0.0000
    P. 156 INSTRUCTIONS   625 But sees, inrag'd, the River flow between.

in's   frequency: 4   relative frequency: 0.0000

inscrib'd   frequency: 1   relative frequency: 0.0000
    P. 186 BRITANNIA   64 Inscrib'd Leviathan the sovereign Lord,

insect   frequency: 1   relative frequency: 0.0000
    P. 178 LOYALL SCOT   272 The Insect Kingdome streight begins to thrive

insects   frequency: 1   relative frequency: 0.0000
    P.   3 LOVELACE   18 Of Insects which against you rise in arms.

insense   frequency: 1   relative frequency: 0.0000
    P. 62 A. HOUSE   110 'With insense of incessant Pray'r.

insinuating   frequency: 1   relative frequency: 0.0000
    P. 164 INSTRUCTIONS   975 Not so does Rust insinuating wear,

insipid   frequency: 1   relative frequency: 0.0000
    P. 175 LOYALL SCOT   142 Howere Insipid Yet the Sawce will mend 'em

inslav'd   frequency: 1   relative frequency: 0.0000
    P. 20 SOUL & BODY   2 A Soul inslav'd so many wayes?

insnar'd   frequency: 1   relative frequency: 0.0000
    P. 49 THE GARDEN   40 Insnar'd with Flow'rs, I fall on Grass.

inspect   frequency: 1   relative frequency: 0.0000
    P. 150 INSTRUCTIONS   372 To forge new Thunder, and inspect their Fires.

inspir'd   frequency: 1   relative frequency: 0.0000
    P. 57 BILL-BOROW   43 Vera the Nymph that him inspir'd,

inspire   frequency: 5   relative frequency: 0.0001
    P. 18 CLORINDA   29 Sing then while he doth us inspire;
    P. 63 A. HOUSE   138 'That me does for your good inspire)
    P. 157 INSTRUCTIONS   674 Inspire, nor would he his own deeds deface.
    P. 172 LOYALL SCOT   40 Inspire, nor cold bee his own Deeds deface;
    P. 205 HISTORICALL   158 The Godly-cheat King-wou'd-be did inspire,

inspires   frequency: 1   relative frequency: 0.0000

P. 154 INSTRUCTIONS 547 Aeolus their Sails inspires with Eastern Wind,

installing   frequency: 1   relative frequency: 0.0000
    P. 32 MOURNING   28 At the installing of a new.

instant   frequency: 3   relative frequency: 0.0000
    P. 27 MISTRESS   36 At every pore with instant Fires,
    P. 67 A. HOUSE   272 Was in one instant dispossest.
    P. 153 INSTRUCTIONS   503 These can, at need, at instant, with a scrip,

instead   frequency: 3   relative frequency: 0.0000
    See also "insted."
    P. 166 KINGS VOWES   22 I will have a new London instead of the old,
    P. 174 LOYALL SCOT   108 Instead of all the Plagues had Bishops come,
    P. 190 STATUE   31 And instead of that markett of herbs and of fruit

insted   frequency: 1   relative frequency: 0.0000
    P. 194 TWO HORSES   104 Insted of a Cudgell Balam wish't for a Sword.

instructions   frequency: 1   relative frequency: 0.0000
    P. 141 INSTRUCTIONS   t The last Instructicns to a Painter.

instructs   frequency: 1   relative frequency: 0.0000
    P. 152 INSTRUCTIONS   451 The first instructs our (Verse the Name abhors)

instrument   frequency: 3   relative frequency: 0.0000
    P. 105 ANNIVERSARY   68 When Cromwell tun'd the ruling Instrument;
    P. 137 HOUSEWARMING   19 He thought (as an Instrument he was most free
                             on)
    P. 142 INSTRUCTIONS   42 Whose Breeches were the Instrument of Peace.

instruments   frequency: 1   relative frequency: 0.0000
    P. 84 FLECKNO   37 Now as two Instruments, tc the same key

insulting   frequency: 2   relative frequency: 0.0000
    P. 28 LOVER   28 That sail'd insulting o're the Wrack,
    P. 158 INSTRUCTIONS   734 With Gamescme Jcy insulting on her Decks.

intail   frequency: 1   relative frequency: 0.0000
    P. 81 A. HOUSE   727 And Goodness doth it self intail

intelligence   frequency: 2   relative frequency: 0.0000
    P. 146 INSTRUCTICNS   240 Without Intelligence, Ccmmand, or Pay:
    P. 150 INSTRUCTIONS   375 Frcm Greenwich (where Intelligence they hold)

intencions   frequency: 1   relative frequency: 0.0000
    P. 185 BRITANNIA   30 Pervert his mind, his good Intencions Choak,

intend   frequency: 2   relative frequency: 0.0000
    P. 86 FLECKNO   114 Did, as he threatned, ere 'twere long intend
    P. 178 LOYALL SCOT   282 Here Douglas smileing said hee did Intend

intent   frequency: 2   relative frequency: 0.0000
    P. 131 PARADISE   6 Held me a while misdoubting his Intent,
    P. 314 CHEQUER INN   76 But was it seems with that intent

intentions. See "intencions."

intercept   frequency: 3   relative frequency: 0.0000
    P.   4 HASTINGS   1 Go, intercept scme Fountain in the Vein,
    P. 66 A. HOUSE   248 And the great Race would intercept.
    P. 98 HOLLAND   106 Or intercept the Western golden Sands:

intercepts   frequency: 1   relative frequency: 0.0000
    P. 106 ANNIVERSARY   142 And intercepts the Beams of Mortal eyes,

interest   frequency: 3   relative frequency: 0.0000
    See also "intrest."
    P. 14 THE CORONET   16 With wreaths of Fame and Interest.
    P. 153 INSTRUCTIONS   500 Greater the Bribe, and that's at Interest.
    P. 178 LOYALL SCCT   259 That senseless Rancour against Interest.

interferes. See "enterfeers."

interline   frequency: 1   relative frequency: 0.0000
    P. 41 THE MOWER   14 And learn'd to interline its cheek:

interpreter   frequency: 1   relative frequency: 0.0000
    P. 93 DR. WITTY   3 The good Interpreter. Scme in this task

intervals   frequency: 1   relative frequency: 0.0000

P. 148 INSTRUCTIONS 296 Without disorder in their Intervals:

interweave   frequency: 2   relative frequency: 0.0000
    P. 62 A. HOUSE   126 'They in their Lives do interweave.
    P. 107 ANNIVERSARY   181 Let this one Sorrow interweave among

interwove   frequency: 1   relative frequency: 0.0000
    P. 162 INSTRUCTIONS   894 With her own Tresses interwove and twin'd:

intire   frequency: 1   relative frequency: 0.0000
    P. 13 DROP OF DEW   38 White, and intire, though congeal'd and chill.

into   frequency: 35   relative frequency: 0.0007

intrails   frequency: 1   relative frequency: 0.0000
    P. 113 BLAKE   9 The new Worlds wounded Intrails they had tore,

intrest   frequency: 1   relative frequency: 0.0000
    P. 187 BRITANNIA   90 When all their Gobling Intrest in Mankind

introduction   frequency: 1   relative frequency: 0.0000
    P. 191 TWO HORSES   t2 Introduction.

intrusion   frequency: 1   relative frequency: 0.0000
    P. 91 MAY'S DEATH   33 At this intrusion. Then with Laurel wand,

intrust   frequency: 2   relative frequency: 0.0000
    P. 58 BILL-BOROW   60 Their prudent Heads too far intrust.
    P. 181 MADE FREE   15 Wou'd intrust their youth to your heeding?

intrusted   frequency: 1   relative frequency: 0.0000
    P. 182 MADE FREE   38 Intrusted him with Cash,

invade   frequency: 6   relative frequency: 0.0001
    P. 57 BILL-BOROW   35 No hostile hand durst ere invade
    P. 98 HOLLAND   117 While, with feign'd Treaties, they invade by
                             stealth
    P. 146 INSTRUCTIONS   234 Who in a time of Treaty durst invade.
    P. 150 INSTRUCTIONS   383 But the just Street does the next House invade,
    P. 153 INSTRUCTIONS   505 When Dutch Invade, when Parliament prepare,
    P. 187 BRITANNIA   93 The Church and state you safely may invade.

invaded   frequency: 1   relative frequency: 0.0000
    P.   4 LOVELACE   43 Mine eyes invaded with a female spight,

invades   frequency: 1   relative frequency: 0.0000
    P. 96 HOLLAND   49 Hence some small Dyke-grave unperceiv'd invades

inveigling   frequency: 1   relative frequency: 0.0000
    P. 154 INSTRUCTIONS   538 And with inveigling Colours Court the Air.

invenom'd   frequency: 1   relative frequency: 0.0000
    P. 198 DUKE   41 Hastning to be invenom'd with the pox

invent   frequency: 3   relative frequency: 0.0000
    P. 30 THE GALLERY   43 In all the Forms thou can'st invent
    P. 60 A. HOUSE   64 Nor Pride invent what to contemn?
    P. 96 HOLLAND   48 Invent a Shov'l and be a Magistrate.

invented   frequency: 1   relative frequency: 0.0000
    P. 150 INSTRUCTIONS   377 A Punishment invented first to awe

inventions   frequency: 1   relative frequency: 0.0000
    P. 138 HOUSEWARMING   25 Thus dayly his Gouty Inventions he pain'd,

inventress   frequency: 1   relative frequency: 0.0000
    P. 142 INSTRUCTIONS   57 Hence Crowder made the rare Inventress free,

inverted   frequency: 1   relative frequency: 0.0000
    P. 76 A. HOUSE   568 I was but an inverted Tree.

inviolate   frequency: 1   relative frequency: 0.0000
    P. 132 PARADISE   34 As them preserves, and Thee inviolate.

invisible   frequency: 2   relative frequency: 0.0000
    P. 35 DAPHNIS   84 And invisible him makes.
    P. 70 A. HOUSE   362 Th' invisible Artilery;

invisibly   frequency: 1   relative frequency: 0.0000
    P. 31 FAIR SINGER   11 Whose subtile Art invisibly can wreath

invite   frequency: 3   relative frequency: 0.0000

```
        See also "t'invite."
        P.  23 NYMPH         42 Of foot, and heart; and did invite,
        P.  84 FLECKNO       55 Nor was I longer to invite him Scant:
        P.  85 FLECKNO      103 To prov't, I said, the place doth us invite
```

invoke   frequency: 1   relative frequency: 0.0000
```
        P. 155 INSTRUCTIONS 591 Th' English from shore the Iron deaf invoke
```

inward   frequency: 1   relative frequency: 0.0000
```
        P. 127 O.C.         181 The Souldier taught that inward Mail to wear,
```

ire   frequency: 1   relative frequency: 0.0000
```
        P. 202 HISTORICALL   47 Which with Religion so enflam'd his ire
```

ireland   frequency: 1   relative frequency: 0.0000
```
        P.  87 ODE            t An Horatian Ode upon Cromwel's Return from
                               Ireland.
```

irish   frequency: 8   relative frequency: 0.0001
```
        P.  89 ODE           73 And now the Irish are asham'd
        P. 171 PROPHECY      46 And think French onely Loyall, Irish wise,
        P. 187 BRITANNIA    106 Of French, Scots, Irish (all my mortall foes):
        P. 187 BRITANNIA    125 Mack James the Irish Pagod does Adore,
        P. 198 DUKE          16 Ile raise my papist and my Irish bands,
        P. 199 DUKE          65 By Irish fools and by a doting pope.
        P. 199 DUKE          73 I'th Irish shambles he first learn'd the trade.
        P. 204 HISTORICALL  148 Bold Irish Ruffins to his Court adress:
```

irish-cattel   frequency: 1   relative frequency: 0.0000
```
        P. 147 INSTRUCTIONS 256 Of Irish-Cattel and Sollicitor.
```

irish-herd   frequency: 1   relative frequency: 0.0000
```
        P. 149 INSTRUCTIONS 351 The Irish-Herd is now let loose, and comes
```

iron   frequency: 5   relative frequency: 0.0001
```
        P.  27 MISTRESS      44 Thorough the Iron gates of Life.
        P.  37 DEFINITION    11 But Fate does Iron wedges drive,
        P.  43 DAMON         71 But, when the Iron blunter grows,
        P. 147 INSTRUCTIONS 279 Ev'n Iron Strangeways, chafing yet gave back,
        P. 155 INSTRUCTIONS 591 Th' English from shore the Iron deaf invoke
```

irrevocable   frequency: 1   relative frequency: 0.0000
```
        P.  92 MAY'S DEATH   97 Thus by irrevocable Sentence cast,
```

is   frequency: 171   relative frequency: 0.0035
```
        See also "here's," "he's," "is't," "it's,"
                "mine's," "minut's," "nimph's,"
                "oat-pipe's," "other's,"
                "reason's," "'s," "she's," "theres,"
                "ther's," "tis," "'tis," "way's,"
                "whats," "what's," "wheres."
```

island   frequency: 4   relative frequency: 0.0000
```
        P. 105 ANNIVERSARY   72 That Island, which the Sea cannot devour:
        P. 113 BLAKE         t2 in the Bay of Sanctacruze, in the Island of
        P. 118 BLAKE        133 Torn Limbs some leagues into the Island fly,
        P. 174 LOYALL SCOT   88 'Tis Holy Island parts us not the Tweed.
```

islands   frequency: 3   relative frequency: 0.0000
```
        P. 112 ANNIVERSARY  359 'Of floting Islands a new Hatched Nest;
        P. 115 BLAKE         51 By that alone those Islands she secures,
        P. 115 BLAKE         63 In vain doth she these Islands free from Ill,
```

isle   frequency: 15   relative frequency: 0.0003
```
        P.  17 BERMUDAS       7 Unto an Isle so long unknown,
        P.  69 A. HOUSE     321 Oh Thou, that dear and happy Isle
        P.  89 ODE           97 What may not then our Isle presume
        P. 114 BLAKE         29 O noble Trust which Heaven on this Isle
                                poures,
        P. 127 O.C.         170 To compass in our Isle; our Tears suffice;
        P. 150 INSTRUCTIONS 398 Off, at the Isle of Candy, Dutch and ships.
        P. 150 INSTRUCTIONS 405 They, by the Name, mistook it for that Isle,
        P. 150 INSTRUCTIONS 410 This Isle of Candy was on Essex Coast.
        P. 154 INSTRUCTIONS 550 Sound the Sea-march, and guide to Sheppy Isle.
        P. 164 INSTRUCTIONS 968 Have strove to Isle the Monarch from his Isle:
        P. 164 INSTRUCTIONS 977 Nor Earthquake so an hollow Isle overwhelm,
        P. 189 BRITANNIA    191 Freed by thy labours, Fortunate blest Isle,
        P. 202 HISTORICALL   38 And Plague and Warre fell heavye on our Isle.
        P. 202 HISTORICALL   55 This Isle was well reform'd and gaind renowne,
```

isles   frequency: 3   relative frequency: 0.0000

```
          See also "isl's."
          P. 114 BLAKE          24 For they behold the sweet Canary Isles;
          P. 114 BLAKE          39 Your worth to all these Isles, a just right
                                   brings,
          P. 188 BRITANNIA     127 The scotch scabbado of one Court, two Isles,

isl's                          frequency:    1    relative frequency: 0.0000
          P.  73 A. HOUSE      472 And Isl's th' astonish'd Cattle round.

israalites                     frequency:    1    relative frequency: 0.0000
          P.  71 A. HOUSE      389 Who seem like Israalites to be,

israel                         frequency:    1    relative frequency: 0.0000
          See also "israell," "is'rel."
          P. 138 HOUSEWARMING   37 And hence like Pharoah that Israel prest

israelites                     frequency:    1    relative frequency: 0.0000
          See also "israalites."
          P.  71 A. HOUSE      406 And cryes, he call'd us Israelites;

israell                        frequency:    1    relative frequency: 0.0000
          P. 174 LOYALL SCOT   109 Pharoah at first would have sent Israell home.

is'rel                         frequency:    1    relative frequency: 0.0000
          P. 109 ANNIVERSARY   252 And Is'rel silent saw him rase the Tow'r;

issu'd                         frequency:    2    relative frequency: 0.0000
          P. 123 O.C.           23 From which those Powers that issu'd the Decree,
          P. 129 O.C.          233 From which he issu'd with that awfull state,

issue                          frequency:    2    relative frequency: 0.0000
          P. 110 ANNIVERSARY   293 Yet such a Chammish issue still does rage,
          P. 201 HISTORICALL    28 To wish her hopeful Issue timely Joy.

issues                         frequency:    1    relative frequency: 0.0000
          P. 105 ANNIVERSARY    73 Then our Amphion issues out and sings,

is't                           frequency:    3    relative frequency: 0.0000

it                             frequency:  237    relative frequency: 0.0050
          See also "for't," "if't," "is't," "it's,"
                   "itt," "know't," "mis't," "on't,"
                   "prov't," "'thad," "tis," "'tis,"
                   "twas," "'twas," "'twere," "'twill,"
                   "'twould," "unless't," "wer't."

italian                        frequency:    1    relative frequency: 0.0000
          P. 184 MADE FREE     120 With a Wife of Religion Italian?

italianated                    frequency:    1    relative frequency: 0.0000
          P.  94 DR. WITTY      23 Her native beauty's not Italianated,

italy                          frequency:    2    relative frequency: 0.0000
          P.  90 ODE           102 To Italy an Hannibal,
          P.  94 DR. WITTY      20 Now learns the tongues of France and Italy;

i'th                           frequency:    3    relative frequency: 0.0000

i'th'                          frequency:    2    relative frequency: 0.0000

its                            frequency:  102    relative frequency: 0.0021

it's                           frequency:    3    relative frequency: 0.0000

itself                         frequency:    3    relative frequency: 0.0000

itt                            frequency:    1    relative frequency: 0.0000

i've                           frequency:    1    relative frequency: 0.0000

ivory.  See "iv'ry."

iv'ry                          frequency:    2    relative frequency: 0.0000
          P. 156 INSTRUCTIONS  635 Scarce can burnt Iv'ry feign an Hair so black,
          P. 162 INSTRUCTIONS  868 Like Knife with Iv'ry haft, and edge of Lead.

ivy                            frequency:    1    relative frequency: 0.0000
          P.  77 A. HOUSE      589 And Ivy, with familiar trails,

ixion's                        frequency:    1    relative frequency: 0.0000
          P.  92 MAY'S DEATH    93 Thou rivited unto Ixion's wheel
```

jacall   frequency: 1   relative frequency: 0.0000
     P. 204 HISTORICALL   139 White liverd Danby for his swift Jacall

jack-pudding   frequency: 1   relative frequency: 0.0000
     P. 180 STOCKSMARKET   42 That to change him into a Jack-pudding you mean,

jackal. See "jacall."

jacket   frequency: 1   relative frequency: 0.0000
     P. 84 FLECKNO   71 Wears a close Jacket of poetick Buff,

jade   frequency: 1   relative frequency: 0.0000
     P. 150 INSTRUCTIONS   384 Mounting the neighbour Couple on lean Jade.

jades   frequency: 2   relative frequency: 0.0000
     P. 192 TWO HORSES   33 And that the two Jades after mutuall Salutes
     P. 196 TWO HORSES   167 But I should have told you, before the Jades
                               parted,

james   frequency: 5   relative frequency: 0.0001
     See also "royal-james."
     P. 184 BRITANNIA   2 To trembling James, would I had yeilded mine.
     P. 185 BRITANNIA   22 Till Charles loves Parliaments, till James
                               hates Rome.
     P. 187 BRITANNIA   125 Mack James the Irish Pagod does Adore,
     P. 195 TWO HORSES   143 Ch. What is thy opinion of James Duke of
                               York?
     P. 201 HISTORICALL   21 Bold James survives, no dangers make him flinch,

james's   frequency: 3   relative frequency: 0.0000
     P. 139 HOUSEWARMING   95 Your Metropolis House is in St. James's
                               Fields,
     P. 140 HOUSEWARMING   112 He comes to be roasted next St. James's Fair.
     P. 142 INSTRUCTIONS   41 He needs no Seal, but to St. James's lease,

jane   frequency: 1   relative frequency: 0.0000
     P. 166 KINGS VOWES   38 As bold as Alce Pierce and as faire as Jane
                               Shore;

janus'   frequency: 1   relative frequency: 0.0000
     P. 129 O.C.   234 It seem'd Mars broke through Janus' double
                               gate;

jarring   frequency: 2   relative frequency: 0.0000
     P. 47 EMPIRE   2 Where Jarring Windes to infant Nature plaid.
     P. 114 BLAKE   35 The jarring Elements no discord know,

jaw   frequency: 1   relative frequency: 0.0000
     P. 144 INSTRUCTIONS   137 Chops off the piece where e're she close the
                               Jaw,

jawes   frequency: 1   relative frequency: 0.0000
     P. 92 MAY'S DEATH   91 The Cerberus with all his Jawes shall gnash,

jaws. See "jawes."

jealous   frequency: 5   relative frequency: 0.0001
     P. 37 DEFINITION   13 For Fate with jealous Eye does see
     P. 73 A. HOUSE   469 For, jealous of its Lords long stay,
     P. 127 O.C.   163 As jealous only here lest all be less,
     P. 131 PARADISE   18 Jealous I was that some less skilful hand
     P. 199 DUKE   48 Better some jealous neighbour of your owne

jealousie   frequency: 1   relative frequency: 0.0000
     P. 25 YOUNG LOVE   4 From cold Jealousie and Fears.

jealousies   frequency: 1   relative frequency: 0.0000
     P.   4 HASTINGS   22 To Earth, and then what Jealousies to Heaven!

jealousy. See "jealousie," "state-jealousie."

jellied. See "gelid."

jellying. See "gellying."

jermyn   frequency: 1   relative frequency: 0.0000
     See also "jermyne."
     P. 143 INSTRUCTIONS   102 And Jermyn straight has leave to come agen.

jermyne   frequency: 1   relative frequency: 0.0000
     P. 200 DUKE   87 Jermyne, Fitzgerald, Loftus, Porter, Scot.

jermyn's. See "germin's."

jessean   frequency: 2   relative frequency: 0.0000
     P. 185 BRITANNIA   48 As the Jessean Herce did appease
     P. 188 BRITANNIA   151 Over the whole: the elect Jessean line

jesse's   frequency: 1   relative frequency: 0.0000
     P. 205 HISTORICALL   168 And Jesse's son plac'd in the Government:

jesuites   frequency: 1   relative frequency: 0.0000
     P. 111 ANNIVERSARY   314 Sorcerers, Atheists, Jesuites, Possess;

jesuits. See "jesuites."

jew   frequency: 2   relative frequency: 0.0000
     P. 106 ANNIVERSARY   116 Nor teach, but traffique with, or burn the Jew.
     P. 201 HISTORICALL   2 Much like the Son of Kish that lofty Jew,

jewel   frequency: 1   relative frequency: 0.0000
     See also "jewell."
     P. 103 ANNIVERSARY   12 And shines the Jewel of the yearly Ring.

jewell   frequency: 1   relative frequency: 0.0000
     P. 131 O.C.   318 His brows, like an imperiall jewell grac'd.

jewels   frequency: 5   relative frequency: 0.0001
     P. 15 EYES   15 And all the Jewels which we prize,
     P. 17 BERMUDAS   20 Jewels more rich than Ormus show's.
     P. 35 DAPHNIS   68 Jewels of so high a rate.
     P. 67 A. HOUSE   262 Only the Jewels there were true.
     P. 158 INSTRUCTIONS 711 The Dutch had robb'd those Jewels of the
                              Crown:

jews   frequency: 2   relative frequency: 0.0000
     P. 26 MISTRESS   10 Till the Conversion of the Jews.
     P. 85 FLECKNO   77 Which by the Jews long hid, and Disesteem'd,

jews-trump   frequency: 1   relative frequency: 0.0000
     P. 137 HOUSEWARMING   20 To build with the Jews-trump of his own tongue.

jigging   frequency: 1   relative frequency: 0.0000
     P. 168 ADVICE   6 The Brittain Jigging it in Mascarade;

jingling. See "gingling."

job   frequency: 1   relative frequency: 0.0000
     P. 161 INSTRUCTIONS 823 Yet Harry must job back and all mature,

john   frequency: 1   relative frequency: 0.0000
     See also "poor-john."
     P. 139 HOUSEWARMING   79 And St. John must now for the Leads be
                              compliant,

join. See "joyn," "joyne."

joined. See "joyn'd," "joyned."

joining. See "joyning."

joint. See "joynt."

jolly   frequency: 2   relative frequency: 0.0000
     P. 162 INSTRUCTIONS 881 At Table, jolly as a Country-Host,
     P. 201 HISTORICAIL   16 His jolly Vassalls treat him day and Night.

joseph   frequency: 2   relative frequency: 0.0000
     P. 138 HOUSEWARMING   35 What Joseph by Famine, he wrought by
                              Sea-Battel;
     P. 195 TWO HORSES   152 W. And our Sir Joseph write news-books, and
                              fiddle.

joshua   frequency: 1   relative frequency: 0.0000
     P. 130 O.C.   293 How soon thou Moses hast, and Joshua found,

jove   frequency: 7   relative frequency: 0.0001
     P. 99 HOLLAND   151 And while Jove governs in the highest Sphere,
     P. 104 ANNIVERSARY   38 But with Astrologers divine, and Jove,
     P. 121 TWO SONGS   53 And Jove himself approves
     P. 129 O.C.   265 When angry Jove darts lightning through the
                              aire,
     P. 139 HOUSEWARMING   77 Like Jove under Aetna o'erwhelming the Gyant,

```
        P. 149 INSTRUCTIONS   356 And sits in State Divine like Jove the
                                  fulminant!
        P. 171 PROPHECY        34 And pray to Jove to take him back againe.

joves                             frequency:    2   relative frequency: 0.0000
        P. 186 BRITANNIA       67 Around her Joves lou'd ravenous Currs complain;
        P. 189 BRITANNIA      185 As Joves great sunn the infested globe did free

jovial                            frequency:    2   relative frequency: 0.0000
        P. 138 HOUSEWARMING    50 The two Allens when jovial, who ply him with
                                  gallons,

jowle                             frequency:    1   relative frequency: 0.0000
        P. 176 LOYALL SCOT    193 The Bishops Nodle Ferks up cheek by Jowle.

joy                               frequency:   16   relative frequency: 0.0003
        P.   5 HASTINGS        41 The gods themselves cannot their Joy conceal,
        P.  32 MOURNING        22 Joy now so much her Master grown,
        P.  34 DAPHNIS         32 Between Joy and Sorrow rent.
        P.  36 DAPHNIS         91 Joy will not with Sorrow weave,
        P. 107 ANNIVERSARY    186 Still as they trickle, glitter in our Joy.
        P. 113 BLAKE           12 But yet in them caus'd as much fear, as Joy.
        P. 116 BLAKE           97 That they with joy their boasting General heard,
        P. 121 TWO SONGS       51 Joy to Endymion,
        P. 122 TWO SONGS       29 Joy to that happy Fair,
        P. 123 TWO SONGS       47 Joy to that happy Fair,
        P. 124 O.C.            49 Or with a Grandsire's joy her Children sees
        P. 157 INSTRUCTIONS    675 And secret Joy, in his calm Soul does rise,
        P. 158 INSTRUCTIONS    734 With Gamesome Joy insulting on her Decks.
        P. 161 INSTRUCTIONS    861 Trembling with joy and fear, Hyde them
                                  Prorogues,
        P. 172 LOYALL SCOT     41 And secrett Joy in his own soul doth Rise
        P. 201 HISTORICALL     28 To wish her hopeful Issue timely Joy.

joy'd                             frequency:    2   relative frequency: 0.0000
        P. 126 O.C.           149 That so who ere would at his Death have joy'd,
        P. 127 O.C.           152 Yet joy'd remembring what he once atchiev'd.

joyes                             frequency:    4   relative frequency: 0.0000
        P.  15 EYES            12 Are the true price of all my Joyes.
        P.  18 CLORINDA         8 C. Seize the short Joyes then, ere they vade.
        P. 111 ANNIVERSARY    334 Did make the Fun'rals sadder by their Joyes.
        P. 130 O.C.           297 And in those joyes dost spend the endlesse day,

joyful                            frequency:    1   relative frequency: 0.0000
        P. 115 BLAKE           69 Never so many with one joyful cry,

joyn                              frequency:    3   relative frequency: 0.0000
        P.  22 NYMPH           11 Thy murder, I will Joyn my Tears
        P.  37 DEFINITION      23 And, us to joyn, the World should all
        P. 173 LOYALL SCOT     74 And Joyn those Lands that seemed to part
                                  before.

joyn'd                            frequency:    2   relative frequency: 0.0000
        P.  34 DAPHNIS         45 Are my Hell and Heaven Joyn'd
        P. 127 O.C.           172 Who once more joyn'd us to the Continent;

joyne                             frequency:    1   relative frequency: 0.0000
        P. 198 DUKE            39 Do's now in popery with his Master joyne.

joyned                            frequency:    1   relative frequency: 0.0000
        P. 198 DUKE             9 Most holy Father, being joyned in league

joyning                           frequency:    3   relative frequency: 0.0000
        P.  31 FAIR SINGER      4 Joyning themselves in fatal Harmony;
        P.  43 DAMON           68 Joyning my Labour to my Pain;
        P. 104 ANNIVERSARY     60 And joyning streight the Theban Tow'r arose;

joynt                             frequency:    3   relative frequency: 0.0000
        P.  96 HOLLAND         51 But for less envy some joynt States endures,
        P. 174 LOYALL SCOT     97 Or to the Joynt stooles reconcile the Chairs?
        P. 187 BRITANNIA      111 With Joynt consent on helpless me they flew,

joys                              frequency:    5   relative frequency: 0.0001
  See also "joyes."
        P.  65 A. HOUSE       194 'Of Joys you see, and may make more!
        P. 143 INSTRUCTIONS    83 Her wonted joys thenceforth and Court she shuns,
        P. 150 INSTRUCTIONS   394 The Joys of State, for the new Peace and Tax.
        P. 176 LOYALL SCOT    201 Shattering the silent Air disturbs our Joys!
        P. 200 DUKE           109 Ends all the Joys of England and thy life.

joy's                             frequency:    1   relative frequency: 0.0000
```

P. 21 SOUL & BODY   37 Joy's chearful Madness does perplex:

jubal   frequency: 2   relative frequency: 0.0000
    P. 47 EMPIRE   5 Jubal first made the wilder Notes agree;
    P. 47 EMPIRE   6 And Jubal tuned Musicks Jubilee:

jubilee   frequency: 1   relative frequency: 0.0000
    P. 47 EMPIRE   6 And Jubal tuned Musicks Jubilee:

judg'd   frequency: 2   relative frequency: 0.0000
    P. 154 INSTRUCTIONS 563 And quickly judg'd the Fort was not tenable,
    P. 172 LOYALL SCOT   10 Hee Judg'd more Clearly now and saw more plain.

judge   frequency: 3   relative frequency: 0.0000
    P. 66 A. HOUSE   232 First from a Judge, then Souldier bred.
    P. 189 BRITANNIA   179 Tarquins just judge and Cesar's Equall Peers
    P. 204 HISTORICALL   152 They'l kill a Judge or Justice of the Peace.

judgement   frequency: 1   relative frequency: 0.0000
    P. 4 LOVELACE   50 His Booke in them finds Judgement, with you
                            Love.

judges   frequency: 3   relative frequency: 0.0000
    P. 86 FLECKNO   119 Turns to recite; though Judges most severe
    P. 92 MAY'S DEATH   63 When the Sword glitters ore the Judges head,
    P. 139 HOUSEWARMING 65 Straight Judges, Priests, Bishops, true sons
                            of the Seal,

judgment   frequency: 2   relative frequency: 0.0000
    See also "judgement."
    P. 32 MOURNING   33 I yet my silent Judgment keep,
    P. 95 DR. WITTY   37 And (if I Judgment have) I censure right;

judicious   frequency: 1   relative frequency: 0.0000
    P. 79 A. HOUSE   653 'Twere shame that such judicious Eyes

juggling. See "jugling."

jugling   frequency: 1   relative frequency: 0.0000
    P. 174 LOYALL SCOT   106 The Jugling Prelate on his hocus calls,

juice   frequency: 2   relative frequency: 0.0000
    P. 116 BLAKE   82 A grief, above the cure of Grapes best juice.
    P. 142 INSTRUCTIONS 66 Can without breaking venom'd juice convey.

julian   frequency: 1   relative frequency: 0.0000
    P. 186 BRITANNIA   58 Outshining Virgo and the Julian Star.

juliana   frequency: 7   relative frequency: 0.0001
    P. 41 DAMON   2 With love of Juliana stung!
    P. 45 GLO-WORMS   14 Since Juliana here is come,
    P. 45 MOWER'S SONG   5 When Juliana came, and She
    P. 45 MOWER'S SONG   11 When Juliana came, and She
    P. 45 MOWER'S SONG   17 When Juliana came, and She
    P. 45 MOWER'S SONG   23 For Juliana comes, and She
    P. 46 MOWER'S SONG   29 For Juliana comes, and She

julianas   frequency: 1   relative frequency: 0.0000
    P. 44 DAMON   86 Whom Julianas Eyes do wound.

juliana's   frequency: 1   relative frequency: 0.0000
    See also "julianas."
    P. 42 DAMON   24 But Juliana's scorching beams.

july   frequency: 1   relative frequency: 0.0000
    P. 42 DAMON   23 Not July causeth these Extremes,

jump   frequency: 1   relative frequency: 0.0000
    P. 142 INSTRUCTIONS 64 There, not behind the Coach, her Pages jump.

junto   frequency: 1   relative frequency: 0.0000
    P. 166 KINGS VOWES   35 I will have a fine Junto to doe what I will,

jupiters   frequency: 1   relative frequency: 0.0000
    P. 195 TWO HORSES   144 W. The Same that the Froggs had of Jupiters
                            Stork.

jury   frequency: 2   relative frequency: 0.0000
    P. 150 INSTRUCTIONS 381 No concern'd Jury for him Damage finds,
    P. 314 CHEQUER INN   84 A Jury right of Wales.

jus   frequency: 2   relative frequency: 0.0000

P. 98 HOLLAND   113 Was this Jus Belli <and> Pacis; could this be
P. 176 LOYALL SCOT   205 And plead their Jus Divinum tho' in Hell.

just   frequency: 23   relative frequency: 0.0004
P. 65 A. HOUSE   210 'One Stone that a just Hand had laid,
P. 67 A. HOUSE   286 In the just Figure of a Fort;
P. 86 FLECKNO   143 To hear his Verses, by so just a curse
P. 89 ODE   79 How good he is, how just,
P. 92 MAY'S DEATH   95 'Tis just what Torments Poets ere did feign,
P. 93 DR. WITTY   2 Where just desert enrolles thy honour'd Name
P. 95 HOLLAND   8 Fell to the Dutch by just Propriety.
P. 103 ANNIVERSARY   10 Is the just Wonder of the Day before.
P. 109 ANNIVERSARY   264 Th' ambitious Shrubs thou in just time didst aw.
P. 114 BLAKE   39 Your worth to all these Isles, a just right
                          brings,
P. 132 PARADISE   43 Just Heav'n Thee, like Tiresias, to requite,
P. 150 INSTRUCTIONS   383 But the just Street does the next House invade,
P. 151 INSTRUCTIONS   422 But Mordant new oblig'd, would sure be just.
P. 160 INSTRUCTIONS   820 Harry came Post just as he shew'd his Watch.
P. 170 PROPHECY   1 The blood of the Just London's firm Doome
                          shall fix
P. 170 PROPHECY   22 When even to rob the Checquer shall be Just,
P. 177 LOYALL SCOT   252 Scotland and England cause of Just uproar!
P. 178 LOYALL SCOT   266 Just soe the prudent Husbandman who sees
P. 179 STOCKSMARKET   28 May be henceforth confiscate for reasons more
                          just.
P. 183 MADE FREE   83 But he may prove more just,
P. 189 BRITANNIA   179 Tarquins just judge and Cesar's Equall Peers
P. 202 HISTORICALL   59 Misguided Monarchs rarely wise or just,
P. 317 CHEQUER INN   181 Just like our Rotten Pump at home

justice   frequency: 13   relative frequency: 0.0002
P. 22 NYMPH   16 Ev'n Beasts must be with justice slain;
P. 66 A. HOUSE   231 For Justice still that Courage led;
P. 88 ODE   37 Though Justice against Fate complain.
P. 107 ANNIVERSARY   153 For the great Justice that did first suspend
P. 108 ANNIVERSARY   207 Justice obstructed lay, and Reason fool'd;
P. 138 HOUSEWARMING   51 The two Allens who serve his blind Justice for
                          ballance,
P. 150 INSTRUCTIONS   382 Nor partial Justice her Behaviour binds;
P. 161 INSTRUCTIONS   827 Up ambles Country Justice on his Pad,
P. 186 BRITANNIA   53 Of Countryes love (by truth and Justice bred).
P. 187 BRITANNIA   118 Had lost all sense of Honour, Justice, fame;
P. 198 DUKE   5 Hateing all justice and resolv'd to fight
P. 199 DUKE   61 To be by justice and by laws confind:
P. 204 HISTORICALL   152 They'l kill a Judge or Justice of the Peace.

justly   frequency: 3   relative frequency: 0.0000
P. 143 INSTRUCTIONS   101 Justly the Rogue was whipt in Porter's Den:
P. 203 HISTORICALL   80 All but religious cheats might justly sweare
P. 314 CHEQUER INN   58 And simper'd (justly to compare)

kate   frequency: 2   relative frequency: 0.0000
P. 185 BRITANNIA   21 Till Kate a happy mother shall become,
P. 201 HISTORICALL   26 To fetch for Charles the floury Lisbon Kate,

keel   frequency: 4   relative frequency: 0.0000
P. 74 A. HOUSE   486 Fit Timber for his Keel have Prest.
P. 154 INSTRUCTIONS   545 And, where the deep Keel on the shallow cleaves,
P. 155 INSTRUCTIONS   593 But with her Sailing weight, the Holland Keel
P. 155 INSTRUCTIONS   613 That sacred Keel, which had, as he, restor'd

keels   frequency: 3   relative frequency: 0.0000
P. 98 HOLLAND   125 While half their banish'd keels the Tempest
                          tost,
P. 148 INSTRUCTIONS   318 To lay the Ships up, cease the Keels begun.
P. 158 INSTRUCTIONS   704 Fraughting their pierced Keels with Oosy
                          Tides.

keen   frequency: 3   relative frequency: 0.0000
P. 29 THE GALLERY   13 Engines more keen than ever yet
P. 147 INSTRUCTIONS   259 Keen Whorwood next, in aid of Damsel frail,
P. 156 INSTRUCTIONS   626 Frustrate Revenge, and Love, by loss more keen,

keener   frequency: 1   relative frequency: 0.0000
P. 88 ODE   59 But with his keener Eye

keep   frequency: 13   relative frequency: 0.0002
P. 18 CLORINDA   6 The Flow'rs I for thy Temples keep.
P. 24 NYMPH   102 Keep these two crystal Tears; and fill
P. 32 MOURNING   33 I yet my silent Judgment keep,
P. 75 A. HOUSE   541 And all the way, to keep it clean,

```
P.  90 ODE          116 Still keep thy Sword erect:
P. 105 ANNIVERSARY   94 And they as Pillars keep the Work upright;
P. 111 ANNIVERSARY  335 His weeping Eyes the doleful Vigils keep,
P. 122 TWO SONGS     25 He so looks as fit to keep
P. 127 O.C.         165 Then let us to our course of Mourning keep:
P. 128 O.C.         218 To keep so deare, so diff'ring minds agreed?
P. 159 INSTRUCTIONS 741 And constant Time, to keep his course yet right,
P. 168 ADVICE        16 To keep his own and loose his sergeants wife.
P. 190 STATUE        32 He will here keep a market of Parliament men.
```

keepers   frequency: 1   relative frequency: 0.0000
```
P. 176 LOYALL SCOT   183 And while hee spared the keepers life hee fail'd.
```

keeping   frequency: 1   relative frequency: 0.0000
```
P. 186 BRITANNIA      75 Who e're grew great by keeping of his word?
```

keeps   frequency: 2   relative frequency: 0.0000
```
P.  22 NYMPH          14 Keeps register of every thing:
P. 132 PARADISE       40 So never Flags, but alwaies keeps on Wing.
```

ken   frequency: 1   relative frequency: 0.0000
```
P. 313 CHEQUER INN    22 Thou'lt ken him out by a white Wand
```

kendal   frequency: 1   relative frequency: 0.0000
```
P. 140 G.-CHILDREN     1 Kendal is dead, and Cambridge riding post.
```

kent   frequency: 2   relative frequency: 0.0000
```
P.   3 LOVELACE       31 And one the Bock prohibits, because Kent
P. 174 LOYALL SCOT    95 For Becketts sake Kent alwayes shall have
                         tails.
```

kept   frequency: 10   relative frequency: 0.0002
```
P.  18 BERMUDAS       40 With falling Oars they kept the time.
P.  36 DAPHNIS       103 This night for Dorinda kept;
P.  40 THE MATCH      21 He kept the several Cells repleat
P.  42 DAMON          15 Only the Snake, that kept within,
P.  65 A. HOUSE      218 'Founded by Folly, kept by Wrong.
P.  66 A. HOUSE      247 Yet, against Fate, his Spouse they kept;
P. 106 ANNIVERSARY   110 The great Designes kept for the latter Dayes!
P. 130 O.C.          309 He, as his father, long was kept from sight
P. 190 STATUE         13 Were these Deales kept in store for sheathing
                         our fleet
P. 201 HISTORICALL     4 And kept his Fathers Asses all the while.
```

kettle   frequency: 1   relative frequency: 0.0000
```
P. 150 INSTRUCTIONS  385 The Distaff knocks, the Grains from Kettle
                         fly,
```

key   frequency: 1   relative frequency: 0.0000
```
P.  84 FLECKNO        37 Now as two Instruments, to the same key
```

kick   frequency: 1   relative frequency: 0.0000
```
P.  73 A. HOUSE      475 How Horses at their Tails do kick,
```

kid   frequency: 1   relative frequency: 0.0000
```
P.  25 YOUNG LOVE     14 Or the wanton Kid does prize,
```

kids   frequency: 1   relative frequency: 0.0000
```
P.  19 THYRSIS         1 Dorinda. When Death, shall part us from these
                         Kids,
```

kill   frequency: 7   relative frequency: 0.0001
```
P.  22 NYMPH           4 To kill thee. Thou neer didst alive
P.  39 PICTURE        37 To kill her Infants in their prime,
P. 107 ANNIVERSARY   174 Our Sins endanger, and shall one day kill.
P. 151 INSTRUCTIONS  432 Uncivil: His unkindness would us kill.
P. 173 LOYALL SCOT    80 That whosoever separates them doth kill.
P. 198 DUKE           27 It is our birthright to have Power to kill.
P. 204 HISTORICALL   152 They'l kill a Judge or Justice of the Peace.
```

kill'd   frequency: 2   relative frequency: 0.0000
```
P.  89 ODE            93 She, having kill'd, no more does search,
P. 156 INSTRUCTIONS  634 Large Limbs, like Ox, not to be kill'd but
                         shown.
```

killegrew   frequency: 1   relative frequency: 0.0000
```
P. 203 HISTORICALL    90 As Killegrew buffoons his Master, they
```

killigrew. See "killegrew."

kills   frequency: 1   relative frequency: 0.0000
```
```

P. 96 HOLLAND   39 For as with Pygmees who best kills the Crane,

kind   frequency: 13   relative frequency: 0.0002
See also "kinde."
P. 34 DAPHNIS   48 But that you must then grow kind?
P. 40 THE MOWER   10 The nutriment did change the kind.
P. 49 THE GARDEN   43 The Mind, that Ocean where each kind
P. 82 A. HOUSE   750 And in your kind your selves preferr;
P. 115 BLAKE   62 Kind Nature had from thence remov'd so far.
P. 125 O.C.   80 Of Halcyons kind, or bleeding Pelicans?
P. 139 HOUSEWARMING   74 Nor would take his beloved Canary in kind:
P. 154 INSTRUCTIONS   548 Puffs them along, and breathes upon them kind.
P. 158 INSTRUCTIONS   703 And the kind River in its Creek them hides,
P. 162 INSTRUCTIONS   901 And with kind hand does the coy Vision press,
P. 186 BRITANNIA   52 And in his heart kind influences shed
P. 188 BRITANNIA   144 With the Doggs bloud his gentle kind convey
P. 189 BRITANNIA   193 And this kind secret for reward shall give:

kinde   frequency: 1   relative frequency: 0.0000
P. 200 DUKE   110 Brothers, its true, by nature should be kinde:

kinder   frequency: 2   relative frequency: 0.0000
P. 17 BERMUDAS   8 And yet far kinder than our own?
P. 125 O.C.   103 Whether some Kinder Pow'rs, that wish us well,

kindly   frequency: 3   relative frequency: 0.0000
P. 98 HOLLAND   123 'Tis true since that (as fortune kindly sports,)
P. 114 BLAKE   36 Fewel and Rain together kindly grow;
P. 128 O.C.   206 Where kindly nature loves itself to lose.

kindred. See "kinred."

king   frequency: 70   relative frequency: 0.0014
P. 14 THE CORONET   12 As never yet the king of Glory wore:
P. 22 NYMPH   13 It cannot dye so. Heavens King
P. 25 YOUNG LOVE   27 In the craddle crown their King,
P. 96 HOLLAND   50 The Pow'r, and grows as 'twere a King of
                          Spades.
P. 103 ANNIVERSARY   22 For one Thing never was by one King don.
P. 108 ANNIVERSARY   226 Then ought below, or yet above a King:
P. 109 ANNIVERSARY   238 But though forewarn'd, o'r-took and wet the
                          King.
P. 109 ANNIVERSARY   255 No King might ever such a Force have done;
P. 110 ANNIVERSARY   297 That their new King might the fifth Scepter
                          shake,
P. 111 ANNIVERSARY   311 Accursed Locusts, whom your King does spit
P. 112 ANNIVERSARY   387 'He seems a King by long Succession born,
P. 112 ANNIVERSARY   388 'And yet the same to be a King does scorn,
P. 112 ANNIVERSARY   389 'Abroad a King he seems, and something more,
P. 148 INSTRUCTIONS   289 Dear Lovers of their King, and Death to meet,
P. 149 INSTRUCTIONS   327 And the lov'd King, and never yet deny'd,
P. 149 INSTRUCTIONS   366 St Albans promis'd him, and he the King.
P. 152 INSTRUCTIONS   468 None but himself must chuse the King a Queen.)
P. 152 INSTRUCTIONS   489 And for their Pay he writes as from the King,
P. 153 INSTRUCTIONS   498 He sucks the King, they him, he them again.
P. 161 INSTRUCTIONS   853 The King, that day rais'd early from his rest,
P. 162 INSTRUCTIONS   885 Paint last the King, and a dead Shade of
                          Night,
P. 163 INSTRUCTIONS   925 The wondrous Night the pensive King revolves,
P. 164 INSTRUCTIONS   948 Himself the Poet and the Painter too. To the
                          King.
P. 164 INSTRUCTIONS   974 Bacchus is Wine, the Country is the King.)
P. 165 INSTRUCTIONS   987 That serve the King with their Estates and
                          Care,
P. 169 ADVICE   35 Thus whilst the King of France with powerfull
                          Armes
P. 170 PROPHECY   12 Give Taxes to the King and Parliament.
P. 171 PROPHECY   44 Make him self rich, his king and People bare,
P. 175 LOYALL SCOT   133 Noe Church! noe Trade! noe king! nce people!
                          noe!
P. 178 LOYALL SCOT   260 One King, one faith, one Language and one Ile:
P. 179 STOCKSMARKET   6 Obliging the city with a king and a steed,
P. 179 STOCKSMARKET   12 That shews him a monster more like than a king.
P. 179 STOCKSMARKET   14 Yet all do affirm that the king is much worse,
P. 179 STOCKSMARKET   16 That he did for the King his own statue erect.
P. 179 STOCKSMARKET   21 But a market, they say, does suit the king well,
P. 180 STOCKSMARKET   44 As if we'd as good have a king made of clouts.
P. 180 STOCKSMARKET   49 Sure the king will ne'er think of repaying his
                          bankers,
P. 180 STOCKSMARKET   56 For 'tis such a king as no chisel can mend.
P. 180 STOCKSMARKET   57 But with all his faults restore us our King,

P. 181 MADE FREE	2 To the King doe present
P. 184 MADE FREE	114 To Charters, our King and Soveraigne.
P. 185 BRITANNIA	33 Thus Fayry like the King they steal away
P. 186 BRITANNIA	69 From th' easie King she truthes bright Mirrour took,
P. 187 BRITANNIA	101 A sacrafice to you, their God and King.
P. 188 BRITANNIA	140 'Tis god-like-good to save a falling King.
P. 190 STATUE	14 When the King in Armado to Portsmouth should saile,
P. 190 STATUE	18 The late King on Horsback is here to be shown:
P. 190 STATUE	28 For the old King on Horseback is but an Halfecrown.
P. 190 STATUE	36 Will you venture soe far to Prorogue the King too?
P. 190 STATUE	37 Let's have a King then, be he new be he old;
P. 190 STATUE	39 Tho' the King be of Copper and Danby of Gold,
P. 191 STATUE	44 And wee've lost both our King, our Hors and our Crupper.
P. 191 STATUE	46 To buy a King is not so wise as to sell,
P. 193 TWO HORSES	58 Yet the King of his debts pay no man a penny;
P. 193 TWO HORSES	59 W. That a King should consume three Realms whole Estates
P. 193 TWO HORSES	68 For restoring the King should be our Rewards.
P. 194 TWO HORSES	89 Ch. But thanks to the whores who have made the King Dogged
P. 194 TWO HORSES	91 W. That a King shou'd endavour to make a warr cease
P. 194 TWO HORSES	95 W. That the King should send for another French whore,
P. 194 TWO HORSES	109 Where is thy King gone? Ch. To see Bishop Laud.
P. 194 TWO HORSES	117 W. Thy Priest-ridden King turn'd desperate Fighter
P. 194 TWO HORSES	122 Ch. Thy King will ne're fight unless't be for Queans.
P. 195 TWO HORSES	124 Ch. The King on thy Back is a Lamentable Tool.
P. 195 TWO HORSES	147 If e're he be King I know Brittains Doome;
P. 200 DUKE	99+ To the King.
P. 202 HISTORICALL	64 The poore Priapus King led by the Nose
P. 204 HISTORICALL	154 Hee'l burne a Citty or destroy a King.
P. 205 HISTORICALL	182 Then how much greater Mischiefe as a King.
P. 315 CHEQUER INN	91 But King (God save him) tho' so cram'd
P. 316 CHEQUER INN	158 Till King both Hostesse kist and Host

king-fisher   frequency: 1   relative frequency: 0.0000
    P. 137 HOUSEWARMING   7 Like the King-fisher chuseth to build in the Broom,

king-wou'd-be   frequency: 1   relative frequency: 0.0000
    P. 205 HISTORICALL   158 The Godly-cheat King-wou'd-be did inspire,

kingdom   frequency: 2   relative frequency: 0.0000
    See also "kingdome."
    P. 108 ANNIVERSARY   218 Unto the Kingdom blest of Peace and Love:
    P. 164 INSTRUCTIONS   971 The Kingdom from the Crown distinct would see,

kingdome   frequency: 4   relative frequency: 0.0000
    P. 88 ODE   35 And cast the Kingdome old
    P. 89 ODE   86 A Kingdome, for his first years rents:
    P. 166 KINGS VOWES   26 If not o're a Kingdome, to raigne ore my Guard;
    P. 178 LOYALL SCOT   272 The Insect Kingdome streight begins to thrive

kingdomes   frequency: 3   relative frequency: 0.0000
    P. 25 YOUNG LOVE   25 Thus as Kingdomes, frustrating
    P. 113 BLAKE   8 With what the Womb of wealthy Kingdomes yield,
    P. 187 BRITANNIA   99 'Tis Royall Game whole Kingdomes to deflower.

kingdoms   frequency: 3   relative frequency: 0.0000
    See also "kingdomes."
    P. 153 INSTRUCTIONS   499 The Kingdoms Farm he lets to them bid least:
    P. 183 MADE FREE   87 To the Duke the Kingdoms Darling?
    P. 195 TWO HORSES   129 Both Infamous Stand in three Kingdoms votes,

kings   frequency: 20   relative frequency: 0.0004
    P. 96 HOLLAND   37 Therefore Necessity, that first made Kings,
    P. 106 ANNIVERSARY   124 Winding his Horn to Kings that chase the Beast.
    P. 109 ANNIVERSARY   250 Yet by the Conquest of two Kings grown great,
    P. 114 BLAKE   40 The best of Lands should have the best of Kings.
    P. 164 INSTRUCTIONS   959 Kings in the Country oft have gone astray,

```
      P. 165 KINGS VOWES       t The Kings Vowes.
      P. 170 PROPHECY         25 When two good Kings shall be att Brantford
                                 knowne
      P. 175 LOYALL SCOT     139 For only Kings can Bishops Exercise.
      P. 176 LOYALL SCOT     191 What Brittain was, betwixt two Kings distrest.
      P. 176 LOYALL SCOT     196 Kings head saith this, But Bishops head that
                                 doe.
      P. 185 BRITANNIA        40 Shew'd him how many Kings in Purple Gore
      P. 186 BRITANNIA        72 'Are thred-bare Virtues Ornaments for Kings?
      P. 188 BRITANNIA       149 Tyrants like Leprous Kings for publick weal
      P. 190 STATUE           19 What a doe with the Kings and the Statues is
                                 here:
      P. 192 TWO HORSES       31 When both the Kings weary of Sitting all day
      P. 192 TWO HORSES       44 And the Kings wicked life say God there is
                                 none;
      P. 195 TWO HORSES      131 Ch. More Tolerable are the Lion Kings
                                 Slaughters
      P. 196 TWO HORSES      162 The Gods have repented the Kings Restoration.
      P. 205 HISTORICALL     180 To give you kings in's Wrath to vex you sore:
      P. 205 HISTORICALL     181 If a Kings Brother can such mischief bring,

king's                        frequency:    5    relative frequency: 0.0001
      P. 139 HOUSEWARMING     83 Who sate heretofore at the King's Receipt;
      P. 160 INSTRUCTIONS    800 To lavish the King's Money more would scorn.
      P. 179 STOCKSMARKET      3 So Sir Robert advanced the King's statue, in
                                 token
      P. 179 STOCKSMARKET     11 Upon the King's birthday to set up a thing
      P. 192 TWO HORSES       42 And the King's Chiefe minister holding the
                                 doore:

kingship                      frequency:    1    relative frequency: 0.0000
      P. 195 TWO HORSES      160 Thy oppression togeather with Kingship shall
                                 dye.

kinred                        frequency:    1    relative frequency: 0.0000
      P.   5 HASTINGS         39 And gladly there can all his Kinred claim,

kips                          frequency:    1    relative frequency: 0.0000
      P. 139 HOUSEWARMING     70 Were shriveled, and Clutterbuck, Eagers <and>
                                 Kips;

kish                          frequency:    1    relative frequency: 0.0000
      P. 201 HISTORICALL       2 Much like the Son of Kish that lofty Jew,

kiss                          frequency:    5    relative frequency: 0.0001
      P.  46 AMETAS           16 And go kiss within the Hay.
      P.  72 A. HOUSE        431 When at their Dances End they kiss,
      P. 106 ANNIVERSARY     106 Kiss the approaching, nor yet angry Son:
      P. 139 HOUSEWARMING     76 No, would the whole Parliament kiss him behind.
      P. 161 INSTRUCTIONS    847 The Girls shall always kiss thee, though grown
                                 old,

kist                          frequency:    2    relative frequency: 0.0000
      P.  86 FLECKNO         138 Yet he first kist them, and after takes pains
      P. 316 CHEQUER INN     158 Till King both Hostesse kist and Host

kites                         frequency:    1    relative frequency: 0.0000
      P.  71 A. HOUSE        403 Greedy as Kites has trust it up,

knave                         frequency:    5    relative frequency: 0.0001
      P. 169 ADVICE          60 To be reproacht with Tearm of Turncoat knave;
      P. 187 BRITANNIA       124 False Finch, Knave Anglesey misguide the
                                 seals;
      P. 191 TWO HORSES        3 When Magpyes and Parratts cry 'walke Knave
                                 walk',
      P. 192 TWO HORSES       18 When Shrines give Answers, say a knave 's in
                                 the Roode;
      P. 193 TWO HORSES       83 W. Four Knights and a Knave, who were
                                 Publicans made,

knaves                        frequency:    3    relative frequency: 0.0000
      P. 192 TWO HORSES       38 When both knaves agreed to be each others
                                 brother.
      P. 194 TWO HORSES      120 By Knaves who cry'd themselves up for the
                                 Church,
      P. 204 HISTORICALL     149 This is the Colony to plant his knaves:

knead                         frequency:    1    relative frequency: 0.0000
      P.  40 THE MOWER        7 And a more luscious Earth for them did knead,

knees                         frequency:    1    relative frequency: 0.0000
```

```
       P.  124 O.C.            50 Hanging about her neck or at his knees.

knew                             frequency:   16    relative frequency: 0.0003
       P.    4 LOVELACE         44 (She knew what pain 'twould be to lose that
                                   sight.)
       P.   33 DAPHNIS           7 But she neither knew t'enjoy,
       P.   33 DAPHNIS          19 Knew not that the Fort to gain
       P.   41 THE MOWER        23 No Plant now knew the Stock from which it came;
       P.   65 A. HOUSE        201 Oft, though he knew it was in vain,
       P.   91 MAY'S DEATH      29 But Ben, who knew not neither foe nor friend,
       P.  116 BLAKE            85 To fight against such Foes, was vain they knew,
       P.  122 TWO SONGS        20 Led our Lambs we knew not where.
       P.  144 INSTRUCTIONS    158 But knew the Word and well could face about;
       P.  146 INSTRUCTIONS    210 Scarce them their Leaders, they their Leaders
                                   knew.
       P.  150 INSTRUCTIONS    387 Prudent Antiquity, that knew by Shame,
       P.  156 INSTRUCTIONS    654 Nor other Courtship knew but to his Cheek.
       P.  163 INSTRUCTIONS    931 Through their feign'd speech their secret hearts
                                   he knew;
       P.  172 LOYALL SCOT      20 Nor other Courtship knew but to his Cheek.
       P.  181 MADE FREE        25 He ne're knew not he
       P.  184 MADE FREE       112 When in Heart you all knew

knife                            frequency:    3    relative frequency: 0.0000
       P.  125 O.C.             94 Chance to be prun'd by an untimely knife,
       P.  162 INSTRUCTIONS    868 Like Knife with Iv'ry haft, and edge of Lead.
       P.  200 DUKE            108 A droppe of poisone or a papish knife

knight                           frequency:    5    relative frequency: 0.0001
       P.  144 INSTRUCTIONS    162 Wood these commands, Knight of the Horn and
                                   Cane.
       P.  180 STOCKSMARKET     33 But, Sir Knight of the Vine, how came't in
                                   your thought
       P.  194 TWO HORSES       94 With an Addleheaded Knight and a Lord without
                                   Brains.
       P.  314 CHEQUER INN      73 This Knight was sent t'america
       P.  315 CHEQUER INN     111 And Lawley Knight of Shropshire

knightly                         frequency:    1    relative frequency: 0.0000
       P.  179 STOCKSMARKET      5 Some thought it a knightly and generous deed,

knights                          frequency:    3    relative frequency: 0.0000
       P.  175 LOYALL SCOT     145 These Templar lords Exceed the Templar
                                   Knights,
       P.  193 TWO HORSES       83 W. Four Knights and a Knave, who were
                                   Publicans made,
       P.  201 HISTORICALL      13 Bishops and Deanes, Peeres, Pimps and Knights
                                   he made,

knit                             frequency:    3    relative frequency: 0.0000
       P.   76 A. HOUSE        574 Then if She were with Lime-twigs knit.
       P.   81 A. HOUSE        731 Nor once at Vice your Brows dare knit
       P.  105 ANNIVERSARY      98 Knit by the Roofs Protecting weight agree.

knits                            frequency:    1    relative frequency: 0.0000
       P.   74 A. HOUSE        505 Dark all without it knits; within

knives                           frequency:    1    relative frequency: 0.0000
       P.  316 CHEQUER INN     169 Candlesticks, Forkes, Saltes Plates Spoones
                                   Knives

knocks                           frequency:    1    relative frequency: 0.0000
       P.  150 INSTRUCTIONS    385 The Distaff knocks, the Grains from Kettle
                                   fly,

knot                             frequency:    1    relative frequency: 0.0000
       P.  124 O.C.             44 Doubling that knot which Destiny had ty'd.

knots                        ,   frequency:    2    relative frequency: 0.0000
       P.   14 THE CORONET      20 Either his slipp'ry knots at once untie,
       P.  112 ANNIVERSARY     384 'And still his Fauchion all our Knots unties.

know                             frequency:   29    relative frequency: 0.0006
       P.    3 LOVELACE         33 But when the beauteous Ladies came to know
       P.   11 DIALOGUE         69 Thou shalt know each hidden Cause;
       P.   19 THYRSIS           7 Dorinda. I know no way, but one, our home;
       P.   21 SOUL & BODY      39 Which Knowledge forces me to know;
       P.   22 NYMPH            29 Gave it to me: nay and I know
       P.   23 NYMPH            47 Had it liv'd long, I do not know
       P.   48 THE GARDEN       21 Little, Alas, they know, or heed,
       P.   58 BILL-BOROW       53 Hence they successes seem to know,
```

```
P.  63 A. HOUSE        147 'Fairfax I know; and long ere this
P.  65 A. HOUSE        219 'I know what Fruit their Gardens yield,
P.  66 A. HOUSE        239 Ill-counsell'd Women, do you know
P.  70 A. HOUSE        379 As, under Water, none does know
P.  86 FLECKNO         154 Should know the contrary. Whereat, I, now
P.  89 ODE              76 That does both act and know.
P.  96 HOLLAND          45 Who best could know to pump an Earth so leak
P. 104 ANNIVERSARY      39 To know how long their Planet yet Reprives
P. 106 ANNIVERSARY     112 They know them not, and what they know not, hate.
P. 114 BLAKE            35 The jarring Elements no discord know,
P. 115 BLAKE            58 Neither the Soyl, nor People quiet know.
P. 116 BLAKE            93 Fond men who know not whilst such works they
                           raise,
P. 143 INSTRUCTIONS    113 But here the Court does its advantage know,
P. 171 PROPHECY         49 Then the English shall a Greater Tyrant Know
P. 173 LOYALL SCOT      79 But this wee knew, tho' that Exceed their skill,
P. 181 MADE FREE        18 Yet know both his Freinds and his Breeding.
P. 188 BRITANNIA       156 From her sage mouth fam'd Principles to know,
P. 195 TWO HORSES      147 If e're he be King I know Brittains Doome;
P. 198 DUKE             19 Prove to the world Ile have ould England know
P. 316 CHEQUER INN     157 They drunke, I know not who had most
```

```
knowes                           frequency:     5    relative frequency: 0.0001
    P.  10 DIALOGUE         29 A Soul that knowes not to presume
    P. 167 KINGS VOWES      51 And who knowes but the Mode may soon bring in
                               the rest?
    P. 170 PROPHECY         21 And no Man knowes in whom to put his trust,
    P. 178 LOYALL SCOT     265 Knowes the last secret how to make them one.
    P. 185 BRITANNIA        14 Till England knowes who did her Citty burn,
```

```
knowest                          frequency:     1    relative frequency: 0.0000
See also "know'st."
    P. 194 TWO HORSES      102 Thou knowest what danger was like to come of it;
```

```
knowing                          frequency:     5    relative frequency: 0.0001
    P.  81 A. HOUSE        719 But knowing where this Ambush lay,
    P. 107 ANNIVERSARY     147 And knowing not where Heavens choice may light,
    P. 111 ANNIVERSARY     336 Not knowing yet the Night was made for sleep:
    P. 124 O.C.             45 While they by sence, not knowing, comprehend
    P. 163 INSTRUCTIONS    929 And they, not knowing, the same thing propose,
```

```
knowledge                        frequency:     5    relative frequency: 0.0001
    P.   4 HASTINGS         21 As that of Knowledge; what Loves had he given
    P.  11 DIALOGUE         74 Of Knowledge, but Humility.
    P.  21 SOUL & BODY      39 Which Knowledge forces me to know;
    P.  81 A. HOUSE        735 When knowledge only could have fill'd
    P.  92 MAY'S DEATH      72 Our spotless knowledge and the studies chast.
```

```
known                            frequency:     8    relative frequency: 0.0001
See also "knowne."
    P.  43 DAMON            41 I am the Mower Damon, known
    P.  68 A. HOUSE        291 The Bee through these known Allies hums,
    P. 108 ANNIVERSARY     196 And the green Grass, and their known Mangers
                               hate,
    P. 117 BLAKE           123 Never so burning was that Climate known,
    P. 130 O.C.            296 (Farr better known above than here below;)
    P. 157 INSTRUCTIONS    672 Or with known Art to try the gentle Wave.
    P. 163 INSTRUCTIONS    913 His mind secure does the known stroke repeat,
    P. 172 LOYALL SCOT      38 Or with known art to try the Gentle Wave.
```

```
knowne                           frequency:     2    relative frequency: 0.0000
    P. 165 KINGS VOWES       8 Where Papist from Protestant shall not be
                               knowne;
    P. 170 PROPHECY         25 When two good Kings shall be att Brantford
                               knowne
```

```
knows                            frequency:     6    relative frequency: 0.0001
See also "knowes," "know's."
    P. 110 ANNIVERSARY     281 But who of both the Bounders knows to lay
    P. 157 INSTRUCTIONS    668 Within its circle, knows himself secure.
    P. 172 LOYALL SCOT      34 Within its Circle knows himselfe secure.
    P. 175 LOYALL SCOT     128 Enough for them, God knows, to Count their
                               Wealth,
    P. 175 LOYALL SCOT     150 None knows what god our Flamen now Adores;
    P. 188 BRITANNIA       139 Who knows what good effects from thence may
                               spring;
```

```
know's                           frequency:     1    relative frequency: 0.0000
    P. 183 MADE FREE        78 He know's not his Trade, nor his Mist'ry.
```

```
know'st                          frequency:     1    relative frequency: 0.0000
```

```
      P. 315 CHEQUER INN      96 For tymes thou know'st grew harder.

know't                            frequency:   1    relative frequency: 0.0000
      P.  90 MAY'S DEATH       2 Tom May was hurry'd hence and did not know't.

label.  See "labell."

labell                            frequency:   1    relative frequency: 0.0000
      P. 198 DUKE              8 Adoreing Roome, this labell in his mouth.

labor                             frequency:   1    relative frequency: 0.0000
      See also "labour."
      P. 109 ANNIVERSARY     259 Though why should others all thy Labor spoil,

labored.  See "labour'd."

laboring.  See "lab'ring."

labors.  See "labours."

labour                            frequency:   6    relative frequency: 0.0001
      See also "labor."
      P.  33 DAPHNIS           4 All his Labour, all his Art.
      P.  43 DAMON            68 Joyning my Labour to my Pain;
      P.  95 HOLLAND          10 They with mad labour fish'd the Land to Shoar;
      P. 105 ANNIVERSARY      80 Nor with such labour from its Center brought;
      P. 116 BLAKE            94 They only Labour to exalt your praise.
      P. 129 O.C.            238 Whose force oft spar'd the labour of his arm:

labour'd                          frequency:   1    relative frequency: 0.0000
      P. 126 O.C.            132 The Universe labour'd beneath their load.

labouring.  See "lab'ring."

labours                           frequency:   4    relative frequency: 0.0000
      P.  48 THE GARDEN        3 And their uncessant Labours see
      P. 131 PARADISE         26 Within thy Labours to pretend a Share.
      P. 153 INSTRUCTIONS    520 Under Herculean Labours he may sink.
      P. 189 BRITANNIA       191 Freed by thy labours, Fortunate blest Isle,

lab'ring                          frequency:   1    relative frequency: 0.0000
      P. 143 INSTRUCTIONS    120 His lab'ring Pencil oft would recreate.

labyrinths                        frequency:   1    relative frequency: 0.0000
      P.  78 A. HOUSE        622 Betwixt two Labyrinths does lead.

lace                              frequency:   3    relative frequency: 0.0000
      P.  78 A. HOUSE        611 And Oh so close your Circles lace,
      P. 111 ANNIVERSARY     316 With the same liberty as Points and Lace;
      P. 143 INSTRUCTIONS     98 More gold in's Fob, more Lace upon his Coat

lack                              frequency:   3    relative frequency: 0.0000
      P. 148 INSTRUCTIONS    324 That Money lack, nor Forts be in repair.
      P. 156 INSTRUCTIONS    636 Or Face so red thine Oker and thy Lack.
      P. 317 CHEQUER INN     184 Soe when mine Host doth Money lack

lackey's.  See "lacquies."

lacquies                          frequency:   1    relative frequency: 0.0000
      P. 143 INSTRUCTIONS     81 She through her Lacquies Drawers as he ran,

laden                             frequency:   2    relative frequency: 0.0000
      P.  60 A. HOUSE         49 Yet thus the laden House does sweat,
      P. 199 DUKE            67 Laden with folly, flesh and Ill got land:

ladies                            frequency:   4    relative frequency: 0.0000
      P.   3 LOVELACE         33 But when the beauteous Ladies came to know
      P.   4 LOVELACE         38 Whose hand so gently melts the Ladies hand.
      P.  16 EYES             34 Nor the chast Ladies pregnant Womb,
      P.  23 NYMPH            62 NAY any Ladies of the Land.

lady                              frequency:   9    relative frequency: 0.0001
      P.  26 MISTRESS          2 This coyness Lady were no crime.
      P.  26 MISTRESS         19 For Lady you deserve this State;
      P.  63 A. HOUSE        131 'By it we would our Lady touch;
      P. 119 TWO SONGS        t2 and the Lady Mary Cromwell.
      P. 137 HOUSEWARMING     13 He had read of Rhodope, a Lady of Thrace,
      P. 141 INSTRUCTIONS      1 After two sittings, now our Lady State,
      P. 314 CHEQUER INN      61 The Lady drest like any Bride
      P. 314 CHEQUER INN      72 His Lady and her Lord
      P. 316 CHEQUER INN     146 That scarce the Lady cou'd edge in
```

laick   frequency: 1   relative frequency: 0.0000
     P. 139 HOUSEWARMING   85 By Subsidies thus both Clerick and Laick,

laid   frequency: 20   relative frequency: 0.0004
     See also "lay'd."
     P.   23 NYMPH   82 It like a bank cf Lillies laid.
     P.   24 NYMPH   119 There at my feet shalt thou be laid,
     P.   29 THE GALLERY   6 Of various Faces, by are laid;
     P.   38 PICTURE   23 Let me be laid,
     P.   56 BILL-BOROW   7 It seems as for a Model laid,
     P.   61 A. HOUSE   78 What she had laid sc sweetly wast;
     P.   65 A. HOUSE   210 'One Stone that a just Hand had laid,
     P.   67 A. HOUSE   285 But laid these Gardens cut in sport
     P.   79 A. HOUSE   665 So when the Shadows laid asleep
     P.   90 MAY'S DEATH   14 Amongst the Chorus of old Poets laid,
     P.   96 HOLLAND   23 Yet still his claim the Injur'd Ocean laid,
     P.   97 HOLLAND   65 More pregnant then their Marg'ret, that laid
                               down
     P. 120 TWO SONGS   31 Yet is her younger Sister laid
     P. 157 INSTRUCTIONS   687 Down on the Deck he laid himself, and dy'd,
     P. 160 INSTRUCTIONS   817 But in the Thames mouth still de Ruyter laid,
     P. 173 LOYALL SCOT   53 Down on the Deck hee laid him down and dy'd
     P. 182 MADE FREE   61 The Plott was sc laid,
     P. 193 TWO HORSES   63 W. Our worm-eaten Navy be laid up at Chatham,
     P. 313 CHEQUER INN   37 And where he might e're now have laid
     P. 314 CHEQUER INN   62 Her Forehead Cloath had laid aside

lamb   frequency: 1   relative frequency: 0.0000
     P.   25 YOUNG LOVE   13 Love as much the snowy Lamb

lambeth   frequency: 1   relative frequency: 0.0000
     P. 177 LOYALL SCOT   218 'Tis necessary Lambeth never wed,

lambs   frequency: 3   relative frequency: 0.0000
     P.   24 NYMPH   108 With milk-white Lambs, and Ermins pure.
     P. 122 TWO SONGS   20 Led our Lambs we knew not where.
     P. 122 TWO SONGS   21 Not our Lambs cwn Fleeces are

lame   frequency: 1   relative frequency: 0.0000
     P. 131 PARADISE   14 C're which lame Faith leads Understanding
                               blind;

lamentable   frequency: 1   relative frequency: 0.0000
     P. 195 TWO HORSES   124 Ch. The King on thy Back is a Lamentable
                               Tool.

lamp   frequency: 1   relative frequency: 0.0000
     P. 120 TWO SONGS   23 My wakeful Lamp all night must move,

lamps   frequency: 3   relative frequency: 0.0000
     P.   17 BERMUDAS   18 Like golden Lamps in a green Night.
     P.   44 GLO-WORMS   1 Ye living Lamps, by whose dear light
     P.   62 A. HOUSE   107 'And our chast Lamps we hourly trim,

lance   frequency: 1   relative frequency: 0.0000
     P. 147 INSTRUCTIONS   276 Broach'd whole Brigades like Larks upon his
                               Lance.

land   frequency: 23   relative frequency: 0.0004
     P.   17 BERMUDAS   26 From Lebanon, he stores the Land.
     P.   23 NYMPH   62 NAY any Ladies cf the Land.
     P.   95 HOLLAND   1 Holland, that scarce deserves the name of Land,
     P.   95 HOLLAND   10 They with mad labour fish'd the Land to Shoar;
     P.   96 HOLLAND   25 As if on purpose it on Land had come
     P.   96 HOLLAND   36 Would throw their Land away at Duck and Drake.
     P.   97 HOLLAND   60 And, as their Land, so them did re-baptize.
     P.   98 HOLLAND   96 When Stagg'ring upon some Land, Snick and
                               Sneer,
     P. 109 ANNIVERSARY   237 Which to the thirsty Land did plenty bring,
     P. 109 ANNIVERSARY   268 And threat'ning Rocks misapprehend for Land;
     P. 110 ANNIVERSARY   294 The Shame and Plague both of the Land and
                               Age,
     P. 112 ANNIVERSARY   370 'But that once took, we Captives are on Land.
     P. 118 BLAKE   156 And the Land owe her peace unto the Sea.
     P. 137 HOUSEWARMING   3 At once three Deluges threatning our Land;
     P. 140 HOUSEWARMING   108 At Tybourn may land, and spare the Tower-Barge.
     P. 144 INSTRUCTIONS   127 Should pay Land Armies, should dissolve the
                               vain
     P. 154 INSTRUCTIONS   562 With panting Heart, lay like a fish on Land,
     P. 185 BRITANNIA   19 Till Atheist Lauderdale shall leave this Land,
     P. 199 DUKE   67 Laden with folly, flesh and Ill got land:

```
        P. 200 DUKE          101 In peace and pleasure this thy native land,
        P. 204 HISTORICALL   119 The most authentik Statutes of the Land,
        P. 205 HISTORICALL   167 From Saul the Land cf Prcmise thus was rent,
        P. 315 CHEQUER INN     97 Holt out of Linnen (as for Land)
```

land-tax   frequency: 1   relative frequency: 0.0000
```
        P. 149 INSTRUCTIONS  331 And to Land-tax from the Excise turn round,
```

landguard. See "languard."

landing   frequency: 1   relative frequency: 0.0000
```
        P. 107 ANNIVERSARY   157 Hence landing Nature tc new Seas is tost,
```

landlord   frequency: 1   relative frequency: 0.0000
```
        P. 315 CHEQUER INN   116 The Landlord Bailes, out eate, out roar'd
```

lands   frequency: 7   relative frequency: 0.0001
```
        P.  17 BERMUDAS       11 He lands us on a grassy Stage;
        P.  96 HCLLAND        44 But who could first discern the rising Lands.
        P. 114 BLAKE          40 The best of Lands shculd have the best of
                                 Kings.
        P. 138 HOUSEWARMING   34 To buy us for Slaves, and purchase our Lands;
        P. 165 KINGS VOWES    15 But if they displease me, I will have all their
                                 Lands.
        P. 173 LOYALL SCOT    74 And Joyn those lands that seemed to part
                                 before.
        P. 185 BRITANNIA      31 Tell him of Golden Indies, Fayry Lands,
```

landscape. See "landskip."

landskip   frequency: 2   relative frequency: 0.0000
```
        P.  73 A. HOUSE      458 A Landskip drawen in Looking-Glass.
        P. 168 ADVICE         12 A Landskip of cur Mottly Parliament;
```

lane   frequency: 3   relative frequency: 0.0000
```
        P.  71 A. HOUSE      392 And crowd a Lane to either Side.
        P.  78 A. HOUSE      618 Where the two Wcods have made a Lane;
        P. 170 PROPHECY        4 As farr as from Whitehall to Pudden lane
```

language   frequency: 6   relative frequency: 0.0001
```
        P.  33 DAPHNIS        25 Till Love in her Language breath'd
        P.  76 A. HOUSE      571 And where I Language want, my Signs
        P.  94 DR. WITTY      26 With other Language doth them fitly fit.
        P. 129 O.C.          237 No more shall heare that powerful language charm,
        P. 167 KINGS VOWES    54 And Quack in their Language still Vive le
                                 Roy.
        P. 178 LOYALL SCOT   260 One King, one faith, one Language and one Ile:
```

languages   frequency: 1   relative frequency: 0.0000
```
        P.  81 A. HOUSE      708 In all the Languages as hers;
```

languard   frequency: 1   relative frequency: 0.0000
```
        P. 159 INSTRUCTIONS  782 Languard, Sheerness, Gravesend, and Upnor?
                                 Pett.
```

languish   frequency: 2   relative frequency: 0.0000
```
        P.  27 MISTRESS       40 Than languish in his slow-chapt pow'r.
        P. 126 O.C.          126 And helpless languish at the tainted Stall.
```

languished   frequency: 1   relative frequency: 0.0000
```
        P.  28 LOVER          39 And languished with doubtful Breath,
```

languishing   frequency: 3   relative frequency: 0.0000
```
        P.  77 A. HOUSE      593 Then, languishing with ease, I toss
        P.  87 ODE            4 His Numbers languishing.
        P. 123 O.C.          29 Streight does a slow and languishing Disease
```

lantern. See "lanthorn."

lanthorn   frequency: 1   relative frequency: 0.0000
```
        P. 139 HOUSEWARMING   90 A Lanthorn, like Faux's surveys the burnt
                                 Town,
```

lap   frequency: 1   relative frequency: 0.0000
```
        P.  82 A. HOUSE      767 You Heaven's Center, Nature's Lap.
```

larder   frequency: 1   relative frequency: 0.0000
```
        P. 315 CHEQUER INN   93 Which Buttry were and Larder
```

large   frequency: 7   relative frequency: 0.0001
```
        P.  98 HOLLAND        99 And carve in their large Bodies, where they
                                                                    please,
```

P. 110 ANNIVERSARY   285 And the large Vale lay subject to thy Will,
P. 118 BLAKE   154 Were buryed in as large, and deep a grave,
P. 142 INSTRUCTIONS   63 With Chanc'lor's Belly, and so large a Rump.
P. 156 INSTRUCTIONS   634 Large Limbs, like Ox, not to be kill'd but
                          shown.
P. 165 INSTRUCTIONS   986 Does with clear Counsels their large Souls
                          supply;
P. 197 DUKE   1 Spread a large canvass, Painter, to containe

largely   frequency: 1   relative frequency: 0.0000
P. 92 MAY'S DEATH   82 Who thy last Reckoning did so largely pay.

larger   frequency: 2   relative frequency: 0.0000
P. 59 A. HOUSE   29 When larger sized Men did stoop
P. 83 FLECKNO   11 Not higher then Seav'n, nor larger then three
                          feet;

larks   frequency: 1   relative frequency: 0.0000
P. 147 INSTRUCTIONS   276 Broach'd whole Brigades like Larks upon his
                          Lance.

lash   frequency: 1   relative frequency: 0.0000
P. 92 MAY'S DEATH   92 Magaera thee with all her Serpents lash.

last   frequency: 43   relative frequency: 0.0008
P. 26 MISTRESS   18 And the last Age should show your Heart.
P. 27 LOVER   13 Till at the last the master-Wave
P. 34 DAPHNIS   43 At the last, this lovers Ghost
P. 34 DAPHNIS   56 For his last and short Delight.
P. 36 DAPHNIS   102 Last night he with Phlogis slept;
P. 55 EPITAPH   15 That ready her last Debt to pay
P. 64 A. HOUSE   168 'Till Miracles it work at last.
P. 65 A. HOUSE   217 'But sure those Buildings last not long,
P. 83 FLECKNO   9 I found at last a Chamber, as 'twas said,
P. 83 FLECKNO   24 To my last Tryal, in a serious thought
P. 83 FLECKNO   28 The last distemper of the sober Brain,
P. 85 FLECKNO   86 But who came last is forc'd first to go out;
P. 88 ODE   23 And Caesars head at last
P. 90 MAY'S DEATH   9 At last while doubtfully he all compares,
P. 90 ODE   115 And for the last effect
P. 92 MAY'S DEATH   82 Who thy last Reckoning did so largely pay.
P. 92 MAY'S DEATH   84 When thou hadst drunk thy last to lead thee home.
P. 109 ANNIVERSARY   236 And down at last thou pow'rdst the fertile
                          Storm;
P. 111 ANNIVERSARY   340 Or why Day last no longer then a Day?
P. 117 BLAKE   118 To give him Lawrel, as the Last did Plate.
P. 123 O.C.   9 And blame the last Act, like Spectators vain,
P. 125 O.C.   75 And with the damp of her last Gasps obscur'd,
P. 127 O.C.   153 And the last minute his victorious Ghost
P. 128 O.C.   216 Their griefs struck deepest, if Eliza's last.
P. 130 O.C.   286 Always thy honour, praise and name, shall last.
P. 139 HOUSEWARMING   87 He finish'd at last his Palace Mosaick,
P. 141 INSTRUCTIONS   t The last Instructions to a Painter.
P. 146 INSTRUCTIONS   213 Last then but one, Powell, that could not ride,
P. 146 INSTRUCTIONS   217 The Lords Sons, last, all these did reinforce:
P. 147 INSTRUCTIONS   277 But strength at last under number bows,
P. 151 INSTRUCTIONS   426 Orders, amaz'd at last gives none at all.
P. 153 INSTRUCTIONS   522 And Hyde's last Project would his Place
                          dispose.
P. 155 INSTRUCTIONS   592 For its last aid: Hold Chain or we are broke.
P. 160 INSTRUCTIONS   812 Blames the last Session, and this more does
                          fear.
P. 161 INSTRUCTIONS   855 At last together Eaton come and he:
P. 162 INSTRUCTIONS   885 Paint last the King, and a dead Shade of
                          Night,
P. 164 INSTRUCTIONS   972 And peal the Bark to burn at last the Tree.
P. 178 LOYALL SCOT   265 Knowes the last secret how to make them one.
P. 179 STOCKSMARKET   9 But now it appears from the first to the last
P. 189 BRITANNIA   189 Her true Crusado shall at last pull down
P. 194 TWO HORSES   119 Till at last on a Scaffold he was left in the
                          lurch
P. 200 DUKE   97 At last to fools and mad men and the pope?
P. 200 DUKE   102 At last take pitty of thy tottering throne,

lasting   frequency: 2   relative frequency: 0.0000
P. 107 ANNIVERSARY   165 Though none does of more lasting Parents grow,
P. 125 O.C.   89 So have I seen a Vine, whose lasting Age

lasts   frequency: 2   relative frequency: 0.0000
P. 74 A. HOUSE   483 And, while it lasts, my self imbark

P. 161 INSTRUCTIONS 846 And long as Cider lasts in Hereford;

late   frequency: 17   relative frequency: 0.0003
P.   18 CLORINDA   2 D. No: 'tis too late they went astray.
P.   18 CLORINDA   19 C. And what late change? D. The other day
P.   31 MOURNING   3 What mean these Infants which of late
P.   35 DAPHNIS   64 By a late Fruition.
P.   44 GLO-WORMS   2 The Nightingale does sit so late,
P.   86 FLECKNO   116 Said 'twas too late, he was already both.
P.   87 FLECKNO   158 But saw with sad dispair that 'twas too late.
P. 112 ANNIVERSARY   351 'Yet rig a Navy while we dress us late;
P. 112 ANNIVERSARY   377 'Him, all the Day, Him, in late Nights I
                            dread,
P. 119 TWO SONGS   3 Only this Shepheard, late and soon,
P. 140 HIS HOUSE   2 Of Paul late gelded of his Stones.
P. 146 INSTRUCTIONS   209 Late and disorder'd out the Drinkers drew;
P. 146 INSTRUCTIONS   223 Nor the late Feather-men, whom Tomkins fierce
P. 160 INSTRUCTIONS   797 But sure his late good Husbandry in Peeter,
P. 161 INSTRUCTIONS   851 Hyde orders Turner that he should come late,
P. 168 ADVICE   15 Unless it be his late Assumed grief
P. 190 STATUE   18 The late King cn Horsback is here to be shown:

lately   frequency: 6   relative frequency: 0.0001
P.   78 A. HOUSE   623 But, where the Floods did lately drown,
P. 107 ANNIVERSARY   161 Whose Saint-like Mother we did lately see
P. 116 BLAKE   98 Wish then for that assault he lately fear'd.
P. 171 PROPHECY   28 Then London lately burnt shall be blowne up,
P. 188 BRITANNIA   146 To the Bleating Flock by him so lately torn.
P. 192 TWO HORSES   24 Of a Dialogue lately between the two Horses,

latest   frequency: 2   relative frequency: 0.0000
P.   34 DAPHNIS   30 Now the latest minut's run
P. 106 ANNIVERSARY   140 And soon precipitate the latest Day.

latine   frequency: 1   relative frequency: 0.0000
P.   93 DR. WITTY   5 Changing the Latine, but do more obscure

latmos   frequency: 1   relative frequency: 0.0000
P. 120 TWO SONGS   35 Here unto Latmos Top I climbe:

latter   frequency: 1   relative frequency: 0.0000
P. 106 ANNIVERSARY   110 The great Designes kept for the latter Dayes!

laud   frequency: 1   relative frequency: 0.0000
P. 194 TWO HORSES   109 Where is thy King gone? Ch. To see Bishop
                            Laud.

lauderdale   frequency: 3   relative frequency: 0.0000
P. 185 BRITANNIA   19 Till Atheist Lauderdale shall leave this Land,
P. 188 BRITANNIA   128 Fiend Lauderdale, with crdure all defiles.
P. 203 HISTORICALL   115 And dos on Gyant Lauderdale reflect.

lauderdales   frequency: 2   relative frequency: 0.0000
P. 174 LOYALL SCOT   94 Never for Burnetts sake the Lauderdales,
P. 189 BRITANNIA   170 The Cleavelands, Osbornes, Barties,
                            Lauderdales.

laugh   frequency: 3   relative frequency: 0.0000
P.   70 A. HOUSE   373 They, in there squeking Laugh, contemn
P. 141 INSTRUCTIONS   17 Where, like the new Controller, all men laugh
P. 171 PROPHECY   36 Whom Wise men Laugh att and the Women Rule,

laughs   frequency: 1   relative frequency: 0.0000
P.   92 MAY'S DEATH   79 Who laughs to see in this thy death renew'd,

laught   frequency: 2   relative frequency: 0.0000
P.   98 HOLLAND   122 While the Sea laught it self into a foam,
P. 145 INSTRUCTIONS   165 The posture strange men laught at of his Poll,

laughter   frequency: 1   relative frequency: 0.0000
P.   15 EYES   14 Yea even Laughter, turns to Tears:

laughters   frequency: 1   relative frequency: 0.0000
P. 152 INSTRUCTIONS   467 (So Spain could not escape his Laughters
                            spleen:

laundress   frequency: 1   relative frequency: 0.0000
P. 174 LOYALL SCOT   117 How a Clean Laundress and noe sermons please.

laurel   frequency: 4   relative frequency: 0.0000
    See also "lawrel."
P.   48 THE GARDEN   30 Only that She might Laurel grow.

P. 90 MAY'S DEATH   13 'Twas Ben that in the dusky Laurel shade
P. 91 MAY'S DEATH   33 At this intrusion. Then with Laurel wand,
P. 91 MAY'S DEATH   58 The sacred Laurel, hence are all these teares?

laurels   frequency: 2   relative frequency: 0.0000
  See also "lawrels."
P. 88 ODE   24 Did through his Laurels blast.
P. 118 BLAKE   146 By which we Laurels reapt ev'n on the Mayn.

laves   frequency: 1   relative frequency: 0.0000
P. 98 HOLLAND   133 Besides that very Agitation laves,

lavish   frequency: 2   relative frequency: 0.0000
P. 160 INSTRUCTIONS   800 To lavish the King's Money more would scorn.
P. 203 HISTORICALL   76 With lavish hands they constant Tributes give

law   frequency: 13   relative frequency: 0.0002
P.   5 HASTINGS   58 And wept, as we, without Redress or Law.
P. 79 A. HOUSE   655 She that already is the Law
P. 109 ANNIVERSARY   263 Therefore first growing to thy self a Law,
P. 113 BLAKE   14 That boundless Empire, where you give the Law,
P. 128 O.C.   222 All law is uselesse, all reward is due.
P. 138 HOUSEWARMING   40 So he could to build but make Policy Law.
P. 145 INSTRUCTIONS   182 The Miter Troop, and with his looks gives Law.
P. 150 INSTRUCTIONS   378 Masculine Wives, transgressing Natures Law.
P. 150 INSTRUCTIONS   388 Better than Law, Domestick Crimes to tame
P. 152 INSTRUCTIONS   455 And that by Law of Arms, in Martial strife,
P. 160 INSTRUCTIONS   802 And ablest Speaker, who of Law has least;
P. 171 PROPHECY   42 And strive by Law to 'stablish Tyrany,
P. 188 BRITANNIA   152 To this firm Law their scepter did resign:

lawes   frequency: 5   relative frequency: 0.0001
P. 36 DAPHNIS   107 For, according to the Lawes,
P. 188 BRITANNIA   154 Eternall Lawes by God for mankind made? Noe!
P. 203 HISTORICALL   108 Thrice wretched they who natures Lawes detest
P. 204 HISTORICALL   117 First temper'd Poison to destroy our Lawes,
P. 205 HISTORICALL   170 And Monarchs are above all human Lawes.

lawful   frequency: 1   relative frequency: 0.0000
P. 66 A. HOUSE   234 The Court him grants the lawful Form;

lawley   frequency: 1   relative frequency: 0.0000
P. 315 CHEQUER INN   111 And Lawley Knight of Shropshire

lawn   frequency: 1   relative frequency: 0.0000
P. 174 LOYALL SCOT   116 How Reverend things are 'lord', Lawn Sleeves
                          and Ease!

lawn-sleeves   frequency: 1   relative frequency: 0.0000
P. 194 TWO HORSES   118 For the Surplice, Lawn-Sleeves, the Cross and
                          the mitre,

lawrel   frequency: 3   relative frequency: 0.0000
P. 117 BLAKE   118 To give him Lawrel, as the Last did Plate.
P. 119 BLAKE   166 Their rich Fleet sunk, and ours with Lawrel
                          fraught.
P. 127 O.C.   156 And slept in Peace under the Lawrel shade.

lawrels   frequency: 1   relative frequency: 0.0000
P.   5 HASTINGS   53 How Sweet and Verdant would these Lawrels be,

laws   frequency: 6   relative frequency: 0.0001
  See also "lawes."
P. 38 PICTURE   11 Yet this is She whose chaster Laws
P. 66 A. HOUSE   230 But reverenceth then the Laws:
P. 111 ANNIVERSARY   315 You who the Scriptures and the Laws deface
P. 196 TWO HORSES   175 Tho' Tyrants make laws which they strictly
                          proclaim
P. 198 DUKE   22 Then to destroy their liberty and laws,
P. 199 DUKE   61 To be by justice and by laws confind:

lawyers   frequency: 1   relative frequency: 0.0000
P. 145 INSTRUCTIONS   185 Next th' Lawyers Mercenary Band appear:

lay   frequency: 25   relative frequency: 0.0005
P.   9 DIALOGUE   13 Lay aside that Warlike Crest,
P. 27 LOVER   11 That my poor Lover floting lay,
P. 32 MOURNING   12 Would strow the ground where Strephon lay.
P. 33 DAPHNIS   14 To lay by her wonted State,
P. 39 THE MATCH   14 What she did separate lay;
P. 45 MOWER'S SONG   16 While I lay trodden under feet?

```
P.  46 AMETAS          15 Then let's both lay by our Rope,
P.  81 A. HOUSE       719 But knowing where this Ambush lay,
P.  89 ODE             90 To lay them at the Publick's skirt.
P.  90 MAY'S DEATH      7 Nor where the Popes head, nor the Mitre lay,
P.  90 ODE            111 Nor lay his Hounds in near
P.  91 MAY'S DEATH     53 And who by Romes example England lay,
P. 103 ANNIVERSARY     19 Their earthy Projects under ground they lay,
P. 108 ANNIVERSARY    207 Justice obstructed lay, and Reason fool'd;
P. 110 ANNIVERSARY    281 But who of both the Bounders knows to lay
P. 110 ANNIVERSARY    285 And the large Vale lay subject to thy Will,
P. 146 INSTRUCTIONS   239 For th' other side all in loose Quarters lay,
P. 148 INSTRUCTIONS   318 To lay the Ships up, cease the Keels begun.
P. 154 INSTRUCTIONS   562 With panting Heart, lay like a fish on Land,
P. 154 INSTRUCTIONS   573 There our sick Ships unrigg'd in Summer lay,
P. 167 KINGS VOWES     55 The Antient Nobility I will lay by,
P. 171 PROPHECY        41 When Bishops shall lay all Religion by
P. 176 LOYALL SCOT    182 But his Lay pitty underneath prevailed
P. 180 STOCKSMARKET    30 Does the fault upon the artificer lay,
P. 185 BRITANNIA       34 And in his place a Lewis Changling lay.
```

lay-men   frequency: 1   relative frequency: 0.0000
```
P. 203 HISTORICALL     88 Riches and honour they from Lay-men reap,
```

lay'd   frequency: 4   relative frequency: 0.0000
```
P. 104 ANNIVERSARY     55 No Note he struck, but a new Story lay'd,
P. 127 O.C.           155 Here ended all his mortal toyles: He lay'd
P. 129 O.C.           258 That still though dead, greater than death he
                          lay'd;
P. 145 INSTRUCTIONS   194 Or in his absence him that first it lay'd.
```

lays   frequency: 1   relative frequency: 0.0000
```
P. 105 ANNIVERSARY     83 And each the Hand that lays him will direct,
```

lazy   frequency: 2   relative frequency: 0.0000
```
P.  79 A. HOUSE       643 Abandoning my lazy Side,
P. 199 DUKE            51 You might have lingred out a lazy age,
```

le   frequency: 1   relative frequency: 0.0000
```
P. 167 KINGS VOWES     54 And Quack in their Language still Vive le
                          Roy.
```

lead   frequency: 14   relative frequency: 0.0002
```
P.  43 DAMON           62 To lead them in their Danses soft;
P.  49 THE GARDEN      33 What wond'rous Life in this I lead!
P.  56 BILL-BOROW      16 Which to securer Glory lead.
P.  64 A. HOUSE       164 'Will soon us to perfection lead.
P.  70 A. HOUSE       382 And show upon their Lead the Ground,
P.  78 A. HOUSE       622 Betwixt two Labyrinths does lead.
P.  92 MAY'S DEATH     84 When thou hadst drunk thy last to lead thee home.
P.  95 HOLLAND          4 By English Pilots when they heav'd the Lead;
P. 106 ANNIVERSARY    108 The path where holy Oracles do lead;
P. 107 ANNIVERSARY    169 Thou, who so oft through Storms of thundring
                          Lead
P. 126 O.C.           121 Then heavy Showres the winged Tempests lead,
P. 158 INSTRUCTIONS   726 To Ruyter's Triumph lead the captive Charles.
P. 162 INSTRUCTIONS   868 Like Knife with Iv'ry haft, and edge of Lead.
P. 189 BRITANNIA      188 In Triumph lead chaind tyrants from afarr.
```

leaden   frequency: 2   relative frequency: 0.0000
```
P. 108 ANNIVERSARY    194 And leaden Sorrow then their flight did stay.
P. 129 O.C.           247 I saw him dead, a leaden slumber lyes,
```

leaders   frequency: 2   relative frequency: 0.0000
```
P. 146 INSTRUCTIONS   210 Scarce them their Leaders, they their Leaders
                          knew.
```

leads   frequency: 7   relative frequency: 0.0001
```
P.  19 THYRSIS         12 That leads to Everlasting day.
P.  82 A. HOUSE       746 Where yet She leads her studious Hours,
P. 105 ANNIVERSARY     91 And they, whose Nature leads them to divide,
P. 117 BLAKE          117 Bold Stainer Leads, this Fleets design'd by
                          fate,
P. 127 O.C.           166 Where Heaven leads, 'tis Piety to weep.
P. 131 PARADISE        14 O're which lame Faith leads Understanding
                          blind;
P. 139 HOUSEWARMING    79 And St. John must now for the Leads be
                          compliant,
```

leaf   frequency: 3   relative frequency: 0.0000
```
P.   9 DIALOGUE        22 Lest one Leaf thy Side should strain.
P.  70 A. HOUSE       357 A prickling leaf it bears, and such
```

P. 76 A. HOUSE   575 No Leaf does tremble in the Wind

league   frequency: 2   relative frequency: 0.0000
P. 115 BLAKE   47 Casting that League off, which she held so long,
P. 198 DUKE   9 Most holy Father, being joyned in league

leaguers   frequency: 1   relative frequency: 0.0000
P. 113 ANNIVERSARY   366 'Whose watry Leaguers all the world surround?

leagues   frequency: 2   relative frequency: 0.0000
P. 98 HOLLAND   107 No, but all ancient Rights and Leagues must
                           vail,
P. 118 BLAKE   133 Torn Limbs some leagues into the Island fly,

leak   frequency: 1   relative frequency: 0.0000
P. 96 HOLLAND   45 Who best could know to pump an Earth so leak

lean   frequency: 2   relative frequency: 0.0000
P. 150 INSTRUCTIONS   384 Mounting the neighbour Couple on lean Jade.
P. 171 PROPHECY   43 When a lean Treasurer shall in one year

leaner   frequency: 1   relative frequency: 0.0000
P. 313 CHEQUER INN   32 And leaner Dick then any Rake

leap   frequency: 1   relative frequency: 0.0000
P.   5 HASTINGS   50 The Golden Harvest, sees his Glasses leap.

leap-frog   frequency: 1   relative frequency: 0.0000
P. 96 HOLLAND   24 And oft at Leap-frog ore their Steeples plaid:

leaper's   frequency: 1   relative frequency: 0.0000
P. 86 FLECKNO   134 Like white fleaks rising from a Leaper's skin!

learn   frequency: 8   relative frequency: 0.0001
See also "learne."
P.   9 DIALOGUE   1 Courage my Soul, now learn to wield
P. 25 YOUNG LOVE   20 And learn Love before we may.
P. 56 BILL-BOROW   9 Here learn ye Mountains more unjust,
P. 56 BILL-BOROW   15 Learn here those humble steps to tread,
P. 94 DR. WITTY   27 Translators learn of her: but stay I slide
P. 112 ANNIVERSARY   385 'Where did he learn those Arts that cost us dear?
P. 164 INSTRUCTIONS   960 Nor of a Peasant scorn'd to learn the way.
P. 174 LOYALL SCOT   123 And learn to pin your faith upon their sleeves.

learn'd   frequency: 6   relative frequency: 0.0001
P. 41 THE MOWER   14 And learn'd to interline its cheek:
P. 116 BLAKE   83 They learn'd with Terrour, that nor Summers
                           heat,
P. 150 INSTRUCTIONS   409 But Morrice learn'd demonstrates, by the Post,
P. 186 BRITANNIA   50 Soe the learn'd Bard with Artfull song represt
P. 188 BRITANNIA   143 As easily learn'd Virtuoso's may
P. 199 DUKE   73 I'th Irish shambles he first learn'd the trade.

learne   frequency: 1   relative frequency: 0.0000
P. 167 KINGS VOWES   47 Miss and I will both learne to live on
                           Exhibition,

learned   frequency: 3   relative frequency: 0.0000
See also "learn'd."
P. 76 A. HOUSE   570 In their most learned Original:
P. 91 MAY'S DEATH   28 Prest for his place among the Learned throng.
P. 196 TWO HORSES   172 As learned men say, came out of their breeches,

learning   frequency: 3   relative frequency: 0.0000
P. 104 ANNIVERSARY   47 Learning a Musique in the Region clear,
P. 174 LOYALL SCOT   118 They wanted zeal and Learning, soe mistook
P. 185 BRITANNIA   41 Were Hurl'd to Hell by Learning Tyrants
                           Lore.

learns   frequency: 1   relative frequency: 0.0000
P. 94 DR. WITTY   20 Now learns the tongues of France and Italy;

lease   frequency: 1   relative frequency: 0.0000
P. 142 INSTRUCTIONS . 41 He needs no Seal, but to St. James's lease,

least   frequency: 14   relative frequency: 0.0002
P. 26 MISTRESS   17 An Age at least to every part,
P. 114 BLAKE   19 They dreaded to behold, Least the Sun's light,
P. 114 BLAKE   27 For least some Gloominess might stain her sky,
P. 115 BLAKE   74 Where you had most of strength, and least of
                           fear.
P. 122 TWO SONGS   11 Let's not then at least be seen

P.	123 O.C.	6	What death might least so fair a Life deface.
P.	123 O.C.	18	For what he least affected was admir'd,
P.	128 O.C.	225	Least others dare to think your zeale a maske,
P.	153 INSTRUCTIONS	499	The Kingdoms Farm he lets to them bid least:
P.	160 INSTRUCTIONS	802	And ablest Speaker, whc cf Law has least;
P.	160 INSTRUCTIONS	804	And for a Ccuns'llcr, he that has least Wit.
P.	170 PROPHECY	18	And whoreing shall be the least sin att Court,
P.	172 LOYALL SCOT	30	Then least Heaven fall ere thither hee Ascend.
P.	188 BRITANNIA	164	Least Court corrupcions should their souls engage.

leathern   frequency: 2   relative frequency: 0.0000
P.	83 A. HOUSE	770	Their Leathern Boats begin to hoist;
P.	144 INSTRUCTIONS	140	And flies like Batts with leathern Wings by Night.

leave   frequency: 19   relative frequency: 0.0003
P.	34 DAPHNIS	44	Thus his Leave resolved took.
P.	55 EPITAPH	1	Enough: and leave the rest to Fame.
P.	61 A. HOUSE	76	As if she said leave this to me.
P.	78 A. HOUSE	612	That I may never leave this Place:
P.	84 FLECKNO	68	Should leave his Soul to wander in the Air,
P.	87 ODE	5	'Tis time to leave the Books in dust,
P.	93 DR. WITTY	4	Take off the Cypress vail, but leave a mask,
P.	103 ANNIVERSARY	21	Well may they strive to leave them to their Son,
P.	112 ANNIVERSARY	372	'Can quickly leave us neither Earth nor Air.
P.	123 O.C.	27	And leave succeeding Ages cause to mourn,
P.	139 HOUSEWARMING	96	And till there you remove, you shall never leave burning
P.	143 INSTRUCTIONS	102	And Jermyn straight has leave to come agen.
P.	155 INSTRUCTIONS	599	Leave him alone when first they hear the Gun;
P.	161 INSTRUCTIONS	858	Nor gave the Commons leave to say their Pray'rs:
P.	169 ADVICE	58	Leave Temple Single to be beat in the Citty.
P.	181 MADE FREE	21	That all the Wcrld there did leave him;
P.	183 MADE FREE	98	Leave his freedome behind
P.	185 BRITANNIA	19	Till Atheist Lauderdale shall leave this Land,
P.	202 HISTORICALL	73	We leave to the repcrt cf Common fame.

leaver   frequency: 1   relative frequency: 0.0000
P.	154 INSTRUCTIONS	546	With Trident's Leaver, and great Shoulder heaves.

leaves   frequency: 10   relative frequency: 0.0002
See also "oak-leaves."
P.	12 DROP OF DEW	23	Shuns the sweat leaves and blossoms green;
P.	29 LOVER	61	Yet dying leaves a Perfume here,
P.	42 DAMON	38	And Oak leaves tipt with hony due.
P.	68 A. HOUSE	315	Their Leaves, that to the stalks are curl'd,
P.	77 A. HOUSE	577	Out of these scatter'd Sibyls Leaves
P.	112 ANNIVERSARY	356	'Of shedding Leaves, that with their Ocean breed.
P.	113 BLAKE	2	Leaves the new Wcrld and hastens for the old:
P.	142 INSTRUCTIONS	71	Ye neighb'ring Elms, that your green leaves did shed,
P.	168 ADVICE	28	For money comes when Seymour leaves the Chair.
P.	201 HISTORICALL	36	So slips away and leaves us in the lurch.

lebanon   frequency: 1   relative frequency: 0.0000
P.	17 BERMUDAS	26	From Lebanon, he stores the Land.

lecher. See "letcher."

led   frequency: 14   relative frequency: 0.0002
P.	17 BERMUDAS	6	That led us thrcugh the watry Maze,
P.	66 A. HOUSE	231	For Justice still that Courage led;
P.	122 TWO SONGS	20	Led our Lambs we knew not where.
P.	130 O.C.	305	And Richard yet, where his great parent led,
P.	144 INSTRUCTIONS	156	That sold their Master, led by Ashburnham.
P.	144 INSTRUCTIONS	160	Thought yet but Picneers, and led by Steward.
P.	146 INSTRUCTIONS	206	Else Talbot offer'd to have led them on.
P.	146 INSTRUCTIONS	214	Led the French Standard, weltring in his stride,
P.	148 INSTRUCTIONS	298	Led by great Garrway, and great Littleton.
P.	158 INSTRUCTIONS	736	Was led about in spcrt, the publick scorn.
P.	161 INSTRUCTIONS	859	But like his Pris'ners to the Bar them led,
P.	184 MADE FREE	122	Led in Hell by the Papes,
P.	187 BRITANNIA	108	Led up by the wise scn-in-law of Hide.
P.	202 HISTORICALL	64	The poore Priapus King led by the Nose

lee   frequency: 1   relative frequency: 0.0000

P. 148 INSTRUCTIONS 299 Lee, equal to obey or to command,

leeches   frequency: 1   relative frequency: 0.0000
See also "horse-leeches."
P.   73 A. HOUSE   476 Turn'd as they hang to Leeches quick;

left   frequency: 22   relative frequency: 0.0004
P.   22 NYMPH   36 Left me his Faun, but took his Heart.
P.   23 NYMPH   67 And when 'thad left me far away,
P.   64 A. HOUSE   188 'Yet Neither should be left behind.
P.   84 FLECKNO   36 Left off, and try'd t' allure me with his Lute.
P.   92 MAY'S DEATH   78 Hast left surviving Davenant still behind
P.   99 HOLLAND   141 Or, what is left, their Carthage overcome
P. 108 ANNIVERSARY   220 Whom thou hadst left beneath with Mantle rent.
P. 110 ANNIVERSARY   284 Left by the Wars Flood on the Mountains crest:
P. 123 O.C.   13 But long his Valour none had left that could
P. 126 O.C.   138 Left to determine now his fatal Hour;
P. 128 O.C.   230 To loathsome life, alas! are left behind.
P. 132 PARADISE   29 So that no room is here for Writers left,
P. 144 INSTRUCTIONS 153 In Loyal haste they left young Wives in Bed,
P. 149 INSTRUCTIONS 340 His Gout (yet still he curst) had left him
                          quite.
P. 158 INSTRUCTIONS 723 Now (nothing more at Chatham left to burn)
P. 159 INSTRUCTIONS 780 And who the Forts left unrepair'd? Pett.
P. 168 ADVICE   17 And place me by the Barr on the left hand
P. 182 MADE FREE   48 And his Creditors all left to Sorrow.
P. 185 BRITANNIA   36 In 's left the scales, in 's right hand plac'd
                          the sword,
P. 186 BRITANNIA   62 Her left Arm bears, the Antient Gallick shield
P. 188 BRITANNIA   130 And none are left these furyes to cast out.
P. 194 TWO HORSES   119 Till at last on a Scaffold he was left in the
                          lurch

legacies   frequency: 1   relative frequency: 0.0000
P.   33 DAPHNIS   27 But then Legacies no more

legal. See "legall."

legall   frequency: 1   relative frequency: 0.0000
P. 187 BRITANNIA   95 Whilst your starv'd power in Legall fetters
                          pines.

legally   frequency: 1   relative frequency: 0.0000
P. 190 STATUE   8 The Mimick so legally seiz'd of Whitehall.

legend   frequency: 1   relative frequency: 0.0000
P.   62 A. HOUSE   122 'Some One the holy Legend reads;

legerdemain'd   frequency: 1   relative frequency: 0.0000
P. 203 HISTORICALL   98 Baals wretched Curates Legerdemain'd it so,

legg   frequency: 1   relative frequency: 0.0000
P. 155 INSTRUCTIONS 605 Oft had he sent, of Duncombe and of Legg

legge. See "legg."

leghorn. See "legorne."

legion   frequency: 1   relative frequency: 0.0000
P. 175 LOYALL SCOT   136 The Legion Devil did but one man possess:

legislators   frequency: 1   relative frequency: 0.0000
P. 170 PROPHECY   9 When Legislators shall their trust betray

legorne   frequency: 1   relative frequency: 0.0000
P. 193 TWO HORSES   66 By pawning for Victualls their Guns at
                          Legorne;

leisure   frequency: 3   relative frequency: 0.0000
See also "leizure."
P.   54 THYESTE   5 In calm Leisure let me rest;
P.   62 A. HOUSE   97 'Within this holy leisure we
P. 106 ANNIVERSARY   120 Leisure to Time, and to my Weakness Strength,

leisurely   frequency: 1   relative frequency: 0.0000
P. 158 INSTRUCTIONS 724 The Holland Squadron leisurely return:

leizure   frequency: 1   relative frequency: 0.0000
P.   98 HOLLAND   127 That ours mean time at leizure might careen,

leness   frequency: 1   relative frequency: 0.0000

```
          P. 177 LOYALL SCOT    232 -leness and all the vice that did abound,

length                          frequency:    4    relative frequency: 0.0000
          P. 106 ANNIVERSARY   119 If gracious Heaven to my Life give length,
          P. 114 BLAKE          23 At length theirs vanishes, and fortune smiles;
          P. 116 BLAKE          95 Yet they by restless toyl, became at Length,
          P. 201 HISTORICALL     5 At length by wonderfull impulse of Fate

lent                            frequency:    3    relative frequency: 0.0000
          P.  27 LOVER          17 The Sea him lent these bitter Tears
          P.  84 FLECKNO        46 Ask'd civilly if he had eat this Lent.
          P. 154 INSTRUCTIONS  543 Old Neptune springs the Tydes, and Water lent:

leprous                         frequency:    1    relative frequency: 0.0000
          P. 188 BRITANNIA     149 Tyrants like Leprous Kings for publick weal

leslie's.  See "lesly's."

lesly's                         frequency:    1    relative frequency: 0.0000
          P. 139 HOUSEWARMING   88 By a Model more excellent than Lesly's Folly.

less                            frequency:   23    relative frequency: 0.0004
          P.  12 DROP OF DEW    26 The greater Heaven in an Heaven less.
          P.  16 EYES           26 That weep the more, and see the less:
          P.  23 NYMPH          44 Its self in me. How could I less
          P.  42 DAMON          34 Esteem me, and my Presents less?
          P.  49 THE GARDEN     41 Mean while the Mind, from pleasure less,
          P.  57 BILL-BOROW     32 Directs, and this no less by Day.
          P.  60 A. HOUSE       44 Things greater are in less contain'd.
          P.  61 A. HOUSE       67 Nor less the Rooms within commends
          P.  82 A. HOUSE      755 Aranjuez, as less, disdain'd;
          P.  82 A. HOUSE      759 Much less the Dead's Elysian Fields,
          P.  88 ODE            42 Allows of penetration less:
          P.  96 HOLLAND        14 Less then what building Swallows bear away;
          P.  96 HOLLAND        51 But for less envy some joynt States endures,
          P. 104 ANNIVERSARY    36 Much less themselves to perfect them begin;
          P. 108 ANNIVERSARY   228 Yielding to Rule, because it made thee Less.
          P. 121 TWO SONGS      47 Less Loves set of each others praise,
          P. 123 O.C.           17 And so less useful where he most desir'd,
          P. 127 O.C.          163 As jealous only here lest all be less,
          P. 131 PARADISE       11 Yet as I read, soon growing less severe,
          P. 131 PARADISE       18 Jealous I was that some less skilful hand
          P. 159 INSTRUCTIONS  756 And were it burnt, yet less would be their pain.
          P. 160 INSTRUCTIONS  803 Who less Estate, for Treasurer most fit;
          P. 165 INSTRUCTIONS  989 (Where few the number, choice is there less hard)

lessen                          frequency:    1    relative frequency: 0.0000
          P. 124 O.C.           62 And He to lessen hers his Sorrow feigns:

lessening.  See "less'ning."

lesser                          frequency:    3    relative frequency: 0.0000
          P.  81 A. HOUSE      706 Disdains to be for lesser prais'd.
          P.  82 A. HOUSE      765 Your lesser World contains the same.
          P. 122 TWO SONGS      35 Now lesser Beauties may take place,

less'ning                       frequency:    1    relative frequency: 0.0000
          P. 127 O.C.          177 And in a valour less'ning Arthur's deeds,

lessons                         frequency:    1    relative frequency: 0.0000
          P. 205 HISTORICALL   156 And brought new Lessons to the Duke from Rome.

lest                            frequency:   31    relative frequency: 0.0006
          P.   5 HASTINGS       24 Lest He become like Them, taste more then one.
          P.   9 DIALOGUE       22 Lest one Leaf thy Side should strain.
          P.  12 DROP OF DEW    16 Trembling lest it grow impure:
          P.  33 DAPHNIS        15 Lest the World should untwine;
          P.  39 PICTURE        36 Lest Flora angry at thy crime,
          P.  41 THE MOWER      28 Lest any Tyrant him out-doe.
          P.  62 A. HOUSE      108 'Lest the great Bridegroom find them dim.
          P.  65 A. HOUSE      224 'Though guiltless lest thou perish there.
          P.  75 A. HOUSE      519 The Thorn, lest it should hurt her, draws
          P.  78 A. HOUSE      613 But, lest your Fetters prove too weak,
          P.  79 A. HOUSE      663 And lest She see him go to Bed;
          P.  81 A. HOUSE      732 Lest the smooth Forehead wrinkled sit:
          P.  84 FLECKNO        67 Lest his too suttle Body, growing rare,
          P.  99 HOLLAND       143 Unless our Senate, lest their Youth disuse,
          P. 124 O.C.           33 And, lest their force the tender burthen wrong,
          P. 124 O.C.           61 She lest He grieve hides what She can her
                                   pains,
          P. 127 O.C.          163 As jealous only here lest all be less,
```

P. 131 PARADISE	15 Lest he perplext the things he would explain,
P. 140 HOUSEWARMING	110 Lest with driving too far his Tallow impair;
P. 142 INSTRUCTIONS	39 Draw no Commission lest the Court should lye,
P. 143 INSTRUCTIONS	89 Fears lest he scorn a Woman once assay'd,
P. 143 INSTRUCTIONS	95 And washing (lest the scent her Crime disclose)
P. 148 INSTRUCTIONS	312 Lest the sure Peace, forsooth, too soon appear.
P. 151 INSTRUCTIONS	447 Yet Lewis writes, and lest our Hearts should break,
P. 157 INSTRUCTIONS	664 Then, lest Heav'n fall, e're thither he ascend.
P. 158 INSTRUCTIONS	712 Our Merchant-men, lest they should burn, we drown.
P. 158 INSTRUCTIONS	722 And shrunk, lest Navigable, to a Ford.
P. 161 INSTRUCTIONS	852 Lest some new Tomkins spring a fresh debate.
P. 178 LOYALL SCOT	284 Forwarn'd him therefore lest in time he were
P. 188 BRITANNIA	150 Must be immur'd, lest their contagion steal
P. 316 CHEQUER INN	173 Lest some shou'd take me for the Man

let   frequency: 41   relative frequency: 0.0008
        See also "lett."

P. 9 DIALOGUE	8 In this day's Combat let it shine:
P. 15 THE CORONET	23 And let these wither, so that he may die,
P. 17 EYES	53 Thus let your Streams o'reflow your Springs,
P. 18 BERMUDAS	33 Oh let our Voice his Praise exalt,
P. 20 THYRSIS	29 I prethee let us spend our time to come
P. 20 THYRSIS	45 Chorus. Then let us give Carillo charge o'th Sheep,
P. 21 SOUL & BODY	18 Has made me live to let me dye.
P. 24 NYMPH	113 Let it be weeping too: but there
P. 27 MISTRESS	37 Now let us sport us while we may;
P. 27 MISTRESS	41 Let us roll all our Strength, and all
P. 33 DAPHNIS	8 Nor yet let her Lover go.
P. 33 DAPHNIS	10 Soon she let that Niceness fall;
P. 38 PICTURE	17 O then let me in time compound,
P. 38 PICTURE	23 Let me be laid,
P. 54 THYESTE	5 In calm Leisure let me rest;
P. 60 A. HOUSE	45 Let others vainly strive t'immure
P. 68 A. HOUSE	298 In fragrant Vollyes they let fly;
P. 73 A. HOUSE	473 Let others tell the Paradox,
P. 85 FLECKNO	111 Let it suffice that we could eat in peace;
P. 97 HOLLAND	81 Let it suffice to give their Country Fame
P. 98 HOLLAND	103 Let this one court'sie witness all the rest;
P. 99 HOLLAND	152 Vainly in Hell let Pluto domineer.
P. 107 ANNIVERSARY	181 Let this one Sorrow interweave among
P. 112 ANNIVERSARY	393 'But let them write his Praise that love him best,
P. 117 BLAKE	109 Of Speedy Victory let no man doubt,
P. 127 O.C.	165 Then let us to cur course of Mourning keep:
P. 149 INSTRUCTIONS	351 The Irish-Herd is now let loose, and comes
P. 153 INSTRUCTIONS	507 Let no Man touch them, or demand his own,
P. 158 INSTRUCTIONS	737 Black Day accurs'd! On thee let no man hale
P. 158 INSTRUCTIONS	740 Thee, the Year's monster, let thy Dam devour.
P. 161 INSTRUCTIONS	826 Let them come up so to go down agen.
P. 163 INSTRUCTIONS	910 But let some other Painter draw the sound:
P. 168 ADVICE	11 Then change the scene and let the next present
P. 168 ADVICE	27 And of his dear Reward let none dispair,
P. 168 ADVICE	29 Change once again and let the next afford
P. 196 TWO HORSES	181 Let the Citty drink Coffee and Quietly groan
P. 199 DUKE	76 Let the beholder by thy Art descrey
P. 199 DUKE	78 Let Belassis Autumnall face be seene,
P. 200 DUKE	104 Let not thy life and crowne togeather end,
P. 202 HISTORICALL	75 Let loose the Raines and give the Realme away:
P. 204 HISTORICALL	135 Let Cromwells Ghost smile with Contempt to see

letanies   frequency: 1   relative frequency: 0.0000
        P. 174 LOYALL SCOT   91 All Letanies in this have wanted faith:

letcher   frequency: 1   relative frequency: 0.0000
        P. 152 INSTRUCTIONS   473 Never old Letcher more repugnance felt,

lethe   frequency: 1   relative frequency: 0.0000
        P. 172 LOYALL SCOT   12 And of wise Lethe hee had took a draught.

lets   frequency: 4   relative frequency: 0.0000
        P. 37 DEFINITION   14 Two perfect Loves; nor lets them close:
        P. 75 A. HOUSE   534 The eldest of its young lets drop,
        P. 122 TWO SONGS   27 Come, lets in some Carol new
        P. 153 INSTRUCTIONS 499 The Kingdoms Farm he lets to them bid least:

let's   frequency: 4   relative frequency: 0.0000
        See also "letts."
        P. 46 AMETAS   15 Then let's both lay by our Rope,

```
P.  83 A. HOUSE       775 Let's in: for the dark Hemisphere
P. 122 TWO SONGS       11 Let's not then at least be seen
P. 190 STATUE          37 Let's have a King then, be he new be he old;
```

lett   frequency: 1   relative frequency: 0.0000
```
P. 200 DUKE            96 And can her Guardian Angell lett her stoope
```

letter   frequency: 1   relative frequency: 0.0000
```
P. 314 CHEQUER INN     52 On backside of their Letter some
```

letters   frequency: 1   relative frequency: 0.0000
```
P. 151 INSTRUCTIONS   449 Two Letters next unto Breda are sent,
```

letts   frequency: 2   relative frequency: 0.0000
```
P. 194 TWO HORSES     108 Letts be true to ourselves; whom then need wee
                              fear?
P. 199 DUKE            75 Letts see the nuntio Arundells sweete face;
```

level   frequency: 1   relative frequency: 0.0000
```
P.  96 HOLLAND         33 Or as they over the new Level rang'd
```

level-coyl   frequency: 1   relative frequency: 0.0000
```
P.  96 HOLLAND         28 The Earth and Water play at Level-coyl;
```

levell'd   frequency: 2   relative frequency: 0.0000
```
P.  72 A. HOUSE       443 A levell'd space, as smooth and plain,
P. 109 ANNIVERSARY    262 Had quickly Levell'd every Cedar's top.
```

levellers   frequency: 1   relative frequency: 0.0000
```
P.  73 A. HOUSE       450 Which Levellers take Pattern at,
```

lever. See "leaver."

leviathan   frequency: 1   relative frequency: 0.0000
```
See also "leviathen."
P. 186 BRITANNIA       64 Inscrib'd Leviathan the sovereign Lord,
```

leviathans   frequency: 1   relative frequency: 0.0000
```
See also "wood-leviathans."
P. 185 BRITANNIA       32 Leviathans and absolute comands.
```

leviathen   frequency: 1   relative frequency: 0.0000
```
P. 175 LOYALL SCOT    147 Leviathen served up and Behemoth.
```

lewd   frequency: 1   relative frequency: 0.0000
```
See also "lew'd."
P. 182 MADE FREE       55 Nay his Company lewd
```

lew'd   frequency: 1   relative frequency: 0.0000
```
P. 185 BRITANNIA       12 Whilest the Lew'd Court in drunken slumbers
                              lyes,
```

lewdness   frequency: 1   relative frequency: 0.0000
```
P. 189 BRITANNIA      172 Yeild to all these in Lewdness, lust, and shame.
```

lewis   frequency: 5   relative frequency: 0.0001
```
P. 151 INSTRUCTIONS   428 To Master Lewis, and tell Coward tale,
P. 151 INSTRUCTIONS   439 But Lewis was of Memory but dull,
P. 151 INSTRUCTIONS   447 Yet Lewis writes, and lest our Hearts should
                              break,
P. 185 BRITANNIA       34 And in his place a Lewis Changling lay.
P. 187 BRITANNIA       94 So boundless Lewis in full Glory shines,
```

lewis's   frequency: 1   relative frequency: 0.0000
```
P. 163 INSTRUCTIONS   914 And finds the Drums Lewis's March did beat.
```

liar. See "lyar."

liars. See "lyers."

liberally   frequency: 2   relative frequency: 0.0000
```
P. 191 STATUE          42 That so liberally treated the members at supper.
P. 193 TWO HORSES      84 For selling their Conscience were Liberally
                              paid.
```

liberties. See "libertyes."

liberty   frequency: 8   relative frequency: 0.0001
```
See also "libertye."
P.  62 A. HOUSE       100 'But hedge our Liberty about.
P.  91 MAY'S DEATH     45 Tell them of Liberty, the Stories fine,
```

```
         P.  96 HOLLAND        54 Nor bear strict service, nor pure Liberty.
         P. 105 ANNIVERSARY    70 Framing a Liberty that still went back;
         P. 110 ANNIVERSARY   288 Of Liberty, not drunken with its Wine.
         P. 110 ANNIVERSARY   289 That sober Liberty which men may have,
         P. 111 ANNIVERSARY   316 With the same liberty as Points and Lace;
         P. 198 DUKE           22 Then to destroy their liberty and laws,

libertye                       frequency:   1    relative frequency: 0.0000
         P. 171 PROPHECY       56 And wish in vain Venetian Libertye.

libertyes                      frequency:   1    relative frequency: 0.0000
         P. 199 DUKE           64 And to destroy our libertyes they hope

liberum                        frequency:   1    relative frequency: 0.0000
         P.  96 HOLLAND        26 To shew them what's their Mare Liberum.

licens'd                       frequency:   1    relative frequency: 0.0000
         P.  66 A. HOUSE      235 Which licens'd either Peace or Force,

lick                           frequency:   2    relative frequency: 0.0000
         P.  78 A. HOUSE      635 And its yet muddy back doth lick,
         P. 315 CHEQUER INN   117 And did his Trencher lick

licks                          frequency:   2    relative frequency: 0.0000
         P.  43 DAMON          46 The Sun himself licks off my Sweat.
         P.  77 A. HOUSE      590 Me licks, and clasps, and curles, and hales.

lids                           frequency:   2    relative frequency: 0.0000
         P.  19 THYRSIS         2 And shut up our divided Lids,
         P. 129 O.C.          249 Those gentle rays under the lids were fled,

lie                            frequency:   4    relative frequency: 0.0000
See also "lye."
         P.  11 DIALOGUE       58 The minted Gold shall lie;
         P.  12 DIALOGUE       77 The rest does lie beyond the Pole,
         P.  38 PICTURE         3 In the green Grass she loves to lie,
         P. 140 HIS HOUSE       3 Here lie Golden Eriberies,

liege                          frequency:   1    relative frequency: 0.0000
         P. 180 STOCKSMARKET   34 That when to the scaffold your liege you had
                                  brought

lies                           frequency:   1    relative frequency: 0.0000
See "lyes."
         P. 140 HIS HOUSE       1 Here lies the sacred Bones

lieutenant                     frequency:   2    relative frequency: 0.0000
         P. 145 INSTRUCTIONS  174 Gentlest of men, and his Lieutenant mild,
         P. 156 INSTRUCTIONS  645 Captain, Lieutenant, Ensign, all make haste,

lieutenants                    frequency:   1    relative frequency: 0.0000
See also "deputy-lieutenants."
         P. 204 HISTORICALL   151 Here for an Ensignes or Lieutenants place

life                           frequency:  29    relative frequency: 0.0006
         P.   4 HASTINGS       20 And on the Tree of Life once made a Feast,
         P.   5 HASTINGS       60 And Art indeed is long, but Life is Short.
         P.  22 NYMPH          40 Could so mine idle Life have spent.
         P.  27 MISTRESS       44 Thorough the Iron gates of Life.
         P.  28 LOVER          40 Th' Amphibium of Life and Death.
         P.  49 THE GARDEN     33 What wond'rous Life in this I lead!
         P.  55 EPITAPH        16 She summ'd her Life up ev'ry day;
         P. 106 ANNIVERSARY   119 If gracious Heaven to my Life give length,
         P. 108 ANNIVERSARY   221 For all delight of Life thou then didst lose,
         P. 123 O.C.            6 What death might least so fair a Life deface.
         P. 125 O.C.           71 And now his Life, suspended by her breath,
         P. 125 O.C.           93 If some dear branch where it extends its life
         P. 128 O.C.          214 For these his life adventur'd every day:
         P. 128 O.C.          230 To loathsome life, alas! are left behind.
         P. 142 INSTRUCTIONS   49 Paint then again Her Highness to the life,
         P. 152 INSTRUCTIONS  456 Who yields his Sword has Title to his Life.
         P. 157 INSTRUCTIONS  671 That precious life he yet disdains to save,
         P. 168 ADVICE         14 Whose life does scarce one Generous Action own,
         P. 172 LOYALL SCOT    32 Hee entertains the while his life too short,
         P. 172 LOYALL SCOT    37 That pretious life hee yet disdaines to save
         P. 173 LOYALL SCOT    78 Where life resides or Understanding dwells:
         P. 175 LOYALL SCOT   156 In faith Erronicus and in life Prophane
         P. 176 LOYALL SCOT   183 And while hee spared the keepers life hee fail'd.
         P. 189 BRITANNIA     182 Balm in their wounds, will fleeting life restore.
         P. 192 TWO HORSES     44 And the Kings wicked life say God there is
                                  none;
         P. 195 TWO HORSES    126 And Free men alike value life and Estate.
```

P. 200	DUKE	104	Let not thy life and crowne togeather end,
P. 200	DUKE	109	Ends all the Joys of England and thy life.
P. 203	HISTORICALL	95	Becomes the Priests Amphitrio dureing Life.

life-blood   frequency: 1   relative frequency: 0.0000
    P. 22   NYMPH   19 In this warm life-blood, which doth part

lift   frequency: 1   relative frequency: 0.0000
    P. 17   BERMUDAS   10 That lift the Deep upon their Backs.

light   frequency: 17   relative frequency: 0.0003

P. 12	DROP OF DEW	12	Shines with a scurnful Light;
P. 12	DROP OF DEW	24	And, recollecting its own Light,
P. 16	EYES	44	But as they seem the Tears of Light.
P. 23	NYMPH	41	For it was full of sport; and light
P. 27	LOVER	5	But soon these Flames do lose their light,
P. 30	THE GALLERY	27	And, by a Light obscure, dost rave
P. 44	GLO-WORMS	1	Ye living Lamps, by whose dear light
P. 49	THE GARDEN	56	Waves in its Plumes the various Light.
P. 77	A. HOUSE	582	I in this light Mosaick read.
P. 107	ANNIVERSARY	147	And knowing not where Heavens choice may light,
P. 111	ANNIVERSARY	328	Pleas'd with that other World of moving Light;
P. 111	ANNIVERSARY	343	So while our Star that gives us Light and Heat,
P. 114	BLAKE	19	They dreaded to behold, Least the Sun's light,
P. 130	O.C.	310	In private, to be view'd by better light;
P. 159	INSTRUCTIONS	746	Thou, and thy Fellows, held'st the odious Light.
P. 162	INSTRUCTIONS	886	Only dispers'd by a weak Tapers light;
P. 164	INSTRUCTIONS	958	Which, in your Splendor hid, Corrode your Light;

lightfoot   frequency: 1   relative frequency: 0.0000
    P. 19   THYRSIS   24 Our Lightfoot we may give away;

lightning   frequency: 6   relative frequency: 0.0001

P. 16	EYES	40	And here the hissing Lightning slakes.
P. 87	ODE	13	And, like the three-fork'd Lightning, first
P. 124	O.C.	69	And frequent lightning to her Soul that flyes,
P. 129	O.C.	265	When angry Jove darts lightning through the aire,
P. 149	INSTRUCTIONS	358	Blasted with Lightning, struck with Thunder fell.
P. 154	INSTRUCTIONS	557	With Thunder and Lightning from each armed Cloud;

lights   frequency: 2   relative frequency: 0.0000
    P. 45   GLO-WORMS   13 Your courteous Lights in vain you wast,
    P. 71   A. HOUSE   405 When on another quick She lights,

ligne. See "ligny."

ligny   frequency: 1   relative frequency: 0.0000
    P. 127   O.C.   154 Gave chase to Ligny on the Belgick Coast.

lik'd   frequency: 3   relative frequency: 0.0000

P. 131	PARADISE	12	I lik'd his Project, the success did fear;
P. 139	HOUSEWARMING	61	He lik'd the advice, and then soon it assay'd;
P. 153	INSTRUCTIONS	504	(This lik'd him best) his Cash beyond Sea whip.

like   frequency: 147   relative frequency: 0.0030
  See also "bee-like," "god-like-good,"
           "image-like," "saint-like,"
           "stork-like," "sun-like."

P. 3	LOVELACE	22	Like the grim consistory on thy Booke;
P. 4	HASTINGS	12	And on Times Wheel sticks like a Remora.
P. 5	HASTINGS	24	Lest He become like Them, taste more then one.
P. 5	HASTINGS	49	Like some sad Chymist, who, prepar'd to reap
P. 10	DIALOGUE	28	Like another God below.
P. 12	DROP OF DEW	13	Like its own Tear,
P. 15	EYES	8	Like wat'ry Lines and Plummets fall.
P. 16	EYES	49	Now like two Clouds dissolving, drop,
P. 16	EYES	51	Now like two Fountains trickle down;
P. 16	EYES	52	Now like two floods o'return and drown.
P. 17	BERMUDAS	18	Like golden Lamps in a green Night.
P. 23	NYMPH	82	It like a bank of Lillies laid.
P. 24	NYMPH	96	Sad, slowly dropping like a Gumme.
P. 27	LOVER	6	Like Meteors of a Summers night:
P. 27	MISTRESS	34	Sits on thy skin like morning dew,
P. 27	MISTRESS	38	And now, like am'rous birds of prey,
P. 28	LOVER	48	Like Ajax, the mad Tempest braves.

```
P.  29 THE GALLERY      18 Like to Aurora in the Dawn;
P.  30 THE GALLERY      25 Like an Enchantress here thou show'st,
P.  30 THE GALLERY      34 Like Venus in her pearly Boat.
P.  32 MOURNING         24 Like Grief, is from her Windows thrown.
P.  35 DAPHNIS          78 Like the Gourmand Hebrew dead,
P.  41 DAMON             5 Like her fair Eyes the day was fair;
P.  41 DAMON             6 But scorching like his am'rous Care.
P.  41 DAMON             7 Sharp like his Sythe his Sorrow was,
P.  41 DAMON             8 And wither'd like his Hopes the Grass.
P.  49 THE GARDEN       53 There like a Bird it sits, and sings,
P.  56 BILL-BOROW        4 A Line more circular and like;
P.  59 A. HOUSE         26 Like Nature, orderly and near:
P.  62 A. HOUSE        106 'Like Virgin Amazons do fight.
P.  64 A. HOUSE        192 'Like Chrystal pure with Cotton warm.
P.  65 A. HOUSE        215 'For like themselves they alter all,
P.  67 A. HOUSE        257 But, waving these aside like Flyes,
P.  67 A. HOUSE        268 Like Gipsies that a Child hath stoln.
P.  70 A. HOUSE        371 Where Men like Grashoppers appear,
P.  71 A. HOUSE        389 Who seem like Israalites to be,
P.  72 A. HOUSE        428 Smells like an Alexanders sweat.
P.  72 A. HOUSE        434 Like a calm Sea it shews the Rocks:
P.  72 A. HOUSE        437 Or, like the Desert Memphis Sand,
P.  74 A. HOUSE        491 It like two Pedigrees appears,
P.  77 A. HOUSE        580 Like Mexique Paintings, all the Plumes.
P.  77 A. HOUSE        592 Like some great Prelate of the Grove,
P.  78 A. HOUSE        619 While, like a Guard on either side,
P.  78 A. HOUSE        621 This, like a long and equal Thread,
P.  78 A. HOUSE        640 Narcissus like, the Sun too pines.
P.  82 A. HOUSE        739 And, like a sprig of Misleto,
P.  83 A. HOUSE        771 And, like Antipodes in Shoes,
P.  83 A. HOUSE        773 How Tortoise like, but not so slow,
P.  83 A. HOUSE        776 Does now like one of them appear.
P.  86 FLECKNO         134 Like white fleaks rising from a Leaper's skin!
P.  86 FLECKNO         152 And roar'd out, like Perillus in's own Bull;
P.  87 ODE             13 And, like the three-fork'd Lightning, first
P.  91 MAY'S DEATH     38 Like Pembroke at the Masque, and then did rate.
P.  96 HOLLAND         38 Something like Government among them brings.
P.  96 HOLLAND         52 Who look like a Commission of the Sewers.
P.  98 HOLLAND         97 They try, like Statuaries, if they can,
P.  98 HOLLAND        132 And, like its own Seas, only Ebbs to flow.
P. 103 ANNIVERSARY      1 Like the vain Curlings of the Watry maze,
P. 105 ANNIVERSARY    101 And in his sev'ral Aspects, like a Star,
P. 106 ANNIVERSARY    123 Like the shrill Huntsman that prevents the
                          East,
P. 107 ANNIVERSARY    183 Like skilful Looms which through the costly
                          thred
P. 109 ANNIVERSARY    234 As a small Cloud, like a Mans hand didst rise;
P. 109 ANNIVERSARY    258 Didst (like thine Olive) still refuse to Reign;
P. 110 ANNIVERSARY    283 Thou, and thine House, like Noah's Eight did
                          rest,
P. 111 ANNIVERSARY    332 And Stars (like Tapers) burn'd upon his Herse:
P. 123 O.C.             9 And blame the last Act, like Spectators vain,
P. 125 O.C.            73 Like polish'd Mirrcurs, so his steely Brest
P. 130 O.C.           300 Wander like ghosts about thy loved tombe;
P. 131 O.C.           318 His brows, like an imperiall jewell grac'd.
P. 132 PARADISE        43 Just Heav'n Thee, like Tiresias, to requite,
P. 132 PARADISE        48 And like a Pack-Horse tires without his Bells.
P. 132 PARADISE        49 Their Fancies like our bushy Points appear,
P. 132 PARADISE        53 Thy verse created like thy Theme sublime,
P. 137 HOUSEWARMING     7 Like the King-fisher chuseth to build in the
                          Broom,
P. 137 HOUSEWARMING     8 And nestles in flames like the Salamander.
P. 138 HOUSEWARMING    37 And hence like Pharoah that Israel prest
P. 138 HOUSEWARMING    56 For his House then would grow like a Vegetable.
P. 139 HOUSEWARMING    77 Like Jove under Aetna o'erwhelming the Gyant,
P. 139 HOUSEWARMING    90 A Ianthorn, like Faux's surveys the burnt
                          Town,
P. 139 HOUSEWARMING    94 Like vain Chymists, a flower from its ashes
                          returning;
P. 140 HOUSEWARMING   111 When like the good Oxe, for publick good chear,
P. 141 INSTRUCTIONS    17 Where, like the new Controller, all men laugh
P. 141 INSTRUCTIONS    34 Member'd like Mules, with Elephantine chine.
P. 143 INSTRUCTIONS   106 The House of Commons clatt'ring like the Men.
P. 144 INSTRUCTIONS   136 And on all Trade like Casawar she feeds:
P. 144 INSTRUCTIONS   140 And flies like Batts with leathern Wings by
                          Night.
P. 144 INSTRUCTIONS   144 And most rapacious, like himself begot.
P. 145 INSTRUCTIONS   166 Hid with his Elbow like the Spice he stole.
P. 146 INSTRUCTIONS   224 Shall with one Breath like thistle-down
                          disperse.
P. 147 INSTRUCTIONS   276 Broach'd whole Brigades like Larks upon his Lance.
```

P. 149 INSTRUCTIONS   333 Thus, like fair Thieves, the Commons Purse they share,
P. 149 INSTRUCTIONS   356 And sits in State Divine like Jove the fulminant!
P. 150 INSTRUCTIONS   370 Like Slaves, shall beg for Peace at Hollands doors.
P. 151 INSTRUCTIONS   445 And so enforc'd, like Enemy or Spy,
P. 153 INSTRUCTIONS   513 If they for nothing ill, like Ashen-wood,
P. 153 INSTRUCTIONS   514 Or think him, like Herb-John, for nothing good.
P. 153 INSTRUCTIONS   533 Like am'rous Victors he begins to shave,
P. 154 INSTRUCTIONS   562 With panting Heart, lay like a fish cn Land,
P. 154 INSTRUCTIONS   574 Like molting Fowl, a weak and easie Prey.
P. 156 INSTRUCTIONS   634 Large Limbs, like Ox, not to be kill'd but shcwn.
P. 156 INSTRUCTIONS   641 And saw himself confin'd, like Sheep in Pen;
P. 156 INSTRUCTIONS   648 Like Shadrack, Mesheck, and Abednego.
P. 157 INSTRUCTIONS   677 Like a glad Lover, the fierce Flames he meets,
P. 157 INSTRUCTIONS   680 Like the Sun's Statue stands of burnish'd Gold.
P. 161 INSTRUCTIONS   859 But like his Pris'ners to the Bar them led,
P. 162 INSTRUCTIONS   868 Like Knife with Iv'ry haft, and edge of Lead.
P. 162 INSTRUCTIONS   871 In Chair, he smoaking sits like Master-Cook,
P. 162 INSTRUCTIONS   872 And a Foll-Bill does like his Apron look.
P. 162 INSTRUCTIONS   877 When Grievance urg'd, he swells like squatted Toad,
P. 162 INSTRUCTIONS   878 Frisks like a Frog to croak a Taxes load.
P. 162 INSTRUCTIONS   880 An Urinal, and sit like any Hen.
P. 162 INSTRUCTIONS   882 And soaks his Sack with Norfolk like a Toast.
P. 167 KINGS VOWES   50 Tho' not rule like the Turk yet I will be so drest,
P. 171 PROPHECY   53 But like the Bellydes shall toyle in vaine
P. 172 LOYALL SCOT   43 Like a glad lover the fierce Flames hee meets
P. 173 LOYALL SCOT   46 Like the sun's Statue stands of burnisht Gold:
P. 174 LOYALL SCOT   90 Noe Scotch was ever like a Bishops feud.
P. 174 LOYALL SCOT   104 A Bishop will like Mahomet tear the Moon
P. 174 LOYALL SCOT   124 Ah! like Lotts wife they still look Back and Halt
P. 174 LOYALL SCOT   125 And surplic'd shew like Pillars too of salt.
P. 175 LOYALL SCOT   171 Like Smutty Storyes in Pure Linnen Wrapt.
P. 176 LOYALL SCOT   177 Like Snake that Swallowes toad doth Dragon swell.
P. 176 LOYALL SCOT   187 With single light like the two Neckt Swan,
P. 176 LOYALL SCOT   208 And would like Chymists fixing Mercury
P. 178 LOYALL SCOT   255 That syllable like a Picts wall devides.
P. 179 STOCKSMARKET   12 That shews him a monster more like than a king.
P. 183 MADE FREE   89 Like Ants at a Straw,
P. 185 BRITANNIA   33 Thus Fayry like the King they steal away
P. 185 BRITANNIA   46 How, like ripe fruit, she dropt from of the Throne
P. 187 BRITANNIA   109 With fury drunke like Backanalls they roar
P. 187 BRITANNIA   119 Like a Tame spinster in 's seraglio sits,
P. 188 BRITANNIA   149 Tyrants like Leprous Kings for publick weal
P. 191 TWO HORSES   10 Would roar like a Devill with a man in his belly:
P. 194 TWO HORSES   102 Thou knowest what danger was like tc come of it;
P. 194 TWO HORSES   111 On ocasions like these he oft steals away
P. 195 TWO HORSES   123 W. He that dyes for Ceremonies dyes like a fool.
P. 195 TWO HORSES   150 None ever Reign'd like old Besse in the Ruffe.
P. 201 HISTORICALL   2 Much like the Son of Kish that lofty Jew,
P. 204 HISTORICALL   129 Like a true Lover for her dying Mate.
P. 204 HISTORICALL   134 Ill luck starts up and thrives like Evil weeds.
P. 313 CHEQUER INN   36 And looks like Bird of Goale
P. 314 CHEQUER INN   59 Like Maidens at a Statute Fair,
P. 314 CHEQUER INN   61 The Lady drest like any Bride
P. 314 CHEQUER INN   86 And popping like an Elder Gun
P. 316 CHEQUER INN   134 Fathers and Sons like Coupl'd Slaves
P. 316 CHEQUER INN   170 Like Sweat Meates, for their Girles and Wives
P. 317 CHEQUER INN   181 Just like our Rotten Pump at home

likely   frequency: 1   relative frequency: 0.0000
P. 67 A. HOUSE   276 'Tis likely better thus fulfill'd.

likeness   frequency: 2   relative frequency: 0.0000
P. 39 THE MATCH   13 But likeness sccn together drew
P. 179 STOCKSMARKET   15 And some by the likeness Sir Robert suspect

likes   frequency: 1   relative frequency: 0.0000
P. 30 THE GALLERY   50 That at the Entrance likes me best:

likewise   frequency: 1   relative frequency: 0.0000

    P. 196 TWO HORSES   174 Have the spirit of Prophecy likewise behind?

liking   frequency: 2   relative frequency: 0.0000
    P. 94 DR. WITTY   34 Liking themselves the worse the more they look,
    P. 94 DR. WITTY   36 Now worth the liking, but thy Book and thee.

lilies. See "lillies," "lillyes."

lillies   frequency: 6   relative frequency: 0.0001
    P. 23 NYMPH   73 And Lillies, that you would it guess
    P. 23 NYMPH   81 For, in the flaxen lillies shade,
    P. 23 NYMPH   82 It like a bank cf Lillies laid.
    P. 24 NYMPH   90 In whitest sheets of Lillies cold.
    P. 24 NYMPH   92 Lillies without, Roses within.
    P. 63 A. HOUSE   142 'On you the Lillies show'ring down:

lilly   frequency: 1   relative frequency: 0.0000
    P. 72 A. HOUSE   444 As Clothes for Lilly strecht to stain.

lillyes   frequency: 1   relative frequency: 0.0000
    P. 23 NYMPH   77 Among the beds of Lillyes, I

lily. See "lilly."

limbs   frequency: 10   relative frequency: 0.0002
    P. 24 NYMPH   89 And its pure virgin Limbs to fold
    P. 118 BLAKE   133 Torn Limbs some leagues into the Island fly,
    P. 124 O.C.   53 A silent fire now wasts those Limbs of Wax,
    P. 149 INSTRUCTIONS   339 And with fresh Age felt his glad Limbs unite;
    P. 156 INSTRUCTIONS   634 Large Limbs, like Ox, not to be kill'd but
                              shown.
    P. 156 INSTRUCTIONS   656 Harden'd and cool'd his Limbs, so soft, so
                              white,
    P. 157 INSTRUCTIONS   686 His alt'ring Form, and soder'd Limbs to melt;
    P. 168 ADVICE   8 Their wearied Limbs and minds to recreate,
    P. 172 LOYALL SCOT   22 Hardned and Cool'd those Limbs soe soft, soe
                              white,
    P. 173 LOYALL SCOT   52 His Altred form and sodred Limbs to Melt,

lime-twigs   frequency: 1   relative frequency: 0.0000
    P. 76 A. HOUSE   574 Then if She were with Lime-twigs knit.

limit. See "limitt."

limits   frequency: 1   relative frequency: 0.0000
    P. 128 O.C.   203 But within one its narrow limits fall,

limitt   frequency: 1   relative frequency: 0.0000
    P. 190 STATUE   6 To Limitt his troop to this Theatre small,

limn   frequency: 1   relative frequency: 0.0000
    P. 141 INSTRUCTIONS   9 Or hast thou mark't how antique Masters limn

limpid   frequency: 1   relative frequency: 0.0000
    P. 80 A. HOUSE   701 And for a Glass the limpid Brook,

lin'd   frequency: 1   relative frequency: 0.0000
    P. 112 ANNIVERSARY   374 'Through double Oak, <and> lin'd with treble
                              Brass;

line   frequency: 9   relative frequency: 0.0001
    P.   3 LOVELACE   23 And on each line cast a reforming eye,
    P. 56 BILL-BOROW   4 A Line more circular and like;
    P. 82 A. HOUSE   738 Supplies beyond her Sex the Line;
    P. 89 ODE   68 The Capitols first Line,
    P. 159 INSTRUCTIONS   750 His Empire old, to their immortal Line!
    P. 174 LOYALL SCOT   100 Stretch for your Line their Circingle Alone,
    P. 188 BRITANNIA   151 Over the whole: the elect Jessean line
    P. 195 TWO HORSES   158 W. When the Reign cf the Line of the Stuarts
                              is ended.
    P. 198 DUKE   38 He who longe since abjured the Royall line

linen. See "linnen."

lines   frequency: 6   relative frequency: 0.0001
    P. 15 EYES   8 Like wat'ry Lines and Plummets fall.
    P. 37 DEFINITION   25 As Lines so Loves oblique may well
    P. 60 A. HOUSE   42 Those short but admirable Lines,
    P. 79 A. HOUSE   648 While at my Lines the Fishes twang!
    P. 116 BLAKE   91 Forts, Lines, and Sconces all the Bay along,
    P. 156 INSTRUCTIONS   638 And all those lines by which men are mistook.

lingered. See "lingred."

lingred   frequency: 1   relative frequency: 0.0000
    P. 199 DUKE   51 You might have lingred out a lazy age,

link'd   frequency: 1   relative frequency: 0.0000
    P.   74 A. HOUSE   490 Link'd in so thick, an Union locks,

links   frequency: 1   relative frequency: 0.0000
    P. 155 INSTRUCTIONS 594 Snapping the brittle links, does thorow reel;

linnen   frequency: 5   relative frequency: 0.0001
    P.   62 A. HOUSE   125 'But what the Linnen can't receive
    P. 175 LOYALL SCOT 157 These Hypocrites their faith and Linnen stain.
    P. 175 LOYALL SCOT 171 Like Smutty Storyes in Pure Linnen Wrapt.
    P. 315 CHEQUER INN   97 Holt out of Linnen (as for Land)
    P. 316 CHEQUER INN 171 And Table Linnen went

linstock   frequency: 1   relative frequency: 0.0000
    P.   98 HOLLAND   116 Should raging bold his Linstock to the Mine?

lion   frequency: 1   relative frequency: 0.0000
    See also "lyon."
    P. 195 TWO HORSES   131 Ch. More Tolerable are the Lion Kings
                             Slaughters

lion's. See "lyons."

lip   frequency: 2   relative frequency: 0.0000
    P.   24 NYMPH   86 And print those Roses on my Lip.
    P. 142 INSTRUCTIONS 61 Paint her with Oyster Lip, and breath of Fame,

lips   frequency: 3   relative frequency: 0.0000
    P.   24 NYMPH   84 Until its Lips ev'n seem'd to bleed:
    P.   29 THE GALLERY   16 Black Eyes, red Lips, and curled Hair.
    P.   94 DR. WITTY   19 And sweet as are her lips that speak it, she

liquid   frequency: 3   relative frequency: 0.0000
    P.   16 EYES   31 Whose liquid Chaines could flowing meet
    P.   18 CLORINDA   13 C. Near this, a Fountaines liquid Bell
    P. 154 INSTRUCTIONS 553 The liquid Region with their Squadrons fill'd,

liquors   frequency: 1   relative frequency: 0.0000
    P. 196 TWO HORSES   184 Chocolet Tea and Coffee are liquors of peace.

lisbon   frequency: 1   relative frequency: 0.0000
    P. 201 HISTORICALL   26 To fetch for Charles the floury Lisbon Kate,

list   frequency: 1   relative frequency: 0.0000
    P. 191 STATUE   50 And his Parliament List withall did produce,

listening. See "listning."

listning   frequency: 4   relative frequency: 0.0000
    P.   17 BERMUDAS   4 The listning Winds receiv'd this Song.
    P.   75 A. HOUSE   518 And listning Elders prick the Ear.
    P. 104 ANNIVERSARY   57 The listning Structures he with Wonder ey'd,
    P. 163 INSTRUCTIONS 907 Express him startling next with listning ear,

litanies. See "letanies."

litle   frequency: 1   relative frequency: 0.0000
    P. 203 HISTORICALL 112 My Muse presum'd a litle to digress

little   frequency: 15   relative frequency: 0.0003
    See also "litle."
    P.   12 DROP OF DEW   7 And in its little Globes Extent,
    P.   23 NYMPH   64 'Twas on those little silver feet.
    P.   23 NYMPH   74 To be a little Wilderness.
    P.   25 YOUNG LOVE   1 Come little Infant, Love me now,
    P.   38 PICTURE   t1 The Picture of little T. C. in a Prospect
    P.   48 THE GARDEN   21 Little, Alas, they know, or heed,
    P.   76 A. HOUSE   563 And little now to make me, wants
    P.   78 A. HOUSE   630 Remains behind our little Nile;
    P.   92 MAY'S DEATH   77 But what will deeper wound thy little mind,
    P. 130 O.C.   276 Seeing how little we confess, how greate;
    P. 141 INSTRUCTIONS   8 'Twill suit our great detauch and little skill.
    P. 143 INSTRUCTIONS 117 Here Painter rest a little, and survey
    P. 152 INSTRUCTIONS 486 Now thinks all but too little for their Fear.
    P. 183 MADE FREE   85 But what little thing,
    P. 195 TWO HORSES   128 Between the two Scourges wee find little odds.

littleton   frequency: 1   relative frequency: 0.0000
    P. 148 INSTRUCTIONS 298 Led by great Garrway, and great Littleton.

liv'd   frequency: 7   relative frequency: 0.0001
    P.   23 NYMPH   47 Had it liv'd long, I do not know
    P.   24 NYMPH   91 Had it liv'd long, it would have been
    P.   55 EPITAPH   9 To say she liv'd a Virgin chast,
    P.   55 THYESTE   9 I have liv'd out all my span,
    P.   88 ODE   30 He liv'd reserved and austere,
    P. 123 O.C.   12 To those that liv'd in War, to dye in Fight.
    P. 177 LOYALL SCOT   233 While they liv'd here, still Haunts them
                              Underground.

live   frequency: 17   relative frequency: 0.0003
    P.   20 THYRSIS   43 Thyrsis. I cannot live, without thee, I
    P.   21 SOUL & BODY   18 Has made me live to let me dye.
    P.   29 LOVER   60 Forced to live in Storms and Warrs:
    P.   49 THE GARDEN   64 To live in Paradise alone.
    P.   62 A. HOUSE   98 'Live innocently as you see.
    P.   62 A. HOUSE   116 'That live without this happy Vow.
    P.   63 A. HOUSE   153 'Here live beloved, and obey'd:
    P. 107 ANNIVERSARY   162 Live out an Age, long as a Pedigree;
    P. 116 BLAKE   88 To all besides, triumphantly do live.
    P. 125 O.C.   86 Not love, not grieve, would neither live nor
                              reign:
    P. 129 O.C.   260 That threatens death, he yet will live again.
    P. 143 INSTRUCTIONS 103 Ah Painter, now could Alexander live,
    P. 164 INSTRUCTIONS 963 Better it were to live in Cloysters Lock,
    P. 167 KINGS VOWES   47 Miss and I will both learne to live on
                              Exhibition,
    P. 175 LOYALL SCOT   148 How can you bear such Miscreants shold live,
    P. 189 BRITANNIA   194 No Poisonous tyrant on thy ground shall live.
    P. 315 CHEQUER INN   119 Should live to sell himself for Meate

liverd   frequency: 1   relative frequency: 0.0000
    P. 204 HISTORICALL   139 White liverd Danby for his swift Jacall

livered. See "liverd."

lives   frequency: 4   relative frequency: 0.0000
    P.   62 A. HOUSE   126 'They in their Lives do interweave.
    P. 104 ANNIVERSARY   40 From the deserved Fate their guilty lives:
    P. 149 INSTRUCTIONS 334 But all the Members Lives, consulting, spare.
    P. 161 INSTRUCTIONS 850 At Court, and so reprieves their guilty Lives.

living   frequency: 4   relative frequency: 0.0000
    P.   44 GLO-WORMS   1 Ye living Lamps, by whose dear light
    P.   55 EPITAPH   3 Courtship, which living she declin'd,
    P. 176 LOYALL SCOT 190 Nature in Living Embleme there Exprest
    P. 193 TWO HORSES   82 Who out of what 's given do get a good living.

livy   frequency: 1   relative frequency: 0.0000
    P. 191 TWO HORSES   7 Livy tells a strang story can hardly be fellow'd

load   frequency: 4   relative frequency: 0.0000
    P. 113 BLAKE   5 For this rich load, of which so proud they are,
    P. 126 O.C.   132 The Universe labour'd beneath their load.
    P. 148 INSTRUCTIONS 326 Load them with Envy, and with Sitting tire:
    P. 162 INSTRUCTIONS 878 Frisks like a Frog to croak a Taxes load.

loaden   frequency: 1   relative frequency: 0.0000
    P.   16 EYES   33 Not full sailes hasting loaden home,

loads   frequency: 1   relative frequency: 0.0000
    P.   96 HOLLAND   13 Collecting anxiously small Loads of Clay,

loadstone   frequency: 1   relative frequency: 0.0000
    P. 174 LOYALL SCOT 102 The friendly Loadstone hath not more Combin'd

loan   frequency: 1   relative frequency: 0.0000
    P. 152 INSTRUCTIONS 491 Of the whole Nation now to ask a Loan.

loath'd   frequency: 1   relative frequency: 0.0000
    P.   86 FLECKNO   132 But how I loath'd to see my Neighbour glean

loathsome   frequency: 1   relative frequency: 0.0000
    P. 128 O.C.   230 To loathsome life, alas! are left behind.

lock   frequency: 2   relative frequency: 0.0000
    P.   28 LOVER   51 While with the other he does lock,
    P. 164 INSTRUCTIONS 963 Better it were to live in Cloysters Lock,

```
lock'd                          frequency:    1    relative frequency: 0.0000
    P.  163 INSTRUCTIONS   924 Through the lock'd door both of them disappear'd.

locked.  See "lock'd," "lockt."

locks                           frequency:   10    relative frequency: 0.0002
    P.   34 DAPHNIS         34 His disorder'd Locks he tare;
    P.   62 A. HOUSE       104 'And, from us, locks on them the Grates.
    P.   74 A. HOUSE       490 Link'd in so thick, an Union locks,
    P.   91 MAY'S DEATH     32 Shook his gray locks, and his own Bayes did tear
    P.  124 O.C.            67 And now Eliza's purple Locks were shorn,
    P.  156 INSTRUCTIONS   653 His yellow Locks curl back themselves to seek,
    P.  157 INSTRUCTIONS   684 His burning Locks adorn his Face Divine.
    P.  172 LOYALL SCOT     19 His shady locks Curl back themselves to seek
    P.  173 LOYALL SCOT     50 His burning Locks Adorn his face divine.
    P.  198 DUKE            40 Then draw the princesse with her golden locks,

lockt                           frequency:    1    relative frequency: 0.0000
    P.  162 INSTRUCTIONS   895 Her mouth lockt up, a blind before her Eyes,

locusts                         frequency:    1    relative frequency: 0.0000
    P.  111 ANNIVERSARY    311 Accursed Locusts, whom your King does spit

lodg'd                          frequency:    1    relative frequency: 0.0000
    P.  151 INSTRUCTIONS   418 In Holland theirs had lodg'd before, and
                               France.

lodge                           frequency:    1    relative frequency: 0.0000
    P.  153 INSTRUCTIONS   502 Their Money lodge; confiscate when he please.

lodging                         frequency:    2    relative frequency: 0.0000
    P.   83 FLECKNO          5 I sought his Lodging; which is at the Sign
    P.  315 CHEQUER INN    124 And wisely lodging at next Doore

lodgings                        frequency:    1    relative frequency: 0.0000
    P.   29 THE GALLERY      3 Now all its several lodgings lye

loftus                          frequency:    1    relative frequency: 0.0000
    P.  200 DUKE            87 Jermyne, Fitzgerald, Loftus, Porter, Scot.

lofty                           frequency:    2    relative frequency: 0.0000
    P.  185 BRITANNIA       43 In Lofty Notes Tudors blest reign to sing,
    P.  201 HISTORICALL      2 Much like the Son of Kish that lofty Jew,

lombard                         frequency:    1    relative frequency: 0.0000
    P.  170 PROPHECY        14 And Checquer dores shall shut up Lombard
                               street,

lombard-street                  frequency:    1    relative frequency: 0.0000
    P.  179 STOCKSMARKET     4 Of bankers defeated and Lombard-street broken.

london                          frequency:    9    relative frequency: 0.0001
    See also "loyal-london."
    P.  155 INSTRUCTIONS   600 (Cornbry the fleetest) and to London run.
    P.  166 KINGS VOWES     22 I will have a new London instead of the old,
    P.  168 ADVICE           2 And draw me in one Scene London and Rome,
    P.  170 PROPHECY        26 And when att London their shall not be One,
    P.  171 PROPHECY        28 Then London lately burnt shall be blowne up,
    P.  171 PROPHECY        31 London shall then see, for it will come to pass,
    P.  182 MADE FREE       69 Which must all be defrayd by London,
    P.  183 MADE FREE       79 Then o London rejoyce!
    P.  184 MADE FREE      126 London beares the Crosse with the Dagger.

londoners                       frequency:    1    relative frequency: 0.0000
    P.  181 MADE FREE        1 The Londoners Gent,

london's                        frequency:    3    relative frequency: 0.0000
    P.  151 INSTRUCTIONS   424 At London's Flame, nor so the Court
                               complain'd.
    P.  158 INSTRUCTIONS   708 Ev'n London's Ashes had been then destroy'd.
    P.  170 PROPHECY         1 The blood of the Just London's firm Doome
                               shall fix

long                            frequency:   68    relative frequency: 0.0014
    See also "longe."
    P.    5 HASTINGS        60 And Art indeed is Long, but Life is Short.
    P.    9 DIALOGUE        18 To bait so long upon the way.
    P.   12 DROP OF DEW     14 Because so long divided from the Sphear.
    P.   14 THE CORONET      1 When for the Thorns with which I long, too
                               long,
    P.   15 EYES             9 Two Tears, which Sorrow long did weigh
```

```
P.  17 BERMUDAS        7 Unto an Isle so long unknown,
P.  23 NYMPH          47 Had it liv'd long, I do not know
P.  24 NYMPH          91 Had it liv'd long, it would have been
P.  26 MISTRESS        4 To walk, and pass our long Loves Day.
P.  26 MISTRESS       28 That long preserv'd Virginity:
P.  30 THE GALLERY    30 How long thou shalt continue fair;
P.  33 DAPHNIS         6 Long had taught her to be coy:
P.  36 DAPHNIS        98 As who long has praying ly'n,
P.  39 THE MATCH       1 Nature had long a Treasure made
P.  39 THE MATCH      17 Love wisely had of long fore-seen
P.  40 THE MATCH      29 Till, by vicinity so long,
P.  42 DAMON          33 How long wilt Thou, fair Shepheardess,
P.  48 THE GARDEN     11 Mistaken long, I sought you then
P.  61 A. HOUSE       96 (As 'twere by Chance) Thoughts long conceiv'd.
P.  63 A. HOUSE      147 'Fairfax I know; and long ere this
P.  65 A. HOUSE      217 'But sure those Buildings last not long,
P.  66 A. HOUSE      245 Till one, as long since prophecy'd,
P.  73 A. HOUSE      469 For, jealous of its Lords long stay,
P.  76 A. HOUSE      557 And yet that Worm triumphs not long,
P.  78 A. HOUSE      621 This, like a long and equal Thread,
P.  85 FLECKNO        77 Which by the Jews long hid, and Disesteem'd,
P.  86 FLECKNO       114 Did, as he threatned, ere 'twere long intend
P.  90 ODE           101 A Caesar he ere long to Gaul,
P. 104 ANNIVERSARY    39 To know how long their Planet yet Reprives
P. 106 ANNIVERSARY   122 Your Regal sloth, and your long Slumbers wake:
P. 107 ANNIVERSARY   162 Live out an Age, long as a Pedigree;
P. 109 ANNIVERSARY   231 But in thine own Fields exercisedst long,
P. 111 ANNIVERSARY   344 Seem'd now a long and gloomy Night to threat,
P. 112 ANNIVERSARY   387 'He seems a King by long Succession born,
P. 114 BLAKE          43 But this great want, will not a long one prove,
P. 114 BLAKE          45 For Spain had better, Shee'l ere long confess,
P. 115 BLAKE          47 Casting that League off, which she held so long,
P. 115 BLAKE          65 But whilst I draw that Scene, where you ere
                         long,
P. 123 O.C.            1 That Providence which had so long the care
P. 123 O.C.           13 But long his Valour none had left that could
P. 123 O.C.           28 As long as Grief shall weep, or Love shall
                         burn.
P. 124 O.C.           68 Where She so long her Fathers fate had worn:
P. 125 O.C.          107 Or rather Heav'n, which us so long foresees,
P. 128 O.C.          201 Friendship, that sacred virtue, long dos claime
P. 130 O.C.          281 As long as rivers to the seas shall runne,
P. 130 O.C.          282 As long as Cynthia shall relieve the sunne,
P. 130 O.C.          285 As long as future time succeeds the past,
P. 130 O.C.          309 He, as his father, long was kept from sight
P. 138 HOUSEWARMING   46 So long as the Yards had a Deal or a Spar:
P. 141 INSTRUCTIONS   21 The Painter so, long having vext his cloth,
P. 144 INSTRUCTIONS  150 Could raise so long for this new Whore of
                         State.
P. 146 INSTRUCTIONS  216 That 'twas so long before he could be drest.
P. 146 INSTRUCTIONS  233 They, that e're long shall the rude Dutch
                         upbraid,
P. 148 INSTRUCTIONS  285 Nor could all these the Field have long
                         maintain'd,
P. 148 INSTRUCTIONS  325 Long thus they could against the House conspire,
P. 156 INSTRUCTIONS  630 Long since were fled on many a feign'd pretence.
P. 161 INSTRUCTIONS  846 And long as Cider lasts in Hereford.
P. 171 PROPHECY       38 To make starcht empty Speeches two hours long.
P. 174 LOYALL SCOT   120 Religion has the World too Long deprav'd
P. 177 LOYALL SCOT   235 Two Nations Neere had mist the Marke soe long.
P. 178 LOYALL SCOT   274 Pardon, Young Heroe, this soe long Transport;
P. 180 STOCKSMARKET   54 For the graver's at work to reform him thus long.
P. 184 BRITANNIA       7 Awake, arise, from thy long blest repose;
P. 188 BRITANNIA     135 Present to his thought his long scorn'd
                         Parliament
P. 188 BRITANNIA     141 Brit: Rawleigh, noe more; too long in vain I've
                         try'd
P. 190 STATUE         33 But why is the worke then soe long at a stand?
P. 193 TWO HORSES     54 And scarce a wise man at a long Councell board;
```

```
long-eard                         frequency:    1    relative frequency: 0.0000
P. 186 BRITANNIA      84 Are proper arts, the long-eard rout t'enslave:

longe                             frequency:    1    relative frequency: 0.0000
P. 198 DUKE          38 He who longe since abjured the Royall line

longer                            frequency:    8    relative frequency: 0.0001
P.  38 PICTURE       32 That Violets may a longer Age endure.
P.  49 THE GARDEN    55 And, till prepar'd for longer flight,
P.  84 FLECKNO       55 Nor was I longer to invite him Scant:
P. 103 ANNIVERSARY   16 Longer, and more Malignant then Saturn:
```

```
     P. 111 ANNIVERSARY      340 Or why Day last no longer then a Day?
     P. 143 INSTRUCTIONS      100 No longer could conceal his Fortune sweet.
     P. 148 INSTRUCTIONS      304 Is longer Work, and harder than to fight.
     P. 162 INSTRUCTIONS      879 His patient Piss, he could hold longer then
```

longest   frequency: 1   relative frequency: 0.0000
```
     P. 120 TWO SONGS         34 Seeks but the honour to have held out longest.
```

look   frequency: 15   relative frequency: 0.0003
     See also "looke."
```
     P.  22 NYMPH             31 Said He, look how your Huntsman here
     P.  30 THE GALLERY       51 Where the same Posture, and the Look
     P.  34 DAPHNIS           41 So did wretched Daphnis look,
     P.  42 DAMON             29 Alas! I lock for Ease in vain,
     P.  62 A. HOUSE         115 'Or Pity, when we look on you
     P.  80 A. HOUSE         702 Where She may all her Beautyes look;
     P.  94 DR. WITTY         34 Liking themselves the worse the more they look,
     P.  96 HOLLAND           52 Who look like a Commission of the Sewers.
     P. 107 ANNIVERSARY      150 Look on, all unconcern'd, or unprepar'd;
     P. 122 TWO SONGS         17 Here She comes; but with a Look
     P. 145 INSTRUCTIONS      170 And follow'd Fox, but with disdainful look.
     P. 152 INSTRUCTIONS      454 Cessation, as the look Adultery.
     P. 156 INSTRUCTIONS      637 Mix a vain Terrour in his Martial lock,
     P. 162 INSTRUCTIONS      872 And a Poll-Bill does like his Apron look.
     P. 174 LOYALL SCOT      124 Ah! like Lotts wife they still lock Back and
                                  Halt
```

looke   frequency: 2   relative frequency: 0.0000
```
     P.   3 LOVELACE          21 The barbed Censurers begin to looke
     P. 313 CHEQUER INN       25 And tho' he now do looke so bigg
```

looked   frequency: 1   relative frequency: 0.0000
```
     P.  43 DAMON             58 If in my Sithe I looked right;
```

lookes   frequency: 3   relative frequency: 0.0000
```
     P. 172 LOYALL SCOT       42 That Monk lookes on to see how Douglass dies.
     P. 186 BRITANNIA         56 How by her Peoples lookes persued from far
     P. 202 HISTORICALL       65 Lookes as one sett up for to scare the Crows.
```

looking   frequency: 2   relative frequency: 0.0000
```
     P. 122 TWO SONGS         38 Looking from high,
     P. 168 ADVICE            24 All looking this way how to give their votes,
```

looking-glass   frequency: 1   relative frequency: 0.0000
```
     P.  73 A. HOUSE         458 A Landskip drawen in Looking-Glass.
```

looks   frequency: 8   relative frequency: 0.0001
     See also "lookes."
```
     P.  34 DAPHNIS           39 Looks distracted back in hast,
     P. 122 TWO SONGS         25 He so looks as fit to keep
     P. 129 O.C.             250 Which through his looks that piercing sweetnesse
                                  shed;
     P. 143 INSTRUCTIONS       88 Her looks, and oft-try'd Beauty now distrusts:
     P. 145 INSTRUCTIONS      182 The Miter Troop, and with his looks gives Law.
     P. 153 INSTRUCTIONS      534 And his new Face looks in the English Wave.
     P. 157 INSTRUCTIONS      676 That Monk looks on to see how Douglas dies.
     P. 313 CHEQUER INN       36 And looks like Bird of Goale
```

looms   frequency: 1   relative frequency: 0.0000
```
     P. 107 ANNIVERSARY      183 Like skilful Looms which through the costly
                                  thred
```

loop   frequency: 1   relative frequency: 0.0000
```
     P.  59 A. HOUSE          30 To enter at a narrow loop;
```

loop-holes   frequency: 1   relative frequency: 0.0000
```
     P.  97 HOLLAND           88 Fumes through the loop-holes of a wooden Square.
```

loose   frequency: 12   relative frequency: 0.0002
```
     P.  13 DROP OF DEW       33 How loose and easie hence to go:
     P.  55 EPITAPH           10 In this Age loose and all unlac't;
     P.  74 A. HOUSE         507 And in as loose an order grows,
     P.  79 A. HOUSE         657 See how loose Nature, in respect
     P. 128 O.C.             200 So loose an enemy, so fast a friend.
     P. 129 O.C.             252 Loose and depriv'd of vigour, stretch'd along:
     P. 146 INSTRUCTIONS      239 For th' other side all in loose Quarters lay,
     P. 149 INSTRUCTIONS      351 The Irish-Herd is now let loose, and comes
     P. 168 ADVICE            16 To keep his own and loose his sergeants wife.
     P. 175 LOYALL SCOT      138 That power Alone Can loose this spell that
                                  tyes,
     P. 179 STOCKSMARKET      19 And so loose in his seat that all men agree
```

```
              P. 202 HISTORICALL       75 Let loose the Raines and give the Realme away:

loosely                                   frequency:    1    relative frequency: 0.0000
              P.  30 THE GALLERY        54 Hangs loosely playing in the Air,

looser                                    frequency:    1    relative frequency: 0.0000
              P.  46 AMETAS             12 Looser then with Ropes of Hay.

lord                                      frequency:   21    relative frequency: 0.0004
              P.   4 HASTINGS            t Upon the Death of the Lord Hastings.
              P.   9 DIALOGUE          12 Lord of Earth, and Heavens Heir.
              P.  56 BILL-BOROW        t2 To the Lord Fairfax.
              P.  59 A. HOUSE           t Upon Appleton House, to my Lord Fairfax.
              P.  61 A. HOUSE          72 Its Lord a while, but not remain.
              P.  64 A. HOUSE         187 'Whom if our Lord at midnight find,
              P.  75 A. HOUSE         536 That Tribute to its Lord to send.
              P.  78 A. HOUSE         620 The Trees before their Lord divide;
              P.  83 FLECKNO            4 (Though he derives himself from my Lord Brooke)
              P.  96 HOLLAND           46 Him they their Lord and Country's Father
                                          speak.
              P. 109 ANNIVERSARY      256 Yet would not he be Lord, nor yet his Son.
              P. 114 BLAKE             42 Unless it be, the having you their Lord;
              P. 119 TWO SONGS         t1 Two Songs at the Marriage of the Lord
                                          Fauconberg
              P. 174 LOYALL SCOT      116 How Reverend things are 'lord', Lawn Sleeves
                                          and Ease!
              P. 186 BRITANNIA         64 Inscrib'd Leviathan the sovereign Lord,
              P. 192 TWO HORSES        36 To see a Lord Major and a Lumbard Street
                                          break,
              P. 193 TWO HORSES        53 Ch. To see a white staffe make a Beggar a Lord
              P. 193 TWO HORSES        56 Lord a Mercy and a Cross might be set on the
                                          doore;
              P. 194 TWO HORSES        94 With an Addleheaded Knight and a Lord without
                                          Brains.
              P. 203 HISTORICALL      104 His God and Lord this preacher did betray.
              P. 314 CHEQUER INN       72 His Lady and her Lord

lords                                     frequency:    6    relative frequency: 0.0001
              P.  73 A. HOUSE         469 For, jealous of its Lords long stay,
              P. 146 INSTRUCTIONS     217 The Lords Sons, last, all these did reinforce:
              P. 161 INSTRUCTIONS     857 The Speaker, Summon'd, to the Lords repairs,
              P. 175 LOYALL SCOT      145 These Templar Lords Exceed the Templar
                                          Knights,
              P. 193 TWO HORSES        76 What a rabble of Rascally Lords have been made.
              P. 198 DUKE             23 Theire house of Commons and their house of
                                          Lords,

lord's                                    frequency:    1    relative frequency: 0.0000
              P.  58 BILL-BOROW        54 And in their Lord's advancement grow;

lordship                                  frequency:    1    relative frequency: 0.0000
              P. 138 HOUSEWARMING      54 Yet his Lordship to finish it would be unable;

lordships                                 frequency:    1    relative frequency: 0.0000
              P. 176 LOYALL SCOT      172 Doe but their Pyebald Lordships once Uncase

lore                                      frequency:    1    relative frequency: 0.0000
              P. 185 BRITANNIA         41 Were Hurl'd to Hell by Learning Tyrants
                                          Lore.

loretto                                   frequency:    1    relative frequency: 0.0000
              P.  91 MAY'S DEATH       50 As Bethlem's House did to Loretto walk.

lose                                      frequency:   10    relative frequency: 0.0002
              P.   4 LOVELACE          44 (She knew what pain 'twould be to lose that
                                          sight.)
              P.  10 DIALOGUE          41 Had I but any time to lose,
              P.  16 EYES              38 Drench'd in these Waves, does lose it fire.
              P.  27 LOVER              5 But soon these Flames do lose their light,
              P.  59 A. HOUSE          20 Where Winds as he themselves may lose.
              P. 108 ANNIVERSARY      221 For all delight of Life thou then didst lose,
              P. 128 O.C.             206 Where kindly nature loves itself to lose.
              P. 146 INSTRUCTIONS     226 For one had much, the other nought to lose.
              P. 149 INSTRUCTIONS     368 To play for Flanders, and the stake to lose.
              P. 166 KINGS VOWES       42 Tho' for't I a branch of Prerogative lose.

losing                                    frequency:    1    relative frequency: 0.0000
              P. 193 TWO HORSES        72 Was after rewarded with losing his own.

loss                                      frequency:    8    relative frequency: 0.0001
              P. 110 ANNIVERSARY      278 Saving himself he does their loss prevent.
```

```
       P.  132 PARADISE       44 Rewards with Prophesie thy loss of Sight.
       P.  156 INSTRUCTIONS   626 Frustrate Revenge, and Love, by loss more keen,
       P.  157 INSTRUCTIONS   697 Each doleful day still with fresh loss returns;
       P.  158 INSTRUCTIONS   710 Our loss, does so much more our loss augment.
       P.  159 INSTRUCTIONS   765 After this loss, to rellish discontent,
       P.  189 STATUE          3 Dear Wheeler impart, for wee're all at a loss
```

losses   frequency: 2   relative frequency: 0.0000
```
       P.   35 DAPHNIS        63 Than my Losses to increase
       P.   98 HOLLAND       131 The Common wealth doth by its losses grow;
```

lost   frequency: 17   relative frequency: 0.0003
```
       P.    3 LOVELACE      12 Our Civill Wars have lost the Civicke crowne.
       P.   44 GLO-WORMS     11 That in the Night have lost their aim,
       P.   90 MAY'S DEATH    8 Signs by which still he found and lost his way.
       P.  104 ANNIVERSARY   26 And will have Wonn, if he no more have Lost;
       P.  107 ANNIVERSARY  158 And good Designes still with their Authors
                                lost.
       P.  111 ANNIVERSARY  337 Still to the West, where he him lost, he turn'd,
       P.  118 BLAKE        160 The certain seeds of many Wars are lost.
       P.  130 O.C.         301 And lost in tears, have neither sight nor mind
       P.  131 PARADISE       t On Mr. Milton's Paradise lost.
       P.  143 INSTRUCTIONS 109 Those having lost the Nation at Trick track,
       P.  144 INSTRUCTIONS 122 And thought all lost that goest not to the
                                Cheats:
       P.  146 INSTRUCTIONS 238 Excise had got the day, and all been lost.
       P.  148 INSTRUCTIONS 310 And what haste lost, recover by delay.
       P.  160 INSTRUCTIONS 790 That lost our Fleet, and did our Flight
                                prevent.
       P.  187 BRITANNIA    118 Had lost all sense of Honour, Justice, fame;
       P.  191 STATUE        44 And wee've lost both our King, our Hors and our
                                Crupper.
       P.  204 HISTORICALL  141 Clifford and Hide before had lost the day,
```

loth   frequency: 1   relative frequency: 0.0000
```
       P.   86 FLECKNO      115 To be both witty and valiant: I loth,
```

lots. See "lotts."

lotts   frequency: 2   relative frequency: 0.0000
```
       P.  145 INSTRUCTIONS 199 Sir Frederick and Sir Salomon draw Lotts
       P.  174 LOYALL SCOT  124 Ah! like Lotts wife they still look Back and
                                Halt
```

loud   frequency: 2   relative frequency: 0.0000
See also "lou'd."
```
       P.  108 ANNIVERSARY  210 And then loud Shreeks the vaulted Marbles rent.
       P.  176 LOYALL SCOT  206 Those whom you hear more Clamerous Yet and
                                Loud
```

lou'd   frequency: 1   relative frequency: 0.0000
```
       P.  186 BRITANNIA     67 Around her Joves lou'd ravenous Currs complain;
```

loudest. See "lowd'st."

loudmouthd   frequency: 1   relative frequency: 0.0000
```
       P.  188 BRITANNIA    160 Shall darken stcry, Ingross loudmouthd fame.
```

loudmouthed. See "loudmouthd."

lov'd   frequency: 8   relative frequency: 0.0001
```
       P.    3 LOVELACE      36 He who lov'd best and them defended best.
       P.    5 HASTINGS      28 Secures his neerest and most lov'd Ally;
       P.  128 O.C.         209 If he Eliza lov'd to that degree,
       P.  128 O.C.         210 (Though who more worthy to be lov'd than she?)
       P.  149 INSTRUCTIONS 327 And the lov'd King, and never yet deny'd,
       P.  152 INSTRUCTIONS 485 And the wise Court, that always lov'd it dear,
       P.  162 INSTRUCTIONS 900 He wonder'd first, then pity'd, then he lov'd:
       P.  185 BRITANNIA     24 Your own lov'd Court and Masters Progeny?
```

love   frequency: 66   relative frequency: 0.0013
```
       P.    4 LOVELACE      50 His Booke in them finds Judgement, with you
                                Love.
       P.   12 DROP OF DEW   32 Here disdaining, there in Love.
       P.   21 SOUL & BODY   35 The Pestilence of Love does heat:
       P.   23 NYMPH         45 Than love it? O I cannot be
       P.   23 NYMPH         53 Thy Love was far more better then
       P.   23 NYMPH         54 The love of false and cruel men.
       P.   25 YOUNG LOVE     t Young Love.
       P.   25 YOUNG LOVE     1 Come little Infant, Love me now,
       P.   25 YOUNG LOVE     6 By young Love old Time beguil'd:
```

P.	25	YOUNG LOVE	12	Yet for Lust, but not for Love.
P.	25	YOUNG LOVE	13	Love as much the snowy Lamb
P.	25	YOUNG LOVE	17	Now then love me: time may take
P.	25	YOUNG LOVE	20	And learn Love before we may.
P.	26	MISTRESS	8	Love you ten years before the Flood:
P.	26	MISTRESS	11	My vegetable Love should grow
P.	26	MISTRESS	20	Nor would I love at lower rate.
P.	26	YOUNG LOVE	30	Now I crown thee with my Love:
P.	26	YOUNG LOVE	31	Crown me with thy Love again,
P.	27	LOVER	2	With whom the Infant Love yet playes!
P.	28	LOVER	45	And Tyrant Love his brest does ply
P.	29	LOVER	58	That ever Love created yet:
P.	31	FAIR SINGER	2	Love did compose so sweet an Enemy,
P.	32	MOURNING	26	To her dead Love this Tribute due;
P.	33	DAPHNIS	25	Till Love in her Language breath'd
P.	35	DAPHNIS	74	All th' Enjoyment of our Love
P.	36	DAPHNIS	85	Gentler times for Love are ment
P.	36	DAPHNIS	90	Which I could from Love receive:
P.	36	DAPHNIS	96	That Love in his Torches had.
P.	36	DEFINITION	t	The Definition of Love.
P.	36	DEFINITION	1	My Love is of a birth as rare
P.	37	DEFINITION	29	Therefore the Love which us doth bind.
P.	38	PICTURE	12	The wanton Love shall one day fear,
P.	39	THE MATCH	17	Love wisely had of long fore-seen
P.	41	DAMON	2	With love of Juliana stung!
P.	43	DAMON	66	Had not Love here his Thistles sow'd!
P.	46	AMETAS	1	Think'st Thou that this Love can stand,
P.	46	AMETAS	3	Love unpaid does soon disband:
P.	46	AMETAS	4	Love binds Love as Hay binds Hay.
P.	46	AMETAS	8	Neither Love will twist nor Hay.
P.	46	AMETAS	11	And Love tyes a Womans Mind
P.	48	THE GARDEN	26	Love hither makes his best retreat.
P.	58	BILL-BOROW	50	As We, of Love and Reverence,
P.	63	A. HOUSE	152	'He your Devoto were, then Love.
P.	82	A. HOUSE	758	For 'twas the Seat of wanton Love;
P.	108	ANNIVERSARY	218	Unto the Kingdom blest of Peace and Love:
P.	112	ANNIVERSARY	393	'But let them write his Praise that love him best,
P.	113	ANNIVERSARY	396	More then our Love and Duty do thee Right.
P.	121	TWO SONGS	55	For he did never love to pair
P.	122	TWO SONGS	28	Pay to Love and Them their due.
P.	122	TWO SONGS	31	What Shepheard could for Love pretend,
P.	123	O.C.	21	To Love and Grief the fatal Writ was sign'd;
P.	123	O.C.	28	As long as Grief shall weep, or Love shall burn.
P.	123	TWO SONGS	42	No more shall need of Love complain;
P.	124	O.C.	36	Which while she drain'd of Milk she fill'd with Love.
P.	125	O.C.	86	Not love, not grieve, would neither live nor reign:
P.	128	O.C.	223	Oh! ill advis'd, if not for love, for shame,
P.	143	INSTRUCTIONS	91	Great Love, how dost thou triumph, and how reign,
P.	151	INSTRUCTIONS	436	To move him out of Pity, if not Love.
P.	156	INSTRUCTIONS	626	Frustrate Revenge, and Love, by loss more keen;
P.	157	INSTRUCTIONS	660	That fly'st Love Fires, reserv'd for other Flame?
P.	164	INSTRUCTIONS	962	Banishing Love, Trust, Ornament and Use;
P.	165	INSTRUCTIONS	988	And, as in Love, on Parliaments can stare:
P.	186	BRITANNIA	53	Of Countryes love (by truth and Justice bred).
P.	188	BRITANNIA	162	To love sobriety and holy truth,
P.	200	DUKE	113	There is no friendship, tenderness nor love:

loved   frequency: 3   relative frequency: 0.0000
See also "lov'd."

P.	23	NYMPH	76	It onely loved to be there.
P.	34	DAPHNIS	42	Frighting her he loved most.
P.	130	O.C.	300	Wander like ghosts about thy loved tombe;

lovelace   frequency: 4   relative frequency: 0.0000

P.	3	LOVELACE	t1	To his Noble Friend Mr. Richard Lovelace,
P.	3	LOVELACE	34	That their deare Lovelace was endanger'd so:
P.	3	LOVELACE	35	Lovelace that thaw'd the most congealed brest,
P.	147	INSTRUCTIONS	262	And Lovelace young, of Chimney-men the Cane.

loveliest   frequency: 1   relative frequency: 0.0000

| P. | 4 | LOVELACE | 41 | And one the loveliest that was yet e're seen, |

lovely   frequency: 7   relative frequency: 0.0001

P.	16	EYES	43	And Stars shew lovely in the Night,
P.	47	EMPIRE	9	Each sought a consort in that lovely place;

P.	48 THE GARDEN	18 So am'rous as this lovely green.
P.	94 DR. WITTY	22 But her own smiles commend that lovely face;
P.	122 TWO SONGS	22 Curl'd so lovely as her Hair:
P.	156 INSTRUCTIONS	649 Not so brave Douglas; on whose lovely chin
P.	172 LOYALL SCCT	15 Not so brave Douglass, or whose Lovely Chin

lover   frequency: 8   relative frequency: 0.0001
P.	27 LOVER	t The unfortunate Lover.
P.	27 LOVER	11 That my poor Lover floting lay,
P.	28 LOVER	55 And all he saies, a Lover drest
P.	29 LOVER	64 In a Field Sable a Lover Gules.
P.	33 DAPHNIS	8 Nor yet let her Lover go.
P.	157 INSTRUCTICNS	677 Like a glad Lover, the fierce Flames he meets,
P.	172 LOYALL SCOT	43 Like a glad lover the fierce Flames hee meets
P.	204 HISTORICALL	129 Like a true Lover for her dying Mate.

lovers   frequency: 3   relative frequency: 0.0000
P.	34 DAPHNIS	43 At the last, this Lovers Ghost
P.	48 THE GARDEN	19 Fond Lovers, cruel as their Flame,
P.	148 INSTRUCTIONS	289 Dear Lovers of their King, and Death to meet,

lover's   frequency: 1   relative frequency: 0.0000
See also "lovers."
| P. | 30 THE GALLERY | 26 Vexing thy restless Lover's Ghost; |

loves   frequency: 20   relative frequency: 0.0004
P.	4 HASTINGS	21 As that of Knowledge; what Loves had he given
P.	18 CLORINDA	10 D. That den? C. Loves Shrine. D. But
		Virtue's Grave.
P.	26 MISTRESS	4 To walk, and pass our long Loves Day.
P.	29 THE GALLERY	24 Sit perfecting their harmless Loves.
P.	37 DEFINITION	14 Two perfect Loves; nor lets them clcse:
P.	37 DEFINITION	19 (Though Loves whole World on us doth wheel)
P.	37 DEFINITION	25 As Lines so Loves oblique may well
P.	38 PICTURE	3 In the green Grass she loves to lie,
P.	44 DAMON	82 To those that dye by Loves despight.
P.	58 BILL-BOROW	80 Nor Height but with Retirement loves.
P.	59 A. HOUSE	15 No Creature loves an empty space;
P.	81 A. HOUSE	716 And Sighs (Loves Cannon charg'd with Wind;)
P.	121 TWO SONGS	47 Less Loves set of each others praise,
P.	121 TWO SONGS	54 With his serenest influence their Loves.
P.	128 O.C.	206 Where kindly nature loves itself to lose.
P.	142 INSTRUCTIONS	74 But in her soft Breast Loves hid Cancer
		smarts.
P.	145 INSTRUCTIONS	175 Brcnkard Loves Squire; through all the field
		array'd,
P.	172 LOYALL SCOT	26 That flyst loves fires reserv'd for other flame?'
P.	185 BRITANNIA	22 Till Charles lcves Parliaments, till James
		hates Rome.
P.	202 HISTORICALL	68 In Loves delights none did him ere excell

love's   frequency: 2   relative frequency: 0.0000
See also "loves."
| P. | 40 THE MATCH | 40 All Love's and Nature's store. |
| P. | 143 INSTRUCTIONS | 82 Discern'd Love's Cause, and a new Flame began. |

loveth   frequency: 1   relative frequency: 0.0000
| P. | 23 NYMPH | 46 Unkind, t' a Beast that lcveth me. |

low   frequency: 8   relative frequency: 0.0001
P.	59 A. HOUSE	13 The low roof'd Tortoises do dwell
P.	60 A. HOUSE	60 But low Things clownishly ascend.
P.	70 A. HOUSE	374 Us as we walk mcre low then then:
P.	75 A. HOUSE	515 Low Shrubs she sits in, and adorns
P.	108 ANNIVERSARY	217 Frcm the low Wcrld, and thankless Men above,
P.	163 INSTRUCTIONS	921 And ghastly Charles, turning his Collar low,
P.	165 KINGS VOWES	1 When the Plate was at pawne, and the fobb att
		low Ebb,
P.	193 TWO HORSES	85 Ch. Yet baser the souls cf those low priced
		Sinners,

lowd'st   frequency: 1   relative frequency: 0.0000
| P. | 66 A. HOUSE | 255 But their lowd'st Cannon were their Lungs; |

lower   frequency: 6   relative frequency: 0.0001
P.	26 MISTRESS	20 Nor would I love at lower rate.
P.	104 ANNIVERSARY	48 To tune this lcwer to that higher Sphere.
P.	104 ANNIVERSARY	53 This took a Lower, that an Higher place,
P.	118 BLAKE	134 Whilst others lcwer, in the Sea do lye.
P.	170 PROPHECY	8 Tho the Walls stand to bring the Citty lower;
P.	316 CHEQUER INN	151 The Host that sate at Lower end

lowness   frequency: 2   relative frequency: 0.0000
    P. 60 A. HOUSE   57 So Honour better Lowness bears,
    P. 71 A. HOUSE   411 When Lowness is unsafe as Hight,

lowse   frequency: 1   relative frequency: 0.0000
    P. 141 INSTRUCTIONS   18 To see a tall Lowse brandish the white Staff.

loyal   frequency: 1   relative frequency: 0.0000
    See also "loyall."
    P. 144 INSTRUCTIONS   153 In Loyal haste they left young Wives in Bed,

loyal-london   frequency: 1   relative frequency: 0.0000
    P. 157 INSTRUCTIONS   698 The Loyal-London, now a third time burns.

loyall   frequency: 4   relative frequency: 0.0000
    P. 171 LOYALL SCOT   t1 The Loyall Scot.
    P. 171 PROPHECY   46 And think French onely Loyall, Irish wise,
    P. 178 LOYALL SCOT   258 For shame extirpate from each loyall brest
    P. 185 BRITANNIA   16 And loyall sufferings by the Court esteem'd,

loyally   frequency: 1   relative frequency: 0.0000
    P. 190 STATUE   21 Does the Treasurer think men so Loyally tame

loyalty   frequency: 1   relative frequency: 0.0000
    P. 180 STOCKSMARKET   50 Whose loyalty now all expires with his spankers.

lucan   frequency: 2   relative frequency: 0.0000
    P. 91 MAY'S DEATH   41 Polydore, Lucan, Allan, Vandale, Goth,
    P. 91 MAY'S DEATH   54 Those but to Lucan do continue May.

lucasta   frequency: 1   relative frequency: 0.0000
    P.   3 LOVELACE   27 Some reading your Lucasta, will alledge

lucifer   frequency: 1   relative frequency: 0.0000
    P. 203 HISTORICALL   84 Not Lucifer himselfe more proud then they,

luck   frequency: 1   relative frequency: 0.0000
    P. 204 HISTORICALL   134 Ill luck starts up and thrives like Evil weeds.

luckless   frequency: 1   relative frequency: 0.0000
    P. 69 A. HOUSE   327 What luckless Apple did we tast,

lucky   frequency: 1   relative frequency: 0.0000
    P. 141 INSTRUCTIONS   27 So may'st thou perfect, by a lucky blow,

luld   frequency: 1   relative frequency: 0.0000
    P. 187 BRITANNIA   121 Luld in security, rouling in lust,

lulled. See "luld."

lumbard   frequency: 2   relative frequency: 0.0000
    P. 182 MADE FREE   43 Throughout Lumbard Streete
    P. 192 TWO HORSES   36 To see a Lord Major and a Lumbard Street
                             break,

luna   frequency: 1   relative frequency: 0.0000
    P. 119 TWO SONGS   t4 Chorus. Endymion. Luna.

lungs   frequency: 2   relative frequency: 0.0000
    P. 66 A. HOUSE   255 But their lowd'st Cannon were their Lungs;
    P. 191 TWO HORSES   5 Nay Statues without either windpipe or Lungs

lurch   frequency: 2   relative frequency: 0.0000
    P. 194 TWO HORSES   119 Till at last on a Scaffold he was left in the
                             lurch
    P. 201 HISTORICALL   36 So slips away and leaves us in the lurch.

lure   frequency: 1   relative frequency: 0.0000
    P. 89 ODE   95 Where, when he first does lure,

luscious   frequency: 2   relative frequency: 0.0000
    P. 40 THE MOWER   7 And a more luscious Earth for them did knead,
    P. 49 THE GARDEN   35 The Luscious Clusters of the Vine

lust   frequency: 7   relative frequency: 0.0001
    P. 25 YOUNG LOVE   12 Yet for Lust, but not for Love.
    P. 26 MISTRESS   30 And into ashes all my Lust.
    P. 171 PROPHECY   51 Their Wives to his Lust expos'd, their Wealth
                             to his spoyle
    P. 187 BRITANNIA   121 Luld in security, rouling in lust,
    P. 189 BRITANNIA   172 Yeild to all these in Lewdness, lust, and shame.

```
       P. 195 TWO HORSES       142 W. But hee 's buryed alive in lust and in
                                    sloath.
       P. 202 HISTORICALL       60 Tainted with Pride or with impetuous lust.

luster.  See "lustre."

lustre                             frequency:    3     relative frequency: 0.0000
       P.  94 DR. WITTY         10 To add such lustre, and so many rayes,
       P. 103 ANNIVERSARY       11 Cromwell alone doth with new Lustre spring,
       P. 124 O.C.              38 And ev'ry minute adds a Lustre new;

lusts                              frequency:    1     relative frequency: 0.0000
       P. 186 BRITANNIA         68 Pale death, lusts, Horrour fill her pompous
                                    train.

lusty                              frequency:    3     relative frequency: 0.0000
       P.  25 YOUNG LOVE        15 As the lusty Bull or Ram,
       P. 110 ANNIVERSARY      273 Some lusty Mate, who with more careful Eye
       P. 169 ADVICE            33 Capacious Bowles with lusty wine repleat

lute                               frequency:    5     relative frequency: 0.0001
       P.  47 EMPIRE            13 Some to the Lute, some to the Viol went,
       P.  84 FLECKNO           36 Left off, and try'd t' allure me with his Lute.
       P.  84 FLECKNO           42 Over the Lute, his murmuring Belly calls,
       P. 104 ANNIVERSARY       49 So when Amphion did the Lute command,
       P. 105 ANNIVERSARY       65 Thus, ere he ceas'd, his sacred Lute creates

luxuriant                          frequency:    1     relative frequency: 0.0000
       P.  45 MOWER'S SONG       8 Grew more luxuriant still and fine;

luxurious                          frequency:    1     relative frequency: 0.0000
       P.  40 THE MOWER          1 Luxurious Man, to bring his Vice in use,

luxury                             frequency:    4     relative frequency: 0.0000
       P. 141 INSTRUCTIONS       14 As th' Indians, draw our Luxury in Plumes.
       P. 144 INSTRUCTIONS      129 Hyde's Avarice, Bennet's Luxury should
                                    suffice,
       P. 177 LOYALL SCOT       230 Luxury malice superstition pride
       P. 203 HISTORICALL        86 'Gainst Avarice and Luxury complaine,

lyar                               frequency:    1     relative frequency: 0.0000
       P. 315 CHEQUER INN       108 That was a greater Lyar.

lye                                frequency:   18     relative frequency: 0.0003
       P.   9 DIALOGUE           19 On these downy Pillows lye,
       P.  18 CLORINDA           11 C. In whose cool bosome we may lye
       P.  19 THYRSIS            10 There the milky way doth lye;
       P.  23 NYMPH              78 Have sought it oft, where it should lye,
       P.  26 MISTRESS           23 And yonder all before us lye
       P.  29 THE GALLERY         3 Now all its several lodgings lye
       P.  41 THE MOWER          32 While the sweet Fields do lye forgot:
       P.  54 THYESTE             3 All I seek is to lye still.
       P.  63 A. HOUSE          159 'How soft the yoke on us would lye,
       P.  64 A. HOUSE          189 'Where you may lye as chast in Bed,
       P.  73 A. HOUSE          462 In Multiplying Glasses lye.
       P.  87 FLECKNO           156 To say that you read false Sir is no Lye.
       P. 117 BLAKE             111 Behold their Navy does at Anchor lye,
       P. 118 BLAKE             134 Whilst others lower, in the Sea do lye.
       P. 128 O.C.              220 Lye weak and easy to the ruler's will;
       P. 142 INSTRUCTIONS       39 Lye nuzz'ling at the Sacramental wart;
       P. 153 INSTRUCTIONS      496 Lye nuzz'ling at the Sacramental wart;
       P. 170 PROPHECY           23 When Declarations lye, when every Oath

lyers                              frequency:    1     relative frequency: 0.0000
       P. 111 ANNIVERSARY      313 Wand'rers, Adult'rers, Lyers, Munser's rest,

lyes                               frequency:   11     relative frequency: 0.0002
       P.  12 DROP OF DEW        10 Scarce touching where it lyes,
       P.  29 THE GALLERY        19 When in the East she slumb'ring lyes,
       P.  57 BILL-BOROW         18 Lyes open to its grassy side;
       P.  72 A. HOUSE          422 Lyes quilted ore with Bodies slain:
       P.  92 MAY'S DEATH        85 If that can be thy home where Spencer lyes
       P. 106 ANNIVERSARY       141 But a thick Cloud about that Morning lyes,
       P. 123 O.C.               25 That they, to whom his Breast still open lyes,
       P. 129 O.C.              247 I saw him dead, a leaden slumber lyes,
       P. 148 INSTRUCTIONS      320 The unpractis'd Saw lyes bury'd in its Dust;
       P. 163 INSTRUCTIONS      912 But again thunders when he lyes in Bed;
       P. 185 BRITANNIA          12 Whilest the Lew'd Court in drunken slumbers
                                    lyes,

lying                              frequency:    1     relative frequency: 0.0000
```

        P. 107 ANNIVERSARY   172 Drawn from the Sheath of lying Prophecies;

ly'n   frequency: 1   relative frequency: 0.0000
        P. 36 DAPHNIS   98 As who long has praying ly'n,

lyon   frequency: 2   relative frequency: 0.0000
        P. 194 TWO HORSES   105 W. Truth 's as Eold as a Lyon, I am not
                                 afraid;
        P. 195 TWO HORSES   125 W. The Goat and the Lyon I Equally hate,

lyons   frequency: 1   relative frequency: 0.0000
        P. 156 INSTRUCTIONS 642 Daniel then thought he was in Lyons Den.

mace's   frequency: 1   relative frequency: 0.0000
        P. 162 INSTRUCTIONS 866 Paint him in Golden Gown, with Mace's Brain:

mack   frequency: 2   relative frequency: 0.0000
        P. 187 BRITANNIA   125 Mack James the Irish Pagod does Adore,
        P. 204 HISTORICALL   153 At his Command Mack will doe any thing,

mad   frequency: 7   relative frequency: 0.0001
        P. 28 LOVER   48 Like Ajax, the mad Tempest braves.
        P. 95 HOLLAND   10 They with mad labour fish'd the Land to Shoar;
        P. 106 ANNIVERSARY   111 But mad with Reason, so miscall'd, of State
        P. 159 INSTRUCTIONS 769 Whose Counsel first did this mad War beget?
        P. 191 STATUE   49 But the Treasurer told her he thought she was
                                 mad
        P. 199 DUKE   59 He proved the mad Cethegus of his age.
        P. 200 DUKE   97 At last to fools and mad men and the pope?

made   frequency: 60   relative frequency: 0.0012
        See also "new-made."
        P.   4 HASTINGS   20 And on the Tree of Life once made a Feast,
        P. 21 SOUL & BODY   18 Has made me live to let me dye.
        P. 22 NYMPH   17 Else Men are made their Deodands.
        P. 24 NYMPH   120 Of purest Alabaster made:
        P. 29 THE GALLERY   5 And the great Arras-hangings, made
        P. 39 THE MATCH   1 Nature had long a Treasure made
        P. 42 DAMON   21 Which made the Dog, and makes the Sun
        P. 47 EMPIRE   1 First was the World as one great Cymbal made,
        P. 47 EMPIRE   5 Jubal first made the wilder Notes agree;
        P. 49 THE GARDEN   47 Annihilating all that's made
        P. 56 BILL-BOROW   8 And that the World by it was made.
        P. 65 A. HOUSE   209 'Were there but, when this House was made,
        P. 67 A. HOUSE   279 Though many a Nun there made her Vow,
        P. 69 A. HOUSE   347 Might once have made our Gardens spring
        P. 78 A. HOUSE   618 Where the two Woods have made a Lane;
        P. 84 FLECKNO   58 But till he had himself a Body made.
        P. 85 FLECKNO   87 I meet one on the Stairs who made me stand,
        P. 85 FLECKNO   95 He gathring fury still made sign to draw;
        P. 86 FLECKNO   113 During the Table; though my new made Friend
        P. 86 FLECKNO   144 That were ill made condemn'd to be read worse:
        P. 86 FLECKNO   145 And how (impossible) he made yet more
        P. 87 FLECKNO   155 Made Mediator, in my room, said, Why?
        P. 87 FLECKNO   169 Have made the Chance be painted; and go now
        P. 96 HOLLAND   37 Therefore Necessity, that first made Kings,
        P. 108 ANNIVERSARY   228 Yielding to Rule, because it made thee Less.
        P. 110 ANNIVERSARY   304 Thy Falling-sickness should have made thee
                                 Reign,
        P. 111 ANNIVERSARY   336 Not knowing yet the Night was made for sleep:
        P. 115 BLAKE   48 She cast off that which only made her strong.
        P. 115 BLAKE   52 Peace made them hers, but War will make them
                                 yours
        P. 116 BLAKE   84 Nor Winters storms, had made your Fleet
                                 retreat.
        P. 116 BLAKE   96 So proud and confident of their made strength,
        P. 117 BLAKE   129 Nature ne'r made Cedars so high aspire,
        P. 123 O.C.   15 And he whom Nature all for Peace had made,
        P. 137 HOUSEWARMING   18 Made Thebes dance aloft while he fidled and
                                 sung,
        P. 142 INSTRUCTIONS   57 Hence Crowder made the rare Inventress free,
        P. 147 INSTRUCTIONS 284 Of Presbyterian Switzers, made a stand.
        P. 165 KINGS VOWES   5 Made these Vowes to his Maker--
        P. 165 KINGS VOWES   13 I will have as fine Bishops as were ere made
                                 with hands,
        P. 168 ADVICE   25 Their new made Band of Pentioners
        P. 169 ADVICE   62 To be at home made such a president!
        P. 180 STOCKSMARKET   44 As if we'd as good have a king made of clouts.
        P. 181 MADE FREE   t Upon his Majesties being made free of the Citty
        P. 182 MADE FREE   53 He still made a Retreate
        P. 183 MADE FREE   81 To have made this Freeman of Spices;

P. 187 BRITANNIA   114 To Boys, Bawds, whores, and made a Publick
                           game.
P. 188 BRITANNIA   154 Eternall Lawes by God for mankind made? Noe!
P. 191 TWO HORSES   11 Fryar Bacon had a head that spoke made of
                           Brass,
P. 193 TWO HORSES   76 What a rabble of Rascally Lords have been made.
P. 193 TWO HORSES   83 W. Four Knights and a Knave, who were
                           Publicans made,
P. 194 TWO HORSES   89 Ch. But thanks to the whores who have made the
                           King Dogged
P. 194 TWO HORSES   96 When one already hath made him soe poor.
P. 195 TWO HORSES   140 Hee made England great and it's enemies tremble.
P. 201 HISTORICALL   13 Bishops and Deanes, Peeres, Pimps and Knights
                           he made,
P. 203 HISTORICALL   83 Who with vain Faith made all their Reason
                           blind:
P. 203 HISTORICALL   105 To have the weaker Vessell made his prey:
P. 204 HISTORICALL   143 'Twas want of Wit and Courage made them fail,
P. 205 HISTORICALL   160 Heaven had him Chieftain of great Britain made,
P. 313 CHEQUER INN   38 Had not the Members most been made
P. 316 CHEQUER INN   138 And made above a Hundred.
P. 316 CHEQUER INN   145 They talkt about and made such Din

madness   frequency: 3   relative frequency: 0.0000
P. 21 SOUL & BODY   37 Joy's chearful Madness does perplex:
P. 21 SOUL & BODY   38 Or Sorrow's other Madness vex.
P. 88 ODE   25 'Tis Madness to resist or blame

madrid. See "madril."

madril   frequency: 1   relative frequency: 0.0000
P. 72 A. HOUSE   448 Ere the Bulls enter at Madril.

magaera   frequency: 1   relative frequency: 0.0000
P. 92 MAY'S DEATH   92 Magaera thee with all her Serpents lash.

magazeen   frequency: 1   relative frequency: 0.0000
P. 69 A. HOUSE   340 Was then the only Magazeen.

magazine   frequency: 1   relative frequency: 0.0000
    See also "magazeen."
P. 39 THE MATCH   19 And therefore stor'd a Magazine,

magdalen   frequency: 1   relative frequency: 0.0000
P. 16 EYES   29 So Magdalen, in Tears more wise

maggot. See "maggott."

maggott   frequency: 1   relative frequency: 0.0000
P. 181 MADE FREE   3 In a Box the Citty Maggott;

magic   frequency: 1   relative frequency: 0.0000
    See also "magick."
P. 149 INSTRUCTIONS   338 With Magic Herbs, rose from the Pot renew'd:

magick   frequency: 2   relative frequency: 0.0000
P. 21 SOUL & BODY   21 What Magick could me thus confine
P. 35 DAPHNIS   82 For the Fern, whose magick Weed

magistrate   frequency: 1   relative frequency: 0.0000
P. 96 HOLLAND   48 Invent a Shov'l and be a Magistrate.

magna   frequency: 2   relative frequency: 0.0000
P. 171 PROPHECY   48 And Magna Carta shall no more appeare,
P. 187 BRITANNIA   110 'Down with that common Magna Charta whore.'

magnanimous   frequency: 1   relative frequency: 0.0000
P. 37 DEFINITION   5 Magnanimous Despair alone

magnetically   frequency: 1   relative frequency: 0.0000
P. 40 THE MATCH   31 And, grown magnetically strong,

magnitude   frequency: 1   relative frequency: 0.0000
P. 60 A. HOUSE   53 More by his Magnitude distrest,

magpies. See "magpyes."

magpyes   frequency: 1   relative frequency: 0.0000
P. 191 TWO HORSES   3 When Magpyes and Parratts cry 'walke Knave
                           walk',

mahomet   frequency: 2   relative frequency: 0.0000

```
        P. 110 ANNIVERSARY    303 Oh Mahomet! now couldst thou rise again,
        P. 174 LOYALL SCOT     104 A Bishop will like Mahomet tear the Moon
```

maid   frequency: 3   relative frequency: 0.0000
```
        P.  63 A. HOUSE        154 'Each one your Sister, each your Maid.
        P. 142 INSTRUCTIONS     54 How after Childbirth to renew a Maid.
        P. 143 INSTRUCTIONS     90 And now first, wisht she e're had been a Maid.
```

maidens   frequency: 1   relative frequency: 0.0000
```
        P. 314 CHEQUER INN      59 Like Maidens at a Statute Fair,
```

maids   frequency: 1   relative frequency: 0.0000
```
        P. 199 DUKE             45 Preserv'd in store for the new sett of maids.
```

mail   frequency: 2   relative frequency: 0.0000
```
        P. 127 O.C.            181 The Souldier taught that inward Mail to wear,
        P. 147 INSTRUCTIONS    260 That pierc't the Gyant Mordant through his
                                   Mail.
```

main   frequency: 2   relative frequency: 0.0000
    See also "mayn."
```
        P. 110 ANNIVERSARY     276 And doubles back unto the safer Main.
        P. 113 BLAKE            13 For now upon the Main, themselves they saw,
```

maintain   frequency: 3   relative frequency: 0.0000
```
        P.  33 DAPHNIS          18 By which men their Siege maintain,
        P.  90 ODE             120 A Pow'r must it maintain.
        P. 144 INSTRUCTIONS    128 Commons, and ever such a Court maintain,
```

maintain'd   frequency: 1   relative frequency: 0.0000
```
        P. 148 INSTRUCTIONS    285 Nor could all these the Field have long
                                   maintain'd,
```

mairmaids   frequency: 1   relative frequency: 0.0000
```
        P.  97 HOLLAND          85 See but their Mairmaids with their Tails of
                                   Fish,
```

majestic. See "majestique."

majesties   frequency: 2   relative frequency: 0.0000
```
        P. 171 LOYALL SCOT      t3 of his Majesties shipps at Chatham.
        P. 181 MADE FREE         t Upon his Majesties being made free of the Citty
```

majestique   frequency: 1   relative frequency: 0.0000
```
        P. 129 O.C.            251 That port which so majestique was and strong,
```

majesty   frequency: 2   relative frequency: 0.0000
```
        P. 132 PARADISE         31 That Majesty which through thy Work doth Reign
        P. 179 STOCKSMARKET     24 Say his Majesty himself is bought too and sold.
```

majesty's. See "majesties."

major   frequency: 1   relative frequency: 0.0000
```
        P. 192 TWO HORSES       36 To see a Lord Major and a Lumbard Street
                                   break,
```

make   frequency: 71   relative frequency: 0.0014
```
        P.  18 CLORINDA         25 D. Clorinda's voice might make it sweet.
        P.  25 YOUNG LOVE       19 Of this Need wee'l Virtue make,
        P.  26 YOUNG LOVE       29 So, to make all Rivals vain,
        P.  27 LOVER             8 To make impression upon Time.
        P.  27 MISTRESS         45 Thus, though we cannot make our Sun
        P.  27 MISTRESS         46 Stand still, yet we will make him run.
        P.  31 FAIR SINGER       1 To make a final conquest of all me,
        P.  38 PICTURE          28 Make that the Tulips may have share
        P.  39 PICTURE          38 Do quickly make th' Example Yours;
        P.  40 THE MATCH        34 To make one fire high:
        P.  61 A. HOUSE         92 Which might Deformity make fair.
        P.  63 A. HOUSE        136 'Enough a thousand Saints to make.
        P.  65 A. HOUSE        194 'Of Joys you see, and may make more!
        P.  65 A. HOUSE        207 'Death only can such Theeves make fast,
        P.  69 A. HOUSE        328 To make us Mortal, and The Wast?
        P.  71 A. HOUSE        407 But now, to make his saying true,
        P.  75 A. HOUSE        513 The Nightingale does here make choice
        P.  76 A. HOUSE        563 And little now to make me, wants
        P.  77 A. HOUSE        606 Can make, or me it toucheth not.
        P.  80 A. HOUSE        693 Nothing could make the River be
        P.  82 A. HOUSE        744 And make their Destiny their Choice.
        P.  84 FLECKNO          56 Happy at once to make him Protestant,
        P.  85 FLECKNO          74 Does make a primitive Sotana fall;
        P.  85 FLECKNO          93 Will make the way here; I said Sir you'l do
```

P.	85	FLECKNO	100	Two make a crowd, ncr can three Persons here
P.	85	FLECKNO	105	He ask'd me pardon; and to make me way
P.	88	ODE	43	And therefore must make room
P.	89	ODE	88	His Fame to make it theirs:
P.	93	DR. WITTY	1	Sit further, and make room for thine own fame,
P.	94	DR. WITTY	8	For ill Translators make the Book their own.
P.	94	DR. WITTY	11	That but to make the Vessel shining, they
P.	96	HOLLAND	47	To make a Bank was a great Plot of State;
P.	103	ANNIVERSARY	15	While heavy Monarchs make a wide Return,
P.	110	ANNIVERSARY	298	And make the World, by his Example, Quake:
P.	111	ANNIVERSARY	334	Did make the Fun'rals sadder by their Joyes.
P.	115	BLAKE	52	Peace made them hers, but War will make them yours
P.	115	BLAKE	64	If fortune can make guilty what she will.
P.	116	BLAKE	80	Make them admire, so much as they did fear.
P.	116	BLAKE	92	They build and act all that can make them strong.
P.	116	BLAKE	100	With winged speed, for Sanctacruze does make.
P.	120	TWO SONGS	26	Can make a Night more bright then Day;
P.	138	HOUSEWARMING	38	To make Mortar and Brick, yet allow'd them no straw,
P.	138	HOUSEWARMING	40	So he could to build but make Policy Law.
P.	142	INSTRUCTIONS	60	To make her glassen D----s once malleable!
P.	151	INSTRUCTIONS	429	How yet the Hollanders do make a noise,
P.	151	INSTRUCTIONS	437	Pray him to make De-Witte, and Ruyter cease,
P.	156	INSTRUCTIONS	645	Captain, Lieutenant, Ensign, all make haste,
P.	162	INSTRUCTIONS	874	And make a sawce fit fcr Whitehall's digestion:
P.	165	INSTRUCTIONS	981	The smallest Vermin make the greatest waste,
P.	166	KINGS VOWES	24	But if they build it too fast, I will soon make them hold.
P.	167	KINGS VOWES	43	Of my Pimp I will make my Minister Premier,
P.	169	ADVICE	34	To make them th' cther Councell board forgett.
P.	169	ADVICE	45	Tis this must make Obryan great in Story,
P.	169	ADVICE	51	Who make it by their mean retreat appear
P.	171	PROPHECY	38	To make starcht empty Speeches two hours long.
P.	171	PROPHECY	44	Make him self rich, his king and People bare,
P.	174	LOYALL SCOT	101	'Twill make a more Inhabitable zone.
P.	178	LOYALL SCOT	265	Knowes the last secret how to make them one.
P.	179	STOCKSMARKET	23	And others to make the similitude hold
P.	185	BRITANNIA	23	Rawl: What fatall crimes make you forever fly
P.	188	BRITANNIA	145	Into the Wolf and make him Guardian turn
P.	189	BRITANNIA	173	Make 'em admire the Sidnies, Talbots, Veres,
P.	192	TWO HORSES	35	W. Quoth the marble white Hors: 'twould make a stone speak
P.	193	TWO HORSES	53	Ch. To see a white staffe make a Beggar a Lord
P.	194	TWO HORSES	91	W. That a King shou'd endavour to make a warr cease
P.	195	TWO HORSES	146	Father Patricks Deciple will make England smart.
P.	196	TWO HORSES	175	Tho' Tyrants make Laws which they strictly proclaim
P.	199	DUKE	69	But nere can make a piller for a church;
P.	201	HISTORICALL	21	Bold James survives, nc dangers make him flinch,
P.	201	HISTORICALL	30	Why not with easy Youngsters make as bold?
P.	313	CHEQUER INN	8	Where all the Berties make their Hay

makeing   frequency: 2   relative frequency: 0.0000

P.	166	KINGS VOWES	25	I will have a fine Son in makeing the marrd,
P.	193	TWO HORSES	67	W. That makeing us slaves by hors and foot Guards

maker--   frequency: 1   relative frequency: 0.0000

P.	165	KINGS VOWES	5	Made these Vowes to his Maker--

makes   frequency: 12   relative frequency: 0.0002

P.	17	BERMUDAS	21	He makes the Figs cur mouths to meet;
P.	17	BERMUDAS	27	And makes the hcllow Seas, that roar,
P.	35	DAPHNIS	84	And invisible him makes.
P.	36	DAPHNIS	99	To his Heads-man makes the Sign,
P.	42	DAMON	21	Which made the Dog, and makes the Sun
P.	48	THE GARDEN	26	Love hither makes his best retreat.
P.	73	A. HOUSE	467	And makes the Meadow truly be
P.	111	ANNIVERSARY	322	Makes you for his sake Tremble one fit more;
P.	121	TWO SONGS	58	Makes Mortals matches fit for Deityes.
P.	174	LOYALL SCOT	107	Shews you first one, then makes that one two Balls.
P.	174	LOYALL SCOT	115	A Bishops Bennett makes the strongest Curd.
P.	196	TWO HORSES	183	'Tis wine and Strong drink makes tumults increase;

makest.   See "mak'st."

maketh   frequency: 1   relative frequency: 0.0000

P. 94 DR. WITTY   15 Of the first Author. Here he maketh blots

making   frequency: 5   relative frequency: 0.0001
    See also "makeing."
    P. 46 AMETAS   t Ametas and Thestylis making Hay-Ropes.
    P. 86 FLECKNO   149 Making the half points and the periods run
    P. 150 INSTRUCTIONS   392 By making them ridiculous to restrain.
    P. 160 INSTRUCTIONS   785 Pett, the Sea Architect, in making Ships,
    P. 195 TWO HORSES   132 Than the Goats making whores of our wives and
                               our Daughters.

mak'st   frequency: 1   relative frequency: 0.0000
    P. 113 ANNIVERSARY   402 Troubling the Waters, yearly mak'st them Heal.

maladies   frequency: 1   relative frequency: 0.0000
    P. 21 SOUL & BODY   32 The Maladies Thou me dost teach;

male   frequency: 3   relative frequency: 0.0000
    P. 81 A. HOUSE   728 On Females, if there want a Male.
    P. 156 INSTRUCTIONS   652 While envious Virgins hope he is a Male.
    P. 172 LOYALL SCOT   18 Whilst Envious virgins hope hee is a Male.

malice   frequency: 7   relative frequency: 0.0001
    P. 36 DAPHNIS   94 As thy Malice could desire;
    P. 91 MAY'S DEATH   56 Misled, but malice fixt and understood.
    P. 106 ANNIVERSARY   118 By Malice some, by Errour more misled;
    P. 113 ANNIVERSARY   400 As far above their Malice as my Praise.
    P. 177 LOYALL SCOT   230 Luxury malice superstition pride
    P. 179 STOCKSMARKET   10 To be all a revenge and a malice forecast,
    P. 205 HISTORICALL   178 And stopt his Malice in its full Careere.

malignant   frequency: 4   relative frequency: 0.0000
    P. 29 LOVER   59 Who though, by the Malignant Starrs,
    P. 91 MAY'S DEATH   42 Malignant Poet and Historian both.
    P. 103 ANNIVERSARY   16 Longer, and more Malignant then Saturn:
    P. 204 HISTORICALL   130 The Royal Evil so malignant growes,

malleable   frequency: 1   relative frequency: 0.0000
    P. 142 INSTRUCTIONS   60 To make her glassen D----s once malleable!

man   frequency: 56   relative frequency: 0.0011
    See also "heads-man."
    P.   4 HASTINGS   13 What man is he, that hath not Heaven beguil'd,
    P.   4 HASTINGS   18 But weigh to Man the Geometrick yeer.
    P.   5 HASTINGS   55 But what could he, good man, although he bruis'd
    P.   5 HASTINGS   59 For Man (alas) is but the Heavens sport;
    P. 14 THE CORONET   17 Ah, foolish Man, that would'st debase with them,
    P. 33 DAPHNIS   28 To a dying Man bequeath'd.
    P. 38 PICTURE   16 Appease this virtuous Enemy of Man!
    P. 40 THE MOWER   1 Luxurious Man, to bring his Vice in use,
    P. 41 THE MOWER   20 To Man, that sov'raign thing and proud;
    P. 49 THE GARDEN   58 While Man there walk'd without a Mate:
    P. 55 THYESTE   11 An old honest Country man.
    P. 59 A. HOUSE   9 Why should of all things Man unrul'd
    P. 60 A. HOUSE   48 In ev'ry Figure equal Man.
    P. 63 A. HOUSE   139 ''Twere Sacriledge a Man t'admit
    P. 64 A. HOUSE   183 'What need is here of Man? unless
    P. 79 A. HOUSE   654 Should with such Toyes a Man surprize;
    P. 83 FLECKNO   1 Oblig'd by frequent visits of this man,
    P. 83 FLECKNO   15 Yet of his State no man could have complain'd;
    P. 84 FLECKNO   63 This Basso Relievo of a Man,
    P. 85 FLECKNO   80 This half transparent Man would soon reflect
    P. 86 FLECKNO   148 As a deaf Man upon a Viol playes,
    P. 88 ODE   28 Much to the Man is due.
    P. 89 ODE   75 So much one Man can do,
    P. 90 MAY'S DEATH   12 But 'twas a man much of another sort;
    P. 92 MAY'S DEATH   71 But thou base man first prostituted hast
    P. 98 HOLLAND   98 Cut out each others Athos to a Man:
    P. 103 ANNIVERSARY   3 So Man, declining alwayes, disappears
    P. 106 ANNIVERSARY   144 If these the Times, then this must be the Man.
    P. 109 ANNIVERSARY   242 Who think those high Decrees by Man design'd.
    P. 111 ANNIVERSARY   325 So when first Man did through the Morning new
    P. 112 ANNIVERSARY   375 'That one Man still, although but nam'd, alarms
    P. 117 BLAKE   109 Of Speedy Victory let no man doubt,
    P. 125 O.C.   84 Nor though a Prince to be a Man refus'd:
    P. 128 O.C.   191 What man was ever so in Heav'n obey'd
    P. 129 O.C.   254 How much another thing, no more that man?
    P. 147 INSTRUCTIONS   271 Believes himself an Army, theirs one Man,
    P. 153 INSTRUCTIONS   507 Let no Man touch them, or demand his own,
    P. 154 INSTRUCTIONS   565 No man can sit there safe, the Cannon pow'rs
    P. 156 INSTRUCTIONS   631 Daniel had there adventur'd, Man of might;

```
P. 158 INSTRUCTIONS  737 Black Day accurs'd! On thee let no man hale
P. 160 INSTRUCTIONS  796 Powder ne're blew man up so soon so high.
P. 164 INSTRUCTIONS  949 So his bold Tube, Man, to the Sun apply'd,
P. 169 ADVICE         44 In this Assault upon a single man.
P. 170 PROPHECY       21 And no Man knowes in whom to put his trust,
P. 175 LOYALL SCOT   136 The Legion Devil did but one man possess:
P. 176 LOYALL SCOT   186 Strange was the Sight the scotch Twin headed
                         man
P. 177 LOYALL SCOT   253 Does man and wife signifie Rogue and Whore?
P. 187 BRITANNIA      92 And by imposters God and man betray'd,
P. 191 TWO HORSES     10 Would roar like a Devill with a man in his
                         belly;
P. 193 TWO HORSES     54 And scarce a wise man at a long Councell board;
P. 193 TWO HORSES     58 Yet the King of his debts pay no man a penny;
P. 194 TWO HORSES    100 Bold speaking hath done both man and beast wrong.
P. 195 TWO HORSES    141 Ch. Thy Ryder puts no man to death in his
                         wrath,
P. 313 CHEQUER INN    14 Is now a Man that was a Mouse
P. 315 CHEQUER INN   130 The Man that gave a woefull Tax
P. 316 CHEQUER INN   173 Lest some shou'd take me for the Man
```

manacled   frequency: 1   relative frequency: 0.0000
  P. 20 SOUL & BODY   4 In Feet; and manacled in Hands.

manag'd   frequency: 2   relative frequency: 0.0000
  P. 146 INSTRUCTIONS   218 Cornbury before them manag'd Hobby-horse.
  P. 198 DUKE   18 Manag'd by wise Fitzgerard and by Scott,

manage   frequency: 1   relative frequency: 0.0000
  P. 160 INSTRUCTIONS   798 Show'd him to manage the Exchequer meeter:

man'd   frequency: 2   relative frequency: 0.0000
  P. 127 O.C.   180 And tim'rous Conscience unto Courage man'd:
  P. 204 HISTORICALL   147 Are man'd by him or by his Holiness.

manes. See "mane's."

mane's   frequency: 1   relative frequency: 0.0000
  P. 108 ANNIVERSARY   198 Nor their round Hoofs, or curled Mane's
                            compare;

mangers   frequency: 1   relative frequency: 0.0000
  P. 108 ANNIVERSARY   196 And the green Grass, and their known Mangers
                            hate,

mankind   frequency: 6   relative frequency: 0.0001
  P. 174 LOYALL SCOT   103 Then Bishops Crampt the Comerce of Mankind.
  P. 187 BRITANNIA   90 When all their Gobling Intrest in Mankind
  P. 188 BRITANNIA   154 Eternall Lawes by God for mankind made? Noe!
  P. 189 BRITANNIA   184 Shall England raise, releive opprest mankind.
  P. 196 TWO HORSES   165 That shall come to pass all mankind may swear
  P. 203 HISTORICALL   82 Priests were the first deluders of Mankind,

manly   frequency: 2   relative frequency: 0.0000
  P. 35 DAPHNIS   70 In a manly stubberness
  P. 47 EMPIRE   10 And Virgin Trebles wed the manly Base.

manna   frequency: 3   relative frequency: 0.0000
  P. 29 THE GALLERY   22 And Manna falls, and Roses spring;
  P. 35 DAPHNIS   79 While with Quailes and Manna fed,
  P. 71 A. HOUSE   408 Rails rain for Quails, for Manna Dew.

manna's   frequency: 1   relative frequency: 0.0000
  P. 13 DROP OF DEW   37 Such did the Manna's sacred Dew destil;

manned. See "man'd."

mannerly   frequency: 1   relative frequency: 0.0000
  P. 314 CHEQUER INN   56 Mannerly rear'd against the Wall

mans   frequency: 2   relative frequency: 0.0000
  P. 109 ANNIVERSARY   234 As a small Cloud, like a Mans hand didst rise;
  P. 192 TWO HORSES   26 Who have told many truths well worth a mans
                            hearing,

man's   frequency: 1   relative frequency: 0.0000
  See also "mans."
  P. 204 HISTORICALL   133 For one man's weakeness a whole Nation bleeds

mansell   frequency: 1   relative frequency: 0.0000
  P. 314 CHEQUER INN   82 Mansell and Morgan and the rest

mansion   frequency: 2   relative frequency: 0.0000
    P.   12 DROP OF DEW   4 Yet careless of its Mansion new;
    P. 130 O.C.   295 How streight canst to each happy mansion goe?

mantle   frequency: 1   relative frequency: 0.0000
    P. 108 ANNIVERSARY   220 Whom thou hadst left beneath with Mantle rent.

mantua's   frequency: 1   relative frequency: 0.0000
    P.   30 THE GALLERY   48 Then or White-hall's, or Mantua's were.

many   frequency: 27   relative frequency: 0.0005
    P.   14 THE CORONET   2 With many a piercing wound,
    P.   20 SOUL & BODY   2 A Soul inslav'd so many wayes?
    P.   67 A. HOUSE   279 Though many a Nun there made her Vow,
    P.   74 A. HOUSE   493 Of whom though many fell in War,
    P.   94 DR. WITTY   10 To add such lustre, and so many rayes,
    P.   97 HOLLAND   58 Th' Apostles were so many Fishermen?
    P. 105 ANNIVERSARY   69 While tedious Statesmen many years did hack,
    P. 110 ANNIVERSARY   305 While Feake and Simpson would in many a Tome,
    P. 115 BLAKE   69 Never so many with one joyful cry,
    P. 118 BLAKE   160 The certain seeds of many Wars are lost.
    P. 125 O.C.   90 Of many a Winter hath surviv'd the rage.
    P. 126 O.C.   124 Offer themselves in many an Hecatomb;
    P. 128 O.C.   221 But to the good (too many or too few)
    P. 129 O.C.   268 So many yeares the shelter of the wood.)
    P. 130 O.C.   277 Thee, many ages hence, in martial verse
    P. 138 HOUSEWARMING   32 Though he had built full many a one for his
                                Master
    P. 147 INSTRUCTIONS   266 And in his Breast wears many Montezumes.
    P. 152 INSTRUCTIONS   471 His Writing-Master many a time he bann'd,
    P. 156 INSTRUCTIONS   630 Long since were fled on many a feign'd pretence.
    P. 175 LOYALL SCOT   164 Abbot one Buck, but he shot many a Doe,
    P. 181 MADE FREE   27 Tho be has past through so many Adventures;
    P. 182 MADE FREE   67 So many are the Debts
    P. 185 BRITANNIA   40 Shew'd him how many Kings in Purple Gore
    P. 191 STATUE   45 Where for so many Earties there are to provide,
    P. 191 STATUE   51 Where he shew'd her that so many voters he had
    P. 192 TWO HORSES   26 Who have told many truths well worth a mans
                                hearing,
    P. 194 TWO HORSES   98 Yet truth many times being punisht for Treason,

map   frequency: 1   relative frequency: 0.0000
    P.   82 A. HOUSE   768 And Paradice's only Map.

marble   frequency: 5   relative frequency: 0.0001
    P.   24 NYMPH   112 Be cut in Marble; and withal,
    P.   26 MISTRESS   26 Nor, in thy marble Vault, shall sound
    P.   59 A. HOUSE   21 What need of all this Marble Crust
    P. 192 TWO HORSES   29 The stately Brass Stallion and the white marble
                                Steed
    P. 192 TWO HORSES   35 W. Quoth the marble white Hors: 'twould make a
                                stone speak

marbles   frequency: 2   relative frequency: 0.0000
    P. 104 ANNIVERSARY   62 The flocking Marbles in a Palace meet;
    P. 108 ANNIVERSARY   210 And then loud Shreeks the vaulted Marbles rent.

march   frequency: 5   relative frequency: 0.0001
    See also "sea-march."
    P.   90 ODE   114 March indefatigably on;
    P. 154 INSTRUCTIONS   572 March straight to Chatham, to increase the fear.
    P. 160 INSTRUCTIONS   792 And march with Punishment in equal pace;
    P. 161 INSTRUCTIONS   837 And Turner gay up to his Pearch does march,
    P. 163 INSTRUCTIONS   914 And finds the Drums Lewis's March did beat.

march'd   frequency: 4   relative frequency: 0.0000
    P. 126 O.C.   146 He march'd, and through deep Severn ending war.
    P. 144 INSTRUCTIONS   151 Of early Wittals first the Troop march'd in,
    P. 145 INSTRUCTIONS   183 He March'd with Beaver cock'd of Bishop's
                                brim,
    P. 152 INSTRUCTIONS   481 First, then he march'd our whole Militia's
                                force,

marched. See "march'd," "marcht," "march't."

marching   frequency: 3   relative frequency: 0.0000
    P. 146 INSTRUCTIONS   212 Apsley and Brotherick, marching hand in hand.
    P. 147 INSTRUCTIONS   281 When, marching in, a seas'nable recruit
    P. 171 LOYALL SCOT   2 Saw Douglass Marching on the Elisian Glades,

marcht   frequency: 1   relative frequency: 0.0000

P. 145 INSTRUCTIONS 191 Then marcht the Troop, whose valiant Acts
                         before,

march't   frequency: 2   relative frequency: 0.0000
    P. 145 INSTRUCTIONS 177 Then march't the Troop of Clarendon, all full,
    P. 314 CHEQUER INN   49 And now they march't all Tagg and Ragg

mare   frequency: 1   relative frequency: 0.0000
    P. 96 HOLLAND   26 To shew them what's their Mare Liberum.

margaret. See "marg'ret."

marg'ret   frequency: 1   relative frequency: 0.0000
    P. 97 HOLLAND   65 More pregnant then their Marg'ret, that laid
                             down

maria   frequency: 2   relative frequency: 0.0000
    P. 79 A. HOUSE   651 The young Maria walks to night:
    P. 80 A. HOUSE   681 Maria such, and so doth hush

marina   frequency: 1   relative frequency: 0.0000
    P. 123 TWO SONGS   45 Marina yields. Who dares be coy?

marina's   frequency: 1   relative frequency: 0.0000
    P. 122 TWO SONGS   34 Before Marina's turn were sped?

mariners. See "marriners."

mark   frequency: 2   relative frequency: 0.0000
    P. 61 A. HOUSE   70 Only as for a Mark of Grace;
    P. 126 O.C.   141 No part of time but bore his mark away

mark'd   frequency: 3   relative frequency: 0.0000
    P. 63 A. HOUSE   148 'Have mark'd the Youth, and what he is.
    P. 76 A. HOUSE   546 As if he mark'd them with the Ax.
    P. 144 INSTRUCTIONS 121 The close Cabal mark'd how the Navy eats,

marke   frequency: 1   relative frequency: 0.0000
    P. 177 LOYALL SCOT   235 Two Nations Neere had mist the Marke soe long.

marked. See "mark'd," "mark't."

market   frequency: 2   relative frequency: 0.0000
See also "markett," "stocks-market."
    P. 179 STOCKSMARKET   21 But a market, they say, does suit the king well,
    P. 190 STATUE   32 He will here keep a market of Parliament men.

markett   frequency: 1   relative frequency: 0.0000
    P. 190 STATUE   31 And instead of that markett of herbs and of fruit

mark't   frequency: 1   relative frequency: 0.0000
    P. 141 INSTRUCTIONS   9 Or hast thou mark't how antique Masters limn

marrd   frequency: 1   relative frequency: 0.0000
    P. 166 KINGS VOWES   25 I will have a fine Son in makeing tho marrd,

marred. See "marrd."

marriage   frequency: 2   relative frequency: 0.0000
    P. 119 TWO SONGS   t1 Two Songs at the Marriage of the Lord
                             Fauconberg
    P. 140 HIS HOUSE   8 The Queens Marriage and all;

married. See "marry'd."

marriners   frequency: 1   relative frequency: 0.0000
    P. 70 A. HOUSE   381 But, as the Marriners that sound,

marry   frequency: 1   relative frequency: 0.0000
    P. 137 HOUSEWARMING   14 Who was dig'd up so often ere she did marry;

marry'd   frequency: 1   relative frequency: 0.0000
    P. 201 HISTORICALL   22 He marry'd Minhier Falmouths pregnant wench.

mars   frequency: 2   relative frequency: 0.0000
    P. 129 O.C.   234 It seem'd Mars broke through Janus' double
                             gate;
    P. 137 HOUSEWARMING   5 Us Mars, and Apollo, and Vulcan consume;

marshall'd   frequency: 1   relative frequency: 0.0000
    P. 153 INSTRUCTIONS 509 The State Affairs thus Marshall'd, for the rest

martial   frequency: 6   relative frequency: 0.0001
    P. 104 ANNIVERSARY   59 Now through the Strings a Martial rage he
                               throws,
    P. 130 O.C.   277 Thee, many ages hence, in martial verse
    P. 148 INSTRUCTIONS   301 The martial Standard Sands displaying, shows
    P. 150 INSTRUCTIONS   376 Comes news of Pastime, Martial and old:
    P. 152 INSTRUCTIONS   455 And that by Law of Arms, in Martial strife,
    P. 156 INSTRUCTIONS   637 Mix a vain Terrour in his Martial lock,

martyr   frequency: 1   relative frequency: 0.0000
    P. 192 TWO HORSES   48 For which his own Father a Martyr did dye.

martyrdom   frequency: 1   relative frequency: 0.0000
    P. 83 FLECKNO   26 And to my Martyrdom prepared Rest.

martyrs   frequency: 1   relative frequency: 0.0000
    P. 145 INSTRUCTIONS   168 And both of them alike French Martyrs were.

marvel   frequency: 1   relative frequency: 0.0000
    P. 41 THE MOWER   18 To find the Marvel of Peru.

mary   frequency: 1   relative frequency: 0.0000
    P. 119 TWO SONGS   t2 and the Lady Mary Cromwell.

mascarade   frequency: 1   relative frequency: 0.0000
    P. 168 ADVICE   6 The Brittain Jigging it in Mascarade;

masculine   frequency: 1   relative frequency: 0.0000
    P. 150 INSTRUCTIONS   378 Masculine Wives, transgressing Natures Law.

mask   frequency: 3   relative frequency: 0.0000
    See also "maske," "masque."
    P. 77 A. HOUSE   586 Could with a Mask my studies hit!
    P. 93 DR. WITTY   4 Take off the Cypress vail, but leave a mask,
    P. 176 LOYALL SCOT   181 The fittest Mask for one that Robs a Crown.

maske   frequency: 1   relative frequency: 0.0000
    P. 128 O.C.   225 Least others dare to think your zeale a maske,

masque   frequency: 2   relative frequency: 0.0000
    P. 28 LOVER   26 This masque of quarrelling Elements;
    P. 91 MAY'S DEATH   38 Like Pembroke at the Masque, and then did rate.

masquerade   frequency: 3   relative frequency: 0.0000
    See also "mascarade."
    P. 175 LOYALL SCOT   167 And their Religion all but Masquerade.
    P. 180 STOCKSMARKET   38 Or is he to Clayton's gone in masquerade?
    P. 194 TWO HORSES   110 W. To Cuckold a Scrivener mine's in
                              Masquerade.

mass   frequency: 2   relative frequency: 0.0000
    P. 30 THE GALLERY   38 A Mass of Ambergris it bears.
    P. 84 FLECKNO   52 So hungry that though ready to say Mass

massacre   frequency: 2   relative frequency: 0.0000
    P. 71 A. HOUSE   394 These Massacre the Grass along:
    P. 106 ANNIVERSARY   114 And her whom they should Massacre adore:

mast   frequency: 1   relative frequency: 0.0000
    P. 57 BILL-BOROW   30 When they salute it from the Mast!

master   frequency: 13   relative frequency: 0.0002
    See "writing-master."
    P. 32 MOURNING   22 Joy now so much her Master grown,
    P. 57 BILL-BOROW   41 Fear of the Master, and respect
    P. 60 A. HOUSE   50 And scarce indures the Master great:
    P. 92 MAY'S DEATH   98 May only Master of these Revels past.
    P. 138 HOUSEWARMING   32 Though he had built full many a one for his
                              Master
    P. 144 INSTRUCTIONS   156 That sold their Master, led by Ashburnham.
    P. 151 INSTRUCTIONS   428 To Master Lewis, and tell Coward tale,
    P. 163 INSTRUCTIONS   933 False to his Master Bristol, Arlington,
    P. 194 TWO HORSES   103 Tho' the beast gave his Master ne're an ill
                              word,
    P. 198 DUKE   39 Do's now in popery with his Master joyne.
    P. 199 DUKE   66 Now Talbott must by his great master stand,
    P. 203 HISTORICALL   90 As Killegrew buffoons his Master, they
    P. 204 HISTORICALL   140 I'hunt down 's Frey and hope to master all.

master-cook   frequency: 1   relative frequency: 0.0000

```
        P. 162 INSTRUCTIONS  871 In Chair, he smeaking sits like Master-Cook,

master-hand                   frequency:    1    relative frequency: 0.0000
        P. 164 INSTRUCTIONS  947 His Master-hand the Ancients shall out-do

master-wave                   frequency:    1    relative frequency: 0.0000
        P.  27 LOVER          13 Till at the last the master-Wave

masters                       frequency:    7    relative frequency: 0.0001
        P.  57 BILL-BOROW      38 Of the great Masters terrour there:
        P. 141 INSTRUCTIONS     9 Or hast thou mark't how antique Masters limn
        P. 155 INSTRUCTIONS   616 Crown'd, for that Merit, with their Masters
                                  Name.
        P. 169 ADVICE          32 Our mighty Masters in a warme debate;
        P. 182 MADE FREE       37 When his Masters too rash
        P. 182 MADE FREE       66 And the Souldiers had all beene your Masters.
        P. 185 BRITANNIA       24 Your own lov'd Court and Masters Progeny?

mastery. See "mast'ry."

mast'ry                       frequency:    1    relative frequency: 0.0000
        P. 150 INSTRUCTIONS   395 So Holland with us had the Mast'ry try'd,

masts                         frequency:    1    relative frequency: 0.0000
        See also "top-masts."
        P. 158 INSTRUCTIONS   728 Her Masts erect, tough Cordage, Timbers
                                  strong,

match                         frequency:    2    relative frequency: 0.0000
        P.  39 THE MATCH        t The Match.
        P. 141 INSTRUCTIONS    13 But if to match our Crimes thy skill presumes,

matches                       frequency:    1    relative frequency: 0.0000
        P. 121 TWO SONGS       58 Makes Mortals matches fit for Deityes.

matchless                     frequency:    2    relative frequency: 0.0000
        P.  44 GLO-WORMS        4 Her matchless Songs does meditate;
        P. 173 LOYALL SCOT     60 That Matchless grace to propagate thy fame,

mate                          frequency:    5    relative frequency: 0.0001
        P.  49 THE GARDEN      58 While Man there walk'd without a Mate:
        P. 110 ANNIVERSARY    273 Some lusty Mate, who with more careful Eye
        P. 170 PROPHECY        19 A Boy shall take his Sister for his Mate
        P. 201 HISTORICALL     29 Her most Uxorious Mate she usd of old;
        P. 204 HISTORICALL    129 Like a true Lover for her dying Mate.

mathematicks                  frequency:    1    relative frequency: 0.0000
        P.  60 A. HOUSE        47 These holy Mathematicks can

matter                        frequency:    3    relative frequency: 0.0000
        P. 104 ANNIVERSARY     34 Nor Matter for succeeding Founders raise;
        P. 105 ANNIVERSARY     77 All other Matter yields, and may be rul'd;
        P. 139 HOUSEWARMING    86 And with matter profane, cemented with holy,

matur'd                       frequency:    1    relative frequency: 0.0000
        P. 142 INSTRUCTIONS    55 And found how Royal Heirs might be matur'd,

mature                        frequency:    1    relative frequency: 0.0000
        P. 161 INSTRUCTIONS   823 Yet Harry must job back and all mature,

maturity                      frequency:    1    relative frequency: 0.0000
        P. 112 ANNIVERSARY    382 'Courage with Age, Maturity with Hast:

maw                           frequency:    2    relative frequency: 0.0000
        P. 144 INSTRUCTIONS   138 Else swallows all down her indented maw.
        P. 158 INSTRUCTIONS   707 And were not Ruyters maw with ravage cloy'd,

maxime                        frequency:    1    relative frequency: 0.0000
        P.   5 HASTINGS        23 But 'tis a Maxime of that State, That none,

may                           frequency:   78    relative frequency: 0.0016
        P.  15 THE CORONET     23 And let these wither, so that he may die,
        P.  15 THE CORONET     26 May crown thy Feet, that could not crown thy
                                  Head.
        P.  18 BERMUDAS        35 Which thence (perhaps) rebounding, may
        P.  18 CLORINDA        11 C. In whose cool bosome we may lye
        P.  19 THYRSIS         13 Dorinda. There Birds may nest, but how can I,
        P.  19 THYRSIS         24 Our Lightfoot we may give away;
        P.  19 THYRSIS         26 May feast with Musick of the Spheres.
        P.  20 THYRSIS         38 And every Nimph's a Queen of May.
        P.  22 NYMPH            9 But, if my simple Pray'rs may yet
```

P.	22 NYMPH	15 And nothing may we use in vain.
P.	24 NYMPH	114 Th' Engraver sure his Art may spare;
P.	25 YOUNG LOVE	17 Now then love me: time may take
P.	25 YOUNG LOVE	20 And learn Love before we may.
P.	27 MISTRESS	37 Now let us sport us while we may;
P.	30 THE GALLERY	39 Nor blows more Wind than what may well
P.	37 DEFINITION	25 As Lines so Loves oblique may well
P.	38 PICTURE	24 Where I may see thy Glories from some shade.
P.	38 PICTURE	28 Make that the Tulips may have share
P.	38 PICTURE	32 That Violets may a longer Age endure.
P.	41 THE MOWER	38 May to adorn the Gardens stand:
P.	42 DAMON	25 Tell me where I may pass the Fires
P.	46 AMETAS	14 Must be taken as you may.
P.	59 A. HOUSE	20 Where Winds as he themselves may lose.
P.	61 A. HOUSE	73 Him Bishops-Hill, or Denton may,
P.	61 A. HOUSE	83 We opportuly may relate
P.	64 A. HOUSE	189 'Where you may lye as chast in Bed,
P.	65 A. HOUSE	194 'Of Joys you see, and may make more!
P.	78 A. HOUSE	612 That I may never leave this Place:
P.	80 A. HOUSE	702 Where She may all her Beautyes look;
P.	89 ODE	87 And, what he may, forbears
P.	89 ODE	97 What may not then our Isle presume
P.	89 ODE	99 What may not others fear
P.	90 MAY'S DEATH	2 Tom May was hurry'd hence and did not know't.
P.	90 MAY'S DEATH	19 But seeing May he varied streight his Song,
P.	91 MAY'S DEATH	25 By this May to himself and them was come,
P.	91 MAY'S DEATH	54 Those but to Lucan do continue May.
P.	92 MAY'S DEATH	98 May only Master of these Revels past.
P.	99 HOLLAND	145 For now of nothing may our State despair,
P.	103 ANNIVERSARY	21 Well may they strive to leave them to their Son,
P.	105 ANNIVERSARY	77 All other Matter yields, and may be rul'd;
P.	107 ANNIVERSARY	147 And knowing not where Heavens choice may light,
P.	108 ANNIVERSARY	187 So with more Modesty we may be True,
P.	110 ANNIVERSARY	289 That sober Liberty which men may have,
P.	110 ANNIVERSARY	292 May shew their own, not see his Nakedness.
P.	111 ANNIVERSARY	319 Well may you act the Adam and the Eve;
P.	113 ANNIVERSARY	398 So that we both alike may miss our End:
P.	118 BLAKE	159 And in one War the present age may boast,
P.	120 TWO SONGS	41 Though I so high may not pretend,
P.	121 TWO SONGS	8 Phillis you may wait the Spring:
P.	122 TWO SONGS	35 Now lesser Beauties may take place,
P.	130 O.C.	304 Onely our sighs, perhaps, may thither reach.
P.	140 HOUSEWARMING	106 That for Name-sake he may with Hyde Park it enlarge,
P.	140 HOUSEWARMING	108 At Tybourn may land, and spare the Tower-Barge.
P.	142 INSTRUCTIONS	62 Wide Mouth that Sparagus may well proclaim:
P.	142 INSTRUCTIONS	67 Or how a mortal Poyson she may draw,
P.	149 INSTRUCTIONS	349 Now Mordant may, within his Castle Tow'r,
P.	149 INSTRUCTIONS	353 And now, now, the Canary-Patent may
P.	150 INSTRUCTIONS	399 Bab May and Arlington did wisely scoff,
P.	151 INSTRUCTIONS	415 Bennet and May, and those of shorter reach,
P.	151 INSTRUCTIONS	427 St. Albans writ to that he may bewail
P.	153 INSTRUCTIONS	520 Under Herculean Labours he may sink.
P.	160 INSTRUCTIONS	805 But the true cause was, that, in 's Brother May,
P.	162 INSTRUCTIONS	865 That may his Body, this his Mind explain.
P.	165 KINGS VOWES	18 And yet call him home again, soon as I may.
P.	167 KINGS VOWES	51 And who knowes but the Mode may soon bring in the rest?
P.	167 KINGS VOWES	53 Where the Ducks and the Drakes may their freedomes enjoy,
P.	167 KINGS VOWES	57 That they may raise Fortunes to my owne frye.
P.	173 LOYALL SCOT	59 Fortunate Boy, if ere my verse may Claim
P.	173 LOYALL SCOT	77 Anatomists may Sooner fix the Cells
P.	179 STOCKSMARKET	28 May be henceforth confiscate for reasons more just.
P.	183 MADE FREE	83 But he may prove more just,
P.	183 MADE FREE	102 The whole Nation may chance to repent it.
P.	187 BRITANNIA	93 The Church and state you safely may invade.
P.	188 BRITANNIA	138 Perhaps that spell may his Erring soul reclaim.
P.	188 BRITANNIA	139 Who knows what good effects from thence may spring;
P.	188 BRITANNIA	143 As easily learn'd Virtuoso's may
P.	191 TWO HORSES	4 It is a clear proofe that birds too may talke;
P.	196 TWO HORSES	165 That shall come to pass all mankind may swear

may-games   frequency: 1   relative frequency: 0.0000
  P.   45 MOWER'S SONG   15 And in your gawdy May-games meet,

mayern   frequency: 2   relative frequency: 0.0000
  P.   5 HASTINGS   48 Himself at once condemneth, and Mayern;

```
        P.    5 HASTINGS        52 Had Mayern once been mixt with Hastings blood!

mayn                               frequency:    1     relative frequency: 0.0000
        P.  118 BLAKE           146 By which we Laurels reapt ev'n on the Mayn.

may's                              frequency:    1     relative frequency: 0.0000
        P.   90 MAY'S DEATH       t Tom May's Death.

may'st                             frequency:    1     relative frequency: 0.0000
        P.  141 INSTRUCTIONS     27 So may'st thou perfect, by a lucky blow,

maze                               frequency:    2     relative frequency: 0.0000
        P.   17 BERMUDAS          6 That led us through the watry Maze,
        P.  103 ANNIVERSARY       1 Like the vain Curlings of the Watry maze,

mazes                              frequency:    1     relative frequency: 0.0000
        P.  203 HISTORICALL     109 To tread the Phantastik Mazes of a Priest,

me                                 frequency:   88     relative frequency: 0.0018
        See also "mee."

mead                               frequency:    2     relative frequency: 0.0000
        P.   14 THE CORONET       5 Through every Garden, every Mead,
        P.   72 A. HOUSE        429 Their Females fragrant as the Mead

meadow                             frequency:    6     relative frequency: 0.0001
        P.   41 THE MOWER        16 That one was for a Meadow sold.
        P.   70 A. HOUSE        377 To see Men through this Meadow Dive,
        P.   73 A. HOUSE        467 And makes the Meadow truly be
        P.   78 A. HOUSE        634 It ev'ry where the Meadow holds;
        P.   80 A. HOUSE        692 To Her the Meadow sweetness owes;
        P.   80 A. HOUSE        699 The Meadow Carpets where to tread;

meadows                            frequency:    7     relative frequency: 0.0001
        See also "medows."
        P.   41 THE MOWER        35 And Fauns and Faryes do the Meadows till,
        P.   42 DAMON            10 Which thus our Sun-burn'd Meadows sear!
        P.   43 DAMON            42 Through all the Meadows I have mown.
        P.   46 MOWER'S SONG     25 And thus, ye Meadows, which have been
        P.   61 A. HOUSE         80 Deep Meadows, and transparent Floods.
        P.   71 A. HOUSE        386 Does oftner then these Meadows change.
        P.   78 A. HOUSE        626 And now the Meadows fresher dy'd;

meads                              frequency:    5     relative frequency: 0.0001
        P.   70 A. HOUSE        367 But ore the Meads below it plays,
        P.   72 A. HOUSE        421 Where, as the Meads with Hay, the Plain
        P.   78 A. HOUSE        632 Among these Meads the only Snake.
        P.   80 A. HOUSE        696 Then Gardens, Woods, Meads, Rivers are.
        P.   82 A. HOUSE        752 So you all Woods, Streams, Gardens, Meads.

meager                             frequency:    1     relative frequency: 0.0000
        P.  204 HISTORICALL     137 His meager Highness now had got astride,

meal                               frequency:    3     relative frequency: 0.0000
        P.  139 HOUSEWARMING     67 Bring in the whole Milk of a year at a meal,
        P.  142 INSTRUCTIONS     68 Out of the cordial meal of the Cacao.
        P.  178 LOYALL SCOT     271 And all themselves in meal and friendship close.

mean                               frequency:   16     relative frequency: 0.0003
        P.   18 CLORINDA         16 Or slake its Drought? C. What is't you mean?
        P.   31 MOURNING          3 What mean these Infants which of late
        P.   38 PICTURE          25 Mean time, whilst every verdant thing
        P.   49 THE GARDEN       41 Mean while the Mind, from pleasure less,
        P.   82 A. HOUSE        745 Mean time ye Fields, Springs, Bushes,
                                    Flow'rs,
        P.   84 FLECKNO          59 I mean till he were drest: for else so thin
        P.   88 ODE              57 He nothing common did or mean
        P.   98 HOLLAND         127 That ours mean time at leizure might careen,
        P.  131 O.C.            319 We find already what those omens mean,
        P.  148 INSTRUCTIONS    317 Mean time through all the Yards their Orders
                                    run
        P.  156 INSTRUCTIONS    619 Now a cheap spoil, and the mean Victor's Slave,
        P.  161 INSTRUCTIONS    849 Mean while the certain News of Peace arrives
        P.  167 KINGS VOWES      58 Some one I will advance from mean descent,
        P.  169 ADVICE           51 Who make it by their mean retreat appear
        P.  180 STOCKSMARKET     42 That to change him into a Jack-pudding you mean,
        P.  192 TWO HORSES       25 The Horses I mean of Woolchurch and Charing,

meaner                             frequency:    1     relative frequency: 0.0000
        P.  122 TWO SONGS        36 And meaner Virtues come in play;

meanest                            frequency:    1     relative frequency: 0.0000
```

P. 129 O.C.   241 Whose meanest acts he would himself advance,

means   frequency: 2   relative frequency: 0.0000
     P. 71 A. HOUSE   404 And forthwith means on it to sup:
     P. 82 A. HOUSE   749 Emplcy the means you have by Her,

meant   frequency: 4   relative frequency: 0.0000
     See also "ment."
     P. 25 YOUNG LOVE   22 And, if good she to us meant,
     P. 81 A. HOUSE   714 Those Trains by Youth against thee meant;
     P. 132 PARADISE   52 And while I meant to Praise thee, must
                             Commend.
     P. 180 STOCKSMARKET 36 As if you had meant it his coffin and shroud?

meas'ring   frequency: 1   relative frequency: 0.0000
     P. 75 A. HOUSE   540 Meas'ring the Timber with his Foot;

measure   frequency: 8   relative frequency: 0.0001
     P.   4 HASTINGS   19 Had he but at this Measure still increast,
     P. 15 EYES   7 These Tears which better measure all,
     P. 59 A. HOUSE   16 Their Bodies measure out their Place.
     P. 61 A. HOUSE   91 Fair beyond Measure, and an Heir
     P. 132 PARADISE   54 In Number, Weight, and Measure, needs not
                             Rhime.
     P. 137 HOUSEWARMING 24 As might carry the measure and name of an Hyde.
     P. 150 INSTRUCTICNS 407 With the Bulls Horn to measure his cwn Head,
     P. 313 CHEQUER INN   24 With which he strikes the Measure.

measures   frequency: 3   relative frequency: 0.0000
     P. 91 MAY'S DEATH   52 How ill the measures of these States agree.
     P. 104 ANNIVERSARY   51 The rougher Stones, unto his Measures hew'd,
     P. 109 ANNIVERSARY 246 Trying the Measures of the Bredth and Height;

measuring. See "meas'ring."

meat   frequency: 1   relative frequency: 0.0000
     See also "meate."
     P. 96 HOLLAND   30 And sat not as a Meat but as a Guest;

meate   frequency: 3   relative frequency: 0.0000
     P. 314 CHEQUER INN   87 Both words and meate did utter
     P. 315 CHEQUER INN 119 Should live tc sell himself for Meate.
     P. 315 CHEQUER INN 122 But wou'd as well as Meate have Cloaths

meates   frequency: 1   relative frequency: 0.0000
     P. 316 CHEQUER INN 170 Like Sweat Meates, for their Girles and Wives

meats. See "meates."

mediator   frequency: 1   relative frequency: 0.0000
     P. 87 FLECKNO   155 Made Mediator, in my room, said, Why?

meditate   frequency: 1   relative frequency: 0.0000
     P. 44 GLC-WORMS   4 Her matchless Scngs dces meditate;

meditates   frequency: 1   relative frequency: 0.0000
     P. 151 INSTRUCTICNS 419 White-hall's unsafe, the Court all meditates

medows   frequency: 2   relative frequency: 0.0000
     P. 45 MOWER'S SONG   2 Of all these Medows fresh and gay;
     P. 45 MOWER'S SONG 13 Unthankful Medcws, could ycu so

medway   frequency: 2   relative frequency: 0.0000
     P. 159 INSTRUCTIONS 744 And Medway chast ravish'd before his Face,
     P. 159 INSTRUCTIONS 759 The Thames roar'd, swouning Medway turn'd her
                             tide,

mee   frequency: 1   relative frequency: 0.0000

meeke   frequency: 1   relative frequency: 0.0000
     P. 199 DUKE   57 Was thought soe meeke, sce prudent and soe wise:

meet   frequency: 19   relative frequency: 0.0003
     See also "meete."
     P. 11 DIALOGUE   53 Shall within one Beauty meet,
     P. 16 EYES   31 Whose liquid Chaines could flowing meet
     P. 17 BERMUDAS   21 He makes the Figs cur mouths to meet;
     P. 18 CLORINDA   26 C. Who would not in Fan's Praises meet?
     P. 37 DEFINITION   28 Though infinite can never meet.
     P. 45 MOWER'S SONG 15 And in your gawdy May-games meet,
     P. 49 THE GARDEN   60 What other Help could yet be meet!

```
P.  64 A. HOUSE       171 'Here Pleasure Piety doth meet;
P.  68 A. HOUSE       306 And round your equal Fires do meet;
P.  85 FLECKNO         87 I meet one on the Stairs who made me stand,
P. 104 ANNIVERSARY     62 The flocking Marbles in a Palace meet;
P. 106 ANNIVERSARY    132 High Grace should meet in one with highest
                          Pow'r,
P. 124 O.C.            42 His hidden Soul at ev'ry turn could meet;
P. 126 O.C.           136 As silent Suns to meet the Night descend.
P. 148 INSTRUCTIONS   289 Dear Lovers of their King, and Death to meet,
P. 149 INSTRUCTIONS   364 United most, else when by turns they meet.
P. 160 INSTRUCTIONS   814 But with a Parliament abhors to meet,
P. 161 INSTRUCTIONS   824 Binding, e're th' Houses meet, the Treaty sure.
P. 202 HISTORICALL     70 As they att Athens, we att Dover meet,
```

```
meete                      frequency:    1    relative frequency: 0.0000
P. 182 MADE FREE       44 Each one he cou'd meete,
```

```
meeter                     frequency:    1    relative frequency: 0.0000
P. 160 INSTRUCTIONS   798 Show'd him to manage the Exchequer meeter:
```

```
meets                      frequency:    2    relative frequency: 0.0000
P. 157 INSTRUCTIONS   677 Like a glad Lover, the fierce Flames he meets,
P. 172 LOYALL SCOT     43 Like a glad lover the fierce Flames hee meets
```

mein herr.   See "minhier."

```
melchizedeck               frequency:    1    relative frequency: 0.0000
P.  83 FLECKNO          3 I for some branch of Melchizedeck took,
```

```
melons                     frequency:    2    relative frequency: 0.0000
P.  17 BERMUDAS        22 And throws the Melons at our feet.
P.  49 THE GARDEN      39 Stumbling on Melons, as I pass,
```

```
melt                       frequency:    5    relative frequency: 0.0001
P.  15 EYES            16 Melt in these Pendants of the Eyes.
P.  24 NYMPH          100 Melt in such Amber Tears as these.
P. 157 INSTRUCTIONS   686 His alt'ring Form, and soder'd Limbs to melt;
P. 173 LOYALL SCOT     52 His Altred form and scdred Limbs to Melt,
P. 191 STATUE          55 Tho of Brass, yet with grief it would melt him
                          away,
```

```
melting                    frequency:    1    relative frequency: 0.0000
P. 173 LOYALL SCOT     72 Our nations Melting thy Colossus Frame,
```

```
melts                      frequency:    1    relative frequency: 0.0000
P.   4 LOVELACE        38 Whose hand so gently melts the Ladies hand.
```

```
member'd                   frequency:    1    relative frequency: 0.0000
P. 141 INSTRUCTIONS    34 Member'd like Mules, with Elephantine chine.
```

```
members                    frequency:    5    relative frequency: 0.0001
P. 149 INSTRUCTIONS   334 But all the Members Lives, consulting, spare.
P. 169 ADVICE          52 Five members need not be demanded here.
P. 191 STATUE          42 That so liberally treated the members at supper.
P. 193 TWO HORSES      75 W. To the bold talking members if the Bastards
                          you adde,
P. 313 CHEQUER INN     38 Had not the Members most been made
```

```
memorable                  frequency:    2    relative frequency: 0.0000
P.  88 ODE             58 Upon that memorable Scene:
P.  89 ODE             65 This was that memorable Hour
```

```
memory                     frequency:    4    relative frequency: 0.0000
P.  21 SOUL & BODY     40 And Memory will not foregoe.
P.  58 BILL-BOROW      55 But in no Memory were seen
P. 127 O.C.           164 That we could to his Memory express.
P. 151 INSTRUCTIONS   439 But Lewis was of Memory but dull,
```

```
memphis                    frequency:    1    relative frequency: 0.0000
P.  72 A. HOUSE       437 Or, like the Desert Memphis Sand,
```

```
men                        frequency:   70    relative frequency: 0.0014
   See also "chimney-men," "feather-men,"
           "lay-men," "merchant-men."
P.   3 LOVELACE        10 To honour not her selfe, but worthy men.
P.   4 LOVELACE        49 Him, valianst men, and fairest Nymphs approve,
P.  22 NYMPH            3 Ungentle men! They cannot thrive
P.  22 NYMPH           17 Else Men are made their Decdands.
P.  23 NYMPH           54 The love of false and cruel men.
P.  33 DAPHNIS         18 By which men their Siege maintain,
P.  48 THE GARDEN       1 How vainly men themselves amaze
```

P.	48 THE GARDEN	12 In busie Companies of Men.
P.	57 BILL-BOROW	39 And Men could hear his Armour still
P.	58 BILL-BOROW	68 And Mountains rais'd of dying Men.
P.	59 A. HOUSE	29 When larger sized Men did stoop
P.	60 A. HOUSE	37 Men will dispute how their Extent
P.	62 A. HOUSE	102 'Of those wild Creatures, called Men.
P.	69 A. HOUSE	334 And Men did rosie Garlands wear?
P.	70 A. HOUSE	371 Where Men like Grashoppers appear,
P.	70 A. HOUSE	377 To see Men through this Meadow Dive,
P.	80 A. HOUSE	679 And Men the silent Scene assist,
P.	88 ODE	40 As Men are strong or weak.
P.	99 HOLLAND	146 Darling of Heaven, and of Men the Care;
P.	105 ANNIVERSARY	78 But who the Minds of stubborn Men can build?
P.	107 ANNIVERSARY	149 But Men alas, as if they nothing car'd,
P.	108 ANNIVERSARY	189 While impious Men deceiv'd with pleasure short,
P.	108 ANNIVERSARY	217 From the low World, and thankless Men above,
P.	110 ANNIVERSARY	289 That sober Liberty which men may have,
P.	110 ANNIVERSARY	299 Whose frantique Army should they want for Men
P.	112 ANNIVERSARY	354 'What Mints of Men, what Union of Designes!
P.	112 ANNIVERSARY	376 'More then all Men, all Navies, and all Arms.
P.	115 BLAKE	59 Which troubles men to raise it when 'tis Oar,
P.	115 BLAKE	71 Deluded men! Fate with you did but sport,
P.	116 BLAKE	93 Fond men who know not whilst such works they raise,
P.	117 BLAKE	127 Thousands of wayes, Thousands of men there dye,
P.	125 O.C.	91 Under whose shady tent Men ev'ry year
P.	126 O.C.	127 Numbers of Men decrease with pains unknown,
P.	128 O.C.	194 He conquer'd God, still ere he fought with men:
P.	141 INSTRUCTIONS	17 Where, like the new Controller, all men laugh
P.	142 INSTRUCTIONS	48 When Men and Women took each others Word.
P.	143 INSTRUCTIONS	106 The House of Commons clatt'ring like the Men.
P.	145 INSTRUCTIONS	165 The posture strange men laught at of his Poll,
P.	145 INSTRUCTIONS	174 Gentlest of men, and his Lieutenant mild,
P.	148 INSTRUCTIONS	307 Broken in Courage, yet the Men the same,
P.	151 INSTRUCTIONS	417 But wiser Men, and well foreseen in chance,
P.	153 INSTRUCTIONS	501 Here Men induc'd by Safety, Gain, and Ease,
P.	156 INSTRUCTIONS	638 And all those lines by which men are mistook.
P.	160 INSTRUCTIONS	795 All men admir'd he to that pitch could fly:
P.	165 KINGS VOWES	17 Yet if Men should clammor I'le pack him away:
P.	169 ADVICE	64 Tis by afflictions passive men grow great.
P.	170 PROPHECY	11 And those false Men the Soveraign People sent
P.	171 PROPHECY	36 Whom Wise men Laugh att and the Women Rule,
P.	171 PROPHECY	45 When the Crowne's Heir shall English Men dispise
P.	174 LOYALL SCOT	110 From Church they need not Censure men Away,
P.	177 LOYALL SCOT	250 And ever since men with a female spite
P.	179 STOCKSMARKET	19 And so loose in his seat that all men agree
P.	189 BRITANNIA	174 Blake, Candish, Drake, (men void of slavish fears)
P.	190 STATUE	21 Does the Treasurer think men so Loyally tame
P.	190 STATUE	32 He will here keep a market of Parliament men.
P.	191 TWO HORSES	6 Have spoken as plainly as men doe with Tongues:
P.	192 TWO HORSES	22 To believe men and beasts have spoke in effigie,
P.	193 TWO HORSES	73 Ch. That Parliament men should rail at the Court,
P.	195 TWO HORSES	126 And Free men alike value life and Estate,
P.	196 TWO HORSES	172 As learned men say, came out of their breeches,
P.	198 DUKE	25 Shall these men dare to contradict my will
P.	198 DUKE	28 Shall these men dare to thinke, shall these decide
P.	200 DUKE	95 When wiser men its ruine undertooke:
P.	200 DUKE	97 At last to fools and mad men and the pope?
P.	203 HISTORICALL	96 Who would such men Heavens messengers believe,
P.	205 HISTORICALL	179 Be wise ye Sons of Men tempt God no more
P.	313 CHEQUER INN	43 But he had Men enough to spare
P.	313 CHEQUER INN	45 Tho' all Men blusht that heard it
P.	315 CHEQUER INN	112 Nay Portman tho' all men cry'd shame
P.	316 CHEQUER INN	166 And for to save the Serving Men,

menalca's   frequency: 2   relative frequency: 0.0000
| P. | 121 TWO SONGS | 4 Has Menalca's daughter won. |
| P. | 122 TWO SONGS | 13 Fear not; at Menalca's Hall |

mend   frequency: 2   relative frequency: 0.0000
| P. | 175 LOYALL SCOT | 142 Howere Insipid Yet the Sawce will mend 'em |
| P. | 180 STOCKSMARKET | 56 For 'tis such a king as no chisel can mend. |

mended   frequency: 1   relative frequency: 0.0000
| P. | 195 TWO HORSES | 157 Ch. But canst thou Divine when things shall be mended? |

mends   frequency: 1   relative frequency: 0.0000

P.   94 DR. WITTY   16 That mends; and added beauties are but spots.

mens   frequency: 2   relative frequency: 0.0000
  P.   47 EMPIRE   16 Tc sing Mens Triumphs, or in Heavens quire.
  P. 178 LOYALL SCOT   256 Rationall mens words pledges are ot peace,

ment   frequency: 4   relative frequency: 0.0000
  P.   36 DAPHNIS   85 Gentler times fcr love are ment
  P.   65 A. HOUSE   213 'And yet, how well scever ment,
  P.   74 A. HOUSE   501 There the huge Bulk takes place, as ment
  P.   84 FLECKNO   45 I, that perceiv'd now what his Musick ment,

mercenary   frequency: 2   relative frequency: 0.0000
  P.   91 MAY'S DEATH   40 Most servil' wit, and Mercenary Pen.
  P. 145 INSTRUCTIONS 185 Next th' Lawyers Mercenary Band appear:

merchant-men   frequency: 1   relative frequency: 0.0000
  P. 158 INSTRUCTIONS 712 Our Merchant-men, lest they should burn, we
                           drcwn.

merchants   frequency: 1   relative frequency: 0.0000
  P. 147 INSTRUCTIONS 282 Of Citizens and Merchants held dispute:

mercury   frequency: 1   relative frequency: 0.0000
  P. 176 LOYALL SCOT   208 And would like Chymists fixing Mercury

mercy   frequency: 2   relative frequency: 0.0000
  P. 193 TWO HORSES   56 Lord a Mercy and a Cross might be set on the
                           docre;
  P. 200 DUKE   100 Great Charles, who full cf mercy wouldst command

meridian   frequency: 1   relative frequency: 0.0000
  P. 124 O.C.   39 When with meridian height her Beauty shin'd,

merit   frequency: 1   relative frequency: 0.0000
  P. 155 INSTRUCTIONS 616 Crcwn'd, for that Merit, with their Masters
                           Name.

merits   frequency: 1   relative frequency: 0.0000
  P. 119 TWO SONGS   15 Nor merits he a Mortal's name,

mermaids. See "mairmaids."

merry   frequency: 2   relative frequency: 0.0000
  P. 121 TWO SONGS   2 Never such a merry day.
  P. 146 INSTRUCTIONS 229 They both accept the Charge with merry glee,

meshach. See "mesheck."

mesheck   frequency: 1   relative frequency: 0.0000
  P. 156 INSTRUCTIONS 648 Like Shadrack, Mesheck, and Abednego.

messe   frequency: 2   relative frequency: 0.0000
  P. 316 CHEQUER INN   141 But Messe was Rickt on Messe

messengers   frequency: 2   relative frequency: 0.0000
  P. 151 INSTRUCTIONS 411 Fresh Messengers still the sad News assure,
  P. 203 HISTORICALL   96 Who would such men Heavens messengers believe,

messiah   frequency: 1   relative frequency: 0.0000
  P. 131 PARADISE   3 Messiah Crown'd, Gods Reconcil'd Decree,

met   frequency: 3   relative frequency: 0.0000
  P.   18 CLORINDA   20 Pan met me. C. What did great Pan say?
  P. 116 BLAKE   81 For here they met with news, which did produce,
  P. 159 INSTRUCTIONS 773 Who the Dutch Fleet with Storms disabled met,

metal   frequency: 2   relative frequency: 0.0000
  See also "mettall."
  P.   94 DR. WITTY   12 Much of the precious Metal rub away.
  P. 155 INSTRUCTIONS 604 Which show the tempting metal in their clutch.

metempsychosed. See "metemsicosd."

metemsicosd   frequency: 1   relative frequency: 0.0000
  P. 178 LOYALL SCOT   285 Metemsicosd to some Scotch Presbyter.

meteor   frequency: 1   relative frequency: 0.0000
  P. 186 BRITANNIA   65 Her Towry front a fiery Meteor bears

meteors   frequency: 1   relative frequency: 0.0000

| | P. 27 LOVER | 6 Like Meteors of a Summers night: |

methinks   frequency: 2   relative frequency: 0.0000
| | P. 77 A. HOUSE | 601 How safe, methinks, and strong, behind |
| | P. 180 STOCKSMARKET | 41 Methinks by the equipage of this vile scene |

metropolis   frequency: 1   relative frequency: 0.0000
| | P. 139 HOUSEWARMING | 95 Your Metropolis House is in St. James's Fields, |

mettall   frequency: 1   relative frequency: 0.0000
| | P. 173 LOYALL SCOT | 71 Mixt in Corinthian Mettall at thy Flame |

mexique   frequency: 2   relative frequency: 0.0000
| | P. 18 BERMUDAS | 36 Eccho beyond the Mexique Bay. |
| | P. 77 A. HOUSE | 580 Like Mexique Paintings, all the Plumes. |

microscope   frequency: 1   relative frequency: 0.0000
| | P. 141 INSTRUCTIONS | 16 With Hook then, through the microscope, take aim |

mid-day   frequency: 1   relative frequency: 0.0000
| | P. 55 EPITAPH | 17 Modest as Morn; as Mid-day bright; |

middle   frequency: 1   relative frequency: 0.0000
| | P. 109 ANNIVERSARY | 244 But walk still middle betwixt War and Peace; |

middleton   frequency: 1   relative frequency: 0.0000
| | P. 160 INSTRUCTIONS | 813 With Boynton or with Middleton 'twere sweet; |

midnight   frequency: 2   relative frequency: 0.0000
| | P. 35 DAPHNIS | 81 Or the Witch that midnight wakes |
| | P. 64 A. HOUSE | 187 'Whom if our Lord at midnight find, |

midwife   frequency: 1   relative frequency: 0.0000
| | P. 144 INSTRUCTIONS | 132 Frighted the Midwife, and the Mother tore. |

mien   frequency: 1   relative frequency: 0.0000
| | P. 141 INSTRUCTIONS | 33 Paint him with Drayman's Shoulders, butchers Mien, |

might   frequency: 63   relative frequency: 0.0013
	P. 15 EYES	4 They might be ready to complain.
	P. 18 CLORINDA	15 D. Might a Soul bath there and be clean,
	P. 18 CLORINDA	25 D. Clorinda's voice might make it sweet.
	P. 23 NYMPH	48 Whether it too might have done so
	P. 23 NYMPH	49 As Sylvio did: his Gifts might be
	P. 31 FAIR SINGER	6 She with her Voice might captivate my Mind.
	P. 31 FAIR SINGER	8 My dis-intangled Soul it self might save,
	P. 31 FAIR SINGER	14 Where Victory might hang in equal choice,
	P. 33 DAPHNIS	24 As to see he might be blest.
	P. 37 DEFINITION	9 And yet I quickly might arrive
	P. 41 THE MOWER	19 And yet these Rarities might be allow'd,
	P. 41 THE MOWER	26 Might put the Palate in dispute.
	P. 43 DAMON	65 How happy might I still have mow'd,
	P. 48 THE GARDEN	30 Only that She might Laurel grow.
	P. 61 A. HOUSE	92 Which might Deformity make fair.
	P. 63 A. HOUSE	160 'Might such fair Hands as yours it tye!
	P. 69 A. HOUSE	333 When Roses only Arms might bear,
	P. 69 A. HOUSE	347 Might once have made our Gardens spring
	P. 69 A. HOUSE	352 Pow'r which the Ocean might command.
	P. 74 A. HOUSE	485 Where the first Carpenter might best
	P. 74 A. HOUSE	487 And where all Creatures might have shares,
	P. 80 A. HOUSE	676 If it might fix her shadow so;
	P. 88 ODE	51 That Charles himself might chase
	P. 88 ODE	54 The Tragick Scaffold might adorn:
	P. 98 HOLLAND	127 That ours mean time at leizure might careen,
	P. 104 ANNIVERSARY	31 If Conquerors, on them they turn their might;
	P. 106 ANNIVERSARY	109 How might they under such a Captain raise
	P. 106 ANNIVERSARY	135 What we might hope, what wonderful Effect
	P. 106 ANNIVERSARY	136 From such a wish'd Conjuncture might reflect.
	P. 107 ANNIVERSARY	163 That she might seem, could we the Fall dispute,
	P. 109 ANNIVERSARY	255 No King might ever such a Force have done;
	P. 110 ANNIVERSARY	297 That their new King might the fifth Scepter shake,
	P. 110 ANNIVERSARY	300 Might muster Heresies, so one were ten.
	P. 112 ANNIVERSARY	392 'So should I hope yet he might Dye as wee.
	P. 113 BLAKE	11 Wealth which all others Avarice might cloy,
	P. 114 BLAKE	22 So that such darkness might suppress their fear;
	P. 114 BLAKE	27 For least some Gloominess might stain her sky,
	P. 123 O.C.	6 What death might least so fair a Life deface.
	P. 124 O.C.	43 Then might y' ha' daily his Affection spy'd,

P. 126 O.C.   139 Which, since they might not hinder, yet they cast
P. 126 O.C.   150 In their own Griefs might find themselves
                             imploy'd;
P. 131 PARADISE   21 Might hence presume the whole Creations day
P. 137 HOUSEWARMING   12 How he might create a House with a Fiat.
P. 137 HOUSEWARMING   24 As might carry the measure and name of an Hyde.
P. 142 INSTRUCTIONS   55 And found how Royal Heirs might be matur'd,
P. 147 INSTRUCTIONS   248 Fighting it single till the rest might arm.
P. 149 INSTRUCTIONS   362 That Peace secur'd, and Money might be sav'd.
P. 155 INSTRUCTIONS   609 He finds wheresoe're he succour might expect,
P. 156 INSTRUCTIONS   631 Daniel had there adventur'd, Man of might;
P. 160 INSTRUCTIONS   791 Then that Reward might in its turn take place,
P. 160 INSTRUCTIONS   806 The Exchequer might the Privy-purse obey.
P. 165 KINGS VOWES   2 And the Spider might weave in our Stomack its
                             web;
P. 179 STOCKSMARKET   7 When with honour he might from his word have gone
                             back;
P. 181 MADE FREE   5 That requires the Might
P. 183 MADE FREE   105 It might deserve a Box and a Gold one;
P. 186 BRITANNIA   85 Bribe hungry Priests to deify your might,
P. 193 TWO HORSES   56 Lord a Mercy and a Cross might be set on the
                             doore;
P. 196 TWO HORSES   173 Why might not our Horses, since words are but
                             wind,
P. 199 DUKE   51 You might have lingred out a lazy age,
P. 203 HISTORICALL   80 All but religious cheats might justly sweare
P. 313 CHEQUER INN   37 And where he might e're now have laid
P. 314 CHEQUER INN   69 She might it well afford

mightst   frequency: 2   relative frequency: 0.0000
P. 110 ANNIVERSARY   307 For soon thou mightst have past among their Rant
P. 132 PARADISE   45 Well mightst thou scorn thy Readers to allure

mighty   frequency: 7   relative frequency: 0.0001
P. 124 O.C.   32 He oft would flourish in his mighty Arms;
P. 131 PARADISE   23 Pardon me, mighty Poet, nor despise
P. 169 ADVICE   32 Our mighty Masters in a warme debate;
P. 184 BRITANNIA   9 Raw: What mighty power has forc'd me from my
                             rest?
P. 184 BRITANNIA   10 Ah! mighty Queen, why so unsemly drest?
P. 186 BRITANNIA   80 Fearing the mighty Projects of the great
P. 192 TWO HORSES   28 For the two mighty Monarchs that doe now
                             bestride 'um.

mild   frequency: 3   relative frequency: 0.0000
P. 86 FLECKNO   120 After th' Assizes dinner mild appear,
P. 129 O.C.   235 Yet always temper'd with an aire so mild,
P. 145 INSTRUCTIONS   174 Gentlest of men, and his Lieutenant mild,

milder   frequency: 2   relative frequency: 0.0000
P. 50 THE GARDEN   67 Where from above the milder Sun
P. 130 O.C.   307 Revives; and by his milder beams assures;

miles   frequency: 1   relative frequency: 0.0000
P. 96 HOLLAND   18 Thorough the Center their new-catched Miles;

militia   frequency: 1   relative frequency: 0.0000
P. 69 A. HOUSE   330 That sweet Militia restore,

militia's   frequency: 1   relative frequency: 0.0000
P. 152 INSTRUCTIONS   481 First, then he march'd our whole Militia's
                             force,

milk   frequency: 3   relative frequency: 0.0000
See also "almond-milk."
P. 23 NYMPH   55 With sweetest milk, and sugar, first
P. 124 O.C.   36 Which while she drain'd of Milk she fill'd with
                             Love.
P. 139 HOUSEWARMING   67 Bring in the whole Milk of a year at a meal,

milk-white   frequency: 1   relative frequency: 0.0000
P. 24 NYMPH   108 With milk-white Lambs, and Ermins pure.

milky   frequency: 2   relative frequency: 0.0000
P. 19 THYRSIS   10 There the milky way doth lye;
P. 29 THE GALLERY   20 And stretches out her milky Thighs;

million   frequency: 1   relative frequency: 0.0000
P. 193 TWO HORSES   57 Ch. That a Million and half should be his
                             revenue,

millions   frequency: 2   relative frequency: 0.0000

```
          P. 149 INSTRUCTIONS   352 By Millions over, not by Hecatombs.
          P. 193 TWO HORSES      78 Should give away Millions at every Summons.

milton's                        frequency:    1    relative frequency: 0.0000
          P. 131 PARADISE         t On Mr. Milton's Paradise lost.

mimick                          frequency:    1    relative frequency: 0.0000
          P. 190 STATUE           8 The Mimick so legally seiz'd of Whitehall.

mimmicks                        frequency:    1    relative frequency: 0.0000
          P. 202 HISTORICALL     66 Yet in the Mimmicks of the Spintrian Sport

mind                            frequency:   34    relative frequency: 0.0007
      See also "minde."
          P.  10 DIALOGUE        43 Cease Tempter. None can chain a mind
          P.  29 THE GALLERY      8 Only your Picture in my Mind.
          P.  31 FAIR SINGER      6 She with her Voice might captivate my Mind.
          P.  37 DEFINITION      31 Is the Conjunction of the Mind,
          P.  40 THE MATCH       24 And all that burns the Mind.
          P.  40 THE MOWER        9 The Pink grew then as double as his Mind;
          P.  45 GLO-WORMS       15 For She my Mind hath so displac'd
          P.  45 MOWER'S SONG     1 My Mind was once the true survey
          P.  46 AMETAS          11 And Love tyes a Womans Mind
          P.  49 THE GARDEN      41 Mean while the Mind, from pleasure less,
          P.  49 THE GARDEN      43 The Mind, that Ocean where each kind
          P.  59 A. HOUSE        28 Of that more sober Age and Mind,
          P.  77 A. HOUSE       602 These Trees have I incamp'd my Mind;
          P.  81 A. HOUSE       715 Tears (watry Shot that pierce the Mind;)
          P.  90 ODE            106 Within his party-colour'd Mind;
          P.  92 MAY'S DEATH     77 But what will deeper wound thy little mind,
          P.  94 DR. WITTY       24 Nor her chast mind into the French translated:
          P. 109 ANNIVERSARY    232 An healthful Mind within a Body strong;
          P. 123 O.C.            22 (Those nobler weaknesses of humane Mind,
          P. 124 O.C.            40 And thorough that sparkled her fairer Mind;
          P. 130 O.C.           301 And lost in tears, have neither sight nor mind
          P. 132 PARADISE        42 Whence furnish such a vast expense of Mind?
          P. 143 INSTRUCTIONS    84 And still within her mind the Footman runs:
          P. 147 INSTRUCTIONS   253 Their former Trophees they recal to mind,
          P. 156 INSTRUCTIONS   622 With present shame compar'd, his mind distraught.
          P. 157 INSTRUCTIONS   685 But, when in his immortal Mind he felt
          P. 162 INSTRUCTIONS   865 That may his Body, this his Mind explain.
          P. 163 INSTRUCTIONS   913 His mind secure does the known stroke repeat,
          P. 163 INSTRUCTIONS   930 Which his hid mind did in its depths inclose.
          P. 173 LOYALL SCOT     51 But when in his Imortall mind hee felt
          P. 177 LOYALL SCOT    228 The Innocentest mind their thirst alone
          P. 185 BRITANNIA       30 Pervert his mind, his good Intencions Choak,
          P. 187 BRITANNIA      104 Strong as your Raigne and beauteous as your
                                    mind.'
          P. 313 CHEQUER INN     46 Therefore I needs must speake my Mind

minde                           frequency:    3    relative frequency: 0.0000
          P.   5 HASTINGS        32 There better recreates his active Minde.
          P. 199 DUKE            60 He and his Duke had both to great a minde
          P. 200 DUKE           111 But to a zealous and ambitious minde,

minds                           frequency:    6    relative frequency: 0.0001
          P. 105 ANNIVERSARY     78 But who the Minds of stubborn Men can build?
          P. 105 ANNIVERSARY     95 While the resistance of opposed Minds,
          P. 109 ANNIVERSARY    266 Hurry the Bark, but more the Seamens minds,
          P. 128 O.C.           218 To keep so deare, so diff'ring minds agreed?
          P. 145 INSTRUCTIONS   179 Gross Bodies, grosser Minds, and grossest
                                    Cheats;
          P. 168 ADVICE          8 Their wearied limbs and minds to recreate,

mine                            frequency:   17    relative frequency: 0.0003
          P.   4 LOVELACE        43 Mine eyes invaded with a female spight,
          P.   4 LOVELACE        48 Above their envy, or mine aid doth clime.
          P.  16 EYES            45 Ope then mine Eyes your double Sluice,
          P.  21 SOUL & BODY     14 That mine own Precipice I go;
          P.  22 NYMPH           40 Could so mine idle Life have spent.
          P.  23 NYMPH           56 I it at mine own fingers nurst.
          P.  23 NYMPH           80 Find it, although before mine Eyes.
          P.  24 NYMPH          103 It till it do o'reflow with mine;
          P.  43 DAMON           51 This Sithe of mine discovers wide
          P.  79 A. HOUSE       660 Starts forth with to its Bonne Mine.
          P.  98 HOLLAND        116 Should raging hold his Linstock to the Mine?
          P. 111 ANNIVERSARY    339 Why did mine Eyes once see so bright a Ray;
          P. 120 TWO SONGS       22 Mine Eyes uncessant deluges.
          P. 148 INSTRUCTIONS   322 The Stores and Wages all are mine and thine.
          P. 184 BRITANNIA        2 To trembling James, would I had yeilded mine.
          P. 192 TWO HORSES      37 Thy founder and mine to Cheat one another,
```

          P. 317 CHEQUER INN   184 Soe when mine Host doth Money lack

miners   frequency: 1   relative frequency: 0.0000
     P. 95 HOLLAND   9 Glad then, as Miners that have found the Oar,

mines   frequency: 2   relative frequency: 0.0000
     P. 76 A. HOUSE   550 And through the tainted Side he mines.
     P. 112 ANNIVERSARY   353 'What Oaken Forrests, and what golden Mines!

mine's   frequency: 1   relative frequency: 0.0000
     P. 194 TWO HORSES   110 W. To Cuckold a Scrivener mine's in
                                Masquerade.

minhier   frequency: 1   relative frequency: 0.0000
     P. 201 HISTORICALL   22 He marry'd Minhier Falmouths pregnant wench.

minion   frequency: 1   relative frequency: 0.0000
     P. 153 INSTRUCTIONS   495 His minion Imps that, in his secret part,

minister   frequency: 3   relative frequency: 0.0000
     P. 167 KINGS VOWES   43 Of my Pimp I will make my Minister Premier,
     P. 171 PROPHECY   37 A Minister able only in his Tongue
     P. 192 TWO HORSES   42 And the King's Chiefe minister holding the
                                doore:

ministers   frequency: 1   relative frequency: 0.0000
     P. 170 PROPHECY   17 When Sodomy is the Premier Ministers sport

mint   frequency: 2   relative frequency: 0.0000
     P. 97 HOLLAND   72 Staple of Sects and Mint of Schisme grew;
     P. 161 INSTRUCTIONS   835 But, fresh as from the Mint, the Courtiers fine

minted   frequency: 1   relative frequency: 0.0000
     P. 11 DIALOGUE   58 The minted Gold shall lie;

mints   frequency: 1   relative frequency: 0.0000
     P. 112 ANNIVERSARY   354 'What Mints of Men, what Union of Designes!

minute   frequency: 6   relative frequency: 0.0001
     P. 34 DAPHNIS   50 Such a wretched minute found,
     P. 35 DAPHNIS   83 In one minute casts the Seed,
     P. 55 EPITAPH   14 No Minute but it came and went;
     P. 124 O.C.   38 And ev'ry minute adds a Lustre new;
     P. 127 O.C.   153 And the last minute his victorious Ghost
     P. 200 DUKE   107 What all thy subjects doe each minute feare:

minute's. See "minut's."

minut's   frequency: 1   relative frequency: 0.0000
     P. 34 DAPHNIS   30 Now the latest minut's run

miracle   frequency: 1   relative frequency: 0.0000
     P. 192 TWO HORSES   19 Those Idolls ne're speak, but the miracle 's
                                dore

miracles   frequency: 1   relative frequency: 0.0000
     P. 64 A. HOUSE   168 'Till Miracles it work at last.

mirror   frequency: 1   relative frequency: 0.0000
     See also "mirrour."
     P. 186 BRITANNIA   59 Whilst in truthes Mirror this Glad scene he
                                spy'd,

mirrors. See "mirrours."

mirrour   frequency: 3   relative frequency: 0.0000
     See also "mirror."
     P. 78 A. HOUSE   636 Till as a Chrystal Mirrour slick;
     P. 125 O.C.   78 But the dear Image fled the Mirrour broke.
     P. 186 BRITANNIA   69 From th' easie King she truthes bright Mirrour
                                took,

mirrours   frequency: 1   relative frequency: 0.0000
     P. 125 O.C.   73 Like polish'd Mirrours, so his steely Brest

misapprehend   frequency: 1   relative frequency: 0.0000
     P. 109 ANNIVERSARY   268 And threat'ning Rocks misapprehend for Land;

miscall'd   frequency: 1   relative frequency: 0.0000
     P. 106 ANNIVERSARY   111 But mad with Reason, so miscall'd, of State

miscarriages   frequency: 1   relative frequency: 0.0000

          P. 159 INSTRUCTIONS 767 All our miscarriages on Pett must fall:

mischeifs   frequency: 1   relative frequency: 0.0000
          P. 175 LOYALL SCOT   134 All Mischeifs Moulded by those state divines:

mischief   frequency: 1   relative frequency: 0.0000
          See also "mischiefe."
          P. 205 HISTORICALL   181 If a Kings Brother can such mischief bring,

mischiefbreeding   frequency: 1   relative frequency: 0.0000
          P. 201 HISTORICALL   33 Her mischiefbreeding breast did so prevaile

mischiefe   frequency: 1   relative frequency: 0.0000
          P. 205 HISTORICALL   182 Then how much greater Mischiefe as a King.

mischiefs. See "mischeifs."

miscreants   frequency: 2   relative frequency: 0.0000
          P. 175 LOYALL SCOT   148 How can you bear such Miscreants shold live,
          P. 204 HISTORICALL   126 Of all the Miscreants ever went to hell

misdoubting   frequency: 1   relative frequency: 0.0000
          P. 131 PARADISE   6 Held me a while misdoubting his Intent,

misfortune   frequency: 1   relative frequency: 0.0000
          P. 110 ANNIVERSARY   301 What thy Misfortune, they the Spirit call,

misguide   frequency: 1   relative frequency: 0.0000
          P. 187 BRITANNIA   124 False Finch, Knave Anglesey misguide the
                                    seals;

misguided   frequency: 1   relative frequency: 0.0000
          P. 202 HISTORICALL   59 Misguided Monarchs rarely wise or just,

mishap   frequency: 1   relative frequency: 0.0000
          P. 201 HISTORICALL   17 But the best times have ever some mishap;

misled   frequency: 4   relative frequency: 0.0000
          P. 65 A. HOUSE   212 'Who first Thee from thy Faith misled.
          P. 91 MAY'S DEATH   56 Misled, but malice fixt and understood.
          P. 106 ANNIVERSARY   118 By Malice some, by Errour more misled;
          P. 175 LOYALL SCOT   162 How oft hath age his hallowing hands Misled

misleto   frequency: 1   relative frequency: 0.0000
          P. 82 A. HOUSE   739 And, like a sprig of Misleto,

mispend   frequency: 1   relative frequency: 0.0000
          P. 190 STATUE   12 Any monument how their time they mispend.

miss   frequency: 4   relative frequency: 0.0000
          See also "mis't."
          P. 97 HOLLAND   56 Came next in order; which they could not miss.
          P. 113 ANNIVERSARY   398 So that we both alike may miss our End:
          P. 167 KINGS VOWES   47 Miss and I will both learne to live on
                                    Exhibition,
          P. 202 HISTORICALL   49 So Philips Son enflamed with a Miss

miss'd   frequency: 2   relative frequency: 0.0000
          P. 111 ANNIVERSARY   329 But thought him when he miss'd his setting beams,
          P. 132 PARADISE   27 Thou hast not miss'd one thought that could be
                                    fit,

missed. See "miss'd," "mist."

mist   frequency: 4   relative frequency: 0.0000
          P. 80 A. HOUSE   680 Charm'd with the Saphir-winged Mist.
          P. 92 MAY'S DEATH   60 Because a Gazet writer mist his aim?
          P. 97 HOLLAND   61 Though Herring for their God few voices mist,
          P. 177 LOYALL SCOT   235 Two Nations Neere had mist the Marke soe long.

mis't   frequency: 1   relative frequency: 0.0000
          P. 19 THYRSIS   6 Thyrsis. A Chast Scul, can never mis't.

mistake   frequency: 4   relative frequency: 0.0000
          P.   4 LOVELACE   45 O no, mistake not, I reply'd, for I
          P. 78 A. HOUSE   631 Unless it self you will mistake,
          P. 90 ODE   110 The English Hunter him mistake;
          P. 96 HOLLAND   35 Nature, it seem'd, asham'd of her mistake,

mistaken   frequency: 4   relative frequency: 0.0000
          P.   4 HASTINGS   14 And is not thence mistaken for a Childe?

```
        P.   48 THE GARDEN       11 Mistaken long, I scught you then
        P.  109 ANNIVERSARY     267 Who with mistaken Course salute the Sand,
        P.  177 LOYALL SCOT     247 Where a Mistaken accent Causeth death.

mistery                         frequency:    1    relative frequency: 0.0000
        P.  189 STATUE            1 What can be the Mistery why Charing Cross

mistletoe.  See "misleto."

mistook                         frequency:    5    relative frequency: 0.0001
        P.   77 A. HOUSE        583 Thrice happy he whc, not mistook,
        P.  150 INSTRUCTIONS    405 They, by the Name, mistook it for that Isle,
        P.  156 INSTRUCTIONS    638 And all those lines by which men are mistook.
        P.  161 INSTRUCTICNS    862 And had almost mistook and call'd them Rogues.
        P.  174 LOYALL SCOT     118 They wanted zeal and Learning, soe mistook

mistress                        frequency:    3    relative frequency: 0.0000
        P.   26 MISTRESS          t To his Coy Mistress.
        P.   48 THE GARDEN       20 Cut in these Trees their Mistress name.
        P.   87 FLECKNO         163 Whc should commend his Mistress now? Or who

mist'ry                         frequency:    1    relative frequency: 0.0000
        P.  183 MADE FREE        78 He know's not his Trade, nor his Mist'ry.

mists                           frequency:    1    relative frequency: 0.0000
        P.  109 ANNIVERSARY     235 Then did thick Mists and Winds the air deform,

miter                           frequency:    1    relative frequency: 0.0000
        P.  145 INSTRUCTIONS    182 The Miter Troop, and with his looks gives Law.

mites                           frequency:    1    relative frequency: 0.0000
        P.  147 INSTRUCTIONS    273 With Heart of Bees so full, and Head of
                                    Mites,

mitre                           frequency:    2    relative frequency: 0.0000
     See also "miter," "mytre."
        P.   90 MAY'S DEATH       7 Nor where the Popes head, nor the Mitre lay,
        P.  194 TWO HORSES      118 For the Surplice, Lawn-Sleeves, the Cross and
                                    the mitre,

mitred                          frequency:    1    relative frequency: 0.0000
        P.  176 LOYALL SCCT     202 The Mitred Hubbub against Pluto Moot

mix                             frequency:    1    relative frequency: 0.0000
        P.  156 INSTRUCTIONS    637 Mix a vain Terrcur in his Martial look,

mix'd                           frequency:    1    relative frequency: 0.0000
        P.  126 O.C.            130 Troubled to part where so exactly mix'd.

mixed.  See "mix'd," "mixt."

mixing                          frequency:    1    relative frequency: 0.0000
        P.  121 TWO SONGS        48 While Stars Eclypse by mixing Bayes.

mixt                            frequency:    3    relative frequency: 0.0000
        P.    5 HASTINGS         52 Had Mayern once been mixt with Hastings blood!
        P.  173 LOYALL SCOT      71 Mixt in Corinthian Mettall at thy Flame
        P.  177 LOYALL SCCT     237 The good, the bad, and those mixt every where.

mixtures                        frequency:    1    relative frequency: 0.0000
        P.   41 THE MOWER        22 Forbidden mixtures there to see.

moan                            frequency:    2    relative frequency: 0.0000
        P.   75 A. HOUSE        526 Sad pair unto the Elms they moan.
        P.  159 INSTRUCTIONS    753 And to each other helpless couple moan,

moar                            frequency:    1    relative frequency: 0.0000
        P.  116 BLAKE            89 With hast they therefore all their Gallions
                                    moar,

mode                            frequency:    2    relative frequency: 0.0000
        P.  132 PARADISE         51 I too transported by the Mode offend,
        P.  167 KINGS VOWES      51 And who knowes but the Mode may soon bring in
                                    the rest?

model                           frequency:    4    relative frequency: 0.0000
        P.   56 BILL-BOROW        7 It seems as for a Model laid,
        P.   59 A. HOUSE          6 Did for a Model vault his Brain,
        P.  138 HOUSEWARMING     49 To proceed in the Model he call'd in his
                                    Allens,
        P.  139 HOUSEWARMING     88 By a Model more excellent than Lesly's Folly.
```

modern   frequency: 2   relative frequency: 0.0000
    P. 150 INSTRUCTIONS   401 Modern Geographers, 'twas there they thought,
    P. 175 LOYALL SCOT   159 But of the Choicest Modern flesh and Bone.

modest   frequency: 6   relative frequency: 0.0001
    P.   3 LOVELACE   9 Modest ambition studi'd only then,
    P. 55 EPITAPH   17 Modest as Morn; as Mid-day bright;
    P. 58 BILL-BOROW   63 Which in their modest Whispers name
    P. 79 A. HOUSE   669 The modest Halcyon comes in sight,
    P. 156 INSTRUCTIONS   651 And modest Beauty yet his Sex did Veil,
    P. 172 LOYALL SCOT   17 And modest beauty yet his sex did vail,

modesty   frequency: 2   relative frequency: 0.0000
    P. 108 ANNIVERSARY   187 So with more Modesty we may be True,
    P. 180 STOCKSMARKET   45 Or do you his beams out of modesty veil

moist   frequency: 2   relative frequency: 0.0000
    P. 83 A. HOUSE   769 But now the Salmon-Fishers moist
    P. 114 BLAKE   34 Where still the Earth is moist, the Air still
                               dry;

moister   frequency: 1   relative frequency: 0.0000
    P. 78 A. HOUSE   627 Whose Grass, with moister colour dasht,

moisture   frequency: 1   relative frequency: 0.0000
    P. 42 DAMON   31 No moisture but my Tears do rest,

mold   frequency: 6   relative frequency: 0.0001
    See also "mould."
    P. 64 A. HOUSE   182 'We mold, as Baits for curious tasts.
    P. 74 A. HOUSE   500 To one great Trunk them all did mold.
    P. 88 ODE   36 Into another Mold.
    P. 107 ANNIVERSARY   160 A Mold was chosen out of better Earth;
    P. 138 HOUSEWARMING   43 Nay ev'n from Tangier have sent back for the
                               mold,
    P. 166 KINGS VOWES   23 with wide streets and uniforme of my owne mold;

molded. See "moulded."

molding   frequency: 1   relative frequency: 0.0000
    P. 32 MOURNING   9 When, molding of the watry Sphears,

molested   frequency: 1   relative frequency: 0.0000
    P. 182 MADE FREE   51 But molested the neighbours with Quarrells,

moloch   frequency: 1   relative frequency: 0.0000
    P. 203 HISTORICALL   81 He true Vicegerent to old Moloch were.

molting   frequency: 1   relative frequency: 0.0000
    P. 154 INSTRUCTIONS   574 Like molting Fowl, a weak and easie Prey.

monarch   frequency: 4   relative frequency: 0.0000
    P. 127 O.C.   169 Your Monarch: We demand not your supplies
    P. 164 INSTRUCTIONS   945 But this great work is for our Monarch fit,
    P. 164 INSTRUCTIONS   968 Have strove to Isle the Monarch from his Isle:
    P. 191 STATUE   48 That a Monarch of Gingerbread would doe as
                               well.

monarchs   frequency: 9   relative frequency: 0.0001
    P. 26 YOUNG LOVE   32 And we both shall monarchs prove.
    P. 103 ANNIVERSARY   15 While heavy Monarchs make a wide Return,
    P. 186 BRITANNIA   74 Doe Monarchs rise by vertues or the sword?
    P. 186 BRITANNIA   78 The Rivall Gods, Monarchs of th' other world,
    P. 192 TWO HORSES   28 For the two mighty Monarchs that doe now
                               bestride 'um.
    P. 200 DUKE   115 Of Monarchs murthered by the Impatient heir:
    P. 201 HISTORICALL   14 Things highly fitting for a Monarchs trade.
    P. 202 HISTORICALL   59 Misguided Monarchs rarely wise or just,
    P. 205 HISTORICALL   170 And Monarchs are above all human Lawes.

monarchys   frequency: 1   relative frequency: 0.0000
    P. 196 TWO HORSES   169 Which Monarchys downfall portended much more

monck   frequency: 1   relative frequency: 0.0000
    P. 99 HOLLAND   150 Steel'd with these piercing Heads, Dean, Monck
                               and Blake.

moneths   frequency: 1   relative frequency: 0.0000
    P. 189 STATUE   2 This five moneths continues still blinded with
                               board?

money   frequency: 12   relative frequency: 0.0002

See also "mony."
P. 138 HOUSEWARMING   33 Already he had got all our Money and Cattel,
P. 148 INSTRUCTIONS 324 That Money lack, nor Forts be in repair.
P. 149 INSTRUCTIONS 362 That Peace secur'd, and Money might be sav'd.
P. 151 INSTRUCTIONS 434 Our Money spent; else 'twere at his command.
P. 153 INSTRUCTIONS 502 Their Money lodge; confiscate when he please.
P. 160 INSTRUCTIONS 800 To lavish the King's Money more would scorn.
P. 168 ADVICE   28 For money comes when Seymour leaves the Chair.
P. 177 LOYALL SCOT 215 To cheat the Plague money Indifferent.
P. 182 MADE FREE   41 The Money he threw
P. 313 CHEQUER INN   20 That now he Money tells by Pecks
P. 317 CHEQUER INN   184 Soe when mine Host doth Money lack
P. 317 CHEQUER INN   185 He Money gives amongst this Pack

mongrel. See "mungrel."

monk   frequency: 5   relative frequency: 0.0001
See also "monck."
P. 153 INSTRUCTIONS 510 Monk in his Shirt against the Dutch is prest.
P. 153 INSTRUCTIONS 518 On Monk and Parliament, yet both do hate.
P. 155 INSTRUCTIONS 596 Monk from the bank the dismal sight does view.
P. 157 INSTRUCTIONS 676 That Monk looks on to see how Douglas dies.
P. 172 LOYALL SCOT   42 That Monk lookes on to see how Douglass dies.

monster   frequency: 7   relative frequency: 0.0001
P. 106 ANNIVERSARY   128 Pursues the Monster thorough every Throne:
P. 144 INSTRUCTIONS 131 Excise, a Monster worse than e're before
P. 147 INSTRUCTIONS 258 Had strecht the monster Patent on the Field.
P. 158 INSTRUCTIONS 740 Thee, the Year's monster, let thy Dam devour.
P. 176 LOYALL SCOT   198 Well that Scotch monster and our Bishops sort
P. 179 STOCKSMARKET   12 That shews him a monster more like than a king.
P. 204 HISTORICALL   116 This haughty Monster with his ugly claws

monsters   frequency: 2   relative frequency: 0.0000
See also "sea-monsters."
P. 185 BRITANNIA   27 Such slimy Monsters ne're approacht a throne
P. 189 BRITANNIA   186 From Noxious Monsters, Hellborn tyranny,

montague. See "mountague."

montezumas. See "montezumes."

montezumes   frequency: 1   relative frequency: 0.0000
P. 147 INSTRUCTIONS 266 And in his Breast wears many Montezumes.

monthly   frequency: 1   relative frequency: 0.0000
P. 204 HISTORICALL   155 From Tybur came the advice boat Monthly home,

months   frequency: 2   relative frequency: 0.0000
See also "moneths."
P. 142 INSTRUCTIONS   56 In fewer months than Mothers once indur'd.
P. 149 INSTRUCTIONS 329 But when this fail'd, and Months enough were
                         spent,

monument   frequency: 1   relative frequency: 0.0000
P. 190 STATUE   12 Any monument how their time they mispend.

mony   frequency: 1   relative frequency: 0.0000
P. 201 HISTORICALL   7 And what is more they send him Mony too,

moon   frequency: 4   relative frequency: 0.0000
P. 43 DAMON   60 As in a crescent Moon the Sun.
P. 119 TWO SONGS   4 Upon this Hill outwakes the Moon.
P. 142 INSTRUCTIONS   70 Moon, that o'recome with the sick steam did'st
                         fail;
P. 174 LOYALL SCOT   104 A Bishop will like Mahomet tear the Moon

moor. See "moar."

moors   frequency: 1   relative frequency: 0.0000
P. 175 LOYALL SCOT   151 One Mytre fitts the Heads of full four Moors.

moot   frequency: 1   relative frequency: 0.0000
P. 176 LOYALL SCOT   202 The Mitred Hubbub against Pluto Moot

morally   frequency: 1   relative frequency: 0.0000
P. 151 INSTRUCTIONS 448 Consoles us morally out of Seneque.

mordant   frequency: 4   relative frequency: 0.0000
P. 147 INSTRUCTIONS 260 That pierc't the Gyant Mordant through his
                         Mail.
P. 149 INSTRUCTIONS 349 Now Mordant may, within his Castle Tow'r,

| | P. | 151 | INSTRUCTIONS | 422 | But Mordant new oblig'd, would sure be just. |
| | P. | 198 | DUKE | 36 | Next, Painter, draw his Mordant by his side, |

more   frequency: 176   relative frequency: 0.0036

	P.	3	LOVELACE	8	Twas more esteemd to give, then weare the Bayes:
	P.	4	HASTINGS	15	While those of growth more sudden, and more bold,
	P.	5	HASTINGS	24	Lest He become like Them, taste more then one.
	P.	12	DIALOGUE	76	The World has not one Pleasure more:
	P.	16	EYES	26	That weep the more, and see the less:
	P.	16	EYES	27	And, to preserve their Sight more true,
	P.	16	EYES	29	So Magdalen, in Tears more wise
	P.	17	BERMUDAS	20	Jewels more rich than Ormus show's.
	P.	20	THYRSIS	44	Will for thee, much more with thee dye.
	P.	23	NYMPH	50	Perhaps as false or more than he.
	P.	23	NYMPH	53	Thy Love was far more better then
	P.	23	NYMPH	58	It wax'd more white and sweet than they.
	P.	23	NYMPH	60	I blusht to see its foot more soft,
	P.	26	MISTRESS	12	Vaster then Empires, and more slow.
	P.	26	MISTRESS	25	Thy Beauty shall no more be found;
	P.	29	THE GALLERY	13	Engines more keen than ever yet
	P.	30	THE GALLERY	39	Nor blows more Wind than what may well
	P.	30	THE GALLERY	41	These Pictures and a thousand more,
	P.	33	DAPHNIS	27	But then Legacies no more
	P.	34	DAPHNIS	46	More to torture him that dies?
	P.	34	DAPHNIS	52	More than all thy Cruelty?
	P.	38	PICTURE	22	And them that yield but more despise.
	P.	39	THE MATCH	4	To beg in vain for more.
	P.	40	THE MOWER	7	And a more luscious Earth for them did knead,
	P.	41	DAMON	4	The Scene more fit for his complaint.
	P.	41	THE MOWER	36	More by their presence then their skill.
	P.	42	DAMON	12	And hamstring'd Frogs can dance no more.
	P.	43	DAMON	52	More ground then all his Sheep do hide.
	P.	43	DAMON	55	And though in Wooll more poor then they,
	P.	45	MOWER'S SONG	8	Grew more luxuriant still and fine;
	P.	46	MOWER'S SONG	26	Companions of my thoughts more green,
	P.	55	EPITAPH	20	'Twere more Significant, She's Dead.
	P.	56	BILL-BOROW	4	A Line more circular and like;
	P.	56	BILL-BOROW	9	Here learn ye Mountains more unjust,
	P.	58	BILL-BOROW	74	More certain Oracles in Oak.
	P.	59	A. HOUSE	18	Demands more room alive then dead.
	P.	59	A. HOUSE	28	Of that more sober Age and Mind,
	P.	60	A. HOUSE	53	More by his Magnitude distrest,
	P.	61	A. HOUSE	77	Art would more neatly have defac'd
	P.	63	A. HOUSE	144	'That something more then humane speaks.
	P.	63	A. HOUSE	151	'Ah, no! and 'twould more Honour prove
	P.	65	A. HOUSE	194	'Of Joys you see, and may make more!
	P.	69	A. HOUSE	329	Unhappy! shall we never more
	P.	69	A. HOUSE	338	And his more gentle Forts did trace.
	P.	70	A. HOUSE	374	Us as we walk more low then them:
	P.	74	A. HOUSE	494	Yet more to Heaven shooting are:
	P.	75	A. HOUSE	522	A Sadder, yet more pleasing Shade:
	P.	76	A. HOUSE	573	And more attentive there doth sit
	P.	80	A. HOUSE	695	She yet more Pure, Sweet, Streight, and Fair,
	P.	82	A. HOUSE	737	Hence She with Graces more divine
	P.	82	A. HOUSE	766	But in more decent Order tame;
	P.	84	FLECKNO	34	Ask'd still for more, and pray'd him to repeat:
	P.	84	FLECKNO	62	Hath sure more flesh and blood then he can boast.
	P.	86	FLECKNO	122	Yet be more strict my sentence doth renew;
	P.	86	FLECKNO	135	More odious then those raggs which the French youth
	P.	86	FLECKNO	145	And how (impossible) he made yet more
	P.	87	ODE	20	Is more then to oppose.
	P.	89	ODE	93	She, having kill'd, no more does search,
	P.	91	MAY'S DEATH	21	Cups more then civil of Emathian wine,
	P.	91	MAY'S DEATH	31	Rose more then ever he was seen severe,
	P.	91	MAY'S DEATH	57	Because some one than thee more worthy weares
	P.	93	DR. WITTY	5	Changing the Latine, but do more obscure
	P.	94	DR. WITTY	13	He is Translations thief that addeth more,
	P.	94	DR. WITTY	17	Caelia whose English doth more richly flow
	P.	94	DR. WITTY	34	Liking themselves the worse the more they look,
	P.	96	HOLLAND	21	Building their watry Babel far more high
	P.	97	HOLLAND	65	More pregnant then their Marg'ret, that laid down
	P.	97	HOLLAND	83	Some Fifteen hundred and more years ago;
	P.	98	HOLLAND	119	Yet of his vain Attempt no more he sees
	P.	103	ANNIVERSARY	16	Longer, and more Malignant then Saturn:
	P.	103	ANNIVERSARY	20	More slow and brittle then the China clay:
	P.	104	ANNIVERSARY	23	Yet some more active for a Frontier Town
	P.	104	ANNIVERSARY	26	And will have Wonn, if he no more have Lost;
	P.	104	ANNIVERSARY	43	Nor more contribute to the state of Things,
	P.	104	ANNIVERSARY	61	Then as he strokes them with a Touch more sweet,

P. 106	ANNIVERSARY	118	By Malice some, by Errour more misled;
P. 107	ANNIVERSARY	165	Though none does of more lasting Parents grow,
P. 108	ANNIVERSARY	187	So with more Modesty we may be True,
P. 108	ANNIVERSARY	192	What could they more? shrunk guiltily aside.
P. 109	ANNIVERSARY	266	Hurry the Bark, but more the Seamens minds,
P. 110	ANNIVERSARY	273	Some lusty Mate, who with more careful Eye
P. 110	ANNIVERSARY	290	That they enjoy, but more they vainly crave:
P. 111	ANNIVERSARY	322	Makes you for his sake Tremble one fit more;
P. 112	ANNIVERSARY	376	'More then all Men, all Navies, and all Arms.
P. 112	ANNIVERSARY	389	'Abroad a King he seems, and something more,
P. 113	ANNIVERSARY	396	More then our Love and Duty do thee Right.
P. 113	BLAKE	10	For wealth wherewith to wound the old once more.
P. 114	BLAKE	16	But much more fearful are your Flags to see.
P. 114	BLAKE	18	More wish't for, and more welcome is then sleep,
P. 115	BLAKE	60	And when 'tis raised, does trouble them much more.
P. 115	BLAKE	73	'Twas more for Englands fame you should dye there,
P. 116	BLAKE	104	We to their Strength are more oblig'd then they.
P. 117	BLAKE	122	Far more enflam'd by it, then by the Sun.
P. 120	TWO SONGS	26	Can make a Night more bright then Day;
P. 122	TWO SONGS	18	Far more catching then my Hook.
P. 123	O.C.	8	Death when more horrid so more noble deem;
P. 123	TWO SONGS	42	No more shall need of love complain;
P. 124	O.C.	60	Answers the touch in Notes more sad more true.
P. 125	O.C.	79	Who now shall tell us more of mournful Swans,
P. 125	O.C.	99	So the dry Stock, no more that spreading Vine,
P. 127	O.C.	161	Which with more Care set forth his Obsequies
P. 127	O.C.	172	Who once more joyn'd us to the Continent;
P. 128	O.C.	197	Pity it seem'd to hurt him more that felt
P. 128	O.C.	207	More strong affections never reason serv'd,
P. 128	O.C.	210	(Though who more worthy to be lov'd than she?)
P. 128	O.C.	217	What prudence more than humane did he need
P. 129	O.C.	231	Where we (so once we us'd) shall now no more,
P. 129	O.C.	237	No more shall heare that powerful language charm,
P. 129	O.C.	239	No more shall follow where he spent the dayes
P. 129	O.C.	254	How much another thing, no more that man?
P. 130	O.C.	274	Detracts from objects than itself more high:
P. 131	O.C.	320	Earth ne'er more glad, nor Heaven more serene.
P. 138	HOUSEWARMING	57	His Rent would no more in arrear run to Worster;
P. 138	HOUSEWARMING	58	He should dwell more noble, and cheap too at-home,
P. 139	HOUSEWARMING	88	By a Model more excellent than Lesly's Folly.
P. 141	INSTRUCTIONS	36	For never Bacon study'd Nature more.
P. 143	INSTRUCTIONS	98	More gold in's Fob, more Lace upon his Coat
P. 145	INSTRUCTIONS	192	(Their publick Acts) oblig'd them still to more.
P. 147	INSTRUCTIONS	267	These and some more with single Valour stay
P. 149	INSTRUCTIONS	343	What an Account to Carteret; that and more
P. 151	INSTRUCTIONS	412	Now tim'rous now we are, than first secure.
P. 152	INSTRUCTIONS	473	Never old Letcher more repugnance felt,
P. 153	INSTRUCTIONS	529	The Sun much brighter, and the Skies more clear,
P. 154	INSTRUCTIONS	569	And swore that he would never more dwell there
P. 155	INSTRUCTIONS	590	Filling his Sails, more force to recollect.
P. 156	INSTRUCTIONS	626	Frustrate Revenge, and Love, by loss more keen,
P. 158	INSTRUCTIONS	710	Our loss, does so much more our loss augment.
P. 158	INSTRUCTIONS	723	Now (nothing more at Chatham left to burn)
P. 160	INSTRUCTIONS	800	To lavish the King's Money more would scorn.
P. 160	INSTRUCTIONS	812	Blames the last Session, and this more does tear.
P. 161	INSTRUCTIONS	828	And Vest bespeaks to be more seemly clad.
P. 161	INSTRUCTIONS	856	No Dial more could with the Sun agree.
P. 162	INSTRUCTIONS	875	Whence ev'ry day, the Palat more to tickle;
P. 162	INSTRUCTIONS	883	At night, than Canticleer more brisk and hot,
P. 166	KINGS VOWES	39	And when I am weary of her, I'le have more.
P. 168	ADVICE	1	Painter once more thy Pencell reassume,
P. 168	ADVICE	9	Do to their more belov'd delights repair,
P. 168	ADVICE	26	That give their votes more by their eyes than ears:
P. 170	PROPHECY	7	Where Vengeance dwells, but there is one trick more
P. 171	PROPHECY	48	And Magna Carta shall no more appeare,
P. 172	LOYALL SCOT	10	Hee Judg'd more Clearly now and saw more plain.
P. 173	LOYALL SCOT	69	Noe more discourse of Scotch or English Race
P. 174	LOYALL SCOT	101	'Twill make a more Inhabitable zone.
P. 174	LOYALL SCOT	102	The friendly Loadstone hath not more Combin'd
P. 176	LOYALL SCOT	206	Those whom you hear more Clamerous Yet and Loud
P. 178	LOYALL SCOT	275	Thy death more noble did the same Extort.
P. 178	LOYALL SCOT	280	My differing Crime doth more thy vertue raise

P.	179	STOCKSMARKET	12	That shews him a monster more like than a king.
P.	179	STOCKSMARKET	18	Who upon their panniers more decently ride,
P.	179	STOCKSMARKET	25	This statue is surely more scandalous far
P.	179	STOCKSMARKET	28	May be henceforth confiscate for reasons more just.
P.	182	MADE FREE	57	But he chanc'd to have more Sobriety,
P.	183	MADE FREE	83	But he may prove more just,
P.	184	BRITANNIA	5	No more of Scottish race thou wouldst complain.
P.	184	BRITANNIA	8	Once more with me partake of mortall woes.
P.	188	BRITANNIA	133	Rawl: Once more, great Queen, thy darling try to save;
P.	188	BRITANNIA	141	Brit: Rawleigh, noe more; too long in vain I've try'd
P.	194	TWO HORSES	90	For giving noe more the Rogues are prorogued.
P.	195	TWO HORSES	131	Ch. More Tolerable are the Lion Kings Slaughters
P.	196	TWO HORSES	169	Which Monarchys downfall portended much more
P.	196	TWO HORSES	188	Theres ten times more Treason in Brandy and ale.
P.	198	DUKE	21	I nere can fight in a more glorious Cause
P.	201	HISTORICALL	7	And what is more they send him Mony too,
P.	203	HISTORICALL	84	Not Lucifer himselfe more proud then they,
P.	205	HISTORICALL	179	Be wise ye Sons of Men tempt God no more
P.	315	CHEQUER INN	94	And of more Provant to dispose
P.	315	CHEQUER INN	114	For something more then Chop Cheere.
P.	316	CHEQUER INN	172	I saw no more but hither ran
P.	317	CHEQUER INN	183	And that way get more cut

morgan　　　　　　　　　　　frequency:　1　relative frequency: 0.0000
P.　314 CHEQUER INN　82 Mansell and Morgan and the rest

morley　　　　　　　　　　　frequency:　1　relative frequency: 0.0000
P.　139 HOUSEWARMING　69 Bulteales, Beakns, Morley, Wrens fingers with telling

morn　　　　　　　　　　　frequency:　3　relative frequency: 0.0000
P.　12 DROP OF DEW　2 Shed from the Bosom of the Morn
P.　43 DAMON　43 On me the Morn her dew distills
P.　55 EPITAPH　17 Modest as Morn; as Mid-day bright;

morning　　　　　　　　　　　frequency:　12　relative frequency: 0.0002
P.　4 HASTINGS　5 Go, stand betwixt the Morning and the Flowers;
P.　22 NYMPH　27 One morning (I remember well)
P.　25 YOUNG LOVE　16 For his morning Sacrifice.
P.　27 MISTRESS　34 Sits on thy skin like morning dew,
P.　29 THE GALLERY　21 While all the morning Quire does sing,
P.　68 A. HOUSE　289 When in the East the Morning Ray
P.　78 A. HOUSE　617 Here in the Morning tye my Chain,
P.　106 ANNIVERSARY　141 But a thick Cloud about that Morning lyes,
P.　111 ANNIVERSARY　325 So when first Man did through the Morning new
P.　146 INSTRUCTIONS　235 Thick was the Morning, and the House was thin,
P.　146 INSTRUCTIONS　244 And undescry'd return'd e're morning peep.
P.　178 LOYALL SCOT　268 The morning dews and flowers Neglected grown,

mornings　　　　　　　　　　　frequency:　1　relative frequency: 0.0000
P.　149 INSTRUCTIONS　345 So the sad Tree shrinks from the Mornings Eye;

morrice　　　　　　　　　　　frequency:　1　relative frequency: 0.0000
P.　150 INSTRUCTIONS　409 But Morrice learn'd demonstrates, by the Post,

mortal　　　　　　　　　　　frequency:　12　relative frequency: 0.0002
See also "mortall."
P.　14 THE CORONET　18 And mortal Glory, Heavens Diadem!
P.　48 THE GARDEN　27 The Gods, that mortal Beauty chase,
P.　64 A. HOUSE　173 'So through the mortal fruit we boyl
P.　69 A. HOUSE　328 To make us Mortal, and The Wast?
P.　106 ANNIVERSARY　142 And intercepts the Beams of Mortal eyes,
P.　107 ANNIVERSARY　179 When thou hadst almost quit thy Mortal cares,
P.　119 TWO SONGS　11 If thou a Mortal, rather sleep;
P.　127 O.C.　155 Here ended all his mortal toyles: He lay'd
P.　129 O.C.　248 And mortal sleep over those wakefull eyes:
P.　142 INSTRUCTIONS　67 Or how a mortal Poyson she may draw,
P.　149 INSTRUCTIONS　342 What to fair Denham mortal Chocolat;
P.　159 INSTRUCTIONS　760 And were they mortal, both for grief had dy'd.

mortall　　　　　　　　　　　frequency:　4　relative frequency: 0.0000
P.　130 O.C.　289 Despoyl'd of mortall robes, in seas of blisse,
P.　184 BRITANNIA　8 Once more with me partake of mortall woes.
P.　186 BRITANNIA　79 This Mortall poyson amongst Princes hurld,
P.　187 BRITANNIA　106 Of French, Scots, Irish (all my mortall foes):

mortalls　　　　　　　　　　　frequency:　1　relative frequency: 0.0000

P. 129 O.C.   266 At mortalls sins, nor his own plant will spare;

mortals   frequency: 2   relative frequency: 0.0000
See also "mortalls."
P. 121 TWO SONGS   58 Makes Mortals matches fit for Deityes.
P. 137 HOUSEWARMING   9 But observing that Mortals run often behind,

mortal's   frequency: 2   relative frequency: 0.0000
P. 49 THE GARDEN   61 But 'twas beyond a Mortal's share
P. 119 TWO SONGS   15 Nor merits he a Mortal's name,

mortar   frequency: 1   relative frequency: 0.0000
P. 138 HOUSEWARMING   38 To make Mortar and Brick, yet allow'd them no
                         straw,

mortgag'd   frequency: 1   relative frequency: 0.0000
P. 315 CHEQUER INN   98 Had Mortgag'd of his Two, one Band

mosaic. See "mosaick," "mosaique."

mosaick   frequency: 2   relative frequency: 0.0000
P. 77 A. HOUSE   582 I in this light Mosaick read.
P. 139 HOUSEWARMING   87 He finish'd at last his Palace Mosaick,

mosaique   frequency: 1   relative frequency: 0.0000
P. 47 EMPIRE   17 Then Musick, the Mosaique of the Air,

moses   frequency: 3   relative frequency: 0.0000
P. 127 O.C.   162 Then those of Moses hid from humane Eyes;
P. 130 O.C.   293 How soon thou Moses hast, and Joshua found,
P. 175 LOYALL SCOT   135 Aaron Casts Calves but Moses them Calcines.

moss   frequency: 1   relative frequency: 0.0000
P. 77 A. HOUSE   594 On Pallets swoln of Velvet Moss;

mossy   frequency: 2   relative frequency: 0.0000
P. 49 THE GARDEN   50 Or at some Fruit-trees mossy root,
P. 77 A. HOUSE   597 Thanks for my Rest ye Mossy Banks,

most   frequency: 46   relative frequency: 0.0009
P.   3 LOVELACE   13 He highest builds, who with most Art destroys,
P.   3 LOVELACE   35 Lovelace that thaw'd the most congealed brest,
P.   5 HASTINGS   28 Secures his neerest and most lov'd Ally;
P.   5 HASTINGS   37 But most he doth th' Eternal Book behold,
P.   5 HASTINGS   40 But most rejoyces at his Mothers name.
P. 15 EYES   13 What in the World most fair appears,
P. 28 LOVER   31 Guardians most fit to entertain
P. 29 THE GALLERY   15 Of which the most tormenting are
P. 34 DAPHNIS   42 Frighting her he loved most.
P. 38 PICTURE   31 But most procure
P. 39 THE MATCH   6 And Essences most pure,
P. 40 THE MOWER   4 Where Nature was most plain and pure.
P. 62 A. HOUSE   112 'Most strangly our Complexion clears.
P. 70 A. HOUSE   356 Which most our Earthly Gardens want.
P. 75 A. HOUSE   537 But most the Hewel's wonders are,
P. 76 A. HOUSE   570 In their most learned Original:
P. 82 A. HOUSE   743 While her glad Parents most rejoice,
P. 86 FLECKNO   119 Turns to recite; though Judges most severe
P. 87 FLECKNO   160 Home, his most furious Satyr to have fir'd
P. 91 MAY'S DEATH   40 Most servil' wit, and Mercenary Pen.
P. 105 ANNIVERSARY   63 But, for he most the graver Notes did try,
P. 105 ANNIVERSARY   93 But the most Equal still sustein the Height,
P. 106 ANNIVERSARY   143 That 'tis the most which we determine can,
P. 111 ANNIVERSARY   317 Oh Race most hypocritically strict!
P. 115 BLAKE   74 Where you had most of strength, and least of
                         fear.
P. 123 O.C.   7 The People, which what most they fear esteem,
P. 123 O.C.   17 And so less useful where he most desir'd,
P. 123 TWO SONGS   41 But what is most, the gentle Swain
P. 126 O.C.   143 But this, of all the most auspicious found,
P. 128 O.C.   208 Yet still affected most what best deserv'd.
P. 137 HOUSEWARMING   19 He thought (as an Instrument he was most free
                         on)
P. 142 INSTRUCTIONS   45 Nor fears he the most Christian should trepan
P. 144 INSTRUCTIONS 143 Black Birch, of all the Earth-born race most
                         hot,
P. 144 INSTRUCTIONS 144 And most rapacious, like himself begot.
P. 149 INSTRUCTIONS 364 United most, else when by turns they meet.
P. 152 INSTRUCTIONS 479 But most rely'd upon this Dutch pretence,
P. 153 INSTRUCTIONS 519 All Causes sure concur, but most they think
P. 158 INSTRUCTIONS 730 And all admires, but most his easie Prey.

```
      P. 159 INSTRUCTIONS  755 But most they for their Darling Charles
                                 complain:
      P. 160 INSTRUCTIONS  803 Who less Estate, for Treasurer most fit;
      P. 198 DUKE            9 Most holy Father, being joyned in league
      P. 201 HISTORICALL    29 Her most Uxorious Mate she usd of old;
      P. 204 HISTORICALL   119 The most authentik Statutes of the Land,
      P. 313 CHEQUER INN    38 Had not the Members most been made
      P. 315 CHEQUER INN   128 Which shoud the other most commend
      P. 316 CHEQUER INN   157 They drunke, I know not who had most

mote                               frequency:    1    relative frequency: 0.0000
      P.  59 A. HOUSE       22 T'impark the wanton Mote of Dust,

mother                             frequency:    6    relative frequency: 0.0001
      P.  27 LOVER          14 Upon the Rock his Mother drave;
      P. 107 ANNIVERSARY   161 Whose Saint-like Mother we did lately see
      P. 144 INSTRUCTIONS  132 Frighted the Midwife, and the Mother tore.
      P. 185 BRITANNIA      21 Till Kate a happy mother shall become,
      P. 201 HISTORICALL    23 The pious Mother Queen heareing her Son
      P. 204 HISTORICALL   125 First brought his Mother for a Prostitute:

mothers                            frequency:    3    relative frequency: 0.0000
      P.   5 HASTINGS       40 But most rejoyces at his Mothers name.
      P. 124 O.C.           35 Then to the Mothers brest her softly move,
      P. 142 INSTRUCTIONS   56 In fewer months than Mothers once indur'd.

moths.  See "wood-moths."

motion                             frequency:    1    relative frequency: 0.0000
      P. 161 INSTRUCTIONS  843 And so, proceeding in his motion warm,

motives                            frequency:    1    relative frequency: 0.0000
      P. 118 BLAKE         141 Far different Motives yet, engag'd them thus,

motley.  See "mottly."

mottly                             frequency:    1    relative frequency: 0.0000
      P. 168 ADVICE         12 A Landskip of our Mottly Parliament;

mould                              frequency:    1    relative frequency: 0.0000
      P. 115 BLAKE          55 They still do yield, such is their pretious
                                 mould,

moulded                            frequency:    1    relative frequency: 0.0000
      P. 175 LOYALL SCOT   134 All Mischeifs Moulded by those state divines:

mount                              frequency:    1    relative frequency: 0.0000
      P. 155 INSTRUCTIONS  602 Unpaid, refuse to mount our Ships for spight:

mountague                          frequency:    1    relative frequency: 0.0000
      P. 314 CHEQUER INN    79 And next him sate George Mountague

mountain                           frequency:    2    relative frequency: 0.0000
      P.  57 BILL-BOROW     33 Upon its crest this Mountain grave
      P. 127 O.C.          189 And where the sandy mountain Fenwick scal'd,

mountains                          frequency:    5    relative frequency: 0.0001
      P.  56 BILL-BOROW      9 Here learn ye Mountains more unjust,
      P.  58 BILL-BOROW     68 And Mountains rais'd of dying Men.
      P. 110 ANNIVERSARY   284 Left by the Wars Flood on the Mountains crest:
      P. 126 O.C.          145 When up the armed Mountains of Dunbar
      P. 169 ADVICE         50 That aime at mountains and bring forth a Mous,

mounted                            frequency:    3    relative frequency: 0.0000
      P. 168 ADVICE         13 Where draw Sir Edward mounted on his throne,
      P. 169 ADVICE         40 Draw me a Champion mounted on his steed,
      P. 186 BRITANNIA      57 Shee mounted up on a triumphall Car

mounting                           frequency:    1    relative frequency: 0.0000
      P. 150 INSTRUCTIONS  384 Mounting the neighbour Couple on lean Jade.

mounts                             frequency:    1    relative frequency: 0.0000
      P.  11 DIALOGUE       73 None thither mounts by the degree

mourn                              frequency:    4    relative frequency: 0.0000
      P.   4 HASTINGS        8 With early Tears must mourn his early Fate.
      P.  75 A. HOUSE      527 O why should such a Couple mourn,
      P. 123 O.C.           27 And leave succeeding Ages cause to mourn,
      P. 160 INSTRUCTIONS  808 Hyde and the Court again begin to mourn.

mourn'd                            frequency:    3    relative frequency: 0.0000
```

P. 108 ANNIVERSARY   202 Or Rock so savage, but it mourn'd for thee:
P. 108 ANNIVERSARY   219 We only mourn'd our selves, in thine Ascent,
P. 111 ANNIVERSARY   338 And with such accents, as Despairing, mourn'd:

mourners   frequency: 1   relative frequency: 0.0000
   P. 127 O.C.   159 For whom the Elements we Mourners see,

mournful   frequency: 2   relative frequency: 0.0000
   P. 12 DROP OF DEW   12 Shines with a mournful Light;
   P. 125 O.C.   79 Who now shall tell us more of mournful Swans,

mourning   frequency: 3   relative frequency: 0.0000
   P. 31 MOURNING   t Mourning.
   P. 127 O.C.   165 Then let us to our course of Mourning keep:
   P. 145 INSTRUCTIONS   198 Mourning his Countess, anxious for his Act.

mourns   frequency: 1   relative frequency: 0.0000
   P. 108 ANNIVERSARY   212 And to deaf Seas, and ruthless Tempests mourns,

mous   frequency: 1   relative frequency: 0.0000
   P. 169 ADVICE   50 That aime at mountains and bring forth a Mous,

mouse   frequency: 1   relative frequency: 0.0000
   See also "mous."
   P. 313 CHEQUER INN   14 Is now a Man that was a Mouse

mouth   frequency: 7   relative frequency: 0.0001
   P. 49 THE GARDEN   36 Upon my Mouth do crush their Wine;
   P. 141 INSTRUCTIONS   22 Of his Hound's Mouth to feign the raging froth,
   P. 142 INSTRUCTIONS   62 Wide Mouth that Sparagus may well proclaim:
   P. 160 INSTRUCTIONS   817 But in the Thames mouth still de Ruyter laid,
   P. 162 INSTRUCTIONS   895 Her mouth lockt up, a blind before her Eyes,
   P. 188 BRITANNIA   156 From her sage mouth fam'd Principles to know,
   P. 198 DUKE   8 Adoreing Roome, this labell in his mouth.

mouths   frequency: 1   relative frequency: 0.0000
   P. 17 BERMUDAS   21 He makes the Figs our mouths to meet;

mov'd   frequency: 2   relative frequency: 0.0000
   P. 84 FLECKNO   40 Mov'd by the Air and hidden Sympathies;
   P. 162 INSTRUCTIONS   899 The Object strange in him no Terrour mov'd:

move   frequency: 6   relative frequency: 0.0001
   P. 25 YOUNG LOVE   10 Such as yours should swifter move;
   P. 73 A. HOUSE   463 They feed so wide, so slowly move,
   P. 77 A. HOUSE   591 Under this antick Cope I move
   P. 120 TWO SONGS   23 My wakeful Lamp all night must move,
   P. 124 O.C.   35 Then to the Mothers brest her softly move,
   P. 151 INSTRUCTIONS   436 To move him out of Pity, if not Love.

moves   frequency: 3   relative frequency: 0.0000
   P. 21 SOUL & BODY   15 And warms and moves this needless Frame:
   P. 112 ANNIVERSARY   380 'Moves the great Bulk, and animates the whole.
   P. 161 INSTRUCTIONS   840 And for three days, thence moves them to adjourn.

moving   frequency: 3   relative frequency: 0.0000
   P. 13 DROP OF DEW   35 Moving but on a point below,
   P. 111 ANNIVERSARY   328 Pleas'd with that other World of moving Light;
   P. 158 INSTRUCTIONS   729 Her moving Shape; all these he does survey,

mow'd   frequency: 2   relative frequency: 0.0000
   P. 43 DAMON   65 How happy might I still have mow'd,
   P. 71 A. HOUSE   399 Fearing the Flesh untimely mow'd

mower   frequency: 9   relative frequency: 0.0001
   P. 40 THE MOWER   t The Mower against Gardens.
   P. 41 DAMON   t Damon the Mower.
   P. 41 DAMON   1 Heark how the Mower Damon Sung,
   P. 42 DAMON   20 Which burns the Fields and Mower both:
   P. 43 DAMON   41 I am the Mower Damon, known
   P. 44 DAMON   80 By his own Sythe, the Mower mown.
   P. 44 DAMON   88 For Death thou art a Mower too.
   P. 44 GLO-WORMS   t The Mower to the Glo-Worms.
   P. 72 A. HOUSE   418 The Mower now commands the Field;

mowers   frequency: 3   relative frequency: 0.0000
   P. 44 GLO-WORMS   10 To wandring Mowers shows the way,
   P. 71 A. HOUSE   388 The tawny Mowers enter next;
   P. 72 A. HOUSE   427 Where every Mowers wholesome Heat

mower's   frequency: 1   relative frequency: 0.0000

```
            See also "mowers."
            P.  45 MOWER'S SONG     t The Mower's Song.

mowing                              frequency:    1    relative frequency: 0.0000
            P.  71 A. HOUSE      402 To bring the mowing Camp their Cates,

mown                                frequency:    2    relative frequency: 0.0000
            P.  43 DAMON          42 Through all the Meadows I have mown.
            P.  44 DAMON          80 By his own Sythe, the Mower mown.

mr.                                 frequency:    2    relative frequency: 0.0000
            P.   3 LOVELACE       t1 To his Noble Friend Mr. Richard Lovelace,
            P. 131 PARADISE        t On Mr. Milton's Paradise lost.

much                                frequency:   60    relative frequency: 0.0012
            P.   3 LOVELACE        1 Our times are much degenerate from those
            P.  20 THYRSIS        44 Will for thee, much more with thee dye.
            P.  23 NYMPH          69 For it was nimbler much than Hindes;
            P.  25 YOUNG LOVE     13 Love as much the snowy Lamb
            P.  32 MOURNING       22 Joy now so much her Master grown,
            P.  33 DAPHNIS        23 That he had not so much Sence
            P.  35 DAPHNIS        61 Absence is too much alone:
            P.  58 BILL-BOROW     65 Much other Groves, say they, then these
            P.  63 A. HOUSE      129 'But much it to our work would add
            P.  63 A. HOUSE      132 'Yet thus She you resembles much.
            P.  82 A. HOUSE      759 Much less the Dead's Elysian Fields,
            P.  88 ODE            28 Much to the Man is due.
            P.  89 ODE            75 So much one Man can do,
            P.  90 MAY'S DEATH    12 But 'twas a man much of another sort;
            P.  94 DR. WITTY      12 Much of the precious Metal rub away.
            P.  94 DR. WITTY      14 As much as he that taketh from the Store
            P.  95 HOLLAND         3 And so much Earth as was contributed
            P. 104 ANNIVERSARY    36 Much less themselves to perfect them begin;
            P. 112 ANNIVERSARY   394 'It grieves me sore to have thus much confest.
            P. 113 BLAKE          12 But yet in them caus'd as much fear, as Joy.
            P. 114 BLAKE          16 But much more fearful are your Flags to see.
            P. 115 BLAKE          60 And when 'tis raised, does trouble them much
                                     more.
            P. 115 BLAKE          76 Yet in their brests, carry a pride much higher.
            P. 116 BLAKE          80 Make them admire, so much as they did fear.
            P. 117 BLAKE         108 Do not so much suppress, as shew their fear.
            P. 119 BLAKE         168 And tells the World, how much to you it owes.
            P. 125 O.C.          110 By nature solemniz'd with so much state.
            P. 129 O.C.          254 How much another thing, no more that man?
            P. 129 O.C.          261 Not much unlike the sacred oak, which shoots
            P. 130 O.C.          308 And yet how much of them his griefe obscures.
            P. 132 PARADISE       36 Thou singst with so much gravity and ease;
            P. 137 HOUSEWARMING   11 His Omnipotence therfore much rather design'd
            P. 137 HOUSEWARMING   15 And wish'd that his Daughter had had as much
                                     grace
            P. 137 HOUSEWARMING   23 That he begg'd for a Pallace so much of his
                                     ground,
            P. 138 HOUSEWARMING   28 And too much resembled his Wives Chocolatte.
            P. 140 HOUSEWARMING  103 And others as much reprehend his Backside,
            P. 145 INSTRUCTIONS  184 And hid much Fraud under an aspect grim.
            P. 146 INSTRUCTIONS  226 For one had much, the other nought to lose.
            P. 153 INSTRUCTIONS  515 Whether his Valour they so much admire,
            P. 153 INSTRUCTIONS  529 The Sun much brighter, and the Skies more
                                     clear,
            P. 157 INSTRUCTIONS  662 And wondred much at those that run away:
            P. 157 INSTRUCTIONS  673 Much him the Honours of his ancient Race
            P. 158 INSTRUCTIONS  710 Our loss, does so much more our loss augment.
            P. 160 INSTRUCTIONS  793 Southampton dead, much of the Treasure's care,
            P. 160 INSTRUCTIONS  811 Grave Primate Shelden (much in Preaching
                                     there)
            P. 172 LOYALL SCOT     9 Much had hee Cur'd the Humor of his vein:
            P. 172 LOYALL SCOT    28 And wonder'd much at those that Runne away,
            P. 172 LOYALL SCOT    39 Much him the glories of his Antient Race
            P. 177 LOYALL SCOT   227 With much adoe preserves his postern Chast.
            P. 179 STOCKSMARKET   14 Yet all do affirm that the king is much worse,
            P. 179 STOCKSMARKET   20 Even Sir William Peake sits much firmer than
                                     he.
            P. 180 STOCKSMARKET   53 But Sir Robert affirms we do him much wrong;
            P. 181 MADE FREE       23 Much worse than before;
            P. 183 MADE FREE     108 For wee have had too much of the Old one.
            P. 192 TWO HORSES     40 My Brass is provok't as much as thy stone
            P. 195 TWO HORSES    154 W. His perfum'd predecessor was never much
                                     fitter.
            P. 196 TWO HORSES    169 Which Monarchys downfall portended much more
            P. 201 HISTORICALL     2 Much like the Son of Kish that lofty Jew,
            P. 203 HISTORICALL    91 Droll on their God but a much duller way:
```

    P. 205 HISTORICALL   182 Then how much greater Mischiefe as a King.

muddy   frequency: 1   relative frequency: 0.0000
    P. 78 A. HOUSE   635 And its yet muddy back doth lick,

mules   frequency: 1   relative frequency: 0.0000
    P. 141 INSTRUCTIONS   34 Member'd like Mules, with Elephantine chine.

multiply   frequency: 1   relative frequency: 0.0000
    P. 147 INSTRUCTIONS   270 And with that thought does multiply his Soul:

multiplying   frequency: 1   relative frequency: 0.0000
    P. 73 A. HOUSE   462 In Multiplying Glasses lye.

multitudes   frequency: 1   relative frequency: 0.0000
    P. 143 INSTRUCTIONS   112 As Chance does still in Multitudes decide.

mungrel   frequency: 1   relative frequency: 0.0000
    P. 144 INSTRUCTIONS   146 Bugger'd in Incest with the mungrel Beast.

munser's   frequency: 1   relative frequency: 0.0000
    P. 111 ANNIVERSARY   313 Wand'rers, Adult'rers, Lyers, Munser's rest,

munzers. See "munser's."

murder   frequency: 1   relative frequency: 0.0000
    P. 22 NYMPH   11 Thy murder, I will Joyn my Tears

murder'd   frequency: 1   relative frequency: 0.0000
    P. 159 INSTRUCTIONS   745 And their dear Off-spring murder'd in their
                              sight;

murdered. See "murthered."

murderess. See "murtheress."

murdering. See "murd'ring."

murd'ring   frequency: 1   relative frequency: 0.0000
    P. 204 HISTORICALL   150 From hence he picks and calls his murd'ring
                              braves:

mure   frequency: 1   relative frequency: 0.0000
    P. 151 INSTRUCTIONS   420 To fly to Windsor, and mure up the Gates.

murm'ring   frequency: 1   relative frequency: 0.0000
    P. 47 EMPIRE   4 To hollow Rocks and murm'ring Fountains bound.

murmur   frequency: 1   relative frequency: 0.0000
    P. 187 BRITANNIA   105 When she had spoke, a confus'd murmur rose

murmuring   frequency: 1   relative frequency: 0.0000
    See also "murm'ring."
    P. 84 FLECKNO   42 Over the Lute, his murmuring Belly calls,

murthered   frequency: 1   relative frequency: 0.0000
    P. 200 DUKE   115 Of Monarchs murthered by the Impatient heir:

murtheress   frequency: 1   relative frequency: 0.0000
    P. 29 THE GALLERY   10 Of an Inhumane Murtheress;

muscle-shell   frequency: 1   relative frequency: 0.0000
    P. 95 HOLLAND   6 Of shipwrackt Cockle and the Muscle-shell;

muscles   frequency: 1   relative frequency: 0.0000
    P. 124 O.C.   34 Slacken the vigour of his Muscles strong;

mus'd   frequency: 1   relative frequency: 0.0000
    P. 153 INSTRUCTIONS   511 Often, dear Painter, have I sate and mus'd

muse   frequency: 9   relative frequency: 0.0001
    P.   3 LOVELACE   2 Which your sweet Muse which your fair Fortune
                              chose,
    P. 92 MAY'S DEATH   61 And for a Tankard-bearing Muse must we
    P. 106 ANNIVERSARY   125 Till then my Muse shall hollow far behind
    P. 144 INSTRUCTIONS   147 Say Muse, for nothing can escape thy sight,
    P. 164 INSTRUCTIONS   957 Blame not the Muse that brought those spots to
                              sight,
    P. 172 LOYALL SCOT   8 His ready muse to Court the Warlike Guest.
    P. 202 HISTORICALL   63 Our muse would on the Readers patience grate.
    P. 203 HISTORICALL   112 My Muse presum'd a litle to digress

P. 204 HISTORICALL   128 Now must my Muse deplore the Nations fate,

muses   frequency: 2   relative frequency: 0.0000
    P. 87 ODE   2 Must now forsake his Muses dear,
    P. 162 INSTRUCTIONS   890 He wakes and Muses of th' uneasie Throne:

musgraves   frequency: 1   relative frequency: 0.0000
    P. 316 CHEQUER INN   133 The Hanmers, Herberts, Sandys, Musgraves

mushroom. See "court-mushrumps."

music. See "musick," "musique."

musician   frequency: 1   relative frequency: 0.0000
    See also "musitian."
    P. 83 FLECKNO   2 Whom as Priest, Poet, and Musician,

musick   frequency: 9   relative frequency: 0.0001
    P. 10 DIALOGUE   37 Heark how Musick then prepares
    P. 19 THYRSIS   26 May feast with Musick of the Spheres.
    P. 29 LOVER   62 And Musick within every Ear:
    P. 47 EMPIRE   3 All Musick was a solitary sound,
    P. 47 EMPIRE   17 Then Musick, the Mosaique of the Air,
    P. 47 EMPIRE   23 Who though He flies the Musick of his praise,
    P. 75 A. HOUSE   516 With Musick high the squatted Thorns.
    P. 75 A. HOUSE   521 But I have for my Musick found
    P. 84 FLECKNO   45 I, that perceiv'd now what his Musick ment,

musicks   frequency: 2   relative frequency: 0.0000
    P. 47 EMPIRE   t Musicks Empire.
    P. 47 EMPIRE   6 And Jubal tuned Musicks Jubilee:

musique   frequency: 1   relative frequency: 0.0000
    P. 104 ANNIVERSARY   47 Learning a Musique in the Region clear,

musitian   frequency: 1   relative frequency: 0.0000
    P. 176 LOYALL SCOT   199 It was Musitian too and dwelt at Court.

must   frequency: 62   relative frequency: 0.0012

muster   frequency: 3   relative frequency: 0.0000
    P. 110 ANNIVERSARY   300 Might muster Heresies, so one were ten.
    P. 138 HOUSEWARMING   59 While into a fabrick the Presents would muster;
    P. 146 INSTRUCTIONS   220 Troop't on to muster in the Tuttle-field.

mute   frequency: 1   relative frequency: 0.0000
    P. 161 INSTRUCTIONS   860 Where mute they stand to hear their Sentence
                               read;

mutiny   frequency: 1   relative frequency: 0.0000
    P.   4 LOVELACE   39 They all in mutiny though yet undrest

mutual. See "mutuall."

mutuall   frequency: 1   relative frequency: 0.0000
    P. 192 TWO HORSES   33 And that the two Jades after mutuall Salutes

my   frequency: 169   relative frequency: 0.0035

myrmidons   frequency: 2   relative frequency: 0.0000
    P. 152 INSTRUCTIONS   488 Of current Myrmidons appear in Arms.
    P. 204 HISTORICALL   145 The Duke now vaunts, with popish Myrmidons;

mysterious   frequency: 1   relative frequency: 0.0000
    P. 106 ANNIVERSARY   137 Sure, the mysterious Work, where none withstand,

mystery. See "mistery," "mist'ry."

mystick   frequency: 1   relative frequency: 0.0000
    P. 77 A. HOUSE   584 Hath read in Natures mystick Book.

mytre   frequency: 1   relative frequency: 0.0000
    P. 175 LOYALL SCOT   151 One Mytre fitts the Heads of full four Moors.

nacion   frequency: 3   relative frequency: 0.0000
    P. 168 ADVICE   20 Sate by the worst Attorney of the Nacion,
    P. 192 TWO HORSES   51 W. That Bondage and Begery should be brought
                               on the Nacion
    P. 195 TWO HORSES   161 W. A Commonwealth a Common-wealth wee proclaim
                               to the Nacion;

nag. See "nagg."

nagg   frequency: 1   relative frequency: 0.0000

         P. 173 LOYALL SCOT   64 Sometimes the Gall'way Proves the better Nagg.

nail   frequency: 1   relative frequency: 0.0000
         P. 78 A. HOUSE   616 And courteous Briars nail me through.

nak'd   frequency: 2   relative frequency: 0.0000
         P. 28 LOVER   49 See how he nak'd and fierce does stand,
         P. 142 INSTRUCTIONS   51 She, rak'd, can Archimedes self put down,

naked   frequency: 3   relative frequency: 0.0000
      See also "nak'd."
         P. 73 A. HOUSE   449 For to this naked equal Flat,
         P. 153 INSTRUCTIONS   526 And Beauties e're this never naked seen.
         P. 162 INSTRUCTIONS   893 Naked as born, and her round Arms behind,

nakedness   frequency: 1   relative frequency: 0.0000
         P. 110 ANNIVERSARY   292 May shew their own, not see his Nakedness.

nam'd   frequency: 2   relative frequency: 0.0000
         P. 112 ANNIVERSARY   375 'That one Man still, although but nam'd, alarms
         P. 132 PARADISE   39 The Bird nam'd from that Paradise you sing

name   frequency: 27   relative frequency: 0.0005
         P.   5 HASTINGS   40 But most rejoyces at his Mothers name.
         P. 18 BERMUDAS   32 A Temple, where to sound his Name.
         P. 18 CLORINDA   23 And his Name swells my slender Oate.
         P. 48 THE GARDEN   20 Cut in these Trees their Mistress name.
         P. 48 THE GARDEN   24 No Name shall but your own be found.
         P. 55 EPITAPH   2 'Tis to commend her but to name.
         P. 57 BILL-BOROW   45 And on these Okes ingrav'd her Name;
         P. 58 BILL-BOROW   63 Which in their modest Whispers name
         P. 82 A. HOUSE   757 But name not the Idalian Grove,
         P. 93 DR. WITTY   2 Where just desert enrolles thy honour'd Name
         P. 95 HOLLAND   1 Holland, that scarce deserves the name of Land,
         P. 97 HOLLAND   82 That it had one Civilis call'd by Name,
         P. 119 TWO SONGS   15 Nor merits he a Mortal's name,
         P. 126 O.C.   148 That had before immortaliz'd his Name?
         P. 128 O.C.   202 The first foundation of his house and name:
         P. 130 O.C.   280 And with the name of Cromwell, armyes fright.
         P. 130 O.C.   286 Always thy honour, praise and name, shall last.
         P. 137 HOUSEWARMING   24 As might carry the measure and name of an Hyde.
         P. 150 INSTRUCTIONS   405 They, by the Name, mistook it for that Isle,
         P. 152 INSTRUCTIONS   451 The first instructs our (Verse the Name abhors)
         P. 155 INSTRUCTIONS   616 Crown'd, for that Merit, with their Masters
                                    Name.
         P. 157 INSTRUCTIONS   694 Or if my Verse can propagate thy Name;
         P. 159 INSTRUCTIONS   768 His Name alone seems fit to answer all.
         P. 161 INSTRUCTIONS   848 And in eternal Healths thy Name be trowl'd.
         P. 177 LOYALL SCOT   246 Nation is all but name as Shibboleth,
         P. 188 BRITANNIA   137 In his deaf ear sound his dead Fathers name;
         P. 189 BRITANNIA   171 Poppea, Tegeline and Acte's name

name-sake   frequency: 1   relative frequency: 0.0000
         P. 140 HOUSEWARMING   106 That for Name-sake he may with Hyde Park it
                                    enlarge,

names   frequency: 5   relative frequency: 0.0001
         P.   5 HASTINGS   38 On which the happie Names do stand enroll'd;
         P. 38 PICTURE   5 The Wilder flow'rs, and gives them names:
         P. 177 LOYALL SCOT   248 In Paradice Names only Nature Shew'd,
         P. 177 LOYALL SCOT   249 At Babel names from pride and discord flow'd,
         P. 177 LOYALL SCOT   251 First call each other names and then they fight.

nan   frequency: 1   relative frequency: 0.0000
         P. 199 DUKE   43 That sent Nan Hide before her under ground,

naphta's   frequency: 1   relative frequency: 0.0000
         P. 40 THE MATCH   23 The Naphta's and the Sulphurs heat,

naphtha's. See "naphta's."

narcissus   frequency: 1   relative frequency: 0.0000
         P. 78 A. HOUSE   640 Narcissus like, the Sun too pines.

narrow   frequency: 7   relative frequency: 0.0001
         P. 48 THE GARDEN   5 Whose short and narrow verged Shade
         P. 59 A. HOUSE   30 To enter at a narrow loop;
         P. 83 FLECKNO   17 And though within one Cell so narrow pent,
         P. 85 FLECKNO   97 As narrow as his Sword's; and I, that was
         P. 88 ODE   52 To Caresbrooks narrow case.
         P. 128 O.C.   203 But within one its narrow limits fall,

```
          P. 140 HOUSEWARMING  104 As too narrow by far for his expatiation,

narrowness                              frequency:    1     relative frequency: 0.0000
          P.  85 FLECKNO        104 By its own narrowness, Sir, to unite.

nation                                  frequency:   14     relative frequency: 0.0002
          See also "nacion."
          P. 111 ANNIVERSARY    349 'Is this, saith one, the Nation that we read
          P. 112 ANNIVERSARY    379 'The Nation had been ours, but his one Soul
          P. 143 INSTRUCTIONS   109 Those having lost the Nation at Trick track,
          P. 152 INSTRUCTIONS   491 Of the whole Nation now to ask a Loan.
          P. 160 INSTRUCTIONS   815 And thinks 'twill ne're be well within this
                                     Nation,
          P. 175 LOYALL SCOT    131 The Nation they devide, their Curates Text.
          P. 177 LOYALL SCOT    246 Nation is all but name as Shibboleth,
          P. 178 LOYALL SCOT    278 I single did against a Nation write,
          P. 178 LOYALL SCOT    279 Against a Nation thou didst singly fight.
          P. 183 MADE FREE      102 The whole Nation may chance to repent it.
          P. 198 DUKE            14 Till all this nation to thy footstoole bend.
          P. 204 HISTORICALL    133 For one man's weakeness a whole Nation bleeds
          P. 315 CHEQUER INN    123 Before he'd sell the Nation,
          P. 317 CHEQUER INN    180 Is to undoe the Nation

nations                                 frequency:    4     relative frequency: 0.0000
          P. 173 LOYALL SCOT     72 Our nations Melting thy Colossus Frame,
          P. 177 LOYALL SCOT    235 Two Nations Neere had mist the Marke soe long.
          P. 177 LOYALL SCOT    236 The world in all doth but two Nations bear,
          P. 204 HISTORICALL    128 Now must my Muse deplore the Nations fate,

nation's                                frequency:    1     relative frequency: 0.0000
          See also "nations."
          P. 200 DUKE            89 And change the order of a nation's fate?

native                                  frequency:    5     relative frequency: 0.0001
          P.  12 DROP OF DEW      8 Frames as it can its native Element.
          P.  94 DR. WITTY       23 Her native beauty's not Italianated,
          P. 198 DUKE             6 To robb their native countrey of its right.
          P. 200 DUKE           101 In peace and pleasure this thy native land,
          P. 203 HISTORICALL    110 Till native Reason's basely forct to yield

nature                                  frequency:   40     relative frequency: 0.0008
          P.   9 DIALOGUE         9 And shew that Nature wants an Art
          P.  15 EYES             1 How wisely Nature did decree,
          P.  28 LOVER           25 While Nature to his Birth presents
          P.  33 DAPHNIS          5 Nature her own Sexes foe,
          P.  33 DAPHNIS         13 Nature so her self does use
          P.  39 PICTURE         34 Whom Nature courts with fruits and flow'rs,
          P.  39 THE MATCH        1 Nature had long a Treasure made
          P.  40 THE MATCH       28 All Nature could inflame.
          P.  40 THE MOWER        4 Where Nature was most plain and pure.
          P.  41 THE MOWER       29 And in the Cherry he does Nature vex,
          P.  41 THE MOWER       33 Where willing Nature does to all dispence
          P.  47 EMPIRE           2 Where Jarring Windes to infant Nature plaid.
          P.  56 BILL-BOROW      14 Nature must a new Center find,
          P.  59 A. HOUSE        26 Like Nature, orderly and near:
          P.  61 A. HOUSE        75 But Nature here hath been so free
          P.  79 A. HOUSE       657 See how loose Nature, in respect
          P.  79 A. HOUSE       672 Admiring Nature does benum.
          P.  80 A. HOUSE       688 Nature is wholly vitrifi'd.
          P.  88 ODE             41 Nature that hateth emptiness,
          P.  96 HOLLAND         35 Nature, it seem'd, asham'd of her mistake,
          P. 105 ANNIVERSARY     91 And they, whose Nature leads them to divide,
          P. 107 ANNIVERSARY    157 Hence landing Nature to new Seas is tost,
          P. 114 BLAKE           25 One of which doubtless is by Nature blest
          P. 115 BLAKE           62 Kind Nature had from thence remov'd so far.
          P. 117 BLAKE          129 Nature ne'r made Cedars so high aspire,
          P. 123 O.C.            15 And be whom Nature all for Peace had made,
          P. 125 O.C.           110 By nature solemniz'd with so much state.
          P. 126 O.C.           112 But oh what pangs that Death did Nature cost!
          P. 126 O.C.           133 Nature it seem'd with him would Nature vye;
          P. 128 O.C.           206 Where kindly nature loves itself to lose.
          P. 141 INSTRUCTIONS    36 For never Bacon study'd Nature more.
          P. 173 LOYALL SCOT     76 Where Nature Scotland doth from England part.
          P. 176 LOYALL SCOT    190 Nature in Living Embleme there Exprest
          P. 177 LOYALL SCOT    248 In Paradice Names only Nature Shew'd,
          P. 187 BRITANNIA      103 Rack nature till new pleasures she shall find,
          P. 200 DUKE           110 Brothers, its true, by nature should be kinde:
          P. 201 HISTORICALL     20 Soft in her Nature and of wanton pride.
          P. 201 HISTORICALL     32 Deludes their plyant Nature with Vain things,
          P. 203 HISTORICALL    106 Hence Death and Sin did human Nature blot:

natures                                 frequency:    7     relative frequency: 0.0001
```

P.	64 A. HOUSE	178 'Still handling Natures finest Parts.
P.	74 A. HOUSE	495 And, as they Natures Cradle deckt,
P.	77 A. HOUSE	584 Hath read in Natures mystick Book.
P.	108 ANNIVERSARY	204 As if that Natures self were overthrown.
P.	123 O.C.	30 Eliza, Natures and his darling, seize.
P.	150 INSTRUCTIONS	378 Masculine Wives, transgressing Natures Law.
P.	203 HISTORICALL	108 Thrice wretched they who natures Lawes detest

nature's   frequency: 5   relative frequency: 0.0001
     See also "natures."
P.	9 DIALOGUE	14 And of Nature's banquet share:
P.	40 THE MATCH	40 All Love's and Nature's store.
P.	82 A. HOUSE	767 You Heaven's Center, Nature's Lap.
P.	128 O.C.	213 For her he once did nature's tribute pay:
P.	128 O.C.	229 And we death's refuse nature's dregs confin'd

naughty   frequency: 1   relative frequency: 0.0000
| P. | 151 INSTRUCTIONS | 430 Threaten to beat us, and are naughty Boys. |

naval   frequency: 2   relative frequency: 0.0000
| P. | 147 INSTRUCTIONS | 264 This Combat truer than the Naval Fight. |
| P. | 160 INSTRUCTIONS | 786 Was the first cause of all these Naval slips: |

navies   frequency: 3   relative frequency: 0.0000
P.	112 ANNIVERSARY	368 'Whose Navies hold the Sluces of the Sea.
P.	112 ANNIVERSARY	376 'More then all Men, all Navies, and all Arms.
P.	118 BLAKE	138 Two dreadful Navies there at Anchor Fight.

navigable   frequency: 1   relative frequency: 0.0000
| P. | 158 INSTRUCTIONS | 722 And shrunk, lest Navigable, to a Ford. |

navy   frequency: 16   relative frequency: 0.0003
P.	98 HOLLAND	104 When their whole Navy they together prest,
P.	98 HOLLAND	121 And the torn Navy stagger'd with him home,
P.	99 HOLLAND	140 Their Navy all our Conquest or our Wreck:
P.	112 ANNIVERSARY	351 'Yet rig a Navy while we dress us late;
P.	117 BLAKE	111 Behold their Navy does at Anchor lye,
P.	138 HOUSEWARMING	47 His Friends in the Navy would not be ingrate,
P.	144 INSTRUCTIONS	121 The close Cabal mark'd how the Navy eats,
P.	150 INSTRUCTIONS	403 While the first year our Navy is but shown,
P.	154 INSTRUCTIONS	535 His sporting Navy all about him swim,
P.	154 INSTRUCTIONS	559 Such up the stream the Belgick Navy glides,
P.	158 INSTRUCTIONS	761 Of all our Navy none should now survive,
P.	159 INSTRUCTIONS	770 Who all Commands sold thro' the Navy? Pett.
P.	159 INSTRUCTIONS	779 Who did advise no Navy out to set?
P.	166 KINGS VOWES	19 I will have a fine Navy to Conquer the Seas,
P.	180 STOCKSMARKET	47 To express how his navy was shattered and torn
P.	193 TWO HORSES	63 W. Our worm-eaten Navy be laid up at Chatham,

nay   frequency: 10   relative frequency: 0.0002

near   frequency: 19   relative frequency: 0.0003
     See also "neare."
P.	18 CLORINDA	13 C. Near this, a Fountaines liquid Bell
P.	26 MISTRESS	22 Times winged Charriot hurrying near:
P.	32 MOURNING	15 Only to soften near her Heart
P.	59 A. HOUSE	26 Like Nature, orderly and near:
P.	61 A. HOUSE	89 Near to this gloomy Cloysters Gates
P.	63 A. HOUSE	158 'Doth your succession near presage.
P.	72 A. HOUSE	435 We wondring in the River near
P.	90 MAY'S DEATH	10 He saw near hand, as he imagin'd Ares.
P.	90 ODE	111 Nor lay his Hourds in near
P.	107 ANNIVERSARY	175 How near they fail'd, and in thy sudden Fall
P.	121 TWO SONGS	46 And cannot, though they would, come near.
P.	140 HOUSEWARMING	109 Or rather how wisely his Stall was built near,
P.	151 INSTRUCTIONS	441 Nor Word, nor near Relation did revere;
P.	158 INSTRUCTIONS	706 The Tow'r it self with the near danger shook.
P.	158 INSTRUCTIONS	714 The Houses were demolish'd near the Tow'r.
P.	160 INSTRUCTIONS	807 But now draws near the Parliament's return;
P.	160 INSTRUCTIONS	822 The Holland Fleet and Parliament so near.
P.	164 INSTRUCTIONS	951 Show'd they obscure him, while too near they please,
P.	190 STATUE	11 And soe near to the Court they will never indure

neare   frequency: 2   relative frequency: 0.0000
| P. | 167 KINGS VOWES | 44 My Bawd shall Embassadors send farr and neare, |
| P. | 200 DUKE | 106 Observe the danger that appeares soe neare, |

nearer   frequency: 8   relative frequency: 0.0001
| P. | 40 THE MATCH | 30 A nearer Way they sought; |
| P. | 64 A. HOUSE | 162 'Shall draw Heav'n nearer, raise us higher. |

```
P.  73 A. HOUSE        454 Is pincht yet nearer by the Beast.
P. 104 ANNIVERSARY      46 And cuts his way still nearer to the Skyes,
P. 138 HOUSEWARMING     44 But that he had nearer the Stones of St.
                           Pauls.
P. 156 INSTRUCTIONS    640 He heard how the wild Cannon nearer roar'd;
P. 156 INSTRUCTIONS    644 Pregnant with Sulphur, to him nearer draw
P. 314 CHEQUER INN      68 And if it had beene nearer yet
```

nearest. See "neerest."

neatly   frequency: 1   relative frequency: 0.0000
```
P.  61 A. HOUSE         77 Art would more neatly have defac'd
```

neatness   frequency: 1   relative frequency: 0.0000
```
P.  60 A. HOUSE         63 Where neatness nothing can condemn,
```

necessary   frequency: 6   relative frequency: 0.0001
```
P. 176 LOYALL SCOT     210 To sit is Necessary in Parliament,
P. 176 LOYALL SCOT     212 To conform's necessary or bee shent,
P. 177 LOYALL SCOT     214 'Tis necessary Bishops have their rent,
P. 177 LOYALL SCOT     216 'Tis necessary to rebabel Pauls,
P. 177 LOYALL SCOT     218 'Tis necessary Lambeth never wed,
P. 177 LOYALL SCOT     221 Not necessary nor Indifferent.
```

necessity   frequency: 4   relative frequency: 0.0000
```
P.  96 HOLLAND          37 Therefore Necessity, that first made Kings,
P. 118 BLAKE           142 Necessity did them, but Choice did us.
P. 161 INSTRUCTIONS    825 And 'twixt Necessity and Spight, till then,
P. 176 LOYALL SCOT     209 Transfuse Indifference with necessity.
```

neck   frequency: 4   relative frequency: 0.0000
```
P.  99 HOLLAND         139 Their Tortoise wants its vainly stretched neck;
P. 124 O.C.            50 Hanging about her neck or at his knees.
P. 163 INSTRUCTIONS    922 The purple thread about his Neck does show:
P. 315 CHEQUER INN     105 His Neck it turn'd on Wyer
```

necks   frequency: 2   relative frequency: 0.0000
```
P.  75 A. HOUSE        523 The Stock-doves, whose fair necks are grac'd
P. 204 HISTORICALL     123 To bring upon our Necks the heavier yoke:
```

neckt   frequency: 1   relative frequency: 0.0000
```
P. 176 LOYALL SCOT     187 With single body like the two Neckt Swan,
```

nectaren   frequency: 1   relative frequency: 0.0000
```
P.  49 THE GARDEN       37 The Nectaren, and curious Peach,
```

nectarine. See "nectaren."

need   frequency: 11   relative frequency: 0.0002
```
P.  19 THYRSIS          23 No need of Dog to fetch our stray,
P.  25 YOUNG LOVE       19 Of this Need wee'l Virtue make,
P.  59 A. HOUSE         21 What need of all this Marble Crust
P.  64 A. HOUSE        183 'What need is here of Man? unless
P. 114 BLAKE            30 Fertile to be, yet never need her showres.
P. 123 TWO SONGS        42 No more shall need of Love complain;
P. 128 O.C.            217 What prudence more than humane did he need
P. 153 INSTRUCTIONS    503 These can, at need, at instant, with a scrip,
P. 169 ADVICE           52 Five members need not be demanded here.
P. 174 LOYALL SCOT     110 From Church they need not Censure men Away,
P. 194 TWO HORSES      108 Letts be true to ourselves; whom then need wee
                           fear?
```

needful   frequency: 1   relative frequency: 0.0000
See also "needfull."
```
P. 155 INSTRUCTIONS    608 Now needful, does for Ammunition call.
```

needfull   frequency: 1   relative frequency: 0.0000
```
P.  19 THYRSIS          25 No Oat-pipe's needfull, there thine Ears
```

needles   frequency: 2   relative frequency: 0.0000
```
P.  62 A. HOUSE        123 'While all the rest with Needles paint
P.  84 FLECKNO          65 The Needles Eye thread without any stich,
```

needless   frequency: 2   relative frequency: 0.0000
```
P.  21 SOUL & BODY      15 And warms and moves this needless Frame:
P. 120 TWO SONGS        39 'Tis needless then that I refuse,
```

needs   frequency: 11   relative frequency: 0.0002
```
P.   4 HASTINGS         10 Needs must he die, that doth out-run his Age.
P.  31 FAIR SINGER      17 And all my Forces needs must be undone,
P.  60 A. HOUSE         61 And yet what needs there here Excuse,
```

```
P. 110 ANNIVERSARY    309 As thou must needs have own'd them of thy band
P. 112 ANNIVERSARY    367 'Needs must we all their Tributaries be,
P. 128 O.C.           193 In all his warrs needs must he triumph, when
P. 132 PARADISE        54 In Number, Weight, and Measure, needs not
                          Rhime.
P. 142 INSTRUCTIONS    41 He needs no Seal, but to St. James's lease,
P. 182 MADE FREE       72 Your Chamber must needs be undone.
P. 204 HISTORICALL    144 But Osborn and the Duke must needs prevail.
P. 313 CHEQUER INN     46 Therefore I needs must speake my Mind
```

needst   frequency: 1   relative frequency: 0.0000
```
P. 173 LOYALL SCOT     63 Skip Sadles: Pegasus thou needst not Bragg,
```

neer   frequency: 3   relative frequency: 0.0000
```
P.  22 NYMPH            4 To kill thee. Thou neer didst alive
P. 116 BLAKE           79 But this stupendious Prospect did not neer,
P. 118 BLAKE          137 Th' all-seeing Sun, neer gaz'd on such a sight,
```

ne'er   frequency: 5   relative frequency: 0.0001
    See also "neer," "neere," "ne'r," "nere,"
             "ne're."
```
P. 131 O.C.           320 Earth ne'er more glad, nor Heaven more serene.
P. 139 HOUSEWARMING    64 The Tribes ne'er contributed so to the Temple.
P. 139 HOUSEWARMING    75 But he swore that the Patent should ne'er be
                          revok'd;
P. 166 KINGS VOWES     28 I will have a fine Court with ne'er an old face,
P. 180 STOCKSMARKET    49 Sure the king will ne'er think of repaying his
                          bankers,
```

neere   frequency: 2   relative frequency: 0.0000
```
P. 177 LOYALL SCOT    235 Two Nations Neere had mist the Marke soe long.
P. 205 HISTORICALL    177 Had not Almighty Providence drawne neere,
```

neerest   frequency: 1   relative frequency: 0.0000
```
P.   5 HASTINGS        28 Secures his neerest and nost lov'd Ally;
```

neglect   frequency: 3   relative frequency: 0.0000
```
P.  66 A. HOUSE       226 Religion, but not Right neglect:
P. 128 O.C.           224 Spare yet your own, if you neglect his fame;
P. 155 INSTRUCTIONS   610 Confusion, folly, treach'ry, fear, neglect.
```

neglected   frequency: 2   relative frequency: 0.0000
```
P. 159 INSTRUCTIONS   774 And rifling Prizes, them neglected? Pett.
P. 178 LOYALL SCOT    268 The morning dews and flowers Neglected grown,
```

negligently   frequency: 1   relative frequency: 0.0000
```
P.  82 A. HOUSE       763 All negligently overthrown,
```

neighbor. See "neighbour."

neighborhood. See "neighbourhood," "neighbr'hood."

neighboring. See "neighbouring," "neighb'ring."

neighbors. See "neighbours."

neighbour   frequency: 4   relative frequency: 0.0000
```
P.  86 FLECKNO        132 But how I loath'd to see my Neighbour glean
P. 150 INSTRUCTIONS   384 Mounting the neighbour Couple on lean Jade.
P. 199 DUKE            48 Better some jealous neighbour of your owne
P. 314 CHEQUER INN     89 Did feed his Neighbour over-thwart
```

neighbour-ruine   frequency: 1   relative frequency: 0.0000
```
P.  61 A. HOUSE        87 And all that Neighbour-Ruine shows
```

neighbourhood   frequency: 1   relative frequency: 0.0000
```
P.  74 A. HOUSE       499 As if their Neighbourhood so old
```

neighbouring   frequency: 2   relative frequency: 0.0000
```
P. 116 BLAKE           90 And flank with Cannon from the Neighbouring
                          shore.
P. 173 LOYALL SCOT     73 Shall fix a foot on either neighbouring Shore
```

neighbours   frequency: 2   relative frequency: 0.0000
```
P. 150 INSTRUCTIONS   396 And our next neighbours France and Flanders
                          ride.
P. 182 MADE FREE       51 But molested the neighbours with Quarrells,
```

neighbr'hood   frequency: 1   relative frequency: 0.0000
```
P. 154 INSTRUCTIONS   567 The neighbr'hood ill, and an unwholesome seat.
```

neighb'ring   frequency: 1   relative frequency: 0.0000

P. 142 INSTRUCTIONS   71 Ye neighb'ring Elms, that your green leaves did
                          shed,

neighings   frequency: 1   relative frequency: 0.0000
    P. 108 ANNIVERSARY   200 And with shrill Neighings ask'd him of the
                             Wood.

neither   frequency: 16   relative frequency: 0.0003
    P. 19 THYRSIS   21 Thyrsis. Oh, ther's, neither hope nor fear
    P. 33 DAPHNIS   7 But she neither knew t'enjoy,
    P. 46 AMETAS   8 Neither Love will twist nor Hay.
    P. 64 A. HOUSE   188 'Yet Neither should be left behind.
    P. 65 A. HOUSE   196 'The Tryal neither Costs, nor Tyes.
    P. 91 MAY'S DEATH   29 But Ben, who knew not neither foe nor friend,
    P. 95 DR. WITTY   40 That handling neither sully nor would guild.
    P. 104 ANNIVERSARY   33 They neither build the Temple in their dayes,
    P. 109 ANNIVERSARY   229 For, neither didst thou from the first apply
    P. 112 ANNIVERSARY   372 'Can quickly leave us neither Earth nor Air.
    P. 115 BLAKE   58 Neither the Soyl, nor People quiet know.
    P. 118 BLAKE   139 And neither have, or power, or will to fly,
    P. 125 O.C.   86 Not love, not grieve, would neither live nor
                             reign:
    P. 130 O.C.   301 And lost in tears, have neither sight nor mind
    P. 141 INSTRUCTIONS   31 Him neither Wit nor Courage did exalt,
    P. 175 LOYALL SCOT   161 Neither before to trust him nor behind.

nell   frequency: 1   relative frequency: 0.0000
    P. 168 KINGS VOWES   66 And Visit Nell when I shold be att Prayers.

nells   frequency: 2   relative frequency: 0.0000
    P. 182 MADE FREE   54 To his Cleavelands, his Nells and his
                             Carwells.
    P. 189 BRITANNIA   169 Teach 'em to scorn the Carwells, Pembrookes,
                             Nells,

neptune   frequency: 3   relative frequency: 0.0000
    P. 99 HOLLAND   149 For while our Neptune doth a Trident shake,
    P. 154 INSTRUCTIONS 543 Old Neptune springs the Tydes, and Water lent:
    P. 159 INSTRUCTIONS 749 And Father Neptune promis'd to resign

ne'r   frequency: 4   relative frequency: 0.0000
    P. 37 DEFINITION   7 Where feeble Hope could ne'r have flown
    P. 55 THYESTE   13 Into his own Heart ne'r pry's,
    P. 117 BLAKE   129 Nature ne'r made Cedars so high aspire,
    P. 146 INSTRUCTIONS 241 A scatter'd Body, which the Foe ne'r try'd,

nere   frequency: 5   relative frequency: 0.0001
    P. 198 DUKE   21 I nere can fight in a more glorious Cause
    P. 199 DUKE   69 But nere can make a piller for a church;
    P. 200 DUKE   90 Ten thousand such as these can nere controule
    P. 200 DUKE   116 Hard fate of princes, who will nere believe,
    P. 200 DUKE   117 Till the stroke is struck which they can nere
                             repreive.

ne're   frequency: 10   relative frequency: 0.0002
    P. 160 INSTRUCTIONS 796 Powder ne're blew man up so soon so high.
    P. 160 INSTRUCTIONS 815 And thinks 'twill ne're be well within this
                             Nation,
    P. 181 MADE FREE   25 He ne're knew not he
    P. 182 MADE FREE   42 As if he shou'd ne're see an end on't.
    P. 185 BRITANNIA   27 Such slimy Monsters ne're approacht a throne
    P. 192 TWO HORSES   17 But they that faith Cathclick ne're understood,
    P. 192 TWO HORSES   19 Those Idolls ne're speak, but the miracle 's
                             done
    P. 194 TWO HORSES   103 Tho' the beast gave his Master ne're an ill
                             word,
    P. 194 TWO HORSES   122 Ch. Thy King will ne're fight unless't be for
                             Queans.
    P. 312 CHEQUER INN   4 But such a Choyce as ne're was found

nero   frequency: 1   relative frequency: 0.0000
    P. 195 TWO HORSES   134 I had rather Bare Nero than Sardanapalus.

nero's   frequency: 1   relative frequency: 0.0000
    P. 86 FLECKNO   126 Then Nero's Poem he calls charity:

nerves   frequency: 1   relative frequency: 0.0000
    P. 20 SOUL & BODY   8 Of Nerves, and Arteries, and Veins.

nest   frequency: 5   relative frequency: 0.0001
    P. 19 THYRSIS   13 Dorinda. There Birds may nest, but how can I,

```
P.  54 THYESTE         4 Settled in some secret Nest
P.  59 A. HOUSE       12 And Birds contrive an equal Nest;
P.  98 HOLLAND       130 Till the dear Halcyon hatch out all its nest.
P. 112 ANNIVERSARY   359 'Of floting Islands a new Hatched Nest;
```

nestles   frequency: 1   relative frequency: 0.0000
```
P. 137 HOUSEWARMING   8 And nestles in flames like the Salamander.
```

net   frequency: 2   relative frequency: 0.0000
```
P.  88 ODE            50 He wove a Net of such a scope,
P. 160 INSTRUCTIONS  783 Who all our Ships expos'd in Chathams Net?
```

never   frequency: 56   relative frequency: 0.0011
See also "neer," "ne'er," "neere," "ne'r,"
         "nere," "ne're."
```
P.    4 HASTINGS        2 Whose Virgin-Source yet never steept the Plain.
P.    4 HASTINGS        4 Of Tears untoucht, and never wept before.
P.   14 THE CORONET    12 As never yet the king of Glory wore:
P.   19 THYRSIS         6 Thyrsis. A Chast Soul, can never mis't.
P.   21 SOUL & BODY    19 A Body that could never rest,
P.   21 SOUL & BODY    31 But Physick yet could never reach
P.   22 NYMPH           7 I'me sure I never wisht them ill;
P.   33 DAPHNIS        26 Words she never spake before;
P.   37 DEFINITION     28 Though infinite can never meet.
P.   42 DAMON          17 This heat the Sun could never raise,
P.   45 GLO-WORMS      16 That I shall never find my home.
P.   55 EPITAPH         5 Where never any could speak ill,
P.   69 A. HOUSE      329 Unhappy! shall we never more
P.   78 A. HOUSE      612 That I may never leave this Place:
P.   84 FLECKNO        49 He never feeds; save only when he tryes
P.   85 FLECKNO        92 I whom the Pallace never has deny'd
P.   97 HOLLAND        63 Faith, that could never Twins conceive before,
P.   97 HOLLAND        64 Never so fertile, spawn'd upon this shore:
P.   97 HOLLAND        84 But surely never any that was so.
P.  103 ANNIVERSARY    22 For one Thing never was by one King don.
P.  107 ANNIVERSARY   166 But never any did them Honor so;
P.  114 BLAKE          30 Fertile to be, yet never need her showres.
P.  114 BLAKE          37 And coolness there, with heat doth never fight,
P.  115 BLAKE          69 Never so many with one joyful cry,
P.  117 BLAKE         123 Never so burning was that Climate known,
P.  121 TWO SONGS       2 Never such a merry day.
P.  121 TWO SONGS      55 For he did never love to pair
P.  125 O.C.          109 But never yet was any humane Fate
P.  128 O.C.          196 Yet him the adverse steel could never pierce.
P.  128 O.C.          207 More strong affections never reason serv'd,
P.  132 PARADISE       40 So never Flags, but alwaies keeps on Wing.
P.  139 HOUSEWARMING   71 Since the Act of Oblivion was never such
                          selling,
P.  139 HOUSEWARMING   96 And till there you remove, you shall never leave
                          burning
P.  141 INSTRUCTIONS   36 For never Bacon study'd Nature more.
P.  146 INSTRUCTIONS  219 Never, before nor since, an Host so steel'd
P.  149 INSTRUCTIONS  327 And the lov'd King, and never yet deny'd,
P.  152 INSTRUCTIONS  473 Never old Letcher more repugnance felt,
P.  153 INSTRUCTIONS  526 And Beauties e're this never naked seen.
P.  154 INSTRUCTIONS  569 And swore that he would never more dwell there
P.  174 LOYALL SCOT    93 Never shall Calvin Pardoned bee for Sales,
P.  174 LOYALL SCOT    94 Never for Burnetts sake the Lauderdales,
P.  177 LOYALL SCOT   218 'Tis necessary Lambeth never wed,
P.  180 STOCKSMARKET   55 But alas! he will never arrive at his end,
P.  182 MADE FREE      50 He never wou'd cease
P.  184 MADE FREE     113 He could never be true
P.  184 MADE FREE     123 Never think in England to swagger,
P.  185 BRITANNIA      13 I stole away; and never will return
P.  190 STATUE         11 And soe near to the Court they will never indure
P.  190 STATUE         34 Such things you should never or Suddainly doe.
P.  195 TWO HORSES    154 W. His perfum'd predecessor was never much
                          fitter.
P.  195 TWO HORSES    156 W. For that very reason hee 's never to rise.
P.  198 DUKE           13 A vow that fire and sword shall never end
P.  200 DUKE           94 Its steady Basis never could bee shooke,
P.  203 HISTORICALL    99 And never durst their tricks above board shew.
P.  314 CHEQUER INN    81 (His Cup he never failes)
P.  316 CHEQUER INN   143 The Reck'ning never will be paid
```

nevill   frequency: 1   relative frequency: 0.0000
```
P. 315 CHEQUER INN   110 Throgmorton, Nevill, Doleman were
```

neville. See "nevill."

new   frequency: 59   relative frequency: 0.0012

P.	10	DIALOGUE	49	Then persevere: for still new Charges sound:
P.	11	DIALOGUE	60	And want new Worlds to buy.
P.	12	DROP OF DEW	4	Yet careless of its Mansion new;
P.	32	MOURNING	28	At the installing of a new.
P.	37	DEFINITION	22	And Earth some new Convulsion tear;
P.	41	THE MOWER	17	Another World was search'd, through Oceans new,
P.	47	EMPIRE	11	From whence the Progeny of numbers new
P.	50	THE GARDEN	66	Of flow'rs and herbes this Dial new;
P.	56	BILL-BOROW	14	Nature must a new Center find,
P.	61	A. HOUSE	68	Daily new Furniture of Friends.
P.	68	A. HOUSE	296	And fills its Flask with Odours new.
P.	72	A. HOUSE	419	In whose new Traverse seemeth wrought
P.	72	A. HOUSE	442	A new and empty Face of things;
P.	78	A. HOUSE	629	No Serpent new nor Crocodile
P.	86	FLECKNO	113	During the Table; though my new made Friend
P.	96	HOLLAND	33	Or as they over the new Level rang'd
P.	98	HOLLAND	118	Our sore new circumcised Common wealth.
P.	103	ANNIVERSARY	11	Cromwell alone doth with new Lustre spring,
P.	104	ANNIVERSARY	55	No Note he struck, but a new Story lay'd,
P.	104	ANNIVERSARY	58	And still new Stopps to various Time apply'd:
P.	107	ANNIVERSARY	157	Hence landing Nature to new Seas is tost,
P.	109	ANNIVERSARY	247	Here pulling down, and there erecting New,
P.	110	ANNIVERSARY	297	That their new King might the fifth Scepter shake,
P.	111	ANNIVERSARY	325	So when first Man did through the Morning new
P.	112	ANNIVERSARY	359	'Of floting Islands a new Hatched Nest;
P.	113	BLAKE	2	Leaves the new World and hastens for the old:
P.	113	BLAKE	9	The new Worlds wounded Intrails they had tore,
P.	122	TWO SONGS	23	Nor our Sheep new Wash'd can be
P.	122	TWO SONGS	27	Come, lets in some Carol new
P.	124	O.C.	38	And ev'ry minute adds a Lustre new;
P.	124	O.C.	59	No trembling String compos'd to numbers new,
P.	141	INSTRUCTIONS	17	Where, like the new Controller, all men laugh
P.	141	INSTRUCTIONS	30	The new Courts pattern, Stallion of the old.
P.	143	INSTRUCTIONS	82	Discern'd Love's Cause, and a new Flame began.
P.	144	INSTRUCTIONS	150	Could raise so long for this new Whore of State.
P.	147	INSTRUCTIONS	254	And to new edge their angry Courage grind.
P.	149	INSTRUCTIONS	355	See how he Reigns in his new Palace culminant,
P.	150	INSTRUCTIONS	372	To forge new Thunder, and inspect their Fires.
P.	150	INSTRUCTIONS	374	All to new Sports their wanton fears release.
P.	150	INSTRUCTIONS	394	The Joys of State, for the new Peace and Tax.
P.	151	INSTRUCTIONS	422	But Mordant new oblig'd, would sure be just.
P.	153	INSTRUCTIONS	534	And his new Face looks in the English Wave.
P.	155	INSTRUCTIONS	598	To be Spectators safe of the new Play,
P.	160	INSTRUCTIONS	818	The Peace not sure, new Army must be paid.
P.	161	INSTRUCTIONS	838	With Face new bleacht, smoothen'd and stiff with starch.
P.	161	INSTRUCTIONS	852	Lest some new Tomkins spring a fresh debate.
P.	166	KINGS VOWES	22	I will have a new London instead of the old,
P.	167	KINGS VOWES	56	And new Ones Create Great Places to supplye,
P.	168	ADVICE	25	Their new made Band of Pentioners
P.	169	ADVICE	46	And add new Beams to Sands's former Glory.
P.	174	LOYALL SCOT	83	Or what new perpendicular doth rise
P.	183	MADE FREE	107	A new Duke to choose,
P.	186	BRITANNIA	82	If not ore aw'd by new found holy cheat.
P.	187	BRITANNIA	103	Rack nature till new pleasures she shall find,
P.	190	STATUE	37	Let's have a King then, be he new be old;
P.	199	DUKE	45	Preserv'd in store for the new sett of maids.
P.	201	HISTORICALL	34	The new got flemish Towne was sett to sale.
P.	205	HISTORICALL	156	And brought new Lessons to the Duke from Rome.
P.	313	CHEQUER INN	9	There stands a House new Painted

new-born   frequency: 1   relative frequency: 0.0000
    P. 80 A. HOUSE   683 No new-born Comet such a Train

new-catched   frequency: 1   relative frequency: 0.0000
    P. 96 HOLLAND   18 Thorough the Center their new-catched Miles;

new-made   frequency: 1   relative frequency: 0.0000
    P. 72 A. HOUSE   432 Their new-made Hay not sweeter is.

new-slain   frequency: 1   relative frequency: 0.0000
    P. 80 A. HOUSE   684 Draws through the Skie, nor Star new-slain.

newcastle's   frequency: 1   relative frequency: 0.0000
    P. 142 INSTRUCTIONS 50 Philosopher beyond Newcastle's Wife.

newly   frequency: 4   relative frequency: 0.0000
    P. 72 A. HOUSE   420 A Camp of Battail newly fought:
    P. 78 A. HOUSE   628 Seems as green Silks but newly washt.

P. 156 INSTRUCTIONS 650 The early Down but newly did begin;
P. 172 LOYALL SCOT   16 The Early down but newly did begin,

news   frequency: 9   relative frequency: 0.0001
P. 33 DAPHNIS   9 But, with this sad News surpriz'd,
P. 116 BLAKE   81 For here they met with news, which did produce,
P. 119 BLAKE   164 And there first brings of his success the news;
P. 119 BLAKE   165 The saddest news that ere to Spain was brought,
P. 150 INSTRUCTIONS   376 Comes news of Pastime, Martial and old:
P. 150 INSTRUCTIONS   397 But a fresh News, the great designment nips,
P. 151 INSTRUCTIONS   411 Fresh Messengers still the sad News assure,
P. 159 INSTRUCTIONS   775 Who with false News prevented the Gazette?
P. 161 INSTRUCTIONS   849 Mean while the certain News of Peace arrives

news-books   frequency: 1   relative frequency: 0.0000
P. 195 TWO HORSES   152 W. And our Sir Joseph write news-bocks, and
                          fiddle.

next   frequency: 28   relative frequency: 0.0005
P. 71 A. HOUSE   388 The tawny Mowers enter next;
P. 89 ODE   94 But on the next green Bow to pearch;
P. 97 HOLLAND   56 Came next in order; which they could not miss.
P. 103 ANNIVERSARY   9 And still the Day which he doth next restore,
P. 140 HOUSEWARMING   112 He comes to be roasted next St. James's Fair.
P. 143 INSTRUCTIONS   105 Draw next a Pair of Tables op'ning, then
P. 144 INSTRUCTIONS   155 Of the old Courtiers next a Squadron came,
P. 145 INSTRUCTIONS   169 Court-Officers, as us'd, the next place took,
P. 145 INSTRUCTIONS   181 C-------n advances next, whose Coife dos awe
P. 145 INSTRUCTIONS   185 Next th' Lawyers Mercenary Band appear:
P. 146 INSTRUCTIONS   207 Bold Duncombe next, of the Projectors chief:
P. 147 INSTRUCTIONS   259 Keen Whorwood next, in aid of Damsel frail,
P. 149 INSTRUCTIONS   359 Next the Twelve Commons are condemn'd to groan,
P. 150 INSTRUCTIONS   383 But the just Street does the next House invade,
P. 150 INSTRUCTIONS   396 And our next neighbours France and Flanders
                          ride.
P. 150 INSTRUCTIONS   404 The next divided, and the third we've none.
P. 151 INSTRUCTIONS   449 Two Letters next unto Breda are sent,
P. 163 INSTRUCTIONS   907 Express him startling next with listning ear,
P. 166 KINGS VOWES   29 And allwayes who beards me shall have the next
                          Grace,
P. 168 ADVICE   11 Then change the scene and let the next present
P. 168 ADVICE   29 Change once again and let the next afford
P. 169 ADVICE   47 Draw our Olimpia next in Councell Sate
P. 191 STATUE   52 As would the next tax reimburse them with use.
P. 198 DUKE   36 Next, Painter, draw his Mordant by his side,
P. 200 DUKE   86 Next, Painter, draw the Rabble of the plott,
P. 314 CHEQUER INN   67 Wheeler at Board, then next her set,
P. 314 CHEQUER INN   79 And next him sate George Mountague
P. 315 CHEQUER INN   124 And wisely lodging at next Doore

nice   frequency: 3   relative frequency: 0.0000
P. 64 A. HOUSE   169 'Nor is our Order yet so nice,
P. 177 LOYALL SCOT   242 The Tryell would however bee too nice
P. 191 STATUE   41 The Huswifely Treasuress sure is grown nice

niceness   frequency: 1   relative frequency: 0.0000
P. 33 DAPHNIS   10 Soon she let that Niceness fall;

nicest   frequency: 1   relative frequency: 0.0000
P. 39 THE MATCH   10 But with the nicest care;

nigh   frequency: 3   relative frequency: 0.0000
P. 30 THE GALLERY   35 The Halcyons, calming all that's nigh,
P. 81 A. HOUSE   725 Where not one cbject can come nigh
P. 195 TWO HORSES   159 Ch. Then, England, Rejoyce, thy Redemption
                          draws nigh; .

night   frequency: 39   relative frequency: 0.0008
See also "summer-night."
P. 16 EYES   43 And Stars shew lovely in the Night,
P. 17 BERMUDAS   18 Like golden Lamps in a green Night.
P. 27 LOVER   6 Like Meteors of a Summers night;
P. 36 DAPHNIS   102 Last night he with Phlogis slept;
P. 36 DAPHNIS   103 This night for Dorinda kept;
P. 44 GLO-WORMS   11 That in the Night have lost their aim,
P. 55 EPITAPH   18 Gentle as Ev'ning; cool as Night;
P. 57 BILL-BOROW   31 By Night the Northern Star their way
P. 64 A. HOUSE   185 'Each Night among us to your side
P. 64 A. HOUSE   191 'All Night embracing Arm in Arm,
P. 65 A. HOUSE   220 'When they it think by Night conceal'd.
P. 74 A. HOUSE   504 As if the Night within were hedg'd.

```
P.  79 A. HOUSE        651 The young Maria walks to night:
P.  79 A. HOUSE        670 Flying betwixt the Day and Night;
P.  90 ODE             118 The Spirits of the shady Night,
P. 111 ANNIVERSARY     336 Not knowing yet the Night was made for sleep:
P. 111 ANNIVERSARY     344 Seem'd now a long and gloomy Night to threat,
P. 114 BLAKE            38 This only rules by day, and that by Night.
P. 117 BLAKE           120 And though it be at Noon, creates a Night.
P. 119 TWO SONGS         6 Thorough the clear and silent Night.
P. 120 TWO SONGS        23 My wakeful Lamp all night must move,
P. 120 TWO SONGS        26 Can make a Night more bright then Day;
P. 124 O.C.             58 Repeated over to the restless Night.
P. 126 O.C.            136 As silent Suns to meet the Night descend.
P. 142 INSTRUCTIONS     69 Witness ye stars of Night, and thou the pale
P. 144 INSTRUCTIONS    140 And flies like Batts with leathern Wings by
                           Night.
P. 146 INSTRUCTIONS    243 And some ran o're each night while others sleep,
P. 147 INSTRUCTIONS    245 But Strangeways, that all Night still walk'd
                           the round,
P. 149 INSTRUCTIONS    346 But blooms all Night, and shoots its branches
                           high.
P. 156 INSTRUCTIONS    655 Oft has he in chill Eske or Seine, by night,
P. 159 INSTRUCTIONS    742 Fill up thy space with a redoubled Night.
P. 162 INSTRUCTIONS    883 At night, than Canticleer more brisk and hot,
P. 162 INSTRUCTIONS    885 Paint last the King, and a dead Shade of
                           Night,
P. 163 INSTRUCTIONS    925 The wondrous Night the pensive King revolves,
P. 172 LOYALL SCOT      21 Oft as hee in Chill Eske or Seyne by night
P. 184 BRITANNIA        11 Brit: Favour'd by night, conceald by this
                           disguise,
P. 192 TWO HORSES       30 One night came togeather by all is agreed,
P. 194 TWO HORSES      113 In every dark night you are sure to find him
P. 201 HISTORICALL      16 His jolly Vassalls treat him day and Night.
```

```
night-mard                       frequency:    1    relative frequency: 0.0000
   P. 188 BRITANNIA    129 Thus the state's night-Mard by this Hellish rout
```

```
nightingale                      frequency:    2    relative frequency: 0.0000
   P.  44 GLO-WORMS      2 The Nightingale does sit so late,
   P.  75 A. HOUSE     513 The Nightingale does here make choice
```

```
nightly                          frequency:    1    relative frequency: 0.0000
   P. 142 INSTRUCTIONS  77 And nightly hears the hated Guards away
```

```
nightmarred.  See "night-mard."
```

```
nights                           frequency:    3    relative frequency: 0.0000
   P. 106 ANNIVERSARY  127 And in dark Nights, and in cold Dayes alone
   P. 112 ANNIVERSARY  377 'Him, all the Day, Him, in late Nights I
                           dread,
   P. 181 MADE FREE     34 And wasts all his Nights
```

```
nile                             frequency:    1    relative frequency: 0.0000
   P.  78 A. HOUSE     630 Remains behind our little Nile;
```

```
nimbler                          frequency:    1    relative frequency: 0.0000
   P.  23 NYMPH         69 For it was nimbler much than Hindes;
```

```
nimph                            frequency:    2    relative frequency: 0.0000
   P.  19 THYRSIS       15 Thyrsis. Do not sigh (fair Nimph) for fire
   P.  38 PICTURE        2 This Nimph begins her golden daies!
```

```
nimph's                          frequency:    1    relative frequency: 0.0000
   P.  20 THYRSIS       38 And every Nimph's a Queen of May.
```

```
nip                              frequency:    1    relative frequency: 0.0000
   P.  39 PICTURE       40 Nip in the blossome all our hopes and Thee.
```

```
nips                             frequency:    1    relative frequency: 0.0000
   P. 150 INSTRUCTIONS 397 But a fresh News, the great designment nips,
```

```
nitre                            frequency:    1    relative frequency: 0.0000
   P.  40 THE MATCH     22 With Nitre thrice refin'd;
```

```
no                               frequency:  108    relative frequency: 0.0022
   See also "noe."
```

```
noah's                           frequency:    1    relative frequency: 0.0000
   P. 110 ANNIVERSARY  283 Thou, and thine House, like Noah's Eight did
                           rest,
```

```
nobility                         frequency:    1    relative frequency: 0.0000
```

P. 167 KINGS VOWES   55 The Antient Nobility I will lay by,

noble   frequency: 8   relative frequency: 0.0001
    P.   3 LOVELACE   t1 To his Noble Friend Mr. Richard Lovelace,
    P. 108 ANNIVERSARY   191 But the poor Beasts wanting their noble Guide,
    P. 114 BLAKE   29 O noble Trust which Heaven on this Isle
                              poures,
    P. 123 O.C.   8 Death when more horrid so more noble deem;
    P. 138 HOUSEWARMING   58 He should dwell more noble, and cheap too
                              at-home,
    P. 178 LOYALL SCOT   275 Thy death more noble did the same Extort.
    P. 188 BRITANNIA   161 Till then, my Rawleigh, teach our noble Youth
    P. 198 DUKE   17 And by a noble well contrived plott,

nobler   frequency: 1   relative frequency: 0.0000
    P. 123 O.C.   22 (Those nobler weaknesses of humane Mind,

noblest   frequency: 2   relative frequency: 0.0000
    P.   16 EYES   46 And practise so your noblest Use.
    P. 117 BLAKE   116 The noblest wreaths, that Victory bestows.

nobly   frequency: 1   relative frequency: 0.0000
    P. 148 INSTRUCTIONS   287 A Gross of English Gentry, nobly born,

nodle   frequency: 1   relative frequency: 0.0000
    P. 176 LOYALL SCOT   193 The Bishops Nodle Perks up cheek by Jowle.

noe   frequency: 21   relative frequency: 0.0004

noise   frequency: 6   relative frequency: 0.0001
    See also "noyse."
    P.   47 EMPIRE   18 Did of all these a solemn noise prepare:
    P.   55 THYESTE   8 Thus when without noise, unknown,
    P. 126 O.C.   135 He without noise still travell'd to his End,
    P. 151 INSTRUCTIONS   429 How yet the Hollanders do make a noise,
    P. 163 INSTRUCTIONS   908 As one that some unusual noise does hear.
    P. 176 LOYALL SCOT   200 Hark! tho' at such a Distance what a Noise

noll   frequency: 1   relative frequency: 0.0000
    P. 195 TWO HORSES   138 W. I freely declare it, I am for old Noll.

none   frequency: 35   relative frequency: 0.0007
    P.   5 HASTINGS   23 But 'tis a Maxime of that State, That none,
    P.   10 DIALOGUE   33 But since none deserves that grace,
    P.   10 DIALOGUE   43 Cease Tempter. None can chain a mind
    P.   11 DIALOGUE   73 None thither mounts by the degree
    P.   26 MISTRESS   32 But none I think do there embrace.
    P.   40 THE MATCH   35 None ever burn'd so hot, so bright;
    P.   68 A. HOUSE   301 None for the Virgin Nymph; for She
    P.   70 A. HOUSE   379 As, under Water, none does know
    P. 105 ANNIVERSARY   81 None to be sunk in the Foundation bends,
    P. 106 ANNIVERSARY   137 Sure, the mysterious Work, where none withstand,
    P. 107 ANNIVERSARY   165 Though none does of more lasting Parents grow,
    P. 121 TWO SONGS   49 That Cave is dark. Endymion. Then none can
                              spy:
    P. 123 O.C.   13 But long his Valour none had left that could
    P. 124 O.C.   51 Hold fast dear Infants, hold them both or none;
    P. 124 O.C.   66 Or on their own redoubled, none can tell.
    P. 127 O.C.   157 O Cromwell, Heavens Favorite! To none
    P. 128 O.C.   195 Hence, though in battle none so brave or fierce,
    P. 131 PARADISE   25 But I am now convinc'd, and none will dare
    P. 138 HOUSEWARMING   30 None sollid enough seem'd for his Thong Caster;
    P. 146 INSTRUCTIONS   205 The Papists, but of those the House had none:
    P. 150 INSTRUCTIONS   404 The next divided, and the third we've none.
    P. 151 INSTRUCTIONS   426 Orders, amaz'd at last gives none at all.
    P. 152 INSTRUCTIONS   468 None but himself must chuse the King a Queen.)
    P. 158 INSTRUCTIONS   701 Of all our Navy none should now survive,
    P. 160 INSTRUCTIONS   787 Had he not built, none of these faults had bin;
    P. 165 KINGS VOWES   9 But if it grow troublesome, I will have none.
    P. 168 ADVICE   27 And of his dear Reward let none dispair,
    P. 175 LOYALL SCOT   150 None knows what god our Flamen now Adores;
    P. 178 LOYALL SCOT   270 Powders them ore till none discern their foes
    P. 188 BRITANNIA   130 And none are left these furyes to cast out.
    P. 192 TWO HORSES   44 And the Kings wicked life say God there is
                              none;
    P. 195 TWO HORSES   150 None ever Reign'd like old Besse in the Ruffe.
    P. 202 HISTORICALL   68 In Loves delights none did him ere excell
    P. 314 CHEQUER INN   60 None went away unhir'd.
    P. 315 CHEQUER INN   121 Yet wot'st thou he was none of those

noodle. See "nodle."

noon   frequency: 2   relative frequency: 0.0000

```
      P.  43 DAMON            45 And, if at Noor my toil me heat,
      P. 117 BLAKE           120 And though it be at Noon, creates a Night.
```

nor   frequency: 133   relative frequency: 0.0027

norfolk   frequency: 1   relative frequency: 0.0000
```
      P. 162 INSTRUCTIONS    882 And soaks his Sack with Norfolk like a Toast.
```

north   frequency: 1   relative frequency: 0.0000
```
      P. 158 INSTRUCTIONS    717 Furrs from the North, and Silver from the
                                 West,
```

northern   frequency: 2   relative frequency: 0.0000
```
      P.  57 BILL-BOROW       31 By Night the Northern Star their way
      P. 121 TWO SONGS         3 For the Northern Shepheards Son.
```

nose   frequency: 4   relative frequency: 0.0000
See also "cut-nose."
```
      P. 148 INSTRUCTIONS    302 St. Dunstan in it, tweaking Satan's Nose.
      P. 166 KINGS VOWES      41 I'll order my Eravo's to cutt off his Nose,
      P. 169 ADVICE           38 The humble fate of a Plebeian nose;
      P. 202 HISTORICALL      64 The poore Priapus King led by the Nose
```

nostradamus's   frequency: 1   relative frequency: 0.0000
```
      P. 170 PROPHECY          t Nostradamus's Prophecy.
```

nostrils   frequency: 3   relative frequency: 0.0000
```
      P.  97 HOLLAND          92 Fills the Priests Nostrils and puts out his
                                 Eyes.
      P. 108 ANNIVERSARY     197 Nor through wide Nostrils snuffe the wanton air,
      P. 140 HOUSEWARMING     99 And to handsel his Altar and Nostrils divine,
```

not   frequency: 226   relative frequency: 0.0047

note   frequency: 7   relative frequency: 0.0001
```
      P.   5 HASTINGS         43 Onely they drooping Hymeneus note,
      P.  18 BERMUDAS         38 An holy and a chearful Note,
      P.  18 CLORINDA         24 C. Sweet must Pan sound in Damons Note.
      P.  71 A. HOUSE        415 Death-Trumpets creak in such a Note,
      P. 104 ANNIVERSARY      55 No Note he struck, but a new Story lay'd,
      P. 143 INSTRUCTIONS      97 But envious Fame, too soon, begun to note
      P. 163 INSTRUCTIONS     937 His Fathers Ghost too whisper'd him one Note,
```

notes   frequency: 5   relative frequency: 0.0001
```
      P.  47 EMPIRE            5 Jubal first made the wilder Notes agree;
      P. 105 ANNIVERSARY      63 But, for he most the graver Notes did try,
      P. 124 O.C.             60 Answers the touch in Notes more sad more true.
      P. 129 O.C.            246 Nor with soft notes shall sing his cares asleep.
      P. 185 BRITANNIA        43 In Lofty Notes Tudors blest reign to sing,
```

nothing   frequency: 18   relative frequency: 0.0003
```
      P.  22 NYMPH            15 And nothing may we use in vain.
      P.  60 A. HOUSE         63 Where neatness nothing can condemn,
      P.  80 A. HOUSE        693 Nothing could make the River be
      P.  84 FLECKNO          57 And Silent. Nothing now Dinner stay'd
      P.  88 ODE              57 He nothing common did or mean
      P.  94 DR. WITTY        35 And so disliking, that they nothing see
      P.  99 HOLLAND         145 For now of nothing may our State despair,
      P. 107 ANNIVERSARY     149 But Men alas, as if they nothing car'd,
      P. 114 BLAKE            41 And these want nothing Heaven can afford,
      P. 127 O.C.            182 And fearing God how they should nothing fear.
      P. 129 O.C.            245 Francisca faire can nothing now but weep,
      P. 144 INSTRUCTIONS    147 Say Muse, for nothing can escape thy sight,
      P. 153 INSTRUCTIONS    513 If they for nothing ill, like Ashen-wood,
      P. 153 INSTRUCTIONS    514 Or think him, like Herb-John, for nothing good.
      P. 158 INSTRUCTIONS    723 Now (nothing more at Chatham left to burn)
      P. 174 LOYALL SCOT      89 Nothing but Clergie cold us two seclude:
      P. 174 LOYALL SCOT      98 Nothing, not Boggs, not Sands, not seas, not
                                 Alpes
      P. 204 HISTORICALL     131 Nothing the dire Contagion can opose.
```

notions   frequency: 1   relative frequency: 0.0000
```
      P. 198 DUKE             34 Ile have these villains in our notions rest;
```

notwithstanding   frequency: 1   relative frequency: 0.0000
```
      P. 182 MADE FREE        70 That Notwithstanding the Care
```

nought   frequency: 3   relative frequency: 0.0000
```
      P.  11 DIALOGUE         62 And that 's worth nought that can be sold.
      P. 146 INSTRUCTIONS    226 For one had much, the other nought to lose.
      P. 317 CHEQUER INN     188 Parli'ments grow nought as they grow old
```

nourisht   frequency: 1   relative frequency: 0.0000
   P. 202 HISTORICALL   39 Pride nourisht folly, folly a Delight

novice   frequency: 1   relative frequency: 0.0000
   P.   91 MAY'S DEATH   43 Go seek the novice Statesmen, and obtrude

now   frequency: 149   relative frequency: 0.0031
   P.   3 LOVELACE   11 These vertues now are banisht out of Towne,
   P.   9 DIALOGUE   1 Courage my Soul, now learn to wield
   P.   9 DIALOGUE   7 Now, if thou bee'st that thing Divine,
   P.   14 THE CORONET   9 And now when I have summ'd up all my store,
   P.   16 EYES   49 Now like two Clouds dissolving, drop,
   P.   16 EYES   51 Now like two Fountains trickle down:
   P.   16 EYES   52 Now like two floods o'return and drown.
   P.   20 THYRSIS   41 Convince me now, that this is true;
   P.   24 NYMPH   105 Now my Sweet Faun is vanish'd to
   P.   25 YOUNG LOVE   1 Come little Infant, Love me now,
   P.   25 YOUNG LOVE   17 Now then love me: time may take
   P.   26 YOUNG LOVE   30 Now I crown thee with my Love:
   P.   27 MISTRESS   33 Now therefore, while the youthful hew
   P.   27 MISTRESS   37 Now let us sport us while we may;
   P.   27 MISTRESS   38 And now, like am'rous birds of prey,
   P.   28 LOVER   41 And now, when angry Heaven wou'd
   P.   29 THE GALLERY   3 Now all its several lodgings lye
   P.   32 MOURNING   22 Joy now so much her Master grown,
   P.   33 DAPHNIS   2 Now is come the dismal Hour
   P.   34 DAPHNIS   30 Now the latest minut's run
   P.   35 DAPHNIS   57 But I will not now begin
   P.   41 THE MOWER   23 No Plant now knew the Stock from which it came;
   P.   42 DAMON   16 Now glitters in its second skin.
   P.   43 DAMON   67 But now I all the day complain,
   P.   45 MOWER'S SONG 20 Shall now by my Revenge be wrought:
   P.   46 MOWER'S SONG 27 Shall now the Heraldry become
   P.   58 BILL-BOROW   57 Yet now no further strive to shoot,
   P.   63 A. HOUSE   157 'Our Abbess too, now far in Age,
   P.   65 A. HOUSE   197 Now Fairfax seek her promis'd faith:
   P.   67 A. HOUSE   280 'Twas no Religious House till now.
   P.   70 A. HOUSE   369 And now to the Abbyss I pass
   P.   71 A. HOUSE   407 But now, to make his saying true,
   P.   71 A. HOUSE   413 And now your Orphan Parents Call
   P.   72 A. HOUSE   418 The Mower now commands the Field;
   P.   72 A. HOUSE   425 And now the careless Victors play,
   P.   73 A. HOUSE   474 How Eels now bellow in the Ox;
   P.   76 A. HOUSE   563 And little now to make me, wants
   P.   78 A. HOUSE   625 For now the Waves are fal'n and dry'd,
   P.   78 A. HOUSE   626 And now the Meadows fresher dy'd;
   P.   79 A. HOUSE   649 But now away my Hooks, my Quills,
   P.   81 A. HOUSE   729 Go now fond Sex that on your Face
   P.   82 A. HOUSE   754 Shall now be scorn'd as obsolete;
   P.   83 A. HOUSE   769 But now the Salmon-Fishers moist
   P.   83 A. HOUSE   776 Does now like one of them appear.
   P.   83 FLECKNO   23 But I, who now imagin'd my self brought
   P.   84 FLECKNO   37 Now as two Instruments, to the same key
   P.   84 FLECKNO   45 I, that perceiv'd now what his Musick ment,
   P.   84 FLECKNO   57 And Silent. Nothing now Dinner stay'd
   P.   85 FLECKNO   83 He drest, and ready to disfurnish now
   P.   86 FLECKNO   117 But now, Alas, my first Tormentor came,
   P.   86 FLECKNO   141 But all his praises could not now appease
   P.   86 FLECKNO   154 Should know the contrary. Whereat, I, now
   P.   87 FLECKNO   163 Who should commend his Mistress now? Or who
   P.   87 FLECKNO   169 Have made the Chance be painted; and go now
   P.   87 ODE   2 Must now forsake his Muses dear,
   P.   89 ODE   73 And now the Irish are asham'd
   P.   90 ODE   105 The Pict no shelter now shall find
   P.   94 DR. WITTY   20 Now learns the tongues of France and Italy;
   P.   94 DR. WITTY   31 Now I reform, and surely so will all
   P.   94 DR. WITTY   36 Now worth the liking, but thy Book and thee.
   P.   98 HOLLAND   135 And now again our armed Bucentore
   P.   99 HOLLAND   137 And now the Hydra of seaven Provinces
   P.   99 HOLLAND   145 For now of nothing may our State despair,
   P. 104 ANNIVERSARY   59 Now through the Strings a Martial rage he
                         throws,
   P. 108 ANNIVERSARY 213 When now they sink, and now the plundring
                         Streams
   P. 110 ANNIVERSARY 303 Oh Mahomet! now couldst thou rise again,
   P. 111 ANNIVERSARY 321 But the great Captain, now the danger's ore,
   P. 111 ANNIVERSARY 344 Seem'd now a long and gloomy Night to threat,
   P. 113 BLAKE   1 Now does Spains Fleet her spatious wings
                         unfold,
   P. 113 BLAKE   13 For now upon the Main, themselves they saw,
   P. 116 BLAKE   99 His wish he has, for now undaunted Blake,

P. 117	BLAKE	110	Our worst works past, now we have found them out.
P. 117	BLAKE	112	And they are ours, for now they cannot fly.
P. 117	BLAKE	119	The Thund'ring Cannon now begins the Fight,
P. 118	BLAKE	149	Our Cannon now tears every Ship and Sconce,
P. 122	TWO SONGS	19	'Twas those Eyes, I now dare swear,
P. 122	TWO SONGS	35	Now lesser Beauties may take place,
P. 123	O.C.	3	Now in its self (the Glass where all appears)
P. 123	TWO SONGS	46	Or who despair, now Damon does enjoy?
P. 124	O.C.	53	A silent fire now wasts those Limbs of Wax,
P. 124	O.C.	67	And now Eliza's purple Locks were shorn,
P. 125	O.C.	71	And now his Life, suspended by her breath,
P. 125	O.C.	79	Who now shall tell us more of mournful Swans,
P. 126	O.C.	138	Left to determine now his fatal Hour:
P. 129	O.C.	231	Where we (so once we us'd) shall now no more,
P. 129	O.C.	245	Francisca faire can nothing now but weep,
P. 131	O.C.	321	Cease now our griefs, calme peace succeeds a war,
P. 131	PARADISE	25	But I am now convinc'd, and none will dare
P. 139	HOUSEWARMING	79	And St. John must now for the Leads be compliant,
P. 139	HOUSEWARMING	84	But receiv'd now and paid the Chancellours Custome.
P. 140	HOUSEWARMING	101	Now some (as all Buildings must censure abide)
P. 141	INSTRUCTIONS	1	After two sittings, now our Lady State,
P. 141	INSTRUCTIONS	37	But Age, allaying now that youthful heat,
P. 142	INSTRUCTIONS	47	But thought the Golden Age was now restor'd,
P. 142	INSTRUCTIONS	65	Express her studying now, if China-clay,
P. 143	INSTRUCTIONS	80	Her, not her Picture, for she now grows old.
P. 143	INSTRUCTIONS	88	Her looks, and oft-try'd Beauty now distrusts:
P. 143	INSTRUCTIONS	90	And now first, wisht she e're had been a Maid.
P. 143	INSTRUCTIONS	103	Ah Painter, now could Alexander live,
P. 143	INSTRUCTIONS	110	These now advent'ring how to win it back.
P. 149	INSTRUCTIONS	349	Now Mordant may, within his Castle Tow'r,
P. 149	INSTRUCTIONS	351	The Irish-Herd is now let loose, and comes
P. 149	INSTRUCTIONS	353	And now, now, the Canary-Patent may
P. 150	INSTRUCTIONS	373	The Court, as once of War, now fond of Peace,
P. 151	INSTRUCTIONS	412	More tim'rous now we are, than first secure.
P. 151	INSTRUCTIONS	431	Now Doleman's disobedient, and they still
P. 152	INSTRUCTIONS	486	Now thinks all but too little for their Fear.
P. 152	INSTRUCTIONS	491	Of the whole Nation now to ask a Loan.
P. 153	INSTRUCTIONS	524	Sail'd now among our Rivers undisturb'd:
P. 155	INSTRUCTIONS	586	And all our hopes now on frail Chain depend:
P. 155	INSTRUCTIONS	608	Now needful, does for Ammunition call.
P. 156	INSTRUCTIONS	619	Now a cheap spoil, and the mean Victor's Slave,
P. 157	INSTRUCTIONS	698	The Loyal-london, now a third time burns.
P. 158	INSTRUCTIONS	701	Of all our Navy none should now survive,
P. 158	INSTRUCTIONS	721	Once a deep River, now with Timber floor'd,
P. 158	INSTRUCTIONS	723	Now (nothing more at Chatham left to burn)
P. 159	INSTRUCTIONS	751	Now with vain grief their vainer hopes they rue,
P. 159	INSTRUCTIONS	758	Now in the Ravisher De-Ruyter's hand,
P. 160	INSTRUCTIONS	807	But now draws near the Parliament's return;
P. 172	LOYALL SCOT	10	Hee Judg'd now Clearly now and saw more plain.
P. 173	LOYALL SCOT	65	Shall not a death soe Generous now when told
P. 175	LOYALL SCOT	150	None knows what god our Flamen now Adores;
P. 176	LOYALL SCOT	192	But now, when one Head doeth both Realmes controule,
P. 179	STOCKSMARKET	9	But now it appears from the first to the last
P. 180	STOCKSMARKET	50	Whose loyalty now all expires with his spankers.
P. 181	MADE FREE	22	And now he's come ore,
P. 183	MADE FREE	76	And tho' he has serv'd now
P. 184	MADE FREE	127	And now Worshipfull Sirs
P. 191	TWO HORSES	13	At Delphos and Rome Stocks and Stones now and then, sirs,
P. 192	TWO HORSES	28	For the two mighty Monarchs that doe now bestride 'um.
P. 198	DUKE	39	Do's now in popery with his Master joyne.
P. 199	DUKE	44	The wound of which now tainted Churchill faids,
P. 199	DUKE	54	Now, Painter, shew us in the blackest dye
P. 199	DUKE	66	Now Talbott must by his great master stand,
P. 200	DUKE	84	And now hath gott his Daughter gott with Child,
P. 202	HISTORICALL	37	Now the Court Sins did every place defile,
P. 202	HISTORICALL	45	But now Yorkes Genitalls grew over hot
P. 203	HISTORICALL	114	Now to the State she tends againe direct,
P. 204	HISTORICALL	128	Now must my Muse deplore the Nations fate,
P. 204	HISTORICALL	137	His meager Highness now had got astride,
P. 204	HISTORICALL	145	The Duke now vaunts, with popish Myrmidons;
P. 313	CHEQUER INN	14	Is now a Man that was a Mouse
P. 313	CHEQUER INN	20	That now he Money tells by Pecks
P. 313	CHEQUER INN	25	And tho' he now do looke so bigg
P. 313	CHEQUER INN	37	And where he might e're now have laid
P. 314	CHEQUER INN	49	And now they march't all Tagg and Ragg
P. 316	CHEQUER INN	164	And now (who wou'd) twas tyme to goe

noxious   frequency: 1   relative frequency: 0.0000
    P. 189 BRITANNIA   186 From Noxious Monsters, Hellborn tyranny,

noyse   frequency: 2   relative frequency: 0.0000
    P. 81 A. HOUSE   710 But for the Wisdome, not the Noyse;
    P. 111 ANNIVERSARY   333 And Owls and Ravens with their screeching noyse

number   frequency: 5   relative frequency: 0.0001
    P.   4 HASTINGS   17 For, there above, They number not as here,
    P. 112 ANNIVERSARY   381 'He Secrecy with Number hath inchas'd,
    P. 132 PARADISE   54 In Number, Weight, and Measure, needs not
                              Rhime.
    P. 147 INSTRUCTIONS   277 But strength at last still under number bows,
    P. 165 INSTRUCTIONS   989 (Where few the number, choice is there less hard)

numbered   frequency: 1   relative frequency: 0.0000
    See also "numbred."
    P. 123 O.C.   2 Of Cromwell's head, and numbered ev'ry hair,

numbers   frequency: 6   relative frequency: 0.0001
    P. 47 EMPIRE   11 From whence the Progeny cf numbers new
    P. 76 A. HOUSE   545 The good he numbers up, and hacks;
    P. 87 ODE   4 His Numbers languishing.
    P. 124 O.C.   59 No trembling String ccmpos'd to numbers new,
    P. 126 O.C.   127 Numbers of Men decrease with pains unknown,
    P. 146 INSTRUCTIONS   231 Pleas'd with their Numbers, yet in Valcur wise,

numbred   frequency: 1   relative frequency: 0.0000
    P. 106 ANNIVERSARY   107 And in their numbred Footsteps humbly tread

numerous   frequency: 1   relative frequency: 0.0000
    See also "num'rous."
    P. 197 DUKE   2 The great assembly and the numerous traine,

num'rous   frequency: 3   relative frequency: 0.0000
    P. 28 LOVER   27 A num'rous fleet of Corm'rants black,
    P. 30 THE GALLERY   46 Art grown a num'rous Colony;
    P. 105 ANNIVERSARY   71 Whose num'rous Gorge could swallow in an hour

nun   frequency: 2   relative frequency: 0.0000
    P. 67 A. HOUSE   279 Though many a Nun there made her Vow,
    P. 192 TWO HORSES   20 By the Devill, a Priest, a Fryar, or Nun.

nunnery   frequency: 1   relative frequency: 0.0000
    P. 61 A. HOUSE   85 A Nunnery first gave it birth.

nunns   frequency: 1   relative frequency: 0.0000
    P. 61 A. HOUSE   94 Discoursing with the Suttle Nunns.

nuns   frequency: 4   relative frequency: 0.0000
    See also "nunns."
    P. 65 A. HOUSE   200 The Nuns smooth Tongue has suckt her in.
    P. 66 A. HOUSE   237 Yet still the Nuns his Right debar'd,
    P. 67 A. HOUSE   266 And to the Nuns bequeaths her Tears:
    P. 67 A. HOUSE   275 And what both Nuns and Founders will'd

nuntio   frequency: 1   relative frequency: 0.0000
    P. 199 DUKE   75 Letts see the nuntio Arundells sweete face;

nuptial   frequency: 2   relative frequency: 0.0000
    P. 75 A. HOUSE   524 With Nuptial Rings their Ensigns chast;
    P. 159 INSTRUCTIONS 748 When all the Rivers grac'd their Nuptial Bed;

nuptials. See "sea-nuptials."

nursed. See "heaven-nursed," "nurst."

nursery   frequency: 1   relative frequency: 0.0000
    P. 69 A. HOUSE   339 The Nursery of all things green

nurses   frequency: 1   relative frequency: 0.0000
    P. 25 YOUNG LOVE   8 As the Nurses with the Child.

nurst   frequency: 3   relative frequency: 0.0000
    P. 23 NYMPH   56 I it at mine own fingers nurst.
    P. 81 A. HOUSE   722 In a Domestick Heaven nurst,
    P. 87 ODE   14 Breaking the Clouds where it was nurst,

nutriment   frequency: 1   relative frequency: 0.0000
    P. 40 THE MOWER   10 The nutriment did change the kind.

nuzz'ling   frequency: 1   relative frequency: 0.0000

          P. 153 INSTRUCTICNS 496 Lye nuzz'ling at the Sacramental wart;

nymph   frequency: 6   relative frequency: 0.0001
     See also "nimph."
     P.   22 NYMPH   t The Nymph complaining for the death of her
                               Faun.
     P.   48 THE GARDEN   32 Not as a Nymph, but for a Reed.
     P.   57 BILL-BOROW   42 Of the great Nymph did it protect;
     P.   57 BILL-BOROW   43 Vera the Nymph that him inspir'd,
     P.   68 A. HOUSE   301 None for the Virgin Nymph; for She
     P.   81 A. HOUSE   713 Blest Nymph! that couldst so soon prevent

nymphs   frequency: 5   relative frequency: 0.0001
     See also "sea-nymphs."
     P.   4 LOVELACE   49 Him, valianst men, and fairest Nymphs approve,
     P. 122 TWO SONGS   32 Whil'st all the Nymphs on Damon's choice
                               attend?
     P. 153 INSTRUCTIONS   527 Through the vain sedge the bashful Nymphs he
                               ey'd;
     P. 156 INSTRUCTIONS   658 The Nymphs would rustle; he would forward swim.
     P. 172 LOYALL SCOT   24 The Nymphs would Rustle, hee would forward
                               swim:

nymph's. See "nimph's."

o   frequency: 23   relative frequency: 0.0004

o'   frequency: 1   relative frequency: 0.0000

oak   frequency: 7   relative frequency: 0.0001
     See also "oake," "oke," "royal-oak."
     P.   42 DAMON   38 And Oak leaves tipt with hony due.
     P.   58 BILL-BOROW   74 More certain Oracles in Oak.
     P.   76 A. HOUSE   548 Does find the hcllcw Oak to speak,
     P.   76 A. HOUSE   551 Who could have thought the tallest Oak
     P.   82 A. HOUSE   740 On the Fairfacian Oak does grow;
     P. 112 ANNIVERSARY   374 'Through double Oak, <and> lin'd with treble
                               Brass;
     P. 129 O.C.   261 Not much unlike the sacred oak, which shoots

oak-leaves   frequency: 1   relative frequency: 0.0000
     P.   77 A. HOUSE   587 The Cak-Leaves me embroyder all,

oake   frequency: 1   relative frequency: 0.0000
     P.   76 A. HOUSE   559 While the Oake seems to fall content,

oaken   frequency: 3   relative frequency: 0.0000
     P. 108 ANNIVERSARY   214 Break up each Deck, and rip the Oaken seams.
     P. 112 ANNIVERSARY   353 'What Oaken Forrests, and what golden Mines!
     P. 155 INSTRUCTICNS   577 Those Oaken Gyants of the ancient Race,

oakes   frequency: 2   relative frequency: 0.0000
     P.   75 A. HOUSE   517 But highest Oakes stoop dcwn to hear,
     P. 117 BLAKE   130 As Oakes did then, Urg'd by the active fire.

oaks. See "oakes," "okes."

oar   frequency: 2   relative frequency: 0.0000
     P.   95 HOLLAND   9 Glad then, as Miners that have found the Oar,
     P. 115 BLAKE   59 Which troubles men to raise it when 'tis Oar,

oars   frequency: 1   relative frequency: 0.0000
     P.   18 BERMUDAS   40 With falling Oars they kept the time.

oat-pipe's   frequency: 1   relative frequency: 0.0000
     P.   19 THYRSIS   25 No Oat-pipe's needfull, there thine Ears

oate   frequency: 1   relative frequency: 0.0000
     P.   18 CLORINDA   23 And his Name swells my slender Oate.

oath   frequency: 2   relative frequency: 0.0000
     See also "oth."
     P. 170 PROPHECY   23 When Declaraticns lye, when every Oath
     P. 183 MADE FREE   73 His word nor his Oath

oathes   frequency: 1   relative frequency: 0.0000
     P. 196 TWO HORSES   185 No Quarrells or oathes amcngst those that drink
                               'um;

oaths. See "oathes."

obdurate   frequency: 1   relative frequency: 0.0000

P. 175 LOYALL SCCT   154 What soe obdurate Pagan Heretique

obey   frequency: 6   relative frequency: 0.0001
    P.   85 FLECKNO   106 Went down, as I him follow'd to obey.
    P.   89 ODE   84 That can so well obey.
    P. 110 ANNIVERSARY   282 Him as their Father must the State obey.
    P. 148 INSTRUCTICNS 299 Lee, equal to obey or to command,
    P. 160 INSTRUCTIONS 806 The Exchequer might the Privy-purse obey.
    P. 203 HISTORICALL   85 And yet perswade the World they must obey:

obey'd   frequency: 4   relative frequency: 0.0000
    P.   63 A. HOUSE   153 'Here live beloved, and obey'd:
    P. 128 O.C.   191 What man was ever so in Heav'n obey'd
    P. 145 INSTRUCTIONS 193 For Chimney's sake they all Sir Pool obey'd,
    P. 200 DUKE   81 And soe should wee, were his advice obey'd.

object   frequency: 4   relative frequency: 0.0000
    P.   15 EYES   3 That, having view'd the object vain,
    P.   36 DEFINITION   2 As 'tis for object strange and high:
    P.   81 A. HOUSE   725 Where not cne cbject can come nigh
    P. 162 INSTRUCTICNS 899 The Cbject strange in him nc Terrour mov'd:

objects   frequency: 1   relative frequency: 0.0000
    P. 130 O.C.   274 Detracts from objects than itself more high:

oblig'd   frequency: 5   relative frequency: 0.0001
    P.   83 FLECKNO   1 Oblig'd by frequent visits of this man,
    P.   85 FLECKNO   108 Oblig'd us, when below, to celebrate
    P. 116 BLAKE   104 We to their Strength are more oblig'd then they.
    P. 145 INSTRUCTIONS 192 (Their publick Acts) oblig'd them still to more.
    P. 151 INSTRUCTIONS 422 But Mordant new oblig'd, would sure be just.

oblige   frequency: 1   relative frequency: 0.0000
    P. 192 TWO HORSES   21 If the Roman Church, good Christians, oblige
                             yee

obliging   frequency: 1   relative frequency: 0.0000
    P. 179 STOCKSMARKET   6 Obliging the city with a king and a steed,

oblique   frequency: 1   relative frequency: 0.0000
    P.   37 DEFINITION   25 As Lines so Loves oblique may well

oblivion   frequency: 1   relative frequency: 0.0000
    P. 139 HOUSEWARMING 71 Since the Act of Oblivion was never such
                             selling,

obryan   frequency: 1   relative frequency: 0.0000
    P. 169 ADVICE   45 Tis this must make Cbryan great in Story,

o'bryan. See "obryan."

obscur'd   frequency: 1   relative frequency: 0.0000
    P. 125 O.C.   75 And with the damp of her last Gasps obscur'd,

obscure   frequency: 5   relative frequency: 0.0001
    P.   30 THE GALLERY   27 And, by a Light cbscure, dost rave
    P.   93 DR. WITTY   5 Changing the Latine, but dc more obscure
    P. 127 O.C.   175 Whose greater Truths obscure the Fables old,
    P. 162 INSTRUCTICNS 867 Bright Hair, fair Face, obscure and dull of
                             Head;
    P. 164 INSTRUCTIONS 951 Show'd they obscure him, while too near they
                             please,

obscurer   frequency: 2   relative frequency: 0.0000
    P.   58 BILL-BOROW   77 Therefore to ycur cbscurer Seats
    P. 120 TWO SONGS   27 Shine thorough this obscurer Brest,

obscures   frequency: 1   relative frequency: 0.0000
    P. 130 O.C.   308 And yet how much of them his griefe cbscures.

obsequies   frequency: 2   relative frequency: 0.0000
    P.   72 A. HOUSE   440 In Hills fcr Scldiers Cbsequies.
    P. 127 O.C.   161 Which with more Care set forth his Obsequies

obsequious   frequency: 1   relative frequency: 0.0000
    P.   98 HCLLAND   129 As the obsequious Air and Waters rest,

observe   frequency: 1   relative frequency: 0.0000
    P. 200 DUKE   106 Observe the danger that appeares soe neare,

observing   frequency: 2   relative frequency: 0.0000

```
        P. 105 ANNIVERSARY    103 While by his Beams observing Princes steer,
        P. 137 HOUSEWARMING     9 But observing that Mortals run often behind,

obsolete                    frequency:    1    relative frequency: 0.0000
        P.  82 A. HOUSE       754 Shall now be scorn'd as obsolete;

obstructed                  frequency:    1    relative frequency: 0.0000
        P. 108 ANNIVERSARY    207 Justice obstructed lay, and Reason fool'd;

obtained                    frequency:    1    relative frequency: 0.0000
        P. 113 BLAKE           t1 On the Victory obtained by Blake over the
                                  Spaniards,

obtrude                     frequency:    1    relative frequency: 0.0000
        P.  91 MAY'S DEATH     43 Go seek the novice Statesmen, and obtrude

ocasions                    frequency:    1    relative frequency: 0.0000
        P. 194 TWO HORSES     111 On ocasions like these he oft steals away

occasion                    frequency:    1    relative frequency: 0.0000
        P. 171 LOYALL SCOT     t2 Upon The occasion of the death of Captain
                                  Douglas burnt in one

occasions.  See "ocasions."

ocean                       frequency:    8    relative frequency: 0.0001
        P.  49 THE GARDEN      43 The Mind, that Ocean where each kind
        P.  69 A. HOUSE       352 Pow'r which the Ocean might command.
        P.  96 HOLLAND         23 Yet still his claim the Injur'd Ocean laid,
        P. 112 ANNIVERSARY    356 'Of shedding Leaves, that with their Ocean
                                  breed.
        P. 112 ANNIVERSARY    369 'The Ocean is the Fountain of Command,
        P. 116 BLAKE           87 Who on the Ocean that does horror give,
        P. 153 INSTRUCTIONS   523 Ruyter the while, that had our Ocean curb'd,
        P. 154 INSTRUCTIONS   576 The Ocean Water, or the Heavens Wind.

oceans                      frequency:    3    relative frequency: 0.0000
        P.  17 BERMUDAS         2 In th' Oceans bosome unespy'd,
        P.  41 THE MOWER       17 Another World was search'd, through Oceans new,
        P.  95 HOLLAND          5 Or what by th' Oceans slow alluvion fell,

ochre.  See "oker."

odds                        frequency:    1    relative frequency: 0.0000
        P. 195 TWO HORSES     128 Between the two Scourges wee find little odds.

ode                         frequency:    1    relative frequency: 0.0000
        P.  87 ODE             t An Horatian Ode upon Cromwel's Return from
                                 Ireland.

odious                      frequency:    3    relative frequency: 0.0000
        P.  86 FLECKNO        135 More odious then those raggs which the French
                                  youth
        P. 152 INSTRUCTIONS   469 But when he came the odious Clause to Pen,
        P. 159 INSTRUCTIONS   746 Thou, and thy Fellows, held'st the odious
                                  Light.

odours                      frequency:    1    relative frequency: 0.0000
        P.  68 A. HOUSE       296 And fills its Flask with Odours new.

o'erwhelming                frequency:    1    relative frequency: 0.0000
        P. 139 HOUSEWARMING    77 Like Jove under Aetna o'erwhelming the Gyant,

oeta                        frequency:    2    relative frequency: 0.0000
        P. 157 INSTRUCTIONS   695 When Oeta and Alcides are forgot,
        P. 173 LOYALL SCOT     61 When Oeta and Alcides are forgott,

of                          frequency:  769    relative frequency: 0.0160
      See also "o'," "of's," "oth," "o'th."

off                         frequency:   15    relative frequency: 0.0003
        P.  43 DAMON           46 The Sun himself licks off my Sweat.
        P.  84 FLECKNO         36 Left off, and try'd t' allure me with his Lute.
        P.  93 DR. WITTY        4 Take off the Cypress vail, but leave a mask,
        P. 115 BLAKE           47 Casting that League off, which she held so long,
        P. 115 BLAKE           48 She cast off that which only made her strong.
        P. 126 O.C.           113 First the great Thunder was shot off, and sent
        P. 139 HOUSEWARMING    80 Or his right hand shall else be cut off with the
                                  Trowel.
        P. 144 INSTRUCTIONS   137 Chops off the piece where e're she close the
                                  Jaw,
        P. 149 INSTRUCTIONS   332 Bought off with Eighteen hundred thousand pound.
```

P. 150 INSTRUCTIONS 398 Off, at the Isle of Candy, Dutch and ships.
P. 150 INSTRUCTIONS 400 And thought all safe if they were so far off.
P. 164 INSTRUCTIONS 954 And hurls them off, e're since, in his Career.
P. 166 KINGS VOWES   41 I'll order my Bravo's to cutt off his Nose,
P. 313 CHEQUER INN   28 Then oh how cou'd I claw him off
P. 316 CHEQUER INN   162 He'd bring him off i' fack.

off-scouring   frequency: 1   relative frequency: 0.0000
P. 95 HCLLAND   2 As but th' Off-scouring cf the Brittish Sand;

off-spring   frequency: 1   relative frequency: 0.0000
P. 159 INSTRUCTIONS 745 And their dear Off-spring murder'd in their
                         sight;

off-springs   frequency: 1   relative frequency: 0.0000
P. 31 MOURNING   2 Of humane Off-springs from the Skies,

offend   frequency: 2   relative frequency: 0.0000
P. 128 O.C.   199 Danger itself refusing to offend
P. 132 PARADISE   51 I too transported by the Mode offend,

offer   frequency: 4   relative frequency: 0.0000
P. 22 NYMPH   24 The World, to offer for their Sin.
P. 55 EPITAPH   4 When dead to offer were unkind.
P. 126 O.C.   124 Offer themselves in many an Hecatomb;
P. 181 MADE FREE   12 You in Chaines offer your freedome.

offer'd   frequency: 1   relative frequency: 0.0000
P. 146 INSTRUCTIONS 206 Else Talbot offer'd to have led them on.

offering   frequency: 1   relative frequency: 0.0000
P. 203 HISTORICALL   79 To the black Idol for an Offering.

officers. See "court-officers."

officious   frequency: 3   relative frequency: 0.0000
P. 44 GLC-WORMS   9 Ye Glo-worms, whose officious Flame
P. 55 EPITAPH   6 Whc would officious Praises spill?
P. 158 INSTRUCTIONS 709 Officious fear, however, to prevent

officiously   frequency: 1   relative frequency: 0.0000
P. 60 A. HOUSE   55 And too officicusly it slights

offspring   frequency: 1   relative frequency: 0.0000
See also "off-spring."
P. 66 A. HOUSE   241 Is not this he whose Offspring fierce

of's   frequency: 1   relative frequency: 0.0000

oft   frequency: 32   relative frequency: 0.0006
P. 10 DIALOGUE   26 Such as oft the Gods appeas'd,
P. 16 EYES   39 Yea oft the Thund'rer pitty takes
P. 21 SOUL & BODY   29 And ready oft the Port to gain,
P. 23 NYMPH   59 It had so sweet a Breath! And oft
P. 23 NYMPH   66 It oft would challenge me the Race:
P. 23 NYMPH   78 Have sought it oft, where it should lye,
P. 32 MOURNING   35 But sure as oft as Women weep,
P. 43 DAMON   61 The deathless Fairyes take me oft
P. 61 A. HOUSE   86 For Virgin Buildings oft brought forth.
P. 61 A. HOUSE   93 And oft She spent the Summer Suns
P. 65 A. HOUSE   201 Oft, though he knew it was in vain,
P. 96 HCLLAND   24 And oft at Leap-frog ore their Steeples plaid:
P. 96 HOLLAND   31 And oft the Tritons and the Sea-Nymphs saw
P. 106 ANNIVERSARY   131 Hence oft I think, if in some happy Hour
P. 107 ANNIVERSARY   169 Thou, who so oft through Storms of thundring
                         Lead
P. 124 O.C.   32 He oft would flcurish in his mighty Arms;
P. 125 O.C.   87 And in himself so cft immortal try'd,
P. 129 O.C.   238 Whose force oft spar'd the labour of his arm:
P. 129 O.C.   264 And honour'd wreaths have oft the victour
                         crcwn'd.
P. 141 INSTRUCTIONS   19 Else shalt thou oft thy guiltless Pencil curse,
P. 142 INSTRUCTIONS   53 She perfected that Engine, oft assay'd,
P. 143 INSTRUCTIONS 120 His lab'ring Pencil oft would recreate.
P. 155 INSTRUCTIONS 605 Oft had he sent, cf Duncombe and of Legg
P. 156 INSTRUCTIONS 618 Secure so oft he had this Foe defy'd:
P. 156 INSTRUCTIONS 655 Oft has he in chill Eske or Seine, by night,
P. 164 INSTRUCTIONS 959 Kings in the Ccuntry oft have gone astray,
P. 172 LOYALL SCOT   21 Oft as hee in Chill Eske or Seyne by night
P. 175 LOYALL SCOT   162 How oft hath age his hallcwing hands Misled
P. 182 MACE FREE   49 Tho' oft bound tc the Peace
P. 185 BRITANNIA   35 How oft have I him to himself restor'd,

```
      P. 194 TWO HORSES    111 On ocasions like these he oft steals away
      P. 317 CHEQUER INN    187 By wise Volke, I have oft been told

oft-times                        frequency:    1    relative frequency: 0.0000
      P.  96 HOLLAND         29 The Fish oft-times the Burger dispossest,

oft-try'd                        frequency:    1    relative frequency: 0.0000
      P. 143 INSTRUCTIONS    88 Her looks, and oft-try'd Beauty now distrusts:

often                            frequency:    7    relative frequency: 0.0001
      See also "oft."
      P.  57 BILL-BOROW      44 To whom he often here retir'd,
      P.  98 HOLLAND        112 We buoy'd so often up their sinking State.
      P. 137 HOUSEWARMING     9 But observing that Mortals run often behind,
      P. 137 HOUSEWARMING    14 Who was dig'd up so often are she did marry;
      P. 153 INSTRUCTIONS   511 Often, dear Painter, have I sate and mus'd
      P. 158 INSTRUCTIONS   727 The pleasing sight he often does prolong:
      P. 313 CHEQUER INN     11 But sure they often there had beene

oftener. See "oftner."

oftner                           frequency:    3    relative frequency: 0.0000
      P.  71 A. HOUSE       386 Does oftner then these Meadows change.
      P. 146 INSTRUCTIONS   242 But oftner did among themselves divide.
      P. 315 CHEQUER INN    125 Was oftner serv'd then the Poor

oh                               frequency:   24    relative frequency: 0.0005
      See also "o."

oil. See "oyl," "oyle."

oke                              frequency:    1    relative frequency: 0.0000
      P.  48 THE GARDEN       2 To win the Palm, the Oke, or Bayes;

oker                             frequency:    1    relative frequency: 0.0000
      P. 156 INSTRUCTIONS   636 Or Face so red thine Oker and thy Lack.

okes                             frequency:    1    relative frequency: 0.0000
      P.  57 BILL-BOROW      45 And on these Okes ingrav'd her Name;

old                              frequency:   46    relative frequency: 0.0009
      See also "ould."
      P.   4 HASTINGS        16 Are hurried hence, as if already old.
      P.  14 THE CORONET     13 Alas I find the Serpent old
      P.  25 YOUNG LOVE       6 By young Love old Time beguil'd:
      P.  39 THE MATCH       18 That he must once grow old;
      P.  55 THYESTE         11 An old honest Country man.
      P.  66 A. HOUSE       252 With their old Holy-Water Brush.
      P.  74 A. HOUSE       499 As if their Neighbourhood so old
      P.  88 ODE             35 And cast the Kingdome old
      P.  90 MAY'S DEATH     14 Amongst the Chorus of old Poets laid,
      P.  91 MAY'S DEATH     49 Transferring old Rome hither in your talk,
      P. 113 BLAKE            2 Leaves the new World and hastens for the old:
      P. 113 BLAKE           10 For wealth wherewith to wound the old once more.
      P. 122 TWO SONGS       16 But when Old he planted Bayes.
      P. 127 O.C.           175 Whose greater Truths obscure the Fables old,
      P. 131 PARADISE         8 The sacred Truths to Fable and old Song,
      P. 141 INSTRUCTIONS    30 The new Courts pattern, Stallion of the old.
      P. 143 INSTRUCTIONS    80 Her, not her Picture, for she now grows old.
      P. 144 INSTRUCTIONS   155 Of the old Courtiers next a Squadron came,
      P. 146 INSTRUCTIONS   208 And old Fitz-Harding of the Eaters Beef.
      P. 147 INSTRUCTIONS   263 Old Waller, Trumpet-gen'ral swore he'd write
      P. 150 INSTRUCTIONS   376 Comes news of Pastime, Martial and old:
      P. 152 INSTRUCTIONS   473 Never old Letcher more repugnance felt,
      P. 153 INSTRUCTIONS   532 Swells his old Veins with fresh Blood, fresh
                               Delight.
      P. 154 INSTRUCTIONS   543 Old Neptune springs the Tydes, and Water lent:
      P. 159 INSTRUCTIONS   750 His Empire old, to their immortal Line!
      P. 161 INSTRUCTIONS   847 The Girls shall always kiss thee, though grown
                               old,
      P. 166 KINGS VOWES     22 I will have a new London instead of the old,
      P. 166 KINGS VOWES     28 I will have a fine Court with ne'er an old face,
      P. 171 LOYALL SCOT      1 Of the old Heroes when the Warlike shades
      P. 171 PROPHECY        39 When an old Scotch Covenanter shall be
      P. 173 LOYALL SCOT     66 Unite our distance, fill the breaches old?
      P. 183 MADE FREE      108 For wee have had too much of the Old one.
      P. 187 BRITANNIA       97 Henceforth be deaf to old witches charmes,
      P. 190 STATUE          16 To repair with such riffe raffe our Churches old
                               Pale?
      P. 190 STATUE          23 And 'tis fourty to one if he Play the old Game
      P. 190 STATUE          28 For the old King on Horseback is but an
                                                                 Halfecrown.
```

P.	190 STATUE	37	Let's have a King then, be he new be he old;
P.	195 TWO HORSES	138	W. I freely declare it, I am for old Noll.
P.	195 TWO HORSES	150	None ever Reign'd like old Besse in the Ruffe.
P.	200 DUKE	92	Old England on its strong foundations stands,
P.	201 HISTORICALL	29	Her most Uxorious Mate she usd of old;
P.	203 HISTORICALL	81	He true Vicegerent to old Moloch were.
P.	204 HISTORICALL	136	Old England truckling under slavery.
P.	315 CHEQUER INN	109	Old Hobbs's Brother, Cheney there
P.	317 CHEQUER INN	188	Parli'ments grow nought as they grow old
P.	317 CHEQUER INN	192	By this old Whitehall Pump.

olimpia   frequency: 1   relative frequency: 0.0000
   P. 169 ADVICE   47 Draw our Olimpia next in Councell Sate

olive   frequency: 1   relative frequency: 0.0000
   P. 109 ANNIVERSARY   258 Didst (like thine Clive) still refuse to Reign;

oliver   frequency: 1   relative frequency: 0.0000
   P. 131 O.C.   322 Rainbows to storms, Richard to Oliver.

omens   frequency: 1   relative frequency: 0.0000
   P. 131 O.C.   319 We find already what those omens mean,

ominous   frequency: 1   relative frequency: 0.0000
   P. 190 STATUE   27 However tis ominous if understood,

omit   frequency: 1   relative frequency: 0.0000
   P. 132 PARADISE   28 And all that was improper dost omit:

omnipotence   frequency: 1   relative frequency: 0.0000
   P. 137 HOUSEWARMING   11 His Omnipotence therfore much rather design'd

on   frequency: 197   relative frequency: 0.0041
   See also "on't."

once   frequency: 60   relative frequency: 0.0012
   P.   4 HASTINGS   20 And on the Tree of Life once made a Feast,
   P.   5 HASTINGS   48 Himself at once condemneth, and Mayern;
   P.   5 HASTINGS   52 Had Mayern once been mixt with Hastings blood!
   P. 14 THE CORONET   8 That once adorn'd my Shepherdesses head.
   P. 14 THE CORONET   20 Either his slipp'ry knots at once untie,
   P. 18 CLORINDA   17 D. These once had been enticing things,
   P. 27 MISTRESS   39 Rather at once our Time devour,
   P. 36 DAPHNIS   108 Why did Chloe once refuse?
   P. 39 THE MATCH   18 That he must once grow old;
   P. 45 MOWER'S SONG   1 My Mind was once the true survey
   P. 58 BILL-BOROW   66 And other Hills him once did please.
   P. 64 A. HOUSE   167 'And that, once sprung, increase so fast
   P. 68 A. HOUSE   319 And sleeps so too: but, if once stir'd,
   P. 69 A. HOUSE   347 Might once have made our Gardens spring
   P. 81 A. HOUSE   731 Nor once at Vice your Brows dare knit
   P. 82 A. HOUSE   761 'Tis not, what once it was, the World;
   P. 84 FLECKNO   56 Happy at once to make him Protestant,
   P. 105 ANNIVERSARY   74 And once he struck, and twice, the pow'rful
                              Strings.
   P. 106 ANNIVERSARY   121 Then shall I once with graver Accents shake
   P. 107 ANNIVERSARY   176 At once assay'd to overturn us all.
   P. 111 ANNIVERSARY   339 Why did mine Eyes once see so bright a Ray;
   P. 112 ANNIVERSARY   370 'But that once took, we Captives are on Land.
   P. 112 ANNIVERSARY   391 'O could I once him with our Title see,
   P. 113 BLAKE   10 For wealth wherewith to wound the old once more.
   P. 114 BLAKE   31 A happy People, which at once do gain
   P. 116 BLAKE   78 At once both to Inhabit Earth and Heaven.
   P. 118 BLAKE   150 And o're two Elements Triumphs at once.
   P. 124 O.C.   52 This will not stay when once the other's gone.
   P. 127 O.C.   152 Yet joy'd remembring what he once atchiev'd.
   P. 127 O.C.   172 Who once more joyn'd us to the Continent;
   P. 128 O.C.   213 For her he once did nature's tribute pay:
   P. 128 O.C.   228 At once with him, and all that's good beside;
   P. 129 O.C.   231 Where we (so once we us'd) shall now no more,
   P. 130 O.C.   291 There thy great soule at once a world does see,
   P. 130 O.C.   311 But open'd once, what splendour does he throw?
   P. 131 O.C.   314 How gently winds at once the ruling reins?
   P. 132 PARADISE   35 At once delight and horrour on us seize,
   P. 137 HOUSEWARMING   3 At once three Deluges threatning our Land;
   P. 139 HOUSEWARMING   63 So the Bribes overlaid her that Rome once
                              betray'd:
   P. 142 INSTRUCTIONS   46 Two Saints at once, St. German, St. Alban.
   P. 142 INSTRUCTIONS   56 In fewer months than Mothers once indur'd.
   P. 142 INSTRUCTIONS   60 To make her glassen D----s once malleable!

P.	142	INSTRUCTIONS	75	While she revolves, at once, Sidney's disgrace,
P.	143	INSTRUCTIONS	89	Fears lest he scorn a Woman once assay'd,
P.	147	INSTRUCTIONS	275	Such once Orlando, famous in Romance,
P.	148	INSTRUCTIONS	293	Candidly credulous for once, nay twice;
P.	150	INSTRUCTIONS	373	The Court, as once of War, now fond of Peace,
P.	155	INSTRUCTIONS	579	The conscious Stag, so once the Forests dread,
P.	158	INSTRUCTIONS	721	Once a deep River, now with Timber floor'd,
P.	165	INSTRUCTIONS	982	And a poor Warren once a City ras'd.
P.	168	ADVICE	1	Painter once more thy Pencell reassume,
P.	168	ADVICE	29	Change once again and let the next afford
P.	176	LOYALL SCOT	172	Doe but their Pyebald Lordships once Uncase
P.	180	STOCKSMARKET	37	Hath Blood him away (as his crown once) conveyed?
P.	184	BRITANNIA	8	Once more with me partake of mortall woes.
P.	187	BRITANNIA	89	And they will fear those powers they once did scorn.
P.	188	BRITANNIA	133	Rawl: Once more, great Queen, thy darling try to save;
P.	188	BRITANNIA	147	If this Imperiall cyl once taint the Blood,
P.	199	DUKE	52	Then in false hopes of being once a Queene
P.	200	DUKE	82	The Hero once gott honour by the sword;

one   frequency: 146   relative frequency: 0.0030

P.	3	LOVELACE	31	And one the Book prohibits, because Kent
P.	4	LOVELACE	41	And one the loveliest that was yet e're seen,
P.	5	HASTINGS	24	Lest He become like Them, taste more then one.
P.	9	DIALOGUE	10	To conquer one resolved Heart.
P.	9	DIALOGUE	22	Lest one Leaf thy Side should strain.
P.	11	DIALOGUE	53	Shall within one Beauty meet,
P.	12	DIALOGUE	76	The World has not one Pleasure more:
P.	19	THYRSIS	7	Dorinda. I know no way, but one, our home;
P.	22	NYMPH	27	One morning (I remember well)
P.	27	MISTRESS	42	Our sweetness, up into one Ball:
P.	28	LOVER	35	And as one Corm'rant fed him, still
P.	28	LOVER	50	Cuffing the Thunder with one hand;
P.	29	THE GALLERY	4	Compos'd into one Gallery;
P.	31	FAIR SINGER	7	I could have fled from One but singly fair:
P.	32	MOURNING	32	And not of one the bottom sound.
P.	34	DAPHNIS	37	As the Soul of one scarce dead,
P.	35	DAPHNIS	83	In one minute casts the Seed,
P.	38	PICTURE	12	The wanton Love shall one day fear,
P.	39	THE MATCH	11	For, with one grain of them diffus'd,
P.	39	THE MATCH	15	Of which one perfect Beauty grew,
P.	40	THE MATCH	27	For, with one Spark of these, he streight
P.	40	THE MATCH	34	To make one fire high:
P.	41	THE MOWER	16	That one was for a Meadow sold.
P.	45	MOWER'S SONG	9	That not one Blade of Grass you spy'd,
P.	45	MOWER'S SONG	22	Will in one common Ruine fall.
P.	46	AMETAS	6	If we both should turn one way?
P.	47	EMPIRE	1	First was the World as one great Cymbal made,
P.	49	THE GARDEN	63	Two Paradises 'twere in one
P.	58	BILL-BOROW	72	The Trophees of one fertile Year.
P.	61	A. HOUSE	95	Whence in these Words one to her weav'd,
P.	62	A. HOUSE	118	'Each one a Spouse, and each a Queen;
P.	62	A. HOUSE	122	'Some One the holy Legend reads;
P.	63	A. HOUSE	135	'And in one Beauty we would take
P.	63	A. HOUSE	154	'Each one your Sister, each your Maid.
P.	64	A. HOUSE	172	'One perfecting the other Sweet.
P.	65	A. HOUSE	210	'One Stone that a just Hand had laid,
P.	66	A. HOUSE	245	Till one, as long since prophecy'd,
P.	67	A. HOUSE	272	Was in one instant dispossest.
P.	67	A. HOUSE	288	As aiming one for ev'ry Sense.
P.	69	A. HOUSE	345	And yet their walks one on the Sod
P.	71	A. HOUSE	395	While one, unkrowing, carves the Rail,
P.	74	A. HOUSE	492	On one hand Fairfax, th' other Veres:
P.	74	A. HOUSE	500	To one great Trunk them all did mold.
P.	77	A. HOUSE	579	And in one History consumes,
P.	81	A. HOUSE	725	Where not one object can come nigh
P.	83	A. HOUSE	776	Does now like one of them appear.
P.	83	FLECKNO	17	And though within one Cell so narrow pent,
P.	84	FLECKNO	38	Being tun'd by Art, if the one touched be
P.	84	FLECKNO	47	He answered yes; with such, and such an one.
P.	85	FLECKNO	87	I meet one on the Stairs who made me stand,
P.	85	FLECKNO	101	Consist but in one substance. Then, to fit
P.	86	FLECKNO	140	Not one Word, thought and swore that they were good.
P.	86	FLECKNO	153	Sir you read false. That any one but you
P.	87	FLECKNO	168	As one scap't strangely from Captivity,
P.	87	ODE	17	For 'tis all one to Courage high
P.	89	ODE	74	To see themselves in one Year tam'd:
P.	89	ODE	75	So much one Man can do,
P.	90	MAY'S DEATH	1	As one put drunk into the Packet-boat,

P.	91	MAY'S DEATH	57 Because some one than thee more worthy weares
P.	97	HOLLAND	70 Each one thence pillag'd the first piece he found:
P.	97	HOLLAND	73 That Bank of Conscience, where not one so strange
P.	97	HOLLAND	82 That it had one Civilis call'd by Name,
P.	98	HOLLAND	103 Let this one court'sie witness all the rest;
P.	103	ANNIVERSARY	14 And in one Year the work of Ages acts:
P.	103	ANNIVERSARY	22 For one Thing never was by one King don.
P.	105	ANNIVERSARY	76 And each one enter'd in the willing Frame;
P.	105	ANNIVERSARY	92 Uphold, this one, and that the other Side;
P.	106	ANNIVERSARY	132 High Grace should meet in one with highest Pow'r,
P.	107	ANNIVERSARY	174 Our Sins endanger, and shall one day kill.
P.	107	ANNIVERSARY	181 Let this one Sorrow interweave among
P.	110	ANNIVERSARY	280 Nor Tyranny, where One does them withstand:
P.	110	ANNIVERSARY	300 Might muster Heresies, so one were ten.
P.	111	ANNIVERSARY	322 Makes you for his sake Tremble one fit more;
P.	111	ANNIVERSARY	349 'Is this, saith one, the Nation that we read
P.	112	ANNIVERSARY	375 'That one Man still, although but nam'd, alarms
P.	112	ANNIVERSARY	379 'The Nation had been ours, but his one Soul
P.	114	BLAKE	25 One of which doubtless is by Nature blest
P.	114	BLAKE	43 But this great want, will not a long one prove,
P.	114	BLAKE	46 Have broken all her Swords, then this one Peace,
P.	115	BLAKE	69 Never so many with one joyful cry,
P.	118	BLAKE	140 There one must Conquer, or there both must dye.
P.	118	BLAKE	159 And in one War the present age may boast,
P.	121	TWO SONGS	44 Rivals each one for thee too strong.
P.	128	O.C.	203 But within one its narrow limits fall,
P.	132	PARADISE	27 Thou hast not miss'd one thought that could be fit,
P.	138	HOUSEWARMING	32 Though he had built full many a one for his Master
P.	144	INSTRUCTIONS	154 And Denham these by one consent did head.
P.	146	INSTRUCTIONS	213 Last then but one, Powell, that could not ride,
P.	146	INSTRUCTIONS	224 Shall with one Breath like thistle-down disperse.
P.	146	INSTRUCTIONS	226 For one had much, the other nought to lose.
P.	147	INSTRUCTIONS	271 Believes himself an Army, theirs one Man,
P.	151	INSTRUCTIONS	414 And the French Army one from Calais spies.
P.	151	INSTRUCTIONS	450 In Cipher one to Harry Excellent.
P.	157	INSTRUCTIONS	690 As one that's warm'd himself and gone to Bed.
P.	159	INSTRUCTIONS	766 Some one must be accus'd by Punishment.
P.	160	INSTRUCTIONS	789 But, his great Crime, one Boat away he sent;
P.	163	INSTRUCTIONS	908 As one that some unusual noise does hear.
P.	163	INSTRUCTIONS	934 And Coventry, falser than any one,
P.	163	INSTRUCTIONS	937 His Fathers Ghost too whisper'd him one Note,
P.	166	KINGS VOWES	36 I will have two fine Secretaryes pisse thro one Quill.
P.	167	KINGS VOWES	58 Some one I will advance from mean descent,
P.	168	ADVICE	2 And draw me in one Scene London and Rome,
P.	168	ADVICE	10 One to his Pathic, th' other to his Player.
P.	168	ADVICE	14 Whose life does scarce one Generous Action own,
P.	170	PROPHECY	7 Where Vengeance dwells, but there is one trick more
P.	170	PROPHECY	26 And when att London their shall not be One,
P.	171	LOYALL SCOT	t2 Upon The occasion of the death of Captain Douglas burnt in one
P.	171	PROPHECY	43 When a lean Treasurer shall in one year
P.	173	LOYALL SCOT	56 As one that Huggs himself in a Warm bed.
P.	173	LOYALL SCOT	82 Whose one bank vertue, th' other vice doth breed?
P.	174	LOYALL SCOT	105 And slip one Half into his sleeve as soon.
P.	174	LOYALL SCOT	107 Shews you first one, then makes that one two Balls.
P.	175	LOYALL SCOT	136 The Legion Devil did but one man possess:
P.	175	LOYALL SCOT	137 One Bishops fiend spirits a whole Diccesse.
P.	175	LOYALL SCOT	151 One Mytre fitts the Heads of full four Moors.
P.	175	LOYALL SCOT	164 Abbot one Buck, but he shot many a Doe,
P.	176	LOYALL SCOT	181 The fittest Mask for one that Robs a Crown.
P.	176	LOYALL SCOT	192 But now, when one Head doeth both Realmes controule,
P.	178	LOYALL SCOT	260 One King, one faith, one Language and one Ile:
P.	178	LOYALL SCOT	265 Knowes the last secret how to make them one.
P.	179	STOCKSMARKET	13 When each one that passes finds fault with the horse,
P.	182	MADE FREE	44 Each one he cou'd meete,
P.	183	MADE FREE	105 It might deserve a Box and a Gold one;
P.	183	MADE FREE	108 For wee have had too much of the Old one.
P.	188	BRITANNIA	127 The scotch scabbado of one Court, two Isles,
P.	190	STATUE	20 Have wee not had enough already of one?

```
       P.  190 STATUE          23 And 'tis fourty to one if he Play the old Game
       P.  192 TWO HORSES      30 One night came togeather by all is agreed,
       P.  192 TWO HORSES      37 Thy founder and mine to Cheat one another,
       P.  194 TWO HORSES      96 When one already hath made him soe poor.
       P.  195 TWO HORSES     135 W. One of the two Tyrants must still be our
                                  case
       P.  195 TWO HORSES     155 Ch. Yet have wee one Secretary honest and wise:
       P.  200 DUKE           112 Bribed by a croune on earth and one above,
       P.  202 HISTORICALL     65 Lockes as one sett up for to scare the Crows.
       P.  204 HISTORICALL    132 In our weal-publik scarce one thing succeeds--
       P.  204 HISTORICALL    133 For one man's weakeness a whole Nation bleeds
       P.  204 HISTORICALL    142 One hang'd himself, the other fled away:
       P.  314 CHEQUER INN     71 When noe one could see Sun betweene
       P.  315 CHEQUER INN     98 Had Mortgag'd of his Two, one Band
       P.  315 CHEQUER INN    107 There was but one cou'd be chose out
       P.  316 CHEQUER INN    150 Not one word of the Wenches.
```

one-ey'd   frequency: 1   relative frequency: 0.0000
```
       P.   96 HOLLAND         41 Among the blind the one-ey'd blinkard reigns,
```

onely   frequency: 12   relative frequency: 0.0002
```
       P.    5 HASTINGS        43 Onely they drooping Hymeneus note,
       P.   23 NYMPH           76 It onely loved to be there.
       P.   58 BILL-BOROW      61 Onely sometimes a flutt'ring Breez
       P.   97 HOLLAND         76 The universal Church is onely there.
       P.  116 BLAKE           77 Onely to this vast hill a power is given,
       P.  123 O.C.             5 And thenceforth onely did attend to trace,
       P.  130 O.C.           304 Onely our sighs, perhaps, may thither reach.
       P.  171 PROPHECY        46 And think French onely Loyall, Irish wise,
       P.  174 LOYALL SCOT    122 Beleive but onely as the Church beleives
       P.  178 LOYALL SCOT    262 Charles our great soul this onely Understands:
       P.  186 BRITANNIA       86 To teach your will 's the onely rule of right,
       P.  192 TWO HORSES      34 Not onely discoursed but fell to disputes.
```

ones   frequency: 1   relative frequency: 0.0000
```
       P.  167 KINGS VOWES     56 And new Ones Create Great Places to supplye,
```

onion   frequency: 1   relative frequency: 0.0000
```
       P.   41 THE MOWER       15 Its Onion root they then so high did hold,
```

only   frequency: 56   relative frequency: 0.0011
    See also "onely."
```
       P.    3 LOVELACE         9 Modest ambition studi'd only then,
       P.   11 DIALOGUE        54 And she be only thine.
       P.   14 THE CORONET      6 I gather flow'rs (my fruits are only flow'rs)
       P.   14 THE CORONET     19 But thou who only could'st the Serpent tame,
       P.   15 EYES            23 But finds the Essence only Showers,
       P.   16 EYES            48 But only humane Eyes can weep.
       P.   21 SOUL & BODY     27 Constrain'd not only to indure
       P.   29 LOVER           57 This is the only Banneret
       P.   29 LOVER           63 And he in Story only rules,
       P.   29 THE GALLERY      8 Only your Picture in my Mind.
       P.   32 MOURNING        15 Only to soften near her Heart
       P.   38 PICTURE          6 But only with the Roses playes;
       P.   42 DAMON           15 Only the Snake, that kept within,
       P.   44 DAMON           85 Only for him no Cure is found,
       P.   48 THE GARDEN      14 Only among the Plants will grow.
       P.   48 THE GARDEN      30 Only that She might Laurel grow.
       P.   57 BILL-BOROW      24 But only strives to raise the Plain.
       P.   61 A. HOUSE        70 Only as for a Mark of Grace;
       P.   65 A. HOUSE       207 'Death only can such Theeves make fast,
       P.   67 A. HOUSE       262 Only the Jewels there were true.
       P.   69 A. HOUSE       331 When Gardens only had their Towrs,
       P.   69 A. HOUSE       333 When Roses only Arms might bear,
       P.   69 A. HOUSE       340 Was then the only Magazeen.
       P.   78 A. HOUSE       632 Among these Meads the only Snake.
       P.   80 A. HOUSE       694 So Chrystal-pure but only She;
       P.   81 A. HOUSE       735 When knowledge only could have fill'd
       P.   82 A. HOUSE       768 And Paradice's only Map.
       P.   83 FLECKNO         12 Only there was nor Seeling, nor a Sheet,
       P.   83 FLECKNO         27 Only this frail Ambition did remain,
       P.   84 FLECKNO         49 He never feeds; save only when he tryes
       P.   84 FLECKNO         54 And th' Ordinance was only Politick.
       P.   84 FLECKNO         60 He stands, as if he only fed had been
       P.   84 FLECKNO         66 (His only impossible is to be rich)
       P.   86 FLECKNO        130 Save only two foul copies for his shirt:
       P.   92 MAY'S DEATH     98 May only Master of these Revels past.
       P.   98 HOLLAND        132 And, like its own Seas, only Ebbs to flow.
       P.  104 ANNIVERSARY     28 And only are against their Subjects strong;
       P.  108 ANNIVERSARY    219 We only mourn'd our selves, in thine Ascent,
       P.  110 ANNIVERSARY    287 And only didst for others plant the Vine
```

P. 110 ANNIVERSARY	302	And their Religion only is to Fall.
P. 114 BLAKE	38	This only rules by day, and that by Night.
P. 115 BLAKE	48	She cast off that which only made her strong.
P. 116 BLAKE	94	They only Labour to exalt your praise.
P. 118 BLAKE	152	The only place where it can cause no Ill.
P. 119 TWO SONGS	3	Only this Shepheard, late and soon,
P. 121 TWO SONGS	10	When She is the only flow'r.
P. 126 O.C.	137	The Stars that for him fought had only pow'r
P. 127 O.C.	163	As jealous only here lest all be less,
P. 128 O.C.	226	And you to govern only Heaven's taske.
P. 162 INSTRUCTIONS	886	Only dispers'd by a weak Tapers light;
P. 164 INSTRUCTIONS	946	And henceforth Charles only to Charles shall sit.
P. 164 INSTRUCTIONS	965	She blames them only who the Court restrain,
P. 171 PROPHECY	37	A Minister able only in his Tongue
P. 175 LOYALL SCOT	139	For only Kings can Bishops Exercise.
P. 177 LOYALL SCOT	248	In Paradice Names only Nature Shew'd,
P. 180 STOCKSMARKET	32	For he counterfeits only in gold, not in stone.

on't   frequency: 3   relative frequency: 0.0000

oosy   frequency: 1   relative frequency: 0.0000
    P. 158 INSTRUCTIONS   704 Fraughting their pierced Keels with Oosy
                              Tides.

oozy. See "oosy."

ope   frequency: 2   relative frequency: 0.0000
    P. 16 EYES   45 Ope then mine Eyes your double Sluice,
    P. 73 A. HOUSE   466 Denton sets ope its Cataracts;

open   frequency: 5   relative frequency: 0.0001
    See also "ope."
    P. 57 BILL-BOROW   18 Lyes open to its grassy side;
    P. 61 A. HOUSE   66 Adorns without the open Door:
    P. 123 O.C.   25 That they, to whom his Breast still open lyes,
    P. 126 O.C.   144 Twice had in open field him Victor crown'd:
    P. 163 INSTRUCTIONS   919 Harry sits down, and in his open side

open'd   frequency: 3   relative frequency: 0.0000
    P. 126 O.C.   120 The deep foundations open'd to the Skyes.
    P. 130 O.C.   311 But open'd once, what splendour does he throw?
    P. 155 INSTRUCTIONS   595 And to the rest the open'd passage shew.

opening. See "op'ning."

opens   frequency: 2   relative frequency: 0.0000
    P. 74 A. HOUSE   506 It opens passable and thin;
    P. 124 O.C.   70 Devides the Air, and opens all the Skyes:

opinion   frequency: 2   relative frequency: 0.0000
    P. 97 HOLLAND   74 Opinion but finds Credit, and Exchange.
    P. 195 TWO HORSES   143 Ch. What is thy opinion of James Duke of
                              York?

op'ning   frequency: 1   relative frequency: 0.0000
    P. 143 INSTRUCTIONS 105 Draw next a Pair of Tables op'ning, then

opose   frequency: 2   relative frequency: 0.0000
    P. 166 KINGS VOWES   40 Which if any bold Commoner dare to opose,
    P. 204 HISTORICALL   131 Nothing the dire Contagion can opose.

opportunly   frequency: 1   relative frequency: 0.0000
    P. 61 A. HOUSE   83 We opportunly may relate

oppose   frequency: 2   relative frequency: 0.0000
    See also "opose."
    P. 66 A. HOUSE   250 Their Wooden Saints in vain oppose.
    P. 87 ODE   20 Is more then to oppose.

opposed   frequency: 1   relative frequency: 0.0000
    P. 105 ANNIVERSARY   95 While the resistance of opposed Minds,

opposite   frequency: 2   relative frequency: 0.0000
    P. 84 FLECKNO   39 The other opposite as soon replies,
    P. 143 INSTRUCTIONS 108 On opposite points, the black against the white.

opposition   frequency: 1   relative frequency: 0.0000
    P. 37 DEFINITION   32 And Opposition of the Stars.

oppression   frequency: 2   relative frequency: 0.0000

P. 177 LOYALL SCOT   231 Oppression Avarice Ambition Id--
P. 195 TWO HORSES   160 Thy oppression togeather with Kingship shall
                          dye.

opprest   frequency: 3   relative frequency: 0.0000
P. 104 ANNIVERSARY   30 This Common Enemy is still opprest;
P. 120 TWO SONGS   28 With shades of deep Despair opprest.
P. 189 BRITANNIA   184 Shall England raise, releive opprest mankind.

optick   frequency: 1   relative frequency: 0.0000
P. 164 INSTRUCTIONS   953 Through Optick Trunk the Planet seem'd to
                          hear,

or   frequency: 180   relative frequency: 0.0037

o'r-took   frequency: 1   relative frequency: 0.0000
P. 109 ANNIVERSARY   238 But though forewarn'd, o'r-took and wet the
                          King.

oracles   frequency: 2   relative frequency: 0.0000
P. 58 BILL-BOROW   74 More certain Oracles in Oak.
P. 106 ANNIVERSARY   108 The path where holy Oracles do lead;

oracular   frequency: 2   relative frequency: 0.0000
P. 191 TWO HORSES   14 Have to Questions return'd oracular Answers:
P. 196 TWO HORSES   171 If the Delphick Sybills oracular speeches,

orange   frequency: 1   relative frequency: 0.0000
P. 17 BERMUDAS   17 He hangs in shades the Orange bright,

orbe   frequency: 1   relative frequency: 0.0000
P. 120 TWO SONGS   36 How far below thine Orbe sublime?

o'rcome   frequency: 1   relative frequency: 0.0000
P. 142 INSTRUCTIONS   70 Moon, that o'rcome with the sick steam did'st
                          fail;

ordain   frequency: 1   relative frequency: 0.0000
P. 125 O.C.   101 A secret Cause does sure those Signs ordain

order   frequency: 12   relative frequency: 0.0002
P. 64 A. HOUSE   169 'Nor is our Order yet so nice,
P. 68 A. HOUSE   311 Each Regiment in order grows,
P. 74 A. HOUSE   507 And in as loose an order grows,
P. 82 A. HOUSE   766 But in more decent Order tame;
P. 97 HOLLAND   56 Came next in order; which they could not miss.
P. 104 ANNIVERSARY   52 Dans'd up in order from the Quarreys rude;
P. 105 ANNIVERSARY   67 Such was that wondrous Order and Consent,
P. 152 INSTRUCTIONS   461 But Harry's Order, if they won't recal
P. 166 KINGS VOWES   41 I'll order my Bravo's to cutt off his Nose,
P. 185 BRITANNIA   45 And Golden dayes in peacefull order rould,
P. 200 DUKE   89 And change the order of a nation's fate?
P. 316 CHEQUER INN   152 The Healths in Order did up send

order'd   frequency: 1   relative frequency: 0.0000
P. 149 INSTRUCTIONS   367 The Count forthwith is order'd all to close,

orderly   frequency: 1   relative frequency: 0.0000
P. 59 A. HOUSE   26 Like Nature, orderly and near:

orders   frequency: 4   relative frequency: 0.0000
P. 148 INSTRUCTIONS   317 Mean time through all the Yards their Orders
                          run
P. 151 INSTRUCTIONS   426 Orders, amaz'd at last gives none at all.
P. 161 INSTRUCTIONS   851 Hyde orders Turner that he should come late,
P. 175 LOYALL SCOT   149 And holy Ordure Holy orders give?

ordinance   frequency: 1   relative frequency: 0.0000
See also "ord'nance."
P. 84 FLECKNO   54 And th' Ordinance was only Politick.

ordinaries   frequency: 1   relative frequency: 0.0000
P. 86 FLECKNO   136 At ordinaries after dinner show'th,

ord'nance   frequency: 1   relative frequency: 0.0000
P. 69 A. HOUSE   344 We Ord'nance Plant and Powder sow.

ordure   frequency: 2   relative frequency: 0.0000
P. 175 LOYALL SCOT   149 And holy Ordure Holy orders give?
P. 188 BRITANNIA   128 Fiend Lauderdale, with ordure all defiles.

ore   frequency: 16   relative frequency: 0.0003

P.	31 MOURNING	5 Her Eyes confus'd, and doubled ore,
P.	42 DAMON	11 The Grass-hopper its pipe gives ore;
P.	70 A. HOUSE	367 But ore the Meads below it plays,
P.	72 A. HOUSE	422 Lyes quilted ore with Bodies slain:
P.	91 MAY'S DEATH	37 As he crowds in he whipt him ore the pate
P.	92 MAY'S DEATH	63 When the Sword glitters ore the Judges head,
P.	96 HOLLAND	24 And oft at Leap-frog ore their Steeples plaid:
P.	107 ANNIVERSARY	184 Of purling Ore, a shining wave do shed:
P.	111 ANNIVERSARY	321 But the great Captain, now the danger's ore,
P.	116 BLAKE	102 Ore Seas as vast as is the Spaniards pride.
P.	126 O.C.	122 And pour the Deluge ore the Chaos head.
P.	127 O.C.	174 And stretch'd our frontire to the Indian Ore;
P.	166 KINGS VOWES	26 If nct o're a Kingdome, to raigne ore my Guard;
P.	178 LOYALL SCOT	270 Powders them ore till none discern their foes
P.	181 MADE FREE	22 And now he's ccme ore,
P.	186 BRITANNIA	82 If not ore aw'd by new found holy cheat.

o're   frequency: 10   relative frequency: 0.0002

o'reflow   frequency: 2   relative frequency: 0.0000
  P.   17 EYES   53 Thus let ycur Streams o'reflow your Springs,
  P.   24 NYMPH   103 It till it do c'reflow with mine;

o'retakes   frequency: 1   relative frequency: 0.0000
  P.   71 A. HOUSE   412 And Chance o'retakes what scapeth spight?

o'rethrown   frequency: 1   relative frequency: 0.0000
  P. 161 INSTRUCTIONS 829 Plain Gentlemen are in Stage-Coach o'rethrown,

o'return   frequency: 1   relative frequency: 0.0000
  P.   16 EYES   52 Now like two flcods o'return and drcwn.

o'rewhelming   frequency: 1   relative frequency: 0.0000
  P. 131 PARADISE   10 The World o'rewhelming to revenge his Sight.

organs   frequency: 1   relative frequency: 0.0000
  P.   47 EMPIRE   8 And built the Crgans City where they dwell.

orient   frequency: 2   relative frequency: 0.0000
  P.   12 DROP OF DEW   1 See how the Orient Dew,
  P.   62 A. HOUSE   109 'Our Orient Ereaths perfumed are

orientest   frequency: 1   relative frequency: 0.0000
  P.   39 THE MATCH   5 Her Orientest Cclours there,

original   frequency: 1   relative frequency: 0.0000
  P.   76 A. HOUSE   570 In their most learned Criginal:

orlando   frequency: 1   relative frequency: 0.0000
  P. 147 INSTRUCTIONS 275 Such once Orlando, famous in Romance,

orleans   frequency: 1   relative frequency: 0.0000
  P. 202 HISTORICALL   71 And gentlier farre the Orleans Dutches treat.

ormus   frequency: 1   relative frequency: 0.0000
  P.   17 BERMUDAS   20 Jewels more rich than Crmus show's.

ornament   frequency: 1   relative frequency: 0.0000
  P. 164 INSTRUCTIONS 962 Banishing Love, Trust, Crnament and Use;

ornaments   frequency: 2   relative frequency: 0.0000
  P.   62 A. HOUSE   128 'That serves for Altar's Ornaments.
  P. 186 BRITANNIA   72 'Are thred-bare Virtues Ornaments for Kings?

orphan   frequency: 2   relative frequency: 0.0000
  P.   28 LOVER   32 The Orphan cf the Hurricane.
  P.   71 A. HOUSE   413 And now your Orphan Parents Call

orphans   frequency: 1   relative frequency: 0.0000
  P. 181 MADE FREE   9 And your Orphans want Bread to feed on,

orthodox   frequency: 1   relative frequency: 0.0000
  P. 175 LOYALL SCOT   152 Noe Wonder if the Crthodox doe Bleed,

osborn   frequency: 3   relative frequency: 0.0000
  P. 185 BRITANNIA   18 Till Golden Osborn cheating shall detect,
  P. 187 BRITANNIA   123 Her Creature Osbcrn the Revenue steals;
  P. 204 HISTORICALL   144 But Csborn and the Duke must needs prevail.

osborne. See "osborn."

osbornes   frequency: 1   relative frequency: 0.0000

```
        P. 189 BRITANNIA     170 The Cleavelands, Osbornes, Barties,
                                 Lauderdales.

osburn                            frequency:    1    relative frequency: 0.0000
        P. 192 TWO HORSES      27 Since Viner and Osburn did buy and provide 'um

osiers                            frequency:    1    relative frequency: 0.0000
        P.  79 A. HOUSE       646 On the Osiers undermined Root,

ostracize                         frequency:    1    relative frequency: 0.0000
        P.   5 HASTINGS        26 And all that Worth from hence did Ostracize.

oth                               frequency:    2    relative frequency: 0.0000
        P. 184 MADE FREE      110 Of the Oth to him read
        P. 198 DUKE            26 And thinke a prince oth blood can ere doe Ill?

o'th                              frequency:    1    relative frequency: 0.0000
        See also "oth."

other                             frequency:   56    relative frequency: 0.0011
        P.   3 LOVELACE         5 That candid Age no other way could tell
        P.  11 DIALOGUE        66 The other half thy Friend.
        P.  18 CLORINDA        19 C. And what late change? D. The other day
        P.  20 SOUL & BODY      9 Tortur'd, besides each other part,
        P.  21 SOUL & BODY     38 Or Sorrow's other Madness vex.
        P.  25 YOUNG LOVE      26 Other Titles to their Crown,
        P.  28 LOVER           51 While with the other he does lock,
        P.  29 THE GALLERY     17 But, on the other side, th' art drawn
        P.  40 THE MATCH       32 Into each other wrought.
        P.  49 THE GARDEN      46 Far other Worlds, and other Seas;
        P.  49 THE GARDEN      60 What other Help could yet be meet!
        P.  58 BILL-BOROW      65 Much other Groves, say they, then these
        P.  58 BILL-BOROW      66 And other Hills him once did please.
        P.  64 A. HOUSE       172 'One perfecting the other Sweet.
        P.  74 A. HOUSE       492 On one hand Fairfax, th' other Veres:
        P.  84 FLECKNO         33 Held him the other; and unchanged yet,
        P.  84 FLECKNO         39 The other opposite as soon replies,
        P.  92 MAY'S DEATH     88 As th' Eagles Plumes from other birds divide.
        P.  94 DR. WITTY       21 But she is Caelia still: no other grace
        P.  94 DR. WITTY       26 With other Language doth them fitly fit.
        P. 104 ANNIVERSARY     29 Their other Wars seem but a feign'd contest,
        P. 104 ANNIVERSARY     37 No other care they bear of things above,
        P. 105 ANNIVERSARY     77 All other Matter yields, and may be rul'd;
        P. 105 ANNIVERSARY     92 Uphold, this one, and that the other Side;
        P. 107 ANNIVERSARY    173 Thee proof beyond all other Force or Skill,
        P. 107 ANNIVERSARY    182 The other Glories of our yearly Song.
        P. 111 ANNIVERSARY    328 Pleas'd with that other World of moving Light;
        P. 111 ANNIVERSARY    345 Up from the other World his Flame he darts,
        P. 112 ANNIVERSARY    360 'A Fleet of Worlds, of other Worlds in quest;
        P. 124 O.C.            46 How on each other both their Fates depend.
        P. 142 INSTRUCTIONS    78 Galloping with the Duke to other Prey.
        P. 144 INSTRUCTIONS   148 (And Painter, wanting other, draw this Fight.)
        P. 145 INSTRUCTIONS   196 Whose Horses each with other enterfeers.
        P. 146 INSTRUCTIONS   226 For one had much, the other nought to lose.
        P. 146 INSTRUCTIONS   239 For th' other side all in loose Quarters lay,
        P. 148 INSTRUCTIONS   308 Resolve henceforth upon their other Game:
        P. 151 INSTRUCTIONS   421 Each does the other blame, and all distrust;
        P. 156 INSTRUCTIONS   654 Nor other Courtship knew but to his Cheek.
        P. 157 INSTRUCTIONS   660 That fly'st Love Fires, reserv'd for other
                                  Flame?
        P. 157 INSTRUCTIONS   663 Nor other fear himself could comprehend,
        P. 159 INSTRUCTIONS   753 And to each other helpless couple moan,
        P. 163 INSTRUCTIONS   910 But let some other Painter draw the sound:
        P. 168 ADVICE          10 One to his Pathic, th' other to his Player.
        P. 169 ADVICE          34 To make them th' other Councell board forgett.
        P. 172 LOYALL SCOT     20 Nor other Courtship knew but to his Cheek.
        P. 172 LOYALL SCOT     26 That flyst loves fires reserv'd for other flame?'
        P. 172 LOYALL SCOT     29 Nor other fear himself cold Comprehend
        P. 173 LOYALL SCOT     82 Whose one bank vertue, th' other vice doth breed?
        P. 177 LOYALL SCOT    251 First call each other names and then they fight.
        P. 185 BRITANNIA       42 The other day fam'd Spencer I did bring
        P. 186 BRITANNIA       78 The Rivall Gods, Monarchs of th' other world,
        P. 199 DUKE            62 Their boyling heads can hear no other sounds
        P. 204 HISTORICALL    142 One hang'd himself, the other fled away:
        P. 315 CHEQUER INN     99 To have the other wash't
        P. 315 CHEQUER INN    128 Which shoud the other most commend

others                            frequency:   27    relative frequency: 0.0005
        P.   3 LOVELACE        14 And against others Fame his owne employs.
        P.  16 EYES            47 For others too can see, or sleep;
        P.  32 MOURNING        21 Nay others, bolder, hence esteem
```

P. 47 EMPIRE	14	And others chose the Cornet eloquent.
P. 55 THYESTE	12	Who expos'd to others Ey's,
P. 60 A. HOUSE	45	Let others vainly strive t'immure
P. 73 A. HOUSE	473	Let others tell the Paradox,
P. 89 ODE	99	What may not others fear
P. 94 DR. WITTY	9	Others do strive with words and forced phrase
P. 98 HOLLAND	98	Cut out each others Athos to a Man:
P. 104 ANNIVERSARY	27	They fight by Others, but in Person wrong,
P. 109 ANNIVERSARY	259	Though why should others all thy Labor spoil,
P. 110 ANNIVERSARY	287	And only didst for others plant the Vine
P. 113 BLAKE	11	Wealth which all others Avarice might cloy,
P. 118 BLAKE	134	Whilst others lower, in the Sea do lye.
P. 121 TWO SONGS	47	Less Loves set of each others praise,
P. 124 O.C.	65	That whether by each others grief they fell,
P. 128 O.C.	198	Each wound himself which he to others delt;
P. 128 O.C.	225	Least others dare to think your zeale a maske,
P. 140 HOUSEWARMING	103	And others as much reprehend his Backside,
P. 142 INSTRUCTIONS	48	When Men and Women took each others Word.
P. 146 INSTRUCTIONS	243	And some ran o're each night while others sleep,
P. 150 INSTRUCTIONS	391	In quick Effigy, others Faults, and feign
P. 177 LOYALL SCOT	224	Others Attempt, to Cool their fervent Chine,
P. 179 STOCKSMARKET	23	And others to make the similitude hold
P. 192 TWO HORSES	38	When both knaves agreed to be each others brother.
P. 200 DUKE	103	Shooke by the faults of others, not thine owne.

other's   frequency: 2   relative frequency: 0.0000
    P. 17 EYES   55 And each the other's difference bears;
    P. 124 O.C.   52 This will not stay when once the other's gone.

ought   frequency: 5   relative frequency: 0.0001
    P. 10 DIALOGUE   24 Conscious of doing what I ought.
    P. 23 NYMPH   51 But I am sure, for ought that I
    P. 45 MOWER'S SONG   19 But what you in Compassion ought,
    P. 108 ANNIVERSARY   226 Then ought below, or yet above a King:
    P. 194 TWO HORSES   99 Wee ought to be wary and Bridle our Tongue;

ould   frequency: 1   relative frequency: 0.0000
    P. 198 DUKE   19 Prove to the world Ile have ould England know

our   frequency: 202   relative frequency: 0.0042

ours   frequency: 6   relative frequency: 0.0001

ourselves   frequency: 2   relative frequency: 0.0000

out   frequency: 55   relative frequency: 0.0011

out-do   frequency: 2   relative frequency: 0.0000
    P. 126 O.C.   115 The Winds receive it, and its force out-do,
    P. 164 INSTRUCTIONS 947 His Master-hand the Ancients shall out-do

out-doe   frequency: 1   relative frequency: 0.0000
    P. 41 THE MOWER   28 Lest any Tyrant him out-doe.

out-run   frequency: 1   relative frequency: 0.0000
    P.   4 HASTINGS   10 Needs must he die, that doth out-run his Age.

outdoes   frequency: 1   relative frequency: 0.0000
    P. 202 HISTORICALL   67 Outdoes Tiberius and his Goatish Court:

outrun   frequency: 1   relative frequency: 0.0000
    See also "out-run."
    P. 314 CHEQUER INN   85 Wild with his Tongue did all outrun

outshining   frequency: 1   relative frequency: 0.0000
    P. 186 BRITANNIA   58 Outshining Virgo and the Julian Star.

outwakes   frequency: 1   relative frequency: 0.0000
    P. 119 TWO SONGS   4 Upon this Hill outwakes the Moon.

outward   frequency: 1   relative frequency: 0.0000
    P. 62 A. HOUSE   103 'The Cloyster outward shuts its Gates,

outwings   frequency: 1   relative frequency: 0.0000
    P. 106 ANNIVERSARY 126 Angelique Cromwell who outwings the wind;

over   frequency: 18   relative frequency: 0.0003
    See also "o'r-took," "ore," "o're."

over-awe   frequency: 1   relative frequency: 0.0000

P. 152 INSTRUCTIONS   478 Their Acts to vitiate, and them over-awe.

over-thwart   frequency: 1   relative frequency: 0.0000
    P. 314 CHEQUER INN   89 Did feed his Neighbour over-thwart

overcome   frequency: 2   relative frequency: 0.0000
    See also "o'rcome."
    P. 89 ODE   78 And have, though overcome, confest
    P. 99 HOLLAND   141 Or, what is left, their Carthage overcome

overcomest. See "overcom'st."

overcom'st   frequency: 1   relative frequency: 0.0000
    P. 10 DIALOGUE   50 And if thou overcom'st thou shalt be crown'd.

overflow. See "o'reflow."

overflows   frequency: 1   relative frequency: 0.0000
    P. 62 A. HOUSE   114 'With which calm Pleasure overflows;

overgrow   frequency: 1   relative frequency: 0.0000
    P. 69 A. HOUSE   343 But war all this doth overgrow:

overlaid   frequency: 1   relative frequency: 0.0000
    P. 139 HOUSEWARMING   63 So the Bribes overlaid her that Rome once
                             betray'd:

overtaken. See "overt'ane."

overtakes. See "o'retakes."

overt'ane   frequency: 1   relative frequency: 0.0000
    P. 80 A. HOUSE   678 As Flies in Chrystal overt'ane;

overthrow   frequency: 1   relative frequency: 0.0000
    P. 169 ADVICE   54 To overthrow the Darby Hous designes,

overthrown   frequency: 2   relative frequency: 0.0000
    See also "o'rethrown."
    P. 82 A. HOUSE   763 All negligently overthrown,
    P. 108 ANNIVERSARY   204 As if that Natures self were overthrown.

overturn   frequency: 1   relative frequency: 0.0000
    See also "o'return," "overturne."
    P. 107 ANNIVERSARY   176 At once assay'd to overturn us all.

overturne   frequency: 1   relative frequency: 0.0000
    P. 200 DUKE   88 Are these fitt hands to overturne a State

overwhelm   frequency: 1   relative frequency: 0.0000
    P. 164 INSTRUCTIONS 977 Nor Earthquake so an hollow Isle overwhelm,

overwhelming. See "o'erwhelming," "o'rewhelming."

owe   frequency: 3   relative frequency: 0.0000
    P. 35 DAPHNIS   59 Nor to my Departure owe
    P. 118 BLAKE   156 And the Land owe her peace unto the Sea.
    P. 189 BRITANNIA   167 Tell em the Generous scorn their Rise to owe

owes   frequency: 3   relative frequency: 0.0000
    See also "ows."
    P. 80 A. HOUSE   692 To Her the Meadow sweetness owes;
    P. 117 BLAKE   115 That Bay they enter, which unto them owes,
    P. 119 BLAKE   168 And tells the World, how much to you it owes.

owls   frequency: 1   relative frequency: 0.0000
    P. 111 ANNIVERSARY   333 And Owls and Ravens with their screeching noyse

own   frequency: 67   relative frequency: 0.0014
    See also "owne."
    P. 10 DIALOGUE   30 Is Heaven's and its own perfume.
    P. 12 DROP OF DEW   13 Like its own Tear,
    P. 12 DROP OF DEW   24 And, recollecting its own Light,
    P. 16 EYES   28 Bath still their Eyes in their own Dew.
    P. 17 BERMUDAS   8 And yet far kinder than our own?
    P. 21 SOUL & BODY   14 That mine own Precipice I go;
    P. 23 NYMPH   56 I it at mine own fingers nurst.
    P. 23 NYMPH   71 I have a Garden of my own,
    P. 28 LOVER   56 In his own Blood does relish best.
    P. 33 DAPHNIS   5 Nature her own Sexes foe,
    P. 42 DAMON   22 Hotter then his own Phaeton.
    P. 44 DAMON   78 Did into his own Ankle glance;
    P. 44 DAMON   80 By his own Sythe, the Mower mown.

P.	48 THE GARDEN	24 No Name shall but your own be found.
P.	49 THE GARDEN	44 Does streight its own resemblance find;
P.	55 THYESTE	13 Into his own Heart ne'r pry's,
P.	58 BILL-BOROW	76 That Courage its own Praises flies.
P.	58 BILL-BOROW	78 From his own Brightness he retreats:
P.	69 A. HOUSE	348 Fresh as his own and flourishing.
P.	81 A. HOUSE	733 Yet your own Face shall at you grin,
P.	84 FLECKNO	70 And swaddled in's own papers seaven times,
P.	85 FLECKNO	104 By its own narrowness, Sir, to unite.
P.	86 FLECKNO	152 And roar'd out, like Perillus in's own Bull;
P.	87 ODE	15 Did thorough his own Side
P.	91 MAY'S DEATH	24 In his own Bowels sheath'd the conquering health.
P.	91 MAY'S DEATH	32 Shook his gray locks, and his own Bayes did tear
P.	93 DR. WITTY	1 Sit further, and make room for thine own fame,
P.	94 DR. WITTY	8 For ill Translators make the Book their own.
P.	94 DR. WITTY	22 But her own smiles commend that lovely face;
P.	98 HOLLAND	132 And, like its own Seas, only Ebbs to flow.
P.	108 ANNIVERSARY	190 On their own Hopes shall find the Fall retort.
P.	109 ANNIVERSARY	231 But in thine own Fields exercisedst long,
P.	110 ANNIVERSARY	292 May shew their own, not see his Nakedness.
P.	117 BLAKE	132 That it return'd to its own Element.
P.	119 TWO SONGS	1 Th' Astrologers own Eyes are set,
P.	120 TWO SONGS	40 Would you but your own Reason use.
P.	122 TWO SONGS	21 Not our Lambs own Fleeces are
P.	124 O.C.	66 Or on their own redoubled, none can tell.
P.	126 O.C.	128 And hasten not to see his Death their own.
P.	126 O.C.	150 In their own Griefs might find themselves imploy'd;
P.	128 O.C.	211 If so indulgent to his own, how deare
P.	128 O.C.	224 Spare yet your own, if you neglect his fame;
P.	129 O.C.	266 At mortalls sins, nor his own plant will spare;
P.	130 O.C.	273 And his own shadows with him fall; the eye
P.	132 PARADISE	46 With tinkling Rhime, of thy own Sense secure;
P.	137 HOUSEWARMING	20 To build with the Jews-trump of his own tongue.
P.	150 INSTRUCTIONS	407 With the Bulls Horn to measure his own Head,
P.	153 INSTRUCTIONS	507 Let no Man touch them, or demand his own.
P.	156 INSTRUCTIONS	627 At her own Breast her useless claws does arm;
P.	157 INSTRUCTIONS	674 Inspire, nor would he his own deeds deface.
P.	161 INSTRUCTIONS	830 And Deputy-Lieutenants in their own.
P.	162 INSTRUCTIONS	894 With her own Tresses interwove and twin'd:
P.	163 INSTRUCTIONS	932 To her own Husband, Castlemain, untrue.
P.	168 ADVICE	14 Whose life does scarce one Generous Action own,
P.	168 ADVICE	16 To keep his own and loose his sergeants wife.
P.	172 LOYALL SCOT	40 Inspire, nor cold hee his own Deeds deface;
P.	172 LOYALL SCOT	41 And secrett Joy in his own soul doth Rise
P.	179 STOCKSMARKET	2 Do at their own charge their citadels build,
P.	179 STOCKSMARKET	16 That he did for the King his own statue erect.
P.	180 STOCKSMARKET	31 And alleges the workmanship was not his own
P.	185 BRITANNIA	24 Your own lov'd Court and Masters Progeny?
P.	192 TWO HORSES	32 Were stolne of Incognito each his own way,
P.	192 TWO HORSES	48 For which his own Father a Martyr did dye.
P.	192 TWO HORSES	50 Not to think his own Father is gone to the Devill.
P.	193 TWO HORSES	72 Was after rewarded with losing his own.
P.	194 TWO HORSES	92 Which Augments and secures his own profitt and peace.
P.	196 TWO HORSES	176 To conceal their own crimes and cover their shame,

own'd   frequency: 1   relative frequency: 0.0000
   P. 110 ANNIVERSARY   309 As thou must needs have own'd them of thy band

owne   frequency: 10   relative frequency: 0.0002
   P.   3 LOVELACE   14 And against others Fame his owne employs.
   P. 165 KINGS VOWES   7 I will have a Religion then all of my owne,
   P. 166 KINGS VOWES   23 with wide streets and uniforme of my owne mold;
   P. 167 KINGS VOWES   57 That they may raise Fortunes to my owne frye.
   P. 182 MADE FREE   39 He us'd as his owne to spend on't
   P. 182 MADE FREE   46 But when they ask't for their owne
   P. 199 DUKE   48 Better some jealous neighbour of your owne
   P. 200 DUKE   103 Shooke by the faults of others, not thine owne.
   P. 315 CHEQUER INN   101 With his owne Gravy fill'd his Plate
   P. 316 CHEQUER INN   153 Nor of his owne took care

ows   frequency: 1   relative frequency: 0.0000
   P.   98 HOLLAND   109 To whom their weather-beaten Province ows

ox   frequency: 3   relative frequency: 0.0000
See also "oxe."
   P.   73 A. HOUSE   474 How Eels now bellow in the Ox;
   P. 156 INSTRUCTIONS 634 Large Limbs, like Ox, not to be kill'd but shown.

P. 191 TWO HORSES   8 That a sacraficed ox, when his Gutts were out,
                         Bellow'd:

oxe   frequency: 1   relative frequency: 0.0000
   P. 140 HOUSEWARMING 111 When like the good Oxe, for publick good chear,

oyl   frequency: 4   relative frequency: 0.0000
   P. 64 A. HOUSE   174 'The Sugars uncerrupting Oyl:
   P. 87 ODE   6 And oyl th' unused Armcurs rust:
   P. 109 ANNIVERSARY   260 And Brambles be anointed with thine Oyl,
   P. 188 BRITANNIA   147 If this Imperiall cyl once taint the Blood,

oyle   frequency: 1   relative frequency: 0.0000
   P. 198 DUKE   32 That extreame unction is but common oyle

oyster   frequency: 1   relative frequency: 0.0000
   P. 142 INSTRUCTIONS   61 Paint her with Oyster lip, and breath of Fame,

pace   frequency: 1   relative frequency: 0.0000
   P. 160 INSTRUCTIONS 792 And march with Punishment in equal pace;

pacifie   frequency: 1   relative frequency: 0.0000
   P. 174 LOYALL SCOT   96 Who sermons ere can pacifie and prayers?

pacify. See "pacifie."

pacis   frequency: 2   relative frequency: 0.0000
   P. 98 HOLLAND   113 Was this Jus Belli <and> Pacis; could this be
   P. 140 HIS HOUSE   9 The Dutchman's Templum Pacis.

pack   frequency: 2   relative frequency: 0.0000
   P. 165 KINGS VOWES   17 Yet if Men should clammcr I'le pack him away:
   P. 317 CHEQUER INN   185 He Money gives amongst this Pack

pack-horse   frequency: 1   relative frequency: 0.0000
   P. 132 PARADISE   48 And like a Pack-Horse tires without his Bells.

packet-boat   frequency: 1   relative frequency: 0.0000
   P. 90 MAY'S DEATH   1 As one put drunk into the Packet-boat,

pad   frequency: 1   relative frequency: 0.0000
   P. 161 INSTRUCTIONS 827 Up ambles Country Justice on his Pad,

pagan   frequency: 1   relative frequency: 0.0000
   See also "turk-christian-pagan-jew."
   P. 175 LOYALL SCOT   154 What soe obdurate Pagan Heretique

page   frequency: 1   relative frequency: 0.0000
   P. 199 DUKE   50 Where twixt a wholsome husband and a page

pages   frequency: 1   relative frequency: 0.0000
   P. 142 INSTRUCTIONS   64 There, not behind the Coach, her Pages jump.

pagod   frequency: 1   relative frequency: 0.0000
   P. 187 BRITANNIA   125 Mack James the Irish Pagcd does Adore,

paid   frequency: 6   relative frequency: 0.0001
   See also "pay'd."
   P. 15 EYES   11 And then paid out in equal Poise,
   P. 139 HOUSEWARMING   84 But receiv'd now and paid the Chancellours
                            Custome.
   P. 160 INSTRUCTIONS 818 The Peace not sure, new Army must be paid.
   P. 193 TWO HORSES   84 For selling their Ccnscience were Liberally
                            paid.
   P. 199 DUKE   72 And will cutt throats againe if he bee paid:
   P. 316 CHEQUER INN   143 The Beck'ning never will be paid

pain   frequency: 8   relative frequency: 0.0001
   P.   4 LOVELACE   44 (She knew what pain 'twould be to lose that
                            sight.)
   P. 12 DROP OF DEW   17 Till the warm Sun pitty it's Pain,
   P. 21 SOUL & BODY   24 I feel, that cannct feel, the pain.
   P. 43 DAMON   68 Joyning my Labour to my Pain;
   P. 59 A. HOUSE   5 Who of his great Design in pain
   P. 125 O.C.   85 But rather then in his Eliza's pain
   P. 153 INSTRUCTIONS 508 Pain of Displeasure of great Clarendon.
   P. 159 INSTRUCTIONS 756 And were it burnt, yet less would be their pain.

pain'd   frequency: 1   relative frequency: 0.0000
   P. 138 HOUSEWARMING   25 Thus dayly his Gouty Inventions he pain'd,

paines   frequency: 2   relative frequency: 0.0000
    P. 177 LOYALL SCOT   222 Incorrigible among all their paines
    P. 316 CHEQUER INN   167 The paines of comeing in agen

pains   frequency: 4   relative frequency: 0.0000
    See also "paines."
    P.   5 HASTINGS   30 And in the choicest Pleasures charms his Pains:
    P.   86 FLECKNO   138 Yet he first kist them, and after takes pains
    P. 124 O.C.   61 She lest He grieve hides what She can her
                               pains,
    P. 126 O.C.   127 Numbers of Men decrease with pains unknown,

paint   frequency: 14   relative frequency: 0.0002
    P.   41 DAMON   3 While ev'ry thing did seem to paint
    P.   41 THE MOWER   12 And Flow'rs themselves were taught to paint.
    P.   62 A. HOUSE   123 'While all the rest with Needles paint
    P. 141 INSTRUCTIONS   5 Canst thou paint without Colours? Then 'tis
                               right:
    P. 141 INSTRUCTIONS   29 Paint then St. Albans full of soup and gold,
    P. 141 INSTRUCTIONS   33 Paint him with Drayman's Shoulders, butchers
                               Mien,
    P. 142 INSTRUCTIONS   49 Paint then again Her Highness to the life,
    P. 142 INSTRUCTIONS   61 Paint her with Oyster Lip, and breath of Fame,
    P. 143 INSTRUCTIONS   79 Paint Castlemaine in Colours that will hold,
    P. 148 INSTRUCTIONS   303 See sudden chance of War! To Paint or Write,
    P. 151 INSTRUCTIONS   444 (His Character was that which thou didst paint)
    P. 156 INSTRUCTIONS   633 Paint him of Person tall, and big of bone,
    P. 162 INSTRUCTIONS   866 Paint him in Golden Gown, with Mace's Brain:
    P. 162 INSTRUCTIONS   885 Paint last the King, and a dead Shade of
                               Night,

painted   frequency: 5   relative frequency: 0.0001
    P.   29 THE GALLERY   9 Here Thou art painted in the Dress
    P.   73 A. HOUSE   455 Such, in the painted World, appear'd
    P.   87 FLECKNO   169 Have made the Chance be painted; and go now
    P. 164 INSTRUCTIONS   944 Poetick Picture, Painted Poetry.
    P. 313 CHEQUER INN   9 There stands a House new Painted

painter   frequency: 22   relative frequency: 0.0004
    P. 141 INSTRUCTIONS   t The last Instructions to a Painter.
    P. 141 INSTRUCTIONS   3 But er'e thou fal'st to work, first Painter see
    P. 141 INSTRUCTIONS   21 The Painter so, long having vext his cloth,
    P. 143 INSTRUCTIONS   103 Ah Painter, now could Alexander live,
    P. 143 INSTRUCTIONS   117 Here Painter rest a little, and survey
    P. 144 INSTRUCTIONS   148 (And Painter, wanting other, draw this Fight.)
    P. 150 INSTRUCTIONS   390 So thou and I, dear Painter, represent
    P. 153 INSTRUCTIONS   511 Often, dear Painter, have I sate and mus'd
    P. 156 INSTRUCTIONS   632 Sweet Painter draw his Picture while I write.
    P. 162 INSTRUCTIONS   863 Dear Painter, draw this Speaker to the foot:
    P. 163 INSTRUCTIONS   910 But let some other Painter draw the sound:
    P. 164 INSTRUCTIONS   943 Painter adieu, how will our Arts agree;
    P. 164 INSTRUCTIONS   948 Himself the Poet and the Painter too. To the
                               King.
    P. 168 ADVICE   t Further Advice to a Painter.
    P. 168 ADVICE   1 Painter once more thy Pencell reassume,
    P. 197 DUKE   t Advice to a Painter to draw the Duke by.
    P. 197 DUKE   1 Spread a large canvass, Painter, to containe
    P. 198 DUKE   36 Next, Painter, draw his Mordant by his side,
    P. 199 DUKE   54 Now, Painter, shew us in the blackest dye
    P. 199 DUKE   74 Then, Painter, shew thy skill and in fitt place
    P. 200 DUKE   86 Next, Painter, draw the Rabble of the plott,
    P. 200 DUKE   98 Noe, Painter, noe; close up this peice and see

paintings   frequency: 1   relative frequency: 0.0000
    P.   77 A. HOUSE   580 Like Mexique Paintings, all the Plumes.

pair   frequency: 6   relative frequency: 0.0001
    P.   75 A. HOUSE   526 Sad pair unto the Elms they moan.
    P. 121 TWO SONGS   55 For he did never love to pair
    P. 122 TWO SONGS   29 Joy to that happy Pair,
    P. 123 TWO SONGS   47 Joy to that happy Fair,
    P. 143 INSTRUCTIONS   105 Draw next a Pair of Tables op'ning, then
    P. 159 INSTRUCTIONS   747 Sad change, since first that happy pair was wed,

paires   frequency: 1   relative frequency: 0.0000
    P.   74 A. HOUSE   488 Although in Armies, not in Paires.

pairs   frequency: 1   relative frequency: 0.0000
    See also "paires."
    P.   27 LOVER   3 Sorted by pairs, they still are seen

palace   frequency: 6   relative frequency: 0.0001

See also "pallace."
```
P.    5  HASTINGS        33 Before the Chrystal Palace where he dwells,
P.   59  A. HOUSE        19 And in his hollcw Palace goes
P.  104  ANNIVERSARY     62 The flocking Marbles in a Palace meet;
P.  108  ANNIVERSARY    209 A dismal Silence through the Palace went,
P.  139  HOUSEWARMING    87 He finish'd at last his Palace Mosaick,
P.  149  INSTRUCTIONS   355 See how he Reigns in his new Palace culminant,
```

palaces. See "pallaces."

palace's   frequency: 1   relative frequency: 0.0000
```
    P. 164 INSTRUCTIONS 979 And through the Palace's Foundations bore,
```

palat   frequency: 1   relative frequency: 0.0000
```
    P. 162 INSTRUCTICNS 875 Whence ev'ry day, the Palat more to tickle;
```

palate   frequency: 1   relative frequency: 0.0000
See also "palat."
```
    P.  41 THE MOWER     26 Might put the Palate in dispute.
```

pale   frequency: 8   relative frequency: 0.0001
```
    P. 129 O.C.         253 All wither'd, all discclour'd, pale and wan,
    P. 142 INSTRUCTIONS  69 Witness ye stars of Night, and thou the pale
    P. 144 INSTRUCTIONS 159 Expectants pale, with hopes of spoil allur'd,
    P. 163 INSTRUCTICNS 917 While, the pale Ghosts, his Eye does fixt
                            admire
    P. 186 BRITANNIA     68 Pale death, lusts, Horrour fill her pompous
                            train.
    P. 190 STATUE        16 To repair with such riffe raffe our Churches old
                            Pale?
    P. 313 CHEQUER INN   33 Envy is not so pale;
    P. 316 CHEQUER INN  160 And prithee why so pale? then swore
```

palestine   frequency: 1   relative frequency: 0.0000
```
    P.  77 A. HOUSE     581 What Rome, Greece, Palestine, ere said
```

pallace   frequency: 3   relative frequency: 0.0000
```
    P.  85 FLECKNO       92 I whcm the Pallace never has deny'd
    P. 137 HOUSEWARMING  23 That he begg'd for a Pallace so much of his
                            grcund,
    P. 202 HISTORICALL   50 Burnt downe the Pallace of Persepolis.
```

pallaces   frequency: 1   relative frequency: 0.0000
```
    P.  88 ODE           22 And Pallaces and Temples rent:
```

pallat   frequency: 1   relative frequency: 0.0000
```
    P. 141 INSTRUCTIONS  20 Stamp on thy Pallat, nor perhaps the worse.
```

pallete. See "pallat."

pallets   frequency: 1   relative frequency: 0.0000
```
    P.  77 A. HOUSE     594 Cn Pallets swoln of Velvet Moss;
```

palm   frequency: 1   relative frequency: 0.0000
```
    P.  48 THE GARDEN     2 Io win the Palm, the Cke, or Bayes;
```

palmer   frequency: 1   relative frequency: 0.0000
```
    P. 150 INSTRUCTIONS 406 Where Pilgrim Palmer travell'd in Exile,
```

palmer's   frequency: 1   relative frequency: 0.0000
```
    P. 201 HISTORICALL   12 And dubd poore Palmer's wife his Royall Whore.
```

palsie   frequency: 1   relative frequency: 0.0000
```
    P.  21 SOUL & BODY   34 And then the Palsie Shakes of Fear.
```

palsy. See "palsie."

pan   frequency: 7   relative frequency: 0.0001
```
    P.  18 CLORINDA      20 Pan met me. C. What did great Pan say?
    P.  18 CLORINDA      24 C. Sweet must Pan sound in Damons Note.
    P.  18 CLORINDA      27 Of Pan the flowry Pastures sing,
    P.  48 THE GARDEN    31 And Pan did after Syrinx speed,
    P.  68 A. HOUSE     295 And dries its Pan yet dank with Dew,
    P. 313 CHEQUER INN   17 But quickly turn'd Catt i'th' Pan
```

pangs   frequency: 1   relative frequency: 0.0000
```
    P. 126 O.C.         112 But oh what pangs that Death did Nature cost!
```

panic. See "panique."

panique   frequency: 1   relative frequency: 0.0000

      P. 108 ANNIVERSARY   203 And all about was heard a Panique groan,

panniers   frequency: 1   relative frequency: 0.0000
      P. 179 STOCKSMARKET   18 Who upon their panniers more decently ride,

pan's   frequency: 2   relative frequency: 0.0000
      P. 18 CLORINDA   26 C. Who would not in Pan's Praises meet?
      P. 18 CLORINDA   30 For all the World is our Pan's Quire.

panting   frequency: 2   relative frequency: 0.0000
      P. 77 A. HOUSE   596 Flatters with Air my panting Brows.
      P. 154 INSTRUCTIONS   562 With panting Heart, lay like a fish on Land,

paper   frequency: 1   relative frequency: 0.0000
      P. 86 FLECKNO   124 Ten quire of paper in which he was drest.

paper-rats   frequency: 1   relative frequency: 0.0000
      P.   3 LOVELACE   19 Word-peckers, Paper-rats, Book-scorpions,

papers   frequency: 2   relative frequency: 0.0000
      P. 84 FLECKNO   70 And swaddled in's own papers seaven times,
      P. 86 FLECKNO   133 Those papers, which he pilled from within

papes   frequency: 1   relative frequency: 0.0000
      P. 184 MADE FREE   122 Led in Hell by the Papes,

papish   frequency: 1   relative frequency: 0.0000
      P. 200 DUKE   108 A droppe of poisone or a papish knife

papist   frequency: 4   relative frequency: 0.0000
      P. 165 KINGS VOWES   8 Where Papist from Protestant shall not be
                                 knowne;
      P. 192 TWO HORSES   47 W. That the Duke should turne Papist and that
                                 Church defy
      P. 198 DUKE   16 Ile raise my papist and my Irish bands,
      P. 316 CHEQUER INN   147 The Papist and the Frenches

papists   frequency: 1   relative frequency: 0.0000
      P. 146 INSTRUCTIONS   205 The Papists, but of those the House had none:

parade   frequency: 1   relative frequency: 0.0000
      P. 68 A. HOUSE   309 See how the Flow'rs, as at Parade,

paradice   frequency: 2   relative frequency: 0.0000
      P. 177 LOYALL SCOT   248 In Paradice Names only Nature Shew'd,
      P. 203 HISTORICALL   100 When our first Parents Paradice did grace,

paradice's   frequency: 1   relative frequency: 0.0000
      P. 82 A. HOUSE   768 And Paradice's only Map.

paradise   frequency: 4   relative frequency: 0.0000
      See also "paradice."
      P. 49 THE GARDEN   64 To live in Paradise alone.
      P. 69 A. HOUSE   323 Thou Paradise of four Seas,
      P. 131 PARADISE   t On Mr. Milton's Paradise lost.
      P. 132 PARADISE   39 The Bird nam'd from that Paradise you sing

paradises   frequency: 1   relative frequency: 0.0000
      P. 49 THE GARDEN   63 Two Paradises 'twere in one

paradise's. See "paradice's."

paradox   frequency: 1   relative frequency: 0.0000
      P. 73 A. HOUSE   473 Let others tell the Paradox,

paralel   frequency: 1   relative frequency: 0.0000
      P. 37 DEFINITION   27 But ours so truly Paralel,

paralell   frequency: 1   relative frequency: 0.0000
      P. 117 LOYALL SCOT   240 And few indeed can paralell our Climes

parallel. See "paralel," "paralell."

parasites. See "parrasites."

parchment   frequency: 1   relative frequency: 0.0000
      P. 198 DUKE   24 Theire parchment presidents and dull records.

pardon   frequency: 4   relative frequency: 0.0000
      P. 85 FLECKNO   105 He ask'd me pardon; and to make me way
      P. 113 ANNIVERSARY   395 Pardon, great Prince, if thus their Fear or Spight

P. 131 PARADISE   23 Pardon me, mighty Poet, nor despise
P. 178 LOYALL SCOT   274 Pardon, Young Heroe, this soe long Transport;

pardoned   frequency: 1   relative frequency: 0.0000
P. 174 LOYALL SCOT   93 Never shall Calvin Pardoned bee for Sales,

parent   frequency: 1   relative frequency: 0.0000
P. 130 O.C.   305 And Richard yet, where his great parent led,

parent-tree   frequency: 1   relative frequency: 0.0000
P. 125 O.C.   95 The Parent-Tree unto the Grief succeeds,

parents   frequency: 6   relative frequency: 0.0001
P. 71 A. HOUSE   413 And now your Orphan Parents Call
P. 82 A. HOUSE   743 While her glad Parents most rejoice,
P. 107 ANNIVERSARY   165 Though none does of more lasting Parents grow,
P. 110 ANNIVERSARY   291 And such as to their Parents Tents do press,
P. 149 INSTRUCTIONS 350 Imprison Parents, and the Child deflowre.
P. 203 HISTORICALL   100 When our first Parents Paradice did grace,

park   frequency: 1   relative frequency: 0.0000
P. 140 HOUSEWARMING 106 That for Name-sake he may with Hyde Park it
                          enlarge,

parley. See "parly."

parliament   frequency: 20   relative frequency: 0.0004
See also "parli'ment."
P. 139 HOUSEWARMING   76 No, would the whole Parliament kiss him behind.
P. 144 INSTRUCTIONS 124 Yet as for War the Parliament should squeeze;
P. 149 INSTRUCTIONS 344 A Parliament is to the Chancellor.
P. 152 INSTRUCTIONS 470 That summons up the Parliament agen;
P. 153 INSTRUCTIONS 505 When Dutch Invade, when Parliament prepare,
P. 153 INSTRUCTIONS 518 On Monk and Parliament, yet both do hate.
P. 160 INSTRUCTIONS 814 But with a Parliament abhors to meet,
P. 160 INSTRUCTIONS 822 The Holland Fleet and Parliament so near.
P. 165 KINGS VOWES   10 I will have a fine Parliament allwayes to
                          Friend,
P. 167 KINGS VOWES   59 So high that he shall brave the Parliament,
P. 168 ADVICE   12 A Landskip of our Mottly Parliament;
P. 169 ADVICE   61 Whom France Esteem'd our Chiefe in
                          Parliament,
P. 170 PROPHECY   12 Give Taxes to the King and Parliament.
P. 176 LOYALL SCOT   210 To sit is Necessary in Parliament,
P. 179 STOCKSMARKET   22 Who the Parliament buys and revenues does sell,
P. 188 BRITANNIA   135 Present to his thought his long scorn'd
                          Parliament
P. 190 STATUE   32 He will here keep a market of Parliament men.
P. 190 STATUE   35 As the Parliament twice was prorogued by your
                          hand,
P. 191 STATUE   50 And his Parliament list withall did produce,
P. 193 TWO HORSES   73 Ch. That Parliament men should rail at the
                          Court,

parliaments   frequency: 2   relative frequency: 0.0000
See also "parli'ments."
P. 165 INSTRUCTIONS 988 And, as in Love, on Parliaments can stare:
P. 185 BRITANNIA   22 Till Charles loves Parliaments, till James
                          hates Rome.

parliament's   frequency: 1   relative frequency: 0.0000
P. 160 INSTRUCTIONS 807 But now draws near the Parliament's return;

parli'ment   frequency: 1   relative frequency: 0.0000
P. 312 CHEQUER INN   2 Where I the Parli'ment have seene

parli'ments   frequency: 1   relative frequency: 0.0000
P. 317 CHEQUER INN   188 Parli'ments grow nought as they grow old

parly   frequency: 2   relative frequency: 0.0000
P. 38 PICTURE   18 And parly with those conquering Eyes;
P. 146 INSTRUCTIONS 232 They feign a parly, better to surprize:

parnassus   frequency: 1   relative frequency: 0.0000
P. 176 LOYALL SCOT   194 They, tho' noe poets, on Parnassus dream,

parrasites   frequency: 1   relative frequency: 0.0000
P. 168 KINGS VOWES   65 And pass my Time with Parrasites and Players,

parratts   frequency: 1   relative frequency: 0.0000

P. 191 TWO HORSES   3 When Magpyes and Parratts cry 'walke Knave
                          walk',

parrots. See "parratts."

part   frequency: 17   relative frequency: 0.0003
     P.   19 THYRSIS   1 Dorinda. When Death, shall part us from these
                              Kids,
     P.   20 SOUL & BODY   9 Tortur'd, besides each other part,
     P.   22 NYMPH   19 In this warm life-blood, which doth part
     P.   26 MISTRESS   17 An Age at least to every part,
     P.   33 DAPHNIS   1 Daphnis must from Chloe part:
     P.   57 BILL-BOROW   47 But ere he well the Barks could part
     P.   88 ODE   47 And Hampton shows what part
     P. 105 ANNIVERSARY   89 The crossest Spirits here do take their part,
     P. 123 O.C.   19 Deserved yet an End whose ev'ry part
     P. 126 O.C.   130 Troubled to part where so exactly mix'd.
     P. 126 O.C.   141 No part of time but bore his mark away
     P. 153 INSTRUCTIONS 495 His minion Imps that, in his secret part,
     P. 168 KINGS VOWES   61 And I will take his part to that degree,
     P. 171 PROPHECY   34+ Second Part.
     P. 172 LOYALL SCOT   14 As of his Satyr this had been a part.
     P. 173 LOYALL SCOT   74 And Joyn those Lands that seemed to part
                              before.
     P. 173 LOYALL SCOT   76 Where Nature Scotland doth from England part.

partake   frequency: 1   relative frequency: 0.0000
     P. 184 BRITANNIA   8 Once more with me partake of mortall woes.

parted   frequency: 1   relative frequency: 0.0000
     P. 196 TWO HORSES   167 But I should have told you, before the Jades
                              parted,

partelot. See "partelott."

partelott   frequency: 1   relative frequency: 0.0000
     P. 162 INSTRUCTIONS 884 And Serjeants Wife serves him for Partelott.

parti-colored. See "party-colour'd."

partial   frequency: 1   relative frequency: 0.0000
     P. 150 INSTRUCTIONS 382 Nor partial Justice her Behaviour binds;

parties   frequency: 1   relative frequency: 0.0000
     P.   46 AMETAS   7 Where both parties so combine,

parting   frequency: 5   relative frequency: 0.0001
     P.   33 DAPHNIS   16 Sudden Parting closer glews,
     P.   33 DAPHNIS   22 With the Grief of Parting thence,
     P.   35 DAPHNIS   77 And I parting should appear
     P.   36 DAPHNIS   86 Who for parting pleasure strain
     P.   36 DAPHNIS   100 And receives the parting stroke.

parts   frequency: 3   relative frequency: 0.0000
     P.   64 A. HOUSE   178 'Still handling Natures finest Parts.
     P. 170 PROPHECY   15 When Players shall use to act the parts of
                              Queens
     P. 174 LOYALL SCOT   88 'Tis Holy Island parts us not the Tweed.

party-colour'd   frequency: 1   relative frequency: 0.0000
     P.   90 ODE   106 Within his party-colour'd Mind;

pasiphae's   frequency: 1   relative frequency: 0.0000
     P. 150 INSTRUCTIONS 408 And on Pasiphae's Tomb to drop a Bead.

pass   frequency: 13   relative frequency: 0.0002
     P.   19 THYRSIS   20 Pass Eternity away?
     P.   20 THYRSIS   48 So shall we smoothly pass away in sleep.
     P.   26 MISTRESS   4 To walk, and pass our long Loves Day.
     P.   42 DAMON   25 Tell me where I may pass the Fires
     P.   49 THE GARDEN   39 Stumbling on Melons, as I pass,
     P.   54 THYESTE   7 Pass away my silent Age.
     P.   70 A. HOUSE   369 And now to the Abbyss I pass
     P.   85 FLECKNO   90 You cannot pass to him but thorow me.
     P.   85 FLECKNO   98 Delightful, said there can no Body pass
     P. 112 ANNIVERSARY 373 'Yet if through these our Fears could find a
                              pass;
     P. 168 KINGS VOWES   65 And pass my Time with Parrasites and Players,
     P. 171 PROPHECY   31 London shall then see, for it will come to pass,
     P. 196 TWO HORSES   165 That shall come to pass all mankind may swear

passable   frequency: 1   relative frequency: 0.0000

P. 74 A. HOUSE   506 It opens passable and thin;

passage   frequency: 3   relative frequency: 0.0000
    P. 85 FLECKNO   88 Stopping the passage, and did him demand:
    P. 126 O.C.   111 He unconcern'd the dreadful passage crost;
    P. 155 INSTRUCTIONS 595 And to the rest the open'd passage shew.

passengers   frequency: 1   relative frequency: 0.0000
    P. 110 ANNIVERSARY   271 The Passengers all wearyed out before,

passes   frequency: 1   relative frequency: 0.0000
    P. 179 STOCKSMARKET   13 When each one that passes finds fault with the
                             horse,

passing   frequency: 1   relative frequency: 0.0000
    P. 84 FLECKNO   50 With gristly Tongue to dart the passing Flyes.

passions   frequency: 3   relative frequency: 0.0000
    P. 48 THE GARDEN   25 When we have run our Passions heat,
    P. 123 O.C.   26 In gentle Passions should his Death disguise:
    P. 186 BRITANNIA   51 The swelling Passions of his Cankred breast,

passive   frequency: 1   relative frequency: 0.0000
    P. 169 ADVICE   64 Tis by afflictions passive men grow great.

past   frequency: 9   relative frequency: 0.0001
    P. 85 FLECKNO   81 Each colour that he past by; and be seen,
    P. 92 MAY'S DEATH   98 May only Master of these Revels past.
    P. 107 ANNIVERSARY   185 So shall the Tears we on past Grief employ,
    P. 110 ANNIVERSARY   307 For soon thou mightst have past among their Rant
    P. 117 BLAKE   110 Our worst works past, now we have found them out.
    P. 126 O.C.   140 To chuse it worthy of his Glories past.
    P. 130 O.C.   285 As long as future time succeeds the past,
    P. 141 INSTRUCTIONS 24 His Anger reacht that rage which past his Art;
    P. 181 MADE FREE   27 Tho he has past through so many Adventures;

pastime   frequency: 1   relative frequency: 0.0000
    P. 150 INSTRUCTIONS 376 Comes news of Pastime, Martial and old:

paston   frequency: 1   relative frequency: 0.0000
    P. 144 INSTRUCTIONS 126 Should Goodrick silence, and strike Paston
                             dumb;

pasts   frequency: 1   relative frequency: 0.0000
    P. 64 A. HOUSE   181 'Balms for the griv'd we draw; and Pasts

pasture   frequency: 1   relative frequency: 0.0000
    P. 73 A. HOUSE   459 And shrunk in the huge Pasture show

pastures   frequency: 3   relative frequency: 0.0000
    P. 18 CLORINDA   18 Clorinda, Pastures, Caves, and Springs.
    P. 18 CLORINDA   27 Of Pan the flowry Pastures sing,
    P. 59 A. HOUSE   4 And Forrests did to Pastures hew;

pate   frequency: 1   relative frequency: 0.0000
    P. 91 MAY'S DEATH   37 As he crowds in he whipt him ore the pate

patent   frequency: 2   relative frequency: 0.0000
    See also "canary-patent."
    P. 139 HOUSEWARMING   75 But he swore that the Patent should ne'er be
                             revok'd;
    P. 147 INSTRUCTIONS 258 Had strecht the monster Patent on the Field.

patentees   frequency: 1   relative frequency: 0.0000
    P. 139 HOUSEWARMING   66 Sinners, Governors, Farmers, Banquers,
                             Patentees.

path   frequency: 2   relative frequency: 0.0000
    P. 57 BILL-BOROW   19 Nor with the rugged path deterrs
    P. 106 ANNIVERSARY   108 The path where holy Oracles do lead;

pathic   frequency: 1   relative frequency: 0.0000
    P. 168 ADVICE   10 One to his Pathic, th' other to his Player.

patience   frequency: 1   relative frequency: 0.0000
    P. 202 HISTORICALL   63 Our muse would on the Readers patience grate.

patient   frequency: 1   relative frequency: 0.0000
    P. 162 INSTRUCTIONS 879 His patient Piss, he could hold longer then

patiently   frequency: 1   relative frequency: 0.0000

    P. 91 MAY'S DEATH   36 And Horace patiently its stroke does take,

patricke   frequency: 1   relative frequency: 0.0000
    P. 198 DUKE   10 With Father Patricke Darby and with Teage,

patricks   frequency: 1   relative frequency: 0.0000
    P. 195 TWO HORSES   146 Father Patricks Deciple will make England
                              smart.

patrol. See "patroul."

patroul   frequency: 1   relative frequency: 0.0000
    P. 68 A. HOUSE   313 But when the vigilant Patroul

pattern   frequency: 4   relative frequency: 0.0000
    P. 73 A. HOUSE   450 Which Levellers take Pattern at,
    P. 106 ANNIVERSARY 105 O would they rather by his Pattern won.
    P. 141 INSTRUCTIONS   30 The new Courts pattern, Stallion of the old.
    P. 147 INSTRUCTIONS 252 And all to pattern his Example boast.

patterns   frequency: 1   relative frequency: 0.0000
    P. 188 BRITANNIA   159 By those great Patterns such a state I'le frame

paul   frequency: 1   relative frequency: 0.0000
    P. 140 HIS HOUSE   2 Of Paul late gelded of his Stones.

pauls   frequency: 2   relative frequency: 0.0000
    P. 138 HOUSEWARMING   44 But that he had nearer the Stones of St.
                              Pauls.
    P. 177 LOYALL SCOT 216 'Tis necessary to rebabel Pauls,

pause   frequency: 1   relative frequency: 0.0000
    P. 194 TWO HORSES 115 Ch. Pause, Brother, a while and calmly
                              consider:

pawne   frequency: 1   relative frequency: 0.0000
    P. 165 KINGS VOWES   1 When the Plate was at pawne, and the fobb att
                              low Ebb,

pawning   frequency: 1   relative frequency: 0.0000
    P. 193 TWO HORSES   66 By pawning for Victualls their Guns at
                              Legorne;

pay   frequency: 10   relative frequency: 0.0002
    P. 55 EPITAPH   15 That ready her last Debt to pay
    P. 92 MAY'S DEATH   82 Who thy last Reckoning did so largely pay.
    P. 122 TWO SONGS   28 Pay to Love and Them their due.
    P. 128 O.C.   213 For her he once did nature's tribute pay:
    P. 144 INSTRUCTIONS 127 Should pay Land Armies, should dissolve the
                              vain
    P. 146 INSTRUCTIONS 240 Without Intelligence, Command, or Pay:
    P. 148 INSTRUCTIONS 314 To cheat their Pay, feign want, the House
                              accuse.
    P. 152 INSTRUCTIONS 489 And for their Pay he writes as from the King,
    P. 155 INSTRUCTIONS 584 Cheated of Pay, was he that show'd them in.
    P. 193 TWO HORSES   58 Yet the King of his debts pay no man a penny;

pay'd   frequency: 1   relative frequency: 0.0000
    P. 145 INSTRUCTIONS 176 No Troop was better clad nor so well pay'd.

payes   frequency: 1   relative frequency: 0.0000
    P. 32 MOURNING   25 Nor that she payes, while she survives,

payments   frequency: 1   relative frequency: 0.0000
    P. 170 PROPHECY   27 When publike faith and Vowes and Payments stop,

pays   frequency: 1   relative frequency: 0.0000
    See also "payes."
    P. 145 INSTRUCTIONS 172 In vain, for always he commands that pays.

peace   frequency: 41   relative frequency: 0.0008
    P. 11 DIALOGUE   64 That War or Peace commend?
    P. 35 DAPHNIS   62 Better 'tis to go in peace,
    P. 58 BILL-BOROW   75 But Peace (if you his favour prize)
    P. 66 A. HOUSE   235 Which licens'd either Peace or Force,
    P. 67 A. HOUSE   283 Who, when retired here to Peace,
    P. 85 FLECKNO   102 Our peace, the Priest said I too had some wit:
    P. 85 FLECKNO   111 Let it suffice that we could eat in peace;
    P. 87 ODE   10 In the inglorious Arts of Peace,
    P. 99 HOLLAND   144 The War, (but who would) Peace if begg'd
                              refuse.
    P. 105 ANNIVERSARY 102 Here shines in Peace, and thither shoots a War.

P. 108 ANNIVERSARY	218 Unto the Kingdom blest of Peace and Love:
P. 109 ANNIVERSARY	244 But walk still middle betwixt War and Peace;
P. 109 ANNIVERSARY	251 He on the Peace extends a Warlike power,
P. 114 BLAKE	46 Have broken all her Swords, then this one Peace,
P. 115 BLAKE	50 Peace, against you, was the sole strength of Spain.
P. 115 BLAKE	52 Peace made them hers, but War will make them yours
P. 118 BLAKE	156 And the Land owe her peace unto the Sea.
P. 118 BLAKE	158 There they destroy, what had destroy'd their Peace.
P. 123 O.C.	15 And he whom Nature all for Peace had made,
P. 127 O.C.	156 And slept in Peace under the Lawrel shade.
P. 131 O.C.	321 Cease now our griefs, calme peace succeeds a war,
P. 140 HOUSEWARMING	97 This Temple, of War and of Peace is the Shrine;
P. 142 INSTRUCTIONS	42 Whose Breeches were the Instrument of Peace.
P. 144 INSTRUCTIONS	123 So therefore secretly for Peace decrees,
P. 148 INSTRUCTIONS	312 Lest the sure Peace, forsooth, too soon appear.
P. 149 INSTRUCTIONS	362 That Peace secur'd, and Money might be sav'd.
P. 150 INSTRUCTIONS	370 Like Slaves, shall beg for Peace at Hollands doors.
P. 150 INSTRUCTIONS	373 The Court, as once of War, now fond of Peace,
P. 150 INSTRUCTIONS	380 And beats the Husband till for peace he prays:
P. 150 INSTRUCTIONS	394 The Joys of State, for the new Peace and Tax.
P. 151 INSTRUCTIONS	438 And whip the Dutch, unless they'l hold their peace.
P. 152 INSTRUCTIONS	476 To work the Peace, and so to send them home.
P. 160 INSTRUCTIONS	818 The Peace not sure, new Army must be paid.
P. 161 INSTRUCTIONS	849 Mean while the certain News of Peace arrives
P. 163 INSTRUCTIONS	906 And he Divin'd 'twas England or the Peace.
P. 178 LOYALL SCOT	256 Rationall mens words pledges are of peace,
P. 182 MADE FREE	49 Tho' oft bound to the Peace
P. 194 TWO HORSES	92 Which Augments and secures his own profitt and peace.
P. 196 TWO HORSES	184 Chocolet Tea and Coffee are liquors of peace.
P. 200 DUKE	101 In peace and pleasure this thy native land,
P. 204 HISTORICALL	152 They'l kill a Judge or Justice of the Peace.

peacefull   frequency: 1   relative frequency: 0.0000
     P. 185 BRITANNIA   45 And Golden dayes in peacefull order rould,

peach   frequency: 2   relative frequency: 0.0000
     P. 49 THE GARDEN   37 The Nectaren, and curious Peach,
     P. 313 CHEQUER INN   40 For whosoe're that Peach him durst

peake   frequency: 1   relative frequency: 0.0000
     P. 179 STOCKSMARKET 20 Even Sir William Peake sits much firmer than he.

peal   frequency: 1   relative frequency: 0.0000
     P. 164 INSTRUCTIONS 972 And peal the Bark to burn at last the Tree.

pearch   frequency: 2   relative frequency: 0.0000
     P. 89 ODE   94 But on the next green Bow to pearch;
     P. 161 INSTRUCTIONS 837 And Turner gay up to his Pearch does march,

pearl   frequency: 2   relative frequency: 0.0000
     P. 17 BERMUDAS   30 The Gospels Pearl upon our Coast.
     P. 32 MOURNING   30 That sink for Pearl through Seas profound,

pearls   frequency: 1   relative frequency: 0.0000
     P. 64 A. HOUSE   190 'As Pearls together billeted.

pearly   frequency: 3   relative frequency: 0.0000
     P. 30 THE GALLERY   34 Like Venus in her pearly Boat.
     P. 131 O.C.   317 A pearly rainbow, where the sun inchas'd
     P. 154 INSTRUCTIONS 549 With Pearly Shell the Tritons all the while

peasant   frequency: 1   relative frequency: 0.0000
     P. 164 INSTRUCTIONS 960 Nor of a Peasant scorn'd to learn the way.

peasants   frequency: 1   relative frequency: 0.0000
     P. 203 HISTORICALL   93 They dazle both the Prince and Peasants sight.

pecks   frequency: 1   relative frequency: 0.0000
     P. 313 CHEQUER INN   20 That now he Money tells by Pecks

pedantick   frequency: 1   relative frequency: 0.0000
     P. 186 BRITANNIA   73 Such poor pedantick toys teach underlings.

pedigree   frequency: 1   relative frequency: 0.0000
     P. 107 ANNIVERSARY   162 Live out an Age, long as a Pedigree;

pedigrees   frequency: 1   relative frequency: 0.0000
     P. 74 A. HOUSE   491 It like two Pedigrees appears,

peek's   frequency: 1   relative frequency: 0.0000
     P. 115 BLAKE   75 The Peek's proud height, the Spaniards all
                               admire,

peel. See "peal."

peeled. See "pilled."

peep   frequency: 1   relative frequency: 0.0000
     P. 146 INSTRUCTIONS   244 And undescry'd return'd e're morning peep.

peeres   frequency: 1   relative frequency: 0.0000
     P. 201 HISTORICALL   13 Bishops and Deanes, Peeres, Pimps and Knights
                               he made,

peers   frequency: 1   relative frequency: 0.0000
     See also "peeres."
     P. 189 BRITANNIA   179 Tarquins just judge and Cesar's Equall Peers

peeter   frequency: 1   relative frequency: 0.0000
     P. 160 INSTRUCTIONS   797 But sure his late good Husbandry in Peeter,

pegasus   frequency: 1   relative frequency: 0.0000
     P. 173 LOYALL SCOT   63 Skip Sadles: Pegasus thou needst not Bragg,

peice   frequency: 1   relative frequency: 0.0000
     P. 200 DUKE   98 Noe, Painter, noe; close up this peice and see

pelican   frequency: 2   relative frequency: 0.0000
     P. 83 FLECKNO   6 Of the sad Pelican; Subject divine
     P. 86 FLECKNO   127 And so the Pelican at his door hung

pelicans   frequency: 1   relative frequency: 0.0000
     P. 125 O.C.   80 Of Halcyons kind, or bleeding Pelicans?

pellets. See "pelletts."

pelletts   frequency: 1   relative frequency: 0.0000
     P. 314 CHEQUER INN   88 The Pelletts which his Choppes did dart

pembroke   frequency: 1   relative frequency: 0.0000
     P. 91 MAY'S DEATH   38 Like Pembroke at the Masque, and then did rate.

pembrokes. See "pembrockes."

pembrookes   frequency: 1   relative frequency: 0.0000
     P. 189 BRITANNIA   169 Teach 'em to scorn the Carwells, Pembrookes,
                               Nells,

pen   frequency: 4   relative frequency: 0.0000
     P. 91 MAY'S DEATH   40 Most servil' wit, and Mercenary Pen.
     P. 152 INSTRUCTIONS   469 But when he came the odious Clause to Pen,
     P. 156 INSTRUCTIONS   641 And saw himself confin'd, like Sheep in Pen;
     P. 162 INSTRUCTIONS   864 Where Pencil cannot, there my Pen shall do't;

penance. See "pennance."

pencell   frequency: 1   relative frequency: 0.0000
     P. 168 ADVICE   1 Painter once more thy Pencell reassume,

pencil   frequency: 4   relative frequency: 0.0000
     See also "pencell," "pensel."
     P. 141 INSTRUCTIONS   19 Else shalt thou oft thy guiltless Pencil curse,
     P. 141 INSTRUCTIONS   23 His desperate Pencil at the work did dart,
     P. 143 INSTRUCTIONS   120 His lab'ring Pencil oft would recreate.
     P. 162 INSTRUCTIONS   864 Where Pencil cannot, there my Pen shall do't;

pencil's   frequency: 1   relative frequency: 0.0000
     P. 157 INSTRUCTIONS   693 Fortunate Boy! if either Pencil's Fame,

pend   frequency: 1   relative frequency: 0.0000
     P. 63 A. HOUSE   155 'And, if our Rule seem strictly pend,

pendants   frequency: 1   relative frequency: 0.0000
     P. 15 EYES   16 Melt in these Pendants of the Eyes.

penetration   frequency: 2   relative frequency: 0.0000
   P.   85 FLECKNO   99 Except by penetration hither, where
   P.   88 ODE   42 Allows of penetration less:

pennance   frequency: 1   relative frequency: 0.0000
   P. 172 LOYALL SCCT   5 And (as a favourable Pennance) Chose

penny   frequency: 1   relative frequency: 0.0000
   P. 193 TWO HORSES   58 Yet the King of his debts pay no man a penny;

pens   frequency: 1   relative frequency: 0.0000
   P. 153 INSTRUCTIONS 493 This done, he Pens a Proclamation stout,

pensel   frequency: 1   relative frequency: 0.0000
   P.   56 BILL-BOROW   5 Nor softest Pensel draw a Brow

pensioners. See "pentioners."

pensions   frequency: 1   relative frequency: 0.0000
   P. 190 STATUE   22 When their Pensions are stopt to be fool'd with
                             a sight?

pensive   frequency: 2   relative frequency: 0.0000
   P. 126 O.C.   125 With pensive head towards the ground they fall,
   P. 163 INSTRUCTIONS 925 The wondrous Night the pensive King revolves,

pent   frequency: 1   relative frequency: 0.0000
   P.   83 FLECKNO   17 And though within one Cell sc narrow pent,

pentioners   frequency: 1   relative frequency: 0.0000
   P. 168 ADVICE   25 Their new made Band of Pentioners

people   frequency: 13   relative frequency: 0.0002
   P.   30 THE GALLERY   45 For thou alcne tc people me,
   P.   94 DR. WITTY   33 I see the people hastning to thy Bock,
   P. 106 ANNIVERSARY 133 And then a seasonable People still
   P. 114 BLAKE   31 A happy People, which at once do gain
   P. 115 BLAKE   58 Neither the Soyl, nor People quiet know.
   P. 123 O.C.   7 The People, which what most they fear esteem,
   P. 170 PROPHECY   11 And those false Men the Soveraign People sent
   P. 171 PROPHECY   44 Make him self rich, his king and People bare,
   P. 175 LOYALL SCCT 133 Noe Church! noe Trade! noe king! noe people!
                             noe!
   P. 188 BRITANNIA   158 To teach my People in their steps to tread.
   P. 196 TWO HORSES   179 When they take from the people the freedome of
                             words,
   P. 201 HISTORICALL   6 The People call him home to helpe the State,
   P. 205 HISTORICALL 176 And all the People been in blood embru'd,

peoples   frequency: 4   relative frequency: 0.0000
   P.   90 MAY'S DEATH   18 Brutus and Cassius the Peoples cheats.
   P. 108 ANNIVERSARY 224 To turn the headstrong Peoples Charioteer;
   P. 186 BRITANNIA   56 How by her Peoples lookes persued from far
   P. 189 BRITANNIA   180 With me I'le bring to dry my peoples tears:

perceiv'd   frequency: 2   relative frequency: 0.0000
   P.   84 FLECKNO   45 I, that perceiv'd now what his Musick ment,
   P. 124 O.C.   63 Yet both perceiv'd, yet both conceal'd their
                             Skills,

perch. See "pearch."

perfect   frequency: 5   relative frequency: 0.0001
   P.   37 DEFINITION   14 Two perfect Loves; nor lets them close:
   P.   39 THE MATCH   15 Of which one perfect Beauty grew,
   P.   56 BILL-BOROW   2 Rise in a perfect Hemisphere!
   P. 104 ANNIVERSARY   36 Much less themselves tc perfect them begin;
   P. 141 INSTRUCTIONS   27 So may'st thou perfect, by a lucky blow,

perfected   frequency: 1   relative frequency: 0.0000
   P. 142 INSTRUCTIONS 53 She perfected that Engine, oft assay'd,

perfecting   frequency: 2   relative frequency: 0.0000
   P.   29 THE GALLERY   24 Sit perfecting their harmless Loves.
   P.   64 A. HOUSE   172 'One perfecting the other Sweet.

perfection   frequency: 1   relative frequency: 0.0000
   P.   64 A. HOUSE   164 'Will soon us to perfection lead.

perfum'd   frequency: 1   relative frequency: 0.0000
   P. 195 TWO HORSES   154 W. His perfum'd predecessor was never much fitter.

perfume   frequency: 4   relative frequency: 0.0000
  P.   10 DIALOGUE   30 Is Heaven's and its own perfume.
  P.   16 EYES   42 Not as a Perfume, but a Tear.
  P.   29 LOVER   61 Yet dying leaves a Perfume here,
  P.   30 THE GALLERY   40 Convoy the Perfume to the Smell.

perfumed   frequency: 1   relative frequency: 0.0000
  See also "perfum'd."
  P.   62 A. HOUSE   109 'Our Orient Breaths perfumed are

perfumes   frequency: 4   relative frequency: 0.0000
  P.   10 DIALOGUE   25 If thou bee'st with Perfumes pleas'd,
  P.   39 THE MATCH   7 With sweetest Perfumes hoarded were,
  P.   41 THE MOWER   11 With strange perfumes he did the Roses taint.
  P. 158 INSTRUCTIONS   718 From the South Perfumes, Spices from the
                             East;

perhaps   frequency: 5   relative frequency: 0.0001
  P.   18 BERMUDAS   35 Which thence (perhaps) rebounding, may
  P.   23 NYMPH   50 Perhaps as false or more than he.
  P. 130 O.C.   304 Onely our sighs, perhaps, may thither reach.
  P. 141 INSTRUCTIONS   20 Stamp on thy Pallat, nor perhaps the worse.
  P. 188 BRITANNIA   138 Perhaps that spell may his Erring soul reclaim.

perillus   frequency: 1   relative frequency: 0.0000
  P.   86 FLECKNO   152 And roar'd out, like Perillus in's own Bull;

period   frequency: 1   relative frequency: 0.0000
  P. 123 O.C.   4 Had seen the period of his golden Years:

periods   frequency: 1   relative frequency: 0.0000
  P.   86 FLECKNO   149 Making the half points and the periods run

perish   frequency: 2   relative frequency: 0.0000
  P.   65 A. HOUSE   224 'Though guiltless lest thou perish there.
  P. 115 BLAKE   72 You scap't the Sea, to perish in your Port.

perisht   frequency: 2   relative frequency: 0.0000
  P.   64 A. HOUSE   175 'And that which perisht while we pull,
  P. 201 HISTORICALL   18 His younger Brother perisht by a clap.

perks   frequency: 1   relative frequency: 0.0000
  P. 176 LOYALL SCOT   193 The Bishops Nodle Perks up cheek by Jowle.

perpendicular   frequency: 1   relative frequency: 0.0000
  P. 174 LOYALL SCOT   83 Or what new perpendicular doth rise

perpetual   frequency: 1   relative frequency: 0.0000
  P.   92 MAY'S DEATH   94 Shalt break, and the perpetual Vulture feel.

perplex   frequency: 1   relative frequency: 0.0000
  P.   21 SOUL & BODY   37 Joy's chearful Madness does perplex:

perplext   frequency: 1   relative frequency: 0.0000
  P. 131 PARADISE   15 Lest he perplext the things he would explain,

persecute   frequency: 1   relative frequency: 0.0000
  P.   84 FLECKNO   35 Till the Tyrant, weary to persecute,

persepolis   frequency: 1   relative frequency: 0.0000
  P. 202 HISTORICALL   50 Burnt downe the Pallace of Persepolis.

persevere   frequency: 1   relative frequency: 0.0000
  P.   10 DIALOGUE   49 Then persevere: for still new Charges sound:

persian   frequency: 1   relative frequency: 0.0000
  P. 189 BRITANNIA   190 The Turkish Crescent and the Persian sun.

person   frequency: 3   relative frequency: 0.0000
  P. 104 ANNIVERSARY   27 They fight by Others, but in Person wrong,
  P. 147 INSTRUCTIONS   269 Each thinks his Person represents the whole,
  P. 156 INSTRUCTIONS   633 Paint him of Person tall, and big of bone,

persons   frequency: 1   relative frequency: 0.0000
  P.   85 FLECKNO   100 Two make a crowd, nor can three Persons here

persuade. See "perswade."

persued   frequency: 1   relative frequency: 0.0000

    P. 186 BRITANNIA   56 How by her Peoples lookes persued from far

persuit   frequency: 1   relative frequency: 0.0000
    P. 202 HISTORICALL   44 Scorning the persuit of such recreant foes.

perswade   frequency: 1   relative frequency: 0.0000
    P. 203 HISTORICALL   85 And yet perswade the World they must obey:

peru   frequency: 1   relative frequency: 0.0000
    P. 41 THE MOWER   18 To find the Marvel of Peru.

perus'd   frequency: 1   relative frequency: 0.0000
    P.   3 LOVELACE   25 Till when in vaine they have thee all perus'd,

pervert   frequency: 1   relative frequency: 0.0000
    P. 185 BRITANNIA   30 Pervert his mind, his good Intencions Choak,

perverted   frequency: 1   relative frequency: 0.0000
    P. 178 LOYALL SCOT   257 Perverted serve dissentions to increase.

pestilence   frequency: 1   relative frequency: 0.0000
    P. 21 SOUL & BODY   35 The Pestilence of Love does heat:

peter. See "peeter."

peter's   frequency: 1   relative frequency: 0.0000
    P. 87 FLECKNO   170 To hang it in Saint Peter's for a Vow.

petition   frequency: 1   relative frequency: 0.0000
    P.   3 LOVELACE   32 Their first Petition by the Authour sent.

pett   frequency: 11   relative frequency: 0.0002
    P. 159 INSTRUCTIONS 767 All our miscarriages on Pett must fall:
    P. 159 INSTRUCTIONS 770 Who all Commands sold thro' the Navy? Pett.
    P. 159 INSTRUCTIONS 772 Who treated out the time at Bergen? Pett.
    P. 159 INSTRUCTIONS 774 And rifling Prizes, them neglected? Pett.
    P. 159 INSTRUCTIONS 776 The Fleet divided? Writ for Rupert? Pett.
    P. 159 INSTRUCTIONS 778 And all our Prizes who did swallow? Pett.
    P. 159 INSTRUCTIONS 780 And who the Forts left unrepair'd? Pett.
    P. 159 INSTRUCTIONS 782 Languard, Sheerness, Gravesend, and Upnor?
                                Pett.
    P. 160 INSTRUCTIONS 784 Who should it be but the Phanatick Pett.
    P. 160 INSTRUCTIONS 785 Pett, the Sea Architect, in making Ships,
    P. 163 INSTRUCTIONS 942 To prove them Traytors, and himself the Pett.

petty   frequency: 1   relative frequency: 0.0000
    P. 199 DUKE   49 Had called you to a sound though petty Throne,

pex   frequency: 1   relative frequency: 0.0000
    P. 183 MADE FREE   96 With the Pex and the Host within it?

phaeton   frequency: 1   relative frequency: 0.0000
    P. 42 DAMON   22 Hotter then his own Phaeton.

phalaris   frequency: 1   relative frequency: 0.0000
    P. 191 TWO HORSES   9 Phalaris had a Bull which grave Authors tell ye

phanatick   frequency: 1   relative frequency: 0.0000
    P. 160 INSTRUCTIONS 784 Who should it be but the Phanatick Pett.

phancy   frequency: 1   relative frequency: 0.0000
    P. 77 A. HOUSE   578 Strange Prophecies my Phancy weaves:

phantastik   frequency: 1   relative frequency: 0.0000
    P. 203 HISTORICALL   109 To tread the Phantastik Mazes of a Priest,

pharaoh. See "pharoah."

pharaoh's. See "pharoh's."

pharoah   frequency: 2   relative frequency: 0.0000
    P. 138 HOUSEWARMING   37 And hence like Pharoah that Israel prest
    P. 174 LOYALL SCOT   109 Pharoah at first would have sent Israell home.

pharoh's   frequency: 1   relative frequency: 0.0000
    P. 185 BRITANNIA   28 Since Pharoh's Reign nor so Defild a Crown.

pharsalian   frequency: 1   relative frequency: 0.0000
    P. 91 MAY'S DEATH   22 I sing (said he) and the Pharsalian Sign,

philips   frequency: 1   relative frequency: 0.0000

P. 202 HISTORICALL   49 So Philips Son enflamed with a Miss

phillis   frequency: 6   relative frequency: 0.0001
    P. 121 TWO SONGS   1 Phillis, Tomalin, away:
    P. 121 TWO SONGS   8 Phillis you may wait the Spring:
    P. 121 TWO SONGS   4+ Phillis.
    P. 121 TWO SONGS   t5+ Hobbinol. Phillis. Tomalin. Hobbinol.
    P. 122 TWO SONGS   10+ Phillis.
    P. 122 TWO SONGS   24+ Phillis.

philomel   frequency: 1   relative frequency: 0.0000
    P. 202 HISTORICALL   69 Not Tereus with his Sister Philomel.

philomela. See "philomel."

philosopher   frequency: 2   relative frequency: 0.0000
    P. 76 A. HOUSE   561 Thus I, easie Philosopher,
    P. 142 INSTRUCTIONS   50 Philosopher beyond Newcastle's Wife.

phlegethon   frequency: 1   relative frequency: 0.0000
    See also "phlegeton."
    P. 177 LOYALL SCOT   229 And Uninforc'd Quaff healths in Phlegethon.

phlegeton   frequency: 1   relative frequency: 0.0000
    P. 92 MAY'S DEATH   90 Where Sulphrey Phlegeton does ever burn.

phlegmatick   frequency: 1   relative frequency: 0.0000
    P.   4 HASTINGS   11 The Phlegmatick and Slowe prolongs his day,

phlogis   frequency: 1   relative frequency: 0.0000
    P. 36 DAPHNIS   102 Last night he with Phlogis slept;

phrase   frequency: 1   relative frequency: 0.0000
    P. 94 DR. WITTY   9 Others do strive with words and forced phrase

phyllis. See "phillis."

physick   frequency: 1   relative frequency: 0.0000
    P. 21 SOUL & BODY   31 But Physick yet could never reach

pick   frequency: 2   relative frequency: 0.0000
    P. 20 THYRSIS   46 And thou and I'le pick poppies and them steep
    P. 130 O.C.   284 While sheep delight the grassy downs to pick,

picking   frequency: 1   relative frequency: 0.0000
    P. 195 TWO HORSES   130 This for picking our Pocketts, that for cutting
                              our Throats.

pickle   frequency: 1   relative frequency: 0.0000
    P. 162 INSTRUCTIONS   876 Court-mushrumps ready are sent in in pickle.

pickled   frequency: 2   relative frequency: 0.0000
    P. 96 HOLLAND   34 For pickled Herring, pickled Heeren chang'd.

picks   frequency: 2   relative frequency: 0.0000
    P. 86 FLECKNO   128 Picks out the tender bosome to its young.
    P. 204 HISTORICALL   150 From hence he picks and calls his murd'ring
                              braves:

pict   frequency: 2   relative frequency: 0.0000
    P. 90 ODE   105 The Pict no shelter now shall find
    P. 111 ANNIVERSARY   318 Bent to reduce us to the ancient Pict;

picts   frequency: 1   relative frequency: 0.0000
    P. 178 LOYALL SCOT   255 That syllable like a Picts wall devides.

picture   frequency: 8   relative frequency: 0.0001
    P. 29 THE GALLERY   8 Only your Picture in my Mind.
    P. 38 PICTURE   t1 The Picture of little T. C. in a Prospect
    P. 43 DAMON   59 In which I see my Picture done,
    P. 141 INSTRUCTIONS   2 To end her Picture, does the third time wait.
    P. 143 INSTRUCTIONS   80 Her, not her Picture, for she now grows old.
    P. 156 INSTRUCTIONS 632 Sweet Painter draw his Picture while I write.
    P. 163 INSTRUCTIONS 904 And th' airy Picture vanisht from his hold.
    P. 164 INSTRUCTIONS 944 Poetick Picture, Painted Poetry.

pictures   frequency: 3   relative frequency: 0.0000
    P. 30 THE GALLERY   41 These Pictures and a thousand more,
    P. 30 THE GALLERY   49 But, of these Pictures and the rest,
    P. 179 STOCKSMARKET   26 Than all the Dutch pictures that caused the war,

piebald. See "pyebald."

piece   frequency: 3   relative frequency: 0.0000

     See also "peice."
P.   95 HOLLAND   11 And div'd as desperately for each piece
P.   97 HOLLAND   70 Each one thence pillag'd the first piece he
                found:
P. 144 INSTRUCTIONS 137 Chops off the piece where e're she close the
                Jaw,

pierce   frequency: 4   relative frequency: 0.0000
P.   81 A. HOUSE   715 Tears (watry Shot that pierce the Mind;)
P. 127 O.C.   183 Those Strokes he said will pierce through all
                below
P. 128 O.C.   196 Yet him the adverse steel could never pierce.
P. 166 KINGS VOWES   38 As bold as Alce Pierce and as faire as Jane
                Shore;

pierced   frequency: 1   relative frequency: 0.0000
     See also "pierc't."
P. 158 INSTRUCTIONS 704 Fraughting their pierced Keels with Oosy
                Tides.

piercing   frequency: 3   relative frequency: 0.0000
P.   14 THE CORONET   2 With many a piercing wound,
P.   99 HOLLAND   150 Steel'd with those piercing Heads, Dean, Monck
                and Blake.
P. 129 O.C.   250 Which through his locks that piercing sweetnesse
                shed;

pierc't   frequency: 1   relative frequency: 0.0000
P. 147 INSTRUCTIONS 260 That pierc't the Gyant Mordant through his
                Mail.

piety   frequency: 2   relative frequency: 0.0000
P.   64 A. HOUSE   171 'Here Pleasure Piety doth meet;
P. 127 O.C.   166 Where Heaven leads, 'tis Piety to weep.

pig-eyed   frequency: 1   relative frequency: 0.0000
P. 168 ADVICE   19 Our Pig-eyed Duncomb in his Dover Fashion

pikes   frequency: 3   relative frequency: 0.0000
P.   58 BILL-BOROW   67 Through Groves of Pikes he thunder'd then,
P.   73 A. HOUSE   480 And Pikes are taken in the Pound.
P. 147 INSTRUCTIONS 283 And, charging all their Pikes, a sullen Band

pil'd   frequency: 1   relative frequency: 0.0000
P.   72 A. HOUSE   433 When after this 'tis pil'd in Cocks,

pile   frequency: 1   relative frequency: 0.0000
P. 178 LOYALL SCOT   261 English and Scotch, 'tis all but Crosse and
                Pile

piles   frequency: 1   relative frequency: 0.0000
P.   96 HOLLAND   17 How did they rivet, with Gigantick Piles,

pilgrim   frequency: 1   relative frequency: 0.0000
P. 150 INSTRUCTIONS 406 Where Pilgrim Palmer travell'd in Exile,

pilgrimage   frequency: 1   relative frequency: 0.0000
P.   60 A. HOUSE   34 Shall hither come in Pilgrimage,

pillag'd   frequency: 1   relative frequency: 0.0000
P.   97 HOLLAND   70 Each one thence pillag'd the first piece he
                found:

pillaging   frequency: 1   relative frequency: 0.0000
P.   72 A. HOUSE   424 Do represent the Pillaging.

pillar. See "piller."

pillars   frequency: 4   relative frequency: 0.0000
P. 105 ANNIVERSARY   94 And they as Pillars keep the Work upright;
P. 174 LOYALL SCOT   125 And surplic'd shew like Pillars too of salt.
P. 175 LOYALL SCOT   158 Seth's Pillars are noe Antique Brick and stone
P. 189 BRITANNIA   175 True sons of Glory, Pillars of the state,

pilled   frequency: 1   relative frequency: 0.0000
P.   86 FLECKNO   133 Those papers, which he pilled from within

piller   frequency: 1   relative frequency: 0.0000
P. 199 DUKE   69 But nere can make a piller for a church;

pillows   frequency: 1   relative frequency: 0.0000

P.   9 DIALOGUE   19 On these downy Pillows lye,

pills   frequency: 2   relative frequency: 0.0000
    P.   96 HOLLAND   15 Or then those Pills which sordid Beetles roul,
    P. 183 MADE FREE   91 If a Box of Pills

pilot   frequency: 1   relative frequency: 0.0000
    P. 155 INSTRUCTIONS 583 An English Pilot too, (O Shame, O Sin!)

pilots   frequency: 1   relative frequency: 0.0000
    P.   95 HOLLAND   4 By English Pilots when they heav'd the Lead;

pimp   frequency: 2   relative frequency: 0.0000
    P. 167 KINGS VOWES   43 Of my Pimp I will make my Minister Premier,
    P. 204 HISTORICALL 124 This is the Savage Pimp without dispute

pimping   frequency: 1   relative frequency: 0.0000
    P. 189 BRITANNIA   168 To Flattery, Pimping, and a gawdy shew:

pimps   frequency: 3   relative frequency: 0.0000
    P. 141 INSTRUCTIONS 12 'Twill serve this race of Drunkards, Pimps, and
                             Fools.
    P. 185 BRITANNIA   26 Pimps, Priests, Buffoones i'th privy chamber
                             sport.
    P. 201 HISTORICALL   13 Bishops and Deanes, Peeres, Pimps and Knights
                             he made,

pimpt   frequency: 1   relative frequency: 0.0000
    P. 200 DUKE   85 And Pimpt to have his family defil'd.

pin   frequency: 1   relative frequency: 0.0000
    P. 174 LOYALL SCOT 123 And learn to pin your faith upon their sleeves.

pinacle   frequency: 1   relative frequency: 0.0000
    P.   54 THYESTE   2 Tottering favors Pinacle;

pincht   frequency: 1   relative frequency: 0.0000
    P.   73 A. HOUSE   454 Is pincht yet nearer by the Beast.

pine   frequency: 3   relative frequency: 0.0000
    P.   21 SOUL & BODY   22 Within anothers Grief to pine?
    P.   35 DAPHNIS   69 Rather I away will pine
    P.   45 MOWER'S SONG   7 But these, while I with Sorrow pine,

pines   frequency: 3   relative frequency: 0.0000
    P.   78 A. HOUSE   640 Narcissus like, the Sun too pines.
    P. 124 O.C.   56 The sad Root pines in secret under ground.
    P. 187 BRITANNIA   95 Whilst your starv'd power in Legall fetters
                             pines.

pink   frequency: 1   relative frequency: 0.0000
    See also "pinke."
    P.   40 THE MOWER   9 The Pink grew then as double as his Mind;

pinke   frequency: 1   relative frequency: 0.0000
    P.   68 A. HOUSE   312 That of the Tulip Pinke and Rose.

pioneers   frequency: 1   relative frequency: 0.0000
    P. 144 INSTRUCTIONS 160 Thought yet but Pioneers, and led by Steward.

pious   frequency: 3   relative frequency: 0.0000
    P. 162 INSTRUCTIONS 869 At Pray'rs, his Eyes turn up the Pious white,
    P. 186 BRITANNIA   83 These pious frauds (too slight t'ensnare the
                             brave)
    P. 201 HISTORICALL   23 The pious Mother Queen heareing her Son

pipe   frequency: 1   relative frequency: 0.0000
    See also "oat-pipe's."
    P.   42 DAMON   11 The Grass-hopper its pipe gives ore;

pipin   frequency: 1   relative frequency: 0.0000
    P. 203 HISTORICALL 103 From the forbidden tree the Pipin take:

piping   frequency: 1   relative frequency: 0.0000
    P.   43 DAMON   49 What, though the piping Shepherd stock

piss   frequency: 1   relative frequency: 0.0000
    See also "pisse."
    P. 162 INSTRUCTIONS 879 His patient Piss, he could hold longer then

pisse   frequency: 1   relative frequency: 0.0000

          P. 166 KINGS VOWES   36 I will have two fine Secretaryes pisse thro one
                                    Quill.

pit   frequency: 1   relative frequency: 0.0000
          P. 111 ANNIVERSARY   312 Cut of the Center of th' unbottom'd Pit;

pitch   frequency: 3   relative frequency: 0.0000
          P. 92 MAY'S DEATH   99 And streight he vanisht in a Cloud of pitch,
          P. 130 O.C.   287 Thou in a pitch how farre beyond the sphere
          P. 160 INSTRUCTIONS   795 All men admir'd he to that pitch could fly:

pitied. See "pity'd."

pitty   frequency: 6   relative frequency: 0.0001
          P. 12 DROP OF DEW   17 Till the warm Sun pitty it's Pain,
          P. 16 EYES   39 Yea oft the Thund'rer pitty takes
          P. 169 ADVICE   57 Thus all imploy themselves, and without pitty
          P. 176 LOYALL SCOT   182 But his Lay pitty underneath prevailed
          P. 200 DUKE   102 At last take pitty of thy tottering throne,
          P. 315 CHEQUER INN   118 What pitty 'tis a Witt so greate

pity   frequency: 4   relative frequency: 0.0000
     See also "pitty."
          P. 15 EYES   24 Which straight in pity back he powers.
          P. 62 A. HOUSE   115 'Or Pity, when we lock cn you
          P. 128 O.C.   197 Pity it seem'd to hurt him more that felt
          P. 151 INSTRUCTIONS   436 To mcve him out of Pity, if not Love.

pity'd   frequency: 1   relative frequency: 0.0000
          P. 162 INSTRUCTIONS   900 He wonder'd first, then pity'd, then he lov'd:

plac'd   frequency: 5   relative frequency: 0.0001
          P. 37 DEFINITION   18 Us as the distant Poles have plac'd,
          P. 156 INSTRUCTIONS   629 The Guards, plac'd for the Chains and Fleets
                                    defence,
          P. 185 BRITANNIA   36 In 's left the scales, in 's right hand plac'd
                                    the sword,
          P. 205 HISTORICALL   166 And in his stead had plac'd him on his Throne.
          P. 205 HISTORICALL   168 And Jesse's son plac'd in the Government:

place   frequency: 38   relative frequency: 0.0007
          P. 24 NYMPH   104 Then place it in Diana's Shrine.
          P. 26 MISTRESS   31 The Grave's a fine and private place,
          P. 32 MOURNING   16 A place to fix another Wound.
          P. 47 EMPIRE   9 Each sought a ccnsort in that lovely place;
          P. 49 THE GARDEN   59 After a Place sc pure, and sweet,
          P. 59 A. HOUSE   16 Their Bodies measure out their Place.
          P. 61 A. HOUSE   69 The House was built upon the Place
          P. 69 A. HOUSE   337 The Gardiner had the Sculdiers place,
          P. 74 A. HOUSE   501 There the huge Bulk takes place, as ment
          P. 78 A. HOUSE   612 That I may never leave this Place:
          P. 81 A. HOUSE   730 Do all your useless Study place,
          P. 85 FLECKNO   85 No empty place for complementing doubt,
          P. 85 FLECKNO   103 To prov't, I said, the place doth us invite
          P. 90 MAY'S DEATH   5 Could not determine in what place he was,
          P. 91 MAY'S DEATH   28 Prest for his place among the Learned throng.
          P. 97 HOLLAND   90 But still does place it at her Western End:
          P. 104 ANNIVERSARY   53 This took a Lower, that an Higher place,
          P. 105 ANNIVERSARY   82 Each in the House the highest Place contends,
          P. 105 ANNIVERSARY   99 When for his Fcct he thus a place had found,
          P. 115 BLAKE   70 That place saluted, where they all must dye.
          P. 118 BLAKE   152 The only place where it can cause no Ill.
          P. 119 BLAKE   167 Whilst fame in every place, her Trumpet blowes,
          P. 122 TWO SONGS   35 Now lesser Beauties may take place,
          P. 145 INSTRUCTIONS   169 Court-Otficers, as us'd, the next place took,
          P. 153 INSTRUCTIONS   522 And Hyde's last Project would his Place
                                    dispose.
          P. 160 INSTRUCTICNS   791 Then that Reward might in its turn take place,
          P. 160 INSTRUCTIONS   794 And place in Ccunsel fell to Duncombes share.
          P. 162 INSTRUCTIONS   892 Though ill agree her Posture, Hour, or Place:
          P. 166 KINGS VOWES   30 And I either will vacate, or buy him a place.
          P. 168 ADVICE   17 And place me by the Barr on the left hand
          P. 168 ADVICE   23 Place Falstaffs Regement of Thread-bare
                                    Coates
          P. 177 LOYALL SCOT   238 Under each pcle place either of the two,
          P. 185 BRITANNIA   34 And in his place a Lewis Changling lay.
          P. 190 STATUE   9 For a Diall the place is too unsecure
          P. 199 DUKE   74 Then, Painter, shew thy skill and in fitt place
          P. 202 HISTORICALL   37 Now the Court Sins did every place defile,
          P. 203 HISTORICALL   101 The Serpent was the Prelat of the place:
          P. 204 HISTORICALL   151 Here for an Ensignes or Lieutenants place

placed   frequency: 1   relative frequency: 0.0000
        See also "plac'd."
        P. 193 TWO HORSES   71 W. On Seventh Harry's head he that placed the
                                    Crown

places   frequency: 2   relative frequency: 0.0000
        P. 60 A. HOUSE   35 These sacred Places to adore,
        P. 167 KINGS VOWES   56 And new Ones Create Great Places to supplye,

plad   frequency: 1   relative frequency: 0.0000
        P. 90 ODE   108 Shrink underneath the Plad:

plague   frequency: 3   relative frequency: 0.0000
        P. 110 ANNIVERSARY   294 The Shame and Plague both of the Land and
                                    Age,
        P. 177 LOYALL SCOT   215 To cheat the Plague money Indifferent.
        P. 202 HISTORICALL   38 And Plague and Warre fell heavye on our Isle.

plagues   frequency: 2   relative frequency: 0.0000
        P. 138 HOUSEWARMING   39 He car'd not though Egypt's Ten Plagues us
                                    distrest,
        P. 174 LOYALL SCOT   108 Instead of all the Plagues had Bishops come,

plaid   frequency: 2   relative frequency: 0.0000
        See also "plad."
        P. 47 EMPIRE   2 Where Jarring windes to infant Nature plaid.
        P. 96 HOLLAND   24 And oft at Leap-frog ore their Steeples plaid:

plain   frequency: 12   relative frequency: 0.0002
        P.   4 HASTINGS   2 Whose Virgin-Source yet never steept the Plain.
        P.   9 DIALOGUE   21 On these Roses strow'd so plain
        P. 31 FAIR SINGER   13 It had been easie fighting in some plain,
        P. 40 THE MOWER   4 Where Nature was most plain and pure.
        P. 57 BILL-BOROW   24 But only strives to raise the Plain.
        P. 72 A. HOUSE   421 Where, as the Meads with Hay, the Plain
        P. 72 A. HOUSE   443 A levell'd space, as smooth and plain,
        P. 80 A. HOUSE   677 The stupid Fishes hang, as plain
        P. 109 ANNIVERSARY   257 Thou with the same strength, and an Heart as
                                    plain,
        P. 144 INSTRUCTIONS   161 Then damming Cowards rang'd the vocal Plain,
        P. 161 INSTRUCTIONS   829 Plain Gentlemen are in Stage-Coach o'rethrown,
        P. 172 LOYALL SCOT   10 Hee Judg'd more Clearly now and saw more plain.

plaines   frequency: 1   relative frequency: 0.0000
        P. 177 LOYALL SCOT   223 Some sue for tyth of the Elyzean plaines:

plainly   frequency: 1   relative frequency: 0.0000
        P. 191 TWO HORSES   6 Have spoken as plainly as men doe with Tongues:

plains   frequency: 1   relative frequency: 0.0000
        See also "plaines."
        P. 43 DAMON   50 The plains with an unnum'red Flock,

plaints   frequency: 1   relative frequency: 0.0000
        P. 119 TWO SONGS   8 Nor scorn Endymions plaints to hear.

planet   frequency: 2   relative frequency: 0.0000
        P. 104 ANNIVERSARY   39 To know how long their Planet yet Reprives
        P. 164 INSTRUCTIONS   953 Through Optick Trunk the Planet seem'd to
                                    hear,

planisphere   frequency: 1   relative frequency: 0.0000
        P. 37 DEFINITION   24 Be cramp'd into a Planisphere.

plank   frequency: 1   relative frequency: 0.0000
        P. 157 INSTRUCTIONS   689 And, on the flaming Plank, so rests his Head,

planks   frequency: 2   relative frequency: 0.0000
        P. 173 LOYALL SCOT   55 And on his flaming Planks soe rests his head
        P. 180 STOCKSMARKET   46 With three shattered planks and the rags of a
                                    sail

plant   frequency: 8   relative frequency: 0.0001
        P. 41 THE MOWER   23 No Plant now knew the Stock from which it came;
        P. 69 A. HOUSE   344 We Ord'nance Plant and Powder sow.
        P. 70 A. HOUSE   355 Conscience, that Heaven-nursed Plant,
        P. 88 ODE   32 To plant the Bergamot,
        P. 110 ANNIVERSARY   287 And only didst for others plant the Vine
        P. 129 O.C.   266 At mortalls sins, nor his own plant will spare;
        P. 204 HISTORICALL   149 This is the Colony to plant his knaves:
        P. 314 CHEQUER INN   77 To Plant with Us his Government

planted   frequency: 4   relative frequency: 0.0000
     P.   5 HASTINGS   54 Had they been planted on that Balsam-tree!
     P.   69 A. HOUSE   324 Which Heaven planted us to please,
     P. 122 TWO SONGS   16 But when Old he planted Bayes.
     P. 127 O.C.   173 Who planted England on the Flandrick shoar,

plants   frequency: 6   relative frequency: 0.0001
     P.   17 BERMUDAS   23 But Apples plants of such a price,
     P.   40 THE MOWER   3 And from the fields the Flow'rs and Plants
                                 allure,
     P.   48 THE GARDEN   13 Your sacred Plants, if here below,
     P.   48 THE GARDEN   14 Only among the Plants will grow.
     P.   69 A. HOUSE   342 Where he the tender Plants removes.
     P.   76 A. HOUSE   564 Cr of the Fowles, or of the Plants.

plate   frequency: 3   relative frequency: 0.0000
     P. 117 BLAKE   118 To give him Lawrel, as the Last did Plate.
     P. 165 KINGS VOWES   1 When the Plate was at pawne, and the fobb att
                                 low Ebb,
     P. 315 CHEQUER INN   101 With his owne Gravy fill'd his Plate

plates   frequency: 1   relative frequency: 0.0000
     P. 316 CHEQUER INN   169 Candlesticks, Forkes, Saltes Plates Spoones
                                 Knives

platonic. See "platonique."

platonique   frequency: 1   relative frequency: 0.0000
     P. 103 ANNIVERSARY   17 And though they all Platonique years should
                                 raign,

play   frequency: 15   relative frequency: 0.0003
     P.   22 NYMPH   37 Thenceforth I set my self to play
     P.   28 LOVER   43 Fortune and He are call'd to play
     P.   72 A. HOUSE   425 And now the careless Victors play,
     P.   77 A. HOUSE   607 But I on it securely play,
     P.   96 HOLLAND   28 The Earth and water play at Level-coyl;
     P. 122 TWO SONGS   36 And meaner Virtues come in play;
     P. 131 PARADISE   22 To change in Scenes, and show it in a Play.
     P. 141 INSTRUCTIONS   38 Fits him in France to play at Cards and treat.
     P. 143 INSTRUCTIONS   118 With what small Arts the publick game they play.
     P. 148 INSTRUCTIONS   309 Where force had fail'd with Stratagem to play,
     P. 149 INSTRUCTIONS   368 To play for Flanders, and the stake to lose.
     P. 154 INSTRUCTIONS   537 Their streaming Silks play through the weather
                                 fair,
     P. 155 INSTRUCTIONS   598 To be Spectators safe of the new Play,
     P. 161 INSTRUCTIONS   854 Expects as at a Play till Turner's drest.
     P. 190 STATUE   23 And 'tis fourty to one if he Play the old Game

playd   frequency: 1   relative frequency: 0.0000
     P. 175 LOYALL SCOT   166 Their Companyes the worst that ever playd

play'd   frequency: 1   relative frequency: 0.0000
     P. 104 ANNIVERSARY   56 And the great Work ascended while he play'd.

played. See "playd," "play'd."

player   frequency: 2   relative frequency: 0.0000
     P. 168 ADVICE   10 One to his Pathic, th' other to his Player.
     P. 182 MADE FREE   71 Of Sir Thomas Player

players   frequency: 2   relative frequency: 0.0000
     P. 168 KINGS VOWES   65 And pass my Time with Parrasites and Players,
     P. 170 PROPHECY   15 When Players shall use to act the parts of
                                 Queens

playes   frequency: 4   relative frequency: 0.0000
     P.   27 LOVER   2 With whom the Infant Love yet playes!
     P.   38 PICTURE   6 But only with the Roses playes;
     P.   86 FLECKNO   148 As a deaf Man upon a Viol playes,
     P. 189 BRITANNIA   166 Imployd the Youth, not Taverns, Stewes and
                                 playes:

playing   frequency: 1   relative frequency: 0.0000
     P.   30 THE GALLERY   54 Hangs loosely playing in the Air,

plays   frequency: 2   relative frequency: 0.0000
     See also "playes."
     P.   70 A. HOUSE   367 But ore the Meads below it plays,
     P. 181 MADE FREE   32 In runing to Plays,

plead   frequency: 2   relative frequency: 0.0000

```
P.   88 ODE              38 And plead the antient Rights in vain:
P.  176 LOYALL SCOT      205 And plead their Jus Divinum tho' in Hell.
```

pleasant   frequency: 3   relative frequency: 0.0000
```
P.   27 LOVER             1 Alas, how pleasant are their dayes
P.   61 A. HOUSE         82 And on each pleasant footstep stay,
P.   73 A. HOUSE        465 Then, to conclude these pleasant Acts,
```

pleasantly   frequency: 1   relative frequency: 0.0000
```
P.  152 INSTRUCTIONS    465 Hyde's flippant Stile there pleasantly curvets;
```

pleas'd   frequency: 3   relative frequency: 0.0000
```
P.   10 DIALOGUE         25 If thou bee'st with Perfumes pleas'd,
P.  111 ANNIVERSARY     328 Pleas'd with that other World of moving Light;
P.  146 INSTRUCTIONS    231 Pleas'd with their Numbers, yet in Valour wise,
```

please   frequency: 12   relative frequency: 0.0002
```
P.   26 MISTRESS          9 And you should if you please refuse
P.   27 LOVER            10 Rul'd, and the Winds did what they please,
P.   30 THE GALLERY      44 Either to please me, or torment:
P.   58 BILL-BOROW       66 And other Hills him once did please.
P.   69 A. HOUSE        324 Which Heaven planted us to please,
P.   98 HOLLAND          99 And carve in their large Bodies, where they
                            please,
P.  153 INSTRUCTIONS    502 Their Money lodge; confiscate when he please.
P.  159 INSTRUCTIONS    761 The Court in Farthing yet it self does please,
P.  164 INSTRUCTIONS    951 Show'd they obscure him, while too near they
                            please,
P.  166 KINGS VOWES      21 But if they should beat me, I will doe what they
                            please.
P.  167 KINGS VOWES      46 If this please not I'lle Raigne upon any
                            Condition,
P.  174 LOYALL SCOT     117 How a Clean Laundress and noe sermons please.
```

pleased   frequency: 1   relative frequency: 0.0000
```
See also "pleas'd."
P.   69 A. HOUSE        346 Who, had it pleased him and God,
```

pleasing   frequency: 3   relative frequency: 0.0000
```
P.   75 A. HOUSE        522 A Sadder, yet more pleasing Sound:
P.  124 O.C.             47 With her each day the pleasing Hours he shares,
P.  158 INSTRUCTIONS    727 The pleasing sight he often does prolong:
```

pleasure   frequency: 19   relative frequency: 0.0003
```
P.    9 DIALOGUE         t2 The Resolved Soul, and Created Pleasure.
P.    9 DIALOGUE        11+ Pleasure.
P.    9 DIALOGUE        18+ Pleasure.
P.   10 DIALOGUE        24+ Pleasure.
P.   10 DIALOGUE        30+ Pleasure.
P.   10 DIALOGUE        36+ Pleasure.
P.   11 DIALOGUE        50+ Pleasure.
P.   11 DIALOGUE        56+ Pleasure.
P.   11 DIALOGUE        62+ Pleasure.
P.   11 DIALOGUE        68+ Pleasure.
P.   12 DIALOGUE        76 The World has not one Pleasure more:
P.   36 DAPHNIS         86 Who for parting pleasure strain
P.   49 THE GARDEN      41 Mean while the Mind, from pleasure less,
P.   62 A. HOUSE       114 'With which calm Pleasure overflows;
P.   64 A. HOUSE       171 'Here Pleasure Piety doth meet;
P.   79 A. HOUSE       641 Oh what a Pleasure 'tis to hedge
P.  108 ANNIVERSARY    189 While impious Men deceiv'd with pleasure short,
P.  141 INSTRUCTIONS    32 But Fortune chose him for her pleasure salt.
P.  200 DUKE           101 In peace and pleasure this thy native land,
```

pleasure-boat   frequency: 1   relative frequency: 0.0000
```
P.  156 INSTRUCTIONS    617 That Pleasure-boat of War, in whose dear side
```

pleasures   frequency: 4   relative frequency: 0.0000
```
P.    5 HASTINGS        30 And in the choicest Pleasures charms his Pains:
P.   27 MISTRESS        43 And tear our Pleasures with rough strife,
P.   79 A. HOUSE       652 Hide trifling Youth thy Pleasures slight.
P.  187 BRITANNIA      103 Rack nature till new pleasures she shall find,
```

plebeian   frequency: 1   relative frequency: 0.0000
```
P.  169 ADVICE          38 The humble fate of a Plebeian nose;
```

pledge   frequency: 1   relative frequency: 0.0000
```
P.  159 INSTRUCTIONS    757 To see that fatal Pledge of Sea-Command,
```

pledges   frequency: 1   relative frequency: 0.0000
```
P.  178 LOYALL SCOT     256 Rationall mens words pledges are of peace,
```

plenipotence   frequency: 1   relative frequency: 0.0000
    P. 142 INSTRUCTIONS   44 Can straight produce them a Plenipotence.

plenipotentiaries. See "plenipotentiaryes."

plenipotentiary   frequency: 1   relative frequency: 0.0000
    P. 152 INSTRUCTIONS   452 Plenipotentiary Ambassadors,

plenipotentiaryes   frequency: 1   relative frequency: 0.0000
    P. 194 TWO HORSES   93 Ch. And Plenipotentiaryes send into France

plenty   frequency: 1   relative frequency: 0.0000
    P. 109 ANNIVERSARY   237 Which to the thirsty Land did plenty bring,

pliant. See "plyant."

plot   frequency: 2   relative frequency: 0.0000
    See also "plott."
    P. 88 ODE   31 As if his highest plot
    P. 96 HOLLAND   47 To make a Bank was a great Plot of State;

plott   frequency: 3   relative frequency: 0.0000
    P. 182 MADE FREE   61 The Plott was so laid,
    P. 198 DUKE   17 And by a noble well contrived plott,
    P. 200 DUKE   86 Next, Painter, draw the Rabble of the plott,

pluck'd   frequency: 1   relative frequency: 0.0000
    P. 152 INSTRUCTIONS   490 With that curs'd Quill pluck'd from a Vulture's
                             Wing:

plume   frequency: 2   relative frequency: 0.0000
    P. 89 ODE   98 While Victory his Crest does plume!
    P. 132 PARADISE   38 With Plume so strong, so equal, and so soft.

plumes   frequency: 6   relative frequency: 0.0001
    P.   9 DIALOGUE   20 Whose soft Plumes will thither fly:
    P. 49 THE GARDEN   56 Waves in its Plumes the various Light.
    P. 77 A. HOUSE   580 Like Mexique Paintings, all the Plumes.
    P. 92 MAY'S DEATH   88 As th' Eagles Plumes from other birds divide.
    P. 125 O.C.   82 Or fan with airy plumes so soft an heat.
    P. 141 INSTRUCTIONS   14 As th' Indians, draw our Luxury in Plumes.

plummets   frequency: 1   relative frequency: 0.0000
    P. 15 EYES   8 Like wat'ry Lines and Plummets fall.

plump   frequency: 1   relative frequency: 0.0000
    P. 57 BILL-BOROW   34 A Plump of aged Trees does wave.

plundering. See "plundring."

plundring   frequency: 1   relative frequency: 0.0000
    P. 108 ANNIVERSARY   213 When now they sink, and now the plundring
                             Streams

plung'd   frequency: 1   relative frequency: 0.0000
    P. 111 ANNIVERSARY   330 Sunk in the Hills, or plung'd below the
                             Streams.

plunging   frequency: 1   relative frequency: 0.0000
    P. 130 O.C.   290 Plunging dost bathe and tread the bright abysse:

pluto   frequency: 2   relative frequency: 0.0000
    P. 99 HOLLAND   152 Vainly in Hell let Pluto domineer.
    P. 176 LOYALL SCOT   202 The Mitred Hubbub against Pluto Moot

ply   frequency: 4   relative frequency: 0.0000
    P. 28 LOVER   45 And Tyrant Love his brest does ply
    P. 70 A. HOUSE   361 The sight does from these Bastions ply,
    P. 138 HOUSEWARMING   50 The two Allens when jovial, who ply him with
                             gallons,

plyant   frequency: 1   relative frequency: 0.0000
    P. 201 HISTORICALL   32 Deludes their plyant Nature with Vain things,

pockets   frequency: 1   relative frequency: 0.0000
    See also "pocketts."
    P. 165 KINGS VOWES   3 Our Pockets as empty as braine;

pocketts   frequency: 1   relative frequency: 0.0000
    P. 195 TWO HORSES   130 This for picking our Pocketts, that for cutting
                             our Throats.

pocus   frequency: 1   relative frequency: 0.0000

P. 203 HISTORICALL   92 With hocus pocus and their heavenly slight

poem   frequency: 3   relative frequency: 0.0000
    P. 86 FLECKNO   126 Then Nero's Poem he calls charity:
    P. 123 O.C.   t A Poem upon the Death of O. C.
    P. 201 HISTORICALL   t An Historicall Poem.

poems   frequency: 3   relative frequency: 0.0000
    P.   3 LOVELACE   t2 upon his Poems.
    P. 85 FLECKNO   112 And that both Poems did and Quarrels cease
    P. 86 FLECKNO   129 Of all his Poems there he stands ungirt

poet   frequency: 8   relative frequency: 0.0001
    P. 83 FLECKNO   2 Whom as Priest, Poet, and Musician,
    P. 86 FLECKNO   151 Thereat the Poet swell'd, with anger full,
    P. 87 FLECKNO   159 For the disdainful Poet was retir'd
    P. 91 MAY'S DEATH   42 Malignant Poet and Historian both.
    P. 92 MAY'S DEATH   81 Poor Poet thou, and grateful Senate they,
    P. 131 PARADISE   1 When I beheld the Poet blind, yet bold,
    P. 131 PARADISE   23 Pardon me, mighty Poet, nor despise
    P. 164 INSTRUCTIONS 948 Himself the Poet and the Painter too. To the
                             King.

poetick   frequency: 2   relative frequency: 0.0000
    P. 84 FLECKNO   71 Wears a close Jacket of poetick Buff,
    P. 164 INSTRUCTIONS 944 Poetick Picture, Painted Poetry.

poetry   frequency: 2   relative frequency: 0.0000
    P. 83 FLECKNO   7 For Poetry: There three Stair-Cases high,
    P. 164 INSTRUCTIONS 944 Poetick Picture, Painted Poetry.

poets   frequency: 7   relative frequency: 0.0001
    P. 87 FLECKNO   166 Ere the fierce Poets anger turn'd to rime.
    P. 90 MAY'S DEATH   14 Amongst the Chorus of old Poets laid,
    P. 92 MAY'S DEATH   65 Then is the Poets time, 'tis then he drawes,
    P. 92 MAY'S DEATH   95 'Tis just what Torments Poets ere did feign,
    P. 132 PARADISE   50 The Poets tag them; we for fashion wear.
    P. 171 LOYALL SCOT   4 Which of their Poets shold his Welcome sing,
    P. 176 LOYALL SCOT 194 They, tho' nce poets, on Parnassus dream,

point   frequency: 4   relative frequency: 0.0000
    P. 13 DROP OF DEW   35 Moving but on a point below,
    P. 70 A. HOUSE   364 To point the Battery of its Beams.
    P. 152 INSTRUCTIONS 457 Presbyter Hollis the first point should clear;
    P. 173 LOYALL SCOT   75 Prick down the point whoever has the Art

points   frequency: 5   relative frequency: 0.0001
    P. 86 FLECKNO   149 Making the half points and the periods run
    P. 111 ANNIVERSARY 316 With the same liberty as Points and Lace;
    P. 132 PARADISE   49 Their Fancies like our bushy Points appear,
    P. 143 INSTRUCTIONS 108 On opposite points, the black against the white.
    P. 169 ADVICE   42 Arm'd at all points ready to reinforce

poise   frequency: 1   relative frequency: 0.0000
    P. 15 EYES   11 And then paid out in equal Poise,

poising. See "poysing."

poison   frequency: 1   relative frequency: 0.0000
    See also "poisone," "poyson."
    P. 204 HISTORICALL 117 First temper'd Poison to destroy our Lawes,

poisone   frequency: 1   relative frequency: 0.0000
    P. 200 DUKE   108 A droppe of poisone or a papish knife

poisoned. See "poyson'd."

poisonous   frequency: 1   relative frequency: 0.0000
    P. 189 BRITANNIA   194 No Poisonous tyrant on thy ground shall live.

poland   frequency: 2   relative frequency: 0.0000
    P. 66 A. HOUSE   244 France, Poland, either Germany;
    P. 67 A. HOUSE   282 Whom France and Poland yet does fame:

pole   frequency: 5   relative frequency: 0.0001
    P. 12 DIALOGUE   77 The rest does lie beyond the Pole,
    P. 19 THYRSIS   17 Till it hit, against the pole,
    P. 68 A. HOUSE   314 Of Stars walks round about the Pole,
    P. 158 INSTRUCTIONS 716 Unloaded here the Birth of either Pole;
    P. 177 LOYALL SCOT 238 Under each pole place either of the two,

poles   frequency: 1   relative frequency: 0.0000

P. 37 DEFINITION   18 Us as the distant Poles have plac'd,

policy   frequency: 1   relative frequency: 0.0000
     P. 138 HOUSEWARMING   40 So he could to build but make Policy Law.

polish'd   frequency: 2   relative frequency: 0.0000
     P. 41 THE MOWER   37 Their Statues polish'd by some ancient hand,
     P. 125 O.C.   73 Like polish'd Mirrcurs, so his steely Brest

polished.   See "polish'd," "polisht."

polisht   frequency: 1   relative frequency: 0.0000
     P. 73 A. HOUSE   457 They seem within the polisht Grass

politick   frequency: 1   relative frequency: 0.0000
     P. 84 FLECKNO   54 And th' Ordinance was only Politick.

politicks   frequency: 1   relative frequency: 0.0000
     P. 145 INSTRUCTIONS 200 For the command of Politicks or Sotts.

poll   frequency: 1   relative frequency: 0.0000
     P. 145 INSTRUCTIONS 165 The posture strange men laught at of his Poll,

poll-bill   frequency: 1   relative frequency: 0.0000
     P. 162 INSTRUCTIONS 872 And a Poll-Bill does like his Apron look.

pollute   frequency: 1   relative frequency: 0.0000
     P. 36 DAPHNIS   92 Nor will I this Grief pollute.

polydore   frequency: 1   relative frequency: 0.0000
     P. 91 MAY'S DEATH   41 Polydore, Lucan, Allan, Vandale, Goth,

pomegranates.   See "pomgranates."

pomgranates   frequency: 1   relative frequency: 0.0000
     P. 17 BERMUDAS   19 And does in the Pomgranates close,

pomp   frequency: 1   relative frequency: 0.0000
     See also "pompe."
     P. 32 MOURNING   17 And, while vain Pomp does her restrain

pompe   frequency: 1   relative frequency: 0.0000
     P. 201 HISTORICALL   25 And that the Fleet was gone in Pompe and state

pompous   frequency: 1   relative frequency: 0.0000
     P. 186 BRITANNIA   68 Pale death, lusts, Horrour fill her pompous
                             train.

pond   frequency: 1   relative frequency: 0.0000
     P. 167 KINGS VOWES   52 I will have a fine pond and a pretty decoy,

poniarding.   See "ponyarding."

ponyarding   frequency: 1   relative frequency: 0.0000
     P. 107 ANNIVERSARY   171 Thy Brest through ponyarding Conspiracies,

pool   frequency: 2   relative frequency: 0.0000
     P. 40 THE MOWER   6 A dead and standing pool of Air:
     P. 145 INSTRUCTIONS 193 For Chimney's sake they all Sir Pool obey'd,

poole   frequency: 1   relative frequency: 0.0000
     P. 315 CHEQUER INN   127 Sir Courtney Poole and he contend

poor   frequency: 15   relative frequency: 0.0003
     See also "poore."
     P. 18 CLORINDA   21 D. Words that transcend poor Shepherds skill,
     P. 27 LOVER   11 That my poor Lover floting lay,
     P. 34 DAPHNIS   31 When poor Daphnis is undone,
     P. 40 THE MATCH   38 Whilst all the World is poor,
     P. 43 DAMON   55 And though in Woell more poor then they,
     P. 61 A. HOUSE   65 A Stately Frontispice of Poor
     P. 92 MAY'S DEATH   81 Poor Poet thou, and grateful Senate they,
     P. 108 ANNIVERSARY   191 But the poor Beasts wanting their noble Guide,
     P. 165 INSTRUCTIONS 982 And a poor Warren once a City ras'd.
     P. 186 BRITANNIA   73 Such poor pedantick toys teach underlings.
     P. 190 STATUE   17 No, to comfort the hearts of the poor Cavaleer
     P. 193 TWO HORSES   55 W. That the bank should be seiz'd yet the
                             Chequer so poor;
     P. 193 TWO HORSES   62 No token should appear but a poor Copper
                             farthing;
     P. 194 TWO HORSES   96 When one already hath made him soe poor.

P. 315 CHEQUER INN   125 Was oftner serv'd then the Poor

poor-john   frequency: 1   relative frequency: 0.0000
    P. 97 HOLLAND   62 And Poor-John to have been th' Evangelist.

poore   frequency: 5   relative frequency: 0.0001
    P. 193 TWO HORSES   60 And yet all his Court be as poore as Church
                             Ratts;
    P. 199 DUKE   46 Poore princess, borne under a sullen starr
    P. 199 DUKE   79 Rich with the Spoile of a poore Algeryne,
    P. 201 HISTORICALL   12 And dubd poore Palmer's wife his Royall Whore.
    P. 202 HISTORICALL   64 The poore Priapus King led by the Nose

pope   frequency: 3   relative frequency: 0.0000
    P. 195 TWO HORSES   145 With the Turk in his head and the Pope in his
                             heart
    P. 199 DUKE   65 By Irish fools and by a doting pope.
    P. 200 DUKE   97 At last to fools and mad men and the pope?

popery   frequency: 2   relative frequency: 0.0000
    P. 198 DUKE   39 Do's now in popery with his Master joyne.
    P. 202 HISTORICALL   58 It has recoild to Popery and Shame,

popes   frequency: 1   relative frequency: 0.0000
    P. 90 MAY'S DEATH   7 Nor where the Popes head, nor the Mitre lay,

popish   frequency: 2   relative frequency: 0.0000
    P. 191 TWO HORSES   15 All Popish beleivers think something divine,
    P. 204 HISTORICALL   145 The Duke now vaunts, with popish Myrmidons;

poppea   frequency: 1   relative frequency: 0.0000
    P. 189 BRITANNIA   171 Poppea, Tegeline and Acte's name

poppies   frequency: 1   relative frequency: 0.0000
    P. 20 THYRSIS   46 And thou and I'le pick poppies and them steep

popping   frequency: 1   relative frequency: 0.0000
    P. 314 CHEQUER INN   86 And popping like an Elder Gun

popular   frequency: 2   relative frequency: 0.0000
    P. 93 DR. WITTY   t2 Translation of the Popular Errors.
    P. 180 STOCKSMARKET   43 Or else thus expose him to popular flouts,

porch   frequency: 1   relative frequency: 0.0000
    P. 199 DUKE   68 He's of a size indeed to fill a porch,

pore   frequency: 1   relative frequency: 0.0000
    P. 27 MISTRESS   36 At every pore with instant Fires,

poreing   frequency: 1   relative frequency: 0.0000
    P. 181 MADE FREE   33 When in his Shop he shou'd be poreing;

poring   frequency: 1   relative frequency: 0.0000
    See also "poreing."
    P. 143 INSTRUCTIONS   87 Poring within her Glass she re-adjusts

port   frequency: 6   relative frequency: 0.0001
    P. 21 SOUL & BODY   29 And ready oft the Port to gain,
    P. 90 MAY'S DEATH   11 Such did he seem for corpulence and port,
    P. 115 BLAKE   72 You scap't the Sea, to perish in your Port.
    P. 129 O.C.   251 That port which so majestique was and strong,
    P. 157 INSTRUCIIONS 670 And safely through its Port the Dutch retire:
    P. 158 INSTRUCTIONS 738 Out of the Port, or dare to hoise a Sail,

portend   frequency: 1   relative frequency: 0.0000
    P. 44 GLO-WORMS   5 Ye Country Comets, that portend

portended   frequency: 1   relative frequency: 0.0000
    P. 196 TWO HORSES   169 Which Monarchys downfall portended much more

porter   frequency: 1   relative frequency: 0.0000
    P. 200 DUKE   87 Jermyne, Fitzgerald, Loftus, Porter, Scot.

porter's   frequency: 1   relative frequency: 0.0000
    P. 143 INSTRUCTIONS 101 Justly the Rogue was whipt in Porter's Den:

porticoes   frequency: 1   relative frequency: 0.0000
    P. 74 A. HOUSE   508 As the Corinthean Porticoes.

portion   frequency: 1   relative frequency: 0.0000
    P. 138 HOUSEWARMING   36 Nay scarce the Priests portion could scape from
                             his hands.

portly   frequency: 1   relative frequency: 0.0000
    P. 161 INSTRUCTIONS   831 The portly Burgess, through the Weather hot,

portman   frequency: 1   relative frequency: 0.0000
    P. 315 CHEQUER INN   112 Nay Portman tho' all men cry'd shame

ports   frequency: 4   relative frequency: 0.0000
    P.   69 A. HOUSE   349 But he preferr'd to the Cinque Ports
    P.   98 HOLLAND   124 A wholesome Danger drove us to our Ports.
    P. 172 LOYALL SCOT   36 And safely through its ports the Dutch retire.
    P. 204 HISTORICALL   146 Our fleets our Ports our Cittyes and our
                               Townes

portsmouth   frequency: 1   relative frequency: 0.0000
    P. 190 STATUE   14 When the King in Armado to Portsmouth should
                               saile,

positive   frequency: 1   relative frequency: 0.0000
    P. 169 ADVICE   55 Whilst Positive walks Woodcock in the dark,

possess   frequency: 2   relative frequency: 0.0000
    P. 175 LOYALL SCOT   136 The Legion Devil did but one man possess:
    P. 185 BRITANNIA   25 Brit: A Colony of French Possess the Court;

possessed. See "possesst," "possest."

possesses   frequency: 1   relative frequency: 0.0000
    P. 191 TWO HORSES   16 When Images speak, possesses the shrine:

possesst   frequency: 1   relative frequency: 0.0000
    P. 205 HISTORICALL   173 Fiends of Ambition here his Soul possesst,

possest   frequency: 5   relative frequency: 0.0001
    P.   21 SOUL & BODY   20 Since this ill Spirit it possest.
    P.   33 DAPHNIS   21 But he came so full possest
    P.   40 THE MATCH   39 And have within our Selves possest
    P.   83 FLECKNO   22 Possest; and sure the Devil brought me there.
    P. 111 ANNIVERSARY   314 Sorcerers, Atheists, Jesuites, Possest;

post   frequency: 4   relative frequency: 0.0000
    See also "sign-post."
    P. 140 G.-CHILDREN   1 Kendal is dead, and Cambridge riding post.
    P. 147 INSTRUCTIONS   251 Each ran, as chance him guides, to sev'ral Post:
    P. 150 INSTRUCTIONS   409 But Morrice learn'd demonstrates, by the Post,
    P. 160 INSTRUCTIONS   820 Harry came Post just as he shew'd his Watch.

postern   frequency: 1   relative frequency: 0.0000
    P. 177 LOYALL SCOT   227 With much adoe preserves his postern Chast.

posting   frequency: 1   relative frequency: 0.0000
    P.   10 DIALOGUE   39 Which the posting Winds recall,

posts   frequency: 1   relative frequency: 0.0000
    P. 131 PARADISE   9 (So Sampson groap'd the Temples Posts in
                               spight)

posture   frequency: 4   relative frequency: 0.0000
    P.   30 THE GALLERY   51 Where the same Posture, and the Look
    P. 103 ANNIVERSARY   18 In the same Posture would be found again.
    P. 145 INSTRUCTIONS   165 The posture strange men laught at of his Poll,
    P. 162 INSTRUCTIONS   892 Though ill agree her Posture, Hour, or Place:

pot   frequency: 2   relative frequency: 0.0000
    P. 149 INSTRUCTIONS   338 With Magic Herbs, rose from the Pot renew'd:
    P. 202 HISTORICALL   46 With Denham and Coneig's infected pot,

potent   frequency: 1   relative frequency: 0.0000
    P. 188 BRITANNIA   148 It 's by noe Potent Antidote withstood.

pothecare   frequency: 1   relative frequency: 0.0000
    P. 316 CHEQUER INN   156 In spight of Pothecare.

poulains   frequency: 1   relative frequency: 0.0000
    P.   86 FLECKNO   137 When they compare their Chancres and Poulains.

poultney   frequency: 1   relative frequency: 0.0000
    P. 137 HOUSEWARMING   22 Of African Poultney, and Tyrian Did'

pound   frequency: 3   relative frequency: 0.0000

```
P.  73 A. HOUSE       480 And Pikes are taken in the Pound.
P. 149 INSTRUCTIONS   332 Bought off with Eighteen hundred thousand pound.
P. 152 INSTRUCTICNS   492 (The Eighteen hundred thcusand pound was gone.)
```

pour   frequency: 1   relative frequency: 0.0000
See also "poure."
```
P. 126 O.C.           122 And pour the Deluge ore the Chaos head.
```

poure   frequency: 1   relative frequency: 0.0000
```
P. 317 CHEQUER INN    182 Wee poure in Water when it won't come
```

pouredest. See "pow'rdst."

poures   frequency: 1   relative frequency: 0.0000
```
P. 114 BLAKE           29 O noble Trust which Heaven on this Isle
                          poures,
```

pours. See "poures."

poverty   frequency: 1   relative frequency: 0.0000
```
P.  92 MAY'S DEATH     80 Right Romane poverty and gratitude.
```

powder   frequency: 5   relative frequency: 0.0001
See also "gun-powder."
```
P.  69 A. HOUSE       344 We Crd'nance Plant and Powder sow.
P. 155 INSTRUCTIONS   606 Cannon and Powder, but in vain, to beg:
P. 159 INSTRUCTIONS   781 Who to supply with Powder, did forget
P. 160 INSTRUCTIONS   796 Powder ne're blew man up so soon so high.
P. 164 INSTRUCTICNS   976 Nor Powder so the vaulted Bastion tear;
```

powders   frequency: 2   relative frequency: 0.0000
```
P. 117 BLAKE          131 Which by quick powders force, so high was sent,
P. 178 LOYALL SCOT    270 Powders them ore till none discern their foes
```

powell   frequency: 1   relative frequency: 0.0000
```
P. 146 INSTRUCTIONS   213 Last then but one, Powell, that could not ride,
```

power   frequency: 10   relative frequency: 0.0002
See also "pow'r."
```
P. 109 ANNIVERSARY    251 He on the Peace extends a Warlike power,
P. 116 BLAKE           77 Onely to this vast hill a power is given,
P. 118 BLAKE          139 And neither have, cr power, or will to fly,
P. 175 LOYALL SCOT    138 That power Alone Can Lcose this spell that
                          tyes,
P. 184 BRITANNIA        9 Raw: What mighty power has forc'd me from my
                          rest?
P. 185 BRITANNIA       44 How Spaines prow'd power her Virgin Armes
                          contrould
P. 187 BRITANNIA       95 Whilst your starv'd power in Legall fetters
                          pires.
P. 187 BRITANNIA       98 Tast the delicicus sweets of sovereign power,
P. 189 BRITANNIA      181 Publicola with healing hand shall power
P. 198 DUKE            27 It is our birthright tc have Power to kill.
```

powerful   frequency: 1   relative frequency: 0.0000
See also "powerfull," "pow'rful."
```
P. 129 O.C.           237 No more shall heare that powerful language charm,
```

powerfull   frequency: 1   relative frequency: 0.0000
```
P. 169 ADVICE          35 Thus whilst the King of France with powerfull
                          Armes
```

powers   frequency: 3   relative frequency: 0.0000
See also "pow'rs."
```
P.  15 EYES            24 Which straight in pity back he powers.
P. 123 O.C.            23 From which those Pcwers that issu'd the Decree,
P. 187 BRITANNIA       89 And they will fear those powers they once did
                          scorn.
```

pow'r   frequency: 11   relative frequency: 0.0002
```
P.  27 MISTRESS        40 Than languish in his slow-chapt pow'r.
P.  37 DEFINITION      16 And her Tyrannick pow'r depose.
P.  69 A. HOUSE       352 Pow'r which the Ocean might command.
P.  89 ODE             66 Which first assur'd the forced Pow'r.
P.  90 ODE            120 A Pow'r must it maintain.
P.  96 HCLLAND         50 The Pow'r, and grows as 'twere a King of
                          Spades.
P. 106 ANNIVERSARY    132 High Grace should meet in one with highest
                          Pow'r,
P. 109 ANNIVERSARY    243 'Twas Heav'n would nct that his Pow'r should
                          cease,
P. 126 O.C.           137 The Stars that for him fought had cnly pow'r
```

```
        P. 131 O.C.          323 Tempt not his clemency to try his pow'r,
        P. 142 INSTRUCTICNS   43 Who, if the French dispute his Pow'r, from
                                 thence

pow'rdst                         frequency:    1    relative frequency: 0.0000
        P. 109 ANNIVERSARY   236 And down at last thou pow'rdst the fertile
                                 Storm;

pow'rful                         frequency:    1    relative frequency: 0.0000
        P. 105 ANNIVERSARY    74 And once he struck, and twice, the pow'rful
                                 Strings.

pow'rs                           frequency:    2    relative frequency: 0.0000
        P. 125 O.C.          103 Whether some Kinder Pow'rs, that wish us well,
        P. 154 INSTRUCTIONS  565 No man can sit there safe, the Cannon pow'rs

pox                              frequency:    1    relative frequency: 0.0000
        P. 198 DUKE           41 Hastning to be invenom'd with the pox

poysing                          frequency:    1    relative frequency: 0.0000
        P. 109 ANNIVERSARY   245 Choosing each Stone, and poysing every weight,

poyson                           frequency:    2    relative frequency: 0.0000
        P. 142 INSTRUCTIONS   67 Or how a mortal Poyson she may draw,
        P. 186 BRITANNIA      79 This Mortall poyson amongst Princes hurld,

poyson'd                         frequency:    1    relative frequency: 0.0000
        P. 188 BRITANNIA     131 Oh Vindex, come, and purge the Poyson'd state;

practic'd                        frequency:    1    relative frequency: 0.0000
        P. 154 INSTRUCTIONS  561 Spray there, thc practic'd in the Sea command,

practise                         frequency:    3    relative frequency: 0.0000
        P.  16 EYES           46 And practise sc your noblest Use.
        P. 170 PROPHECY       20 And practise Incest between Seven and Eight,
        P. 203 HISTORICALL    87 And practise all the Vices they araigne:

practising                       frequency:    3    relative frequency: 0.0000
        P.  47 EMPIRE         15 These practising the Wind, and those the Wire,
        P.  59 A. HOUSE       31 As practising, in doors so strait,
        P. 126 O.C.          116 As practising how they could thunder too:

prais'd                          frequency:    1    relative frequency: 0.0000
        P.  81 A. HOUSE      706 Disdains to be for lesser prais'd.

praise                           frequency:   16    relative frequency: 0.0003
        See also "prayse."
        P.  17 BERMUDAS        5 What should we do but sing his Praise
        P.  18 BERMUDAS       33 Ch let our Voice his Praise exalt,
        P.  26 MISTRESS       13 An hundred years should go to praise
        P.  47 EMPIRE         23 Who though He flies the Musick of his praise,
        P.  81 A. HOUSE      717 True Praise (That breaks through all defence;)
        P.  87 FLECKNO       164 Praise him? both difficult indeed to do
        P. 112 ANNIVERSARY   393 'But let them write his Praise that love him
                                 best,
        P. 113 ANNIVERSARY   400 As far above their Malice as my Praise.
        P. 116 BLAKE          94 They only Labour to exalt your praise.
        P. 121 TWO SONGS      47 Less Loves set cf each others praise,
        P. 129 O.C.          240 In warre, in ccunsell, or in pray'r, and praise;
        P. 129 O.C.          271 So shall his praise to after times encrease,
        P. 130 O.C.          286 Always thy honour, praise and name, shall last.
        P. 132 PARADISE       52 And while I meant to Praise thee, must
                                 Commend.
        P. 152 INSTRUCTIONS  484 These; and in Standing-Armies praise declaims.
        P. 178 LOYALL SCOT   281 And such my Rashness best thy valour praise.

praises                          frequency:    6    relative frequency: 0.0001
        P.  18 CLORINDA       26 C. Who would not in Pan's Praises meet?
        P.  55 EPITAPH         6 Who would officicus Praises spill?
        P.  58 BILL-BOROW     76 That Courage its own Fraises flies.
        P.  86 FLECKNO       141 But all his praises could nct now appease
        P.  89 ODE            77 They can affirm his Fraises best,
        P. 108 ANNIVERSARY   188 And speak as of the Dead the Praises due:

prat                             frequency:    1    relative frequency: 0.0000
        P. 139 HOUSEWARMING   81 For surveying the building, Prat did the feat,

pray                             frequency:    2    relative frequency: 0.0000
        P. 151 INSTRUCTIONS  437 Pray him tc make De-Witte, and Ruyter cease,
        P. 171 PROPHECY       34 And pray to Jove tc take him back againe.

pray'd                           frequency:    1    relative frequency: 0.0000
```

```
    P.  84 FLECKNO        34 Ask'd still for more, and pray'd him to repeat:

prayed                            frequency:   1    relative frequency: 0.0000
    See also "pray'd."
    P.  62 A. HOUSE      121 'When we have prayed all our Beads,

prayer                            frequency:   1    relative frequency: 0.0000
    See also "pray'r."
    P. 127 O.C.          186 And cityes strong were stormed by his prayer;

prayers                           frequency:   2    relative frequency: 0.0000
    See also "pray'rs."
    P. 168 KINGS VOWES    66 And Visit Nell when I shold be att Prayers.
    P. 174 LOYALL SCOT    96 Who sermons ere can pacifie and prayers?

praying                           frequency:   1    relative frequency: 0.0000
    P.  36 DAPHNIS        98 As whc long has praying ly'n,

pray'r                            frequency:   3    relative frequency: 0.0000
    P.  62 A. HOUSE      110 'With insense of incessant Pray'r.
    P. 127 O.C.          190 The sea between, yet hence his pray'r prevail'd.
    P. 129 O.C.          240 In warre, in ccunsell, or in pray'r, and praise;

pray'rs                           frequency:   3    relative frequency: 0.0000
    P.  22 NYMPH          9 But, if my simple Fray'rs may yet
    P. 161 INSTRUCTICNS  858 Nor gave the Commons leave to say their
                             Pray'rs:
    P. 162 INSTRUCTIONS  869 At Pray'rs, his Eyes turn up the Pious white,

prays                             frequency:   1    relative frequency: 0.0000
    P. 150 INSTRUCTIONS  380 And beats the Husband till for peace he prays:

prayse                            frequency:   2    relative frequency: 0.0000
    P.   3 LOVELACE       7 Who best cculd prayse, had then the greatest
                             prayse,

preach                            frequency:   1    relative frequency: 0.0000
    P. 176 LOYALL SCOT   211 To preach in diccesse Indifferent.

preacher                          frequency:   1    relative frequency: 0.0000
    P. 203 HISTORICALL   1C4 His God and Lord this preacher did betray.

preaching                         frequency:   1    relative frequency: 0.0000
    P. 160 INSTRUCTIONS  811 Grave Primate Shelden (much in Preaching
                             there)

precedent.  See "presedent," "president."

precedents.  See "presidents."

precedes.  See "preceds."

preceds                           frequency:   1    relative frequency: 0.0000
    P.  82 A. HOUSE      751 That, as all Virgins She preceds,

precepts                          frequency:   1    relative frequency: 0.0000
    P. 205 HISTORICALL   157 Here with curst precepts and with Councels dire

precious                          frequency:   3    relative frequency: 0.0000
    See also "pretious."
    P.  32 MOURNING       11 As it she, with thcse precious Tears,
    P.  94 DR. WITTY      12 Much of the precicus Metal rub away.
    P. 157 INSTRUCTICNS  671 That precious life he yet disdains tc save,

precipice                         frequency:   1    relative frequency: 0.0000
    P.  21 SOUL & BODY    14 That mine own Precipice I go;

precipices                        frequency:   2    relative frequency: 0.0000
    P.  70 A. HOUSE      375 And, from the Precipices tall
    P.  82 A. HOUSE      764 Gulfes, Deserts, Precipices, Stone.

precipitate                       frequency:   1    relative frequency: 0.0000
    P. 106 ANNIVERSARY   140 And soon precipitate the latest Day.

predecessor                       frequency:   1    relative frequency: 0.0000
    P. 195 TWO HORSES    154 W. His perfum'd predecessor was never much
                             fitter.

prefer.  See "preferr."

preferment                        frequency:   1    relative frequency: 0.0000
```

    P. 193 TWO HORSES   74 And get good preferment Imediately for't.

preferr   frequency: 1   relative frequency: 0.0000
    P. 82 A. HOUSE   750 And in your kind your selves preferr;

preferr'd   frequency: 1   relative frequency: 0.0000
    P. 69 A. HOUSE   349 But he preferr'd to the Cinque Ports

preferring   frequency: 1   relative frequency: 0.0000
    P. 145 INSTRUCTIONS   178 Haters of Fowl, to Teal preferring Bull.

pregnant   frequency: 4   relative frequency: 0.0000
    P. 16 EYES   34 Nor the chast Ladies pregnant Womb,
    P. 97 HOLLAND   65 More pregnant then their Marg'ret, that laid
                                      down
    P. 156 INSTRUCTIONS   644 Pregnant with Sulphur, to him nearer draw
    P. 201 HISTORICALL   22 He marry'd Minhier Falmouths pregnant wench.

preists   frequency: 1   relative frequency: 0.0000
    P. 176 LOYALL SCOT   184 With the preists vestments had hee but put on

prelat   frequency: 1   relative frequency: 0.0000
    P. 203 HISTORICALL   101 The Serpent was the Prelat of the place:

prelate   frequency: 4   relative frequency: 0.0000
    See also "prelat."
    P. 70 A. HOUSE   366 Th' Ambition of its Prelate great.
    P. 77 A. HOUSE   592 Like some great Prelate of the Grove,
    P. 174 LOYALL SCOT   106 The Jugling Prelate on his hocus calls,
    P. 175 LOYALL SCOT   168 The Conscious Prelate therefore did not Err,

prelate's. See "prelat's."

prelat's   frequency: 1   relative frequency: 0.0000
    P. 17 BERMUDAS   12 Safe from the Storms, and Prelat's rage.

premier   frequency: 2   relative frequency: 0.0000
    P. 167 KINGS VOWES   43 Of my Pimp I will make my Minister Premier,
    P. 170 PROPHECY   17 When Sodomy is the Premier Ministers sport

prentiships   frequency: 1   relative frequency: 0.0000
    P. 183 MADE FREE   77 Two Prentiships through,

prepar'd   frequency: 4   relative frequency: 0.0000
    P. 5 HASTINGS   49 Like some sad Chymist, who, prepar'd to reap
    P. 9 DIALOGUE   16 Stand prepar'd to heighten yours.
    P. 49 THE GARDEN   55 And, till prepar'd for longer flight,
    P. 131 O.C.   315 Heav'n to this choice prepar'd a diadem,

prepare   frequency: 3   relative frequency: 0.0000
    P. 47 EMPIRE   18 Did of all these a solemn noise prepare:
    P. 127 O.C.   185 Astonish'd armyes did their flight prepare,
    P. 153 INSTRUCTIONS   505 When Dutch Invade, when Parliament prepare,

prepared   frequency: 1   relative frequency: 0.0000
    See also "prepar'd."
    P. 83 FLECKNO   26 And to my Martyrdom prepared Rest.

prepares   frequency: 1   relative frequency: 0.0000
    P. 10 DIALOGUE   37 Heark how Musick then prepares

prerogative   frequency: 1   relative frequency: 0.0000
    P. 166 KINGS VOWES   42 Tho' for't I a branch of Prerogative lose.

presage   frequency: 5   relative frequency: 0.0001
    P. 4 HASTINGS   9 Alas, his Vertues did his Death presage:
    P. 44 GLO-WORMS   8 Then to presage the Grasses fall;
    P. 63 A. HOUSE   158 'Doth your succession near presage.
    P. 125 O.C.   105 Or the great World do by consent presage,
    P. 196 TWO HORSES   164 Prodigious events did surely presage,

presbyter   frequency: 2   relative frequency: 0.0000
    P. 152 INSTRUCTIONS   457 Presbyter Hollis the first point should clear;
    P. 178 LOYALL SCOT   285 Metemsicosd to some Scotch Presbyter.

presbyterian   frequency: 1   relative frequency: 0.0000
    P. 147 INSTRUCTIONS   284 Of Presbyterian Switzers, made a stand.

presbytery   frequency: 1   relative frequency: 0.0000
    P. 3 LOVELACE   24 Severer then the yong Presbytery.

presedent   frequency: 1   relative frequency: 0.0000

P. 169 ADVICE   62 To be at home made such a presedent!

presence   frequency: 2   relative frequency: 0.0000
  P. 35 DAPHNIS   60 What my Presence could not win.
  P. 41 THE MOWER   36 More by their presence then their skill.

present   frequency: 8   relative frequency: 0.0001
  P. 80 A. HOUSE   698 They gratefully again present.
  P. 83 FLECKNO   29 That there had been some present to assure
  P. 115 BLAKE   66 Shall conquests act, your present are unsung.
  P. 118 BLAKE   159 And in one War the present age may boast,
  P. 156 INSTRUCTIONS   622 With present shame compar'd, his mind distraught.
  P. 168 ADVICE   11 Then change the scene and let the next present
  P. 181 MADE FREE   2 To the King doe present
  P. 188 BRITANNIA   135 Present to his thought his long scorn'd
                           Parliament

presents   frequency: 5   relative frequency: 0.0001
  P. 28 LOVER   25 While Nature to his Birth presents
  P. 42 DAMON   34 Esteem me, and my Presents less?
  P. 89 ODE   85 He to the Commons Feet presents
  P. 138 HOUSEWARMING   59 While into a fabrick the Presents would muster;
  P. 139 HOUSEWARMING   62 And Presents croud headlong to give good
                           example:

preserv'd   frequency: 2   relative frequency: 0.0000
  P. 26 MISTRESS   28 That long preserv'd Virginity:
  P. 199 DUKE   45 Preserv'd in store for the new sett of maids.

preserve   frequency: 2   relative frequency: 0.0000
  P. 16 EYES   27 And, to preserve their Sight more true,
  P. 21 SOUL & BODY   26 That to preserve, which me destroys:

preserved   frequency: 1   relative frequency: 0.0000
  See also "preserv'd."
  P. 64 A. HOUSE   176 'Is thus preserved clear and full.

preserves   frequency: 2   relative frequency: 0.0000
  P. 132 PARADISE   34 As them preserves, and Thee inviolate.
  P. 177 LOYALL SCOT   227 With much adoe preserves his postern Chast.

preside   frequency: 1   relative frequency: 0.0000
  P. 188 BRITANNIA   163 Watch and Preside over their tender age

president   frequency: 1   relative frequency: 0.0000
  P. 137 HOUSEWARMING   21 Yet a President fitter in Virgil he found,

presidents   frequency: 1   relative frequency: 0.0000
  P. 198 DUKE   24 Theire parchment presidents and dull records.

press   frequency: 3   relative frequency: 0.0000
  See also "presse."
  P. 68 A. HOUSE   300 Again as great a charge they press:
  P. 110 ANNIVERSARY   291 And such as to their Parents Tents do press,
  P. 162 INSTRUCTIONS   901 And with kind hand does the coy Vision press,

presse   frequency: 1   relative frequency: 0.0000
  P. 129 O.C.   232 To fetch day, presse about his chamber-door;

prest   frequency: 7   relative frequency: 0.0001
  P. 60 A. HOUSE   54 Then he is by its straitness prest:
  P. 74 A. HOUSE   486 Fit Timber for his Keel have Prest.
  P. 91 MAY'S DEATH   28 Prest for his place among the Learned throng.
  P. 98 HOLLAND   104 When their whole Navy they together prest,
  P. 106 ANNIVERSARY   146 Who in his Age has always forward prest:
  P. 138 HOUSEWARMING   37 And hence like Pharoah that Israel prest
  P. 153 INSTRUCTIONS   510 Monk in his Shirt against the Dutch is prest.

preston's   frequency: 1   relative frequency: 0.0000
  P. 127 O.C.   187 Of that for ever Preston's field shall tell

presum'd   frequency: 1   relative frequency: 0.0000
  P. 203 HISTORICALL   112 My Muse presum'd a litle to digress

presume   frequency: 4   relative frequency: 0.0000
  P. 10 DIALOGUE   29 A Soul that knowes not to presume
  P. 89 ODE   97 What may not then our Isle presume
  P. 131 PARADISE   21 Might hence presume the whole Creations day
  P. 198 DUKE   30 Shall they presume to say that bread is bread,

presumes   frequency: 2   relative frequency: 0.0000

P. 141 INSTRUCTIONS   13 But if to match our Crimes thy skill presumes,
P. 147 INSTRUCTIONS   265 Of Birth, State, Wit, Strength, Courage,
                          How'rd presumes,

pretence   frequency: 3   relative frequency: 0.0000
     P. 152 INSTRUCTIONS   479 But most rely'd upon this Dutch pretence,
     P. 156 INSTRUCTIONS   630 Long since were fled or many a feign'd pretence.
     P. 164 INSTRUCTIONS   969 And to improve themselves, on false pretence,

pretend   frequency: 5   relative frequency: 0.0001
     P. 75 A. HOUSE   535 As if it Stork-like did pretend
     P. 91 MAY'S DEATH   30 Sworn Enemy to all that do pretend,
     P. 120 TWO SONGS   41 Though I so high may not pretend,
     P. 122 TWO SONGS   31 What Shepheard could for Love pretend,
     P. 131 PARADISE   26 Within thy Labours to pretend a Share.

pretending   frequency: 1   relative frequency: 0.0000
     P. 32 MOURNING   13 Yet some affirm, pretending Art,

prethee   frequency: 2   relative frequency: 0.0000
     P. 19 THYRSIS   3 Tell me Thyrsis, prethee do,
     P. 20 THYRSIS   29 I prethee let us spend our time to come

pretious   frequency: 2   relative frequency: 0.0000
     P. 115 BLAKE   55 They still do yield, such is their pretious
                                mould,
     P. 172 LOYALL SCOT   37 That pretious life hee yet disdaines to save

pretty   frequency: 3   relative frequency: 0.0000
     P. 23 NYMPH   65 With what a pretty skipping grace,
     P. 25 YOUNG LOVE   5 Pretty surely 'twere to see
     P. 167 KINGS VOWES   52 I will have a fine pond and a pretty decoy,

prevail   frequency: 2   relative frequency: 0.0000
See also "prevaile."
     P. 22 NYMPH   10 Prevail with Heaven to forget
     P. 204 HISTORICALL   144 But Osborn and the Duke must needs prevail.

prevail'd   frequency: 1   relative frequency: 0.0000
     P. 127 O.C.   190 The sea between, yet hence his pray'r prevail'd.

prevaile   frequency: 1   relative frequency: 0.0000
     P. 201 HISTORICALL   33 Her mischiefbreeding breast did so prevaile

prevailed   frequency: 1   relative frequency: 0.0000
See also "prevail'd."
     P. 176 LOYALL SCOT   182 But his Lay pitty underneath prevailed

prevent   frequency: 7   relative frequency: 0.0001
     P. 25 YOUNG LOVE   24 Or, if ill, that Ill prevent.
     P. 81 A. HOUSE   713 Blest Nymph! that couldst so soon prevent
     P. 110 ANNIVERSARY   278 Saving himself he does their loss prevent.
     P. 125 O.C.   104 What they above cannot prevent, foretell;
     P. 158 INSTRUCTIONS   709 Officious fear, however, to prevent
     P. 160 INSTRUCTIONS   790 That lost our Fleet, and did our Flight
                                prevent.
     P. 167 KINGS VOWES   60 And all their bills for publike good prevent.

prevented   frequency: 1   relative frequency: 0.0000
     P. 159 INSTRUCTIONS   775 Who with false News prevented the Gazette?

prevents   frequency: 1   relative frequency: 0.0000
     P. 106 ANNIVERSARY   123 Like the shrill Huntsman that prevents the
                                East,

prey   frequency: 7   relative frequency: 0.0001
     P. 27 MISTRESS   38 And now, like am'rous birds of prey,
     P. 30 THE GALLERY   32 To be the greedy Vultur's prey.
     P. 142 INSTRUCTIONS   78 Galloping with the Duke to other Prey.
     P. 154 INSTRUCTIONS   574 Like molting Fowl, a weak and easie Prey.
     P. 158 INSTRUCTIONS   730 And all admires, but most his easie Prey.
     P. 203 HISTORICALL   105 To have the weaker Vessell made his prey:
     P. 204 HISTORICALL   140 T'hunt down 's Prey and hope to master all.

preys   frequency: 1   relative frequency: 0.0000
     P. 144 INSTRUCTIONS   141 She wastes the Country and on Cities preys.

priapus   frequency: 1   relative frequency: 0.0000
     P. 202 HISTORICALL   64 The poore Priapus King led by the Nose

price   frequency: 5   relative frequency: 0.0001

```
P.  11 DIALOGUE        61 Wer't not a price who'ld value Gold?
P.  15 EYES            12 Are the true price of all my Joyes.
P.  17 BERMUDAS        23 But Apples plants of such a price,
P. 140 HIS HOUSE        4 The price of ruin'd Families:
P. 191 STATUE          43 She thinks nct convenient to goe to the price,
```

priced   frequency: 1   relative frequency: 0.0000
```
P. 193 TWO HORSES      85 Ch. Yet baser the sculs cf those low priced
                          Sinners,
```

prick   frequency: 2   relative frequency: 0.0000
```
P.  75 A. HOUSE       518 And listning Elders prick the Ear.
P. 173 LOYALL SCCT     75 Prick down the point whoever has the Art
```

prickling   frequency: 1   relative frequency: 0.0000
```
P.  70 A. HOUSE       357 A prickling leaf it bears, and such
```

pride   frequency: 10   relative frequency: 0.0002
```
P.  18 CLORINDA         4 Where Flora blazons all her pride.
P.  60 A. HOUSE        64 Nor Eride invent what to contemn?
P. 115 BLAKE           76 Yet in their brests, carry a pride much higher.
P. 116 BLAKE          102 Ore Seas as vast as is the Spaniards pride.
P. 177 LOYALL SCOT    230 Luxury malice superstition pride
P. 177 LOYALL SCCT    249 At Babel names frcm pride and discord flow'd,
P. 186 BRITANNIA       60 Entred a Dame bedeckt with spotted pride;
P. 201 HISTORICALL     20 Soft in her Nature and of wanton pride.
P. 202 HISTORICALL     39 Pride nourisht folly, folly a Delight
P. 202 HISTORICALL     60 Tainted with Pride cr with impetuous lust.
```

pries. See "prys," "pry's."

priest   frequency: 8   relative frequency: 0.0001
```
P.  82 A. HOUSE       742 The Priest shall cut the sacred Bud;
P.  83 FLECKNO          t Fleckno, an English Priest at Rome.
P.  83 FLECKNO          2 Whom as Priest, Poet, and Musician,
P.  85 FLECKNO        102 Our peace, the Priest said I too had some wit:
P.  85 FLECKNC        107 But the propitiatory Priest had straight
P. 192 TWO HORSES      20 By the Devill, a Priest, a Fryar, or Nun.
P. 203 HISTORICALL    109 To tread the Phantastik Mazes of a Priest,
P. 205 HISTORICALL    163 A Priest should dce it, from whose sacred stroke
```

priest-ridden   frequency: 1   relative frequency: 0.0000
```
P. 194 TWO HORSES     117 W. Thy Priest-ridden King turn'd desperate
                          Fighter
```

priests   frequency: 7   relative frequency: 0.0001
```
P.  97 HOLLAND         92 Fills the Priests Nostrils and puts out his
                          Eyes.
P. 138 HOUSEWARMING    36 Nay scarce the Priests porticn could scape from
                          his hands.
P. 139 HOUSEWARMING    65 Straight Judges, Priests, Bishops, true sons
                          of the Seal,
P. 185 BRITANNIA       26 Pimps, Priests, Buffoones i'th privy chamber
                          sport.
P. 186 BRITANNIA       85 Bribe hungry Priests to deify your might,
P. 203 HISTORICALL     82 Priests were the first deluders of Mankind,
P. 203 HISTORICALL     95 Beccmes the Priests Amphitrio dureing Life.
```

primate   frequency: 1   relative frequency: 0.0000
```
P. 160 INSTRUCTIONS   811 Grave Primate Shelden (much in Preaching
                          there)
```

prime   frequency: 1   relative frequency: 0.0000
```
P.  39 PICTURE         37 To kill her Infants in their prime,
```

primitive   frequency: 1   relative frequency: 0.0000
```
P.  85 FLECKNO         74 Does make a primitive Sotana fall;
```

prince   frequency: 9   relative frequency: 0.0001
```
P.   5 HASTINGS        27 Yet as some Prince, that, for State-Jealousie,
P. 113 ANNIVERSARY    395 Pardon, great Prince, if thus their Fear or
                          Spight
P. 123 O.C.            10 Unless the Prince whom they applaud be slain.
P. 125 O.C.            84 Nor though a Prince to be a Man refus'd:.
P. 130 O.C.           312 A Cromwell in an houre a prince will grow.
P. 164 INSTRUCTIONS   970 About the Commcn Prince have rais'd a Fence;
P. 190 STATUE          40 Shall a Treasurer cf Guinny a Prince Grudge
                          of Token?
P. 198 DUKE            26 And thinke a prince oth blood can ere doe Ill?
P. 203 HISTORICAIL     93 They dazle both the Prince and Peasants sight.
```

princes   frequency: 11   relative frequency: 0.0002

P.   44 GLO-WORMS   6 No War, nor Princes funeral,
P. 105 ANNIVERSARY   103 While by his Beams observing Princes steer,
P. 106 ANNIVERSARY   117 Unhappy Princes, ignorantly bred,
P. 111 ANNIVERSARY   346 And Princes shining through their windows
                          starts;
P. 125 O.C.   102 Pore boding Princes falls, and seldom vain.
P. 152 INSTRUCTIONS 466 Still his sharp Wit on States and Princes
                          whets.
P. 175 LOYALL SCOT   140 Will you bee treated Princes? here fall to:
P. 184 BRITANNIA   4 Of Earles, of Dukes, and Princes of the blood,
P. 186 BRITANNIA   79 This Mortall poyson amongst Princes hurld,
P. 200 DUKE   116 Hard fate of princes, who will nere believe,
P. 202 HISTORICALL   74 The Senate which should headstrong Princes stay

princess   frequency: 1   relative frequency: 0.0000
   See also "princesse."
   P. 199 DUKE   46 Poore princess, borne under a sullen starr

princesse   frequency: 1   relative frequency: 0.0000
   P. 198 DUKE   40 Then draw the princesse with her golden locks,

principles   frequency: 1   relative frequency: 0.0000
   P. 188 BRITANNIA   156 From her sage mouth fam'd Principles to know,

print   frequency: 1   relative frequency: 0.0000
   P.   24 NYMPH   86 And print those Roses on my Lip.

pris'ners   frequency: 1   relative frequency: 0.0000
   P. 161 INSTRUCTIONS 859 But like his Pris'ners to the Bar them led,

prison   frequency: 2   relative frequency: 0.0000
   P.   65 A. HOUSE   206 'Who though in prison yet inchant!
   P.   98 HOLLAND   126 Half bound at home in Prison to the frost:

prisoners. See "pris'ners."

prithee   frequency: 1   relative frequency: 0.0000
   See also "prethee."
   P. 316 CHEQUER INN 160 And prithee why so pale? then swore

privacy   frequency: 1   relative frequency: 0.0000
   P. 108 ANNIVERSARY 223 Resigning up thy Privacy so dear,

private   frequency: 3   relative frequency: 0.0000
   P.   26 MISTRESS   31 The Grave's a fine and private place,
   P.   88 ODE   29 Who, from his private Gardens, where
   P. 130 O.C.   310 In private, to be view'd by better light;

private-bill's   frequency: 1   relative frequency: 0.0000
   P. 162 INSTRUCTIONS 870 But all the while his Private-Bill's in sight.

privateers   frequency: 1   relative frequency: 0.0000
   P. 145 INSTRUCTIONS 195 Then comes the thrifty Troop of Privateers,

priviledge   frequency: 2   relative frequency: 0.0000
   P.   3 LOVELACE   28 You wrong'd in her the Houses Priviledge.
   P. 145 INSTRUCTIONS 187 The Troop of Priviledge, a Rabble bare

privilege. See "priviledge."

privy   frequency: 3   relative frequency: 0.0000
   P. 166 KINGS VOWES 34 I will have a Privy Councell to sit allwayes
                          still,
   P. 185 BRITANNIA   26 Pimps, Priests, Buffoones i'th privy chamber
                          sport.
   P. 190 STATUE   10 Since the privy garden could not it defend,

privy-purse   frequency: 2   relative frequency: 0.0000
   P. 160 INSTRUCTIONS 806 The Exchequer might the Privy-purse obey.
   P. 166 KINGS VOWES 31 I will have a Privy-purse without a Controll,

priz'd   frequency: 1   relative frequency: 0.0000
   P.   10 DIALOGUE   35 When the Creator's skill is priz'd,

prize   frequency: 5   relative frequency: 0.0001
   P.   15 EYES   15 And all the Jewels which we prize,
   P.   25 YOUNG LOVE   14 Or the wanton Kid does prize,
   P.   58 BILL-BOROW   75 But Peace (if you his favour prize)
   P.   67 A. HOUSE   267 Who guiltily their Prize bemoan,
   P. 113 ANNIVERSARY 397 I yield, nor further will the Prize contend;

prizes   frequency: 2   relative frequency: 0.0000

P. 159 INSTRUCTIONS 774 And rifling Prizes, them neglected? Pett.
P. 159 INSTRUCTIONS 778 And all our Prizes who did swallow? Pett.

probable   frequency: 1   relative frequency: 0.0000
    P.   97 HOLLAND   55 'Tis probable Religion after this

proceed   frequency: 2   relative frequency: 0.0000
    P. 112 ANNIVERSARY   355 'Unless their Ships, &c, as their Fowle proceed
    P. 138 HOUSEWARMING   49 To proceed in the Model he call'd in his
                             Allens,

proceeding   frequency: 1   relative frequency: 0.0000
    P. 161 INSTRUCTIONS 843 And so, proceeding in his motion warm,

process   frequency: 1   relative frequency: 0.0000
    P. 140 HOUSEWARMING 105 But do not consider how in process of times,

processioning   frequency: 1   relative frequency: 0.0000
    P. 183 MADE FREE   95 A Processioning goe,

proclaim   frequency: 3   relative frequency: 0.0000
    See also "proclaime."
    P. 142 INSTRUCTIONS   62 Wide Mouth that Sparagus may well proclaim:
    P. 195 TWO HORSES   161 W. A Commonwealth a Common-wealth wee proclaim
                             to the Nacion;
    P. 196 TWO HORSES   175 Tho' Tyrants make Laws which they strictly
                             proclaim

proclaime   frequency: 1   relative frequency: 0.0000
    P.   17 BERMUDAS   28 Proclaime the Ambergris on shoar.

proclamation   frequency: 2   relative frequency: 0.0000
    P. 152 INSTRUCTIONS 463 The Dutch are then in Proclamation shent,
    P. 153 INSTRUCTIONS 493 This done, he Pens a Proclamation stout,

procreate   frequency: 1   relative frequency: 0.0000
    P.   41 THE MOWER   30 To procreate without a Sex.

procure   frequency: 1   relative frequency: 0.0000
    P.   38 PICTURE   31 But most procure

procurers   frequency: 1   relative frequency: 0.0000
    P. 145 INSTRUCTIONS 173 Then the Procurers under Progers fil'd,

prodigious   frequency: 2   relative frequency: 0.0000
    P. 141 INSTRUCTIONS   11 Sketching in shady smoke prodigious tools,
    P. 196 TWO HORSES   164 Prodigious events did surely presage,

produce   frequency: 3   relative frequency: 0.0000
    P. 116 BLAKE   81 For here they met with news, which did produce,
    P. 142 INSTRUCTIONS   44 Can straight produce them a Plenipotence.
    P. 191 STATUE   50 And his Parliament List withall did produce,

profane   frequency: 3   relative frequency: 0.0000
    See also "prophane."
    P. 132 PARADISE   32 Draws the Devout, deterring the Profane.
    P. 139 HOUSEWARMING   86 And with matter profane, cemented with holy,
    P. 191 TWO HORSES   1 Wee read in profane and Sacred records

proffer   frequency: 1   relative frequency: 0.0000
    P. 149 INSTRUCTIONS 330 They with the first days proffer seem content:

profit   frequency: 1   relative frequency: 0.0000
    See also "profitt."
    P. 114 BLAKE   33 Both health and profit, Fate cannot deny;

profitt   frequency: 1   relative frequency: 0.0000
    P. 194 TWO HORSES   92 Which Augments and secures his own profitt and
                             peace.

profound   frequency: 1   relative frequency: 0.0000
    P.   32 MOURNING   30 That sink for Pearl through Seas profound,

progeny   frequency: 3   relative frequency: 0.0000
    P.   47 EMPIRE   11 From whence the Progeny of numbers new
    P. 121 TWO SONGS   56 His Progeny above the Air;
    P. 185 BRITANNIA   24 Your own lov'd Court and Masters Progeny?

progers   frequency: 1   relative frequency: 0.0000
    P. 145 INSTRUCTIONS 173 Then the Procurers under Progers fil'd,

progress   frequency: 1   relative frequency: 0.0000

P. 61 A. HOUSE   84 The Progress of this Houses Fate.

prohibits   frequency: 1   relative frequency: 0.0000
    P.   3 LOVELACE   31 And one the Bock prohibits, because Kent

project   frequency: 3   relative frequency: 0.0000
    P. 131 PARADISE   12 I lik'd his Project, the success did fear;
    P. 153 INSTRUCTIONS   522 And Hyde's last Project would his Place
                             dispose.
    P. 202 HISTORICALL   61 Should we the Blackheath Project here relate,

projectors   frequency: 1   relative frequency: 0.0000
    P. 146 INSTRUCTIONS   207 Bold Duncombe next, of the Projectors chief:

projects   frequency: 3   relative frequency: 0.0000
    P. 103 ANNIVERSARY   19 Their earthy Projects under ground they lay,
    P. 169 ADVICE   56 Contriving Projects with a Brewers Clerk.
    P. 186 BRITANNIA   80 Fearing the mighty Projects of the great

prolong   frequency: 2   relative frequency: 0.0000
    P. 158 INSTRUCTIONS   727 The pleasing sight he often does prolong:
    P. 160 INSTRUCTIONS   810 All Arts they try how to prolong its Date.

prolongs   frequency: 1   relative frequency: 0.0000
    P.   4 HASTINGS   11 The Phlegmatick and Slowe prolongs his day,

promis'd   frequency: 4   relative frequency: 0.0000
    P. 65 A. HOUSE   197 Now Fairfax seek her promis'd faith:
    P. 149 INSTRUCTIONS   365 France had St. Albans promis'd (so they sing)
    P. 149 INSTRUCTIONS   366 St Albans promis'd him, and he the King.
    P. 159 INSTRUCTIONS   749 And Father Neptune promis'd to resign

promise   frequency: 1   relative frequency: 0.0000
    P. 205 HISTORICALL   167 From Saul the Land of Promise thus was rent,

promises   frequency: 1   relative frequency: 0.0000
    P. 86 FLECKNO   131 Yet these he promises as soon as clean.

promontories   frequency: 1   relative frequency: 0.0000
    P. 112 ANNIVERSARY   358 'And beaked Promontories sail'd from far;

proof   frequency: 1   relative frequency: 0.0000
    See also "proofe."
    P. 107 ANNIVERSARY   173 Thee proof beyond all other Force or Skill,

proofe   frequency: 1   relative frequency: 0.0000
    P. 191 TWO HORSES   4 It is a clear proofe that birds too may talke;

propagate   frequency: 2   relative frequency: 0.0000
    P. 157 INSTRUCTIONS   694 Or if my Verse can propagate thy Name;
    P. 173 LOYALL SCOT   60 That Matchless grace to propagate thy fame,

proper   frequency: 1   relative frequency: 0.0000
    P. 186 BRITANNIA   84 Are proper arts, the long-eard rout t'enslave:

property   frequency: 1   relative frequency: 0.0000
    P. 83 FLECKNO   8 Which signifies his triple property,

prophane   frequency: 1   relative frequency: 0.0000
    P. 175 LOYALL SCOT   156 In faith Erronicus and in life Prophane

prophecies   frequency: 4   relative frequency: 0.0000
    P. 77 A. HOUSE   578 Strange Prophecies my Phancy weaves:
    P. 104 ANNIVERSARY   35 Nor sacred Prophecies consult within,
    P. 107 ANNIVERSARY   172 Drawn from the Sheath of lying Prophecies;
    P. 110 ANNIVERSARY   310 For prophecies fit to be Alcorand.

prophecy   frequency: 2   relative frequency: 0.0000
    See also "prophesie."
    P. 170 PROPHECY   t Nostradamus's Prophecy.
    P. 196 TWO HORSES   174 Have the spirit of Prophecy likewise behind?

prophecy'd   frequency: 1   relative frequency: 0.0000
    P. 66 A. HOUSE   245 Till one, as long since prophecy'd,

prophesie   frequency: 1   relative frequency: 0.0000
    P. 132 PARADISE   44 Rewards with Prophesie thy loss of Sight.

prophesied. See "prophecy'd."

prophesy   frequency: 1   relative frequency: 0.0000

P. 196 TWO HORSES   178 Will publish their faults and prophesy their
                           fall.

prophet   frequency: 2   relative frequency: 0.0000
P. 191 TWO HORSES   12 And Balam the Prophet was reprov'd by his
                           Asse:

P. 194 TWO HORSES   101 When the Asse so bouldly rebuked the Prophet,

propitiatory   frequency: 1   relative frequency: 0.0000
P. 85 FLECKNO   107 But the propitiatory Priest had straight

propitious   frequency: 2   relative frequency: 0.0000
P. 122 TWO SONGS   40 Our Flocks and us with a propitious Eye.
P. 146 INSTRUCTIONS   237 Propitious Heavens, had not you them crost,

proportions   frequency: 1   relative frequency: 0.0000
P. 109 ANNIVERSARY   248 Founding a firm State by Proportions true.

propose   frequency: 1   relative frequency: 0.0000
P. 163 INSTRUCTIONS   929 And they, not knowing, the same thing propose,

propriety   frequency: 2   relative frequency: 0.0000
P. 95 HOLLAND   8 Fell to the Dutch by just Propriety.
P. 182 MADE FREE   60 They had Burglard all your Propriety.

prorogu'd   frequency: 1   relative frequency: 0.0000
P. 149 INSTRUCTIONS   336 The House Prorogu'd, the Chancellor rebounds.

prorogue   frequency: 1   relative frequency: 0.0000
P. 190 STATUE   36 Will you venture soe far to Prorogue the King
                           too?

prorogued   frequency: 2   relative frequency: 0.0000
See also "prorogu'd."
P. 190 STATUE   35 As the Parliament twice was prorogued by your
                           hand,

P. 194 TWO HORSES   90 For giving noe more the Rogues are prorogued.

prorogues   frequency: 1   relative frequency: 0.0000
P. 161 INSTRUCTIONS   861 Trembling with joy and fear, Hyde them
                           Prorogues,

proserpine   frequency: 1   relative frequency: 0.0000
P. 177 LOYALL SCOT   225 The second time to Ravish Proserpine.

prospect   frequency: 2   relative frequency: 0.0000
P. 38 PICTURE   t1 The Picture of little T. C. in a Prospect
P. 116 BLAKE   79 But this stupendious Prospect did not neer,

prosperous   frequency: 1   relative frequency: 0.0000
P. 118 BLAKE   147 So prosperous Stars, though absent to the sence,

prostitute   frequency: 1   relative frequency: 0.0000
P. 204 HISTORICALL   125 First brought his Mother for a Prostitute:

prostituted   frequency: 1   relative frequency: 0.0000
P. 92 MAY'S DEATH   71 But thou base man first prostituted hast

prostrate   frequency: 1   relative frequency: 0.0000
P. 198 DUKE   7 First draw him falling prostrate to the South,

protect   frequency: 1   relative frequency: 0.0000
P. 57 BILL-BOROW   42 Of the great Nymph did it protect;

protecting   frequency: 1   relative frequency: 0.0000
P. 105 ANNIVERSARY   98 Knit by the Roofs Protecting weight agree.

protestant   frequency: 2   relative frequency: 0.0000
P. 84 FLECKNO   56 Happy at once to make him Protestant,
P. 165 KINGS VOWES   8 Where Papist from Protestant shall not be
                           knowne;

proud   frequency: 9   relative frequency: 0.0001
P. 41 THE MOWER   20 To Man, that sov'raign thing and proud;
P. 55 EPITAPH   12 Of Virtue or asham'd, or proud;
P. 70 A. HOUSE   363 And at proud Cawood Castle seems
P. 113 BLAKE   5 For this rich load, of which so proud they are,
P. 115 BLAKE   75 The Peek's proud height, the Spaniards all
                           admire,
P. 116 BLAKE   96 So proud and confident of their made strength,
P. 186 BRITANNIA   71 And, frowning, thus with proud disdain she spoke.

```
        P. 186 BRITANNIA        81 Should drive them from their proud Celestiall
                                   seat,
        P. 203 HISTORICALL      84 Not Lucifer himselfe more proud then they,

provant                            frequency:    1    relative frequency: 0.0000
        P. 315 CHEQUER INN      94 And of more Provant to dispose

provd                              frequency:    1    relative frequency: 0.0000
        P. 202 HISTORICALL      53 But here his french bred Prowes provd in Vain,

prov'd                             frequency:    1    relative frequency: 0.0000
        P.  67 A. HOUSE        277 For if the Virgin prov'd not theirs,

prove                              frequency:   12    relative frequency: 0.0002
    See also "prov't."
        P.  26 YOUNG LOVE       32 And we both shall monarchs prove.
        P.  35 DAPHNIS          75 But the ravishment would prove
        P.  63 A. HOUSE        151 'Ah, no! and 'twould more Honour prove
        P.  70 A. HOUSE        384 And prove they've at the Bottom been.
        P.  78 A. HOUSE        613 But, lest your Fetters prove too weak,
        P. 114 BLAKE            43 But this great want, will not a long one prove,
        P. 151 INSTRUCTIONS    435 Summon him therefore of his Word, and prove
        P. 152 INSTRUCTIONS    453 To prove by Scripture, Treaty does imply
        P. 163 INSTRUCTIONS    942 To prove them Traytors, and himself the Pett.
        P. 183 MADE FREE        83 But he may prove more just,
        P. 194 TWO HORSES      106 I'le prove every tittle of what I have said.
        P. 198 DUKE             19 Prove to the world Ile have ould England know

proved                             frequency:    1    relative frequency: 0.0000
    See also "provd," "prov'd."
        P. 199 DUKE             59 He proved the mad Cethegus of his age.

provender.  See "provant."

proves                             frequency:    1    relative frequency: 0.0000
        P. 173 LOYALL SCOT      64 Sometimes the Gall'way Proves the better Nagg.

provide                            frequency:    2    relative frequency: 0.0000
        P. 191 STATUE           45 Where for so many Parties there are to provide,
        P. 192 TWO HORSES       27 Since Viner and Osburn did buy and provide 'um

provided                           frequency:    1    relative frequency: 0.0000
        P.  99 HOLLAND         147 Provided that they be what they have been,

providence                         frequency:    2    relative frequency: 0.0000
        P. 123 O.C.              1 That Providence which had so long the care
        P. 205 HISTORICALL     177 Had not Almighty Providence drawne neere,

provident                          frequency:    1    relative frequency: 0.0000
        P. 154 INSTRUCTIONS    544 (The Gods themselves do help the provident.)

province                           frequency:    1    relative frequency: 0.0000
        P.  98 HOLLAND         109 To whom their weather-beaten Province ows

provinces                          frequency:    3    relative frequency: 0.0000
        P.  98 HOLLAND         100 The Armes of the United Provinces
        P.  99 HOLLAND         137 And now the Hydra of seaven Provinces
        P. 166 KINGS VOWES      20 And the Dutch shall give Caution for their
                                   Provinces;

provok'd                           frequency:    1    relative frequency: 0.0000
        P. 163 INSTRUCTIONS    941 While Hyde provok'd his foaming tusk does whet,

provoked.  See "provok'd," "provok't."

provok't                           frequency:    2    relative frequency: 0.0000
        P.  86 FLECKNO         142 The provok't Author, whom it did displease
        P. 192 TWO HORSES       40 My Brass is provok't as much as thy stone

prov't                             frequency:    1    relative frequency: 0.0000
        P.  85 FLECKNO         103 To prov't, I said, the place doth us invite

prow'd                             frequency:    1    relative frequency: 0.0000
        P. 185 BRITANNIA        44 How Spaines prow'd power her Virgin Armes
                                   contrould

prowes                             frequency:    1    relative frequency: 0.0000
        P. 202 HISTORICALL      53 But here his french bred Prowes provd in Vain,

prowess.  See "prowes."

proxie                             frequency:    1    relative frequency: 0.0000
```

P. 104 ANNIVERSARY   24 Took in by Proxie, beggs a false Renown;

proxy. See "proxie."

prudence   frequency: 3   relative frequency: 0.0000
    P. 128 O.C.   217 What prudence more than humane did he need
    P. 128 O.C.   227 Valour, religion, friendship, prudence dy'd
    P. 188 BRITANNIA   157 With her the Prudence of the Antients read

prudent   frequency: 5   relative frequency: 0.0001
    P. 58 BILL-BOROW   60 Their prudent Heads too far intrust.
    P. 150 INSTRUCTIONS 387 Prudent Antiquity, that knew by Shame,
    P. 178 LOYALL SCOT   266 Just soe the prudent Husbandman who sees
    P. 190 STATUE   30 That the Treasurer thought prudent to Try it
                             again,
    P. 199 DUKE   57 Was thought soe meeke, soe prudent and soe wise:

prudently   frequency: 1   relative frequency: 0.0000
    P. 48 THE GARDEN   6 Does prudently their Toyles upbraid;

prun'd   frequency: 1   relative frequency: 0.0000
    P. 125 O.C.   94 Chance to be prun'd by an untimely knife,

prys   frequency: 1   relative frequency: 0.0000
    P. 144 INSTRUCTIONS 134 Breaks into Shops, and into Cellars prys.

pry's   frequency: 1   relative frequency: 0.0000
    P. 55 THYESTE   13 Into his own Heart ne'r pry's,

public. See "publick," "publike," "publique," "weal-publik."

publicans   frequency: 1   relative frequency: 0.0000
    P. 193 TWO HORSES   83 W. Four Knights and a Knave, who were
                             Publicans made,

publick   frequency: 10   relative frequency: 0.0002
    P. 54 THYESTE   6 And far of the publick Stage
    P. 92 MAY'S DEATH   83 And with the publick gravity would come,
    P. 104 ANNIVERSARY   25 Another triumphs at the publick Cost,
    P. 140 HOUSEWARMING 111 When like the good Oxe, for publick good chear,
    P. 143 INSTRUCTIONS 118 With what small Arts the publick game they play.
    P. 145 INSTRUCTIONS 192 (Their publick Acts) oblig'd them still to more.
    P. 149 INSTRUCTIONS 328 Is brought to beg in publick and to chide.
    P. 158 INSTRUCTIONS 736 Was led about in sport, the publick scorn.
    P. 187 BRITANNIA   114 To Boys, Bawds, whores, and made a Publick
                             game.
    P. 188 BRITANNIA   149 Tyrants like Leprous Kings for publick weal

publick's   frequency: 1   relative frequency: 0.0000
    P. 89 ODE   90 To lay them at the Publick's skirt.

publicola   frequency: 1   relative frequency: 0.0000
    P. 189 BRITANNIA   181 Publicola with healing hand shall power

public's. See "publick's."

publike   frequency: 2   relative frequency: 0.0000
    P. 167 KINGS VOWES   60 And all their bills for publike good prevent.
    P. 170 PROPHECY   27 When publike faith and Vowes and Payments stop,

publique   frequency: 2   relative frequency: 0.0000
    P. 105 ANNIVERSARY   88 Draw the Circumf'rence of the publique Wall;
    P. 192 TWO HORSES   23 Why should wee not credit the publique discourses

publish   frequency: 1   relative frequency: 0.0000
    P. 196 TWO HORSES   178 Will publish their faults and prophesy their
                             fall.

puchinello   frequency: 1   relative frequency: 0.0000
    P. 189 STATUE   4 Unless Puchinello be to be restor'd.

pudden   frequency: 1   relative frequency: 0.0000
    P. 170 PROPHECY   4 As farr as from Whitehall to Pudden lane

pudding. See "jack-pudding."

puffs   frequency: 1   relative frequency: 0.0000
    P. 154 INSTRUCTIONS 548 Puffs them along, and breathes upon them kind.

pull   frequency: 2   relative frequency: 0.0000
    P. 64 A. HOUSE   175 'And that which perisht while we pull,

```
        P.  189 BRITANNIA       189 Her true Crusado shall at last pull down

pulling                         frequency:    1    relative frequency: 0.0000
        P.  109 ANNIVERSARY     247 Here pulling down, and there erecting New,

pulpit                          frequency:    2    relative frequency: 0.0000
        P.  175 LOYALL SCOT     126 Who that is wise would pulpit Toyl Indure?
        P.  203 HISTORICALL      97 Who from the sacred Pulpit dare decieve?

pump                            frequency:    3    relative frequency: 0.0000
        P.   96 HOLLAND          45 Who best could know to pump an Earth so leak
        P.  317 CHEQUER INN     181 Just like our Rotten Pump at home
        P.  317 CHEQUER INN     192 By this old Whitehall Pump.

punchinello.  See "puchinello."

punishment                      frequency:    4    relative frequency: 0.0000
        P.   76 A. HOUSE        560 Viewing the Treason's Punishment.
        P.  150 INSTRUCTIONS    377 A Punishment invented first to awe
        P.  159 INSTRUCTIONS    766 Some one must be accus'd by Punishment.
        P.  160 INSTRUCTIONS    792 And march with Punishment in equal pace;

punisht                         frequency:    1    relative frequency: 0.0000
        P.  194 TWO HORSES       98 Yet truth many times being punisht for Treason,

purchase                        frequency:    2    relative frequency: 0.0000
        P.   11 DIALOGUE         59 Till thou purchase all below,
        P.  138 HOUSEWARMING     34 To buy us for Slaves, and purchase our Lands;

pure                            frequency:   15    relative frequency: 0.0003
        See "chrystal-pure."
        P.    5 HASTINGS         42 But draw their Veils, and their pure Beams
                                    reveal:
        P.   12 DROP OF DEW      25 Does, in its pure and circling thoughts, express
        P.   24 NYMPH            89 And its pure virgin limbs to fold
        P.   24 NYMPH           108 With milk-white Lambs, and Ermins pure.
        P.   39 THE MATCH         6 And Essences most pure,
        P.   40 THE MOWER         4 Where Nature was most plain and pure.
        P.   49 THE GARDEN       59 After a Place so pure, and sweet,
        P.   64 A. HOUSE        192 'Like Chrystal pure with Cotton warm.
        P.   72 A. HOUSE        446 Was such a Table rase and pure.
        P.   80 A. HOUSE        695 She yet more Pure, Sweet, Streight, and Fair,
        P.   81 A. HOUSE        726 But pure, and spotless as the Eye;
        P.   93 DR. WITTY         6 That sence in English which was bright and pure
        P.   96 HOLLAND          54 Nor bear strict service, nor pure Liberty.
        P.  130 O.C.            292 Spacious enough, and pure enough for thee.
        P.  175 LOYALL SCOT     171 Like Smutty Storyes in Pure Linnen Wrapt.

purer                           frequency:    1    relative frequency: 0.0000
        P.   94 DR. WITTY        18 Then Tagus, purer then dissolved snow,

purest                          frequency:    1    relative frequency: 0.0000
        P.   24 NYMPH           120 Of purest Alabaster made:

purgatory                       frequency:    1    relative frequency: 0.0000
        P.  198 DUKE             31 Or that theres not a purgatory for the dead?

purge                           frequency:    1    relative frequency: 0.0000
        P.  188 BRITANNIA       131 Oh Vindex, come, and purge the Poyson'd state;

purges                          frequency:    1    relative frequency: 0.0000
        P.   98 HOLLAND         134 And purges out the corruptible waves.

purling                         frequency:    1    relative frequency: 0.0000
        P.  107 ANNIVERSARY     184 Of purling Ore, a shining wave do shed:

purple                          frequency:    6    relative frequency: 0.0001
        P.    5 HASTINGS         44 Who for sad Purple, tears his Saffron-coat;
        P.   12 DROP OF DEW       9 How it the purple flow'r does slight,
        P.   22 NYMPH            22 Is dy'd in such a Purple Grain.
        P.  124 O.C.             67 And now Eliza's purple Locks were shorn,
        P.  163 INSTRUCTIONS    922 The purple thread about his Neck does show:
        P.  185 BRITANNIA        40 Shew'd him how many Kings in Purple Gore

purpose                         frequency:    1    relative frequency: 0.0000
        P.   96 HOLLAND          25 As if on purpose it on Land had come

purse                           frequency:    3    relative frequency: 0.0000
        See also "privy-purse," "shepherds-purse."
        P.  149 INSTRUCTIONS    333 Thus, like fair Thieves, the Commons Purse
                                    they share,
        P.  163 INSTRUCTIONS    938 That who does cut his Purse will cut his Throat.
```

P. 317 CHEQUER INN   191 That suck and draine thus ev'ry Purse

pursue   frequency: 1   relative frequency: 0.0000
    P. 111 ANNIVERSARY   326 See the bright Sun his shining Race pursue,

pursues   frequency: 2   relative frequency: 0.0000
    P. 106 ANNIVERSARY   128 Pursues the Monster thorough every Throne:
    P. 119 BLAKE   163 His Seige of Spain he then again pursues,

push   frequency: 1   relative frequency: 0.0000
    P. 66 A. HOUSE   251 Another bolder stands at push

push'd   frequency: 1   relative frequency: 0.0000
    P. 109 ANNIVERSARY   239 What since he did, an higher Force him push'd

put   frequency: 8   relative frequency: 0.0001
    P. 41 THE MOWER   26 Might put the Palate in dispute.
    P. 90 MAY'S DEATH   1 As one put drunk into the Packet-boat,
    P. 127 O.C.   179 He first put Armes into Religions hand,
    P. 142 INSTRUCTIONS   51 She, nak'd, can Archimedes self put down,
    P. 154 INSTRUCTIONS   570 Until the City put it in repair.
    P. 167 KINGS VOWES   48 And I'lle first put the Church then my Crowne
                             in Commission.
    P. 170 PROPHECY   21 And no Man knowes in whom to put his trust,
    P. 176 LOYALL SCOT   184 With the preists vestments had hee but put on

putrid   frequency: 1   relative frequency: 0.0000
    P. 80 A. HOUSE   686 Which from the putrid Earth exhale,

puts   frequency: 2   relative frequency: 0.0000
    P. 97 HOLLAND   92 Fills the Priests Nostrils and puts out his
                             Eyes.
    P. 195 TWO HORSES   141 Ch. Thy Ryder puts no man to death in his
                             wrath,

pyebald   frequency: 1   relative frequency: 0.0000
    P. 176 LOYALL SCOT   172 Doe but their Pyebald Lordships once Uncase

pygmees   frequency: 1   relative frequency: 0.0000
    P. 96 HOLLAND   39 For as with Pygmees who best kills the Crane,

pygmies. See "pygmees."

pyramid   frequency: 1   relative frequency: 0.0000
    P. 137 HOUSEWARMING   16 To erect him a Pyramid out of her Quarry.

pyramids   frequency: 1   relative frequency: 0.0000
    P. 72 A. HOUSE   438 Short Pyramids of Hay do stand.

pyx. See "pex."

quack   frequency: 1   relative frequency: 0.0000
    P. 167 KINGS VOWES   54 And Quack in their Language still Vive le
                             Roy.

quadrature   frequency: 1   relative frequency: 0.0000
    P. 60 A. HOUSE   46 The Circle in the Quadrature!

quaff   frequency: 1   relative frequency: 0.0000
    P. 177 LOYALL SCOT   229 And Uninforc'd Quaff healths in Phlegethon.

quailes   frequency: 1   relative frequency: 0.0000
    P. 35 DAPHNIS   79 While with Quailes and Manna fed,

quails   frequency: 1   relative frequency: 0.0000
    See also "quailes."
    P. 71 A. HOUSE   408 Rails rain for Quails, for Manna Dew.

quaint   frequency: 1   relative frequency: 0.0000
    P. 26 MISTRESS   29 And your quaint Honour turn to dust;

quake   frequency: 2   relative frequency: 0.0000
    P. 91 MAY'S DEATH   35 At whose dread Whisk Virgil himself does quake,
    P. 110 ANNIVERSARY   298 And make the World, by his Example, Quake:

quarrel   frequency: 1   relative frequency: 0.0000
    P. 145 INSTRUCTIONS   201 Thence fell to Words, but, quarrel to adjourn,

quarrell'd   frequency: 1   relative frequency: 0.0000
    P. 70 A. HOUSE   365 As if it quarrell'd in the Seat

```
quarrelling                     frequency:   1    relative frequency: 0.0000
    P.  28 LOVER          26 This masque of quarrelling Elements;

quarrells                       frequency:   2    relative frequency: 0.0000
    P. 182 MADE FREE      51 But molested the neighbours with Quarrells,
    P. 196 TWO HORSES    185 No Quarrells or oathes amongst those that drink
                            'um;

quarrels                        frequency:   1    relative frequency: 0.0000
    See also "quarrells."
    P.  85 FLECKNO       112 And that both Poems did and Quarrels cease

quarreys                        frequency:   1    relative frequency: 0.0000
    P. 104 ANNIVERSARY    52 Dans'd up in order from the Quarreys rude;

quarries                        frequency:   2    relative frequency: 0.0000
    See also "quarreys."
    P.  59 A. HOUSE        3 That unto Caves the Quarries drew,
    P.  61 A. HOUSE       88 The Quarries whence this dwelling rose.

quarry                          frequency:   2    relative frequency: 0.0000
    P. 105 ANNIVERSARY    79 No Quarry bears a Stone so hardly wrought,
    P. 137 HOUSEWARMING   16 To erect him a Pyramid cut of her Quarry.

quarter                         frequency:   1    relative frequency: 0.0000
    P. 313 CHEQUER INN    29 For all his slender Quarter Staffe

quarters                        frequency:   2    relative frequency: 0.0000
    P.  69 A. HOUSE      341 The Winter Quarters were the Stoves,
    P. 146 INSTRUCTIONS  239 For th' other side all in loose Quarters lay,

queans                          frequency:   1    relative frequency: 0.0000
    P. 194 TWO HORSES    122 Ch. Thy King will ne're fight unless't be for
                            Queans.

queen                           frequency:   6    relative frequency: 0.0001
    See also "queene."
    P.  20 THYRSIS        38 And every Nimph's a Queen of May.
    P.  62 A. HOUSE      118 'Each one a Spouse, and each a Queen;
    P. 152 INSTRUCTIONS  468 None but himself must chuse the King a Queen.)
    P. 184 BRITANNIA      10 Ah! mighty Queen, why so unsemly drest?
    P. 188 BRITANNIA     133 Rawl: Once more, great Queen, thy darling try
                            to save;
    P. 201 HISTORICALL    23 The pious Mother Queen heareing her Son

queene                          frequency:   1    relative frequency: 0.0000
    P. 199 DUKE           52 Then in false hopes of being once a Queene

queens                          frequency:   2    relative frequency: 0.0000
    P. 140 HIS HOUSE       8 The Queens Marriage and all;
    P. 170 PROPHECY       15 When Players shall use to act the parts of
                            Queens

quench                          frequency:   1    relative frequency: 0.0000
    P.  63 A. HOUSE      137 'And (for I dare not quench the Fire

quest                           frequency:   1    relative frequency: 0.0000
    P. 112 ANNIVERSARY   360 'A Fleet of Worlds, of other Worlds in quest;

question                        frequency:   1    relative frequency: 0.0000
    P. 162 INSTRUCTIONS  873 Well was he skill'd to season any question,

questiond                       frequency:   1    relative frequency: 0.0000
    P. 166 KINGS VOWES    33 And if any be Questiond, I'lle answer the
                            whole.

questioned.  See "questiond."

questions                       frequency:   1    relative frequency: 0.0000
    P. 191 TWO HORSES     14 Have to Questions return'd oracular Answers:

quick                           frequency:   4    relative frequency: 0.0000
    P.  71 A. HOUSE      405 When on another quick She lights,
    P.  73 A. HOUSE      476 Turn'd as they hang to Leeches quick;
    P. 117 BLAKE         131 Which by quick powders force, so high was sent,
    P. 150 INSTRUCTIONS  391 In quick Effigy, others Faults, and feign

quickly                         frequency:   7    relative frequency: 0.0001
    P.  37 DEFINITION      9 And yet I quickly might arrive
    P.  39 PICTURE        38 Do quickly make th' Example Yours;
    P. 109 ANNIVERSARY   262 Had quickly Levell'd every Cedar's top.
```

P.	112 ANNIVERSARY	372	'Can quickly leave us neither Earth nor Air.
P.	154 INSTRUCTIONS	563	And quickly judg'd the Fort was not tenable,
P.	201 HISTORICALL	19	And his Dutch Sister quickly after dy'd,
P.	313 CHEQUER INN	17	But quickly turn'd Catt i'th' Pan

quiet   frequency: 2   relative frequency: 0.0000
P. 48 THE GARDEN   9 Fair quiet, have I found thee here,
P. 115 BLAKE   58 Neither the Soyl, nor People quiet know.

quietly   frequency: 1   relative frequency: 0.0000
P. 196 TWO HORSES   181 Let the Citty drink Coffee and Quietly groan

quill   frequency: 2   relative frequency: 0.0000
P. 152 INSTRUCTIONS 490 With that curs'd Quill pluck'd from a Vulture's
                             Wing:
P. 166 KINGS VOWES   36 I will have two fine Secretaryes pisse thro one
                             Quill.

quills   frequency: 1   relative frequency: 0.0000
See also "quils."
P. 79 A. HOUSE   649 But now away my Hocks, my Quills,

quils   frequency: 1   relative frequency: 0.0000
P. 71 A. HOUSE   396 Whose yet unfeather'd Quils her fail.

quilted   frequency: 1   relative frequency: 0.0000
P. 72 A. HOUSE   422 Lyes quilted ore with Bodies slain:

quire   frequency: 5   relative frequency: 0.0001
P. 18 CLORINDA   30 For all the World is our Pan's Quire.
P. 29 THE GALLERY   21 While all the morning Quire does sing,
P. 47 EMPIRE   16 To sing Mens Triumphs, or in Heavens quire.
P. 64 A. HOUSE   161 'Your voice, the sweetest of the Quire,
P. 86 FLECKNO   124 Ten quire of paper in which he was drest.

quires   frequency: 1   relative frequency: 0.0000
P. 74 A. HOUSE   511 And underneath the winged Quires

quit   frequency: 2   relative frequency: 0.0000
P. 107 ANNIVERSARY   179 When thou hadst almost quit thy Mortal cares,
P. 174 LOYALL SCCT   113 At Bishops Lung the Foxes quit the feild.

quite   frequency: 2   relative frequency: 0.0000
P. 22 NYMPH   35 And quite regardless of my Smart,
P. 149 INSTRUCTIONS 340 His Gout (yet still he curst) had left him
                             quite.

quoth   frequency: 3   relative frequency: 0.0000
P. 161 INSTRUCTIONS 841 Not so, quoth Tomkins; and straight drew his
                             Tongue,
P. 192 TWO HORSES   35 W. Quoth the marble white Hors: 'twould make a
                             stone speak
P. 317 CHEQUER INN   177 Quoth Dick with Indignation

rabble   frequency: 3   relative frequency: 0.0000
P. 145 INSTRUCTIONS 187 The Troop of Priviledge, a Rabble bare
P. 193 TWO HORSES   76 What a rabble of Rascally Lords have been made.
P. 200 DUKE   86 Next, Painter, draw the Rabble of the plott,

race   frequency: 17   relative frequency: 0.0003
P.   5 HASTINGS   51 For, how Immortal must their race have stood,
P. 23 NYMPH   66 It oft would challenge me the Race:
P. 48 THE GARDEN   28 Still in a Tree did end their race.
P. 66 A. HOUSE   248 And the great Race would intercept.
P. 111 ANNIVERSARY   317 Oh Race most hypocritically strict!
P. 111 ANNIVERSARY   326 See the bright Sun his shining Race pursue,
P. 126 O.C.   123 The Race of warlike Horses at his Tomb
P. 141 INSTRUCTIONS   12 'Twill serve this race of Drunkards, Pimps, and
                             Fools.
P. 143 INSTRUCTIONS   86 She slights) his Feet shapt for a smoother race.
P. 144 INSTRUCTIONS 143 Black Birch, of all the Earth-born race most
                             hot,
P. 155 INSTRUCTIONS 577 Those Oaken Gyants of the ancient Race,
P. 157 INSTRUCTIONS 673 Much him the Honours of his ancient Race
P. 172 LOYALL SCOT   39 Much him the glories of his Antient Race
P. 173 LOYALL SCOT   69 Noe more discourse of Scotch or English Race
P. 184 BRITANNIA   5 No more of Scottish race thou wouldst complain;
P. 195 TWO HORSES   136 Under all that shall Reign of the false
                             Scottish race.
P. 202 HISTORICALL   57 But since the ill gott race of Stewarts came,

rack   frequency: 1   relative frequency: 0.0000

```
       P.  187 BRITANNIA       103 Rack nature till new pleasures she shall find,

racks                              frequency:    1    relative frequency: 0.0000
       P.  124 O.C.            54 And him within his tortur'd Image racks.

raffe                              frequency:    1    relative frequency: 0.0000
       P.  190 STATUE          16 To repair with such riffe raffe our Churches old
                                  Pale?

rag                                frequency:    1    relative frequency: 0.0000
     See also "ragg."
       P.  180 STOCKSMARKET    52 They will scarce afford him a rag to his breech.

rage                               frequency:   12    relative frequency: 0.0002
       P.   17 BERMUDAS        12 Safe from the Storms, and Prelat's rage.
       P.  104 ANNIVERSARY     59 Now through the Strings a Martial rage he
                                  throws,
       P.  110 ANNIVERSARY    293 Yet such a Chammish issue still does rage,
       P.  114 BLAKE           15 Of winds and waters rage, they fearful be,
       P.  116 BLAKE           86 Which did the rage of Elements subdue.
       P.  125 O.C.            90 Of many a Winter hath surviv'd the rage.
       P.  125 O.C.           106 As hollow Seas with future Tempests rage:
       P.  141 INSTRUCTIONS    24 His Anger reacht that rage which past his Art;
       P.  145 INSTRUCTIONS   189 Their Fortune's error they supply'd in rage,
       P.  155 INSTRUCTIONS   611 But when the Royal Charles, what Rage, what
                                  Grief,
       P.  185 BRITANNIA       49 Sauls stormy rage and Check his black disease,
       P.  186 BRITANNIA       70 And on the ground in spitefull rage it broak,

ragg                               frequency:    1    relative frequency: 0.0000
       P.  314 CHEQUER INN     49 And now they march't all Tagg and Ragg

ragg'd                             frequency:    1    relative frequency: 0.0000
       P.   28 LOVER           54 Torn into Flames, and ragg'd with Wounds.

raggs                              frequency:    1    relative frequency: 0.0000
       P.   86 FLECKNO        135 More odious then those raggs which the French
                                  youth

raging                             frequency:    2    relative frequency: 0.0000
       P.   98 HOLLAND        116 Should raging hold his Linstock to the Mine?
       P.  141 INSTRUCTIONS    22 Of his Hound's Mouth to feign the raging froth,

rags                               frequency:    1    relative frequency: 0.0000
     See also "raggs."
       P.  180 STOCKSMARKET    46 With three shattered planks and the rags of a
                                  sail

raign                              frequency:    2    relative frequency: 0.0000
       P.  103 ANNIVERSARY     17 And though they all Platonique years should
                                  raign,
       P.  118 BLAKE          145 For your resistless genious there did Raign,

raigne                             frequency:    4    relative frequency: 0.0000
       P.  166 KINGS VOWES     26 If not o're a Kingdome, to raigne ore my Guard;
       P.  167 KINGS VOWES     46 If this please not I'lle Raigne upon any
                                  Condition,
       P.  187 BRITANNIA      104 Strong as your Raigne and beauteous as your
                                  mind.'
       P.  201 HISTORICALL     10 But in his thirtieth yeare began to Raigne.

raigning                           frequency:    1    relative frequency: 0.0000
       P.  130 O.C.           288 Of humane glory tow'rst, and raigning there

rail                               frequency:    2    relative frequency: 0.0000
     See also "raile."
       P.   71 A. HOUSE       395 While one, unknowing, carves the Rail,
       P.  193 TWO HORSES      73 Ch. That Parliament men should rail at the
                                  Court,

raile                              frequency:    1    relative frequency: 0.0000
       P.  316 CHEQUER INN    148 On them she was allowed to raile

rails                              frequency:    1    relative frequency: 0.0000
       P.   71 A. HOUSE       408 Rails rain for Quails, for Manna Dew.

rain                               frequency:    6    relative frequency: 0.0001
       P.   32 MOURNING        19 She courts her self in am'rous Rain:
       P.   36 DAPHNIS         87 Gather Roses in the rain,
       P.   71 A. HOUSE       408 Rails rain for Quails, for Manna Dew.
       P.  114 BLAKE           32 The benefits without the ills of rain.
```

P. 114 BLAKE   36 Fewel and Rain together kindly grow;
P. 176 LOYALL SCOT   197 Doth Charles the second rain or Charles the
                          two?

rainbow   frequency: 1   relative frequency: 0.0000
    P. 131 O.C.   317 A pearly rainbow, where the sun inchas'd

rainbows   frequency: 1   relative frequency: 0.0000
    P. 131 O.C.   322 Rainbows to storms, Richard to Oliver.

raines   frequency: 1   relative frequency: 0.0000
    P. 202 HISTORICALL   75 Let loose the Raines and give the Realme away:

rais'd   frequency: 8   relative frequency: 0.0001
    P. 58 BILL-BOROW   68 And Mountains rais'd of dying Men.
    P. 59 A. HOUSE   7 Whose Columnes should so high be rais'd
    P. 81 A. HOUSE   705 For She, to higher Beauties rais'd,
    P. 113 BLAKE   6 Was rais'd by Tyranny, and rais'd for War;
    P. 161 INSTRUCTIONS 844 Th' Army soon rais'd, he doth as soon disarm.
    P. 161 INSTRUCTIONS 853 The King, that day rais'd early from his rest,
    P. 164 INSTRUCTIONS 970 About the Common Prince have rais'd a Fence;

raise   frequency: 24   relative frequency: 0.0005
    P. 20 SOUL & BODY   1 O who shall, from this Dungeon, raise
    P. 33 DAPHNIS   20 Better 'twas the Siege to raise.
    P. 42 DAMON   17 This heat the Sun could never raise,
    P. 47 EMPIRE   24 Would with you Heavens Hallelujahs raise.
    P. 57 BILL-BOROW   24 But only strives to raise the Plain.
    P. 64 A. HOUSE   162 'Shall draw Heav'n nearer, raise us higher.
    P. 68 A. HOUSE   293 Then Flow'rs their drowsie Eylids raise,
    P. 86 FLECKNO   147 For he his untun'd voice did fall or raise
    P. 103 ANNIVERSARY   2 Which in smooth streams a sinking Weight does
                             raise;
    P. 104 ANNIVERSARY   34 Nor Matter for succeeding Founders raise;
    P. 106 ANNIVERSARY   109 How might they under such a Captain raise
    P. 113 ANNIVERSARY   399 While thou thy venerable Head dost raise
    P. 115 BLAKE   59 Which troubles men to raise it when 'tis Oar,
    P. 116 BLAKE   93 Fond men who know not whilst such works they
                             raise,
    P. 138 HOUSEWARMING   42 He would have demolisht to raise up his Walls;
    P. 144 INSTRUCTIONS 150 Could raise so long for this new Whore of
                             State.
    P. 152 INSTRUCTIONS 480 To raise a two-edg'd Army for's defence.
    P. 161 INSTRUCTIONS 834 And threaten Hyde to raise a greater Dust.
    P. 162 INSTRUCTIONS 891 Raise up a sudden Shape with Virgins Face,
    P. 167 KINGS VOWES   57 That they may raise Fortunes to my owne frye.
    P. 178 LOYALL SCOT   280 My differing Crime doth more thy vertue raise
    P. 189 BRITANNIA   184 Shall England raise, releive opprest mankind.
    P. 198 DUKE   16 Ile raise my papist and my Irish bands,
    P. 317 CHEQUER INN   178 They are but Engines to raise Tax

raised   frequency: 1   relative frequency: 0.0000
    See also "rais'd."
    P. 115 BLAKE   60 And when 'tis raised, does trouble them much
                             more.

rake   frequency: 1   relative frequency: 0.0000
    P. 313 CHEQUER INN   32 And leaner Dick then any Rake

raleigh. See "rawl.," "rawleigh."

ram   frequency: 1   relative frequency: 0.0000
    P. 25 YOUNG LOVE   15 As the lusty Bull or Ram,

ram'd   frequency: 2   relative frequency: 0.0000
    P. 98 HOLLAND   115 Ram'd with Gun-powder, flaming with Brand wine,
    P. 315 CHEQUER INN   92 The Cheere into his Breeches ram'd

rammed. See "ram'd."

rampant   frequency: 1   relative frequency: 0.0000
    P. 204 HISTORICALL   127 This Villin Rampant bares away the bell.

ran   frequency: 6   relative frequency: 0.0001
    P. 125 O.C.   72 Ran out impetuously to hasting Death.
    P. 143 INSTRUCTIONS   81 She through her Lacquies Drawers as he ran,
    P. 146 INSTRUCTIONS 243 And some ran o're each night while others sleep,
    P. 147 INSTRUCTIONS 251 Each ran, as chance him guides, to sev'ral Post:
    P. 181 MADE FREE   20 Where such Riott he ran,
    P. 316 CHEQUER INN   172 I saw no more but hither ran

rancour   frequency: 1   relative frequency: 0.0000

         P. 178 LOYALL SCOT   259 That senseless Rancour against Interest.

rang'd   frequency: 2   relative frequency: 0.0000
         P. 96 HOLLAND   33 Or as they over the new Level rang'd
         P. 144 INSTRUCTIONS   161 Then damming Cowards rang'd the vocal Plain,

rank   frequency: 1   relative frequency: 0.0000
         P. 174 LOYALL SCOT   114 Their Rank Ambition all this heat hath stir'd

rant   frequency: 1   relative frequency: 0.0000
         P. 110 ANNIVERSARY   307 For soon thou mightst have past among their Rant

rapacious   frequency: 1   relative frequency: 0.0000
         P. 144 INSTRUCTIONS   144 And most rapacious, like himself begot.

rare   frequency: 3   relative frequency: 0.0000
         P. 36 DEFINITION   1 My Love is of a birth as rare
         P. 84 FLECKNO   67 Lest his too suttle Body, growing rare,
         P. 142 INSTRUCTIONS   57 Hence Crowder made the rare Inventress free,

rarely   frequency: 2   relative frequency: 0.0000
         P. 40 THE MATCH   26 And rarely thither came;
         P. 202 HISTORICALL   59 Misguided Monarchs rarely wise or just,

rarities   frequency: 1   relative frequency: 0.0000
         P. 41 THE MOWER   19 And yet these Rarities might be allow'd,

rascally   frequency: 1   relative frequency: 0.0000
         P. 193 TWO HORSES   76 What a rabble of Rascally Lords have been made.

ras'd   frequency: 1   relative frequency: 0.0000
         P. 165 INSTRUCTIONS   982 And a poor Warren once a City ras'd.

rase   frequency: 4   relative frequency: 0.0000
         P. 72 A. HOUSE   446 Was such a Table rase and pure.
         P. 73 A. HOUSE   452 Their Cattle, which it closer rase;
         P. 109 ANNIVERSARY   252 And Is'rel silent saw him rase the Tow'r;
         P. 112 ANNIVERSARY   352 'And ere we Dine, rase and rebuild their State.

rash   frequency: 1   relative frequency: 0.0000
         P. 182 MADE FREE   37 When his Masters too rash

rashness   frequency: 1   relative frequency: 0.0000
         P. 178 LOYALL SCOT   281 And such my Rashness best thy valour praise.

rat   frequency: 2   relative frequency: 0.0000
         P. 149 INSTRUCTIONS   341 What Frosts to Fruit, what Ars'nick to the
                                   Rat,
         P. 176 LOYALL SCOT   174 A Hungry Chaplain and a Starved Rat

rate   frequency: 5   relative frequency: 0.0001
         P. 26 MISTRESS   20 Nor would I love at lower rate.
         P. 35 DAPHNIS   68 Jewels of so high a rate.
         P. 91 MAY'S DEATH   38 Like Pembroke at the Masque, and then did rate.
         P. 137 HOUSEWARMING   10 (So unreasonable are the rate they buy-at)
         P. 138 HOUSEWARMING   45 His Wood would come in at the easier rate,

rather   frequency: 17   relative frequency: 0.0003
         P. 17 BERMUDAS   29 He cast (of which we rather boast)
         P. 22 NYMPH   12 Rather then fail. But, O my fears!
         P. 27 MISTRESS   39 Rather at once our Time devour,
         P. 35 DAPHNIS   69 Rather I away will pine
         P. 72 A. HOUSE   447 Or rather such is the Toril
         P. 98 HOLLAND   108 Rather then to the English strike their sail;
         P. 106 ANNIVERSARY   105 O would they rather by his Pattern won.
         P. 108 ANNIVERSARY   227 Therefore thou rather didst thy Self depress,
         P. 112 ANNIVERSARY   357 'Theirs are not Ships, but rather Arks of War,
         P. 119 TWO SONGS   11 If thou a Mortal, rather sleep;
         P. 120 TWO SONGS   21 Rather restrain these double Seas,
         P. 125 O.C.   85 But rather then in his Eliza's pain
         P. 125 O.C.   107 Or rather Heav'n, which us so long foresees,
         P. 137 HOUSEWARMING   11 His Omnipotence therfore much rather design'd
         P. 140 HOUSEWARMING   109 Or rather how wisely his Stall was built near,
         P. 175 LOYALL SCOT   132 Noe Bishop Rather then it shold bee soe!
         P. 195 TWO HORSES   134 I had rather Bare Nero than Sardanapalus.

rational   frequency: 1   relative frequency: 0.0000
         See also "rationall."
         P. 83 A. HOUSE   774 These rational Amphibii go?

rationall   frequency: 1   relative frequency: 0.0000

P. 178 LOYALL SCOT   256 Rationall mens words pledges are of peace,

ratling   frequency: 2   relative frequency: 0.0000
    P.   28 LOVER   23 While round the ratling Thunder hurl'd,
    P.   57 BILL-BOROW   40 Ratling through all the Grove and Hill.

rats. See "paper-rats," "ratts."

rattling. See "ratling."

ratts   frequency: 1   relative frequency: 0.0000
    P. 193 TWO HORSES   60 And yet all his Court be as poore as Church
                             Ratts;

ravage   frequency: 1   relative frequency: 0.0000
    P. 158 INSTRUCTIONS 707 And were not Ruyters maw with ravage cloy'd,

rave   frequency: 1   relative frequency: 0.0000
    P.   30 THE GALLERY   27 And, by a Light obscure, dost rave

ravenous   frequency: 1   relative frequency: 0.0000
    P. 186 BRITANNIA   67 Around her Joves lou'd ravenous Currs complain;

ravens   frequency: 1   relative frequency: 0.0000
    P. 111 ANNIVERSARY   333 And Owls and Ravens with their screeching noyse

ravish   frequency: 1   relative frequency: 0.0000
    P. 177 LOYALL SCOT   225 The second time to Ravish Proserpine.

ravish'd   frequency: 1   relative frequency: 0.0000
    P. 159 INSTRUCTIONS 744 And Medway chast ravish'd before his Face,

ravisher   frequency: 1   relative frequency: 0.0000
    P. 159 INSTRUCTIONS 758 Now in the Ravisher De-Ruyter's hand,

ravishment   frequency: 1   relative frequency: 0.0000
    P.   35 DAPHNIS   75 But the ravishment would prove

raw   frequency: 1   relative frequency: 0.0000
    P. 184 BRITANNIA   9 Raw: What mighty power has forc'd me from my
                             rest?

rawl.   frequency: 2   relative frequency: 0.0000
    P. 185 BRITANNIA   23 Rawl: What fatall crimes make you forever fly
    P. 188 BRITANNIA   133 Rawl: Once more, great Queen, thy darling try
                             to save;

rawleigh   frequency: 4   relative frequency: 0.0000
    See also "rawl."
    P. 184 BRITANNIA   t BRITANNIA and RAWLEIGH.
    P. 184 BRITANNIA   1 Brit: Ah! Rawleigh, when thy Breath thou didst
                             resign
    P. 188 BRITANNIA   141 Brit: Rawleigh, noe more; too long in vain I've
                             try'd
    P. 188 BRITANNIA   161 Till then, my Rawleigh, teach our noble Youth

ray   frequency: 5   relative frequency: 0.0001
    P.   12 DROP OF DEW   19 So the Soul, that Drop, that Ray
    P.   15 EYES   22 Distills the World with Chymick Ray;
    P.   68 A. HOUSE   289 When in the East the Morning Ray
    P. 111 ANNIVERSARY   339 Why did mine Eyes once see so bright a Ray;
    P. 120 TWO SONGS   25 If therefore thy resplendent Ray

rayes   frequency: 2   relative frequency: 0.0000
    P.   94 DR. WITTY   10 To add such lustre, and so many rayes,
    P. 121 TWO SONGS   48 While Stars Eclypse by mixing Rayes.

rays   frequency: 1   relative frequency: 0.0000
    See also "rayes."
    P. 129 O.C.   249 Those gentle rays under the lids were fled,

raze. See "rase."

razed. See "ras'd."

re   frequency: 1   relative frequency: 0.0000
    P. 152 INSTRUCTIONS 460 Then to return home straight infecta re.

re-adjusts   frequency: 1   relative frequency: 0.0000
    P. 143 INSTRUCTIONS   87 Poring within her Glass she re-adjusts

re-baptize   frequency: 1   relative frequency: 0.0000

     P.   97 HOLLAND   60 And, as their Land, so them did re-baptize.

reach   frequency: 7   relative frequency: 0.0001
     P.   21 SOUL & BODY   31 But Physick yet could never reach
     P.   49 THE GARDEN   38 Into my hands themselves do reach;
     P.   96 HOLLAND   22 To reach the Sea, then those to scale the Sky.
     P. 120 TWO SONGS   38 Have I not Armes that reach to thee?
     P. 125 O.C.   77 Fate could not either reach with single stroke,
     P. 130 O.C.   304 Onely our sighs, perhaps, may thither reach.
     P. 151 INSTRUCTIONS   415 Bennet and May, and those of shorter reach,

reacht   frequency: 1   relative frequency: 0.0000
     P. 141 INSTRUCTIONS   24 His Anger reacht that rage which past his Art;

read   frequency: 14   relative frequency: 0.0002
     P.   33 DAPHNIS   17 He, well read in all the wayes
     P.   77 A. HOUSE   582 I in this light Mosaick read.
     P.   77 A. HOUSE   584 Hath read in Natures mystick Book.
     P.   86 FLECKNO   139 To read; and then, because he understood
     P.   86 FLECKNO   144 That were ill made condemn'd to be read worse:
     P.   86 FLECKNO   153 Sir you read false. That any one but you
     P.   87 FLECKNO   156 To say that you read false Sir is no Lye.
     P. 111 ANNIVERSARY   349 'Is this, saith one, the Nation that we read
     P. 131 PARADISE   11 Yet as I read, soon growing less severe,
     P. 137 HOUSEWARMING   13 He had read of Rhodope, a Lady of Thrace,
     P. 161 INSTRUCTIONS   860 Where mute they stand to hear their Sentence
                              read;
     P. 184 MADE FREE   110 Of the Oth to him read
     P. 188 BRITANNIA   157 With her the Prudence of the Antients read
     P. 191 TWO HORSES   1 Wee read in profane and Sacred records

readers   frequency: 2   relative frequency: 0.0000
     P. 132 PARADISE   45 Well mightst thou scorn thy Readers to allure
     P. 202 HISTORICALL   63 Our muse would on the Readers patience grate.

reading   frequency: 1   relative frequency: 0.0000
     P.   3 LOVELACE   27 Some reading your Lucasta, will alledge

reads   frequency: 1   relative frequency: 0.0000
     P.   62 A. HOUSE   122 'Some One the holy Legend reads;

ready   frequency: 11   relative frequency: 0.0002
     P.   13 DROP OF DEW   34 How girt and ready to ascend.
     P.   15 EYES   4 They might be ready to complain.
     P.   21 SOUL & BODY   29 And ready oft the Port to gain,
     P.   55 EPITAPH   15 That ready her last Debt to pay
     P.   84 FLECKNO   52 So hungry that though ready to say Mass
     P.   85 FLECKNO   83 He drest, and ready to disfurnish now
     P. 107 ANNIVERSARY   148 Girds yet his Sword, and ready stands to fight;
     P. 161 INSTRUCTIONS   842 Trusty as Steel, that always ready hung;
     P. 162 INSTRUCTIONS   876 Court-mushrumps ready are sent in in pickle.
     P. 169 ADVICE   42 Arm'd at all points ready to reinforce
     P. 172 LOYALL SCOT   8 His ready muse to Court the Warlike Guest.

realm   frequency: 1   relative frequency: 0.0000
     See also "realme."
     P. 164 INSTRUCTIONS   978 As scratching Courtiers undermine a Realm:

realme   frequency: 1   relative frequency: 0.0000
     P. 202 HISTORICALL   75 Let loose the Raines and give the Realme away:

realmes   frequency: 1   relative frequency: 0.0000
     P. 176 LOYALL SCOT   192 But now, when one Head doeth both Realmes
                              controule,

realms   frequency: 1   relative frequency: 0.0000
     See also "realmes."
     P. 193 TWO HORSES   59 W. That a King should consume three Realms
                              whole Estates

reap   frequency: 2   relative frequency: 0.0000
     P.   5 HASTINGS   49 Like some sad Chymist, who, prepar'd to reap
     P. 203 HISTORICALL   88 Riches and honour they from Lay-men reap,

reapt   frequency: 1   relative frequency: 0.0000
     P. 118 BLAKE   146 By which we Laurels reapt ev'n on the Mayn.

rear   frequency: 2   relative frequency: 0.0000
     P. 145 INSTRUCTIONS   186 Finch, in the Front, and Thurland in the Rear.
     P. 154 INSTRUCTIONS   571 So he in Front, his Garrison in Rear,

rear'd   frequency: 2   relative frequency: 0.0000

P. 105 ANNIVERSARY   64 Therefore the Temples rear'd their Columns high:
P. 314 CHEQUER INN   56 Mannerly rear'd against the Wall

reason   frequency: 8   relative frequency: 0.0001
See also "reason's."
P. 106 ANNIVERSARY   111 But mad with Reason, so miscall'd, of State
P. 108 ANNIVERSARY   207 Justice obstructed lay, and Reason fool'd;
P. 120 TWO SONGS   40 Would you but your own Reason use.
P. 128 O.C.   207 More strong affections never reason serv'd,
P. 175 LOYALL SCOT   160 Who views but Gilberts Toyls will reason find
P. 194 TWO HORSES   97 Ch. Enough, dear Brother, for tho' we have reason,
P. 195 TWO HORSES   156 W. For that very reason hee 's never to rise.
P. 203 HISTORICALL   83 Who with vain Faith made all their Reason blind:

reasons   frequency: 1   relative frequency: 0.0000
P. 179 STOCKSMARKET   28 May be henceforth confiscate for reasons more just.

reason's   frequency: 1   relative frequency: 0.0000
P. 203 HISTORICALL   110 Till native Reason's basely forct to yield

reassume   frequency: 1   relative frequency: 0.0000
P. 168 ADVICE   1 Painter once more thy Pencell reassume,

rebabel   frequency: 1   relative frequency: 0.0000
P. 177 LOYALL SCOT   216 'Tis necessary to rebabel Pauls,

rebel   frequency: 2   relative frequency: 0.0000
See also "rebell."
P. 87 FLECKNO   161 Against the Rebel; who, at this struck dead,
P. 149 INSTRUCTIONS   357 First Buckingham, that durst to him Rebel,

rebell   frequency: 1   relative frequency: 0.0000
P. 176 LOYALL SCOT   204 Strange boldness! even bishops there rebell

rebelling   frequency: 1   relative frequency: 0.0000
P. 131 PARADISE   4 Rebelling Angels, the Forbidden Tree,

rebel's   frequency: 1   relative frequency: 0.0000
P. 90 MAY'S DEATH   16 The Subjects Safety, and the Rebel's Fear.

rebounding   frequency: 1   relative frequency: 0.0000
P. 18 BERMUDAS   35 Which thence (perhaps) rebounding, may

rebounds   frequency: 2   relative frequency: 0.0000
P. 28 LOVER   53 From which he with each Wave rebounds,
P. 149 INSTRUCTIONS   336 The House Prorogu'd, the Chancellor rebounds.

rebuild   frequency: 1   relative frequency: 0.0000
P. 112 ANNIVERSARY   352 'And ere we Dine, rase and rebuild their State.

rebuked   frequency: 1   relative frequency: 0.0000
P. 194 TWO HORSES   101 When the Asse so bouldly rebuked the Prophet,

recal   frequency: 3   relative frequency: 0.0000
P. 147 INSTRUCTIONS   253 Their former Trophees they recal to mind,
P. 151 INSTRUCTIONS   425 The Bloodworth-Chanc'lor gives, then does recal
P. 152 INSTRUCTIONS   461 But Harry's Order, if they won't recal

recall   frequency: 2   relative frequency: 0.0000
See also "recal."
P. 10 DIALOGUE   39 Which the posting Winds recall,
P. 196 TWO HORSES   187 Then, Charles, thy edict against Coffee recall;

recanters   frequency: 1   relative frequency: 0.0000
P. 169 ADVICE   49 Two of the five recanters of the Hous

receipt   frequency: 1   relative frequency: 0.0000
P. 139 HOUSEWARMING   83 Who sate heretofore at the King's Receipt;

receiv'd   frequency: 3   relative frequency: 0.0000
P. 17 BERMUDAS   4 The listning Winds receiv'd this Song.
P. 28 LOVER   29 Receiv'd into their cruel Care,
P. 139 HOUSEWARMING   84 But receiv'd now and paid the Chancellours Custome.

receive   frequency: 5   relative frequency: 0.0001
See also "recieve."
P. 36 DAPHNIS   90 Which I could from love receive:

```
P.    62  A. HOUSE       125  'But what the Linnen can't receive
P.   126  O.C.           115  The Winds receive it, and its force out-do,
P.   181  MADE FREE       24  Oh what Fooles were you to receive him.
P.   199  DUKE            42  And in her youthfull veines receive the wound
```

receives   frequency: 2   relative frequency: 0.0000
```
P.    36  DAPHNIS        100  And receives the parting stroke.
P.   148  INSTRUCTIONS   306  And the Excise receives a total Rout.
```

receiving   frequency: 1   relative frequency: 0.0000
```
P.    12  DROP OF DEW     30  Yet receiving in the Day.
```

recess   frequency: 1   relative frequency: 0.0000
```
P.   149  INSTRUCTIONS   347  So, at the Suns recess, again returns,
```

recieve   frequency: 1   relative frequency: 0.0000
```
P.   203  HISTORICALL     77  And annual Stypends for their guilt recieve:
```

recite   frequency: 1   relative frequency: 0.0000
```
P.    86  FLECKNO        119  Turns to recite; though Judges most severe
```

reck'ning   frequency: 1   relative frequency: 0.0000
```
P.   316  CHEQUER INN    143  The Reck'ning never will be paid
```

reckon'd   frequency: 1   relative frequency: 0.0000
```
P.    50  THE GARDEN      72  Be reckon'd but with herbs and flow'rs!
```

reckoning   frequency: 1   relative frequency: 0.0000
```
     See also "reck'ning."
P.    92  MAY'S DEATH     82  Who thy last Reckoning did so largely pay.
```

reclaim   frequency: 1   relative frequency: 0.0000
```
P.   188  BRITANNIA      138  Perhaps that spell may his Erring soul reclaim.
```

recoild   frequency: 1   relative frequency: 0.0000
```
P.   202  HISTORICALL     58  It has recoild to Popery and Shame,
```

recoiled. See "recoild."

recollect   frequency: 2   relative frequency: 0.0000
```
P.    79  A. HOUSE       658  To her, it self doth recollect;
P.   155  INSTRUCTIONS   590  Filling his Sails, more force to recollect.
```

recollecting   frequency: 2   relative frequency: 0.0000
```
P.    12  DROP OF DEW     24  And, recollecting its own Light,
P.   137  HOUSEWARMING    17  But then recollecting how the Harper Amphyon
```

reconcil'd   frequency: 1   relative frequency: 0.0000
```
P.   131  PARADISE         3  Messiah Crown'd, Gods Reconcil'd Decree,
```

reconcile   frequency: 1   relative frequency: 0.0000
```
P.   174  LOYALL SCOT     97  Or to the Joynt stooles reconcile the Chairs?
```

records   frequency: 2   relative frequency: 0.0000
```
P.   191  TWO HORSES       1  Wee read in profane and Sacred records
P.   198  DUKE            24  Theire parchment presidents and dull records.
```

recover   frequency: 1   relative frequency: 0.0000
```
P.   148  INSTRUCTIONS   310  And what haste lost, recover by delay.
```

recreant   frequency: 1   relative frequency: 0.0000
```
P.   202  HISTORICALL     44  Scorning the persuit of such recreant foes.
```

recreate   frequency: 2   relative frequency: 0.0000
```
P.   143  INSTRUCTIONS   120  His lab'ring Pencil oft would recreate.
P.   168  ADVICE           8  Their wearied Limbs and minds to recreate,
```

recreates   frequency: 1   relative frequency: 0.0000
```
P.     5  HASTINGS        32  There better recreates his active Minde.
```

recruit   frequency: 1   relative frequency: 0.0000
```
P.   147  INSTRUCTIONS   281  When, marching in, a seas'nable recruit
```

red   frequency: 5   relative frequency: 0.0001
```
P.    15  EYES            18  Amongst the Red, the White, the Green;
P.    29  THE GALLERY     16  Black Eyes, red Lips, and curled Hair.
P.    48  THE GARDEN      17  No white nor red was ever seen
P.   154  INSTRUCTIONS   539  While the red Flags breath on their Top-masts
                              high
P.   156  INSTRUCTIONS   636  Or Face so red thine Oker and thy Lack.
```

redeem   frequency: 1   relative frequency: 0.0000

P. 98 HOLLAND   105 Not Christian Captives to redeem from Bands:

redeem'd   frequency: 1   relative frequency: 0.0000
   P. 85 FLECKNO   78 He heard of by Tradition, and redeem'd.

redeemers   frequency: 1   relative frequency: 0.0000
   P. 16 EYES   32 To fetter her Redeemers feet.

redemption   frequency: 1   relative frequency: 0.0000
   P. 195 TWO HORSES   159 Ch. Then, England, Rejoyce, thy Redemption
                             draws nigh;

redoubled   frequency: 2   relative frequency: 0.0000
   P. 124 O.C.   66 Or on their own redoubled, none can tell.
   P. 159 INSTRUCTIONS   742 Fill up thy space with a redoubled Night.

redress   frequency: 2   relative frequency: 0.0000
   P.   5 HASTINGS   58 And wept, as we, without Redress or Law.
   P. 14 THE CORONET   4 I seek with Garlands to redress that Wrong:

reduce   frequency: 3   relative frequency: 0.0000
   P. 111 ANNIVERSARY   318 Bent to reduce us to the ancient Pict;
   P. 164 INSTRUCTIONS   961 Would she the unattended Throne reduce,
   P. 190 STATUE   24 Hee'l shortly reduce us to fourty and eight.

reed   frequency: 1   relative frequency: 0.0000
   P. 48 THE GARDEN   32 Not as a Nymph, but for a Reed.

reeds   frequency: 2   relative frequency: 0.0000
   P. 156 INSTRUCTIONS   657 Among the Reeds, to be espy'd by him,
   P. 172 LOYALL SCOT   23 Among the Reeds to bee espy'd by him

reeking   frequency: 1   relative frequency: 0.0000
   P. 97 HOLLAND   86 Reeking at Church over the Chafing-Dish.

reel   frequency: 1   relative frequency: 0.0000
   P. 155 INSTRUCTIONS   594 Snapping the brittle links, does thorow reel;

refin'd   frequency: 1   relative frequency: 0.0000
   P. 40 THE MATCH   22 With Nitre thrice refin'd;

reflect   frequency: 4   relative frequency: 0.0000
   P. 85 FLECKNO   80 This half transparent Man would soon reflect
   P. 106 ANNIVERSARY   136 From such a wish'd Conjuncture might reflect.
   P. 177 LOYALL SCOT   244 Or whether the same vertue would reflect
   P. 203 HISTORICALL   115 And dos on Gyant Lauderdale reflect.

reform   frequency: 4   relative frequency: 0.0000
   P. 38 PICTURE   27 Reform the errours of the Spring;
   P. 94 DR. WITTY   31 Now I reform, and surely so will all
   P. 176 LOYALL SCOT   213 But to reform is all Indifferent
   P. 180 STOCKSMARKET   54 For the graver's at work to reform him thus long.

reform'd   frequency: 1   relative frequency: 0.0000
   P. 202 HISTORICALL   55 This Isle was well reform'd and gaind renowne,

reforming   frequency: 1   relative frequency: 0.0000
   P.   3 LOVELACE   23 And on each line cast a reforming eye,

refrain'd   frequency: 1   relative frequency: 0.0000
   P. 107 ANNIVERSARY   168 And always hast thy Tongue from fraud refrain'd;

refuge   frequency: 1   relative frequency: 0.0000
   P. 112 ANNIVERSARY   365 'What refuge to escape them can be found,

refus'd   frequency: 1   relative frequency: 0.0000
   P. 125 O.C.   84 Nor though a Prince to be a Man refus'd:

refuse   frequency: 9   relative frequency: 0.0001
   P. 26 MISTRESS   9 And you should if you please refuse
   P. 36 DAPHNIS   108 Why did Chloe once refuse?
   P. 99 HOLLAND   144 The War, (but who would) Peace if begg'd
                             refuse.
   P. 109 ANNIVERSARY   258 Didst (like thine Clive) still refuse to Reign;
   P. 111 ANNIVERSARY   347 Who their suspected Counsellors refuse,
   P. 120 TWO SONGS   39 'Tis needless then that I refuse,
   P. 123 O.C.   11 Nor Fate indeed can well refuse that right
   P. 128 O.C.   229 And we death's refuse nature's dregs confin'd
   P. 155 INSTRUCTIONS   602 Unpaid, refuse to mount our Ships for spight:

refusing   frequency: 1   relative frequency: 0.0000

                  P. 128 O.C.   199 Danger itself refusing to offend

regain'd   frequency: 1   relative frequency: 0.0000
          P. 176 LOYALL SCOT   178 When daring Blood to have his rents regain'd

regal   frequency: 2   relative frequency: 0.0000
          P. 106 ANNIVERSARY   122 Your Regal sloth, and your long Slumbers wake:
          P. 139 HOUSEWARMING   91 And shews on the top by the Regal Gilt Ball,

regardless   frequency: 1   relative frequency: 0.0000
          P. 22 NYMPH   35 And quite regardless of my Smart,

regement   frequency: 1   relative frequency: 0.0000
          P. 168 ADVICE   23 Place Falstaffs Regement of Thread-bare
                                         Coates

regiment   frequency: 1   relative frequency: 0.0000
          See also "regement."
          P. 68 A. HOUSE   311 Each Regiment·in order grows,

region   frequency: 5   relative frequency: 0.0001
          P. 12 DROP OF DEW   5 For the clear Region where 'twas born
          P. 27 LOVER   7 Nor can they to that Region climb,
          P. 104 ANNIVERSARY   47 Learning a Musique in the Region clear,
          P. 130 O.C.   302 To guide us upward through this region blinde.
          P. 154 INSTRUCTIONS 553 The liquid Region with their Squadrons fill'd,

register   frequency: 1   relative frequency: 0.0000
          P. 22 NYMPH   14 Keeps register of every thing:

rehearse   frequency: 1   relative frequency: 0.0000
          P. 130 O.C.   278 Shall th' English souldier, ere he charge,
                                         rehearse;

reign   frequency: 11   relative frequency: 0.0002
          See also "raign," "raigne," "rain."
          P. 109 ANNIVERSARY   258 Didst (like thine Olive) still refuse to Reign;
          P. 110 ANNIVERSARY   304 Thy Falling-sickness should have made thee
                                         Reign,
          P. 125 O.C.   86 Not love, not grieve, would neither live nor
                                         reign:
          P. 132 PARADISE   31 That Majesty which through thy Work doth Reign
          P. 143 INSTRUCTIONS   91 Great Love, how dost thou triumph, and how
                                         reign,
          P. 164 INSTRUCTIONS 966 And, where all England serves, themselves would
                                         reign.
          P. 184 BRITANNIA   6 Those would be Blessings in this spurious reign,
          P. 185 BRITANNIA   28 Since Pharoh's Reign nor so Defild a Crown.
          P. 185 BRITANNIA   43 In Lofty Notes Tudors blest reign to sing,
          P. 195 TWO HORSES   136 Under all that shall Reign of the false
                                         Scottish race.
          P. 195 TWO HORSES   158 W. When the Reign of the Line of the Stuarts
                                         is ended.

reign'd   frequency: 2   relative frequency: 0.0000
          P. 151 INSTRUCTIONS 423 Not such a fatal stupefaction reign'd
          P. 195 TWO HORSES   150 None ever Reign'd like old Besse in the Ruffe.

reigning. See "raigning."

reigns   frequency: 2   relative frequency: 0.0000
          P. 96 HOLLAND   41 Among the blind the one-ey'd blinkard reigns,
          P. 149 INSTRUCTIONS 355 See how he Reigns in his new Palace culminant,

reimburse   frequency: 1   relative frequency: 0.0000
          P. 191 STATUE   52 As would the next tax reimburse them with use.

reinforce   frequency: 2   relative frequency: 0.0000
          P. 146 INSTRUCTIONS 217 The Lords Sons, last, all these did reinforce:
          P. 169 ADVICE   42 Arm'd at all points ready to reinforce

reins   frequency: 1   relative frequency: 0.0000
          See also "raines."
          P. 131 O.C.   314 How gently winds at once the ruling reins?

reject   frequency: 1   relative frequency: 0.0000
          P. 185 BRITANNIA   17 Till Howard and Garway shall a bribe reject,

rejoice   frequency: 1   relative frequency: 0.0000
          See also "rejoyce."
          P. 82 A. HOUSE   743 While her glad Parents most rejoice,

rejoices. See "rejoyces."

rejoicing. See "rejoycing."

rejoyce   frequency: 2   relative frequency: 0.0000
    P. 183 MADE FREE   79 Then o London rejoyce!
    P. 195 TWO HORSES   159 Ch. Then, England, Rejoyce, thy Redemption
                              draws nigh;

rejoyces   frequency: 1   relative frequency: 0.0000
    P.   5 HASTINGS   40 But most rejoyces at his Mothers name.

rejoycing   frequency: 1   relative frequency: 0.0000
    P. 110 ANNIVERSARY   296 Rejoycing when thy Foot had slipt aside;

relate   frequency: 3   relative frequency: 0.0000
    P. 61 A. HOUSE   83 We opportuny may relate
    P. 92 MAY'S DEATH   76 Before thou couldst great Charles his death
                              relate.
    P. 202 HISTORICALL   61 Should we the Blackheath Project here relate,

relation   frequency: 1   relative frequency: 0.0000
    P. 151 INSTRUCTIONS   441 Nor Word, ncr near Relation did revere;

relax   frequency: 1   relative frequency: 0.0000
    P. 150 INSTRUCTIONS   393 With homely sight, they chose thus tc relax

release   frequency: 1   relative frequency: 0.0000
    P. 150 INSTRUCTIONS   374 All to new Sports their wanton fears release.

releive   frequency: 1   relative frequency: 0.0000
    P. 189 BRITANNIA   184 Shall England raise, releive opprest mankind.

relented   frequency: 1   relative frequency: 0.0000
    P. 87 FLECKNO   157 Thereat the waxen Youth relented straight;

relicks   frequency: 2   relative frequency: 0.0000
    P. 67 A. HOUSE   261 The Relicks false were set to view;
    P. 157 INSTRUCTIONS   691 His Ship burns down, and with his Relicks
                              sinks,

relics. See "relicks," "reliques."

relied. See "rely'd."

relief   frequency: 1   relative frequency: 0.0000
    P. 155 INSTRUCTIONS   612 He saw seiz'd, and could give her no Relief!

relieve   frequency: 1   relative frequency: 0.0000
    See also "releive."
    P. 130 O.C.   282 As long as Cynthia shall relieve the sunne,

relievo   frequency: 1   relative frequency: 0.0000
    P. 84 FLECKNO   63 This Basso Relievo of a Man,

religion   frequency: 16   relative frequency: 0.0003
    P. 65 A. HOUSE   198 Religion that dispensed hath;
    P. 66 A. HOUSE   226 Religion, but nct Right neglect:
    P. 66 A. HOUSE   227 For first Religion taught him Right,
    P. 97 HCLLAND   55 'Tis probable Religion after this
    P. 97 HOLLAND   67 Sure when Religion did it self imbark,
    P. 108 ANNIVERSARY   208 Courage disheartned, and Religion cocl'd.
    P. 110 ANNIVERSARY   302 And their Religion only is to Pall.
    P. 128 O.C.   227 Valour, religion, friendship, prudence dy'd
    P. 165 KINGS VOWES   7 I will have a Religion then all of my owne,
    P. 171 PROPHECY   41 When Bishops shall lay all Religion by
    P. 174 LOYALL SCOT   120 Religion has the World too Long deprav'd
    P. 175 LOYALL SCOT   167 And their Religion all but Masquerade.
    P. 184 MADE FREE   120 With a Wife of Religion Italian?
    P. 192 TWO HORSES   49 Ch. Tho he chang'd his Religion I hope hee 's
                              so civill
    P. 198 DUKE   37 Conveying his Religion and his bride:
    P. 202 HISTORICAIL   47 Which with Religicr so enilam'd his ire

religions   frequency: 1   relative frequency: 0.0000
    P. 127 O.C.   179 He first put Armes intc Religions hand,

religious   frequency: 2   relative frequency: 0.0000
    P. 67 A. HOUSE   280 'Twas no Religicus House till now.
    P. 203 HISTOBICALL   80 All but religious cheats might justly sweare

reliques   frequency: 1   relative frequency: 0.0000

         P. 173 LOYALL SCOT   57 The ship burnes down and with his reliques sinks,

relish   frequency: 1   relative frequency: 0.0000
         See also "rellish."
         P. 28 LOVER   56 In his own Blood does relish best.

rellish   frequency: 1   relative frequency: 0.0000
         P. 159 INSTRUCTIONS 765 After this loss, to rellish discontent,

rely'd   frequency: 2   relative frequency: 0.0000
         P. 139 HOUSEWARMING   82 But for the expence he rely'd upon Worstenholm,
         P. 152 INSTRUCTIONS 479 But most rely'd upon this Dutch pretence,

remain   frequency: 2   relative frequency: 0.0000
         P. 61 A. HOUSE   72 Its Lord a while, but not remain.
         P. 83 FLECKNO   27 Only this frail Ambition did remain,

remain'd   frequency: 1   relative frequency: 0.0000
         P. 148 INSTRUCTIONS 286 But for th' unknown Reserve that still remain'd:

remained   frequency: 1   relative frequency: 0.0000
         See also "remain'd."
         P. 67 A. HOUSE   278 The Cloyster yet remained hers.

remains   frequency: 2   relative frequency: 0.0000
         P. 30 THE GALLERY   52 Remains, with which I first was took.
         P. 78 A. HOUSE   630 Remains behind our little Nile;

remedies   frequency: 1   relative frequency: 0.0000
         P. 42 DAMON   30 When Remedies themselves complain.

remember   frequency: 1   relative frequency: 0.0000
         P. 22 NYMPH   27 One morning (I remember well)

remembering. See "remembring."

remembring   frequency: 2   relative frequency: 0.0000
         P. 12 DROP OF DEW   22 Remembring still its former height,
         P. 127 O.C.   152 Yet joy'd remembring what he once atchiev'd.

remora   frequency: 1   relative frequency: 0.0000
         P.   4 HASTINGS   12 And on Times Wheel sticks like a Remora.

remote   frequency: 1   relative frequency: 0.0000
         P. 17 BERMUDAS   1 Where the remote Bermudas ride

remount   frequency: 1   relative frequency: 0.0000
         P. 194 TWO HORSES   112 And returns to remount about break of Day.

remov'd   frequency: 1   relative frequency: 0.0000
         P. 115 BLAKE   62 Kind Nature had from thence remov'd so far.

remove   frequency: 2   relative frequency: 0.0000
         P. 114 BLAKE   44 Your Conquering Sword will soon that want
                                  remove.
         P. 139 HOUSEWARMING   96 And till there you remove, you shall never leave
                                  burning

removed   frequency: 1   relative frequency: 0.0000
         See also "remov'd."
         P. 180 STOCKSMARKET   40 Or have you to the Compter removed him for debt?

removes   frequency: 1   relative frequency: 0.0000
         P. 69 A. HOUSE   342 Where he the tender Plants removes.

removing   frequency: 1   relative frequency: 0.0000
         P. 87 ODE   7 Removing from the Wall

render   frequency: 2   relative frequency: 0.0000
         P. 99 HOLLAND   142 Would render fain unto our better Rome.
         P. 131 PARADISE   16 And what was easie he should render vain.

rends   frequency: 1   relative frequency: 0.0000
         P. 67 A. HOUSE   270 The Castle vanishes or rends)

renew   frequency: 3   relative frequency: 0.0000
         P. 86 FLECKNO   122 Yet he more strict my sentence doth renew;
         P. 142 INSTRUCTIONS   54 How after Childbirth to renew a Maid.
         P. 148 INSTRUCTIONS 316 How strong the Dutch their Equipage renew.

renew'd   frequency: 2   relative frequency: 0.0000

```
         P.  92 MAY'S DEATH     79 Who laughs to see in this thy death renew'd,
         P. 149 INSTRUCTIONS   338 With Magic Herbs, rose from the Pot renew'd:

                                   frequency:    1    relative frequency: 0.0000
renews
         P. 202 HISTORICALL     52 And with the Dutch a second Warr renews.

rennet.  See "rennett."

                                   frequency:    1    relative frequency: 0.0000
rennett
         P. 174 LOYALL SCOT    115 A Bishops Bennett makes the strongest Curd.

                                   frequency:    1    relative frequency: 0.0000
renounce
         P. 205 HISTORICALL    165 God did renounce him and his Cause disowne

                                   frequency:    3    relative frequency: 0.0000
renown
      See also "renowne."
         P. 104 ANNIVERSARY     24 Took in by Proxie, beggs a false Rencwn;
         P. 116 BLAKE          101 For your renown, his conquering Fleet does ride,
         P. 185 BRITANNIA       47 Full of Gray Hairs, good deeds, endless renown.

                                   frequency:    3    relative frequency: 0.0000
renown'd
         P. 130 O.C.           294 And David, for the sword and harpe renown'd;
         P. 144 INSTRUCTIONS   152 For Diligence rencwn'd, and Discipline:
         P. 147 INSTRUCTIONS   246 (For Vigilance and Courage both renown'd)

                                   frequency:    1    relative frequency: 0.0000
renowne
         P. 202 HISTORICALL     55 This Isle was well reform'd and gaind renowne,

                                   frequency:    8    relative frequency: 0.0001
rent
         P.  34 DAPHNIS         32 Between Joy and Sorrow rent.
         P.  88 ODE             22 And Pallaces and Temples rent:
         P. 108 ANNIVERSARY    210 And then loud Shreeks the vaulted Marbles rent.
         P. 108 ANNIVERSARY    220 Whom thou hadst left beneath with Mantle rent.
         P. 127 O.C.           171 Since him away the dismal Tempest rent,
         P. 138 HOUSEWARMING    57 His Rent would rc more in arrear run to
                                      Worster;
         P. 177 LOYALL SCOT    214 'Tis necessary Bishops have their rent,
         P. 205 HISTORICALL    167 From Saul the Land cf Promise thus was rent,

                                   frequency:    2    relative frequency: 0.0000
rents
         P.  89 ODE             86 A Kingdome, for his first years rents:
         P. 176 LOYALL SCOT    178 When daring Blccd tc have his rents regain'd

                                   frequency:    5    relative frequency: 0.0001
repair
         P.  39 THE MATCH       12 She could the World repair.
         P. 148 INSTRUCTIONS   324 That Money lack, ncr Forts be in repair.
         P. 154 INSTRUCTIONS   570 Until the City put it in repair.
         P. 168 ADVICE           9 Do to their more belov'd delights repair,
         P. 190 STATUE          16 To repair with such riffe raffe our Churches old
                                      Pale?

                                   frequency:    1    relative frequency: 0.0000
repairs
         P. 161 INSTRUCTIONS   857 The Speaker, Summon'd, tc the Lords repairs,

                                   frequency:    1    relative frequency: 0.0000
repaying
         P. 180 STOCKSMARKET    49 Sure the king will ne'er think of repaying his
                                      bankers,

                                   frequency:    2    relative frequency: 0.0000
repeat
         P.  84 FLECKNO         34 Ask'd still for more, and pray'd him to repeat:
         P. 163 INSTRUCTIONS   913 His mind secure does the known stroke repeat,

                                   frequency:    1    relative frequency: 0.0000
repeated
         P. 124 O.C.            58 Repeated over to the restless Night.

                                   frequency:    1    relative frequency: 0.0000
repent
         P. 183 MADE FREE      102 The whole Naticn may chance to repent it.

                                   frequency:    1    relative frequency: 0.0000
repented
         P. 196 TWO HORSES     162 The Gods have repented the Kings Restoration.

                                   frequency:    1    relative frequency: 0.0000
repin'd
         P.  84 FLECKNO         44 In Echo to the trembling Strings repin'd.

                                   frequency:    2    relative frequency: 0.0000
repleat
         P.  40 THE MATCH       21 He kept the several Cells repleat
         P. 169 ADVICE          33 Capacious Bowles with lusty wine repleat

replete.  See "repleat."

replied.  See "reply'd."

                                   frequency:    1    relative frequency: 0.0000
replies
```

P.   84 FLECKNO   39 The other opposite as soon replies,

reply'd   frequency: 2   relative frequency: 0.0000
P.   4 LOVELACE   45 O no, mistake not, I reply'd, for I
P.   85 FLECKNO   91 He thought himself affronted; and reply'd,

report   frequency: 2   relative frequency: 0.0000
P.   68 A. HOUSE   307 Whose shrill report no Ear can tell,
P. 202 HISTORICALL   73 We leave to the report of Common fame.

repose   frequency: 4   relative frequency: 0.0000
P.   48 THE GARDEN   8 To weave the Garlands of repose.
P. 120 TWO SONGS   24 Securing their Repose above.
P. 184 BRITANNIA   7 Awake, arise, from thy long blest repose;
P. 202 HISTORICALL   43 The dreadfull Victor tooke his soft repose,

reposing   frequency: 2   relative frequency: 0.0000
P. 157 INSTRUCTIONS 688 With his dear Sword reposing by his Side.
P. 173 LOYALL SCOT   54 With his dear sword reposing by his side,

reprehend   frequency: 1   relative frequency: 0.0000
P. 140 HOUSEWARMING 103 And others as much reprehend his Backside,

repreive   frequency: 1   relative frequency: 0.0000
P. 200 DUKE   117 Till the stroke is struck which they can nere
                             repreive.

represent   frequency: 2   relative frequency: 0.0000
P.   72 A. HOUSE   424 Do represent the Pillaging.
P. 150 INSTRUCTIONS 390 So thou and I, dear Painter, represent

representatives   frequency: 1   relative frequency: 0.0000
P. 317 CHEQUER INN 175 Curse on such Representatives

represents   frequency: 2   relative frequency: 0.0000
P.   62 A. HOUSE   127 'This Work the Saints best represents;
P. 147 INSTRUCTIONS 269 Each thinks his Person represents the whole,

represt   frequency: 1   relative frequency: 0.0000
P. 186 BRITANNIA   50 Soe the learn'd Bard with Artfull song represt

repriev'd   frequency: 1   relative frequency: 0.0000
P. 163 INSTRUCTIONS 940 As Thieves repriev'd for Executioners;

reprieve. See "repreive."

reprieves   frequency: 1   relative frequency: 0.0000
See also "reprives."
P. 161 INSTRUCTIONS 850 At Court, and so reprieves their guilty Lives.

reprives   frequency: 1   relative frequency: 0.0000
P. 104 ANNIVERSARY   39 To know how long their Planet yet Reprives

reproachful   frequency: 1   relative frequency: 0.0000
P. 156 INSTRUCTIONS 621 Of former Glories the reproachful thought,

reproacht   frequency: 1   relative frequency: 0.0000
P. 169 ADVICE   60 To be reproacht with Tearm of Turncoat knave;

reprov'd   frequency: 1   relative frequency: 0.0000
P. 191 TWO HORSES   12 And Balam the Prophet was reprov'd by his
                             Asse:

republick's   frequency: 1   relative frequency: 0.0000
P.   89 ODE   82 But still in the Republick's hand:

repugnance   frequency: 1   relative frequency: 0.0000
P. 152 INSTRUCTIONS 473 Never old Letcher more repugnance felt,

repute   frequency: 1   relative frequency: 0.0000
P. 190 STATUE   29 But his brother-in-law's horse had gain'd such
                             repute

requires   frequency: 1   relative frequency: 0.0000
P. 181 MADE FREE   5 That requires the Might

requite   frequency: 1   relative frequency: 0.0000
P. 132 PARADISE   43 Just Heav'n Thee, like Tiresias, to requite,

requited. See "requitted."

requitted   frequency: 1   relative frequency: 0.0000

P. 313 CHEQUER INN   42 Had they too beene requitted

rescue   frequency: 3   relative frequency: 0.0000
    P. 146 INSTRUCTIONS   222 To rescue Albemarle from the Sea-Cod:
    P. 153 INSTRUCTIONS   494 In rescue of the Banquiers Banquerout:
    P. 188 BRITANNIA   134 Rescue him again from scandall and the Grave.

resemblance   frequency: 1   relative frequency: 0.0000
    P. 49 THE GARDEN   44 Does streight its cwn resemblance find;

resemble   frequency: 1   relative frequency: 0.0000
    P. 195 TWO HORSES   139 Tho' his Government did a Tyrants resemble,

resembled   frequency: 1   relative frequency: 0.0000
    P. 138 HOUSEWARMING   28 And too much resembled his Wives Chocolatte.

resembles   frequency: 1   relative frequency: 0.0000
    P. 63 A. HOUSE   132 'Yet thus She ycu resembles much.

reserv'd   frequency: 2   relative frequency: 0.0000
    P. 157 INSTRUCTIONS   660 That fly'st Love Fires, reserv'd for other
                              Flame?
    P. 172 LOYALL SCOT   26 That flyst loves fires reserv'd for other flame?'

reserve   frequency: 1   relative frequency: 0.0000
    P. 148 INSTRUCTIONS   286 But for th' unknown Reserve that still remain'd:

reserved   frequency: 1   relative frequency: 0.0000
    See also "reserv'd."
    P. 88 ODE   30 He liv'd reserved and austere,

resides   frequency: 1   relative frequency: 0.0000
    P. 173 LOYALL SCOT   78 Where life resides or Understanding dwells:

resign   frequency: 3   relative frequency: 0.0000
    P. 159 INSTRUCTIONS   749 And Father Neptune promis'd to resign
    P. 184 BRITANNIA   1 Brit: Ah! Rawleigh, when thy Breath thou didst
                              resign
    P. 188 BRITANNIA   152 To this firm Law their scepter did resign:

resign'd   frequency: 1   relative frequency: 0.0000
    P. 187 BRITANNIA   91 By hirelings sculd to you shall be resign'd

resigning   frequency: 1   relative frequency: 0.0000
    P. 108 ANNIVERSARY   223 Resigning up thy Privacy so dear,

resigns   frequency: 1   relative frequency: 0.0000
    P. 187 BRITANNIA   122 Resigns his Crown to Angell Carwells trust.

resist   frequency: 2   relative frequency: 0.0000
    P. 66 A. HOUSE   240 Whcm you resist, or what you do?
    P. 88 ODE   25 'Tis Madness to resist or blame

resistance   frequency: 2   relative frequency: 0.0000
    P. 31 FAIR SINGER   15 But all resistance against her is vain,
    P. 105 ANNIVERSARY   95 While the resistance of cpposed Minds,

resistless   frequency: 1   relative frequency: 0.0000
    P. 118 BLAKE   145 For your resistless genious there did Raign,

resolv'd   frequency: 2   relative frequency: 0.0000
    P. 66 A. HOUSE   229 Sometimes resolv'd his Sword he draws,
    P. 198 DUKE   5 Hateing all justice and resolv'd to fight

resolve   frequency: 1   relative frequency: 0.0000
    P. 148 INSTRUCTIONS   308 Resolve henceforth upcn their cther Game:

resolved   frequency: 3   relative frequency: 0.0000
    See also "resolv'd."
    P.   9 DIALOGUE   t2 The Resolved Scul, and Created Pleasure.
    P.   9 DIALOGUE   10 To conquer cne resolved Heart.
    P. 34 DAPHNIS   44 Thus his Leave resolved tcok.

resolves   frequency: 2   relative frequency: 0.0000
    P. 154 INSTRUCTIONS   568 So at the first Salute resclves Retreat,
    P. 163 INSTRUCTIONS   926 And rising, straight cn Hyde's Disgrace
                              resolves.

respect   frequency: 4   relative frequency: 0.0000
    P. 57 BILL-BOROW   41 Fear of the Master, and respect
    P. 66 A. HOUSE   225 What should he dc? He would respect

                P. 79 A. HOUSE   657 See how loose Nature, in respect
                P. 155 INSTRUCTIONS   589 A Skipper rude shocks it without respect,

resplendent   frequency: 1   relative frequency: 0.0000
                P. 120 TWO SONGS   25 If therefore thy resplendent Ray

rest   frequency: 31   relative frequency: 0.0006
                P. 10 DIALOGUE   23 My gentler Rest is on a Thought,
                P. 10 DIALOGUE   36 The rest is all but Earth disguis'd.
                P. 12 DIALOGUE   77 The rest does lie beyond the Pole,
                P. 21 SOUL & BODY   19 A Body that could never rest,
                P. 26 MISTRESS   16 But thirty thousand to the rest.
                P. 30 THE GALLERY   49 But, of these Pictures and the rest,
                P. 40 THE MATCH   37 So we alone the happy rest,
                P. 42 DAMON   31 No moisture but my Tears do rest,
                P. 54 THYESTE   5 In calm Leisure let me rest;
                P. 55 EPITAPH   1 Enough: and leave the rest to Fame.
                P. 62 A. HOUSE   123 'While all the rest with Needles paint
                P. 67 A. HOUSE   271 The wasting Cloister with the rest
                P. 77 A. HOUSE   597 Thanks for my Rest ye Mossy Banks,
                P. 83 FLECKNO   26 And to my Martyrdom prepared Rest.
                P. 98 HOLLAND   103 Let this one court'sie witness all the rest;
                P. 98 HOLLAND   129 As the obsequious Air and Waters rest,
                P. 110 ANNIVERSARY   283 Thou, and thine House, like Noah's Eight did
                                           rest,
                P. 111 ANNIVERSARY   313 Wand'rers, Adult'rers, Lyers, Munser's rest,
                P. 114 BLAKE   26 Above both Worlds, since 'tis above the rest.
                P. 143 INSTRUCTIONS   117 Here Painter rest a little, and survey
                P. 147 INSTRUCTIONS   248 Fighting it single till the rest might arm.
                P. 153 INSTRUCTIONS   509 The State Affairs thus Marshall'd, for the
                                           rest
                P. 155 INSTRUCTIONS   595 And to the rest the open'd passage shew.
                P. 161 INSTRUCTIONS   853 The King, that day rais'd early from his rest,
                P. 167 KINGS VOWES   51 And who knowes but the Mode may soon bring in
                                           the rest?
                P. 170 PROPHECY   10 Hir'd for their share to give the rest away
                P. 184 BRITANNIA   9 Raw: What mighty power has forc'd me from my
                                           rest?
                P. 189 BRITANNIA   192 The Earth shall rest, the Heavens shall on thee
                                           smile,
                P. 198 DUKE   34 Ile have these villains in our notions rest;
                P. 314 CHEQUER INN   54 The rest were bid by Cooper.
                P. 314 CHEQUER INN   82 Mansell and Morgan and the rest

restauracion   frequency: 1   relative frequency: 0.0000
                P. 192 TWO HORSES   52 By a Curst hous of Commons and a blest
                                           Restauracion;

restless   frequency: 6   relative frequency: 0.0001
                P. 12 DROP OF DEW   15 Restless it roules and unsecure,
                P. 30 THE GALLERY   26 Vexing thy restless Lover's Ghost;
                P. 87 ODE   9 So restless Cromwel could not cease
                P. 108 ANNIVERSARY   199 With wandring Eyes, and restless Ears they
                                           stood,
                P. 116 BLAKE   95 Yet they by restless toyl, became at Length,
                P. 124 O.C.   58 Repeated over to the restless Night.

restoration   frequency: 1   relative frequency: 0.0000
                See also "restauracion."
                P. 196 TWO HORSES   162 The Gods have repented the Kings Restoration.

restor'd   frequency: 4   relative frequency: 0.0000
                P. 142 INSTRUCTIONS   47 But thought the Golden Age was now restor'd,
                P. 155 INSTRUCTIONS   613 That sacred Keel, which had, as he, restor'd
                P. 185 BRITANNIA   35 How oft have I him to himself restor'd,
                P. 189 STATUE   4 Unless Puchinello be to be restor'd.

restore   frequency: 6   relative frequency: 0.0001
                P. 31 MOURNING   7 Seem bending upwards, to restore
                P. 69 A. HOUSE   330 That sweet Militia restore,
                P. 98 HOLLAND   136 Doth yearly their Sea-Nuptials restore.
                P. 103 ANNIVERSARY   9 And still the Day which he doth next restore,
                P. 180 STOCKSMARKET   57 But with all his faults restore us our King,
                P. 189 BRITANNIA   182 Balm in their wounds, will fleeting life restore.

restored   frequency: 1   relative frequency: 0.0000
                See also "restor'd."
                P. 180 STOCKSMARKET   48 The day that he was both restored and born?

restoring   frequency: 1   relative frequency: 0.0000
                P. 193 TWO HORSES   68 For restoring the King should be our Rewards.

restrain   frequency: 5   relative frequency: 0.0001
  P.   32 MOURNING   17 And, while vain Pomp does her restrain
  P.   62 A. HOUSE   99 'These Walls restrain the World without,
  P. 120 TWO SONGS   21 Rather restrain these double Seas,
  P. 150 INSTRUCTIONS 392 By making them ridiculous to restrain.
  P. 164 INSTRUCTIONS 965 She blames them only who the Court restrain,

rests   frequency: 2   relative frequency: 0.0000
  P. 157 INSTRUCTIONS 689 And, on the flaming Plank, so rests his Head,
  P. 173 LOYALL SCOT   55 And on his flaming Planks soe rests his head

retir'd   frequency: 2   relative frequency: 0.0000
  P.   57 BILL-BOROW   44 To whom he often here retir'd,
  P.   87 FLECKNO   159 For the disdainful Poet was retir'd

retire   frequency: 4   relative frequency: 0.0000
  P. 118 BLAKE   162 Victorious Blake, does from the Bay retire,
  P. 153 INSTRUCTIONS 516 Or that for Cowardice they all retire.
  P. 157 INSTRUCTIONS 670 And safely through its Port the Dutch retire:
  P. 172 LOYALL SCOT   36 And safely through its ports the Dutch retire.

retired   frequency: 1   relative frequency: 0.0000
  See also "retir'd."
  P.   67 A. HOUSE   283 Who, when retired here to Peace,

retirement   frequency: 1   relative frequency: 0.0000
  P.   58 BILL-BOROW   80 Nor Height but with Retirement loves.

retires   frequency: 1   relative frequency: 0.0000
  P. 150 INSTRUCTIONS 371 This done, among his Cyclops he retires,

retiring   frequency: 2   relative frequency: 0.0000
  P.   74 A. HOUSE   481 But I, retiring from the Flood,
  P. 148 INSTRUCTIONS 295 The Van and Battel, though retiring, falls

retort   frequency: 1   relative frequency: 0.0000
  P. 108 ANNIVERSARY   190 On their own Hopes shall find the Fall retort.

retreat   frequency: 6   relative frequency: 0.0001
  See also "retreate."
  P.   48 THE GARDEN   26 Love hither makes his best retreat.
  P. 109 ANNIVERSARY   249 When Gideon so did from the War retreat,
  P. 116 BLAKE   84 Nor Winters storms, had made your Fleet
                             retreat.
  P. 154 INSTRUCTIONS 568 So at the first Salute resolves Retreat,
  P. 169 ADVICE   51 Who make it by their mean retreat appear
  P. 169 ADVICE   63 Tis hard; yet this he has for safe retreat:

retreate   frequency: 1   relative frequency: 0.0000
  P. 182 MADE FREE   53 He still made a Retreate

retreats   frequency: 1   relative frequency: 0.0000
  P.   58 BILL-BOROW   78 From his own Brightness he retreats:

return   frequency: 9   relative frequency: 0.0001
  P.   87 ODE   t An Horatian Ode upon Cromwel's Return from
                             Ireland.
  P.   92 MAY'S DEATH   89 Nor here thy shade must dwell, Return, Return,
  P. 103 ANNIVERSARY   15 While heavy Monarchs make a wide Return,
  P. 152 INSTRUCTIONS 460 Then to return home straight infecta re.
  P. 158 INSTRUCTIONS 724 The Holland Squadron leisurely return:
  P. 160 INSTRUCTIONS 807 But now draws near the Parliament's return;
  P. 185 BRITANNIA   13 I stole away; and never will return
  P. 189 BRITANNIA   178 Back to my dearest Country I'le return:

return'd   frequency: 3   relative frequency: 0.0000
  P. 117 BLAKE   132 That it return'd to its own Element.
  P. 146 INSTRUCTIONS 244 And undescry'd return'd e're morning peep.
  P. 191 TWO HORSES   14 Have to Questions return'd cracular Answers:

returning   frequency: 3   relative frequency: 0.0000
  P.   76 A. HOUSE   576 Which I returning cannot find.
  P. 111 ANNIVERSARY   323 And, to your spight, returning yet alive
  P. 139 HOUSEWARMING   94 Like vain Chymists, a flower from its ashes
                             returning;

returns   frequency: 3   relative frequency: 0.0000
  P. 149 INSTRUCTIONS 347 So, at the Suns recess, again returns,
  P. 157 INSTRUCTIONS 697 Each doleful day still with fresh loss returns;
  P. 194 TWO HORSES   112 And returns to remount about break of Day.

reveal   frequency: 1   relative frequency: 0.0000

P.   5 HASTINGS   42 But draw their Veils, and their pure Beams
                             reveal:

reveals   frequency: 1   relative frequency: 0.0000
     P. 163 INSTRUCTIONS 920 The grizly Wound reveals, of which he dy'd.

revelling   frequency: 1   relative frequency: 0.0000
     P. 181 MADE FREE   36 Of Revelling, Drinking and Whoreing.

revels   frequency: 1   relative frequency: 0.0000
     P. 92 MAY'S DEATH   98 May only Master of these Revels past.

revenge   frequency: 7   relative frequency: 0.0001
     P. 45 MOWER'S SONG   20 Shall now by my Revenge be wrought:
     P. 131 PARADISE   10 The World o'rewhelming to revenge his Sight.
     P. 149 INSTRUCTIONS 361 But still he car'd, while in Revenge he brav'd,
     P. 149 INSTRUCTIONS 363 Gain and Revenge, Revenge and Gain are sweet:
     P. 156 INSTRUCTIONS 626 Frustrate Revenge, and Love, by loss more keen,
     P. 179 STOCKSMARKET   10 To be all a revenge and a malice forecast,

revenue   frequency: 4   relative frequency: 0.0000
     P. 144 INSTRUCTIONS 125 And fix to the Revenue such a Summ,
     P. 166 KINGS VOWES   32 I will winke all the while my Revenue is stole,
     P. 187 BRITANNIA   123 Her Creature Osborn the Revenue steals;
     P. 193 TWO HORSES   57 Ch. That a Million and half should be his
                             revenue,

revenues   frequency: 1   relative frequency: 0.0000
     P. 179 STOCKSMARKET   22 Who the Parliament buys and revenues does sell,

revere   frequency: 1   relative frequency: 0.0000
     P. 151 INSTRUCTIONS 441 Nor Word, nor near Felation did revere;

reverence   frequency: 1   relative frequency: 0.0000
     P. 58 BILL-BOROW   50 As We, of Love and Reverence,

reverenceth   frequency: 1   relative frequency: 0.0000
     P. 66 A. HOUSE   230 But reverenceth then the Laws:

reverend   frequency: 3   relative frequency: 0.0000
     P. 92 MAY'S DEATH   86 And reverend Chaucer, but their dust does rise
     P. 174 LOYALL SCOT   116 How Reverend things are 'lord', Lawn Sleeves
                             and Ease!
     P. 187 BRITANNIA   113 My reverend head expos'd to scorn and shame,

reversed   frequency: 1   relative frequency: 0.0000
     P.   5 HASTINGS   46 Reversed, at his Darlings Funeral.

revive   frequency: 1   relative frequency: 0.0000
     P. 111 ANNIVERSARY   324 Does with himself all that is good revive.

revives   frequency: 1   relative frequency: 0.0000
     P. 130 O.C.   307 Revives; and by his milder beams assures;

revok'd   frequency: 1   relative frequency: 0.0000
     P. 139 HOUSEWARMING   75 But he swore that the Patent should ne'er be
                             revok'd;

revolves   frequency: 2   relative frequency: 0.0000
     P. 142 INSTRUCTIONS   75 While she revolves, at once, Sidney's disgrace,
     P. 163 INSTRUCTIONS 925 The wondrous Night the pensive King revolves,

reward   frequency: 4   relative frequency: 0.0000
     P. 128 O.C.   222 All law is uselesse, all reward is due.
     P. 160 INSTRUCTIONS 791 Then that Reward might in its turn take place,
     P. 168 ADVICE   27 And of his dear Reward let none dispair,
     P. 189 BRITANNIA   193 And this kind secret for reward shall give:

rewarded   frequency: 1   relative frequency: 0.0000
     P. 193 TWO HORSES   72 Was after rewarded with losing his own.

rewards   frequency: 2   relative frequency: 0.0000
     P. 132 PARADISE   44 Rewards with Prophesie thy loss of Sight.
     P. 193 TWO HORSES   68 For restoring the King should be our Rewards.

rhime   frequency: 2   relative frequency: 0.0000
     P. 132 PARADISE   46 With tinkling Rhime, of thy own Sense secure;
     P. 132 PARADISE   54 In Number, Weight, and Measure, needs not
                             Rhime.

rhodope   frequency: 1   relative frequency: 0.0000

P. 137 HOUSEWARMING   13 He had read of Rhodope, a Lady of Thrace,

rhyme. See "rhime," "rime."

rhymes. See "rimes."

rich   frequency: 10   relative frequency: 0.0002
P.   14 THE CORONET   11 So rich a Chaplet thence to weave
P.   17 BERMUDAS   20 Jewels more rich than Ormus show's.
P.   84 FLECKNO   66 (His only impossible is to be rich)
P. 113 BLAKE   5 For this rich load, of which so proud they are,
P. 115 BLAKE   53 There the indulgent Soil that rich Grape
                             breeds,
P. 119 BLAKE   166 Their rich Fleet sunk, and ours with Lawrel
                             fraught.
P. 125 O.C.   92 At its rich bloods expence their Scrrows chear,
P. 146 INSTRUCTIONS   203 Carteret the rich did the Accomptants guide,
P. 171 PROPHECY   44 Make him self rich, his king and People bare,
P. 199 DUKE   79 Rich with the Spoile cf a poore Algeryne,

richard   frequency: 3   relative frequency: 0.0000
P.   3 LOVELACE   t1 To his Noble Friend Mr. Richard Lovelace,
P. 130 O.C.   305 And Richard yet, where his great parent led,
P. 131 O.C.   322 Rainbows to storms, Richard to Oliver.

richer   frequency: 2   relative frequency: 0.0000
P.   43 DAMON   56 Yet am I richer far in Hay.
P. 131 O.C.   316 Richer than any eastern silk, or gemme;

riches   frequency: 1   relative frequency: 0.0000
P. 203 HISTORICALL   88 Riches and honcur they from Lay-men reap,

richest   frequency: 1   relative frequency: 0.0000
P.   5 HASTINGS   29 His Thought with richest Triumphs entertains,

richly   frequency: 1   relative frequency: 0.0000
P.   94 DR. WITTY   17 Caelia whose English dcth more richly flow

richmond   frequency: 1   relative frequency: 0.0000
P. 159 INSTRUCTICNS   764 And Richmond here commands, as Ruyter those.

rickt   frequency: 1   relative frequency: 0.0000
P. 316 CHEQUER INN   141 But Messe was Rickt on Messe

rid   frequency: 1   relative frequency: 0.0000
P.   36 DAPHNIS   104 And but rid to take the Air.

riddle   frequency: 1   relative frequency: 0.0000
P. 112 ANNIVERSARY   383 'The Valiants Terror, Riddle of the Wise;

ride   frequency: 8   relative frequency: 0.0001
P.   17 BERMUDAS   1 Where the remote Bermudas ride
P.   66 A. HOUSE   246 His Horse through ccnquer'd Britain ride?
P. 112 ANNIVERSARY   364 'And sink the Earth that does at Anchor ride.
P. 116 BLAKE   101 For your renown, his conquering Fleet does ride,
P. 146 INSTRUCTICNS   213 Last then but cne, Powell, that could not ride,
P. 150 INSTRUCTIONS   396 And our next neighbours France and Flanders
                             ride.
P. 179 STOCKSMARKET   18 Who upon their panniers more decently ride,
P. 204 HISTORICALL   138 Dos cn Brittania as cn Churchill ride:

rider   frequency: 1   relative frequency: 0.0000
See also "ryder."
P. 194 TWO HORSES   116 What hast thou to say of my Royall Rider?

riders   frequency: 1   relative frequency: 0.0000
P. 194 TWO HORSES   107 Our riders are absent; who is't that can hear?

rides   frequency: 1   relative frequency: 0.0000
P. 145 INSTRUCTIONS   197 Before them Higgins rides with brow compact,

ridiculous   frequency: 1   relative frequency: 0.0000
P. 150 INSTRUCTIONS   392 By making them ridiculcus to restrain.

riding   frequency: 2   relative frequency: 0.0000
P.   22 NYMPH   1 The wanton Troopers riding by
P. 140 G.-CHILDREN   1 Kendal is dead, and Cambridge riding post.

riffe   frequency: 1   relative frequency: 0.0000
P. 190 STATUE   16 To repair with such riffe raffe our Churches old
                             Pale?

riffraff. See "riffe" or "raffe."

rifling   frequency: 1   relative frequency: 0.0000

P. 159 INSTRUCTIONS   774 And rifling Prizes, them neglected? Pett.

rig   frequency: 1   relative frequency: 0.0000
    P. 112 ANNIVERSARY   351 'Yet rig a Navy while we dress us late;

right   frequency: 19   relative frequency: 0.0003
    P. 43 DAMON   58 If in my Sithe I looked right;
    P. 66 A. HOUSE   226 Religion, but not Right neglect:
    P. 66 A. HOUSE   227 For first Religion taught him Right,
    P. 66 A. HOUSE   237 Yet still the Nuns his Right debar'd,
    P. 89 ODE   62 To vindicate his helpless Right,
    P. 92 MAY'S DEATH   80 Right Romane poverty and gratitude.
    P. 95 DR. WITTY   37 And (if I Judgment have) I censure right;
    P. 113 ANNIVERSARY   396 More then our Love and Duty do thee Right.
    P. 114 BLAKE   39 Your worth to all these Isles, a just right
                             brings,
    P. 123 O.C.   11 Nor Fate indeed can well refuse that right
    P. 139 HOUSEWARMING   80 Or his right hand shall else be cut off with the
                             Trowel.
    P. 141 INSTRUCTIONS   5 Canst thou paint without Colours? Then 'tis
                             right:
    P. 143 INSTRUCTIONS 107 Describe the Court and Country, both set right,
    P. 159 INSTRUCTIONS 741 And constant Time, to keep his course yet right,
    P. 185 BRITANNIA   36 In 's left the scales, in 's right hand plac'd
                             the sword,
    P. 186 BRITANNIA   63 (By her usurpt), her right a bloudy sword
    P. 186 BRITANNIA   86 To teach your will 's the onely rule of right,
    P. 198 DUKE   6 To robb their native countrey of its right.
    P. 314 CHEQUER INN   84 A Jury right of Wales.

rights   frequency: 3   relative frequency: 0.0000
    P. 88 ODE   38 And plead the antient Rights in vain:
    P. 92 MAY'S DEATH   69 Sings still of ancient Rights and better Times,
    P. 98 HOLLAND   107 No, but all ancient Rights and Leagues must
                             vail,

rime   frequency: 1   relative frequency: 0.0000
    See also "rhime."
    P. 87 FLECKNO   166 Ere the fierce Poets anger turn'd to rime.

rimes   frequency: 1   relative frequency: 0.0000
    P. 84 FLECKNO   69 He therefore circumscribes himself in rimes;

rind   frequency: 1   relative frequency: 0.0000
    P. 58 BILL-BOROW   51 And underneath the Courser Rind

ring   frequency: 4   relative frequency: 0.0000
    P. 18 CLORINDA   28 Caves eccho, and the Fountains ring.
    P. 43 DAMON   64 About me they contract their Ring.
    P. 103 ANNIVERSARY   12 And shines the Jewel of the yearly Ring.
    P. 171 LOYALL SCOT   3 They streight Consulting gather'd in a Ring

rings   frequency: 1   relative frequency: 0.0000
    P. 75 A. HOUSE   524 With Nuptial Rings their Ensigns chast;

riot. See "riott."

riott   frequency: 1   relative frequency: 0.0000
    P. 181 MADE FREE   20 Where such Riott he ran,

rip   frequency: 1   relative frequency: 0.0000
    P. 108 ANNIVERSARY   214 Break up each Deck, and rip the Oaken seams.

ripe   frequency: 2   relative frequency: 0.0000
    P. 49 THE GARDEN   34 Ripe Apples drop about my head;
    P. 185 BRITANNIA   46 How, like ripe fruit, she dropt from of the
                             Throne

riper   frequency: 1   relative frequency: 0.0000
    P. 124 O.C.   37 But as with riper Years her Virtue grew,

rise   frequency: 21   relative frequency: 0.0004
    P.   3 LOVELACE   18 Of Insects which against you rise in arms.
    P.   5 HASTINGS   25 Therefore the Democratick Stars did rise,
    P. 23 NYMPH   79 Yet could not, till it self would rise,
    P. 56 BILL-BOROW   2 Rise in a perfect Hemisphere!
    P. 67 A. HOUSE   258 Young Fairfax through the Wall does rise.
    P. 70 A. HOUSE   378 We wonder how they rise alive.
    P. 72 A. HOUSE   439 And such the Roman Camps do rise
    P. 92 MAY'S DEATH   86 And reverend Chaucer, but their dust does rise
    P. 97 HOLLAND   59 Besides the Waters of themselves did rise,

P. 109 ANNIVERSARY   234 As a small Cloud, like a Mans hand didst rise;
P. 110 ANNIVERSARY   303 Ch Mahomet! now couldst thou rise again,
P. 126 O.C.   119 Or of huge Trees, whose growth with his did
                          rise,
P. 157 INSTRUCTIONS   675 And secret Joy, in his calm Soul does rise,
P. 162 INSTRUCTICNS   896 Yet from beneath the Veil her blushes rise;
P. 163 INSTRUCTIONS   911 Thrice did he rise, thrice the vain Tumult fled,
P. 170 PROPHECY   5 To turne the Cittye which againe shall rise
P. 172 LOYALL SCOT   41 And secrett Joy in his own soul doth Rise
P. 174 LOYALL SCCT   83 Or what new perpendicular doth rise
P. 186 BRITANNIA   74 Doe Monarchs rise by vertues or the sword?
P. 189 BRITANNIA   167 Tell em the Generous scorn their Rise to owe
P. 195 TWO HORSES   156 W. For that very reason hee 's never to rise.

rises   frequency: 1   relative frequency: 0.0000
P. 57 BILL-BOROW   22 And all the way it rises bends;

rising   frequency: 5   relative frequency: 0.0001
P. 20 THYRSIS   35 There, alwayes is, a rising Sun,
P. 86 FLECKNO   134 Like white fleaks rising from a Leaper's skin!
P. 96 HOLLAND   43 Not who first see the rising Sun commands,
P. 96 HOLLAND   44 But who could first discern the rising Lands.
P. 163 INSTRUCTICNS   926 And rising, straight on Hyde's Disgrace
                          resolves.

rival   frequency: 1   relative frequency: 0.0000
See also "rivall."
P. 63 A. HOUSE   149 'But can he such a Rival seem

rivall   frequency: 1   relative frequency: 0.0000
P. 186 BRITANNIA   78 The Rivall Gods, Monarchs of th' cther world,

rivals   frequency: 2   relative frequency: 0.0000
P. 26 YOUNG LOVE   29 So, to make all Rivals vain,
P. 121 TWO SONGS   44 Rivals each one for thee tco strong.

river   frequency: 8   relative frequency: 0.0001
P. 72 A. HOUSE   435 We wondring in the River near
P. 73 A. HOUSE   471 The River in it self is drown'd,
P. 79 A. HOUSE   667 And on the River as it flows
P. 80 A. HOUSE   693 Nothing could make the River be
P. 156 INSTRUCTIONS   625 But sees, inrag'd, the River flow between.
P. 158 INSTRUCTIONS   703 And the kind River in its Creek them hides,
P. 158 INSTRUCTIONS   721 Once a deep River, now with Timber floor'd,
P. 173 LOYALL SCCT   81 What Ethick River is this Wondrous Tweed

rivers   frequency: 6   relative frequency: 0.0001
P. 10 DIALOGUE   40 And suspend the Rivers Fall.
P. 80 A. HOUSE   696 Then Gardens, Wcods, Meads, Rivers are.
P. 130 O.C.   281 As long as rivers to the seas shall runne,
P. 153 INSTRUCTIONS   524 Sail'd now among cur Rivers undisturb'd:
P. 155 INSTRUCTIONS   582 They sail securely through the Rivers track.
P. 159 INSTRUCTIONS   748 When all the Rivers grac'd their Nuptial Bed;

rives   frequency: 1   relative frequency: 0.0000
P. 154 INSTRUCTIONS   556 When, all on sudden, their calm boscme rives

rivet   frequency: 1   relative frequency: 0.0000
P. 96 HOLLAND   17 How did they rivet, with Gigantick Piles,

riveted. See "rivited."

rivited   frequency: 1   relative frequency: 0.0000
P. 92 MAY'S DEATH   93 Thou rivited untc Ixion's wheel

roar   frequency: 4   relative frequency: 0.0000
P. 17 BERMUDAS   27 And makes the hcllcw Seas, that roar,
P. 27 LOVER   20 Which through his surging Breast do roar.
P. 187 BRITANNIA   109 With fury drunke like Backanalls they roar
P. 191 TWO HORSES   10 Would roar like a Devill with a man in his
                          belly:

roar'd   frequency: 4   relative frequency: 0.0000
P. 86 FLECKNO   152 And roar'd out, like Perillus in's cwn Bull;
P. 156 INSTRUCTICNS   640 He heard how the wild Cannon nearer roar'd;
P. 159 INSTRUCTIONS   759 The Thames roar'd, swouning Medway turn'd her
                          tide,
P. 315 CHEQUER INN   116 The Landlord Bailes, out eate, out roar'd

roasted   frequency: 1   relative frequency: 0.0000
P. 140 HOUSEWARMING   112 He comes to be roasted next St. James's Fair.

rob   frequency: 3   relative frequency: 0.0000
    See also "robb."
    P. 65 A. HOUSE   208 'As rob though in the Dungeon cast.
    P. 170 PROPHECY   22 When even to rob the Checquer shall be Just,
    P. 177 LOYALL SCOT   217 Indifferent to Rob Churches of their Coals.

robb   frequency: 1   relative frequency: 0.0000
    P. 198 DUKE   6 To robb their native ccuntrey of its right.

robb'd   frequency: 1   relative frequency: 0.0000
    P. 158 INSTRUCTIONS   711 The Dutch had robb'd those Jewels of the
                               Crown:

robbers   frequency: 1   relative frequency: 0.0000
    P. 156 INSTRUCTIONS   624 After the Robbers, for her Whelps does yell:

robert   frequency: 4   relative frequency: 0.0000
    P. 179 STOCKSMARKET   3 So Sir Robert advanced the King's statue, in
                               token
    P. 179 STOCKSMARKET   15 And some by the likeness Sir Robert suspect
    P. 180 STOCKSMARKET   29 But Sir Robert to take all the scandal away
    P. 180 STOCKSMARKET   53 But Sir Robert affirms we do him much wrong;

robes   frequency: 2   relative frequency: 0.0000
    P. 62 A. HOUSE   120 'Our brighter Robes and Crowns of Gold?
    P. 130 O.C.   289 Despoyl'd of mortall robes, in seas of blisse,

robs   frequency: 1   relative frequency: 0.0000
    P. 176 LOYALL SCOT   181 The fittest Mask for one that Robs a Crown.

rochets   frequency: 1   relative frequency: 0.0000
    P. 176 LOYALL SCOT   173 Of Rochets Tippets Copes, and wheres theire
                               Grace?

rock   frequency: 3   relative frequency: 0.0000
    P. 27 LOVER   14 Upon the Rock his Mother drave;
    P. 28 LOVER   52 And grapple, with the stubborn Rock:
    P. 108 ANNIVERSARY   202 Or Rock so savage, but it mourn'd for thee:

rockets   frequency: 1   relative frequency: 0.0000
    P. 80 A. HOUSE   685 For streight those giddy Rockets fail,

rocks   frequency: 5   relative frequency: 0.0001
    P. 18 BERMUDAS   31 And in these Rocks for us did frame
    P. 47 EMPIRE   4 To hollow Rocks and murm'ring Fountains bound.
    P. 72 A. HOUSE   434 Like a calm Sea it shews the Rocks:
    P. 109 ANNIVERSARY   268 And threat'ning Rocks misapprehend for Land;
    P. 181 MADE FREE   11 Set with Stones of both Rocks

rodds   frequency: 1   relative frequency: 0.0000
    P. 195 TWO HORSES   127 Tho Father and Sonne are different Rodds,

rods.   See "rodds."

rogue   frequency: 2   relative frequency: 0.0000
    P. 143 INSTRUCTIONS   101 Justly the Rogue was whipt in Porter's Den:
    P. 177 LOYALL SCOT   253 Does man and wife signifie Rogue and Whore?

rogues   frequency: 2   relative frequency: 0.0000
    P. 161 INSTRUCTIONS   862 And had almost mistook and call'd them Rogues.
    P. 194 TWO HORSES   90 For giving nce more the Rogues are prorogued.

roll   frequency: 1   relative frequency: 0.0000
    See also "roul."
    P. 27 MISTRESS   41 Let us roll all our Strength, and all

rolled. See "rould."

rolling. See "rouling," "rowling."

rolls. See "roules."

roman   frequency: 8   relative frequency: 0.0001
    See also "romane."
    P. 72 A. HOUSE   439 And such the Roman Camps do rise
    P. 106 ANNIVERSARY   129 Which shrinking to her Roman Den impure,
    P. 147 INSTRUCTIONS   249 Such Roman Cocles strid: before the Foe,
    P. 168 ADVICE   5 The Roman takeing up the fencers trade,
    P. 173 LOYALL SCOT   67 Such in the Roman forum Curtius brave
    P. 189 BRITANNIA   183 Greek arts and Roman armes in her conjoynd
    P. 192 TWO HORSES   21 If the Roman Church, good Christians, oblige yee

P. 198 DUKE   33 And not Infallible the Roman Soyle?

romance   frequency: 1   relative frequency: 0.0000
P. 147 INSTRUCTIONS   275 Such once Orlando, famous in Romance,

romane   frequency: 2   relative frequency: 0.0000
P. 91 MAY'S DEATH   44 On them some Romane cast similitude,
P. 92 MAY'S DEATH   80 Right Romane poverty and gratitude.

rome   frequency: 10   relative frequency: 0.0002
P. 77 A. HOUSE   581 What Rome, Greece, Palestine, ere said
P. 83 FLECKNO   t Fleckno, an English Priest at Rome.
P. 91 MAY'S DEATH   49 Transferring old Rome hither in your talk,
P. 99 HOLLAND   142 Would render fain unto our better Rome.
P. 139 HOUSEWARMING   63 So the Bribes overlaid her that Rome once
                          betray'd:
P. 168 ADVICE   2 And draw me in one Scene London and Rome,
P. 185 BRITANNIA   22 Till Charles loves Parliaments, till James
                          hates Rome.
P. 191 TWO HORSES   13 At Delphos and Rome Stocks and Stones now and
                          then, sirs,
P. 195 TWO HORSES   148 Wee must all to the Stake or be Converts to
                          Rome.
P. 205 HISTORICALL   156 And brought new Lessons to the Duke from Rome.

romes   frequency: 2   relative frequency: 0.0000
P. 91 MAY'S DEATH   53 And who by Romes example England lay,
P. 196 TWO HORSES   163 If Speech from Brute Animals in Romes first
                          age

romulus   frequency: 1   relative frequency: 0.0000
P. 60 A. HOUSE   40 As Romulus his Bee-like Cell.

roode   frequency: 1   relative frequency: 0.0000
P. 192 TWO HORSES   18 When Shrines give Answers, say a knave 's in
                          the Roode;

roof   frequency: 1   relative frequency: 0.0000
P. 141 INSTRUCTIONS   10 The Aly roof, with snuff of Candle dimm,

roof'd   frequency: 1   relative frequency: 0.0000
P. 59 A. HOUSE   13 The low roof'd Tortoises do dwell

roofs   frequency: 1   relative frequency: 0.0000
P. 105 ANNIVERSARY   98 Knit by the Roofs Protecting weight agree.

room   frequency: 7   relative frequency: 0.0001
See also "roome."
P. 59 A. HOUSE   18 Demands more room alive then dead.
P. 83 FLECKNO   14 Turn in, and shew to Wainscot half the Room.
P. 87 FLECKNO   155 Made Mediator, in my room, said, Why?
P. 88 ODE   43 And therefore must make room
P. 93 DR. WITTY   1 Sit further, and make room for thine own fame,
P. 132 PARADISE   29 So that no room is here for Writers left,
P. 163 INSTRUCTIONS   915 Shake then the room, and all his Curtains tear,

roome   frequency: 2   relative frequency: 0.0000
P. 198 DUKE   8 Adoreing Roome, this labell in his mouth.
P. 314 CHEQUER INN   64 Tho they had dirted so the Roome

rooms   frequency: 1   relative frequency: 0.0000
P. 61 A. HOUSE   67 Nor less the Rooms within commends

root   frequency: 8   relative frequency: 0.0001
P. 41 THE MOWER   15 Its Onion root they then so high did hold,
P. 44 DAMON   76 Each stroke between the Earth and Root,
P. 49 THE GARDEN   50 Or at some Fruit-trees mossy root,
P. 58 BILL-BOROW   58 Contented if they fix their Root.
P. 71 A. HOUSE   410 To build below the Grasses Root;
P. 75 A. HOUSE   539 He walks still upright from the Root,
P. 79 A. HOUSE   646 On the Osiers undermined Root,
P. 124 O.C.   56 The sad Root pines in secret under ground.

roots   frequency: 1   relative frequency: 0.0000
P. 129 O.C.   262 To Heav'n its branches, and through earth its
                          roots:

rope   frequency: 3   relative frequency: 0.0000
P. 46 AMETAS   5 Think'st Thou that this Rope would twine
P. 46 AMETAS   15 Then let's both lay by our Rope,

          P. 154 INSTRUCTIONS 542 And wanton Boys on every Rope do cling.

ropes   frequency: 2   relative frequency: 0.0000
     See also "hay-ropes."
     P.   46 AMETAS   12 Looser then with Ropes of Hay.
     P. 148 INSTRUCTIONS 321 The busie Hammer sleeps, the Ropes untwine;

rose   frequency: 5   relative frequency: 0.0001
     P.   61 A. HOUSE   88 The Quarries whence this dwelling rose.
     P.   68 A. HOUSE   312 That of the Tulip Pinke and Rose.
     P.   91 MAY'S DEATH   31 Rose more then ever he was seen severe,
     P. 149 INSTRUCTIONS 338 With Magic Herbs, rose from the Pot renew'd:
     P. 187 BRITANNIA   105 When she had spoke, a confus'd murmur rose

rosen   frequency: 1   relative frequency: 0.0000
     P. 313 CHEQUER INN   18 The way they all have rosen.

roses   frequency: 13   relative frequency: 0.0002
     P.   9 DIALOGUE   21 On these Roses strow'd so plain
     P.   12 DROP OF DEW   3 Into the blowing Roses,
     P.   23 NYMPH   72 But so with Roses over grown,
     P.   24 NYMPH   83 Upon the Roses it would feed,
     P.   24 NYMPH   86 And print those Roses on my Lip.
     P.   24 NYMPH   88 On Roses thus its self to fill:
     P.   24 NYMPH   92 Lillies without, Roses within.
     P.   29 THE GALLERY   22 And Manna falls, and Roses spring;
     P.   36 DAPHNIS   87 Gather Roses in the rain,
     P.   38 PICTURE   6 But only with the Roses playes;
     P.   38 PICTURE   30 And Roses of their thorns disarm:
     P.   41 THE MOWER   11 With strange perfumes he did the Roses taint.
     P.   69 A. HOUSE   333 When Roses only Arms might bear,

rosie   frequency: 1   relative frequency: 0.0000
     P.   69 A. HOUSE   334 And Men did rosie Garlands wear?

rosy. See "rosie."

rot. See "rott."

rots   frequency: 1   relative frequency: 0.0000
     P. 148 INSTRUCTIONS 319 The Timber rots, and useless Ax does rust,

rott   frequency: 1   relative frequency: 0.0000
     P. 199 DUKE   53 Dy before twenty, or rott before sixteene.

rotten   frequency: 1   relative frequency: 0.0000
     P. 317 CHEQUER INN   181 Just like our Rotten Pump at home

rough   frequency: 1   relative frequency: 0.0000
     P.   27 MISTRESS   43 And tear our Pleasures with rough strife,

rougher   frequency: 1   relative frequency: 0.0000
     P. 104 ANNIVERSARY   51 The rougher Stones, unto his Measures hew'd,

roughest   frequency: 1   relative frequency: 0.0000
     P.   81 A. HOUSE   720 She scap'd the safe, but roughest Way.

roul   frequency: 2   relative frequency: 0.0000
     P.   96 HOLLAND   15 Or then those Pills which sordid Beetles roul,
     P. 149 INSTRUCTIONS 360 And roul in vain at Sisyphus's Stone.

rould   frequency: 1   relative frequency: 0.0000
     P. 185 BRITANNIA   45 And Golden dayes in peacefull order rould,

roules   frequency: 1   relative frequency: 0.0000
     P.   12 DROP OF DEW   15 Restless it roules and unsecure,

rouling   frequency: 2   relative frequency: 0.0000
     P.   34 DAPHNIS   35 And with rouling Eyes did glare,
     P. 187 BRITANNIA   121 Luld in security, rouling in lust,

round   frequency: 19   relative frequency: 0.0003
     P.   12 DROP OF DEW   6 Round in its self incloses:
     P.   12 DROP OF DEW   29 So the World excluding round,
     P.   28 LOVER   23 While round the ratling Thunder hurl'd,
     P.   44 DAMON   73 While thus he threw his Elbow round,
     P.   63 A. HOUSE   143 'And round about you Glory breaks,
     P.   68 A. HOUSE   306 And round your equal Fires do meet;
     P.   68 A. HOUSE   314 Of Stars walks round about the Pole,
     P.   73 A. HOUSE   472 And Isl's th' astonish'd Cattle round.
     P.   88 ODE   55 While round the armed Bands
     P. 105 ANNIVERSARY   100 He hurles e'r since the World about him round;

P.	108 ANNIVERSARY	198	Nor their round Hoofs, or curled Mane's compare;
P.	111 ANNIVERSARY	331	While dismal blacks hung round the Universe,
P.	129 O.C.	263	Whose spacious boughs are hung with trophies round,
P.	147 INSTRUCTIONS	245	But Strangeways, that all Night still walk'd the round,
P.	149 INSTRUCTIONS	331	And to Land-tax from the Excise turn round,
P.	157 INSTRUCTIONS	681	Round the transparent Fire about him glows,
P.	162 INSTRUCTIONS	893	Naked as born, and her round Arms behind,
P.	169 ADVICE	31	At Arlingtons, and round about it sate
P.	173 LOYALL SCOT	47	Round the Transparent fire about him Gloves

rout   frequency: 6   relative frequency: 0.0001
P.	4 LOVELACE	42	Thinking that I too of the rout had been,
P.	144 INSTRUCTIONS	157	To them succeeds a despicable Rout,
P.	148 INSTRUCTIONS	306	And the Excise receives a total Rout.
P.	186 BRITANNIA	84	Are proper arts, the long-eard rout t'enslave:
P.	188 BRITANNIA	129	Thus the state's night-Mard by this Hellish rout
P.	315 CHEQUER INN	106	And Berkenhead of all the Rout

row   frequency: 2   relative frequency: 0.0000
| P. | 156 INSTRUCTIONS | 647 | Three Children tall, unsing'd, away they row, |
| P. | 158 INSTRUCTIONS | 739 | Or row a Boat in thy unlucky hour: |

row'd   frequency: 1   relative frequency: 0.0000
| P. | 17 BERMUDAS | 3 | From a small Boat, that row'd along, |

rowling   frequency: 1   relative frequency: 0.0000
| P. | 30 THE GALLERY | 37 | Or, if some rowling Wave appears, |

rows   frequency: 1   relative frequency: 0.0000
| P. | 144 INSTRUCTIONS | 135 | With hundred rows of Teeth the Shark exceeds, |

roy   frequency: 1   relative frequency: 0.0000
| P. | 167 KINGS VOWES | 54 | And Quack in their Language still Vive le Roy. |

royal   frequency: 5   relative frequency: 0.0001
See also "royall."
P.	88 ODE	53	That thence the Royal Actor born
P.	142 INSTRUCTIONS	55	And found how Royal Heirs might be matur'd,
P.	142 INSTRUCTIONS	58	Of's Highnesses Royal Society.
P.	155 INSTRUCTIONS	611	But when the Royal Charles, what Rage, what Grief,
P.	204 HISTORICALL	130	The Royal Evil so malignant growes,

royal-james   frequency: 1   relative frequency: 0.0000
| P. | 157 INSTRUCTIONS | 699 | And the true Royal-Oak, and Royal-James, |

royal-oak   frequency: 1   relative frequency: 0.0000
| P. | 157 INSTRUCTIONS | 699 | And the true Royal-Oak, and Royal-James, |

royall   frequency: 5   relative frequency: 0.0001
P.	187 BRITANNIA	99	'Tis Royall Game whole Kingdomes to deflower.
P.	194 TWO HORSES	116	What hast thou to say of my Royall Rider?
P.	198 DUKE	38	He who longe since abjured the Royall line
P.	201 HISTORICALL	12	And dubd poore Palmer's wife his Royall Whore.
P.	315 CHEQUER INN	113	And Cholmley of Vale Royall came

rub   frequency: 2   relative frequency: 0.0000
| P. | 94 DR. WITTY | 12 | Much of the precious Metal rub away. |
| P. | 143 INSTRUCTIONS | 94 | Nor scorns to rub him down with those fair Hands; |

rubbish   frequency: 1   relative frequency: 0.0000
| P. | 139 HOUSEWARMING | 93 | Fond City, its Rubbish and Ruines that builds, |

rubens   frequency: 1   relative frequency: 0.0000
| P. | 143 INSTRUCTIONS | 119 | For so too Rubens, with affairs of State, |

rubies   frequency: 1   relative frequency: 0.0000
| P. | 26 MISTRESS | 6 | Should'st Rubies find: I by the Tide |

rude   frequency: 7   relative frequency: 0.0001
P.	48 THE GARDEN	15	Society is all but rude,
P.	82 A. HOUSE	762	But a rude heap together hurl'd;
P.	104 ANNIVERSARY	52	Dans'd up in order from the Quarreys rude;
P.	146 INSTRUCTIONS	233	They, that e're long shall the rude Dutch upbraid,
P.	155 INSTRUCTIONS	589	A Skipper rude shocks it without respect,

```
        P.  158 INSTRUCTIONS   733 Then with rude shouts, secure, the Air they vex;
        P.  182 MADE FREE       56 Were thrice growne so rude,

rudely                           frequency:    1    relative frequency: 0.0000
        P.    4 LOVELACE         37 Whose hand so rudely grasps the steely brand,

rue                              frequency:    1    relative frequency: 0.0000
        P.  159 INSTRUCTIONS    751 Now with vain grief their vainer hopes they rue,

ruffe                            frequency:    1    relative frequency: 0.0000
        P.  195 TWO HORSES      150 None ever Reign'd like old Besse in the Ruffe.

ruffians.  See "ruffins."

ruffins                          frequency:    1    relative frequency: 0.0000
        P.  204 HISTORICALL     148 Bold Irish Ruffins to his Court adress:

rugged                           frequency:    3    relative frequency: 0.0000
        P.   19 THYRSIS          11 'Tis a sure but rugged way,
        P.   57 BILL-BOROW       19 Nor with the rugged path deterrs
        P.  130 O.C.            306 Beats on the rugged track: he, vertue dead,

ruin.  See "neighbour-ruine," "ruine."

ruin'd                           frequency:    1    relative frequency: 0.0000
        P.  140 HIS HOUSE         4 The price of ruin'd Families:

ruine                            frequency:    7    relative frequency: 0.0001
        P.   37 DEFINITION       15 Their union would her ruine be,
        P.   45 MOWER'S SONG     22 Will in one common Ruine fall.
        P.   65 A. HOUSE        223 'Fly from their Ruine. How I fear
        P.   88 ODE              34 To ruine the great Work of Time,
        P.  131 PARADISE          7 That he would ruine (for I saw him strong)
        P.  200 DUKE             95 When wiser men its ruine undertooke:
        P.  205 HISTORICALL     175 Hence Ruine and Destruction had ensu'd,

ruines                           frequency:    1    relative frequency: 0.0000
        P.  139 HOUSEWARMING     93 Fond City, its Rubbish and Ruines that builds,

ruins.  See "ruines."

rul'd                            frequency:    3    relative frequency: 0.0000
        P.   27 LOVER            10 Rul'd, and the Winds did what they please,
        P.  105 ANNIVERSARY      77 All other Matter yields, and may be rul'd;
        P.  155 INSTRUCTIONS    578 That rul'd all Seas, and did our Channel grace.

rule                             frequency:    8    relative frequency: 0.0001
        P.   63 A. HOUSE        155 'And, if our Rule seem strictly pend,
        P.   63 A. HOUSE        156 'The Rule it self to you shall bend.
        P.  108 ANNIVERSARY     228 Yielding to Rule, because it made thee Less.
        P.  164 INSTRUCTIONS    964 Or in fair Fields to rule the easie Flock.
        P.  165 INSTRUCTIONS    990 Give us this Court, and rule without a Guard.
        P.  167 KINGS VOWES      50 Tho' not rule like the Turk yet I will be so
                                    drest,
        P.  171 PROPHECY         36 Whom Wise men Laugh att and the Women Rule,
        P.  186 BRITANNIA        86 To teach your will 's the onely rule of right,

ruler's                          frequency:    1    relative frequency: 0.0000
        P.  128 O.C.            220 Lye weak and easy to the ruler's will;

rules                            frequency:    4    relative frequency: 0.0000
        P.   29 LOVER            63 And he in Story only rules,
        P.   96 HOLLAND          42 So rules among the drowned he that draines.
        P.  114 BLAKE            38 This only rules by day, and that by Night.
        P.  159 INSTRUCTIONS    762 And female Stewart, there, Rules the four
                                    Seas.

ruling                           frequency:    3    relative frequency: 0.0000
        P.  105 ANNIVERSARY      68 When Cromwell tun'd the ruling Instrument;
        P.  120 TWO SONGS        18 Ruling the Waves that Ebb and flow.
        P.  131 O.C.            314 How gently winds at once the ruling reins?

rump                             frequency:    2    relative frequency: 0.0000
        P.  142 INSTRUCTIONS     63 With Chanc'lor's Belly, and so large a Rump.
        P.  317 CHEQUER INN     189 Wee groan'd under the Rump

run                              frequency:   17    relative frequency: 0.0003
        See also "out-run," "runne."
        P.   13 DROP OF DEW      39 Congeal'd on Earth: but does, dissolving, run
        P.   23 NYMPH            68 'Twould stay, and run again, and stay.
        P.   24 NYMPH           109 O do not run too fast: for I
        P.   27 MISTRESS         46 Stand still, yet we will make him run.
```

```
P.  34 DAPHNIS          30 Now the latest minut's run
P.  48 THE GARDEN       25 When we have run our Passions heat,
P.  50 THE GARDEN       68 Does through a fragrant Zodiack run;
P.  86 FLECKNO         149 Making the half points and the periods run
P.  89 ODE              70 Did fright the Architects to run;
P. 117 BLAKE           105 Wer't not for that, they from their Fate would
                           run,
P. 137 HOUSEWARMING      9 But observing that Mortals run often behind,
P. 138 HOUSEWARMING     57 His Rent would no more in arrear run to
                           Worster;
P. 148 INSTRUCTIONS    317 Mean time through all the Yards their Orders
                           run
P. 150 INSTRUCTIONS    386 And Boys and Girls in Troops run houting by;
P. 155 INSTRUCTIONS    600 (Cornbry the fleetest) and to London run.
P. 157 INSTRUCTIONS    662 And wondred much at those that run away:
P. 182 MADE FREE        45 He wou'd run on the score and borrow;
```

runing   frequency: 1   relative frequency: 0.0000
```
P. 181 MADE FREE        32 In runing to Plays,
```

runne   frequency: 2   relative frequency: 0.0000
```
P. 130 O.C.            281 As long as rivers to the seas shall runne,
P. 172 LOYALL SCOT      28 And wonder'd much at those that Runne away,
```

running. See "runing."

runs   frequency: 5   relative frequency: 0.0001
```
P.  68 A. HOUSE        320 She runs you through, or askes the Word.
P. 103 ANNIVERSARY       7 Cromwell alone with greater Vigour runs,
P. 143 INSTRUCTIONS     84 And still within her mind the Footman runs:
P. 171 PROPHECY         54 For that still fill'd runs out as fast againe;
P. 317 CHEQUER INN     186 And then it runs full spout
```

rupert   frequency: 1   relative frequency: 0.0000
```
P. 159 INSTRUCTIONS    776 The Fleet divided? Writ for Rupert? Pett.
```

ruperts   frequency: 1   relative frequency: 0.0000
```
P. 158 INSTRUCTIONS    725 And spight of Ruperts and of Albemarles,
```

rupture   frequency: 1   relative frequency: 0.0000
```
P. 152 INSTRUCTIONS    474 Consenting, for his Rupture, to be Gelt;
```

rush   frequency: 1   relative frequency: 0.0000
```
P.  80 A. HOUSE        682 The World, and through the Ev'ning rush.
```

rush'd   frequency: 1   relative frequency: 0.0000
```
P. 109 ANNIVERSARY     240 Still from behind, and it before him rush'd,
```

rust   frequency: 3   relative frequency: 0.0000
```
P.  87 ODE               6 And oyl th' unused Armours rust:
P. 148 INSTRUCTIONS    319 The Timber rots, and useless Ax does rust,
P. 164 INSTRUCTIONS    975 Not so does Rust insinuating wear,
```

rustle   frequency: 2   relative frequency: 0.0000
```
P. 156 INSTRUCTIONS    658 The Nymphs would rustle; he would forward swim.
P. 172 LOYALL SCOT      24 The Nymphs would Rustle, hee would forward
                           swim:
```

ruthless   frequency: 1   relative frequency: 0.0000
```
P. 108 ANNIVERSARY     212 And to deaf Seas, and ruthless Tempests mourns,
```

ruyter   frequency: 6   relative frequency: 0.0001
```
P. 151 INSTRUCTIONS    437 Pray him to make De-Witte, and Ruyter cease,
P. 153 INSTRUCTIONS    523 Ruyter the while, that had our Ocean curb'd,
P. 155 INSTRUCTIONS    581 Ruyter forthwith a Squadron does untack,
P. 159 INSTRUCTIONS    764 And Richmond here commands, as Ruyter those.
P. 160 INSTRUCTIONS    817 But in the Thames mouth still de Ruyter laid,
P. 202 HISTORICALL      54 De Ruyter claps him in Solbay again.
```

ruyters   frequency: 1   relative frequency: 0.0000
```
P. 158 INSTRUCTIONS    707 And were not Ruyters maw with ravage cloy'd,
```

ruyter's   frequency: 1   relative frequency: 0.0000
See also "de-ruyter's," "ruyters."
```
P. 158 INSTRUCTIONS    726 To Ruyter's Triumph lead the captive Charles.
```

ryder   frequency: 1   relative frequency: 0.0000
```
P. 195 TWO HORSES      141 Ch. Thy Ryder puts no man to death in his
                           wrath,
```

's   frequency: 17   relative frequency: 0.0003

```
P.  11 DIALOGUE        62 And that 's worth nought that can be sold.
P.  55 THYESTE         14 Death to him 's a Strange surprise.
P. 160 INSTRUCTIONS   805 But the true cause was, that, in 's Brother
                         May,
P. 185 BRITANNIA       36 In 's left the scales, in 's right hand plac'd
                         the sword,
P. 186 BRITANNIA       86 To teach your will 's the onely rule of right,
P. 187 BRITANNIA      119 Like a Tame spinster in 's seraglio sits,
P. 187 BRITANNIA      120 Beseig'd by 's whores, Buffoones, and Bastard
                         Chitts;
P. 188 BRITANNIA      148 It 's by noe Potent Antidote withstood.
P. 192 TWO HORSES      18 When Shrines give Answers, say a knave 's in
                         the Roode;
P. 192 TWO HORSES      19 Those Idolls ne're speak, but the miracle 's
                         done
P. 192 TWO HORSES      49 Ch. Tho he chang'd his Religion I hope hee 's
                         so civill
P. 193 TWO HORSES      82 Who out of what 's given do get a good living.
P. 194 TWO HORSES     105 W. Truth 's as Bold as a Lyon, I am not
                         afraid,
P. 195 TWO HORSES     142 W. But hee 's buryed alive in lust and in
                         sloath.
P. 195 TWO HORSES     156 W. For that very reason hee 's never to rise.
P. 204 HISTORICALL    140 T'hunt down 's Prey and hope to master all.
```

sabbath. See "sabboth."

```
sabboth                      frequency:    1    relative frequency: 0.0000
    P.  92 MAY'S DEATH   100 Such as unto the Sabboth bears the Witch.

sable                        frequency:    2    relative frequency: 0.0000
    P.  29 LOVER          64 In a Field Sable a Lover Gules.
    P. 201 HISTORICALL     1 Of a tall Stature and of sable hue,

sack                         frequency:    1    relative frequency: 0.0000
    P. 162 INSTRUCTIONS  882 And soaks his Sack with Norfolk like a Toast.

sacrafice                    frequency:    1    relative frequency: 0.0000
    P. 187 BRITANNIA     101 A sacrafice to you, their God and King.

sacraficed                   frequency:    1    relative frequency: 0.0000
    P. 191 TWO HORSES      8 That a sacraficed ox, when his Gutts were out,
                         Bellow'd:

sacramental                  frequency:    1    relative frequency: 0.0000
    P. 153 INSTRUCTIONS  496 Lye nuzz'ling at the Sacramental wart;

sacred                       frequency:   19    relative frequency: 0.0003
    P.  13 DROP OF DEW    37 Such did the Manna's sacred Dew destil;
    P.  48 THE GARDEN     13 Your sacred Plants, if here below,
    P.  57 BILL-BOROW     36 With impious Steel the sacred Shade.
    P.  60 A. HOUSE       35 These sacred Places to adore,
    P.  82 A. HOUSE      742 The Priest shall cut the sacred Bud;
    P.  91 MAY'S DEATH    58 The sacred Laurel, hence are all these teares?
    P. 104 ANNIVERSARY    35 Nor sacred Prophecies consult within,
    P. 105 ANNIVERSARY    65 Thus, ere he ceas'd, his sacred Lute creates
    P. 110 ANNIVERSARY   306 Have writ the Comments of thy sacred Foame:
    P. 128 O.C.          201 Friendship, that sacred virtue, long dos claime
    P. 129 O.C.          261 Not much unlike the sacred oak, which shoots
    P. 131 PARADISE        8 The sacred Truths to Fable and old Song,
    P. 140 HIS HOUSE       1 Here lies the sacred Bones
    P. 155 INSTRUCTIONS  613 That sacred Keel, which had, as he, restor'd
    P. 185 BRITANNIA      29 I'th sacred ear Tyranick Arts they Croak,
    P. 191 TWO HORSES      1 Wee read in profane and Sacred records
    P. 198 DUKE           11 Throwne att thy sacred feete I humbly bow,
    P. 203 HISTORICALL    97 Who from the sacred Pulpit dare decieve?
    P. 205 HISTORICALL   163 A Priest should doe it, from whose sacred stroke

sacrifice                    frequency:    5    relative frequency: 0.0001
See also "sacrafice."
    P.  25 YOUNG LOVE     16 For his morning Sacrifice.
    P.  97 HOLLAND        91 While the fat steam of Female Sacrifice
    P. 119 TWO SONGS      14 And Sheep are both thy Sacrifice.
    P. 140 G.-CHILDREN     2 What fitter Sacrifice for Denham's Ghost?
    P. 140 HOUSEWARMING  100 Great Buckingham's Sacrifice must be the first.
```

sacrificed. See "sacraficed."

```
sacriledge                   frequency:    1    relative frequency: 0.0000
    P.  63 A. HOUSE      139 ''Twere Sacriledge a Man t'admit
```

sacrilege. See "sacriledge."

```
sad                          frequency:   20    relative frequency: 0.0004
```

P.	5 HASTINGS	44	Who for sad Purple, tears his Saffron-coat;
P.	5 HASTINGS	49	Like some sad Chymist, who, prepar'd to reap
P.	24 NYMPH	96	Sad, slowly dropping like a Gumme.
P.	33 DAPHNIS	9	But, with this sad News surpriz'd,
P.	36 DAPHNIS	93	Fate I come, as dark, as sad,
P.	75 A. HOUSE	526	Sad pair unto the Elms they moan.
P.	83 FLECKNO	6	Of the sad Pelican; Subject divine
P.	87 FLECKNO	158	But saw with sad dispair that 'twas too late.
P.	90 ODE	107	But from this Valour sad
P.	119 TWO SONGS	5	Heark how he sings, with sad delight,
P.	124 O.C.	56	The sad Root pines in secret under ground.
P.	124 O.C.	60	Answers the touch in Notes more sad more true.
P.	149 INSTRUCTIONS	345	So the sad Tree shrinks from the Mornings Eye;
P.	151 INSTRUCTIONS	411	Fresh Messengers still the sad News assure,
P.	157 INSTRUCTIONS	692	And the sad Stream beneath his Ashes drinks.
P.	159 INSTRUCTIONS	747	Sad change, since first that happy pair was wed,
P.	159 INSTRUCTIONS	754	As the sad Tortoise for the Sea does groan.
P.	173 LOYALL SCOT	58	And the sad stream beneath his Ashes drinks.
P.	187 BRITANNIA	116	And to his care did my sad state commend.
P.	202 HISTORICALL	72	What sad events attended on the same

sadder   frequency: 2   relative frequency: 0.0000
P.	75 A. HOUSE	522	A Sadder, yet more pleasing Sound:
P.	111 ANNIVERSARY	334	Did make the Fun'rals sadder by their Joyes.

saddest   frequency: 1   relative frequency: 0.0000
P.	119 BLAKE	165	The saddest news that ere to Spain was brought,

saddles.   See "sadles."

sadles   frequency: 1   relative frequency: 0.0000
P.	173 LOYALL SCOT	63	Skip Sadles: Pegasus thou needst not Bragg,

sadly   frequency: 1   relative frequency: 0.0000
P.	127 O.C.	151	But those that sadly his departure griev'd,

safe   frequency: 8   relative frequency: 0.0001
P.	17 BERMUDAS	12	Safe from the Storms, and Prelat's rage.
P.	18 CLORINDA	12	Safe from the Sun. D. not Heaven's Eye.
P.	77 A. HOUSE	601	How safe, methinks, and strong, behind
P.	81 A. HOUSE	720	She scap'd the safe, but roughest Way.
P.	150 INSTRUCTIONS	400	And thought all safe if they were so far off.
P.	154 INSTRUCTIONS	565	No man can sit there safe, the Cannon pow'rs
P.	155 INSTRUCTIONS	598	To be Spectators safe of the new Play,
P.	169 ADVICE	63	Tis hard; yet this he has for safe retreat:

safely   frequency: 5   relative frequency: 0.0001
P.	72 A. HOUSE	436	How Boats among them safely steer.
P.	115 BLAKE	68	And safely there casts Anchor in the Bay.
P.	157 INSTRUCTIONS	670	And safely through its Port the Dutch retire:
P.	172 LOYALL SCOT	36	And safely through its ports the Dutch retire.
P.	187 BRITANNIA	93	The Church and state you safely may invade.

safer   frequency: 1   relative frequency: 0.0000
P.	110 ANNIVERSARY	276	And doubles back unto the safer Main.

safety   frequency: 2   relative frequency: 0.0000
P.	90 MAY'S DEATH	16	The Subjects Safety, and the Rebel's Fear.
P.	153 INSTRUCTIONS	501	Here Men induc'd by Safety, Gain, and Ease,

saffron-coat   frequency: 1   relative frequency: 0.0000
P.	5 HASTINGS	44	Who for sad Purple, tears his Saffron-coat;

sage   frequency: 1   relative frequency: 0.0000
P.	188 BRITANNIA	156	From her sage mouth fam'd Principles to know,

said   frequency: 28   relative frequency: 0.0005
P.	22 NYMPH	30	What he said then; I'me sure I do.
P.	22 NYMPH	31	Said He, look how your Huntsman here
P.	44 DAMON	81	Alas! said He, these hurts are slight
P.	55 EPITAPH	19	'Tis true: but all so weakly said;
P.	61 A. HOUSE	76	As if she said leave this to me.
P.	77 A. HOUSE	581	What Rome, Greece, Palestine, ere said
P.	83 FLECKNO	9	I found at last a Chamber, as 'twas said,
P.	84 FLECKNO	53	Would break his fast before, said he was Sick,
P.	85 FLECKNO	93	Will make the way here; I said Sir you'l do
P.	85 FLECKNO	98	Delightful, said there can no Body pass
P.	85 FLECKNO	102	Our peace, the Priest said I too had some wit:
P.	85 FLECKNO	103	To prov't, I said, the place doth us invite
P.	86 FLECKNO	116	Said 'twas too late, he was already both.
P.	87 FLECKNO	155	Made Mediator, in my room, said, Why?

P. 91 MAY'S DEATH   22 I sing (said he) and the Pharsalian Sign,
P. 117 BLAKE   113 This said, the whole Fleet gave it their
                         applause,
P. 127 O.C.   183 Those Strokes he said will pierce through all
                         below
P. 138 HOUSEWARMING   53 They approve it thus far, and said it was fine;
P. 157 INSTRUCTIONS   659 They sigh'd and said, Fond Boy, why so untame,
P. 172 LOYALL SCOT   25 They sigh'd and said 'fond boy why soe Untame,
P. 178 LOYALL SCOT   282 Here Douglas smileing said hee did Intend
P. 191 STATUE   47 And however, she said, it could not be denyed
P. 194 TWO HORSES   106 I'le prove every tittle of what I have said.
P. 195 TWO HORSES   153 Ch. Troth, Brother, well said, but thats
                         somewhat bitter:
P. 205 HISTORICALL   171 Thus said the Scarlet Whore to her gallant,
P. 315 CHEQUER INN   104 For words not to be said but sung
P. 316 CHEQUER INN   163 They all said I who had said noe

saies   frequency: 1   relative frequency: 0.0000
P. 28 LOVER   55 And all he saies, a Lover drest

sail   frequency: 6   relative frequency: 0.0001
See also "saile."
P. 73 A. HOUSE   477 How Boats can over Bridges sail;
P. 98 HOLLAND   108 Rather then to the English strike their sail;
P. 114 BLAKE   17 Day, that to those who sail upon the deep,
P. 155 INSTRUCTIONS   582 They sail securely through the Rivers track.
P. 158 INSTRUCTIONS   738 Out of the Port, or dare to hoise a Sail,
P. 180 STOCKSMARKET   46 With three shattered planks and the rags of a
                         sail

sail'd   frequency: 3   relative frequency: 0.0000
P. 28 LOVER   28 That sail'd insulting o're the Wrack,
P. 112 ANNIVERSARY   358 'And beaked Promontories sail'd from far;
P. 153 INSTRUCTIONS   524 Sail'd now among our Rivers undisturb'd:

saile   frequency: 2   relative frequency: 0.0000
P. 190 STATUE   14 When the King in Armado to Portsmouth should
                         saile,
P. 314 CHEQUER INN   63 And smileing through did Saile

sailes   frequency: 1   relative frequency: 0.0000
P. 16 EYES   33 Not full sailes hasting loaden home,

sailing   frequency: 2   relative frequency: 0.0000
P. 154 INSTRUCTIONS   552 A Fleet of Clouds, sailing along the Skies:
P. 155 INSTRUCTIONS   593 But with her Sailing weight, the Holland Keel

sails   frequency: 2   relative frequency: 0.0000
See also "sailes."
P. 154 INSTRUCTIONS   547 Aeolus their Sails inspires with Eastern Wind,
P. 155 INSTRUCTIONS   590 Filling his Sails, more force to recollect.

saint   frequency: 3   relative frequency: 0.0000
P. 24 NYMPH   94 And dye as calmely as a Saint.
P. 62 A. HOUSE   124 'The Face and Graces of the Saint.
P. 87 PLECKNO   170 To hang it in Saint Peter's for a Vow.

saint-like   frequency: 1   relative frequency: 0.0000
P. 107 ANNIVERSARY   161 Whose Saint-like Mother we did lately see

saints   frequency: 6   relative frequency: 0.0001
P. 62 A. HOUSE   127 'This Work the Saints best represents;
P. 63 A. HOUSE   136 'Enough a thousand Saints to make.
P. 66 A. HOUSE   250 Their Wooden Saints in vain oppose.
P. 70 A. HOUSE   360 That in the Crowns of Saints do shine.
P. 127 O.C.   176 Whether of British Saints or Worthy's told;
P. 142 INSTRUCTIONS   46 Two Saints at once, St. German, St. Alban.

saith   frequency: 4   relative frequency: 0.0000
P. 111 ANNIVERSARY   349 'Is this, saith one, the Nation that we read
P. 160 INSTRUCTIONS   819 Hyde saith he hourly waits for a Dispatch;
P. 176 LOYALL SCOT   196 Kings head saith this, But Bishops head that
                         doe.
P. 192 TWO HORSES   46 Who beleives not a word, the word of God saith;

sake   frequency: 5   relative frequency: 0.0001
P. 111 ANNIVERSARY   322 Makes you for his sake Tremble one fit more;
P. 145 INSTRUCTIONS   193 For Chimney's sake they all Sir Pool obey'd,
P. 174 LOYALL SCOT   94 Never for Burnetts sake the Lauderdales,
P. 174 LOYALL SCOT   95 For Becketts sake Kent alwayes shall have
                         tails.
P. 203 HISTORICALL   102 Fond Eve did for this subtle Tempters sake

salamander   frequency: 1   relative frequency: 0.0000
    P. 137 HOUSEWARMING   8 And nestles in flames like the Salamander.

sale   frequency: 1   relative frequency: 0.0000
    P. 201 HISTORICALL   34 The new got flemish Towne was sett to sale.

sales   frequency: 1   relative frequency: 0.0000
    P. 174 LOYALL SCOT   93 Never shall Calvin Pardoned bee for Sales,

sallied. See "sally'd."

sally'd   frequency: 1   relative frequency: 0.0000
    P.   4 LOVELACE   40 Sally'd, and would in his defence contest.

salmon-fishers   frequency: 1   relative frequency: 0.0000
    P.   83 A. HOUSE   769 But now the Salmon-Fishers moist

salmons   frequency: 1   relative frequency: 0.0000
    P.   73 A. HOUSE   479 How Salmons trespassing are found;

salomon   frequency: 1   relative frequency: 0.0000
    P. 145 INSTRUCTIONS   199 Sir Frederick and Sir Salomon draw Lotts

salt   frequency: 2   relative frequency: 0.0000
    P. 141 INSTRUCTIONS   32 But Fortune chose him for her pleasure salt.
    P. 174 LOYALL SCOT   125 And surplic'd shew like Pillars too of salt.

saltes   frequency: 1   relative frequency: 0.0000
    P. 316 CHEQUER INN   169 Candlesticks, Forkes, Saltes Plates Spoones
                                     Knives

saltpeter. See "peeter."

salts. See "saltes."

salute   frequency: 6   relative frequency: 0.0001
    P.   57 BILL-BOROW   30 When they salute it from the Mast!
    P.   68 A. HOUSE   299 And to salute their Governess
    P. 109 ANNIVERSARY   267 Who with mistaken Course salute the Sand,
    P. 114 BLAKE   20 With English Streamers, should salute their
                                     sight:
    P. 154 INSTRUCTIONS   568 So at the first Salute resolves Retreat,
    P. 161 INSTRUCTIONS   836 Salute them, smiling at their vain design.

saluted   frequency: 1   relative frequency: 0.0000
    P. 115 BLAKE   70 That place saluted, where they all must dye.

salutes   frequency: 1   relative frequency: 0.0000
    P. 192 TWO HORSES   33 And that the two Jades after mutuall Salutes

same   frequency: 25   relative frequency: 0.0005
    P.   15 EYES   2 With the same Eyes to weep and see!
    P.   17 EYES   54 Till Eyes and Tears be the same things:
    P.   21 SOUL & BODY   16 (A Fever could but do the same.)
    P.   30 THE GALLERY   51 Where the same Posture, and the Look
    P.   82 A. HOUSE   765 Your lesser World contains the same.
    P.   84 FLECKNO   37 Now as two Instruments, to the same key
    P.   84 FLECKNO   43 Whose hungry Guts to the same streightness
                                     twin'd
    P.   90 ODE   119 The same Arts that did gain
    P.   98 HOLLAND   111 A Cock-boat tost with the same wind and fate;
    P. 103 ANNIVERSARY   18 In the same Posture would be found again.
    P. 107 ANNIVERSARY   154 The World by Sin, does by the same extend.
    P. 109 ANNIVERSARY   257 Thou with the same strength, and an Heart as
                                     plain,
    P. 111 ANNIVERSARY   316 With the same liberty as Points and Lace;
    P. 112 ANNIVERSARY   388 'And yet the same to be a King does scorn.
    P. 120 TWO SONGS   42 It is the same so you descend.
    P. 126 O.C.   147 What day should him eternize but the same
    P. 148 INSTRUCTIONS   307 Broken in Courage, yet the Men the same,
    P. 163 INSTRUCTIONS   929 And they, not knowing, the same thing propose,
    P. 177 LOYALL SCOT   244 Or whether the same vertue would reflect
    P. 177 LOYALL SCOT   245 From Scotch or English heart the same effect.
    P. 178 LOYALL SCOT   275 Thy death more noble did the same Extort.
    P. 181 MADE FREE   29 ('tis the same to be Crown'd)
    P. 195 TWO HORSES   144 W. The Same that the Froggs had of Jupiters
                                     Stork.
    P. 202 HISTORICALL   72 What sad events attended on the same
    P. 313 CHEQUER INN   13 The Host, that dwells in that same House

sampson   frequency: 1   relative frequency: 0.0000

P. 131 PARADISE   9 (So Sampson groap'd the Temples Posts in
                          spight)

samson. See "sampson."

sanctacruze   frequency: 3   relative frequency: 0.0000
    P. 113 BLAKE   t2 in the Bay of Sanctacruze, in the Island of
    P. 115 BLAKE   67 For Sanctacruze the glad Fleet takes her way,
    P. 116 BLAKE   100 With winged speed, for Sanctacruze does make.

sanctity   frequency: 2   relative frequency: 0.0000
    P. 64 A. HOUSE   166 'Will straight grow Sanctity when here:
    P. 65 A. HOUSE   203 'Is this that Sanctity so great,

sanctuary   frequency: 1   relative frequency: 0.0000
    P. 74 A. HOUSE   482 Take Sanctuary in the Wood;

sand   frequency: 3   relative frequency: 0.0000
    P. 72 A. HOUSE   437 Or, like the Desert Memphis Sand,
    P. 95 HOLLAND   2 As but th' Off-scouring of the Brittish Sand;
    P. 109 ANNIVERSARY 267 Who with mistaken Course salute the Sand,

sands   frequency: 3   relative frequency: 0.0000
    P. 98 HOLLAND   106 Or intercept the Western golden Sands:
    P. 148 INSTRUCTIONS 301 The martial Standard Sands displaying, shows
    P. 174 LOYALL SCCT 98 Nothing, not Boggs, not Sands, not seas, not
                            Alpes

sands's   frequency: 1   relative frequency: 0.0000
    P. 169 ADVICE   46 And add new Beams to Sands's former Glory.

sandy   frequency: 1   relative frequency: 0.0000
    P. 127 O.C.   189 And where the sandy mountain Fenwick scal'd,

sandys   frequency: 1   relative frequency: 0.0000
    P. 316 CHEQUER INN 133 The Hanmers, Herberts, Sandys, Musgraves

santa cruz. See "sanctacruze."

saphir-winged   frequency: 1   relative frequency: 0.0000
    P. 80 A. HOUSE   680 Charm'd with the Saphir-winged Mist.

saracen   frequency: 1   relative frequency: 0.0000
    P. 204 HISTORICALL 122 This Saracen his Countryes freedom broke

sardanapalus   frequency: 1   relative frequency: 0.0000
    P. 195 TWO HORSES   134 I had rather Bare Nero than Sardanapalus.

sash   frequency: 1   relative frequency: 0.0000
    P. 167 KINGS VOWES 49 I will have a fine Tunick a Sash and a Vest,

sat   frequency: 2   relative frequency: 0.0000
    See also "sate."
    P. 96 HOLLAND   30 And sat not as a Meat but as a Guest;
    P. 141 INSTRUCTIONS 26 And he sat smiling how his Dog did grinn.

satan's   frequency: 1   relative frequency: 0.0000
    P. 148 INSTRUCTIONS 302 St. Dunstan in it, tweaking Satan's Nose.

sate   frequency: 8   relative frequency: 0.0001
    P. 139 HOUSEWARMING 83 Who sate heretofore at the King's Receipt;
    P. 153 INSTRUCTIONS 511 Often, dear Painter, have I sate and mus'd
    P. 168 ADVICE   3 There holy Charles, here good Aurelius Sate,
    P. 168 ADVICE   20 Sate by the worst Attorney of the Nacion,
    P. 169 ADVICE   31 At Arlingtons, and round about it sate
    P. 169 ADVICE   47 Draw our Olimpia next in Councell Sate
    P. 314 CHEQUER INN 79 And next him sate George Mountague
    P. 316 CHEQUER INN 151 The Host that sate at Lower end

satire. See "satyr."

satisfied. See "satisfy'd."

satisfy'd   frequency: 1   relative frequency: 0.0000
    P. 86 FLECKNO   118 Who satisfy'd with eating, but not tame

saturn   frequency: 1   relative frequency: 0.0000
    P. 103 ANNIVERSARY 16 Longer, and more Malignant then Saturn:

satyr   frequency: 3   relative frequency: 0.0000
    P. 87 FLECKNO   160 Home, his most furious Satyr to have fir'd

P. 172 LOYALL SCOT   14 As of his Satyr this had been a part.
P. 178 LOYALL SCOT   276 My former satyr for this verse forget,

sauce. See "sawce."

saul   frequency: 1   relative frequency: 0.0000
    P. 205 HISTORICALL   167 From Saul the Land of Promise thus was rent,

sauls   frequency: 1   relative frequency: 0.0000
    P. 185 BRITANNIA   49 Sauls stormy rage and Check his black disease,

savage   frequency: 2   relative frequency: 0.0000
    P. 108 ANNIVERSARY   202 Or Rock so savage, but it mourn'd for thee:
    P. 204 HISTORICALL   124 This is the Savage Pimp without dispute

sav'd   frequency: 2   relative frequency: 0.0000
    P. 149 INSTRUCTIONS   362 That Peace secur'd, and Money might be sav'd.
    P. 174 LOYALL SCOT   121 A shorter Way's to bee by Clergie sav'd.

save   frequency: 12   relative frequency: 0.0002
    P. 31 FAIR SINGER   8 My dis-intangled Soul it self might save,
    P. 39 THE MATCH   20 To save him from the cold.
    P. 83 FLECKNO   13 Save that th' ingenious Door did as you come
    P. 84 FLECKNO   49 He never feeds; save only when he tryes
    P. 86 FLECKNO   130 Save only two foul copies for his shirt:
    P. 138 HOUSEWARMING   26 And all for to save the expences of Brickbat,
    P. 157 INSTRUCTIONS   671 That precious life he yet disdains to save,
    P. 172 LOYALL SCOT   37 That precious life hee yet disdaines to save
    P. 188 BRITANNIA   133 Rawl: Once more, great Queen, thy darling try
                                    to save;
    P. 188 BRITANNIA   140 'Tis god-like-good to save a falling King.
    P. 315 CHEQUER INN   91 But King (God save him) tho' so cram'd
    P. 316 CHEQUER INN   166 And for to save the Serving Men,

saving   frequency: 1   relative frequency: 0.0000
    P. 110 ANNIVERSARY   278 Saving himself he does their loss prevent.

saviours   frequency: 1   relative frequency: 0.0000
    P. 14 THE CORONET   3 My Saviours head have crown'd,

saw   frequency: 19   relative frequency: 0.0003
    P.   5 HASTINGS   57 All he had try'd, but all in vain, he saw,
    P. 15 EYES   19 And yet, from all the flow'rs I saw,
    P. 28 LOVER   21 No Day he saw but that which breaks,
    P. 85 FLECKNO   96 But himself there clos'd in a Scabbard saw
    P. 87 FLECKNO   158 But saw with sad dispair that 'twas too late.
    P. 90 MAY'S DEATH   10 He saw near hand, as he imagin'd Ares.
    P. 96 HOLLAND   31 And oft the Tritons and the Sea-Nymphs saw
    P. 109 ANNIVERSARY   252 And Is'rel silent saw him rase the Tow'r;
    P. 113 BLAKE   13 For now upon the Main, themselves they saw,
    P. 119 TWO SONGS   13 The Shepheard, since he saw thine Eyes,
    P. 129 O.C.   247 I saw him dead, a leaden slumber lyes,
    P. 131 PARADISE   7 That he would ruine (for I saw him strong)
    P. 148 INSTRUCTIONS   320 The unpractis'd Saw lyes bury'd in its Dust;
    P. 155 INSTRUCTIONS   612 He saw seiz'd, and could give her no Relief!
    P. 156 INSTRUCTIONS   641 And saw himself confin'd, like Sheep in Pen;
    P. 156 INSTRUCTIONS   643 But when the frightful Fire-ships he saw,
    P. 171 LOYALL SCOT   2 Saw Douglass Marching on the Elisian Glades,
    P. 172 LOYALL SCOT   10 Hee Judg'd more Clearly now and saw more plain.
    P. 316 CHEQUER INN   172 I saw no more but hither ran

sawce   frequency: 3   relative frequency: 0.0000
    P. 162 INSTRUCTIONS   874 And make a sawce fit for Whitehall's digestion:
    P. 175 LOYALL SCOT   142 Howere Insipid Yet the Sawce will mend 'em
    P. 315 CHEQUER INN   102 That Band with Sawce too dasht.

say   frequency: 20   relative frequency: 0.0004
    P. 18 CLORINDA   20 Pan met me. C. What did great Pan say?
    P. 23 NYMPH   61 And white, (shall I say then my hand?)
    P. 46 AMETAS   2 Whilst Thou still dost say me nay?
    P. 55 EPITAPH   9 To say she liv'd a Virgin chast,
    P. 58 BILL-BOROW   65 Much other Groves, say they, then these
    P. 84 FLECKNO   52 So hungry that though ready to say Mass
    P. 87 FLECKNO   156 To say that you read false Sir is no Lye.
    P. 116 BLAKE   103 Whose Fleet and Trenches view'd, he soon did
                                    say,
    P. 121 TWO SONGS   43 These Stars would say I do them wrong,
    P. 144 INSTRUCTIONS   147 Say Muse, for nothing can escape thy sight,
    P. 161 INSTRUCTIONS   858 Nor gave the Commons leave to say their
                                    Pray'rs:
    P. 178 LOYALL SCOT   254 Say but a Scot and streight wee fall to sides:

```
        P.  179 STOCKSMARKET      21 But a market, they say, does suit the king well,
        P.  179 STOCKSMARKET      24 Say his Majesty himself is bought too and sold.
        P.  192 TWO HORSES        18 When Shrines give Answers, say a knave 's in
                                     the Roode;
        P.  192 TWO HORSES        44 And the Kings wicked life say God there is
                                     none;
        P.  194 TWO HORSES       116 What hast thou to say of my Royall Rider?
        P.  196 TWO HORSES       172 As learned men say, came out of their breeches,
        P.  198 DUKE              30 Shall they presume to say that bread is bread,
        P.  198 DUKE              35 You and I say itt: therefore its the best.
```

saying   frequency: 1   relative frequency: 0.0000
```
        P.   71 A. HOUSE         407 But now, to make his saying true,
```

says.   See "saies."

scabbado   frequency: 1   relative frequency: 0.0000
```
        P.  188 BRITANNIA        127 The scotch scabbado of one Court, two Isles,
```

scabbard   frequency: 1   relative frequency: 0.0000
```
        P.   85 FLECKNO           96 But himself there clos'd in a Scabbard saw
```

scaffold   frequency: 3   relative frequency: 0.0000
```
        P.   88 ODE               54 The Tragick Scaffold might adorn:
        P.  180 STOCKSMARKET      34 That when to the scaffold your liege you had
                                     brought
        P.  194 TWO HORSES       119 Till at last on a Scaffold he was left in the
                                     lurch
```

scal'd   frequency: 1   relative frequency: 0.0000
```
        P.  127 O.C.             189 And where the sandy mountain Fenwick scal'd,
```

scale   frequency: 2   relative frequency: 0.0000
```
        P.   73 A. HOUSE         478 And Fishes do the Stables scale.
        P.   96 HOLLAND           22 To reach the Sea, then those to scale the Sky.
```

scales   frequency: 2   relative frequency: 0.0000
```
        P.   15 EYES              10 Within the Scales of either Eye,
        P.  185 BRITANNIA         36 In 's left the scales, in 's right hand plac'd
                                     the sword,
```

scalpes   frequency: 1   relative frequency: 0.0000
```
        P.  174 LOYALL SCOT       99 Seperate the world soe as the Bishops scalpes.
```

scalps.   See "scalpes."

scandal   frequency: 1   relative frequency: 0.0000
    See also "scandall."
```
        P.  180 STOCKSMARKET      29 But Sir Robert to take all the scandal away
```

scandall   frequency: 1   relative frequency: 0.0000
```
        P.  188 BRITANNIA        134 Rescue him again from scandall and the Grave.
```

scandalous   frequency: 2   relative frequency: 0.0000
```
        P.  179 STOCKSMARKET      25 This statue is surely more scandalous far
        P.  194 TWO HORSES        87 W. 'Tis they who brought on us the Scandalous
                                     Yoak
```

scandal's   frequency: 1   relative frequency: 0.0000
```
        P.  169 ADVICE            59 What Scandal's this! Temple, the wise, the
                                     Brave,
```

scant   frequency: 1   relative frequency: 0.0000
```
        P.   84 FLECKNO           55 Nor was I longer to invite him Scant:
```

scap'd   frequency: 1   relative frequency: 0.0000
```
        P.   81 A. HOUSE         720 She scap'd the safe, but roughest Way.
```

scape   frequency: 1   relative frequency: 0.0000
```
        P.  138 HOUSEWARMING      36 Nay scarce the Priests portion could scape from
                                     his hands.
```

scapeth   frequency: 1   relative frequency: 0.0000
```
        P.   71 A. HOUSE         412 And Chance o'retakes what scapeth spight?
```

scap't   frequency: 2   relative frequency: 0.0000
```
        P.   87 FLECKNO          168 As one scap't strangely from Captivity,
        P.  115 BLAKE             72 You scap't the Sea, to perish in your Port.
```

scaramouch.   See "scaramuchio."

scaramuchio   frequency: 1   relative frequency: 0.0000

```
           P. 190 STATUE          5 'Twere to Scaramuchio too great disrespect

scarce                            frequency:   14     relative frequency: 0.0002
    P.  12 DROP OF DEW           10 Scarce touching where it lyes,
    P.  34 DAPHNIS               37 As the Soul of cne scarce dead,
    P.  60 A. HOUSE             50 And scarce indures the Master great:
    P.  95 HCLLAND               1 Holland, that scarce deserves the name of Land,
    P. 118 BLAKE               135 Scarce souls frcm bodies sever'd are so far,
    P. 138 HOUSEWARMING         36 Nay scarce the Priests portion could scape from
                                    his hands.
    P. 146 INSTRUCTIONS        210 Scarce them their Leaders, they their Leaders
                                    knew.
    P. 154 INSTRUCTIONS        575 For whose strong bulk Earth scarce could Timber
                                    find,
    P. 156 INSTRUCTIONS        635 Scarce can burnt Iv'ry feign an Hair so black,
    P. 168 ADVICE               14 Whose life does scarce one Generous Action own,
    P. 180 STOCKSMARKET         52 They will scarce afford him a rag to his breech.
    P. 193 TWO HORSES           54 And scarce a wise man at a long Councell board;
    P. 204 HISTORICALL         132 In our weal-publik scarce one thing succeeds--
    P. 316 CHEQUER INN         146 That scarce the Lady cou'd edge in

scare                             frequency:    1     relative frequency: 0.0000
    P. 202 HISTORICALL          65 Lockes as one sett up for to scare the Crows.

scarlet                           frequency:    1     relative frequency: 0.0000
    P. 205 HISTORICALL         171 Thus said the Scarlet Whore tc her gallant,

scars                             frequency:    1     relative frequency: 0.0000
    P.  88 ODE                  46 Where his were not the deepest Scars?

scatter'd                         frequency:    3     relative frequency: 0.0000
    P.  77 A. HOUSE            577 Out of these scatter'd Sibyls Leaves
    P. 103 ANNIVERSARY          13 'Tis he the force of scatter'd Time contracts,
    P. 146 INSTRUCTIONS        241 A scatter'd Body, which the Foe ne'r try'd,

scatteringly                      frequency:    1     relative frequency: 0.0000
    P.  11 DIALOGUE             52 Which scatteringly doth shine,

scene                             frequency:   10     relative frequency: 0.0002
    P.  41 DAMON                 4 The Scene more fit for his complaint.
    P.  71 A. HOUSE            385 No Scene that turns with Engines strange
    P.  72 A. HOUSE            441 This Scene again withdrawing brings
    P.  80 A. HOUSE            679 And Men the silent Scene assist,
    P.  88 ODE                  58 Upon that memorable Scene:
    P. 115 BLAKE                65 But whilst I draw that Scene, where you ere
                                    long,
    P. 168 ADVICE                2 And draw me in cne Scene London and Rome,
    P. 168 ADVICE               11 Then change the scene and let the next present
    P. 180 STOCKSMARKET         41 Methinks by the equipage of this vile scene
    P. 186 BRITANNIA            59 Whilst in truthes Mirror this Glad scene he
                                    spy'd,

scenes                            frequency:    2     relative frequency: 0.0000
    P. 131 PARADISE             22 To change in Scenes, and show it in a Play.
    P. 170 PROPHECY             16 Within the Curtains and behind the Scenes,

scent                             frequency:    1     relative frequency: 0.0000
    P. 143 INSTRUCTIONS         95 And washing (lest the scent her Crime disclose)

scepter                           frequency:    4     relative frequency: 0.0000
    P. 104 ANNIVERSARY          42 And with vain Scepter, strike the hourly Bell;
    P. 110 ANNIVERSARY         297 That their new King might the fifth Scepter
                                    shake,
    P. 139 HOUSEWARMING         92 Where you are tc expect the Scepter and Crown.
    P. 188 BRITANNIA           152 To this firm Law their scepter did resign:

schisme                           frequency:    1     relative frequency: 0.0000
    P.  97 HOLLAND              72 Staple of Sects and Mint of Schisme grew;

scholar. See "scholler."

scholler                          frequency:    1     relative frequency: 0.0000
    P. 199 DUKE                 71 Although no schcller, yet can act the cooke:

scoff                             frequency:    1     relative frequency: 0.0000
    P. 150 INSTRUCTIONS        399 Bab May and Arlington did wisely scoff,

sconce                            frequency:    1     relative frequency: 0.0000
    P. 118 BLAKE               149 Our Cannon now tears every Ship and Sconce,

sconces                           frequency:    1     relative frequency: 0.0000
```

        P. 116 BLAKE   91 Forts, Lines, and Sconces all the Bay along,

scope   frequency: 1   relative frequency: 0.0000
        P. 88 ODE   50 He wove a Net of such a scope,

scorching   frequency: 2   relative frequency: 0.0000
        P. 41 DAMON   6 But scorching like his am'rous Care.
        P. 42 DAMON   24 But Juliana's scorching beams.

scor'd   frequency: 1   relative frequency: 0.0000
        P. 316 CHEQUER INN   137 On Chequer Tally was scor'd up

score   frequency: 2   relative frequency: 0.0000
        P. 141 INSTRUCTIONS   15 Or if to score out our compendious Fame,
        P. 182 MADE FREE   45 He wou'd run on the score and borrow;

scorn   frequency: 11   relative frequency: 0.0002
        P. 112 ANNIVERSARY   388 'And yet the same to be a King does scorn.
        P. 119 TWO SONGS   8 Nor scorn Endymions plaints to hear.
        P. 132 PARADISE   45 Well mightst thou scorn thy Readers to allure
        P. 143 INSTRUCTIONS   89 Fears lest he scorn a Woman once assay'd,
        P. 158 INSTRUCTIONS   736 Was led about in sport, the publick scorn.
        P. 160 INSTRUCTIONS   800 To lavish the King's Money more would scorn.
        P. 187 BRITANNIA   89 And they will fear those powers they once did
                                    scorn.
        P. 187 BRITANNIA   113 My reverend head expos'd to scorn and shame,
        P. 189 BRITANNIA   167 Tell em the Generous scorn their Rise to owe
        P. 189 BRITANNIA   169 Teach 'em to scorn the Carwells, Pembrookes,
                                    Nells,
        P. 193 TWO HORSES   65 Ch. And our few ships abroad become Tripoly's
                                    scorn

scorn'd   frequency: 4   relative frequency: 0.0000
        P. 82 A. HOUSE   754 Shall now be scorn'd as obsolete;
        P. 142 INSTRUCTIONS   76 And her self scorn'd for emulous Denham's Face;
        P. 164 INSTRUCTIONS   960 Nor of a Peasant scorn'd to learn the way.
        P. 188 BRITANNIA   135 Present to his thought his long scorn'd
                                    Parliament

scorning   frequency: 1   relative frequency: 0.0000
        P. 202 HISTORICALL   44 Scorning the persuit of such recreant foes.

scorns   frequency: 1   relative frequency: 0.0000
        P. 143 INSTRUCTIONS   94 Nor scorns to rub him down with those fair
                                    Hands;

scot   frequency: 4   relative frequency: 0.0000
    See also "scott."
        P. 157 INSTRUCTIONS   696 Our English youth shall sing the Valiant Scot.
        P. 171 LOYALL SCOT   t1 The Loyall Scot.
        P. 178 LOYALL SCOT   254 Say but a Scot and streight wee fall to sides:
        P. 200 DUKE   87 Jermyne, Fitzgerald, Loftus, Porter, Scot.

scotch   frequency: 11   relative frequency: 0.0002
        P. 138 HOUSEWARMING   41 The Scotch Forts <and> Dunkirk, but that they
                                    were sold,
        P. 171 PROPHECY   39 When an old Scotch Covenanter shall be
        P. 173 LOYALL SCOT   69 Noe more discourse of Scotch or English Race
        P. 174 LOYALL SCOT   90 Noe Scotch was ever like a Bishops feud.
        P. 176 LOYALL SCOT   186 Strange was the Sight the scotch Twin headed
                                    man
        P. 176 LOYALL SCOT   198 Well that Scotch monster and our Bishops sort
        P. 177 LOYALL SCOT   243 Which stronger were, a Scotch or English vice,
        P. 177 LOYALL SCOT   245 From Scotch or English heart the same effect.
        P. 178 LOYALL SCOT   261 English and Scotch, 'tis all but Crosse and
                                    Pile
        P. 178 LOYALL SCOT   285 Metemsicosd to some Scotch Presbyter.
        P. 188 BRITANNIA   127 The scotch scabbado of one Court, two Isles,

scotland   frequency: 3   relative frequency: 0.0000
        P. 173 LOYALL SCOT   76 Where Nature Scotland doth from England part.
        P. 177 LOYALL SCOT   252 Scotland and England cause of Just uproar!
        P. 204 HISTORICALL   120 Sets up in Scotland alamode de France,

scots   frequency: 1   relative frequency: 0.0000
        P. 187 BRITANNIA   106 Of French, Scots, Irish (all my mortall foes):

scott   frequency: 2   relative frequency: 0.0000
        P. 173 LOYALL SCOT   62 Our English youth shall sing the valiant Scott.
        P. 198 DUKE   18 Manag'd by wise Fitzgerard and by Scott,

scottish   frequency: 4   relative frequency: 0.0000

P. 184 BRITANNIA   5 No more of Scottish race thou wouldst complain;
P. 185 BRITANNIA   39 The Bloody scottish Chronicle turnd o're
P. 188 BRITANNIA   153 And shall this stinking Scottish brood evade
P. 195 TWO HORSES   136 Under all that shall Reign of the false
                           Scottish race.

scourges   frequency: 1   relative frequency: 0.0000
    P. 195 TWO HORSES   128 Between the two Scourges wee find little odds.

scouring. See "off-scouring."

scratching   frequency: 1   relative frequency: 0.0000
    P. 164 INSTRUCTIONS   978 As scratching Courtiers undermine a Realm:

screeching   frequency: 1   relative frequency: 0.0000
    P. 111 ANNIVERSARY   333 And Owls and Ravens with their screeching noyse

screen. See "skreen."

scrip   frequency: 1   relative frequency: 0.0000
    P. 153 INSTRUCTIONS   503 These can, at need, at instant, with a scrip,

scripture   frequency: 2   relative frequency: 0.0000
    P. 152 INSTRUCTIONS   453 To prove by Scripture, Treaty does imply
    P. 205 HISTORICALL   169 The holy Scripture vindicates his Cause,

scriptures   frequency: 1   relative frequency: 0.0000
    P. 111 ANNIVERSARY   315 You who the Scriptures and the Laws deface

scrivener   frequency: 1   relative frequency: 0.0000
    P. 194 TWO HORSES   110 W. To Cuckold a Scrivener mine's in
                               Masquerade.

scutcheon   frequency: 1   relative frequency: 0.0000
    P. 18 CLORINDA   3 C. I have a grassy Scutcheon spy'd,

scythe. See "sith," "sithe," "sythe."

sea   frequency: 25   relative frequency: 0.0005
    P. 27 LOVER   17 The Sea him lent these bitter Tears
    P. 71 A. HOUSE   390 Walking on foot through a green Sea.
    P. 72 A. HOUSE   434 Like a calm Sea it shews the Rocks:
    P. 73 A. HOUSE   468 (What it but seem'd before) a Sea.
    P. 95 HOLLAND   7 This indigested vomit of the Sea
    P. 96 HOLLAND   22 To reach the Sea, then those to scale the Sky.
    P. 98 HOLLAND   114 Cause why their Burgomaster of the Sea
    P. 98 HOLLAND   122 While the Sea laught it self into a foam,
    P. 105 ANNIVERSARY   72 That Island, which the Sea cannot devour:
    P. 109 ANNIVERSARY   265 So have I seen at Sea, when whirling Winds,
    P. 112 ANNIVERSARY   368 'Whose Navies hold the Sluces of the Sea.
    P. 115 BLAKE   72 You scap't the Sea, to perish in your Port.
    P. 118 BLAKE   134 Whilst others lower, in the Sea do lye.
    P. 118 BLAKE   151 Their Gallions sunk, their wealth the Sea does
                               fill,
    P. 118 BLAKE   156 And the Land owe her peace unto the Sea.
    P. 118 BLAKE   161 All the Foes Ships destroy'd, by Sea or fire,
    P. 127 O.C.   190 The sea between, yet hence his pray'r prevail'd.
    P. 152 INSTRUCTIONS   459 But, would they not be argu'd back from Sea,
    P. 153 INSTRUCTIONS   504 (This lik'd him best) his Cash beyond Sea whip.
    P. 154 INSTRUCTIONS   561 Sprag there, the practic'd in the Sea command,
    P. 155 INSTRUCTIONS   587 Engine so slight to guard us from the Sea,
    P. 159 INSTRUCTIONS   754 As the sad Tortoise for the Sea does groan.
    P. 160 INSTRUCTIONS   785 Pett, the Sea Architect, in making Ships,
    P. 181 MADE FREE   19 Beyond Sea he began,
    P. 187 BRITANNIA   126 His French and Teagues comand on sea and shoar.

sea-battel   frequency: 1   relative frequency: 0.0000
    P. 138 HOUSEWARMING   35 What Joseph by Famine, he wrought by
                               Sea-Battel;

sea-born   frequency: 1   relative frequency: 0.0000
    P. 64 A. HOUSE   180 'The Sea-born Amber we compose;

sea-cod   frequency: 1   relative frequency: 0.0000
    P. 146 INSTRUCTIONS   222 To rescue Albemarle from the Sea-Cod:

sea-command   frequency: 1   relative frequency: 0.0000
    P. 159 INSTRUCTIONS   757 To see that fatal Pledge of Sea-Command,

sea-march   frequency: 1   relative frequency: 0.0000
    P. 154 INSTRUCTIONS   550 Sound the Sea-march, and guide to Sheppy Isle.

```
sea-monsters                    frequency:    1    relative frequency: 0.0000
    P.   17 BERMUDAS         9 Where he the huge Sea-Monsters wracks,

sea-nuptials                    frequency:    1    relative frequency: 0.0000
    P.   98 HOLLAND        136 Doth yearly their Sea-Nuptials restore.

sea-nymphs                      frequency:    1    relative frequency: 0.0000
    P.   96 HOLLAND         31 And oft the Tritons and the Sea-Nymphs saw

seal                            frequency:    4    relative frequency: 0.0000
    P.   44 DAMON           84 The Blood I stanch, and Wound I seal.
    P.  139 HOUSEWARMING    65 Straight Judges, Priests, Bishops, true sons
                              of the Seal,
    P.  142 INSTRUCTIONS    41 He needs no Seal, but to St. James's lease,
    P.  168 KINGS VOWES     63 Under my hand and Seal shall have Indemnity.

seals                           frequency:    1    relative frequency: 0.0000
    P.  187 BRITANNIA      124 False Finch, Knave Anglesey misguide the
                              seals;

seal's                          frequency:    1    relative frequency: 0.0000
    P.  171 PROPHECY        35 When the Seal's given to a talking fool

seamen                          frequency:    5    relative frequency: 0.0001
    P.   57 BILL-BOBOW      29 How glad the weary Seamen hast
    P.  154 INSTRUCTIONS   541 Among the Shrowds the Seamen sit and sing,
    P.  155 INSTRUCTIONS   601 Our Seamen, whom no Dangers shape could fright,
    P.  158 INSTRUCTIONS   731 The Seamen search her all, within, without:
    P.  159 INSTRUCTIONS   777 Who all our Seamen cheated of their Debt?

seamens                         frequency:    2    relative frequency: 0.0000
    P.  109 ANNIVERSARY    266 Hurry the Bark, but more the Seamens minds,
    P.  148 INSTRUCTIONS   313 The Seamens Clamour to three ends they use;

seams                           frequency:    1    relative frequency: 0.0000
    P.  108 ANNIVERSARY    214 Break up each Deck, and rip the Oaken seams.

sear                            frequency:    1    relative frequency: 0.0000
    P.   42 DAMON           10 Which thus our Sun-burn'd Meadows sear!

search                          frequency:    2    relative frequency: 0.0000
    P.   89 ODE             93 She, having kill'd, no more does search,
    P.  158 INSTRUCTIONS   731 The Seamen search her all, within, without:

search'd                        frequency:    1    relative frequency: 0.0000
    P.   41 THE MOWER       17 Another World was search'd, through Oceans new,

seas                            frequency:   19    relative frequency: 0.0003
    P.   17 BERMUDAS        27 And makes the hollow Seas, that roar,
    P.   27 LOVER            9 'Twas in a Shipwrack, when the Seas
    P.   32 MOURNING        30 That sink for Pearl through Seas profound,
    P.   49 THE GARDEN      46 Far other Worlds, and other Seas;
    P.   69 A. HOUSE       323 Thou Paradise of four Seas,
    P.   98 HOLLAND        132 And, like its own Seas, only Ebbs to flow.
    P.  107 ANNIVERSARY    157 Hence landing Nature to new Seas is tost,
    P.  108 ANNIVERSARY    212 And to deaf Seas, and ruthless Tempests mourns,
    P.  116 BLAKE          102 Ore Seas as vast as is the Spaniards pride.
    P.  120 TWO SONGS       21 Rather restrain these double Seas,
    P.  125 O.C.           106 As hollow Seas with future Tempests rage:
    P.  127 O.C.           167 Stand back ye Seas, and shrunk beneath the vail
    P.  130 O.C.           281 As long as rivers to the seas shall runne,
    P.  130 O.C.           289 Despoyl'd of mortall robes, in seas of blisse,
    P.  155 INSTRUCTIONS   578 That rul'd all Seas, and did our Channel grace.
    P.  159 INSTRUCTIONS   762 And female Stewart, there, Rules the four
                              Seas.
    P.  166 KINGS VOWES     19 I will have a fine Navy to Conquer the Seas,
    P.  174 LOYALL SCOT     98 Nothing, not Boggs, not Sands, not seas, not
                              Alpes
    P.  193 TWO HORSES      61 Ch. That of four Seas dominion and Guarding

seas'nable                      frequency:    1    relative frequency: 0.0000
    P.  147 INSTRUCTIONS   281 When, marching in, a seas'nable recruit

season                          frequency:    2    relative frequency: 0.0000
    P.  137 HOUSEWARMING     4 'Twas the season he thought to turn Architect.
    P.  162 INSTRUCTIONS   873 Well was he skill'd to season any question,

seasonable                      frequency:    1    relative frequency: 0.0000
    See also "seas'nable."
    P.  106 ANNIVERSARY    133 And then a seasonable People still

seat                            frequency:    8    relative frequency: 0.0001
```

```
        See also "seate."
        P.   67 A. HOUSE      273 At the demolishing, this Seat
        P.   70 A. HOUSE      365 As if it quarrell'd in the Seat
        P.   82 A. HOUSE      753 For you Thessalian Tempe's Seat
        P.   82 A. HOUSE      758 For 'twas the Seat of wanton Love;
        P.  131 O.C.          313 How he becomes that seat, how strongly streigns,
        P.  154 INSTRUCTIONS  567 The neighbr'hood ill, and an unwholesome seat.
        P.  179 STOCKSMARKET   19 And so loose in his seat that all men agree
        P.  186 BRITANNIA      81 Should drive them from their proud Celestiall
                                  seat,
```

```
seate                         frequency:    1   relative frequency: 0.0000
        P.  130 O.C.          275 But when death takes them from that envy'd seate,
```

```
seats                         frequency:    2   relative frequency: 0.0000
        P.   58 BILL-BOROW     77 Therefore to your obscurer Seats
        P.  145 INSTRUCTIONS  180 And bloated Wren conducts them to their seats.
```

```
seaven                        frequency:    2   relative frequency: 0.0000
        P.   84 FLECKNO        70 And swaddled in's own papers seaven times,
        P.   99 HOLLAND       137 And now the Hydra of seaven Provinces
```

```
seav'n                        frequency:    1   relative frequency: 0.0000
        P.   83 FLECKNO        11 Not higher then Seav'n, nor larger then three
                                  feet;
```

```
seclude                       frequency:    1   relative frequency: 0.0000
        P.  174 LOYALL SCOT    89 Nothing but Clergie cold us two seclude:
```

```
second                        frequency:    7   relative frequency: 0.0001
        P.   42 DAMON          16 Now glitters in its second skin.
        P.  121 TWO SONGS      t5 Second Song.
        P.  152 INSTRUCTIONS  458 The second Coventry the Cavalier.
        P.  171 PROPHECY      34+ Second Part.
        P.  176 LOYALL SCOT   197 Doth Charles the second rain or Charles the
                                  two?
        P.  177 LOYALL SCOT   225 The second time to Ravish Proserpine.
        P.  202 HISTORICALL    52 And with the Dutch a second Warr renews.
```

```
secrecy                       frequency:    1   relative frequency: 0.0000
        P.  112 ANNIVERSARY   381 'He Secrecy with Number hath inchas'd,
```

```
secret                        frequency:    9   relative frequency: 0.0001
        See also "secrett."
        P.   54 THYESTE         4 Settled in some secret Nest
        P.  124 O.C.           56 The sad Root pines in secret under ground.
        P.  125 O.C.          101 A secret Cause does sure those Signs ordain
        P.  153 INSTRUCTIONS  495 His minion Imps that, in his secret part,
        P.  157 INSTRUCTIONS  675 And secret Joy, in his calm Soul does rise,
        P.  162 INSTRUCTIONS  897 And silent tears her secret anguish speak,
        P.  163 INSTRUCTIONS  931 Through their feign'd speech their secret hearts
                                  he knew;
        P.  178 LOYALL SCOT   265 Knowes the last secret how to make them one.
        P.  189 BRITANNIA     193 And this kind secret for reward shall give:
```

```
secretaries.  See "secretaryes."
```

```
secretary                     frequency:    1   relative frequency: 0.0000
        P.  195 TWO HORSES    155 Ch. Yet have wee one Secretary honest and wise:
```

```
secretaryes                   frequency:    1   relative frequency: 0.0000
        P.  166 KINGS VOWES    36 I will have two fine Secretaryes pisse thro one
                                  Quill.
```

```
secretly                      frequency:    1   relative frequency: 0.0000
        P.  144 INSTRUCTIONS  123 So therefore secretly for Peace decrees,
```

```
secrett                       frequency:    1   relative frequency: 0.0000
        P.  172 LOYALL SCOT    41 And secrett Joy in his own soul doth Rise
```

```
section                       frequency:    1   relative frequency: 0.0000
        P.   27 LOVER          16 In a Cesarian Section.
```

```
sects                         frequency:    1   relative frequency: 0.0000
        P.   97 HOLLAND        72 Staple of Sects and Mint of Schisme grew;
```

```
secur'd                       frequency:    1   relative frequency: 0.0000
        P.  149 INSTRUCTIONS  362 That Peace secur'd, and Money might be sav'd.
```

```
secure                        frequency:   11   relative frequency: 0.0002
        P.    4 LOVELACE       47 But he secure of glory and of time
```

```
P.  39 THE MATCH        8 All as she thought secure.
P. 106 ANNIVERSARY    130 Gnashes her Goary teeth; nor there secure.
P. 132 PARADISE        46 With tinkling Rhime, of thy own Sense secure;
P. 151 INSTRUCTIONS   412 More tim'rous now we are, than first secure.
P. 156 INSTRUCTIONS   618 Secure so oft he had this Foe defy'd:
P. 157 INSTRUCTIONS   668 Within its circle, knows himself secure.
P. 158 INSTRUCTIONS   733 Then with rude shouts, secure, the Air they vex;
P. 163 INSTRUCTIONS   913 His mind secure does the known stroke repeat,
P. 172 LOYALL SCOT     34 Within its Circle knows himselfe secure.
P. 193 TWO HORSES      64 Not our trade to secure but foes to come at 'um,
```

securely   frequency: 3   relative frequency: 0.0000
```
P.  77 A. HOUSE       607 But I on it securely play,
P. 107 ANNIVERSARY    170 Hast born securely thine undaunted Head,
P. 155 INSTRUCTIONS   582 They sail securely through the Rivers track.
```

securer   frequency: 1   relative frequency: 0.0000
```
P.  56 BILL-BOROW      16 Which to securer Glory lead.
```

secures   frequency: 3   relative frequency: 0.0000
```
P.   5 HASTINGS        28 Secures his neerest and most lov'd Ally;
P. 115 BLAKE           51 By that alone those Islands she secures,
P. 194 TWO HORSES      92 Which Augments and secures his own profitt and
                          peace.
```

securing   frequency: 1   relative frequency: 0.0000
```
P. 120 TWO SONGS       24 Securing their Repose above.
```

security   frequency: 1   relative frequency: 0.0000
```
P. 187 BRITANNIA      121 Luld in security, rouling in lust,
```

sedge   frequency: 2   relative frequency: 0.0000
```
P.  79 A. HOUSE       642 My Temples here with heavy sedge;
P. 153 INSTRUCTIONS   527 Through the vain sedge the bashful Nymphs he
                          ey'd;
```

seduce   frequency: 1   relative frequency: 0.0000
```
P.  40 THE MOWER        2 Did after him the World seduce:
```

see   frequency: 84   relative frequency: 0.0017
```
P.   3 LOVELACE        15 I see the envious Caterpillar sit
P.   9 DIALOGUE         5 See where an Army, strong as fair,
P.  11 DIALOGUE        56 What Heavens are those we cannot see?
P.  11 DIALOGUE        70 And see the future Time:
P.  12 DROP OF DEW      1 I see how the Orient Dew,
P.  15 EYES            2 With the same Eyes to weep and see!
P.  16 EYES           26 That weep the more, and see the less:
P.  16 EYES           47 For others too can see, or sleep;
P.  23 NYMPH          60 I blusht to see its foot more soft,
P.  24 NYMPH          93 O help! O help! I see it faint:
P.  24 NYMPH          95 See how it weeps. The Tears do come
P.  25 YOUNG LOVE      5 Pretty surely 'twere to see
P.  28 LOVER          49 See how he nak'd and fierce does stand,
P.  33 DAPHNIS        24 As to see he might be blest.
P.  37 DEFINITION     13 For Fate with jealous Eye does see
P.  38 PICTURE         1 I see with what simplicity
P.  38 PICTURE        14 See his Bow broke and Ensigns torn.
P.  38 PICTURE        24 Where I may see thy Glories from some shade.
P.  39 PICTURE        39 And, ere we see,
P.  41 THE MOWER      22 Forbidden mixtures there to see.
P.  43 DAMON          59 In which I see my Picture done,
P.  45 MOWER'S SONG    4 Did see its Hopes as in a Glass;
P.  48 THE GARDEN      3 And their uncessant Labours see
P.  56 BILL-BOROW      1 See how the arched Earth does here
P.  57 BILL-BOROW     17 See what a soft access and wide
P.  57 BILL-BOROW     21 See then how courteous it ascends,
P.  62 A. HOUSE       98 'Live innocently as you see.
P.  63 A. HOUSE      141 'I see the Angels in a Crown
P.  65 A. HOUSE      194 'Of Joys you see, and may make more!
P.  68 A. HOUSE      309 See how the Flow'rs, as at Parade,
P.  70 A. HOUSE      377 To see Men through this Meadow Dive,
P.  76 A. HOUSE      567 Or turn me but, and you shall see
P.  77 A. HOUSE      585 And see how Chance's better Wit
P.  78 A. HOUSE      633 See in what wanton harmless folds
P.  79 A. HOUSE      657 See how loose Nature, in respect
P.  79 A. HOUSE      663 And lest She see him go to Bed;
P.  85 FLECKNO        89 I answer'd he is here Sir; but you see
P.  86 FLECKNO       132 But how I loath'd to see my Neighbour glean
P.  89 ODE            74 To see themselves in one Year tam'd:
P.  91 MAY'S DEATH    51 Foul Architect that hadst not Eye to see
P.  92 MAY'S DEATH    79 Who laughs to see in this thy death renew'd,
```

P.	94	DR. WITTY	33	I see the people hastning to thy Book,
P.	94	DR. WITTY	35	And so disliking, that they nothing see
P.	96	HOLLAND	43	Not who first see the rising Sun commands,
P.	97	HCLLAND	85	See but their Mairmaids with their Tails of Fish,
P.	107	ANNIVERSARY	161	Whose Saint-like Mother we did lately see
P.	108	ANNIVERSARY	195	See how they each his towring Crest abate,
P.	110	ANNIVERSARY	292	May shew their own, not see his Nakedness.
P.	111	ANNIVERSARY	326	See the bright Sun his shining Race pursue,
P.	111	ANNIVERSARY	339	Why did mine Eyes once see so bright a Ray;
P.	112	ANNIVERSARY	391	'O could I once him with our Title see,
P.	114	BLAKE	16	But much more fearful are your Flags to see.
P.	120	TWO SONGS	37	O why, as well as Eyes to see,
P.	126	O.C.	128	And hasten not to see his Death their own.
P.	127	O.C.	159	For whom the Elements we Mourners see,
P.	130	O.C.	291	There thy great soule at once a world does see,
P.	141	INSTRUCTIONS	3	But er'e thou fal'st to work, first Painter see
P.	141	INSTRUCTIONS	18	To see a Lowse brandish the white Staff.
P.	143	INSTRUCTIONS	93	Stript to her Skin, see how she stooping stands,
P.	148	INSTRUCTICNS	303	See sudden chance of War! To Paint or Write,
P.	149	INSTRUCTIONS	355	See how he Reigns in his new Palace culminant,
P.	157	INSTRUCTIONS	676	That Monk looks cn to see how Douglas dies.
P.	159	INSTRUCTIONS	757	To see that fatal Pledge of Sea-Command,
P.	164	INSTRUCTIONS	971	The Kingdom from the Crown distinct would see,
P.	165	KINGS VOWES	6	If ere I see England againe,
P.	168	ADVICE	4	Weeping to see their Scnns degenerate,
P.	170	PROPHECY	3	Fireballs shall flye and but few see the traine
P.	171	PROPHECY	31	London shall then see, for it will come to pass,
P.	171	PROPHECY	55	Then They with envious Eyes shall Belgium See
P.	172	LOYALL SCOT	42	That Monk lookes cn to see how Douglass dies.
P.	179	STOCKSMARKET	17	To see him so disfigured the herbwomen chide,
P.	182	MADE FREE	42	As if he shcu'd ne're see an end on't.
P.	184	MADE FREE	130	I see who e're is freed,
P.	192	TWO HORSES	36	To see a Lord Major and a Lumbard Street break,
P.	192	TWO HORSES	41	To see Church and state bow down to a whore
P.	192	TWO HORSES	43	W. To see dei Gratia writ on the Throne,
P.	193	TWO HORSES	53	Ch. To see a white staffe make a Beggar a Lord
P.	194	TWO HORSES	109	Where is thy King gone? Ch. To see Bishop Laud.
P.	199	DUKE	75	Letts see the nuntio Arundells sweete face;
P.	200	DUKE	98	Noe, Painter, noe; close up this peice and see
P.	200	DUKE	114	See in all ages what examples are
P.	204	HISTORICAIL	135	Let Cromwells Ghost smile with Contempt to see
P.	313	CHEQUER INN	10	Where I cou'd see 'em Crowding in
P.	314	CHEQUER INN	71	When noe one cculd see Sun betweene

seed   frequency: 1   relative frequency: 0.0000
P. 35 DAPHNIS   83 In one minute casts the Seed,

seeds   frequency: 2   relative frequency: 0.0000
P. 118 BLAKE   160 The certain seeds of many Wars are lost.
P. 314 CHEQUER INN   78 Frcm thence he brought his Seeds.

seeing   frequency: 4   relative frequency: 0.0000
See also "all-seeing."
P. 17 EYES   56 These weeping Eyes, those seeing Tears.
P. 38 PICTURE   29 Cf sweetness, seeing they are fair;
P. 90 MAY'S DEATH   19 But seeing May he varied streight his Song,
P. 130 O.C.   276 Seeing how little we confess, how greate;

seek   frequency: 10   relative frequency: 0.0002
P. 14 THE CORONET   4 I seek with Garlands to redress that Wrong:
P. 41 THE MOWER   13 The Tulip, white, did for complexion seek;
P. 42 DAMON   14 And Grass-hoppers seek out the shades.
P. 54 THYESTE   3 All I seek is tc lye still.
P. 65 A. HOUSE   197 Now Fairfax seek her promis'd faith:
P. 85 FLECKNO   94 Me a great favour, for I seek to go.
P. 91 MAY'S DEATH   43 Go seek the novice Statesmen, and obtrude
P. 117 BLAKE   106 And a third World seek out our Armes to shun.
P. 156 INSTRUCTIONS   653 His yellow Locks curl back themselves to seek,
P. 172 LOYALL SCOT   19 His shady locks Curl back themselves to seek

seeks   frequency: 2   relative frequency: 0.0000
P. 92 MAY'S DEATH   70 Seeks wretched good, arraigns successful Crimes.
P. 120 TWO SONGS   34 Seeks but the hcnour tc have held out longest.

seeling   frequency: 1   relative frequency: 0.0000
P. 83 FLECKNO   12 Only there was nor Seeling, nor a Sheet,

seem   frequency: 16   relative frequency: 0.0003

```
P.   10 DIALOGUE        31 Every thing does seem to vie
P.   16 EYES            44 But as they seem the Tears of Light.
P.   31 MOURNING         7 Seem bending upwards, to restore
P.   32 MOURNING        23 That whatsoever does but seem
P.   41 DAMON            3 While ev'ry thing did seem to paint
P.   58 BILL-BOROW      53 Hence they successes seem to know,
P.   63 A. HOUSE       149 'But can he such a Rival seem
P.   63 A. HOUSE       155 'And, if our Rule seem strictly pend,
P.   68 A. HOUSE       316 Seem to their Staves the Ensigns furl'd.
P.   71 A. HOUSE       389 Who seem like Israalites to be,
P.   73 A. HOUSE       457 They seem within the polisht Grass
P.   90 MAY'S DEATH     11 Such did he seem for corpulence and port,
P.  104 ANNIVERSARY     29 Their other Wars seem but a feign'd contest,
P.  107 ANNIVERSARY    163 That she might seem, could we the Fall dispute,
P.  149 INSTRUCTIONS   330 They with the first days proffer seem content:
P.  164 INSTRUCTIONS   952 And seem his Courtiers, are but his disease.
```

seem'd   frequency: 16   relative frequency: 0.0003
```
P.   23 NYMPH           43 Me to its game: it seem'd to bless
P.   24 NYMPH           84 Until its Lips ev'n seem'd to bleed:
P.   73 A. HOUSE       468 (What it but seem'd before) a Sea.
P.   83 FLECKNO         10 But seem'd a Coffin set on the Stairs head.
P.   96 HOLLAND         35 Nature, it seem'd, asham'd of her mistake,
P.  108 ANNIVERSARY    205 It seem'd the Earth did from the Center tear;
P.  108 ANNIVERSARY    206 It seem'd the Sun was faln out of the Sphere:
P.  111 ANNIVERSARY    344 Seem'd now a long and gloomy Night to threat,
P.  126 O.C.           133 Nature it seem'd with him would Nature vye;
P.  128 O.C.           197 Pity it seem'd to hurt him more that felt
P.  129 O.C.           234 It seem'd Mars broke through Janus' double
                          gate;
P.  138 HOUSEWARMING    30 None sollid enough seem'd for his Thong Caster;
P.  155 INSTRUCTIONS   588 It fitter seem'd to captivate a Flea.
P.  162 INSTRUCTIONS   902 Whose Beauty greater seem'd by her distress;
P.  164 INSTRUCTIONS   953 Through Optick Trunk the Planet seem'd to
                          hear,
P.  313 CHEQUER INN     12 They seem'd so well acquainted
```

seemed   frequency: 1   relative frequency: 0.0000
      See also "seem'd."
```
P.  173 LOYALL SCOT     74 And Joyn those Lands that seemed to part
                          before.
```

seemeth   frequency: 1   relative frequency: 0.0000
```
P.   72 A. HOUSE       419 In whose new Traverse seemeth wrought
```

seeming   frequency: 1   relative frequency: 0.0000
```
P.   91 MAY'S DEATH     55 But the nor Ignorance nor seeming good
```

seemly   frequency: 1   relative frequency: 0.0000
```
P.  161 INSTRUCTIONS   828 And Vest bespeaks to be more seemly clad.
```

seems   frequency: 14   relative frequency: 0.0002
```
P.   56 BILL-BOROW       7 It seems as for a Model laid,
P.   68 A. HOUSE       302 Seems with the Flow'rs a Flow'r to be.
P.   70 A. HOUSE       363 And at proud Cawood Castle seems
P.   70 A. HOUSE       368 Or innocently seems to gaze.
P.   74 A. HOUSE       498 It seems indeed as Wood not Trees:
P.   76 A. HOUSE       559 While the Oake seems to fall content,
P.   78 A. HOUSE       628 Seems as green Silks but newly washt.
P.   79 A. HOUSE       662 Seems to descend with greater Care;
P.  112 ANNIVERSARY    378 'And still his Sword seems hanging o're my head.
P.  112 ANNIVERSARY    387 'He seems a King by long Succession born,
P.  112 ANNIVERSARY    389 'Abroad a King he seems, and something more,
P.  145 INSTRUCTIONS   163 Still his Hook-shoulder seems the blow to dread,
P.  159 INSTRUCTIONS   768 His Name alone seems fit to answer all.
P.  314 CHEQUER INN     76 But was it seems with that intent
```

seen   frequency: 17   relative frequency: 0.0003
      See also "seene."
```
P.    4 LOVELACE        41 And one the loveliest that was yet e're seen,
P.   12 DROP OF DEW     21 Could it within the humane flow'r be seen,
P.   27 LOVER            3 Sorted by pairs, they still are seen
P.   48 THE GARDEN      17 No white nor red was ever seen
P.   58 BILL-BOROW      55 But in no Memory were seen
P.   62 A. HOUSE       117 'How should we grieve that must be seen,
P.   70 A. HOUSE       383 They bring up Flow'rs so to be seen,
P.   80 A. HOUSE       703 But, since She would not have them seen,
P.   85 FLECKNO         81 Each colour that he past by; and be seen,
P.   91 MAY'S DEATH     31 Rose more then ever he was seen severe,
P.  109 ANNIVERSARY    265 So have I seen at Sea, when whirling Winds,
P.  122 TWO SONGS       11 Let's not then at least be seen
```

P.	123	O.C.	4	Had seen the period of his golden Years:
P.	125	O.C.	89	So have I seen a Vine, whose lasting Age
P.	153	INSTRUCTIONS	526	And Beauties e're this never naked seen.
P.	154	INSTRUCTIONS	551	So have I seen in April's bud, arise
P.	184	BRITANNIA	3	Cubbs, didst thou call 'um? hadst thou seen this Brood

seene   frequency: 2   relative frequency: 0.0000
P. 199 DUKE   78 Let Belassis Autumnall face be seene,
P. 312 CHEQUER INN   2 Where I the Parli'ment have seene

s'eer   frequency: 1   relative frequency: 0.0000
P.   48 THE GARDEN   23 Fair Trees! where s'eer your barkes I wound,

sees   frequency: 6   relative frequency: 0.0001
P.   5 HASTINGS   50 The Golden Harvest, sees his Glasses leap.
P.   74 A. HOUSE   497 When first the Eye this Forrest sees
P.   98 HOLLAND   119 Yet of his vain Attempt no more he sees
P. 124 O.C.   49 Or with a Grandsire's joy her Children sees
P. 156 INSTRUCTIONS   625 But sees, inrag'd, the River flow between.
P. 178 LOYALL SCOT   266 Just soe the prudent Husbandman who sees

seest   frequency: 1   relative frequency: 0.0000
P.   18 CLORINDA   9 Seest thou that unfrequented Cave?

seige   frequency: 1   relative frequency: 0.0000
P. 119 BLAKE   163 His Seige of Spain he then again pursues,

seine   frequency: 1   relative frequency: 0.0000
See also "seyne."
P. 156 INSTRUCTIONS   655 Oft has he in chill Eske or Seine, by night,

seiz'd   frequency: 3   relative frequency: 0.0000
P. 155 INSTRUCTIONS   612 He saw seiz'd, and could give her no Relief!
P. 190 STATUE   8 The Mimick so legally seiz'd of Whitehall.
P. 193 TWO HORSES   55 W. That the bank should be seiz'd yet the Chequer so poor;

seize   frequency: 4   relative frequency: 0.0000
P.   18 CLORINDA   8 C. Seize the short Joyes then, ere they vade.
P. 123 O.C.   30 Eliza, Natures and his darling, seize.
P. 132 PARADISE   35 At once delight and horrour on us seize,
P. 152 INSTRUCTIONS   472 And wish'd himself the Gout, to seize his hand.

seldom   frequency: 2   relative frequency: 0.0000
P.   39 THE MATCH   9 She seldom them unlock'd, or us'd,
P. 125 O.C.   102 Fore boding Princes falls, and seldom vain.

self   frequency: 42   relative frequency: 0.0008
See also "selfe," "selve."
P.   11 DIALOGUE   67 What Friends, if to my self untrue?
P.   12 DROP OF DEW   6 Round in its self incloses:
P.   14 THE CORONET   10 Thinking (so I my self deceive)
P.   21 SOUL & BODY   25 And all my Care its self employes,
P.   22 NYMPH   37 Thenceforth I set my self to play
P.   23 NYMPH   44 Its self in me. How could I less
P.   23 NYMPH   79 Yet could not, till it self would rise,
P.   24 NYMPH   88 On Roses thus its self to fill:
P.   31 FAIR SINGER   8 My dis-intangled Soul it self might save,
P.   32 MOURNING   19 She courts her self in am'rous Rain;
P.   32 MOURNING   20 Her self both Danae and the Showr.
P.   33 DAPHNIS   13 Nature so her self does use
P.   37 DEFINITION   12 And alwaies crouds it self betwixt.
P.   38 PICTURE   26 It self does at thy Beauty charm,
P.   43 DAMON   63 And, when I tune my self to sing,
P.   57 BILL-BOROW   23 Nor for it self the height does gain,
P.   60 A. HOUSE   56 That in it self which him delights.
P.   63 A. HOUSE   156 'The Rule it self to you shall bend.
P.   73 A. HOUSE   471 The River in it self is drown'd,
P.   74 A. HOUSE   483 And, while it lasts, my self imbark
P.   78 A. HOUSE   631 Unless it self you will mistake,
P.   79 A. HOUSE   658 To her, it self doth recollect;
P.   81 A. HOUSE   709 Nor yet in those her self imployes
P.   81 A. HOUSE   727 And Goodness doth it self intail
P.   83 FLECKNO   23 But I, who now imagin'd my self brought
P.   87 FLECKNO   167 He hasted; and I, finding my self free,
P.   97 HOLLAND   67 Sure when Religion did it self imbark,
P.   98 HOLLAND   110 It self, when as some greater Vessel tows
P.   98 HOLLAND   122 While the Sea laught it self into a foam,
P. 108 ANNIVERSARY   204 As if that Natures self were overthrown.
P. 108 ANNIVERSARY   222 When to Command, thou didst thy self Depose;

```
         P. 108 ANNIVERSARY     227 Therefore thou rather didst thy Self depress,
         P. 109 ANNIVERSARY     263 Therefore first growing to thy self a Law,
         P. 123 O.C.              3 Now in its self (the Glass where all appears)
         P. 127 O.C.            160 And Heav'n it self would the great Herald be;
         P. 142 INSTRUCTIONS     51 She, nak'd, can Archimedes self put down,
         P. 142 INSTRUCTIONS     76 And her self scorn'd for emulous Denham's Face;
         P. 158 INSTRUCTIONS    706 The Tow'r it self with the near danger shook.
         P. 159 INSTRUCTIONS    761 The Court in Farthing yet it self does please,
         P. 171 PROPHECY         44 Make him self rich, his king and People bare,
         P. 174 LOYALL SCOT     111 A Bishops self is an Anathama.
         P. 187 BRITANNIA        88 Thus Heavens designs against heavens self youl
                                    turn
```

self-deluding   frequency: 1   relative frequency: 0.0000
```
         P.  15 EYES              5 And, since the Self-deluding Sight,
```

selfe   frequency: 1   relative frequency: 0.0000
```
         P.   3 LOVELACE         10 To honour not her selfe, but worthy men.
```

sell   frequency: 5   relative frequency: 0.0001
```
         P. 179 STOCKSMARKET     22 Who the Parliament buys and revenues does sell,
         P. 191 STATUE           46 To buy a King is not so wise as to sell,
         P. 315 CHEQUER INN     119 Should live to sell himself for Meate
         P. 315 CHEQUER INN     123 Before he'd sell the Nation,
         P. 317 CHEQUER INN     176 They sell us all our Barnes and Wives
```

selling   frequency: 3   relative frequency: 0.0000
```
         P. 139 HOUSEWARMING     71 Since the Act of Oblivion was never such
                                    selling,
         P. 193 TWO HORSES       84 For selling their Conscience were Liberally
                                    paid.
         P. 313 CHEQUER INN      34 And tho' by selling of Us all
```

sells   frequency: 1   relative frequency: 0.0000
```
         P. 202 HISTORICALL      48 He sells the Citty where 'twas sett on fire.
```

selve   frequency: 1   relative frequency: 0.0000
```
         P.  46 AMETAS           10 Which your selve and us delay:
```

selves   frequency: 4   relative frequency: 0.0000
```
         P.  40 THE MATCH        39 And have within our Selves possest
         P.  82 A. HOUSE        750 And in your kind your selves preferr;
         P.  97 HOLLAND          75 In vain for Catholicks our selves we bear;
         P. 108 ANNIVERSARY     219 We only mourn'd our selves, in thine Ascent,
```

senate   frequency: 5   relative frequency: 0.0001
```
         P.  92 MAY'S DEATH      81 Poor Poet thou, and grateful Senate they,
         P.  99 HOLLAND         143 Unless our Senate, lest their Youth disuse,
         P. 105 ANNIVERSARY      97 Which on the Basis of a Senate free,
         P. 144 INSTRUCTIONS    149 Who, in an English Senate, fierce debate,
         P. 202 HISTORICALL      74 The Senate which should headstrong Princes stay
```

sence   frequency: 4   relative frequency: 0.0000
```
         P.  33 DAPHNIS          23 That he had not so much Sence
         P.  93 DR. WITTY         6 That sence in English which was bright and pure
         P. 118 BLAKE           147 So prosperous Stars, though absent to the sence,
         P. 124 O.C.             45 While they by sence, not knowing, comprehend
```

send   frequency: 8   relative frequency: 0.0001
```
         P.  75 A. HOUSE        536 That Tribute to its Lord to send.
         P. 152 INSTRUCTIONS    476 To work the Peace, and so to send them home.
         P. 167 KINGS VOWES      44 My Bawd shall Embassadors send farr and neare,
         P. 187 BRITANNIA       115 Frequent adresses to my Charles I send,
         P. 194 TWO HORSES       93 Ch. And Plenipotentiaryes send into France
         P. 194 TWO HORSES       95 W. That the King should send for another
                                    French whore,
         P. 201 HISTORICALL       7 And what is more they send him Mony too,
         P. 316 CHEQUER INN     152 The Healths in Order did up send
```

sends   frequency: 1   relative frequency: 0.0000
```
         P.  17 BERMUDAS         15 And sends the Fowl's to us in care,
```

senec   frequency: 1   relative frequency: 0.0000
```
         P.  54 THYESTE           t Senec. Traged. ex Thyeste Chor. 2.
```

seneca. See "senec," "seneque."

seneque   frequency: 1   relative frequency: 0.0000
```
         P. 151 INSTRUCTIONS    448 Consoles us morally out of Seneque.
```

sense   frequency: 7   relative frequency: 0.0001

```
      See also "sence."
      P.   10  DIALOGUE       47 The Batteries of alluring Sense,
      P.   58  BILL-BOROW      49 For they ('tis credible) have sense,
      P.   67  A. HOUSE       288 As aiming one for ev'ry Sense.
      P.  132  PARADISE        46 With tinkling Rhime, of thy own Sense secure;
      P.  187  BRITANNIA      118 Had lost all sense of Honour, Justice, fame;
      P.  198  DUKE            20 That common sense is my eternall foe.
      P.  199  DUKE            77 His sense, his soul as squinting as his eye.

senseless                       frequency:    1    relative frequency: 0.0000
      P.  178  LOYALL SCOT    259 That senseless Rancour against Interest.

sent                            frequency:   16    relative frequency: 0.0003
      P.    3  LOVELACE        32 Their first Petition by the Authour sent.
      P.   36  DAPHNIS         88 Wet themselves and spoil their Sent.
      P.  117  BLAKE          131 Which by quick powders force, so high was sent,
      P.  126  O.C.           113 First the great Thunder was shot off, and sent
      P.  138  HOUSEWARMING    43 Nay ev'n from Tangier have sent back for the
                                  mold,
      P.  148  INSTRUCTIONS   311 St. Albans straight is sent to, to forbear,
      P.  151  INSTRUCTIONS   449 Two Letters next unto Breda are sent,
      P.  155  INSTRUCTIONS   605 Oft had he sent, of Duncombe and of Legg
      P.  160  INSTRUCTIONS   789 But, his great Crime, one Boat away he sent;
      P.  162  INSTRUCTIONS   876 Court-mushrumps ready are sent in in pickle.
      P.  170  PROPHECY        11 And those false Men the Soveraign People sent
      P.  174  LOYALL SCOT    109 Pharoah at first would have sent Israell home.
      P.  183  MADE FREE       99 And in this Box you have sent it;
      P.  199  DUKE            43 That sent Nan Hide before her under ground,
      P.  314  CHEQUER INN     73 This Knight was sent t'america
      P.  314  CHEQUER INN     74 And was as soone sent for away

sentence                        frequency:    3    relative frequency: 0.0000
      P.   86  FLECKNO        122 Yet he more strict my sentence doth renew;
      P.   92  MAY'S DEATH     97 Thus by irrevocable Sentence cast,
      P.  161  INSTRUCTIONS   860 Where mute they stand to hear their Sentence
                                  read;

sentinel                        frequency:    1    relative frequency: 0.0000
      P.   68  A. HOUSE       318 Each Bee as Sentinel is shut;

separate                        frequency:    2    relative frequency: 0.0000
      See also "seperate."
      P.   33  DAPHNIS         15 Lest the World should separate;
      P.   39  THE MATCH       14 What she did separate lay;

separates                       frequency:    1    relative frequency: 0.0000
      P.  173  LOYALL SCOT     80 That whosoever separates them doth kill.

seperate                        frequency:    2    relative frequency: 0.0000
      P.  174  LOYALL SCOT     99 Seperate the world soe as the Bishops scalpes.
      P.  185  BRITANNIA       38 To those that try'd to seperate these two.

sequestration                   frequency:    1    relative frequency: 0.0000
      P.    3  LOVELACE        29 Some that you under sequestration are,

seraglio                        frequency:    2    relative frequency: 0.0000
      P.   41  THE MOWER       27 His green Seraglio has its Eunuchs too;
      P.  187  BRITANNIA      119 Like a Tame spinster in 's seraglio sits,

serene                          frequency:    4    relative frequency: 0.0000
      P.   98  HOLLAND        128 In a calm Winter, under Skies Serene.
      P.  124  O.C.            41 When She with Smiles serene and Words discreet
      P.  131  O.C.           320 Earth ne'er more glad, nor Heaven more serene.
      P.  188  BRITANNIA      155 To the serene Venetian state I'le goe

serenely                        frequency:    1    relative frequency: 0.0000
      P.  111  ANNIVERSARY    342 Smiling serenely from the further side.

serenest                        frequency:    1    relative frequency: 0.0000
      P.  121  TWO SONGS       54 With his serenest influence their Loves.

sergeants                       frequency:    1    relative frequency: 0.0000
      P.  168  ADVICE          16 To keep his own and loose his sergeants wife.

sergeant's.  See "sergeants," "serjeants."

serious                         frequency:    1    relative frequency: 0.0000
      P.   83  FLECKNO         24 To my last Tryal, in a serious thought

serjeants                       frequency:    1    relative frequency: 0.0000
      P.  162  INSTRUCTIONS   884 And Serjeants Wife serves him for Partelott.
```

sermons   frequency: 2   relative frequency: 0.0000
    P. 174 LOYALL SCOT   96 Who sermons ere can pacifie and prayers?
    P. 174 LOYALL SCOT   117 How a Clean Laundress and noe sermons please.

serpent   frequency   5   relative frequency: 0.0001
    P. 14 THE CORONET   13 Alas I find the Serpent old
    P. 14 THE CORONET   19 But thou who only could'st the Serpent tame,
    P. 78 A. HOUSE   629 No Serpent new nor Crocodile
    P. 111 ANNIVERSARY   320 Ay, and the Serpent too that did deceive.
    P. 203 HISTORICALL   101 The Serpent was the Prelat of the place:

serpents   frequency: 1   relative frequency: 0.0000
    P. 92 MAY'S DEATH   92 Magaera thee with all her Serpents lash.

serv'd   frequency: 4   relative frequency: 0.0000
    P. 96 HOLLAND   32 Whole sholes of Dutch serv'd up for Cabillau;
    P. 128 O.C.   207 More strong affections never reason serv'd,
    P. 183 MADE FREE   76 And tho' he has serv'd now
    P. 315 CHEQUER INN   125 Was oftner serv'd then the Poor

serve   frequency: 6   relative frequency: 0.0001
    P. 138 HOUSEWARMING   51 The two Allens who serve his blind Justice for
                               ballance,
    P. 138 HOUSEWARMING   52 The two Allens who serve his Injustice for
                               Tallons.
    P. 141 INSTRUCTIONS   12 'Twill serve this race of Drunkards, Pimps, and
                               Fools.
    P. 165 INSTRUCTIONS   987 That serve the King with their Estates and
                               Care,
    P. 178 LOYALL SCOT   257 Perverted serve dissentions to increase.
    P. 181 MADE FREE   26 How to serve or be free,

served   frequency: 1   relative frequency: 0.0000
    See also "serv'd."
    P. 175 LOYALL SCOT   147 Leviathen served up and Behemoth.

serves   frequency: 4   relative frequency: 0.0000
    P. 62 A. HOUSE   128 'That serves for Altar's Ornaments.
    P. 76 A. HOUSE   558 But serves to feed the Hewels young.
    P. 162 INSTRUCTIONS   884 And Serjeants Wife serves him for Partelott.
    P. 164 INSTRUCTIONS   966 And, where all England serves, themselves would
                               reign.

service   frequency: 2   relative frequency: 0.0000
    P. 96 HOLLAND   54 Nor bear strict service, nor pure Liberty.
    P. 174 LOYALL SCOT   119 The Bible and Grammar for the service Book.

servil'   frequency: 1   relative frequency: 0.0000
    P. 91 MAY'S DEATH   40 Most servil' wit, and Mercenary Pen.

servile. See "servil'."

serving   frequency: 1   relative frequency: 0.0000
    P. 316 CHEQUER INN   166 And for to save the Serving Men,

sesse   frequency: 1   relative frequency: 0.0000
    P. 316 CHEQUER INN   144 Without another Sesse.

session   frequency: 1   relative frequency: 0.0000
    P. 160 INSTRUCTIONS   812 Blames the last Session, and this more does
                               fear.

set   frequency: 16   relative frequency: 0.0003
    See also "sett."
    P. 15 THE CORONET   24 Though set with Skill and chosen out with Care.
    P. 22 NYMPH   37 Thenceforth I set my self to play
    P. 67 A. HOUSE   261 The Relicks false were set to view;
    P. 83 FLECKNO   10 But seem'd a Coffin set on the Stairs head.
    P. 91 MAY'S DEATH   59 Must therefore all the World be set on flame,
    P. 119 TWO SONGS   1 Th' Astrologers own Eyes are set,
    P. 121 TWO SONGS   47 Less Loves set of each others praise,
    P. 127 O.C.   161 Which with more Care set forth his Obsequies
    P. 143 INSTRUCTIONS   107 Describe the Court and Country, both set right,
    P. 159 INSTRUCTIONS   779 Who did advise no Navy out to set?
    P. 179 STOCKSMARKET   11 Upon the King's birthday to set up a thing
    P. 180 STOCKSMARKET   39 Or is he in cabal in his cabinet set?
    P. 181 MADE FREE   11 Set with Stones of both Rocks
    P. 183 MADE FREE   101 For himself up to set,
    P. 193 TWO HORSES   56 Lord a Mercy and a Cross might be set on the
                               doore;
    P. 314 CHEQUER INN   67 Wheeler at Board, then next her set,

seth's   frequency: 1   relative frequency: 0.0000
    P. 175 LOYALL SCOT   158 Seth's Pillars are noe Antique Brick and stone

sets   frequency: 2   relative frequency: 0.0000
    P.   73 A. HOUSE   466 Denton sets ope its Cataracts;
    P. 204 HISTORICALL   120 Sets up in Scotland alamode de France,

sett   frequency: 5   relative frequency: 0.0001
    P. 178 LOYALL SCOT   277 The hare's head 'gainst the goose gibletts sett.
    P. 199 DUKE   45 Preserv'd in store for the new sett of maids.
    P. 201 HISTORICALL   34 The new got flemish Towne was sett to sale.
    P. 202 HISTORICALL   48 He sells the Citty where 'twas sett on fire.
    P. 202 HISTORICALL   65 Lockes as one sett up for to scare the Crows.

setting   frequency: 2   relative frequency: 0.0000
    P. 111 ANNIVERSARY   329 But thought him when he miss'd his setting beams,
    P. 186 BRITANNIA   55 To him I shew'd this Glorious setting sun,

settled   frequency: 1   relative frequency: 0.0000
    P.   54 THYESTE   4 Settled in some secret Nest

seven   frequency: 2   relative frequency: 0.0000
    See also "seaven," "seav'n."
    P. 105 ANNIVERSARY   66 Th' harmonious City of the seven Gates.
    P. 170 PROPHECY   20 And practise Incest between Seven and Eight,

seventh   frequency: 2   relative frequency: 0.0000
    P. 109 ANNIVERSARY   233 Till at the Seventh time thou in the Skyes,
    P. 193 TWO HORSES   71 W. On Seventh Harry's head he that placed the
                               Crown

several   frequency: 3   relative frequency: 0.0000
    See also "sev'ral."
    P.   29 THE GALLERY   3 Now all its several lodgings lye
    P.   40 THE MATCH   21 He kept the several Cells repleat
    P.   69 A. HOUSE   335 Tulips, in several Colours barr'd,

sever'd   frequency: 1   relative frequency: 0.0000
    P. 118 BLAKE   135 Scarce souls from bodies sever'd are so far,

severe   frequency: 5   relative frequency: 0.0001
    P.   38 PICTURE   13 And, under her command severe,
    P.   81 A. HOUSE   723 Under the Discipline severe
    P.   86 FLECKNO   119 Turns to recite; though Judges most severe
    P.   91 MAY'S DEATH   31 Rose more then ever he was seen severe,
    P. 131 PARADISE   11 Yet as I read, soon growing less severe,

severer   frequency: 1   relative frequency: 0.0000
    P.   3 LOVELACE   24 Severer then the yong Presbytery.

severn   frequency: 1   relative frequency: 0.0000
    P. 126 O.C.   146 He march'd, and through deep Severn ending war.

sev'ral   frequency: 3   relative frequency: 0.0000
    P.   98 HOLLAND   95 Tunn'd up with all their sev'ral Towns of Beer;
    P. 105 ANNIVERSARY   101 And in his sev'ral Aspects, like a Star,
    P. 147 INSTRUCTIONS   251 Each ran, as chance him guides, to sev'ral Post:

sewed. See "sowd."

sewers   frequency: 1   relative frequency: 0.0000
    P.   96 HOLLAND   52 Who look like a Commission of the Sewers.

sex   frequency: 6   relative frequency: 0.0001
    P.   41 THE MOWER   30 To procreate without a Sex.
    P.   79 A. HOUSE   656 Of all her Sex, her Ages Aw.
    P.   81 A. HOUSE   729 Go now fond Sex that on your Face
    P.   82 A. HOUSE   738 Supplies beyond her Sex the Line;
    P. 156 INSTRUCTIONS   651 And modest Beauty yet his Sex did Veil,
    P. 172 LOYALL SCOT   17 And modest beauty yet his sex did vail,

sexes   frequency: 1   relative frequency: 0.0000
    P.   33 DAPHNIS   5 Nature her own Sexes foe,

seymour   frequency: 3   relative frequency: 0.0000
    P. 147 INSTRUCTIONS   257 Then daring Seymour, that with Spear and
                               Shield,
    P. 168 ADVICE   28 For money comes when Seymour leaves the Chair.
    P. 169 ADVICE   48 With Cupid Seymour and the Tool of State,

seyne   frequency: 1   relative frequency: 0.0000

        P. 172 LOYALL SCOT   21 Oft as hee in Chill Eske or Seyne by night

shaddy   frequency: 1   relative frequency: 0.0000
        P. 61 A. HOUSE   79 In fragrant Gardens, shaddy Woods,

shade   frequency: 11   relative frequency: 0.0002
        P. 23 NYMPH   81 For, in the flaxen Lillies shade,
        P. 38 PICTURE   24 Where I may see thy Glories from some shade.
        P. 48 THE GARDEN   5 Whose short and narrow verged Shade
        P. 49 THE GARDEN   48 To a green Thought in a green Shade.
        P. 57 BILL-BOROW   36 With impious Steel the sacred Shade.
        P. 78 A. HOUSE   639 And for his shade which therein shines,
        P. 90 MAY'S DEATH   13 'Twas Ben that in the dusky Laurel shade
        P. 92 MAY'S DEATH   89 Nor here thy shade must dwell, Return, Return,
        P. 120 TWO SONGS   32 Sporting with him in Ida's shade:
        P. 127 O.C.   156 And slept in Peace under the Lawrel shade.
        P. 162 INSTRUCTIONS   885 Paint last the King, and a dead Shade of
                                  Night,

shades   frequency: 5   relative frequency: 0.0001
        P. 17 BERMUDAS   17 He hangs in shades the Orange bright,
        P. 42 DAMON   14 And Grass-hoppers seek out the shades.
        P. 91 MAY'S DEATH   39 Far from these blessed shades tread back agen
        P. 120 TWO SONGS   28 With shades of deep Despair opprest.
        P. 171 LOYALL SCOT   1 Of the old Heroes when the Warlike shades

shadow   frequency: 1   relative frequency: 0.0000
        P. 80 A. HOUSE   676 If it might fix her shadow so;

shadows   frequency: 4   relative frequency: 0.0000
        P. 27 LOVER   4 By Fountains cool, and Shadows green.
        P. 79 A. HOUSE   665 So when the Shadows laid asleep
        P. 87 ODE   3 Nor in the Shadows sing
        P. 130 O.C.   273 And his own shadows with him fall; the eye

shadrach. See "shadrack."

shadrack   frequency: 1   relative frequency: 0.0000
        P. 156 INSTRUCTIONS   648 Like Shadrack, Mesheck, and Abednego.

shady   frequency: 4   relative frequency: 0.0000
        See also "shaddy."
        P. 90 ODE   118 The Spirits of the shady Night,
        P. 125 O.C.   91 Under whose shady tent Men ev'ry year
        P. 141 INSTRUCTIONS   11 Sketching in shady smoke prodigious tools,
        P. 172 LOYALL SCOT   19 His shady locks Curl back themselves to seek

shake   frequency: 5   relative frequency: 0.0001
        P. 99 HOLLAND   149 For while our Neptune doth a Trident shake,
        P. 106 ANNIVERSARY   121 Then shall I once with graver Accents shake
        P. 110 ANNIVERSARY   297 That their new King might the fifth Scepter
                                  shake,
        P. 163 INSTRUCTIONS 915 Shake then the room, and all his Curtains tear,
        P. 187 BRITANNIA   96 Shake of those Baby bonds from your strong
                                  Armes,

shakes   frequency: 1   relative frequency: 0.0000
        P. 21 SOUL & BODY   34 And then the Palsie Shakes of Fear.

shall   frequency: 143   relative frequency: 0.0029

shallow   frequency: 1   relative frequency: 0.0000
        P. 154 INSTRUCTIONS 545 And, where the deep Keel cn the shallow cleaves,

shalt   frequency: 7   relative frequency: 0.0001

shambles   frequency: 1   relative frequency: 0.0000
        P. 199 DUKE   73 I'th Irish shambles he first learn'd the trade.

shame   frequency: 15   relative frequency: 0.0003
        P. 79 A. HOUSE   653 'Twere shame that such judicious Eyes
        P. 110 ANNIVERSARY   294 The Shame and Plague both of the Land and
                                  Age,
        P. 128 O.C.   223 Oh! ill advis'd, if not for love, for shame,
        P. 150 INSTRUCTIONS 387 Prudent Antiquity, that knew by Shame,
        P. 155 INSTRUCTIONS 583 An English Pilot too, (O Shame, O Sin!)
        P. 156 INSTRUCTIONS 622 With present shame compar'd, his mind distraught.
        P. 156 INSTRUCTIONS 639 But when, by shame constrain'd to go on Board,
        P. 162 INSTRUCTIONS 898 Her heart throbs, and with very shame would
                                  break.
        P. 178 LOYALL SCOT   258 For shame extirpate from each loyall brest

P. 187 BRITANNIA   107 Some English tco disguis'd (oh shame) I spy'd
P. 187 BRITANNIA   113 My reverend head expos'd to scorn and shame,
P. 189 BRITANNIA   172 Yeild to all these in Lewdness, lust, and shame.
P. 196 TWO HORSES   176 To conceal their own crimes and cover their
                          shame,
P. 202 HISTORICALL   58 It has recoild tc Fopery and Shame,
P. 315 CHEQUER INN   112 Nay Portman tho' all men cry'd shame

shameful. See "shamefull."

shamefull   frequency: 1   relative frequency: 0.0000
P. 313 CHEQUER INN   48 For such a shamefull Verdict.

shap'd   frequency: 1   relative frequency: 0.0000
P. 73 A. HOUSE   460 As Spots, so shap'd, on Faces do.

shape   frequency: 7   relative frequency: 0.0001
P. 125 O.C.   97 Trickling in watry drops, whose flowing shape
P. 129 O.C.   257 Yet dwelt that greatnesse in his shape decay'd,
P. 155 INSTRUCTIONS   601 Our Seamen, whcm nc Dangers shape could fright,
P. 157 INSTRUCTIONS   679 His shape exact, which the bright flames infold,
P. 158 INSTRUCTIONS   729 Her moving Shape; all these he does survey,
P. 162 INSTRUCTIONS   891 Raise up a sudden Shape with Virgins Face,
P. 173 LOYALL SCOT   45 His shape Exact which the bright flames enfold

shaped. See "shap'd," "shapt."

shapt   frequency: 1   relative frequency: 0.0000
P. 143 INSTRUCTICNS   86 She slights) his Feet shapt for a smoother race.

share   frequency: 11   relative frequency: 0.0002
P.   9 DIALOGUE   14 And of Nature's banquet share:
P. 38 PICTURE   28 Make that the Tulips may have share
P. 49 THE GARDEN   61 But 'twas beyond a Mortal's share
P. 112 ANNIVERSARY   371 'And those that have the Waters for their share,
P. 120 TWO SONGS   19 Since thou disdain'st not then to share
P. 131 PARADISE   26 Within thy Labours to pretend a Share.
P. 143 INSTRUCTIONS   116 Can strike the Die, and still with them goes
                          share.
P. 149 INSTRUCTIONS   333 Thus, like fair Thieves, the Commons Purse
                          they share,
P. 160 INSTRUCTIONS   794 And place in Ccunsel fell to Duncombes share.
P. 164 INSTRUCTIONS   955 And you, Great Sir, that with him Empire
                          share,
P. 170 PROPHECY   10 Hir'd for their share to give the rest away

shares   frequency: 2   relative frequency: 0.0000
P. 74 A. HOUSE   487 And where all Creatures might have shares,
P. 124 O.C.   47 With her each day the pleasing Hours he shares,

shark   frequency: 1   relative frequency: 0.0000
P. 144 INSTRUCTIONS   135 With hundred rcws cf Teeth the Shark exceeds,

sharp   frequency: 3   relative frequency: 0.0000
P. 28 LOVER   44 At sharp before it all the day:
P. 41 DAMON   7 Sharp like his Sythe his Sorrow was,
P. 152 INSTRUCTIONS   466 Still his sharp Wit on States and Princes
                          whets.

sharpest   frequency: 1   relative frequency: 0.0000
P. 66 A. HOUSE   256 And sharpest Weapons were their Tongues.

shatter   frequency: 1   relative frequency: 0.0000
P. 14 THE CORONET   22 Or shatter too with him my curious frame:

shattered   frequency: 2   relative frequency: 0.0000
P. 180 STOCKSMARKET   46 With three shattered planks and the rags of a
                          sail
P. 180 STOCKSMARKET   47 To express how his navy was shattered and torn

shattering   frequency: 1   relative frequency: 0.0000
P. 176 LOYALL SCOT   201 Shattering the silent Air disturbs our Joys!

shave   frequency: 1   relative frequency: 0.0000
P. 153 INSTRUCTICNS   533 Like am'rous Victors he begins to shave,

she   frequency: 118   relative frequency: 0.0024
See also "shee," "shee'l," "she's."

shear   frequency: 1   relative frequency: 0.0000
P. 43 DAMON   53 With this the gclden fleece I shear

sheath   frequency: 1   relative frequency: 0.0000
     P. 107 ANNIVERSARY   172 Drawn from the Sheath of lying Prophecies;

sheath'd   frequency: 1   relative frequency: 0.0000
     P. 91 MAY'S DEATH   24 In his own Bowels sheath'd the conquering
                              health.

sheathing   frequency: 1   relative frequency: 0.0000
     P. 190 STATUE   13 Were these Deales kept in store for sheathing
                              our fleet

sheaves   frequency: 1   relative frequency: 0.0000
     P. 126 O.C.   117 Out of the Binders Hand the Sheaves they tore,

shed   frequency: 6   relative frequency: 0.0001
     P. 12 DROP OF DEW   2 Shed from the Bosom of the Morn
     P. 77 A. HOUSE   599 Who, as my Hair, my Thoughts too shed,
     P. 107 ANNIVERSARY   184 Of purling Ore, a shining wave do shed:
     P. 129 O.C.   250 Which through his looks that piercing sweetnesse
                              shed;
     P. 142 INSTRUCTIONS   71 Ye neighb'ring Elms, that your green leaves did
                              shed,
     P. 186 BRITANNIA   52 And in his heart kind influences shed

shedding   frequency: 1   relative frequency: 0.0000
     P. 112 ANNIVERSARY   356 'Of shedding Leaves, that with their Ocean
                              breed.

shee   frequency: 1   relative frequency: 0.0000

shee'l   frequency: 1   relative frequency: 0.0000

sheep   frequency: 12   relative frequency: 0.0002
     P. 18 CLORINDA   5 The Grass I aim to feast thy Sheep:
     P. 20 THYRSIS   31 Thyrsis. Then I'le go on: There, sheep are
                              full
     P. 20 THYRSIS   45 Chorus. Then let us give Carillo charge o'th
                              Sheep,
     P. 43 DAMON   52 More ground then all his Sheep do hide.
     P. 119 TWO SONGS   2 And even Wolves the Sheep forget;
     P. 119 TWO SONGS   12 Or if a Shepheard, watch thy Sheep.
     P. 119 TWO SONGS   14 And Sheep are both thy Sacrifice.
     P. 122 TWO SONGS   23 Nor our Sheep new Wash'd can be
     P. 122 TWO SONGS   26 Somewhat else then silly Sheep.
     P. 130 O.C.   284 While sheep delight the grassy downs to pick,
     P. 156 INSTRUCTIONS   641 And saw himself confin'd, like Sheep in Pen;
     P. 203 HISTORICALL   89 And with dull Crambo feed the silly sheep.

sheerness   frequency: 2   relative frequency: 0.0000
     P. 154 INSTRUCTIONS   560 And at Sheerness unloads its stormy sides.
     P. 159 INSTRUCTIONS   782 Languard, Sheerness, Gravesend, and Upnor?
                              Pett.

sheet   frequency: 1   relative frequency: 0.0000
     P. 83 FLECKNO   12 Only there was nor Seeling, nor a Sheet,

sheets   frequency: 3   relative frequency: 0.0000
     P. 24 NYMPH   90 In whitest sheets of Lillies cold.
     P. 157 INSTRUCTIONS   678 And tries his first embraces in their Sheets.
     P. 172 LOYALL SCOT   44 And tries his first Imbraces in their sheets.

shelden   frequency: 1   relative frequency: 0.0000
     P. 160 INSTRUCTIONS   811 Grave Primate Shelden (much in Preaching
                              there)

sheldon   frequency: 1   relative frequency: 0.0000
     See also "shelden."
     P. 175 LOYALL SCOT   165 Nor is our Sheldon whiter then his Snow.

shell   frequency: 2   relative frequency: 0.0000
     See also "muscle-shell," "tortoise-shell."
     P. 18 CLORINDA   14 Tinkles within the concave Shell.
     P. 154 INSTRUCTIONS   549 With Pearly Shell the Tritons all the while

shelter   frequency: 2   relative frequency: 0.0000
     P. 90 ODE   105 The Pict no shelter now shall find
     P. 129 O.C.   268 So many yeares the shelter of the wood.)

shent   frequency: 3   relative frequency: 0.0000
     P. 152 INSTRUCTIONS   463 The Dutch are then in Proclamation shent,
     P. 176 LOYALL SCOT   212 To conform's necessary or bee shent,

P. 316 CHEQUER INN   174 And I for them be shent.

shepheard   frequency: 5   relative frequency: 0.0001
  P. 119 TWO SONGS   3 Only this Shepheard, late and soon,
  P. 119 TWO SONGS   12 Or if a Shepheard, watch thy Sheep.
  P. 119 TWO SONGS   13 The Shepheard, since he saw thine Eyes,
  P. 120 TWO SONGS   30 Anchises was a Shepheard too;
  P. 122 TWO SONGS   31 What Shepheard could for Love pretend,

shepheardess   frequency: 1   relative frequency: 0.0000
  P. 42 DAMON   33 How long wilt Thou, fair Shepheardess,

shepheards   frequency: 2   relative frequency: 0.0000
  P. 20 THYRSIS   37 Shepheards there, bear equal sway,
  P. 121 TWO SONGS   3 For the Northern Shepheards Son.

shepherd   frequency: 1   relative frequency: 0.0000
  See also "shepheard."
  P. 43 DAMON   49 What, though the piping Shepherd stock

shepherdess   frequency: 2   relative frequency: 0.0000
  See also "shepheardess."
  P. 30 THE GALLERY   53 A tender Shepherdess, whose Hair
  P. 122 TWO SONGS   33 What Shepherdess could hope to wed

shepherdesses   frequency: 1   relative frequency: 0.0000
  P. 14 THE CORONET   8 That once adorn'd my Shepherdesses head.

shepherds   frequency: 2   relative frequency: 0.0000
  See also "shepheards."
  P. 18 CLORINDA   21 D. Words that transcend poor Shepherds skill,
  P. 154 INSTRUCTIONS   558 Shepherds themselves in vain in bushes shrowd.

shepherd's. see also "shepheards."

shepherds-purse   frequency: 1   relative frequency: 0.0000
  P. 44 DAMON   83 With Shepherds-purse, and Clowns-all-heal,

sheppy   frequency: 1   relative frequency: 0.0000
  P. 154 INSTRUCTIONS   550 Sound the Sea-march, and guide to Sheppy Isle.

she's   frequency: 1   relative frequency: 0.0000
  P. 55 EPITAPH   20 'Twere more Significant, She's Dead.

shew   frequency: 15   relative frequency: 0.0003
  P.   9 DIALOGUE   9 And shew that Nature wants an Art
  P. 10 DIALOGUE   45 Earth cannot shew so brave a Sight
  P. 16 EYES   43 And Stars shew lovely in the Night,
  P. 83 FLECKNO   14 Turn in, and shew to Wainscot half the Room.
  P. 96 HOLLAND   26 To shew them what's their Mare Liberum.
  P. 110 ANNIVERSARY   292 May shew their own, not see his Nakedness.
  P. 117 BLAKE   108 Do not so much suppress, as shew their fear.
  P. 155 INSTRUCTIONS 595 And to the rest the open'd passage shew.
  P. 171 PROPHECY   50 Then either Greek or Gallick Story shew,
  P. 174 LOYALL SCOT   125 And surplic'd shew like Pillars too of salt.
  P. 180 STOCKSMARKET   59 For though the whole world cannot shew such
              another,
  P. 189 BRITANNIA   168 To Flattery, Pimping, and a gawdy shew:
  P. 199 DUKE   54 Now, Painter, shew us in the blackest dye
  P. 199 DUKE   74 Then, Painter, shew thy skill and in fitt place
  P. 203 HISTORICALL   99 And never durst their tricks above board shew.

shew'd   frequency: 5   relative frequency: 0.0001
  P. 160 INSTRUCTIONS   820 Harry came Post just as he shew'd his Watch.
  P. 177 LOYALL SCOT   248 In Paradice Names only Nature Shew'd,
  P. 185 BRITANNIA   40 Shew'd him how many Kings in Purple Gore
  P. 186 BRITANNIA   55 To him I shew'd this Glorious setting sun,
  P. 191 STATUE   51 Where he shew'd her that so many voters he had

shews   frequency: 6   relative frequency: 0.0001
  P. 72 A. HOUSE   434 Like a calm Sea it shews the Rocks:
  P. 129 O.C.   270 When fall'n shews taller yet than as it grew:
  P. 139 HOUSEWARMING   91 And shews on the top by the Regal Gilt Ball,
  P. 174 LOYALL SCOT   107 Shews you first one, then makes that one two
              Balls.
  P. 179 STOCKSMARKET   12 That shews him a monster more like than a king.
  P. 184 MADE FREE   111 Shews how fit he is to Governe;

shibboleth   frequency: 1   relative frequency: 0.0000
  P. 177 LOYALL SCOT   246 Nation is all but name as Shibboleth,

shield   frequency: 3   relative frequency: 0.0000

```
         P.   9 DIALOGUE          2 The weight of thine immortal Shield.
         P. 147 INSTRUCTIONS     257 Then daring Seymour, that with Spear and
                                     Shield,
         P. 186 BRITANNIA         62 Her left Arm bears, the Antient Gallick shield
```

shillings   frequency: 1   relative frequency: 0.0000
```
         P. 193 TWO HORSES        80 As not to be trusted for twice fifty shillings.
```

shin'd   frequency: 1   relative frequency: 0.0000
```
         P. 124 O.C.              39 When with meridian height her Beauty shin'd,
```

shine   frequency: 8   relative frequency: 0.0001
```
         P.   9 DIALOGUE          8 In this day's Combat let it shine:
         P.  11 DIALOGUE         52 Which scatteringly doth shine,
         P.  70 A. HOUSE        360 That in the Crowns of Saints do shine.
         P. 118 BLAKE           148 Bless those they shine for, by their Influence.
         P. 120 TWO SONGS        27 Shine thorough this obscurer Brest,
         P. 121 TWO SONGS        50 Or shine Thou there and 'tis the Sky.
         P. 157 INSTRUCTIONS    683 And, as on Angels Heads their Glories shine,
         P. 173 LOYALL SCOT      49 And as on Angells head their Glories shine
```

shines   frequency: 5   relative frequency: 0.0001
```
         P.  12 DROP OF DEW       12 Shines with a mournful Light;
         P.  78 A. HOUSE        639 And for his shade which therein shines,
         P. 103 ANNIVERSARY      12 And shines the Jewel of the yearly Ring.
         P. 105 ANNIVERSARY     102 Here shines in Peace, and thither shoots a War.
         P. 187 BRITANNIA        94 So boundless Lewis in full Glory shines,
```

shining   frequency: 7   relative frequency: 0.0001
```
         P.  44 GLO-WORMS         7 Shining unto no higher end
         P.  62 A. HOUSE        105 'Here we, in shining Armour white,
         P.  75 A. HOUSE        532 The hatching Thrastles shining Eye,
         P.  94 DR. WITTY        11 That but to make the Vessel shining, they
         P. 107 ANNIVERSARY     184 Of purling Ore, a shining wave do shed:
         P. 111 ANNIVERSARY     326 See the bright Sun his shining Race pursue,
         P. 111 ANNIVERSARY     346 And Princes shining through their windows
                                     starts;
```

ship   frequency: 5   relative frequency: 0.0001
```
         P. 118 BLAKE           149 Our Cannon now tears every Ship and Sconce,
         P. 157 INSTRUCTIONS    661 Fixt on his Ship, he fac'd that horrid Day,
         P. 157 INSTRUCTIONS    691 His Ship burns down, and with his Relicks
                                     sinks,
         P. 172 LOYALL SCOT      27 Fix'd on his ship hee fac'd the horrid day
         P. 173 LOYALL SCOT      57 The ship burnes down and with his reliques sinks,
```

shipps   frequency: 1   relative frequency: 0.0000
```
         P. 171 LOYALL SCOT      t3 of his Majesties shipps at Chatham.
```

ships   frequency: 16   relative frequency: 0.0003
```
See also "fire-ships," "shipps."
         P. 112 ANNIVERSARY     355 'Unless their Ships, do, as their Fowle proceed
         P. 112 ANNIVERSARY     357 'Theirs are not Ships, but rather Arks of War,
         P. 117 BLAKE           128 Some Ships are sunk, some blown up in the skie.
         P. 118 BLAKE           161 All the Foes Ships destroy'd, by Sea or fire,
         P. 148 INSTRUCTIONS    318 To lay the Ships up, cease the Keels begun.
         P. 150 INSTRUCTIONS    398 Off, at the Isle of Candy, Dutch and ships.
         P. 151 INSTRUCTIONS    433 Tell him our Ships unrigg'd, our Forts unman'd,
         P. 152 INSTRUCTIONS    482 (As if, alas, we Ships or Dutch had Horse.)
         P. 154 INSTRUCTIONS    573 There our sick Ships unrigg'd in Summer lay,
         P. 155 INSTRUCTIONS    585 Our wretched Ships within their Fate attend,
         P. 155 INSTRUCTIONS    602 Unpaid, refuse to mount our Ships for spight:
         P. 158 INSTRUCTIONS    702 But that the Ships themselves were taught to
                                     dive:
         P. 158 INSTRUCTIONS    715 Those Ships, that yearly from their teeming
                                     Howl,
         P. 160 INSTRUCTIONS    783 Who all our Ships expos'd in Chathams Net?
         P. 160 INSTRUCTIONS    785 Pett, the Sea Architect, in making Ships,
         P. 193 TWO HORSES       65 Ch. And our few ships abroad become Tripoly's
                                     scorn
```

shipwrack   frequency: 2   relative frequency: 0.0000
```
         P.  27 LOVER             9 'Twas in a Shipwrack, when the Seas
         P. 109 ANNIVERSARY     269 While baleful Tritons to the shipwrack guide.
```

shipwrackt   frequency: 2   relative frequency: 0.0000
```
         P.  21 SOUL & BODY      30 Am Shipwrackt into Health again.
         P.  95 HOLLAND           6 Of shipwrackt Cockle and the Muscle-shell;
```

shipwreck. See "shipwrack."

shipwrecked. See "shipwrackt."

shire   frequency: 1   relative frequency: 0.0000

P. 312 CHEQUER INN   6 In Burrough or in Shire.

shirt   frequency: 2   relative frequency: 0.0000
P. 86 FLECKNO   130 Save only two foul copies for his shirt:
P. 153 INSTRUCTIONS   510 Monk in his Shirt against the Dutch is prest.

shoal. See "shole."

shoals. See "sholes."

shoar   frequency: 4   relative frequency: 0.0000
P. 17 BERMUDAS   28 Proclaime the Ambergris on shoar.
P. 95 HOLLAND   10 They with mad labour fish'd the Land to Shoar;
P. 127 O.C.   173 Who planted England on the Flandrick shoar,
P. 187 BRITANNIA   126 His French and Teagues comand on sea and shoar.

shoare   frequency: 1   relative frequency: 0.0000
P. 201 HISTORICALL   11 In a slasht doublet then he came to shoare,

shocks   frequency: 1   relative frequency: 0.0000
P. 155 INSTRUCTIONS   589 A Skipper rude shocks it without respect,

shod   frequency: 2   relative frequency: 0.0000
P. 83 A. HOUSE   772 Have shod their Heads in their Canoos.
P. 146 INSTRUCTIONS   221 Not the first Cock-horse, that with Cork were
                            shod

shoes   frequency: 1   relative frequency: 0.0000
See also "shoos."
P. 83 A. HOUSE   771 And, like Antipodes in Shoes,

shold   frequency: 5   relative frequency: 0.0001

shole   frequency: 1   relative frequency: 0.0000
P. 112 ANNIVERSARY   361 'An hideous shole of wood-Leviathans,

sholes   frequency: 1   relative frequency: 0.0000
P. 96 HOLLAND   32 Whole sholes of Dutch serv'd up for Cabillau;

shook   frequency: 2   relative frequency: 0.0000
See also "shooke."
P. 91 MAY'S DEATH   32 Shook his gray locks, and his own Bayes did tear
P. 158 INSTRUCTIONS   706 The Tow'r it self with the near danger shook.

shooke   frequency: 2   relative frequency: 0.0000
P. 200 DUKE   94 Its steady Basis never could bee shocke,
P. 200 DUKE   103 Shooke by the faults of others, not thine owne.

shoos   frequency: 2   relative frequency: 0.0000
P. 171 PROPHECY   29 And Wooden shoos shall come to be the weare
P. 171 PROPHECY   47 Then wooden Shoos shall be the English weare

shoot   frequency: 2   relative frequency: 0.0000
P. 58 BILL-BOROW   57 Yet now no further strive to shoot,
P. 112 ANNIVERSARY   363 'That through the Center shoot their thundring
                            side

shooting   frequency: 1   relative frequency: 0.0000
P. 74 A. HOUSE   494 Yet more to Heaven shooting are:

shoots   frequency: 4   relative frequency: 0.0000
P. 16 EYES   37 The sparkling Glance that shoots Desire,
P. 105 ANNIVERSARY   102 Here shines in Peace, and thither shoots a War.
P. 129 O.C.   261 Not much unlike the sacred oak, which shoots
P. 149 INSTRUCTIONS   346 But blooms all Night, and shoots its branches
                            high.

shop   frequency: 2   relative frequency: 0.0000
P. 29 THE GALLERY   12 Thy fertile Shop of cruel Arts:
P. 181 MADE FREE   33 When in his Shop he shou'd be poreing;

shops   frequency: 1   relative frequency: 0.0000
P. 144 INSTRUCTIONS   134 Breaks into Shops, and into Cellars prys.

shore   frequency: 6   relative frequency: 0.0001
See also "shoar," "shoare."
P. 97 HOLLAND   64 Never so fertile, spawn'd upon this shore:
P. 110 ANNIVERSARY   272 Giddy, and wishing for the fatal Shore;
P. 116 BLAKE   90 And flank with Cannon from the Neighbouring
                            shore.
P. 155 INSTRUCTIONS   591 Th' English from shore the Iron deaf invoke

P. 166 KINGS VOWES   38 As bold as Alce Pierce and as faire as Jane
                          Shore;
P. 173 LOYALL SCOT   73 Shall fix a foot on either neighbouring Shore

shorn   frequency: 2   relative frequency: 0.0000
P. 124 O.C.   67 And now Eliza's purple Locks were shorn,
P. 158 INSTRUCTIONS   735 Such the fear'd Hebrew, captive, blinded, shorn,

short   frequency: 12   relative frequency: 0.0002
P.   5 HASTINGS   60 And Art indeed is Long, but Life is Short.
P. 18 CLORINDA   8 C. Seize the short Joyes then, ere they vade.
P. 23 NYMPH   52 Could in so short a time espie,
P. 34 DAPHNIS   56 For his last and short Delight.
P. 48 THE GARDEN   5 Whose short and narrow verged Shade
P. 60 A. HOUSE   42 Those short but admirable Lines,
P. 72 A. HOUSE   438 Short Pyramids of Hay do stand.
P. 103 ANNIVERSARY   5 And his short Tumults of themselves Compose,
P. 108 ANNIVERSARY   189 While impious Men deceiv'd with pleasure short,
P. 157 INSTRUCTIONS   665 But entertains, the while, his time too short
P. 158 INSTRUCTIONS   720 Take a short Voyage underneath the Thames.
P. 172 LOYALL SCOT   32 Hee entertains the while his life too short,

shorter   frequency: 2   relative frequency: 0.0000
P. 151 INSTRUCTIONS   415 Bennet and May, and those of shorter reach,
P. 174 LOYALL SCOT   121 A shorter Way's to bee by Clergie sav'd.

shortly   frequency: 1   relative frequency: 0.0000
P. 190 STATUE   24 Hee'l shortly reduce us to fourty and eight.

shot   frequency: 7   relative frequency: 0.0001
See also "chain-shot," "gun-shot."
P. 22 NYMPH   2 Have shot my Faun and it will dye.
P. 68 A. HOUSE   305 Well shot ye Firemen! Oh how sweet,
P. 77 A. HOUSE   605 And where the World no certain Shot
P. 81 A. HOUSE   715 Tears (watry Shot that pierce the Mind;)
P. 98 HOLLAND   120 Then of Case-Butter shot and Bullet-Cheese.
P. 126 O.C.   113 First the great Thunder was shot off, and sent
P. 175 LOYALL SCOT   164 Abbot one Buck, but he shot many a Doe,

shoud   frequency: 1   relative frequency: 0.0000
P. 315 CHEQUER INN   128 Which shoud the other most commend

shou'd   frequency: 5   relative frequency: 0.0001

should   frequency: 98   relative frequency: 0.0020
See also "shold," "shoud," "shou'd."

shoulder   frequency: 1   relative frequency: 0.0000
See also "hook-shoulder."
P. 154 INSTRUCTIONS   546 With Trident's leaver, and great Shoulder
                           heaves.

shoulders   frequency: 1   relative frequency: 0.0000
P. 141 INSTRUCTIONS   33 Paint him with Drayman's Shoulders, butchers
                           Mien,

shouldest. See "shouldst," "should'st."

shouldst   frequency: 1   relative frequency: 0.0000

should'st   frequency: 1   relative frequency: 0.0000

shouts   frequency: 1   relative frequency: 0.0000
P. 158 INSTRUCTIONS   733 Then with rude shouts, secure, the Air they vex;

shovel. See "shov'l."

shov'l   frequency: 1   relative frequency: 0.0000
P. 96 HOLLAND   48 Invent a Shov'l and be a Magistrate.

show   frequency: 9   relative frequency: 0.0001
See also "shew."
P. 10 DIALOGUE   27 Thou in fragrant Clouds shalt show
P. 26 MISTRESS   18 And the last Age should show your Heart.
P. 37 DEFINITION   6 Could show me so divine a thing,
P. 70 A. HOUSE   382 And show upon their Lead the Ground,
P. 73 A. HOUSE   459 And shrunk in the huge Pasture show
P. 131 PARADISE   22 To change in Scenes, and show it in a Play.
P. 155 INSTRUCTIONS   604 Which show the tempting metal in their clutch.
P. 163 INSTRUCTIONS   922 The purple thread about his Neck does show:
P. 183 MADE FREE   94 Or does your fayre show

show'd   frequency: 4   relative frequency: 0.0000

```
P.  98 HOLLAND        101 But when such Amity at home is show'd;
P. 155 INSTRUCTIONS   584 Cheated of Pay, was he that show'd them in.
P. 160 INSTRUCTIONS   798 Show'd him to manage the Exchequer meeter:
P. 164 INSTRUCTIONS   951 Show'd they obscure him, while too near they
                          please,
```

showed. See "shew'd," "show'd."

shower. See "showr," "showre."

showering. See "show'ring."

```
showers                      frequency:    2    relative frequency: 0.0000
    See also "showres," "show'rs."
    P.   4 HASTINGS        6 And, ere they fall, arrest the early Showers.
    P.  15 EYES           23 But finds the Essence only Showers,
```

```
shown                        frequency:    5    relative frequency: 0.0001
    P. 127 O.C.          158 Have such high honours from above been shown:
    P. 150 INSTRUCTIONS  403 While the first year our Navy is but shown,
    P. 156 INSTRUCTIONS  634 Large Limbs, like Ox, not to be kill'd but
                             shown.
    P. 178 LOYALL SCOT   283 After such Frankness shown to bee his friend,
    P. 190 STATUE         18 The late King on Horsback is here to be shown:
```

```
showr                        frequency:    1    relative frequency: 0.0000
    P.  32 MOURNING       20 Her self both Danae and the Showr.
```

```
showre                       frequency:    1    relative frequency: 0.0000
    P. 131 O.C.          324 He threats no deluge, yet foretells a showre.
```

```
showres                      frequency:    2    relative frequency: 0.0000
    P. 114 BLAKE          30 Fertile to be, yet never need her showres.
    P. 126 O.C.          121 Then heavy Showres the winged Tempests lead,
```

```
show'ring                    frequency:    1    relative frequency: 0.0000
    P.  63 A. HOUSE      142 'On you the Lillies show'ring down:
```

```
show'rs                      frequency:    1    relative frequency: 0.0000
    P. 154 INSTRUCTIONS  566 Through the Walls untight, and Bullet show'rs:
```

```
shows                        frequency:    4    relative frequency: 0.0000
    See also "shews," "show's."
    P.  44 GLO-WORMS      10 To wandring Mowers shows the way,
    P.  61 A. HOUSE       87 And all that Neighbour-Ruine shows
    P.  88 ODE            47 And Hampton shows what part
    P. 148 INSTRUCTIONS  301 The martial Standard Sands displaying, shows
```

```
show's                       frequency:    2    relative frequency: 0.0000
    P.  16 EYES           35 Nor Cynthia Teeming show's so fair,
    P.  17 BERMUDAS       20 Jewels more rich than Ormus show's.
```

```
show'st                      frequency:    1    relative frequency: 0.0000
    P.  30 THE GALLERY    25 Like an Enchantress here thou show'st,
```

```
show'th                      frequency:    1    relative frequency: 0.0000
    P.  86 FLECKNO       136 At ordinaries after dinner show'th,
```

```
shreeks                      frequency:    1    relative frequency: 0.0000
    P. 108 ANNIVERSARY   210 And then loud Shreeks the vaulted Marbles rent.
```

```
shrieks                      frequency:    1    relative frequency: 0.0000
    See also "shreeks."
    P.  34 DAPHNIS        38 With the shrieks of Friends aghast,
```

```
shrill                       frequency:    3    relative frequency: 0.0000
    P.  68 A. HOUSE      307 Whose shrill report no Ear can tell,
    P. 106 ANNIVERSARY   123 Like the shrill Huntsman that prevents the
                             East,
    P. 108 ANNIVERSARY   200 And with shrill Neighings ask'd him of the
                             Wood.
```

```
shrine                       frequency:    5    relative frequency: 0.0001
    P.  18 CLORINDA       10 D. That den? C. Loves Shrine. D. But
                             Virtue's Grave.
    P.  24 NYMPH         104 Then place it in Diana's Shrine.
    P.  63 A. HOUSE      134 'Through ev'ry Shrine should be bestow'd.
    P. 140 HOUSEWARMING   97 This Temple, of War and of Peace is the
                             Shrine;
    P. 191 TWO HORSES     16 When Images speak, possesses the shrine:
```

```
shrines                      frequency:    1    relative frequency: 0.0000
```

     P. 192 TWO HORSES   18 When Shrines give Answers, say a knave 's in
                                 the Roode;

shrink   frequency: 1   relative frequency: 0.0000
     P. 90 ODE   108 Shrink underneath the Plad:

shrinking   frequency: 1   relative frequency: 0.0000
     P. 106 ANNIVERSARY   129 Which shrinking to her Roman Den impure,

shrinks   frequency: 2   relative frequency: 0.0000
     P. 70 A. HOUSE   358 As that which shrinks at ev'ry touch;
     P. 149 INSTRUCTIONS   345 So the sad Tree shrinks from the Mornings Eye;

shriveled   frequency: 1   relative frequency: 0.0000
     P. 139 HOUSEWARMING   70 Were shriveled, and Clutterbuck, Eagers <and>
                                 Kips;

shropshire   frequency: 1   relative frequency: 0.0000
     P. 315 CHEQUER INN   111 And Lawley Knight of Shropshire

shroud   frequency: 1   relative frequency: 0.0000
See also "shrowd."
     P. 180 STOCKSMARKET   36 As if you had meant it his coffin and shroud?

shrouds. See "shrowds."

shrowd   frequency: 1   relative frequency: 0.0000
     P. 154 INSTRUCTIONS   558 Shepherds themselves in vain in bushes shrowd.

shrowds   frequency: 1   relative frequency: 0.0000
     P. 154 INSTRUCTIONS   541 Among the Shrowds the Seamen sit and sing,

shrubs   frequency: 2   relative frequency: 0.0000
     P. 75 A. HOUSE   515 Low Shrubs she sits in, and adorns
     P. 109 ANNIVERSARY   264 Th' ambitious Shrubs thou in just time didst aw.

shrunk   frequency: 5   relative frequency: 0.0001
     P. 73 A. HOUSE   459 And shrunk in the huge Pasture show
     P. 108 ANNIVERSARY   192 What could they more? shrunk guiltily aside.
     P. 127 O.C.   167 Stand back ye Seas, and shrunk beneath the vail
     P. 158 INSTRUCTIONS   722 And shrunk, lest Navigable, to a Ford.
     P. 163 INSTRUCTIONS   903 But soon shrunk back, chill'd with her touch so
                                 cold,

shrunken   frequency: 1   relative frequency: 0.0000
     P. 75 A. HOUSE   520 Within the Skin its shrunken claws.

shun   frequency: 2   relative frequency: 0.0000
     P. 117 BLAKE   106 And a third World seek out our Armes to shun.
     P. 191 STATUE   54 But to turn the face to Whitehall you must
                                 Shun;

shuns   frequency: 2   relative frequency: 0.0000
     P. 12 DROP OF DEW   23 Shuns the sweat leaves and blossoms green;
     P. 143 INSTRUCTIONS   83 Her wonted joys thenceforth and Court she shuns,

shut   frequency: 3   relative frequency: 0.0000
     P. 19 THYRSIS   2 And shut up our divided lids,
     P. 68 A. HOUSE   318 Each Bee as Sentinel is shut;
     P. 170 PROPHECY   14 And Checquer dores shall shut up Lombard
                                 street,

shuts   frequency: 2   relative frequency: 0.0000
     P. 62 A. HOUSE   103 'The Cloyster outward shuts its Gates,
     P. 79 A. HOUSE   668 With Eben Shuts begin to close;

sibyls   frequency: 1   relative frequency: 0.0000
See also "sybills."
     P. 77 A. HOUSE   577 Out of these scatter'd Sibyls Leaves

sick   frequency: 5   relative frequency: 0.0001
     P. 20 THYRSIS   40 Dorinda. I'm sick, I'm sick, and fain would
                                 dye:
     P. 84 FLECKNO   53 Would break his fast before, said he was Sick,
     P. 142 INSTRUCTIONS   70 Moon, that o'rccme with the sick steam did'st
                                 fail;
     P. 154 INSTRUCTIONS   573 There our sick Ships unrigg'd in Summer lay,

sickness. See "faint-green-sickness," "falling-sickness."

side   frequency: 23   relative frequency: 0.0004

P.	9	DIALOGUE	22	Lest one Leaf thy Side should strain.
P.	26	MISTRESS	5	Thou by the Indian Ganges side
P.	29	THE GALLERY	17	But, on the other side, th' art drawn
P.	45	MOWER'S SONG	10	But had a Flower on either side;
P.	57	BILL-BOROW	18	Lyes open to its grassy side;
P.	64	A. HOUSE	185	'Each Night among us to your side
P.	71	A. HOUSE	392	And crowd a Lane to either Side.
P.	76	A. HOUSE	550	And through the tainted Side he mines.
P.	78	A. HOUSE	619	While, like a Guard on either side,
P.	79	A. HOUSE	643	Abandoning my lazy Side,
P.	87	ODE	15	Did thorough his own Side
P.	90	MAY'S DEATH	3	But was amaz'd on the Elysian side,
P.	92	MAY'S DEATH	87	Against thee, and expels thee from their side,
P.	105	ANNIVERSARY	92	Uphold, this one, and that the other Side;
P.	111	ANNIVERSARY	342	Smiling serenely from the further side.
P.	112	ANNIVERSARY	363	'That through the Center shoot their thundring side
P.	146	INSTRUCTIONS	239	For th' other side all in loose Quarters lay,
P.	156	INSTRUCTIONS	617	That Pleasure-boat of War, in whose dear side
P.	157	INSTRUCTIONS	688	With his dear Sword reposing by his Side.
P.	163	INSTRUCTIONS	919	Harry sits down, and in his open side
P.	168	ADVICE	22	The spoyls of England; and along that side
P.	173	LOYALL SCOT	54	With his dear sword reposing by his side,
P.	198	DUKE	36	Next, Painter, draw his Mordant by his side,

sides   frequency: 2   relative frequency: 0.0000
| P. | 154 | INSTRUCTIONS | 560 | And at Sheerness unloads its stormy sides. |
| P. | 178 | LOYALL SCOT | 254 | Say but a Scot and streight wee fall to sides: |

sidneys. See "sidnies."

sidney's   frequency: 1   relative frequency: 0.0000
| P. | 142 | INSTRUCTIONS | 75 | While she revolves, at once, Sidney's disgrace, |

sidnies   frequency: 1   relative frequency: 0.0000
| P. | 189 | BRITANNIA | 173 | Make 'em admire the Sidnies, Talbots, Veres, |

siege   frequency: 2   relative frequency: 0.0000
| P. | 33 | DAPHNIS | 18 | By which men their Siege maintain, |
| P. | 33 | DAPHNIS | 20 | Better 'twas the Siege to raise. |

sigh   frequency: 2   relative frequency: 0.0000
| P. | 19 | THYRSIS | 15 | Thyrsis. Do not sigh (fair Nimph) for fire |
| P. | 124 | O.C. | 57 | Each Groan he doubled and each Sigh he sigh'd, |

sigh'd   frequency: 3   relative frequency: 0.0000
P.	124	O.C.	57	Each Groan he doubled and each Sigh he sigh'd,
P.	157	INSTRUCTIONS	659	They sigh'd and said, Fond Boy, why so untame,
P.	172	LOYALL SCOT	25	They sigh'd and said 'fond boy why see Untame,

sighing   frequency: 1   relative frequency: 0.0000
| P. | 43 | DAMON | 72 | Sighing I whet my Sythe and Woes. |

sighs   frequency: 3   relative frequency: 0.0000
P.	27	LOVER	19	And from the Winds the Sighs he bore,
P.	81	A. HOUSE	716	And Sighs (Loves Cannon charg'd with Wind;)
P.	130	O.C.	304	Onely our sighs, perhaps, may thither reach.

sight   frequency: 28   relative frequency: 0.0005
P.	4	LOVELACE	44	(She knew what pain 'twould be to lose that sight.)
P.	10	DIALOGUE	45	Earth cannot shew so brave a Sight
P.	11	DIALOGUE	55	If things of Sight such Heavens be,
P.	15	EYES	5	And, since the Self-deluding Sight,
P.	16	EYES	27	And, to preserve their Sight more true,
P.	43	DAMON	57	Nor am I so deform'd to sight,
P.	66	A. HOUSE	228	And dazled not but clear'd his sight.
P.	70	A. HOUSE	361	The sight does from these Bastions fly,
P.	79	A. HOUSE	669	The modest Halcyon comes in sight,
P.	111	ANNIVERSARY	327	All day he follow'd with unwearied sight,
P.	114	BLAKE	20	With English Streamers, should salute their sight:
P.	118	BLAKE	137	Th' all-seeing Sun, neer gaz'd on such a sight,
P.	130	O.C.	301	And lost in tears, have neither sight nor mind
P.	130	O.C.	309	He, as his father, long was kept from sight
P.	131	PARADISE	10	The World o'rewhelming to revenge his Sight.
P.	132	PARADISE	44	Rewards with Prophesie thy loss of Sight.
P.	144	INSTRUCTIONS	139	She stalks all day in Streets conceal'd from sight,
P.	144	INSTRUCTIONS	147	Say Muse, for nothing can escape thy sight,
P.	150	INSTRUCTIONS	393	With homely sight, they chose thus to relax

```
     P. 153 INSTRUCTIONS    531 The sudden change, and such a tempting sight,
     P. 155 INSTRUCTIONS    596 Monk from the bank the dismal sight does view.
     P. 158 INSTRUCTIONS    727 The pleasing sight he often does prolong:
     P. 159 INSTRUCTIONS    745 And their dear Off-spring murder'd in their
                                sight;
     P. 162 INSTRUCTIONS    870 But all the while his Private-Bill's in sight.
     P. 164 INSTRUCTIONS    957 Blame not the Muse that brought those spots to
                                sight,
     P. 176 LOYALL SCOT     186 Strange was the Sight the scotch Twin headed
                                man
     P. 190 STATUE           22 When their Pensions are stopt to be fool'd with
                                a sight?
     P. 203 HISTORICALL      93 They dazle both the Prince and Peasants sight.

sign                          frequency:    5    relative frequency: 0.0001
     P.  36 DAPHNIS          99 To his Heads-man makes the Sign,
     P.  83 FLECKNO           5 I sought his Lodging; which is at the Sign
     P.  85 FLECKNO          95 He gathring fury still made sign to draw;
     P.  91 MAY'S DEATH      22 I sing (said he) and the Pharsalian Sign,
     P.  91 MAY'S DEATH      34 The awful Sign of his supream command.

sign-post                     frequency:    1    relative frequency: 0.0000
     P. 141 INSTRUCTIONS      7 Or canst thou dawb a Sign-post, and that ill?

signal                        frequency:    1    relative frequency: 0.0000
     P. 126 O.C.            114 The Signal from the starry Battlement.

sign'd                        frequency:    1    relative frequency: 0.0000
     P. 123 O.C.             21 To Love and Grief the fatal Writ was sign'd;

significant                   frequency:    1    relative frequency: 0.0000
     P.  55 EPITAPH          20 'Twere more Significant, She's Dead.

signifie                      frequency:    2    relative frequency: 0.0000
     P.  91 MAY'S DEATH      20 Gently to signifie that he was wrong.
     P. 177 LOYALL SCOT     253 Does man and wife signifie Rogue and Whore?

signifies                     frequency:    1    relative frequency: 0.0000
     P.  83 FLECKNO           8 Which signifies his triple property,

signify. See "signifie."

signs                         frequency:    3    relative frequency: 0.0000
     P.  76 A. HOUSE        571 And where I Language want, my Signs
     P.  90 MAY'S DEATH       8 Signs by which still he found and lost his way.
     P. 125 O.C.            101 A secret Cause does sure those Signs ordain

silence                       frequency:    3    relative frequency: 0.0000
     P. 108 ANNIVERSARY     209 A dismal Silence through the Palace went,
     P. 144 INSTRUCTIONS    126 Should Goodrick silence, and strike Paston
                                dumb;
     P. 192 TWO HORSES       39 Ch. Here Charing broke silence and thus he went
                                on:

silenced                      frequency:    1    relative frequency: 0.0000
     P.  92 MAY'S DEATH      64 And fear has Coward Churchmen silenced,

silent                        frequency:   12    relative frequency: 0.0002
     P.  20 THYRSIS          28 By silent thinking, Antidate:
     P.  32 MOURNING         33 I yet my silent Judgment keep,
     P.  54 THYESTE           7 Pass away my silent Age.
     P.  80 A. HOUSE        679 And Men the silent Scene assist,
     P.  84 FLECKNO          31 And how I, silent, turn'd my burning Ear
     P.  84 FLECKNO          57 And Silent. Nothing now Dinner stay'd
     P. 109 ANNIVERSARY     252 And Is'rel silent saw him rase the Tow'r;
     P. 119 TWO SONGS         6 Thorough the clear and silent Night.
     P. 124 O.C.             53 A silent fire now wasts those Limbs of Wax,
     P. 126 O.C.            136 As silent Suns to meet the Night descend.
     P. 162 INSTRUCTIONS    897 And silent tears her secret anguish speak,
     P. 176 LOYALL SCOT     201 Shattering the silent Air disturbs our Joys!

silk                          frequency:    1    relative frequency: 0.0000
     P. 131 O.C.            316 Richer than any eastern silk, or gemme;

silken                        frequency:    3    relative frequency: 0.0000
     P.   9 DIALOGUE          6 With silken Banners spreads the air.
     P.  68 A. HOUSE        294 Their Silken Ensigns each displayes,
     P.  78 A. HOUSE        614 Ere I your Silken Bondage break,

silks                         frequency:    2    relative frequency: 0.0000
     P.  78 A. HOUSE        628 Seems as green Silks but newly washt.
```

P. 154 INSTRUCTIONS 537 Their streaming Silks play through the weather
                         fair,

silly   frequency: 2   relative frequency: 0.0000
P. 122 TWO SONGS   26 Somewhat else then silly Sheep.
P. 203 HISTORICALL   89 And with dull Crambo feed the silly sheep.

silver   frequency: 6   relative frequency: 0.0001
P. 22 NYMPH   28 Ty'd in this silver Chain and Bell,
P. 23 NYMPH   64 'Twas on those little silver feet.
P. 49 THE GARDEN   54 Then whets, and combs its silver Wings;
P. 107 ANNIVERSARY 180 And soyl'd in Dust thy Crown of silver Hairs.
P. 119 TWO SONGS   10 The fleecy Clouds with silver wand.
P. 158 INSTRUCTIONS 717 Furrs from the North, and Silver from the
                         West,

similitude   frequency: 2   relative frequency: 0.0000
P. 91 MAY'S DEATH   44 On them some Romane cast similitude,
P. 179 STOCKSMARKET 23 And others to make the similitude hold

simpathies   frequency: 1   relative frequency: 0.0000
P. 178 LOYALL SCOT 264 And, where twin Simpathies cannot atone,

simper'd   frequency: 1   relative frequency: 0.0000
P. 314 CHEQUER INN   58 And simper'd (justly to compare)

simple   frequency: 1   relative frequency: 0.0000
P. 22 NYMPH   9 But, if my simple Pray'rs may yet

simplicity   frequency: 1   relative frequency: 0.0000
P. 38 PICTURE   1 See with what simplicity

simpson   frequency: 1   relative frequency: 0.0000
P. 110 ANNIVERSARY 305 While Peake and Simpson would in many a Tome,

sin   frequency: 9   relative frequency: 0.0001
P. 21 SOUL & BODY   42 To build me up for Sin so fit?
P. 22 NYMPH   24 The World, to offer for their Sin.
P. 76 A. HOUSE   556 Tempts impotent and bashful Sin.
P. 107 ANNIVERSARY 154 The World by Sin, does by the same extend.
P. 152 INSTRUCTIONS 464 For Sin against th' Eleventh Commandment.
P. 155 INSTRUCTIONS 583 An English Pilot too, (O Shame, O Sin!)
P. 160 INSTRUCTIONS 788 If no Creation, there had been no Sin.
P. 170 PROPHECY   18 And whoreing shall be the least sin att Court,
P. 203 HISTORICALL 106 Hence Death and Sin did human Nature blot:

since   frequency: 35   relative frequency: 0.0007
P. 10 DIALOGUE   33 But since none deserves that grace,
P. 15 EYES   5 And, since the Self-deluding Sight,
P. 18 CLORINDA   22 But He ere since my Songs does fill:
P. 21 SOUL & BODY   20 Since this ill Spirit it possest.
P. 45 GLO-WORMS   14 Since Juliana here is come,
P. 66 A. HOUSE   245 Till one, as long since prophecy'd,
P. 80 A. HOUSE   703 But, since She would nct have them seen,
P. 98 HOLLAND   123 'Tis true since that (as fortune kindly sports,)
P. 105 ANNIVERSARY 100 He hurles e'r since the World about him round;
P. 109 ANNIVERSARY 239 What since he did, an higher Force him push'd
P. 114 BLAKE   26 Above both Worlds, since 'tis above the rest.
P. 119 TWO SONGS   13 The Shepheard, since he saw thine Eyes,
P. 120 TWO SONGS   19 Since thou disdain'st not then to share
P. 126 O.C.   139 Which, since they might not hinder, yet they cast
P. 127 O.C.   171 Since him away the dismal Tempest rent,
P. 128 O.C.   192 Since the commanded sun o're Gibeon stay'd?
P. 130 O.C.   299 For we, since thou art gone, with heavy doome,
P. 130 O.C.   303 Since thou art gone, who best that way could'st
                         teach,
P. 139 HOUSEWARMING 71 Since the Act of Oblivion was never such
                         selling,
P. 146 INSTRUCTIONS 219 Never, before nor since, an Host so steel'd
P. 156 INSTRUCTIONS 628 She tears herself since him she cannot harm.
P. 156 INSTRUCTIONS 630 Long since were fled or many a feign'd pretence.
P. 159 INSTRUCTIONS 747 Sad change, since first that happy pair was wed,
P. 164 INSTRUCTIONS 954 And hurls them off, e're since, in his Career.
P. 177 LOYALL SCOT 250 And ever since men with a female spite
P. 180 STOCKSMARKET 35 With canvas and deals you e'er since do him
                         cloud,
P. 181 MADE FREE   28 But e're since he was bound
P. 185 BRITANNIA   28 Since Pharoh's Reign nor so Defild a Crown.
P. 190 STATUE   10 Since the privy garden could not it defend,
P. 192 TWO HORSES   27 Since Viner and Osburn did buy and provide 'um
P. 195 TWO HORSES   133 The Debauch'd and the Bloody since they Equally
                         Gall us,

P. 196	TWO HORSES	173	Why might not our Horses, since words are but wind,
P. 198	DUKE	38	He who longe since abjured the Royall line
P. 202	HISTORICALL	57	But since the ill gott race of Stewarts came,
P. 313	CHEQUER INN	19	And ever since he did so wex

sine-cure   frequency: 1 relative frequency: 0.0000
P. 175 LOYALL SCOT 127 A Bishoprick is a great sine-Cure.

sinecure. See "sine-cure."

sing   frequency: 19 relative frequency: 0.0003

P. 17	BERMUDAS	5	What should we do but sing his Praise
P. 18	CLORINDA	27	Of Pan the flowry Pastures sing,
P. 18	CLORINDA	29	Sing then while he doth us inspire;
P. 20	THYRSIS	33	There, birds sing Consorts, garlands grow,
P. 29	THE GALLERY	21	While all the morning Quire does sing,
P. 43	DAMON	63	And, when I tune my self to sing,
P. 47	EMPIRE	16	To sing Mens Triumphs, or in Heavens quire.
P. 75	A. HOUSE	514	To sing the Tryals of her Voice.
P. 87	ODE	3	Nor in the Shadows sing
P. 91	MAY'S DEATH	22	I sing (said he) and the Pharsalian Sign,
P. 106	ANNIVERSARY	113	Hence still they sing Hosanna to the Whore,
P. 129	O.C.	246	Nor with soft notes shall sing his cares asleep.
P. 132	PARADISE	39	The Bird nam'd from that Paradise you sing
P. 149	INSTRUCTIONS	365	France had St. Albans promis'd (so they sing)
P. 154	INSTRUCTIONS	541	Among the Shrowds the Seamen sit and sing,
P. 157	INSTRUCTIONS	696	Our English youth shall sing the Valiant Scot.
P. 171	LOYALL SCOT	4	Which of their Poets shold his Welcome sing,
P. 173	LOYALL SCOT	62	Our English youth shall sing the valiant Scott.
P. 185	BRITANNIA	43	In Lofty Notes Tudors blest reign to sing,

singer   frequency: 1 relative frequency: 0.0000
P. 31 FAIR SINGER t The Fair Singer.

singest. See "singst."

singing   frequency: 1 relative frequency: 0.0000
P. 130 O.C. 279 Singing of thee, inflame themselves to fight,

single   frequency: 10 relative frequency: 0.0002

P. 10	DIALOGUE	46	As when a single Soul does fence
P. 48	THE GARDEN	4	Crown'd from some single Herb or Tree.
P. 92	MAY'S DEATH	66	And single fights forsaken Vertues cause.
P. 125	O.C.	77	Fate could not either reach with single stroke,
P. 147	INSTRUCTIONS	248	Fighting it single till the rest might arm.
P. 147	INSTRUCTIONS	267	These and some more with single Valour stay
P. 169	ADVICE	44	In this Assault upon a single man.
P. 169	ADVICE	58	Leave Temple Single to be beat in the Citty.
P. 176	LOYALL SCOT	187	With single body like the two Neckt Swan,
P. 178	LOYALL SCOT	278	I single did against a Nation write,

singly   frequency: 2 relative frequency: 0.0000
P. 31 FAIR SINGER 7 I could have fled from One but singly fair:
P. 178 LOYALL SCOT 279 Against a Nation thou didst singly fight.

sings   frequency: 5 relative frequency: 0.0001

P. 49	THE GARDEN	53	There like a Bird it sits, and sings,
P. 92	MAY'S DEATH	69	Sings still of ancient Rights and better Times,
P. 105	ANNIVERSARY	73	Then our Amphion issues out and sings,
P. 108	ANNIVERSARY	211	Such as the dying Chorus sings by turns,
P. 119	TWO SONGS	5	Heark how he sings, with sad delight,

singst   frequency: 1 relative frequency: 0.0000
P. 132 PARADISE 36 Thou singst with so much gravity and ease;

sink   frequency: 5 relative frequency: 0.0001

P. 32	MOURNING	30	That sink for Pearl through Seas profound,
P. 108	ANNIVERSARY	213	When now they sink, and now the plundring Streams
P. 112	ANNIVERSARY	364	'And sink the Earth that does at Anchor ride.
P. 153	INSTRUCTIONS	520	Under Herculean Labours he may sink.
P. 196	TWO HORSES	186	Tis Bacchus and the Brewer swear Dam 'um and sink 'um.

sinking   frequency: 2 relative frequency: 0.0000
P. 98 HOLLAND 112 We buoy'd so often up their sinking State.
P. 103 ANNIVERSARY 2 Which in smooth streams a sinking Weight does raise;

sinks   frequency: 2 relative frequency: 0.0000

P. 157 INSTRUCTIONS   691 His Ship burns down, and with his Relicks
                          sinks,
P. 173 LOYALL SCOT   57 The ship burnes down and with his reliques sinks,

sinners   frequency: 2   relative frequency: 0.0000
    P. 139 HOUSEWARMING   66 Sinners, Governors, Farmers, Banquers,
                              Patentees.
    P. 193 TWO HORSES   85 Ch. Yet baser the souls of those low priced
                              Sinners,

sins   frequency: 5   relative frequency: 0.0001
    P. 64 A. HOUSE   184 'These as sweet Sins we should confess.
    P. 107 ANNIVERSARY   174 Our Sins endanger, and shall one day kill.
    P. 129 O.C.   266 At mortalls sins, nor his own plant will spare;
    P. 201 HISTORICALL   35 For those and Germin's sins she founds a
                              Church,
    P. 202 HISTORICALL   37 Now the Court Sins did every place defile,

sir   frequency: 20   relative frequency: 0.0004
    P.   3 LOVELACE   t1+ Sir,
    P. 85 FLECKNO   89 I answer'd he is here Sir; but you see
    P. 85 FLECKNO   93 Will make the way here; I said Sir you'l do
    P. 85 FLECKNO   104 By its own narrcwness, Sir, to unite.
    P. 86 FLECKNO   153 Sir you read false. That any one but you
    P. 87 FLECKNO   156 To say that you read false Sir is no Lye.
    P. 145 INSTRUCTIONS   193 For Chimney's sake they all Sir Pool obey'd,
    P. 145 INSTRUCTIONS   199 Sir Frederick and Sir Salomon draw Lotts
    P. 164 INSTRUCTIONS   955 And you, Great Sir, that with him Empire
                              share,
    P. 168 ADVICE   13 Where draw Sir Edward mounted on his throne,
    P. 179 STOCKSMARKET   3 So Sir Robert advanced the King's statue, in
                              token
    P. 179 STOCKSMARKET   15 And some by the likeness Sir Robert suspect
    P. 179 STOCKSMARKET   20 Even Sir William Peake sits much firmer than
                              he.
    P. 180 STOCKSMARKET   29 But Sir Robert to take all the scandal away
    P. 180 STOCKSMARKET   33 But, Sir Knight of the Vine, how came't in
                              your thought
    P. 180 STOCKSMARKET   53 But Sir Robert affirms we do him much wrong;
    P. 182 MADE FREE   71 Of Sir Thomas Player
    P. 195 TWO HORSES   152 W. And our Sir Joseph write news-books, and
                              fiddle.
    P. 315 CHEQUER INN   127 Sir Courtney Pocle and he contend

sire   frequency: 1   relative frequency: 0.0000
    P. 163 INSTRUCTIONS   918 Of Grandsire Harry, and of Charles his Sire.

sirs   frequency: 2   relative frequency: 0.0000
    P. 184 MADE FREE   127 And now Worshipfull Sirs
    P. 191 TWO HORSES   13 At Delphos and Rome Stocks and Stones now and
                              then, sirs,

sister   frequency: 6   relative frequency: 0.0001
    P. 48 THE GARDEN   10 And Innocence thy Sister dear!
    P. 63 A. HOUSE   154 'Each one your Sister, each your Maid.
    P. 120 TWO SONGS   31 Yet is her younger Sister laid
    P. 170 PROPHECY   19 A Boy shall take his Sister for his Mate
    P. 201 HISTORICALL   19 And his Dutch Sister quickly after dy'd,
    P. 202 HISTORICALL   69 Not Tereus with his Sister Philomel.

sisyphus's   frequency: 1   relative frequency: 0.0000
    P. 149 INSTRUCTIONS   360 And roul in vain at Sisyphus's Stone.

sit   frequency: 14   relative frequency: 0.0002
    See also "sitte."
    P.   3 LOVELACE   15 I see the envious Caterpillar sit
    P. 26 MISTRESS   3 We would sit down, and think which way
    P. 29 THE GALLERY   24 Sit perfecting their harmless Loves.
    P. 44 GLO-WORMS   2 The Nightingale does sit so late,
    P. 76 A. HOUSE   573 And more attentive there doth sit
    P. 81 A. HOUSE   732 Lest the smooth Forehead wrinkled sit:
    P. 93 DR. WITTY   1 Sit further, and make room for thine own fame,
    P. 154 INSTRUCTIONS   541 Among the Shrowds the Seamen sit and sing,
    P. 154 INSTRUCTIONS   565 No man can sit there safe, the Cannon pow'rs
    P. 162 INSTRUCTIONS   880 An Urinal, and sit like any Hen.
    P. 164 INSTRUCTIONS   946 And henceforth Charles only to Charles shall
                              sit.
    P. 166 KINGS VOWES   34 I will have a Privy Councell to sit allwayes
                              still,
    P. 176 LOYALL SCOT   210 To sit is Necessary in Parliament,
    P. 314 CHEQUER INN   57 Till to sit downe were desir'd

sith   frequency: 1   relative frequency: 0.0000

P. 73 A. HOUSE   453 And what below the Sith increast

sithe   frequency: 3   relative frequency: 0.0000
P. 43 DAMON   51 This Sithe of mine discovers wide
P. 43 DAMON   58 If in my Sithe I looked right;
P. 71 A. HOUSE   393 With whistling Sithe, and Elbow strong,

sits   frequency: 9   relative frequency: 0.0001
P. 27 MISTRESS   34 Sits on thy skin like morning dew,
P. 49 THE GARDEN   53 There like a Bird it sits, and sings,
P. 75 A. HOUSE   515 Low Shrubs she sits in, and adorns
P. 140 HOUSEWARMING   98 Where this Idol of State sits ador'd and
                             accurst:
P. 149 INSTRUCTIONS   356 And sits in State Divine like Jove the
                             fulminant!
P. 162 INSTRUCTIONS   871 In Chair, he smoaking sits like Master-Cook,
P. 163 INSTRUCTIONS   919 Harry sits down, and in his open side
P. 179 STOCKSMARKET   20 Even Sir William Peake sits much firmer than
                             he.
P. 187 BRITANNIA   119 Like a Tame spinster in 's seraglio sits,

sit'st   frequency: 1   relative frequency: 0.0000
P. 30 THE GALLERY   33 But, against that, thou sit'st a float

sitte   frequency: 1   relative frequency: 0.0000
P. 197 DUKE   3 Who all in triumph shall about him sitte

sitting   frequency: 2   relative frequency: 0.0000
P. 148 INSTRUCTIONS   326 Load them with Envy, and with Sitting tire:
P. 192 TWO HORSES   31 When both the Kings weary of Sitting all day

sittings   frequency: 1   relative frequency: 0.0000
P. 141 INSTRUCTIONS   1 After two sittings, now our Lady State,

situation   frequency: 1   relative frequency: 0.0000
P. 140 HOUSEWARMING   102 Throw dust in its Front, and blame situation:

six   frequency: 1   relative frequency: 0.0000
P. 170 PROPHECY   2 And cover it in flames in sixty six;

sixteene   frequency: 1   relative frequency: 0.0000
P. 199 DUKE   53 Dy before twenty, or rott before sixteene.

sixty   frequency: 1   relative frequency: 0.0000
P. 170 PROPHECY   2 And cover it in flames in sixty six;

size   frequency: 1   relative frequency: 0.0000
P. 199 DUKE   68 He's of a size indeed to fill a porch,

sized   frequency: 1   relative frequency: 0.0000
P. 59 A. HOUSE   29 When larger sized Men did stoop

sketching   frequency: 1   relative frequency: 0.0000
P. 141 INSTRUCTIONS   11 Sketching in shady smoke prodigious tools,

skie   frequency: 3   relative frequency: 0.0000
P. 19 THYRSIS   9 Thyrsis. Turn thine Eye to yonder Skie,
P. 80 A. HOUSE   684 Draws through the Skie, nor Star new-slain.
P. 117 BLAKE   128 Some Ships are sunk, some blown up in the skie.

skies   frequency: 6   relative frequency: 0.0001
See also "skyes."
P. 12 DROP OF DEW   11 But gazing back upon the Skies,
P. 12 DROP OF DEW   18 And to the Skies exhale it back again.
P. 31 MOURNING   2 Of humane Off-springs from the Skies,
P. 98 HOLLAND   128 In a calm Winter, under Skies Serene.
P. 153 INSTRUCTIONS   529 The Sun much brighter, and the Skies more
                             clear,
P. 154 INSTRUCTIONS   552 A Fleet of Clouds, sailing along the Skies:

skilful   frequency: 3   relative frequency: 0.0000
P. 50 THE GARDEN   65 How well the skilful Gardner drew
P. 107 ANNIVERSARY   183 Like skilful Looms which through the costly
                             thred
P. 131 PARADISE   18 Jealous I was that some less skilful hand

skill   frequency: 10   relative frequency: 0.0002
P. 10 DIALOGUE   35 When the Creator's skill is priz'd,
P. 15 THE CORONET   24 Though set with Skill and chosen out with Care.
P. 18 CLORINDA   21 D. Words that transcend poor Shepherds skill,
P. 41 THE MOWER   36 More by their presence then their skill.

```
    P.  70 A. HOUSE       353 For he did, with his utmost Skill,
    P. 107 ANNIVERSARY    173 Thee proof beyond all other Force or Skill,
    P. 141 INSTRUCTIONS     8 'Twill suit our great debauch and little skill.
    P. 141 INSTRUCTIONS    13 But if to match our Crimes thy skill presumes,
    P. 173 LOYALL SCOT     79 But this wee know, tho' that Exceed their skill,
    P. 199 DUKE            74 Then, Painter, shew thy skill and in fitt place
```

skill'd   frequency: 1   relative frequency: 0.0000
```
    P. 162 INSTRUCTIONS   873 Well was he skill'd to season any question,
```

skills   frequency: 1   relative frequency: 0.0000
```
    P. 124 O.C.            63 Yet both perceiv'd, yet both conceal'd their
                             Skills,
```

skin   frequency: 6   relative frequency: 0.0001
```
    P.  27 MISTRESS        34 Sits on thy skin like morning dew,
    P.  42 DAMON           16 Now glitters in its second skin.
    P.  75 A. HOUSE       520 Within the Skin its shrunken claws.
    P.  81 A. HOUSE       734 Thorough the Black-bag of your Skin;
    P.  86 FLECKNO        134 Like white fleaks rising from a Leaper's skin!
    P. 143 INSTRUCTIONS    93 Stript to her Skin, see how she stooping stands,
```

skip   frequency: 1   relative frequency: 0.0000
```
    P. 173 LOYALL SCOT     63 Skip Sadles: Pegasus thou needst not Bragg,
```

skipper   frequency: 2   relative frequency: 0.0000
```
    P.  97 HOLLAND         93 Or what a Spectacle the Skipper gross,
    P. 155 INSTRUCTIONS   589 A Skipper rude shocks it without respect,
```

skipping   frequency: 1   relative frequency: 0.0000
```
    P.  23 NYMPH          65 With what a pretty skipping grace,
```

skirt   frequency: 1   relative frequency: 0.0000
```
    P.  89 ODE            90 To lay them at the Publick's skirt.
```

skreen   frequency: 1   relative frequency: 0.0000
```
    P.  80 A. HOUSE      704 The Wood about her draws a Skreen.
```

sky   frequency: 4   relative frequency: 0.0000
See also "skie."
```
    P.  89 ODE            92 Falls heavy from the Sky,
    P.  96 HOLLAND        22 To reach the Sea, then those to scale the Sky.
    P. 114 BLAKE          27 For least some Gloominess might stain her sky,
    P. 121 TWO SONGS      50 Or shine Thou there and 'tis the Sky.
```

skyes   frequency: 5   relative frequency: 0.0001
```
    P. 104 ANNIVERSARY    46 And cuts his way still nearer to the Skyes,
    P. 109 ANNIVERSARY   233 Till at the Seventh time thou in the Skyes,
    P. 124 O.C.           70 Devides the Air, and opens all the Skyes:
    P. 126 O.C.          120 The deep foundations open'd to the Skyes.
    P. 170 PROPHECY        6 With high aspireing head towards those Skyes
```

sky's   frequency: 1   relative frequency: 0.0000
```
    P. 174 LOYALL SCOT    84 Up from her Stream Continued to the Sky's,
```

slacken   frequency: 1   relative frequency: 0.0000
```
    P. 124 O.C.           34 Slacken the vigour of his Muscles strong;
```

slain   frequency: 3   relative frequency: 0.0000
See also "new-slain."
```
    P.  22 NYMPH          16 Ev'n Beasts must be with justice slain;
    P.  72 A. HOUSE      422 Lyes quilted ore with Bodies slain:
    P. 123 O.C.           10 Unless the Prince whom they applaud be slain.
```

slake   frequency: 1   relative frequency: 0.0000
```
    P.  18 CLORINDA       16 Or slake its Drought? C. What is't you mean?
```

slakes   frequency: 1   relative frequency: 0.0000
```
    P.  16 EYES           40 And here the hissing Lightning slakes.
```

slasht   frequency: 1   relative frequency: 0.0000
```
    P. 201 HISTORICALL    11 In a slasht doublet then he came to shoare,
```

slaughters   frequency: 1   relative frequency: 0.0000
```
    P. 195 TWO HORSES    131 Ch. More Tolerable are the Lion Kings
                             Slaughters
```

slave   frequency: 3   relative frequency: 0.0000
```
    P.  11 DIALOGUE       65 Half the World shall be thy Slave
    P.  31 FAIR SINGER    10 But how should I avoid to be her Slave,
    P. 156 INSTRUCTIONS  619 Now a cheap spoil, and the mean Victor's Slave,
```

slavery   frequency: 1   relative frequency: 0.0000
    P. 204 HISTORICAII   136 Old England truckling under slavery.

slaves   frequency: 8   relative frequency: 0.0001
    P. 11 DIALOGUE   68 What Slaves, unless I captive you?
    P. 32 MOURNING   29 How wide they dream! The Indian Slaves
    P. 138 HOUSEWARMING   34 To buy us for Slaves, and purchase our Lands;
    P. 150 INSTRUCTIONS   370 Like Slaves, shall beg for Peace at Hollands
                              doors.
    P. 184 MADE FREE   131 You for Slaves are decreed,
    P. 193 TWO HORSES   67 W. That makeing us slaves by hors and foot
                              Guards
    P. 196 TWO HORSES   182 They that Conquered the Father won't be slaves
                              to the Son:
    P. 316 CHEQUER INN   134 Fathers and Sons like Coupl'd Slaves

slavish   frequency: 1   relative frequency: 0.0000
    P. 189 BRITANNIA   174 Blake, Candish, Drake, (men void of slavish
                              fears)

sleep   frequency: 7   relative frequency: 0.0001
    P. 16 EYES   47 For others too can see, or sleep;
    P. 20 THYRSIS   48 So shall we smoothly pass away in sleep.
    P. 111 ANNIVERSARY   336 Not knowing yet the Night was made for sleep:
    P. 114 BLAKE   18 More wish't for, and more welcome is then sleep,
    P. 119 TWO SONGS   11 If thou a Mortal, rather sleep;
    P. 129 O.C.   248 And mortal sleep over those wakefull eyes:
    P. 146 INSTRUCTIONS   243 And some ran o're each night while others sleep,

sleeps   frequency: 2   relative frequency: 0.0000
    P. 68 A. HOUSE   319 And sleeps so too: but, if once stir'd,
    P. 148 INSTRUCTICNS   321 The busie Hammer sleeps, the Ropes untwine;

sleeve   frequency: 1   relative frequency: 0.0000
    P. 174 LOYALL SCOT   105 And slip one Half into his sleeve as soon.

sleeves   frequency: 2   relative frequency: 0.0000
    See also "lawn-sleeves."
    P. 174 LOYALL SCOT   116 How Reverend things are 'lord', Lawn Sleeves
                              and Ease!
    P. 174 LOYALL SCOT   123 And learn to pin your faith upon their sleeves.

slender   frequency: 3   relative frequency: 0.0000
    P. 18 CLORINDA   23 And his Name swells my slender Oate.
    P. 131 PARADISE   2 In slender Book his vast Design unfold,
    P. 313 CHEQUER INN   29 For all his slender Quarter Staffe

slept   frequency: 2   relative frequency: 0.0000
    P. 36 DAPHNIS   102 Last night he with Phlogis slept;
    P. 127 O.C.   156 And slept in Peace under the Lawrel shade.

slick   frequency: 1   relative frequency: 0.0000
    P. 78 A. HOUSE   636 Till as a Chrystal Mirrour slick;

slide   frequency: 2   relative frequency: 0.0000
    P. 94 DR. WITTY   27 Translators learn of her: but stay I slide
    P. 109 ANNIVERSARY   270 And Corposants along the Tacklings slide.

sliding   frequency: 2   relative frequency: 0.0000
    P. 49 THE GARDEN   49 Here at the Fountains sliding foot,
    P. 79 A. HOUSE   645 Or to suspend my sliding Foot

slight   frequency: 7   relative frequency: 0.0001
    P. 12 DROP OF DEW   9 How it the purple flow'r does slight,
    P. 44 DAMON   81 Alas! said He, these hurts are slight
    P. 79 A. HOUSE   652 Hide trifling Youth thy Pleasures slight.
    P. 141 INSTRUCTIONS   4 It be'nt too slight grown, or too hard for thee.
    P. 155 INSTRUCTIONS 587 Engine so slight to guard us from the Sea,
    P. 186 BRITANNIA   83 These pious frauds (too slight t'ensnare the
                              brave)
    P. 203 HISTORICALL   92 With hocus pocus and their heavenly slight

slights   frequency: 2   relative frequency: 0.0000
    P. 60 A. HOUSE   55 And too officiously it slights
    P. 143 INSTRUCTIONS   86 She slights) his Feet shapt for a smoother race.

slimy   frequency: 1   relative frequency: 0.0000
    P. 185 BRITANNIA   27 Such slimy Monsters ne're approacht a throne

slip   frequency: 1   relative frequency: 0.0000
    P. 174 LOYALL SCOT   105 And slip one Half into his sleeve as soon.

slippery. See "slipp'ry."

slipp'ry   frequency: 1   relative frequency: 0.0000
    P.   14 THE CORONET   20 Either his slipp'ry knots at once untie,

slips   frequency: 2   relative frequency: 0.0000
    P. 160 INSTRUCTIONS   786 Was the first cause of all these Naval slips:
    P. 201 HISTORICALL   36 So slips away and leaves us in the lurch.

slipt   frequency: 1   relative frequency: 0.0000
    P. 110 ANNIVERSARY   296 Rejoycing when thy Foot had slipt aside;

sloath   frequency: 1   relative frequency: 0.0000
    P. 195 TWO HORSES   142 W. But hee 's buryed alive in lust and in
                                slcath.

sloth   frequency: 1   relative frequency: 0.0000
    See also "sloath."
    P. 106 ANNIVERSARY   122 Your Regal sloth, and your long Slumbers wake:

slow   frequency: 7   relative frequency: 0.0001
    See also "slowe."
    P.   26 MISTRESS   12 Vaster then Empires, and more slow.
    P.   32 MOURNING   10 Slcw drops unty themselves away;
    P.   61 A. HOUSE   81 While with slow Eyes we these survey,
    P.   83 A. HOUSE   773 How Tortoise like, but not so slow,
    P.   95 HOLLAND   5 Or what by th' Oceans slcw alluvion fell,
    P. 103 ANNIVERSARY   20 More slow and brittle then the China clay:
    P. 123 O.C.   29 Streight does a slcw and languishing Disease

slow-chapt   frequency: 1   relative frequency: 0.0000
    P.   27 MISTRESS   40 Than languish in his slow-chapt pow'r.

slowe   frequency: 1   relative frequency: 0.0000
    P.   4 HASTINGS   11 The Phlegmatick and Slowe prolongs his day,

slowly   frequency: 3   relative frequency: 0.0000
    P.   24 NYMPH   96 Sad, slowly dropping like a Gumme.
    P.   73 A. HOUSE   463 They feed so wide, so slcwly move,
    P. 113 BLAKE   3 But though the wind was fair, they slowly swoome

slowness   frequency: 1   relative frequency: 0.0000
    P. 146 INSTRUCTIONS   215 He, to excuse his slowness, truth ccnfest

sluces   frequency: 1   relative frequency: 0.0000
    P. 112 ANNIVERSARY   368 'Whose Navies hold the Sluces of the Sea.

sluice   frequency: 1   relative frequency: 0.0000
    P.   16 EYES   45 Ope then mine Eyes your double Sluice,

sluices. See "sluces."

slumber   frequency: 1   relative frequency: 0.0000
    P. 129 O.C.   247 I saw him dead, a leaden slumber lyes,

slumbering. See "slumb'ring."

slumbers   frequency: 2   relative frequency: 0.0000
    P. 106 ANNIVERSARY   122 Your Regal sloth, and your long Slumbers wake:
    P. 185 BRITANNIA   12 Whilest the Lew'd Court in drunken slumbers
                                lyes,

slumb'ring   frequency: 1   relative frequency: 0.0000
    P.   29 THE GALLERY   19 When in the East she slumb'ring lyes,

smalest   frequency: 1   relative frequency: 0.0000
    P. 200 DUKE   91 The smalest atcme cf an English soul.

small   frequency: 9   relative frequency: 0.0001
    P.   17 BERMUDAS   3 From a small Bcat, that row'd along,
    P.   66 A. HOUSE   233 Small Honour would be in the Storm.
    P.   96 HOLLAND   13 Collecting anxiously small Loads of Clay,
    P.   96 HOLLAND   49 Hence some small Dyke-grave unperceiv'd invades
    P. 109 ANNIVERSARY   234 As a small Cloud, like a Mans hand didst rise;
    P. 143 INSTRUCTIONS   118 With what small Arts the publick game they play.
    P. 183 MADE FREE   90 Tho' too small fcr the Carriage of Starling.
    P. 190 STATUE   6 To Limitt his trocp to this Theatre small,
    P. 201 HISTORICALL   9 Nor did he such small favours then disdain

smallest   frequency: 1   relative frequency: 0.0000
    See also "smalest."
    P. 165 INSTRUCTIONS   981 The smallest Vermin make the greatest waste,

smart   frequency: 2   relative frequency: 0.0000
    P. 22 NYMPH   35 And quite regardless of my Smart.
    P. 195 TWO HORSES   146 Father Patricks Deciple will make England
                              smart.

smarts   frequency: 1   relative frequency: 0.0000
    P. 142 INSTRUCTIONS   74 But in her soft Breast Loves hid Cancer
                              smarts.

smell   frequency: 3   relative frequency: 0.0000
    P. 30 THE GALLERY   40 Convoy the Perfume to the Smell.
    P. 38 PICTURE   8 What Colour best becomes them, and what Smell.
    P. 68 A. HOUSE   308 But Ecchoes to the Eye and smell.

smells   frequency: 1   relative frequency: 0.0000
    P. 72 A. HOUSE   428 Smells like an Alexanders sweat.

smelt   frequency: 1   relative frequency: 0.0000
    P. 107 ANNIVERSARY   164 T'have smelt the Blosscme, and not eat the
                              Fruit;

smil'd   frequency: 1   relative frequency: 0.0000
    P. 129 O.C.   236 No April sunns that e'er so gently smil'd;

smile   frequency: 3   relative frequency: 0.0000
    P. 60 A. HOUSE   39 And some will smile at this, as well
    P. 189 BRITANNIA   192 The Earth shall rest, the Heavens shall on thee
                              smile,
    P. 204 HISTORICALL   135 Let Cromwells Ghost smile with Contempt to see

smileing   frequency: 2   relative frequency: 0.0000
    P. 178 LOYALL SCOT   282 Here Douglas smileing said hee did Intend
    P. 314 CHEQUER INN   63 And smileing through did Saile

smiles   frequency: 3   relative frequency: 0.0000
    P. 94 DR. WITTY   22 But her own smiles commend that lovely face;
    P. 114 BLAKE   23 At length theirs vanishes, and fortune smiles;
    P. 124 O.C.   41 When She with Smiles serene and Words discreet

smiling   frequency: 3   relative frequency: 0.0000
    See also "smileing."
    P. 111 ANNIVERSARY   342 Smiling serenely from the further side.
    P. 141 INSTRUCTIONS   26 And he sat smiling how his Dog did grinn.
    P. 161 INSTRUCTIONS   836 Salute them, smiling at their vain design.

smoak   frequency: 1   relative frequency: 0.0000
    P. 194 TWO HORSES   88 Of Exciseing our Cups and Taxing our Smoak.

smoakd   frequency: 1   relative frequency: 0.0000
    P. 139 HOUSEWARMING   73 'Twas then that the Chimny-Contractors he smoakd,

smoake   frequency: 1   relative frequency: 0.0000
    P. 315 CHEQUER INN   132 Excise Us for our Smoake.

smoaking   frequency: 1   relative frequency: 0.0000
    P. 162 INSTRUCTIONS   871 In Chair, he smoaking sits like Master-Cook,

smoke   frequency: 1   relative frequency: 0.0000
    See also "smoak," "smoake."
    P. 141 INSTRUCTIONS   11 Sketching in shady smoke prodigious tools,

smoked. See "smoakd."

smoking. See "smoaking."

smooth   frequency: 4   relative frequency: 0.0000
    P. 65 A. HOUSE   200 The Nuns smooth Tongue has suckt her in.
    P. 72 A. HOUSE   443 A levell'd space, as smooth and plain,
    P. 81 A. HOUSE   732 Lest the smooth Forehead wrinkled sit:
    P. 103 ANNIVERSARY   2 Which in smooth streams a sinking Weight does
                              raise;

smoothen'd   frequency: 1   relative frequency: 0.0000
    P. 161 INSTRUCTIONS   838 With Face new bleacht, smoothen'd and stiff with
                              starch.

smoother   frequency: 1   relative frequency: 0.0000
    P. 143 INSTRUCTIONS   86 She slights) his Feet shapt for a smoother race.

smoothly   frequency: 1   relative frequency: 0.0000
    P. 20 THYRSIS   48 So shall we smoothly pass away in sleep.

smutty   frequency: 1   relative frequency: 0.0000
    P. 175 LOYALL SCOT   171 Like Smutty Storyes in Pure Linnen Wrapt.

smyrna   frequency: 1   relative frequency: 0.0000
    P. 180 STOCKSMARKET   51 If the Indies and Smyrna do not him enrich,

snake   frequency: 4   relative frequency: 0.0000
    P. 42 DAMON   15 Only the Snake, that kept within,
    P. 42 DAMON   35 To Thee the harmless Snake I bring,
    P. 78 A. HOUSE   632 Among these Meads the only Snake.
    P. 176 LOYALL SCOT   177 Like Snake that Swallowes toad doth Dragon
                             swell.

snapping   frequency: 1   relative frequency: 0.0000
    P. 155 INSTRUCTIONS 594 Snapping the brittle links, does thorow reel;

snare   frequency: 1   relative frequency: 0.0000
    P. 14 THE CORONET   21 And disintangle all his winding Snare:

sneaking   frequency: 1   relative frequency: 0.0000
    P. 205 HISTORICALL   162 His Brother sneaking Heretik should dye,

sneer   frequency: 1   relative frequency: 0.0000
    P. 98 HOLLAND   96 When Stagg'ring upon some Land, Snick and
                             Sneer,

snick   frequency: 1   relative frequency: 0.0000
    P. 98 HOLLAND   96 When Stagg'ring upon some Land, Snick and
                             Sneer,

snips   frequency: 1   relative frequency: 0.0000
    P. 139 HOUSEWARMING   72 As at this Benevolence out of the Snips.

snow   frequency: 2   relative frequency: 0.0000
    P. 94 DR. WITTY   18 Then Tagus, purer then dissolved snow,
    P. 175 LOYALL SCOT   165 Nor is our Sheldon whiter then his Snow.

snowy   frequency: 1   relative frequency: 0.0000
    P. 25 YOUNG LOVE   13 Love as much the snowy Lamb

snuff   frequency: 1   relative frequency: 0.0000
    See also "snuffe."
    P. 141 INSTRUCTIONS   10 The Aly roof, with snuff of Candle dimm,

snuffe   frequency: 1   relative frequency: 0.0000
    P. 108 ANNIVERSARY   197 Nor through wide Nostrils snuffe the wanton air,

so   frequency: 312   relative frequency: 0.0065
    See also "soe."

soaks   frequency: 1   relative frequency: 0.0000
    P. 162 INSTRUCTIONS 882 And soaks his Sack with Norfolk like a Toast.

soar   frequency: 1   relative frequency: 0.0000
    P. 132 PARADISE   37 And above humane flight dost soar aloft,

sober   frequency: 5   relative frequency: 0.0001
    P. 59 A. HOUSE   1 Within this sober Frame expect
    P. 59 A. HOUSE   28 Of that more sober Age and Mind,
    P. 83 FLECKNO   28 The last distemper of the sober Brain,
    P. 109 ANNIVERSARY   230 Thy sober Spirit unto things too High,
    P. 110 ANNIVERSARY   289 That sober Liberty which men may have,

sobriety   frequency: 2   relative frequency: 0.0000
    P. 182 MADE FREE   57 But he chanc'd to have more Sobriety,
    P. 188 BRITANNIA   162 To love sobriety and holy truth,

society   frequency: 2   relative frequency: 0.0000
    P. 48 THE GARDEN   15 Society is all but rude,
    P. 142 INSTRUCTIONS   58 Of's Highnesses Royal Society.

sod   frequency: 1   relative frequency: 0.0000
    P. 69 A. HOUSE   345 And yet their walks one on the Sod

soder'd   frequency: 1   relative frequency: 0.0000
    P. 157 INSTRUCTIONS 686 His alt'ring Form, and soder'd Limbs to melt;

sodomy   frequency: 1   relative frequency: 0.0000
    P. 170 PROPHECY   17 When Sodomy is the Premier Ministers sport

sodred   frequency: 1   relative frequency: 0.0000

          P. 173 LOYALL SCOT   52 His Altred form and sodred Limbs to Melt,

soe   frequency: 25   relative frequency: 0.0005

soever   frequency: 1   relative frequency: 0.0000

soft   frequency: 15   relative frequency: 0.0003
    P.   9 DIALOGUE   20 Whose soft Plumes will thither fly:
    P. 11 DIALOGUE   51 All this fair, and soft, and sweet,
    P. 23 NYMPH   60 I blusht to see its foot more soft,
    P. 43 DAMON   62 To lead them in their Danses soft;
    P. 57 BILL-BOROW   17 See what a soft access and wide
    P. 63 A. HOUSE   159 'How soft the yoke on us would lye,
    P. 125 O.C.   82 Or fan with airy plumes so soft an heat.
    P. 129 O.C.   246 Nor with soft notes shall sing his cares asleep.
    P. 132 PARADISE   38 With Plume so strong, so equal, and so soft.
    P. 142 INSTRUCTIONS   74 But in her soft Breast Loves hid Cancer
                              smarts.
    P. 156 INSTRUCTIONS   656 Harden'd and cool'd his limbs, so soft, so
                              white,
    P. 172 LOYALL SCOT   11 For those soft Airs had temper'd every thought,
    P. 172 LOYALL SCOT   22 Hardned and Cool'd those Limbs soe soft, soe
                              white,
    P. 201 HISTORICALL   20 Soft in her Nature and of wanton pride.
    P. 202 HISTORICALL   43 The dreadfull Victor tooke his soft repose,

soften   frequency: 1   relative frequency: 0.0000
    P. 32 MOURNING   15 Only to soften near her Heart

softest   frequency: 3   relative frequency: 0.0000
    P. 20 THYRSIS   32 Of sweetest grass, and softest wooll;
    P. 56 BILL-BOROW   5 Nor softest Pensel draw a Brow
    P. 141 INSTRUCTIONS   28 What all thy softest touches cannot do.

softly   frequency: 1   relative frequency: 0.0000
    P. 124 O.C.   35 Then to the Mothers brest her softly move,

softness   frequency: 1   relative frequency: 0.0000
    P. 123 O.C.   20 Should speak the wondrous softness of his Heart.

soil   frequency: 1   relative frequency: 0.0000
    See also "soyl," "scyle."
    P. 115 BLAKE   53 There the indulgent Soil that rich Grape
                              breeds,

soiled. See "soyl'd."

solac'd   frequency: 1   relative frequency: 0.0000
    P. 152 INSTRUCTIONS   475 But still in hope he solac'd, e're they come,

solaced. See "solac'd."

solbay   frequency: 1   relative frequency: 0.0000
    P. 202 HISTORICALL   54 De Ruyter claps him in Solbay again.

sold   frequency: 6   relative frequency: 0.0001
    See also "sould."
    P. 11 DIALOGUE   62 And that 's worth nought that can be sold.
    P. 41 THE MOWER   16 That one was for a Meadow sold.
    P. 138 HOUSEWARMING   41 The Scotch Forts <and> Dunkirk, but that they
                              were sold,
    P. 144 INSTRUCTIONS   156 That sold their Master, led by Ashburnham.
    P. 159 INSTRUCTIONS   770 Who all Commands sold thro' the Navy? Pett.
    P. 179 STOCKSMARKET   24 Say his Majesty himself is bought too and sold.

soldered. See "soder'd," "sodred."

soldier. See "souldier."

soldiers   frequency: 1   relative frequency: 0.0000
    See also "souldiers."
    P. 72 A. HOUSE   440 In Hills for Soldiers Obsequies.

sole   frequency: 1   relative frequency: 0.0000
    P. 115 BLAKE   50 Peace, against you, was the sole strength of
                              Spain.

solebay. See "solbay."

solemn   frequency: 1   relative frequency: 0.0000
    P. 47 EMPIRE   18 Did of all these a solemn noise prepare:

solemniz'd   frequency: 1   relative frequency: 0.0000
    P. 125 O.C.   110 By nature solemniz'd with so much state.

solicitor.   See "sollicitor."

solid.   See "sollid."

solitary   frequency: 4   relative frequency: 0.0000
    P. 22 NYMPH   38 My solitary time away,
    P. 32 MOURNING   18 Within her solitary Bowr,
    P. 47 EMPIRE   3 All Musick was a solitary sound,
    P. 49 THE GARDEN   62 To wander solitary there:

solitude   frequency: 1   relative frequency: 0.0000
    P. 48 THE GARDEN   16 To this delicious Solitude.

sollicitor   frequency: 1   relative frequency: 0.0000
    P. 147 INSTRUCTIONS 256 Of Irish-Cattel and Sollicitor.

sollid   frequency: 1   relative frequency: 0.0000
    P. 138 HOUSEWARMING   30 None sollid enough seem'd for his Thong Caster;

some   frequency: 71   relative frequency: 0.0014
    P.   3 LOVELACE   27 Some reading your Lucasta, will alledge
    P.   3 LOVELACE   29 Some that you under sequestration are,
    P.   4 HASTINGS   1 Go, intercept some Fountain in the Vein,
    P.   5 HASTINGS   27 Yet as some Prince, that, for State-Jealousie,
    P.   5 HASTINGS   49 Like some sad Chymist, who, prepar'd to reap
    P. 30 THE GALLERY   37 Or, if some rowling Wave appears,
    P. 31 FAIR SINGER   13 It had been easie fighting in some plain,
    P. 32 MOURNING   13 Yet some affirm, pretending Art,
    P. 37 DEFINITION   22 And Earth some new Convulsion tear;
    P. 38 PICTURE   24 Where I may see thy Glories from some shade.
    P. 41 THE MOWER   37 Their Statues polish'd by some ancient hand,
    P. 47 EMPIRE   13 Some to the Lute, some to the Viol went,
    P. 48 THE GARDEN   4 Crown'd from some single Herb or Tree.
    P. 49 THE GARDEN   50 Or at some Fruit-trees mossy root,
    P. 54 THYESTE   4 Settled in some secret Nest
    P. 60 A. HOUSE   39 And some will smile at this, as well
    P. 62 A. HOUSE   122 'Some One the holy Legend reads;
    P. 63 A. HOUSE   133 'Some of your Features, as we sow'd,
    P. 66 A. HOUSE   249 Some to the Breach against their Foes
    P. 68 A. HOUSE   317 Then in some Flow'rs beloved Hut
    P. 75 A. HOUSE   525 Yet always, for some Cause unknown,
    P. 77 A. HOUSE   592 Like some great Prelate of the Grove,
    P. 77 A. HOUSE   604 Bends in some Tree its useless Dart;
    P. 82 A. HOUSE   741 Whence, for some universal good,
    P. 83 FLECKNO   3 I for some branch of Melchizedeck took,
    P. 83 FLECKNO   29 That there had been some present to assure
    P. 85 FLECKNO   102 Our peace, the Priest said I too had some wit:
    P. 91 MAY'S DEATH   44 On them some Romane cast similitude,
    P. 91 MAY'S DEATH   57 Because some one than thee more worthy weares
    P. 93 DR. WITTY   3 The good Interpreter. Some in this task
    P. 96 HOLLAND   49 Hence some small Dyke-grave unperceiv'd invades
    P. 96 HOLLAND   51 But for less envy some joynt States endures,
    P. 97 HOLLAND   83 Some Fifteen hundred and more years ago;
    P. 98 HOLLAND   96 When Stagg'ring upon some Land, Snick and
                             Sneer,
    P. 98 HOLLAND   110 It self, when as some greater Vessel tows
    P. 104 ANNIVERSARY   23 Yet some more active for a Frontier Town
    P. 105 ANNIVERSARY   84 And some fall back upon the Architect;
    P. 106 ANNIVERSARY   118 By Malice some, by Errour more misled;
    P. 106 ANNIVERSARY   131 Hence oft I think, if in some happy Hour
    P. 110 ANNIVERSARY   273 Some lusty Mate, who with more careful Eye
    P. 114 BLAKE   27 For least some Gloominess might stain her sky,
    P. 117 BLAKE   128 Some Ships are sunk, some blown up in the skie.
    P. 118 BLAKE   133 Torn Limbs some leagues into the Island fly,
    P. 121 TWO SONGS   5 Stay till I some flow'rs ha' ty'd
    P. 122 TWO SONGS   27 Come, lets in some Carol new
    P. 125 O.C.   93 If some dear branch where it extends its life
    P. 125 O.C.   103 Whether some Kinder Pow'rs, that wish us well,
    P. 131 PARADISE   18 Jealous I was that some less skilful hand
    P. 138 HOUSEWARMING   48 To grudge him some Timber who fram'd them the
                             War.
    P. 140 HOUSEWARMING 101 Now some (as all Buildings must censure abide)
    P. 143 INSTRUCTIONS 115 As some from Boxes, he so from the Chair
    P. 146 INSTRUCTIONS 243 And some ran o're each night while others sleep,
    P. 147 INSTRUCTIONS 267 These and some more with single Valour stay
    P. 159 INSTRUCTIONS 766 Some one must be accus'd by Punishment.
    P. 161 INSTRUCTIONS 852 Lest some new Tomkins spring a fresh debate.
    P. 163 INSTRUCTIONS 908 As one that some unusual noise does hear.

```
          P.  163 INSTRUCTIONS   910 But let some other Painter draw the sound:
          P.  167 KINGS VOWES      58 Some one I will advance from mean descent,
          P.  177 LOYALL SCOT     223 Some sue for tyth of the Elyzean plaines:
          P.  178 LOYALL SCOT     285 Metemsicosd to some Scotch Presbyter.
          P.  179 STOCKSMARKET      5 Some thought it a knightly and generous deed,
          P.  179 STOCKSMARKET     15 And some by the likeness Sir Robert suspect
          P.  187 BRITANNIA       107 Some English too disguis'd (oh shame) I spy'd
          P.  193 TWO HORSES       79 W. Yet some of those givers such beggerly
                                      Villains
          P.  199 DUKE             48 Better some jealous neighbour of your owne
          P.  201 HISTORICALL      17 But the best times have ever some mishap;
          P.  313 CHEQUER INN      39 For some had been Indicted
          P.  314 CHEQUER INN      52 On backside of their Letter some
          P.  316 CHEQUER INN     173 Lest some shou'd take me for the Man

something                    frequency:     8    relative frequency: 0.0001
          P.   57 BILL-BOROW      37 For something alwaies did appear
          P.   63 A. HOUSE       144 'That something more then humane speaks.
          P.   95 DR. WITTY       38 For something guides my hand that I must write.
          P.   96 HOLLAND         38 Something like Government among them brings.
          P.  112 ANNIVERSARY    389 'Abroad a King he seems, and something more,
          P.  129 O.C.           259 And in his alter'd face you something faigne
          P.  191 TWO HORSES      15 All Popish beleivers think something divine,
          P.  315 CHEQUER INN    114 For something more then Chop Cheere.

sometimes                    frequency:     3    relative frequency: 0.0000
          P.   58 BILL-BOROW      61 Onely sometimes a flutt'ring Breez
          P.   66 A. HOUSE       229 Sometimes resolv'd his Sword he draws,
          P.  173 LOYALL SCOT     64 Sometimes the Gall'way Proves the better Nagg.

somewhat                     frequency:     2    relative frequency: 0.0000
          P.  122 TWO SONGS       26 Somewhat else then silly Sheep.
          P.  195 TWO HORSES     153 Ch. Troth, Brother, well said, but thats
                                      somewhat bitter:

son                          frequency:    13    relative frequency: 0.0002
          See also "sonne."
          P.   90 ODE            113 But thou the Wars and Fortunes Son
          P.  103 ANNIVERSARY     21 Well may they strive to leave them to their Son,
          P.  106 ANNIVERSARY    106 Kiss the approaching, nor yet angry Son;
          P.  109 ANNIVERSARY    256 Yet would not he be Lord, nor yet his Son.
          P.  121 TWO SONGS        3 For the Northern Shepheards Son.
          P.  163 INSTRUCTIONS   923 Then, whisp'ring to his Son in Words unheard,
          P.  166 KINGS VOWES     25 I will have a fine Son in makeing tho marrd,
          P.  191 STATUE          56 To behold every day such a Court, such a son.
          P.  196 TWO HORSES     182 They that Conquered the Father won't be slaves
                                      to the Son:
          P.  201 HISTORICALL      2 Much like the Son of Kish that lofty Jew,
          P.  201 HISTORICALL     23 The pious Mother Queen heareing her Son
          P.  202 HISTORICALL     49 So Philips Son enflamed with a Miss
          P.  205 HISTORICALL    168 And Jesse's son plac'd in the Government:

son-in-law                   frequency:     1    relative frequency: 0.0000
          P.  187 BRITANNIA      108 Led up by the wise son-in-law of Hide.

song                         frequency:     9    relative frequency: 0.0001
          P.   17 BERMUDAS         4 The listning Winds receiv'd this Song.
          P.   26 MISTRESS        27 My ecchoing Song: then Worms shall try
          P.   45 MOWER'S SONG     t The Mower's Song.
          P.   90 MAY'S DEATH     19 But seeing May he varied streight his Song,
          P.  105 ANNIVERSARY     85 Yet all compos'd by his attractive Song,
          P.  107 ANNIVERSARY    182 The other Glories of our yearly Song.
          P.  121 TWO SONGS       t5 Second Song.
          P.  131 PARADISE         8 The sacred Truths to Fable and old Song,
          P.  186 BRITANNIA       50 Soe the learn'd Bard with Artfull song represt

songs                        frequency:     3    relative frequency: 0.0000
          P.   18 CLORINDA        22 But He ere since my Songs does fill:
          P.   44 GLO-WORMS        4 Her matchless Songs does meditate;
          P.  119 TWO SONGS       t1 Two Songs at the Marriage of the Lord
                                      Fauconberg

sonne                        frequency:     1    relative frequency: 0.0000
          P.  195 TWO HORSES     127 Tho Father and Sonne are different Rodds,

sonns                        frequency:     1    relative frequency: 0.0000
          P.  168 ADVICE          4 Weeping to see their Sonns degenerate,

sons                         frequency:     6    relative frequency: 0.0001
          See also "sonns."
          P.    3 LOVELACE        20 Of wit corrupted, the unfashion'd Sons.
```

P. 139	HOUSEWARMING	65	Straight Judges, Priests, Bishops, true sons of the Seal,
P. 146	INSTRUCTIONS	217	The Lords Sons, last, all these did reinforce:
P. 189	BRITANNIA	175	True sons of Glory, Pillars of the state,
P. 205	HISTORICALL	179	Be wise ye Sons of Men tempt God no more
P. 316	CHEQUER INN	134	Fathers and Sons like Coupl'd Slaves

soon   frequency: 34   relative frequency: 0.0007
See also "soone."

P. 22	NYMPH	33	But Sylvio soon had me beguil'd.
P. 27	LOVER	5	But soon these Flames do lose their light,
P. 28	LOVER	34	Which soon digested to Despair.
P. 33	DAPHNIS	10	Soon she let that Niceness fall;
P. 39	THE MATCH	13	But likeness seen together drew
P. 46	AMETAS	3	Love unpaid does scon disband:
P. 64	A. HOUSE	164	'Will soon us to perfection lead.
P. 65	A. HOUSE	214	'With them 'twould soon grow fraudulent:
P. 81	A. HOUSE	713	Blest Nymph! that couldst so soon prevent
P. 84	FLECKNO	39	The other opposite as soon replies,
P. 85	FLECKNO	80	This half transparent Man would soon reflect
P. 86	FLECKNO	131	Yet these he promises as soon as clean.
P. 106	ANNIVERSARY	140	And soon precipitate the latest Day.
P. 110	ANNIVERSARY	307	For soon thou mightst have past among their Rant
P. 114	BLAKE	44	Your Conquering Sword will soon that want remove.
P. 115	BLAKE	49	Forces and art, she soon will feel, are vain,
P. 116	BLAKE	103	Whose Fleet and Trenches view'd, he soon did say,
P. 117	BLAKE	121	The Air was soon after the fight begun,
P. 119	TWO SONGS	3	Only this Shepheard, late and soon,
P. 130	O.C.	293	How soon thou Moses hast, and Joshua found,
P. 131	PARADISE	11	Yet as I read, soon growing less severe,
P. 139	HOUSEWARMING	61	He lik'd the advice, and then soon it assay'd;
P. 140	HOUSEWARMING	107	And with that convenience he soon for his Crimes
P. 143	INSTRUCTIONS	97	But envious Fame, too soon, begun to note
P. 148	INSTRUCTIONS	312	Lest the sure Peace, forsooth, too soon appear.
P. 153	INSTRUCTIONS	521	Soon then the Independent Troops would close,
P. 160	INSTRUCTIONS	796	Powder ne're blew man up so soon so high.
P. 161	INSTRUCTIONS	844	Th' Army soon rais'd, he doth as soon disarm.
P. 163	INSTRUCTIONS	903	But soon shrunk back, chill'd with her touch so cold,
P. 165	KINGS VOWES	18	And yet call him home again, soon as I may.
P. 166	KINGS VOWES	24	But if they build it too fast, I will soon make them hold.
P. 167	KINGS VOWES	51	And who knowes but the Mode may soon bring in the rest?
P. 174	LOYALL SCOT	105	And slip one Half into his sleeve as soon.

soone   frequency: 1   relative frequency: 0.0000
P. 314	CHEQUER INN	74	And was as soone sent for away

sooner   frequency: 3   relative frequency: 0.0000
P. 72	A. HOUSE	417	Or sooner hatch or higher build:
P. 173	LOYALL SCOT	77	Anatomists may Sooner fix the Cells
P. 196	TWO HORSES	180	They teach them the Sooner to fall to their Swords.

sorcerers   frequency: 1   relative frequency: 0.0000
P. 111	ANNIVERSARY	314	Sorcerers, Atheists, Jesuites, Possest;

sordid   frequency: 1   relative frequency: 0.0000
P. 96	HOLLAND	15	Or then those Pills which sordid Beetles roul,

sore   frequency: 3   relative frequency: 0.0000
P. 98	HOLLAND	118	Our sore new circumcised Common wealth.
P. 112	ANNIVERSARY	394	'It grieves me sore to have thus much confest.
P. 205	HISTORICALL	180	To give you kings in's Wrath to vex you sore:

sorrow   frequency: 9   relative frequency: 0.0001
P. 15	EYES	9	Two Tears, which Sorrow long did weigh
P. 34	DAPHNIS	32	Between Joy and Sorrow rent.
P. 36	DAPHNIS	91	Joy will not with Sorrow weave,
P. 41	DAMON	7	Sharp like his Sythe his Sorrow was,
P. 45	MOWER'S SONG	7	But these, while I with Sorrow pine,
P. 107	ANNIVERSARY	181	Let this one Sorrow interweave among
P. 108	ANNIVERSARY	194	And leaden Sorrow then their flight did stay.
P. 124	O.C.	62	And He to lessen hers his Sorrow feigns:
P. 182	MADE FREE	48	And his Creditors all left to Sorrow.

sorrows   frequency: 1   relative frequency: 0.0000
P. 125	O.C.	92	At its rich bloods expence their Sorrows chear,

sorrow's   frequency: 1   relative frequency: 0.0000
     P.   21 SOUL & BODY   38 Or Sorrow's other Madness vex.

sort   frequency: 3   relative frequency: 0.0000
     P.   90 MAY'S DEATH   12 But 'twas a man much of another sort;
     P. 128 O.C.   219 The worser sort, so conscious of their ill,
     P. 176 LOYALL SCOT   198 Well that Scotch monster and our Bishops sort

sorted   frequency: 1   relative frequency: 0.0000
     P.   27 LOVER   3 Sorted by pairs, they still are seen

sotana   frequency: 1   relative frequency: 0.0000
     P.   85 FLECKNO   74 Does make a primitive Sotana fall;

sots. See "sotts."

sottana. See "sotana."

sotts   frequency: 1   relative frequency: 0.0000
     P. 145 INSTRUCTIONS   200 For the command of Politicks or Sotts.

sought   frequency: 6   relative frequency: 0.0001
     P.   23 NYMPH   78 Have sought it oft, where it should lye,
     P.   40 THE MATCH   30 A nearer Way they sought;
     P.   42 DAMON   39 Yet Thou ungrateful hast not sought
     P.   47 EMPIRE   9 Each sought a consort in that lovely place;
     P.   48 THE GARDEN   11 Mistaken long, I sought you then
     P.   83 FLECKNO   5 I sought his Lodging; which is at the Sign

soul   frequency: 47   relative frequency: 0.0009
     See also "soule."
     P.   9 DIALOGUE   1 Courage my Soul, now learn to wield
     P.   9 DIALOGUE   t2 The Resolved Soul, and Created Pleasure.
     P.   9 DIALOGUE   16+ Soul.
     P.   10 DIALOGUE   29 A Soul that knows not to presume
     P.   10 DIALOGUE   46 As when a single Soul does fence
     P.   10 DIALOGUE   22+ Soul.
     P.   10 DIALOGUE   28+ Soul.
     P.   10 DIALOGUE   34+ Soul.
     P.   10 DIALOGUE   40+ Soul.
     P.   11 DIALOGUE   54+ Soul.
     P.   11 DIALOGUE   60+ Soul.
     P.   11 DIALOGUE   66+ Soul.
     P.   11 DIALOGUE   72+ Soul.
     P.   12 DIALOGUE   75 Triumph, triumph, victorious Soul;
     P.   12 DROP OF DEW   19 So the Soul, that Drop, that Ray
     P.   18 CLORINDA   15 D. Might a Soul bath there and be clean,
     P.   19 THYRSIS   6 Thyrsis. A Chast Soul, can never mis't.
     P.   19 THYRSIS   18 Heaven's the Center of the Soul.
     P.   20 SOUL & BODY   t A Dialogue between the Soul and Body.
     P.   20 SOUL & BODY   2 A Soul inslav'd so many wayes?
     P.   20 SOUL & BODY   7 A Soul hung up, as 'twere, in Chains
     P.   20 SOUL & BODY   t+ Soul.
     P.   21 SOUL & BODY   12 From bonds of this Tyrannic Soul?
     P.   21 SOUL & BODY   41 What but a Soul could have the wit
     P.   21 SOUL & BODY   20+ Soul.
     P.   27 MISTRESS   35 And while thy willing Soul transpires
     P.   29 THE GALLERY   1 Clora come view my Soul, and tell
     P.   31 FAIR SINGER   8 My dis-intangled Soul it self might save,
     P.   34 DAPHNIS   37 As the Soul of one scarce dead,
     P.   37 DEFINITION   10 Where my extended Soul is fixt,
     P.   49 THE GARDEN   52 My Soul into the boughs does glide:
     P.   55 EPITAPH   13 That her Soul was on Heaven so bent
     P.   84 FLECKNO   68 Should leave his Soul to wander in the Air,
     P.   96 HOLLAND   16 Tranfusing into them their Dunghil Soul.
     P. 112 ANNIVERSARY   379 'The Nation had been ours, but his one Soul
     P. 124 O.C.   42 His hidden Soul at ev'ry turn could meet;
     P. 124 O.C.   69 And frequent lightning to her Soul that flyes,
     P. 147 INSTRUCTIONS   270 And with that thought does multiply his Soul:
     P. 157 INSTRUCTIONS   675 And secret Joy, in his calm Soul does rise,
     P. 172 LOYALL SCOT   41 And secrett Joy in his own soul doth Rise
     P. 178 LOYALL SCOT   262 Charles our great soul this onely Understands:
     P. 187 BRITANNIA   117 But his fair soul, transform'd by that French
                                Dame,
     P. 188 BRITANNIA   138 Perhaps that spell may his Erring soul reclaim.
     P. 195 TWO HORSES   137 Ch. De Witt and Cromwell had each a brave
                                soul.
     P. 199 DUKE   77 His sense, his soul as squinting as his eye.
     P. 200 DUKE   91 The smalest atome of an English soul.
     P. 205 HISTORICALL   173 Fiends of Ambition here his Soul possesst,

sould   frequency: 1   relative frequency: 0.0000

P. 187 BRITANNIA   91 By hirelings sould to you shall be resign'd

souldier   frequency: 3   relative frequency: 0.0000
  P. 66 A. HOUSE   232 First from a Judge, then Souldier bred.
  P. 127 O.C.   181 The Souldier taught that inward Mail to wear,
  P. 130 O.C.   278 Shall th' English souldier, ere he charge,
    rehearse;

souldiers   frequency: 2   relative frequency: 0.0000
  P. 69 A. HOUSE   337 The Gardiner had the Souldiers place,
  P. 182 MADE FREE   66 And the Souldiers had all beene your Masters.

soule   frequency: 2   relative frequency: 0.0000
  P. 128 O.C.   205 And that deep scule through every channell flows,
  P. 130 O.C.   291 There thy great soule at once a world does see,

souls   frequency: 7   relative frequency: 0.0001
  P.   9 DIALOGUE   15 Where the Souls of fruits and flow'rs
  P. 118 BLAKE   135 Scarce souls from bodies sever'd are so far,
  P. 165 INSTRUCTIONS   986 Does with clear Counsels their large Souls
    supply;
  P. 186 BRITANNIA   76 Virtues a faint-green-sickness of the souls,
  P. 188 BRITANNIA   164 Least Court corrupcions should their souls
    engage.
  P. 189 BRITANNIA   177 When with fierce Ardour their brave souls do
    burn,
  P. 193 TWO HORSES   85 Ch. Yet baser the souls of those low priced
    Sinners,

sound   frequency: 13   relative frequency: 0.0002
  P. 10 DIALOGUE   49 Then persevere: for still new Charges sound:
  P. 18 BERMUDAS   32 A Temple, where to sound his Name.
  P. 18 CLORINDA   24 C. Sweet must Pan sound in Damons Note.
  P. 26 MISTRESS   26 Nor, in thy marble Vault, shall sound
  P. 32 MOURNING   32 And not of one the bottom sound.
  P. 47 EMPIRE   3 All Musick was a solitary sound,
  P. 70 A. HOUSE   381 But, as the Marriners that sound,
  P. 75 A. HOUSE   522 A Sadder, yet more pleasing Sound:
  P. 154 INSTRUCTIONS   550 Sound the Sea-march, and guide to Sheppy Isle.
  P. 163 INSTRUCTIONS   910 But let some other Painter draw the sound:
  P. 186 BRITANNIA   87 To sound damnacion to those dare deny't.
  P. 188 BRITANNIA   137 In his deaf ear sound his dead Pathers name;
  P. 199 DUKE   49 Had called you to a sound though petty Throne,

sounding   frequency: 1   relative frequency: 0.0000
  P. 90 MAY'S DEATH   15 Sounding of ancient Heroes, such as were

sounds   frequency: 3   relative frequency: 0.0000
  P. 47 EMPIRE   21 Victorious sounds! yet here your Homage do
  P. 71 A. HOUSE   414 Sounds your untimely Funeral.
  P. 199 DUKE   62 Their boyling heads can hear no other sounds

soup   frequency: 1   relative frequency: 0.0000
  P. 141 INSTRUCTIONS   29 Paint then St. Albans full of soup and gold,

source. See "virgin-source."

sourdine   frequency: 1   relative frequency: 0.0000
  P. 71 A. HOUSE   416 And 'tis the Scurdine in their Throat.

south   frequency: 2   relative frequency: 0.0000
  P. 158 INSTRUCTIONS   718 From the South Perfumes, Spices from the
    East;
  P. 198 DUKE   7 First draw him falling prostrate to the South,

southampton   frequency: 1   relative frequency: 0.0000
  P. 160 INSTRUCTIONS   793 Southampton dead, much of the Treasure's care,

soveraign   frequency: 1   relative frequency: 0.0000
  P. 170 PROPHECY   11 And those false Men the Soveraign People sent

soveraigne   frequency: 1   relative frequency: 0.0000
  P. 184 MADE FREE   114 To Charters, our King and Soveraigne.

sovereign   frequency: 2   relative frequency: 0.0000
  See also "soveraign," "soveraigne," "sov'raign."
  P. 186 BRITANNIA   64 Inscrib'd Leviathan the sovereign Lord,
  P. 187 BRITANNIA   98 Tast the delicious sweets of sovereign power,

sov'raign   frequency: 2   relative frequency: 0.0000
  P. 41 THE MOWER   20 To Man, that sov'raign thing and proud;

P. 155 INSTRUCTIONS 614 His exil'd Sov'raign on its happy Board;

sow   frequency: 1   relative frequency: 0.0000
    P. 69 A. HOUSE   344 We Ord'nance Plant and Powder sow.

sowd   frequency: 1   relative frequency: 0.0000
    P. 315 CHEQUER INN 95 Had sowd on too his double Hose

sow'd   frequency: 2   relative frequency: 0.0000
    P. 43 DAMON   66 Had not Love here his Thistles sow'd!
    P. 63 A. HOUSE   133 'Some of your Features, as we sow'd,

soyl   frequency: 1   relative frequency: 0.0000
    P. 115 BLAKE   58 Neither the Soyl, nor People quiet know.

soyl'd   frequency: 1   relative frequency: 0.0000
    P. 107 ANNIVERSARY 180 And soyl'd in Dust thy Crown of silver Hairs.

soyle   frequency: 1   relative frequency: 0.0000
    P. 198 DUKE   33 And not Infallible the Roman Soyle?

space   frequency: 3   relative frequency: 0.0000
    P. 59 A. HOUSE   15 No Creature loves an empty space;
    P. 72 A. HOUSE   443 A levell'd space, as smooth and plain,
    P. 159 INSTRUCTIONS 742 Fill up thy space with a redoubled Night.

spacious   frequency: 2   relative frequency: 0.0000
    See also "spatious."
    P. 129 O.C.   263 Whose spacious boughs are hung with trophies
                           round,
    P. 130 O.C.   292 Spacious enough, and pure enough for thee.

spades   frequency: 1   relative frequency: 0.0000
    P. 96 HOLLAND   50 The Pow'r, and grows as 'twere a King of
                           Spades.

spain   frequency: 5   relative frequency: 0.0001
    P. 114 BLAKE   45 For Spain had better, Shee'l ere long confess,
    P. 115 BLAKE   50 Peace, against you, was the sole strength of
                           Spain.
    P. 119 BLAKE   163 His Seige of Spain he then again pursues,
    P. 119 BLAKE   165 The saddest news that ere to Spain was brought,
    P. 152 INSTRUCTIONS 467 (So Spain could not escape his Laughters
                           spleen:

spaines   frequency: 1   relative frequency: 0.0000
    P. 185 BRITANNIA   44 How Spaines prow'd power her Virgin Armes
                           contrould

spains   frequency: 1   relative frequency: 0.0000
    P. 113 BLAKE   1 Now does Spains Fleet her spatious wings
                           unfold,

spain's. See "spaines," "spains."

spake   frequency: 1   relative frequency: 0.0000
    P. 33 DAPHNIS   26 Words she never spake before;

span   frequency: 1   relative frequency: 0.0000
    P. 55 THYESTE   9 I have liv'd out all my span,

spaniards   frequency: 3   relative frequency: 0.0000
    P. 113 BLAKE   t1 On the Victory obtained by Blake over the
                           Spaniards,
    P. 115 BLAKE   75 The Peek's proud height, the Spaniards all
                           admire,
    P. 116 BLAKE   102 Ore Seas as vast as is the Spaniards pride.

spankers   frequency: 1   relative frequency: 0.0000
    P. 180 STOCKSMARKET 50 Whose loyalty now all expires with his spankers.

spann'd   frequency: 2   relative frequency: 0.0000
    P. 69 A. HOUSE   351 And, in those half-dry Trenches, spann'd
    P. 131 PARADISE   17 Or if a Work so infinite be spann'd,

spar   frequency: 1   relative frequency: 0.0000
    P. 138 HOUSEWARMING 46 So long as the Yards had a Deal or a Spar:

sparagus   frequency: 1   relative frequency: 0.0000
    P. 142 INSTRUCTIONS 62 Wide Mouth that Sparagus may well proclaim:

spar'd   frequency: 1   relative frequency: 0.0000

```
         P. 129 O.C.           238 Whose force oft spar'd the labour of his arm:

spare                              frequency:    8   relative frequency: 0.0001
         P.  24 NYMPH          114 Th' Engraver sure his Art may spare;
         P.  39 PICTURE         35 Gather the Flow'rs, but spare the Buds;
         P. 128 O.C.           224 Spare yet your own, if you neglect his fame;
         P. 129 O.C.           266 At mortalls sins, nor his own plant will spare;
         P. 140 HOUSEWARMING   108 At Tybourn may land, and spare the Tower-Barge.
         P. 149 INSTRUCTIONS   334 But all the Members Lives, consulting, spare.
         P. 153 INSTRUCTIONS   506 How can he Engines so convenient spare?
         P. 313 CHEQUER INN     43 But he had Men enough to spare

spared                             frequency:    1   relative frequency: 0.0000
         See also "spar'd."
         P. 176 LOYALL SCOT    183 And while hee spared the keepers life hee fail'd.

spark                              frequency:    1   relative frequency: 0.0000
         P.  40 THE MATCH       27 For, with one Spark of these, he streight

sparkled                           frequency:    1   relative frequency: 0.0000
         P. 124 O.C.            40 And thorough that sparkled her fairer Mind;

sparkling                          frequency:    2   relative frequency: 0.0000
         P.  16 EYES            37 The sparkling Glance that shoots Desire,
         P.  94 DR. WITTY       25 Her thoughts are English, though her sparkling
                                   wit

spartacus                          frequency:    1   relative frequency: 0.0000
         P.  92 MAY'S DEATH     74 To turn the Chronicler to Spartacus.

spatious                           frequency:    1   relative frequency: 0.0000
         P. 113 BLAKE            1 Now does Spains Fleet her spatious wings
                                   unfold,

spawn'd                            frequency:    1   relative frequency: 0.0000
         P.  97 HOLLAND         64 Never so fertile, spawn'd upon this shore:

speak                              frequency:   12   relative frequency: 0.0002
         See also "speake."
         P.  55 EPITAPH          5 Where never any could speak ill,
         P.  76 A. HOUSE       548 Does find the hollow Oak to speak,
         P.  88 ODE             27 And, if we would speak true,
         P.  94 DR. WITTY       19 And sweet as are her lips that speak it, she
         P.  96 HOLLAND         46 Him they their Lord and Country's Father
                                   speak.
         P. 108 ANNIVERSARY    188 And speak as of the Dead the Praises due:
         P. 123 O.C.            20 Should speak the wondrous softness of his Heart.
         P. 148 INSTRUCTIONS   291 To speak not forward, but in Action brave;
         P. 162 INSTRUCTIONS   897 And silent tears her secret anguish speak,
         P. 191 TWO HORSES      16 When Images speak, possesses the shrine:
         P. 192 TWO HORSES      19 Those Idolls ne're speak, but the miracle 's
                                   done
         P. 192 TWO HORSES      35 W. Quoth the marble white Hors: 'twould make a
                                   stone speak

speake                             frequency:    1   relative frequency: 0.0000
         P. 313 CHEQUER INN     46 Therefore I needs must speake my Mind

speaker                            frequency:    4   relative frequency: 0.0000
         P. 146 INSTRUCTIONS   236 The Speaker early, when they all fell in.
         P. 160 INSTRUCTIONS   802 And ablest Speaker, who of Law has least;
         P. 161 INSTRUCTIONS   857 The Speaker, Summon'd, to the Lords repairs,
         P. 162 INSTRUCTIONS   863 Dear Painter, draw this Speaker to the foot:

speaking                           frequency:    2   relative frequency: 0.0000
         P.   3 LOVELACE         6 To be ingenious, but by speaking well.
         P. 194 TWO HORSES     100 Bold speaking hath done both man and beast wrong.

speaks                             frequency:    1   relative frequency: 0.0000
         P.  63 A. HOUSE       144 'That something more then humane speaks.

spear                              frequency:    1   relative frequency: 0.0000
         P. 147 INSTRUCTIONS   257 Then daring Seymour, that with Spear and
                                   Shield,

speckled                           frequency:    1   relative frequency: 0.0000
         P.  14 THE CORONET     14 That, twining in his speckled breast,

spectacle                          frequency:    3   relative frequency: 0.0000
         P.  28 LOVER           42 Behold a spectacle of Blood,
         P.  97 HOLLAND         93 Or what a Spectacle the Skipper gross,
```

        P. 150 INSTRUCTIONS   389 And taught Youth by Spectacle Innocent!

spectators   frequency: 2   relative frequency: 0.0000
        P. 123 O.C.   9 And blame the last Act, like Spectators vain,
        P. 155 INSTRUCTICNS   598 To be Spectators safe of the new Play,

sped   frequency: 1   relative frequency: 0.0000
        P. 122 TWO SONGS   34 Before Marina's turn were sped?

speech   frequency: 2   relative frequency: 0.0000
        P. 163 INSTRUCTIONS   931 Through their feign'd speech their secret hearts
                                  he knew;
        P. 196 TWO HORSES   163 If Speech from Erute Animals in Romes first
                                  age

speeches   frequency: 2   relative frequency: 0.0000
        P. 171 PROPHECY   38 To make starcht empty Speeches two hours long.
        P. 196 TWO HORSES   171 If the Delphick Sybills cracular speeches,

speed   frequency: 2   relative frequency: 0.0000
        P. 48 THE GARDEN   31 And Pan did after Syrinx speed,
        P. 116 BLAKE   100 With winged speed, for Sanctacruze does make.

speedy   frequency: 1   relative frequency: 0.0000
        P. 117 BLAKE   109 Of Speedy Victory let no man doubt,

spell   frequency: 2   relative frequency: 0.0000
        P. 175 LOYALL SCOT   138 That power Alone Can Loose this spell that
                                  tyes,
        P. 188 BRITANNIA   138 Perhaps that spell may his Erring soul reclaim.

spells   frequency: 1   relative frequency: 0.0000
        P. 132 PARADISE   47 While the Town-Bays writes all the while and
                                  spells,

spencer   frequency: 2   relative frequency: 0.0000
        P. 92 MAY'S DEATH   85 If that can be thy home where Spencer lyes
        P. 185 BRITANNIA   42 The other day fam'd Spencer I did bring

spend   frequency: 4   relative frequency: 0.0000
        P. 20 THYRSIS   29 I prethee let us spend our time to come
        P. 130 O.C.   297 And in those joyes dost spend the endlesse day,
        P. 165 KINGS VOWES   11 That shall furnish me Treasure as fast as I
                                  spend;
        P. 182 MADE FREE   39 He us'd as his cwne to spend on't

spends   frequency: 1   relative frequency: 0.0000
        P. 181 MADE FREE   31 He spends all his Days

spenser. See "spencer."

spent   frequency: 9   relative frequency: 0.0001
        P. 22 NYMPH   40 Could so mine idle Life have spent.
        P. 34 DAPHNIS   29 For, Alas, the time was spent,
        P. 61 A. HOUSE   93 And oft She spent the Summer Suns
        P. 80 A. HOUSE   697 Therefore what first She on them spent,
        P. 111 ANNIVERSARY   350 'Spent with both Wars, under a Captain dead?
        P. 129 O.C.   239 No more shall fcllcw where he spent the dayes
        P. 147 INSTRUCTIONS   280 Spent with fatigue, tc breath a while Toback.
        P. 149 INSTRUCTICNS   329 But when this fail'd, and Months enough were
                                  spent,
        P. 151 INSTRUCTIONS   434 Our Money spent; else 'twere at his command.

sphear   frequency: 2   relative frequency: 0.0000
        P. 12 DROP OF DEW   14 Because so long divided from the Sphear.
        P. 47 EMPIRE   20 Including all between the Earth and Sphear.

sphears   frequency: 1   relative frequency: 0.0000
        P. 32 MOURNING   9 When, molding of the watry Sphears,

sphere   frequency: 6   relative frequency: 0.0001
        See also "sphear."
        P. 99 HOLLAND   151 And while Jcve governs in the highest Sphere,
        P. 104 ANNIVERSARY   48 To tune this lower to that higher Sphere.
        P. 108 ANNIVERSARY   206 It seem'd the Sun was faln out of the Sphere:
        P. 112 ANNIVERSARY   386 'Where below Earth, or where above the Sphere?
        P. 121 TWO SONGS   45 The Stars are fix'd unto their Sphere,
        P. 130 O.C.   287 Thou in a pitch how farre beyond the sphere

spheres   frequency: 1   relative frequency: 0.0000
        See also "sphears."
        P. 19 THYRSIS   26 May feast with Musick cf the Spheres.

spherical   frequency: 1   relative frequency: 0.0000
    P. 60 A. HOUSE   52 Stirs, and the Square grows Spherical;

spice   frequency: 1   relative frequency: 0.0000
    P. 145 INSTRUCTIONS 166 Hid with his Elbow like the Spice he stole.

spices   frequency: 2   relative frequency: 0.0000
    P. 158 INSTRUCTIONS 718 From the South Perfumes, Spices from the
                           East;
    P. 183 MADE FREE   81 To have made this Freeman of Spices;

spider   frequency: 1   relative frequency: 0.0000
    P. 165 KINGS VOWES   2 And the Spider might weave in our Stomack its
                           web;

spied. See "spy'd."

spies   frequency: 1   relative frequency: 0.0000
    P. 151 INSTRUCTIONS 414 And the French Army one from Calais spies.

spight   frequency: 12   relative frequency: 0.0002
    P.   4 LOVELACE   43 Mine eyes invaded with a female spight,
    P. 21 SOUL & BODY   17 And, wanting where its spight to try,
    P. 71 A. HOUSE   412 And Chance o'retakes what scapeth spight?
    P. 89 ODE   61 Nor call'd the Gods with vulgar spight
    P. 104 ANNIVERSARY   32 If Conquered, on them they wreak their Spight:
    P. 111 ANNIVERSARY 323 And, to your spight, returning yet alive
    P. 113 ANNIVERSARY 395 Pardon, great Prince, if thus their Fear or
                           Spight
    P. 131 PARADISE   9 (So Sampson grcap'd the Temples Posts in
                           spight)
    P. 155 INSTRUCTIONS 602 Unpaid, refuse to mount our Ships for spight:
    P. 158 INSTRUCTIONS 725 And spight of Ruperts and of Albemarles,
    P. 161 INSTRUCTIONS 825 And 'twixt Necessity and Spight, till then,
    P. 316 CHEQUER INN 156 In spight of Pothecare.

spill   frequency: 1   relative frequency: 0.0000
    P. 55 EPITAPH   6 Who would officious Praises spill?

spinster   frequency: 1   relative frequency: 0.0000
    P. 187 BRITANNIA   119 Like a Tame spinster in 's seraglio sits,

spintrian   frequency: 1   relative frequency: 0.0000
    P. 202 HISTORICALL   66 Yet in the Mimmicks of the Spintrian Sport

spires. See "spir's."

spirit   frequency: 4   relative frequency: 0.0000
    P. 21 SOUL & BODY   20 Since this ill Spirit it possest.
    P. 109 ANNIVERSARY 230 Thy sober Spirit unto things too High,
    P. 110 ANNIVERSARY 301 What thy Misfortune, they the Spirit call,
    P. 196 TWO HORSES   174 Have the spirit cf Prophecy likewise behind?

spirits   frequency: 5   relative frequency: 0.0001
    P. 88 ODE   44 Where greater Spirits come.
    P. 90 ODE   118 The Spirits of the shady Night,
    P. 105 ANNIVERSARY   89 The crossest Spirits here do take their part,
    P. 126 O.C.   131 And as through Air his wasting Spirits flow'd,
    P. 175 LOYALL SCOT 137 One Bishops fiend spirits a whole Diocese.

spir's   frequency: 1   relative frequency: 0.0000
    P. 70 A. HOUSE   376 Of the green spir's, to us do call.

spit   frequency: 1   relative frequency: 0.0000
    P. 111 ANNIVERSARY 311 Accursed Locusts, whom your King does spit

spite   frequency: 1   relative frequency: 0.0000
    P. 177 LOYALL SCOT 250 And ever since men with a female spite

spiteful. See "spitefull."

spitefull   frequency: 1   relative frequency: 0.0000
    P. 186 BRITANNIA   70 And on the ground in spitefull rage it broak,

spleen   frequency: 1   relative frequency: 0.0000
    P. 152 INSTRUCTIONS 467 (So Spain could not escape his Laughters
                           spleen:

splendor   frequency: 1   relative frequency: 0.0000
    See also "splendour."
    P. 164 INSTRUCTIONS 958 Which, in your Splendor hid, Ccrrode your Light;

splendour   frequency: 1   relative frequency: 0.0000
   See also "splendor."
   P. 130 O.C.   311 But open'd once, what splendour does he throw?

split   frequency: 2   relative frequency: 0.0000
   P. 27 LOVER   15 And there she split against the Stone,
   P. 174 LOYALL SCOT   86 And split the Influence of Every star?

splitting   frequency: 1   relative frequency: 0.0000
   P. 97 HCLLAND   69 It struck, and splitting on this unknown ground,

spoil   frequency: 4   relative frequency: 0.0000
   See also "spoile," "spoyle."
   P. 36 DAPHNIS   88 Wet themselves and spoil their Sent.
   P. 109 ANNIVERSARY   259 Though why should others all thy Labor spoil,
   P. 144 INSTRUCTIONS 159 Expectants pale, with hopes of spoil allur'd,
   P. 156 INSTRUCTIONS 619 Now a cheap spoil, and the mean Victor's Slave,

spoile   frequency: 1   relative frequency: 0.0000
   P. 199 DUKE   79 Rich with the Spoile of a poore Algeryne,

spoils   frequency: 1   relative frequency: 0.0000
   See also "spoyls."
   P. 15 THE CORONET   25 That they, while Thou on both their Spoils dost
                            tread,

spoke   frequency: 6   relative frequency: 0.0001
   P. 58 BILL-BOROW   73 'Tis true, ye Trees nor ever spoke
   P. 186 BRITANNIA   71 And, frowning, thus with proud disdain she spoke.
   P. 187 BRITANNIA   105 When she had spoke, a confus'd murmur rose
   P. 191 TWO HORSES   11 Fryar Bacon had a head that spoke made of
                            Brass,
   P. 192 TWO HORSES   22 To beleive men and beasts have spoke in effigie,
   P. 315 CHEQUER INN   129 For what that Day they spoke

spoken   frequency: 2   relative frequency: 0.0000
   P. 191 TWO HORSES   6 Have spoken as plainly as men doe with Tongues:
   P. 196 TWO HORSES   170 Than all that the beasts had spoken before.

spoones   frequency: 1   relative frequency: 0.0000
   P. 316 CHEQUER INN   169 Candlesticks, Forkes, Saltes Plates Spoones
                            Knives

spoons. See "spoones."

sport   frequency: 11   relative frequency: 0.0002
   P.   5 HASTINGS   59 For Man (alas) is but the Heavens sport;
   P. 23 NYMPH   41 For it was full of sport; and light
   P. 27 MISTRESS   37 Now let us sport us while we may;
   P. 67 A. HOUSE   285 But laid these Gardens out in sport
   P. 115 BLAKE   71 Deluded men! Fate with you did but sport,
   P. 157 INSTRUCTIONS 666 With birding at the Dutch, as if in sport:
   P. 158 INSTRUCTIONS 736 Was led about in sport, the publick scorn.
   P. 170 PROPHECY   17 When Sodomy is the Premier Ministers sport
   P. 172 LOYALL SCOT   31 With birding at the Dutch, as though in sport,
   P. 185 BRITANNIA   26 Pimps, Priests, Buffoones i'th privy chamber
                            sport.
   P. 202 HISTORICALL   66 Yet in the Mimmicks of the Spintrian Sport

sporting   frequency: 2   relative frequency: 0.0000
   P. 120 TWO SONGS   32 Sporting with him in Ida's shade:
   P. 154 INSTRUCTIONS 535 His sporting Navy all about him swim,

sportings   frequency: 1   relative frequency: 0.0000
   P. 25 YOUNG LOVE   7 While our Sportings are as free

sports   frequency: 2   relative frequency: 0.0000
   P. 98 HCLLAND   123 'Tis true since that (as fortune kindly sports,)
   P. 150 INSTRUCTIONS 374 All to new Sports their wanton fears release.

spotless   frequency: 3   relative frequency: 0.0000
   P. 81 A. HOUSE   726 But pure, and spotless as the Eye;
   P. 92 MAY'S DEATH   72 Our spotless knowledge and the studies chast.
   P. 187 BRITANNIA   100 Three spotless virgins to your bed I bring,

spots   frequency: 4   relative frequency: 0.0000
   P. 73 A. HOUSE   460 As Spots, so shap'd, on Faces do.
   P. 94 DR. WITTY   16 That mends; and added beauties are but spots.
   P. 164 INSTRUCTIONS 950 And Spots unknown to the bright Star descry'd;

P. 164 INSTRUCTIONS 957 Blame not the Muse that brought those spots to
                         sight,

spotted   frequency: 1   relative frequency: 0.0000
    P. 186 BRITANNIA   60 Entred a Dame bedeckt with spotted pride;

spouse   frequency: 2   relative frequency: 0.0000
    P. 62 A. HOUSE   118 'Each one a Spouse, and each a Queen;
    P. 66 A. HOUSE   247 Yet, against Fate, his Spouse they kept;

spout   frequency: 1   relative frequency: 0.0000
    P. 317 CHEQUER INN   186 And then it runs full spout

spoyle   frequency: 1   relative frequency: 0.0000
    P. 171 PROPHECY   51 Their Wives to his Lust expos'd, their Wealth
                              to his spoyle

spoyls   frequency: 2   relative frequency: 0.0000
    P. 89 ODE   89 And has his Sword and Spoyls ungirt,
    P. 168 ADVICE   22 The spoyls of England; and along that side

sprag   frequency: 1   relative frequency: 0.0000
    P. 154 INSTRUCTIONS   561 Sprag there, the practic'd in the Sea command,

spread   frequency: 2   relative frequency: 0.0000
    P. 59 A. HOUSE   17 But He, superfluously spread,
    P. 197 DUKE   1 Spread a large canvass, Painter, to containe

spreading   frequency: 1   relative frequency: 0.0000
    P. 125 O.C.   99 So the dry Stock, no more that spreading Vine,

spreads   frequency: 1   relative frequency: 0.0000
    P.   9 DIALOGUE   6 With silken Banners spreads the air.

sprig   frequency: 2   relative frequency: 0.0000
    P. 82 A. HOUSE   739 And, like a sprig of Misleto,
    P. 122 TWO SONGS   12 Without each a Sprig of Green.

spring   frequency: 12   relative frequency: 0.0002
    See also "off-spring."
    P. 17 BERMUDAS   13 He gave us this eternal Spring,
    P. 23 NYMPH   75 And all the Spring time of the year
    P. 29 THE GALLERY   22 And Manna falls, and Roses spring;
    P. 31 MOURNING   4 Spring from the Starrs of Chlora's Eyes?
    P. 38 PICTURE   27 Reform the errours of the Spring;
    P. 69 A. HOUSE   347 Might once have made our Gardens spring
    P. 103 ANNIVERSARY   11 Cromwell alone doth with new Lustre spring,
    P. 121 TWO SONGS   8 Phillis you may wait the Spring:
    P. 161 INSTRUCTIONS   852 Lest some new Tomkins spring a fresh debate.
    P. 164 INSTRUCTIONS   973 (But Ceres Corn, and Flora is the Spring,
    P. 180 STOCKSMARKET   58 As ever you hope in December for Spring,
    P. 188 BRITANNIA   139 Who knows what good effects from thence may
                              spring;

springs   frequency: 5   relative frequency: 0.0001
    See also "off-springs."
    P. 17 EYES   53 Thus let your Streams o'reflow your Springs,
    P. 18 CLORINDA   18 Clorinda, Pastures, Caves, and Springs.
    P. 20 THYRSIS   34 Cool winds do whisper, springs do flow.
    P. 82 A. HOUSE   745 Mean time ye Fields, Springs, Bushes,
                              Flow'rs,
    P. 154 INSTRUCTIONS   543 Old Neptune springs the Tydes, and Water lent:

sprung   frequency: 1   relative frequency: 0.0000
    P. 64 A. HOUSE   167 'And that, once sprung, increase so fast

spurious   frequency: 1   relative frequency: 0.0000
    P. 184 BRITANNIA   6 Those would be Blessings in this spurious reign,

sputter   frequency: 1   relative frequency: 0.0000
    P. 314 CHEQUER INN   90 That gap'd to heare him sputter

spy   frequency: 3   relative frequency: 0.0000
    P. 110 ANNIVERSARY   274 Counted the Hours, and ev'ry Star did spy,
    P. 121 TWO SONGS   49 That Cave is dark. Endymion. Then none can
                              spy:
    P. 151 INSTRUCTIONS   445 And so enforc'd, like Enemy or Spy,

spy'd   frequency: 6   relative frequency: 0.0001
    P. 18 CLORINDA   3 C. I have a grassy Scutcheon spy'd,
    P. 45 MOWER'S SONG   9 That not one Blade of Grass you spy'd,

```
        P.  124 O.C.            43 Then might y' ha' daily his Affection spy'd,
        P.  147 INSTRUCTIONS   247 First spy'd the Enemy and gave th' Alarm:
        P.  186 BRITANNIA       59 Whilst in truthes Mirror this Glad scene he
                                   spy'd,
        P.  187 BRITANNIA      107 Some English too disguis'd (oh shame) I spy'd
```

squadron   frequency: 3   relative frequency: 0.0000
```
        P.  144 INSTRUCTIONS   155 Of the old Courtiers next a Squadron came,
        P.  155 INSTRUCTIONS   581 Ruyter forthwith a Squadron does untack,
        P.  158 INSTRUCTIONS   724 The Holland Squadron leisurely return:
```

squadrons   frequency: 1   relative frequency: 0.0000
```
        P.  154 INSTRUCTIONS   553 The liquid Region with their Squadrons fill'd,
```

square   frequency: 4   relative frequency: 0.0000
```
        P.   21 SOUL & BODY     43 So Architects do square and hew,
        P.   40 THE MOWER        5 He first enclos'd within the Gardens square
        P.   60 A. HOUSE        52 Stirs, and the Square grows Spherical;
        P.   97 HOLLAND         88 Fumes through the loop-holes of a wooden Square.
```

squatted   frequency: 2   relative frequency: 0.0000
```
        P.   75 A. HOUSE       516 With Musick high the squatted Thorns.
        P.  162 INSTRUCTIONS   877 When Grievance urg'd, he swells like squatted
                                   Toad,
```

squeaking. See "squeking."

squeeze   frequency: 1   relative frequency: 0.0000
```
        P.  144 INSTRUCTIONS   124 Yet as for War the Parliament should squeeze;
```

squeking   frequency: 1   relative frequency: 0.0000
```
        P.   70 A. HOUSE       373 They, in there squeking Laugh, contemn
```

squinting   frequency: 1   relative frequency: 0.0000
```
        P.  199 DUKE            77 His sense, his soul as squinting as his eye.
```

squire   frequency: 1   relative frequency: 0.0000
```
        P.  145 INSTRUCTIONS   175 Bronkard Loves Squire; through all the field
                                   array'd,
```

st.   frequency: 16   relative frequency: 0.0003
```
        P.  138 HOUSEWARMING    44 But that he had nearer the Stones of St.
                                   Pauls.
        P.  139 HOUSEWARMING    79 And St. John must now for the Leads be
                                   compliant,
        P.  139 HOUSEWARMING    95 Your Metropolis House is in St. James's
                                   Fields,
        P.  140 HOUSEWARMING   112 He comes to be roasted next St. James's Fair.
        P.  141 INSTRUCTIONS    29 Paint then St. Albans full of soup and gold,
        P.  141 INSTRUCTIONS    35 Well he the Title of St. Albans bore,
        P.  142 INSTRUCTIONS    41 He needs no Seal, but to St. James's lease,
        P.  142 INSTRUCTIONS    46 Two Saints at once, St. German, St. Alban.
        P.  145 INSTRUCTIONS   167 Headless St. Dennis so his Head does bear;
        P.  148 INSTRUCTIONS   302 St. Dunstan in it, tweaking Satan's Nose.
        P.  148 INSTRUCTIONS   311 St. Albans straight is sent to, to forbear,
        P.  149 INSTRUCTIONS   365 France had St. Albans promis'd (so they sing)
        P.  149 INSTRUCTIONS   366 St Albans promis'd him, and he the King.
        P.  151 INSTRUCTIONS   427 St. Albans writ to that he may bewail
        P.  151 INSTRUCTIONS   440 And to St. Albans too undutiful;
```

stables   frequency: 1   relative frequency: 0.0000
```
        P.   73 A. HOUSE       478 And Fishes do the Stables scale.
```

'stablish   frequency: 1   relative frequency: 0.0000
```
        P.  171 PROPHECY        42 And strive by law to 'stablish Tyrany,
```

stacks   frequency: 1   relative frequency: 0.0000
```
        P.  315 CHEQUER INN    131 And sweeping all our Chimney Stacks
```

staff   frequency: 1   relative frequency: 0.0000
        See also "staffe."
```
        P.  141 INSTRUCTIONS    18 To see a tall lowse brandish the white Staff.
```

staffe   frequency: 2   relative frequency: 0.0000
```
        P.  193 TWO HORSES      53 Ch. To see a white staffe make a Beggar a Lord
        P.  313 CHEQUER INN     29 For all his slender Quarter Staffe
```

stag   frequency: 1   relative frequency: 0.0000
```
        P.  155 INSTRUCTIONS   579 The conscious Stag, so once the Forests dread,
```

stage   frequency: 3   relative frequency: 0.0000
```
```

```
            P.   17 BERMUDAS        11 He lands us on a grassy Stage;
            P.   54 THYESTE          6 And far of the publick Stage
            P.  199 DUKE            58 But when he came to act upon the stage,

stage-coach                         frequency:    1    relative frequency: 0.0000
            P.  161 INSTRUCTICNS   829 Plain Gentlemen are in Stage-Coach o'rethrown,

stages                              frequency:    1    relative frequency: 0.0000
            P.  103 ANNIVERSARY      8 (Sun-like) the Stages of succeeding Suns:

stagger'd                           frequency:    1    relative frequency: 0.0000
            P.   98 HOLLAND        121 And the torn Navy stagger'd with him home,

staggering.  See "stagg'ring."

stagg'ring                          frequency:    1    relative frequency: 0.0000
            P.   98 HOLLAND         96 When Stagg'ring upon some Land, Snick and
                                       Sneer,

staggs                              frequency:    1    relative frequency: 0.0000
            P.  130 O.C.           283 While staggs shall fly unto the forests thick,

stags.  See "staggs."

stain                               frequency:    4    relative frequency: 0.0000
            P.   22 NYMPH           21 Yet could they not be clean: their Stain
            P.   72 A. HOUSE       444 As Clothes for Lilly strecht to stain.
            P.  114 BLAKE           27 For least some Gloominess might stain her sky,
            P.  175 LOYALL SCOT    157 These Hypocrites their faith and Linnen stain.

stainer                             frequency:    1    relative frequency: 0.0000
            P.  117 BLAKE          117 Bold Stainer Leads, this Fleets design'd by
                                       fate,

staines                             frequency:    1    relative frequency: 0.0000
            P.  125 O.C.            76 Had drawn such staines as were not to be cur'd.

stains.  See "staines."

stair-cases                         frequency:    1    relative frequency: 0.0000
            P.   83 FLECKNO          7 For Poetry: There three Stair-Cases high,

stairs                              frequency:    2    relative frequency: 0.0000
            P.   83 FLECKNO         10 But seem'd a Coffin set on the Stairs head.
            P.   85 FLECKNO         87 I meet one on the Stairs who made me stand,

stake                               frequency:    5    relative frequency: 0.0001
            P.   78 A. HOUSE       624 There at the Ev'ning stake me down.
            P.   96 HOLLAND         19 And to the stake a strugling Country bound,
            P.  149 INSTRUCTIONS   368 To play for Flanders, and the stake to lose.
            P.  195 TWO HORSES     148 Wee must all to the Stake or be Converts to
                                       Rome.
            P.  313 CHEQUER INN     31 He is as stiff as any Stake

stale                               frequency:    1    relative frequency: 0.0000
            P.  187 BRITANNIA      102 As these grow stale weel Harass humankind,

stalks                              frequency:    2    relative frequency: 0.0000
            P.   68 A. HOUSE       315 Their Leaves, that to the stalks are curl'd,
            P.  144 INSTRUCTIONS   139 She stalks all day in Streets conceal'd from
                                       sight,

stall                               frequency:    2    relative frequency: 0.0000
            P.  126 O.C.           126 And helpless languish at the tainted Stall.
            P.  140 HOUSEWARMING   109 Or rather how wisely his Stall was built near,

stallion                            frequency:    2    relative frequency: 0.0000
            P.  141 INSTRUCTIONS    30 The new Courts pattern, Stallion of the old.
            P.  192 TWO HORSES      29 The stately Brass Stallion and the white marble
                                       Steed

stamp                               frequency:    1    relative frequency: 0.0000
            P.  141 INSTRUCTIONS    20 Stamp on thy Pallat, nor perhaps the worse.

stamps                              frequency:    1    relative frequency: 0.0000
            P.  152 INSTRUCTICNS   487 Hyde Stamps, and straight upon the ground the
                                       swarms

stanch                              frequency:    1    relative frequency: 0.0000
            P.   44 DAMON           84 The Blood I stanch, and Wound I seal.

stand                               frequency:   18    relative frequency: 0.0003
```

```
P.    4 HASTINGS          5 Go, stand betwixt the Morning and the Flowers;
P.    5 HASTINGS         38 On which the happie Names do stand enroll'd;
P.    9 DIALOGUE         16 Stand prepar'd to heighten yours.
P.   27 MISTRESS         46 Stand still, yet we will make him run.
P.   28 LOVER            49 See how he nak'd and fierce does stand,
P.   41 THE MOWER        38 May to adorn the Gardens stand:
P.   46 AMETAS            1 Think'st Thou that this Love can stand,
P.   68 A. HOUSE        310 Under their Colcurs stand displaid:
P.   72 A. HOUSE        438 Short Pyramids cf Hay do stand.
P.   75 A. HOUSE        544 Which fit to stand and which to fell.
P.   85 FLECKNO          87 I meet one on the Stairs who made me stand,
P.  127 O.C.            167 Stand back ye Seas, and shrunk beneath the vail
P.  147 INSTRUCTIONS    284 Of Presbyterian Switzers, made a stand.
P.  161 INSTRUCTIONS    860 Where mute they stand to hear their Sentence
                            read;
P.  170 PROPHECY          8 Tho the Walls stand to bring the Citty lower;
P.  190 STATUE           33 But why is the worke then soe long at a stand?
P.  195 TWO HORSES      129 Both Infamous Stand in three Kingdoms votes,
P.  199 DUKE             66 Now Talbott must by his great master stand,
```

standard   frequency: 2   relative frequency: 0.0000
```
P.  146 INSTRUCTIONS    214 Led the French Standard, weltring in his
                            stride,
P.  148 INSTRUCTIONS    301 The martial Standard Sands displaying, shows
```

standing   frequency: 2   relative frequency: 0.0000
```
P.   40 THE MOWER         6 A dead and standing pocl of Air:
P.   66 A. HOUSE        238 Standing upon their holy Guard.
```

standing-armies   frequency: 1   relative frequency: 0.0000
```
P.  152 INSTRUCTIONS    484 These; and in Standing-Armies praise declaims.
```

stands   frequency: 12   relative frequency: 0.0002
```
P.   20 SOUL & BODY       3 With bolts cf Bcnes, that fetter'd stands
P.   57 BILL-BOROW       26 And in unenvy'd Greatness stands,
P.   66 A. HOUSE        251 Another bolder stands at push
P.   84 FLECKNO          60 He stands, as if he orly fed had been
P.   86 FLECKNO         129 Of all his Poems there he stands ungirt
P.  107 ANNIVERSARY     148 Girds yet his Sword, and ready stands to fight;
P.  143 INSTRUCTIONS     93 Stript to her Skin, see how she stooping stands,
P.  157 INSTRUCTIONS    680 Like the Sun's Statue stands of burnish'd
                            Gold.
P.  173 LOYALL SCOT      46 Like the sun's Statue stands of burnisht Gold:
P.  175 LOYALL SCOT     153 Whilst Arrius stands at th' Athanasian Creed.
P.  200 DUKE             92 Old England on its strcng foundations stands,
P.  313 CHEQUER INN       9 There stands a House new Painted
```

stanzas. See "stanza's."

stanza's   frequency: 1   relative frequency: 0.0000
```
P.   83 FLECKNO          18 He'd Stanza's for a whole Appartement.
```

staple   frequency: 1   relative frequency: 0.0000
```
P.   97 HCLLAND          72 Staple of Sects and Mint of Schisme grew;
```

star   frequency: 9   relative frequency: 0.0001
See also "dog-star," "starr."
```
P.   57 BILL-BOROW       31 By Night the Ncrthern Star their way
P.   80 A. HOUSE        684 Draws through the Skie, nor Star new-slain.
P.   87 ODE              12 Urged his active Star.
P.  105 ANNIVERSARY     101 And in his sev'ral Aspects, like a Star,
P.  110 ANNIVERSARY     274 Counted the Hours, and ev'ry Star did spy,
P.  111 ANNIVERSARY     343 So while our Star that gives us Light and
                            Heat,
P.  164 INSTRUCTIONS    950 And Spots unkncwn to the bright Star descry'd;
P.  174 LOYALL SCOT      86 And split the Influence of Every star?
P.  186 BRITANNIA        58 Outshining Virgc and the Julian Star.
```

starch   frequency: 1   relative frequency: 0.0000
```
P.  161 INSTRUCTIONS    838 With Face new bleacht, smoothen'd and stiff with
                            starch.
```

starcht   frequency: 1   relative frequency: 0.0000
```
P.  171 PROPHECY         38 To make starcht empty Speeches two hcurs long.
```

stare   frequency: 1   relative frequency: 0.0000
```
P.  165 INSTRUCTIONS    988 And, as in Love, on Parliaments can stare:
```

starling   frequency: 1   relative frequency: 0.0000
```
P.  183 MADE FREE        90 Tho' too small for the Carriage of Starling.
```

starr   frequency: 1   relative frequency: 0.0000

```
        P. 199 DUKE            46 Poore princess, borne under a sullen starr

starrs                            frequency:    2    relative frequency: 0.0000
        P.  29 LOVER           59 Who though, by the Malignant Starrs,
        P.  31 MOURNING         4 Spring from the Starrs of Chlora's Eyes?

starry                            frequency:    3    relative frequency: 0.0000
        P.   5 HASTINGS        45 And trails his Torches th'row the Starry Hall
        P.  81 A. HOUSE       724 Of Fairfax, and the starry Vere;
        P. 126 O.C.           114 The Signal from the starry Battlement.

stars                             frequency:   12    relative frequency: 0.0002
        See also "starrs."
        P.   5 HASTINGS        25 Therefore the Democratick Stars did rise,
        P.  16 EYES            43 And Stars shew lovely in the Night,
        P.  37 DEFINITION      32 And Opposition of the Stars.
        P.  68 A. HOUSE       314 Of Stars walks round about the Pole,
        P. 107 ANNIVERSARY    151 And Stars still fall, and still the Dragons
                                  Tail
        P. 111 ANNIVERSARY    332 And Stars (like Tapers) burn'd upon his Herse:
        P. 118 BLAKE          147 So prosperous Stars, though absent to the sence,
        P. 121 TWO SONGS       43 These Stars would say I do them wrong,
        P. 121 TWO SONGS       45 The Stars are fix'd unto their Sphere,
        P. 121 TWO SONGS       48 While Stars Eclypse by mixing Rayes.
        P. 126 O.C.           137 The Stars that for him fought had only pow'r
        P. 142 INSTRUCTIONS    69 Witness ye stars of Night, and thou the pale

startling                         frequency:    1    relative frequency: 0.0000
        P. 163 INSTRUCTIONS   907 Express him startling next with listning ear,

starts                            frequency:    3    relative frequency: 0.0000
        P.  79 A. HOUSE       660 Starts forth with to its Bonne Mine.
        P. 111 ANNIVERSARY    346 And Princes shining through their windows
                                  starts;
        P. 204 HISTORICALL    134 Ill luck starts up and thrives like Evil weeds.

starv'd                           frequency:    1    relative frequency: 0.0000
        P. 187 BRITANNIA       95 Whilst your starv'd power in Legall fetters
                                  pines.

starved                           frequency:    1    relative frequency: 0.0000
        See also "starv'd."
        P. 176 LOYALL SCOT    174 A Hungry Chaplain and a Starved Rat

state                             frequency:   42    relative frequency: 0.0008
        See also "garden-state."
        P.   5 HASTINGS        23 But 'tis a Maxime of that State, That none,
        P.  20 THYRSIS         27 Dorinda. Oh sweet! oh sweet! How I my future
                                  state
        P.  26 MISTRESS        19 For Lady you deserve this State;
        P.  33 DAPHNIS         14 To lay by her wonted State,
        P.  65 A. HOUSE       221 'Fly from their Vices. 'tis thy state,
        P.  83 FLECKNO         15 Yet of his State no man could have complain'd;
        P.  89 ODE             71 And yet in that the State
        P.  96 HOLLAND         47 To make a Bank was a great Plot of State;
        P.  98 HOLLAND        112 We buoy'd so often up their sinking State.
        P.  99 HOLLAND        145 For now of nothing may our State despair,
        P. 104 ANNIVERSARY     43 Nor more contribute to the state of Things,
        P. 106 ANNIVERSARY    111 But mad with Reason, so miscall'd, of State
        P. 109 ANNIVERSARY    248 Founding a firm State by Proportions true.
        P. 110 ANNIVERSARY    282 Him as their Father must the State obey.
        P. 112 ANNIVERSARY    352 'And ere we Dine, rase and rebuild their State.
        P. 125 O.C.           110 By nature solemniz'd with so much state.
        P. 129 O.C.           233 From which he issu'd with that awful state,
        P. 132 PARADISE        33 And things divine thou treatst of in such state
        P. 140 HOUSEWARMING    98 Where this Idol of State sits ador'd and
                                  accurst:
        P. 141 INSTRUCTIONS     1 After two sittings, now our Lady State,
        P. 143 INSTRUCTIONS   119 For so too Rubens, with affairs of State,
        P. 144 INSTRUCTIONS   150 Could raise so long for this new Whore of
                                  State.
        P. 147 INSTRUCTIONS   265 Of Birth, State, Wit, Strength, Courage,
                                  How'rd presumes,
        P. 149 INSTRUCTIONS   356 And sits in State Divine like Jove the
                                  fulminant!
        P. 150 INSTRUCTIONS   394 The Joys of State, for the new Peace and Tax.
        P. 153 INSTRUCTIONS   509 The State Affairs thus Marshall'd, for the
                                  rest
        P. 153 INSTRUCTIONS   517 As Heav'n in Storms, they call, in gusts of
                                  State,
        P. 168 ADVICE           7 Whilest the brave youths tired with the work of
                                  State
```

```
      P. 168 KINGS VOWES      64 I wholly will abandon State affaires,
      P. 169 ADVICE           48 With Cupid Seymour and the Tool of State,
      P. 175 LOYALL SCOT     134 All Mischeifs Moulded by those state divines:
      P. 187 BRITANNIA        93 The Church and state you safely may invade.
      P. 187 BRITANNIA       116 And to his care did my sad state commend.
      P. 188 BRITANNIA       131 Oh Vindex, come, and purge the Poyson'd state;
      P. 188 BRITANNIA       155 To the serene Venetian state I'le goe
      P. 188 BRITANNIA       159 By those great Patterns such a state I'le frame
      P. 189 BRITANNIA       175 True sons of Glory, Pillars of the state,
      P. 192 TWO HORSES       41 To see Church and state bow down to a whore
      P. 200 DUKE             88 Are these fitt hands to overturne a State
      P. 201 HISTORICALL       6 The People call him home to helpe the State,
      P. 201 HISTORICALL      25 And that the Fleet was gone in Pompe and state
      P. 203 HISTORICALL     114 Now to the State she tends againe direct,
```

state--   frequency: 1   relative frequency: 0.0000
      P. 202 HISTORICALL   62 Or count the various blemishes of State--

state-jealousie   frequency: 1   relative frequency: 0.0000
      P.   5 HASTINGS   27 Yet as some Prince, that, for State-Jealousie,

stately   frequency: 2   relative frequency: 0.0000
      P. 61 A. HOUSE   65 A Stately Frontispice of Poor
      P. 192 TWO HORSES   29 The stately Brass Stallion and the white marble
                                  Steed

states   frequency: 4   relative frequency: 0.0000
      P. 90 ODE   103 And to all States not free
      P. 91 MAY'S DEATH   52 How ill the measures of these States agree.
      P. 96 HOLLAND   51 But for less envy some joynt States endures,
      P. 152 INSTRUCTIONS   466 Still his sharp Wit on States and Princes
                                  whets.

state's   frequency: 1   relative frequency: 0.0000
      P. 188 BRITANNIA   129 Thus the state's night-Mard by this Hellish rout

statesmen   frequency: 2   relative frequency: 0.0000
      P. 91 MAY'S DEATH   43 Go seek the novice Statesmen, and obtrude
      P. 105 ANNIVERSARY   69 While tedious Statesmen many years did hack,

statuaries   frequency: 1   relative frequency: 0.0000
      P. 98 HOLLAND   97 They try, like Statuaries, if they can,

statue   frequency: 9   relative frequency: 0.0001
      P. 24 NYMPH   111 First my unhappy Statue made
      P. 157 INSTRUCTIONS   680 Like the Sun's Statue stands of burnish'd
                                  Gold.
      P. 173 LOYALL SCOT   46 Like the sun's Statue stands of burnisht Gold:
      P. 179 STOCKSMARKET   t The Statue in Stocks-Market.
      P. 179 STOCKSMARKET   3 So Sir Robert advanced the King's statue, in
                                  token
      P. 179 STOCKSMARKET   16 That he did for the King his own statue erect.
      P. 179 STOCKSMARKET   25 This statue is surely more scandalous far
      P. 189 STATUE   t The Statue at Charing Cross.
      P. 191 STATUE   53 So the Statue will up after all this delay,

statues   frequency: 3   relative frequency: 0.0000
      P. 41 THE MOWER   37 Their Statues polish'd by some ancient hand,
      P. 190 STATUE   19 What a doe with the Kings and the Statues is
                                  here:
      P. 191 TWO HORSES   5 Nay Statues without either windpipe or Lungs

stature   frequency: 1   relative frequency: 0.0000
      P. 201 HISTORICALL   1 Of a tall Stature and of sable hue,

statute   frequency: 1   relative frequency: 0.0000
      P. 314 CHEQUER INN   59 Like Maidens at a Statute Fair,

statutes   frequency: 2   relative frequency: 0.0000
      P. 95 DR. WITTY   39 You have Translations statutes best fulfil'd.
      P. 204 HISTORICALL   119 The most authentik Statutes of the Land,

staves   frequency: 1   relative frequency: 0.0000
      P. 68 A. HOUSE   316 Seem to their Staves the Ensigns furl'd.

stay   frequency: 17   relative frequency: 0.0003
      P.   9 DIALOGUE   17 I sup above, and cannot stay
      P. 10 DIALOGUE   38 For thy Stay these charming Aires;
      P. 23 NYMPH   68 'Twould stay, and run again, and stay.
      P. 25 YOUNG LOVE   9 Common Beauties stay fifteen;
      P. 33 DAPHNIS   12 So it had his stay compriz'd.
      P. 34 DAPHNIS   33 At that Why, that Stay my Dear,
```
```

```
     P.  61 A. HOUSE          82 And on each pleasant footstep stay,
     P.  73 A. HOUSE         469 For, jealous of its Lords long stay,
     P.  94 DR. WITTY         27 Translators learn of her: but stay I slide
     P. 106 ANNIVERSARY      139 Fore-shortned Time its useless Course would
                                 stay,
     P. 108 ANNIVERSARY      194 And leaden Sorrow then their flight did stay.
     P. 121 TWO SONGS          5 Stay till I some flow'rs ha' ty'd
     P. 124 O.C.              52 This will not stay when once the other's gone.
     P. 147 INSTRUCTIONS     267 These and some more with single Valour stay
     P. 202 HISTORICALL       74 The Senate which should headstrong Princes stay
     P. 316 CHEQUER INN      165 For Grace they did not stay
```

stay'd   frequency: 2   relative frequency: 0.0000
```
     P.  84 FLECKNO           57 And Silent. Nothing now Dinner stay'd
     P. 128 O.C.             192 Since the commanded sun o're Gibeon stay'd?
```

stead   frequency: 1   relative frequency: 0.0000
```
     P. 205 HISTORICALL      166 And in his stead had plac'd him on his Throne.
```

steady   frequency: 1   relative frequency: 0.0000
```
     P. 200 DUKE             94 Its steady Basis never could bee shooke,
```

steal   frequency: 2   relative frequency: 0.0000
```
     P. 185 BRITANNIA         33 Thus Fayry like the King they steal away
     P. 188 BRITANNIA        150 Must be immur'd, lest their contagion steal
```

steals   frequency: 2   relative frequency: 0.0000
```
     P. 187 BRITANNIA        123 Her Creature Osborn the Revenue steals;
     P. 194 TWO HORSES       111 On ocasions like these he oft steals away
```

stealth   frequency: 2   relative frequency: 0.0000
```
     P.  98 HOLLAND          117 While, with feign'd Treaties, they invade by
                                 stealth
     P. 165 INSTRUCTIONS     984 Nor Guilt to flatt'ry binds, nor want to
                                 stealth;
```

steam   frequency: 2   relative frequency: 0.0000
```
     P.  97 HOLLAND           91 While the fat steam of Female Sacrifice
     P. 142 INSTRUCTIONS      70 Moon, that o'rccme with the sick steam did'st
                                 fail;
```

steed   frequency: 3   relative frequency: 0.0000
```
     P. 169 ADVICE            40 Draw me a Champion mounted on his steed,
     P. 179 STOCKSMARKET       6 Obliging the city with a king and a steed,
     P. 192 TWO HORSES        29 The stately Brass Stallion and the white marble
                                 Steed
```

steeds   frequency: 1   relative frequency: 0.0000
```
     P. 108 ANNIVERSARY      216 And firy Steeds had born out of the Warr,
```

steel   frequency: 4   relative frequency: 0.0000
```
     See also "stele."
     P.  37 DEFINITION        17 And therefore her Decrees of Steel
     P.  57 BILL-BOROW        36 With impious Steel the sacred Shade.
     P. 128 O.C.             196 Yet him the adverse steel could never pierce.
     P. 161 INSTRUCTIONS     842 Trusty as Steel, that always ready hung;
```

steel'd   frequency: 2   relative frequency: 0.0000
```
     P.  99 HOLLAND          150 Steel'd with those piercing Heads, Dean, Monck
                                 and Blake.
     P. 146 INSTRUCTIONS     219 Never, before nor since, an Host so steel'd
```

steely   frequency: 2   relative frequency: 0.0000
```
     P.   4 LOVELACE          37 Whose hand so rudely grasps the steely brand,
     P. 125 O.C.              73 Like polish'd Mirrcurs, so his steely Brest
```

steep   frequency: 1   relative frequency: 0.0000
```
     P.  20 THYRSIS           46 And thou and I'le pick poppies and them steep
```

steeples   frequency: 1   relative frequency: 0.0000
```
     P.  96 HOLLAND           24 And oft at Leap-frog ore their Steeples plaid:
```

steept   frequency: 1   relative frequency: 0.0000
```
     P.   4 HASTINGS           2 Whose Virgin-Source yet never steept the Plain.
```

steer   frequency: 5   relative frequency: 0.0001
```
     P.  72 A. HOUSE         436 How Boats among them safely steer.
     P.  97 HOLLAND           68 And from the East would Westward steer its
                                 Ark,
     P. 105 ANNIVERSARY      103 While by his Beams observing Princes steer,
     P. 114 BLAKE             21 In thickest darkness they would choose to steer,
```

```
              P. 154 INSTRUCTIONS  555 And gentle Gales them steer, and Heaven drives,

steers                              frequency:    1    relative frequency: 0.0000
     P. 146 INSTRUCTIONS  228 While Hector Harry steers by Will the Wit:

steersman                           frequency:    1    relative frequency: 0.0000
     P. 110 ANNIVERSARY   275 The Helm does from the artless Steersman
                             strain,

stele                               frequency:    1    relative frequency: 0.0000
     P.  44 DAMON          77 The edged Stele by careless chance

step                                frequency:    1    relative frequency: 0.0000
     P. 163 INSTRUCTIONS  927 At his first step, he Castlemain does find,

steps                               frequency:    2    relative frequency: 0.0000
     P.  56 BILL-BOROW     15 Learn here those humble steps to tread,
     P. 188 BRITANNIA     158 To teach my People in their steps to tread.

stern                               frequency:    1    relative frequency: 0.0000
     P.   5 HASTINGS       47 And Aesculapius, who, asham'd and stern,

sterns                              frequency:    1    relative frequency: 0.0000
     P. 154 INSTRUCTIONS  554 The airy Sterns the Sun behind does guild;

stevens                             frequency:    1    relative frequency: 0.0000
     P.  90 MAY'S DEATH     6 For whence in Stevens ally Trees or Grass?

steward                             frequency:    1    relative frequency: 0.0000
     P. 144 INSTRUCTIONS  160 Thought yet but Pioneers, and led by Steward.

stewart                             frequency:    1    relative frequency: 0.0000
     See also "steward."
     P. 159 INSTRUCTIONS  762 And female Stewart, there, Rules the four
                             Seas.

stewarts                            frequency:    1    relative frequency: 0.0000
     P. 202 HISTORICALL    57 But since the ill gott race of Stewarts came,

stew'd                              frequency:    1    relative frequency: 0.0000
     P. 149 INSTRUCTIONS  337 Not so decrepid Aeson, hash'd and stew'd

stewes                              frequency:    1    relative frequency: 0.0000
     P. 189 BRITANNIA     166 Imployd the Youth, not Taverns, Stewes and
                             playes:

stews.  See "stewes."

stich                               frequency:    1    relative frequency: 0.0000
     P.  84 FLECKNO        65 The Needles Eye thread without any stich,

sticks                              frequency:    1    relative frequency: 0.0000
     P.   4 HASTINGS       12 And on Times Wheel sticks like a Remora.

stiff                               frequency:    2    relative frequency: 0.0000
     P. 161 INSTRUCTIONS  838 With Face new bleacht, smoothen'd and stiff with
                             starch.
     P. 313 CHEQUER INN    31 He is as stiff as any Stake

stiffer                             frequency:    1    relative frequency: 0.0000
     P.  89 ODE            81 Nor yet grown stiffer with Command,

stiffest                            frequency:    1    relative frequency: 0.0000
     P.  56 BILL-BOROW      3 The stiffest Compass could not strike

stile                               frequency:    1    relative frequency: 0.0000
     P. 152 INSTRUCTIONS  465 Hyde's flippant Stile there pleasantly curvets;

still                               frequency:   94    relative frequency: 0.0019
     P.   4 HASTINGS       19 Had he but at this Measure still increast,
     P.  10 DIALOGUE       49 Then persevere: for still new Charges sound:
     P.  12 DROP OF DEW    22 Remembring still its former height,
     P.  16 EYES           28 Bath still their Eyes in their own Dew.
     P.  24 NYMPH          87 But all its chief delight was still
     P.  24 NYMPH         117 Until my Tears, still dropping, wear
     P.  27 LOVER           3 Sorted by pairs, they still are seen
     P.  27 MISTRESS       46 Stand still, yet we will make him run.
     P.  28 LOVER          35 And as their Corm'rant fed him, still
     P.  43 DAMON          65 How happy might I still have mov'd,
     P.  43 DAMON          70 Yet still my Grief is where it was:
     P.  45 MOWER'S SONG    8 Grew more luxuriant still and fine;
```

P.	46	AMETAS	2	Whilst Thou still dost say me nay?
P.	48	THE GARDEN	28	Still in a Tree did end their race.
P.	54	THYESTE	3	All I seek is to lye still.
P.	57	BILL-BOROW	39	And Men could hear his Armour still
P.	64	A. HOUSE	178	'Still handling Natures finest Parts.
P.	66	A. HOUSE	231	For Justice still that Courage led;
P.	66	A. HOUSE	237	Yet still the Nuns his Right debar'd,
P.	68	A. HOUSE	303	And think so still! though not compare
P.	74	A. HOUSE	503	And stretches still so closely wedg'd
P.	75	A. HOUSE	539	He walks still upright from the Root,
P.	84	FLECKNO	34	Ask'd still for more, and pray'd him to repeat:
P.	85	FLECKNO	95	He gathring fury still made sign to draw;
P.	89	ODE	82	But still in the Republick's hand:
P.	90	MAY'S DEATH	8	Signs by which still he found and lost his way.
P.	90	ODE	116	Still keep thy Sword erect:
P.	92	MAY'S DEATH	69	Sings still of ancient Rights and better Times,
P.	92	MAY'S DEATH	78	Hast left surviving Davenant still behind
P.	94	DR. WITTY	21	But she is Caelia still: no other grace
P.	96	HOLLAND	20	Where barking Waves still bait the forced Ground;
P.	96	HOLLAND	23	Yet still his claim the Injur'd Ocean laid,
P.	97	HOLLAND	90	But still does place it at her Western End:
P.	99	HOLLAND	148	Watchful abroad, and honest still within.
P.	103	ANNIVERSARY	9	And still the Day which he doth next restore,
P.	104	ANNIVERSARY	30	This Common Enemy is still opprest;
P.	104	ANNIVERSARY	46	And cuts his way still nearer to the Skyes,
P.	104	ANNIVERSARY	58	And still new Stopps to various Time apply'd:
P.	105	ANNIVERSARY	70	Framing a Liberty that still went back.
P.	105	ANNIVERSARY	93	But the most Equal still sustein the Height,
P.	106	ANNIVERSARY	113	Hence still they sing Hosanna to the Whore,
P.	106	ANNIVERSARY	133	And then a seasonable People still
P.	107	ANNIVERSARY	151	And Stars still fall, and still the Dragons Tail
P.	107	ANNIVERSARY	155	Hence that blest Day still counterpoysed wastes,
P.	107	ANNIVERSARY	158	And good Designes still with their Authors lost.
P.	107	ANNIVERSARY	167	Though thou thine Heart from Evil still unstain'd,
P.	107	ANNIVERSARY	186	Still as they trickle, glitter in our Joy.
P.	109	ANNIVERSARY	240	Still from behind, and it before him rush'd,
P.	109	ANNIVERSARY	244	But walk still middle betwixt War and Peace;
P.	109	ANNIVERSARY	258	Didst (like thine Olive) still refuse to Reign;
P.	110	ANNIVERSARY	293	Yet such a Chammish issue still does rage,
P.	111	ANNIVERSARY	337	Still to the West, where he him lost, he turn'd,
P.	112	ANNIVERSARY	375	'That one Man still, although but nam'd, alarms
P.	112	ANNIVERSARY	378	'And still his Sword seems hanging o're my head.
P.	112	ANNIVERSARY	384	'And still his Fauchion all our Knots unties.
P.	114	BLAKE	34	Where still the Earth is moist, the Air still dry;
P.	115	BLAKE	55	They still do yield, such is their pretious mould,
P.	115	BLAKE	57	With fatal Gold, for still where that does grow,
P.	123	O.C.	25	That they, to whom his Breast still open lyes,
P.	126	O.C.	135	He without noise still travell'd to his End,
P.	128	O.C.	194	He conquer'd God, still ere he fought with men:
P.	128	O.C.	208	Yet still affected most what best deserv'd.
P.	129	O.C.	258	That still though dead, greater than death he lay'd;
P.	143	INSTRUCTIONS	84	And still within her mind the Footman runs:
P.	143	INSTRUCTIONS	112	As Chance does still in Multitudes decide.
P.	143	INSTRUCTIONS	116	Can strike the Die, and still with them goes share.
P.	145	INSTRUCTIONS	163	Still his Hook-shoulder seems the blow to dread,
P.	145	INSTRUCTIONS	192	(Their publick Acts) oblig'd them still to more.
P.	147	INSTRUCTIONS	245	But Strangeways, that all Night still walk'd the round,
P.	147	INSTRUCTIONS	277	But strength at last still under number bows,
P.	148	INSTRUCTIONS	286	But for th' unknown Reserve that still remain'd:
P.	148	INSTRUCTIONS	300	Adjutant-General was still at hand.
P.	149	INSTRUCTIONS	340	His Gout (yet still he curst) had left him quite.
P.	149	INSTRUCTIONS	361	But still he car'd, while in Revenge he brav'd,
P.	151	INSTRUCTIONS	411	Fresh Messengers still the sad News assure,
P.	151	INSTRUCTIONS	431	Now Doleman's disobedient, and they still
P.	152	INSTRUCTIONS	466	Still his sharp Wit on States and Princes whets.
P.	152	INSTRUCTIONS	475	But still in hope he solac'd, e're they come,
P.	153	INSTRUCTIONS	512	Why he should still b'on all adventures us'd.
P.	157	INSTRUCTIONS	697	Each doleful day still with fresh loss returns;
P.	159	INSTRUCTIONS	763	But Fate does still accumulate our Woes,
P.	160	INSTRUCTIONS	817	But in the Thames mouth still de Ruyter laid,

P. 166 KINGS VOWES   34 I will have a Privy Councell to sit allwayes
                             still,
P. 167 KINGS VOWES   54 And Quack in their Language still Vive le
                             Roy.
P. 171 PROPHECY   54 For that still fill'd runs out as fast againe;
P. 174 LOYALL SCOT   124 Ah! like Lotts wife they still look Back and
                             Halt
P. 177 LOYALL SCOT   233 While they liv'd here, still Haunts them
                             Underground.
P. 182 MADE FREE   53 He still made a Retreate
P. 184 MADE FREE   118 Who still doth advance
P. 189 STATUE   2 This five moneths continues still blinded with
                             board?
P. 193 TWO HORSES   81 Ch. No wonder that Beggers should still be for
                             giving
P. 195 TWO HORSES   135 W. One of the two Tyrants must still be our
                             case

sting   frequency: 1   relative frequency: 0.0000
     P. 42 DAMON   36 Disarmed of its teeth and sting.

stinking   frequency: 1   relative frequency: 0.0000
     P. 188 BRITANNIA   153 And shall this stinking Scottish brood evade

stint   frequency: 1   relative frequency: 0.0000
     P. 94 DR. WITTY   30 Stint them to Cawdles, Almond-milk, and Broth.

stipends. See "stypends."

stir'd   frequency: 2   relative frequency: 0.0000
     P. 68 A. HOUSE   319 And sleeps so too: but, if once stir'd,
     P. 174 LOYALL SCOT   114 Their Rank Ambition all this heat hath stir'd

stirred. See "stir'd."

stirs   frequency: 1   relative frequency: 0.0000
     P. 60 A. HOUSE   52 Stirs, and the Square grows Spherical;

stitch. See "stich."

stock   frequency: 3   relative frequency: 0.0000
     P. 41 THE MOWER   23 No Plant now knew the Stock from which it came;
     P. 43 DAMON   49 What, though the piping Shepherd stock
     P. 125 O.C.   99 So the dry Stock, no more that spreading Vine,

stock-doves   frequency: 1   relative frequency: 0.0000
     P. 75 A. HOUSE   523 The Stock-doves, whose fair necks are grac'd

stocks   frequency: 2   relative frequency: 0.0000
     P. 74 A. HOUSE   489 The double Wood of ancient Stocks
     P. 191 TWO HORSES   13 At Delphos and Rome Stocks and Stones now and
                              then, sirs,

stocks-market   frequency: 1   relative frequency: 0.0000
     P. 179 STOCKSMARKET   t The Statue in Stocks-Market.

stole   frequency: 3   relative frequency: 0.0000
     P. 145 INSTRUCTIONS   166 Hid with his Elbow like the Spice he stole.
     P. 166 KINGS VOWES   32 I will winke all the while my Revenue is stole,
     P. 185 BRITANNIA   13 I stole away; and never will return

stolen. See "stoln," "stolne."

stoln   frequency: 1   relative frequency: 0.0000
     P. 67 A. HOUSE   268 Like Gipsies that a Child hath stoln.

stolne   frequency: 1   relative frequency: 0.0000
     P. 192 TWO HORSES   32 Were stolne of Incognito each his own way,

stomach   frequency: 1   relative frequency: 0.0000
     See also "stomack."
     P. 86 FLECKNO   121 And on full stomach do condemn but few:

stomack   frequency: 1   relative frequency: 0.0000
     P. 165 KINGS VOWES   2 And the Spider might weave in our Stomack its
                              web;

stone   frequency: 11   relative frequency: 0.0002
     P. 24 NYMPH   116 That I shall weep though I be Stone:
     P. 27 LOVER   15 And there she split against the Stone,
     P. 65 A. HOUSE   210 'One Stone that a just Hand had laid,

P.	82 A. HOUSE	764 Gulfes, Deserts, Precipices, Stone.
P.	105 ANNIVERSARY	79 No Quarry bears a Stone so hardly wrought,
P.	109 ANNIVERSARY	245 Choosing each Stone, and poysing every weight,
P.	149 INSTRUCTIONS	360 And roul in vain at Sisyphus's Stone.
P.	175 LOYALL SCOT	158 Seth's Pillars are noe Antique Brick and stone
P.	180 STOCKSMARKET	32 For he counterfeits only in gold, not in stone.
P.	192 TWO HORSES	35 W. Quoth the marble white Hors: 'twould make a stone speak
P.	192 TWO HORSES	40 My Brass is provok't as much as thy stone

stones   frequency: 6   relative frequency: 0.0001
P.	104 ANNIVERSARY	51 The rougher Stones, unto his Measures hew'd,
P.	138 HOUSEWARMING	44 But that he had nearer the Stones of St. Pauls.
P.	140 HIS HOUSE	2 Of Paul late gelded of his Stones.
P.	181 MADE FREE	11 Set with Stones of both Rocks
P.	191 TWO HORSES	13 At Delphos and Rome Stocks and Stones now and then, sirs,
P.	196 TWO HORSES	177 Yet the beasts of the field or the stones in the wall

stood   frequency: 4   relative frequency: 0.0000
P.	5 HASTINGS	51 For, how Immortal must their race have stood,
P.	108 ANNIVERSARY	199 With wandring Eyes, and restless Ears they stood,
P.	129 O.C.	267 (It groanes, and bruises all below that stood
P.	314 CHEQUER INN	55 They stood (when enter'd in the Hall)

stooles   frequency: 1   relative frequency: 0.0000
P.   174 LOYALL SCOT   97 Or to the Joynt stooles reconcile the Chairs?

stools. See "stooles."

stoop   frequency: 2   relative frequency: 0.0000
See also "stoope."
P.	59 A. HOUSE	29 When larger sized Men did stoop
P.	75 A. HOUSE	517 But highest Oakes stoop down to hear,

stoope   frequency: 1   relative frequency: 0.0000
P.   200 DUKE   96 And can her Guardian Angell lett her stoope

stooping   frequency: 1   relative frequency: 0.0000
P.   143 INSTRUCTIONS   93 Stript to her Skin, see how she stooping stands,

stop   frequency: 3   relative frequency: 0.0000
P.	16 EYES	50 And at each Tear in distance stop:
P.	109 ANNIVERSARY	261 Whose climbing Flame, without a timely stop,
P.	170 PROPHECY	27 When publike faith and Vowes and Payments stop,

stopping   frequency: 1   relative frequency: 0.0000
P.   85 FLECKNO   88 Stopping the passage, and did him demand:

stopps   frequency: 1   relative frequency: 0.0000
P.   104 ANNIVERSARY   58 And still new Stopps to various Time apply'd:

stops. See "stopps."

stopt   frequency: 2   relative frequency: 0.0000
P.	190 STATUE	22 When their Pensions are stopt to be fool'd with a sight?
P.	205 HISTORICALL	178 And stopt his Malice in its full Careere.

stor'd   frequency: 1   relative frequency: 0.0000
P.   39 THE MATCH   19 And therefore stor'd a Magazine,

store   frequency: 11   relative frequency: 0.0002
P.	4 HASTINGS	3 Hastings is dead, and we must finde a Store
P.	12 DIALOGUE	78 And is thine everlasting Store.
P.	14 THE CORONET	9 And now when I have summ'd up all my store,
P.	30 THE GALLERY	42 Of Thee, my Gallery do store;
P.	39 THE MATCH	2 Of all her choisest store;
P.	40 THE MATCH	40 All Love's and Nature's store.
P.	65 A. HOUSE	193 'But what is this to all the store
P.	94 DR. WITTY	14 As much as he that taketh from the Store
P.	164 INSTRUCTIONS	980 Burr'wing themselves to hoard their guilty Store.
P.	190 STATUE	13 Were these Deales kept in store for sheathing our fleet
P.	199 DUKE	45 Preserv'd in store for the new sett of maids.

stores   frequency: 2   relative frequency: 0.0000

P. 17 BERMUDAS   26 From Lebanon, he stores the Land.
P. 148 INSTRUCTIONS   322 The Stores and Wages all are mine and thine.

stories   frequency: 1   relative frequency: 0.0000
   See also "storyes."
P. 91 MAY'S DEATH   45 Tell them of Liberty, the Stories fine,

stork   frequency: 1   relative frequency: 0.0000
P. 195 TWO HORSES   144 W. The Same that the Froggs had of Jupiters
                          Stork.

stork-like   frequency: 1   relative frequency: 0.0000
P. 75 A. HOUSE   535 As if it Stork-like did pretend

storm   frequency: 2   relative frequency: 0.0000
P. 66 A. HOUSE   233 Small Honour would be in the Storm.
P. 109 ANNIVERSARY   236 And down at last thou pow'rdst the fertile
                          Storm;

stormed   frequency: 1   relative frequency: 0.0000
P. 127 O.C.   186 And cityes strong were stormed by his prayer;

storms   frequency: 7   relative frequency: 0.0001
P. 17 BERMUDAS   12 Safe from the Storms, and Prelat's rage.
P. 29 LOVER   60 Forced to live in Storms and Warrs:
P. 107 ANNIVERSARY   169 Thou, who so oft through Storms of thundring
                          Lead
P. 116 BLAKE   84 Nor Winters storms, had made your Fleet
                          retreat.
P. 131 O.C.   322 Rainbows to storms, Richard to Oliver.
P. 153 INSTRUCTIONS   517 As Heav'n in Storms, they call, in gusts of
                          State,
P. 159 INSTRUCTIONS   773 Who the Dutch Fleet with Storms disabled met,

stormy   frequency: 2   relative frequency: 0.0000
P. 154 INSTRUCTIONS   560 And at Sheerness unloads its stormy sides.
P. 185 BRITANNIA   49 Sauls stormy rage and Check his black disease,

story   frequency: 7   relative frequency: 0.0001
P. 29 LOVER   63 And he in Story only rules,
P. 104 ANNIVERSARY   55 No Note he struck, but a new Story lay'd,
P. 127 O.C.   188 The story, and impregnable Clonmell.
P. 169 ADVICE   45 Tis this must make Obryan great in Story,
P. 171 PROPHECY   50 Then either Greek or Gallick Story shew,
P. 188 BRITANNIA   160 Shall darken story, Ingross loudmouthd fame.
P. 191 TWO HORSES   7 Livy tells a strang story can hardly be fellow'd

storyes   frequency: 1   relative frequency: 0.0000
P. 175 LOYALL SCOT   171 Like Smutty Storyes in Pure Linnen Wrapt.

stout   frequency: 1   relative frequency: 0.0000
P. 153 INSTRUCTIONS   493 This done, he Pens a Proclamation stout,

stoves   frequency: 1   relative frequency: 0.0000
P. 69 A. HOUSE   341 The Winter Quarters were the Stoves,

straight   frequency: 14   relative frequency: 0.0002
P. 15 EYES   24 Which straight in pity back he powers.
P. 64 A. HOUSE   166 'Will straight grow Sanctity when here:
P. 83 FLECKNO   19 Straight without further information,
P. 85 FLECKNO   107 But the propitiatory Priest had straight
P. 87 FLECKNO   157 Thereat the waxen Youth relented straight;
P. 139 HOUSEWARMING   65 Straight Judges, Priests, Bishops, true sons
                          of the Seal,
P. 142 INSTRUCTIONS   44 Can straight produce them a Plenipotence.
P. 143 INSTRUCTIONS   102 And Jermyn straight has leave to come agen.
P. 148 INSTRUCTIONS   311 St. Albans straight is sent to, to forbear,
P. 152 INSTRUCTIONS   460 Then to return home straight infecta re.
P. 152 INSTRUCTIONS   487 Hyde Stamps, and straight upon the ground the
                          swarms
P. 154 INSTRUCTIONS   572 March straight to Chatham, to increase the fear.
P. 161 INSTRUCTIONS   841 Not so, quoth Tomkins; and straight drew his
                          Tongue,
P. 163 INSTRUCTIONS   926 And rising, straight on Hyde's Disgrace
                          resolves.

strain   frequency: 4   relative frequency: 0.0000
P.   9 DIALOGUE   22 Lest one Leaf thy Side should strain.
P. 36 DAPHNIS   86 Who for parting pleasure strain
P. 59 A. HOUSE   32 To strain themselves through Heavens Gate.
P. 110 ANNIVERSARY   275 The Helm does from the artless Steersman

strain,

strains. See "streigns."

strait   frequency: 3   relative frequency: 0.0000
     See also "streight."
     P. 59 A. HOUSE   31 As practising, in doors so strait,
     P. 205 HISTORICALL   164 All England strait should fall beneath his
                               yoake,
     P. 205 HISTORICALL   172 Who strait design'd his Brother to supplant.

straitness   frequency: 1   relative frequency: 0.0000
     See also "streightness."
     P. 60 A. HOUSE   54 Then he is by its straitness prest:

strang   frequency: 1   relative frequency: 0.0000
     P. 191 TWO HORSES   7 Livy tells a strang story can hardly be fellow'd

strange   frequency: 10   relative frequency: 0.0002
     See also "strang."
     P. 36 DEFINITION   2 As 'tis for object strange and high:
     P. 41 THE MOWER   11 With strange perfumes he did the Roses taint.
     P. 55 THYESTE   14 Death to him 's a Strange surprise.
     P. 71 A. HOUSE   385 No Scene that turns with Engines strange
     P. 77 A. HOUSE   578 Strange Prophecies my Fhancy weaves:
     P. 97 HOLLAND   73 That Bank of Conscience, where not one so
                               strange
     P. 145 INSTRUCTIONS   165 The posture strange men laught at of his Poll,
     P. 162 INSTRUCTIONS   899 The Object strange in him no Terrour mov'd:
     P. 176 LOYALL SCOT   186 Strange was the Sight the scotch Twin headed
                               man
     P. 176 LOYALL SCOT   204 Strange boldness! even bishops there rebell

strangely   frequency: 1   relative frequency: 0.0000
     See also "strangly."
     P. 87 FLECKNO   168 As one scap't strangely from Captivity,

strangeways   frequency: 2   relative frequency: 0.0000
     P. 147 INSTRUCTIONS   245 But Strangeways, that all Night still walk'd
                               the round,
     P. 147 INSTRUCTIONS   279 Ev'n Iron Strangeways, chafing yet gave back,

strangled   frequency: 1   relative frequency: 0.0000
     P. 99 HOLLAND   138 Is strangled by our Infant Hercules.

strangly   frequency: 1   relative frequency: 0.0000
     P. 62 A. HOUSE   112 'Most strangly our Complexion clears.

stratagem   frequency: 1   relative frequency: 0.0000
     P. 148 INSTRUCTIONS   309 Where force had fail'd with Stratagem to play,

straw   frequency: 2   relative frequency: 0.0000
     P. 138 HOUSEWARMING   38 To make Mortar and Brick, yet allow'd them no
                               straw,
     P. 183 MADE FREE   89 Like Ants at a Straw,

straw-berryes   frequency: 1   relative frequency: 0.0000
     P. 75 A. HOUSE   530 Of gelid Straw-berryes do tread,

stray   frequency: 2   relative frequency: 0.0000
     P. 19 THYRSIS   23 No need of Dog to fetch our stray,
     P. 44 GLO-WORMS   12 And after foolish Fires do stray;

streaks   frequency: 2   relative frequency: 0.0000
     P. 28 LOVER   22 Through frighted Clouds in forked streaks.
     P. 163 INSTRUCTIONS   916 And with blue streaks infect the Taper clear:

stream   frequency: 6   relative frequency: 0.0001
     P. 80 A. HOUSE   675 The gellying Stream compacts below,
     P. 147 INSTRUCTIONS   250 The falling Bridge behind, the Stream below.
     P. 154 INSTRUCTIONS   559 Such up the stream the Belgick Navy glides,
     P. 157 INSTRUCTIONS   692 And the sad Stream beneath his Ashes drinks.
     P. 173 LOYALL SCOT   58 And the sad stream beneath his Ashes drinks.
     P. 174 LOYALL SCOT   84 Up from her Stream Continued to the Sky's,

streamers   frequency: 1   relative frequency: 0.0000
     P. 114 BLAKE   20 With English Streamers, should salute their
                               sight:

streaming   frequency: 1   relative frequency: 0.0000
     P. 154 INSTRUCTIONS   537 Their streaming Silks play through the weather
                                                               fair,

```
streams                              frequency:    6    relative frequency: 0.0001
     P.   17 EYES            53 Thus let your Streams o'reflow your Springs,
     P.   82 A. HOUSE       752 So you all Woods, Streams, Gardens, Meads.
     P.  103 ANNIVERSARY      2 Which in smooth streams a sinking Weight does
                                raise;
     P.  108 ANNIVERSARY    213 When now they sink, and now the plundring
                                Streams
     P.  111 ANNIVERSARY    330 Sunk in the Hills, or plung'd below the
                                Streams.
     P.  153 INSTRUCTIONS   525 Survey'd their Crystal Streams, and Banks so
                                green,

strecht                              frequency:    2    relative frequency: 0.0000
     P.   72 A. HOUSE       444 As Clothes for Lilly strecht to stain.
     P.  147 INSTRUCTIONS   258 Had strecht the monster Patent on the Field.

street                               frequency:    3    relative frequency: 0.0000
See also "lombard-street," "streete."
     P.  150 INSTRUCTIONS   383 But the just Street does the next House invade,
     P.  170 PROPHECY        14 And Checquer dcres shall shut up Lombard
                                street,
     P.  192 TWO HORSES      36 To see a Lord Major and a Lumbard Street
                                break,

streete                              frequency:    1    relative frequency: 0.0000
     P.  182 MADE FREE       43 Throughout Lumbard Streete

streets                              frequency:    2    relative frequency: 0.0000
     P.  144 INSTRUCTIONS   139 She stalks all day in Streets conceal'd from
                                sight,
     P.  166 KINGS VOWES     23 with wide streets and uniforme of my owne mold;

streight                             frequency:   16    relative frequency: 0.0003
     P.   34 DAPHNIS         40 And then streight again is fled.
     P.   40 THE MATCH       27 For, with cne Spark of these, he streight
     P.   49 THE GARDEN      44 Does streight its cwn resemblance find;
     P.   58 BILL-BOROW      56 As under this sc streight and green.
     P.   76 A. HOUSE       566 Streight floting on the Air shall fly:
     P.   80 A. HOUSE       685 For streight those giddy Rockets fail,
     P.   80 A. HOUSE       695 She yet more Pure, Sweet, Streight, and Fair,
     P.   90 MAY'S DEATH     19 But seeing May he varied streight his Song,
     P.   92 MAY'S DEATH     99 And streight he vanisht in a Cloud of pitch,
     P.  104 ANNIVERSARY     60 And joyning streight the Theban Tow'r arose;
     P.  111 ANNIVERSARY    341 When streight the Sun behind him he descry'd,
     P.  123 O.C.            29 Streight does a slcw and languishing Disease
     P.  130 O.C.           295 How streight canst to each happy mansion goe?
     P.  171 LOYALL SCOT      3 They streight Consulting gather'd in a Ring
     P.  178 LOYALL SCOT    254 Say but a Scot and streight wee fall to sides:
     P.  178 LOYALL SCOT    272 The Insect Kingdome streight begins to thrive

streightness                         frequency:    2    relative frequency: 0.0000
     P.   80 A. HOUSE       691 She streightness on the Woods bestows;
     P.   84 FLECKNO         43 Whcse hungry Guts to the same streightness
                                twin'd

streigns                             frequency:    1    relative frequency: 0.0000
     P.  131 O.C.           313 How he becomes that seat, how strongly streigns,

strength                             frequency:   10    relative frequency: 0.0002
     P.   27 MISTRESS        41 Let us roll all our Strength, and all
     P.  106 ANNIVERSARY    120 Leisure to Time, and tc my Weakness Strength,
     P.  109 ANNIVERSARY    257 Thou with the same strength, and an Heart as
                                plain,
     P.  115 BLAKE           50 Peace, against you, was the sole strength of
                                Spain.
     P.  115 BLAKE           74 Where you had mcst of strength, and least of
                                fear.
     P.  116 BLAKE           96 So proud and confident of their made strength,
     P.  116 BLAKE          104 We to their Strength are mcre oblig'd then they.
     P.  147 INSTRUCTIONS   265 Of Birth, State, Wit, Strength, Courage,
                                How'rd presumes,
     P.  147 INSTRUCTIONS   277 But strength at last still under number bows,
     P.  158 INSTRUCTIONS   732 Viewing her strength, they yet their Conquest
                                doubt.

strephon                             frequency:    1    relative frequency: 0.0000
     P.   32 MOURNING        12 Would strcw the grcund where Strephon lay.

stretch                              frequency:    1    relative frequency: 0.0000
```

P. 174 LOYALL SCOT   100 Stretch for your Line their Circingle Alone,

stretch'd   frequency: 2   relative frequency: 0.0000
    P. 127 O.C.   174 And stretch'd our frontire to the Indian Ore;
    P. 129 O.C.   252 Loose and depriv'd cf vigour, stretch'd along:

stretched   frequency: 1   relative frequency: 0.0000
    See also "stretch'd," "stretcht."
    P. 99 HOLLAND   139 Their Tortoise wants its vainly stretched neck;

stretches   frequency: 2   relative frequency: 0.0000
    P. 29 THE GALLERY   20 And stretches cut her milky Thighs;
    P. 74 A. HOUSE   503 And stretches still sc closely wedg'd

stretcht   frequency: 2   relative frequency: 0.0000
    P. 21 SOUL & BOLY   13 Which, stretcht upright, impales me so,
    P. 79 A. HOUSE   644 Stretcht as a Bank untc the Tide;

strict   frequency: 3   relative frequency: 0.0000
    P. 86 FLECKNO   122 Yet he more strict my sentence doth renew;
    P. 96 HOLLAND   54 Nor bear strict service, nor pure Liberty.
    P. 111 ANNIVERSARY   317 Oh Race most hypocritically strict!

strictly   frequency: 2   relative frequency: 0.0000
    P. 63 A. HOUSE   155 'And, if our Rule seem strictly pend,
    P. 196 TWO HORSES   175 Tho' Tyrants make Laws which they strictly
                              proclaim

strid   frequency: 1   relative frequency: 0.0000
    P. 147 INSTRUCTIONS   249 Such Roman Cocles strid: before the Foe,

stride   frequency: 1   relative frequency: 0.0000
    P. 146 INSTRUCTIONS   214 Led the French Standard, weltring in his
                              stride,

strife   frequency: 2   relative frequency: 0.0000
    P. 27 MISTRESS   43 And tear our Pleasures with rough strife,
    P. 152 INSTRUCTIONS   455 And that by Law cf Arms, in Martial strife,

strike   frequency: 6   relative frequency: 0.0001
    P. 56 BILL-BOROW   3 The stiffest Compass could not strike
    P. 98 HOLLAND   108 Rather then to the English strike their sail;
    P. 104 ANNIVERSARY   42 And with vain Scepter, strike the hourly Bell;
    P. 127 O.C.   184 Where those that strike from Heaven fetch their
                              Blcw.
    P. 143 INSTRUCTIONS   116 Can strike the Die, and still with them goes
                              share.
    P. 144 INSTRUCTIONS   126 Should Goodrick silence, and strike Paston
                              dumb;

strikes   frequency: 1   relative frequency: 0.0000
    P. 313 CHEQUER INN   24 With which he strikes the Measure.

string   frequency: 1   relative frequency: 0.0000
    P. 124 O.C.   59 No trembling String cospc'd to numbers new,

strings   frequency: 4   relative frequency: 0.0000
    P. 84 FLECKNO   44 In Echo to the trembling Strings repin'd.
    P. 104 ANNIVERSARY   44 Then wooden Heads untc the Viols strings.
    P. 104 ANNIVERSARY   59 Now through the Strings a Martial rage he
                              throws,
    P. 105 ANNIVERSARY   74 And once he struck, and twice, the pow'rful
                              Strings.

stript   frequency: 1   relative frequency: 0.0000
    P. 143 INSTRUCTIONS   93 Stript to her Skin, see how she stooping stands,

strive   frequency: 6   relative frequency: 0.0001
    P. 38 PICTURE   21 In Triumph cver Hearts that strive,
    P. 58 BILL-BOROW   57 Yet now nc further strive tc shoot,
    P. 60 A. HOUSE   45 Let others vainly strive t'immure
    P. 94 DR. WITTY   9 Others do strive with words and forced phrase
    P. 103 ANNIVERSARY   21 Well may they strive tc leave them to their Son,
    P. 171 PROPHECY   42 And strive by Law tc 'stablish Tyrany,

strives   frequency: 1   relative frequency: 0.0000
    P. 57 BILL-BOROW   24 But only strives to raise the Plain.

strok'   frequency: 1   relative frequency: 0.0000
    P. 76 A. HOUSE   552 Should fall by such a feeble Strok'!

stroke   frequency: 8   relative frequency: 0.0001

```
      P.   36 DAPHNIS      100 And receives the parting stroke.
      P.   44 DAMON         76 Each stroke between the Earth and Root,
      P.   71 A. HOUSE     398 He draws, and does his stroke detest;
      P.   91 MAY'S DEATH   36 And Horace patiently its stroke does take,
      P.  125 O.C.          77 Fate could not either reach with single stroke,
      P.  163 INSTRUCTIONS 913 His mind secure does the known stroke repeat,
      P.  200 DUKE         117 Till the stroke is struck which they can nere
                               repreive.
      P.  205 HISTORICALL  163 A Priest should doe it, from whose sacred stroke
```

strokes   frequency: 2   relative frequency: 0.0000
```
      P.  104 ANNIVERSARY   61 Then as he strokes them with a Touch more sweet,
      P.  127 O.C.         183 Those Strokes he said will pierce through all
                               below
```

strong   frequency: 25   relative frequency: 0.0005
```
      P.    9 DIALOGUE       5 See where an Army, strong as fair,
      P.   40 THE MATCH     31 And, grown magnetically strong,
      P.   71 A. HOUSE     393 With whistling Sithe, and Elbow strong,
      P.   77 A. HOUSE     601 How safe, methinks, and strong, behind
      P.   88 ODE           40 As Men are strong or weak.
      P.  104 ANNIVERSARY   28 And only are against their Subjects strong;
      P.  109 ANNIVERSARY  232 An healthful Mind within a Body strong;
      P.  115 BLAKE         48 She cast off that which only made her strong.
      P.  116 BLAKE         92 They build and act all that can make them strong.
      P.  117 BLAKE        107 Those Forts, which there, so high and strong
                               appear,
      P.  121 TWO SONGS     44 Rivals each one for thee too strong.
      P.  124 O.C.          34 Slacken the vigour of his Muscles strong;
      P.  127 O.C.         186 And cityes strong were stormed by his prayer;
      P.  128 O.C.         207 More strong affections never reason serv'd,
      P.  129 O.C.         251 That port which so majestique was and strong,
      P.  131 PARADISE       7 That he would ruine (for I saw him strong)
      P.  132 PARADISE      38 With Plume so strong, so equal, and so soft.
      P.  148 INSTRUCTIONS 316 How strong the Dutch their Equipage renew.
      P.  154 INSTRUCTIONS 575 For whose strong bulk Earth scarce could Timber
                               find,
      P.  158 INSTRUCTIONS 728 Her Masts erect, tough Cordage, Timbers
                               strong,
      P.  177 LOYALL SCOT  234 Had it not been for such a Biass Strong,
      P.  187 BRITANNIA     96 Shake of those Baby bonds from your strong
                               Armes,
      P.  187 BRITANNIA    104 Strong as your Raigne and beauteous as your
                               mind.'
      P.  196 TWO HORSES   183 'Tis wine and Strong drink makes tumults
                               increase;
      P.  200 DUKE          92 Old England on its strong foundations stands,
```

stronger   frequency: 2   relative frequency: 0.0000
```
      P.  105 ANNIVERSARY   96 The Fabrick as with Arches stronger binds,
      P.  177 LOYALL SCOT  243 Which stronger were, a Scotch or English vice,
```

strongest   frequency: 2   relative frequency: 0.0000
```
      P.  120 TWO SONGS     33 And Cynthia, though the strongest,
      P.  174 LOYALL SCOT  115 A Bishops Bennett makes the strongest Curd.
```

strongly   frequency: 1   relative frequency: 0.0000
```
      P.  131 O.C.         313 How he becomes that seat, how strongly streigns,
```

strook   frequency: 1   relative frequency: 0.0000
```
      P.  158 INSTRUCTIONS 705 Up to the Bridge contagious Terrour strook:
```

strove   frequency: 1   relative frequency: 0.0000
```
      P.  164 INSTRUCTIONS 968 Have strove to Isle the Monarch from his Isle:
```

strow   frequency: 1   relative frequency: 0.0000
```
      P.   32 MOURNING      12 Would strow the ground where Strephon lay.
```

strow'd   frequency: 1   relative frequency: 0.0000
```
      P.    9 DIALOGUE      21 On these Roses strow'd so plain
```

struck   frequency: 7   relative frequency: 0.0001
```
      See also "strook."
      P.   87 FLECKNO      161 Against the Rebel; who, at this struck dead,
      P.   97 HOLLAND       69 It struck, and splitting on this unknown ground,
      P.  104 ANNIVERSARY   55 No Note he struck, but a new Story lay'd,
      P.  105 ANNIVERSARY   74 And once he struck, and twice, the pow'rful
                               Strings.
      P.  128 O.C.         216 Their griefs struck deepest, if Eliza's last.
      P.  149 INSTRUCTIONS 358 Blasted with Lightning, struck with Thunder
                               fell.
      P.  200 DUKE         117 Till the stroke is struck which they can nere
                               repreive.
```

structures   frequency: 1   relative frequency: 0.0000
    P. 104 ANNIVERSARY   57 The listning Structures he with Wonder ey'd,

struggling. See "strugling."

strugling   frequency: 2   relative frequency: 0.0000
    P. 96 HOLLAND   19 And to the stake a strugling Country bound,
    P. 107 ANNIVERSARY   177 Our brutish fury strugling to be Free,

strumpets. See "strumpetts."

strumpetts   frequency: 1   relative frequency: 0.0000
    P. 182 MADE FREE   64 All your Wives had been Strumpetts

stuart   frequency: 1   relative frequency: 0.0000
    P. 188 BRITANNIA   142 The Stuart from the Tyrant to devide.

stuarts   frequency: 2   relative frequency: 0.0000
    P. 195 TWO HORSES   149 A Tudor a Tudor! wee've had Stuarts enough;
    P. 195 TWO HORSES   158 W. When the Reign of the Line of the Stuarts
                            is ended.

stubborn   frequency: 2   relative frequency: 0.0000
    P. 28 LOVER   52 And grapple, with the stubborn Rock:
    P. 105 ANNIVERSARY   78 But who the Minds of stubborn Men can build?

stubborness   frequency: 1   relative frequency: 0.0000
    P. 35 DAPHNIS   70 In a manly stubberness

studi'd   frequency: 1   relative frequency: 0.0000
    P.   3 LOVELACE   9 Modest ambition studi'd only then,

studied. See "studi'd," "study'd."

studies   frequency: 3   relative frequency: 0.0000
    P. 67 A. HOUSE   284 His warlike Studies could not cease;
    P. 77 A. HOUSE   586 Could with a Mask my studies hit!
    P. 92 MAY'S DEATH   72 Our spotless knowledge and the studies chast.

studious   frequency: 1   relative frequency: 0.0000
    P. 82 A. HOUSE   746 Where yet She leads her studious Hours,

study   frequency: 2   relative frequency: 0.0000
    P. 81 A. HOUSE   730 Do all your useless Study place,
    P. 175 LOYALL SCOT   129 To Excommunicate and Study health.

study'd   frequency: 1   relative frequency: 0.0000
    P. 141 INSTRUCTIONS   36 For never Bacon study'd Nature more.

studying   frequency: 2   relative frequency: 0.0000
    P. 44 GLO-WORMS   3 And studying all the Summer-night,
    P. 142 INSTRUCTIONS   65 Express her studying now, if China-clay,

stuff   frequency: 1   relative frequency: 0.0000
    P. 85 FLECKNO   72 With which he doth his third Dimension Stuff.

stumbling   frequency: 2   relative frequency: 0.0000
    P. 49 THE GARDEN   39 Stumbling on Melons, as I pass,
    P. 91 MAY'S DEATH   27 Yet then with foot as stumbling as his tongue

stung   frequency: 1   relative frequency: 0.0000
    P. 41 DAMON   2 With love of Juliana stung!

stupefaction   frequency: 1   relative frequency: 0.0000
    P. 151 INSTRUCTIONS 423 Not such a fatal stupefaction reign'd

stupendious   frequency: 1   relative frequency: 0.0000
    P. 116 BLAKE   79 But this stupendious Prospect did not neer,

stupendous. See "stupendious."

stupid   frequency: 2   relative frequency: 0.0000
    P. 80 A. HOUSE   677 The stupid Fishes hang, as plain
    P. 108 ANNIVERSARY   201 Thou Cromwell falling, not a stupid Tree,

stupifi'd   frequency: 1   relative frequency: 0.0000
    P. 40 THE MOWER   8 Which stupifi'd them while it fed.

style. See "stile."

styled   frequency: 1   relative frequency: 0.0000

          P. 192 TWO HORSES   45 Ch. That he should be styled defender o' th
                                    faith,

stypends   frequency: 1   relative frequency: 0.0000
          P. 203 HISTORICALL   77 And annual Stypends for their guilt recieve:

subdue   frequency: 2   relative frequency: 0.0000
          P. 106 ANNIVERSARY   115 But Indians whom they should convert, subdue;
          P. 116 BLAKE   86 Which did the rage of Elements subdue.

subject   frequency: 3   relative frequency: 0.0000
          P. 83 FLECKNO   6 Of the sad Pelican; Subject divine
          P. 110 ANNIVERSARY   285 And the large Vale lay subject to thy Will,
          P. 112 ANNIVERSARY   390 'At Home a Subject on the equal Floor.

subjects   frequency: 4   relative frequency: 0.0000
          P. 90 MAY'S DEATH   16 The Subjects Safety, and the Rebel's Fear.
          P. 97 HOLLAND   80 Themselves the Hogs as all their Subjects
                                    Bores!
          P. 104 ANNIVERSARY   28 And only are against their Subjects strong;
          P. 200 DUKE   107 What all thy subjects doe each minute feare:

sublime   frequency: 2   relative frequency: 0.0000
          P. 120 TWO SONGS   36 How far below thine Orbe sublime?
          P. 132 PARADISE   53 Thy verse created like thy Theme sublime,

sublunary   frequency: 2   relative frequency: 0.0000
          P.   5 HASTINGS   36 Of all these Sublunary Elements.
          P. 120 TWO SONGS   20 On Sublunary things thy care;

subsidies   frequency: 1   relative frequency: 0.0000
          P. 139 HOUSEWARMING   85 By Subsidies thus both Clerick and Laick,

substance   frequency: 1   relative frequency: 0.0000
          P. 85 FLECKNO   101 Consist but in one substance. Then, to fit

subtile   frequency: 2   relative frequency: 0.0000
          P. 31 FAIR SINGER   11 Whose subtile Art invisibly can wreath
          P. 88 ODE   49 Where, twining subtile fears with hope,

subtle   frequency: 1   relative frequency: 0.0000
See also "subtile," "suttle."
          P. 203 HISTORICALL   102 Fond Eve did for this subtle Tempters sake

succeeding   frequency: 3   relative frequency: 0.0000
          P. 103 ANNIVERSARY   8 (Sun-like) the Stages of succeeding Suns:
          P. 104 ANNIVERSARY   34 Nor Matter for succeeding Founders raise;
          P. 123 O.C.   27 And leave succeeding Ages cause to mourn,

succeeds   frequency: 4   relative frequency: 0.0000
See also "succeeds--."
          P. 125 O.C.   95 The Parent-Tree unto the Grief succeeds,
          P. 130 O.C.   285 As long as future time succeeds the past,
          P. 131 O.C.   321 Cease now our griefs, calme peace succeeds a war,
          P. 144 INSTRUCTIONS   157 To them succeeds a despicable Rout,

succeeds--   frequency: 1   relative frequency: 0.0000
          P. 204 HISTORICALL   132 In our weal-publik scarce one thing succeeds--

success   frequency: 3   relative frequency: 0.0000
          P. 118 BLAKE   144 And was attended by as high success.
          P. 119 BLAKE   164 And there first brings of his success the news;
          P. 131 PARADISE   12 I lik'd his Project, the success did fear;

successes   frequency: 1   relative frequency: 0.0000
          P. 58 BILL-BOROW   53 Hence they successes seem to know,

successful   frequency: 1   relative frequency: 0.0000
          P. 92 MAY'S DEATH   70 Seeks wretched good, arraigns successful Crimes.

succession   frequency: 2   relative frequency: 0.0000
          P. 63 A. HOUSE   158 'Doth your succession near presage.
          P. 112 ANNIVERSARY   387 'He seems a King by long Succession born,

successive   frequency: 1   relative frequency: 0.0000
          P. 66 A. HOUSE   243 And with successive Valour try

successor   frequency: 1   relative frequency: 0.0000
          P. 166 KINGS VOWES   27 And Successor be, if not to me, to Gerrard.

succoths   frequency: 1   relative frequency: 0.0000

P. 109 ANNIVERSARY   253 And how he Succctbs Elders durst suppress,

succour   frequency: 1   relative frequency: 0.0000
    P. 155 INSTRUCTIONS   609 He finds wheresce're he succour might expect,

such   frequency: 112   relative frequency: 0.0023

suck   frequency: 1   relative frequency: 0.0000
    P. 317 CHEQUER INN   191 That suck and draine thus ev'ry Purse

sucks   frequency: 2   relative frequency: 0.0000
    P. 80 A. HOUSE   674 Follcws and sucks her Azure dy;
    P. 153 INSTRUCTIONS   498 He sucks the King, they him, he them again.

suckt   frequency: 1   relative frequency: 0.0000
    P. 65 A. HOUSE   200 The Nuns smooth Tongue has suckt her in.

suddainly   frequency: 2   relative frequency: 0.0000
    P. 190 STATUE   34 Such things you should never or Suddainly doe.
    P. 202 HISTORICALL   41 But the Dutch fleet fled suddainly with feare;

sudden   frequency: 7   relative frequency: 0.0001
    P.   4 HASTINGS   15 While those of growth more sudden, and more bold,
    P. 33 DAPHNIS   16 Sudden Parting closer glews.
    P. 107 ANNIVERSARY   175 How near they fail'd, and in thy sudden Fall
    P. 148 INSTRUCTIONS   303 See sudden chance cf War! To Paint or Write,
    P. 153 INSTRUCTIONS   531 The sudden change, and such a tempting sight,
    P. 154 INSTRUCTICNS   556 When, all on sudden, their calm boscme rives
    P. 162 INSTRUCTIONS   891 Raise up a sudden Shape with Virgins Face,

suddenly. See "suddainly."

sue   frequency: 1   relative frequency: 0.0000
    P. 177 LOYALL SCOT   223 Some sue for tyth of the Elyzean plaines:

suffer'd   frequency: 1   relative frequency: 0.0000
    P. 201 HISTORICALL   3 Twelve Yeares ccmpleat he suffer'd in Exile

sufferings   frequency: 1   relative frequency: 0.0000
    P. 185 BRITANNIA   16 And loyall sufferings by the Court esteem'd,

suffice   frequency: 5   relative frequency: 0.0001
    P. 34 DAPHNIS   47 Could departure not suffice,
    P. 85 FLECKNO   111 Let it suffice that we could eat in peace;
    P. 97 HOLLAND   81 Let it suffice to give their Ccuntry Fame
    P. 127 O.C.   170 To compass in cur Isle; our Tears suffice;
    P. 144 INSTRUCTICNS   129 Hyde's Avarice, Bennet's Luxury should
                              suffice,

sugar   frequency: 1   relative frequency: 0.0000
    P. 23 NYMPH   55 With sweetest milk, and sugar, first

sugars   frequency: 1   relative frequency: 0.0000
    P. 64 A. HOUSE   174 'The Sugars unccrrupting Oyl:

suit   frequency: 2   relative frequency: 0.0000
    P. 141 INSTRUCTIONS   8 'Twill suit our great debauch and little skill.
    P. 179 STOCKSMARKET   21 But a market, they say, does suit the king well,

sullen   frequency: 3   relative frequency: 0.0000
    P. 47 EMPIRE   7 He call'd the Ecchoes frcm their sullen Cell,
    P. 147 INSTRUCTIONS   283 And, charging all their Pikes, a sullen Band
    P. 199 DUKE   46 Poore princess, bcrne under a sullen starr

sully   frequency: 1   relative frequency: 0.0000
    P. 95 DR. WITTY   40 That handling neither sully nor would guild.

sulphrey   frequency: 1   relative frequency: 0.0000
    P. 92 MAY'S DEATH   90 Where Sulphrey Fhlegeton does ever burn.

sulphur   frequency: 1   relative frequency: 0.0000
    P. 156 INSTRUCTIONS   644 Pregnant with Sulphur, to him nearer draw

sulphurs   frequency: 1   relative frequency: 0.0000
    P. 40 THE MATCH   23 The Naphta's and the Sulphurs heat,

sulphury. See "sulphrey."

sum. See "summ."

summ   frequency: 1   relative frequency: 0.0000

P. 144 INSTRUCTIONS   125 And fix to the Revenue such a Summ,

summ'd   frequency: 2   relative frequency: 0.0000
   P. 14 THE CORONET   9 And now when I have summ'd up all my store,
   P. 55 EPITAPH   16 She summ'd her Life up ev'ry day;

summer   frequency: 2   relative frequency: 0.0000
   P. 61 A. HOUSE   93 And oft She spent the Summer Suns
   P. 154 INSTRUCTIONS 573 There our sick Ships unrigg'd in Summer lay,

summer-night   frequency: 1   relative frequency: 0.0000
   P. 44 GLO-WORMS   3 And studying all the Summer-night,

summers   frequency: 2   relative frequency: 0.0000
   P. 27 LOVER   6 Like Meteors of a Summers night:
   P. 116 BLAKE   83 They learn'd with Terrour, that nor Summers
                           heat,

summon   frequency: 1   relative frequency: 0.0000
   P. 151 INSTRUCTIONS 435 Summon him therefore of his Word, and prove

summon'd   frequency: 1   relative frequency: 0.0000
   P. 161 INSTRUCTIONS 857 The Speaker, Summon'd, to the Lords repairs,

summons   frequency: 2   relative frequency: 0.0000
   P. 152 INSTRUCTIONS 470 That summons up the Parliament agen;
   P. 193 TWO HORSES   78 Should give away Millions at every Summons.

sun   frequency: 33   relative frequency: 0.0006
   See also "sunn," "sunne."
   P. 12 DROP OF DEW   17 Till the warm Sun pitty it's Pain,
   P. 13 DROP OF DEW   40 Into the Glories of th' Almighty Sun.
   P. 15 EYES   21 So the all-seeing Sun each day
   P. 18 CLORINDA   12 Safe from the Sun. D. not Heaven's Eye.
   P. 20 THYRSIS   35 There, alwayes is, a rising Sun,
   P. 27 MISTRESS   45 Thus, though we cannot make our Sun
   P. 31 FAIR SINGER   18 She having gained both the Wind and Sun.
   P. 42 DAMON   17 This heat the Sun could never raise,
   P. 42 DAMON   21 Which made the Dog, and makes the Sun
   P. 43 DAMON   46 The Sun himself licks off my Sweat.
   P. 43 DAMON   60 As in a crescent Moon the Sun.
   P. 50 THE GARDEN   67 Where from above the milder Sun
   P. 71 A. HOUSE   387 For when the Sun the Grass hath vext,
   P. 78 A. HOUSE   640 Narcissus like, the Sun too pines.
   P. 79 A. HOUSE   661 The Sun himself, of Her aware,
   P. 86 FLECKNO   150 Confus'der then the atomes in the Sun.
   P. 96 HOLLAND   43 Not who first see the rising Sun commands,
   P. 108 ANNIVERSARY 206 It seem'd the Sun was faln out of the Sphere.
   P. 111 ANNIVERSARY 326 See the bright Sun his shining Race pursue,
   P. 111 ANNIVERSARY 341 When streight the Sun behind him he descry'd,
   P. 117 BLAKE   122 Far more enflam'd by it, then by the Sun.
   P. 118 BLAKE   137 Th' all-seeing Sun, neer gaz'd on such a sight,
   P. 128 O.C.   192 Since the commanded sun o're Gibeon stay'd?
   P. 131 O.C.   317 A pearly rainbow, where the sun inchas'd
   P. 153 INSTRUCTIONS 529 The Sun much brighter, and the Skies more
                           clear,
   P. 154 INSTRUCTIONS 554 The airy Sterns the Sun behind does guild;
   P. 161 INSTRUCTIONS 833 And all with Sun and Choler come adust;
   P. 161 INSTRUCTIONS 856 No Dial more could with the Sun agree.
   P. 164 INSTRUCTIONS 949 So his bold Tube, Man, to the Sun apply'd,
   P. 164 INSTRUCTIONS 956 Sun of our World, as he the Charles is there.
   P. 186 BRITANNIA   55 To him I shew'd this Glorious setting sun,
   P. 189 BRITANNIA   190 The Turkish Crescent and the Persian sun.
   P. 314 CHEQUER INN   71 When noe one could see Sun betweene

sun-burn'd   frequency: 1   relative frequency: 0.0000
   P. 42 DAMON   10 Which thus our Sun-burn'd Meadows sear!

sun-like   frequency: 1   relative frequency: 0.0000
   P. 103 ANNIVERSARY   8 (Sun-like) the Stages of succeeding Suns:

sunder'd   frequency: 1   relative frequency: 0.0000
   P. 316 CHEQUER INN 135 They were not to be sunder'd

sung   frequency: 4   relative frequency: 0.0000
   P. 18 BERMUDAS   37 Thus sung they, in the English boat,
   P. 41 DAMON   1 Heark how the Mower Damon Sung,
   P. 137 HOUSEWARMING 18 Made Thebes dance aloft while he fidled and
                           sung,
   P. 315 CHEQUER INN 104 For words not to be said but sung

sunk   frequency: 6   relative frequency: 0.0001

P. 105 ANNIVERSARY   81 None to be sunk in the Foundation bends,
P. 111 ANNIVERSARY   330 Sunk in the Hills, or plung'd below the
                         Streams.
P. 117 BLAKE   128 Some Ships are sunk, some blown up in the skie.
P. 118 BLAKE   151 Their Gallicns sunk, their wealth the Sea does
                         fill,
P. 119 BLAKE   166 Their rich Fleet sunk, and ours with Lawrel
                         fraught.
P. 139 HOUSEWARMING   78 For foundaticn he Bristol sunk in the Earth's
                         bowel;

sunn   frequency: 1   relative frequency: 0.0000
    P. 189 BRITANNIA   185 As Joves great sunn the infested glcbe did free

sunne   frequency: 1   relative frequency: 0.0000
    P. 130 O.C.   282 As long as Cynthia shall relieve the sunne,

sunns   frequency: 1   relative frequency: 0.0000
    P. 129 O.C.   236 No April sunns that e'er so gently smil'd;

suns   frequency: 4   relative frequency: 0.0000
    See also "sunns."
    P. 61 A. HOUSE   93 And oft She spent the Summer Suns
    P. 103 ANNIVERSARY   8 (Sun-like) the Stages cf succeeding Suns:
    P. 126 O.C.   136 As silent Suns to meet the Night descend.
    P. 149 INSTRUCTIONS 347 So, at the Suns recess, again returns,

sun's   frequency: 3   relative frequency: 0.0000
    P. 114 BLAKE   19 They dreaded to behold, Least the Sun's light,
    P. 157 INSTRUCTIONS 680 Like the Sun's Statue stands of burnish'd
                         Gold.
    P. 173 LOYALL SCOT 46 Like the sun's Statue stands of burnish't Gold:

sup   frequency: 3   relative frequency: 0.0000
    P.   9 DIALOGUE   17 I sup above, and cannot stay
    P. 71 A. HOUSE   404 And forthwith means on it to sup:
    P. 316 CHEQUER INN 136 The tale of all that there did sup

superfluously   frequency: 1   relative frequency: 0.0000
    P. 59 A. HOUSE   17 But He, superflucusly spread,

superstition   frequency: 1   relative frequency: 0.0000
    P. 177 LOYALL SCCT 230 Luxury malice superstiticn pride

superstitions   frequency: 1   relative frequency: 0.0000
    P. 67 A. HOUSE   260 And superstiticns vainly fear'd.

supper   frequency: 2   relative frequency: 0.0000
    P. 191 STATUE   42 That so liberally treated the members at supper.
    P. 314 CHEQUER INN 51 Over a Gallant Supper

supplant   frequency: 1   relative frequency: 0.0000
    P. 205 HISTORICALL 172 Who strait design'd his Brother to supplant.

supplied. See "supply'd."

supplies   frequency: 2   relative frequency: 0.0000
    P. 82 A. HOUSE   738 Supplies beyond her Sex the Line;
    P. 127 O.C.   169 Your Monarch: We demand not your supplies

supply   frequency: 4   relative frequency: 0.0000
    See also "supplye."
    P. 114 BLAKE   28 Trees there the duty of the Clouds supply;
    P. 142 INSTRUCTIONS 40 That, disavowing Treaty, ask supply.
    P. 159 INSTRUCTIONS 781 Whc to supply with Powder, did forget
    P. 165 INSTRUCTIONS 986 Does with clear Counsels their large Souls
                         supply;

supply'd   frequency: 1   relative frequency: 0.0000
    P. 145 INSTRUCTIONS 189 Their Fortune's error they supply'd in rage,

supplye   frequency: 1   relative frequency: 0.0000
    P. 167 KINGS VOWES 56 And new Ones Create Great Places to supplye,

support   frequency: 1   relative frequency: 0.0000
    P. 118 BLAKE   155 Wars chief support with them would buried be,

suppos'd   frequency: 1   relative frequency: 0.0000
    P. 32 MOURNING   36 It is to be suppos'd they grieve.

suppress   frequency: 4   relative frequency: 0.0000

```
        P. 109 ANNIVERSARY     253 And tow he Succcths Elders durst suppress,
        P. 114 BLAKE            22 So that such darkness might suppress their fear;
        P. 117 BLAKE           108 Do not so much suppress, as shew their fear.

supream                            frequency:    2    relative frequency: 0.0000
        P.  91 MAY'S DEATH      34 The awful Sign of his supream command.
        P. 176 LOYALL SCCT     195 And in their Causes think themselves supream.

supreme.  See "supream."

surcingle.  See "circingle."

sure                               frequency:   27    relative frequency: 0.0005
        P.  19 THYRSIS          11 'Tis a sure but rugged way,
        P.  22 NYMPH             7 I'me sure I never wisht them ill;
        P.  22 NYMPH            30 What he said then; I'me sure I do.
        P.  23 NYMPH            51 But I am sure, for ought that I
        P.  24 NYMPH           114 Th' Engraver sure his Art may spare;
        P.  32 MOURNING         35 But sure as oft as Women weep,
        P.  65 A. HOUSE        217 'But sure those Buildings last not long,
        P.  72 A. HOUSE        445 The World when first created sure
        P.  83 FLECKNO          22 Possest; and sure the Devil brought me there.
        P.  84 FLECKNO          62 Hath sure more flesh and blood then he can boast.
        P.  89 ODE              96 The Falckner has her sure.
        P.  97 HCLLAND          67 Sure when Religicn did it self imbark,
        P. 106 ANNIVERSARY     137 Sure, the mysterious Wcrk, where none withstand,
        P. 125 O.C.            101 A secret Cause does sure those Signs ordain
        P. 148 INSTRUCTIONS    294 But sure the Devil cannot cheat them thrice.
        P. 148 INSTRUCTIONS    312 Lest the sure Peace, forsooth, too soon appear.
        P. 151 INSTRUCTIONS    422 But Mordant new oblig'd, would sure be just.
        P. 153 INSTRUCTIONS    519 All Causes sure concur, but most they think
        P. 160 INSTRUCTIONS    797 But sure his late good Husbandry in Peeter,
        P. 160 INSTRUCTIONS    818 The Peace not sure, new Army must be paid.
        P. 161 INSTRUCTIONS    824 Binding, e're th' Houses meet, the Treaty sure.
        P. 180 STOCKSMARKET     49 Sure the king will ne'er think of repaying his
                                    bankers,
        P. 181 MADE FREE         4 'Tis a thing sure of Weight,
        P. 191 STATUE           41 The Huswifely Treasuress sure is grown nice
        P. 194 TWO HORSES      113 In every dark night you are sure to find him
        P. 313 CHEQUER INN      11 But sure they often there had beene
        P. 317 CHEQUER INN     190 But sure this is a heavier Curse

surely                             frequency:    6    relative frequency: 0.0001
        P.  25 YOUNG LOVE        5 Pretty surely 'twere to see
        P.  60 A. HOUSE         33 And surely when the after Age
        P.  94 DR. WITTY        31 Now I reform, and surely so will all
        P.  97 HOLLAND          84 But surely never any that was so.
        P. 179 STOCKSMARKET     25 This statue is surely more scandalous far
        P. 196 TWO HORSES      164 Prodigious events did surely presage,

surenesse                          frequency:    1    relative frequency: 0.0000
        P. 314 CHEQUER INN      53 For surenesse Cited were to come

surging                            frequency:    1    relative frequency: 0.0000
        P.  27 LOVER            20 Which through his surging Breast do roar.

surly                              frequency:    1    relative frequency: 0.0000
        P. 147 INSTRUCTICNS    261 And surly Williams, the Accomptants bane:

surmise                            frequency:    1    relative frequency: 0.0000
        P. 131 PARADISE         24 My causeless, yet not impious, surmise.

surplic'd                          frequency:    1    relative frequency: 0.0000
        P. 174 LOYALL SCOT     125 And surplic'd shew like Pillars too of salt.

surplice                           frequency:    1    relative frequency: 0.0000
        P. 194 TWO HORSES      118 For the Surplice, Lawn-Sleeves, the Cross and
                                    the mitre,

surprise                           frequency:    1    relative frequency: 0.0000
        See also "surprize."
        P.  55 THYESTE          14 Death to him 's a Strange surprise.

surprised.  See "surpriz'd."

surpriz'd                          frequency:    1    relative frequency: 0.0000
        P.  33 DAPHNIS           9 But, with this sad News surpriz'd,

surprize                           frequency:    2    relative frequency: 0.0000
        P.  79 A. HOUSE        654 Should with such Tcyes a Man surprize;
        P. 146 INSTRUCTIONS    232 They feign a parly, better to surprize:
```

surround   frequency: 2   relative frequency: 0.0000
    P. 113 ANNIVERSARY   366 'Whose watry Leaguers all the world surround?
    P. 163 INSTRUCTIONS   909 With Canon, Trumpets, Drums, his door
                               surround,

survey   frequency: 4   relative frequency: 0.0000
    P. 45 MOWER'S SONG   1 My Mind was once the true survey
    P. 61 A. HOUSE   81 While with slow Eyes we these survey,
    P. 143 INSTRUCTIONS   117 Here Painter rest a little, and survey
    P. 158 INSTRUCTIONS   729 Her moving Shape; all these he does survey,

survey'd   frequency: 1   relative frequency: 0.0000
    P. 153 INSTRUCTIONS   525 Survey'd their Crystal Streams, and Banks so
                               green,

surveying   frequency: 1   relative frequency: 0.0000
    P. 139 HOUSEWARMING   81 For surveying the building, Prat did the feat,

surveys   frequency: 1   relative frequency: 0.0000
    P. 139 HOUSEWARMING   90 A Lanthorn, like Faux's surveys the burnt
                               Town,

surviv'd   frequency: 1   relative frequency: 0.0000
    P. 125 O.C.   90 Of many a Winter hath surviv'd the rage.

survive   frequency: 1   relative frequency: 0.0000
    P. 158 INSTRUCTIONS   701 Of all our Navy none should now survive,

survives   frequency: 2   relative frequency: 0.0000
    P. 32 MOURNING   25 Nor that she payes, while she survives,
    P. 201 HISTORICALL   21 Bold James survives, no dangers make him flinch,

surviving   frequency: 1   relative frequency: 0.0000
    P. 92 MAY'S DEATH   78 Hast left surviving Davenant still behind

suspect   frequency: 1   relative frequency: 0.0000
    P. 179 STOCKSMARKET   15 And some by the likeness Sir Robert suspect

suspected   frequency: 1   relative frequency: 0.0000
    P. 111 ANNIVERSARY   347 Who their suspected Counsellors refuse,

suspend   frequency: 3   relative frequency: 0.0000
    P. 10 DIALOGUE   40 And suspend the Rivers Fall.
    P. 79 A. HOUSE   645 Or to suspend my sliding Foot
    P. 107 ANNIVERSARY   153 For the great Justice that did first suspend

suspended   frequency: 2   relative frequency: 0.0000
    P. 31 MOURNING   6 With Tears suspended ere they flow;
    P. 125 O.C.   71 And now his Life, suspended by her breath,

sustain   frequency: 1   relative frequency: 0.0000
    See also "sustein."
    P. 92 MAY'S DEATH   96 Thou first Historically shouldst sustain.

sustein   frequency: 1   relative frequency: 0.0000
    P. 105 ANNIVERSARY   93 But the most Equal still sustein the Height,

suttle   frequency: 2   relative frequency: 0.0000
    P. 61 A. HOUSE   94 Discoursing with the Suttle Nunns.
    P. 84 FLECKNO   67 Lest his too suttle Body, growing rare,

swaddled   frequency: 1   relative frequency: 0.0000
    P. 84 FLECKNO   70 And swaddled in's own papers seaven times,

swagger   frequency: 1   relative frequency: 0.0000
    P. 184 MADE FREE   123 Never think in England to swagger,

swain   frequency: 1   relative frequency: 0.0000
    P. 123 TWO SONGS   41 But what is most, the gentle Swain

swallow   frequency: 2   relative frequency: 0.0000
    P. 105 ANNIVERSARY   71 Whose num'rous Gorge could swallow in an hour
    P. 159 INSTRUCTIONS   778 And all our Prizes who did swallow? Pett.

swallowes   frequency: 1   relative frequency: 0.0000
    P. 176 LOYALL SCOT   177 Like Snake that Swallowes toad doth Dragon
                               swell.

swallows   frequency: 2   relative frequency: 0.0000
    See also "swallowes."
    P. 96 HOLLAND   14 Less then what building Swallows bear away;

P. 144 INSTRUCTIONS 138 Else swallows all down her indented maw.

swan   frequency: 1   relative frequency: 0.0000
P. 176 LOYALL SCOT   187 With single body like the two Neckt Swan,

swans   frequency: 2   relative frequency: 0.0000
P. 24 NYMPH   106 Whether the Swans and Turtles go:
P. 125 O.C.   79 Who now shall tell us more of mournful Swans,

swarms   frequency: 2   relative frequency: 0.0000
P.   3 LOVELACE   17 The Ayre's already tainted with the swarms
P. 152 INSTRUCTIONS 487 Hyde Stamps, and straight upon the ground the
                         swarms

sway   frequency: 3   relative frequency: 0.0000
P. 20 THYRSIS   37 Shepheards there, bear equal sway,
P. 89 ODE   83 How fit he is to sway
P. 165 KINGS VOWES   16 I will have a fine Chancelor beare all the sway,

sway'd   frequency: 1   relative frequency: 0.0000
P. 123 O.C.   16 But angry Heaven unto War had sway'd,

swear   frequency: 3   relative frequency: 0.0000
See also "sweare."
P. 122 TWO SONGS   19 'Twas those Eyes, I now dare swear,
P. 196 TWO HORSES   165 That shall come to pass all mankind may swear
P. 196 TWO HORSES   186 Tis Bacchus and the Brewer swear Dam 'um and
                         sink 'um.

sweare   frequency: 2   relative frequency: 0.0000
P. 184 MADE FREE   115 And how cou'd he sweare
P. 203 HISTORICALL   80 All but religious cheats might justly sweare

sweat   frequency: 7   relative frequency: 0.0001
See also "sweate."
P. 12 DROP OF DEW   23 Shuns the sweat leaves and blossoms green;
P. 43 DAMON   46 The Sun himself licks off my Sweat.
P. 60 A. HOUSE   49 Yet thus the laden House does sweat,
P. 72 A. HOUSE   428 Smells like an Alexanders sweat.
P. 147 INSTRUCTIONS 278 And the faint sweat trickled down Temples
                         Brows.
P. 161 INSTRUCTIONS 832 Does for his Corporation sweat and trot.
P. 316 CHEQUER INN   170 Like Sweat Meates, for their Girles and Wives

sweate   frequency: 1   relative frequency: 0.0000
P. 315 CHEQUER INN   100 And tho' his Sweate the while he eate

sweaty   frequency: 1   relative frequency: 0.0000
P. 143 INSTRUCTIONS   96 His sweaty Hooves, tickles him 'twixt the Toes.

sweeping   frequency: 1   relative frequency: 0.0000
P. 315 CHEQUER INN   131 And sweeping all our Chimney Stacks

sweet   frequency: 31   relative frequency: 0.0006
See also "sweat," "sweete."
P.   3 LOVELACE   2 Which your sweet Muse which your fair Fortune
                         chose,
P.   5 HASTINGS   53 How Sweet and Verdant would these Lawrels be,
P. 10 DIALOGUE   44 Whom this sweet Chordage cannot bind.
P. 11 DIALOGUE   51 All this fair, and soft, and sweet,
P. 18 CLORINDA   24 C. Sweet must Pan sound in Damons Note.
P. 18 CLORINDA   25 D. Clorinda's voice might make it sweet.
P. 20 THYRSIS   27 Dorinda. Oh sweet! oh sweet! How I my future
                         state
P. 23 NYMPH   58 It wax'd more white and sweet than they.
P. 23 NYMPH   59 It had so sweet a Breath! And oft
P. 24 NYMPH   105 Now my Sweet Faun is vanish'd to
P. 31 FAIR SINGER   2 Love did compose so sweet an Enemy,
P. 41 THE MOWER   32 While the sweet Fields do lye forgot:
P. 43 DAMON   47 While, going home, the Ev'ning sweet
P. 49 THE GARDEN   59 After a Place so pure, and sweet,
P. 50 THE GARDEN   71 How could such sweet and wholsome Hours
P. 64 A. HOUSE   172 'One perfecting the other Sweet.
P. 64 A. HOUSE   184 'These as sweet Sins we should confess.
P. 68 A. HOUSE   304 With Breath so sweet, or Cheek so faire.
P. 68 A. HOUSE   305 Well shot ye Firemen! Oh how sweet,
P. 69 A. HOUSE   330 That sweet Militia restore,
P. 80 A. HOUSE   695 She yet more Pure, Sweet, Streight, and Fair,
P. 94 DR. WITTY   19 And sweet as are her lips that speak it, she
P. 104 ANNIVERSARY   61 Then as he strokes them with a Touch more sweet,
P. 114 BLAKE   24 For they behold the sweet Canary Isles;

```
P. 122 TWO SONGS        24 Half so white or sweet as She.
P. 143 INSTRUCTIONS    100 No longer could conceal his Fortune sweet.
P. 148 INSTRUCTIONS    290 For Countrys Cause, that Glorious think and
                          sweet:
P. 149 INSTRUCTIONS    363 Gain and Revenge, Revenge and Gain are sweet:
P. 156 INSTRUCTIONS    632 Sweet Painter draw his Picture while I write.
P. 160 INSTRUCTIONS    813 With Boynton or with Middleton 'twere sweet;
```

sweete   frequency: 1   relative frequency: 0.0000
```
P. 199 DUKE             75 Letts see the nuntic Arundells sweete face;
```

sweeter   frequency: 2   relative frequency: 0.0000
```
P.  72 A. HOUSE        432 Their new-made Hay not sweeter is.
P. 153 INSTRUCTIONS    530 He finds the Air, and all things, sweeter here.
```

sweetest   frequency: 4   relative frequency: 0.0000
```
P.  20 THYRSIS          32 Of sweetest grass, and softest wooll;
P.  23 NYMPH            55 With sweetest milk, and sugar, first
P.  39 THE MATCH         7 With sweetest Perfumes hoarded were,
P.  64 A. HOUSE        161 'Your voice, the sweetest of the Quire,
```

sweetly   frequency: 1   relative frequency: 0.0000
```
P.  61 A. HOUSE         78 What she had laid so sweetly wast;
```

sweetness   frequency: 3   relative frequency: 0.0000
See also "sweetnesse."
```
P.  27 MISTRESS         42 Our sweetness, up into one Ball:
P.  38 PICTURE         29 Of sweetness, seeing they are fair;
P.  80 A. HOUSE        692 To Her the Meadow sweetness owes;
```

sweetnesse   frequency: 1   relative frequency: 0.0000
```
P. 129 O.C.            250 Which through his locks that piercing sweetnesse
                          shed;
```

sweets   frequency: 1   relative frequency: 0.0000
```
P. 187 BRITANNIA        98 Tast the delicious sweets of sovereign power,
```

swell   frequency: 1   relative frequency: 0.0000
```
P. 176 LOYALL SCOT     177 Like Snake that Swallowes toad doth Dragon
                          swell.
```

swell'd   frequency: 2   relative frequency: 0.0000
```
P.  58 BILL-BOROW       64 Those Acts that swell'd the Cheek of Fame.
P.  86 FLECKNO         151 Thereat the Poet swell'd, with anger full,
```

swelling   frequency: 2   relative frequency: 0.0000
```
P.  60 A. HOUSE         51 But where he comes the swelling Hall
P. 186 BRITANNIA        51 The swelling Passions of his Cankred breast,
```

swells   frequency: 3   relative frequency: 0.0000
```
P.  18 CLORINDA         23 And his Name swells my slender Oate.
P. 153 INSTRUCTIONS    532 Swells his old Veins with fresh Blood, fresh
                          Delight.
P. 162 INSTRUCTIONS    877 When Grievance urg'd, he swells like squatted
                          Toad,
```

swift   frequency: 1   relative frequency: 0.0000
```
P. 204 HISTORICALL     139 White liverd Danby for his swift Jacall
```

swifter   frequency: 1   relative frequency: 0.0000
```
P.  25 YOUNG LOVE       10 Such as yours should swifter move;
```

swim   frequency: 4   relative frequency: 0.0000
```
P. 154 INSTRUCTIONS    535 His sporting Navy all about him swim,
P. 155 INSTRUCTIONS    603 Or to their fellows swim on board the Dutch,
P. 156 INSTRUCTIONS    658 The Nymphs would rustle; he would forward swim.
P. 172 LOYALL SCOT      24 The Nymphs would Rustle, hee would forward
                          swim:
```

swinges   frequency: 1   relative frequency: 0.0000
```
P. 107 ANNIVERSARY     152 Swinges the Volumes of its horrid Flail.
```

switzers   frequency: 2   relative frequency: 0.0000
```
P.  69 A. HOUSE        336 Were then the Switzers of our Guard.
P. 147 INSTRUCTIONS    284 Of Presbyterian Switzers, made a stand.
```

swollen. See "swoln."

swoln   frequency: 2   relative frequency: 0.0000
```
P.  16 EYES             36 As two Eyes swoln with weeping are.
P.  77 A. HOUSE        594 On Pallets swoln of Velvet Moss;
```

swoome   frequency: 1   relative frequency: 0.0000
     P. 113 BLAKE   3 But though the wind was fair, they slowly swoome

swooning. See "swouning."

sword   frequency: 22   relative frequency: 0.0004
     P.   9 DIALOGUE   4 Ballance thy Sword against the Fight.
     P. 66 A. HOUSE   229 Sometimes resolv'd his Sword he draws,
     P. 69 A. HOUSE   326 With watry if not flaming Sword;
     P. 89 ODE   89 And has his Sword and Spoyls ungirt,
     P. 90 ODE   116 Still keep thy Sword erect:
     P. 92 MAY'S DEATH   63 When the Sword glitters ore the Judges head,
     P. 107 ANNIVERSARY 148 Girds yet his Sword, and ready stands to fight;
     P. 112 ANNIVERSARY 378 'And still his Sword seems hanging o're my head.
     P. 114 BLAKE   44 Your Conquering Sword will soon that want
                            remove.
     P. 130 O.C.   294 And David, for the sword and harpe renown'd;
     P. 152 INSTRUCTICNS 456 Who yields his Sword has Title to his Life.
     P. 157 INSTRUCTIONS 667 Or Waves his Sword, and could he them conjure
     P. 157 INSTRUCTIONS 688 With his dear Sword reposing by his Side.
     P. 172 LOYALL SCOT   33 Or waves his sword and, Cou'd hee them Conjure,
     P. 173 LOYALL SCOT   54 With his dear sword reposing by his side,
     P. 185 BRITANNIA   36 In 's left the scales, in 's right hand plac'd
                            the sword,
     P. 186 BRITANNIA   63 (By her usurpt), her right a bloudy sword
     P. 186 BRITANNIA   74 Doe Monarchs rise by vertues or the sword?
     P. 194 TWO HORSES   104 Insted of a Cudgell Balam wish't for a Sword.
     P. 198 DUKE   13 A vow that fire and sword shall never end
     P. 199 DUKE   70 His sword is all his argument, and his book;
     P. 200 DUKE   82 The Hero once gott honour by the sword;

swords   frequency: 2   relative frequency: 0.0000
     P. 114 BLAKE   46 Have broken all her Swords, then this one
                            Peace,
     P. 196 TWO HORSES   180 They teach them the Sooner to fall to their
                            Swords.

sword's   frequency: 1   relative frequency: 0.0000
     P. 85 FLECKNO   97 As narrow as his Sword's; and I, that was

swore   frequency: 5   relative frequency: 0.0001
     P. 86 FLECKNC   140 Not one Word, thought and swore that they were
                            good.
     P. 139 HOUSEWARMING 75 But he swore that the Patent should ne'er be
                            revok'd;
     P. 147 INSTRUCTICNS 263 Old Waller, Trumpet-gen'ral swore he'd write
     P. 154 INSTRUCTIONS 569 And swore that he would never more dwell there
     P. 316 CHEQUER INN 160 And prithee why so pale? then swore

sworn   frequency: 2   relative frequency: 0.0000
     P. 91 MAY'S DEATH   30 Sworn Enemy to all that do pretend,
     P. 148 INSTRUCTIONS 288 Of clear Estates, and to no Faction sworn;

swouning   frequency: 1   relative frequency: 0.0000
     P. 159 INSTRUCTIONS 759 The Thames roar'd, swouning Medway turn'd her
                            tide,

swum. See "swoome."

sybills   frequency: 1   relative frequency: 0.0000
     P. 196 TWO HORSES   171 If the Delphick Sybills oracular speeches,

syllable   frequency: 1   relative frequency: 0.0000
     P. 178 LOYALL SCOT 255 That syllable like a Picts wall devides.

sylvio   frequency: 3   relative frequency: 0.0000
     P. 22 NYMPH   25 Unconstant Sylvio, when yet
     P. 22 NYMPH   33 But Sylvio soon had me beguil'd.
     P. 23 NYMPH   49 As Sylvio did: his Gifts might be

sympathies   frequency: 1   relative frequency: 0.0000
     See also "simpathies."
     P. 84 FLECKNO   40 Mov'd by the Air and hidden Sympathies;

syrinx   frequency: 1   relative frequency: 0.0000
     P. 48 THE GARDEN   31 And Pan did after Syrinx speed,

sythe   frequency: 5   relative frequency: 0.0001
     P. 41 DAMON   7 Sharp like his Sythe his Sorrow was,
     P. 43 DAMON   69 And with my Sythe cut down the Grass,
     P. 43 DAMON   72 Sighing I whet my Sythe and Woes.

P. 44 DAMON   75 And, with his whistling Sythe, does cut
P. 44 DAMON   80 By his own Sythe, the Mower mown.

t.   frequency: 1   relative frequency: 0.0000
P. 38 PICTURE   t1 The Picture of little T. C. in a Prospect

t'   frequency: 2   relative frequency: 0.0000

table   frequency: 4   relative frequency: 0.0000
P. 72 A. HOUSE   446 Was such a Table rase and pure.
P. 86 FLECKNO   113 During the Table; though my new made Friend
P. 162 INSTRUCTIONS 881 At Table, jolly as a Country-Host,
P. 316 CHEQUER INN   171 And Table Linnen went

tables   frequency: 1   relative frequency: 0.0000
P. 143 INSTRUCTIONS 105 Draw next a Pair of Tables op'ning, then

tacklings   frequency: 1   relative frequency: 0.0000
P. 109 ANNIVERSARY   270 And Corposants along the Tacklings slide.

t'admit   frequency: 1   relative frequency: 0.0000
P. 63 A. HOUSE   139 ''Twere Sacriledge a Man t'admit

tag   frequency: 1   relative frequency: 0.0000
See also "tagg."
P. 132 PARADISE   50 The Poets tag them; we for fashion wear.

tagg   frequency: 1   relative frequency: 0.0000
P. 314 CHEQUER INN   49 And now they march't all Tagg and Ragg

tagus   frequency: 1   relative frequency: 0.0000
P. 94 DR. WITTY   18 Then Tagus, purer then dissolved snow,

tail   frequency: 1   relative frequency: 0.0000
See also "taile."
P. 107 ANNIVERSARY   151 And Stars still fall, and still the Dragons
                        Tail

taile   frequency: 1   relative frequency: 0.0000
P. 314 CHEQUER INN   66 To carry up her Taile.

tails   frequency: 3   relative frequency: 0.0000
P. 73 A. HOUSE   475 How Horses at their Tails do kick,
P. 97 HOLLAND   85 See but their Mairmaids with their Tails of
                        Fish,
P. 174 LOYALL SCOT   95 For Becketts sake Kent alwayes shall have
                        tails.

taint   frequency: 2   relative frequency: 0.0000
P. 41 THE MOWER   11 With strange perfumes he did the Roses taint.
P. 188 BRITANNIA   147 If this Imperiall cyl once taint the Blood,

tainted   frequency: 5   relative frequency: 0.0001
P. 3 LOVELACE   17 The Ayre's already tainted with the swarms
P. 76 A. HOUSE   550 And through the tainted Side he mines.
P. 126 O.C.   126 And helpless languish at the tainted Stall.
P. 199 DUKE   44 The wound of which now tainted Churchill faids,
P. 202 HISTORICALL   60 Tainted with Pride or with impetuous lust.

take   frequency: 23   relative frequency: 0.0004
P. 25 YOUNG LOVE   17 Now then love me: time may take
P. 36 DAPHNIS   104 And but rid to take the Air.
P. 43 DAMON   61 The deathless Fairyes take me oft
P. 63 A. HOUSE   135 'And in one Beauty we would take
P. 73 A. HOUSE   450 Which Levellers take Pattern at,
P. 74 A. HOUSE   482 Take Sanctuary in the Wood;
P. 91 MAY'S DEATH   36 And Horace patiently its stroke does take,
P. 93 DR. WITTY   4 Take oft the Cypress vail, but leave a mask,
P. 105 ANNIVERSARY   89 The crossest Spirits here do take their part,
P. 122 TWO SONGS   35 Now lesser Beauties may take place,
P. 139 HOUSEWARMING 74 Nor would take his beloved Canary in kind:
P. 141 INSTRUCTIONS 16 With Hook then, through the microscope, take aim
P. 148 INSTRUCTIONS 323 Along the Coast and Harbours they take care
P. 158 INSTRUCTIONS 720 Take a short Voyage underneath the Thames.
P. 160 INSTRUCTIONS 791 Then that Reward might in its turn take place,
P. 168 KINGS VOWES   61 And I will take his part to that degree,
P. 170 PROPHECY   19 A Boy shall take his Sister for his Mate
P. 171 PROPHECY   34 And pray to Jove to take him back againe.
P. 180 STOCKSMARKET 29 But Sir Robert to take all the scandal away
P. 196 TWO HORSES   179 When they take from the people the freedome of
                        words,
P. 200 DUKE   102 At last take pitty of thy tottering throne,

P. 203 HISTORICALL   103 From the forbidden tree the Pipin take:
P. 316 CHEQUER INN   173 Lest some shou'd take me for the Man

takeing   frequency: 1   relative frequency: 0.0000
    P. 168 ADVICE   5 The Roman takeing up the fencers trade,

taken   frequency: 4   relative frequency: 0.0000
    P. 46 AMETAS   14 Must be taken as you may.
    P. 73 A. HOUSE   480 And Pikes are taken in the Pound.
    P. 92 MAY'S DEATH   75 Yet wast thou taken hence with equal fate,
    P. 124 O.C.   31 Her when an infant, taken with her Charms,

takes   frequency: 6   relative frequency: 0.0001
    P. 15 EYES   6 In a false Angle takes each hight;
    P. 16 EYES   39 Yea oft the Thund'rer fitty takes
    P. 74 A. HOUSE   501 There the huge Bulk takes place, as went
    P. 86 FLECKNO   138 Yet he first kist them, and after takes pains
    P. 115 BLAKE   67 For Sanctacruze the glad Fleet takes her way,
    P. 130 O.C.   275 But when death takes them from that envy'd seate,

taketh   frequency: 1   relative frequency: 0.0000
    P. 94 DR. WITTY   14 As much as he that taketh from the Store

taking. See "takeing."

talbot   frequency: 1   relative frequency: 0.0000
    See also "talbott."
    P. 146 INSTRUCTIONS 206 Else Talbot offer'd to have led them on.

talbots   frequency: 1   relative frequency: 0.0000
    P. 189 BRITANNIA   173 Make 'em admire the Sidnies, Talbots, Veres,

talbott   frequency: 1   relative frequency: 0.0000
    P. 199 DUKE   66 Now Talbott must by his great master stand,

tale   frequency: 4   relative frequency: 0.0000
    P. 148 INSTRUCTIONS 315 Each day they bring the Tale, and that too true,
    P. 151 INSTRUCTIONS 428 To Master Lewis, and tell Coward tale,
    P. 316 CHEQUER INN   136 The tale of all that there did sup
    P. 316 CHEQUER INN   149 But (and thereby doth hange a Tale)

talk   frequency: 1   relative frequency: 0.0000
    See also "talke."
    P. 91 MAY'S DEATH   49 Transferring old Rome hither in your talk,

talke   frequency: 1   relative frequency: 0.0000
    P. 191 TWO HORSES   4 It is a clear proofe that birds too may talke;

talking   frequency: 3   relative frequency: 0.0000
    P. 20 THYRSIS   30 In talking of Elizium.
    P. 171 PROPHECY   35 When the Seal's given to a talking fool
    P. 193 TWO HORSES   75 W. To the bold talking members if the Bastards
                             you adde,

talkt   frequency: 1   relative frequency: 0.0000
    P. 316 CHEQUER INN   145 They talkt about and made such Din

tall   frequency: 6   relative frequency: 0.0001
    P. 70 A. HOUSE   375 And, from the Precipices tall
    P. 84 FLECKNO   64 Who as a Camel tall, yet easly can
    P. 141 INSTRUCTIONS   18 To see a tall Lowse brandish the white Staff.
    P. 156 INSTRUCTIONS 633 Paint him of Person tall, and big of bone,
    P. 156 INSTRUCTIONS 647 Three Children tall, unsing'd, away they row,
    P. 201 HISTORICALL   1 Of a tall Stature and of sable hue,

taller   frequency: 1   relative frequency: 0.0000
    P. 129 O.C.   270 When fall'n shews taller yet than as it grew:

tallest   frequency: 1   relative frequency: 0.0000
    P. 76 A. HOUSE   551 Who could have thought the tallest Oak

tallons   frequency: 1   relative frequency: 0.0000
    P. 138 HOUSEWARMING   52 The two Allens who serve his Injustice for
                             Tallons.

tallow   frequency: 1   relative frequency: 0.0000
    P. 140 HOUSEWARMING 110 Lest with driving too far his Tallow impair;

tally   frequency: 1   relative frequency: 0.0000
    P. 316 CHEQUER INN   137 On Chequer Tally was scor'd up

tam'd   frequency: 1   relative frequency: 0.0000

```
           P.   89 ODE               74 To see themselves in one Year tam'd:

tame                                    frequency:    8    relative frequency: 0.0001
           P.   14 THE CORONET        19 But thou who only could'st the Serpent tame,
           P.   22 NYMPH             34 This waxed tame, while he grew wild,
           P.   41 THE MOWER         24 He grafts upon the Wild the Tame:
           P.   82 A. HOUSE         766 But in more decent Order tame;
           P.   86 FLECKNO          118 Who satisfy'd with eating, but not tame
           P.  150 INSTRUCTIONS     388 Better than Law, Domestick Crimes to tame
           P.  187 BRITANNIA        119 Like a Tame spinster in 's seraglio sits,
           P.  190 STATUE            21 Does the Treasurer think men so Loyally tame

t'america                               frequency:    1    relative frequency: 0.0000
           P.  314 CHEQUER INN       73 This Knight was sent t'america

tames                                   frequency:    1    relative frequency: 0.0000
           P.   38 PICTURE            4 And there with her fair Aspect tames

tangier                                 frequency:    1    relative frequency: 0.0000
           P.  138 HOUSEWARMING      43 Nay ev'n from Tangier have sent back for the
                                        mold,

tangier-hall                            frequency:    1    relative frequency: 0.0000
           P.  140 HIS HOUSE          7 Here's Dunkirk-Town and Tangier-Hall,

tankard-bearing                         frequency:    1    relative frequency: 0.0000
           P.   92 MAY'S DEATH       61 And for a Tankard-bearing Muse must we

taper                                   frequency:    1    relative frequency: 0.0000
           P.  163 INSTRUCTIONS     916 And with blue streaks infect the Taper clear:

tapers                                  frequency:    2    relative frequency: 0.0000
           P.  111 ANNIVERSARY      332 And Stars (like Tapers) burn'd upon his Herse:
           P.  162 INSTRUCTIONS     886 Only dispers'd by a weak Tapers light;

tare                                    frequency:    1    relative frequency: 0.0000
           P.   34 DAPHNIS           34 His disorder'd Locks he tare;

tarquins                                frequency:    1    relative frequency: 0.0000
           P.  189 BRITANNIA        179 Tarquins just judge and Cesar's Equall Peers

tarras                                  frequency:    1    relative frequency: 0.0000
           P.  139 HOUSEWARMING      89 And upon the Tarras, to consummate all,

task                                    frequency:    2    relative frequency: 0.0000
        See also "taske."
           P.   93 DR. WITTY          3 The good Interpreter. Some in this task
           P.  172 LOYALL SCOT        6 Cleavland on whom they would the Task Impose.

taske                                   frequency:    1    relative frequency: 0.0000
           P.  128 O.C.             226 And you to govern only Heaven's taske.

tast                                    frequency:    2    relative frequency: 0.0000
           P.   69 A. HOUSE         327 What luckless Apple did we tast,
           P.  187 BRITANNIA         98 Tast the delicious sweets of sovereign power,

taste                                   frequency:    1    relative frequency: 0.0000
        See also "tast."
           P.    5 HASTINGS          24 Lest He become like Them, taste more then one.

tastes.  See "tasts."

tasts                                   frequency:    1    relative frequency: 0.0000
           P.   64 A. HOUSE         182 'We mold, as Baits for curious tasts.

taught                                  frequency:    9    relative frequency: 0.0001
           P.   22 NYMPH             32 Hath taught a Faun to hunt his Dear.
           P.   33 DAPHNIS            6 Long had taught her to be coy:
           P.   41 THE MOWER         12 And Flow'rs themselves were taught to paint.
           P.   66 A. HOUSE         227 For first Religion taught him Right,
           P.  127 O.C.             181 The Souldier taught that inward Mail to wear,
           P.  150 INSTRUCTIONS     389 And taught Youth by Spectacle Innocent!
           P.  156 INSTRUCTIONS     620 Taught the Dutch Colours from its top to wave;
           P.  158 INSTRUCTIONS     702 But that the Ships themselves were taught to
                                        dive:
           P.  185 BRITANNIA         37 Taught him their use, what dangers would ensue

taverns                                 frequency:    1    relative frequency: 0.0000
           P.  189 BRITANNIA        166 Imploy'd the Youth, not Taverns, Stewes and
                                        playes:

tawny                                   frequency:    1    relative frequency: 0.0000
```

P. 71 A. HOUSE   388 The tawny Mowers enter next;

tax   frequency: 4   relative frequency: 0.0000
    See also "land-tax."
    P. 150 INSTRUCTIONS 394 The Joys of State, for the new Peace and Tax.
    P. 191 STATUE   52 As would the next tax reimburse them with use.
    P. 315 CHEQUER INN   130 The Man that gave a woefull Tax
    P. 317 CHEQUER INN   178 They are but Engines to raise Tax

taxes   frequency: 3   relative frequency: 0.0000
    P. 162 INSTRUCTIONS 878 Frisks like a Frog to croak a Taxes load.
    P. 170 PROPHECY   12 Give Taxes to the King and Parliament.
    P. 204 HISTORICALL   121 Taxes Excise and Armyes dos advance.

taxing   frequency: 1   relative frequency: 0.0000
    P. 194 TWO HORSES   88 Of Exciseing our Cups and Taxing our Smoak.

te   frequency: 1   relative frequency: 0.0000
    P. 201 HISTORICALL   27 She chants Te Deum and so comes away

tea   frequency: 1   relative frequency: 0.0000
    P. 196 TWO HORSES   184 Chocolet Tea and Coffee are liquors of peace.

teach   frequency: 10   relative frequency: 0.0002
    P. 21 SOUL & BODY   32 The Maladies Thou me dost teach;
    P. 94 DR. WITTY   29 Women must not teach here: the Doctor doth
    P. 106 ANNIVERSARY   116 Nor teach, but traffique with, or burn the Jew.
    P. 130 O.C.   303 Since thou art gone, who best that way could'st
                             teach,
    P. 186 BRITANNIA   73 Such poor pedantick toys teach underlings.
    P. 186 BRITANNIA   86 To teach your will 's the onely rule of right,
    P. 188 BRITANNIA   158 To teach my People in their steps to tread.
    P. 188 BRITANNIA   161 Till then, my Rawleigh, teach our noble Youth
    P. 189 BRITANNIA   169 Teach 'em to scorn the Carwells, Pembrookes,
                             Nells,
    P. 196 TWO HORSES   180 They teach them the Sooner to fall to their
                             Swords.

teage   frequency: 1   relative frequency: 0.0000
    P. 198 DUKE   10 With Father Patricke Darby and with Teage,

teague.   See "teage," "teagues."

teagues   frequency: 1   relative frequency: 0.0000
    P. 187 BRITANNIA   126 His French and Teagues comand on sea and shoar.

teal   frequency: 1   relative frequency: 0.0000
    P. 145 INSTRUCTIONS 178 Haters of Fowl, to Teal preferring Bull.

teame   frequency: 1   relative frequency: 0.0000
    P. 181 MADE FREE   6 Of the whole Guild-Hall Teame to dragg it.

tear   frequency: 11   relative frequency: 0.0002
    P. 12 DROP OF DEW   13 Like its own Tear,
    P. 16 EYES   42 Not as a Perfume, but a Tear.
    P. 16 EYES   50 And at each Tear in distance stop:
    P. 21 SOUL & BODY   33 Whom first the Cramp of Hope does Tear:
    P. 27 MISTRESS   43 And tear our Pleasures with rough strife,
    P. 37 DEFINITION   22 And Earth some new Convulsion tear;
    P. 91 MAY'S DEATH   32 Shook his gray locks, and his own Bayes did tear
    P. 108 ANNIVERSARY   205 It seem'd the Earth did from the Center tear;
    P. 163 INSTRUCTIONS 915 Shake then the room, and all his Curtains tear,
    P. 164 INSTRUCTIONS 976 Nor Powder so the vaulted Bastion tear;
    P. 174 LOYALL SCOT   104 A Bishop will like Mahomet tear the Moon

teares   frequency: 1   relative frequency: 0.0000
    P. 91 MAY'S DEATH   58 The sacred Laurel, hence are all these teares?

tearm   frequency: 1   relative frequency: 0.0000
    P. 169 ADVICE   60 To be reproacht with Tearm of Turncoat knave;

tears   frequency: 34   relative frequency: 0.0007
    See also "teares."
    P.   4 HASTINGS   4 Of Tears untoucht, and never wept before.
    P.   4 HASTINGS   8 With early Tears must mourn his early Fate.
    P.   5 HASTINGS   44 Who for sad Purple, tears his Saffron-coat;
    P. 15 EYES   t Eyes and Tears.
    P. 15 EYES   7 These Tears which better measure all,
    P. 15 EYES   9 Two Tears, which Sorrow long did weigh
    P. 15 EYES   14 Yea even Laughter, turns to Tears:
    P. 15 EYES   20 No Hony, but these Tears could draw.

P.	16	EYES	29	So Magdalen, in Tears more wise
P.	16	EYES	44	But as they seem the Tears of Light.
P.	17	EYES	54	Till Eyes and Tears be the same things:
P.	17	EYES	56	These weeping Eyes, those seeing Tears.
P.	22	NYMPH	11	Thy murder, I will Jcyn my Tears
P.	24	NYMPH	95	See how it weeps. The Tears do come
P.	24	NYMPH	100	Melt in such Amber Tears as these.
P.	24	NYMPH	102	Keep these two crystal Tears; and fill
P.	24	NYMPH	117	Until my Tears, still dropping, wear
P.	27	LOVER	17	The Sea him lent these bitter Tears
P.	31	MOURNING	6	With Tears suspended ere they flow;
P.	32	MOURNING	11	As if she, with these precious Tears,
P.	32	MOURNING	31	Would find her Tears yet deeper Waves
P.	42	DAMON	31	No moisture but my Tears do rest,
P.	62	A. HOUSE	111	'And Holy-water of our Tears
P.	62	A. HOUSE	113	'Not Tears of Grief; but such as those
P.	67	A. HOUSE	266	And to the Nuns bequeaths her Tears:
P.	81	A. HOUSE	715	Tears (watry Shct that pierce the Mind;)
P.	107	ANNIVERSARY	185	So shall the Tears we on past Grief employ,
P.	118	BLAKE	149	Our Cannon now tears every Ship and Sconce,
P.	127	O.C.	170	To compass in our Isle; our Tears suffice;
P.	130	O.C.	301	And lost in tears, have neither sight nor mind
P.	156	INSTRUCTIONS	628	She tears herself since him she cannot harm.
P.	162	INSTRUCTIONS	897	And silent tears her secret anguish speak,
P.	186	BRITANNIA	66	From Exhalation bred of bloud and tears.
P.	189	BRITANNIA	180	With me I'le bring to dry my peoples tears:

tedious   frequency: 1   relative frequency: 0.0000
     P. 105 ANNIVERSARY   69 While tedious Statesmen many years did hack,

teeming   frequency: 2   relative frequency: 0.0000
     P. 16 EYES   35 Nor Cynthia Teeming shcw's so fair,
     P. 158 INSTRUCTIONS   715 Those Ships, that yearly from their teeming
                                Howl,

teeth   frequency: 3   relative frequency: 0.0000
     P. 42 DAMON   36 Disarmed of its teeth and sting.
     P. 106 ANNIVERSARY   130 Gnashes her Goary teeth; nor there secure.
     P. 144 INSTRUCTIONS   135 With hundred rcws cf Teeth the Shark exceeds,

tegeline   frequency: 1   relative frequency: 0.0000
     P. 189 BRITANNIA   171 Poppea, Tegeline and Acte's name

tell   frequency: 19   relative frequency: 0.0003
     P.   3 LOVELACE   5 That candid Age no cther way could tell
     P. 19 THYRSIS   3 Tell me Thyrsis, prethee do,
     P. 29 THE GALLERY   1 Clora come view my Soul, and tell
     P. 38 PICTURE   7 And them does tell
     P. 42 DAMON   25 Tell me where I may pass the Fires
     P. 68 A. HOUSE   3C7 Whose shrill report no Ear can tell,
     P. 73 A. HOUSE   473 Let others tell the Paradox,
     P. 91 MAY'S DEATH   45 Tell them of Liberty, the Stories fine,
     P. 104 ANNIVERSARY   41 Thus (Image-like) an useless time they tell,
     P. 124 O.C.   66 Or on their cwn redoubled, none can tell.
     P. 125 O.C.   79 Who now shall tell us mcre of mournful Swans,
     P. 127 O.C.   187 Cf that for ever Preston's field shall tell
     P. 151 INSTRUCTIONS   428 To Master Lewis, and tell Coward tale,
     P. 151 INSTRUCTIONS   433 Tell him our Ships unrigg'd, our Ports unman'd,
     P. 185 BRITANNIA   31 Tell him of Golden Indies, Fayry Lands,
     P. 189 BRITANNIA   165 Tell 'em how arts and Arms in thy ycung dayes
     P. 189 BRITANNIA   167 Tell em the Generous scorn chimer their Rise to owe
     P. 191 TWO HORSES   9 Phalaris had a Bull which grave Authors tell ye
     P. 312 CHEQUER INN   1 I'll tell thee Dick where I have beene

telling   frequency: 1   relative frequency: 0.0000
     P. 139 HOUSEWARMING   69 Bulteales, Beakns, Morley, Wrens fingers with
                                telling

tells   frequency: 5   relative frequency: 0.0001
     P. 119 BLAKE   168 And tells the wcrld, how much to you it owes.
     P. 161 INSTRUCTICNS   839 Tells them he at Whitehall had tcok a turn,
     P. 191 TWO HORSES   7 Livy tells a strang stcry can hardly be fellow'd
     P. 205 HISTORICALL   159 Tells him the hcly Church demands his aide,
     P. 313 CHEQUER INN   20 That now he Money tells by Pecks

temperate   frequency: 1   relative frequency: 0.0000
     P. 117 BLAKE   124 War turn'd the temperate, to the Torrid Zone.

temper'd   frequency: 3   relative frequency: 0.0000
     P. 129 O.C.   235 Yet always temper'd with an aire so mild,
     P. 172 LOYALL SCOT   11 For those soft Airs had temper'd every thought,

```
         P. 204 HISTORICALL    117 First temper'd Poison to destroy our Lawes,

tempe's                             frequency:    1    relative frequency: 0.0000
         P.  82 A. HOUSE        753 For you Thessalian Tempe's Seat

tempest                             frequency:    3    relative frequency: 0.0000
         P.  28 LOVER           48 Like Ajax, the mad Tempest braves.
         P.  98 HOLLAND        125 While half their banish'd keels the Tempest
                                    tost,
         P. 127 O.C.           171 Since him away the dismal Tempest rent,

tempests                            frequency:    3    relative frequency: 0.0000
         P. 108 ANNIVERSARY    212 And to deaf Seas, and ruthless Tempests mourns,
         P. 125 O.C.           106 As hollow Seas with future Tempests rage:
         P. 126 O.C.           121 Then heavy Showres the winged Tempests lead,

templar                             frequency:    2    relative frequency: 0.0000
         P. 175 LOYALL SCOT    145 These Templar Lords Exceed the Templar
                                    Knights,

temple                              frequency:    9    relative frequency: 0.0001
         P.  18 BERMUDAS        32 A Temple, where to sound his Name.
         P.  74 A. HOUSE       510 The Columnes of the Temple green;
         P.  97 HOLLAND         89 Each to the Temple with these Altars tend,
         P. 104 ANNIVERSARY     33 They neither build the Temple in their dayes,
         P. 139 HOUSEWARMING    64 The Tribes ne'er contributed so to the Temple.
         P. 140 HOUSEWARMING    97 This Temple, of War and of Peace is the
                                    Shrine;
         P. 147 INSTRUCTIONS   255 First enter'd forward Temple, Conqueror
         P. 169 ADVICE          58 Leave Temple Single to be beat in the Citty.
         P. 169 ADVICE          59 What Scandal's this! Temple, the wise, the
                                    Brave,

temples                             frequency:    6    relative frequency: 0.0001
         P.  18 CLORINDA         6 The Flow'rs I for thy Temples keep.
         P.  79 A. HOUSE       642 My Temples here with heavy sedge;
         P.  88 ODE             22 And Pallaces and Temples rent:
         P. 105 ANNIVERSARY     64 Therefore the Temples rear'd their Columns
                                    high:
         P. 131 PARADISE         9 (So Sampson groap'd the Temples Posts in
                                    spight)
         P. 147 INSTRUCTIONS   278 And the faint sweat trickled down Temples
                                    Brows.

templum                             frequency:    1    relative frequency: 0.0000
         P. 140 HIS HOUSE        9 The Dutchman's Templum Pacis.

tempt                               frequency:    3    relative frequency: 0.0000
         P. 131 O.C.           323 Tempt not his clemency to try his pow'r,
         P. 175 LOYALL SCOT    144 If Wealth or vice can tempt your appetites,
         P. 205 HISTORICALL    179 Be wise ye Sons of Men tempt God no more

tempter                             frequency:    1    relative frequency: 0.0000
         P.  10 DIALOGUE        43 Cease Tempter. None can chain a mind

tempters                            frequency:    1    relative frequency: 0.0000
         P. 203 HISTORICALL    102 Fond Eve did for this subtle Tempters sake

tempting                            frequency:    2    relative frequency: 0.0000
         P. 153 INSTRUCTIONS   531 The sudden change, and such a tempting sight,
         P. 155 INSTRUCTIONS   604 Which show the tempting metal in their clutch.

tempts                              frequency:    1    relative frequency: 0.0000
         P.  76 A. HOUSE       556 Tempts impotent and bashful Sin.

ten                                 frequency:    6    relative frequency: 0.0001
         P.  26 MISTRESS         8 Love you ten years before the Flood.
         P.  86 FLECKNO        124 Ten quire of paper in which he was drest.
         P. 110 ANNIVERSARY    300 Might muster Heresies, so one were ten.
         P. 138 HOUSEWARMING    39 He car'd not though Egypt's Ten Plagues us
                                    distrest,
         P. 196 TWO HORSES     188 Theres ten times more Treason in Brandy and
                                    ale.
         P. 200 DUKE            90 Ten thousand such as these can nere controule

tenable                             frequency:    1    relative frequency: 0.0000
         P. 154 INSTRUCTIONS   563 And quickly judg'd the Fort was not tenable,

tenantable                          frequency:    1    relative frequency: 0.0000
         P. 154 INSTRUCTIONS   564 Which, if a House, yet were not tenantable.

tend                                frequency:    1    relative frequency: 0.0000
```

P. 97 HOLLAND   89 Each to the Temple with these Altars tend,

tender   frequency: 5   relative frequency: 0.0001
  P. 30 THE GALLERY   53 A tender Shepherdess, whose Hair
  P. 69 A. HOUSE   342 Where he the tender Plants removes.
  P. 86 FLECKNO   128 Picks out the tender bosome to its young.
  P. 124 O.C.   33 And, lest their force the tender burthen wrong,
  P. 188 BRITANNIA   163 Watch and Preside over their tender age

tenderness   frequency: 1   relative frequency: 0.0000
  See also "tendernesse."
  P. 200 DUKE   113 There is no friendship, tenderness nor love:

tendernesse   frequency: 1   relative frequency: 0.0000
  P. 128 O.C.   204 His tendernesse extended unto all.

tends   frequency: 1   relative frequency: 0.0000
  P. 203 HISTORICALL 114 Now to the State she tends againe direct,

tenerife. See "teneriff."

teneriff   frequency: 2   relative frequency: 0.0000
  P. 57 BILL-BOROW   28 Of Heaven-daring Teneriff.
  P. 113 BLAKE   t3 Teneriff. !?.

t'enjoy   frequency: 1   relative frequency: 0.0000
  P. 33 DAPHNIS   7 But she neither knew t'enjoy,

t'enslave   frequency: 1   relative frequency: 0.0000
  P. 186 BRITANNIA   84 Are proper arts, the long-eard rout t'enslave:

t'ensnare   frequency: 1   relative frequency: 0.0000
  P. 186 BRITANNIA   83 These pious frauds (too slight t'ensnare the
                         brave)

tent   frequency: 1   relative frequency: 0.0000
  P. 125 O.C.   91 Under whose shady tent Men ev'ry year

tents   frequency: 1   relative frequency: 0.0000
  P. 110 ANNIVERSARY 291 And such as to their Parents Tents do press,

tereus   frequency: 1   relative frequency: 0.0000
  P. 202 HISTORICALL   69 Not Tereus with his Sister Philomel.

term. See "tearm."

terrace. See "tarras."

terrible   frequency: 1   relative frequency: 0.0000
  P. 202 HISTORICALL   42 Death and the Duke so terrible apeare.

terror   frequency: 1   relative frequency: 0.0000
  See also "terrour."
  P. 112 ANNIVERSARY 383 'The Valiants Terror, Riddle of the Wise;

terrors   frequency: 1   relative frequency: 0.0000
  P. 151 INSTRUCTIONS 413 False Terrors our believing Fears devise:

terrour   frequency: 6   relative frequency: 0.0001
  See also "terror."
  P. 57 BILL-BOROW   38 Of the great Masters terrour there:
  P. 116 BLAKE   83 They learn'd with Terrour, that nor Summers
                         heat,
  P. 154 INSTRUCTIONS 540 Terrour and War, but want an Enemy.
  P. 156 INSTRUCTIONS 637 Mix a vain Terrour in his Martial look,
  P. 158 INSTRUCTIONS 705 Up to the Bridge contagious Terrour strook:
  P. 162 INSTRUCTIONS 899 The Object strange in him no Terrour mov'd:

terrours. See "terrors."

text   frequency: 1   relative frequency: 0.0000
  P. 175 LOYALL SCOT 131 The Nation they devide, their Curates Text.

th   frequency: 1   relative frequency: 0.0000
  P. 192 TWO HORSES   45 Ch. That he should be styled defender o' th
                         faith,

th'   frequency: 52   relative frequency: 0.0010
  P.   3 LOVELACE   4 Our wits have drawne th' infection of our times.
  P.   5 HASTINGS   37 But most he doth th' Eternal Book behold,
  P. 13 DROP OF DEW   40 Into the Glories of th' Almighty Sun.

P.	17	BERMUDAS	2	In th' Oceans bosome unespy'd,
P.	24	NYMPH	114	Th' Engraver sure his Art may spare;
P.	28	LOVER	30	Th' unfortunate and abject Heir:
P.	28	LOVER	40	Th' Amphibium of Life and Death.
P.	29	THE GALLERY	17	But, on the other side, th' art drawn
P.	31	FAIR SINGER	16	Who has th' advantage both of Eyes and Voice,
P.	35	DAPHNIS	74	All th' Enjoyment of our Love
P.	39	PICTURE	38	Do quickly make th' Example Yours;
P.	50	THE GARDEN	69	And, as it works, th' industrious Bee
P.	67	A. HOUSE	259	Then th' unfrequented Vault appear'd,
P.	67	A. HOUSE	269	Thenceforth (as when th' Inchantment ends
P.	70	A. HOUSE	362	Th' invisible Artilery;
P.	70	A. HOUSE	366	Th' Ambition of its Prelate great.
P.	73	A. HOUSE	456	Davenant with th' Universal Heard.
P.	73	A. HOUSE	472	And Isl's th' astonish'd Cattle round.
P.	74	A. HOUSE	492	On one hand Fairfax, th' other Veres:
P.	83	FLECKNO	13	Save that th' ingenious Door did as you come
P.	84	FLECKNO	54	And th' Ordinance was only Politick.
P.	86	FLECKNO	120	After th' Assizes dinner mild appear,
P.	87	ODE	6	And oyl th' unused Armours rust:
P.	92	MAY'S DEATH	88	As th' Eagles Plumes from other birds divide.
P.	95	HOLLAND	2	As but th' Off-scouring of the Brittish Sand;
P.	95	HOLLAND	5	Or what by th' Oceans slow alluvion fell,
P.	97	HOLLAND	58	Th' Apostles were so many Fishermen?
P.	97	HOLLAND	62	And Poor-john to have been th' Evangelist.
P.	105	ANNIVERSARY	66	Th' harmonious City of the seven Gates.
P.	109	ANNIVERSARY	264	Th' ambitious Shrubs thou in just time didst aw.
P.	111	ANNIVERSARY	312	Out of the Center of th' unbottom'd Pit;
P.	118	BLAKE	137	Th' all-seeing Sun, neer gaz'd on such a sight,
P.	119	TWO SONGS	1	Th' Astrologers own Eyes are set,
P.	130	O.C.	278	Shall th' English souldier, ere he charge, rehearse;
P.	141	INSTRUCTIONS	14	As th' Indians, draw our Luxury in Plumes.
P.	145	INSTRUCTIONS	185	Next th' Lawyers Mercenary Band appear:
P.	146	INSTRUCTIONS	239	For th' other side all in loose Quarters lay,
P.	147	INSTRUCTIONS	247	First spy'd the Enemy and gave th' Alarm:
P.	148	INSTRUCTIONS	286	But for th' unknown Reserve that still remain'd:
P.	152	INSTRUCTIONS	464	For Sin against th' Eleventh Commandment.
P.	155	INSTRUCTIONS	591	Th' English from shore the Iron deaf invoke
P.	161	INSTRUCTIONS	824	Binding, e're th' Houses meet, the Treaty sure.
P.	161	INSTRUCTIONS	844	Th' Army soon rais'd, he doth as soon disarm.
P.	162	INSTRUCTIONS	890	He wakes and Muses of th' uneasie Throne:
P.	163	INSTRUCTIONS	904	And th' airy Picture vanisht from his hold.
P.	168	ADVICE	10	One to his Pathic, th' other to his Player.
P.	169	ADVICE	34	To make them th' other Councell board forgett.
P.	173	LOYALL SCOT	82	Whose one bank vertue, th' other vice doth breed?
P.	175	LOYALL SCOT	153	Whilst Arrius stands at th' Athanasian Creed.
P.	186	BRITANNIA	69	From th' easie King she truthes bright Mirrour took,
P.	186	BRITANNIA	78	The Rivall Gods, Monarchs of th' other world,
P.	202	HISTORICALL	56	Whilst the brave Tudors wore th' Imperial Crowne:

'thad   frequency: 1   relative frequency: 0.0000
   P. 23 NYMPH   67 And when 'thad left me far away,

thames   frequency: 4   relative frequency: 0.0000
   P. 158 INSTRUCTIONS 720 Take a short Voyage underneath the Thames.
   P. 159 INSTRUCTIONS 743 When aged Thames was bound with Fetters base,
   P. 159 INSTRUCTIONS 759 The Thames roar'd, swouning Medway turn'd her tide,
   P. 160 INSTRUCTIONS 817 But in the Thames mouth still de Ruyter laid,

than   frequency: 39   relative frequency: 0.0008

thankless   frequency: 1   relative frequency: 0.0000
   P. 108 ANNIVERSARY   217 From the low World, and thankless Men above,

thanks   frequency: 3   relative frequency: 0.0000
   P. 77 A. HOUSE   597 Thanks for my Rest ye Mossy Banks,
   P. 77 A. HOUSE   598 And unto you cool Zephyr's Thanks,
   P. 194 TWO HORSES   89 Ch. But thanks to the whores who have made the King Dogged

that   frequency: 549   relative frequency: 0.0114

thats   frequency: 1   relative frequency: 0.0000

that's   frequency: 5   relative frequency: 0.0001
   See also "thats."

t'have   frequency: 1   relative frequency: 0.0000

thaw'd   frequency: 1   relative frequency: 0.0000
    P.   3 LOVELACE   35 lovelace that thaw'd the most congealed brest,

the   frequency: 2481   relative frequency: 0.0518
    See also "i'th," "i'th'," "o'th," "th,"
        "th'," "th'elected."

theatre   frequency: 2   relative frequency: 0.0000
    P. 175 LOYALL SCOT   169 When for a Church hee built a Theatre.
    P. 190 STATUE   6 To Limitt his troop to this Theatre small,

theban   frequency: 1   relative frequency: 0.0000
    P. 104 ANNIVERSARY   60 And joyning streight the Theban Tow'r arose;

thebes   frequency: 1   relative frequency: 0.0000
    P. 137 HOUSEWARMING   18 Made Thebes dance aloft while he fidled and
        sung,

thee   frequency: 46   relative frequency: 0.0009

theeves   frequency: 1   relative frequency: 0.0000
    P. 65 A. HOUSE   207 'Death only can such Theeves make fast,

theft   frequency: 1   relative frequency: 0.0000
    P. 132 PARADISE   30 But to detect their Igncrance or Theft.

their   frequency: 358   relative frequency: 0.0074
    See also "theire."

theire   frequency: 3   relative frequency: 0.0000

theirs   frequency: 7   relative frequency: 0.0001

th'elected   frequency: 1   relative frequency: 0.0000
    P. 107 ANNIVERSARY   156 The Ill delaying, what th'elected hastes;

them   frequency: 139   relative frequency: 0.0029
    See also "em," "'em," "'um."

theme   frequency: 1   relative frequency: 0.0000
    P. 132 PARADISE   53 Thy verse created like thy Theme sublime,

themselves   frequency: 42   relative frequency: 0.0008

then   frequency: 212   relative frequency: 0.0044

thence   frequency: 14   relative frequency: 0.0002

thenceforth   frequency: 4   relative frequency: 0.0000

there   frequency: 102   relative frequency: 0.0021
    See also "theres," "ther's."

thereat   frequency: 2   relative frequency: 0.0000

thereby   frequency: 1   relative frequency: 0.0000

therefore   frequency: 25   relative frequency: 0.0005

therein   frequency: 1   relative frequency: 0.0000

theres   frequency: 3   relative frequency: 0.0000

therfore   frequency: 1   relative frequency: 0.0000
    P. 137 HOUSEWARMING   11 His Omnipotence therfore much rather design'd

ther's   frequency: 2   relative frequency: 0.0000

these   frequency: 108   relative frequency: 0.0022

thessalian   frequency: 1   relative frequency: 0.0000
    P. 82 A. HOUSE   753 For you Thessalian Tempe's Seat

thestylis   frequency: 4   relative frequency: 0.0000
    P. 46 AMETAS   t Ametas and Thestylis making Hay-Ropes.
    P. 46 AMETAS   4+ Thestylis.
    P. 46 AMETAS   12+ Thestylis.
    P. 71 A. HOUSE   401 But bloody Thestylis, that waites

they   frequency: 298   relative frequency: 0.0062

they'l   frequency: 2   relative frequency: 0.0000 they've   frequency: 1   relative frequency: 0.0000

thick   frequency: 6   relative frequency: 0.0001
    P.   74 A. HOUSE   490 Link'd in so thick, an Union locks,
    P.   75 A. HOUSE   531 And through the Hazles thick espy
    P. 106 ANNIVERSARY   141 But a thick Cloud about that Morning lyes,
    P. 109 ANNIVERSARY   235 Then did thick Mists and Winds the air deform,
    P. 130 O.C.   283 While staggs shall fly unto the forests thick,
    P. 146 INSTRUCTIONS   235 Thick was the Morning, and the House was thin,

thickest   frequency: 1   relative frequency: 0.0000
    P. 114 BLAKE   21 In thickest darkness they would choose to steer,

thief   frequency: 2   relative frequency: 0.0000
    P.   94 DR. WITTY   13 He is Translations thief that addeth more,
    P. 171 PROPHECY   32 A Greater Thief then Alexander was.

thieves   frequency: 2   relative frequency: 0.0000
    See also "theeves."
    P. 149 INSTRUCTIONS   333 Thus, like fair Thieves, the Commons Purse
                               they share,
    P. 163 INSTRUCTIONS   940 As Thieves repriev'd for Executioners;

thighs   frequency: 2   relative frequency: 0.0000
    P.   29 THE GALLERY   20 And stretches out her silky Thighs;
    P. 143 INSTRUCTIONS   85 His brazen Calves, his brawny Thighs, (the
                               Face

thin   frequency: 3   relative frequency: 0.0000
    P.   74 A. HOUSE   506 It opens passable and thin;
    P.   84 FLECKNO   59 I mean till he were drest: for else so thin
    P. 146 INSTRUCTIONS   235 Thick was the Morning, and the House was thin,

thine   frequency: 26   relative frequency: 0.0005

thing   frequency: 20   relative frequency: 0.0004
    P.   9 DIALOGUE   7 Now, if thou bee'st that thing Divine,
    P.   10 DIALOGUE   31 Every thing does seem to vie
    P.   17 BERMUDAS   14 Which here enamells every thing;
    P.   22 NYMPH   14 Keeps register of every thing:
    P.   23 NYMPH   63 It is a wond'rous thing, how fleet
    P.   37 DEFINITION   6 Could show me so divine a thing,
    P.   38 PICTURE   25 Mean time, whilst every verdant thing
    P.   41 DAMON   3 While ev'ry thing did seem to paint
    P.   41 THE MOWER   20 To Man, that sov'raign thing and proud;
    P.   60 A. HOUSE   62 Where ev'ry Thing does answer Use?
    P.   79 A. HOUSE   659 And every thing so whisht and fine,
    P. 103 ANNIVERSARY   22 For one Thing never was by one King don.
    P. 108 ANNIVERSARY   225 For to be Cromwell was a greater thing,
    P. 129 O.C.   254 How much another thing, no more that man?
    P. 163 INSTRUCTIONS   929 And they, not knowing, the same thing propose,
    P. 179 STOCKSMARKET   11 Upon the King's birthday to set up a thing
    P. 181 MADE FREE   4 'Tis a thing sure of Weight,
    P. 183 MADE FREE   85 But what little thing,
    P. 204 HISTORICALL   132 In our weal-publik scarce one thing succeeds--
    P. 204 HISTORICALL   153 At his Command Mack will doe any thing,

things   frequency: 24   relative frequency: 0.0005
    P.   11 DIALOGUE   55 If things of Sight such Heavens be,
    P.   17 EYES   54 Till Eyes and Tears be the same things:
    P.   18 CLORINDA   17 D. These once had been enticing things,
    P.   59 A. HOUSE   9 Why should of all things Man unrul'd
    P.   59 A. HOUSE   25 But all things are composed here
    P.   60 A. HOUSE   44 Things greater are in less contain'd.
    P.   60 A. HOUSE   60 But low Things clownishly ascend.
    P.   63 A. HOUSE   140 'To holy things, for Heaven fit.
    P.   69 A. HOUSE   339 The Nursery of all things green
    P.   72 A. HOUSE   442 A new and empty Face of things;
    P.   78 A. HOUSE   637 Where all things gaze themselves, and doubt
    P. 104 ANNIVERSARY   37 No other care they bear of things above,
    P. 104 ANNIVERSARY   43 Nor more contribute to the state of Things,
    P. 109 ANNIVERSARY   230 Thy sober Spirit unto things too High,
    P. 120 TWO SONGS   20 On Sublunary things thy care;
    P. 129 O.C.   256 Oh! worthlesse world! oh transitory things!
    P. 131 PARADISE   15 Lest he perplext the things he would explain,
    P. 132 PARADISE   33 And things divine thou treatst of in such state
    P. 153 INSTRUCTIONS   530 He finds the Air, and all things, sweeter here.
    P. 174 LOYALL SCOT   116 How Reverend things are 'lord', Lawn Sleeves
                               and Ease!
    P. 190 STATUE   34 Such things you should never or Suddainly doe.
    P. 195 TWO HORSES   157 Ch. But canst thou Divine when things shall be
                                                                      mended?

P. 201 HISTORICALL   14 Things highly fitting for a Monarchs trade.
P. 201 HISTORICALL   32 Deludes their plyant Nature with Vain things,

think   frequency: 17   relative frequency: 0.0003
See also "thinke."
P. 26 MISTRESS   3 We would sit down, and think which way
P. 26 MISTRESS   32 But none I think do there embrace.
P. 65 A. HOUSE   220 'When they it think by Night conceal'd.
P. 68 A. HOUSE   303 And think so still! though not compare
P. 106 ANNIVERSARY   131 Hence ott I think, if in some happy Hour
P. 109 ANNIVERSARY   242 Who think those high Decrees by Man design'd.
P. 128 O.C.   225 Least others dare to think your zeale a maske,
P. 148 INSTRUCTIONS   290 For Countrys Cause, that Glorious think and
                          sweet:
P. 153 INSTRUCTIONS   514 Or think him, like Herb-John, for nothing good.
P. 153 INSTRUCTIONS   519 All Causes sure concur, but most they think
P. 171 PROPHECY   46 And think French onely Loyall, Irish wise,
P. 176 LOYALL SCOT   195 And in their Causes think themselves supream.
P. 180 STOCKSMARKET   49 Sure the king will ne'er think of repaying his
                          bankers,
P. 184 MADE FREE   123 Never think in England to swagger,
P. 190 STATUE   21 Does the Treasurer think men so Loyally tame
P. 191 TWO HORSES   15 All Popish beleivers think something divine,
P. 192 TWO HORSES   50 Not to think his own Father is gone to the
                          Devill.

thinke   frequency: 2   relative frequency: 0.0000
P. 198 DUKE   26 And thinke a prince oth blood can ere doe Ill?
P. 198 DUKE   28 Shall these men dare to thinke, shall these
                          decide

thinkest. See "think'st."

thinking   frequency: 3   relative frequency: 0.0000
P.   4 LOVELACE   42 Thinking that I too of the rout had been,
P. 14 THE CORONET   10 Thinking (so I my self deceive)
P. 20 THYRSIS   28 By silent thinking, Antidate:

thinks   frequency: 5   relative frequency: 0.0001
P. 59 A. HOUSE   23 That thinks by Breadth the World t'unite
P. 147 INSTRUCTIONS   269 Each thinks his Person represents the whole,
P. 152 INSTRUCTIONS   486 Now thinks all but too little for their Fear.
P. 160 INSTRUCTIONS   815 And thinks 'twill ne're be well within this
                          Nation,
P. 191 STATUE   43 She thinks not convenient to goe to the price,

think'st   frequency: 2   relative frequency: 0.0000
P. 46 AMETAS   1 Think'st Thou that this Iove can stand,
P. 46 AMETAS   5 Think'st Thou that this Rope would twine

third   frequency: 5   relative frequency: 0.0001
P. 85 FLECKNO   72 With which he doth his third Dimension Stuff.
P. 117 BLAKE   106 And a third World seek out our Armes to shun.
P. 141 INSTRUCTIONS   2 To end her Picture, does the third time wait.
P. 150 INSTRUCTIONS   404 The next divided, and the third we've none.
P. 157 INSTRUCTIONS   698 The Loyal-london, now a third time burns.

thirst   frequency: 2   relative frequency: 0.0000
P. 177 LOYALL SCOT   228 The Innocentest mind their thirst alone
P. 205 HISTORICALL   174 And thirst of Empire Calentur'd his Breast.

thirsty   frequency: 1   relative frequency: 0.0000
P. 109 ANNIVERSARY   237 Which to the thirsty Land did plenty bring,

thirtieth   frequency: 1   relative frequency: 0.0000
P. 201 HISTORICALL   10 But in his thirtieth yeare began to Raigne.

thirty   frequency: 1   relative frequency: 0.0000
P. 26 MISTRESS   16 But thirty thousand to the rest.

this   frequency: 206   relative frequency: 0.0043

thistle-down   frequency: 1   relative frequency: 0.0000
P. 146 INSTRUCTIONS   224 Shall with one Breath like thistle-down
                          disperse.

thistles   frequency: 1   relative frequency: 0.0000
P. 43 DAMON   66 Had not Love here his Thistles sow'd!

thither   frequency: 8   relative frequency: 0.0001 tho   frequency: 9   relative frequency: 0.0001

tho'   frequency: 24   relative frequency: 0.0005

thomas   frequency: 1   relative frequency: 0.0000
   P. 182 MADE FREE   71 Of Sir Thomas Player

thong   frequency: 1   relative frequency: 0.0000
   P. 138 HOUSEWARMING   30 None sollid enough seem'd for his Thong Caster:

thorn   frequency: 1   relative frequency: 0.0000
   P.   75 A. HOUSE   519 The Thorn, lest it should hurt her, draws

thorns   frequency: 4   relative frequency: 0.0000
   P.   14 THE CORONET   1 When for the Thorns with which I long, too
                    long,
   P.   38 PICTURE   30 And Roses of their thorns disarm:
   P.   75 A. HOUSE   516 With Musick high the squatted Thorns.
   P. 109 ANNIVERSARY   254 With Thorns and Briars of the Wilderness.

thorough   frequency: 8   relative frequency: 0.0001
   See also "thorow," "th'row."

thorow   frequency: 2   relative frequency: 0.0000

those   frequency: 89   relative frequency: 0.0018

thou   frequency: 96   relative frequency: 0.0020

though   frequency: 56   relative frequency: 0.0011
   See also "tho," "tho'."

thought   frequency: 27   relative frequency: 0.0005
   P.   5 HASTINGS   29 His Thought with richest Triumphs entertains,
   P.   10 DIALOGUE   23 My gentler Rest is on a Thought,
   P.   39 THE MATCH   8 All as she thought secure.
   P.   49 THE GARDEN   48 To a green Thought in a green Shade.
   P.   76 A. HOUSE   551 Who could have thought the tallest Oak
   P.   83 FLECKNO   24 To my last Tryal, in a serious thought
   P.   85 FLECKNO   91 He thought himself affronted; and reply'd,
   P.   86 FLECKNO   140 Not one Word, thought and swore that they were
                    good.
   P. 111 ANNIVERSARY   329 But thought him when he miss'd his setting beams,
   P. 132 PARADISE   27 Thou hast not miss'd one thought that could be
                    fit,
   P. 137 HOUSEWARMING   4 'Twas the season he thought to turn Architect.
   P. 137 HOUSEWARMING   19 He thought (as an Instrument he was most free
                    on)
   P. 142 INSTRUCTIONS   47 But thought the Golden Age was now restor'd,
   P. 144 INSTRUCTIONS   122 And thought all lost that goest not to the
                    Cheats:
   P. 144 INSTRUCTIONS   160 Thought yet but Picneers, and led by Steward.
   P. 147 INSTRUCTIONS   270 And with that thought does multiply his Soul:
   P. 150 INSTRUCTIONS   400 And thought all safe if they were so far off.
   P. 150 INSTRUCTIONS   401 Modern Geographers, 'twas there they thought,
   P. 156 INSTRUCTIONS   621 Of former Glories the reproachful thought,
   P. 156 INSTRUCTIONS   642 Daniel then thought he was in Lyons Den.
   P. 172 LOYALL SCOT   11 For those soft Airs had temper'd every thought,
   P. 179 STOCKSMARKET   5 Some thought it a knightly and generous deed,
   P. 180 STOCKSMARKET   33 But, Sir Knight of the Vine, how came't in
                    your thought
   P. 188 BRITANNIA   135 Present to his thought his long scorn'd
                    Parliament
   P. 190 STATUE   30 That the Treasurer thought prudent to Try it
                    again,
   P. 191 STATUE   49 But the Treasurer told her he thought she was
                    mad
   P. 199 DUKE   57 Was thought soe meeke, soe prudent and soe wise:

thoughts   frequency: 12   relative frequency: 0.0002
   P.   12 DROP OF DEW   25 Does, in its pure and circling thoughts, express
   P.   45 MOWER'S SONG   6 What I do to the Grass, does to my Thoughts
                    and Me.
   P.   45 MOWER'S SONG   12 What I do to the Grass, does to my Thoughts
                    and Me.
   P.   45 MOWER'S SONG   18 What I do to the Grass, does to my Thoughts
                    and Me.
   P.   45 MOWER'S SONG   24 What I do to the Grass, does to my Thoughts
                    and Me.
   P.   46 MOWER'S SONG   26 Companions of my thoughts more green,
   P.   46 MOWER'S SONG   30 What I do to the Grass, does to my Thoughts
                    and Me.

```
P.   61 A. HOUSE       96 (As 'twere by Chance) Thoughts long conceiv'd.
P.   77 A. HOUSE      599 Who, as my Hair, my Thoughts too shed,
P.   94 DR. WITTY      25 Her thoughts are English, though her sparkling
                          wit
P.  128 O.C.          215 And 'twould be found, could we his thoughts have
                          cast,
P.  163 INSTRUCTIONS  905 In his deep thoughts the wonder did increase,
```

thou'lt   frequency: 1   relative frequency: 0.0000
```
P.  313 CHEQUER INN    22 Thou'lt ken him out by a white Wand
```

thousand   frequency: 9   relative frequency: 0.0001
```
P.    5 HASTINGS       56 All Herbs, and them a thousand ways infus'd?
P.   26 MISTRESS       16 But thirty thousand to the rest.
P.   30 THE GALLERY    41 These Pictures and a thousand more,
P.   63 A. HOUSE      136 'Enough a thousand Saints to make.
P.  144 INSTRUCTIONS  133 A thousand Hands she has and thousand Eyes,
P.  149 INSTRUCTIONS  332 Bought off with Eighteen hundred thousand pound.
P.  152 INSTRUCTIONS  492 (The Eighteen hundred thousand pound was gone.)
P.  200 DUKE           90 Ten thousand such as these can nere controule
```

thousands   frequency: 2   relative frequency: 0.0000
```
P.  117 BLAKE         127 Thousands of wayes, Thousands of men there dye,
```

thrace   frequency: 1   relative frequency: 0.0000
```
P.  137 HOUSEWARMING   13 He had read of Rhodope, a Lady of Thrace,
```

thrash'd   frequency: 1   relative frequency: 0.0000
```
P.  126 O.C.         118 And thrash'd the Harvest in the airy floore;
```

thrastles   frequency: 1   relative frequency: 0.0000
```
P.   75 A. HOUSE     532 The hatching Thrastles shining Eye,
```

thread   frequency: 3   relative frequency: 0.0000
```
See also "thred."
P.   78 A. HOUSE     621 This, like a long and equal Thread,
P.   84 FLECKNO       65 The Needles Eye thread without any stich,
P.  163 INSTRUCTIONS 922 The purple thread about his Neck does show:
```

thread-bare   frequency: 1   relative frequency: 0.0000
```
P.  168 ADVICE       23 Place Falstaffs Regement of Thread-bare
                        Coates
```

threadbare. See "thread-bare," "thred-bare."

threads   frequency: 1   relative frequency: 0.0000
```
P.   66 A. HOUSE     253 While the disjointed Abbess threads
```

threat   frequency: 1   relative frequency: 0.0000
```
P.  111 ANNIVERSARY  344 Seem'd now a long and gloomy Night to threat,
```

threaten   frequency: 3   relative frequency: 0.0000
```
P.  151 INSTRUCTIONS 430 Threaten to beat us, and are naughty Boys.
P.  152 INSTRUCTIONS 462 Their Fleet, to threaten, we will give them all.
P.  161 INSTRUCTIONS 834 And threaten Hyde to raise a greater Dust.
```

threatening. See "threatning," "threat'ning."

threatens   frequency: 1   relative frequency: 0.0000
```
P.  129 O.C.        260 That threatens death, he yet will live again.
```

threatned   frequency: 1   relative frequency: 0.0000
```
P.   86 FLECKNO     114 Did, as he threatned, ere 'twere long intend
```

threatning   frequency: 1   relative frequency: 0.0000
```
P.  137 HOUSEWARMING  3 At once three Deluges threatning our Land;
```

threat'ning   frequency: 1   relative frequency: 0.0000
```
P.  109 ANNIVERSARY 268 And threat'ring Rocks misapprehend for Land;
```

threats   frequency: 1   relative frequency: 0.0000
```
P.  131 O.C.        324 He threats no deluge, yet foretells a showre.
```

thred   frequency: 1   relative frequency: 0.0000
```
P.  107 ANNIVERSARY 183 Like skilful Looms which through the costly
                        thred
```

thred-bare   frequency: 1   relative frequency: 0.0000
```
P.  186 BRITANNIA    72 'Are thred-bare Virtues Ornaments for Kings?
```

three   frequency: 12   relative frequency: 0.0002

P.   83 FLECKNO   7 For Poetry: There three Stair-Cases high,
P.   83 FLECKNO   11 Not higher then Seav'n, nor larger then three
                            feet;
P.   85 FLECKNO   100 Two make a crowd, nor can three Persons here
P. 112 ANNIVERSARY   362 'Arm'd with three Tire of brazen Hurricans;
P. 137 HOUSEWARMING   3 At once three Deluges threatning our Land;
P. 148 INSTRUCTIONS   313 The Seamens Clamour to three ends they use;
P. 156 INSTRUCTIONS   647 Three Children tall, unsing'd, away they row,
P. 161 INSTRUCTIONS   840 And for three days, thence moves them to adjourn.
P. 180 STOCKSMARKET   46 With three shattered planks and the rags of a
                            sail
P. 187 BRITANNIA   100 Three spotless virgins to your bed I bring,
P. 193 TWO HORSES   59 W. That a King should consume three Realms
                            whole Estates
P. 195 TWO HORSES   129 Both Infamous Stand in three Kingdoms votes,

three-fork'd   frequency: 1   relative frequency: 0.0000
P.   87 ODE   13 And, like the three-fork'd Lightning, first

threw   frequency: 3   relative frequency: 0.0000
P.   44 DAMON   73 While thus he threw his Elbow round,
P. 182 MADE FREE   41 The Money he threw
P. 316 CHEQUER INN   154 But downe the Visick Bottle threw

thrice   frequency: 7   relative frequency: 0.0001
P.   40 THE MATCH   22 With Nitre thrice refin'd;
P.   77 A. HOUSE   583 Thrice happy he whc, not mistook,
P. 148 INSTRUCTIONS   294 But sure the Devil cannot cheat them thrice.
P. 163 INSTRUCTIONS   911 Thrice did he rise, thrice the vain Tumult fled,
P. 182 MADE FREE   56 Were thrice growne so rude,
P. 203 HISTORICALL   108 Thrice wretched they who natures Lawes detest

thrifty   frequency: 1   relative frequency: 0.0000
P. 145 INSTRUCTIONS   195 Then comes the thrifty Troop of Privateers,

thrive   frequency: 2   relative frequency: 0.0000
P.   22 NYMPH   3 Ungentle men! They cannot thrive
P. 178 LOYALL SCOT   272 The Insect Kingdome streight begins to thrive

thrives   frequency: 1   relative frequency: 0.0000
P. 204 HISTORICALL   134 Ill luck starts up and thrives like Evil weeds.

thro   frequency: 1   relative frequency: 0.0000

thro'   frequency: 1   relative frequency: 0.0000

throat   frequency: 2   relative frequency: 0.0000
P.   71 A. HOUSE   416 And 'tis the Sourdine in their Throat.
P. 163 INSTRUCTIONS   938 That who does cut his Purse will cut his
                            Throat.

throats   frequency: 2   relative frequency: 0.0000
P. 195 TWO HORSES   130 This for picking our Pocketts, that for cutting
                            our Throats.
P. 199 DUKE   72 And will cutt throats againe if he bee paid:

throbs   frequency: 1   relative frequency: 0.0000
P. 162 INSTRUCTIONS   898 Her heart throbs, and with very shame would
                            break.

throgmorton   frequency: 1   relative frequency: 0.0000
P. 315 CHEQUER INN   110 Throgmorton, Nevill, Doleman were

throne   frequency: 11   relative frequency: 0.0002
P. 106 ANNIVERSARY   128 Pursues the Monster thorough every Throne:
P. 162 INSTRUCTIONS   890 He wakes and Muses of th' uneasie Throne:
P. 164 INSTRUCTIONS   961 Would she the unattended Throne reduce,
P. 168 ADVICE   13 Where draw Sir Edward mounted on his throne,
P. 185 BRITANNIA   27 Such slimy Monsters ne're approacht a throne
P. 185 BRITANNIA   46 How, like ripe fruit, she dropt from of the
                            Throne
P. 188 BRITANNIA   136 (The Bassis of his throne and Government);
P. 192 TWO HORSES   43 W. To see dei Gratia writ on the Throne,
P. 199 DUKE   49 Had called you tc a sound though petty Throne,
P. 200 DUKE   102 At last take pitty of thy tottering throne,
P. 205 HISTORICALL   166 And in his stead had plac'd him on his Throne.

throng   frequency: 2   relative frequency: 0.0000
P.   91 MAY'S DEATH   28 Prest for his place among the Learned throng.
P. 105 ANNIVERSARY   86 Into the Animated City throng.

throstle's. See "thrastles."

through   frequency: 78   relative frequency: 0.0016

See also "thro," "thro'."

throughout   frequency: 1   relative frequency: 0.0000

throw   frequency: 4   relative frequency: 0.0000
    P. 96 HOLLAND   36 Would throw their Land away at Duck and Drake.
    P. 130 O.C.   311 But open'd once, what splendour does he throw?
    P. 140 HOUSEWARMING 102 Throw dust in its Front, and blame situation:
    P. 143 INSTRUCTIONS 114 For the Cheat Turner for them both must throw.

th'row   frequency: 1   relative frequency: 0.0000

throwest. See "throw'st."

thrown   frequency: 1   relative frequency: 0.0000
    See also "throwne."
    P. 32 MOURNING   24 Like Grief, is from her Windows thrown.

throwne   frequency: 1   relative frequency: 0.0000
    P. 198 DUKE   11 Throwne att thy sacred feete I humbly bow,

throws   frequency: 2   relative frequency: 0.0000
    P. 17 BERMUDAS   22 And throws the Melons at our feet.
    P. 104 ANNIVERSARY   59 Now through the Strings a Martial rage he
                            throws,

throw'st   frequency: 1   relative frequency: 0.0000
    P. 30 THE GALLERY   31 And (when inform'd) them throw'st away,

thrust   frequency: 2   relative frequency: 0.0000
    P. 56 BILL-BOROW   10 Which to abrupter greatness thrust,
    P. 74 A. HOUSE   502 To thrust up a Fifth Element;

thunder   frequency: 7   relative frequency: 0.0001
    P. 28 LOVER   23 While round the ratling Thunder hurl'd,
    P. 28 LOVER   50 Cuffing the Thunder with one hand;
    P. 126 O.C.   113 First the great Thunder was shot off, and sent
    P. 126 O.C.   116 As practising how they could thunder too:
    P. 149 INSTRUCTIONS 358 Blasted with Lightning, struck with Thunder
                            fell.
    P. 150 INSTRUCTIONS 372 To forge new Thunder, and inspect their Fires.
    P. 154 INSTRUCTIONS 557 With Thunder and Lightning from each armed
                            Cloud;

thunder'd   frequency: 1   relative frequency: 0.0000
    P. 58 BILL-BOROW   67 Through Groves of Pikes he thunder'd then,

thunderer. See "thund'rer."

thundering. See "thundring," "thund'ring."

thunders   frequency: 1   relative frequency: 0.0000
    P. 163 INSTRUCTIONS 912 But again thunders when he lyes in Bed;

thund'rer   frequency: 1   relative frequency: 0.0000
    P. 16 EYES   39 Yea oft the Thund'rer pitty takes

thundring   frequency: 2   relative frequency: 0.0000
    P. 107 ANNIVERSARY   169 Thou, who so oft through Storms of thundring
                            Lead
    P. 112 ANNIVERSARY   363 'That through the Center shoot their thundring
                            side

thund'ring   frequency: 1   relative frequency: 0.0000
    P. 117 BLAKE   119 The Thund'ring Cannon now begins the Fight,

t'hunt   frequency: 1   relative frequency: 0.0000
    P. 204 HISTORICALL   140 T'hunt down 's Prey and hope to master all.

thurland   frequency: 1   relative frequency: 0.0000
    P. 145 INSTRUCTIONS 186 Finch, in the Front, and Thurland in the Rear.

thus   frequency: 53   relative frequency: 0.0011

thwaites   frequency: 2   relative frequency: 0.0000
    See also "thwates."
    P. 67 A. HOUSE   263 But truly bright and holy Thwaites
    P. 82 A. HOUSE   748 And find a Fairfax for our Thwaites)

thwart   frequency: 1   relative frequency: 0.0000
    See also "over-thwart."
    P. 105 ANNIVERSARY   90 Fast'ning the Contignation which they thwart;

thwates   frequency: 1   relative frequency: 0.0000
    P.   61 A. HOUSE   90 There dwelt the blooming Virgin Thwates;

thy   frequency: 132   relative frequency: 0.0027

thyeste   frequency: 1   relative frequency: 0.0000
    P.   54 THYESTE   t Senec. Traged. ex Thyeste Chor. 2.

thyrsis   frequency: 10   relative frequency: 0.0002
    P.   19 THYRSIS   t A Dialogue between Thyrsis and Dorinda.
    P.   19 THYRSIS   3 Tell me Thyrsis, prethee do,
    P.   19 THYRSIS   5 Thyrsis. To the Elizium: (Dorinda) oh where
                              i'st?
    P.   19 THYRSIS   6 Thyrsis. A Chast Soul, can never mis't.
    P.   19 THYRSIS   9 Thyrsis. Turn thine Eye to yonder Skie,
    P.   19 THYRSIS   15 Thyrsis. Do not sigh (fair Nimph) for fire
    P.   19 THYRSIS   21 Thyrsis. Oh, ther's, neither hope nor fear
    P.   20 THYRSIS   31 Thyrsis. Then I'le go on: There, sheep are
                              full
    P.   20 THYRSIS   39 Dorinda. Ah me, ah me. (Thyrsis.) Dorinda, why
                              do'st Cry?
    P.   20 THYRSIS   43 Thyrsis. I cannot live, without thee, I

tiber. See "tybur."

tiberius   frequency: 1   relative frequency: 0.0000
    P. 202 HISTORICALL   67 Outdoes Tiberius and his Goatish Court:

tickle   frequency: 1   relative frequency: 0.0000
    P. 162 INSTRUCTIONS   875 Whence ev'ry day, the Palat more to tickle;

tickles   frequency: 1   relative frequency: 0.0000
    P. 143 INSTRUCTIONS   96 His sweaty Hooves, tickles him 'twixt the Toes.

tide   frequency: 4   relative frequency: 0.0000
    P.   26 MISTRESS   6 Should'st Rubies find: I by the Tide
    P.   79 A. HOUSE   644 Stretcht as a Bank unto the Tide;
    P.   94 DR. WITTY   28 Down into Error with the Vulgar tide;
    P. 159 INSTRUCTIONS   759 The Thames roar'd, swouning Medway turn'd her
                              tide,

tides   frequency: 1   relative frequency: 0.0000
    See also "tydes."
    P. 158 INSTRUCTIONS   704 Fraughting their pierced Keels with Oosy
                              Tides.

tie. See "tye."

ties. See "tyes."

tigellinus. See "tegeline."

tigress. See "tygress."

till   frequency: 54   relative frequency: 0.0011
    P.   3 LOVELACE   25 Till when in vaine they have thee all perus'd,
    P.   11 DIALOGUE   59 Till thou purchase all below,
    P.   12 DROP OF DEW   17 Till the warm Sun pitty it's Pain,
    P.   17 EYES   54 Till Eyes and Tears be the same things:
    P.   18 BERMUDAS   34 Till it arrive at Heavens Vault:
    P.   19 THYRSIS   17 Till it hit, against the pole,
    P.   20 THYRSIS   47 In wine, and drink on't even till we weep,
    P.   23 NYMPH   79 Yet could not, till it self would rise,
    P.   24 NYMPH   103 It till it do o'reflow with mine;
    P.   26 MISTRESS   10 Till the Conversion of the Jews.
    P.   27 LOVER   13 Till at the last the master-Wave
    P.   33 DAPHNIS   25 Till Love in her Language breath'd
    P.   40 THE MATCH   29 Till, by vicinity so long,
    P.   41 THE MOWER   35 And Fauns and Faryes do the Meadows till,
    P.   49 THE GARDEN   55 And, till prepar'd for longer flight,
    P.   64 A. HOUSE   168 'Till Miracles it work at last.
    P.   66 A. HOUSE   245 Till one, as long since prophecy'd,
    P.   67 A. HOUSE   280 'Twas no Religicus House till now.
    P.   70 A. HOUSE   354 Ambition weed, but Conscience till.
    P.   78 A. HOUSE   636 Till as a Chrystal Mirrour slick;
    P.   82 A. HOUSE   747 (Till Fate her worthily translates,
    P.   84 FLECKNO   35 Till the Tyrant, weary to persecute,
    P.   84 FLECKNO   58 But till he had himself a Body made.
    P.   84 FLECKNO   59 I mean till he were drest: for else so thin
    P.   98 HOLLAND   130 Till the dear Halcyon hatch out all its nest.
    P. 106 ANNIVERSARY   125 Till then my Muse shall hollow far behind

P.	109	ANNIVERSARY	233	Till at the Seventh time thou in the Skyes,
P.	110	ANNIVERSARY	286	Which thou but as an Husbandman wouldst Till:
P.	121	TWO SONGS	5	Stay till I some flow'rs ha' ty'd
P.	139	HOUSEWARMING	96	And till there you remove, you shall never leave burning
P.	147	INSTRUCTIONS	248	Fighting it single till the rest might arm.
P.	150	INSTRUCTIONS	380	And beats the Husband till for peace he prays:
P.	160	INSTRUCTIONS	816	Till it be govern'd by a Convocation.
P.	161	INSTRUCTIONS	825	And 'twixt Necessity and Spight, till then,
P.	161	INSTRUCTIONS	854	Expects as at a Play till Turner's drest.
P.	178	LOYALL SCOT	270	Powders them ore till none discern their foes
P.	185	BRITANNIA	14	Till England knowes who did her Citty burn,
P.	185	BRITANNIA	15	Till Cavaleers shall favorites be Deem'd
P.	185	BRITANNIA	17	Till Howard and Garway shall a bribe reject,
P.	185	BRITANNIA	18	Till Golden Osborn cheating shall detect,
P.	185	BRITANNIA	19	Till Atheist Lauderdale shall leave this Land,
P.	185	BRITANNIA	20	Till commons votes shall cut-nose guards disband,
P.	185	BRITANNIA	21	Till Kate a happy mother shall become,
P.	185	BRITANNIA	22	Till Charles loves Parliaments, till James hates Rome.
P.	187	BRITANNIA	103	Rack nature till new pleasures she shall find,
P.	188	BRITANNIA	161	Till then, my Rawleigh, teach our noble Youth
P.	194	TWO HORSES	119	Till at last on a Scaffold he was left in the lurch
P.	198	DUKE	14	Till all this nation to thy footstoole bend.
P.	200	DUKE	117	Till the stroke is struck which they can nere repreive.
P.	203	HISTORICALL	110	Till native Reason's basely forct to yield
P.	313	CHEQUER INN	15	Till he was Burgesse chosen
P.	314	CHEQUER INN	57	Till to sit downe were desir'd
P.	316	CHEQUER INN	158	Till King both Hostesse kist and Host

tillage   frequency: 1   relative frequency: 0.0000
P.	97	HOLLAND	77	Nor can Civility there want for Tillage,

till'd   frequency: 1   relative frequency: 0.0000
P.	81	A. HOUSE	736	And Virtue all those Furrows till'd.

timber   frequency: 7   relative frequency: 0.0001
P.	74	A. HOUSE	486	Fit Timber for his Keel have Prest.
P.	75	A. HOUSE	540	Meas'ring the Timber with his Foot;
P.	138	HOUSEWARMING	48	To grudge him some Timber who fram'd them the War.
P.	148	INSTRUCTIONS	319	The Timber rots, and useless Ax does rust,
P.	154	INSTRUCTIONS	575	For whose strong bulk Earth scarce could Timber find,
P.	158	INSTRUCTIONS	721	Once a deep River, now with Timber floor'd,
P.	316	CHEQUER INN	140	The Belly Timber that they fell'd

timbers   frequency: 1   relative frequency: 0.0000
P.	158	INSTRUCTIONS	728	Her Masts erect, tough Cordage, Timbers strong,

time   frequency: 47   relative frequency: 0.0009
See also "tyme."
P.	4	LOVELACE	47	But he secure of glory and of time
P.	10	DIALOGUE	41	Had I but any time to lose,
P.	11	DIALOGUE	70	And see the future Time:
P.	18	BERMUDAS	40	With falling Oars they kept the time.
P.	20	THYRSIS	29	I prethee let us spend our time to come
P.	22	NYMPH	38	My solitary time away,
P.	23	NYMPH	52	Could in so short a time espie,
P.	23	NYMPH	75	And all the Spring time of the year
P.	25	YOUNG LOVE	6	By young Love old Time beguil'd:
P.	25	YOUNG LOVE	17	Now then love me: time may take
P.	25	YOUNG LOVE	18	Thee before thy time away:
P.	26	MISTRESS	1	Had we but World enough, and Time,
P.	27	LOVER	8	To make impression upon Time.
P.	27	MISTRESS	39	Rather at once our Time devour,
P.	34	DAPHNIS	29	For, Alas, the time was spent,
P.	38	PICTURE	17	O then let me in time compound,
P.	38	PICTURE	25	Mean time, whilst every verdant thing
P.	50	THE GARDEN	70	Computes its time as well as we.
P.	82	A. HOUSE	745	Mean time ye Fields, Springs, Bushes, Flow'rs,
P.	87	FLECKNO	165	With truth. I counsell'd him to go in time,
P.	87	ODE	5	'Tis time to leave the Books in dust,
P.	88	ODE	34	To ruine the great Work of Time,
P.	92	MAY'S DEATH	65	Then is the Poets time, 'tis then he drawes,
P.	98	HOLLAND	127	That ours mean time at leizure might careen,
P.	103	ANNIVERSARY	6	While flowing Time above his Head does close.

```
P. 103 ANNIVERSARY      13 'Tis he the force cf scatter'd Time contracts,
P. 104 ANNIVERSARY      41 Thus (Image-like) an useless time they tell,
P. 104 ANNIVERSARY      58 And still new Stopps to various Time apply'd:
P. 106 ANNIVERSARY     120 Leisure to Time, and to my Weakness Strength,
P. 106 ANNIVERSARY     139 Fore-shortned Time its useless Course would
                          stay,
P. 109 ANNIVERSARY     233 Till at the Seventh time thou in the Skyes,
P. 109 ANNIVERSARY     264 Th' ambitious Shrubs thou in just time didst aw.
P. 126 O.C.            141 No part of time but bore his mark away
P. 130 O.C.            285 As long as future time succeeds the past,
P. 141 INSTRUCTIONS      2 To end her Picture, does the third time wait.
P. 146 INSTRUCTIONS    234 Who in a time cf Treaty durst invade.
P. 148 INSTRUCTIONS    317 Mean time through all the Yards their Orders
                          run
P. 152 INSTRUCTIONS    471 His Writing-Master many a time he bann'd,
P. 157 INSTRUCTIONS    665 But entertains, the while, his time too short
P. 157 INSTRUCTIONS    698 The Loyal-lcndcn, now a third time burns.
P. 159 INSTRUCTIONS    741 And constant Time, to keep his course yet right,
P. 159 INSTRUCTIONS    772 Whc treated out the time at Bergen? Pett.
P. 168 KINGS VOWES      65 And pass my Time with Parrasites and Players,
P. 177 LOYALL SCOT     225 The second time to Bavish Proserpine.
P. 178 LOYALL SCOT     284 Forwarn'd him therefore lest in time he were
P. 190 STATUE           12 Any monument hcw their time they mispend.
P. 314 CHEQUER INN      70 For ev'n at Bed the time has beene
```

timely   frequency: 2   relative frequency: 0.0000
```
P. 109 ANNIVERSARY     261 Whose climbing Flame, withcut a timely stop,
P. 201 HISTORICALL      28 To wish her hopeful Issue timely Joy.
```

times   frequency: 13   relative frequency: 0.0002
See also "oft-times," "tymes."
```
P.   3 LOVELACE          1 Our times are much degenerate from those
P.   3 LOVELACE          4 Our wits have drawne th' infection of our times.
P.   4 HASTINGS         12 And cn Times Wheel sticks like a Remora.
P.  26 MISTRESS         22 Times winged Charriot hurrying near:
P.  36 DAPHNIS          85 Gentler times fcr Love are ment
P.  84 FLECKNO          70 And swaddled in's cwn papers seaven times,
P.  92 MAY'S DEATH      69 Sings still of ancient Rights and better Times,
P. 106 ANNIVERSARY     144 If these the Times, then this must be the Man.
P. 129 O.C.            271 So shall his praise to after times encrease,
P. 140 HOUSEWARMING    105 But do not consider how in process of times,
P. 194 TWO HORSES       98 Yet truth many times being punisht for Treason,
P. 196 TWO HORSES      188 Theres ten times mcre Treason in Brandy and
                          ale.
P. 201 HISTORICALL      17 But the best times have ever some mishap;
```

t'immure   frequency: 1   relative frequency: 0.0000
```
P.  60 A. HOUSE         45 Let others vainly strive t'immure
```

timorous. See "tim'rous."

t'impark   frequency: 1   relative frequency: 0.0000
```
P.  59 A. HOUSE         22 T'impark the wantcn Mcte of Dust,
```

tim'rous   frequency: 2   relative frequency: 0.0000
```
P. 127 O.C.            180 And tim'rous Ccnscience unto Courage man'd:
P. 151 INSTRUCTIONS    412 More tim'rous ncw we are, than first secure.
```

tinkles   frequency: 1   relative frequency: 0.0000
```
P.  18 CLORINDA         14 Tinkles within the concave Shell.
```

tinkling   frequency: 2   relative frequency: 0.0000
```
P.  76 A. HOUSE        547 But where he, tinkling with his Beak,
P. 132 PARADISE         46 With tinkling Rhime, cf thy own Sense secure;
```

tinsel   frequency: 1   relative frequency: 0.0000
```
P.  37 DEFINITION        8 But vainly flapt its Tinsel Wing.
```

t'invite   frequency: 1   relative frequency: 0.0000
```
P.  73 A. HOUSE        470 It try's t'invite him thus away.
```

tippets   frequency: 1   relative frequency: 0.0000
```
P. 176 LOYALL SCOT     173 Cf Rochets Tippets Copes, and wheres theire
                          Grace?
```

tipt   frequency: 1   relative frequency: 0.0000
```
P.  42 DAMON            38 And Oak leaves tipt with hony due.
```

tire   frequency: 2   relative frequency: 0.0000
```
P. 112 ANNIVERSARY     362 'Arm'd with three Tire cf brazen Hurricans;
P. 148 INSTRUCTIONS    326 Load them with Envy, and with Sitting tire:
```

tired   frequency: 1   relative frequency: 0.0000
      P. 168 ADVICE   7 Whilest the brave youths tired with the work of
                                 State

tires   frequency: 1   relative frequency: 0.0000
      P. 132 PARADISE   48 And like a Pack-Horse tires without his Bells.

tiresias   frequency: 1   relative frequency: 0.0000
      P. 132 PARADISE   43 Just Heav'n Thee, like Tiresias, to requite,

tis   frequency: 6   relative frequency: 0.0001

'tis   frequency: 51   relative frequency: 0.0010
      See also "tis."

tithe. See "tyth."

title   frequency: 4   relative frequency: 0.0000
      P. 97 HOLLAND   79 How fit a Title clothes their Governours,
      P. 112 ANNIVERSARY   391 'O could I once him with our Title see,
      P. 141 INSTRUCTIONS   35 Well he the Title of St. Albans bore,
      P. 152 INSTRUCTIONS   456 Who yields his Sword has Title to his Life.

titles   frequency: 1   relative frequency: 0.0000
      P. 25 YOUNG LOVE   26 Other Titles to their Crown,

tittle   frequency: 1   relative frequency: 0.0000
      P. 194 TWO HORSES   106 I'le prove every tittle of what I have said.

to   frequency: 1047   relative frequency: 0.0219
      See also "t'," "t'admit," "t'america,"
               "t'enjoy," "t'enslave,"
               "t'ensnare," "t'have," "t'hunt,"
               "t'immure," "t'impark," "t'invite,"
               "t'unite."

toad   frequency: 2   relative frequency: 0.0000
      P. 162 INSTRUCTIONS   877 When Grievance urg'd, he swells like squatted
                                 Toad,
      P. 176 LOYALL SCOT   177 Like Snake that Swallowes toad doth Dragon
                                 swell.

toast   frequency: 1   relative frequency: 0.0000
      P. 162 INSTRUCTIONS   882 And soaks his Sack with Norfolk like a Toast.

toback   frequency: 1   relative frequency: 0.0000
      P. 147 INSTRUCTIONS   280 Spent with fatigue, to breath a while Toback.

toes   frequency: 1   relative frequency: 0.0000
      P. 143 INSTRUCTIONS   96 His sweaty Hooves, tickles him 'twixt the Toes.

togeather   frequency: 3   relative frequency: 0.0000
      P. 192 TWO HORSES   30 One night came togeather by all is agreed,
      P. 195 TWO HORSES   160 Thy oppression togeather with Kingship shall
                                 dye.
      P. 200 DUKE   104 Let not thy life and crowne togeather end,

together   frequency: 9   relative frequency: 0.0001
      See also "togeather."
      P. 39 THE MATCH   13 But likeness soon together drew
      P. 64 A. HOUSE   190 'As Pearls together billeted.
      P. 82 A. HOUSE   762 But a rude heap together hurl'd;
      P. 85 FLECKNO   109 Together our attonement: so increas'd
      P. 98 HOLLAND   104 When their whole Navy they together prest,
      P. 105 ANNIVERSARY   75 The Commonwealth then first together came,
      P. 114 BLAKE   36 Fewel and Rain together kindly grow;
      P. 150 INSTRUCTIONS   369 While Chain'd together two Ambassadors
      P. 161 INSTRUCTIONS   855 At last together Eaten come and he:

toil   frequency: 1   relative frequency: 0.0000
      See also "toyl," "toyle."
      P. 43 DAMON   45 And, if at Noon my toil me heat,

toils. See "toyles," "toyls."

token   frequency: 3   relative frequency: 0.0000
      P. 179 STOCKSMARKET   3 So Sir Robert advanced the King's statue, in
                                 token
      P. 190 STATUE   40 Shall a Treasurer of Guinny a Prince Grudge
                                 of Token?
      P. 193 TWO HORSES   62 No token should appear but a poor Copper farthing;

```
told                              frequency:   6     relative frequency: 0.0001
     P.  127 O.C.          176 Whether of British Saints or Worthy's told;
     P.  173 LOYALL SCOT    65 Shall not a death soe Generous now when told
     P.  191 STATUE         49 But the Treasurer told her he thought she was
                               mad
     P.  192 TWO HORSES     26 Who have told many truths well worth a mans
                               hearing,
     P.  196 TWO HORSES    167 But I should have told ycu, before the Jades
                               parted,
     P.  317 CHEQUER INN   187 By wise Volke, I have oft been told

tolerable                         frequency:   1     relative frequency: 0.0000
     P.  195 TWO HORSES    131 Ch. More Tolerable are the Lion Kings
                               Slaughters

tom                               frequency:   2     relative frequency: 0.0000
     P.   90 MAY'S DEATH     t Tom May's Death.
     P.   90 MAY'S DEATH     2 Tom May was hurry'd hence and did not know't.

tomalin                           frequency:   4     relative frequency: 0.0000
     P.  121 TWO SONGS       1 Phillis, Tomalin, away:
     P.  121 TWO SONGS      6+ Tomalin.
     P.  121 TWO SONGS     t5+ Hobbinol. Phillis. Tomalin. Hobbinol.
     P.  122 TWO SONGS     16+ Tomalin.

tomb                              frequency:   3     relative frequency: 0.0000
     See also "tombe."
     P.   46 MOWER'S SONG   28 With which I shall adorn my Tomb;
     P.  126 O.C.          123 The Race of warlike Horses at his Tomb
     P.  150 INSTRUCTIONS  408 And on Pasiphae's Tomb tc drop a Bead.

tombe                             frequency:   1     relative frequency: 0.0000
     P.  130 O.C.          300 Wander like ghosts about thy loved tombe;

tome                              frequency:   1     relative frequency: 0.0000
     P.  110 ANNIVERSARY   305 While Feake and Simpson would in many a Tome,

tomkins                           frequency:   3     relative frequency: 0.0000
     P.  146 INSTRUCTIONS  223 Nor the late Feather-men, whom Tomkins fierce
     P.  161 INSTRUCTIONS  841 Not so, quoth Tcmkins; and straight drew his
                               Tongue,
     P.  161 INSTRUCTIONS  852 Lest some new Tcmkins spring a fresh debate.

tone                              frequency:   1     relative frequency: 0.0000
     P.   83 FLECKNO        20 In hideous verse, he, and a dismal tone,

tongue                            frequency:  10     relative frequency: 0.0002
     P.   65 A. HOUSE      200 The Nuns smooth Tcngue has suckt her in.
     P.   84 FLECKNO        50 With gristly Tcngue to dart the passing Flyes.
     P.   91 MAY'S DEATH    27 Yet then with fcot as stumbling as his tongue
     P.  107 ANNIVERSARY   168 And always hast thy Tongue from fraud refrain'd;
     P.  137 HOUSEWARMING    20 To build with the Jews-trump of his cwn tongue.
     P.  143 INSTRUCTIONS    99 And he, unwary, and of Tongue too fleet,
     P.  161 INSTRUCTIONS   841 Not so, quoth Tomkins; and straight drew his
                               Tcngue,
     P.  171 PROPHECY        37 A Minister able only in his Tongue
     P.  194 TWO HORSES      99 Wee ought to be wary and Bridle our Tongue;
     P.  314 CHEQUER INN     85 Wild with his Tcngue did all outrun

tongues                           frequency:   4     relative frequency: 0.0000
     P.   66 A. HOUSE      256 And sharpest Weapons were their Tongues.
     P.   94 DR. WITTY      20 Now learns the tcngues of France and Italy;
     P.  189 BRITANNIA     176 On whose fam'd Deeds all tongues, all writers
                               wait.
     P.  191 TWO HORSES      6 Have spoken as plainly as men doe with Tongues:

too                               frequency:  75     relative frequency: 0.0015

took                              frequency:  14     relative frequency: 0.0002
     See also "o'r-took," "tooke."
     P.   22 NYMPH          36 Left me his Faun, but took his Heart.
     P.   30 THE GALLERY    52 Remains, with which I first was took.
     P.   34 DAPHNIS        44 Thus his Leave resolved tcok.
     P.   83 FLECKNO         3 I tor some branch cf Melchizedeck took,
     P.  104 ANNIVERSARY    24 Took in ty Proxie, beggs a false Renown;
     P.  104 ANNIVERSARY    53 This took a Lower, that an Higher place,
     P.  112 ANNIVERSARY   370 'But that once tcok, we Captives are on Land.
     P.  142 INSTRUCTIONS    48 When Men and Women took each others Word.
     P.  145 INSTRUCTIONS   169 Court-Officers, as us'd, the next place took,
```

```
      P. 161 INSTRUCTIONS  839 Tells them he at Whitehall had took a turn,
      P. 172 LOYALL SCCT    12 And of wise Lethe hee had tcok a draught.
      P. 179 STOCKSMARKET   27 And what the exchequer for that took on trust
      P. 186 BRITANNIA      69 From th' easie King she truthes bright Mirrour
                               took,
      P. 316 CHEQUER INN   153 Nor of his cwne tcok care

tooke                         frequency:    3    relative frequency: 0.0000
      P. 202 HISTORICALL    43 The dreadfull Victcr tcoke his soft repose,
      P. 316 CHEQUER INN   155 And tooke his Wine when it was due
      P. 316 CHEQUER INN   168 The Guests tcoke all away

tool                          frequency:    2    relative frequency: 0.0000
      P. 169 ADVICE         48 With Cupid Seymcur and the Tool of State,
      P. 195 TWO HORSES    124 Ch. The King on thy Back is a Lamentable
                               Tool.

tools                         frequency:    1    relative frequency: 0.0000
      P. 141 INSTRUCTIONS   11 Sketching in shady smoke prodigious tools,

top                           frequency:    5    relative frequency: 0.0001
      P.  75 A. HOUSE      533 The Heron from the Ashes top,
      P. 109 ANNIVERSARY   262 Had quickly Levell'd every Cedar's top.
      P. 120 TWO SONGS      35 Here unto Latmcs Tcp I climbe:
      P. 139 HOUSEWARMING   91 And shews on the tcp by the Regal Gilt Ball,
      P. 156 INSTRUCTIONS  620 Taught the Dutch Cclours from its top to wave;

top-masts                     frequency:    1    relative frequency: 0.0000
      P. 154 INSTRUCTIONS  539 While the red Flags breath on their Top-masts
                               high

topics.  See "topiks."

topiks                        frequency:    1    relative frequency: 0.0000
      P. 201 HISTORICALL    31 From the french Court she haughty Topiks
                               brings,

torches                       frequency:    2    relative frequency: 0.0000
      P.   5 HASTINGS       45 And trails his Tcrches th'row the Starry Hall
      P.  36 DAPHNIS        96 That Love in his Torches had.

tore                          frequency:    3    relative frequency: 0.0000
      See also "tare."
      P. 113 BLAKE           9 The new Worlds wcunded Intrails they had tore,
      P. 126 O.C.          117 Out of the Binders Hand the Sheaves they tore,
      P. 144 INSTRUCTIONS  132 Frighted the Midwife, and the Mother tore.

toril                         frequency:    1    relative frequency: 0.0000
      P.  72 A. HOUSE      447 Or rather such is the Toril

torment                       frequency:    1    relative frequency: 0.0000
      P.  30 THE GALLERY    44 Either to please me, cr tcrment:

tormenting                    frequency:    1    relative frequency: 0.0000
      P.  29 THE GALLERY    15 Cf which the mcst tormenting are

tormentor                     frequency:    1    relative frequency: 0.0000
      P.  86 FLECKNO       117 But now, Alas, my first Tcrmentor came,

torments                      frequency:    1    relative frequency: 0.0000
      P.  92 MAY'S DEATH    95 'Tis just what Torments Poets ere did feign,

torn                          frequency:    6    relative frequency: 0.0001
      P.  28 LOVER          54 Torn into Flames, and ragg'd with Wcunds.
      P.  38 PICTURE        14 See his Bow brcke and Ensigns torn.
      P.  98 HCLLAND       121 And the torn Navy stagger'd with him home,
      P. 118 BLAKE         133 Torn Limbs scme leagues into the Island fly,
      P. 180 STOCKSMARKET   47 To express how his navy was shattered and torn
      P. 188 BRITANNIA     146 To the Bleating Flcck by him so lately torn.

torrid                        frequency:    1    relative frequency: 0.0000
      P. 117 BLAKE         124 War turn'd the temperate, to the Torrid Zone.

tortoise                      frequency:    3    relative frequency: 0.0000
      P.  83 A. HOUSE      773 How Tortoise like, but nct so slow,
      P.  99 HOLLAND       139 Their Tortcise wants its vainly stretched neck;
      P. 159 INSTRUCTIONS  754 As the sad Tortoise for the Sea does groan.

tortoise-shell                frequency:    1    relative frequency: 0.0000
      P.  59 A. HOUSE       14 In cases fit of Tortoise-shell:

tortoises                     frequency:    1    relative frequency: 0.0000
```

```
        P.  59 A. HOUSE        13 The low roof'd Tortoises do dwell

tortur'd                      frequency:     2    relative frequency: 0.0000
        P.  20 SOUL & BODY      9 Tortur'd, besides each other part,
        P. 124 O.C.            54 And him within his tortur'd Image racks.

torture                       frequency:     1    relative frequency: 0.0000
        P.  34 DAPHNIS         46 More to torture him that dies?

tortures                      frequency:     1    relative frequency: 0.0000
        P. 126 O.C.           129 Such Tortures all the Elements unfix'd,

toss                          frequency:     1    relative frequency: 0.0000
        P.  77 A. HOUSE       593 Then, languishing with ease, I toss

tost                          frequency:     3    relative frequency: 0.0000
        P.  98 HOLLAND        111 A Cock-boat tost with the same wind and fate;
        P.  98 HOLLAND        125 While half their banish'd keels the Tempest
                                  tost,
        P. 107 ANNIVERSARY    157 Hence landing Nature to new Seas is tost,

total                         frequency:     1    relative frequency: 0.0000
        P. 148 INSTRUCTIONS   306 And the Excise receives a total Rout.

tottering                     frequency:     2    relative frequency: 0.0000
        P.  54 THYESTE          2 Tottering favors Pinacle;
        P. 200 DUKE           102 At last take pitty of thy tottering throne,

touch                         frequency:     7    relative frequency: 0.0001
        P.  63 A. HOUSE       131 'By it we would our Lady touch;
        P.  70 A. HOUSE       358 As that which shrinks at ev'ry touch;
        P. 104 ANNIVERSARY     61 Then as he strokes them with a Touch more sweet,
        P. 124 O.C.            60 Answers the touch in Notes more sad more true.
        P. 153 INSTRUCTIONS   507 Let no Man touch them, or demand his own,
        P. 163 INSTRUCTIONS   903 But soon shrunk back, chill'd with her touch so
                                  cold,
        P. 203 HISTORICALL    113 And touch the holy function with her Verse:

touched                       frequency:     1    relative frequency: 0.0000
        P.  84 FLECKNO         38 Being tun'd by Art, if the one touched be

touches                       frequency:     1    relative frequency: 0.0000
        P. 141 INSTRUCTIONS    28 What all thy softest touches cannot do.

toucheth                      frequency:     1    relative frequency: 0.0000
        P.  77 A. HOUSE       606 Can make, or me it toucheth not.

touching                      frequency:     1    relative frequency: 0.0000
        P.  12 DROP OF DEW     10 Scarce touching where it lyes,

tough                         frequency:     2    relative frequency: 0.0000
        P.  79 A. HOUSE       647 And in its Branches tough to hang,
        P. 158 INSTRUCTIONS   728 Her Masts erect, tough Cordage, Timbers
                                  strong,

tournaments. See "turraments."

towards                       frequency:     3    relative frequency: 0.0000

tower. See "tow'r."

tower-barge                   frequency:     1    relative frequency: 0.0000
        P. 140 HOUSEWARMING   108 At Tybourn may land, and spare the Tower-Barge.

towerest. See "tow'rst."

towering. See "towring."

towers                        frequency:     1    relative frequency: 0.0000
        See also "towrs."
        P.  14 THE CORONET      7 Dismantling all the fragrant Towers

towery. See "towry."

town                          frequency:     4    relative frequency: 0.0000
        See also "dunkirk-town," "hans-town," "towne."
        P. 104 ANNIVERSARY     23 Yet some more active for a Frontier Town
        P. 139 HOUSEWARMING    90 A Lanthorn, like Faux's surveys the burnt
                                  Town,
        P. 161 INSTRUCTIONS   845 True Trojan! while this Town can Girls afford,
        P. 190 STATUE          26 Had within it an Army that burnt up the Town:
```

town-bays   frequency: 1   relative frequency: 0.0000
    P. 132 PARADISE   47 While the Town-Bays writes all the while and
                              spells,

towne   frequency: 2   relative frequency: 0.0000
    P.   3 LOVELACE   11 These vertues now are banisht out of Towne,
    P. 201 HISTORICALL   34 The new got flemish Towne was sett to sale.

townes   frequency: 1   relative frequency: 0.0000
    P. 204 HISTORICALL   146 Our fleets our Forts our Cittyes and our
                              Townes

towns   frequency: 1   relative frequency: 0.0000
    See also "townes."
    P. 98 HOLLAND   95 Tunn'd up with all their sev'ral Towns of Beer;

tow'r   frequency: 5   relative frequency: 0.0001
    P. 104 ANNIVERSARY   60 And joyning streight the Theban Tow'r arose;
    P. 109 ANNIVERSARY   252 And Is'rel silent saw him rase the Tow'r;
    P. 149 INSTRUCTIONS   349 Now Mordant may, within his Castle Tow'r,
    P. 158 INSTRUCTIONS   706 The Tow'r it self with the near danger shook.
    P. 158 INSTRUCTIONS   714 The Houses were demolish'd near the Tow'r.

towring   frequency: 1   relative frequency: 0.0000
    P. 108 ANNIVERSARY   195 See how they each his towring Crest abate,

towrs   frequency: 1   relative frequency: 0.0000
    P. 69 A. HOUSE   331 When Gardens only had their Towrs,

tow'rst   frequency: 1   relative frequency: 0.0000
    P. 130 O.C.   288 Of humane glory tow'rst, and raigning there

towry   frequency: 1   relative frequency: 0.0000
    P. 186 BRITANNIA   65 Her Towry front a fiery Meteor bears

tow'ry. See "towry."

tows   frequency: 1   relative frequency: 0.0000
    P. 98 HOLLAND   110 It self, when as some greater Vessel tows

toy   frequency: 1   relative frequency: 0.0000
    P. 183 MADE FREE   103 And yet if our Toy

toyes   frequency: 1   relative frequency: 0.0000
    P. 79 A. HOUSE   654 Should with such Toyes a Man surprize;

toyl   frequency: 2   relative frequency: 0.0000
    P. 116 BLAKE   95 Yet they by restless toyl, became at Length,
    P. 175 LOYALL SCOT   126 Who that is wise would pulpit Toyl Indure?

toyle   frequency: 2   relative frequency: 0.0000
    P. 171 PROPHECY   52 With groans to fill his Treasure they must
                              toyle,
    P. 171 PROPHECY   53 But like the Bellydes shall toyle in vaine

toyles   frequency: 2   relative frequency: 0.0000
    P. 48 THE GARDEN   6 Does prudently their Toyles upbraid;
    P. 127 O.C.   155 Here ended all his mortal toyles: He lay'd

toyls   frequency: 1   relative frequency: 0.0000
    P. 175 LOYALL SCOT   160 Who views but Gilberts Toyls will reason find

toys   frequency: 1   relative frequency: 0.0000
    See also "toyes."
    P. 186 BRITANNIA   73 Such poor pedantick toys teach underlings.

trace   frequency: 2   relative frequency: 0.0000
    P. 69 A. HOUSE   338 And his more gentle Forts did trace.
    P. 123 O.C.   5 And thenceforth onely did attend to trace,

track   frequency: 3   relative frequency: 0.0000
    P. 130 O.C.   306 Beats on the rugged track: he, vertue dead,
    P. 143 INSTRUCTIONS   109 Those having lost the Nation at Trick track,
    P. 155 INSTRUCTIONS   582 They sail securely through the Rivers track.

trade   frequency: 7   relative frequency: 0.0001
    P. 144 INSTRUCTIONS   136 And on all Trade like Casawar she feeds:
    P. 168 ADVICE   5 The Roman takeing up the fencers trade,
    P. 175 LOYALL SCOT   133 Noe Church! noe Trade! noe king! noe people!
                              noe!
    P. 183 MADE FREE   78 He know's not his Trade, nor his Mist'ry.

P. 193 TWO HORSES	64	Not our trade to secure but foes to come at 'um,
P. 199 DUKE	73	I'th Irish shambles he first learn'd the trade.
P. 201 HISTORICALL	14	Things highly fitting for a Monarchs trade.

tradition   frequency: 1   relative frequency: 0.0000
    P. 85 FLECKNO   78 He heard of by Tradition, and redeem'd.

traffic. See "traffique."

traffique   frequency: 1   relative frequency: 0.0000
    P. 106 ANNIVERSARY 116 Nor teach, but traffique with, or burn the Jew.

traged.   frequency: 1   relative frequency: 0.0000
    P. 54 THYESTE   t Senec. Traged. ex Thyeste Chor. 2.

tragedy. See "traged."

tragick   frequency: 1   relative frequency: 0.0000
    P. 88 ODE   54 The Tragick Scaffold might adorn:

trails   frequency: 2   relative frequency: 0.0000
    P.   5 HASTINGS   45 And trails his Torches th'row the Starry Hall
    P. 77 A. HOUSE   589 And Ivy, with familiar trails,

train   frequency: 2   relative frequency: 0.0000
    See also "traine."
    P. 80 A. HOUSE   683 No new-born Comet such a Train
    P. 186 BRITANNIA   68 Pale death, lusts, Horrour fill her pompous
                            train.

traine   frequency: 2   relative frequency: 0.0000
    P. 170 PROPHECY   3 Fireballs shall flye and but few see the traine
    P. 197 DUKE   2 The great assembly and the numerous traine,

trains   frequency: 1   relative frequency: 0.0000
    P. 81 A. HOUSE   714 Those Trains by Youth against thee meant;

traitor-worm   frequency: 1   relative frequency: 0.0000
    P. 76 A. HOUSE   554 A Traitor-worm, within it bred.

traitors   frequency: 1   relative frequency: 0.0000
    See also "traytors."
    P. 193 TWO HORSES   77 Ch. That Traitors to their Country in a
                            Erib'd Hous of Commons

trammels   frequency: 1   relative frequency: 0.0000
    P. 31 FAIR SINGER   9 Breaking the curled trammels of her hair.

tranfusing   frequency: 1   relative frequency: 0.0000
    P. 96 HOLLAND   16 Tranfusing into them their Dunghil Soul.

transcend   frequency: 1   relative frequency: 0.0000
    P. 18 CLORINDA   21 D. Words that transcend poor Shepherds skill,

transcending   frequency: 1   relative frequency: 0.0000
    P. 49 THE GARDEN   45 Yet it creates, transcending these,

transferring   frequency: 1   relative frequency: 0.0000
    P. 91 MAY'S DEATH   49 Transferring old Rome hither in your talk,

transform   frequency: 1   relative frequency: 0.0000
    P. 175 LOYALL SCOT 155 But will Transform for an Archbishoprick.

transform'd   frequency: 1   relative frequency: 0.0000
    P. 187 BRITANNIA   117 But his fair soul, transform'd by that French
                            Dame,

transfuse   frequency: 1   relative frequency: 0.0000
    P. 176 LOYALL SCOT 209 Transfuse Indifferrence with necessity.

transfusing. See "tranfusing."

transgressing   frequency: 1   relative frequency: 0.0000
    P. 150 INSTRUCTIONS 378 Masculine Wives, transgressing Natures Law.

transitory   frequency: 1   relative frequency: 0.0000
    P. 129 O.C.   256 Oh! worthlesse world! oh transitory things!

translated   frequency: 2   relative frequency: 0.0000
    P. 91 MAY'S DEATH   26 He found he was translated, and by whom.
    P. 94 DR. WITTY   24 Nor her chast mird into the French translated:

translates   frequency: 1   relative frequency: 0.0000
    P. 82 A. HOUSE   747 (Till Fate her worthily translates,

translation   frequency: 2   relative frequency: 0.0000
    P. 93 DR. WITTY   t2 Translation of the Popular Errors.
    P. 94 DR. WITTY   32 Whose happy Eyes on thy Translation fall,

translations   frequency: 2   relative frequency: 0.0000
    P. 94 DR. WITTY   13 He is Translations thief that addeth more,
    P. 95 DR. WITTY   39 You have Translations statutes best fulfil'd.

translators   frequency: 3   relative frequency: 0.0000
    P. 94 DR. WITTY   7 So of Translators they are Authors grown,
    P. 94 DR. WITTY   8 For ill Translators make the Book their own.
    P. 94 DR. WITTY   27 Translators learn of her: but stay I slide

transparent   frequency: 4   relative frequency: 0.0000
    P. 61 A. HOUSE   80 Deep Meadows, and transparent Floods.
    P. 85 FLECKNO   80 This half transparent Man would soon reflect
    P. 157 INSTRUCTIONS 681 Round the transparent Fire about him glows,
    P. 173 LOYALL SCOT   47 Round the Transparent fire about him Glowes

transpires   frequency: 1   relative frequency: 0.0000
    P. 27 MISTRESS   35 And while thy willing Soul transpires

transplanting   frequency: 1   relative frequency: 0.0000
    P. 30 THE GALLERY   55 Transplanting Flow'rs from the green Hill,

transport   frequency: 1   relative frequency: 0.0000
    P. 178 LOYALL SCOT   274 Pardon, Young Heroe, this soe long Transport;

transported   frequency: 1   relative frequency: 0.0000
    P. 132 PARADISE   51 I too transported by the Mode offend,

transports   frequency: 1   relative frequency: 0.0000
    P. 108 ANNIVERSARY   193 First winged Fear transports them far away,

travell'd   frequency: 2   relative frequency: 0.0000
    P. 126 O.C.   135 He without noise still travell'd to his End,
    P. 150 INSTRUCTIONS 406 Where Pilgrim Palmer travell'd in Exile,

travellers   frequency: 1   relative frequency: 0.0000
    P. 57 BILL-BOROW   20 The feet of breathless Travellers.

traverse   frequency: 1   relative frequency: 0.0000
    P. 72 A. HOUSE   419 In whose new Traverse seemeth wrought

traytors   frequency: 2   relative frequency: 0.0000
    P. 163 INSTRUCTIONS 942 To prove them Traytors, and himself the Pett.
    P. 200 DUKE   99 This band of traytors hang'd in Effigie.

treachery. See "treach'ry."

treach'ry   frequency: 1   relative frequency: 0.0000
    P. 155 INSTRUCTIONS 610 Confusion, folly, treach'ry, fear, neglect.

tread   frequency: 10   relative frequency: 0.0002
    P. 15 THE CORONET   25 That they, while Thou on both their Spoils dost
                             tread,
    P. 56 BILL-BOROW   15 Learn here those humble steps to tread,
    P. 72 A. HOUSE   430 Which they in Fairy Circles tread:
    P. 75 A. HOUSE   530 Of gelid Straw-berryes do tread,
    P. 80 A. HOUSE   699 The Meadow Carpets where to tread;
    P. 91 MAY'S DEATH   39 Far from these blessed shades tread back agen
    P. 106 ANNIVERSARY   107 And in their numbred Footsteps humbly tread
    P. 130 O.C.   290 Plunging dost bathe and tread the bright abysse:
    P. 188 BRITANNIA   158 To teach my People in their steps to tread.
    P. 203 HISTORICALL   109 To tread the Phantastik Mazes of a Priest,

treason   frequency: 2   relative frequency: 0.0000
    P. 194 TWO HORSES   98 Yet truth many times being punisht for Treason,
    P. 196 TWO HORSES   188 Theres ten times more Treason in Brandy and
                             ale.

treason's   frequency: 1   relative frequency: 0.0000
    P. 76 A. HOUSE   560 Viewing the Treason's Punishment.

treasure   frequency: 4   relative frequency: 0.0000
    P. 39 THE MATCH   1 Nature had long a Treasure made
    P. 165 KINGS VOWES   11 That shall furnish me Treasure as fast as I
                             spend;
    P. 171 PROPHECY   52 With groans to fill his Treasure they must toyle,

P. 313 CHEQUER INN   21 And heapes up all our Treasure

treasurer   frequency: 8   relative frequency: 0.0001
    P. 160 INSTRUCTIONS 803 Who less Estate, for Treasurer most fit;
    P. 171 PROPHECY   30 When Cerberus shall be the Treasurer.
    P. 171 PROPHECY   43 When a lean Treasurer shall in one year
    P. 190 STATUE   15 Or the Bishops and Treasurer did they Agree't
    P. 190 STATUE   21 Does the Treasurer think men so Loyally tame
    P. 190 STATUE   30 That the Treasurer thought prudent to Try it
                             again,
    P. 190 STATUE   40 Shall a Treasurer of Guinny a Prince Grudge
                             of Token?
    P. 191 STATUE   49 But the Treasurer told her he thought she was
                             mad

treasures   frequency: 2   relative frequency: 0.0000
    P. 96 HOLLAND   40 Among the hungry he that treasures Grain,
    P. 118 BLAKE   153 Ah would those Treasures which both Indies
                             have,

treasure's   frequency: 1   relative frequency: 0.0000
    P. 160 INSTRUCTIONS 793 Southampton dead, much of the Treasure's care,

treasuress   frequency: 1   relative frequency: 0.0000
    P. 191 STATUE   41 The Huswifely Treasuress sure is grown nice

treat   frequency: 3   relative frequency: 0.0000
    P. 141 INSTRUCTIONS   38 Fits him in France to play at Cards and treat.
    P. 201 HISTORICALL   16 His jolly Vassalls treat him day and Night.
    P. 202 HISTORICALL   71 And gentlier farre the Orleans Dutches treat.

treated   frequency: 3   relative frequency: 0.0000
    P. 159 INSTRUCTIONS 772 Who treated out the time at Bergen? Pett.
    P. 175 LOYALL SCOT   140 Will you bee treated Princes? here fall to:
    P. 191 STATUE   42 That so liberally treated the members at supper.

treatest. See "treatst."

treaties   frequency: 1   relative frequency: 0.0000
    P. 98 HOLLAND   117 While, with feign'd Treaties, they invade by
                             stealth

treatst   frequency: 1   relative frequency: 0.0000
    P. 132 PARADISE   33 And things divine thou treatst of in such state

treaty   frequency: 4   relative frequency: 0.0000
    P. 142 INSTRUCTIONS   40 That, disavowing Treaty, ask supply.
    P. 146 INSTRUCTIONS 234 Who in a time of Treaty durst invade.
    P. 152 INSTRUCTIONS 453 To prove by Scripture, Treaty does imply
    P. 161 INSTRUCTIONS 824 Binding, e're th' Houses meet, the Treaty sure.

treble   frequency: 2   relative frequency: 0.0000
    P. 104 ANNIVERSARY   54 As he the Treble alter'd, or the Base:
    P. 112 ANNIVERSARY   374 'Through double Oak, <and> lin'd with treble
                             Brass;

trebles   frequency: 1   relative frequency: 0.0000
    P. 47 EMPIRE   10 And Virgin Trebles wed the manly Base.

tredenham   frequency: 1   relative frequency: 0.0000
    P. 315 CHEQUER INN   103 His Braine and Face Tredenham wrung

tree   frequency: 14   relative frequency: 0.0002
    See also "balsam-tree," "parent-tree."
    P.   4 HASTINGS   20 And on the Tree of Life once made a Feast,
    P. 17 BERMUDAS   24 No Tree could ever bear them twice.
    P. 41 THE MOWER   21 Had he not dealt between the Bark and Tree,
    P. 48 THE GARDEN   4 Crown'd from some single Herb or Tree.
    P. 48 THE GARDEN   28 Still in a Tree did end their race.
    P. 76 A. HOUSE   553 Nor would it, had the Tree not fed
    P. 76 A. HOUSE   568 I was but an inverted Tree.
    P. 77 A. HOUSE   604 Bends in some Tree its useless Dart;
    P. 108 ANNIVERSARY   201 Thou Cromwell falling, not a stupid Tree,
    P. 129 O.C.   269 The tree ere while foreshortned to our view,
    P. 131 PARADISE   4 Rebelling Angels, the Forbidden Tree,
    P. 149 INSTRUCTIONS 345 So the sad Tree shrinks from the Mornings Eye;
    P. 164 INSTRUCTIONS 972 And peal the Bark to burn at last the Tree.
    P. 203 HISTORICALL   103 From the forbidden tree the Pipin take:

trees   frequency: 14   relative frequency: 0.0002

```
P.  21 SOUL & BODY      44 Green Trees that in the Forest grew.
P.  48 THE GARDEN        7 While all Flow'rs and all Trees do close
P.  48 THE GARDEN       20 Cut in these Trees their Mistress name.
P.  48 THE GARDEN       23 Fair Trees! where s'eer your barkes I wound,
P.  57 BILL-BOROW       34 A Plump of aged Trees does wave.
P.  58 BILL-BOROW       62 Discourses with the breathing Trees;
P.  58 BILL-BOROW       73 'Tis true, ye Trees nor ever spoke
P.  74 A. HOUSE        498 It seems indeed as Wood not Trees:
P.  76 A. HOUSE        562 Among the Birds and Trees confer:
P.  77 A. HOUSE        602 These Trees have I incamp'd my Mind;
P.  78 A. HOUSE        620 The Trees before their Lord divide;
P.  90 MAY'S DEATH       6 For whence in Stevens ally Trees or Grass?
P. 114 BLAKE            28 Trees there the duty of the Clouds supply;
P. 126 O.C.            119 Or of huge Trees, whose growth with his did
                          rise,
```

tree's. See "fruit-trees."

```
trelawny's                    frequency:    1    relative frequency: 0.0000
P. 145 INSTRUCTIONS 188 Of Debtors deep, fell to Trelawny's Care.
```

```
tremble                       frequency:    3    relative frequency: 0.0000
P.  76 A. HOUSE        575 No Leaf does tremble in the Wind
P. 111 ANNIVERSARY     322 Makes you for his sake Tremble one fit more;
P. 195 TWO HORSES      140 Hee made England great and it's enemies tremble.
```

```
trembling                     frequency:    5    relative frequency: 0.0001
P.  12 DROP OF DEW      16 Trembling lest it grow impure:
P.  84 FLECKNO         44 In Echo to the trembling Strings repin'd.
P. 124 O.C.            59 No trembling String compos'd to numbers new,
P. 161 INSTRUCTIONS   861 Trembling with joy and fear, Hyde them
                          Prorogues,
P. 184 BRITANNIA        2 To trembling James, would I had yeilded mine.
```

```
trencher                      frequency:    1    relative frequency: 0.0000
P. 315 CHEQUER INN    117 And did his Trencher lick
```

```
trenches                      frequency:    2    relative frequency: 0.0000
P.  69 A. HOUSE       351 And, in those half-dry Trenches, spann'd
P. 116 BLAKE          103 Whose Fleet and Trenches view'd, he soon did
                          say,
```

```
trepan                        frequency:    1    relative frequency: 0.0000
P. 142 INSTRUCTIONS    45 Nor fears he the most Christian should trepan
```

```
trespassing                   frequency:    1    relative frequency: 0.0000
P.  73 A. HOUSE       479 How Salmons trespassing are found;
```

```
tresses                       frequency:    1    relative frequency: 0.0000
P. 162 INSTRUCTIONS   894 With her own Tresses interwove and twin'd:
```

trial. See "tryal," "tryell."

trials. See "tryals."

```
tribes                        frequency:    1    relative frequency: 0.0000
P. 139 HOUSEWARMING    64 The Tribes ne'er contributed so to the Temple.
```

```
tributaries                   frequency:    1    relative frequency: 0.0000
P. 112 ANNIVERSARY    367 'Needs must we all their Tributaries be,
```

```
tribute                       frequency:    3    relative frequency: 0.0000
P.  32 MOURNING       26 To her dead Love this Tribute due;
P.  75 A. HOUSE       536 That Tribute to its lord to send.
P. 128 O.C.           213 For her he once did nature's tribute pay:
```

```
tributes                      frequency:    1    relative frequency: 0.0000
P. 203 HISTORICALL     76 With lavish hands they constant Tributes give
```

```
trick                         frequency:    2    relative frequency: 0.0000
P. 143 INSTRUCTIONS   109 Those having lost the Nation at Trick track,
P. 170 PROPHECY         7 Where Vengeance dwells, but there is one trick
                          more
```

```
trickle                       frequency:    2    relative frequency: 0.0000
P.  16 EYES            51 Now like two Fountains trickle down:
P. 107 ANNIVERSARY    186 Still as they trickle, glitter in our Joy.
```

```
trickled                      frequency:    1    relative frequency: 0.0000
P. 147 INSTRUCTIONS   278 And the faint sweat trickled down Temples
                          Brows.
```

```
trickling                     frequency:    1    relative frequency: 0.0000
```

P. 125 O.C.   97 Trickling in watry drops, whose flowing shape

tricks   frequency: 1   relative frequency: 0.0000
    P. 203 HISTORICALL   99 And never durst their tricks above board shew.

trident   frequency: 1   relative frequency: 0.0000
    P. 99 HOLLAND   149 For while our Neptune doth a Trident shake,

trident's   frequency: 1   relative frequency: 0.0000
    P. 154 INSTRUCTIONS 546 With Trident's Leaver, and great Shoulder
                             heaves.

tried. See "oft-try'd," "try'd."

tries   frequency: 2   relative frequency: 0.0000
    See also "tryes," "trys," "try's."
    P. 157 INSTRUCTIONS 678 And tries his first embraces in their Sheets.
    P. 172 LOYALL SCOT   44 And tries his first Imbraces in their sheets.

trifling   frequency: 1   relative frequency: 0.0000
    P. 79 A. HOUSE   652 Hide trifling Youth thy Pleasures slight.

trim   frequency: 2   relative frequency: 0.0000
    P. 62 A. HOUSE   107 'And our chast lamps we hourly trim,
    P. 154 INSTRUCTIONS 536 And witness their complaisence in their trim.

trip   frequency: 1   relative frequency: 0.0000
    P. 24 NYMPH   85 And then to me 'twould boldly trip,

triple   frequency: 1   relative frequency: 0.0000
    P. 83 FLECKNO   8 Which signifies his triple property,

tripoli's. See "tripoly's."

tripoly's   frequency: 1   relative frequency: 0.0000
    P. 193 TWO HORSES   65 Ch. And our few ships abroad become Tripoly's
                             scorn

tritons   frequency: 3   relative frequency: 0.0000
    P. 96 HOLLAND   31 And oft the Tritons and the Sea-Nymphs saw
    P. 109 ANNIVERSARY   269 While baleful Tritons to the shipwrack guide.
    P. 154 INSTRUCTIONS 549 With Pearly Shell the Tritons all the while

triumph   frequency: 8   relative frequency: 0.0001
    P. 12 DIALOGUE   75 Triumph, triumph, victorious Soul;
    P. 38 PICTURE   21 In Triumph over Hearts that strive,
    P. 128 O.C.   193 In all his warrs needs must he triumph, when
    P. 143 INSTRUCTIONS   91 Great Love, how dost thou triumph, and how
                             reign,
    P. 158 INSTRUCTIONS 726 To Ruyter's Triumph lead the captive Charles.
    P. 189 BRITANNIA   188 In Triumph lead chaind tyrants from afarr.
    P. 197 DUKE   3 Who all in triumph shall about him sitte

triumphal. See "triumphall."

triumphall   frequency: 1   relative frequency: 0.0000
    P. 186 BRITANNIA   57 Shee mounted up on a triumphall Car

triumphant   frequency: 1   relative frequency: 0.0000
    P. 108 ANNIVERSARY   215 But thee triumphant hence the firy Carr,

triumphantly   frequency: 1   relative frequency: 0.0000
    P. 116 BLAKE   88 To all besides, triumphantly do live.

triumphs   frequency: 6   relative frequency: 0.0001
    P.   5 HASTINGS   29 His Thought with richest Triumphs entertains,
    P. 47 EMPIRE   16 To sing Mens Triumphs, or in Heavens quire.
    P. 72 A. HOUSE   426 Dancing the Triumphs of the Hay;
    P. 76 A. HOUSE   557 And yet that Worm triumphs not long,
    P. 104 ANNIVERSARY   25 Another triumphs at the publick Cost,
    P. 118 BLAKE   150 And o're two Elements Triumphs at once.

triumvirate   frequency: 1   relative frequency: 0.0000
    P. 168 ADVICE   21 This great triumvirate that can devide

trod   frequency: 2   relative frequency: 0.0000
    P. 23 NYMPH   70 And trod, as on the four Winds.
    P. 60 A. HOUSE   36 By Vere and Fairfax trod before,

trodden   frequency: 1   relative frequency: 0.0000
    P. 45 MOWER'S SONG   16 While I lay trodden under feet?

trojan   frequency: 2   relative frequency: 0.0000
    P. 161 INSTRUCTIONS   845 True Trojan! while this Town can Girls afford,
    P. 190 STATUE   25 The Trojan Horse, tho' not of Brass but of
                              wood,

troop   frequency: 8   relative frequency: 0.0001
    P. 144 INSTRUCTIONS   151 Of early Wittals first the Troop march'd in,
    P. 145 INSTRUCTIONS   176 No Troop was better clad nor so well pay'd.
    P. 145 INSTRUCTIONS   177 Then march't the Troop of Clarendon, all full,
    P. 145 INSTRUCTIONS   182 The Miter Troop, and with his looks gives Law.
    P. 145 INSTRUCTIONS   187 The Troop of Priviledge, a Rabble bare
    P. 145 INSTRUCTIONS   191 Then marcht the Troop, whose valiant Acts
                              before,
    P. 145 INSTRUCTIONS   195 Then comes the thrifty Troop of Privateers,
    P. 190 STATUE   6 To Limitt his troop to this Theatre small,

troopers   frequency: 1   relative frequency: 0.0000
    P.   22 NYMPH   1 The wanton Troopers riding by

troops   frequency: 3   relative frequency: 0.0000
    P. 147 INSTRUCTIONS   268 The adverse Troops, and hold them all at Bay.
    P. 150 INSTRUCTIONS   386 And Boys and Girls in Troops run houting by;
    P. 153 INSTRUCTIONS   521 Soon then the Independent Troops would close,

troop't   frequency: 1   relative frequency: 0.0000
    P. 146 INSTRUCTIONS   220 Troop't on to muster in the Tuttle-field.

trophees   frequency: 2   relative frequency: 0.0000
    P.   58 BILL-BOROW   72 The Trophees of one fertile Year.
    P. 147 INSTRUCTIONS   253 Their former Trophees they recal to mind,

trophies   frequency: 1   relative frequency: 0.0000
    See also "trophees."
    P. 129 O.C.   263 Whose spacious boughs are hung with trophies
                              round,

trot   frequency: 1   relative frequency: 0.0000
    P. 161 INSTRUCTIONS   832 Does for his Corporation sweat and trot.

troth   frequency: 3   relative frequency: 0.0000
    P. 170 PROPHECY   24 Shall be in use at Court but faith and Troth,
    P. 183 MADE FREE   74 Cannot bind him to Troth,
    P. 195 TWO HORSES   153 Ch. Troth, Brother, well said, but thats
                              somewhat bitter:

trouble   frequency: 1   relative frequency: 0.0000
    P. 115 BLAKE   60 And when 'tis raised, does trouble them much
                              more.

troubled   frequency: 1   relative frequency: 0.0000
    P. 126 O.C.   130 Troubled to part where so exactly mix'd.

troubles   frequency: 1   relative frequency: 0.0000
    P. 115 BLAKE   59 Which troubles men to raise it when 'tis Oar,

troublesome   frequency: 1   relative frequency: 0.0000
    P. 165 KINGS VOWES   9 But if it grow troublesome, I will have none.

troubling   frequency: 1   relative frequency: 0.0000
    P. 113 ANNIVERSARY   402 Troubling the Waters, yearly mak'st them Heal.

trowel   frequency: 1   relative frequency: 0.0000
    P. 139 HOUSEWARMING   80 Or his right hand shall else be cut off with the
                              Trowel.

trowl'd   frequency: 1   relative frequency: 0.0000
    P. 161 INSTRUCTIONS   848 And in eternal Healths thy Name be trowl'd.

truckling   frequency: 1   relative frequency: 0.0000
    P. 204 HISTORICALL   136 Old England truckling under slavery.

true   frequency: 27   relative frequency: 0.0005
    P.   15 EYES   12 Are the true price of all my Joyes.
    P.   16 EYES   27 And, to preserve their Sight more true,
    P.   20 THYRSIS   41 Convince me now, that this is true;
    P.   45 MOWER'S SONG   1 My Mind was once the true survey
    P.   45 MOWER'S SONG   14 A fellowship so true forego,
    P.   55 EPITAPH   19 'Tis true: but all so weakly said;
    P.   58 BILL-BOROW   73 'Tis true, ye Trees nor ever spoke
    P.   67 A. HOUSE   262 Only the Jewels there were true.
    P.   71 A. HOUSE   407 But now, to make his saying true,

```
P.  81 A. HOUSE      717 True Praise (That breaks through all defence;)
P.  88 ODE            27 And, if we would speak true,
P.  98 HOLLAND       123 'Tis true since that (as fortune kindly sports,)
P. 108 ANNIVERSARY   187 So with more Modesty we may be True,
P. 109 ANNIVERSARY   248 Founding a firm State by Proportions true.
P. 124 O.C.           60 Answers the touch in Notes more sad more true.
P. 139 HOUSEWARMING   65 Straight Judges, Priests, Bishops, true sons
                         of the Seal,
P. 148 INSTRUCTIONS  315 Each day they bring the Tale, and that too true,
P. 157 INSTRUCTIONS  699 And the true Royal-Oak, and Royal-James,
P. 160 INSTRUCTIONS  805 But the true cause was, that, in 's Brother
                         May,
P. 161 INSTRUCTIONS  845 True Trojan! while this Town can Girls afford,
P. 184 MADE FREE     113 He could never be true
P. 189 BRITANNIA     175 True sons of Glory, Pillars of the state,
P. 189 BRITANNIA     189 Her true Crusado shall at last pull down
P. 194 TWO HORSES    108 Letts be true to ourselves; whom then need wee
                         fear?
P. 200 DUKE          110 Brothers, its true, by nature should be kinde:
P. 203 HISTORICALL    81 He true Vicegerent to old Moloch were.
P. 204 HISTORICALL   129 Like a true Lover for her dying Mate.
```

truer   frequency: 1   relative frequency: 0.0000
```
P. 147 INSTRUCTIONS  264 This Combat truer than the Naval Fight.
```

truest   frequency: 1   relative frequency: 0.0000
```
P.  55 EPITAPH         7 Nor can the truest Wit or Friend,
```

truly   frequency: 4   relative frequency: 0.0000
```
P.  24 NYMPH         115 For I so truly thee bemoane,
P.  37 DEFINITION     27 But ours so truly Paralel,
P.  67 A. HOUSE      263 But truly bright and holy Thwaites
P.  73 A. HOUSE      467 And makes the Meadow truly be
```

trumpet   frequency: 1   relative frequency: 0.0000
```
P. 119 BLAKE         167 Whilst fame in every place, her Trumpet blowes,
```

trumpet-gen'ral   frequency: 1   relative frequency: 0.0000
```
P. 147 INSTRUCTIONS  263 Old Waller, Trumpet-gen'ral swore he'd write
```

trumpets   frequency: 1   relative frequency: 0.0000
See also "death-trumpets," "trumpetts."
```
P. 163 INSTRUCTIONS  909 With Canon, Trumpets, Drums, his door
                         surround,
```

trumpetts   frequency: 1   relative frequency: 0.0000
```
P. 182 MADE FREE      65 To his Highnesses's Trumpetts
```

trunk   frequency: 2   relative frequency: 0.0000
```
P.  74 A. HOUSE      500 To one great Trunk them all did mold.
P. 164 INSTRUCTIONS  953 Through Optick Trunk the Planet seem'd to
                         hear,
```

trunks   frequency: 1   relative frequency: 0.0000
```
P.  58 BILL-BOROW     71 Nor are our Trunks enow to bear
```

trusses   frequency: 1   relative frequency: 0.0000
```
P. 151 INSTRUCTIONS  446 Trusses his baggage, and the Camp does fly.
```

trust   frequency: 9   relative frequency: 0.0001
```
P.  71 A. HOUSE      403 Greedy as Kites has trust it up,
P.  89 ODE            80 And fit for highest Trust:
P. 114 BLAKE          29 O noble Trust which Heaven on this Isle
                         poures,
P. 164 INSTRUCTIONS  962 Banishing Love, Trust, Ornament and Use;
P. 170 PROPHECY        9 When Legislators shall their trust betray
P. 170 PROPHECY       21 And no Man knowes in whom to put his trust,
P. 175 LOYALL SCOT   161 Neither before to trust him nor behind.
P. 179 STOCKSMARKET   27 And what the exchequer for that took on trust
P. 187 BRITANNIA     122 Resigns his Crown to Angell Carwells trust.
```

trusted   frequency: 1   relative frequency: 0.0000
```
P. 193 TWO HORSES     80 As not to be trusted for twice fifty shillings.
```

trusting   frequency: 1   relative frequency: 0.0000
```
P. 200 DUKE           80 Who trusting in him was by him betray'd,
```

trusts   frequency: 1   relative frequency: 0.0000
```
P. 163 INSTRUCTIONS  936 Nor therefore trusts himself to such as they.
```

trusty   frequency: 1   relative frequency: 0.0000

P. 161 INSTRUCTIONS 842 Trusty as Steel, that always ready hung;

truth   frequency: 7   relative frequency: 0.0001
    P. 87 FLECKNO   165 With truth. I ccunsell'd him to go in time,
    P. 129 O.C.   272 When truth shall be allow'd, and faction cease,
    P. 146 INSTRUCTIONS 215 He, to excuse his slowness, truth confest
    P. 186 BRITANNIA   53 Of Ccuntryes love (by truth and Justice bred).
    P. 188 BRITANNIA   162 To love sobriety and holy truth,
    P. 194 TWO HORSES   98 Yet truth many times being punisht for Treason,
    P. 194 TWO HORSES   105 W. Truth 's as Bold as a Lyon, I am not
                             afraid;

truthes   frequency: 2   relative frequency: 0.0000
    P. 186 BRITANNIA   59 Whilst in truthes Mirror this Glad scene he
                             spy'd,
    P. 186 BRITANNIA   69 From th' easie King she truthes bright Mirrour
                             took,

truths   frequency: 3   relative frequency: 0.0000
    See also "truthes."
    P. 127 O.C.   175 Whose greater Truths obscure the Fables old,
    P. 131 PARADISE   8 The sacred Truths to Fable and old Song,
    P. 192 TWO HORSES   26 Who have told many truths well worth a mans
                             hearing,

try   frequency: 14   relative frequency: 0.0002
    P. 11 DIALOGUE   71 Try what depth the Centre draws;
    P. 21 SOUL & BODY   17 And, wanting where its spight to try,
    P. 26 MISTRESS   27 My ecchoing Song: then Worms shall try
    P. 65 A. HOUSE   195 'Try but a while, if you be wise:
    P. 66 A. HOUSE   243 And with successive Valour try
    P. 88 ODE   60 The Axes edge did try:
    P. 98 HOLLAND   97 They try, like Statuaries, if they can,
    P. 105 ANNIVERSARY   63 But, for he most the graver Notes did try,
    P. 131 O.C.   323 Tempt not his clemency to try his pow'r,
    P. 157 INSTRUCTIONS 672 Or with known Art to try the gentle Wave.
    P. 160 INSTRUCTIONS 810 All Arts they try to prolong its Date.
    P. 172 LOYALL SCOT   38 Or with known art to try the Gentle Wave.
    P. 188 BRITANNIA   133 Rawl: Once more, great Queen, thy darling try
                             to save;
    P. 190 STATUE   30 That the Treasurer thought prudent to Try it
                             again,

tryal   frequency: 2   relative frequency: 0.0000
    P. 65 A. HOUSE   196 'The Tryal neither Costs, nor Tyes.
    P. 83 FLECKNO   24 To my last Tryal, in a serious thought

tryals   frequency: 1   relative frequency: 0.0000
    P. 75 A. HOUSE   514 To sing the Tryals of her Voice.

try'd   frequency: 9   relative frequency: 0.0001
    P.   5 HASTINGS   57 All he had try'd, but all in vain, he saw,
    P. 38 PICTURE   19 Ere they have try'd their force to wound,
    P. 80 A. HOUSE   687 But by her Flames, in Heaven try'd,
    P. 84 FLECKNO   36 Left off, and try'd t' allure me with his Lute.
    P. 125 O.C.   87 And in himself so oft immortal try'd,
    P. 146 INSTRUCTIONS 241 A scatter'd Body, which the Foe ne'r try'd,
    P. 150 INSTRUCTIONS 395 So Holland with us had the Mast'ry try'd,
    P. 185 BRITANNIA   38 To those that try'd to seperate these two.
    P. 188 BRITANNIA   141 Brit: Rawleigh, noe more; too long in vain I've
                             try'd

tryell   frequency: 1   relative frequency: 0.0000
    P. 177 LOYALL SCOT   242 The Tryell would however bee too nice

tryes   frequency: 1   relative frequency: 0.0000
    P. 84 FLECKNO   49 He never feeds; save only when he tryes

trying   frequency: 1   relative frequency: 0.0000
    P. 109 ANNIVERSARY   246 Trying the Measures of the Bredth and Height;

trys   frequency: 1   relative frequency: 0.0000
    P. 142 INSTRUCTIONS   73 Not unprovok'd she trys forbidden Arts,

try's   frequency: 1   relative frequency: 0.0000
    P. 73 A. HOUSE   470 It try's t'invite him thus away.

tube   frequency: 1   relative frequency: 0.0000
    P. 164 INSTRUCTIONS 949 So his bold Tube, Man, to the Sun apply'd,

tudor   frequency: 2   relative frequency: 0.0000

        P. 195 TWO HORSES   149 A Tudor a Tudor! wee've had Stuarts enough;

tudors   frequency: 2   relative frequency: 0.0000
        P. 185 BRITANNIA   43 In Lofty Notes Tudors blest reign to sing,
        P. 202 HISTORICALL   56 Whilst the brave Tudors wore th' Imperial
                                     Crowne:

tufted   frequency: 1   relative frequency: 0.0000
        P. 90 ODE   109 Happy if in the tufted brake

tulip   frequency: 2   relative frequency: 0.0000
        P. 41 THE MOWER   13 The Tulip, white, did for complexion seek;
        P. 68 A. HOUSE   312 That of the Tulip Pinke and Rose.

tulipant   frequency: 1   relative frequency: 0.0000
        P. 110 ANNIVERSARY   308 Wer't but for thine unmoved Tulipant;

tulips   frequency: 2   relative frequency: 0.0000
        P. 38 PICTURE   28 Make that the Tulips may have share
        P. 69 A. HOUSE   335 Tulips, in several Colours barr'd,

tumult   frequency: 3   relative frequency: 0.0000
        P. 109 ANNIVERSARY   241 Though undiscern'd among the tumult blind,
        P. 163 INSTRUCTIONS   911 Thrice did he rise, thrice the vain Tumult fled,
        P. 178 LOYALL SCOT   267 The Idle tumult of his factious bees,

tumults   frequency: 2   relative frequency: 0.0000
        P. 103 ANNIVERSARY   5 And his short Tumults of themselves Compose,
        P. 196 TWO HORSES   183 'Tis wine and Strong drink makes tumults
                                     increase;

tun'd   frequency: 2   relative frequency: 0.0000
        P. 84 FLECKNO   38 Being tun'd by Art, if the one touched be
        P. 105 ANNIVERSARY   68 When Cromwell tun'd the ruling Instrument;

tune   frequency: 2   relative frequency: 0.0000
        P. 43 DAMON   63 And, when I tune my self to sing,
        P. 104 ANNIVERSARY   48 To tune this lower to that higher Sphere.

tuned   frequency: 2   relative frequency: 0.0000
        See also "tun'd."
        P. 47 EMPIRE   6 And Jubal tuned Musicks Jubilee:
        P. 74 A. HOUSE   512 Echo about their tuned Fires.

tunick   frequency: 1   relative frequency: 0.0000
        P. 167 KINGS VOWES   49 I will have a fine Tunick a Sash and a Vest,

t'unite   frequency: 1   relative frequency: 0.0000
        P. 59 A. HOUSE   23 That thinks by Breadth the World t'unite

tunn'd   frequency: 1   relative frequency: 0.0000
        P. 98 HOLLAND   95 Tunn'd up with all their sev'ral Towns of Beer;

turf   frequency: 1   relative frequency: 0.0000
        P. 97 HOLLAND   87 A vestal Turf enshrin'd in Earthen Ware

turk   frequency: 3   relative frequency: 0.0000
        P. 150 INSTRUCTIONS   402 Where Venice twenty years the Turk had fought:
        P. 167 KINGS VOWES   50 Tho' not rule like the Turk yet I will be so
                                     drest,
        P. 195 TWO HORSES   145 With the Turk in his head and the Pope in his
                                     heart

turk-christian-pagan-jew   frequency: 1   relative frequency: 0.0000
        P. 97 HOLLAND   71 Hence Amsterdam, Turk-Christian-Pagan-Jew,

turkish   frequency: 1   relative frequency: 0.0000
        P. 189 BRITANNIA   190 The Turkish Crescent and the Persian sun.

turn   frequency: 21   relative frequency: 0.0004
        See also "turne."
        P. 19 THYRSIS   9 Thyrsis. Turn thine Eye to yonder Skie,
        P. 26 MISTRESS   29 And your quaint Honour turn to dust;
        P. 46 AMETAS   6 If we both should turn one way?
        P. 76 A. HOUSE   567 Or turn me but, and you shall see
        P. 83 FLECKNO   14 Turn in, and shew to Wainscot half the Room.
        P. 92 MAY'S DEATH   74 To turn the Chronicler to Spartacus.
        P. 104 ANNIVERSARY   31 If Conquerors, on them they turn their might;
        P. 108 ANNIVERSARY   224 To turn the headstrong Peoples Charioteer;
        P. 119 TWO SONGS   7 Cynthia, O Cynthia, turn thine Ear,
        P. 122 TWO SONGS   34 Before Marina's turn were sped?

```
P. 124 O.C.           42 His hidden Scul at ev'ry turn could meet;
P. 137 HOUSEWARMING    4 'Twas the season he thought to turn Architect.
P. 145 INSTRUCTIONS  202 Their Friends agreed they should command by
                         turn.
P. 149 INSTRUCTIONS  331 And to Land-tax from the Excise turn round,
P. 160 INSTRUCTIONS  791 Then that Reward might in its turn take place,
P. 161 INSTRUCTIONS  839 Tells them he at Whitehall had took a turn,
P. 162 INSTRUCTIONS  869 At Pray'rs, his Eyes turn up the Pious white,
P. 176 LOYALL SCOT   175 Eating their brethren Bishop Turn and Cat
P. 187 BRITANNIA      88 Thus Heavens designs against heavens self youl
                         turn
P. 188 BRITANNIA     145 Into the Wolf and make him Guardian turn
P. 191 STATUE         54 But to turn the face to Whitehall you must
                         Shun;
```

turnaments   frequency: 1   relative frequency: 0.0000
```
P.   5 HASTINGS       35 And underneath, he views the Turnaments
```

turncoat   frequency: 1   relative frequency: 0.0000
```
P. 169 ADVICE         60 To be reproacht with Tearm cf Turncoat knave;
```

turnd   frequency: 1   relative frequency: 0.0000
```
P. 185 BRITANNIA      39 The Bloody scottish Chronicle turnd o're
```

turn'd   frequency: 9   relative frequency: 0.0001
```
P.  73 A. HOUSE      476 Turn'd as they hang tc Leeches quick;
P.  84 FLECKNO        31 And how I, silent, turn'd my burning Ear
P.  87 FLECKNO       166 Ere the fierce Poets anger turn'd to rime.
P. 111 ANNIVERSARY   337 Still to the West, where he him lost, he turn'd,
P. 117 BLAKE         124 War turn'd the temperate, to the Torrid Zone.
P. 159 INSTRUCTIONS  759 The Thames roar'd, swouning Medway turn'd her
                         tide,
P. 194 TWO HORSES    117 W. Thy Priest-ridden King turn'd desperate
                         Fighter
P. 313 CHEQUER INN    17 But quickly turn'd Catt i'th' Pan
P. 315 CHEQUER INN   105 His Neck it turn'd on Wyer
```

turne   frequency: 3   relative frequency: 0.0000
```
P. 184 MADE FREE     129 And turne again Viner, turne again;
P. 192 TWO HORSES     47 W. That the Duke should turne Papist and that
                         Church defy
```

turned. See "turnd," "turn'd."

turner   frequency: 2   relative frequency: 0.0000
```
See also "turnor."
P. 161 INSTRUCTIONS  837 And Turner gay up to his Pearch does march,
P. 161 INSTRUCTIONS  851 Hyde orders Turner that he should come late,
```

turner's   frequency: 1   relative frequency: 0.0000
```
P. 161 INSTRUCTIONS  854 Expects as at a Play till Turner's drest.
```

turning   frequency: 1   relative frequency: 0.0000
```
P. 163 INSTRUCTIONS  921 And ghastly Charles, turning his Collar low,
```

turnor   frequency: 1   relative frequency: 0.0000
```
P. 143 INSTRUCTIONS  114 For the Cheat Turner for them both must throw.
```

turns   frequency: 6   relative frequency: 0.0001
```
P.  12 DROP OF DEW    28 Every way it turns away:
P.  15 EYES           14 Yea even Laughter, turns to Tears:
P.  71 A. HOUSE      385 No Scene that turns with Engines strange
P.  86 FLECKNO       119 Turns to recite; though Judges most severe
P. 108 ANNIVERSARY   211 Such as the dying Chcrus sings by turns,
P. 149 INSTRUCTIONS  364 United most, else when by turns they meet.
```

turtles   frequency: 1   relative frequency: 0.0000
```
P.  24 NYMPH         106 Whether the Swans and Turtles go:
```

tusk   frequency: 1   relative frequency: 0.0000
```
P. 163 INSTRUCTIONS  941 While Hyde provck'd his foaming tusk does whet,
```

tuttle-field   frequency: 1   relative frequency: 0.0000
```
P. 146 INSTRUCTIONS  220 Troop't on to muster in the Tuttle-field.
```

twang   frequency: 1   relative frequency: 0.0000
```
P.  79 A. HOUSE      648 While at my Lires the Fishes twang!
```

twas   frequency: 3   relative frequency: 0.0000

'twas   frequency: 23   relative frequency: 0.0004

See also "twas."

tweaking   frequency: 1   relative frequency: 0.0000
     P. 148 INSTRUCTIONS   302 St. Dunstan in it, tweaking Satan's Nose.

tweed   frequency: 2   relative frequency: 0.0000
     P. 173 LOYALL SCOT   81 What Ethick River is this Wondrous Tweed
     P. 174 LOYALL SCOT   88 'Tis Holy Island parts us not the Tweed.

twelve   frequency: 2   relative frequency: 0.0000
     P. 149 INSTRUCTIONS   359 Next the Twelve Commons are condemn'd to groan,
     P. 201 HISTORICALL   3 Twelve Yeares compleat he suffer'd in Exile

twenty   frequency: 2   relative frequency: 0.0000
     P. 150 INSTRUCTIONS   402 Where Venice twenty years the Turk had fought:
     P. 199 DUKE   53 Dy before twenty, cr rott before sixteene.

'twere   frequency: 12   relative frequency: 0.0002

twice   frequency: 6   relative frequency: 0.0001
     P. 17 BERMUDAS   24 No Tree could ever bear them twice.
     P. 105 ANNIVERSARY   74 And once he struck, and twice, the pow'rful
                               Strings.
     P. 126 O.C.   144 Twice had in open field him Victor crown'd:
     P. 148 INSTRUCTIONS   293 Candidly credulcus for once, nay twice;
     P. 190 STATUE   35 As the Parliament twice was prorogued by your
                               hand,
     P. 193 TWO HORSES   8C As not to be trusted for twice fifty shillings.

twig. See "twigg."

twigg   frequency: 1   relative frequency: 0.0000
     P. 313 CHEQUER INN   26 And beare himself on such a Twigg

twigs. See "lime-twigs."

'twill   frequency: 5   relative frequency: 0.0001

twin   frequency: 2   relative frequency: 0.0000
     P. 176 LOYALL SCOT   186 Strange was the Sight the scotch Twin headed
                               man
     P. 178 LOYALL SCOT   264 And, where twin Simpathies cannot atcne,

twin'd   frequency: 2   relative frequency: 0.0000
     P. 84 FLECKNO   43 Whose hungry Guts to the same streightness
                               twin'd
     P. 162 INSTRUCTIONS   894 With her own Tresses interwove and twin'd:

twine   frequency: 1   relative frequency: 0.0000
     P. 46 AMETAS   5 Think'st Thou that this Rope would twine

'twines   frequency: 1   relative frequency: 0.0000
     P. 78 A. HOUSE   609 Bind me ye Woodbines in your 'twines,

twining   frequency: 2   relative frequency: 0.0000
     P. 14 THE CORONET   14 That, twining in his speckled breast,
     P. 88 ODE   49 Where, twining subtile fears with hope,

twins   frequency: 1   relative frequency: 0.0000
     P. 97 HOLLAND   63 Faith, that could never Twins conceive before,

twist   frequency: 1   relative frequency: 0.0000
     P. 46 AMETAS   8 Neither Love will twist nor Hay.

twixt   frequency: 1   relative frequency: 0.0000

'twixt   frequency: 2   relative frequency: 0.0000
     See also "twixt."

two   frequency: 55   relative frequency: 0.0011
     P. 15 EYES   9 Two Tears, which Scrrow long did weigh
     P. 16 EYES   36 As two Eyes swoln with weeping are.
     P. 16 EYES   49 Now like two Clcuds dissolving, drop,
     P. 16 EYES   51 Now like twc Fountains trickle down:
     P. 16 EYES   52 Now like two flccds o'return and drcwn.
     P. 24 NYMPH   102 Keep these two crystal Tears; and fill
     P. 26 MISTRESS   15 Two hundred to adore each Breast:
     P. 37 DEFINITION   14 Two perfect Loves; nor lets them close:
     P. 49 THE GARDEN   63 Two Faradises 'twere in cne
     P. 74 A. HOUSE   491 It like two Pedigrees appears,
     P. 78 A. HOUSE   618 Where the two Wcods have made a Lane;

P.	78 A. HOUSE	622 Betwixt two Labyrinths does lead.
P.	84 PLECKNO	37 Now as two Instruments, to the same key
P.	85 FLECKNO	100 Two make a crowd, nor can three Persons here
P.	85 FLECKNO	110 Betwixt us two the Dinner to a Feast.
P.	86 FLECKNO	130 Save only two foul copies for his shirt:
P.	109 ANNIVERSARY	250 Yet by the Conquest of two Kings grown great,
P.	117 BLAKE	125 Fate these two Fleets, between both Worlds had brought.
P.	118 BLAKE	138 Two dreadful Navies there at Anchor Fight.
P.	118 BLAKE	150 And o're two Elements Triumphs at once.
P.	119 TWO SONGS	t1 Two Songs at the Marriage of the Lord Fauconberg
P.	138 HOUSEWARMING	50 The two Allens when jovial, who ply him with gallons,
P.	138 HOUSEWARMING	51 The two Allens who serve his blind Justice for ballance,
P.	138 HOUSEWARMING	52 The two Allens who serve his Injustice for Tallons.
P.	141 INSTRUCTIONS	1 After two sittings, now our Lady State,
P.	142 INSTRUCTIONS	46 Two Saints at once, St. German, St. Alban.
P.	146 INSTRUCTIONS	225 All the two Coventrys their Gen'rals chose:
P.	150 INSTRUCTIONS	369 While Chain'd together two Ambassadors
P.	151 INSTRUCTIONS	449 Two Letters next unto Breda are sent,
P.	166 KINGS VOWES	36 I will have two fine Secretaryes pisse thro one Quill.
P.	169 ADVICE	49 Two of the five recanters of the Hous
P.	170 PROPHECY	25 When two good Kings shall be att Brantford knowne
P.	171 PROPHECY	38 To make starcht empty Speeches two hours long.
P.	174 LOYALL SCOT	89 Nothing but Clergie cold us two seclude:
P.	174 LOYALL SCOT	107 Shews you first one, then makes that one two Balls.
P.	176 LOYALL SCOT	187 With single body like the two Neckt Swan,
P.	176 LOYALL SCOT	189 Where but two hands to Act, two feet to goe.
P.	176 LOYALL SCOT	191 What Brittain was, betwixt two Kings distrest.
P.	176 LOYALL SCOT	197 Doth Charles the second rain or Charles the two?
P.	177 LOYALL SCOT	235 Two Nations Neere had mist the Marke soe long.
P.	177 LOYALL SCOT	236 The world in all doth but two Nations bear,
P.	177 LOYALL SCOT	238 Under each pole place either of the two,
P.	183 MADE FREE	77 Two Prentiships through,
P.	185 BRITANNIA	38 To those that try'd to seperate these two.
P.	188 BRITANNIA	127 The scotch scabbado of one Court, two Isles.
P.	191 TWO HORSES	t1 A Dialogue between the Two Horses.
P.	192 TWO HORSES	24 Of a Dialogue lately between the two Horses,
P.	192 TWO HORSES	28 For the two mighty Monarchs that doe now bestride 'um.
P.	192 TWO HORSES	33 And that the two Jades after mutuall Salutes
P.	195 TWO HORSES	128 Between the two Scourges wee find little odds.
P.	195 TWO HORSES	135 W. One of the two Tyrants must still be our case
P.	196 TWO HORSES	166 Which two inanimate Horses declare.
P.	315 CHEQUER INN	98 Had Mortgag'd of his Two, one Band

two-edg'd   frequency: 1   relative frequency: 0.0000
  P. 152 INSTRUCTIONS   480 To raise a two-edg'd Army for's defence.

'twould   frequency: 7   relative frequency: 0.0001

tybourn   frequency: 1   relative frequency: 0.0000
  P. 140 HOUSEWARMING   108 At Tybourn may land, and spare the Tower-Barge.

tybur   frequency: 1   relative frequency: 0.0000
  P. 204 HISTORICALL   155 From Tybur came the advice boat Monthly home,

tyburn. See "tybourn."

ty'd   frequency: 3   relative frequency: 0.0000
  P. 22 NYMPH   28 Ty'd in this silver Chain and Bell,
  P. 121 TWO SONGS   5 Stay till I some flow'rs ha' ty'd
  P. 124 O.C.   44 Doubling that knot which Destiny had ty'd.

tydes   frequency: 1   relative frequency: 0.0000
  P. 154 INSTRUCTIONS   543 Old Neptune springs the Tydes, and Water lent:

tye   frequency: 2   relative frequency: 0.0000
  P. 63 A. HOUSE   160 'Might such fair Hands as yours it tye!
  P. 78 A. HOUSE   617 Here in the Morning tye my Chain,

tyes   frequency: 3   relative frequency: 0.0000
  P. 46 AMETAS   11 And Love tyes a Womans Mind
  P. 65 A. HOUSE   196 'The Tryal neither Costs, nor Tyes.

P. 175 LOYALL SCOT   138 That power Alone Can Loose this spell that
                          tyes,

tygress   frequency: 1   relative frequency: 0.0000
       P. 156 INSTRUCTIONS   623 Such from Euphrates bank, a Tygress fell,

tyme   frequency: 1   relative frequency: 0.0000
       P. 316 CHEQUER INN   164 And now (who wou'd) twas tyme to goe

tymes   frequency: 1   relative frequency: 0.0000
       P. 315 CHEQUER INN   96 For tymes thou know'st grew harder.

tyranick   frequency: 1   relative frequency: 0.0000
       P. 185 BRITANNIA   29 I'th sacred ear Tyranick Arts they Croak,

tyrannic   frequency: 1   relative frequency: 0.0000
See also "tyranick," "tyrannick."
       P. 21 SOUL & BODY   12 From bonds of this Tyrannic Soul?

tyrannick   frequency: 1   relative frequency: 0.0000
       P. 37 DEFINITION   16 And her Tyrannick pow'r depose.

tyranny   frequency: 3   relative frequency: 0.0000
See also "tyrany."
       P. 110 ANNIVERSARY   280 Nor Tyranny, where One does them withstand:
       P. 113 BLAKE   6 Was rais'd by Tyranny, and rais'd for War;
       P. 189 BRITANNIA   186 From Noxious Monsters, Hellborn tyranny,

tyrant   frequency: 6   relative frequency: 0.0001
       P. 28 LOVER   45 And Tyrant Love his brest does ply
       P. 41 THE MOWER   28 Lest any Tyrant him out-doe.
       P. 84 FLECKNO   35 Till the Tyrant, weary to persecute,
       P. 171 PROPHECY   49 Then the English shall a Greater Tyrant Know
       P. 188 BRITANNIA   142 The Stuart from the Tyrant to devide.
       P. 189 BRITANNIA   194 No Poisonous tyrant on thy ground shall live.

tyrants   frequency: 8   relative frequency: 0.0001
       P. 29 THE GALLERY   14 Adorned Tyrants Cabinet;
       P. 185 BRITANNIA   41 Were Hurl'd to Hell by Learning Tyrants
                                   Lore.
       P. 188 BRITANNIA   149 Tyrants like Leprous Kings for publick weal
       P. 189 BRITANNIA   188 In Triumph lead chaind tyrants from afarr.
       P. 193 TWO HORSES   70 But Tyrants ingratefull are always afeard.
       P. 195 TWO HORSES   135 W. One of the two Tyrants must still be our
                                   case
       P. 195 TWO HORSES   139 Tho' his Government did a Tyrants resemble,
       P. 196 TWO HORSES   175 Tho' Tyrants make laws which they strictly
                                   proclaim

tyrany   frequency: 1   relative frequency: 0.0000
       P. 171 PROPHECY   42 And strive by Law to 'stablish Tyrany,

tyrian   frequency: 1   relative frequency: 0.0000
       P. 137 HOUSEWARMING   22 Of African Foultney, and Tyrian Did'

tyth   frequency: 1   relative frequency: 0.0000
       P. 177 LOYALL SCOT   223 Some sue for tyth of the Elyzean plaines:

ugly   frequency: 1   relative frequency: 0.0000
       P. 204 HISTORICALL   116 This haughty Monster with his ugly claws

ulcer   frequency: 1   relative frequency: 0.0000
       P. 21 SOUL & BODY   36 Or Hatred's hidden Ulcer eat.

'um   frequency: 7   relative frequency: 0.0001
       P. 184 BRITANNIA   3 Cubbs, didst thou call 'um? hadst thou seen this
                                   Brood
       P. 192 TWO HORSES   27 Since Viner and Osburn did buy and provide 'um
       P. 192 TWO HORSES   28 For the two mighty Monarchs that doe now
                                   bestride 'um.
       P. 193 TWO HORSES   64 Not our trade to secure but foes to come at 'um,
       P. 196 TWO HORSES   185 No Quarrells or oathes amongst those that drink
                                   'um;
       P. 196 TWO HORSES   186 Tis Bacchus and the Brewer swear Dam 'um and
                                   sink 'um.

unable   frequency: 1   relative frequency: 0.0000
       P. 138 HOUSEWARMING   54 Yet his Lordship to finish it would be unable;

unattended   frequency: 1   relative frequency: 0.0000
       P. 164 INSTRUCTIONS   961 Would she the unattended Throne reduce,

unbottom'd   frequency: 1   relative frequency: 0.0000
    P. 111 ANNIVERSARY   312 Cut of the Center of th' unbottom'd Pit;

unbuilt   frequency: 1   relative frequency: 0.0000
    P. 181 MADE FREE   7 Whil'st your Churches unbuilt

uncase   frequency: 1   relative frequency: 0.0000
    P. 176 LOYALL SCOT   172 Doe but their Fyebald lordships once Uncase

uncertain   frequency: 3   relative frequency: 0.0000
    P. 41 THE MOWER   25 That the uncertain and adult'rate fruit
    P. 58 BILL-BOROW   59 Nor to the winds uncertain gust,
    P. 90 MAY'S DEATH   4 And with an Eye uncertain, gazing wide,

uncessant   frequency: 2   relative frequency: 0.0000
    P. 48 THE GARDEN   3 And their uncessant Labours see
    P. 120 TWO SONGS   22 Mine Eyes uncessant deluges.

unchanged   frequency: 1   relative frequency: 0.0000
    P. 84 FLECKNO   33 Held him the other; and unchanged yet,

uncivil   frequency: 1   relative frequency: 0.0000
    P. 151 INSTRUCTIONS   432 Uncivil: His unkindness would us kill.

unconcern'd   frequency: 2   relative frequency: 0.0000
    P. 107 ANNIVERSARY   150 Look on, all unconcern'd, or unprepar'd;
    P. 126 O.C.   111 He unconcern'd the dreadful passage crost;

unconstant   frequency: 1   relative frequency: 0.0000
    P. 22 NYMPH   25 Unconstant Sylvio, when yet

unconstrain'd   frequency: 1   relative frequency: 0.0000
    P. 60 A. HOUSE   43 By which, ungirt and unconstrain'd,

uncorrupting   frequency: 1   relative frequency: 0.0000
    P. 64 A. HOUSE   174 'The Sugars uncorrupting Oyl:

unction   frequency: 1   relative frequency: 0.0000
    P. 198 DUKE   32 That extreame unction is but common cyle

undaunted   frequency: 2   relative frequency: 0.0000
    P. 107 ANNIVERSARY   170 Hast born securely thine undaunted Head,
    P. 116 BLAKE   99 His wish he has, for now undaunted Blake,

under   frequency: 30   relative frequency: 0.0006

underground   frequency: 1   relative frequency: 0.0000
    P. 177 LOYALL SCOT   233 While they liv'd here, still Haunts them
                                Underground.

underlings   frequency: 1   relative frequency: 0.0000
    P. 186 BRITANNIA   73 Such poor pedantick toys teach underlings.

undermine   frequency: 1   relative frequency: 0.0000
    P. 164 INSTRUCTIONS   978 As scratching Courtiers undermine a Realm:

undermined   frequency: 1   relative frequency: 0.0000
    P. 79 A. HOUSE   646 On the Osiers undermined Root,

underneath   frequency: 8   relative frequency: 0.0001
    P.   5 HASTINGS   35 And underneath, he views the Turnaments
    P. 58 BILL-BOROW   51 And underneath the Courser Rind
    P. 74 A. HOUSE   511 And underneath the winged Quires
    P. 79 A. HOUSE   666 From underneath these Banks do creep,
    P. 85 FLECKNO   73 Thus armed underneath, he over all
    P. 90 ODE   108 Shrink underneath the Plad:
    P. 158 INSTRUCTIONS   720 Take a short Vcyage underneath the Thames.
    P. 176 LOYALL SCOT   182 But his Lay pitty underneath prevailed

under's   frequency: 1   relative frequency: 0.0000
    P. 145 INSTRUCTIONS   164 And under's Armpit he defends his Head.

understanding   frequency: 2   relative frequency: 0.0000
    P. 131 PARADISE   14 O're which lame Faith leads Understanding
                                blind;
    P. 173 LOYALL SCOT   78 Where life resides or Understanding dwells:

understands   frequency: 1   relative frequency: 0.0000
    P. 178 LOYALL SCOT   262 Charles our great soul this onely Understands:

understood   frequency: 5   relative frequency: 0.0001

P. 86 FLECKNO	139	To read; and then, because he understood
P. 91 MAY'S DEATH	56	Misled, but malice fixt and understood.
P. 172 LOYALL SCOT	7	Hee Understood and Willingly Addrest
P. 190 STATUE	27	However tis ominous if understood,
P. 192 TWO HORSES	17	But they that faith Cathclick ne're understood,

undertooke   frequency: 1   relative frequency: 0.0000
   P. 200 DUKE   95 When wiser men its ruine undertooke:

undescry'd   frequency: 1   relative frequency: 0.0000
   P. 146 INSTRUCTIONS 244 And undescry'd return'd e're morning peep.

undiscern'd   frequency: 1   relative frequency: 0.0000
   P. 109 ANNIVERSARY 241 Though undiscern'd among the tumult blind,

undisturb'd   frequency: 1   relative frequency: 0.0000
   P. 153 INSTRUCTIONS 524 Sail'd now among our Rivers undisturb'd:

undoe   frequency: 1   relative frequency: 0.0000
   P. 317 CHEQUER INN 180 Is to undoe the Nation

undone   frequency: 3   relative frequency: 0.0000
   P. 31 FAIR SINGER   17 And all my Forces needs must be undone,
   P. 34 DAPHNIS   31 When poor Daphnis is undone,
   P. 182 MADE FREE   72 Your Chamber must needs be undone.

undrest   frequency: 1   relative frequency: 0.0000
   P.   4 LOVELACE   39 They all in mutiny though yet undrest

undutiful   frequency: 1   relative frequency: 0.0000
   P. 151 INSTRUCTIONS 440 And to St. Albans too undutiful;

undwelt   frequency: 1   relative frequency: 0.0000
   P. 181 MADE FREE   8 And your Houses undwelt

uneasie   frequency: 1   relative frequency: 0.0000
   P. 162 INSTRUCTIONS 890 He wakes and Muses of th' uneasie Throne:

uneasy. See "uneasie."

unenvied. See "unenvy'd."

unenvy'd   frequency: 1   relative frequency: 0.0000
   P. 57 BILL-BOROW   26 And in unenvy'd Greatness stands,

unespied. See "unespy'd."

unespy'd   frequency: 1   relative frequency: 0.0000
   P. 17 BERMUDAS   2 In th' Oceans bosome unespy'd,

unfashion'd   frequency: 1   relative frequency: 0.0000
   P.   3 LOVELACE   20 Of wit corrupted, the unfashion'd Sons.

unfathomable   frequency: 1   relative frequency: 0.0000
   P. 70 A. HOUSE   370 Of that unfathomable Grass,

unfeather'd   frequency: 1   relative frequency: 0.0000
   P. 71 A. HOUSE   396 Whose yet unfeather'd Quils her fail.

unfix'd   frequency: 1   relative frequency: 0.0000
   P. 126 O.C.   129 Such Tortures all the Elements unfix'd,

unfold   frequency: 2   relative frequency: 0.0000
   P. 113 BLAKE   1 Now does Spains Fleet her spatious wings
                    unfold,
   P. 131 PARADISE   2 In slender Book his vast Design unfold,

unfortunate   frequency: 2   relative frequency: 0.0000
   P. 27 LOVER   t The unfortunate Lover.
   P. 28 LOVER   30 Th' unfortunate and abject Heir:

unfrequented   frequency: 2   relative frequency: 0.0000
   P. 18 CLORINDA   9 Seest thou that unfrequented Cave?
   P. 67 A. HOUSE   259 Then th' unfrequented Vault appear'd,

ungentle   frequency: 1   relative frequency: 0.0000
   P. 22 NYMPH   3 Ungentle men! They cannot thrive

ungirt   frequency: 4   relative frequency: 0.0000
   P. 60 A. HOUSE   43 By which, ungirt and unconstrain'd,
   P. 86 FLECKNO   129 Of all his Poems there he stands ungirt

```
P.   89 ODE              89 And has his Sword and Spoyls ungirt,
P.  129 O.C.            242 As ungirt David to the arke did dance.

ungrateful                       frequency:    1    relative frequency: 0.0000
P.   42 DAMON           39 Yet Thou ungrateful hast not sought

unhappy                          frequency:    4    relative frequency: 0.0000
P.   24 NYMPH          111 First my unhappy Statue shall
P.   69 A. HOUSE       329 Unhappy! shall we never more
P.   71 A. HOUSE       409 Unhappy Birds! what does it boot
P.  106 ANNIVERSARY    117 Unhappy Princes, ignorantly bred,

unheard                          frequency:    1    relative frequency: 0.0000
P.  163 INSTRUCTIONS   923 Then, whisp'ring to his Son in Words unheard,

unhir'd                          frequency:    1    relative frequency: 0.0000
P.  314 CHEQUER INN     60 None went away unhir'd.

uniforme                         frequency:    1    relative frequency: 0.0000
P.  166 KINGS VOWES     23 with wide streets and uniforme of my owne mold;

uninforc'd                       frequency:    1    relative frequency: 0.0000
P.  177 LOYALL SCOT    229 And Uninforc'd Quaff healths in Phlegethon.

union                            frequency:    3    relative frequency: 0.0000
P.   37 DEFINITION      15 Their union would her ruine be,
P.   74 A. HOUSE       490 Link'd in so thick, an Union locks,
P.  112 ANNIVERSARY    354 'What Mints of Men, what Union of Designes!

unite                            frequency:    5    relative frequency: 0.0001
See also "t'unite."
P.   40 THE MATCH       33 Thus all his fewel did unite
P.   74 A. HOUSE       509 The arching Boughs unite between
P.   85 FLECKNO        104 By its own narrcwness, Sir, to unite.
P.  149 INSTRUCTIONS   339 And with fresh Age felt his glad Limbs unite;
P.  173 LOYALL SCOT     66 Unite our distance, fill the breaches old?

united                           frequency:    4    relative frequency:'0.0000
P.   98 HOLLAND        100 The Armes of the United Provinces.
P.  122 TWO SONGS       30 Whose Hopes united banish our Despair.
P.  123 TWO SONGS       48 Whose Hopes united banish our Despair.
P.  149 INSTRUCTIONS   364 United most, else when by turns they meet.

universal                        frequency:    3    relative frequency: 0.0000
P.   73 A. HOUSE       456 Davenant with th' Universal Heard.
P.   82 A. HOUSE       741 Whence, for some universal good,
P.   97 HOLLAND         76 The universal Church is onely there.

universe                         frequency:    3    relative frequency: 0.0000
P.   66 A. HOUSE       242 Shall fight through all the Universe;
P.  111 ANNIVERSARY    331 While dismal blacks hung round the Universe,
P.  126 O.C.           132 The Universe labour'd beneath their load.

unjust                           frequency:    2    relative frequency: 0.0000
P.   56 BILL-BOROW       9 Here learn ye Mountains more unjust,
P.   66 A. HOUSE       236 To hinder the unjust Divorce.

unkind                           frequency:    2    relative frequency: 0.0000
P.   23 NYMPH           46 Unkind, t' a Beast that loveth me.
P.   55 EPITAPH          4 When dead to offer were unkind.

unkindness                       frequency:    1    relative frequency: 0.0000
P.  151 INSTRUCTIONS   432 Uncivil: His unkindness would us kill.

unknowing                        frequency:    1    relative frequency: 0.0000
P.   71 A. HOUSE       395 While one, unknowing, carves the Rail,

unknown                          frequency:    7    relative frequency: 0.0001
P.   17 BERMUDAS         7 Unto an Isle so long unknown,
P.   55 THYESTE          8 Thus when without noise, unknown,
P.   75 A. HOUSE       525 Yet always, for some Cause unknown,
P.   97 HOLLAND         69 It struck, and splitting on this unknown ground,
P.  126 O.C.           127 Numbers of Men decrease with pains unknown,
P.  148 INSTRUCTIONS   286 But for th' unknown Reserve that still remain'd:
P.  164 INSTRUCTIONS   950 And Spots unknown to the bright Star descry'd;

unlac't                          frequency:    1    relative frequency: 0.0000
P.   55 EPITAPH         10 In this Age loose and all unlac't;

unless                           frequency:   13    relative frequency: 0.0002
P.   11 DIALOGUE        68 What Slaves, unless I captive you?
```

```
    P.  37 DEFINITION     21 Unless the giddy Heaven fall,
    P.  64 A. HOUSE      183 'What need is here of Man? unless
    P.  78 A. HOUSE      631 Unless it self you will mistake,
    P.  99 HOLLAND       143 Unless our Senate, lest their Youth disuse,
    P. 112 ANNIVERSARY   355 'Unless their Ships, do, as their Fowle proceed
    P. 114 BLAKE          42 Unless it be, the having you their Lord;
    P. 123 O.C.           10 Unless the Prince whom they applaud be slain.
    P. 138 HOUSEWARMING   55 Unless all abroad he divulg'd the design,
    P. 151 INSTRUCTIONS  438 And whip the Dutch, unless they'l hold their
                            peace.
    P. 168 ADVICE         15 Unless it be his late Assumed grief
    P. 184 MADE FREE     132 Unless you all turne again, burne again.
    P. 189 STATUE          4 Unless Puchinello be to be restor'd.
```

unless't   frequency: 1   relative frequency: 0.0000
    P. 194 TWO HORSES   122 Ch. Thy King will ne're tight unless't be for
                            Queans.

unlike   frequency: 1   relative frequency: 0.0000
    P. 129 O.C.   261 Not much unlike the sacred oak, which shoots

unloaded   frequency: 1   relative frequency: 0.0000
    P. 158 INSTRUCTIONS 716 Unloaded here the Birth of either Pole;

unloads   frequency: 1   relative frequency: 0.0000
    P. 154 INSTRUCTIONS 560 And at Sheerness unloads its stormy sides.

unlock'd   frequency: 1   relative frequency: 0.0000
    P. 39 THE MATCH   9 She seldom them unlock'd, or us'd,

unlocks   frequency: 1   relative frequency: 0.0000
    P. 184 MADE FREE   124 He will find who unlocks,

unlucky   frequency: 1   relative frequency: 0.0000
    P. 158 INSTRUCTIONS 739 Or row a Boat in thy unlucky hour:

unman'd   frequency: 1   relative frequency: 0.0000
    P. 151 INSTRUCTIONS 433 Tell him our Ships unrigg'd, our Forts unman'd,

unmanned. See "unman'd."

unmoved   frequency: 1   relative frequency: 0.0000
    P. 110 ANNIVERSARY   308 Wer't but for thine unmoved Tulipant;

unnumbered. See "unnum'red."

unnum'red   frequency: 1   relative frequency: 0.0000
    P. 43 DAMON   50 The plains with an unnum'red Flock,

unpaid   frequency: 2   relative frequency: 0.0000
    P. 46 AMETAS   3 Love unpaid does soon disband:
    P. 155 INSTRUCTIONS 602 Unpaid, refuse to mount our Ships for spight:

unperceiv'd   frequency: 1   relative frequency: 0.0000
    P. 96 HOLLAND   49 Hence some small Dyke-grave unperceiv'd invades

unpractis'd   frequency: 1   relative frequency: 0.0000
    P. 148 INSTRUCTIONS 320 The unpractis'd Saw lyes bury'd in its Dust;

unprepar'd   frequency: 1   relative frequency: 0.0000
    P. 107 ANNIVERSARY   150 Look on, all unconcern'd, or unprepar'd;

unproportion'd   frequency: 1   relative frequency: 0.0000
    P. 59 A. HOUSE   10 Such unproportion'd dwellings build?

unprovok'd   frequency: 1   relative frequency: 0.0000
    P. 142 INSTRUCTIONS   73 Not unprovok'd she trys forbidden Arts,

unreasonable   frequency: 1   relative frequency: 0.0000
    P. 137 HOUSEWARMING   10 (So unreasonable are the rate they buy-at)

unrepair'd   frequency: 1   relative frequency: 0.0000
    P. 159 INSTRUCTIONS 780 And who the Forts left unrepair'd? Pett.

unriddle   frequency: 1   relative frequency: 0.0000
    P. 195 TWO HORSES   151 Ch. Her Walsingham could dark Councells
                            unriddle,

unrigg'd   frequency: 2   relative frequency: 0.0000
    P. 151 INSTRUCTIONS 433 Tell him our Ships unrigg'd, our Forts unman'd,
    P. 154 INSTRUCTIONS 573 There our sick Ships unrigg'd in Summer lay,

unrul'd   frequency: 1   relative frequency: 0.0000
    P.   59 A. HOUSE   9 Why should of all things Man unrul'd

unsafe   frequency: 2   relative frequency: 0.0000
    P.   71 A. HOUSE   411 When Lowness is unsafe as Hight,
    P. 151 INSTRUCTIONS 419 White-hall's unsafe, the Court all meditates

unsecure   frequency: 2   relative frequency: 0.0000
    P.   12 DROP OF DEW   15 Restless it roules and unsecure,
    P. 190 STATUE   9 For a Diall the place is too unsecure

unseemly. See "unsemly."

unsemly   frequency: 1   relative frequency: 0.0000
    P. 184 BRITANNIA   10 Ah! mighty Queen, why so unsemly drest?

unsing'd   frequency: 1   relative frequency: 0.0000
    P. 156 INSTRUCTIONS 647 Three Children tall, unsing'd, away they row,

unstain'd   frequency: 1   relative frequency: 0.0000
    P. 107 ANNIVERSARY   167 Though thou thine Heart from Evil still
                              unstain'd,

unsung   frequency: 1   relative frequency: 0.0000
    P. 115 BLAKE   66 Shall conquests act, your present are unsung.

unsuspected   frequency: 1   relative frequency: 0.0000
    P.   25 YOUNG LOVE   2 While thine unsuspected years

untack   frequency: 1   relative frequency: 0.0000
    P. 155 INSTRUCTIONS 581 Ruyter forthwith a Squadron does untack,

untame   frequency: 2   relative frequency: 0.0000
    P. 157 INSTRUCTIONS 659 They sigh'd and said, Fond Boy, why so untame,
    P. 172 LOYALL SCOT   25 They sigh'd and said 'fond boy why sce Untame,

unthankful   frequency: 1   relative frequency: 0.0000
    P.   45 MOWER'S SONG   13 Unthankful Medows, could you so

untie   frequency: 1   relative frequency: 0.0000
    See also "unty."
    P.   14 THE CORONET   20 Either his slipp'ry knots at once untie,

unties   frequency: 1   relative frequency: 0.0000
    P. 112 ANNIVERSARY   384 'And still his Fauchion all our Knots unties.

untight   frequency: 1   relative frequency: 0.0000
    P. 154 INSTRUCTIONS 566 Through the Walls untight, and Bullet show'rs:

until   frequency: 4   relative frequency: 0.0000
    P.   24 NYMPH   84 Until its Lips ev'n seem'd to bleed:
    P.   24 NYMPH   117 Until my Tears, still dropping, wear
    P.   91 MAY'S DEATH   46 Until you all grow Consuls in your wine.
    P. 154 INSTRUCTIONS 570 Until the City put it in repair.

untimely   frequency: 3   relative frequency: 0.0000
    P.   71 A. HOUSE   399 Fearing the Flesh untimely mow'd
    P.   71 A. HOUSE   414 Sounds your untimely Funeral.
    P. 125 O.C.   94 Chance to be prun'd by an untimely knife,

unto   frequency: 26   relative frequency: 0.0005

untoucht   frequency: 1   relative frequency: 0.0000
    P.   4 HASTINGS   4 Of Tears untoucht, and never wept before.

untrue   frequency: 3   relative frequency: 0.0000
    P.   11 DIALOGUE   67 What Friends, if to my self untrue?
    P. 159 INSTRUCTIONS 752 Themselves dishonour'd, and the Gods untrue:
    P. 163 INSTRUCTIONS 932 To her own Husband, Castlemain, untrue.

untun'd   frequency: 1   relative frequency: 0.0000
    P.   86 FLECKNO   147 For he his untun'd voice did fall or raise

untwine   frequency: 1   relative frequency: 0.0000
    P. 148 INSTRUCTIONS 321 The busie Hammer sleeps, the Ropes untwine;

unty   frequency: 1   relative frequency: 0.0000
    P.   32 MOURNING   10 Slow drops unty themselves away;

unused   frequency: 1   relative frequency: 0.0000
    P.   87 ODE   6 And oyl th' unused Armours rust:

unusual   frequency: 2   relative frequency: 0.0000
     P.   42 DAMON   9 Oh what unusual Heats are here,
     P. 163 INSTRUCTIONS 908 As one that some unusual noise does hear.

unwary   frequency: 1   relative frequency: 0.0000
     P. 143 INSTRUCTIONS   99 And he, unwary, and of Tongue too fleet,

unwearied   frequency: 1   relative frequency: 0.0000
     P. 111 ANNIVERSARY   327 All day he follow'd with unwearied sight,

unwholesome   frequency: 1   relative frequency: 0.0000
     P. 154 INSTRUCTIONS 567 The neighbr'hood ill, and an unwholesome seat.

unwonted   frequency: 1   relative frequency: 0.0000
     P.   60 A. HOUSE   58 Then That unwonted Greatness wears.

up   frequency: 61   relative frequency: 0.0012
     P.   14 THE CORONET   9 And now when I have summ'd up all my store,
     P.   19 THYRSIS   2 And shut up our divided Lids,
     P.   20 SOUL & BODY   7 A Soul hung up, as 'twere, in Chains
     P.   21 SOUL & BODY   42 To build me up for Sin so fit?
     P.   27 MISTRESS   42 Our sweetness, up into one Ball:
     P.   28 LOVER   33 They fed him up with Hopes and Air,
     P.   35 DAPHNIS   71 Than be fatted up express
     P.   55 EPITAPH   16 She summ'd her Life up ev'ry day;
     P.   70 A. HOUSE   383 They bring up Flow'rs so to be seen,
     P.   71 A. HOUSE   403 Greedy as Kites has trust it up,
     P.   74 A. HOUSE   502 To thrust up a Fifth Element;
     P.   76 A. HOUSE   545 The good he numbers up, and hacks;
     P.   96 HOLLAND   32 Whole sholes of Dutch serv'd up for Cabillau;
     P.   98 HOLLAND   95 Tunn'd up with all their sev'ral Towns of Beer;
     P.   98 HOLLAND   112 We buoy'd so often up their sinking State.
     P. 104 ANNIVERSARY   52 Dans'd up in order from the Quarreys rude;
     P. 108 ANNIVERSARY   214 Break up each Deck, and rip the Oaken seams.
     P. 108 ANNIVERSARY   223 Resigning up thy Privacy so dear,
     P. 111 ANNIVERSARY   345 Up from the other World his Flame he darts,
     P. 117 BLAKE   128 Some Ships are sunk, some blown up in the skie.
     P. 126 O.C.   145 When up the armed Mountains of Dunbar
     P. 137 HOUSEWARMING   14 Who was dig'd up so often ere she did marry;
     P. 138 HOUSEWARMING   42 He would have demclisht to raise up his Walls;
     P. 148 INSTRUCTIONS 318 To lay the Ships up, cease the Keels begun.
     P. 151 INSTRUCTIONS 420 To fly to Windsor, and mure up the Gates.
     P. 152 INSTRUCTIONS 470 That summons up the Parliament agen;
     P. 154 INSTRUCTIONS 559 Such up the stream the Belgick Navy glides,
     P. 158 INSTRUCTIONS 705 Up to the Bridge contagious Terrour strook:
     P. 159 INSTRUCTIONS 742 Fill up thy space with a redoubled Night.
     P. 160 INSTRUCTIONS 796 Powder ne're blew man up so soon so high.
     P. 161 INSTRUCTIONS 826 Let them come up so to go dcwn agen.
     P. 161 INSTRUCTIONS 827 Up ambles Ccuntry Justice on his Pad,
     P. 161 INSTRUCTIONS 837 And Turner gay up to his Pearch does march,
     P. 162 INSTRUCTIONS 869 At Pray'rs, his Eyes turn up the Pious white,
     P. 162 INSTRUCTIONS 891 Raise up a sudden Shape with Virgins Face,
     P. 162 INSTRUCTIONS 895 Her mouth lockt up, a blind before her Eyes,
     P. 168 ADVICE   5 The Roman takeing up the fencers trade,
     P. 170 PROPHECY   14 And Checquer dcres shall shut up Lombard
                               street,
     P. 171 PROPHECY   28 Then London lately burnt shall be blowne up,
     P. 173 LOYALL SCCT   68 Galloping down Clos'd up the Gaping Cave.
     P. 174 LOYALL SCOT   84 Up from her Stream Continued to the Sky's,
     P. 175 LOYALL SCCT   147 Leviathen served up and Behemoth.
     P. 176 LOYALL SCOT   193 The Bishops Nodle Perks up cheek by Jowle.
     P. 179 STOCKSMARKET   11 Upon the King's birthday to set up a thing
     P. 183 MADE FREE   101 For himself up tc set,
     P. 184 MADE FREE   128 Goe fold up your Furrs,
     P. 186 BRITANNIA   57 Shee mounted up on a triumphall Car
     P. 187 BRITANNIA   108 Led up by the wise son-in-law of Hide.
     P. 190 STATUE   26 Had within it an Army that burnt up the Town:
     P. 191 STATUE   53 So the Statue will up after all this delay,
     P. 193 TWO HORSES   63 W. Our worm-eaten Navy be laid up at Chatham,
     P. 194 TWO HORSES   114 With an Harlot got up cn my Crupper behind him.
     P. 194 TWO HORSES   120 By Knaves who cry'd themselves up for the
                               Church,
     P. 200 DUKE   98 Noe, Painter, nce; close up this peice and see
     P. 202 HISTORICALL   65 Lookes as one sett up fcr to scare the Crows.
     P. 204 HISTORICALL   120 Sets up in Scotland alamode de France,
     P. 204 HISTORICALL   134 Ill luck starts up and thrives like Evil weeds.
     P. 313 CHEQUER INN   21 And heapes up all cur Treasure
     P. 314 CHEQUER INN   66 To carry up her Taile.
     P. 316 CHEQUER INN   137 On Chequer Tally was scor'd up
     P. 316 CHEQUER INN   152 The Healths in Order did up send

upbraid   frequency: 2   relative frequency: 0.0000

```
        P.  48 THE GARDEN      6 Does prudently their Toyles upbraid;
        P. 146 INSTRUCTIONS  233 They, that e're long shall the rude Dutch
                               upbraid,

uphold                          frequency:    1    relative frequency: 0.0000
        P. 105 ANNIVERSARY    92 Uphold, this one, and that the other Side;

upnor                           frequency:    1    relative frequency: 0.0000
        P. 159 INSTRUCTIONS  782 Languard, Sheerness, Gravesend, and Upnor?
                               Pett.

upnor-castle's                  frequency:    1    relative frequency: 0.0000
        P. 155 INSTRUCTIONS  607 And Upnor-Castle's ill-deserted Wall,

upon                            frequency:   57    relative frequency: 0.0011
        See also "upon----."

upon----                        frequency:    1    relative frequency: 0.0000
        P.  55 EPITAPH         t An Epitaph upon----

upright                         frequency:    3    relative frequency: 0.0000
        P.  21 SOUL & BODY    13 Which, stretcht upright, impales me so,
        P.  75 A. HOUSE      539 He walks still upright from the Root,
        P. 105 ANNIVERSARY    94 And they as Pillars keep the Work upright;

uproar                          frequency:    1    relative frequency: 0.0000
        P. 177 LOYALL SCOT   252 Scotland and England cause of Just uproar!

upstart                         frequency:    1    relative frequency: 0.0000
        P. 203 HISTORICALL   111 And hosts of upstart Errours gaine the field.

upward                          frequency:    1    relative frequency: 0.0000
        P. 130 O.C.          302 To guide us upward through this region blinde.

upwards                         frequency:    2    relative frequency: 0.0000
        P.  13 DROP OF DEW    36 It all about does upwards bend.
        P.  31 MOURNING        7 Seem bending upwards, to restore

urg'd                           frequency:    2    relative frequency: 0.0000
        P. 117 BLAKE         130 As Oakes did then, Urg'd by the active fire.
        P. 162 INSTRUCTIONS  877 When Grievance urg'd, he swells like squatted
                               Toad,

urged                           frequency:    1    relative frequency: 0.0000
        See also "urg'd."
        P.  87 ODE            12 Urged his active Star.

urinal                          frequency:    1    relative frequency: 0.0000
        P. 162 INSTRUCTIONS  880 An Urinal, and sit like any Hen.

us                              frequency:   76    relative frequency: 0.0015
        See also "for's," "let's," "letts."

usd                             frequency:    1    relative frequency: 0.0000
        P. 201 HISTORICALL    29 Her most Uxorious Mate she usd of old;

us'd                            frequency:    5    relative frequency: 0.0001
        P.  39 THE MATCH       9 She seldom them unlock'd, or us'd,
        P. 129 O.C.          231 Where we (so once we us'd) shall now no more,
        P. 145 INSTRUCTIONS  169 Court-Officers, as us'd, the next place took,
        P. 153 INSTRUCTIONS  512 Why he should still b'on all adventures us'd.
        P. 182 MADE FREE      39 He us'd as his owne to spend on't

use                             frequency:   13    relative frequency: 0.0002
        P.  16 EYES           46 And practise so your noblest Use.
        P.  22 NYMPH          15 And nothing may we use in vain.
        P.  33 DAPHNIS        13 Nature so her self does use
        P.  40 THE MOWER       1 Luxurious Man, to bring his Vice in use,
        P.  60 A. HOUSE       62 Where ev'ry Thing does answer Use?
        P. 120 TWO SONGS      40 Would you but your own Reason use.
        P. 148 INSTRUCTIONS  313 The Seamens Clamour to three ends they use;
        P. 164 INSTRUCTIONS  962 Banishing Love, Trust, Ornament and Use;
        P. 170 PROPHECY       15 When Players shall use to act the parts of
                               Queens
        P. 170 PROPHECY       24 Shall be in use at Court but faith and Troth,
        P. 183 MADE FREE     106 In Ballating it use
        P. 185 BRITANNIA      37 Taught him their use, what dangers would ensue
        P. 191 STATUE         52 As would the next tax reimburse them with use.

used.   See "usd," "us'd."

useful                          frequency:    1    relative frequency: 0.0000
```

P. 123 O.C.   17 And so less useful where he most desir'd,

useless   frequency: 6   relative frequency: 0.0001
See also "uselesse."
P. 77 A. HOUSE   604 Bends in some Tree its useless Dart;
P. 81 A. HOUSE   730 Do all your useless Study place,
P. 104 ANNIVERSARY   41 Thus (Image-like) an useless time they tell,
P. 106 ANNIVERSARY   139 Fore-shortned Time its useless Course would
                         stay,
P. 148 INSTRUCTIONS 319 The Timber rots, and useless Ax does rust,
P. 156 INSTRUCTIONS 627 At her own Breast her useless claws does arm;

uselesse   frequency: 1   relative frequency: 0.0000
P. 128 O.C.   222 All law is uselesse, all reward is due.

usual   frequency: 1   relative frequency: 0.0000
P. 152 INSTRUCTIONS 483 Then, from the usual Common-place, he blames

usurpt   frequency: 1   relative frequency: 0.0000
P. 186 BRITANNIA   63 (By her usurpt), her right a bloudy sword

utensils   frequency: 1   relative frequency: 0.0000
P. 79 A. HOUSE   650 And Angles, idle Utensils.

utmost   frequency: 1   relative frequency: 0.0000
P. 70 A. HOUSE   353 For he did, with his utmost Skill,

utter   frequency: 1   relative frequency: 0.0000
P. 314 CHEQUER INN   87 Both words and meate did utter

uttered   frequency: 1   relative frequency: 0.0000
P. 191 TWO HORSES   2 Of Beasts that have uttered Articulate words:

uxorious   frequency: 1   relative frequency: 0.0000
P. 201 HISTORICALL   29 Her most Uxoricus Mate she usd of old;

vacate   frequency: 1   relative frequency: 0.0000
P. 166 KINGS VOWES   30 And I either will vacate, or buy him a place.

vade   frequency: 1   relative frequency: 0.0000
P. 18 CLORINDA   8 C. Seize the short Joyes then, ere they vade.

vail   frequency: 4   relative frequency: 0.0000
P. 93 DR. WITTY   4 Take off the Cypress vail, but leave a mask,
P. 98 HOLLAND   107 No, but all ancient Rights and Leagues must
                         vail,
P. 127 O.C.   167 Stand back ye Seas, and shrunk beneath the vail
P. 172 LOYALL SCOT   17 And modest beauty yet his sex did vail,

vain   frequency: 40   relative frequency: 0.0008
See also "vaine."
P.   5 HASTINGS   57 All he had try'd, but all in vain, he saw,
P. 15 EYES   3 That, having view'd the object vain,
P. 20 SOUL & BODY   10 In a vain Head, and double Heart.
P. 22 NYMPH   15 And nothing may we use in vain.
P. 26 YOUNG LOVE   29 So, to make all Rivals vain,
P. 31 FAIR SINGER   15 But all resistance against her is vain,
P. 32 MOURNING   17 And, while vain Pomp does her restrain
P. 39 THE MATCH   4 To beg in vain for more.
P. 42 DAMCN   29 Alas! I look for Ease in vain,
P. 45 GLO-WORMS   13 Your courteous Lights in vain you wast,
P. 46 AMETAS   9 Thus you vain Excuses find,
P. 65 A. HOUSE   201 Oft, though he knew it was in vain,
P. 66 A. HOUSE   250 Their Wooden Saints in vain oppose.
P. 88 ODE   38 And plead the antient Rights in vain:
P. 97 HOLLAND   75 In vain for Catholicks our selves we bear;
P. 98 HOLLAND   119 Yet of his vain Attempt no more he sees
P. 103 ANNIVERSARY   1 Like the vain Curlings of the Watry maze,
P. 104 ANNIVERSARY   42 And with vain Scepter, strike the hourly Bell;
P. 115 BLAKE   49 Forces and art, she soon will feel, are vain,
P. 115 BLAKE   63 In vain doth she these Islands free from Ill,
P. 116 BLAKE   85 To fight against such Foes, was vain they knew,
P. 123 O.C.   9 And blame the last Act, like Spectators vain,
P. 125 O.C.   102 Fore boding Princes falls, and seldom vain.
P. 131 PARADISE   16 And what was easie he should render vain.
P. 139 HOUSEWARMING   94 Like vain Chymists, a flower from its ashes
                         returning;
P. 144 INSTRUCTIONS 127 Should pay Land Armies, should dissolve the
                         vain
P. 145 INSTRUCTIONS 172 In vain, for always he commands that pays.
P. 149 INSTRUCTIONS 360 And roul in vain at Sisyphus's Stone.

```
P. 153 INSTRUCTIONS  527 Through the vain sedge the bashful Nymphs he
                          ey'd;
P. 154 INSTRUCTIONS  558 Shepherds themselves in vain in bushes shrowd.
P. 155 INSTRUCTIONS  606 Cannon and Powder, but in vain, to beg:
P. 156 INSTRUCTIONS  637 Mix a vain Terrour in his Martial look,
P. 159 INSTRUCTIONS  751 Now with vain grief their vainer hopes they rue,
P. 161 INSTRUCTIONS  836 Salute them, smiling at their vain design.
P. 163 INSTRUCTIONS  911 Thrice did he rise, thrice the vain Tumult fled,
P. 171 PROPHECY       56 And wish in vain Venetian Libertye.
P. 188 BRITANNIA     141 Brit: Rawleigh, noe more; too long in vain I've
                          try'd
P. 201 HISTORICALL    32 Deludes their plyant Nature with Vain things,
P. 202 HISTORICALL    53 But here his french bred Prowes provd in Vain,
P. 203 HISTORICALL    83 Who with vain Faith made all their Reason
                          blind:
```

```
vaine                       frequency:    3     relative frequency: 0.0000
P.    3 LOVELACE      25 Till when in vaine they have thee all perus'd,
P. 129 O.C.         255 Oh! humane glory, vaine, oh! death, oh! wings,
P. 171 PROPHECY      53 But like the Bellydes shall toyle in vaine
```

```
vainer                      frequency:    1     relative frequency: 0.0000
P. 159 INSTRUCTIONS 751 Now with vain grief their vainer hopes they rue,
```

```
vainly                      frequency:    7     relative frequency: 0.0001
P.   37 DEFINITION    8 But vainly flapt its Tinsel Wing.
P.   48 THE GARDEN    1 How vainly men themselves amaze
P.   60 A. HOUSE     45 Let others vainly strive t'immure
P.   67 A. HOUSE    260 And superstitions vainly fear'd.
P.   99 HOLLAND     139 Their Tortoise wants its vainly stretched neck;
P.   99 HOLLAND     152 Vainly in Hell let Pluto domineer.
P. 110 ANNIVERSARY  290 That they enjoy, but more they vainly crave:
```

```
vale                        frequency:    2     relative frequency: 0.0000
P. 110 ANNIVERSARY  285 And the large Vale lay subject to thy Will,
P. 315 CHEQUER INN  113 And Cholmley of Vale Royall came
```

```
valianst                    frequency:    1     relative frequency: 0.0000
P.    4 LOVELACE     49 Him, valianst men, and fairest Nymphs approve,
```

```
valiant                     frequency:    5     relative frequency: 0.0001
P.   86 FLECKNO     115 To be both witty and valiant: I loth,
P. 121 TWO SONGS     57 But to be honest, valiant, wise,
P. 145 INSTRUCTIONS 191 Then marcht the Troop, whose valiant Acts
                          before,
P. 157 INSTRUCTIONS 696 Our English youth shall sing the Valiant Scot.
P. 173 LOYALL SCOT   62 Our English youth shall sing the valiant Scott.
```

valiantest. See "valianst."

```
valiantly                   frequency:    1     relative frequency: 0.0000
P.   65 A. HOUSE    202 Yet would he valiantly complain.
```

```
valiants                    frequency:    1     relative frequency: 0.0000
P. 112 ANNIVERSARY  383 'The Valiants Terror, Riddle of the Wise;
```

```
valour                      frequency:   10     relative frequency: 0.0002
P.   66 A. HOUSE    243 And with successive Valour try
P.   88 ODE          33 Could by industrious Valour climbe
P.   90 ODE         107 But from this Valour sad
P. 123 O.C.          13 But long his Valour none had left that could
P. 127 O.C.         177 And in a valour less'ning Arthur's deeds,
P. 128 O.C.         227 Valour, religion, friendship, prudence dy'd
P. 146 INSTRUCTIONS 231 Pleas'd with their Numbers, yet in Valour wise,
P. 147 INSTRUCTIONS 267 These and some more with single Valour stay
P. 153 INSTRUCTIONS 515 Whether his Valour they so much admire,
P. 178 LOYALL SCOT  281 And such my Rashness best thy valour praise.
```

```
value                       frequency:    2     relative frequency: 0.0000
P.   11 DIALOGUE     61 Wer't not a price who'ld value Gold?
P. 195 TWO HORSES   126 And Free men alike value life and Estate.
```

```
values                      frequency:    1     relative frequency: 0.0000
P. 183 MADE FREE     75 He values not Credit nor Hist'ry,
```

```
van                         frequency:    2     relative frequency: 0.0000
P. 148 INSTRUCTIONS 295 The Van and Battel, though retiring, falls
P. 169 ADVICE        43 The body of foot that was to have the van
```

```
vandale                     frequency:    1     relative frequency: 0.0000
P.   91 MAY'S DEATH  41 Polydore, Lucan, Allan, Vandale, Goth,
```

vanish'd   frequency: 1   relative frequency: 0.0000
    P.   24 NYMPH   105 Now my Sweet Faun is vanish'd to

vanishes   frequency: 2   relative frequency: 0.0000
    P.   67 A. HOUSE   270 The Castle vanishes or rends)
    P. 114 BLAKE   23 At length theirs vanishes, and fortune smiles;

vanisht   frequency: 2   relative frequency: 0.0000
    P.   92 MAY'S DEATH   99 And streight he vanisht in a Cloud of pitch,
    P. 163 INSTRUCTIONS 904 And th' airy Picture vanisht from his hold.

vanity   frequency: 1   relative frequency: 0.0000
    P.   35 DAPHNIS   66 'Tis a Vanity tc wear,

varied   frequency: 1   relative frequency: 0.0000
    P.   90 MAY'S DEATH   19 But seeing May he varied streight his Song,

various   frequency: 4   relative frequency: 0.0000
    P.   29 THE GALLERY   6 Of various Faces, by are laid;
    P.   49 THE GARDEN   56 Waves in its Plumes the various Light.
    P. 104 ANNIVERSARY   58 And still new Stopps to various Time apply'd:
    P. 202 HISTORICALL   62 Cr count the various blemishes of State--

vassalls   frequency: 1   relative frequency: 0.0000
    P. 201 HISTORICALL   16 His jolly Vassalls treat him day and Night.

vassals. See "vassalls."

vast   frequency: 5   relative frequency: 0.0001
    P.   26 MISTRESS   24 Desarts of vast Eternity.
    P. 116 BLAKE   77 Onely to this vast hill a power is given,
    P. 116 BLAKE   102 Ore Seas as vast as is the Spaniards pride.
    P. 131 PARADISE   2 In slender Book his vast Design unfold,
    P. 132 PARADISE   42 Whence furnish such a vast expense of Mind?

vaster   frequency: 1   relative frequency: 0.0000
    P.   26 MISTRESS   12 Vaster then Empires, and more slow.

vault   frequency: 4   relative frequency: 0.0000
    P.   18 BERMUDAS   34 Till it arrive at Heavens Vault:
    P.   26 MISTRESS   26 Nor, in thy marble Vault, shall sound
    P.   59 A. HOUSE   6 Did for a Model vault his Brain,
    P.   67 A. HOUSE   259 Then th' unfrequented Vault appear'd,

vaulted   frequency: 2   relative frequency: 0.0000
    P. 108 ANNIVERSARY 210 And then loud Shreeks the vaulted Marbles rent.
    P. 164 INSTRUCTIONS 976 Ncr Powder so the vaulted Bastion tear;

vaunts   frequency: 1   relative frequency: 0.0000
    P. 204 HISTORICALL 145 The Duke now vaunts, with popish Myrmidons;

vegetable   frequency: 2   relative frequency: 0.0000
    P.   26 MISTRESS   11 My vegetable Love should grow
    P. 138 HOUSEWARMING 56 For his House then would grow like a Vegetable.

veil   frequency: 3   relative frequency: 0.0000
    P. 156 INSTRUCTIONS 651 And modest Beauty yet his Sex did Veil,
    P. 162 INSTRUCTIONS 896 Yet from beneath the Veil her blushes rise;
    P. 180 STOCKSMARKET 45 Cr do you his beams out of modesty veil

veils   frequency: 1   relative frequency: 0.0000
    P.   5 HASTINGS   42 But draw their Veils, and their pure Beams
                             reveal:

vein   frequency: 3   relative frequency: 0.0000
    P.   4 HASTINGS   1 Go, intercept scme Fountain in the Vein,
    P. 153 INSTRUCTIONS 497 Horse-leeches circling at the Hem'roid Vein;
    P. 172 LOYALL SCOT   9 Much had hee Cur'd the Humor cf his vein:

veines   frequency: 1   relative frequency: 0.0000
    P. 199 DUKE   42 And in her youthfull veines receive the wound

veins   frequency: 2   relative frequency: 0.0000
    See also "veines."
    P.   20 SOUL & BODY   8 Of Nerves, and Arteries, and Veins.
    P. 153 INSTRUCTIONS 532 Swells his old Veins with fresh Blood, fresh
                             Delight.

velvet   frequency: 1   relative frequency: 0.0000
    P.   77 A. HOUSE   594 Cn Pallets swoln cf Velvet Moss;

venerable   frequency: 1   relative frequency: 0.0000

```
         P. 113 ANNIVERSARY    399 While thou thy venerable Head dost raise

venetian                          frequency:    2    relative frequency: 0.0000
         P. 171 PROPHECY        56 And wish in vain Venetian Libertye.
         P. 188 BRITANNIA      155 To the serene Venetian state I'le goe

vengeance                         frequency:    1    relative frequency: 0.0000
         P. 170 PROPHECY         7 Where Vengeance dwells, but there is one trick
                                   more

venice                            frequency:    1    relative frequency: 0.0000
         P. 150 INSTRUCTIONS   402 Where Venice twenty years the Turk had fought:

venom'd                           frequency:    1    relative frequency: 0.0000
         P. 142 INSTRUCTIONS    66 Can without breaking venom'd juice convey.

venture                           frequency:    1    relative frequency: 0.0000
         P. 190 STATUE          36 Will you venture soe far to Prorogue the King
                                   too?

venus                             frequency:    2    relative frequency: 0.0000
         P.  30 THE GALLERY     34 Like Venus in her pearly Boat.
         P. 202 HISTORICALL     51 Foil'd thus by Venus he Bellona woes,

vera                              frequency:    1    relative frequency: 0.0000
         P.  57 BILL-BOROW      43 Vera the Nymph that him inspir'd,

verdant                           frequency:    2    relative frequency: 0.0000
         P.   5 HASTINGS        53 How Sweet and Verdant would these Lawrels be,
         P.  38 PICTURE         25 Mean time, whilst every verdant thing

verdict                           frequency:    1    relative frequency: 0.0000
         P. 313 CHEQUER INN     48 For such a shamefull Verdict.

vere                              frequency:    2    relative frequency: 0.0000
         P.  60 A. HOUSE        36 By Vere and Fairfax trod before,
         P.  81 A. HOUSE       724 Of Fairfax, and the starry Vere;

veres                             frequency:    2    relative frequency: 0.0000
         P.  74 A. HOUSE       492 On one hand Fairfax, th' other Veres:
         P. 189 BRITANNIA      173 Make 'em admire the Sidnies, Talbots, Veres,

verged                            frequency:    1    relative frequency: 0.0000
         P.  48 THE GARDEN       5 Whose short and narrow verged Shade

vermin                            frequency:    1    relative frequency: 0.0000
         P. 165 INSTRUCTIONS   981 The smallest Vermin make the greatest waste,

verse                             frequency:    9    relative frequency: 0.0001
         P.  83 FLECKNO         20 In hideous verse, he, and a dismal tone,
         P.  84 FLECKNO         32 Towards the Verse; and when that could not hear,
         P. 130 O.C.           277 Thee, many ages hence, in martial verse
         P. 132 PARADISE        53 Thy verse created like thy Theme sublime,
         P. 152 INSTRUCTIONS   451 The first instructs our (Verse the Name abhors)
         P. 157 INSTRUCTIONS   694 Or if my Verse can propagate thy Name;
         P. 173 LOYALL SCOT     59 Fortunate Boy, if ere my verse may Claim
         P. 178 LOYALL SCOT    276 My former satyr for this verse forget,
         P. 203 HISTORICALL    113 And touch the holy function with her Verse:

verses                            frequency:    1    relative frequency: 0.0000
         P.  86 FLECKNO        143 To hear his Verses, by so just a curse

vertue                            frequency:    4    relative frequency: 0.0000
         P. 130 O.C.           306 Beats on the rugged track: he, vertue dead,
         P. 173 LOYALL SCOT     82 Whose one bank vertue, th' other vice doth breed?
         P. 177 LOYALL SCOT    244 Or whether the same vertue would reflect
         P. 178 LOYALL SCOT    280 My differing Crime doth more thy vertue raise

vertues                           frequency:    4    relative frequency: 0.0000
         P.   3 LOVELACE        11 These vertues now are banisht out of Towne,
         P.   4 HASTINGS         9 Alas, his Vertues did his Death presage:
         P.  92 MAY'S DEATH     66 And single fights forsaken Vertues cause.
         P. 186 BRITANNIA       74 Doe Monarchs rise by vertues or the sword?

very                              frequency:    8    relative frequency: 0.0001
         P.  22 NYMPH           39 With this: and very well content,
         P.  31 FAIR SINGER     12 My Fetters of the very Air I breath?
         P.  65 A. HOUSE       216 'And vice infects the very Wall.
         P.  98 HOLLAND        133 Besides that very Agitation laves,
         P. 162 INSTRUCTIONS   898 Her heart throbs, and with very shame would
                                   break.
         P. 175 LOYALL SCOT    143 Bishops are very good when in Commendum.
```

```
      P. 184 MADE FREE      109 The very First Head
      P. 195 TWO HORSES     156 W. For that very reason hee 's never to rise.

vessel                        frequency:    2    relative frequency: 0.0000
      See also "vessell."
      P.  94 DR. WITTY       11 That but to make the Vessel shining, they
      P.  98 HOLLAND        110 It self, when as scme greater Vessel tows

vessell                       frequency:    1    relative frequency: 0.0000
      P. 203 HISTORICALL    105 To have the weaker Vessell made his prey:

vest                          frequency:    3    relative frequency: 0.0000
      P.  49 THE GARDEN      51 Casting the Bodies Vest aside,
      P. 161 INSTRUCTICNS   828 And Vest bespeaks to be more seemly clad.
      P. 167 KINGS VOWES     49 I will have a fine Tunick a Sash and a Vest,

vestal                        frequency:    1    relative frequency: 0.0000
      P.  97 HOLLAND         87 A vestal Turf enshrin'd in Earthen Ware

vestments                     frequency:    1    relative frequency: 0.0000
      P. 176 LOYALL SCOT    184 With the preists vestments had hee but put on

vex                           frequency:    4    relative frequency: 0.0000
      P.  21 SOUL & BODY     38 Cr Sorrow's other Madness vex.
      P.  41 THE MOWER       29 And in the Cherry he does Nature vex,
      P. 158 INSTRUCTIONS   733 Then with rude shouts, secure, the Air they vex;
      P. 205 HISTORICALL    180 To give you kings in's Wrath to vex you sore:

vexing                        frequency:    1    relative frequency: 0.0000
      P.  30 THE GALLERY     26 Vexing thy restless Lover's Ghost;

vext                          frequency:    2    relative frequency: 0.0000
      P.  71 A. HOUSE       387 For when the Sun the Grass hath vext,
      P. 141 INSTRUCTIONS    21 The Painter so, long having vext his cloth,

vial                          frequency:    1    relative frequency: 0.0000
      P.  24 NYMPH          101 I in a golden Vial will

viands.  See "vyands."

vice                          frequency:    9    relative frequency: 0.0001
      P.  40 THE MOWER        1 Luxurious Man, to bring his Vice in use,
      P.  55 EPITAPH         11 Nor was, when Vice is so allow'd,
      P.  64 A. HOUSE       170 'Delight to banish as a Vice.
      P.  65 A. HOUSE       216 'And vice infects the very Wall.
      P.  81 A. HOUSE       731 Nor once at Vice your Brows dare knit
      P. 173 LOYALL SCOT     82 Whose one bank vertue, th' other vice doth breed?
      P. 175 LOYALL SCOT    144 If Wealth or vice can tempt your appetites,
      P. 177 LOYALL SCOT    232 -leness and all the vice that did abound,
      P. 177 LOYALL SCOT    243 Which stronger were, a Scotch or English vice,

vicegerent                    frequency:    1    relative frequency: 0.0000
      P. 203 HISTORICALL     81 He true Vicegerent to cld Moloch were.

vices                         frequency:    3    relative frequency: 0.0000
      P.  65 A. HOUSE       221 'Fly from their Vices. 'tis thy state,
      P. 183 MADE FREE       84 For his virtues exceed all his vices.
      P. 203 HISTORICALL     87 And practise all the Vices they araigne:

vicinity                      frequency:    1    relative frequency: 0.0000
      P.  40 THE MATCH       29 Till, by vicinity so long,

victor                        frequency:    2    relative frequency: 0.0000
      See also "victour."
      P. 126 O.C.           144 Twice had in open field him Victor crown'd:
      P. 202 HISTORICALL     43 The dreadfull Victcr tooke his soft repose,

victorious                    frequency:    4    relative frequency: 0.0000
      P.  12 DIALOGUE        75 Triumph, triumph, victorious Soul;
      P.  47 EMPIRE          21 Victorious sounds! yet here your Homage do
      P. 118 BLAKE          162 Victorious Blake, does from the Bay retire,
      P. 127 O.C.           153 And the last minute his victorious Ghost

victors                       frequency:    2    relative frequency: 0.0000
      P.  72 A. HOUSE       425 And now the careless Victors play,
      P. 153 INSTRUCTIONS   533 Like am'rous Victors he begins to shave,

victor's                      frequency:    1    relative frequency: 0.0000
      P. 156 INSTRUCTIONS   619 Now a cheap spcil, and the mean Victor's Slave,

victory                       frequency:    5    relative frequency: 0.0001
```

P. 31 FAIR SINGER   14 Where Victory might hang in equal choice,
P. 89 ODE   98 While Victory his Crest does plume!
P. 113 BLAKE   t1 On the Victory obtained by Blake over the
                         Spaniards,
P. 117 BLAKE   109 Of Speedy Victory let no man doubt,
P. 117 BLAKE   116 The noblest wreaths, that Victory bestows.

victour   frequency: 1   relative frequency: 0.0000
P. 129 O.C.   264 And honour'd wreaths have oft the victour
                         crown'd.

victualls   frequency: 1   relative frequency: 0.0000
P. 193 TWO HORSES   66 By pawning for Victualls their Guns at
                         Legorne;

victuals. See "victualls."

vie   frequency: 1   relative frequency: 0.0000
   See also "vye."
P. 10 DIALOGUE   31 Every thing does seem to vie

view   frequency: 5   relative frequency: 0.0001
P. 10 DIALOGUE   34 In this Crystal view thy face.
P. 29 THE GALLERY   1 Clora come view my Soul, and tell
P. 67 A. HOUSE   261 The Relicks false were set to view;
P. 129 O.C.   269 The tree ere while foreshortned to our view,
P. 155 INSTRUCTIONS 596 Monk from the tank the dismal sight does view.

view'd   frequency: 3   relative frequency: 0.0000
P. 15 EYES   3 That, having view'd the object vain,
P. 116 BLAKE   103 Whose Fleet and Trenches view'd, he soon did
                         say,
P. 130 O.C.   310 In private, to be view'd by better light;

viewing   frequency: 2   relative frequency: 0.0000
P. 76 A. HOUSE   560 Viewing the Treason's Punishment.
P. 158 INSTRUCTIONS 732 Viewing her strength, they yet their Conquest
                         doubt.

views   frequency: 3   relative frequency: 0.0000
P.   5 HASTINGS   35 And underneath, he views the Turnaments
P. 10 DIALOGUE   48 And Heaven views it with delight.
P. 175 LOYALL SCOT   160 Who views but Gilberts Toyls will reason find

vigilance   frequency: 1   relative frequency: 0.0000
P. 147 INSTRUCTIONS 246 (For Vigilance and Courage both renown'd)

vigilant   frequency: 1   relative frequency: 0.0000
P. 68 A. HOUSE   313 But when the vigilant Patroul

vigils   frequency: 1   relative frequency: 0.0000
P. 111 ANNIVERSARY   335 His weeping Eyes the doleful Vigils keep,

vigor. See "vigour."

vigour   frequency: 3   relative frequency: 0.0000
P. 103 ANNIVERSARY   7 Cromwell alone with greater Vigour runs,
P. 124 O.C.   34 Slacken the vigour of his Muscles strong;
P. 129 O.C.   252 Loose and depriv'd of vigour, stretch'd along:

vile   frequency: 1   relative frequency: 0.0000
P. 180 STOCKSMARKET   41 Methinks by the equipage of this vile scene

village   frequency: 1   relative frequency: 0.0000
P. 97 HOLLAND   78 Where wisely for their Court they chose a
                         Village.

villagers   frequency: 1   relative frequency: 0.0000
P. 73 A. HOUSE   451 The Villagers in common chase

villain. See "villin."

villains   frequency: 2   relative frequency: 0.0000
P. 193 TWO HORSES   79 W. Yet some of those givers such beggerly
                         Villains
P. 198 DUKE   34 Ile have these villains in our notions rest;

villany   frequency: 2   relative frequency: 0.0000
P. 170 PROPHECY   13 When bare fac'd Villany shall not blush to cheat
P. 199 DUKE   55 The Counsellors of all this villany.

villin   frequency: 1   relative frequency: 0.0000

P. 204 HISTORICALL   127 This Villin Rampant bares away the bell.

vindex   frequency: 1   relative frequency: 0.0000
     P. 188 BRITANNIA   131 Oh Vindex, come, and purge the Poyson'd state;

vindicate   frequency: 1   relative frequency: 0.0000
     P. 89 ODE   62 To vindicate his helpless Right,

vindicates   frequency: 1   relative frequency: 0.0000
     P. 205 HISTORICALL   169 The holy Scripture vindicates his Cause,

vine   frequency: 5   relative frequency: 0.0001
     P. 49 THE GARDEN   35 The Luscious Clusters of the Vine
     P. 110 ANNIVERSARY 287 And only didst for cthers plant the Vine
     P. 125 O.C.   89 So have I seen a Vine, whose lasting Age
     P. 125 O.C.   99 So the dry Stock, nc more that spreading Vine,
     P. 180 STOCKSMARKET 33 But, Sir Knight of the Vine, how came't in
                             your thought

viner   frequency: 3   relative frequency: 0.0000
     P. 184 MADE FREE   129 And turne again Viner, turne again;
     P. 190 STATUE   38 Not Viner delayed us so, tho' he was brooken
     P. 192 TWO HORSES   27 Since Viner and Csburn did buy and provide 'um

vines   frequency: 1   relative frequency: 0.0000
     P. 78 A. HOUSE   610 Curle me about ye gadding Vines,

viol   frequency: 2   relative frequency: 0.0000
     P. 47 EMPIRE   13 Some to the Lute, some to the Viol went,
     P. 86 FLECKNO   148 As a deaf Man upon a Viol playes,

violets   frequency: 1   relative frequency: 0.0000
     P. 38 PICTURE   32 That Violets may a longer Age endure.

viols   frequency: 1   relative frequency: 0.0000
     P. 104 ANNIVERSARY   44 Then wooden Heads unto the Viols strings.

virgil   frequency: 2   relative frequency: 0.0000
     P. 91 MAY'S DEATH   35 At whose dread Whisk Virgil himself does quake,
     P. 137 HOUSEWARMING 21 Yet a President fitter in Virgil he found,

virgin   frequency: 10   relative frequency: 0.0002
     P. 24 NYMPH   89 And its pure virgin Limbs to fold
     P. 47 EMPIRE   10 And Virgin Trebles wed the manly Base.
     P. 55 EPITAPH   9 To say she liv'd a Virgin chast,
     P. 61 A. HOUSE   86 For Virgin Buildings oft brought forth.
     P. 61 A. HOUSE   90 There dwelt the blcoming Virgin Thwates;
     P. 62 A. HOUSE   106 'Like Virgin Amazcns do fight.
     P. 64 A. HOUSE   186 'Appoint a fresh and Virgin Bride;
     P. 67 A. HOUSE   277 For if the Virgin prov'd not theirs,
     P. 68 A. HOUSE   301 None for the Virgin Nymph; for She
     P. 185 BRITANNIA   44 How Spaines prcw'd power her Virgin Armes
                             contrould

virgin-source   frequency: 1   relative frequency: 0.0000
     P.   4 HASTINGS   2 Whose Virgin-Source yet never steept the Plain.

virginity   frequency: 1   relative frequency: 0.0000
     P. 26 MISTRESS   28 That long preserv'd Virginity:

virgins   frequency: 6   relative frequency: 0.0001
     P. 36 DAPHNIS   101 But hence Virgins all beware.
     P. 82 A. HOUSE   751 That, as all Virgins She preceds,
     P. 156 INSTRUCTIONS 652 While envious Virgins hope he is a Male.
     P. 162 INSTRUCTIONS 891 Raise up a sudden Shape with Virgins Face,
     P. 172 LOYALL SCOT   18 Whilst Envious Virgins hope hee is a Male.
     P. 187 BRITANNIA   100 Three spotless virgins to your bed I bring,

virgo   frequency: 1   relative frequency: 0.0000
     P. 186 BRITANNIA   58 Outshining Virgc and the Julian Star.

virtue   frequency: 7   relative frequency: 0.0001
  See also "vertue."
     P. 25 YOUNG LOVE   19 Of this Need wee'l Virtue make,
     P. 55 EPITAPH   12 Of Virtue or asham'd, cr proud;
     P. 81 A. HOUSE   736 And Virtue all thcse Furrows till'd.
     P. 123 TWO SONGS   43 But Virtue shall be Beauties hire,
     P. 124 O.C.   37 But as with riper Years her Virtue grew,
     P. 128 O.C.   201 Friendship, that sacred virtue, long dos claime
     P. 165 INSTRUCTIONS 983 But they whcm born to Virtue and to Wealth,

virtues   frequency: 5   relative frequency: 0.0001

See also "vertues."
P. 64 A. HOUSE   165 'Those Virtues to us all so dear,
P. 122 TWO SONGS   36 And meaner Virtues come in play;
P. 183 MADE FREE   84 For his virtues exceed all his vices.
P. 186 BRITANNIA   72 'Are thred-bare Virtues Ornaments for Kings?
P. 186 BRITANNIA   76 Virtues a faint-green-sickness of the souls,

virtue's   frequency: 1   relative frequency: 0.0000
P. 18 CLORINDA   10 D. That den? C. Loves Shrine. D. But
                             Virtue's Grave.

virtuoso's   frequency: 1   relative frequency: 0.0000
P. 188 BRITANNIA   143 As easily learn'd Virtuoso's may

virtuous   frequency: 1   relative frequency: 0.0000
P. 38 PICTURE   16 Appease this virtuous Enemy of Man!

viscous   frequency: 1   relative frequency: 0.0000
P. 80 A. HOUSE   673 The viscous Air, wheres'ere She fly,

visick   frequency: 1   relative frequency: 0.0000
P. 316 CHEQUER INN   154 But downe the Visick Bottle threw

vision   frequency: 1   relative frequency: 0.0000
P. 162 INSTRUCTIONS   901 And with kind hand does the coy Vision press,

visit   frequency: 1   relative frequency: 0.0000
P. 168 KINGS VOWES   66 And Visit Nell when I shold be att Prayers.

visits   frequency: 2   relative frequency: 0.0000
P. 17 BERMUDAS   16 On daily Visits through the Air.
P. 83 FLECKNO   1 Oblig'd by frequent visits of this man,

vital   frequency: 1   relative frequency: 0.0000
P. 125 O.C.   96 And through the Wound its vital humour bleeds;

vitiate   frequency: 1   relative frequency: 0.0000
P. 152 INSTRUCTIONS   478 Their Acts to vitiate, and them over-awe.

vitrifi'd   frequency: 1   relative frequency: 0.0000
P. 80 A. HOUSE   688 Nature is wholly vitrifi'd.

vitrified. See "vitrifi'd."

vive   frequency: 1   relative frequency: 0.0000
P. 167 KINGS VOWES   54 And Quack in their Language still Vive le
                             Roy.

vocal   frequency: 1   relative frequency: 0.0000
P. 144 INSTRUCTIONS   161 Then damming Cowards rang'd the vocal Plain,

voice   frequency: 7   relative frequency: 0.0001
P. 18 BERMUDAS   33 Oh let our Voice his Praise exalt,
P. 18 CLORINDA   25 D. Clorinda's voice might make it sweet.
P. 31 FAIR SINGER   6 She with her Voice might captivate my Mind.
P. 31 FAIR SINGER   16 Who has th' advantage both of Eyes and Voice,
P. 64 A. HOUSE   161 'Your voice, the sweetest of the Quire,
P. 75 A. HOUSE   514 To sing the Tryals of her Voice.
P. 86 FLECKNO   147 For he his untun'd voice did fall or raise

voices   frequency: 1   relative frequency: 0.0000
P. 97 HOLLAND   61 Though Herring for their God few voices mist,

void   frequency: 1   relative frequency: 0.0000
P. 189 BRITANNIA   174 Blake, Candish, Drake, (men void of slavish
                             fears)

volke   frequency: 1   relative frequency: 0.0000
P. 317 CHEQUER INN   187 By wise Volke, I have oft been told

volleys. See "vollyes."

vollyes   frequency: 1   relative frequency: 0.0000
P. 68 A. HOUSE   298 In fragrant Vollyes they let fly;

volumes   frequency: 1   relative frequency: 0.0000
P. 107 ANNIVERSARY   152 Swinges the Volumes of its horrid Flail.

vomit   frequency: 1   relative frequency: 0.0000
P. 95 HOLLAND   7 This indigested vomit of the Sea

vote   frequency: 1   relative frequency: 0.0000

```
         P. 193 TWO HORSES      86 Who vote with the Court for drink and for
                                   Dinners.

voters                             frequency:    1    relative frequency: 0.0000
         P. 191 STATUE          51 Where he shew'd her that so many voters he had

votes                              frequency:    4    relative frequency: 0.0000
         P. 168 ADVICE         24 All looking this way how to give their votes,
         P. 168 ADVICE         26 That give their votes more by their eyes than
                                   ears:
         P. 185 BRITANNIA      20 Till commons votes shall cut-nose guards disband,
         P. 195 TWO HORSES    129 Both Infamous Stand in three Kingdoms votes,

vouchsafe                          frequency:    1    relative frequency: 0.0000
         P. 160 INSTRUCTIONS  799 And who the Forts would not vouchsafe a corn,

vow                                frequency:    5    relative frequency: 0.0001
         P.  62 A. HOUSE      116 'That live without this happy Vow.
         P.  67 A. HOUSE      279 Though many a Nun there made her Vow,
         P.  87 FLECKNO       170 To hang it in Saint Peter's for a Vow.
         P. 198 DUKE           12 I and the wise associates of my vow,
         P. 198 DUKE           13 A vow that fire and sword shall never end

vowes                              frequency:    3    relative frequency: 0.0000
         P. 165 KINGS VOWES     t The Kings Vowes.
         P. 165 KINGS VOWES     5 Made these Vowes to his Maker--
         P. 170 PROPHECY       27 When publike faith and Vowes and Payments stop,

vows                               frequency:    1    relative frequency: 0.0000
         See also "vowes."
         P. 179 STOCKSMARKET    8 He that vows for a calm is absolved by a wreck.

voyage                             frequency:    1    relative frequency: 0.0000
         P. 158 INSTRUCTIONS  720 Take a short Voyage underneath the Thames.

vulcan                             frequency:    1    relative frequency: 0.0000
         P. 137 HOUSEWARMING    5 Us Mars, and Apollo, and Vulcan consume;

vulgar                             frequency:    2    relative frequency: 0.0000
         P.  89 ODE            61 Nor call'd the Gods with vulgar spight
         P.  94 DR. WITTY      28 Down into Error with the Vulgar tide;

vulture                            frequency:    2    relative frequency: 0.0000
         P.  90 MAY'S DEATH    17 But how a double headed Vulture Eats,
         P.  92 MAY'S DEATH    94 Shalt break, and the perpetual Vulture feel.

vulture's                          frequency:    1    relative frequency: 0.0000
         See also "vultur's."
         P. 152 INSTRUCTIONS  490 With that curs'd Quill pluck'd from a Vulture's
                                   Wing:

vultur's                           frequency:    1    relative frequency: 0.0000
         P.  30 THE GALLERY    32 To be the greedy Vultur's prey.

vyands                             frequency:    1    relative frequency: 0.0000
         P. 201 HISTORICALL    15 With Women, Wire and Vyands of delight

vye                                frequency:    1    relative frequency: 0.0000
         P. 126 O.C.          133 Nature it seem'd with him would Nature vye:

W.                                 frequency:   29    relative frequency: 0.0006
         P. 192 TWO HORSES     35 W. Quoth the marble white Hors: 'twould make a
                                   stone speak
         P. 192 TWO HORSES     43 W. To see dei Gratia writ on the Throne,
         P. 192 TWO HORSES     47 W. That the Duke should turne Papist and that
                                   Church defy
         P. 192 TWO HORSES     51 W. That Bondage and Begery should be brought
                                   on the Nacion
         P. 193 TWO HORSES     55 W. That the bank should be seiz'd yet the
                                   Chequer so poor;
         P. 193 TWO HORSES     59 W. That a King should consume three Realms
                                   whole Estates
         P. 193 TWO HORSES     63 W. Our worm-eaten Navy be laid up at Chatham,
         P. 193 TWO HORSES     67 W. That makeing us slaves by hors and foot
                                   Guards
         P. 193 TWO HORSES     71 W. On Seventh Harry's head he that placed the
                                   Crown
         P. 193 TWO HORSES     75 W. To the bold talking members if the Bastards
                                   you adde,
         P. 193 TWO HORSES     79 W. Yet some of those givers such beggerly
                                   Villains
         P. 193 TWO HORSES     83 W. Four Knights and a Knave, who were Publicans
                                                                        made,
```

```
P. 194 TWO HORSES      87 W. 'tis they who brought on us the Scandalous
                              Yoak
P. 194 TWO HORSES      91 W. That a King shou'd endavour to make a warr
                              cease
P. 194 TWO HORSES      95 W. That the King should send for another
                              French where,
P. 194 TWO HORSES     105 W. Truth 's as Bold as a Lyon, I am not
                              afraid;
P. 194 TWO HORSES     110 W. To Cuckold a Scrivener mine's in
                              Masquerade.
P. 194 TWO HORSES     117 W. Thy Priest-ridden King turn'd desperate
                              Fighter
P. 195 TWO HORSES     123 W. He that dyes for Ceremonies dyes like a
                              fool.
P. 195 TWO HORSES     125 W. The Goat and the Lyon I Equally hate,
P. 195 TWO HORSES     135 W. One of the two Tyrants must still be our
                              case
P. 195 TWO HORSES     138 W. I freely declare it, I am for old Noll.
P. 195 TWO HORSES     142 W. But hee 's buryed alive in lust and in
                              sloath.
P. 195 TWO HORSES     144 W. The Same that the Froggs had of Jupiters
                              Stork.
P. 195 TWO HORSES     152 W. And our Sir Joseph write news-books, and
                              fiddle.
P. 195 TWO HORSES     154 W. His perfum'd predecessor was never much
                              fitter.
P. 195 TWO HORSES     156 W. For that very reason hee 's never to rise.
P. 195 TWO HORSES     158 W. When the Reign of the Line of the Stuarts
                              is ended.
P. 195 TWO HORSES     161 W. A Commonwealth a Common-wealth wee proclaim
                              to the Nacion;
```

```
wades                         frequency:   1    relative frequency: 0.0000
   P.  42 DAMON           13 But in the brock the green Frog wades;

wafers                        frequency:   1    relative frequency: 0.0000
   P.  84 FLECKNO         61 With consecrated Wafers: and the Host

wages                         frequency:   1    relative frequency: 0.0000
   P. 148 INSTRUCTIONS   322 The Stores and Wages all are mine and thine.

wainscot                      frequency:   1    relative frequency: 0.0000
   P.  83 FLECKNO         14 Turn in, and shew to Wainscot half the Room.

wait                          frequency:   3    relative frequency: 0.0000
   P. 121 TWO SONGS        8 Phillis you may wait the Spring:
   P. 141 INSTRUCTIONS     2 To end her Picture, does the third time wait.
   P. 189 BRITANNIA      176 On whose fam'd Deeds all tongues, all writers
                              wait.

waites                        frequency:   2    relative frequency: 0.0000
   P.  67 A. HOUSE       264 That weeping at the Altar waites.
   P.  71 A. HOUSE       401 But bloody Thestylis, that waites

waits                         frequency:   1    relative frequency: 0.0000
   See also "waites."
   P. 160 INSTRUCTIONS   819 Hyde saith he hourly waits for a Dispatch;

wake                          frequency:   1    relative frequency: 0.0000
   P. 106 ANNIVERSARY    122 Your Regal sloth, and your long Slumbers wake:

wakeful                       frequency:   1    relative frequency: 0.0000
   See also "wakefull."
   P. 120 TWO SONGS       23 My wakeful Lamp all night must move,

wakefull                      frequency:   1    relative frequency: 0.0000
   P. 129 O.C.           248 And mortal sleep over those wakefull eyes:

wakes                         frequency:   2    relative frequency: 0.0000
   P.  35 DAPHNIS         81 Or the Witch that midnight wakes
   P. 162 INSTRUCTIONS   890 He wakes and Muses of th' uneasie Throne:

wales                         frequency:   1    relative frequency: 0.0000
   P. 314 CHEQUER INN     84 A Jury right of Wales.

walk                          frequency:   5    relative frequency: 0.0001
   See also "walke."
   P.  26 MISTRESS         4 To walk, and pass our long Loves Day.
   P.  70 A. HOUSE       374 Us as we walk more low then them:
   P.  91 MAY'S DEATH     50 As Bethlem's House did to Loretto walk.
```

```
      P. 109 ANNIVERSARY    244 But walk still middle betwixt War and Peace;
      P. 191 TWO HORSES       3 When Magpyes and Parratts cry 'walke Knave
                                walk',
```

walk'd   frequency: 2   relative frequency: 0.0000
```
      P.  49 THE GARDEN       58 While Man there walk'd without a Mate:
      P. 147 INSTRUCTIONS    245 But Strangeways, that all Night still walk'd
                                the round,
```

walke   frequency: 1   relative frequency: 0.0000
```
      P. 191 TWO HORSES       3 When Magpyes and Parratts cry 'walke Knave
                                walk',
```

walking   frequency: 1   relative frequency: 0.0000
```
      P.  71 A. HOUSE        390 Walking on foot through a green Sea.
```

walks   frequency: 5   relative frequency: 0.0001
```
      P.  68 A. HOUSE        314 Of Stars walks round about the Pole,
      P.  69 A. HOUSE        345 And yet their walks one on the Sod
      P.  75 A. HOUSE        539 He walks still upright from the Root,
      P.  79 A. HOUSE        651 The young Maria walks to night:
      P. 169 ADVICE          55 Whilst Positive walks Woodcock in the dark,
```

wall   frequency: 8   relative frequency: 0.0001
See also "debenter-wall."
```
      P.  65 A. HOUSE        216 'And vice infects the very Wall.
      P.  67 A. HOUSE        258 Young Fairfax through the Wall does rise.
      P.  87 ODE              7 Removing from the Wall
      P. 105 ANNIVERSARY     88 Draw the Circumf'rence of the publique Wall;
      P. 155 INSTRUCTIONS    607 And Upnor-Castle's ill-deserted Wall,
      P. 178 LOYALL SCOT     255 That syllable like a Picts wall devides.
      P. 196 TWO HORSES      177 Yet the beasts of the field or the stones in the
                                wall
      P. 314 CHEQUER INN      56 Mannerly rear'd against the Wall
```

waller   frequency: 1   relative frequency: 0.0000
```
      P. 147 INSTRUCTIONS    263 Old Waller, Trumpet-gen'ral swore he'd write
```

walls   frequency: 4   relative frequency: 0.0000
```
      P.  62 A. HOUSE        99 'These Walls restrain the World without,
      P. 138 HOUSEWARMING    42 He would have demclisht to raise up his Walls;
      P. 154 INSTRUCTIONS    566 Through the Walls untight, and Bullet show'rs:
      P. 170 PROPHECY         8 Tho the Walls stand to bring the Citty lower;
```

walsingham   frequency: 1   relative frequency: 0.0000
```
      P. 195 TWO HORSES      151 Ch. Her Walsingham could dark Councells
                                unriddle,
```

wan   frequency: 1   relative frequency: 0.0000
```
      P. 129 O.C.            253 All wither'd, all discolour'd, pale and wan,
```

wand   frequency: 4   relative frequency: 0.0000
```
      P.  91 MAY'S DEATH     33 At this intrusion. Then with Laurel wand,
      P. 119 TWO SONGS       10 The fleecy Clouds with silver wand.
      P. 168 ADVICE          18 Circean Clifford with his charming Wand,
      P. 313 CHEQUER INN      22 Thou'lt ken him out by a white Wand
```

wander   frequency: 3   relative frequency: 0.0000
```
      P.  49 THE GARDEN      62 To wander solitary there:
      P.  84 FLECKNO         68 Should leave his Soul to wander in the Air,
      P. 130 O.C.           300 Wander like ghosts about thy loved tombe;
```

wanderers. See "wand'rers."

wandering. See "wandring."

wand'rers   frequency: 1   relative frequency: 0.0000
```
      P. 111 ANNIVERSARY    313 Wand'rers, Adult'rers, Lyers, Munser's rest,
```

wandring   frequency: 2   relative frequency: 0.0000
```
      P.  44 GLO-WORMS       10 To wandring Mowers shows the way,
      P. 108 ANNIVERSARY    199 With wandring Eyes, and restless Ears they
                                stood,
```

want   frequency: 14   relative frequency: 0.0002
```
      P.  11 DIALOGUE        60 And want new Worlds to buy.
      P.  70 A. HOUSE       356 Which most our Earthly Gardens want.
      P.  76 A. HOUSE       571 And where I Language want, my Signs
      P.  81 A. HOUSE       728 On Females, if there want a Male.
      P.  97 HOLLAND         77 Nor can Civility there want for Tillage,
      P. 110 ANNIVERSARY    299 Whose frantique Army should they want for Men
```

```
P. 114 BLAKE          41 And these want nothing Heaven can afford,
P. 114 BLAKE          43 But this great want, will not a long one prove,
P. 114 BLAKE          44 Your Conquering Sword will soon that want
                         remove.
P. 148 INSTRUCTIONS  314 To cheat their Pay, feign want, the House
                         accuse.
P. 154 INSTRUCTIONS  540 Terrour and War, but want an Enemy.
P. 165 INSTRUCTIONS  984 Nor Guilt to flatt'ry binds, nor want to
                         stealth;
P. 181 MADE FREE       9 And your Orphans want Bread to feed on,
P. 204 HISTORICALL   143 'Twas want of Wit and Courage made them fail,
```

wanted   frequency: 2   relative frequency: 0.0000
```
P. 174 LOYALL SCOT    91 All Letanies in this have wanted faith:
P. 174 LOYALL SCOT   118 They wanted zeal and Learning, see mistook
```

wanting   frequency: 3   relative frequency: 0.0000
```
P.  21 SOUL & BODY    17 And, wanting where its spight to try,
P. 108 ANNIVERSARY   191 But the poor Beasts wanting their noble Guide,
P. 144 INSTRUCTIONS  148 (And Painter, wanting other, draw this Fight.)
```

wanton   frequency: 10   relative frequency: 0.0002
```
P.  22 NYMPH           1 The wanton Troopers riding by
P.  25 YOUNG LOVE     14 Or the wanton Kid does prize,
P.  38 PICTURE        12 The wanton Love shall one day fear,
P.  59 A. HOUSE       22 T'impark the wanton Mote of Dust,
P.  78 A. HOUSE      633 See in what wanton harmless folds
P.  82 A. HOUSE      758 For 'twas the Seat of wanton Love;
P. 108 ANNIVERSARY   197 Nor through wide Nostrils snuffe the wanton air,
P. 150 INSTRUCTIONS  374 All to new Sports their wanton fears release.
P. 154 INSTRUCTIONS  542 And wanton Boys on every Rope do cling.
P. 201 HISTORICALL    20 Soft in her Nature and of wanton pride.
```

wants   frequency: 3   relative frequency: 0.0000
```
P.   9 DIALOGUE        9 And shew that Nature wants an Art
P.  76 A. HOUSE      563 And little now to make me, wants
P.  99 HOLLAND       139 Their Tortoise wants its vainly stretched neck;
```

war   frequency: 29   relative frequency: 0.0006
```
See also "warr," "warre."
P.  11 DIALOGUE       64 That War or Peace commend?
P.  44 GLO-WORMS       6 No War, nor Princes funeral,
P.  69 A. HOUSE      343 But war all this doth overgrow:
P.  74 A. HOUSE      493 Of whom though many fell in War,
P.  87 ODE            11 But through adventrous War
P.  99 HOLLAND       144 The War, (but who would) Peace if begg'd
                         refuse.
P. 105 ANNIVERSARY   102 Here shines in Peace, and thither shoots a War.
P. 109 ANNIVERSARY   244 But walk still middle betwixt War and Peace;
P. 109 ANNIVERSARY   249 When Gideon so did from the War retreat,
P. 112 ANNIVERSARY   357 'Theirs are not Ships, but rather Arks of War,
P. 113 BLAKE           6 Was rais'd by Tyranny, and rais'd for War;
P. 115 BLAKE          52 Peace made them hers, but War will make them
                         yours
P. 115 BLAKE          61 Ah, why was thither brought that cause of War,
P. 117 BLAKE         124 War turn'd the temperate, to the Torrid Zone.
P. 118 BLAKE         136 By death, as bodies there were by the War.
P. 118 BLAKE         159 And in one War the present age may boast,
P. 123 O.C.           12 To those that liv'd in War, to dye in Fight.
P. 123 O.C.           16 But angry Heaven unto War had sway'd,
P. 126 O.C.          146 He march'd, and through deep Severn ending war.
P. 131 O.C.          321 Cease now our griefs, calme peace succeeds a war,
P. 138 HOUSEWARMING   48 To grudge him some Timber who fram'd them the
                         War.
P. 140 HOUSEWARMING   97 This Temple, of War and of Peace is the
                         Shrine;
P. 144 INSTRUCTIONS  124 Yet as for War the Parliament should squeeze;
P. 148 INSTRUCTIONS  303 See sudden chance of War! To Paint or Write,
P. 150 INSTRUCTIONS  373 The Court, as once of War, now fond of Peace,
P. 154 INSTRUCTIONS  540 Terrour and War, but want an Enemy.
P. 156 INSTRUCTIONS  617 That Pleasure-boat of War, in whose dear side
P. 159 INSTRUCTIONS  769 Whose Counsel first did this mad War beget?
P. 179 STOCKSMARKET   26 Than all the Dutch pictures that caused the war,
```

ware   frequency: 1   relative frequency: 0.0000
```
P.  97 HOLLAND        87 A vestal Turf enshrin'd in Earthen Ware
```

warlike   frequency: 6   relative frequency: 0.0001
```
P.   9 DIALOGUE       13 Lay aside that Warlike Crest,
P.  67 A. HOUSE      284 His warlike Studies could not cease;
P. 109 ANNIVERSARY   251 He on the Peace extends a Warlike power,
```

P. 126 O.C.   123 The Race of warlike Horses at his Tomb
P. 171 LOYALL SCCT   1 Of the old Feroes when the Warlike shades
P. 172 LOYALL SCOT   8 His ready muse to Court the Warlike Guest.

warm   frequency: 6   relative frequency: 0.0001
   See also "warme."
P.   12 DROP OF DEW   17 Till the warm Sun pitty it's Pain,
P.   22 NYMPH   19 In this warm life-blood, which doth part
P.   35 DAPHNIS   76 Of a Body dead while warm.
P.   64 A. HOUSE   192 'Like Chrystal pure with Cotton warm.
P. 161 INSTRUCTIONS   843 And so, proceeding in his motion warm,
P. 173 LOYALL SCOT   56 As one that Huggs himself in a Warm bed.

warm'd   frequency: 1   relative frequency: 0.0000
P. 157 INSTRUCTIONS   690 As one that's warm'd himself and gone to Bed.

warme   frequency: 1   relative frequency: 0.0000
P. 169 ADVICE   32 Our mighty Masters in a warme debate;

warming. See "house-warming."

warms   frequency: 1   relative frequency: 0.0000
P.   21 SOUL & BODY   15 And warms and moves this needless Frame:

warr   frequency: 4   relative frequency: 0.0000
P. 108 ANNIVERSARY   216 And firy Steeds had born cut of the Warr,
P. 189 BRITANNIA   187 Soe shall my England by a Holy Warr
P. 194 TWO HORSES   91 W. That a King shou'd endavour to make a warr
                           cease
P. 202 HISTORICALL   52 And with the Dutch a second Warr renews.

warre   frequency: 3   relative frequency: 0.0000
P.   3 LOVELACE   30 Because you write when going to the Warre,
P. 129 O.C.   240 In warre, in ccunsell, or in pray'r, and praise;
P. 202 HISTORICALL   38 And Plague and Warre fell heavye on our Isle.

warren   frequency: 1   relative frequency: 0.0000
P. 165 INSTRUCTIONS   982 And a poor Warren once a City ras'd.

warrs   frequency: 2   relative frequency: 0.0000
P.   29 LOVER   60 Forced to live in Storms and Warrs:
P. 128 O.C.   193 In all his warrs needs must he triumph, when

wars   frequency: 8   relative frequency: 0.0001
   See also "warrs."
P.   3 LOVELACE   12 Our Civill Wars have lost the Civicke crowne.
P.   88 ODE   45 What Field of all the Civil Wars,
P.   90 ODE   113 But thou the Wars and Fortunes Son
P. 104 ANNIVERSARY   29 Their other Wars seem but a feign'd contest,
P. 110 ANNIVERSARY   284 Left by the Wars Flood on the Mountains crest:
P. 111 ANNIVERSARY   350 'Spent with both Wars, under a Captain dead?
P. 118 BLAKE   155 Wars chief support with them would buried be,
P. 118 BLAKE   160 The certain seeds cf many Wars are lost.

wart   frequency: 1   relative frequency: 0.0000
P. 153 INSTRUCTIONS   496 Lye nuzz'ling at the Sacramental wart;

wary   frequency: 1   relative frequency: 0.0000
P. 194 TWO HORSES   99 Wee ought tc be wary and Bridle our Tongue;

was   frequency: 161   relative frequency: 0.0033
   See also "twas," "'twas."

wash   frequency: 1   relative frequency: 0.0000
P.   22 NYMPH   18 Though they should wash their guilty hands

wash'd   frequency: 1   relative frequency: 0.0000
P. 122 TWO SONGS   23 Nor our Sheep new Wash'd can be

washed. See "wash'd," "washt," "wash't."

washing   frequency: 1   relative frequency: 0.0000
P. 143 INSTRUCTIONS   95 And washing (lest the scent her Crime disclose)

washt   frequency: 1   relative frequency: 0.0000
P.   78 A. HOUSE   628 Seems as green Silks but newly washt.

wash't   frequency: 1   relative frequency: 0.0000
P. 315 CHEQUER INN   99 To have the other wash't

wast   frequency: 4   relative frequency: 0.0000

P. 45 GLO-WORMS   13 Your courteous Lights in vain you wast,
P. 61 A. HOUSE   78 What she had laid so sweetly Wast;
P. 69 A. HOUSE   328 To make us Mortal, and The Wast?
P. 92 MAY'S DEATH   75 Yet wast thou taken hence with equal fate,

waste   frequency: 1   relative frequency: 0.0000
   See also "wast."
   P. 165 INSTRUCTIONS 981 The smallest Vermin make the greatest waste,

wastes   frequency: 2   relative frequency: 0.0000
   See also "wasts."
   P. 107 ANNIVERSARY   155 Hence that blest Day still counterpoysed wastes,
   P. 144 INSTRUCTIONS 141 She wastes the Country and on Cities preys.

wasting   frequency: 2   relative frequency: 0.0000
   P. 67 A. HOUSE   271 The wasting Cloister with the rest
   P. 126 O.C.   131 And as through Air his wasting Spirits flow'd,

wasts   frequency: 2   relative frequency: 0.0000
   P. 124 O.C.   53 A silent fire now wasts those Limbs of Wax,
   P. 181 MADE FREE   34 And wasts all his Nights

watch   frequency: 3   relative frequency: 0.0000
   P. 119 TWO SONGS   12 Or if a Shepheard, watch thy Sheep.
   P. 160 INSTRUCTIONS 820 Harry came Post just as he shew'd his Watch.
   P. 188 BRITANNIA   163 Watch and Preside over their tender age

watch'd   frequency: 1   relative frequency: 0.0000
   P. 110 ANNIVERSARY   295 Who watch'd thy halting, and thy Fall deride,

watchful   frequency: 1   relative frequency: 0.0000
   P. 99 HOLLAND   148 Watchful abroad, and honest still within.

water   frequency: 6   relative frequency: 0.0001
   See also "cowslip-water," "holy-water."
   P. 30 THE GALLERY   36 Betwixt the Air and Water fly.
   P. 70 A. HOUSE   379 As, under Water, none does know
   P. 96 HOLLAND   28 The Earth and Water play at Level-coyl;
   P. 154 INSTRUCTIONS 543 Old Neptune springs the Tydes, and Water lent:
   P. 154 INSTRUCTIONS 576 The Ocean Water, or the Heavens Wind.
   P. 317 CHEQUER INN   182 Wee poure in Water when it won't come

water-hercules   frequency: 1   relative frequency: 0.0000
   P. 97 HOLLAND   94 A Water-Hercules Butter-Coloss,

waters   frequency: 5   relative frequency: 0.0001
   P. 97 HOLLAND   59 Besides the Waters of themselves did rise,
   P. 98 HOLLAND   129 As the obsequious Air and Waters rest,
   P. 112 ANNIVERSARY   371 'And those that have the Waters for their share,
   P. 113 ANNIVERSARY   402 Troubling the Waters, yearly mak'st them Heal.
   P. 114 BLAKE   15 Of winds and waters rage, they fearful be,

watery.   See "watry," "wat'ry."

watry   frequency: 8   relative frequency: 0.0001
   P. 17 BERMUDAS   6 That led us through the watry Maze,
   P. 32 MOURNING   9 When, molding of the watry Sphears,
   P. 69 A. HOUSE   326 With watry if not flaming Sword;
   P. 81 A. HOUSE   715 Tears (watry Shot that pierce the Mind;)
   P. 96 HOLLAND   21 Building their watry Babel far more high
   P. 103 ANNIVERSARY   1 Like the vain Curlings of the Watry maze,
   P. 113 ANNIVERSARY   366 'Whose watry Leaguers all the world surround?
   P. 125 O.C.   97 Trickling in watry drops, whose flowing shape

wat'ry   frequency: 1   relative frequency: 0.0000
   P. 15 EYES   8 Like wat'ry Lines and Plummets fall.

wave   frequency: 8   relative frequency: 0.0001
   P. 28 LOVER   53 From which he with each Wave rebounds,
   P. 30 THE GALLERY   37 Or, if some rowling Wave appears,
   P. 57 BILL-BOROW   34 A Plump of aged Trees does wave.
   P. 107 ANNIVERSARY   184 Of purling Ore, a shining wave do shed:
   P. 153 INSTRUCTIONS 534 And his new Face looks in the English Wave.
   P. 156 INSTRUCTIONS 620 Taught the Dutch Colours from its top to wave;
   P. 157 INSTRUCTIONS 672 Or with known Art to try the gentle Wave.
   P. 172 LOYALL SCOT   38 Or with known art to try the Gentle Wave.

waves   frequency: 10   relative frequency: 0.0002
   P. 16 EYES   38 Drench'd in these Waves, does lose it fire.
   P. 28 LOVER   47 Whilst he, betwixt the Flames and Waves,
   P. 32 MOURNING   31 Would find her Tears yet deeper Waves

```
P.   49 THE GARDEN      56 Waves in its Plumes the various Light.
P.   78 A. HOUSE       625 For now the Waves are fal'n and dry'd,
P.   96 HOLLAND         20 Where barking Waves still bait the forced
                           Ground;
P.   98 HOLLAND        134 And purges out the corruptible waves.
P.  120 TWO SONGS       18 Ruling the Waves that Ebb and flow.
P.  157 INSTRUCTIONS   667 Or Waves his Sword, and could he them conjure
P.  172 LOYALL SCOT     33 Or waves his sword and, Cou'd hee them Conjure,
```

waving   frequency: 1   relative frequency: 0.0000
```
P.   67 A. HOUSE       257 But, waving these aside like Flyes,
```

wax   frequency: 1   relative frequency: 0.0000
See also "wex."
```
P.  124 O.C.            53 A silent fire now wasts those Limbs of Wax,
```

wax'd   frequency: 1   relative frequency: 0.0000
```
P.   23 NYMPH           58 It wax'd more white and sweet than they.
```

waxed   frequency: 1   relative frequency: 0.0000
See also "wax'd."
```
P.   22 NYMPH           34 This waxed tame, while he grew wild,
```

waxen   frequency: 1   relative frequency: 0.0000
```
P.   87 FLECKNO        157 Thereat the waxen Youth relented straight;
```

way   frequency: 32   relative frequency: 0.0006
```
P.    3 LOVELACE         5 That candid Age no other way could tell
P.    9 DIALOGUE        18 To bait so long upon the way.
P.   12 DROP OF DEW     28 Every way it turns away:
P.   18 BERMUDAS        39 And all the way, to guide their Chime,
P.   18 CLORINDA         1 C. Damon come drive thy flocks this way.
P.   19 THYRSIS          7 Dorinda. I know no way, but one, our home;
P.   19 THYRSIS         10 There the milky way doth lye;
P.   19 THYRSIS         11 'Tis a sure but rugged way,
P.   26 MISTRESS         3 We would sit down, and think which way
P.   40 THE MATCH       30 A nearer Way they sought;
P.   44 GLO-WORMS       10 To wandring Mowers shows the way,
P.   46 AMETAS           6 If we both should turn one way?
P.   57 BILL-BOROW      22 And all the way it rises bends;
P.   57 BILL-BOROW      31 By Night the Northern Star their way
P.   75 A. HOUSE       541 And all the way, to keep it clean,
P.   81 A. HOUSE       720 She scap'd the safe, but roughest Way.
P.   85 FLECKNO         93 Will make the way here; I said Sir you'l do
P.   85 FLECKNO        105 He ask'd me pardon; and to make me way
P.   87 ODE             16 His fiery way divide.
P.   90 MAY'S DEATH      8 Signs by which still he found and lost his way.
P.  104 ANNIVERSARY     46 And cuts his way still nearer to the Skyes,
P.  115 BLAKE           67 For Sanctacruze the glad Fleet takes her way,
P.  130 O.C.           303 Since thou art gone, who best that way could'st
                           teach,
P.  131 PARADISE        13 Through that wide Field how he his way should
                           find
P.  164 INSTRUCTIONS   960 Nor of a Peasant scorn'd to learn the way.
P.  168 ADVICE          24 All looking this way how to give their votes,
P.  192 TWO HORSES      32 Were stolne of Incognito each his own way,
P.  198 DUKE            29 The way to heaven and who shall be my guide?
P.  203 HISTORICALL     91 Droll on their God but a much duller way:
P.  313 CHEQUER INN      7 At Chareing Crosse hard by the way
P.  313 CHEQUER INN     18 The way they all have rosen.
P.  317 CHEQUER INN    183 And that way get more out
```

wayes   frequency: 3   relative frequency: 0.0000
```
P.   20 SOUL & BODY      2 A Soul inslav'd so many wayes?
P.   33 DAPHNIS         17 He, well read in all the wayes
P.  117 BLAKE          127 Thousands of wayes, Thousands of men there dye,
```

ways   frequency: 1   relative frequency: 0.0000
See also "wayes."
```
P.    5 HASTINGS        56 All Herbs, and them a thousand ways infus'd?
```

way's   frequency: 1   relative frequency: 0.0000
```
P.  174 LOYALL SCOT    121 A shorter Way's to bee by Clergie sav'd.
```

we   frequency: 100   relative frequency: 0.0020
See also "we'd," "wee," "weel," "wee'l," "wee're," "wee've," "we've."

weak   frequency: 6   relative frequency: 0.0001
```
P.   78 A. HOUSE       613 But, lest your Fetters prove too weak,
P.   88 ODE             40 As Men are strong or weak.
P.  103 ANNIVERSARY      4 In the weak Circles of increasing Years;
```

```
P. 128 O.C.              220 Lye weak and easy to the ruler's will;
P. 154 INSTRUCTIONS      574 Like molting Fowl, a weak and easie Prey.
P. 162 INSTRUCTIONS      886 Only dispers'd by a weak Tapers light;
```

weakeness   frequency: 1   relative frequency: 0.0000
```
P. 204 HISTORICALL       133 For one man's weakeness a whole Nation bleeds
```

weaker   frequency: 1   relative frequency: 0.0000
```
P. 203 HISTORICALL       105 To have the weaker Vessell made his prey:
```

weakly   frequency: 1   relative frequency: 0.0000
```
P.  55 EPITAPH            19 'Tis true: but all so weakly said;
```

weakness   frequency: 1   relative frequency: 0.0000
See also "weakeness."
```
P. 106 ANNIVERSARY       120 Leisure to Time, and to my Weakness Strength,
```

weaknesses   frequency: 1   relative frequency: 0.0000
```
P. 123 O.C.               22 (Those nobler weaknesses of humane Mind,
```

weal   frequency: 1   relative frequency: 0.0000
```
P. 188 BRITANNIA         149 Tyrants like Leprous Kings for publick weal
```

weal-publik   frequency: 1   relative frequency: 0.0000
```
P. 204 HISTORICALL       132 In our weal-publik scarce one thing succeeds--
```

wealth   frequency: 11   relative frequency: 0.0002
```
P.  98 HOLLAND           118 Our sore new circumcised Common wealth.
P.  98 HOLLAND           131 The Common wealth doth by its losses grow;
P. 113 BLAKE              10 For wealth wherewith to wound the old once more.
P. 113 BLAKE              11 Wealth which all others Avarice might cloy,
P. 118 BLAKE             151 Their Gallicns sunk, their wealth the Sea does
                             fill,
P. 165 INSTRUCTIONS      983 But they whom torn to Virtue and to Wealth,
P. 171 PROPHECY           51 Their Wives to his Lust expos'd, their Wealth
                             to his spoyle
P. 175 LOYALL SCOT       128 Enough for them, God knows, to Count their
                             Wealth,
P. 175 LOYALL SCOT       144 If Wealth or vice can tempt your appetites,
P. 200 DUKE               83 He gott his wealth by breaking of his word;
P. 202 HISTORICALL        40 With the Batavian common Wealth to fight.
```

wealthy   frequency: 1   relative frequency: 0.0000
```
P. 113 BLAKE               8 With what the Womb of wealthy Kingdomes yield,
```

weapons   frequency: 1   relative frequency: 0.0000
```
P.  66 A. HOUSE          256 And sharpest Weapons were their Tongues.
```

wear   frequency: 6   relative frequency: 0.0001
See also "weare."
```
P.  24 NYMPH             117 Until my Tears, still dropping, wear
P.  35 DAPHNIS            66 'Tis a Vanity to wear,
P.  69 A. HOUSE          334 And Men did rosie Garlands wear?
P. 127 O.C.              181 The Souldier taught that inward Mail to wear,
P. 132 PARADISE           50 The Poets tag them; we for fashion wear.
P. 164 INSTRUCTIONS      975 Not so does Rust insinuating wear,
```

weare   frequency: 3   relative frequency: 0.0000
```
P.   3 LOVELACE            8 Twas more esteemd to give, then weare the Bayes:
P. 171 PROPHECY           29 And Wooden shoos shall come to be the weare
P. 171 PROPHECY           47 Then wooden Shoos shall be the English weare
```

weares   frequency: 1   relative frequency: 0.0000
```
P.  91 MAY'S DEATH        57 Because some one than thee more worthy weares
```

wearied   frequency: 1   relative frequency: 0.0000
See also "wearyed."
```
P. 168 ADVICE              8 Their wearied limbs and minds to recreate,
```

wears   frequency: 3   relative frequency: 0.0000
See also "weares."
```
P.  60 A. HOUSE           58 Then That unwonted Greatness wears.
P.  84 FLECKNO            71 Wears a close Jacket cf poetick Buff,
P. 147 INSTRUCTIONS      266 And in his Breast wears many Montezumes.
```

weary   frequency: 5   relative frequency: 0.0001
```
P.  57 BILL-BOROW         29 How glad the weary Seamen hast
P.  84 FLECKNO            35 Till the Tyrant, weary to persecute,
P. 166 KINGS VOWES        39 And when I am weary of her, I'le have more.
P. 171 PROPHECY           33 The Frogs shall then grow weary of their Crane
P. 192 TWO HORSES         31 When both the Kings weary of Sitting all day
```

wearyed   frequency: 1   relative frequency: 0.0000
    P. 110 ANNIVERSARY   271 The Passengers all wearyed out before,

weather   frequency: 2   relative frequency: 0.0000
    P. 154 INSTRUCTIONS   537 Their streaming Silks play through the weather
                              fair,
    P. 161 INSTRUCTIONS   831 The portly Burgess, through the Weather hot,

weather-beaten   frequency: 1   relative frequency: 0.0000
    P. 98 HOLLAND   109 To whom their weather-beaten Province ows

weav'd   frequency: 1   relative frequency: 0.0000
    P. 61 A. HOUSE   95 Whence in these Words one to her weav'd,

weave   frequency: 4   relative frequency: 0.0000
    P. 14 THE CORONET   11 So rich a Chaplet thence to weave
    P. 36 DAPHNIS   91 Joy will not with Sorrow weave,
    P. 48 THE GARDEN   8 To weave the Garlands of repose.
    P. 165 KINGS VOWES   2 And the Spider might weave in our Stomack its
                              web;

weaves   frequency: 1   relative frequency: 0.0000
    P. 77 A. HOUSE   578 Strange Prophecies my Phancy weaves:

web   frequency: 1   relative frequency: 0.0000
    P. 165 KINGS VOWES   2 And the Spider might weave in our Stomack its
                              web;

wed   frequency: 4   relative frequency: 0.0000
    P. 47 EMPIRE   10 And Virgin Trebles wed the manly Base.
    P. 122 TWO SONGS   33 What Shepherdess could hope to wed
    P. 159 INSTRUCTIONS   747 Sad change, since first that happy pair was wed,
    P. 177 LOYALL SCOT   218 'Tis necessary Lambeth never wed,

we'd   frequency: 2   relative frequency: 0.0000

wedg'd   frequency: 1   relative frequency: 0.0000
    P. 74 A. HOUSE   503 And stretches still so closely wedg'd

wedges   frequency: 1   relative frequency: 0.0000
    P. 37 DEFINITION   11 But Fate does Iron wedges drive,

wee   frequency: 17   relative frequency: 0.0003

weed   frequency: 2   relative frequency: 0.0000
    P. 35 DAPHNIS   82 For the Fern, whose magick Weed
    P. 70 A. HOUSE   354 Ambition weed, but Conscience till.

weeds   frequency: 1   relative frequency: 0.0000
    P. 204 HISTORICALL   134 Ill luck starts up and thrives like Evil weeds.

weel   frequency: 1   relative frequency: 0.0000

wee'l   frequency: 1   relative frequency: 0.0000

weep   frequency: 9   relative frequency: 0.0001
    P. 15 EYES   2 With the same Eyes to weep and see!
    P. 16 EYES   26 That weep the more, and see the less:
    P. 16 EYES   48 But only humane Eyes can weep.
    P. 20 THYRSIS   47 In wine, and drink on't even till we weep,
    P. 24 NYMPH   116 That I shall weep though I be Stone:
    P. 32 MOURNING   35 But sure as oft as Women weep,
    P. 123 O.C.   28 As long as Grief shall weep, or Love shall
                              burn.
    P. 127 O.C.   166 Where Heaven leads, 'tis Piety to weep.
    P. 129 O.C.   245 Francisca faire can nothing now but weep,

weeping   frequency: 6   relative frequency: 0.0001
    P. 16 EYES   36 As two Eyes swoln with weeping are.
    P. 17 EYES   56 These weeping Eyes, those seeing Tears.
    P. 24 NYMPH   113 Let it be weeping too: but there
    P. 67 A. HOUSE   264 That weeping at the Altar waites.
    P. 111 ANNIVERSARY   335 His weeping Eyes the doleful Vigils keep,
    P. 168 ADVICE   4 Weeping to see their Scenns degenerate,

weeps   frequency: 3   relative frequency: 0.0000
    P. 24 NYMPH   95 See how it weeps. The Tears do come
    P. 24 NYMPH   97 So weeps the wounded Balsome: so
    P. 125 O.C.   98 Weeps that it falls ere fix'd into a Grape.

wee're   frequency: 1   relative frequency: 0.0000

| | P. 189 STATUE | 3 Dear Wheeler impart, for wee're all at a loss |

wee've   frequency: 2   relative frequency: 0.0000
    P. 191 STATUE   44 And wee've lost both our King, our Hors and our Crupper.
    P. 195 TWO HORSES   149 A Tudor a Tudor! wee've had Stuarts enough;

weigh   frequency: 2   relative frequency: 0.0000
    P.   4 HASTINGS   18 But weigh to Man the Geometrick yeer.
    P. 15 EYES   9 Two Tears, which Sorrow long did weigh

weight   frequency: 7   relative frequency: 0.0001
    P.   9 DIALOGUE   2 The weight of thine immortal Shield.
    P. 103 ANNIVERSARY   2 Which in smooth streams a sinking Weight does raise;
    P. 105 ANNIVERSARY   98 Knit by the Roofs Protecting weight agree.
    P. 109 ANNIVERSARY   245 Choosing each Stone, and poysing every weight,
    P. 132 PARADISE   54 In Number, Weight, and Measure, needs not Rhime.
    P. 155 INSTRUCTIONS   593 But with her Sailing weight, the Holland Keel
    P. 181 MADE FREE   4 'Tis a thing sure of Weight,

welcome   frequency: 3   relative frequency: 0.0000
    See also "wellcome."
    P.   9 DIALOGUE   11 Welcome the Creations Guest,
    P. 114 BLAKE   18 More wish't for, and more welcome is then sleep,
    P. 171 LOYALL SCOT   4 Which of their Poets shold his Welcome sing,

well   frequency: 44   relative frequency: 0.0009
    P.   3 LOVELACE   6 To be ingenious, but by speaking well.
    P. 22 NYMPH   27 One morning (I remember well)
    P. 22 NYMPH   39 With this: and very well content,
    P. 29 THE GALLERY   2 Whether I have contriv'd it well.
    P. 30 THE GALLERY   39 Nor blows more Wind than what may well
    P. 33 DAPHNIS   17 He, well read in all the wayes
    P. 37 DEFINITION   25 As Lines so Loves oblique may well
    P. 50 THE GARDEN   65 How well the skilful Gardner drew
    P. 50 THE GARDEN   70 Computes its time as well as we.
    P. 57 BILL-BOROW   47 But ere he well the Barks could part
    P. 60 A. HOUSE   39 And some will smile at this, as well
    P. 65 A. HOUSE   213 'And yet, how well soever ment,
    P. 68 A. HOUSE   305 Well shot ye Firemen! Oh how sweet,
    P. 75 A. HOUSE   543 He, with his Beak, examines well
    P. 89 ODE   84 That can so well obey.
    P. 103 ANNIVERSARY   21 Well may they strive to leave them to their Son,
    P. 106 ANNIVERSARY   145 And well he therefore does, and well has guest,
    P. 111 ANNIVERSARY   319 Well may you act the Adam and the Eve;
    P. 120 TWO SONGS   37 O why, as well as Eyes to see,
    P. 123 O.C.   11 Nor Fate indeed can well refuse that right
    P. 125 O.C.   103 Whether some Kinder Pow'rs, that wish us well,
    P. 131 PARADISE   19 (Such as disquiet alwayes what is well,
    P. 132 PARADISE   45 Well mightst thou scorn thy Readers to allure
    P. 141 INSTRUCTIONS   35 Well he the Title of St. Albans bore,
    P. 142 INSTRUCTIONS   62 Wide Mouth that Sparagus may well proclaim:
    P. 144 INSTRUCTIONS   158 But knew the Word and well could face about;
    P. 145 INSTRUCTIONS   176 No Troop was better clad nor so well pay'd.
    P. 151 INSTRUCTIONS   417 But wiser Men, and well foreseen in chance,
    P. 160 INSTRUCTIONS   815 And thinks 'twill ne're be well within this Nation,
    P. 162 INSTRUCTIONS   873 Well was he skill'd to season any question,
    P. 174 LOYALL SCOT   87 But who Considers well will find indeed
    P. 176 LOYALL SCOT   198 Well that Scotch monster and our Bishops sort
    P. 179 STOCKSMARKET   21 But a market, they say, does suit the king well,
    P. 182 MADE FREE   58 And the House was well barr'd,
    P. 186 BRITANNIA   54 Then, to confirm the cure so well begun,
    P. 191 STATUE   48 That a Monarch of Gingerbread would doe as well.
    P. 192 TWO HORSES   26 Who have told many truths well worth a mans hearing,
    P. 195 TWO HORSES   153 Ch. Troth, Brother, well said, but thats somewhat bitter:
    P. 198 DUKE   17 And by a noble well contrived plott,
    P. 202 HISTORICALL   55 This Isle was well reform'd and gaind renowne,
    P. 313 CHEQUER INN   12 They seem'd so well acquainted
    P. 314 CHEQUER INN   69 She might it well afford
    P. 315 CHEQUER INN   122 But wou'd as well as Meate have Cloaths

wellcome   frequency: 1   relative frequency: 0.0000
    P. 199 DUKE   47 To finde such wellcome when you come soe farr.

weltering. See "weltring."

weltring   frequency: 1   relative frequency: 0.0000

        P. 146 INSTRUCTIONS   214 Led the French Standard, weltring in his
                                  stride,

wench   frequency: 3   relative frequency: 0.0000
        P. 167 KINGS VOWES   45 And my Wench shall dispose of the Conge
                                  d'eslire.
        P. 177 LOYALL SCOT   219 Indifferent to have a Wench in bed.
        P. 201 HISTORICALL   22 He marry'd Minhier Falmouths pregnant wench.

wenches   frequency: 1   . 'ative frequency: 0.0000
        P. 316 CHEQUER INN   150 Not one word of the Wenches.

went   frequency: 12   relative frequency: 0.0002
        P. 18 CLORINDA   2 D. No: 'tis too late they went astray.
        P. 47 EMPIRE   13 Some to the Lute, some to the Viol went,
        P. 55 EPITAPH   14 No Minute but it came and went;
        P. 60 A. HOUSE   38 Within such dwarfish Confines went:
        P. 85 FLECKNO   106 Went down, as I him follow'd to obey.
        P. 88 ODE   21 Then burning through the Air he went,
        P. 105 ANNIVERSARY   70 Framing a Liberty that still went back;
        P. 108 ANNIVERSARY   209 A dismal Silence through the Palace went,
        P. 192 TWO HORSES   39 Ch. here Charing broke silence and thus he went
                                  on:
        P. 204 HISTORICALL   126 Of all the Miscreants ever went to hell
        P. 314 CHEQUER INN   60 None went away unhir'd.
        P. 316 CHEQUER INN   171 And Table Linnen went

wept   frequency: 3   relative frequency: 0.0000
        P.   4 HASTINGS   4 Of Tears untoucht, and never wept before.
        P.   5 HASTINGS   58 And wept, as we, without Redress or Law.
        P. 87 FLECKNO   162 Wept bitterly as disinherited.

were   frequency: 77   relative frequency: 0.0016
        See also "'twere."

wer't   frequency: 3   relative frequency: 0.0000

west   frequency: 2   relative frequency: 0.0000
        P. 111 ANNIVERSARY   337 Still to the West, where he him lost, he turn'd,
        P. 158 INSTRUCTIONS   717 Furrs from the North, and Silver from the
                                  West,

western   frequency: 2   relative frequency: 0.0000
        See also "westerne."
        P. 97 HOLLAND   90 But still does place it at her Western End:
        P. 98 HOLLAND   106 Or intercept the Western golden Sands:

westerne   frequency: 1   relative frequency: 0.0000
        P. 315 CHEQUER INN   115 The Westerne Glory, Harry Ford

westward   frequency: 1   relative frequency: 0.0000
        P. 97 HOLLAND   68 And from the East would Westward steer its
                                  Ark,

wet   frequency: 3   relative frequency: 0.0000
        P. 36 DAPHNIS   88 Wet themselves and spoil their Sent.
        P. 96 HOLLAND   53 For these Half-anders, half wet, and half dry,
        P. 109 ANNIVERSARY   238 But though forewarn'd, o'r-took and wet the
                                  King.

we've   frequency: 1   relative frequency: 0.0000

wex   frequency: 1   relative frequency: 0.0000
        P. 313 CHEQUER INN   19 And ever since he did so wex

what   frequency: 159   relative frequency: 0.0033

whats   frequency: 1   relative frequency: 0.0000

what's   frequency: 1   relative frequency: 0.0000

whatsoever   frequency: 2   relative frequency: 0.0000

wheel   frequency: 4   relative frequency: 0.0000
        P.   4 HASTINGS   12 And on Times Wheel sticks like a Remora.
        P. 37 DEFINITION   19 (Though Loves whole World on us doth wheel)
        P. 92 MAY'S DEATH   67 He, when the wheel of Empire, whirleth back,
        P. 92 MAY'S DEATH   93 Thou rivited unto Ixion's wheel

wheeler   frequency: 2   relative frequency: 0.0000
        P. 189 STATUE   3 Dear Wheeler impart, for wee're all at a loss

```
       P. 314 CHEQUER INN      67 Wheeler at Board, then next her set,

wheels                            frequency:    1    relative frequency: 0.0000
       P.  38 PICTURE          20 Ere, with their glancing wheels, they drive

whelps                            frequency:    1    relative frequency: 0.0000
       P. 156 INSTRUCTIONS     624 After the Robbers, for her Whelps does yell:

when                              frequency:  190    relative frequency: 0.0039

whence                            frequency:    8    relative frequency: 0.0001

where                             frequency:  140    relative frequency: 0.0029

whereat                           frequency:    1    relative frequency: 0.0000

wheres                            frequency:    1    relative frequency: 0.0000

wheres'ere                        frequency:    1    relative frequency: 0.0000

wheresoe're                       frequency:    1    relative frequency: 0.0000

wheresoever.  see also "wheres'ere," "wheresoe're."

wherewith                         frequency:    1    relative frequency: 0.0000

whet                              frequency:    2    relative frequency: 0.0000
       P.  43 DAMON            72 Sighing I whet my Sythe and Woes.
       P. 163 INSTRUCTIONS     941 While Hyde provck'd his foaming tusk does whet,

whether                           frequency:    9    relative frequency: 0.0001

whets                             frequency:    2    relative frequency: 0.0000
       P.  49 THE GARDEN       54 Then whets, and combs its silver Wings;
       P. 152 INSTRUCTIONS     466 Still his sharp Wit on States and Princes
                                  whets.

which                             frequency:  164    relative frequency: 0.0034

while                             frequency:  112    relative frequency: 0.0023
       P.   4 HASTINGS         15 While those of growth more sudden, and more bold,
       P.  15 THE CORONET      25 That they, while Thou on both their Spoils dost
                                  tread,
       P.  18 CLORINDA         29 Sing then while he doth us inspire;
       P.  22 NYMPH            34 This waxed tame, while he grew wild,
       P.  25 YOUNG LOVE        2 While thine unsuspected years
       P.  25 YOUNG LOVE        7 While our Sportings are as free
       P.  27 MISTRESS         33 Now therefore, while the youthful hew
       P.  27 MISTRESS         35 And while thy willing Soul transpires
       P.  27 MISTRESS         37 Now let us sport us while we may;
       P.  28 LOVER            23 While round the ratling Thunder hurl'd,
       P.  28 LOVER            25 While Nature to his Birth presents
       P.  28 LOVER            37 Thus while they famish him, and feast,
       P.  28 LOVER            51 While with the other he does lock,
       P.  29 THE GALLERY      21 While all the morning Quire does sing,
       P.  31 FAIR SINGER       5 That while she with her Eyes my Heart does
                                  bind,
       P.  32 MOURNING        17 And, while vain Pomp does her restrain
       P.  32 MOURNING        25 Nor that she payes, while she survives,
       P.  35 DAPHNIS         76 Of a Body dead while warm.
       P.  35 DAPHNIS         79 While with Quailes and Manna fed,
       P.  40 THE MOWER        8 Which stupifi'd them while it fed.
       P.  41 DAMON            3 While ev'ry thing did seem to paint
       P.  41 THE MOWER       32 While the sweet Fields do lye forgot:
       P.  43 DAMON           47 While, going home, the Ev'ning sweet
       P.  44 DAMON           73 While thus he threw his Elbow round,
       P.  45 MOWER'S SONG      7 But these, while I with Sorrow pine,
       P.  45 MOWER'S SONG     16 While I lay trodden under feet?
       P.  48 THE GARDEN       7 While all Flow'rs and all Trees do close
       P.  49 THE GARDEN      41 Mean while the Mind, from pleasure less,
       P.  49 THE GARDEN      58 While Man there walk'd without a Mate:
       P.  61 A. HOUSE        72 Its Lord a while, but not remain.
       P.  61 A. HOUSE        81 While with slow Eyes we these survey,
       P.  62 A. HOUSE       123 'While all the rest with Needles paint
       P.  64 A. HOUSE       175 'And that which perisht while we pull,
       P.  65 A. HOUSE       195 'Try but a while, if you be wise:
       P.  66 A. HOUSE       253 While the disjointed Abbess threads
       P.  69 A. HOUSE       322 The Garden of the World ere while,
       P.  71 A. HOUSE       395 While one, unknowing, carves the Rail,
       P.  74 A. HOUSE       483 And, while it lasts, my self imbark
       P.  76 A. HOUSE       559 While the Oake seems to fall content,
```

P.	77	A. HOUSE	595	While the Wind, cooling through the Boughs,
P.	78	A. HOUSE	619	While, like a Guard on either side,
P.	79	A. HOUSE	648	While at my Lines the Fishes twang!
P.	82	A. HOUSE	743	While her glad Parents most rejoice,
P.	84	FLECKNO	41	So while he with his gouty Fingers craules
P.	88	ODE	55	While round the armed Bands
P.	89	ODE	98	While Victory his Crest does plume!
P.	90	MAY'S DEATH	9	At last while doubtfully he all compares,
P.	97	HOLLAND	91	While the fat steam of Female Sacrifice
P.	98	HOLLAND	117	While, with feign'd Treaties, they invade by stealth
P.	98	HOLLAND	122	While the Sea laught it self into a foam,
P.	98	HOLLAND	125	While half their banish'd keels the Tempest tost,
P.	99	HOLLAND	149	For while our Neptune doth a Trident shake,
P.	99	HOLLAND	151	And while Jove governs in the highest Sphere,
P.	103	ANNIVERSARY	6	While flowing Time above his Head does close.
P.	103	ANNIVERSARY	15	While heavy Monarchs make a wide Return,
P.	104	ANNIVERSARY	45	While indefatigable Cromwell hyes,
P.	104	ANNIVERSARY	56	And the great Work ascended while he play'd.
P.	105	ANNIVERSARY	69	While tedious Statesmen many years did hack,
P.	105	ANNIVERSARY	95	While the resistance of opposed Minds,
P.	105	ANNIVERSARY	103	While by his Beams observing Princes steer,
P.	107	ANNIVERSARY	178	Hurry'd thy Horses while they hurry'd thee.
P.	108	ANNIVERSARY	189	While impious Men deceiv'd with pleasure short,
P.	109	ANNIVERSARY	269	While baleful Tritons to the shipwrack guide.
P.	110	ANNIVERSARY	277	What though a while they grumble discontent,
P.	110	ANNIVERSARY	305	While Feake and Simpson would in many a Tome,
P.	111	ANNIVERSARY	331	While dismal blacks hung round the Universe,
P.	111	ANNIVERSARY	343	So while our Star that gives us Light and Heat,
P.	112	ANNIVERSARY	351	'Yet rig a Navy while we dress us late;
P.	113	ANNIVERSARY	399	While thou thy venerable Head dost raise
P.	121	TWO SONGS	48	While Stars Eclipse by mixing Rayes.
P.	122	TWO SONGS	37	While they,
P.	124	O.C.	36	Which while she drain'd of Milk she fill'd with Love.
P.	124	O.C.	45	While they by sence, not knowing, comprehend
P.	125	O.C.	108	Their fun'rals celebrate while it decrees.
P.	129	O.C.	269	The tree ere while foreshortned to our view,
P.	130	O.C.	283	While staggs shall fly unto the forests thick,
P.	130	O.C.	284	While sheep delight the grassy downs to pick,
P.	131	PARADISE	6	Held me a while misdoubting his Intent,
P.	132	PARADISE	47	While the Town-Bays writes all the while and spells,
P.	132	PARADISE	52	And while I meant to Praise thee, must Commend.
P.	137	HOUSEWARMING	6	While he the Betrayer of England and Flander,
P.	137	HOUSEWARMING	18	Made Thebes dance aloft while he fidled and sung,
P.	138	HOUSEWARMING	29	But while these devices he all doth compare,
P.	138	HOUSEWARMING	59	While into a fabrick the Presents would muster;
P.	142	INSTRUCTIONS	75	While she revolves, at once, Sidney's disgrace,
P.	146	INSTRUCTIONS	228	While Hector Harry steers by Will the Wit:
P.	146	INSTRUCTIONS	243	And some ran o're each night while others sleep,
P.	147	INSTRUCTIONS	280	Spent with fatigue, to breath a while Toback.
P.	149	INSTRUCTIONS	361	But still he car'd, while in Revenge he brav'd,
P.	150	INSTRUCTIONS	369	While Chain'd together two Ambassadors
P.	150	INSTRUCTIONS	403	While the first year our Navy is but shown,
P.	153	INSTRUCTIONS	523	Ruyter the while, that had our Ocean curb'd,
P.	154	INSTRUCTIONS	539	While the red Flags breath on their Top-masts high
P.	154	INSTRUCTIONS	549	With Pearly Shell the Tritons all the while
P.	156	INSTRUCTIONS	632	Sweet Painter draw his Picture while I write.
P.	156	INSTRUCTIONS	652	While envious Virgins hope he is a Male.
P.	157	INSTRUCTIONS	665	But entertains, the while, his time too short
P.	161	INSTRUCTIONS	845	True Trojan! while this Town can Girls afford,
P.	161	INSTRUCTIONS	849	Mean while the certain News of Peace arrives
P.	162	INSTRUCTIONS	870	But all the while his Private-Bill's in sight.
P.	163	INSTRUCTIONS	917	While, the pale Ghosts, his Eye does fixt admire
P.	163	INSTRUCTIONS	941	While Hyde provok'd his foaming tusk does whet,
P.	164	INSTRUCTIONS	951	Show'd they obscure him, while too near they please,
P.	164	INSTRUCTIONS	967	Bold and accurs'd are they, that all this while
P.	166	KINGS VOWES	32	I will winke all the while my Revenue is stole,
P.	172	LOYALL SCOT	32	Hee entertains the while his life too short,
P.	176	LOYALL SCOT	183	And while hee spared the keepers life hee fail'd.
P.	177	LOYALL SCOT	233	While they liv'd here, still Haunts them Underground.
P.	194	TWO HORSES	115	Ch. Pause, Brother, a while and calmly consider:

P. 201 HISTORICALL   4 And kept his Fathers Asses all the while.
P. 315 CHEQUER INN   100 And tho' his Sweate the while he eate

whilest   frequency: 2   relative frequency: 0.0000
P. 168 ADVICE   7 Whilest the brave youths tired with the work of
                         State
P. 185 BRITANNIA   12 Whilest the Lew'd Court in drunken slumbers
                         lyes,

whilst   frequency: 16   relative frequency: 0.0003
See also "whilest," "whil'st."
P. 28 LOVER   47 Whilst he, betwixt the Flames and Waves,
P. 35 DAPHNIS   73 Whilst this grief does thee disarm,
P. 38 PICTURE   25 Mean time, whilst every verdant thing
P. 40 THE MATCH   38 Whilst all the World is poor,
P. 46 AMETAS   2 Whilst Thou still dost say me nay?
P. 115 BLAKE   65 But whilst I draw that Scene, where you ere
                         long,
P. 116 BLAKE   93 Fond men who know not whilst such works they
                         raise,
P. 118 BLAKE   134 Whilst others lower, in the Sea do lye.
P. 119 BLAKE   167 Whilst fame in every place, her Trumpet blowes,
P. 169 ADVICE   35 Thus whilst the King of France with powerfull
                         Armes
P. 169 ADVICE   55 Whilst Positive walks Woodcock in the dark,
P. 172 LOYALL SCOT   18 Whilst Envious virgins hope hee is a Male.
P. 175 LOYALL SCOT   153 Whilst Arrius stands at th' Athanasian Creed.
P. 186 BRITANNIA   59 Whilst in truthes Mirror this Glad scene he
                         spy'd,
P. 187 BRITANNIA   95 Whilst your starv'd power in Legall fetters
                         pines.
P. 202 HISTORICALL   56 Whilst the brave Tudors wore th' Imperial
                         Crowne:

whil'st   frequency: 2   relative frequency: 0.0000
P. 122 TWO SONGS   32 Whil'st all the Nymphs on Damon's choice
                         attend?
P. 181 MADE FREE   7 Whil'st your Churches unbuilt

whip   frequency: 2   relative frequency: 0.0000
P. 151 INSTRUCTIONS 438 And whip the Dutch, unless they'l hold their
                         peace.
P. 153 INSTRUCTIONS 504 (This lik'd him best) his Cash beyond Sea whip.

whipt   frequency: 2   relative frequency: 0.0000
P. 91 MAY'S DEATH   37 As he crowds in he whipt him ore the pate
P. 143 INSTRUCTIONS 101 Justly the Rogue was whipt in Porter's Den:

whirleth   frequency: 1   relative frequency: 0.0000
P. 92 MAY'S DEATH   67 He, when the wheel of Empire, whirleth back,

whirling   frequency: 1   relative frequency: 0.0000
P. 109 ANNIVERSARY   265 So have I seen at Sea, when whirling Winds,

whisht   frequency: 1   relative frequency: 0.0000
P. 79 A. HOUSE   659 And every thing so whisht and fine,

whisk   frequency: 1   relative frequency: 0.0000
P. 91 MAY'S DEATH   35 At whose dread Whisk Virgil himself does quake,

whisper   frequency: 1   relative frequency: 0.0000
P. 20 THYRSIS   34 Cool winds do whisper, springs do flow.

whisper'd   frequency: 1   relative frequency: 0.0000
P. 163 INSTRUCTIONS 937 His Fathers Ghost too whisper'd him one Note,

whispering. See "whisp'ring."

whispers   frequency: 1   relative frequency: 0.0000
P. 58 BILL-BOROW   63 Which in their modest Whispers name

whisp'ring   frequency: 1   relative frequency: 0.0000
P. 163 INSTRUCTIONS 923 Then, whisp'ring to his Son in Words unheard,

whistling   frequency: 2   relative frequency: 0.0000
P. 44 DAMON   75 And, with his whistling Sythe, does cut
P. 71 A. HOUSE   393 With whistling Sithe, and Elbow strong,

white   frequency: 20   relative frequency: 0.0004
See also "milk-white."
P. 13 DROP OF DEW   38 White, and intire, though congeal'd and chill.

```
P.   15 EYES              18 Amongst the Red, the White, the Green;
P.   23 NYMPH             58 It wax'd more white and sweet than they.
P.   23 NYMPH             61 And white, (shall I say then my hand?)
P.   24 NYMPH            122 White as I can, though not as Thee.
P.   41 THE MOWER         13 The Tulip, white, did for complexion seek;
P.   48 THE GARDEN        17 No white nor red was ever seen
P.   62 A. HOUSE         105 'Here we, in shining Armour white,
P.   86 FLECKNO          134 Like white fleaks rising from a Leaper's skin!
P.  122 TWO SONGS         24 Half so white or sweet as She.
P.  141 INSTRUCTIONS      18 To see a tall Lowse brandish the white Staff.
P.  143 INSTRUCTIONS     108 On opposite points, the black against the white.
P.  156 INSTRUCTIONS     656 Harden'd and cool'd his Limbs, so soft, so
                            white,
P.  162 INSTRUCTIONS     869 At Pray'rs, his Eyes turn up the Pious white,
P.  172 LOYALL SCOT       22 Hardned and Cool'd those Limbs soe soft, soe
                            white,
P.  192 TWO HORSES        29 The stately Brass Stallion and the white marble
                            Steed
P.  192 TWO HORSES        35 W. Quoth the marble white Hors: 'twould make a
                            stone speak
P.  193 TWO HORSES        53 Ch. To see a white staffe make a Beggar a Lord
P.  204 HISTORICALL      139 White liverd Danby for his swift Jacall
P.  313 CHEQUER INN       22 Thou'lt ken him out by a white Wand
```

white-hall's   frequency: 2   relative frequency: 0.0000
```
P.   30 THE GALLERY       48 Then or White-hall's, or Mantua's were.
P.  151 INSTRUCTIONS     419 White-hall's unsafe, the Court all meditates
```

whitehall   frequency: 7   relative frequency: 0.0001
```
P.  161 INSTRUCTIONS     839 Tells them he at Whitehall had took a turn,
P.  170 PROPHECY           4 As farr as from Whitehall to Pudden lane
P.  190 STATUE             8 The Mimick so legally seiz'd of Whitehall.
P.  191 STATUE            54 But to turn the face to Whitehall you must
                            Shun;
P.  196 TWO HORSES       168 Both Gallopt to Whitehall and there Horribly
                            farted,
P.  313 CHEQUER INN       35 Has wrought himself into Whitehall
P.  317 CHEQUER INN      192 By this old Whitehall Pump.
```

whitehall's   frequency: 1   relative frequency: 0.0000
See also "white-hall's."
```
P.  162 INSTRUCTIONS     874 And make a sawce fit for Whitehall's digestion:
```

whiter   frequency: 1   relative frequency: 0.0000
```
P.  175 LOYALL SCOT      165 Nor is our Sheldon whiter then his Snow.
```

whitest   frequency: 1   relative frequency: 0.0000
```
P.   24 NYMPH             90 In whitest sheets of Lillies cold.
```

whither   frequency: 1   relative frequency: 0.0000

who   frequency: 146   relative frequency: 0.0030

whoever   frequency: 1   relative frequency: 0.0000

who'ld   frequency: 1   relative frequency: 0.0000

whole   frequency: 26   relative frequency: 0.0005
```
P.   21 SOUL & BODY       11 O who shall me deliver whole,
P.   37 DEFINITION        19 (Though Loves whole World on us doth wheel)
P.   83 FLECKNO           18 He'd Stanza's for a whole Appartement.
P.   96 HOLLAND           32 Whole sholes of Dutch serv'd up for Cabillau;
P.   97 HOLLAND           66 For Hans-in-Kelder of a whole Hans-Town.
P.   98 HOLLAND          104 When their whole Navy they together prest,
P.  112 ANNIVERSARY      380 'Moves the great Bulk, and animates the whole.
P.  117 BLAKE            113 This said, the whole Fleet gave it their
                            applause,
P.  131 PARADISE          21 Might hence presume the whole Creations day
P.  139 HOUSEWARMING      67 Bring in the whole Milk of a year at a meal,
P.  139 HOUSEWARMING      76 No, would the whole Parliament kiss him behind.
P.  147 INSTRUCTIONS     269 Each thinks his Person represents the whole,
P.  147 INSTRUCTIONS     276 Broach'd whole Brigades like Larks upon his
                            Lance.
P.  152 INSTRUCTIONS     481 First, then he march'd our whole Militia's
                            force,
P.  152 INSTRUCTIONS     491 Of the whole Nation now to ask a Loan.
P.  166 KINGS VOWES       33 And if any be Questiond, I'lle answer the
                            whole.
P.  175 LOYALL SCOT      137 One Bishops fiend spirits a whole Diocesse.
P.  180 STOCKSMARKET      59 For though the whole world cannot shew such
                            another,
P.  181 MADE FREE          6 Of the whole Guild-Hall Teame to dragg it.
```

P. 183 MADE FREE   102 The whole Nation may chance to repent it.
P. 187 BRITANNIA   99 'Tis Royall Game whole Kingdomes to deflower.
P. 188 BRITANNIA   151 Over the whole: the elect Jessean line
P. 193 TWO HORSES   59 W. That a King should consume three Realms
                           whole Estates
P. 204 HISTORICALL   133 For one man's weakeness a whole Nation bleeds
P. 315 CHEQUER INN   126 With his whole Generation
P. 317 CHEQUER INN   179 And the whole business of their Acts

wholesome   frequency: 2   relative frequency: 0.0000
    See also "wholsome."
    P. 72 A. HOUSE   427 Where every Mowers wholesome Heat
    P. 98 HOLLAND   124 A wholesome Danger drove us to our Ports.

wholly   frequency: 2   relative frequency: 0.0000
    P. 80 A. HOUSE   688 Nature is wholly vitrifi'd.
    P. 168 KINGS VOWES   64 I wholly will abandon State affaires,

wholsome   frequency: 2   relative frequency: 0.0000
    P. 50 THE GARDEN   71 How could such sweet and wholsome Hours
    P. 199 DUKE   50 Where twixt a wholsome husband and a page

whom   frequency: 35   relative frequency: 0.0007

whore   frequency: 9   relative frequency: 0.0001
    P. 106 ANNIVERSARY   113 Hence still they sing Hosanna to the Whore,
    P. 144 INSTRUCTIONS   150 Could raise so long for this new Whore of
                               State.
    P. 166 KINGS VOWES   37 But what ever it cost I will have a fine Whore,
    P. 177 LOYALL SCOT   253 Does man and wife signifie Rogue and Whore?
    P. 187 BRITANNIA   110 'Down with that common Magna Charta whore.'
    P. 192 TWO HORSES   41 To see Church and state bow down to a whore
    P. 194 TWO HORSES   95 W. That the King should send for another
                               French whore,
    P. 201 HISTORICALL   12 And dubd poore Palmer's wife his Royall Whore.
    P. 205 HISTORICALL   171 Thus said the Scarlet Whore to her gallant,

whoreing   frequency: 2   relative frequency: 0.0000
    P. 170 PROPHECY   18 And whoreing shall be the least sin att Court,
    P. 181 MADE FREE   36 Of Revelling, Drinking and Whoreing.

whores   frequency: 4   relative frequency: 0.0000
    P. 187 BRITANNIA   114 To Boys, Bawds, whores, and made a Publick
                               game.
    P. 187 BRITANNIA   120 Beseig'd by 's whores, Buffoones, and Bastard
                               Chitts;
    P. 194 TWO HORSES   89 Ch. But thanks to the whores who have made the
                               King Dogged
    P. 195 TWO HORSES   132 Than the Goats making whores of our wives and
                               our Daughters.

whoring. See "whoreing."

whorwood   frequency: 1   relative frequency: 0.0000
    P. 147 INSTRUCTIONS   259 Keen Whorwood next, in aid of Damsel frail,

whose   frequency: 64   relative frequency: 0.0013

whosoe're   frequency: 1   relative frequency: 0.0000

whosoever   frequency: 1   relative frequency: 0.0000
    See also "whosoe're."

why   frequency: 23   relative frequency: 0.0004

wicked   frequency: 1   relative frequency: 0.0000
    P. 192 TWO HORSES   44 And the Kings wicked life say God there is
                               none;

wide   frequency: 10   relative frequency: 0.0002
    P. 32 MOURNING   29 How wide they dream! The Indian Slaves
    P. 43 DAMON   51 This Sithe of mine discovers wide
    P. 57 BILL-BOROW   17 See what a soft access and wide
    P. 73 A. HOUSE   463 They feed so wide, so slowly move,
    P. 90 MAY'S DEATH   4 And with an Eye uncertain, gazing wide,
    P. 103 ANNIVERSARY   15 While heavy Monarchs make a wide Return,
    P. 108 ANNIVERSARY   197 Nor through wide Nostrils snuffe the wanton air,
    P. 131 PARADISE   13 Through that wide Field how he his way should
                               find
    P. 142 INSTRUCTIONS   62 Wide Mouth that Sparagus may well proclaim:
    P. 166 KINGS VOWES   23 with wide streets and uniforme of my owne mold;

wider   frequency: 1   relative frequency: 0.0000
    P.   62 A. HOUSE   101 'These Bars inclose that wider Den

wield   frequency: 1   relative frequency: 0.0000
    P.   9 DIALOGUE   1 Courage my Soul, now learn to wield

wife   frequency: 8   relative frequency: 0.0001
    P. 142 INSTRUCTIONS   50 Philosopher beyond Newcastle's Wife.
    P. 162 INSTRUCTIONS   884 And Serjeants Wife serves him for Partelott.
    P. 168 ADVICE   16 To keep his own and loose his sergeants wife.
    P. 174 LOYALL SCOT   124 Ah! like Lotts wife they still look Back and
                               Halt
    P. 177 LOYALL SCOT   253 Does man and wife signifie Rogue and Whore?
    P. 184 MADE FREE   120 With a Wife of Religion Italian?
    P. 201 HISTORICALL   12 And dubd poore Palmer's wife his Royall Whore.
    P. 203 HISTORICALL   94 Who ever has an over zealous wife

wight   frequency: 1   relative frequency: 0.0000
    P.   34 DAPHNIS   53 So to the condemned Wight

wild   frequency: 9   relative frequency: 0.0001
    P.   22 NYMPH   34 This waxed tame, while he grew wild,
    P.   41 THE MOWER   24 He grafts upon the Wild the Tame:
    P.   41 THE MOWER   34 A wild and fragrant Innocence:
    P.   62 A. HOUSE   102 'Of those wild Creatures, called Men.
    P. 129 O.C.   244 In horses fierce, wild deer, or armour bright;
    P. 156 INSTRUCTIONS   640 He heard how the wild Cannon nearer roar'd;
    P. 176 LOYALL SCOT   188 And wild disputes betwixt those heads must Grow,
    P. 182 MADE FREE   40 And amongst his Wild Crew
    P. 314 CHEQUER INN   85 Wild with his Tongue did all outrun

wilder   frequency: 2   relative frequency: 0.0000
    P.   38 PICTURE   5 The Wilder flow'rs, and gives them names:
    P.   47 EMPIRE   5 Jubal first made the wilder Notes agree;

wilderness   frequency: 2   relative frequency: 0.0000
    P.   23 NYMPH   74 To be a little Wilderness.
    P. 109 ANNIVERSARY   254 With Thorns and Briars of the Wilderness.

will   frequency: 112   relative frequency: 0.0023
    See also "hee'l," "shee'l," "they'l,"
             "'twill," "weel," "wee'l," "youl,"
             "you'l."
    P.   3 LOVELACE   27 Some reading your Lucasta, will alledge
    P.   9 DIALOGUE   20 Whose soft Plumes will thither fly:
    P.   20 THYRSIS   44 Will for thee, much more with thee dye.
    P.   21 SOUL & BODY   40 And Memory will not foregoe.
    P.   22 NYMPH   2 Have shot my Faun and it will dye.
    P.   22 NYMPH   8 Nor do I for all this; nor will:
    P.   22 NYMPH   11 Thy murder, I will Joyn my Tears
    P.   24 NYMPH   101 I in a golden Vial will
    P.   24 NYMPH   110 Will but bespeak thy Grave, and dye.
    P.   27 MISTRESS   46 Stand still, yet we will make him run.
    P.   34 DAPHNIS   55 And allow him all he will,
    P.   35 DAPHNIS   57 But I will not now begin
    P.   35 DAPHNIS   69 Rather I away will pine
    P.   36 DAPHNIS   91 Joy will not with Sorrow weave,
    P.   36 DAPHNIS   92 Nor will I this Grief pollute.
    P.   45 MOWER'S SONG   22 Will in one common Ruine fall.
    P.   46 AMETAS   8 Neither Love will twist nor Hay.
    P.   48 THE GARDEN   14 Only among the Plants will grow.
    P.   54 THYESTE   1 Climb at Court for me that will
    P.   60 A. HOUSE   37 Men will dispute how their Extent
    P.   60 A. HOUSE   39 And some will smile at this, as well
    P.   64 A. HOUSE   164 'Will soon us to perfection lead.
    P.   64 A. HOUSE   166 'Will straight grow Sanctity when here:
    P.   74 A. HOUSE   496 Will in green Age her Hearse expect.
    P.   78 A. HOUSE   631 Unless it self you will mistake,
    P.   85 FLECKNO   93 Will make the way here; I said Sir you'l do
    P.   92 MAY'S DEATH   77 But what will deeper wound thy little mind,
    P.   94 DR. WITTY   31 Now I reform, and surely so will all
    P. 104 ANNIVERSARY   26 And will have known, if he no more have Lost;
    P. 105 ANNIVERSARY   83 And each the Hand that lays him will direct,
    P. 106 ANNIVERSARY   134 Should bend to his, as he to Heavens will,
    P. 110 ANNIVERSARY   285 And the large Vale lay subject to thy Will,
    P. 113 ANNIVERSARY   397 I yield, nor further will the Prize contend;
    P. 114 BLAKE   43 But this great want, will not a long one prove,
    P. 114 BLAKE   44 Your Conquering Sword will soon that want
                               remove.
    P. 115 BLAKE   49 Forces and art, she soon will feel, are vain,
    P. 115 BLAKE   52 Peace made them hers, but War will make them

yours

P.	115	BLAKE	64 If fortune can make guilty what she will.
P.	118	BLAKE	139 And neither have, or power, or will to fly,
P.	118	BLAKE	157 Ages to come, your conquering Arms will bless,
P.	124	O.C.	52 This will not stay when once the other's gone.
P.	127	O.C.	183 Those Strokes he said will pierce through all below
P.	128	O.C.	220 Lye weak and easy to the ruler's will;
P.	129	O.C.	260 That threatens death, he yet will live again.
P.	129	O.C.	266 At mortalls sins, nor his own plant will spare;
P.	130	O.C.	312 A Cromwell in an houre a prince will grow.
P.	131	PARADISE	25 But I am now cervinc'd, and none will dare
P.	143	INSTRUCTIONS	79 Paint Castlemaine in Colcurs that will hold,
P.	146	INSTRUCTIONS	228 While Hector Harry steers by Will the Wit:
P.	152	INSTRUCTIONS	462 Their Fleet, to threaten, we will give them all.
P.	163	INSTRUCTIONS	938 That who does cut his Purse will cut his Throat.
P.	164	INSTRUCTIONS	943 Painter adieu, how will our Arts agree;
P.	165	KINGS VOWES	7 I will have a Religion then all of my owne,
P.	165	KINGS VOWES	9 But if it grow troublesome, I will have none.
P.	165	KINGS VOWES	10 I will have a fine Parliament allwayes to Friend,
P.	165	KINGS VOWES	12 But when they will not, they shall be att an end.
P.	165	KINGS VOWES	13 I will have as fine Bishops as were ere made with hands,
P.	165	KINGS VOWES	15 But if they displease me, I will have all their Lands.
P.	165	KINGS VOWES	16 I will have a fine Chancelor beare all the sway,
P.	166	KINGS VOWES	19 I will have a fine Navy to Ccnquer the Seas,
P.	166	KINGS VOWES	21 But if they should beat me, I will doe what they please.
P.	166	KINGS VOWES	22 I will have a new Londcn instead of the old,
P.	166	KINGS VOWES	24 But if they build it too fast, I will soon make them hold.
P.	166	KINGS VOWES	25 I will have a fine Son in makeing the marrd,
P.	166	KINGS VOWES	28 I will have a fine Court with ne'er an old face,
P.	166	KINGS VOWES	30 And I either will vacate, or buy him a place.
P.	166	KINGS VOWES	31 I will have a Privy-purse without a Controll,
P.	166	KINGS VOWES	32 I will winke all the while my Revenue is stole,
P.	166	KINGS VOWES	34 I will have a Privy Councell to sit allwayes still,
P.	166	KINGS VOWES	35 I will have a fine Junto to doe what I will,
P.	166	KINGS VOWES	36 I will have two fine Secretaryes pisse thro one Quill.
P.	166	KINGS VOWES	37 But what ever it cost I will have a fine Whore,
P.	167	KINGS VOWES	43 Of my Pimp I will make my Minister Premier,
P.	167	KINGS VOWES	47 Miss and I will both learne to live cn Exhibition,
P.	167	KINGS VOWES	49 I will have a fine Tunick a Sash and a Vest,
P.	167	KINGS VOWES	50 Tho' not rule like the Turk yet I will be so drest,
P.	167	KINGS VOWES	52 I will have a fine pond and a pretty decoy,
P.	167	KINGS VOWES	55 The Antient Nobility I will lay by,
P.	167	KINGS VOWES	58 Some one I will advance from mean descent,
P.	168	KINGS VOWES	61 And I will take his part to that degree,
P.	168	KINGS VOWES	64 I wholly will abandon State affaires,
P.	171	PROPHECY	31 London shall then see, for it will come to pass,
P.	174	LOYALL SCOT	87 But who Considers well will find indeed
P.	174	LOYALL SCOT	104 A Bishop will like Mahomet tear the Moon
P.	175	LOYALL SCOT	140 Will you bee treated Princes? here fall to:
P.	175	LOYALL SCOT	142 Howere Insipid Yet the Sawce will mend 'em
P.	175	LOYALL SCOT	155 But will Transform for an Archbishoprick.
P.	175	LOYALL SCOT	160 Who views but Gilberts Toyls will reason find
P.	177	LOYALL SCOT	239 The good will bravely, bad will basely doe;
P.	178	LOYALL SCOT	263 Hee our Affection both and will Comands,
P.	180	STOCKSMARKET	49 Sure the king will ne'er think of repaying his bankers,
P.	180	STOCKSMARKET	52 They will scarce afford him a rag to his breech.
P.	180	STOCKSMARKET	55 But alas! he will never arrive at his end,
P.	184	MADE FREE	124 He will find whc unlocks,
P.	185	BRITANNIA	13 I stole away; and never will return
P.	186	BRITANNIA	86 To teach your will 's the onely rule of right,
P.	187	BRITANNIA	89 And they will fear those powers they once did scorn.
P.	189	BRITANNIA	182 Balm in their wounds, will fleeting life restore.
P.	190	STATUE	11 And soe near to the Court they will never indure
P.	190	STATUE	32 He will here keep a market of Parliament men.
P.	190	STATUE	36 Will you venture soe far to Prorogue the King too?
P.	191	STATUE	53 So the Statue will up after all this delay,
P.	194	TWO HORSES	122 Ch. Thy King will ne're fight unless't be for

```
                                        Queans.
        P.  195 TWO HORSES      146 Father Patricks Deciple will make England
                                        smart.
        P.  196 TWO HORSES      178 Will publish their faults and prophesy their
                                        fall.
        P.  198 DUKE             25 Shall these men dare to contradict my will
        P.  199 DUKE             72 And will cutt throats againe if he bee paid:
        P.  200 DUKE            116 Hard fate of princes, who will nere believe,
        P.  204 HISTORICALL     153 At his Command Mack will doe any thing,
        P.  316 CHEQUER INN     143 The Beck'ning never will be paid


will'd                                  frequency:    1    relative frequency: 0.0000
        P.   67 A. HOUSE        275 And what both Nuns and Founders will'd


william                                 frequency:    1    relative frequency: 0.0000
        P.  179 STOCKSMARKET     20 Even Sir William Peake sits much firmer than
                                        he.


williams                                frequency:    1    relative frequency: 0.0000
        P.  147 INSTRUCTIONS    261 And surly Williams, the Accomptants bane:


willing                                 frequency:    3    relative frequency: 0.0000
        P.   27 MISTRESS         35 And while thy willing Soul transpires
        P.   41 THE MOWER        33 Where willing Nature does to all dispence
        P.  105 ANNIVERSARY      76 And each one enter'd in the willing Frame;


willingly                               frequency:    1    relative frequency: 0.0000
        P.  172 LOYALL SCOT       7 Hee Understood and Willingly Addrest


wilt                                    frequency:    2    relative frequency: 0.0000
        P.   11 DIALOGUE         63 Wilt thou all the Glory have
        P.   42 DAMON            33 How long wilt Thou, fair Shepheardess,


win                                     frequency:    4    relative frequency: 0.0000
        P.   25 YOUNG LOVE       21 So we win of doubtful Fate;
        P.   35 DAPHNIS          60 What my Presence could not win.
        P.   48 THE GARDEN        2 To win the Palm, the Oke, or Bayes;
        P.  143 INSTRUCTIONS     110 These now advent'ring how to win it back.


wind                                    frequency:   12    relative frequency: 0.0002
        P.   30 THE GALLERY      39 Nor blows more Wind than what may well
        P.   31 FAIR SINGER      18 She having gained both the Wind and Sun.
        P.   47 EMPIRE           15 These practising the Wind, and those the Wire,
        P.   76 A. HOUSE        575 No Leaf does tremble in the Wind
        P.   77 A. HOUSE        595 While the Wind, cooling through the Boughs,
        P.   81 A. HOUSE        716 And Sighs (Loves Cannon charg'd with Wind;)
        P.   98 HOLLAND         111 A Cock-boat tost with the same wind and fate;
        P.  106 ANNIVERSARY     126 Angelique Cromwell who outwings the wind;
        P.  113 BLAKE             3 But though the wind was fair, they slowly swoome
        P.  154 INSTRUCTIONS     547 Aeolus their Sails inspires with Eastern Wind,
        P.  154 INSTRUCTIONS     576 The Ocean Water, or the Heavens Wind.
        P.  196 TWO HORSES      173 Why might not our Horses, since words are but
                                        wind,


windes                                  frequency:    1    relative frequency: 0.0000
        P.   47 EMPIRE            2 Where Jarring Windes to infant Nature plaid.


winding                                 frequency:    2    relative frequency: 0.0000
        P.   14 THE CORONET      21 And disintangle all his winding Snare:
        P.  106 ANNIVERSARY     124 Winding his Horn to Kings that chase the
                                        Beast.


windows                                 frequency:    2    relative frequency: 0.0000
        P.   32 MOURNING         24 Like Grief, is from her Windows thrown.
        P.  111 ANNIVERSARY     346 And Princes shining through their windows
                                        starts;


windpipe                                frequency:    1    relative frequency: 0.0000
        P.  191 TWO HORSES        5 Nay Statues without either windpipe or Lungs


winds                                   frequency:   13    relative frequency: 0.0002
        See also "windes."
        P.   10 DIALOGUE         39 Which the posting Winds recall,
        P.   17 BERMUDAS          4 The listning Winds receiv'd this Song.
        P.   20 THYRSIS          34 Cool winds do whisper, springs do flow.
        P.   23 NYMPH            70 And trod, as on the four Winds.
        P.   27 LOVER            10 Bul'd, and the Winds did what they please,
        P.   27 LOVER            19 And from the Winds the Sighs he bore,
        P.   58 BILL-BOROW       59 Nor to the winds uncertain gust,
        P.   59 A. HOUSE         20 Where Winds as he themselves may lose.
        P.  109 ANNIVERSARY     235 Then did thick Mists and Winds the air deform,
```

```
         P. 109 ANNIVERSARY   265 So have I seen at Sea, when whirling Winds,
         P. 114 BLAKE          15 Of winds and waters rage, they fearful be,
         P. 126 O.C.          115 The Winds receive it, and its force out-do,
         P. 131 O.C.          314 How gently winds at once the ruling reins?
```

windsor   frequency: 1   relative frequency: 0.0000
```
         P. 151 INSTRUCTIONS   420 To fly to Windscr, and mure up the Gates.
```

wine   frequency: 12   relative frequency: 0.0002
```
         P.  20 THYRSIS         47 In wine, and drirk cn't even till we weep,
         P.  49 THE GARDEN      36 Upon my Mouth do crush their Wine;
         P.  91 MAY'S DEATH     21 Cups more then civil of Emathian wine,
         P.  91 MAY'S DEATH     46 Until you all grow Consuls in your wine.
         P.  98 HOLLAND        115 Ram'd with Gun-powder, flaming with Brand wine,
         P. 110 ANNIVERSARY    288 Of Liberty, not drunken with its Wine.
         P. 125 O.C.           100 Frustrates the Autumn and the hopes cf Wine.
         P. 164 INSTRUCTIONS   974 Bacchus is Wine, the Ccuntry is the King.)
         P. 169 ADVICE          33 Capacious Bowles with Lusty wine repleat
         P. 196 TWO HORSES     183 'Tis wine and Strong drink makes tumults
                                   increase;
         P. 201 HISTORICALL     15 With Women, Wine and Vyands of delight
         P. 316 CHEQUER INN    155 And tooke his Wine when it was due
```

wing   frequency: 3   relative frequency: 0.0000
```
         P.  37 DEFINITION       8 But vainly flapt its Tinsel Wing.
         P. 132 PARADISE        40 So never Flags, but alwaies keeps on Wing.
         P. 152 INSTRUCTIONS    490 With that curs'd Quill pluck'd from a Vulture's
                                   Wing:
```

wing'd   frequency: 1   relative frequency: 0.0000
```
         P.  28 LOVER           46 With all his wing'd Artillery.
```

winged   frequency: 5   relative frequency: 0.0001
See also "saphir-winged," "wing'd."
```
         P.  26 MISTRESS        22 Times winged Charriot hurrying near:
         P.  74 A. HOUSE       511 And underneath the winged Quires
         P. 108 ANNIVERSARY    193 First winged Fear transports them far away,
         P. 116 BLAKE          100 With winged speed, for Sanctacruze does make.
         P. 126 O.C.           121 Then heavy Showres the winged Tempests lead,
```

wings   frequency: 7   relative frequency: 0.0001
```
         P.  19 THYRSIS         14 That have no wings and cannot fly?
         P.  19 THYRSIS         16 Hath no wings, yet doth aspire
         P.  49 THE GARDEN      54 Then whets, and combs its silver Wings;
         P.  76 A. HOUSE       565 Give me but Wings as they, and I
         P. 113 BLAKE            1 Now does Spains Fleet her spatious wings
                                   unfold,
         P. 129 O.C.           255 Oh! humane glcry, vaine, oh! death, oh! wings,
         P. 144 INSTRUCTICNS   140 And flies like Eatts with leathern Wings by
                                   Night.
```

wink. See "winke."

winke   frequency: 1   relative frequency: 0.0000
```
         P. 166 KINGS VOWES     32 I will winke all the while my Revenue is stole,
```

winnow   frequency: 1   relative frequency: 0.0000
```
         P.  77 A. HOUSE       600 And winncw from the Chaff my Head.
```

winter   frequency: 3   relative frequency: 0.0000
```
         P.  69 A. HOUSE       341 The Winter Quarters were the Stoves,
         P.  98 HOLLAND        128 In a calm Winter, under Skies Serene.
         P. 125 O.C.            90 Of many a Winter hath surviv'd the rage.
```

winters   frequency: 1   relative frequency: 0.0000
```
         P. 116 BLAKE           84 Nor Winters storms, had made your Fleet
                                   retreat.
```

wire   frequency: 1   relative frequency: 0.0000
See also "wyer."
```
         P.  47 EMPIRE          15 These practising the Wind, and those the Wire,
```

wisdome   frequency: 3   relative frequency: 0.0000
```
         P.  81 A. HOUSE       710 But for the Wisdome, nct the Noyse;
         P.  81 A. HOUSE       711 Nor yet that Wisdome would affect,
         P. 197 DUKE             4 Abhoring wisdome and dispising witt,
```

wise   frequency: 22   relative frequency: 0.0004
```
         P.  16 EYES            29 So Magdalen, in Tears more wise
         P.  65 A. HOUSE       195 'Try but a while, if you be wise:
         P. 112 ANNIVERSARY    383 'The Valiants Terror, Riddle of the Wise;
```

```
      P.  121 TWO SONGS      57 But to be honest, valiant, wise,
      P.  146 INSTRUCTIONS  231 Pleas'd with their Numbers, yet in Valour wise,
      P.  152 INSTRUCTIONS  485 And the wise Court, that always lov'd it dear,
      P.  163 INSTRUCTIONS  939 But in wise anger he their Crimes forbears,
      P.  169 ADVICE         59 What Scandal's this! Temple, the wise, the
                                Brave,
      P.  171 PROPHECY       36 Whom Wise men Laugh att and the Women Rule,
      P.  171 PROPHECY       46 And think French onely Loyall, Irish wise,
      P.  172 LOYALL SCOT    12 And of wise Lethe hee had took a draught.
      P.  175 LOYALL SCOT   126 Who that is wise would pulpit Toyl Indure?
      P.  187 BRITANNIA     108 Led up by the wise son-in-law of Hide.
      P.  191 STATUE         46 To buy a King is not so wise as to sell,
      P.  193 TWO HORSES     54 And scarce a wise man at a long Councell board;
      P.  195 TWO HORSES    155 Ch. Yet have wee one Secretary honest and wise:
      P.  198 DUKE           12 I and the wise associates of my vow,
      P.  198 DUKE           18 Manag'd by wise Fitzgerald and by Scott,
      P.  199 DUKE           57 Was thought soe meeke, soe prudent and soe wise:
      P.  202 HISTORICALL    59 Misguided Monarchs rarely wise or just,
      P.  205 HISTORICALL   179 Be wise ye Sons of Men tempt God no more
      P.  317 CHEQUER INN    187 By wise Volke, I have oft been told

wisely                          frequency:   8    relative frequency: 0.0001
      P.   15 EYES            1 How wisely Nature did decree,
      P.   39 THE MATCH      17 Love wisely had of long fore-seen
      P.   97 HOLLAND        78 Where wisely for their Court they chose a
                                Village.
      P.  105 ANNIVERSARY   104 And wisely court the Influence they fear;
      P.  140 HOUSEWARMING  109 Or rather how wisely his Stall was built near,
      P.  150 INSTRUCTIONS  399 Bab May and Arlington did wisely scoff,
      P.  183 MADE FREE     104 You would wisely employ,
      P.  315 CHEQUER INN   124 And wisely lodging at next Doore

wiser                           frequency:   3    relative frequency: 0.0000
      P.   88 ODE            48 He had of wiser Art.
      P.  151 INSTRUCTIONS  417 But wiser Men, and well foreseen in chance,
      P.  200 DUKE           95 When wiser men its ruine undertooke:

wish                            frequency:   5    relative frequency: 0.0001
      P.  116 BLAKE          98 Wish then for that assault he lately fear'd.
      P.  116 BLAKE          99 His wish he has, for now undaunted Blake,
      P.  125 O.C.          103 Whether some Kinder Pow'rs, that wish us well,
      P.  171 PROPHECY       56 And wish in vain Venetian Libertye.
      P.  201 HISTORICALL    28 To wish her hopeful Issue timely Joy.

wish'd                          frequency:   3    relative frequency: 0.0000
      P.  106 ANNIVERSARY   136 From such a wish'd Conjuncture might reflect.
      P.  137 HOUSEWARMING   15 And wish'd that his Daughter had had as much
                                grace
      P.  152 INSTRUCTIONS  472 And wish'd himself the Gout, to seize his hand.

wished.  See "wish'd," "wisht," "wish't."

wishing                         frequency:   1    relative frequency: 0.0000
      P.  110 ANNIVERSARY   272 Giddy, and wishing for the fatal Shore;

wisht                           frequency:   2    relative frequency: 0.0000
      P.   22 NYMPH           7 I'me sure I never wisht them ill;
      P.  143 INSTRUCTIONS   90 And now first, wisht she e're had been a Maid.

wish't                          frequency:   2    relative frequency: 0.0000
      P.  114 BLAKE          18 More wish't for, and more welcome is then sleep,
      P.  194 TWO HORSES    104 Insted of a Cudgell Balam wish't for a Sword.

wit                             frequency:  14    relative frequency: 0.0002
   See also "witt."
      P.    3 LOVELACE       16 On the faire blossome of each growing wit.
      P.    3 LOVELACE       20 Of wit corrupted, the unfashion'd Sons.
      P.   21 SOUL & BODY    41 What but a Soul could have the wit
      P.   55 EPITAPH         7 Nor can the truest Wit or Friend,
      P.   77 A. HOUSE      585 And see how Chance's better Wit
      P.   85 FLECKNO       102 Our peace, the Priest said I too had some wit:
      P.   91 MAY'S DEATH    40 Most servil' wit, and Mercenary Pen.
      P.   94 DR. WITTY      25 Her thoughts are English, though her sparkling
                                wit
      P.  141 INSTRUCTIONS   31 Him neither Wit nor Courage did exalt,
      P.  146 INSTRUCTIONS  228 While Hector Harry steers by Will the Wit:
      P.  147 INSTRUCTIONS  265 Of Birth, State, Wit, Strength, Courage,
                                How'rd presumes,
      P.  152 INSTRUCTIONS  466 Still his sharp Wit on States and Princes
                                whets.
      P.  160 INSTRUCTIONS  804 And for a Couns'llor, he that has least Wit.
```

P. 204 HISTORICALL   143 'Twas want of Wit and Courage made them fail,

witch   frequency: 2   relative frequency: 0.0000
  P. 35 DAPHNIS   81 Or the Witch that midnight wakes
  P. 92 MAY'S DEATH   100 Such as unto the Sabboth bears the Witch.

witches   frequency: 2   relative frequency: 0.0000
  P. 65 A. HOUSE   205 'Hypocrite Witches, hence avant,
  P. 187 BRITANNIA   97 Henceforth be deaf to that old witches charmes,

with   frequency: 500   relative frequency: 0.0104

withal   frequency: 1   relative frequency: 0.0000
  See also "withall."
  P. 24 NYMPH   112 Be cut in Marble; and withal,

withall   frequency: 1   relative frequency: 0.0000
  P. 191 STATUE   50 And his Parliament List withall did produce,

withdrawing   frequency: 1   relative frequency: 0.0000
  P. 72 A. HOUSE   441 This Scene again withdrawing brings

withdraws   frequency: 1   relative frequency: 0.0000
  P. 49 THE GARDEN   42 Withdraws into its happiness:

withdrew   frequency: 1   relative frequency: 0.0000
  P. 47 EMPIRE   12 Into harmonious Colonies withdrew.

wither   frequency: 1   relative frequency: 0.0000
  P. 15 THE CORONET   23 And let these wither, so that he may die,

wither'd   frequency: 2   relative frequency: 0.0000
  P. 41 DAMON   8 And wither'd like his Hopes the Grass.
  P. 129 O.C.   253 All wither'd, all discolour'd, pale and wan,

withering. See "with'ring."

withers   frequency: 1   relative frequency: 0.0000
  P. 18 CLORINDA   7 D. Grass withers; and the Flow'rs too fade.

within   frequency: 42   relative frequency: 0.0008
  P. 11 DIALOGUE   53 Shall within one Beauty meet,
  P. 12 DROP OF DEW   21 Could it within the humane flow'r be seen,
  P. 15 EYES   10 Within the Scales of either Eye,
  P. 18 CLORINDA   14 Tinkles within the concave Shell.
  P. 21 SOUL & BODY   22 Within anothers Grief to pine?
  P. 24 NYMPH   92 Lillies without, Roses within.
  P. 29 LOVER   62 And Musick within every Ear:
  P. 32 MOURNING   18 Within her solitary Bowr,
  P. 40 THE MATCH   39 And have within our Selves possest
  P. 40 THE MOWER   5 He first enclos'd within the Gardens square
  P. 42 DAMON   15 Only the Snake, that kept within,
  P. 46 AMETAS   16 And go kiss within the Hay.
  P. 59 A. HOUSE   1 Within this sober Frame expect
  P. 60 A. HOUSE   38 Within such dwarfish Confines went:
  P. 61 A. HOUSE   67 Nor less the Rooms within commends
  P. 62 A. HOUSE   97 'Within this holy leisure we
  P. 73 A. HOUSE   457 They seem within the polisht Grass
  P. 74 A. HOUSE   504 As if the Night within were hedg'd.
  P. 74 A. HOUSE   505 Dark all without it knits; within
  P. 75 A. HOUSE   520 Within the Skin its shrunken claws.
  P. 76 A. HOUSE   554 A Traitor-worm, within it bred.
  P. 76 A. HOUSE   555 (As first our Flesh corrupt within
  P. 83 FLECKNO   17 And though within one Cell so narrow pent,
  P. 86 FLECKNO   133 Those papers, which he pilled from within
  P. 90 ODE   106 Within his party-colour'd Mind;
  P. 99 HOLLAND   148 Watchful abroad, and honest still within.
  P. 104 ANNIVERSARY   35 Nor sacred Prophecies consult within,
  P. 109 ANNIVERSARY   232 An healthful Mind within a Body strong;
  P. 124 O.C.   54 And him within his tortur'd Image racks.
  P. 128 O.C.   203 But within one its narrow limits fall,
  P. 131 PARADISE   26 Within thy Labours to pretend a Share.
  P. 143 INSTRUCTIONS   84 And still within her mind the Footman runs:
  P. 143 INSTRUCTIONS   87 Poring within her Glass she re-adjusts
  P. 149 INSTRUCTIONS   349 Now Mordant may, within his Castle Tow'r,
  P. 155 INSTRUCTIONS   585 Our wretched Ships within their Fate attend,
  P. 157 INSTRUCTIONS   668 Within its circle, knows himself secure.
  P. 158 INSTRUCTIONS   731 The Seamen search her all, within, without:
  P. 160 INSTRUCTIONS   815 And thinks 'twill ne're be well within this
                            Nation,
  P. 170 PROPHECY   16 Within the Curtains and behind the Scenes,

P. 172 LOYALL SCOT   34 Within its Circle knows himselfe secure.
P. 183 MADE FREE   96 With the Pex and the Host within it?
P. 190 STATUE   26 Had within it an Army that burnt up the Town:

without   frequency: 38   relative frequency: 0.0007
P.   5 HASTINGS   58 And wept, as we, without Redress or Law.
P. 20 THYRSIS   43 Thyrsis. I cannot live, without thee, I
P. 24 NYMPH   92 Lillies without, Roses within.
P. 36 DAPHNIS   106 Nor indeed without a Cause.
P. 41 THE MOWER   30 To procreate without a Sex.
P. 49 THE GARDEN   58 While Man there walk'd without a Mate:
P. 55 EPITAPH   8 Without Detracting, her commend.
P. 55 THYESTE   8 Thus when without noise, unknown,
P. 55 THYESTE   10 I shall dye, without a groan,
P. 58 BILL-BOROW   79 Nor he the Hills without the Groves,
P. 61 A. HOUSE   66 Adorns without the open Door:
P. 62 A. HOUSE   99 'These Walls restrain the World without,
P. 62 A. HOUSE   116 'That live without this happy Vow.
P. 74 A. HOUSE   505 Dark all without it knits; within
P. 78 A. HOUSE   638 If they be in it or without.
P. 83 FLECKNO   19 Straight without further information,
P. 84 FLECKNO   65 The Needles Eye thread without any stich,
P. 109 ANNIVERSARY   261 Whose climbing Flame, without a timely stop,
P. 114 BLAKE   32 The benefits without the ills of rain.
P. 122 TWO SONGS   12 Without each a Sprig of Green.
P. 126 O.C.   135 He without noise still travell'd to his End,
P. 132 PARADISE   48 And like a Pack-Horse tires without his Bells.
P. 141 INSTRUCTIONS   5 Canst thou paint without Colours? Then 'tis
                          right:
P. 141 INSTRUCTIONS   6 For so we too without a Fleet can fight.
P. 142 INSTRUCTIONS   66 Can without breaking venom'd juice convey.
P. 146 INSTRUCTIONS   240 Without Intelligence, Command, or Pay:
P. 148 INSTRUCTIONS   296 Without disorder in their Intervals:
P. 155 INSTRUCTIONS   589 A Skipper rude shocks it without respect,
P. 158 INSTRUCTIONS   731 The Seamen search her all, within, without:
P. 165 INSTRUCTIONS   990 Give us this Court, and rule without a Guard.
P. 165 KINGS VOWES   4 Then Charles without acre
P. 166 KINGS VOWES   31 I will have a Privy-purse without a Controll,
P. 169 ADVICE   57 Thus all imploy themselves, and without pitty
P. 177 LOYALL SCOT   220 Such Bishops are Without a Complement
P. 191 TWO HORSES   5 Nay Statues without either windpipe or Lungs
P. 194 TWO HORSES   94 With an Addleheaded Knight and a Lord without
                          Brains.
P. 204 HISTORICALL   124 This is the Savage Pimp without dispute
P. 316 CHEQUER INN   144 Without another Sesse.

with'ring   frequency: 1   relative frequency: 0.0000
P. 124 O.C.   55 So the Flowr with'ring which the Garden
                          crown'd,

withstand   frequency: 2   relative frequency: 0.0000
P. 106 ANNIVERSARY   137 Sure, the mysterious Work, where none withstand,
P. 110 ANNIVERSARY   280 Nor Tyranny, where One does them withstand:

withstood   frequency: 1   relative frequency: 0.0000
P. 188 BRITANNIA   148 It 's by noe Potent Antidote withstood.

witness   frequency: 3   relative frequency: 0.0000
P. 98 HOLLAND   103 Let this one court'sie witness all the rest;
P. 142 INSTRUCTIONS   69 Witness ye stars of Night, and thou the pale
P. 154 INSTRUCTIONS   536 And witness their complaisence in their trim.

wits   frequency: 1   relative frequency: 0.0000
See also "witts."
P.   3 LOVELACE   4 Our wits have drawne th' infection of our times.

witt   frequency: 3   relative frequency: 0.0000
See also "de-witte."
P. 195 TWO HORSES   137 Ch. De Witt and Cromwell had each a brave
                          soul.
P. 197 DUKE   4 Abhoring wisdome and dispising witt,
P. 315 CHEQUER INN   118 What pitty 'tis a Witt so greate

wittals   frequency: 1   relative frequency: 0.0000
P. 144 INSTRUCTIONS   151 Of early Wittals first the Troop march'd in,

wittols. See "wittals."

witts   frequency: 1   relative frequency: 0.0000
P. 181 MADE FREE   14 Who henceforth in their Witts

witty   frequency: 2   relative frequency: 0.0000

P. 86 FLECKNO   115 To be both witty and valiant: I loth,
P. 93 DR. WITTY   t1 To his worthy Friend Doctor Witty upon his

wives   frequency: 9   relative frequency: 0.0001
P. 138 HOUSEWARMING   28 And too much resembled his Wives Chocolatte.
P. 144 INSTRUCTIONS   153 In Loyal haste they left young Wives in Bed,
P. 150 INSTRUCTIONS   378 Masculine Wives, transgressing Natures Law.
P. 171 PROPHECY   51 Their Wives to his Lust expos'd, their Wealth
                          to his spoyle
P. 182 MADE FREE   64 All your Wives had been Strumpetts
P. 195 TWO HORSES   132 Than the Goats making whores of our wives and
                          our Daughters.
P. 203 HISTORICALL   78 Corrupt with Gold they Wives and Daughters
                          bring
P. 316 CHEQUER INN   170 Like Sweat Meates, for their Girles and Wives
P. 317 CHEQUER INN   176 They sell us all our Barnes and Wives

woe   frequency: 1   relative frequency: 0.0000
P. 31 MOURNING   8 To Heaven, whence it came, their Woe.

woeful. See "woefull."

woefull   frequency: 1   relative frequency: 0.0000
P. 315 CHEQUER INN   130 The Man that gave a woefull Tax

woes   frequency: 5   relative frequency: 0.0001
P. 43 DAMON   72 Sighing I whet my Sythe and Woes.
P. 125 O.C.   74 Had ev'ry figure of her woes exprest;
P. 159 INSTRUCTIONS   763 But Fate does still accumulate our Woes,
P. 184 BRITANNIA   8 Once more with me partake of mortall woes.
P. 202 HISTORICALL   51 Foil'd thus by Venus he Bellona woes,

wolf   frequency: 2   relative frequency: 0.0000
P. 19 THYRSIS   22 Ther's no Wolf, no Fox, nor Bear.
P. 188 BRITANNIA   145 Into the Wolf and make him Guardian turn

wolves   frequency: 1   relative frequency: 0.0000
P. 119 TWO SONGS   2 And even Wolves the Sheep forget;

woman   frequency: 1   relative frequency: 0.0000
P. 143 INSTRUCTIONS   89 Fears lest he scorn a Woman once assay'd,

womans   frequency: 1   relative frequency: 0.0000
P. 46 AMETAS   11 And Love tyes a Womans Mind

womb   frequency: 4   relative frequency: 0.0000
P. 16 EYES   34 Nor the chast Ladies pregnant Womb,
P. 113 BLAKE   7 Every capatious Gallions womb was fill'd,
P. 113 BLAKE   8 With what the Womb of wealthy Kingdomes yield,
P. 142 INSTRUCTIONS   72 And Fawns, that from the womb abortive fled.

women   frequency: 8   relative frequency: 0.0001
P. 32 MOURNING   35 But sure as oft as Women weep,
P. 66 A. HOUSE   239 Ill-counsell'd Women, do you know
P. 72 A. HOUSE   423 The Women that with forks it fling,
P. 94 DR. WITTY   29 Women must not teach here: the Doctor doth
P. 142 INSTRUCTIONS   48 When Men and Women took each others Word.
P. 142 INSTRUCTIONS   59 Happy'st of Women, if she were but able
P. 171 PROPHECY   36 Whom Wise men Laugh att and the Women Rule,
P. 201 HISTORICALL   15 With Women, Wine and Vyands of delight

won   frequency: 3   relative frequency: 0.0000
See also "wonn."
P. 106 ANNIVERSARY   105 O would they rather by his Pattern won.
P. 121 TWO SONGS   4 Has Menalca's daughter won.
P. 121 TWO SONGS   52 For he has Cynthia's favour won.

wonder   frequency: 6   relative frequency: 0.0001
P. 70 A. HOUSE   378 We wonder how they rise alive.
P. 103 ANNIVERSARY   10 Is the just Wonder of the Day before.
P. 104 ANNIVERSARY   57 The listning Structures he with Wonder ey'd,
P. 163 INSTRUCTIONS   905 In his deep thoughts the wonder did increase,
P. 175 LOYALL SCOT   152 Noe Wonder if the Orthodox doe Bleed,
P. 193 TWO HORSES   81 Ch. No wonder that Beggers should still be for
                          giving

wonder'd   frequency: 2   relative frequency: 0.0000
P. 162 INSTRUCTIONS   900 He wonder'd first, then pity'd, then he lov'd:
P. 172 LOYALL SCOT   28 And wonder'd much at those that Runne away,

wondered. See "wonder'd," "wondred."

wonderful   frequency: 1   relative frequency: 0.0000

See also "wonderfull."
P. 106 ANNIVERSARY   135 What we might hope, what wonderful Effect

wonderfull   frequency: 1   relative frequency: 0.0000
P. 201 HISTORICALL   5 At length by wonderfull impulse of Fate

wondering. See "wondring."

wonders   frequency: 1   relative frequency: 0.0000
P. 75 A. HOUSE   537 But most the Hewel's wonders are,

wondred   frequency: 1   relative frequency: 0.0000
P. 157 INSTRUCTIONS 662 And wondred much at those that run away:

wondring   frequency: 1   relative frequency: 0.0000
P. 72 A. HOUSE   435 We wondring in the River near

wondrous   frequency: 5   relative frequency: 0.0001
See also "wond'rous."
P. 80 A. HOUSE   690 That wondrous Beauty which they have,
P. 105 ANNIVERSARY   67 Such was that wondrous Order and Consent,
P. 123 O.C.   20 Should speak the wondrous softness of his Heart.
P. 163 INSTRUCTIONS 925 The wondrous Night the pensive King revolves,
P. 173 LOYALL SCOT   81 What Ethick River is this Wondrous Tweed

wond'rous   frequency: 2   relative frequency: 0.0000
P. 23 NYMPH   63 It is a wond'rous thing, how fleet
P. 49 THE GARDEN   33 What wond'rous Life in this I lead!

wonn   frequency: 1   relative frequency: 0.0000
P. 104 ANNIVERSARY   26 And will have Wonn, if he no more have Lost;

won't   frequency: 3   relative frequency: 0.0000
P. 152 INSTRUCTIONS 461 But Harry's Order, if they won't recal
P. 196 TWO HORSES   182 They that Conquered the Father won't be slaves
                         to the Son:
P. 317 CHEQUER INN   182 Wee poure in Water when it won't come

wonted   frequency: 2   relative frequency: 0.0000
P. 33 DAPHNIS   14 To lay by her wonted State,
P. 143 INSTRUCTIONS   83 Her wonted joys thenceforth and Court she shuns,

woo   frequency: 1   relative frequency: 0.0000
P. 120 TWO SONGS   29 Courage, Endymion, boldly Woo,

wood   frequency: 10   relative frequency: 0.0002
P. 74 A. HOUSE   482 Take Sanctuary in the Wood;
P. 74 A. HOUSE   489 The double Wood of ancient Stocks
P. 74 A. HOUSE   498 It seems indeed as Wood not Trees:
P. 80 A. HOUSE   704 The Wood about her draws a Skreen.
P. 108 ANNIVERSARY   200 And with shrill Neighings ask'd him of the
                         Wood.
P. 129 O.C.   268 So many yeares the shelter of the wood.)
P. 138 HOUSEWARMING   45 His Wood would come in at the easier rate,
P. 144 INSTRUCTIONS 162 Wood these commands, Knight of the Horn and
                         Cane.
P. 155 INSTRUCTIONS 580 Flies to the Wood, and hides his armless Head.
P. 190 STATUE   25 The Trojan Horse, tho' not of Brass but of
                         wood,

wood-leviathans   frequency: 1   relative frequency: 0.0000
P. 112 ANNIVERSARY   361 'An hideous shole of wood-Leviathans,

wood-moths   frequency: 1   relative frequency: 0.0000
P. 75 A. HOUSE   542 Doth from the Bark the Wood-moths glean.

woodbines   frequency: 1   relative frequency: 0.0000
P. 78 A. HOUSE   609 Bind me ye Woodbines in your 'twines,

woodcock   frequency: 1   relative frequency: 0.0000
P. 169 ADVICE   55 Whilst Positive walks Woodcock in the dark,

wooden   frequency: 5   relative frequency: 0.0001
P. 66 A. HOUSE   250 Their Wooden Saints in vain oppose.
P. 97 HOLLAND   88 Fumes through the loop-holes of a wooden Square.
P. 104 ANNIVERSARY   44 Then wooden Heads unto the Viols strings.
P. 171 PROPHECY   29 And Wooden shoos shall come to be the weare
P. 171 PROPHECY   47 Then wooden Shoos shall be the English weare

woods   frequency: 7   relative frequency: 0.0001
P. 39 PICTURE   33 But O young beauty of the Woods,

```
P.  57 BILL-BOROW     46 Such Wounds alone these Woods became:
P.  61 A. HOUSE       79 In fragrant Gardens, shaddy Woods,
P.  78 A. HOUSE      618 Where the two Woods have made a Lane;
P.  80 A. HOUSE      691 She streightness on the Woods bestows;
P.  80 A. HOUSE      696 Then Gardens, Woods, Meads, Rivers are.
P.  82 A. HOUSE      752 So you all Woods, Streams, Gardens, Meads.
```

wooing   frequency: 1   relative frequency: 0.0000
```
P.  29 THE GALLERY    23 And, at thy Feet, the wooing Doves
```

wool. See "wooll."

woolchurch   frequency: 1   relative frequency: 0.0000
   See also "w."
```
P. 192 TWO HORSES     25 The Horses I mean of Woolchurch and Charing,
```

wooll   frequency: 2   relative frequency: 0.0000
```
P.  20 THYRSIS        32 Of sweetest grass, and softest wooll;
P.  43 DAMON          55 And though in Wooll more poor then they,
```

worcester. See "worster."

word   frequency: 14   relative frequency: 0.0002
```
P.  68 A. HOUSE      320 She runs you through, or askes the Word.
P.  86 FLECKNO       140 Not one Word, thought and swore that they were
                         good.
P. 142 INSTRUCTIONS   48 When Men and Women took each others Word.
P. 144 INSTRUCTIONS  158 But knew the Word and well could face about;
P. 151 INSTRUCTIONS  435 Summon him therefore of his Word, and prove
P. 151 INSTRUCTIONS  441 Nor Word, nor near Relation did revere;
P. 179 STOCKSMARKET    7 When with honour he might from his word have gone
                         back;
P. 183 MADE FREE      73 His word nor his Oath
P. 186 BRITANNIA      75 Who e're grew great by keeping of his word?
P. 192 TWO HORSES     46 Who believes not a word, the word of God saith;
P. 194 TWO HORSES    103 Tho' the beast gave his Master ne're an ill
                         word,
P. 200 DUKE           83 He gott his wealth by breaking of his word;
P. 316 CHEQUER INN   150 Not one word of the Wenches.
```

word-peckers   frequency: 1   relative frequency: 0.0000
```
P.   3 LOVELACE       19 Word-peckers, Paper-rats, Book-scorpions,
```

words   frequency: 15   relative frequency: 0.0003
```
P.  18 CLORINDA       21 D. Words that transcend poor Shepherds skill,
P.  33 DAPHNIS        26 Words she never spake before;
P.  36 DAPHNIS        97 At these words away he broke;
P.  61 A. HOUSE       95 Whence in these Words one to her weav'd,
P.  94 DR. WITTY       9 Others do strive with words and forced phrase
P. 124 O.C.           41 When She with Smiles serene and Words discreet
P. 132 PARADISE       41 Where couldst thou Words of such a compass find?
P. 145 INSTRUCTIONS  201 Thence fell to Words, but, quarrel to adjourn,
P. 163 INSTRUCTIONS  923 Then, whisp'ring to his Son in Words unheard,
P. 178 LOYALL SCOT   256 Rationall mens words pledges are of peace,
P. 191 TWO HORSES      2 Of Beasts that have uttered Articulate words:
P. 196 TWO HORSES    173 Why might not our Horses, since words are but
                         wind,
P. 196 TWO HORSES    179 When they take from the people the freedome of
                         words,
P. 314 CHEQUER INN    87 Both words and meate did utter
P. 315 CHEQUER INN   104 For words not to be said but sung
```

wore   frequency: 2   relative frequency: 0.0000
```
P.  14 THE CORONET    12 As never yet the king of Glory wore:
P. 202 HISTORICALL    56 Whilst the brave Tudors wore th' Imperial
                         Crowne:
```

work   frequency: 19   relative frequency: 0.0003
   See also "worke."
```
P.  59 A. HOUSE        2 Work of no Forrain Architect;
P.  62 A. HOUSE      127 'This Work the Saints best represents;
P.  63 A. HOUSE      129 'But much it to our work would add
P.  64 A. HOUSE      168 'Till Miracles it work at last.
P.  88 ODE            34 To ruine the great Work of Time,
P. 103 ANNIVERSARY    14 And in one Year the work of Ages acts:
P. 104 ANNIVERSARY    56 And the great Work ascended while he play'd.
P. 105 ANNIVERSARY    94 And they as Pillars keep the Work upright;
P. 106 ANNIVERSARY   137 Sure, the mysterious Work, where none withstand,
P. 131 PARADISE       17 Or if a Work so infinite he spann'd,
P. 132 PARADISE       31 That Majesty which through thy Work doth Reign
P. 141 INSTRUCTIONS    3 But er'e thou fal'st to work, first Painter see
```

P. 141 INSTRUCTIONS   23 His desperate Pencil at the work did dart,
P. 148 INSTRUCTIONS   304 Is longer Work, and harder then to fight.
P. 152 INSTRUCTIONS   476 To work the Peace, and so to send them home.
P. 164 INSTRUCTIONS   945 But this great work is for our Monarch fit,
P. 168 ADVICE   7 Whilest the brave youths tired with the work of
                          State
P. 175 LOYALL SCOT   130 A higher work is to their Court Annext:
P. 180 STOCKSMARKET   54 For the graver's at work to reform him thus long.

worke   frequency: 1   relative frequency: 0.0000
P. 190 STATUE   33 But why is the worke then soe long at a stand?

workmanship   frequency: 1   relative frequency: 0.0000
P. 180 STOCKSMARKET   31 And alleges the workmanship was not his own

works   frequency: 4   relative frequency: 0.0000
P. 50 THE GARDEN   69 And, as it works, th' industrious Bee
P. 116 BLAKE   93 Fond men who know not whilst such works they
                          raise,
P. 117 BLAKE   110 Our worst works past, now we have found them out.
P. 178 LOYALL SCOT   273 And Each works bony for the Common Hive.

world   frequency: 54   relative frequency: 0.0011
P. 11 DIALOGUE   65 Half the World shall be thy Slave
P. 12 DIALOGUE   76 The World has not one Pleasure more:
P. 12 DROP OF DEW   29 So the World excluding round,
P. 15 EYES   13 What in the World most fair appears,
P. 15 EYES   22 Distills the World with Chymick Ray;
P. 18 CLORINDA   30 For all the World is our Pan's Quire.
P. 22 NYMPH   24 The World, to offer for their Sin.
P. 26 MISTRESS   1 Had we but World enough, and Time,
P. 28 LOVER   24 As at the Fun'ral of the World.
P. 33 DAPHNIS   15 Lest the World should separate;
P. 37 DEFINITION   19 (Though Loves whole World on us doth wheel)
P. 37 DEFINITION   23 And, us to joyn, the World should all
P. 39 THE MATCH   12 She could the World repair.
P. 40 THE MATCH   38 Whilst all the World is poor,
P. 40 THE MOWER   2 Did after him the World seduce:
P. 41 THE MOWER   17 Another World was search'd, through Oceans new,
P. 47 EMPIRE   1 First was the World as one great Cymbal made,
P. 56 BILL-BOROW   8 And that the World by it was made.
P. 59 A. HOUSE   23 That thinks by Breadth the World t'unite
P. 62 A. HOUSE   99 'These Walls restrain the World without,
P. 69 A. HOUSE   322 The Garden of the World ere while,
P. 69 A. HOUSE   325 But, to exclude the World, did guard
P. 72 A. HOUSE   445 The World when first created sure
P. 73 A. HOUSE   455 Such, in the painted World, appear'd
P. 77 A. HOUSE   605 And where the World no certain Shot
P. 80 A. HOUSE   682 The World, and through the Ev'ning rush.
P. 82 A. HOUSE   761 'Tis not, what once it was, the World;
P. 82 A. HOUSE   765 Your lesser World contains the same.
P. 91 MAY'S DEATH   59 Must therefore all the World be set on flame,
P. 105 ANNIVERSARY   100 He hurles e'r since the World about him round;
P. 107 ANNIVERSARY   154 The World by Sin, does by the same extend.
P. 108 ANNIVERSARY   217 From the low World, and thankless Men above,
P. 110 ANNIVERSARY   298 And make the World, by his Example, Quake:
P. 111 ANNIVERSARY   328 Pleas'd with that other World of moving Light;
P. 111 ANNIVERSARY   345 Up from the other World his Flame he darts,
P. 113 ANNIVERSARY   366 'Whose watry Leaguers all the world surround?
P. 113 BLAKE   2 Leaves the new World and hastens for the old:
P. 117 BLAKE   106 And a third World seek out our Armes to shun.
P. 119 BLAKE   168 And tells the World, how much to you it owes.
P. 125 O.C.   105 Or the great World do by consent presage,
P. 129 O.C.   256 Oh! worthlesse world! oh transitory things!
P. 130 O.C.   291 There thy great soule at once a world does see,
P. 131 PARADISE   10 The World o'rewhelming to revenge his Sight.
P. 138 HOUSEWARMING   60 As by hook and by crook the world cluster'd of
                          Atome.
P. 146 INSTRUCTIONS   204 And in ill English all the World defy'd.
P. 164 INSTRUCTIONS   956 Sun of our World, as he the Charles is there.
P. 174 LOYALL SCOT   99 Seperate the world soe as the Bishops scalpes.
P. 174 LOYALL SCOT   120 Religion has the World too Long deprav'd
P. 177 LOYALL SCOT   236 The world in all doth but two Nations bear,
P. 180 STOCKSMARKET   59 For though the whole world cannot shew such
                          another,
P. 181 MADE FREE   21 That all the World there did leave him;
P. 186 BRITANNIA   78 The Rivall Gods, Monarchs of th' other world,
P. 198 DUKE   19 Prove to the world Ile have ould England know
P. 203 HISTORICALL   85 And yet perswade the World they must obey:

worlds   frequency: 8   relative frequency: 0.0001

P.   11 DIALOGUE   60 And want new Worlds to buy.
P.   49 THE GARDEN   46 Far other Worlds, and other Seas;
P. 112 ANNIVERSARY 360 'A Fleet of Worlds, of other Worlds in quest;
P. 113 BLAKE   9 The new Worlds wounded Intrails they had tore,
P. 114 BLAKE   26 Above both Worlds, since 'tis above the rest.
P. 117 BLAKE   125 Fate these two Fleets, between both Worlds had
                        brought.
P. 117 BLAKE   126 Who fight, as if for both those Worlds they
                        fought.

world's   frequency: 1   relative frequency: 0.0000
P.   92 MAY'S DEATH 68 And though the World's disjointed Axel crack,

worm   frequency: 1   relative frequency: 0.0000
See also "traitor-worm."
P.   76 A. HOUSE   557 And yet that Worm triumphs not long,

worm-eaten   frequency: 1   relative frequency: 0.0000
P. 193 TWO HORSES   63 W. Our worm-eaten Navy be laid up at Chatham,

worms   frequency: 1   relative frequency: 0.0000
See also "glo-worms."
P.   26 MISTRESS   27 My ecchoing Song: then Worms shall try

worn   frequency: 2   relative frequency: 0.0000
P.   85 FLECKNO   76 Worn at the first Counsel of Antioch;
P. 124 O.C.   68 Where She so long her Fathers fate had worn:

worse   frequency: 7   relative frequency: 0.0001
P.   21 SOUL & BODY 28 Diseases, but, whats worse, the Cure:
P.   86 FLECKNO   144 That were ill made condemn'd to be read worse:
P.   94 DR. WITTY   34 Liking themselves the worse the more they look,
P. 141 INSTRUCTIONS 20 Stamp on thy Pallat, nor perhaps the worse.
P. 144 INSTRUCTIONS 131 Excise, a Monster worse than e're before
P. 179 STOCKSMARKET 14 Yet all do affirm that the king is much worse,
P. 181 MADE FREE   23 Much worse than before;

worser   frequency: 1   relative frequency: 0.0000
P. 128 O.C.   219 The worser sort, so conscious of their ill,

worshipful. See "worshipfull."

worshipfull   frequency: 1   relative frequency: 0.0000
P. 184 MADE FREE   127 And now Worshipfull Sirs

worst   frequency: 3   relative frequency: 0.0000
P. 117 BLAKE   110 Our worst works past, now we have found them out.
P. 168 ADVICE   20 Sate by the worst Attorney of the Nacion,
P. 175 LOYALL SCOT 166 Their Companyes the worst that ever playd

worstenholm   frequency: 1   relative frequency: 0.0000
P. 139 HOUSEWARMING 82 But for the expence he rely'd upon Worstenholm,

worster   frequency: 1   relative frequency: 0.0000
P. 138 HOUSEWARMING 57 His Rent would no more in arrear run to
                        Worster;

worth   frequency: 7   relative frequency: 0.0001
P.   5 HASTINGS   26 And all that Worth from hence did Ostracize.
P.   11 DIALOGUE   62 And that 's worth nought that can be sold.
P.   94 DR. WITTY   36 Now worth the liking, but thy Book and thee.
P. 114 BLAKE   39 Your worth to all these Isles, a just right
                        brings,
P. 118 BLAKE   143 A choice which did the highest worth express,
P. 177 LOYALL SCOT 241 For Worth Heroick or Heroick Crimes.
P. 192 TWO HORSES   26 Who have told many truths well worth a mans
                        hearing,

worthily   frequency: 1   relative frequency: 0.0000
P.   82 A. HOUSE   747 (Till Fate her worthily translates,

worthlesse   frequency: 1   relative frequency: 0.0000
P. 129 O.C.   256 Oh! worthlesse world! oh transitory things!

worthy   frequency: 5   relative frequency: 0.0001
P.   3 LOVELACE   10 To honour not her selfe, but worthy men.
P.   91 MAY'S DEATH 57 Because some one than thee more worthy weares
P.   93 DR. WITTY   t1 To his worthy Friend Doctor Witty upon his
P. 126 O.C.   140 To chuse it worthy of his Glories past.
P. 128 O.C.   210 (Though who more worthy to be lov'd than she?)

worthy's   frequency: 1   relative frequency: 0.0000

P. 127 O.C.   176 Whether of British Saints or Worthy's told;

wotest. See "wot'st."

wot'st   frequency: 1   relative frequency: 0.0000
    P. 315 CHEQUER INN   121 Yet wot'st thou he was none of those

wou'd   frequency: 7   relative frequency: 0.0001

would   frequency: 121   relative frequency: 0.0025
    See also "he'd," "king-wou'd-be," "'twould,"
            "we'd," "who'ld," "wou'd."

wouldest. See "wouldst," "would'st."

wouldst   frequency: 3   relative frequency: 0.0000

would'st   frequency: 2   relative frequency: 0.0000

wound   frequency: 16   relative frequency: 0.0003
    P.   12 DROP OF DEW   27 In how coy a Figure wound,
    P.   14 THE CORONET   2 With many a piercing wound,
    P.   22 NYMPH   20 From thine, and wound me to the Heart,
    P.   32 MOURNING   16 A place to fix another Wound.
    P.   34 DAPHNIS   51 When thy Favours should me wound
    P.   38 PICTURE   19 Ere they have try'd their force to wound,
    P.   44 DAMON   84 The Blood I stanch, and Wound I seal.
    P.   44 DAMON   86 Whom Julianas Eyes do wound.
    P.   48 THE GARDEN   23 Fair Trees! where s'eer your barkes I wound,
    P.   92 MAY'S DEATH   77 But what will deeper wound thy little mind,
    P. 113 BLAKE   10 For wealth wherewith to wound the old once more.
    P. 125 O.C.   96 And through the Wound its vital humour bleeds;
    P. 128 O.C.   198 Each wound himself which he to others delt;
    P. 163 INSTRUCTIONS   920 The grizly Wound reveals, of which he dy'd.
    P. 199 DUKE   42 And in her youthfull veines receive the wound
    P. 199 DUKE   44 The wound of which now tainted Churchill faids,

wounded   frequency: 2   relative frequency: 0.0000
    P.   24 NYMPH   97 So weeps the wounded Balsome: so
    P. 113 BLAKE   9 The new Worlds wounded Intrails they had tore,

wounds   frequency: 4   relative frequency: 0.0000
    P.   28 LOVER   54 Torn into Flames, and ragg'd with Wounds.
    P.   57 BILL-BOROW   46 Such Wounds alone these Woods became:
    P. 189 BRITANNIA   182 Balm in their wounds, will fleeting life restore.
    P. 199 DUKE   63 Then Fleets and Armyes, battles, blood and
                             wounds;

wove   frequency: 1   relative frequency: 0.0000
    P.   88 ODE   50 He wove a Net of such a scope,

wrack   frequency: 1   relative frequency: 0.0000
    P.   28 LOVER   28 That sail'd insulting o're the Wrack,

wracks   frequency: 1   relative frequency: 0.0000
    P.   17 BERMUDAS   9 Where he the huge Sea-Monsters wracks,

wrangle   frequency: 1   relative frequency: 0.0000
    P. 176 LOYALL SCOT   207 Of Ceremonyes Wrangle in the Crow'd,

wrapt   frequency: 1   relative frequency: 0.0000
    P. 175 LOYALL SCOT   171 Like Smutty Storyes in Pure Linnen Wrapt.

wrath   frequency: 3   relative frequency: 0.0000
    P. 174 LOYALL SCOT   92 Theres noe 'deliver us from a Bishops Wrath'.
    P. 195 TWO HORSES   141 Ch. Thy Ryder puts no man to death in his
                             wrath,
    P. 205 HISTORICALL   180 To give you kings in's Wrath to vex you sore:

wreak   frequency: 1   relative frequency: 0.0000
    P. 104 ANNIVERSARY   32 If Conquered, on them they wreak their Spight:

wreath   frequency: 1   relative frequency: 0.0000
    P.   31 FAIR SINGER   11 Whose subtile Art invisibly can wreath

wreaths   frequency: 3   relative frequency: 0.0000
    P.   14 THE CORONET   16 With wreaths of Fame and Interest.
    P. 117 BLAKE   116 The noblest wreaths, that Victory bestows.
    P. 129 O.C.   264 And honour'd wreaths have oft the victour
                             crown'd.

wreck   frequency: 2   relative frequency: 0.0000

```
         See also "wrack."
         P.  99 HOLLAND        140 Their Navy all our Conquest or our Wreck:
         P. 179 STOCKSMARKET     8 He that vows for a calm is absolved by a wreck.

wrecks. See "wracks."

wren                             frequency:   1    relative frequency: 0.0000
         P. 145 INSTRUCTIONS    180 And bloated Wren conducts them to their seats.

wrens                            frequency:   1    relative frequency: 0.0000
         P. 139 HOUSEWARMING     69 Bulteales, Beakrs, Morley, Wrens fingers with
                                    telling

wretched                         frequency:   6    relative frequency: 0.0001
         P.  34 DAPHNIS          41 So did wretched Daphnis look,
         P.  34 DAPHNIS          50 Such a wretched minute found,
         P.  92 MAY'S DEATH      70 Seeks wretched good, arraigns successful Crimes.
         P. 155 INSTRUCTIONS     585 Our wretched Ships within their Fate attend,
         P. 203 HISTORICALL      98 Baals wretched Curates Legerdemain'd it so,
         P. 203 HISTORICALL     108 Thrice wretched they who natures Lawes detest

wrinkled                         frequency:   1    relative frequency: 0.0000
         P.  81 A. HOUSE        732 Lest the smooth Forehead wrinkled sit:

writ                             frequency:   6    relative frequency: 0.0001
         P.  57 BILL-BOROW       48 'Twas writ already in their Heart.
         P. 110 ANNIVERSARY     306 Have writ the Comments of thy sacred Foame:
         P. 123 O.C.             21 To Love and Grief the fatal Writ was sign'd;
         P. 151 INSTRUCTIONS     427 St. Albans writ to that he may bewail
         P. 159 INSTRUCTIONS     776 The Fleet divided? Writ for Rupert? Pett.
         P. 192 TWO HORSES       43 W. To see dei Gratia writ on the Throne,

write                            frequency:   8    relative frequency: 0.0001
         P.   3 LOVELACE         30 Because you write when going to the Warre,
         P.  95 DR. WITTY        38 For something guides my hand that I must write.
         P. 112 ANNIVERSARY     393 'But let them write his Praise that love him
                                    best,
         P. 147 INSTRUCTIONS     263 Old Waller, Trumpet-gen'ral swore he'd write
         P. 148 INSTRUCTIONS     303 See sudden chance of War! To Paint or Write,
         P. 156 INSTRUCTIONS     632 Sweet Painter draw his Picture while I write.
         P. 178 LOYALL SCOT      278 I single did against a Nation write,
         P. 195 TWO HORSES      152 W. And our Sir Joseph write news-books, and
                                    fiddle.

writer                           frequency:   1    relative frequency: 0.0000
         P.  92 MAY'S DEATH      60 Because a Gazet writer mist his aim?

writers                          frequency:   2    relative frequency: 0.0000
         P. 132 PARADISE         29 So that no room is here for Writers left,
         P. 189 BRITANNIA       176 On whose fam'd Deeds all tongues, all writers
                                    wait.

writes                           frequency:   3    relative frequency: 0.0000
         P. 132 PARADISE         47 While the Town-Bays writes all the while and
                                    spells,
         P. 151 INSTRUCTIONS     447 Yet Lewis writes, and lest our Hearts should
                                    break,
         P. 152 INSTRUCTIONS     489 And for their Pay he writes as from the King,

writing-master                   frequency:   1    relative frequency: 0.0000
         P. 152 INSTRUCTIONS     471 His Writing-Master many a time he bann'd,

written. See "writ."

wrong                            frequency:   8    relative frequency: 0.0001
         P.  14 THE CORONET       4 I seek with Garlands to redress that Wrong:
         P.  65 A. HOUSE        218 'Founded by Folly, kept by Wrong.
         P.  91 MAY'S DEATH      20 Gently to signifie that he was wrong.
         P. 104 ANNIVERSARY      27 They fight by Others, but in Person wrong,
         P. 121 TWO SONGS        43 These Stars would say I do them wrong,
         P. 124 O.C.             33 And, lest their force the tender burthen wrong,
         P. 180 STOCKSMARKET     53 But Sir Robert affirms we do him much wrong;
         P. 194 TWO HORSES      100 Bold speaking hath done both man and beast wrong.

wrong'd                          frequency:   1    relative frequency: 0.0000
         P.   3 LOVELACE         28 You wrong'd in her the Houses Priviledge.

wrought                          frequency:   6    relative frequency: 0.0001
         P.  40 THE MATCH        32 Into each other wrought.
         P.  45 MOWER'S SONG     20 Shall now by my Revenge be wrought:
         P.  72 A. HOUSE        419 In whose new Traverse seemeth wrought
```

P. 105 ANNIVERSARY   79 No Quarry bears a Stone so hardly wrought,
P. 138 HOUSEWARMING   35 What Joseph by Famine, he wrought by
                           Sea-Battel;
P. 313 CHEQUER INN   35 Has wrought himself into Whitehall

wrung   frequency: 1   relative frequency: 0.0000
P. 315 CHEQUER INN   103 His Braine and Face Tredenham wrung

wyer   frequency: 1   relative frequency: 0.0000
P. 315 CHEQUER INN   105 His Neck it turn'd on Wyer

y'   frequency: 1   relative frequency: 0.0000

yards   frequency: 2   relative frequency: 0.0000
P. 138 HOUSEWARMING   46 So long as the Yards had a Deal or a Spar:
P. 148 INSTRUCTIONS   317 Mean time through all the Yards their Orders
                           run

ye   frequency: 17   relative frequency: 0.0003
    See also "y'," "yee."

yea   frequency: 2   relative frequency: 0.0000

year   frequency: 11   relative frequency: 0.0002
    See also "yeare," "yeer."
P. 23 NYMPH   75 And all the Spring time of the year
P. 43 DAMON   54 Of all these Closes ev'ry Year.
P. 58 BILL-BOROW   72 The Trophees of one fertile Year.
P. 89 ODE   74 To see themselves in one Year tam'd:
P. 89 ODE   100 If thus he crown each Year!
P. 103 ANNIVERSARY   14 And in one Year the work of Ages acts:
P. 125 O.C.   91 Under whose shady tent Men ev'ry year
P. 126 O.C.   142 Of honour; all the Year was Cromwell's day:
P. 139 HOUSEWARMING   67 Bring in the whole Milk of a year at a meal,
P. 150 INSTRUCTIONS   403 While the first year our Navy is but shown,
P. 171 PROPHECY   43 When a lean Treasurer shall in one year

yeare   frequency: 2   relative frequency: 0.0000
P. 201 HISTORICALL   10 But in his thirtieth yeare began to Raigne.
P. 313 CHEQUER INN   27 'Twill faile him in a yeare

yeares   frequency: 2   relative frequency: 0.0000
P. 129 O.C.   268 So many yeares the shelter of the wood.)
P. 201 HISTORICALL   3 Twelve Yeares compleat he suffer'd in Exile

yearly   frequency: 5   relative frequency: 0.0001
P. 98 HOLLAND   136 Doth yearly their Sea-Nuptials restore.
P. 103 ANNIVERSARY   12 And shines the Jewel of the yearly Ring.
P. 107 ANNIVERSARY   182 The other Glories of our yearly Song.
P. 113 ANNIVERSARY   402 Troubling the Waters, yearly mak'st them Heal.
P. 158 INSTRUCTIONS   715 Those Ships, that yearly from their teeming
                           Howl,

years   frequency: 11   relative frequency: 0.0002
    See also "yeares."
P. 25 YOUNG LOVE   2 While thine unsuspected years
P. 26 MISTRESS   8 Love you ten years before the Flood:
P. 26 MISTRESS   13 An hundred years should go to praise
P. 89 ODE   86 A Kingdome, for his first years rents:
P. 97 HOLLAND   83 Some Fifteen hundred and more years ago;
P. 103 ANNIVERSARY   4 In the weak Circles of increasing Years;
P. 103 ANNIVERSARY   17 And though they all Platonique years should
                           raign,
P. 105 ANNIVERSARY   69 While tedious Statesmen many years did hack,
P. 123 O.C.   4 Had seen the period of his golden Years:
P. 124 O.C.   37 But as with riper Years her Virtue grew,
P. 150 INSTRUCTIONS   402 Where Venice twenty years the Turk had fought:

year's   frequency: 1   relative frequency: 0.0000
P. 158 INSTRUCTIONS   740 Thee, the Year's monster, let thy Dam devour.

yee   frequency: 1   relative frequency: 0.0000

yeer   frequency: 1   relative frequency: 0.0000
P.   4 HASTINGS   18 But weigh to Man the Geometrick yeer.

yeild   frequency: 2   relative frequency: 0.0000
P. 174 LOYALL SCOT   112 Where Foxes Dung their earths the Badgers
                           yeild;
P. 189 BRITANNIA   172 Yeild to all these in lewdness, lust, and shame.

yeilded   frequency: 1   relative frequency: 0.0000

| | P. | 184 | BRITANNIA | 2 | To trembling James, would I had yeilded mine. |

yell   frequency: 1   relative frequency: 0.0000
| | P. | 156 | INSTRUCTIONS | 624 | After the Robbers, for her Whelps does yell: |

yellow   frequency: 2   relative frequency: 0.0000
| | P. | 85 | FLECKNO | 82 | As the Chamelion, yellow, blew, or green. |
| | P. | 156 | INSTRUCTIONS | 653 | His yellow Locks curl back themselves to seek, |

yes   frequency: 1   relative frequency: 0.0000
| | P. | 84 | FLECKNO | 47 | He answered yes; with such, and such an one. |

yet   frequency: 177   relative frequency: 0.0036
P.	4	HASTINGS	2	Whose Virgin-Source yet never steept the Plain.
P.	4	LOVELACE	39	They all in mutiny though yet undrest
P.	4	LOVELACE	41	And one the loveliest that was yet e're seen,
P.	5	HASTINGS	27	Yet as some Prince, that, for State-Jealousie,
P.	12	DROP OF DEW	4	Yet careless of its Mansion new;
P.	12	DROP OF DEW	30	Yet receiving in the Day.
P.	14	THE CORONET	12	As never yet the king of Glory wore:
P.	15	EYES	19	And yet, from all the flow'rs I saw,
P.	16	EYES	25	Yet happy they whom Grief doth bless,
P.	17	BERMUDAS	8	And yet far kinder than our own?
P.	19	THYRSIS	16	Hath no wings, yet doth aspire
P.	21	SOUL & BODY	31	But Physick yet could never reach
P.	22	NYMPH	6	Thy death yet do them any good.
P.	22	NYMPH	9	But, if my simple Pray'rs may yet
P.	22	NYMPH	21	Yet could they not be clean: their Stain
P.	22	NYMPH	25	Unconstant Sylvio, when yet
P.	23	NYMPH	79	Yet could not, till it self would rise,
P.	25	YOUNG LOVE	12	Yet for Lust, but not for Love.
P.	27	LOVER	2	With whom the Infant Love yet playes!
P.	27	MISTRESS	46	Stand still, yet we will make him run.
P.	29	LOVER	58	That ever Love created yet:
P.	29	LOVER	61	Yet dying leaves a Perfume here,
P.	29	THE GALLERY	13	Engines more keen than ever yet
P.	32	MOURNING	13	Yet some affirm, pretending Art,
P.	32	MOURNING	31	Would find her Tears yet deeper Waves
P.	32	MOURNING	33	I yet my silent Judgment keep,
P.	33	DAPHNIS	8	Nor yet let her Lover go.
P.	36	DAPHNIS	95	Yet bring with me all the Fire
P.	36	DAPHNIS	105	Yet he does himself excuse;
P.	37	DEFINITION	9	And yet I quickly might arrive
P.	38	PICTURE	11	Yet this is She whose chaster Laws
P.	41	THE MOWER	19	And yet these Rarities might be allow'd,
P.	42	DAMON	39	Yet Thou ungrateful hast not sought
P.	43	DAMON	56	Yet am I richer far in Hay.
P.	43	DAMON	70	Yet still my Grief is where it was:
P.	47	EMPIRE	21	Victorious sounds! yet here your Homage do
P.	49	THE GARDEN	45	Yet it creates, transcending these,
P.	49	THE GARDEN	60	What other Help could yet be meet!
P.	57	BILL-BOROW	25	Yet thus it all the field commands,
P.	58	BILL-BOROW	57	Yet now no further strive to shoot,
P.	60	A. HOUSE	49	Yet thus the laden House does sweat,
P.	60	A. HOUSE	61	And yet what needs there here Excuse,
P.	63	A. HOUSE	132	'Yet thus She you resembles much.
P.	64	A. HOUSE	169	'Nor is our Order yet so nice,
P.	64	A. HOUSE	188	'Yet Neither should be left behind.
P.	65	A. HOUSE	202	Yet would he valiantly complain.
P.	65	A. HOUSE	206	'Who though in prison yet inchant!
P.	65	A. HOUSE	213	'And yet, how well soever ment,
P.	66	A. HOUSE	237	Yet still the Nuns his Right debar'd,
P.	66	A. HOUSE	247	Yet, against Fate, his Spouse they kept;
P.	67	A. HOUSE	278	The Cloyster yet remained hers.
P.	67	A. HOUSE	282	Whom France and Poland yet does fame:
P.	68	A. HOUSE	295	And dries its Pan yet dank with Dew,
P.	69	A. HOUSE	345	And yet their walks one on the Sod
P.	71	A. HOUSE	396	Whose yet unfeather'd Quils her fail.
P.	73	A. HOUSE	454	Is pincht yet nearer by the Beast.
P.	74	A. HOUSE	484	In this yet green, yet growing Ark;
P.	74	A. HOUSE	494	Yet more to Heaven shooting are:
P.	75	A. HOUSE	522	A Sadder, yet more pleasing Sound:
P.	75	A. HOUSE	525	Yet always, for some Cause unknown,
P.	76	A. HOUSE	557	And yet that Worm triumphs not long,
P.	78	A. HOUSE	635	And its yet muddy back doth lick,
P.	80	A. HOUSE	695	She yet more Pure, Sweet, Streight, and Fair,
P.	81	A. HOUSE	709	Nor yet in those her self imployes
P.	81	A. HOUSE	711	Nor yet that Wisdome would affect,
P.	81	A. HOUSE	733	Yet your own Face shall at you grin,
P.	82	A. HOUSE	746	Where yet She leads her studious Hours,
P.	82	A. HOUSE	760	Yet nor to them your Beauty yields.

P.	83	FLECKNO	15	Yet of his State no man could have complain'd;
P.	84	FLECKNO	33	Held him the other; and unchanged yet,
P.	84	FLECKNO	64	Who as a Camel tall, yet easly can
P.	85	FLECKNO	75	And above that yet casts an antick Cloak,
P.	86	FLECKNO	122	Yet he more strict my sentence doth renew;
P.	86	FLECKNO	125	Yet that which was a greater cruelty
P.	86	FLECKNO	131	Yet these he promises as soon as clean.
P.	86	FLECKNO	138	Yet he first kist them, and after takes pains
P.	86	FLECKNO	145	And how (impossible) he made yet more
P.	89	ODE	71	And yet in that the State
P.	89	ODE	81	Nor yet grown stiffer with Command,
P.	91	MAY'S DEATH	27	Yet then with foot as stumbling as his tongue
P.	92	MAY'S DEATH	75	Yet wast thou taken hence with equal fate,
P.	96	HOLLAND	23	Yet still his claim the Injur'd Ocean laid,
P.	98	HOLLAND	119	Yet of his vain Attempt no more he sees
P.	104	ANNIVERSARY	23	Yet some more active for a Frontier Town
P.	104	ANNIVERSARY	39	To know how long their Planet yet Reprives
P.	105	ANNIVERSARY	85	Yet all compos'd by his attractive Song,
P.	106	ANNIVERSARY	106	Kiss the approaching, nor yet angry Son;
P.	107	ANNIVERSARY	148	Girds yet his Sword, and ready stands to fight;
P.	108	ANNIVERSARY	226	Then ought below, or yet above a King:
P.	109	ANNIVERSARY	250	Yet by the Conquest of two Kings grown great,
P.	109	ANNIVERSARY	256	Yet would not he be Lord, nor yet his Son.
P.	110	ANNIVERSARY	293	Yet such a Chammish issue still does rage,
P.	111	ANNIVERSARY	323	And, to your spight, returning yet alive
P.	111	ANNIVERSARY	336	Not knowing yet the Night was made for sleep:
P.	112	ANNIVERSARY	351	'Yet rig a Navy while we dress us late;
P.	112	ANNIVERSARY	373	'Yet if through these our Fears could find a pass;
P.	112	ANNIVERSARY	388	'And yet the same to be a King does scorn.
P.	112	ANNIVERSARY	392	'So should I hope yet he might Dye as wee.
P.	113	BLAKE	12	But yet in them caus'd as much fear, as Joy.
P.	114	BLAKE	30	Fertile to be, yet never need her showres.
P.	115	BLAKE	76	Yet in their brests, carry a pride much higher.
P.	116	BLAKE	95	Yet they by restless toyl, became at Length,
P.	118	BLAKE	141	Far different Motives yet, engag'd them thus,
P.	120	TWO SONGS	31	Yet is her younger Sister laid
P.	123	O.C.	19	Deserved yet an End whose ev'ry part
P.	124	O.C.	63	Yet both perceiv'd, yet both conceal'd their Skills,
P.	125	O.C.	88	Yet in compassion of another dy'd.
P.	125	O.C.	109	But never yet was any humane Fate
P.	126	O.C.	139	Which, since they might not hinder, yet they cast
P.	127	O.C.	152	Yet joy'd remembring what he once atchiev'd.
P.	127	O.C.	190	The sea between, yet hence his pray'r prevail'd.
P.	128	O.C.	196	Yet him the adverse steel could never pierce.
P.	128	O.C.	208	Yet still affected most what best deserv'd.
P.	128	O.C.	224	Spare yet your own, if you neglect his fame;
P.	129	O.C.	235	Yet always temper'd with an aire so mild,
P.	129	O.C.	257	Yet dwelt that greatnesse in his shape decay'd,
P.	129	O.C.	260	That threatens death, he yet will live again.
P.	129	O.C.	270	When fall'n shews taller yet than as it grew:
P.	130	O.C.	305	And Richard yet, where his great parent led,
P.	130	O.C.	308	And yet how much of them his griefe obscures.
P.	131	O.C.	324	He threats no deluge, yet foretells a showre.
P.	131	PARADISE	1	When I beheld the Poet blind, yet bold,
P.	131	PARADISE	11	Yet as I read, soon growing less severe,
P.	131	PARADISE	24	My causeless, yet not impious, surmise.
P.	137	HOUSEWARMING	21	Yet a President fitter in Virgil he found,
P.	138	HOUSEWARMING	38	To make Mortar and Brick, yet allow'd them no straw,
P.	138	HOUSEWARMING	54	Yet his Lordship to finish it would be unable;
P.	144	INSTRUCTIONS	124	Yet as for War the Parliament should squeeze;
P.	144	INSTRUCTIONS	160	Thought yet but Picneers, and led by Steward.
P.	146	INSTRUCTIONS	231	Pleas'd with their Numbers, yet in Valour wise,
P.	147	INSTRUCTIONS	279	Ev'n Iron Strangeways, chafing yet gave back,
P.	148	INSTRUCTIONS	307	Broken in Courage, yet the Men the same,
P.	149	INSTRUCTIONS	327	And the lov'd King, and never yet deny'd,
P.	149	INSTRUCTIONS	340	His Gout (yet still he curst) had left him quite.
P.	151	INSTRUCTIONS	429	How yet the Hollanders do make a noise,
P.	151	INSTRUCTIONS	447	Yet Lewis writes, and lest our Hearts should break,
P.	153	INSTRUCTIONS	518	On Monk and Parliament, yet both do hate.
P.	154	INSTRUCTIONS	564	Which, if a House, yet were not tenantable.
P.	156	INSTRUCTIONS	651	And modest Beauty yet his Sex did Veil,
P.	157	INSTRUCTIONS	671	That precious life he yet disdains to save,
P.	158	INSTRUCTIONS	732	Viewing her strength, they yet their Conquest doubt.
P.	159	INSTRUCTIONS	741	And constant Time, to keep his course yet right,
P.	159	INSTRUCTIONS	756	And were it burnt, yet less would be their pain.

P. 159 INSTRUCTIONS   761 The Court in Farthing yet it self does please,
P. 161 INSTRUCTIONS   823 Yet Harry must job back and all mature,
P. 162 INSTRUCTIONS   888 From his clear Eyes, yet these too dark with
                           Care.
P. 162 INSTRUCTIONS   896 Yet from beneath the Veil her blushes rise;
P. 165 KINGS VOWES   17 Yet if Men should clammor I'le pack him away:
P. 165 KINGS VOWES   18 And yet call him home again, soon as I may.
P. 167 KINGS VOWES   50 Tho' not rule like the Turk yet I will be so
                           drest,
P. 169 ADVICE   63 Tis hard; yet this he has for safe retreat:
P. 172 LOYALL SCOT   17 And modest beauty yet his sex did vail,
P. 172 LOYALL SCOT   37 That pretious life hee yet disdaines to save
P. 175 LOYALL SCOT   142 Howere Insipid Yet the Sawce will mend 'em
P. 176 LOYALL SCOT   206 Those whom you hear more Clamerous Yet and
                           Loud
P. 179 STOCKSMARKET   14 Yet all do affirm that the king is much worse,
P. 180 STOCKSMARKET   60 Yet we'd better by far have him than his brother.
P. 181 MADE FREE   18 Yet know both his Freinds and his Breeding.
P. 183 MADE FREE   82 Yet I doe not distrust
P. 183 MADE FREE   103 And yet if our Toy
P. 191 STATUE   55 Tho of Brass, yet with grief it would melt him
                           away,
P. 193 TWO HORSES   55 W. That the bank should be seiz'd yet the
                           Chequer so poor;
P. 193 TWO HORSES   58 Yet the King of his debts pay no man a penny;
P. 193 TWO HORSES   60 And yet all his Court be as poore as Church
                           Ratts;
P. 193 TWO HORSES   79 W. Yet some of those givers such beggerly
                           Villains
P. 193 TWO HORSES   85 Ch. Yet baser the souls of those low priced
                           Sinners,
P. 194 TWO HORSES   98 Yet truth many times being punisht for Treason,
P. 195 TWO HORSES   155 Ch. Yet have wee one Secretary honest and wise:
P. 196 TWO HORSES   177 Yet the beasts of the field or the stones in the
                           wall
P. 199 DUKE   71 Although no scholler, yet can act the cooke:
P. 202 HISTORICALL   66 Yet in the Mimmicks of the Spintrian Sport
P. 203 HISTORICALL   85 And yet perswade the World they must obey:
P. 314 CHEQUER INN   68 And if it had beene nearer yet
P. 315 CHEQUER INN   121 Yet wot'st thou he was none of those

yield   frequency: 8   relative frequency: 0.0001
    See also "yeild."
    P. 33 DAPHNIS   11 And would gladly yield to all,
    P. 38 PICTURE   22 And them that yield but more despise.
    P. 65 A. HOUSE   219 'I know what Fruit their Gardens yield,
    P. 113 ANNIVERSARY 397 I yield, nor further will the Prize contend;
    P. 113 BLAKE   8 With what the Womb of wealthy Kingdomes yield,
    P. 115 BLAKE   55 They still do yield, such is their pretious
                           mould,
    P. 179 STOCKSMARKET   1 As cities that to the fierce conquerors yield
    P. 203 HISTORICALL 110 Till native Reason's basely forct to yield

yielded. See "yeilded."

yielding   frequency: 1   relative frequency: 0.0000
    P. 108 ANNIVERSARY 228 Yielding to Rule, because it made thee Less.

yields   frequency: 4   relative frequency: 0.0000
    P. 82 A. HOUSE   760 Yet nor to them your Beauty yields.
    P. 105 ANNIVERSARY   77 All other Matter yields, and may be rul'd;
    P. 123 TWO SONGS   45 Marina yields. Who dares be coy?
    P. 152 INSTRUCTIONS 456 Who yields his Sword has Title to his Life.

yoak   frequency: 1   relative frequency: 0.0000
    P. 194 TWO HORSES   87 W. 'Tis they who brought on us the Scandalous
                           Yoak

yoake   frequency: 1   relative frequency: 0.0000
    P. 205 HISTORICALL 164 All England strait should fall beneath his
                           yoake,

yoke   frequency: 2   relative frequency: 0.0000
    See also "yoak," "yoake."
    P. 63 A. HOUSE   159 'How soft the yoke on us would lye,
    P. 204 HISTORICALL 123 To bring upon our Necks the heavier yoke:

yonder   frequency: 2   relative frequency: 0.0000
    P. 19 THYRSIS   9 Thyrsis. Turn thine Eye to yonder Skie,
    P. 26 MISTRESS   23 And yonder all before us lye

yong   frequency: 1   relative frequency: 0.0000

```
        P.   3 LOVELACE       24 Severer then the yong Presbytery.

york                              frequency:    1    relative frequency: 0.0000
        P. 195 TWO HORSES     143 Ch. What is thy opinion of James Duke of
                                  York?

yorkes                            frequency:    1    relative frequency: 0.0000
        P. 202 HISTORICALL     45 But now Yorkes Genitalls grew over hot

york's.  See "yorkes."

you                               frequency:  123   relative frequency: 0.0025

youl                              frequency:    1    relative frequency: 0.0000

you'l                             frequency:    2    relative frequency: 0.0000

young                             frequency:   13   relative frequency: 0.0002
        See also "yong."
        P.  25 YOUNG LOVE       t Young Love.
        P.  25 YOUNG LOVE       6 By young Love old Time beguil'd:
        P.  39 PICTURE         33 But O young beauty of the Woods,
        P.  67 A. HOUSE       258 Young Fairfax through the Wall does rise.
        P.  75 A. HOUSE       534 The eldest of its young lets drop,
        P.  76 A. HOUSE       558 But serves to feed the Hewels young.
        P.  79 A. HOUSE       651 The young Maria walks to night:
        P.  86 FLECKNO        128 Picks out the tender bosome to its young.
        P. 122 TWO SONGS       15 He when Young as we did graze,
        P. 144 INSTRUCTIONS   153 In Loyal haste they left young Wives in Bed,
        P. 147 INSTRUCTIONS   262 And Lovelace young, of Chimney-men the Cane.
        P. 178 LOYALL SCOT    274 Pardon, Young Heroe, this soe long Transport;
        P. 189 BRITANNIA      165 Tell 'em how arts and Arms in thy young dayes

younger                           frequency:    2    relative frequency: 0.0000
        P. 120 TWO SONGS       31 Yet is her younger Sister laid
        P. 201 HISTORICALL     18 His younger Brother perisht by a clap.

youngsters                        frequency:    1    relative frequency: 0.0000
        P. 201 HISTORICALL     30 Why not with easy Youngsters make as bold?

your                              frequency:  102   relative frequency: 0.0021

yours                             frequency:    5    relative frequency: 0.0001

youth                             frequency:   15   relative frequency: 0.0003
        P.  63 A. HOUSE       148 'Have mark'd the Youth, and what he is.
        P.  67 A. HOUSE       265 But the glad Youth away her bears,
        P.  79 A. HOUSE       652 Hide trifling Youth thy Pleasures slight.
        P.  81 A. HOUSE       714 Those Trains by Youth against thee meant;
        P.  86 FLECKNO        135 More odious then those raggs which the French
                                  youth
        P.  87 FLECKNO        157 Thereat the waxen Youth relented straight:
        P.  87 ODE             1 The forward Youth that would appear
        P.  99 HOLLAND        143 Unless our Senate, lest their Youth disuse,
        P. 145 INSTRUCTIONS   171 His Birth, his Youth, his Brokage all
                                  dispraise,
        P. 150 INSTRUCTIONS   389 And taught Youth by Spectacle Innocent!
        P. 157 INSTRUCTIONS   696 Our English youth shall sing the Valiant Scot.
        P. 173 LOYALL SCOT     62 Our English youth shall sing the valiant Scott.
        P. 181 MADE FREE       15 Wou'd intrust their youth to your heeding?
        P. 188 BRITANNIA      161 Till then, my Rawleigh, teach our noble Youth
        P. 189 BRITANNIA      166 Imploy'd the Youth, not Taverns, Stewes and
                                  playes:

youthful                          frequency:    3    relative frequency: 0.0000
        See also "youthfull."
        P.  27 MISTRESS        33 Now therefore, while the youthful hew
        P.  83 FLECKNO         25 Calm'd the disorders of my youthful Breast,
        P. 141 INSTRUCTIONS    37 But Age, allaying now that youthful heat,

youthfull                         frequency:    1    relative frequency: 0.0000
        P. 199 DUKE            42 And in her youthfull veines receive the wound

youths                            frequency:    1    relative frequency: 0.0000
        P. 168 ADVICE          7 Whilest the brave youths tired with the work of
                                  State

zeal                              frequency:    1    relative frequency: 0.0000
        See also "zeale."
        P. 174 LOYALL SCOT    118 They wanted zeal and Learning, soe mistook

zeale                             frequency:    2    relative frequency: 0.0000
```

```
         P. 128 O.C.          225 Least others dare to think your zeale a maske,
         P. 198 DUKE           15 Armed with boold zeale and blessing with thy
                                  hands

zealous                            frequency:    2    relative frequency: 0.0000
         P. 200 DUKE          111 But to a zealous and ambitious minde,
         P. 203 HISTORICALL    94 Who ever has an over zealous wife

zephyr's                           frequency:    1    relative frequency: 0.0000
         P.  77 A. HOUSE      598 And unto you cocl Zephyr's Thanks,

zodiack                            frequency:    1    relative frequency: 0.0000
         P.  50 THE GARDEN     68 Does through a fragrant Zodiack run;

zone                               frequency:    2    relative frequency: 0.0000
         P. 117 BLAKE         124 War turn'd the temperate, to the Torrid Zone.
         P. 174 LOYALL SCCT   101 'Twill make a more Inhatitable zone.
```

2481 the	196 at	121 if would	68 each long
1789 and	190 when	118 she	67 own
1047 to	186 him	112 such while will	66 love
769 of	184 did	110 are	64 whose
727 a	182 from	108 no these	63 might
682 in	180 or	102 its there your	62 great must
648 his	177 yet	101 do	61 up
549 that	176 more	100 we	60 both made much once
500 with	171 is	98 should	59 day new
489 but	169 my	96 thou	57 upon
472 he	167 have	95 could	56 man never only other though
416 for	164 which	94 still	55 out two
383 all	161 was	90 first	54 till world
367 as	159 what	89 can those	53 thus
358 their	156 does	88 an me	52 th'
312 so	151 had	84 see	51 'tis
298 they	149 now	78 may through	50 doth
269 i	147 like	77 were	49 head
244 by	146 one who	76 us	47 soul time
237 it	143 shall	75 too	46 away most old thee
226 not	140 where	73 here	45 eyes
212 then	139 them	71 make some	44 well
209 be	133 nor	70 king men	
208 her	132 thy		
206 this	128 how		
202 our	123 you		
197 on			

43
before
last

42
self
state
themselves
within

41
let
peace

40
court
ere
himself
nature
vain

39
night
than

38
come
good
place
without

37
has

36
death
every
fate

35
into
none
since
whom

34
fair
hand
heaven
mind
soon.
tears

33
been
down
fall
find
sun

32
oft
way

31
fear
lest
rest
sweet

30
air
earth
english
far
hence
under

29
high
know

life
w.
war

28
again
against
ch.
draw
give
green
hee
next
said
sight

27
about
age
cannot
flow'rs
house
many
name
others
sure
thought
true

26
above
back
dear
dutch
thine
unto
whole

25
any
art
bishops
came
ever
found
grow
ill
lay
same
sea
soe
strong
therefore

24
best
face
fight
oh
raise
things
tho'

23
better
go
grass
just
land
less
o
side
take
'twas
why

22
after
among
care
crown

eye
fit
heart
left
painter
sword
wise

21
cause
charles
dead
england
fleet
happy
hath
heavens
holy
lord
noe
rise
turn

20
bring
dye
equal
e're
kings
laid
loves
parliament
sad
say
sir
thing
white

19
alone
behind
doe
fame
grief
home
leave
meet
near
pleasure
right
round
sacred
saw
seas
sing
tell
work

18
beauty
bright
command
ev'ry
god
lye
nothing
over
stand

17
below
between
brought
false
fine
fly
full
greater
hold
late
light

live
lost
mine
part
race
rather
run
's
seen
stay
think
wee
ye

16
another
bee
breast
church
clear
close
courage
either
fire
foot
golden
joy
knew
mean
navy
neither
ore
praise
religion
seem
seem'd
sent
set
ships
st.
streight
whilst
wound

15
bold
common
enough
fell
force
free
gold
gone
ground
hands
hope
isle
little
look
off
play
poor
pure
shame
shew
soft
words
youth

14
alas
arts
bed
blood
brave
brother
c.
end
faith
feet
french
grace

lead
least
led
nation
paint
read
scarce
seems
sit
straight
thence
took
tree
trees
try
want
wit
word

13
appear
body
cromwell
didst
divine
field
gardens
hast
hear
heat
hopes
justice
keep
kind
law
master
pass
people
roses
son
sound
times
unless
use
winds
young

12
bear
begin
build
call
cast
deep
delight
father
flame
flames
france
fresh
gave
glory
gods
grew
half
heav'n
height
honour
loose
makes
money
morning
mortal
onely
order
plain
please
prove
rage
save
sheep

short
silent
speak
spight
spring
stands
stars
thoughts
three
'twere
went
wind
wine

11
act
ah
already
always
betwixt
beyond
black
cease
chance
change
comes
complain
country
cynthia
dare
dorinda
duke
else
endymion
fierce
fill
grown
hay
higher
humane
lyes
need
needs
pett
pow'r
princes
ready
reign
scorn
scotch
secure
shade
share
sport
stone
store
tear
throne
wealth
year
years

10
along
am
att
bears
blest
born
breath
chast
choice
chorus
commons
d.
dark
dost
double
draws
ear
enemy

fairfax
friend
gentle
glad
horses
kept
leaves
limbs
locks
lose
nay
ne're
o're
owne
pay
power
pride
publick
rich
rome
scene
seek
single
skill
strange
strength
teach
thyrsis
tongue
tread
valour
virgin
wanton
waves
wide
wood

9
agree
arms
beams
board
book
break
burn
calm
chose
cold
cou'd
crimes
crown'd
cut
drest
dy'd
fast
fatal
fears
fled
forts
guard
heads
highest
hyde
i'le
indeed
lady
line
london
monarchs
mower
muse
musick
news
past
prince
proud
refuse
return
secret
show
sin

sits
small
song
sorrow
spent
star
statue
taught
temple
tho
thousand
together
trust
try'd
turn'd
verse
vice
weep
whether
whore
wild
wives

8
acts
ancient
armes
army
bank
beauties
beneath
birds
blind
broke
call'd
cannon
center
cheat
citty
clouds
colours
commands
commend
dayes
despair
dew
due
dust
early
easie
ev'n
few
fields
finds
fires
fond
fruit
further
gain
garden
glories
grave
hair
hour
irish
known
learn
liberty
longer
looks
loss
lov'd
lover
low
measure
nearer
noble
ocean
pain
pale
picture

plant	excise	truth	lately
poet	express	'twould	laws
present	fix	'um	learn'd
priest	flesh	unknown	lightning
put	flow	vainly	lillies
rais'd	foe	virtue	lines
reason	foes	voice	lords
rent	fortune	weight	lower
ride	forward	whitehall	mankind
river	fragrant	wings	martial
roman	frame	woods	meadow
root	gives	worse	minds
rule	goe	worth	minute
safe	got	wou'd	modest
sate	government		mold
seat	guide	**6**	mother
send	harry	abroad	move
shine	heard	againe	necessary
slaves	hell	although	noise
something	hid	amongst	numbers
spare	holland	arm	nymph
stroke	hollow	ashes	obey
tame	host	aside	ours
thither	hot	ask'd	paid
thorough	hundred	bark	pair
treasurer	immortal	beast	palace
triumph	increase	beene	parents
troop	jove	begun	phillis
tyrants	juliana	bend	pitty
underneath	kill	bind	plants
very	lands	boat	plumes
wall	large	bosome	port
wars	leads	bound	praises
watry	liv'd	brass	purple
wave	lovely	bred	queen
whence	lust	built	rain
wife	mad	burning	ran
wisely	malice	burns	restless
women	masters	chain	restore
worlds	meadows	charge	retreat
write	mighty	chase	rivers
wrong	monster	cheek	rout
yield	mouth	conscience	ruyter
	narrow	damon	sail
7	natures	deaf	saints
ages	note	deeds	salute
albans	oak	descend	sees
ambition	often	design'd	serve
angry	pan	dialogue	sex
armed	poets	dismal	shed
band	prest	dispute	shews
bay	prevent	drew	shore
beasts	prey	drink	silver
because	priests	drop	sister
behold	quickly	even	skies
being	reach	example	skin
besides	revenge	fathers	sold
birth	room	feast	sons
bodies	rude	fed	sought
box	ruine	feed	sphere
brest	second	feign	spoke
burnt	sense	female	spy'd
city	shalt	fill'd	stones
cool	shape	folly	stream
darling	shining	former	streams
divide	shot	four	strike
done	sleep	game	strive
durst	slight	ghost	sunk
dwell	slow	groan	surely
elements	souls	growing	takes
'em	storms	grows	tall
empire	story	having	temples
	struck	hearts	ten
	sudden	held	terrour
	sweat	hide	thick
	theirs	hill	tis
	thrice	indifferent	told
	thunder	invade	torn
	timber	knows	triumphs
	touch	labour	turns
	trade	language	twice

tyrant	eternal	nature's	third
useless	fail	ne'er	top
virgins	fail'd	nere	tow'r
warlike	faire	nest	trembling
warm	falling	notes	'twill
water	falls	number	understood
weak	farr	nymphs	unite
wear	faults	oblig'd	us'd
weeping	faun	obscure	valiant
wonder	feign'd	open	vast
wretched	felt	ought	victory
writ	fertile	painted	view
wrought	figure	parting	vine
	five	perfect	virtues
5	fixt	perhaps	vow
active	fleets	plac'd	walk
admire	flies	points	walks
adorn	flight	pole	waters
advice	forth	poore	weary
afford	fought	possest	winged
agen	fountain	powder	wish
alive	fountains	presage	woes
allens	friends	presents	wondrous
alwaies	fright	pretend	wooden
am'rous	front	price	worthy
answer	future	prize	yearly
appears	garlands	prudent	yours
architect	gates	quire	
base	gently	rate	**4**
bayes	glass	ray	adore
beat	gott	receive	advance
began	grassy	red	agreed
begins	guilty	region	aim
bell	hadst	repair	airy
binds	hall	restrain	allow'd
bishop	hang	rising	alwayes
blake	hard	rocks	amber
blame	heaven's	rose	ametas
bloody	heavy	royal	anchor
bow	heir	royall	angels
boy	henceforth	runs	anger
brings	hers	sacrifice	antient
brows	hither	safely	armyes
buy	hobbinol	sake	ascend
captain	horrid	seamen	asham'd
casts	horse	sell	assay'd
cave	hours	senate	avarice
certain	houses	serpent	bare
chosen	hung	sett	become
clean	hungry	severe	beg
cloud	increast	shades	belly
compare	infant	shake	betray
conquering	inspire	shepheard	betray'd
couldst	iron	shew'd	bird
councell	james	shines	bless
counsel	jealous	ship	boast
coy	jewels	shold	bore
crest	joys	shou'd	boughs
crime	king's	shown	boys
cruel	kiss	shrine	branches
cure	knave	shrunk	breaking
danger	knight	sick	breaks
dart	knowes	sign	bride
defence	knowing	sings	brit.
den	knowledge	sink	broken
design	lawes	sins	building
destroy	lewis	skyes	bull
devour	linnen	sober	burne
dispose	lute	spain	calls
door	making	spirits	canst
dos	marble	springs	castle
dread	march	stake	cell
dying	mate	steer	chair
ease	meads	suffice	chamber
east	melt	swore	charing
eat	members	sythe	chatham
edge	mistook	tainted	cheats
effect	monk	tells	child
elizium	mountains	tender	chloe
empty	names	that's	chrystal
envious	native	thinks	coast

colour	hills	pregnant	town
conquest	honest	prelate	transparent
conscious	hors	prepar'd	treasure
consent	hous	presume	treaty
constant	however	promis'd	truly
cost	huge	prophecies	ungirt
count	humble	punishment	unhappy
course	hyde's	quick	united
courtiers	ile	raigne	until
created	indure	rase	vail
cross	influence	rawleigh	various
crowne	in's	reflect	vault
curse	island	reform	vertue
curst	joyes	repose	vertues
daily	keel	respect	vex
dangers	kingdome	restor'd	victorious
daphnis	labours	retire	votes
days	ladies	revenue	walls
de	laurel	reward	wand
debate	lay'd	ring	warr
debt	length	roar	wast
decrees	lets	roar'd	weave
deface	let's	robert	wed
delights	lie	rules	wheel
denham	listning	saith	whores
designes	lives	scepter	win
dick	living	scorn'd	womb
dinner	load	scot	works
divided	lovelace	scottish	wounds
dog	loyall	seal	yields
doubt	luxury	seeing	
douglas	malignant	seize	3
dress	march'd	selves	add
drive	meant	sence	affirm
drown	memory	serene	aged
dry	ment	serv'd	aid
dull	misled	serves	alike
dwells	miss	shadows	allure
engines	mist	shady	allwayes
ensigns	mistake	shoar	ambassadors
enter	mistaken	shoots	answers
enter'd	model	show'd	appease
envy	monarch	shows	armour
erect	moon	sky	arrive
ev'ning	mordant	smooth	aspect
exceed	mortall	snake	attend
expect	mourn	solitary	authors
expos'd	nations	speaker	bands
fearing	necessity	spend	banish
feel	neck	spirit	banks
fetch	neighbour	spoil	basis
fetters	ne'r	spots	battel
fish	newly	square	became
fitter	nose	stain	becomes
flaming	nuns	states	beguil'd
flow'r	obey'd	steel	believe
forbidden	object	stood	beloved
forced	offer	strain	bends
forget	orders	strings	bid
forthwith	oyl	subjects	blames
fortunate	pains	succeeds	blinded
freedome	papist	sung	blossome
frequent	paradise	suns	blow
friendship	pardon	supply	boats
generous	pattern	suppress	brain
get	pen	survey	branch
given	pencil	sweetest	bread
glorious	peoples	swim	breeches
grieve	perfume	table	bribe
grove	perfumes	taken	brittish
guards	pierce	tale	brow
guest	pillars	tax	buildings
guilt	pity	thames	bulk
hastings	planted	thenceforth	camp
hate	playes	thestylis	captive
health	pleasures	thorns	car'd
he'd	ply	throw	careless
help	point	tide	cares
helpless	ports	title	carry
herbs	post	tomalin	carwells
hidden	posture	tongues	case

caves
censure
character
chequer
chief
children
chill
choyce
churches
circle
circles
claim
claws
clifford
climb
clothes
coffee
colony
commission
common-wealth
compass
compos'd
compose
comprehend
conceal
conceal'd
confess
confest
confin'd
conquer
conquer'd
constrain'd
content
cool'd
couple
courteous
courts
courtship
coventry
creates
credit
crosse
cruelty
cry
crystal
curious
curled
dance
darkness
daughter
deare
deck
decree
degree
delay
delicious
deluge
demand
departure
desert
designs
desperate
destroy'd
determine
devide
devil
devill
diadem
die
dies
disarm
disdain
disease
disguis'd
distance
distrest
doome
doore
douglass
downe
drawn
drunken

duty
dwelt
dy
ears
eight
elbow
element
eliza
eliza's
employ
ends
engine
enjoy
entertains
escape
estates
esteem
evil
exalt
exceeds
exchequer
excuse
exprest
fac'd
faint
fam'd
favour
fear'd
fence
fingers
firm
firy
fishes
fix'd
flags
flock
flocks
flood
floods
flora
flcting
flowers
flcwing
flyes
fold
follow'd
fools
forces
forehead
form
fort
foundation
foundations
frail
fruits
funeral
fury
gallery
gallions
gate
gather
gaze
gen'rous
gentler
giddy
girls
giving
goes
grac'd
grain
greatest
greatness
griefs
gross
groves
gyant
ha'
hangs
harmless
haste
healths

heark
heroe
hew
hides
hit
hony
hook
hcrn
horrour
hourly
hurl'd
hurry'd
husband
idle
i'lle
ills
i'm
image
impious
inclose
indian
indies
infants
innocence
instant
instead
instrument
intercept
interest
invent
invite
islands
isles
is't
i'th
it's
itself
james's
joyn
joyning
joynt
judge
judges
justly
keels
keen
kindly
kingdomes
kingdoms
knaves
knife
knights
knit
lace
lack
lambs
lamps
lane
languishing
lauderdale
laugh
lawrel
leaf
learned
learning
leisure
lent
lesser
lik'd
lips
liquid
london's
lookes
loved
lovers
lustre
lusty
madness
maid
maintain
male

manna
marching
mark'd
mask
masquerade
matter
meal
measures
meate
met
mild
milk
minde
minister
mirrour
mistress
mixt
morn
moses
mothers
mounted
mourn'd
mourning
moves
moving
mowers
muster
nacion
naked
navies
neer
neglect
neptune
nice
nigh
nights
nostrils
nought
num'rous
nurst
oaken
oceans
odious
officious
oftner
on't
open'd
opprest
osborn
owe
owes
ox
pallace
parts
passage
passions
pastures
pearly
person
pictures
piece
piercing
pikes
pimps
pine
pines
pious
pitch
plague
plate
pleasant
pleas'd
pleasing
plott
poem
poems
pope
pound
powers
practise
practising

pray'r	smell	ty'd	ale
pray'rs	smile	tyes	alexander
precious	smiles	tyranny	all-seeing
prepare	smiling	uncertain	allow
press	softest	undone	ally
pretence	sometimes	union	almighty
pretty	songs	universal	almost
private	sooner	universe	aloft
privy	sore	untimely	altar
proclaim	sort	untrue	altars
produce	souldier	upright	alter
profane	sounds	vaine	alter'd
progeny	space	veil	amaz'd
project	spaniards	veil	ambergris
projects	spectacle	vein	ambitious
provinces	spotless	vest	amphion
prudence	spy	vices	angell
pump	squadron	view'd	angle
purse	stage	views	antick
quoth	starry	vigour	antique
rabble	starts	viner	apollo
rare	statues	vowes	appear'd
recal	steed	wait	apples
receiv'd	stock	wander	apply'd
reduce	stole	wanting	approve
relate	stop	wants	architects
renew	strait	warre	argument
renown	street	watch	arise
renown'd	strict	wayes	ark
rescue	studies	weare	arlington
resign	subject	wears	arm'd
resolved	succeeding	weeps	armies
return'd	success	welcome	ask
returning	sullen	wench	asleep
returns	sun's	wept	aspire
reverend	sup	wer't	assault
richard	suspend	wet	asse
rights	sway	willing	assist
rob	swear	wing	assure
rock	sweetness	winter	as't
rope	swells	wisdome	astonish'd
rugged	sylvio	wiser	astray
rul'd	tails	wish'd	astrologers
ruling	talking	witness	atome
rust	taxes	witt	attempt
sail'd	teeth	won	attended
saint	temper'd	won't	author
sanctacruze	tempest	worst	aw
sand	tempests	wouldst	awe
sands	tempt	wrath	ax
satyr	thanks	wreaths	azure
sawce	theire	writes	babel
scaffold	theres	youthful	bacchus
scatter'd	thin		backside
scotland	thinking	2	bacon
securely	thread	abbess	bad
secures	threaten	abhors	bait
seiz'd	threw	able	balam
selling	togeather	absence	ball
sentence	token	absent	ballance
several	tomb	abysse	banisht
sev'ral	tomkins	accents	bankers
seymour	tooke	accomptants	bar
sharp	tore	accurs'd	barr'd
sheets	tortoise	accus'd	barties
shent	tost	accuse	basely
shield	towards	action	bashful
shrill	track	adieu	bastards
shut	translators	adjourn	bastions
sigh'd	treat	admir'd	bath
sighs	treated	adorns	beads
signs	tremble	advantage	beak
silence	tribute	adventur'd	beare
silken	tritons	adventures	beats
sithe	troops	adverse	beauteous
skie	troth	affairs	bees
skilful	truths	affected	bee'st
slain	tumult	affection	begg'd
slave	turk	afraid	beleive
slender	turne	aiming	beleives
slowly	twas	aire	belgick
		alarms	believing
		alcides	

ben	chaos	coward	discourses
bennet	charm	crane	disdainful
bent	charming	create	disdains
bermudas	charms	creations	disgrace
bestows	cheap	creature	disguise
bewail	chear	creatures	disjointed
birding	chearful	credulous	disorder'd
bitter	cheated	crescent	dispair
bleed	checquer	crew	displease
bleeding	cheere	croak	dispossest
bleeds	chide	cromwell's	disputes
blessings	chiefe	crost	dissolving
blew	chin	crowd	distills
blossoms	chine	crowns	distrust
bloud	choicest	crupper	dive
blusht	choose	cry'd	divines
boards	christian	cup	doctor
bolder	churchill	cups	doleful
boldly	chuse	curates	domestick
bondage	chymists	cur'd	doors
bonds	circingle	curl	doubled
bone	circling	curl'd	doubtful
bones	cities	curtains	dover
booke	civil	cutt	downy
bottom	civill	dam	drake
bought	clad	dame	drawne
boundless	clap	danby	dreadful
boyl	clarendon	daniel	dream
bragg	clay	darby	drinks
braine	cleavelands	daring	dropping
brambles	clemency	darts	drops
brand	clergie	dasht	drown'd
braves	climbe	daughters	drums
brawny	climes	davenant	drunk
brazen	cloath	david	drunke
breed	clorinda	debts	dukes
briars	clos'd	decay'd	dumb
brick	closer	deceive	duncombe
bridge	cloven	decide	dung
brighter	cloyster	declare	dungeon
bristol	cloysters	decreed	dyes
britain	coffin	deeper	eas'ly
brittain	columnes	deepest	eastern
brittle	comands	deer	easy
broach'd	combat	defac'd	eate
brood	comet	deform	eating
brook	commonwealth	defy'd	eats
bud	compassion	degenerate	ebb
buffoones	complain'd	deliver	ecchc
builds	complexion	deluges	ecchoes
bulls	conclusion	demands	echo
burn'd	condemn	denham's	e'er
buryed	condemn'd	denton	effigie
bushes	confiscate	deny'd	eighteen
busie	confus'd	depend	elders
cabal	congeal'd	depose	elms
cabinet	conjure	descry'd	elysian
caelia	conquered	deserv'd	emulous
called	conqueror	deserve	enamour'd
calves	conquerors	deserved	ended
canary	consecrate	deserves	endure
candy	consider	desir'd	enflam'd
cane	consulting	desire	enforc'd
captivate	consume	despise	enrich
captives	contagion	destiny	enroll'd
carteret	contemn	destroys	entertain
cash	contend	detect	equally
casting	contest	detest	equipage
castlemain	continue	devides	err
cattle	contributed	dial	error
causes	controule	different	errours
causeth	convenient	dine	eske
cedars	convey	diocesse	espy'd
celia	copper	dire	estate
cells	corn	direct	esteem'd
cerberus	corrupt	disband	eternall
chaines	could'st	discern	eternity
chains	counsellors	discern'd	eve
champion	countrey	discipline	events
chancellor	countryes	discontent	everlasting
chang'd	cover	discord	exact

excell	ganges	honours	leaders
excellent	garland	horror	league
exercise	gaul	hounds	leagues
exhale	gawdy	human	lean
exile	gay	humbly	leathern
expence	gaz'd	humility	letts
explain	gazing	hunt	level'd
extended	gelid	huntsman	liberally
extends	ghosts	hurt	lick
extent	gladly	husbandman	licks
ey'd	glance	idol	lids
fabrick	glare	ignorance	lieutenant
faces	glasses	i'll	lights
faction	glean	imagin'd	likeness
fain	glitters	imbark	liking
fall'n	glo-worms	i'me	lip
farre	gloomy	imperiall	lock
farthing	going	impossible	lodging
fashion	gout	impure	lofty
fatall	gouty	incest	looke
fault	govern	inchas'd	looking
favours	gown	indians	losses
fayry	graces	indulgent	lotts
feare	grape	industrious	loud
fearful	grashoppers	infinite	love's
feeble	grasses	inflame	lowness
feeds	graver	ingenious	lucan
fellows	gravity	injustice	lumbard
females	gray	inn	lungs
fewel	greate	innocently	lurch
fiend	greedy	insulting	luscious
fiery	greek	intelligence	lyon
fifteen	grim	intend	mack
fifth	growth	intent	magick
fighting	grudge	interweave	magna
fights	guardian	intrust	mahomet
fills	guides	invisible	mail
finch	guild	issu'd	main
finde	guiltily	issue	majesties
finish	guiltless	italy	majesty
fitt	gun	i'th'	makeing
flanders	gyants	iv'ry	manag'd
flow'd	hairs	jades	manly
flower	halcyon	jarring	mans
flowrs	halcyons	jessean	mansion
flows	handling	jew	marbles
follow	hang'd	jews	march't
fool	hanging	jolly	maria
fool'd	harder	joseph	mark
foolish	hardly	joves	market
forbears	harm	jovial	marriage
forc'd	harmonious	joy'd	mars
ford	harry's	joyn'd	masque
forests	harvest	jubal	mass
foretel	hasting	judg'd	massacre
forgot	hastning	judgment	match
forrests	hatch	juice	matchless
for't	haughty	jury	maw
fortunes	headed	jus	mayern
foul	headstrong	kate	maze
founders	heare	keeps	mead
fourty	heavier	kent	means
fowl	hebrew	kill'd	medows
fox	hedge	kinder	medway
foxes	hee'l	kingdom	meets
fraud	helpe	kist	melons
freed	hemisphere	knots	memorable
frighted	heroes	knowne	menalca's
frog	heroick	laden	mend
frogs	herring	landskip	mens
fryar	he's	languish	mercenary
fun'rals	hideous	larger	mercy
furnish	highness	lasting	merry
furniture	hight	lasts	messe
furrs	himselfe	latest	messengers
gain'd	hinder	lauderdales	metal
'gainst	historian	laught	methinks
gallant	hive	laurels	mexique
gallick	hocus	lavish	midnight
gallons	holy-water	lazy	mightst
galloping	honour'd	leaden	

milder	panting	prospect	riding
milky	papers	protestant	ripe
millions	paradice	provide	rivals
mines	parliaments	providence	robes
mint	parly	provok't	rogue
miscreants	patent	publike	rogues
miss'd	path	publique	romane
mitre	pauls	pull	romes
moan	peach	pulpit	roome
mode	pearch	purchase	ropes
modern	pearl	pursues	roul
modesty	pelican	puts	rouling
moist	penetration	quake	row
monsters	pensive	quarrells	rub
months	perceiv'd	quarries	rump
mortals	perfecting	quarry	runne
mortal's	perish	quarters	rustle
mosaick	perisht	queens	sable
mossy	pharoah	quiet	sadder
mountain	philosopher	quill	safety
mournful	pick	quit	saile
mov'd	pickled	quite	sailing
mow'd	picks	raging	sails
mown	pict	raign	salt
mr.	piety	rail	sanctity
muses	pills	ram'd	sat
musicks	pimp	rang'd	savage
myrmidons	places	rarely	sav'd
nak'd	plagues	rat	scale
nam'd	plaid	ratling	scales
naval	planet	rawl.	scandalous
neare	planks	rayes	scap't
necks	player	readers	scenes
needles	players	reap	scorching
needless	plays	rear	score
neere	plead	rear'd	scott
neglected	plot	rebel	scripture
neighbouring	plume	rebounds	seamens
neighbours	pluto	recall	search
nells	poetick	receives	season
net	poetry	recollect	seats
nightingale	poland	recollecting	seaven
nimph	polish'd	records	sedge
noblest	pool	recreate	seeds
noon	popery	redoubled	seeks
northern	popish	redress	seene
noyse	popular	reeds	seldom
nun	possess	regal	separate
nuptial	pot	reign'd	seperate
oakes	powders	reigns	seraglio
oar	pow'rs	reinforce	sermons
oath	poyson	rejoyce	service
obscurer	pray	relicks	sets
obsequies	prayers	religious	setting
observing	prayse	rely'd	seven
oeta	precipices	remain	seventh
offend	premier	remains	shares
ope	presbyter	remembring	shattered
opens	presence	remove	sheerness
opinion	preserv'd	render	shell
opose	preserve	renew'd	shelter
oppose	preserves	rents	shepheards
opposite	presumes	repeat	shepherdess
oppression	prethee	repleat	shepherds
oracles	pretious	reply'd	shipwrack
oracular	prevail	report	shipwrackt
ordure	prick	reposing	shirt
o'reflow	prison	represent	shod
orient	priviledge	represents	shook
ornaments	privy-purse	reserv'd	shooke
orphan	prizes	resist	shoos
oth	proceed	resistance	shoot
other's	proclamation	resolv'd	shop
ourselves	prodigious	resolves	shorn
out-do	prolong	rests	shorter
overcome	propagate	retir'd	showers
overthrown	prophecy	retiring	showres
pacis	prophet	revolves	show's
pack	propitious	rewards	shrinks
paines	propriety	rhime	shrubs
pan's	prorogued	richer	shun

shuns	stores	throng	vanishes
shuts	storm	throws	vanisht
sides	stormy	thrust	vaulted
siege	strangeways	thundring	vegetable
sigh	straw	thwaites	veins
signifie	stray	timely	venetian
silks	streaks	tim'rous	venus
silly	strecht	tinkling	verdant
similitude	streets	tire	vere
singly	streightness	toad	veres
sinking	stretch'd	tom	vessel
sinks	stretches	tool	vext
sinners	stretcht	torches	victor
sirs	strictly	tortur'd	victors
sitting	strife	tottering	viewing
skipper	strokes	tough	villains
sleeps	stronger	towne	villany
sleeves	strongest	toyl	viol
slept	strugling	toyle	virgil
slide	stuarts	toyles	visits
sliding	stubborn	trace	vulgar
slights	study	trails	vulture
slips	studying	train	waites
slumbers	stumbling	traine	wakes
smart	stupid	translated	walk'd
smileing	subdue	translation	wandring
snow	sublime	translations	wanted
sobriety	sublunary	travell'd	warrs
society	subtile	traytors	wastes
somewhat	succession	treason	wasting
souldiers	sucks	treasures	wasts
soule	suddainly	treble	weather
south	suit	trenches	we'd
soveregin	summ'd	trick	weed
sov'raign	summer	trickle	wee've
sow'd	summers	tries	weigh
spacious	summons	trim	west
spann'd	supper	trod	western
sparkling	supplies	trojan	whatsoever
speaking	supream	trophees	wheeler
spectators	surprize	trunk	whet
speech	surround	truthes	whets
speeches	survives	tryal	whilest
speed	suspended	tudor	whil'st
spell	suttle	tudors	whip
spencer	swallow	tulip	whipt
sphear	swallows	tulips	whistling
spices	swans	tumults	white-hall's
split	swarms	tun'd	wholesome
spoken	sweare	tune	wholly
sporting	sweeter	tuned	wholsome
sports	swell'd	turner	whoreing
spouse	swelling	tweed	wilder
spoyls	switzers	twelve	wilderness
spread	swoln	twenty	wilt
sprig	swords	twin	winding
squatted	sworn	twin'd	windows
staffe	t'	twining	wisht
stairs	taint	'twixt	wish't
stalks	tapers	tye	witch
stall	task	uncessant	witches
stallion	tast	unconcern'd	wither'd
standard	teeming	undaunted	withstand
standing	templar	understanding	witty
starrs	tempting	unfold	wolf
stately	teneriff	unfortunate	wonder'd
statesmen	theatre	unfrequented	wond'rous
statutes	thereat	unjust	wonted
stay'd	ther's	unkind	wooll
steal	they'l	unpaid	wore
steals	thief	unrigg'd	worn
stealth	thieves	unsafe	would'st
steam	thighs	unsecure	wounded
steel'd	thinke	untame	wreck
steely	think'st	unusual	writers
steps	thirst	upbraid	yards
stiff	thorow	upwards	yea
stir'd	thousands	urg'd	yeare
stocks	thrive	vale	yeares
stoop	throat	value	yeild
stopt	throats	van	yellow

yoke
yonder
you'l
younger
zeale
zealous
zone

1

aaron
abandon
abandoning
abate
abbot
abbyss
abednego
abhoring
abide
abject
abjured
ablest
abortive
abound
abrupter
abruptly
absolute
absolved
absurdityes
accent
accept
access
accidents
according
account
accumulate
accursed
accurst
acquainted
acre
acted
acte's
actor
adam
adam's
adapt
adde
added
addeth
addle-brain'd
addleheaded
addrest
adds
adjutant-general
admirable
admiral
admires
admiring
adoe
ador'd
adoreing
adores
adorn'd
adorned
adress
adresses
adultery
adult'rate
adult'rers
adust
advanced
advancement
advances
advent'ring
adventrous
advis'd
advise
aeolus
aesculapius
aeson
aetna
afarr

afeard
affaires
affect
affections
affirms
afflictions
affronted
african
aghast
agitation
ago
agree't
aide
aime
aires
airs
ajax
alabaster
a la mode
alarm
alban
albemarle
albemarles
alce
alcorand
alexanders
algeryne
alien
allan
allaying
alledge
alleges
allies
allowed
allows
allur'd
alluring
alluvion
ally'd
almond-milk
alpes
altar's
altred
alt'ring
aly
amaze
amazons
ambergreece
ambigue
ambles
ambush
amity
ammunition
amphibii
amphibium
amphitrio
amphyon
amsterdam
anathama
anatomists
anchises
ancients
anew
angel
angelique
angells
angles
anglesey
anguish
animals
animated
animates
ankle
annext
annihilating
anniversary
annual
anointed
anothers
answer'd
answered

antedate
antidate
antidote
antients
antioch
antidodes
antiquity
ants
anxious
anxiously
apeare
apelles
apes
apochriphall
apostatizing
apostles
appartement
appeare
appeared
appeares
appeas'd
appetites
applaud
applause
apple
appleton
apply
appoint
approach
approaching
approacht
approves
april
april's
apron
apsley
araigne
aranjuez
arch
arch-bishops
arch-deacons
archbishopp
archbishoprick
arched
arches
archimedes
arching
ardour
ares
argu'd
arke
arks
arlingtons
armado
armepitts
armless
armours
armpit
arose
around
arraigns
arras-hangings
array'd
arrear
arrest
arrius
arrives
ars'nick
arteries
artfull
arthur's
articles
articulate
artificer
artilery
artillery
artless
arundells
ascended
ascends
ascent

ashburnham
ashen-wood
askes
ask't
aspects
aspireing
assembly
asses
assizes
associates
assumed
assumes
assur'd
assures
astride
at-home
atchiev'd
athanasian
atheist
atheists
athens
athos
atomes
atone
attentive
attonement
attorney
attract
attractive
augment
augments
aurelius
aurora
auspicious
austere
authentik
authour
autumn
autumnall
avant
avoid
awake
aware
aw'd
awful
awfull
axel
axes
ay
ayre's
baals
bab
baby
bacchanals
backanalls
backs
badgers
baggage
bailes
baits
baleful
ballad
ballating
balls
balm
balms
balsam-tree
balsome
bane
banish'd
banishing
bann'd
banneret
banners
banquerout
banquers
banquet
banquiers
barbed
bard
bares

barkes
barking
barks
barne
barnes
baron
barr
bars
baser
basest
basket
bassis
basso
bastard
bastion
batavian
bathe
bathes
battail
batteries
battery
battle
battlement
battles
batts
bawd
bawds
bead
beaked
beakns
beards
beares
beate
beating
beautyes
beauty's
beaver
becketts
bedeckt
beds
bee-like
beef
beer
beere
beetles
beforehand
begery
beget
beggar
beggerly
beggers
beggs
begot
begotten
behaviour
beheld
behemoth
behoulder
bel-retiro
belassis
beleivers
belgium
believes
belli
bellona
bellow
bellow'd
bells
bellydes
belov'd
bemoan
bemoane
bending
benefits
benevolence
bennet's
be'nt
benum
bequeath'd
bequeaths
bergamot

bergen
berkenhead
berties
beseig'd
beside
bespeak
bespeaks
besse
bestow
bestow'd
bestride
bet
bethlem's
betrayer
betweene
beware
biass
bible
bidding
big
bigg
bilbrough
bill
bill-borow
billeted
bills
bin
binders
binding
birch
birthday
birthright
bishoprick
bishop's
bishops-hill
bitterly
black-bag
blackest
blackheath
blacks
blade
blast
blasted
blazons
bleacht
bleating
blemishes
blessed
blessing
blinde
blinkard
blisse
blither
bloated
bloods
bloodworth-
   chanc'lor
blooming
blooms
blot
blots
bloudy
blowes
blowing
blown
blowne
blows
blue
blunter
bluntly
blush
blushes
blushing
boasting
boding
boggs
boldness
bolts
b'on
bonne

book-scorpions
books
boold
boot
bores
borne
borrow
bosom
bosomes
bottle
bottome
bough
bouldly
bounders
bow'd
bowel
bowels
bowles
bowr
bows
boxes
boyling
boynton
brain'd
brains
brake
brandish
brandy
brantford
brat
brav'd
bravely
bravo's
breach
breaches
breadth
breasts
breath'd
breathes
breathing
breathless
breaths
breda
bredth
breech
breeding
breeds
breez
bregade
brests
brethren
brewer
brewers
brib'd
bribed
briberies
bribes
brickbat
bridegroom
bridges
bridle
brigades
brightness
brim
brisk
britannia
british
brittains
brittania
broak
brokage
bronkard
brooke
brooken
broom
broth
brother-in-law's
brotherick
brotherless
brothers
bruis'd

bruises
brush
brute
brutish
brutus
bucentore
buck
buckingham
buckingham's
buds
buff
buffoons
bugger'd
builders
bullet
bullet-cheese
bulteales
bun
buoy'd
burger
burgess
burgesse
burglard
burgomaster
buried
burnes
burnetts
burnish'd
burnisht
burrough
burr'wing
burthen
bury'd
bushy
business
butchers
butter-coloss
butterd
buttry
buy-at
buys
c-------n
cabillau
cacao
caesar
caesars
calais
calcines
caledonian
calentur'd
calm'd
calme
calmely
calming
calmly
calms
calvin
cambridge
camel
came't
campaspe
camps
canary-patent
cancelld
cancer
candid
candidly
candish
candle
candlesticks
canibal
cankred
canon
canoos
can'st
can't
canticleer
canvas
canvass
capacious
capatious

capitols	chancelor	circumf'rence	combin'd
captivating	chance's	circumscribes	combine
captivity	chanc'lor's	citadels	combs
car	chancres	cited	comeing
cards	changing	citizens	comely
careen	changing-hue	citts	comerce
career	changling	cittye	comets
careere	channel	cittyes	comfort
careful	channell	cityes	commanded
caresbrooks	chants	civick	commandment
carillo	chaplain	civicke	commends
carless	chaplet	civilis	commendum
carol	chaplin	civility	comments
carouzels	chareing	civilly	common-place
carpenter	charg'd	claime	commoner
carpets	charges	claims	commonweal
carr	charging	clamerous	compact
carriage	charioteer	clammor	compactness
carta	charity	clamour	compacts
carthage	charm'd	claps	companies
carve	charmes	clap't	companions
carves	charriot	clarindon	company
casawar	charta	clarindon's	companyes
case-butter	charters	clasps	compar'd
cases	chaster	clatt'ring	compares
cassius	chathams	clause	compendious
cassock	chaucer	claw	complaine
caster	chaunt	clayton's	complaining
castlemaine	cheating	clear'd	complaint
cat	check	cleare	complaisence
cataracts	chedder	clearly	compleat
catching	cheese	clears	complement
caterpillar	cheney	cleaves	complementing
caterpillars	cherry	cleavland	complexions
cates	chiefest	clerick	compliant
catholick	chieftain	clerk	complying
catholicks	childbirth	cliff	composed
cato	childe	climate	compound
catt	chill'd	climbing	compriz'd
cattel	chime	clime	compter
caus'd	chimney	cling	computes
caused	chimney-men	cloak	concave
causeless	chimneys	cloaths	conceald
caution	chimney's	cloister	conceales
cavaleer	chimny-contractors	clonmell	conceiv'd
cavaleers	china	clora	conceive
cavalier	china-clay	clorinda's	concern'd
cavaliers	chisel	closely	conclude
cawdles	chitts	closes	concur
cawood	chivy	closing	condemned
ceas'd	chlora's	cloth	condemneth
cedar's	choak	clouts	condition
celebrate	chocolat	clownishly	conducts
celebrates	chocolatte	clowns-all-heal	coneig's
celestiall	chocolet	cloy	confederacies
cellars	choicer	cloy'd	confer
cemented	choisest	club	confessor
censurers	choler	cluster'd	confident
centers	cholmley	clusters	confind
centre	choosing	clutch	confine
ceremonies	chop	clutterbuck	confines
ceremonyes	choppes	clymacterick	confirm
ceres	chops	coach	confirming
cesarian	chor,	coals	conform's
cesar's	chordage	coat	confus'der
cessation	christendome	coates	confusion
cethegus	christians	cock-boat	conge
chaff	chronicle	cock-horse	congealed
chafing	chronicler	cock'd	congruous
chafing-dish	chrystal-pure	cockle	conjoynd
chain-shot	churchmen	cocks	conjunction
chaind	chuseth	cccles	conjuncture
chain'd	chymick	coife	conquests
chairs	chymist	collar	consciences
challenge	cicero	collecting	consecrated
chamber-door	cider	collection	consenting
chameleons	cinque	colonies	considers
chamelion	cipher	colossus	consist
chammish	circean	columns	consistory
chanc'd	circular	comand	consoles
chancellours	circumcised	comb	consort

consorts	ccuns'llor	cuts	deeps
conspiracies	counted	cutting	defeated
conspire	counterfeit	cyclops	defend
constellations	counterfeits	cymbal	defended
consuls	countermines	cynthia's	defender
consult	counterpoysed	cypress	defends
consumed	countess	d----s	defild
consumes	country-host	daffadils	defil'd
consummate	countrys	dagger	defile
contagious	country's	daies	defiles
contain'd	counts	dairys	definition
containe	coupl'd	damage	deflower
contains	courser	damming	deflowre
contempt	court-mushrumps	damnacion	deform'd
contends	court-officers	damons	deformity
contented	courtney	damon's	defray
contignation	court'sie	damp	defrayd
continent	covenanter	damsel	defy
continued	coventrys	danae	defye
continues	cover'd	dances	defying
contract	cowardice	dancing	dei
contracts	cowards	dandles	deify
contradict	cowslip-water	danger's	deityes
contrary	coyness	dank	delayed
contribute	crack	dans'd	delaying
contriv'd	craddle	danses	delightful
contrive	cradle	daphne	delphick
contrived	crambo	dareing	delphos
contriving	cram'd	dares	delt
controll	cramp	darken	deluded
controller	cramp'd	darlings	deluders
contrould	crampt	dastards	deludes
controules	craules	date	demanded
convenience	crave	dawb	democratick
converse	crawl	dawn	demolish'd
conversion	creak	dayly	demolishing
convert	creation	day's	demolisht
converted	creator's	dazle	demonstrates
converts	credible	dazled	dennis
conveyed	creditors	de-ruyter's	denns
conveying	creed	de-witte	deny
convinc'd	creek	dead's	denyed
convince	creep	deal	deny't
convocation	crocodile	deales	deodands
convoy	cromwel	deals	deplore
convulsion	cromwells	dealt	depopulating
cooke	cromwel's	dean	deprav'd
cooling	crook	deanes	depress
coolness	crossest	deans	depriv'd
cooper	croud	dearest	depth
cope	crouds	death-trumpets	depths
copes	croune	deathless	deputy-lieutenants
copies	crow'd	death's	deride
cordage	crowder	debar'd	derives
cordial	crowding	debarrs	desarts
corinthean	crowds	debase	descent
corinthian	crowne's	debauch	descrey
cork	crows	debauch'd	describe
corm'rant	crusado	debenter-wall	deserts
corm'rants	crush	debtors	designment
cornbry	crust	deceiv'd	desires
cornbury	cryes	december	d'eslire
cornet	cubbs	decent	despairing
coronet	cuckold	decently	desperately
corporation	cudgell	decieve	despicable
corposants	cuffing	decipher	despight
corpulence	culminant	deciple	despoyl'd
corrode	cupid	decks	destil
corrupcions	curb'd	deckt	destroyd
corrupted	curd	deck't	destruction
corruptible	cures	declaims	deterring
corslet	curle	declarations	deterrs
costly	curles	declares	detracting
costs	curlings	declin'd	detracts
cotton	current	declining	deum
councel	currs	decoy	device's
councells	curs'd	decrease	devise
councels	curtius	decrepid	devoto
counsell	curvets	deed	devout
counsell'd	custome	deem	dews
counsels	cut-nose	deem'd	dialect

diall
diamonds
dian
diana's
dice
dictator
did'
did'st
difference
differing
difficult
diff'ring
diffus'd
dig'd
digested
digestion
digress
diligence
dim
dimension
dimensions
diminishing
dimm
din
dinners
directs
dirted
dis
dis-intangled
disabled
disappear'd
disappears
disarmed
disasters
disavowing
discerning
disclose
discolour'd
disconsolate
discourse
discoursed
discoursing
discovers
discreet
disdain'd
disdaines
disdaining
disdain'st
diseases
disesteem
disesteem'd
disfigured
disfurnish
disguising
disheartned
dishonour'd
disinherited
disintangle
disliking
dismantling
disobedient
disobeys
disorder
disorders
discwne
dispatch
dispence
dispensed
dispers'd
disperse
dispise
dispising
displac'd
displaid
displayes
displaying
displeasure
dispraise
disputing
disquiet
disrespect

dissentions
dissolv'd
dissolve
dissolved
distaff
distant
distemper
distinct
distracted
distrain'd
distraught
distress
distrusts
disturbs
disuse
div'd
divin'd
divining
divinum
divorce
divulg'd
doeth
dog-star
dogged
doggs
dcing
doleman
doleman's
domineer
dominion
don
donatives
dores
do's
do'st
do't
doting
dcubles
doublet
doubling
doubtfully
doubtless
doves
dcwnfall
downs
dragg
dragon
dragons
drain'd
draine
draines
drakes
draught
drave
drawen
drawers
drawes
drayman's
dreaded
dreadfull
dregs
drench'd
dries
drinkers
drinking
drives
driving
droll
drone
drooping
droppe
dropt
drought
drove
drowned
drowsie
drumming
drumms
drunkards
dry'd
dubd

duck
ducks
duelling
duller
dunbar
duncomb
duncombes
dunghil
dunkirk
dunkirk-town
dunstan
dureing
during
dusky
dutches
dutchman's
dwarfish
dwelling
dwellings
dyke-grave
eagers
eagles
earles
earnest
earth-born
earthen
earthly
earthquake
earths
earth's
earthy
easier
easily
easly
eaters
eaton
ebbs
eben
eccentrick
ecchoing
eclypse
edged
edict
edicts
edward
eels
effects
effigy
egypt's
eject
elder
eldest
elect
elephantine
eleventh
elisian
eloquent
elyzean
em
emathian
embassadors
embleme
embrac'd
embrace
embraces
embracing
embroyder
embru'd
empires
employes
employs
emptiness
enamells
enchantress
enclos'd
encrease
endanger
endanger'd
endavour
ending
endless

endlesse
endures
endymions
enemies
enflamed
enfold
engag'd
engage
englands
engraver
engraving
enjoyment
enlarge
enow
enrolles
enshrin'd
ensign
ensignes
ensu'd
ensue
enterfeers
entertain'd
enticing
entrails
entrance
entred
enviously
envy'd
epitaph
equall
e'r
erecting
ermins
erring
erronious
errors
errour
escap'd
escheat
espie
espy
essence
essences
essex
esteemd
eternize
ethick
eunuchs
euphrates
evade
evangelist
ex
exactly
examines
examining
examples
excel
except
exchange
exciseing
exclude
excluding
excommunicate
excrescence
excus'd
excuses
executioner
executioners
exercisedst
exhalation
exhibition
exil'd
expatiation
expectants
expects
expels
expences
expense
experiment
expires
expose

expressing
extend
extirpate
extort
extreame
extremes
eylids
ey's
fable
fables
fabulous
fack
factious
fade
faids
faigne
faile
failes
faint-green-
  sickness
fairer
fairest
fairfacian
fairy
fairyes
falckner
falcon
falling-sickness
falmouths
faln
fal'n
falser
fal'st
falstaffs
familiar
families
family
famine
famish
famous
fan
fancied
fancies
farewel
farm
farmers
farted
faryes
fast'ning
fat
fates
fatigue
fatted
fauchion
fauconberg
faultlesse
fauns
faux's
favorite
favorites
favors
favourable
favour'd
fawns
fayre
feake
feat
feather-men
feather'd
features
feete
feigns
feild
fell'd
fellow'd
fellcwship
fencers
fenwick
fern
fervent
fetter

fetter'd
feud
fever
fewer
fiat
fiddle
fidled
fiends
fifty
fighter
figs
figures
fil'd
filling
final
fin'd
finding
finest
finish'd
finisht
finly'r
fir'd
fire-ships
fireballs
firemen
firmer
fish'd
fishermen
fitly
fits
fittest
fitting
fitts
fitz-harding
fitzgerald
fitzgerard
fixing
flail
flamen
flander
flandrick
flank
flapt
flask
flat
flatters
flattery
flatt'ry
flaw
flaxen
flea
fleaks
fleas
fleckno
fleece
fleeces
fleecy
fleetest
fleeting
flemish
flew
flexible
flinch
fling
flippant
float
flocking
floor
floor'd
floore
flourish
flourishing
floury
flouts
flower-deluces
flcwn
flowr
flcwry
flutt'ring
flye
flying

flyst
fly'st
foam
foame
foaming
fob
fobb
foil'd
folds
follows
fooles
footman
footstep
footsteps
foctstoole
forbear
forbeare
forct
forc't
fore
fore-seen
fore-shortned
forebode
forecast
forego
foregoe
foreman
foresaw
foreseen
foresees
foreshortned
forest
foretell
foretells
forever
forewarn'd
forge
forgett
forgott
forked
forkes
forks
forms
forraign
forrain
forrest
for's
forsake
forsaken
forsooth
forswear
fortifi'd
fortune's
forum
forwarn'd
founded
founder
founding
founds
fountaines
fowle
fowles
fowl's
fram'd
frames
framing
francisca
frankincense
frankness
frantique
frauds
fraudulent
fraught
fraughting
frayted
frederick
freedom
freedomes
freely
freeman
freind

freinds
frenches
fresher
friendly
frightens
frightful
frighting
frisks
froggs
frontier
frontire
frontispice
frost
frosts
froth
frowning
fruit-trees
fruition
frustrate
frustrates
frustrating
frye
fulfil'd
fulfill'd
fulminant
fumes
function
fun'ral
furious
furl'd
furnace
furrows
furyes
gadding
gaind
gaine
gained
gales
gall
gallants
gallopt
gall'way
gambo
gamesome
gap'd
gaping
garden-state
gardiner
gardner
garrison
garrisons
garrway
garway
gasps
gather'd
gathring
gazet
gazette
gelded
gellying
gelt
gemme
gems
general
generation
genious
genitalls
genius
gen'rals
gent
gentlemen
gentlest
gentlier
gentry
geographers
gecmetrick
george
german
germany
germin's
gerrard

gets
ghastly
gibellines
gibeon
gibletts
gideon
gifts
gigantick
gilberts
gilt
gingerbread
gingling
gipsies
girds
girles
girt
givers
glades
glancing
glassen
gleams
glee
glews
glide
glides
glitter
globe
globes
glcominess
glowes
glows
gnash
gnashes
goal
goale
goary
goat
goatish
goats
gobling
god-like-good
godly-cheat
goest
goodness
goodrick
goose
gore
gorge
gospels
goth
gourmand
govern'd
governe
governess
governors
governour
governours
governs
gracious
grafts
grains
grammar
grand
grand-children
grandsire
grandsire's
grants
grapes
grapling
grapple
grappling
grasps
grass-hopper
grass-hoppers
grate
grateful
gratefully
grates
gratia
gratitude
gravell'd

graver's
grave's
gravesend
gravy
graze
greatnesse
greece
greenness
greenwich
greet
griefe
grievance
griev'd
grieves
grin
grind
grinn
gristly
griv'd
grizly
groan'd
groanes
groans
groap'd
groom
groome
grosser
grossest
grot
growes
growne
grow'th
grumble
guardians
guarding
guelphs
guess
guests
guild-hall
guinea's
guinny
guise
gules
gulfes
gumme
gun-powder
gun-shot
guns
gust
gusts
guts
gutts
habit
hack
hacks
haft
hale
hales
half-anders
half-dry
halfecrown
hallelujahs
hallowing
halt
halting
hammer
hampton
hamstring'd
handsel
handyworke
hange
hanmers
hannibal
hans-in-kelder
hans-town
happie
happiness
happy'st
harass
harbours
harden'd

hardned
hare
hare's
hark
harlot
harmony
harpe
harper
harpy
hash'd
hasted
hasten
hastens
hastes
hasty
hatched
hatching
hated
hateing
haters
hates
hateth
hatred's
haunts
hay-ropes
hazles
headless
headlong
heads-man
heal
healing
healthful
heap
heapes
heareing
hearing
hears
hearse
heats
heav'd
heaven-daring
heaven-nursed
heavenly
heaves
heavye
hecatomb
hecatombs
hector
hedg'd
heed
heeding
heeren
heighten
heirs
held'st
heliades
hellborn
hellish
helm
helmet
hem'roid
hen
herald
heraldry
herb
herb-john
herberts
herbes
herbwomen
herculean
hercules
hereford
here's
heresies
heretik
heretique
heretofore
hero
heron
herse
herself

hew'd
hewels
hewel's
hierarchye
higgins
highly
highnesses
highnesses's
hindes
hir'd
hire
hirelings
hissing
histcricall
historically
history
hist'ry
hoard
hoarded
hobbs's
hobby-horse
hogs
hoise
hoist
holding
holds
holiness
hollanders
hollands
hollis
holt
holt-felsters
holy-day
holyness
homage
homely
honor
hocfs
hook-shoulder
hook-shoulder'd
hooks
hooves
hopeful
horace
horatian
horribly
horsback
horse-leeches
horseback
horsemen
hosanna
hose
hostesse
hostile
hosts
hotter
hound's
houre
house-warming
houting
howard
howere
howl
how'rd
howso'ere
hubbub
hue
hugg
huggs
humankind
humber
humor
humour
hums
hunted
hunter
hurld
hurles
hurls
hurricane
hurricans

hurried	induc'd	israelites	lab'ring
hurry	indur'd	israell	labyrinths
hurrying	indures	is'rel	lacquies
hurts	infallible	issues	laick
husbandry	infamous	italian	lamb
hush	infect	italianated	lambeth
huswifely	infecta	itt	lame
hut	infected	i've	lamentable
hydra	infection	ivy	lamp
hyes	infects	ixion's	lance
hymeneus	infested	jacall	land-tax
hypocrite	inflame's	jack-pudding	landing
hypocrites	influences	jacket	landlord
hypocritically	infold	jade	languages
i'	information	jane	languard
icy	inform'd	janus'	languished
id--	infus'd	jaw	lanthorn
idalian	ingage	jawes	lap
ida's	inglorious	jealousie	larder
idolls	ingrate	jealousies	largely
if't	ingratefull	jermyn	larks
ignorantly	ingratitude	jermyne	lash
ill-counsell'd	ingrav'd	jesse's	latine
ill-deserted	ingross	jesuites	latmos
image-like	inhabit	jewel	latter
images	inhabitable	jewell	laud
imaginary	inhumane	jews-trump	laughs
imbraces	injur'd	jigging	laughter
imediately	innocent	job	laughters
imitating	innocentest	john	laundresse
immortaliz'd	inquest	joshua	laves
immur'd	inrag'd	jowle	lawful
imortall	inscrib'd	joyful	lawley
impair	insect	joyne	lawn
impales	insects	jcyned	lawn-sleeves
impart	insense	joy's	lawrels
impatient	insinuating	jubilee	lawyers
imperial	insipid	judgement	lay-men
impetuous	inslav'd	judicious	lays
impetuously	insnar'd	jugling	le
imploy	inspect	julian	leaguers
imployd	inspir'd	julianas	leak
imploy'd	inspires	juliana's	leaner
imployes	installing	july	leap
imply	insted	jump	leap-frog
impose	instructions	junto	leaper's
impossibility	instructs	jupiters	learne
imposters	instruments	keener	learns
impotent	intail	keepers	lease
impregnable	intencions	keeping	leaver
impression	intercepts	ken	lebanon
imprison	interline	kendal	lee
improper	interpreter	kettle	leeches
improve	intervals	key	legacies
imps	interwove	kick	legall
impulse	intire	kid	legally
inanimate	intrails	kids	legend
incamp'd	intrest	killegrew	legerdemain'd
incense	introduction	kills	legg
incessant	intrusion	kinde	legion
inchant	intrusted	king-fisher	legislators
inchantment	invaded	king-wou'd-be	legorne
incloses	invades	kingship	leisurely
including	inveigling	kinred	leizure
incognito	invenom'd	kips	leness
incorporate	invented	kish	leprous
incorrigible	inventions	kites	lesly's
increas'd	inventress	knead	lessen
increasing	inverted	knees	less'ning
indanger	inviolate	knightly	lessons
indefatigable	invisibly	knits	letanies
indefatigably	invoke	knives	letcher
indemnity	inward	knocks	lethe
indented	ire	knot	lett
indentures	ireland	kncwest	letter
independent	irish-cattel	know's	letters
indicted	irish-herd	know'st	level
indiferrence	irrevocable	know't	level-coyl
indigested	isl's	labell	levellers
indignation	israalites	labor	leviathan
indite	israel	labour'd	leviathans

leviathen	loyally	mathematicks	misleto
lewd	loyalty	matur'd	mispend
lew'd	lucasta	mature	mis't
lewdness	lucifer	maturity	mistery
lewis's	luck	maxime	mist'ry
libertye	luckless	may-games	mists
libertyes	lucky	mayn	miter
liberum	luld	may's	mites
licens'd	luna	may'st	mitred
liege	lure	mazes	mix
lies	lusts	meager	mix'd
lieutenants	luxuriant	meaner	mixing
life-blood	luxurious	meanest	mixtures
lift	lyar	meas'ring	moar
lightfoot	lyers	meat	moister
ligny	lying	meates	moisture
likely	ly'n	mediator	molding
likes	lyons	meditate	molested
likewise	mace's	meditates	moloch
lilly	madril	mee	molting
lillyes	magaera	meeke	monarchys
lime-twigs	magazeen	meete	monck
limits	magazine	meeter	moneths
limitt	magdalen	melchizedeck	montezumes
limn	maggott	melting	monthly
limpid	magic	melts	monument
lin'd	magistrate	member'd	mony
lingred	magnanimous	memphis	moors
link'd	magnetically	mended	moot
links	magnitude	mends	morally
linstock	magpyes	merchant-men	morgan
lion	maidens	merchants	morley
liquors	maids	mercury	mornings
lisbon	maintain'd	meridian	morrice
list	mairmaids	merit	mortalls
litle	majestique	merits	mortar
littleton	major	mesheck	mortgag'd
liverd	maker--	messiah	mosaique
livy	maketh	metemsicosd	moss
loaden	mak'st	meteor	mote
loads	maladies	meteors	motion
loadstone	malleable	metropolis	motives
loan	manacled	mettall	mottly
loath'd	manage	microscope	mould
loathsome	mane's	mid-day	moulded
lock'd	mangers	middle	mount
lockt	manna's	middleton	mountague
locusts	mannerly	midwife	mounting
lodg'd	man's	mien	mounts
lodge	mansell	miles	mourners
lodgings	mantle	militia	mourns
loftus	mantua's	militia's	mous
lombard	map	milk-white	mouse
lombard-street	marcht	million	mouths
londoners	mare	milton's	mower's
long-eard	marg'ret	mimick	mowing
longe	marina	mimmicks	muddy
longest	marina's	miners	mules
locked	marke	mine's	multiply
looking-glass	markett	minhier	multiplying
looms	mark't	minion	multitudes
loop	marrd	ministers	mungrel
loop-holes	marriners	minted	munser's
loosely	marry	mints	murder
looser	marry'd	minut's	murder'd
lord's	marshall'd	miracle	murd'ring
lordship	martyr	miracles	mure
lordships	martyrdom	mirror	murm'ring
lore	martyrs	mirrours	murmur
loretto	marvel	misapprehend	murmuring
losing	mary	miscall'd	murthered
loth	mascarade	miscarriages	muttheress
lou'd	masculine	mischeifs	muscle-shell
loudmouthd	maske	mischief	muscles
loveliest	mast	mischiefbreeding	mus'd
lover's	master-cook	mischiefe	musgraves
loveth	master-hand	misdoubting	musician
lowd'st	master-wave	misfortune	musique
lowse	mast'ry	misguide	musitian
loyal	masts	misguided	mute
loyal-london	matches	mishap	mutiny

perverted	plung'd	predecessor	prosperous
pestilence	plunging	preferment	prostitute
peter's	plyant	preferr	prostituted
petition	pockets	preferr'd	prostrate
petty	pocketts	preferring	protect
pex	pocus	preists	protecting
phaeton	poise	prelat	provant
phalaris	poison	prelat's	provd
phanatick	poisone	prentiships	prov'd
phancy	poisonous	prepared	proved
phantastik	poles	prepares	proves
pharoh's	policy	prerogative	provided
pharsalian	polisht	presbyterian	provident
philips	politick	presbytery	province
philomel	politicks	presedent	provok'd
phlegethon	poll	preserved	prov't
phlegeton	poll-bill	preside	prow'd
phlegmatick	pollute	president	prowes
phlogis	polydore	presidents	proxie
phrase	pomgranates	presse	prudently
physick	pomp	preston's	prun'd
picking	pompe	presum'd	prys
pickle	pompous	pretending	pry's
picts	pond	prevail'd	publicans
pierced	ponyarding	prevaile	publick's
pierc't	poole	prevailed	publicola
pig-eyed	poor-john	prevented	publish
pil'd	popes	prevents	puchinello
pile	poppea	preys	pudden
piles	poppies	priapus	puffs
pilgrim	popping	priced	pulling
pilgrimage	porch	prickling	punisht
pillag'd	pore	priest-ridden	purer
pillaging	poreing	primate	purest
pilled	poring	prime	purgatory
piller	portend	primitive	purge
pillows	portended	princess	purges
pilot	porter	princesse	purling
pilots	porter's	principles	purpose
pimping	porticoes	print	pursue
pimpt	portion	pris'ners	push
pin	portly	prithee	push'd
pinacle	portman	privacy	putrid
pincht	portsmouth	private-bill's	pyebald
pink	positive	privateers	pygmees
pinke	possesses	priz'd	pyramid
pioneers	possesst	probable	pyramids
pipe	postern	proceeding	quack
pipin	posting	process	quadrature
piping	posts	processioning	quaff
piss	potent	proclaime	quailes
pisse	pothecare	procreate	quails
pit	poulains	procure	quaint
pity'd	poultney	procurers	quarrel
placed	pour	proffer	quarrell'd
plad	poure	profit	quarrelling
plaines	poures	profitt	quarrels
plainly	poverty	profound	quarreys
plains	powell	progers	quarter
plaints	powerful	progress	queans
planisphere	powerfull	prohibits	queene
plank	pow'rdst	projectors	quench
plates	pow'rful	prolongs	quest
platonique	pox	promise	question
playd	poysing	promises	questiond
play'd	poyson'd	promontories	questions
playing	practic'd	proof	quietly
pleasantly	prais'd	proofe	quills
pleased	prat	proper	quils
pleasure-boat	pray'd	property	quilted
plebeian	prayed	prophane	quires
pledge	prayer	prophecy'd	rack
pledges	praying	prophesie	racks
plenipotence	prays	prophesy	raffe
plenipotentiary	preach	propitiatory	rag
plenipotentiaryes	preacher	proportions	ragg
plenty	preaching	propose	ragg'd
pluck'd	preceds	prorogu'd	raggs
plummets	precepts	prorogue	rags
plump	precipice	prorogues	raigning
plundring	precipitate	proserpine	raile

rails
rainbow
rainbows
raines
raised
rake
ram
rampant
rancour
rank
rant
rapacious
rarities
rascally
ras'd
rash
rashness
rational
rationall
ratts
ravage
rave
ravenous
ravens
ravish
ravish'd
ravisher
ravishment
raw
rays
re
re-adjusts
re-baptize
reacht
reading
reads
realm
realme
realmes
realms
reapt
reasons
reason's
reassume
rebabel
rebell
rebelling
rebel's
rebounding
rebuild
rebuked
recanters
receipt
receiving
recess
recieve
recite
reck'ning
reckon'd
reckoning
reclaim
recoild
reconcil'd
reconcile
recover
recreant
recreates
recruit
redeem
redeem'd
redeemers
redemption
reed
reeking
reel
refin'd
reform'd
reforming
refrain'd
refuge
refus'd

refusing
regain'd
regardless
regement
regiment
register
rehearse
reimburse
reins
reject
rejoice
rejoyces
rejoycing
relation
relax
release
releive
relented
relief
relieve
relievo
religions
reliques
relish
rellish
remain'd
remained
remedies
remember
remora
remote
remount
remov'd
removed
removes
removing
rends
renews
rennett
renounce
renowne
repairs
repaying
repeated
repent
repented
repin'd
replies
reprehend
repreive
representatives
represt
repriev'd
reprieves
reprives
reproachful
reproacht
reprov'd
republick's
repugnance
repute
requires
requite
requitted
resemblance
resemble
resembled
resembles
reserve
reserved
resides
resign'd
resigning
resigns
resistless
resolve
resplendent
restauracion
restoration
restored
restoring

retired
retirement
retires
retort
retreate
retreats
reveal
reveals
revelling
revels
revenues
revere
reverence
reverenceth
reversed
revive
revives
revok'd
rewarded
rhodope
riches
richest
richly
richmond
rickt
rid
riddle
rider
riders
rides
ridiculous
riffe
rifling
rig
rime
rimes
rind
rings
riott
rip
riper
rises
rival
rivall
rives
rivet
rivited
roasted
robb
robb'd
robbers
robs
rochets
rockets
rodds
roll
romance
romulus
roode
roof
roof'd
roofs
rooms
roots
rosen
rosie
rots
rott
rotten
rough
rougher
roughest
rould
roules
row'd
rowling
rows
roy
royal-james
royal-oak
rubbish

rubens
rubies
rudely
rue
ruffe
ruffins
ruin'd
ruines
ruler's
runing
rupert
ruperts
rupture
rush
rush'd
ruthless
ruyters
ruyter's
ryder
sabboth
sack
sacrafice
sacraficed
sacramental
sacriledge
saddest
sadles
sadly
safer
saffron-coat
sage
saies
sailes
saint-like
salamander
sale
sales
sally'd
salmon-fishers
salmons
salomon
saltes
saluted
salutes
sampson
sanctuary
sands's
sandy
sandys
saphir-winged
saracen
sardanapalus
sash
satan's
satisfy'd
saturn
saul
sauls
saving
saviours
saying
scabbado
scabbard
scal'd
scalpes
scandal
scandall
scandal's
scant
scap'd
scape
scapeth
scaramuchio
scare
scarlet
scars
scatteringly
scent
schisme
scholler
scoff

sconce	sewers	silk	sodomy
sconces	sexes	simpathies	sodred
scope	seyne	simper'd	soever
scor'd	shaddy	simple	soften
scorning	shadow	simplicity	softly
scorns	shadrack	simpson	softness
scots	shakes	sine-cure	soil
scourges	shallow	singer	solac'd
scratching	shambles	singing	solbay
screeching	shamefull	singst	soldiers
scrip	shap'd	sire	sole
scriptures	shapt	sisyphus's	solemn
scrivener	shark	sith	solemniz'd
scutcheon	sharpest	sit'st	solitude
sea-battel	shatter	sitte	scllicitor
sea-born	shattering	sittings	sollid
sea-cod	shave	situation	son-in-law
sea-command	shear	six	sonne
sea-march	sheath	sixteene	sonns
sea-monsters	sheath'd	sixty	soone
sea-nuptials	sheathing	size	sorcerers
sea-nymphs	sheaves	sized	sordid
seals	shedding	sketching	sorrows
seal's	shee	skill'd	sorrow's
seams	shee'l	skills	sorted
sear	sheet	skip	sotana
search'd	shelden	skipping	sotts
seas'nable	sheldon	skirt	sould
seasonable	shepheardess	skreen	scunding
seate	shepherd	sky's	soup
seav'n	shepherdesses	slacken	sourdine
seclude	shepherds-purse	slake	southampton
secrecy	sheppy	slakes	soveraign
secretary	she's	slasht	soveraigne
secretaryes	shibboleth	slaughters	sow
secretly	shillings	slavery	sowd
secrett	shin'd	slavish	soyl
section	shipps	sleeve	soyl'd
sects	shire	slick	soyle
secur'd	shoare	slimy	spades
securer	shocks	slip	spaines
securing	shoes	slipp'ry	spains
security	shole	slipt	spake
seduce	sholes	sloath	span
seed	shooting	sloth	spankers
seeling	shops	slow-chapt	spar
seemed	shortly	slowe	sparagus
seemeth	shoud	slowness	spar'd
seeming	shoulder	sluces	spared
seemly	shoulders	sluice	spark
s'eer	shouldst	slumber	sparkled
seest	should'st	slumb'ring	spartacus
seige	shouts	smalest	spatious
seine	shov'l	smallest	spawn'd
self-deluding	showr	smarts	speake
selfe	showre	smells	speaks
sells	show'ring	smelt	spear
selve	show'rs	smil'd	speckled
sends	show'st	smoak	sped
senec	show'th	smoakd	speedy
seneque	shreeks	smoake	spells
senseless	shrieks	smoaking	spends
sentinel	shrines	smoke	sphears
separates	shrink	smoothen'd	spheres
sequestration	shrinking	smoother	spherical
serenely	shriveled	smoothly	spice
serenest	shropshire	smutty	spider
sergeants	shroud	smyrna	spies
serious	shrowd	snapping	spill
serjeants	shrowds	snare	spinster
serpents	shrunken	sneaking	spintrian
served	sibyls	sneer	spir's
scrvil'	sidney's	snick	spit
serving	sidnies	snips	spite
sesse	sighing	snowy	spitefull
session	sign-post	snuff	spleen
seth's	signal	snuffe	splendor
settled	sign'd	scaks	splendour
sever'd	significant	soar	splitting
severer	signifies	sod	spoile
severn	silenced	soder'd	spoils

spoones
sportings
spotted
spout
spoyle
sprag
spreading
spreads
sprung
spurious
sputter
squadrons
squeeze
squeking
squinting
squire
stables
'stablish
stacks
staff
stag
stage-coach
stages
stagger'd
stagg'ring
staggs
stainer
staines
stair-cases
stale
stamp
stamps
stanch
standing-armies
stanza's
staple
starch
starcht
stare
starling
starr
startling
starv'd
starved
state--
state-jealousie
state's
statuaries
stature
statute
staves
stead
steady
steeds
steep
steeples
steept
steers
steersman
stele
step
stern
sterns
stevens
steward
stewart
stewarts
stew'd
stewes
stich
sticks
stiffer
stiffest
stile
sting
stinking
stint
stirs
stock-doves
stocks-market
stoln

stolne
stomach
stomack
stooles
stoope
stooping
stopping
stopps
stor'd
stories
stork
stork-like
stormed
storyes
stout
stoves
straitness
strang
strangely
strangled
strangly
stratagem
straw-berryes
streamers
streaming
streete
streigns
strephon
stretch
stretched
strid
stride
strikes
string
stript
strives
strok'
strongly
strook
strove
strow
strow'd
structures
strumpetts
stuart
stubborness
studi'd
studious
stud y'd
stuff
stung
stupefaction
stupendious
stupifi'd
styled
stypends
subsidies
substance
subtle
succeeds--
successes
successful
successive
successor
succoths
succour
suck
suckt
sue
suffer'd
sufferings
sugar
sugars
sully
sulphrey
sulphur
sulphurs
summ
summer-night
summon
summon'd

sun-burn'd
sun-like
sunder'd
sunn
sunne
sunns
superfluously
supersti tion
superstitions
supplant
supply'd
supplye
support
suppos'd
surenesse
surging
surly
surmise
surplic'd
surplice
surprise
surpriz'd
survey'd
surveying
surveys
survi v'd
survive
surviving
suspect
suspected
sustain
sustein
swaddled
swagger
swain
swallowes
swan
sway'd
sweate
sweaty
sweeping
sweete
sweetly
sweetnesse
sweets
swell
swift
swifter
swinges
swoome
sword's
swouning
sybills
syllable
sympathies
syrinx
t.
tables
tacklings
t'admit
tag
tagg
tagus
tail
taile
takeing
taketh
talbot
talbots
talbott
talk
talke
talkt
taller
tallest
tallons
tallow
tally
tam'd
t'america
tames

tangier
tangier-hall
tankard-bearing
taper
tare
tarquins
tarras
taske
taste
tasts
taverns
tawny
taxing
te
tea
teage
teagues
teal
teame
teares
tearm
tedious
tegeline
telling
temperate
tempe's
templum
tempter
tempters
tempts
tenable
tenantable
tend
tenderness
tendernesse
tends
t'enjoy
t'enslave
t'ensnare
tent
tents
tereus
terrible
terror
terrors
text
th
'thad
thankless
thats
t'have
thaw'd
theban
thebes
theeves
theft
th'elected
theme
thereby
therein
therfore
thessalian
they've
thickest
thirsty
thirtieth
thirty
thistle-down
thistles
thomas
thong
thorn
thou'lt
thrace
thrash'd
thrastles
thread-bare
threads
threat
threatens
threatned

threatning	tows	trusting	unfeather'd
threat'ning	toy	trusts	unfix'd
threats	toyes	trusty	ungentle
thred	toyls	tryals	ungrateful
thred-bare	toys	tryell	unheard
three-fork'd	tradition	tryes	unhir'd
thrifty	traffique	trying	uniforme
thrives	traged.	trys	uninforc'd
thro	tragick	try's	unkindness
thro'	trains	tube	unknowing
throbs	traitor-worm	tufted	unlac't
throgmorton	traitors	tulipant	unless't
throughout	trammels	tunick	unlike
th'row	tranfusing	t'unite	unloaded
thrown	transcend	tunn'd	unloads
throwne	transcending	turf	unlock'd
throw'st	transferring	turk-christian-	unlocks
thunder'd	transform	pagan-jew	unlucky
thunders	transform'd	turkish	unman'd
thund'rer	transfuse	turnaments	unmoved *
thund'ring	transgressing	turncoat	unnum'red
t'hunt	transitory	turnd	unperceiv'd
thurland	translates	turner's	unpractis'd
thwart	transpires	turning	unprepar'd
thwates	transplanting	turnor	unproportion'd
thyeste	transport	turtles	unprovok'd
tiberius	transported	tusk	unreasonable
tickle	transports	tuttle-field	unrepair'd
tickles	travellers	twang	unriddle
tides	traverse	tweaking	unrul'd
tillage	treach'ry	twigg	unsemly
till'd	treason's	twine	unsing'd
timbers	treasure's	'twines	unstain'd
t'immure	treasuress	twins	unsung
t'impark	treaties	twist	unsuspected
tinkles	treatst	twixt	untack
tinsel	trebles	two-edg'd	unthankful
t'invite	tredenham	tybourn	untie
tippets	trelawny's	tybur	unties
tipt	trencher	tydes	untight
tired	trepan	tygress	untoucht
tires	trespassing	tyme	untun'd
tiresias	tresses	tymes	untwine
titles	tribes	tyranick	unty
tittle	tributaries	tyrannic	unused
toast	tributes	tyrannick	unwary
toback	trickled	tyrany	unwearied
toes	trickling	tyrian	unwhclesome
toil	tricks	tyth	unwonted
tclerable	trident	ugly	uphold
tombe	trident's	ulcer	upnor
tome	trifling	unable	upnor-castle's
tone	trip	unattended	upon----
tools	triple	unbottom'd	uproar
top-masts	tripoly's	unbuilt	upstart
topiks	triumphall	uncase	upward
toril	triumphant	unchanged	urged
torment	triumphantly	uncivil	urinal
tormenting	triumvirate	unconstant	usd
tormentor	trodden	unconstrain'd	useful
torments	troopers	uncorrupting	uselesse
torrid	troop't	unction	usual
tortoise-shell	trophies	underground	usurpt
tortoises	trot	underlings	utensils
torture	trouble	undermine	utmost
tortures	troubled	undermined	utter
toss	troubles	under's	uttered
total	troublesome	understands	uxorious
touched	troubling	undertooke	vacate
touches	trowel	undescry'd	vade
toucheth	trowl'd	undiscern'd	vainer
touching	truckling	undisturb'd	valianst
tower-barge	truer	undoe	valiantly
towers	truest	undrest	valiants
town-bays	trumpet	undutiful	values
townes	trumpet-gen'ral	undwelt	vandale
towns	trumpets	uneasie	vanish'd
towring	trumpetts	unenvy'd	vanity
towrs	trunks	unespy'd	varied
tow'rst	trusses	unfashion'd	vassalls
towry	trusted	unfathomable	vaster

vaunts	walsingham	whosoever	yeer
veils	wan	wicked	yeilded
veines	wand'rers	wider	yell
velvet	ware	wield	yes
venerable	warm'd	wight	yielding
vengeance	warme	will'd	yoak
venice	warms	william	yoake
venom'd	warren	williams	yong
venture	wart	willingly	york
vera	wary	windes	yorkes
verdict	wash	windpipe	youl
verged	wash'd	windsor	youngsters
vermin	washing	wing'd	youthfull
verses	washt	winke	youths
vessell	wash't	winnow	zeal
vestal	waste	winters	zephyr's
vestments	watch'd	wire	zodiack
vexing	watchful	wishing	
vial	water-hercules	withal	
vicegerent	wat'ry	withall	
vicinity	waving	withdrawing	
victor's	wax	withdraws	
victour	wax'd	withdrew	
victualls	waxed	wither	
vie	waxen	withers	
vigilance	ways	with'ring	
vigilant	way's	withstood	
vigils	weakeness	wits	
vile	weaker	wittals	
village	weakly	witts	
villagers	weakness	woe	
villin	weaknesses	woefull	
vindex	weal	wolves	
vindicate	weal-publik	woman	
vindicates	wealthy	womans	
vines	weapons	wonderful	
violets	weares	wonderfull	
viols	wearied	wonders	
virgin-source	wearyed	wondred	
virginity	weather-beaten	wondring	
virgo	weav'd	wonn	
virtue's	weaves	woo	
virtuoso's	web	wood-leviathans	
virtuous	wedg'd	wood-moths	
viscous	wedges	woodbines	
visick	weeds	woodcock	
vision	weel	wooing	
visit	wee'l	woolchurch	
vital	wee're	word-peckers	
vitiate	wellcome	worke	
vitrifi'd	weltring	workmanship	
vive	wenches	world's	
vocal	westerne	worm	
voices	westward	worm-eaten	
void	we've	worms	
volke	wex	worser	
vollyes	whats	worshipfull	
volumes	what's	worstenholm	
vomit	wheels	worster	
vote	whelps	worthily	
voters	whereat	worthlesse	
vouchsafe	wheres	worthy's	
vows	wheres'ere	wot'st	
voyage	wheresoe're	wove	
vulcan	wherewith	wrack	
vulture's	whirleth	wracks	
vultur's	whirling	wrangle	
vyands	whisht	wrapt	
vye	whisk	wreak	
wades	whisper	wreath	
wafers	whisper'd	wren	
wages	whispers	wrens	
wainscot	whisp'ring	wrinkled	
waits	whitehall's	writer	
wake	whiter	writing-master	
wakeful	whitest	wrong'd	
wakefull	whither	wrung	
wales	whoever	wyer	
walke	who'ld	y'	
walking	whorwood	year's	
waller	whosoe're	yee